Barron's
How to Prepare
for the College-Level
Examination Program

CLEP

General Examinations

Fifth Edition

ENGLISH COMPOSITION
William C. Doster, EDITOR College of DuPage, Glen Ellyn, Illinois

HUMANITIES
Ruth Ward Miami-Dade Community College, Miami, Florida

MATHEMATICS
Shirley O. Hockett Ithaca College, Ithaca, New York

NATURAL SCIENCES
Adrian W. Poitras Miami-Dade Community College, Miami, Florida (retired)

SOCIAL SCIENCES — HISTORY
Robert Bjork George Peabody College for Teachers, Nashville, Tennessee

Barron's Educational Series, Inc.
New York / London / Toronto / Sydney

Printed in 1988

© Copyright 1985 by Barron's Educational Series, Inc.

Prior edition © Copyright 1983, 1979, 1975 by Barron's Educational Series, Inc.

All inquiries should be addressed to:
Barron's Educational Series, Inc.
250 Wireless Boulevard
Hauppauge, New York 11788

Library of Congress Catalog Card No. 83-12276
International Standard Book No. 0-8120-2980-1

Library of Congress Cataloging in Publication Data
Main entry under title:

Barron's How to prepare for the college-level
  examination program, CLEP, general examinations.

  1. College Entrance Examination Board. College-Level
Examination Program. I. Doster, William C.
II. Title: How to prepare for the college-level
examination program.
LB2353.68.B37   1983   378'.1664   83-12276
ISBN 0-8120-2980-1

TABLE OF CONTENTS

ACKNOWLEDGMENTS

The authors are grateful to the following copyright owners for permission to reprint materials:

The *Chicago Tribune* for permission to reprint and adapt paragraphs on pages 40, 41, 92, 93, 122, 123, 156, 167, 168, 191 and 192. These paragraphs reprinted, courtesy of the *Chicago Tribune*.

GayLife: The Midwest Gay Newsleader for permission to reprint paragraphs on pages 42, 91, 95-97. These paragraphs reprinted, courtesy of *GayLife*.

The two sample CLEP essay questions (page 94 and page 97), the sample essays (pages 95-97), and questions one to four on African/Asian Civilizations (page 616) are from *Guide to the CLEP Examinations,* College Entrance Examination Board, 1982. Reprinted by permission of Educational Testing Service, copyright owner of the sample questions. Permission to reprint CLEP sample questions and related directions does not constitute review or endorsement by Educational Testing Service or the College Board of this publication as a whole or of any other sample questions or testing information it may contain.

Photographic Credits

Grateful acknowledgment is made to the following photographers, agents, and museums for permission to reprint their materials: British Crown Copyright (reproduced with the permission of the Controller of Her Britannic Majesty's Stationery Office); Hirmer Fotoarchiv Munchen; Jerry Frank; Marlborough Gallery (Estate of David Smith); Metropolitan Museum of Art (Rogers Fund); Metropolitan Museum of Art (Levi Hale Willard Bequest); Mexican-National Tourist Council; Museum of Modern Art (on extended loan from the artist); Museum of Modern Art (acquired through the Lillie P. Bliss Bequest); Museum of Primitive Art; National Gallery of Art (Andrew Mellon Collection); Photo Alinari; Roger Viollet; Solomon R. Guggenheim Museum.

An Introduction to the College-Level Examination Program

Several years ago, the College Entrance Examination Board and Educational Testing Service decided to develop a new examination battery—the College-Level Examination Program (CLEP)—for a variety of purposes:

1.   Many adults were returning to the classroom after a number of years working or in the home rearing a family. During these years, these people continued their educational growth in many ways: reading magazines and other periodicals, watching television, joining discussion groups, reading books, and often just thinking about what had happened to them during these years. On their return to college, these students wanted a valid, standardized examination to demonstrate their self-development; and the colleges wanted an examination in order to be able to advise students properly about possible courses of study and often about the level of difficulty the students might want to attempt.

2.   Between 1945 and 1985, the number of locally controlled two-year colleges more than tripled so that in some states over half of all freshmen and sophomores enrolled in college were enrolled in a two-year institution. Since these colleges are, for the most part, autonomous and develop curriculums to suit the needs of their own communities, and since many of their graduates want to transfer to an upper division college or university, there was a problem: how could the receiving institution be sure of the quality of applicants for admission? The CLEP General Examinations battery provides scores which a college might consider in its decision to accept or reject an applicant.

3.   For one reason or another, many students attend educational institutions which are not accredited by one of the regional accrediting associations. Often the lack of accreditation is a technical matter which in no way reflects upon the quality of instruction obtainable there; but if the student wants to transfer any or all of his credits to another college, the receiving college needs some instrument to validate that earlier education.

4.   Some government agencies have determined that a standardized test covering a variety of subject areas often reveals more about a person applying for a position or for a promotion from one position to another than a transcript of grades or a personal interview. Also, such a required test makes all applicants equal, for their scores are theirs alone and cannot be qualified by prejudices which might influence an interviewer.

5. Many people, interested in self-education, would like to know how they rate on a comparative scale developed by scoring the CLEP General Examinations of thousands of individuals all over the country. They may never want to attend a college or university, but they are interested in their own growth and development through their own activities.

6. Many students who have come through excellent high schools wish to skip one or more required courses in nearly every college's curriculum: English composition, social sciences, various natural sciences, and basic mathematics. Some colleges now accept certain scores on the CLEP General Examinations sections as demonstration of a student's competence in these areas and do not require him or her to enroll in required courses.

For these reasons, and to aid these individuals and institutions, the CLEP battery was developed by panels of scholars and teachers in five broad subject-matter fields.

The Content of the CLEP General Examination Battery

In 1978, new forms of the CLEP General Examination battery were introduced. Now each examination is in two separately timed parts, according to the following table:

CONTENTS OF GENERAL EXAMINATION BATTERY

(NOTE: Percentages are approximate in every instance and may vary from test to test.)

TEST	PART	CONTENT OR ITEM TYPES		TIME/NUMBER OF QUESTIONS
English Composition	I	45%	Sentence Variety	45 minutes
		15–20%	Sentence Completion	60–65 questions
		33%	Construction Shift	
		5–10%	Ambiguous Sentences	
	II (all-multiple-choice version)	33%	Illogical Statement	45 minutes
		15–20%	Attitude Discerning	60–65 questions
		33%	Sentence Relationship	
		15–20%	Paragraph Organization	
	II (essay version)	Written Composition		45 minutes
Humanities	I & II	50%	Literature	45 minutes each section
			10% Drama	75 questions each section
			15–20% Poetry	
			10–15% Fiction	
			10% Nonfiction	
		50%	Fine Arts	
			20% Visual Arts (painting, sculpture, etc.)	
			15% Music	
			10% Performing Arts (film, dance, etc.)	
			5% Architecture	

Note: On the Humanities examination, questions from all 8 categories are mixed together.

TEST	PART	CONTENT OR ITEM TYPES		TIME/NUMBER OF QUESTIONS
Mathematics	I (Basic Skills and Concepts)	30% Arithmetic 35% Algebra 15–20% Geometry 15–20% Data Interpretation (graphs and charts)		30 minutes 40 questions
	II (Content)	10% Sets 10% Logic 30% Real Number System 20% Functions and Their Graphs 15% Probability and Statistics 15% Miscellaneous Topics		60 minutes 50 questions
Natural Sciences	I	50% Biological Science		45 minutes 60 questions
			10% Origin and evolution of life, classification of organisms	
			10% Cell organization, cell division, chemical nature of the gene, bio-energetics, biosynthesis	
			20% Structure, function, and development in organisms; patterns of heredity	
			10% Concepts of population biology with emphasis on ecology	
	II	50% Physical Science		45 minutes 60 questions
			7% Atomic and nuclear structure and properties, elementary particles, nuclear reactions	
			10% Chemical elements, compounds and re-actions; molecular structure and bonding	
			12% Heat, thermodynamics, and states of matter; classical mechanics; relativity	
			4% Electricity and mag-netism, waves, light and sound	
			7% The universe: galaxies, stars, the solar system	
			10% The Earth: atmosphere, hydrosphere, structure, properties, surface features, geological processes, history	

TEST	PART	CONTENT OR ITEM TYPES	TIME/NUMBER OF QUESTIONS
Social Sciences and History	I & II	35% History 10–15% United States History 10–15% Western Civilization 5–10% African/Asian Civilizations 65% Social Sciences 25–30% Sociology 15–20% Economics 15–20% Political Science 3–5% Social Psychology	45 minutes each section 60–65 questions each section
Note: On the Social Sciences and History examination, questions from all 7 categories are mixed together.			

The emphasis of each of the sections of the battery is on the general principles of the subject area being tested, not the mere facts anyone might remember from a specific course. More specific discussion of examination coverage is given in each of the five major parts of this book. In general, however, it is possible to say that the whole battery covers what anyone might be expected to know from the first two years of college work or the equivalent. Most colleges have a required series of courses which provide the type of general information and educational experience that every educated person should have as he or she goes into a specialized area in the third year, and the CLEP General Examination battery does not go beyond the content of these "general education" courses, as they are so often called. Obviously, not every college provides the same content in each of these courses, and some schools have no such "general education" requirements. Those who have been following their own plans for their own education may find themselves deficient in one area but very good in another, and for most purposes, it is the overall, total score of each test which is meaningful.

Note: NO ONE IS REQUIRED TO TAKE ALL FIVE EXAMINATIONS IN THE CLEP BATTERY UNLESS THE COLLEGE WILL ACCEPT ALL FIVE FOR CREDIT. ANYONE MAY TAKE ONE OR MORE OF THE GENERAL EXAMINATIONS, AND IT IS CERTAINLY NOT ADVISABLE FOR ANYONE TO PLAN TO TAKE MORE THAN TWO ON ANY TESTING DAY.

Organization of the CLEP Examinations

On all of the CLEP General Examinations except the Mathematics each question is a multiple-choice type with five choices given; the questions on the Mathematics Examination have only four answer choices. Only one answer is possible for each question. Often the student's reading comprehension is tested indirectly in all the tests, for he or she must be sure to understand the question before attempting to answer it. There are no "trick" questions, however, for each item has been carefully screened by teachers in the subject field working with test construction experts from Educational Testing Service. An answer sheet will be provided at the time the examination is given, and the examinee should be very careful to follow instructions exactly, or the answers will not be registered by the machine which does the scoring by an optical scanning method. The answer sheet consists of rows of small boxes, and to indicate an answer, the examinee should fill in the appropriate box completely.

FOR EXAMPLE:

An apple is
   (A) a fruit   (B) an animal   (C) a flower   (D) a fish
   (E) a reptile

Ⓐ Ⓑ Ⓒ Ⓓ Ⓔ

The obvious answer is A; therefore, box A should be filled in completely.

There are separate answer sheets for each examination, and all should be returned to the supervisor of the examination when he or she calls for them.

The Scoring of the Examinations

For each of the examinations in the CLEP General Examination battery (except English Composition), a total score and two sub-scores are provided:

English Composition: a single score
Humanities: sub-scores for Fine Arts and Literature, as well as a total score
Mathematics: sub-scores for Basic Skills and Concepts and for Content, as well as a total score
Natural Sciences: sub-scores for Biological Sciences and Physical Sciences, as well as a total score
Social Sciences–History: sub-scores for Social Sciences and History, as well as a total score

The result sheet that will be sent to the examinee will list these thirteen scores, scaled to a range of (a low of) 200 to (a high of) 800 for the total scores, and a range of 20 to 80 for the sub-scores. Average scores and sub-scores are considered to be 500 and 50, respectively.

Caution: THERE IS NO SUCH THING AS A PASSING OR A FAILING SCORE ON THE CLEP GENERAL EXAMINATION BATTERY.

The College Entrance Examination Board merely provides the examinations and the scoring of these examinations; how any school or college interprets these scores is the sole responsibility of the particular institution. Nor does the College Entrance Examination Board offer "credit" for certain scores on the CLEP battery. Before anyone takes the tests, it would be wise to consult the institution which has requested the test to know exactly what will be done with the scores and how that institution will evaluate them for its own purposes.

Penalty for Guessing: The total scores and the sub-scores are derived by subtracting a percentage of the number of incorrect answers from the number of correct answers given on a test; this figure is converted to the scaled score. Thus, there is a penalty for guessing answers if one guesses incorrectly; and pure guessing, that is answering when one has no idea of the correct answer, will probably lower the score on the test. However, if the process of elimination discards two or three of the listed choices, the examinee might consider choosing among the remaining ones. Omitted answers are not counted in this computation.

No one is expected to finish any one of the examinations in the CLEP General Examination battery within the time limit; therefore if you do not finish, don't worry too much about it. Correct answers to about one-half of the questions on any examination will provide a score above the average score obtained by college sophomores from whose scores the scales were developed.

At the time of the examination, you will be asked to fill out a form which indicates to whom your scores should be sent; if at any time you wish additional transcripts of these scores, they may be obtained by sending $4 for each transcript to the College Board, Box 1822, Princeton, New Jersey 08541, Attention: CLEP Transcript Service.

How to Arrange to Take the CLEP Examinations

Educational Testing Service has established test centers at major colleges in all parts of the United States, and information on when and where the CLEP battery is available may be obtained by writing directly to Educational Testing Service, Princeton, New Jersey 08540; by consulting the admissions officer or academic counselling office at any college; or by writing or calling one of the College Entrance Examination Board regional offices listed below:

New England

(Connecticut, Maine, Massachusetts, New Hampshire, Rhode Island, Vermont)
College Board Regional Office
470 Totten Pond Road
Waltham, MA 02154
(617) 890-9150

Middle States

(Delaware, District of Columbia, Maryland, New Jersey, New York, Pennsylvania)
College Board Regional Office
Suite 410, 3440 Market Street
Philadelphia, PA 19104
(215) 387-7600

South

(Alabama, Florida, Georgia, Kentucky, Louisiana, Mississippi, North Carolina, South Carolina, Tennessee, Virginia)
College Board Regional Office
Suite 200, 17 Executive Park Drive, N.E.
Atlanta, GA 30329
(404) 636-9465

Southwest

(Arkansas, New Mexico, Oklahoma, Texas)
College Board Regional Office
Suite 922, 211 East 7th Street
Austin, TX 78701
(512) 472-0231

Midwest

(*Illinois, Indiana, Iowa, Kansas, Michigan, Minnesota, Missouri, Nebraska, North Dakota, Ohio, South Dakota, West Virginia, Wisconsin*)
College Board Regional Office
Suite 605, 500 Davis Street
Evanston, IL 60201
(312) 866–1700

West

(*Alaska, Arizona, California, Colorado, Hawaii, Idaho, Montana, Nevada, Oregon, Utah, Washington, Wyoming*)
College Board Regional Office
Suite 228, 2700 Augustine Drive
Santa Clara, CA 95051
(408) 427–0406
    or
College Board Regional Office
Suite 705, 4155 East Jewell Avenue
Denver, CO 80222
(303) 759–1800

Subject Examinations

There are a number of special examinations in the College Level Examination Program that test the content of specific college courses, such as chemistry, English literature, or world history. Information on these course examinations is also available from College Board Regional Offices or from college admissions officers or college academic advising officers. Many colleges will now permit students to submit scores on these specific course examinations for transcript credit, but these specialized tests are not related to the CLEP General Examinations battery.

Final Caution

Before you plan to take the CLEP battery, consult the person at the institution to which you will direct the scores be sent. You should know exactly how the scores will be interpreted, what uses will be made of the scores, and what specific total scores or sub-scores are required by that institution for admission or for validation of any prior educational experiences. Let us repeat: NEITHER THE COLLEGE ENTRANCE EXAMINATION BOARD NOR EDUCATIONAL TESTING SERVICE EVALUATES THE SCORES YOU RECEIVE; THAT EVALUATION IS THE SOLE PROVINCE OF THE INSTITUTION TO WHICH THE SCORES WILL BE SUBMITTED. Since most institutions have different policies on these matters, important to you, you should have that information before you take the examinations.

Note: The format and content of the CLEP General Examination Battery are changed periodically, and you should write or call the CEEB regional office nearest you for information about the current content and format.

How to Use This Book in Preparing for the CLEP General Examinations

How to Study for the CLEP General Examinations Battery

The CLEP Examinations represent a survey of five basic subjects. When the test is constructed, each subject is outlined or divided up into a number of main topics. Questions are written which fall under the main headings. In each test, an approximately equal number of questions are drawn from each of the main categories. This is true even though some categories may seem more important than others. For instance, in American History, there are likely to be no more questions on the Civil War than there will be on the Late Nineteenth Century. Because the test has only a limited number of questions, these questions will, for the most part, cover only the main points of any one category. Therefore, in studying for the examination the student should survey the entire subject, draw up an outline of the subject, review the main points in familiar areas, and study those topics with which he is less familiar.

This book helps you get used to the actual process of taking multiple-choice tests. At the same time each sample question reveals a topic or subject area that may be on the actual test. Because these questions and those presented on the actual test are not identical, it may be best not to simply memorize answers to the questions in this book. Instead when you run across questions you can't answer, check them off. When you find the answer, try to understand the concept or idea involved. You might keep track of the questions you miss and see if they fall in the same category. In this way you can direct your review toward those areas in which you are least proficient. You may have difficulty with a question because the question contains words you do not know. In this case, write the words down as you confront them and find out what they mean in a dictionary or other reference book.

Because the CLEP General Examinations battery covers a wide area of general knowledge, it would be difficult to start from scratch, learning everything that might be included in the test. However, you should realize that you are not starting from scratch. If you are a recent high school graduate, you will discover that most of the material on the tests is material with which you are already familiar from high school and elementary school courses. If you have been out of school for some time, you will find that much of the material on the actual examination is familiar to you from newspapers, magazines, and your general experience.

In preparing for the test it is best to use books that outline the material to be covered in a brief but concise way. You need to know the main points of a subject. If you do not already have extensive knowledge in a field, it is unreasonable to expect to acquire it now and for the most part it will be unnecessary in terms of this particular examination. Main points you should know include the major persons in a field, the main events, principles involved, and the vocabulary of each field.

The General Examination in Mathematics covers material that is generally taught in a college course for non-mathematics majors. It also tests skills usually acquired in high school: arithmetic, algebra, geometry, and data interpretation. The bibliography given in Chapter 10 will be helpful if you feel the need for a general review of mathematics.

It is important to remember that survey courses for freshmen and sophomores in college, for the most part, repeat a good deal of material that the student should have learned in high school. To be sure, college courses are more compact or concise and may go into the subject in greater depth. Nevertheless, many of the main topics covered are the same as those covered in high school. Do not be overwhelmed by the idea that these are "college" examinations for they are designed for the person who has acquired a basic education on his own. Working out the items offered in this book and answering the questions will be one way in which you can review what you have already learned, either in a classroom or on your own.

A Strategy for Taking the CLEP Examination

Different strategies work for different people in taking exams. You should follow whatever procedure seems best for you. Because each test is timed, however, you should not linger too long on any single question. As soon as it becomes obvious to you that you do not know the answer, you should move on to the next question. Many poor test takers get bogged down on one or two questions and don't have time to complete all the questions they could have answered.

A strategy for taking multiple-choice examinations which seems to work for many people is as follows: (1) Read the statement and try to recall the correct answer. (2) See if the answer you recalled is listed among the choices and mark it immediately. (3) If you were not able to *recall* the correct answer, but on the first reading of the choices you *recognize* the correct answer, mark it immediately. (4) If you cannot answer the question on the first reading, immediately go on to the next question. This way you will be spending your time on what you know. The secret of taking this type of test is to decide immediately whether or not you know the answer. If you cannot decide quickly, go on to the next item so that no time is wasted.

After having completed all the questions that you were sure of, you may have time to go back and check some of the questions you did not complete the first time round. When you go back and check the questions that you skipped the first time, you will immediately recognize some of the answers. For the items that still give you difficulty, you might proceed to eliminate the obviously incorrect answers.

FOR EXAMPLE:
The man who invented the first usable electric light was:
(A) Benjamin Franklin   (B) George Washington
(C) Thomas Edison   (D) Henry Ford   (E) Max Planck

You may not know a thing about electricity but certainly you can eliminate the names of George Washington and Henry Ford. You have bettered your odds. Your chances are now one-in-three instead of one-in-five. If you still are not sure which is correct, but have a hunch, then play that hunch. Often, you will have heard or read the correct answer without remembering. You will feel or think a statement is true without knowing why. Play your hunch. If, after having chosen an answer, you still aren't sure, it is best to leave the first answer. Research studies have demonstrated that the first guess is more likely to be correct than a revised guess later on.

The questions on the General Examination in Mathematics can frequently be answered using shortcuts which make pencil and paper unnecessary. These methods will be discussed in detail in Chapter 10. That is, there is often a "trick" by which the answer can be figured out in one's head. The goal is to avoid excessive computation. Since the test places little emphasis on arithmetic calculations, you should not waste time on long computations on any single question. Instead, answer those items that come quickly. Go back to the others if you still have time after you have done the items that come easier.

Hints for Success:

1. Get plenty of sleep. An important factor in taking an examination is to rest the night before. Fatigue can lower your self-confidence, your ability to concentrate, your speed in taking the examination, and ultimately can lower your score.

2. Arrive early. Arrive at the designated place at least ten or fifteen minutes before the test is scheduled to begin. Be sure you have allowed yourself time to take care of all last minute details. It is important to arrive early so you will not feel rushed and will have time to get adjusted to the surroundings. It is best that whatever shuffling and rearranging you might feel inclined to do be done before the test begins, rather than during the first ten minutes of actual test time. When it is time to start working on the test questions, you should be able to begin immediately with no confusion or warm-up period.

3. Do not assume anything in regard to test directions. Time will be given to read the test directions before the test begins. Even if you feel completely familiar with the directions from other experiences, you should take time to read them on this particular test so that you know exactly what to expect and don't start out with a false assumption.

4. Relax. Don't let last minute nervousness get the better of you. Almost everyone is a little tense before an examination. If you freeze or clutch during the examination, then forget the questions for a few moments and concentrate on something else. Don't worry about the few minutes you

will be losing. You'll waste more time and will be less efficient if you try to struggle through the test with that "locked up" feeling. Relax and be cool. Remind yourself that you're pretty smart and you have what it takes. Then, when you're calmer, pick up your exam and go to it.

When you finish this book with the illustrative and sample test items we have prepared for you, you will have worked through more than 3500 different test items:

English Composition	675
Humanities	680
Mathematics	700
Natural Sciences	750
Social Sciences – History	630

Why so many? We believe that this much practice is necessary for anyone to do well on the CLEP battery, and, of course, we do not expect that anyone will attempt to finish the whole book within a few days. Take your time, and you will be better off.

For example: from the following four statements, several different questions might be written:

1. William Shakespeare was a playwright of the English Renaissance.
2. One of his best and most famous tragedies is *Hamlet*.
3. "To be or not to be—that is the question" is the first line of one of Hamlet's soliloquies.
4. By definition, a soliloquy is a speech which a character says aloud, alone on stage, and which may represent what he is thinking at the moment.

Now, look at just a few of the different questions which might be derived from these facts:

1. William Shakespeare, author of *Hamlet,* was a playwright during the English   1. Ⓐ Ⓑ Ⓒ Ⓓ Ⓔ
   (A) Renaissance   (B) Medieval period   (C) Neo-Classic period
   (D) Romantic period   (E) Victorian period

2. One of Shakespeare's best and most famous tragedies is   2. Ⓐ Ⓑ Ⓒ Ⓓ Ⓔ
   (A) *All for Love*   (B) *Tammarlane the Great*   (C) *Dr. Faustus*
   (D) *Hamlet*   (E) *Cavalcade*

3. "To be or not to be—that is the question" is the first line of one of Shakespeare's   3. Ⓐ Ⓑ Ⓒ Ⓓ Ⓔ
   (A) dramatic monologues   (B) soliloquies   (C) sonnets
   (D) epic poems   (E) lyric poems

4. One of Shakespeare's famous soliloquies begins   4. Ⓐ Ⓑ Ⓒ Ⓓ Ⓔ
   (A) "What have I got now that I did not have?"
   (B) "To be or not to be—that is the question"
   (C) "A girl's best friend is her mother, not dad."
   (D) "These are the times that sorely try men's souls."
   (E) "Of man's first disobedience, and the fruit"

5. A speech which an actor speaks alone on the stage and which perhaps represents his thoughts at the moment, merely verbalized, is called
(A) an epic poem   (B) an aside   (C) a soliloquy
(D) an interruption   (E) a dramatic monologue

We could go on formulating additional questions using the given facts, but you get the idea. If you will note these apparent repetitions, which have been included primarily to reinforce your remembering certain information, you can more easily recall facts if you are confronted with a similar question on an actual examination. Indeed, it is not too much to say that anyone who knows the answer to every question in this book has achieved an educational level which few other people can match, whether they have ever attended college or not.

Review materials for the CLEP battery are primarily of a factual nature, then, except in English Composition and Mathematics. In these two examinations, you will be asked to make applications of certain general principles from the subject area to sentences or problems which you have never seen before—the sentences and problems may be new, but each one incorporates a principle which is illustrated and explained in this book. If you find a question whose answer eludes you, check the answer and answer explanation.

This book is organized into five major parts, one part for each of the five examinations of the CLEP battery. Each part opens with a Trial Examination, which gives you an idea of what the examination is like and lets you determine how you would score on the examination without any specific preparation or practice. Then there is a chapter which provides general information about the examination and a number of items illustrating the basic principles of the subject area as well as the different kinds of information you will need to have or the different responses you might be called upon to make. These sample items you will find in small groups, and we have provided answers and explanations of these answers immediately following each group of questions. We recommend that you work through these groups of items at whatever speed suits you best. We also believe that you can deduce the principles being illustrated from the questions which we have given you to answer.

At the end of each part is a chapter containing three sample examinations, and we suggest, when you do some of these samples, that you follow the time limit that will be imposed during an actual CLEP examination, just to get into the habit of having that limitation as part of the test procedure. An answer key is included at the end of each test so that you can check yourself almost immediately. Answer explanations are also provided; these explanations can help you learn how to read the question carefully and answer exactly what is asked as well as help you recognize your weak spots and plan your studies.

Some teachers of "cram" courses on test taking allege that someone taking a test can figure out a certain pattern of answers and urge students to mark answers according to that pattern. Thus, these teachers say, if the answer to a question is (A), the answer to the next question will probably be (D), and the correct response to the following question might be (B). YOU SHOULD NOT MARK ANSWERS AT RANDOM ACCORDING TO ANY SYSTEM OF RESPONSES WHICH YOU MIGHT DEDUCE. REMEMBER, THERE IS A PENALTY FOR INCORRECT ANSWERS, AND SUCH GUESSING WILL CERTAINLY INCREASE YOUR NUMBER OF INCORRECT RESPONSES.

Here are a few other suggestions about using this book:

1. Skip around among parts. For instance, do not work through the whole part on English Composition and then move to the Humanities part. You will find that shifting from part to part will provide some break for you as you work.

2. Do not attempt any of the complete sample examinations at the end of each part until you have worked through all the sample items. As you try the small groups of questions, you will see that each of these groups deals with just one part of the subject area, while in the complete examinations, questions are arranged in an almost random order to cover the whole subject area.

3. Before attempting to answer any of the questions, read the directions carefully. These directions are repeated before each small group of questions and within the complete examinations. Know exactly what each group of questions requires you to do. All the practice questions except those for the Mathematics Examination have five answer choices. The practice questions for the Mathematics Examination contain only four answer choices. This agrees with the number of answer choices on the actual CLEP General Examinations: four for mathematics, five for each of the other subjects.

4. Do not despair if you discover that you do not finish each sample examination within the indicated time limit. Test experts tell us that many people do not finish tests for many reasons, but do the best you can, for if you get about 50% of each test correct, your score will be above the average score of all college sophomores in the United States.

5. The vocabulary level of the test items is about Grade 14, which means that the words used are those which any college sophomore should recognize and understand from his or her reading. Sentence structure and syntax are at the same level, and it might be a good idea for you to have a good desk dictionary available in case you find words in the practice groups of questions which you do not know.

6. If you would prefer not to fill out the answer blanks in this book so that you can work through the sample questions more than once, you can easily make some answer sheets to use as you practice and review.

7. Within each part, there is a brief bibliography of reference works and textbooks which you might want to review if you find that you are weak in one of the subject areas. Most of these books are available in a good public library.

Each of the following five parts of this book opens with a trial test, followed by a description of the CLEP test which that part covers. Read these descriptions carefully and work through each of the sample exercises and examinations just as carefully. When you finish this book, look back through the questions, and check to see just how much factual information you can recall from your experiences with the sample items. We think that you will be pleasantly surprised.

Good luck!

NOTE: No sample question in this book has ever appeared on an actual CLEP examination. The examinations are security tests, and all material on those tests is protected by copyright in the name of the Educational Testing Service. The test items in this book are meant to be similar in format to an actual CLEP examination, *not* actual items that you might find when you take one or more of the examinations.

Chart of Progress

	Total Possible	Trial Test	Exam 1	Exam 2	Exam 3
English Comp 90 minutes	130				
Humanities 90 minutes	150				
Mathematics 90 minutes	90				
Natural Sciences 90 minutes	120				
Social Science— History 90 minutes	125				

To calculate your raw score on each sample examination use the following formula:

$$RS = C - \frac{I}{n - 1}$$

in which RS = raw score

    C = number of correct answers

    I = number of incorrect answers

    n = number of answer choices. (Each of the examinations, except the Mathematics examination, has five answer choices; the Mathematics examination has only four choices.)

Note: Omitted items are not counted in the formula.

Example: If you have answered 80 questions correctly and 28 incorrectly on the all-multiple-choice English Composition examination, your raw score is

$$RS = C - \frac{I}{n - 1}$$

$$RS = 80 - \frac{28}{4}$$

$$RS = 80 - 7$$

$$RS = 73$$

Only total scores are used to calculate the raw score, not the scores on parts of a single examination.

The raw score on an actual CLEP examination is converted to a three-digit scale score using a complicated statistical formula.

PART ONE
THE ENGLISH COMPOSITION EXAMINATION

Trial Test

This chapter contains a trial English Composition test, which you should take to get an idea of what the examination is like and to determine how you would score before any practice or review. The test contains 130 multiple-choice questions, organized into two parts.

Part I

Number of Items: 65
Time: 45 minutes

Directions: For each of these questions, you are to choose the version of the underlined sentence or part of the sentence that not only has the same or nearly the same meaning as the original but follows the requirements of standard written English. That is, in selecting the version that matches the underlined part in meaning, pay attention to grammar, choice of words, sentence structure, and punctuation. The answer you select should, when inserted in the original sentence, produce an effective sentence—clear and exact, without awkwardness or ambiguity.

1. <u>There were fewer people in the auditorium than</u> we had expected; there were seats for everyone.
   (A) There were less people in the auditorium as
   (B) There were no more people in the auditorium than
   (C) In the auditorium, there were a lot more people than
   (D) There were not as many people in the auditorium as
   (E) A great deal fewer people showed up in the auditorium as

   1. Ⓐ Ⓑ Ⓒ Ⓓ Ⓔ

2. During the Renaissance, <u>the Italian peasants could hardly find enough food</u> to keep their families alive and healthy.
   (A) the Italian peasants couldn't hardly find enough food
   (B) the Italian peasants could hardly locate in the country more food than necessary
   (C) the Italian peasants could scarcely find sufficient food
   (D) the Italian peasants starved themselves with enough food
   (E) the Italian peasants could not have found more than enough food

   2. Ⓐ Ⓑ Ⓒ Ⓓ Ⓔ

3. To make their children realize the significance of wise decision making, sometimes parents <u>should let them suffer the consequences of their actions.</u>
   (A) should let them stew in the juice of their own concoction

   3. Ⓐ Ⓑ Ⓒ Ⓓ Ⓔ

(B) should allow them to receive whatever penalties ensue
(C) should reduce the penalties for their deviant behavior
(D) should let them stew in their own consequences
(E) should tell them to get lost

4. A good plumber can connect one pipe with another so completely that there will be no leak from the joint.   **4.** Ⓐ Ⓑ Ⓒ Ⓓ Ⓔ
   (A) with another as completely as there
   (B) into another with such a high degree of skill as
   (C) with another so that there will be completely
   (D) with another with such little skill that
   (E) with another with such accuracy that

5. My old dog Bruce who is out there lying in the sun has served me well for the past twelve years.   **5.** Ⓐ Ⓑ Ⓒ Ⓓ Ⓔ
   (A) Bruce, lying out there in the sun,
   (B) Bruce that foolishly is not lying in the sun
   (C) Bruce, on the alert out there in the sun,
   (D) Bruce, working hard for his daily cookie treats,
   (E) Bruce whom we found out in the bright sun of noon

6. Many others who are not so fortunate will lose all the money they have invested in the stock market.   **6.** Ⓐ Ⓑ Ⓒ Ⓓ Ⓔ
   (A) others not as fortunate
   (B) others who have had more fortunes
   (C) others who have fewer fortunes
   (D) others whom we find to be among the more unfortunate
   (E) others who have had too many fortunes

7. Marguerite spoke French with a charming accent for she had studied the language with a former Russian countess in Paris.   **7.** Ⓐ Ⓑ Ⓒ Ⓓ Ⓔ
   (A) The reason Marguerite spoke French with such a charming accent was because she had
   (B) Marguerite spoke French with a very unique accent because she had
   (C) Marguerite, speaking French with a charming accent, had
   (D) Marguerite had often spoken French with a charming accent so that she had
   (E) Marguerite, speaking French with a charming accent, for she had

8. Frightened by the sound of footsteps, Jane ran upstairs and hid in the closet.   **8.** Ⓐ Ⓑ Ⓒ Ⓓ Ⓔ
   (A) ran upstairs and that she hid in the closet
   (B) ran upstairs, having hidden in the closet
   (C) ran upstairs; they went away
   (D) ran upstairs, which was hiding in the closet
   (E) ran upstairs and into the closet

9. The more money Mr. Getty accumulated, the more he wanted.   **9.** Ⓐ Ⓑ Ⓒ Ⓓ Ⓔ
   (A) he wanted more
   (B) he increased his desires
   (C) the more he accumulated

(D) the greater quantity he desired

(E) the larger in number became his dependents

10. No one doubts Lorraine Hansbury's skill as a <u>dramatist, but there are some critics who believe</u> that her plays lack poetic dialogue and skillful exposition.

    (A) dramatist, but some critics doubt

    (B) dramatist; they say

    (C) dramatist, although some critics believe

    (D) dramatist, believing

    (E) dramatist, who some critics believe

10. Ⓐ Ⓑ Ⓒ Ⓓ Ⓔ

11. The bus driver is always <u>pleasant to us riders even though</u> he must become impatient with some of us who never have the correct change.

    (A) pleasant to we riders even though

    (B) affable to us riders although

    (C) pleasant to us riders so that

    (D) pleasantly to us riders even though

    (E) impatient to those riders who

11. Ⓐ Ⓑ Ⓒ Ⓓ Ⓔ

12. <u>The clever orator's presenting a specious argument caused his audience to become restless and inattentive.</u>

    (A) When the clever orator presented a specious argument, his audience became restless and inattentive.

    (B) When the clever orator presented a specious argument, they became restless and attentive.

    (C) The clever orator's presentation of a specious argument, causing his audience to become restless and inattentive.

    (D) The clever orator's presenting a specious argument was when his audience became restless and inattentive.

    (E) The clever orator presented a specious argument because his audience became restless and inattentive.

12. Ⓐ Ⓑ Ⓒ Ⓓ Ⓔ

13. <u>That type of person always strongly resents</u> any attempt by anyone to limit his actions.

    (A) That type person always strongly resents

    (B) That type of person who always strongly resents

    (C) That type person which strongly resents

    (D) Those same people always strongly resist

    (E) Some people always resent

13. Ⓐ Ⓑ Ⓒ Ⓓ Ⓔ

14. Because he was growing marijuana, Jerry was <u>picked up</u> by the police.

    (A) arrested

    (B) arrested, being taken

    (C) arrested, and they were

    (D) arrested; they held

    (E) arrested, without charge

14. Ⓐ Ⓑ Ⓒ Ⓓ Ⓔ

15. While glancing through today's newspaper, I read that the cost of living has risen another four points.

    (A) Glancing through today's newspaper, the cost of living has risen another four points.

15. Ⓐ Ⓑ Ⓒ Ⓓ Ⓔ

(B) Today's newspaper contained an item that the cost of living has risen another four points.

(C) The cost of living having risen another four points, I read in today's newspaper.

(D) I read in today's newspaper where the cost of living has risen another four points.

(E) I was glancing through today's newspaper when the cost of living rose another four points.

16. Each time Leonard Bernstein sits down at the piano, he plays at least one song from one of his musical hits. 16.
    (A) piano, playing at least
    (B) piano, he always performs at least
    (C) piano, and he plays at least one
    (D) piano, having played at least
    (E) piano, which he always plays at least

17. While making a pathetic attempt to explain their behavior to the policeman, the young thief along with his accomplices was unfortunately caught in a web of contradictions. 17.
    (A) thief and his accomplices was unfortunately
    (B) thief together with his accomplices were unfortunately
    (C) thief and his accomplices were unfortunately
    (D) thief; along with his accomplices; were unfortunately
    (E) thief who had a few accomplices were unfortunately

18. Rudolph acts like a foolish child because he trusts anyone who can tell a story in a believable manner. 18.
    (A) , trusting anyone who can tell their story
    (B) because he trusts anyone who can tell their story
    (C) so that he trusts anyone whom can tell a story
    (D) , having trusted anyone who can tell a story
    (E) , trusting anyone who can tell a story

19. Shirley remains convinced that she is as young as, if not younger than, her friend Molly. 19.
    (A) Shirley may be younger than her friend Molly.
    (B) Shirley is convinced that Molly is much older than she is.
    (C) Molly is really much older than Shirley.
    (D) Shirley remains convinced that she is as young, if not younger than, her friend Molly.
    (E) Shirley remains convinced that she is as young as, if not younger as her friend Molly.

20. I cannot talk or write in class without the teacher correcting and embarrassing me. 20.
    (A) I cannot talk or write anything without the teacher corrects and embarrasses me in class.
    (B) Whenever I talk or write in class, the teacher corrects and embarrasses me.
    (C) I cannot talk or write anything in class unless the teacher corrects and embarrasses me.

(D) Whatever I talk or write in class, the teacher is always correcting and embarrassing me.

(E) Correcting and embarrassing me in class is the result whenever I talk or write.

21. The young woman strolled into the department store, looked at some blouses, <u>tried on some shoes, and walked out without</u> buying anything.

21. Ⓐ Ⓑ Ⓒ Ⓓ Ⓔ

(A) , and tried on some shoes; she walked out without
(B) , tried on some shoes; and walked out without
(C) ; tried on some shoes, and walked out without
(D) , and tried on some shoes, and walked out without
(E) , tried on some shoes; and she walked out without

22. <u>Looking up from the top of the high hill, we thought the DC-10 seemed larger than it did parked at the loading ramp.</u>

22. Ⓐ Ⓑ Ⓒ Ⓓ Ⓔ

(A) Watching the DC-10 from the top of the high hill, it seemed larger than it had at the loading ramp.
(B) Looking up from the top of the high hill, the DC-10 seemed larger than it did parked at the loading ramp.
(C) Seeming larger that it did parked at the loading ramp, we were watching the DC-10 from the top of a high hill.
(D) We looked up from the top of a high hill and thought the DC-10 seemed larger than it had parked at the loading ramp.
(E) The DC-10 at the loading ramp seemed larger from the top of the high hill.

23. In her lecture, the novelist alluded to difficulties with her publisher who had insisted that all four-letter words be removed from the manuscript.

23. Ⓐ Ⓑ Ⓒ Ⓓ Ⓔ

(A) In her lecture, the publisher insisted that all four-letter words be removed from the author's manuscript.
(B) No four-letter words were in the manuscript; therefore, the publisher refused to print it.
(C) All four-letter words were deleted by the author before he published the book.
(D) Without eliminating the four-letter words, the publisher produced the book.
(E) The author said that her publisher had insisted that all four-letter words be removed from the manuscript she submitted.

24. Rather than purchase common stocks, many investors prefer real estate, municipal bonds, or convertible debentures.

24. Ⓐ Ⓑ Ⓒ Ⓓ Ⓔ

(A) Rather than purchase common stocks, many investors prefer to buy real estate, municipal bonds, or put their money into convertible debentures.
(B) Buying common stocks is preferable to many investors rather than their investing in municipal bonds, real estate, or convertible debentures.
(C) When investors buy real estate, municipal bonds or convertible debentures, they also purchase common stocks.
(D) Many investors avoid common stocks; instead, they buy real estate, municipal bonds, or convertible debentures.

(E) Buying real estate, municipal bonds, or convertible debentures is not as attractive as common stocks.

25. <u>We could only wonder if he were going to attend college or if he were planning to seek immediate employment.</u> 25. Ⓐ Ⓑ Ⓒ Ⓓ Ⓔ
    (A) We could only wonder whether he was going to college or to seek immediate employment.
    (B) We could only wonder if he was going to college or seeking immediate employment.
    (C) His decision between two alternatives—going to college or seeking immediate employment—concerned us.
    (D) That he was going to attend college and seek immediate employment was a question that bothered us.
    (E) We could only wonder about both his attending college and seeking immediate employment.

26. Because I know so little about the subject, I have no opinion about sensitivity training, and I will keep <u>a disinterested</u> attitude until I have more facts. 26. Ⓐ Ⓑ Ⓒ Ⓓ Ⓔ
    (A) an uninterested
    (B) an impartial
    (C) an interested
    (D) a prejudiced
    (E) a malevolent

27. Hunter is an expert athlete, for he enjoys swimming, bowling, and tennis. 27. Ⓐ Ⓑ Ⓒ Ⓓ Ⓔ
    (A) Hunter is an expert athlete, to enjoy swimming, bowling, and playing tennis.
    (B) Hunter, an expert athlete, enjoys swimming, bowling, and playing tennis.
    (C) To swim, to bowl, and to play tennis—in these games lie Hunter's pleasure.
    (D) Swimming, bowling, and tennis are all enjoyed by Hunter, who isn't very good at any of them.
    (E) An expert athlete, Hunter enjoys to swim, to bowl, and playing tennis.

28. Each of you can do the <u>problem if you will put your minds</u> to work and not give up too easily. 28. Ⓐ Ⓑ Ⓒ Ⓓ Ⓔ
    (A) problem, provided you put your minds
    (B) , problem, and you will put your minds
    (C) problem if you put their minds
    (D) problem, and if you put their minds
    (E) problem; you will put your minds

29. <u>Louis XIV's closest advisors were nobles of the Catholic Church whose loyalty might have been suspected by impartial observers.</u> 29. Ⓐ Ⓑ Ⓒ Ⓓ Ⓔ
    (A) Even though Louis XIV's closest advisors were nobles of the Catholic Church, their loyalty could not be questioned by impartial observers.
    (B) When Louis XIV's closest advisors were revealed as nobles of the Catholic Church, they questioned their loyalty.

(C) Their loyalty was questionable; Louis XIV's closest advisors were nobles of the Catholic Church.

(D) Louis XIV's closest advisors were nobles of the Catholic Church and whose loyalty was questionable by impartial observers.

(E) That Louis XIV's closest advisors were nobles of the Catholic Church made their loyalty to him questionable to many unprejudiced observers.

Directions: For each of these sentences, select the answer that, when inserted in the blank in the original sentence, produces the best sentence. Pay attention to meaning and to choice of words.

30. Walking up four flights of stairs is not _____ for anyone who has heart trouble.
    (A) a thing to be done unthinkingly
    (B) a truly easy procedure
    (C) easily tiring
    (D) simple
    (E) worth the time and effort

    30. Ⓐ Ⓑ Ⓒ Ⓓ Ⓔ

31. _____ is that George has no chance of winning first prize in the poetry contest.
    (A) The consensus of the group's opinion
    (B) Our conclusion
    (C) We all thought
    (D(Our recently arrived at attitude
    (E) Our truth

    31. Ⓐ Ⓑ Ⓒ Ⓓ Ⓔ

32. A brilliant future lies ahead for any young person who _____ at many difficult tasks.
    (A) can succeed
    (B) has achieved a modicum of success
    (C) can be even rather moderately successful
    (D) can successfully work
    (E) can accomplish somewhat successfully

    32. Ⓐ Ⓑ Ⓒ Ⓓ Ⓔ

33. No parents enjoy the prospect of their child's secretly confiding his plans for life to _____
    (A) an uninteresting counsellor
    (B) an advisor who may not really care
    (C) a disinterested neighbor
    (D) persons outside the uninterested home
    (E) a confessor behind a curtain

    33. Ⓐ Ⓑ Ⓒ Ⓓ Ⓔ

34. No law can actually _____ an addict from getting the drugs he must have every day.
    (A) resist
    (B) veto
    (C) prevent
    (D) relieve
    (E) prohibit

    34. Ⓐ Ⓑ Ⓒ Ⓓ Ⓔ

35. Since Old Mother Hubbard _____ enough food for herself, her friends wondered how she expected to feed her pets.

    (A) had not much more than

    (B) had little

    (C) had not really sufficient

    (D) had rather

    (E) had scarcely

35. Ⓐ Ⓑ Ⓒ Ⓓ Ⓔ

36. Among nuclear scientists, Enrico Fermi's name is revered, for his research achieved _____ other physicists with the Manhattan Project.

    (A) greater results than many

    (B) more commercial products than many

    (C) most fruitful outcomes of all

    (D) more success than that of

    (E) much more resounding success than that of

36. Ⓐ Ⓑ Ⓒ Ⓓ Ⓔ

37. The chairperson was not really _____ the other members of the committee.

    (A) congruent with

    (B) compassionate for

    (C) in complete tune and harmony with

    (D) congenial with

    (E) sympathetic among

37. Ⓐ Ⓑ Ⓒ Ⓓ Ⓔ

38. The meal was _____ to satisfy our hunger pangs, but I should not have eaten a third piece of pie.

    (A) ample enough

    (B) just about sufficient

    (C) worthy enough

    (D) more than overly adequate

    (E) most acceptable

38. Ⓐ Ⓑ Ⓒ Ⓓ Ⓔ

39. After Jill and Harold attended the exhibition, she told him that it was one of the most _____ she had ever seen.

    (A) nearly complete

    (B) delighting

    (C) unique

    (D) thoughtful

    (E) perfect

39. Ⓐ Ⓑ Ⓒ Ⓓ Ⓔ

Directions: Revise each of the following sentences according to the directions which follow it. Rephrase the sentence mentally to save time, making notes in your book if you wish. Although the directions may at times require you to change the relationship between parts of the sentence or to make slight changes in other ways, *make only those changes that the directions require.*

Below each sentence and its directions are listed words or phrases that may occur in your revised sentence. When you have thought out a good sentence, look at the choices A through E for the word or entire phrase that is included in your revised sentence.

Of course, a number of different sentences can be obtained if the sentence is revised according to directions, and not all of these possibilities can be included in only five choices. If you should find that you have thought of a sentence that contains none of the words listed in the choices, rephrase the sentence again to include a word or phrase that *is* listed.

40. Insomnia, especially if long standing, is both one of the most troublesome of man's afflictions and one of the most difficult to treat without special medication.

Eliminate <u>both</u>.

(A) so   (B) so well as   (C) as well as   (D) as much as
(E) thus

40. Ⓐ Ⓑ Ⓒ Ⓓ Ⓔ

41. Few Americans have been allowed to visit mainland China since 1948 when the Communists caused Chiang to flee to the island of Formosa.

Begin with <u>Communists have permitted</u>.

(A) Chiang fled   (B) Communists drove Chiang
(C) Chiang allowed   (D) Communists were permitted
(E) Chiang was fled

41. Ⓐ Ⓑ Ⓒ Ⓓ Ⓔ

42. No one can possibly comprehend that I can eat and relish fried squid or boiled seaweed, but I am not afraid to sample exotic dishes from strange places.

Change <u>No one can possibly</u> to <u>Everyone finds it</u>.

(A) possible that I can
(B) comprehending that I can
(C) comprehensible that I can
(D) uncomprehending that I can
(E) incomprehensible that I can

42. Ⓐ Ⓑ Ⓒ Ⓓ Ⓔ

43. Some unstable women suffer irreversible traumas when their marriages fail and they are bereft of a husband at a fairly early age.

Begin with <u>Some unstable women whose</u>.

(A) whose husbands are bereft
(B) who are bereft
(C) who suffer irreversible traumas
(D) whose age is young
(E) they are bereft

43. Ⓐ Ⓑ Ⓒ Ⓓ Ⓔ

44. The doleful sound of the funeral bell reverberated through the village, and we could see the dismal cortege winding its way to the local cemetery.

Begin with <u>With the doleful.</u>

(A) reverberating through the village, so we
(B) reverberating through the village; we
(C) reverberating through the village, we
(D) reverberating through the village, and we
(E) reverberating through the village, thus we

44. Ⓐ Ⓑ Ⓒ Ⓓ Ⓔ

45. A birth rate that continues to increase is no blessing to an island like Java, one of the most densely populated areas in the world with more than twelve hundred people per square mile.

Begin with Java, one of the most.

(A) needs an increasing birth rate
(B) does not increase its birth rate each year
(C) blesses an increasing birth rate
(D) does not need an increasing birth rate
(E) is not overpopulated

45. Ⓐ Ⓑ Ⓒ Ⓓ Ⓔ

46. Old timers say that a job well done is its own reward, but I would rather have my satisfaction in hard cash.

Begin with Hard cash pleases me more.
(A) in spite of what old timers say
(B) by which the old timers worked
(C) under which the old timers worked
(D) and what the old timers say
(E) in spite of what the old timers did

46. Ⓐ Ⓑ Ⓒ Ⓓ Ⓔ

47. When the sun's rays illuminate each small piece of colored glass in that translucent stained glass window and radiate glorious hues throughout the cathedral, a really spectacular effect is created.

Eliminate When, and change illuminate to illuminating.

(A) creates a really spectacular effect
(B) a really spectacular effect is created
(C) a really spectacular sight is effected
(D) create a really spectacular effect
(E) affect a really spectacular sight

47. Ⓐ Ⓑ Ⓒ Ⓓ Ⓔ

48. If the population of the United States ever becomes predominantly submissive and passive, an enemy could quite easily conquer us, for there would be no one willing to fight.

Begin with An enemy could quite easily.

(A) States, if the population of the United States
(B) States with its population
(C) States, unless its population
(D) States, because its population
(E) States, if its population

48. Ⓐ Ⓑ Ⓒ Ⓓ Ⓔ

49. Paul McCartney has had more influence upon contemporary popular music than almost any other composer with the possible exception of Johann Sebastian Bach.

Change more to as much.
(A) if not more than almost
(B) as, if not more than, almost
(C) so, if not more than, almost
(D) also, if not more than, almost
(E) just as, if not more than, almost

49. Ⓐ Ⓑ Ⓒ Ⓓ Ⓔ

50. A constant repression of his feelings and the continued sublimation of his desires can distort a man's real personality, so say psychiatrists.

   Begin with <u>If a man constantly represses.</u>

   (A) his real personality can be sublimated
   (B) his real personality can be continued
   (C) his real personality can become distorted
   (D) his real personality can be desired
   (E) his real personality can be realized

   50. Ⓐ Ⓑ Ⓒ Ⓓ Ⓔ

51. The slow evaporation of underground waters has left some beautiful gypsum deposits on the walls of Kentucky's Mammoth Cave.

   Begin with <u>Some beautiful gypsum.</u>

   (A) have resulted from
   (B) have left
   (C) has remained from
   (D) have left from
   (E) has resulted from

   51. Ⓐ Ⓑ Ⓒ Ⓓ Ⓔ

52. The advent of new techniques for identifying deafness in babies has completely altered some traditional ideas about the possibility of teaching a deaf child to speak.

   Begin with <u>Some traditional ideas.</u>

   (A) has been altered
   (B) has altered
   (C) have been altered
   (D) have altered
   (E) will alter

   52. Ⓐ Ⓑ Ⓒ Ⓓ Ⓔ

53. The hiker was weary after his twenty-mile walk; he rested for half an hour, then picked up his pack, and walked off into the west again.

   Change <u>The hiker was</u> to <u>The hiker.</u>

   (A) hour, then   (B) hour, and then   (C) hour, so then
   (D) hour; then he   (E) hour; then his pack

   53. Ⓐ Ⓑ Ⓒ Ⓓ Ⓔ

54. There are some doctors who attribute about half of their patients' problems to psychosomatic causes rather than to any actual diseases.

   Change <u>who attribute</u> to <u>who say that.</u>

   (A) are psychosomatic in origin
   (B) are caused by actual diseases
   (C) are not health problems
   (D) are not just imaginary
   (E) are attributable to psychosomatic causes

   54. Ⓐ Ⓑ Ⓒ Ⓓ Ⓔ

55. On the whole, a literary critic is not likely to praise a novel unless it provides both some new twists on a traditional plot and writing that is free of clichés.

   Begin with <u>If an author expects a literary critic.</u>

   (A) novel; he must provide
   (B) novel, he must provide

   55. Ⓐ Ⓑ Ⓒ Ⓓ Ⓔ

(C) novel, must provide
(D) novel, and he must provide
(E) novel; therefore, he must provide

56. A good recipe not only lists each ingredient of a dish but also tells the cook the exact amounts of each he should use.

56. Ⓐ Ⓑ Ⓒ Ⓓ Ⓔ

Eliminate not only.

(A) as well as the exact
(B) as well as tells the cook
(C) along with telling the cook
(D) besides tells the cook
(E) or tells the cook

57. About five percent of all American school children exhibit certain learning difficulties which are due to minimal brain dysfunction.

57. Ⓐ Ⓑ Ⓒ Ⓓ Ⓔ

Begin with Minimal brain dysfunction.

(A) exhibits certain
(B) are certain
(C) learn
(D) is difficult
(E) causes certain

58. Researchers drew one startling conclusion from data accumulated during the Head Start program: ghetto children of pre-kindergarten age learn rapidly in school but soon regress if nothing is done to improve their home situations.

58. Ⓐ Ⓑ Ⓒ Ⓓ Ⓔ

Begin with That ghetto children.

(A) drew one startling conclusion
(B) one startling conclusion was drawn
(C) draw one startling conclusion
(D) was one startling conclusion drawn
(E) were one startling conclusion

59. The president announced that labor leaders had given him a tacit commitment not to demand exorbitant wage increases when current union contracts expire.

59. Ⓐ Ⓑ Ⓒ Ⓓ Ⓔ

Change when to upon.

(A) which current union contracts expire
(B) his cancellation of current union contracts
(C) the expiration of current union contracts
(D) current union contracts expire
(E) his expiration of current union contracts

60. As a young man, James Baldwin fled to Europe from the United States because of the bigotry and intolerance which he as a black met everywhere he went.

60. Ⓐ Ⓑ Ⓒ Ⓓ Ⓔ

Begin with As a black, James Baldwin met.

(A) therefore, he fled   (B) so, therefore, he fled   (C) ; fled
(D) , he fled   (E) ; therefore, he fled

Directions: For each of the following choose the one phrasing that makes the intended meaning clear; that is, the one that avoids ambiguity, that does not leave the actual meaning open to question or that does not leave the reader guessing about what is intended.

61. (A) The real charm of their productions lie in poor photography, bad acting, and sleazy sets, according to many cinema buffs.
    (B) Many cinema buffs who overpraise the films of certain underground directors consider bad acting, poor photography, and sleazy sets the real charm of the productions.
    (C) Bad acting, poor photography, and sleazy sets, the real charms of underground films, have been the cause of their overpraise by certain cinema buffs.
    (D) It is clear that certain underground film directors make them with bad acting, poor photography, and sleazy sets.
    (E) The overpraise of the films of certain underground directors by many cinema buffs is the reason why they are filled with poor technical qualities.

61. 　Ⓐ Ⓑ Ⓒ Ⓓ Ⓔ

62. (A) The United States Supreme Court has ruled that they may not ban films until critics have rated them for obscenity.
    (B) Critics having rated the film for obscenity, the United States Supreme Court then can censor it.
    (C) Without viewing a film, the United States Supreme Court has stated that it may not be called obscene.
    (D) Until critics have rated a film for obscenity, the United States Supreme Court has held that no censor may ban it.
    (E) No film may be banned, the United States Supreme Court has ruled, without a critic's having rated it for obscenity.

62. 　Ⓐ Ⓑ Ⓒ Ⓓ Ⓔ

63. (A) John who was running down the street rapidly turned the corner.
    (B) John who was running down the street turned rapidly the corner.
    (C) John who was running rapidly down the street turned the corner.
    (D) Rapidly John who was running down the street turned the corner.
    (E) John who was running down the street turned the rapid corner.

63. 　Ⓐ Ⓑ Ⓒ Ⓓ Ⓔ

64. (A) Mary likes oranges more better than bananas.
    (B) More than bananas, oranges are liked by Mary.
    (C) Bananas are less favored by Mary than oranges.
    (D) Oranges are more likable to Mary than are bananas.
    (E) Mary likes oranges better than she likes bananas.

64. 　Ⓐ Ⓑ Ⓒ Ⓓ Ⓔ

65. (A) When only five years old, my parents died in an automobile accident.
    (B) An automobile accident killed my parents at the age of five.
    (C) What with an automobile accident, my parents died, only five.
    (D) When my parents died in an automobile accident, I was only five years old.
    (E) At the age of five, my parents died, the result of an automobile accident.

65. 　Ⓐ Ⓑ Ⓒ Ⓓ Ⓔ

Directions: Questions 66–87 are each based on a short passage. Read the passage and then select the one best answer to the questions that follow the passage, using the information provided by or suggested in the passage.

66. A student said, "I didn't take my final examination today because I know the instructor doesn't like me and will fail me no matter how good my answers are or how much I write."

66. Ⓐ Ⓑ Ⓒ Ⓓ Ⓔ

The student is

(A) convinced that the teacher does not let her attitudes interfere with her evaluation of students
(B) blaming the teacher for something the teacher is not responsible for
(C) asking for a delay in the date of the examination for an illogical reason
(D) too ill to take the final examination
(E) too dumb to pass the examination anyhow

67. A radio pastor attacked the sin of adultery in many of his recorded messages aired nationwide. At least three of his followers admitted that they had committed adultery with him.

67. Ⓐ Ⓑ Ⓒ Ⓓ Ⓔ

The pastor

(A) covered up his own sin by attacking the sin in other people
(B) was not successful in raising money
(C) was a sinner, in his own opinion
(D) was not upset by the testimony of his three followers
(E) was an oversexed individual

68. The girl said, "If my father really liked me, he would allow me to date Billy, who really loves me. But my father never lets me do anything I want to do."

68. Ⓐ Ⓑ Ⓒ Ⓓ Ⓔ

The girl assumes that

(A) Billy has made a positive impression on her father
(B) her needs are very important to her father
(C) her father does not like young men
(D) Billy may not be in love with her
(E) her father has no reason to dislike Billy

69. The little boy said, "If you don't play by my rules, I am going to pick up my ball and go home. I won't play with you again."

69. Ⓐ Ⓑ Ⓒ Ⓓ Ⓔ

The little boy

(A) lives near the playing field
(B) is afraid of his playmates
(C) avoids a quarrel by leaving
(D) owns a very expensive ball
(E) is usually not hard to get along with

Questions 70-71 are based on the following:

The district attorney ordered all off-track betting parlors to close immediately. A survey of four of these parlors, the official revealed, showed that they were owned by members of an organized crime syndicate, and he concluded that the other 143 parlors were also controlled by the same group.

70. The district attorney
    (A) was acting within the law to close the betting parlors
    (B) closed all the betting parlors on the basis of accurate information
    (C) was only trying to impress the governor with his anti-crime program
    (D) made a decision based upon insufficient evidence
    (E) is planning to run for governor next year

71. The conclusion of the district attorney was that
    (A) the off-track betting parlors were taking too much money away from race tracks in the area
    (B) his chances for promotion would be improved if he could get a big case onto the front pages
    (C) all off-track betting parlors are controlled by the organized crime syndicate
    (D) working hard for convictions would make his reputation better
    (E) the governor would praise him for his anti-crime activities

72. A television commercial says, "Eat Mumbly-Wumblies, the new all-natural cereal. Mumbly-Wumblies contains more natural vitamin A than any other cereal tested."

A viewer is supposed to conclude that

    (A) the producers of the new cereal have used a large number of other cereals in the testing program
    (B) vitamin A may be insignificant in anyone's diet
    (C) an all-natural cereal provides a basis for a testing program
    (D) the cereal company has added nutrients to the cereal
    (E) testing of new cereals is not very important

Questions 73-74 are based on the following:

"Anyone who rides around in a Cadillac must be wealthy. I could never enjoy seeing anyone in that kind of car."

73. The person who made the statement
    (A) does not like Cadillacs
    (B) prefers European-made cars to those made in the United States
    (C) does not work for General Motors which makes the Cadillac
    (D) has rather negative feelings toward all luxury cars
    (E) does not like wealthy people

74. What assumption must we accept if we accept the statement as true?
    (A) The Cadillac is a car often found on the nation's highways.
    (B) Many wealthy people drive Cadillacs.
    (C) The speaker does not know much about luxury automobiles.
    (D) The Cadillac consumes too much gas.
    (E) The speaker has very few pleasures in his life.

75. A reporter wrote, "A noisy crowd clad in ragged blue jeans listened while their dirty, long-haired freak of a leader vomited his hatred of the United States over the whole mob."

Just through his choices of words, the reporter

(A) shows that he can write vividly
(B) demonstrates that he is sympathetic to the speaker
(C) implies that he did not want the assignment
(D) joined in to harass the speaker
(E) makes a negative comment about the speaker and the crowd

75. Ⓐ Ⓑ Ⓒ Ⓓ Ⓔ

76. "Sure my child broke a window in the school, but it was only a harmless prank. Now—that kid across the street—he's a real vandal. He broke two windows."

In this statement, the parent is

(A) not trying to excuse the child's behavior
(B) defending the kid across the street
(C) expressing an intense dislike for the kid across the street
(D) prepared to replace the window the child broke
(E) spoiling the child too much

76. Ⓐ Ⓑ Ⓒ Ⓓ Ⓔ

77. The speaker said, "We must strike the plant now for higher wages before we strike out in the battle against the decreasing purchasing power of our pay checks."

In this statement, the word *strike* is used twice. The word

(A) does not have exactly the same meaning in both places
(B) means the same thing in both places
(C) may have several different meanings in both places
(D) would be understood by his listeners
(E) should have been used by the speaker

77. Ⓐ Ⓑ Ⓒ Ⓓ Ⓔ

78. The owner of a small business complained that the government required him to fill out so many forms that he did not have time to look after his inventory or pay attention to the needs of his employees. Therefore, he hired a person whose sole responsibility was filling out forms, increasing prices in his store to pay the person's salary. The owner of the business was

(A) demonstrating a reasonable reaction to the situation
(B) increasing prices unnecessarily, thus adding to the nation's concerns about inflation
(C) caught between confusing government regulations
(D) not smart enough to handle paperwork
(E) opposed to all government regulations

78. Ⓐ Ⓑ Ⓒ Ⓓ Ⓔ

79. An advertisement says, "Buy a Denmark—the better car."

The writer of the ad

(A) tells a possible customer much about the quality of the car
(B) knows exactly how the reader will interpret *better*
(C) wants the reader to be impressed with the word *better*

79. Ⓐ Ⓑ Ⓒ Ⓓ Ⓔ

(D) has chosen to emphasize specific details rather than vagueness

(E) is not a very skillful writer

80. The old man said, "Things aren't what they used to be. Times were better then cause prices were lower, automobiles were not as expensive, and we didn't have television. Give me the good old days."

80. Ⓐ Ⓑ Ⓒ Ⓓ Ⓔ

The old man

(A) is at least ninety years old

(B) may remember only Mom's apple pie and not the spankings she gave him

(C) is obviously senile

(D) remembers that wages were also lower in the "Old days"

(E) has chosen to live for the rest of his life in a retirement home

81. "Everybody knows why we have had such wet springs and dry falls for the past ten years. It's the fault of those Chinese who have been testing atomic and hydrogen bombs in Tibet."

81. Ⓐ Ⓑ Ⓒ Ⓓ Ⓔ

The speaker

(A) knows all there is to know about weather forecasting

(B) is satisfied with the first answer that comes to his mind

(C) is an atomic scientist

(D) is a weatherperson for a local television station

(E) wants simple answers for complex questions

Questions 82-83 are based on the following dialogue:

John Birch Society (JBS) Member: "The whole government is full of Communists and Communist sympathizers. Just look at the amount of our trade with Russia."
Man: "What does your statement prove?"
JBS Member: "No country would advocate trade with Russia unless it were about to be swallowed up by Communism."

82. The John Birch Society Member

82. Ⓐ Ⓑ Ⓒ Ⓓ Ⓔ

(A) has considered all the evidence before reaching a conclusion

(B) uses words with neutral meanings to make his point

(C) has been an anti-Communist since the 1920s

(D) makes trading policies the equivalent of political ideas

(E) knows exactly what he is talking about

83. If we accept the conclusion of the JBS Member, we must also accept the conclusion that

83. Ⓐ Ⓑ Ⓒ Ⓓ Ⓔ

(A) our trade with Israel is anti-Arab

(B) our trade with South Africa means that we support segregation by race

(C) our trade with Arabs is anti-Israel

(D) our trade with Sweden means that we support a Socialist government

(E) all of the above

84. In one scene in *It Happened One Night*, Clark Gable appeared without an undershirt. The sales of undershirts dropped dramatically. These facts demonstrate that
    (A) many men refused to wear undershirts for no good reason
    (B) all men refuse to follow the leader
    (C) the film first played during the summer when it was too hot for men to wear undershirts
    (D) many men copied Clark Gable and refused to wear undershirts
    (E) many men found wearing undershirts detracted from their sex appeal.

84. Ⓐ Ⓑ Ⓒ Ⓓ Ⓔ

85. Chairperson: "No, I can't support our usual gift to the hospital this year."
    Club Member: "Why?"
    Chairperson: "Oh, I have several reasons."
    Club Member: "How many is several—two, four, six, eight?"

    In this dialogue, the club member is attempting

    (A) to obtain the gift for the hospital
    (B) to become chairperson next year
    (C) to save money for the club
    (D) to be as mean as possible
    (E) to make the chairperson be more specific

85. Ⓐ Ⓑ Ⓒ Ⓓ Ⓔ

86. "I cannot favor the plan to convert Main Street into an enclosed shopping mall, because I just heard that the architect who designed the project cheats at cards when he plays with friends."

    The speaker assumes that

    (A) his taxes will increase if the mall is built
    (B) a man, perhaps unethical in one area of his life, could not be trusted to do a good professional job
    (C) cheaters may be poor architects
    (D) his employer (another architect) should be given the job
    (E) one should always choose an architect on the basis of his card-playing ability

86. Ⓐ Ⓑ Ⓒ Ⓓ Ⓔ

87. The senator said, "You must support my bill to provide free breakfast for all poor children in our public and private schools. Voting against such a bill can only mean that you don't like poor children."

    The senator

    (A) has been a member of the Senate for many years
    (B) is not dealing with the possible cost of the proposal
    (C) is chairperson of a powerful subcommittee
    (D) has very few poor children in his state
    (E) does not often make statements he cannot support

87. Ⓐ Ⓑ Ⓒ Ⓓ Ⓔ

Directions: In questions 88–97, you are to compare various statements in the light of the questions posed. Pay attention to the tone, emphasis, and implications of each of the statements as you select the one response that is best in each case.

88. Which of the following sentences is the clearest statement of Sandy's attitude toward her boyfriend, Bob?
    (A) I love to ride in Bob's Corvette, especially when the top is down.
    (B) Bob always has his hair trimmed by the most expensive hair stylist in town.

88. Ⓐ Ⓑ Ⓒ Ⓓ Ⓔ

(C) As long as he gives me presents, who cares about anything else?

(D) Bob's clothes are always in the latest fashion.

(E) My mother doesn't think much of Bob as a possible son-in-law.

89. Which of the following advertising slogans tells the *least* about the quality of the product?

(A) "Merit Cigarettes are low in tar and nicotine."

(B) "The Dodge Omni is a new automobile, imported from Europe."

(C) "The Beef and Barrel Beltbuster, its largest hamburger, contains only Grade A ground beef."

(D) "Some Fords have been driven over 100,000 miles without major repairs."

(E) "The Michelin Guide gives The Bakery three stars for its excellent food and service."

90. Which of the following sentences makes the most negative comment about a new record album?

(A) This album is just another of the long series of disappointments from this group.

(B) The group's harmonies are all borrowed from old Beatle records.

(C) The lyrics and the music seem not to match very well.

(D) All of the songs have been recorded previously.

(E) The record jacket is very poorly designed.

91. Which of the following advertising slogans tells a consumer the *most* about the quality of the product?

(A) "Product K contains many vitamins."

(B) "Bon Ami hasn't scratched yet."

(C) "The Mercedes-Benz—the best engineered car on the road."

(D) "That's one of Ford's bright ideas."

(E) "Prudential Insurance—buy a piece of the rock."

92. Which of the following sentences represents most clearly Paul's attitude toward a tax increase for schools?

(A) All the school officials say that a tax increase is necessary to support education.

(B) Those deadbeats in the school's administration want another tax increase.

(C) If the schools would really teach, I would consider voting for a tax increase.

(D) A tax increase for schools right now has the support of the community.

(E) My accountant tells me that the increase, if approved, will not be great.

93. Which of the following sentences states Carl's strongest characteristic as president of a large corporation?

(A) Carl's leadership has created no great problems for the company.

(B) The company's profits have increased 10% during the past year.

(C) The company has bought out two competing companies within the past five years.

(D) The company's stock has risen 15% in price within the past six months.

(E) Carl knows how to get the best from his subordinates.

94. Which of the following sentences makes the most *positive* statement about Jill's ability as a cook?

94. Ⓐ Ⓑ Ⓒ Ⓓ Ⓔ

(A) Jill has memorized many famous recipes.

(B) Jill always uses the freshest ingredients available.

(C) Jill uses many recipes that she inherited from her grandmother.

(D) Jill can make a light-as-air soufflé when she wants to.

(E) Jill knows how to take the simplest ingredients and prepare a marvelous dish.

95. Which of the following sentences makes the most *negative* statement about Jill's ability as a cook?

95. Ⓐ Ⓑ Ⓒ Ⓓ Ⓔ

(A) Jill can only follow step-by-step directions in a recipe, adding little of her own.

(B) Jill does not always use the freshest ingredients in her dishes.

(C) Jill has only a few methods for disguising leftovers.

(D) Jill has every cookbook Myra Breckenridge ever published.

(E) Jill can't tell the differences among several types of pepper used in recipes.

96. Which of the following suggests that Shaun is *not* an unusually talented singer?

96. Ⓐ Ⓑ Ⓒ Ⓓ Ⓔ

(A) His supporting band played off-key once in a while.

(B) The drummer overpowered Shaun's voice with his pounding.

(C) He hits all the notes with little vocal expression.

(D) Shaun has the appearance of an immature teenager.

(E) Shaun's voice is not heavy enough for the selections he chose to sing.

97. Which of the following most clearly suggests a speaker's opinion about a new novel?

97. Ⓐ Ⓑ Ⓒ Ⓓ Ⓔ

(A) The dust jacket carries little information about the author.

(B) The publisher used a cheap, gray paper for the book.

(C) The book consists of six hundred tedious pages.

(D) I found eight typographical errors in one chapter.

(E) The author used at least two plot twists that amazed me.

Directions: In this group of questions, two underlined sentences are followed by a question or incomplete statement about them. Read each group of sentences and then choose the best answer to the question or the best completion of the statement.

98. Nat Cole made a fortune from his recordings.
"Paradise" was one of his best sellers.

98. Ⓐ Ⓑ Ⓒ Ⓓ Ⓔ

Sentence two

(A) makes an exception

(B) gives a contrast

(C) presents a conclusion

(D) provides an illustration

(E) draws a conclusion

99. The Rockefellers spent millions of dollars restoring the buildings in Williamsburg, Virginia.
The Governor's Mansion there is a masterpiece of colonial architecture.

What is a conclusion to be drawn from these two sentences?

(A) The Rockefellers wasted their money.
(B) Williamsburg, Virginia, is a small city.
(C) The Rockefellers are interested only in restoring colonial architecture.
(D) The Governor's Mansion may have been restored with Rockefeller money.
(E) The Governor's Mansion did not need to be restored.

100. Carolyn and Mark married very suddenly.
Five months later, Carolyn had an eight-pound boy.

A conclusion that could be drawn from these statements is

(A) Carolyn does not believe in abortion
(B) Carolyn was pregnant when she was married
(C) Mark was the father of the child
(D) Carolyn's parents forced Mark to marry her
(E) Mark can provide for a wife and child

101. Carrie Nation hated alcoholic beverages of all kinds.
She used a hatchet to wreck several saloons.

Sentence two

(A) makes a comparison
(B) states a result
(C) states a cause
(D) provides an illustration
(E) makes an exception

102. Most truck drivers who steer the big rigs belong to the Teamsters Union.
Jack Brophy owns his own truck and is an independent.

Sentence two

(A) provides an exception
(B) implies a comparison
(C) draws a conclusion
(D) defines a concept
(E) gives an illustration

103. Only bankers dress in dark-gray or black suits.
Josie Washichek wears a black pants suit to work every day.

A conclusion that could be drawn from these two sentences is

(A) Josie Washichek is a banker
(B) black suits are unattractive on women
(C) bankers frown on pastel-colored clothing
(D) bankers dress too conservatively
(E) women should not be bankers

104. John was sitting next to his mother on the front seat.
Mary was sitting next to her sister on the back seat.

The four persons in these two sentences are categorized by

(A) their blood relationship to each other
(B) how old they are
(C) how they look
(D) what they are sharing
(E) where they are located

105. Ford produces automobiles which last longer than those produced by other automakers.
My 1948 Ford is still running.

105. Ⓐ Ⓑ Ⓒ Ⓓ Ⓔ

What is happening in these two sentences?

(A) A generalization is supported with an example.
(B) A comparison is implied.
(C) A concept is being defined.
(D) An exception is stated.
(E) A working relationship is established.

106. The number of people on welfare in the United States is much too high.
My next door neighbor is on welfare.

106. Ⓐ Ⓑ Ⓒ Ⓓ Ⓔ

A reader could conclude that I think

(A) welfare checks are too high
(B) all people on welfare are deserving
(C) my neighbor has earned his welfare check
(D) my neighbor should not collect a welfare check
(E) welfare checks are wasted on the poor

107. Fresh orange juice contains vitamin C.
Everyone needs some vitamin C every day.

107. Ⓐ Ⓑ Ⓒ Ⓓ Ⓔ

A possible conclusion to be drawn from these two sentences is

(A) there are better sources than orange juice for vitamin C
(B) orange juice from California is better than orange juice from Florida
(C) too much vitamin C is bad for the kidneys
(D) some people may be allergic to vitamin C
(E) everyone should drink fresh orange juice

108. There are many varieties of Christianity.
All of the churches believe in Christ as a Supreme Being.

108. Ⓐ Ⓑ Ⓒ Ⓓ Ⓔ

What is happening in these sentences?

(A) Two objects are being compared.
(B) A conclusion is not implied.
(C) A concept is defined.
(D) No generalization is given.
(E) An example is given.

109. The Boeing 747 seats about 350 passengers.
The Douglas DC-10 seats about the same number.

109. Ⓐ Ⓑ Ⓒ Ⓓ Ⓔ

What is happening in these two sentences?

(A) Facts are arranged on the basis of passenger comfort.
(B) Facts are organized according to capacity.

(C) Facts are contrasted according to manufacturer.

(D) A conclusion is drawn on the basis of capacity.

(E) A concept is being defined.

110. My apple tree produced a poor crop this year.
My neighbor's plum tree produced an excellent crop.

110. Ⓐ Ⓑ Ⓒ Ⓓ Ⓔ

What is happening in these two sentences?

(A) A comparison is made on the basis of variety.

(B) A conclusion is being drawn.

(C) A recommendation is made on the basis of quantity.

(D) A contrast is made according to quality.

(E) A generalization is given.

111. Michigan produces a huge blueberry crop each summer.
Michigan also produces apples and cauliflower.

111. Ⓐ Ⓑ Ⓒ Ⓓ Ⓔ

The objects in these sentences are organized by

(A) cost of production

(B) kinds of fruits

(C) varieties of vegetables

(D) time of production

(E) source

112. I have gained twenty pounds within the past year.
None of my clothes fit me anymore.

112. Ⓐ Ⓑ Ⓒ Ⓓ Ⓔ

What is the relationship between these two sentences?

(A) Cause—effect

(B) Generalization—example

(C) An organization of facts by shapes

(D) Comparison—contrast

(E) Effect—cause

113. Cooking is my favorite hobby.
I have all of Julia Child's cookbooks.

113. Ⓐ Ⓑ Ⓒ Ⓓ Ⓔ

Sentence one

(A) produces an effect

(B) provides a cause

(C) makes a comparison

(D) implies a contrast

(E) makes a generalization

114. Yves St. Laurent designed many high fashion gowns.
Calvin Klein has many customers for his dresses.

114. Ⓐ Ⓑ Ⓒ Ⓓ Ⓔ

What is happening in these two sentences?

(A) An exception is being made.

(B) A contrast is established.

(C) A comparison is implied.

(D) A conclusion is being drawn.

(E) A concept is being defined.

115. If wishes were horses, all persons would ride.
I wish I had a Rolls Royce Silver Cloud.

What is happening in these two sentences?

(A) The Roll Royce is being compared to a horse.
(B) The speaker may be hoping a Rolls Royce will appear in his garage.
(C) A concept is being defined.
(D) A contrast between the Rolls Royce and a horse is established.
(E) An exception is being made.

115. A B C D E

116. The cinnamon is stored in a blue shaker.
The black pepper is kept in a red jar.

How are the spices organized in these sentences?

(A) According to their origins.
(B) According to their uses.
(C) According to their cost.
(D) According to their potency.
(E) According to the color of their containers.

116. A B C D E

117. Some department stores sell cheap merchandise.
Weiboldt's is a department store chain which has stores in the Chicago area.

What is the only logical conclusion which can be drawn from these statements?

(A) Wieboldt's sells cheap merchandise.
(B) Wieboldt's is a department store.
(C) Wieboldt's has a good reputation as a department store.
(D) Wieboldt's merchandise is questionable in quality.
(E) Wieboldt's probably does not sell cheap merchandise.

117. A B C D E

118. Inflation hurts everyone's pocketbook.
Inflation occurs when prices rise faster than wages do.

What is the function of sentence two?

(A) It provides a contrast.
(B) It draws a conclusion.
(C) It defines a concept.
(D) It makes a comparison.
(E) It makes a generalization.

118. A B C D E

Directions: Each of the questions or incomplete statements in questions 119–130 is followed by five suggested answers or completions. Select the one that is best in each case, paying attention to grammar, usage, diction, idiom, and tone.

Questions 119-121 are based on the following passage:

[1]Writing in the June 28 *Tribune*, David Rockefeller asserts that "rather than serving as the catalyst for free enterprise and individual industry, government increasingly stands as a roadblock." [2]Mr. Rockefeller goes on to cite the enormous cost of government regulation, and he applauds the efforts of various business lobbying organizations that are attempting to stem the tide of encroaching government with economic freedom. [3]The defeat of the Consumer Protection Agency, Mr. Rockefeller especially

praised. [4]It appears that Mr. Rockefeller fails to grasp the real reason for this government interference, and consequently he fails to see how business can very easily and very cheaply put a stop to the interference.

Adapted from the *Chicago Tribune*, July 19, 1978. Courtesy of the *Chicago Tribune*.

119. Sentence three might be phrased to read
   (A) Mr. Rockefeller especially praised the defeat of the Consumer Protection Agency.
   (B) The defeat of the Consumer Protection Agency had been especially not praised by Mr. Rockefeller.
   (C) Especially praising the defeat of the Consumer Protection Agency by Rockefeller.
   (D) The Consumer Protection Agency was praised for the defeat of the special Mr. Rockefeller.
   (E) The especial defeat of Mr. Rockefeller was praised by the Consumer Protection Agency.

119. Ⓐ Ⓑ Ⓒ Ⓓ Ⓔ

120. If the passage were divided into two paragraphs, the most logical point for paragraph two to begin is
   (A) sentence 2
   (B) sentence 3
   (C) sentence 4
   (D) either sentence 2 or sentence 3
   (E) either sentence 3 or sentence 4

120. Ⓐ Ⓑ Ⓒ Ⓓ Ⓔ

121. What should be done with sentence 2?
   (A) It should be omitted.
   (B) It should be replaced by sentence 4.
   (C) It should be left as it is.
   (D) It should come after sentence 4.
   (E) It should come after sentence 3.

121. Ⓐ Ⓑ Ⓒ Ⓓ Ⓔ

Questions 122-124 are based on the following passage:

[1]Is there a malevolent force that snares ships and planes in the Bermuda Triangle? [2]Has the Earth been visited by intelligent extraterrestial beings in UFOs? [3]Proponents ask people to believe in these phenomena as a matter of faith, since there has been no good scientific evidence to support their existence. [4]But then there have been crackpots around for thousands of years! [5]The newest addition to this list of unsubstantiated claims is the contention by David Rorvik that a human baby has been cloned (*In His Image: The Cloning of a Man:* J. B. Lippincott Co.; $8.95). [6]Cloning involves the genetic manipulation of cells to produce identical genetic copies of an organism.

Adapted from the *Chicago Tribune*, July 19, 1978. Courtesy of the *Chicago Tribune*.

122. What should be done with sentence 4?
   (A) It should be left as it is.

122. Ⓐ Ⓑ Ⓒ Ⓓ Ⓔ

(B) It should be combined with sentence 3.
(C) It should be omitted.
(D) It should be placed after sentence 6.
(E) It should be placed before sentence 1.

123. If the question in sentence 2 were changed to a statement, it would logically begin

123. Ⓐ Ⓑ Ⓒ Ⓓ Ⓔ

(A) By intelligent beings
(B) In UFOs
(C) Intelligent beings
(D) Working with UFOs
(E) The Earth has been visited

124. If the passage were divided into three paragraphs, the sentences which would logically begin those two new paragraphs are, respectively,

124. Ⓐ Ⓑ Ⓒ Ⓓ Ⓔ

(A) sentences 3 and 4
(B) sentences 5 and 6
(C) sentences 3 and 6
(D) sentences 3 and 5
(E) sentences 4 and 5

Questions 125-127 are based on the following passage:

[1]A few issues back I discussed some of the questions raised for the gay community by the presence of openly gay candidates. [2]Beyond this area of community/candidate interaction, however, there is the vital topic of a candidate's position on the issues. [3]Even given the ideal community/ candidate relationship, a candidate with a "bad" opinion on the issues should not be supported just because she/he is gay. [4]What's a good position? [5]That's what I'd like to explore here. [6]The gay movement and most, if not all, gay candidates have taken a "human rights" approach to gay issues; slogans like "gay rights are human rights" have appeared regularly in gay media and campaigns. [7]In such a situation the phrase "human rights" can easily become just a code word for gay rights, even as "gay" was once a code word. [8]But if movements and candidates are to remain honest and principled, clearly a "human rights" campaign has to encompass more than just support for gay rights—after all, there are many other groups, as we should all know, who have been denied their human rights, and gay people go beyond this (slogan).

Reprinted from *GayLife*, February 17, 1978, by permission.

125. If this passage were to be divided into two paragraphs, paragraph two would logically begin with

125. Ⓐ Ⓑ Ⓒ Ⓓ Ⓔ

(A) sentence 5
(B) sentence 6
(C) sentence 2
(D) sentence 8
(E) sentence 7

126. Sentences 7 and 8 might be joined together. Which of the following revisions is correct?

126. Ⓐ Ⓑ Ⓒ Ⓓ Ⓔ

(A) a code word, if movements

(B) a code word, but if movements

(C) a code word; movements and

(D) a code word, therefore if movements

(E) a code word, but, therefore and however, if

127. Which of the following would serve as a logical conclusion for this passage? 127. Ⓐ Ⓑ Ⓒ Ⓓ Ⓔ

(A) Therefore, let us look at a candidate's whole platform, not just his position on gay rights.

(B) Who cares whether a candidate can interact with the community?

(C) "Human rights" is just a slogan that does not mean much for a candidate for public office.

(D) Gay rights are of lesser importance than human rights.

(E) Let's all support any candidate who says he/she will support gay rights.

Questions 128-130 are based on the following passage:

[1]Through your years of high school you have been exposed to a number of courses labeled "English" or something of the sort. [2]Beginning about the fifth grade in most schools, the rules of grammar are stressed again and again, and it is quite possible that you became bored with the whole process of learning "English." [3]The stated aim of most of these courses was to teach you how to use the English language effectively in speaking and writing as well as in listening and reading. [4]In many instances you were assigned rules to learn, exercises to prepare, perhaps some sentences to diagram or analyze, themes to write, and so on. [5]In many instances, you have learned how to use the English language to a degree, but many of you may believe that you could improve your English skills in many ways.

128. Sentence 2 should 128. Ⓐ Ⓑ Ⓒ Ⓓ Ⓔ

(A) come before sentence 1

(B) come after sentence 5

(C) come just after sentence 1

(D) come after sentence 4

(E) come before sentence 4

129. The section of sentence 5 beginning *but many of you* seems to introduce an idea which has not been introduced earlier in the passage. That section of sentence 5 129. Ⓐ Ⓑ Ⓒ Ⓓ Ⓔ

(A) should be left as it is

(B) should be revised so that the material introduced is more logically connected with the rest of the passage

(C) should be omitted

(D) should be moved to be a part of sentence 1

(E) should be made a part of sentence 2

130. *to teach you how to use* in sentence 3 might be reworded. Which of the following is the correct new version? 130. Ⓐ Ⓑ Ⓒ Ⓓ Ⓔ

(A) teaching you the using

(B) to teach you how the using

(C) teaching you how to use

(D) to teach you about the usefulness

(E) to teach you about using

ANSWER KEY — TRIAL TEST

Part I

1.	D	14.	A	27.	B	40.	C	53.	D
2.	C	15.	B	28.	A	41.	A	54.	A
3.	B	16.	B	29.	E	42.	E	55.	B
4.	E	17.	C	30.	D	43.	B	56.	A
5.	A	18.	E	31.	B	44.	C	57.	E
6.	A	19.	A	32.	A	45.	D	58.	D
7.	C	20.	B	33.	C	46.	A	59.	C
8.	E	21.	A	34.	C	47.	D	60.	E
9.	D	22.	D	35.	E	48.	E	61.	B
10.	C	23.	E	36.	D	49.	B	62.	D
11.	B	24.	D	37.	D	50.	C	63.	C
12.	A	25.	C	38.	A	51.	A	64.	E
13.	E	26.	B	39.	A	52.	C	65.	D

Part II

66.	B	77.	A	88.	C	99.	D	110.	D	121.	B
67.	A	78.	A	89.	B	100.	B	111.	E	122.	C
68.	E	79.	C	90.	A	101.	B	112.	A	123.	E
69.	C	80.	B	91.	C	102.	A	113.	B	124.	D
70.	D	81.	E	92.	B	103.	A	114.	C	125.	B
71.	C	82.	D	93.	E	104.	E	115.	B	126.	B
72.	A	83.	E	94.	E	105.	A	116.	E	127.	A
73.	E	84.	D	95.	A	106.	D	117.	B	128.	D
74.	B	85.	E	96.	C	107.	E	118.	C	129.	C
75.	E	86.	B	97.	C	108.	C	119.	A	130.	E
76.	C	87.	B	98.	D	109.	B	120.	C		

SCORING CHART—TRIAL TEST

After you have scored your Trial Test, enter the results in the chart below (the Raw Score computation is explained on page 14); then transfer your Raw Score to the Progress Chart on page 14. As you complete the Sample Examinations later in this part, you should be able to achieve increasingly higher Raw Scores.

Total Test	Number Right	Number Wrong	Number Omitted	Raw Score
Part I:				
Part II:				
Total:				

ANSWER EXPLANATIONS—TRIAL TEST

Part I

1. D. (A) is incorrect because less is a poor choice of words. (B) and (E) are wordy and inexact. (C) is incorrect because the meaning is changed.

2. C. (A) is incorrect; it contains a double negative (couldn't hardly). (B) is wordy and awkward. (D) changes the meaning of the original. (E) is wordy and awkward.

3. B. (A) contains a cliché (stew in the juice) and is too slangy. (C) and (E) change the meaning of the original. (D) contains a mixed metaphor (stew in their own consequences).

4. E. (A) is incorrect because as completely as is not an effective idiom in written English. (C) is wordy and ambiguous. (B) and (D) are not clear.

5. A. (B) changes the meaning of the original sentence. (C) is incorrect because there is no indication in the original sentence that Bruce is alert. (D) and (E) add details that are not in the original sentence.

6. A. (B), (C), and (E) are incorrect because fortunes and fortunate are not synonyms. (D) is incorrect because it changes the meaning of the original.

7. C. (A) is incorrect, for the reason is . . . because is redundant, therefore wordy. (B) contains very unique, an incorrect comparison form; unique means different from anything else; therefore, it cannot be compared. (D) changes the meaning of the original sentence. (E) incorrectly reduces an independent clause to a modifier.

8. E. (A) contains and that she which destroys the correct parallelism (two verb phrases) of the original. In (B) the phrase having hidden in the closet is a dangling modifier. In (C) they has no specific antecedent. In (D), the clause beginning with which is another dangling modifier.

9. D. (A) (B) and (C) are ambiguous, therefore vague. (E) adds information that is not in the original.

10. C. (A) is incorrect because it changes the meaning of the original (notice the word doubt). (B) is incorrect because they has no specific antecedent. (D) contains a dangling modifier, beginning believing. (E) is incorrect because of the misplaced who.

11. B. In (A) we is an incorrect case form. In (C) so that creates an ambiguous clause. In (D) pleasantly is an adverb; the adjective form pleasant is required. (E) changes the meaning of the original sentence.

12. A. In (B) they has no specific antecedent. (C) is a sentence fragment. In (D) the construction was when is incorrect. (E) changes the meaning of the original.

13. E. In (A) that type person is not a correct idiom in written English. Choices (B) and (C) would create a sentence fragment. In (D) those same people is unclear because those has no specific antecedent.

14. A. Choice (B) would create a sentence fragment. In (C) and (D) they has no specific antecedent. In (E) the phrase without charge is ambiguous.

15. B. In (A) the introductory phrase is a dangling modifier. (C) is a confused awkward sentence. In (D) where is an incorrect choice of words; that would be correct. (E) establishes an incorrect cause-effect relationship.

16. B. Choice (A), (D), and (E) would create a sentence fragment. (C) would contain incorrect parallel structures before and after and.

17. C. (A) contains a plural subject (thief and his accomplices) and a singular verb (was), an error in agreement. (B) contains a singular subject (thief) and a plural verb (were), an agreement error. In (D), both semi-colons are used incorrectly. In (E), there is a singular subject (thief) and a plural verb (were), an error in agreement.

18. E. In (A) and (B) anyone and their represent an error in agreement. (C) contains whom, an incorrect case form; who would be correct. In (D) the phrase beginning having could modify Rudolph or child, a squinting modifier.

19. A. (B) changes the meaning of the original sentence. (C) is not an exact statement of the original. In (D) the phrase must be as young as to establish a correct comparison. (E) is incorrect because not younger as is illogical.

20. B. (A) is incorrect because without is not a conjunction and what follows is a complete dependent clause. (C) is incorrect because unless creates an ambiguous sentence. (D) is incorrect; Whatever I talk is illogical. (E) is ambiguous when that version is compared to the original sentence.

21. A. The semi-colons are used incorrectly in (B), (C), and (E). (D) is wordy because of the unnecessary repetition of <u>and</u>. Besides, if <u>and</u> were used, the commas would be incorrect.

22. D. In (A), (B), and (C), the introductory phrase is a dangling modifier, an illogical sentence structure. (E) is an ambiguous sentence.

23. E. (A), (B), and (D) change the meaning of the original sentence. In (C), <u>he</u> has no antecedent; in the original sentence, the novelist is identified as female.

24. D. (A) is incorrect because <u>real estate, municipal bonds, or put</u> . . . are not parallel in structure. (B) is wordy and awkward in construction. (C) changes the meaning of the original sentence. In (E) <u>as common stock</u> omits the word <u>buying</u> after <u>as</u>, which would make the phrase correct.

25. C. In (A) the two groups of words after <u>whether</u> are not parallel in structure: a subject-verb and an infinitive. In (B) there is a similar lack of parallelism after <u>if</u>. (D) is confused and awkward. In (E) <u>his</u> inserted before <u>seeking</u> would make the choice correct.

26. B. In (A), <u>uninterested</u> is an incorrect word choice. (C), (D), and (E) are incorrect. Note the difference in meaning between <u>uninterested</u> and <u>disinterested</u>; the two words are not synonyms and are often confused.

27. B. In (A), <u>to enjoy</u> creates an ambiguous sentence. In (C) the group of words after the dash is ambiguous. (D) adds some information not included in the original sentence. In (E) the three phrases after <u>enjoys</u> are not parallel in structure.

28. A. In (B) the comma before <u>problem</u> is incorrect. In (C) <u>their</u> (third person) represents a shift in person from <u>you</u> (second person). (D) adds <u>and which</u> creates an error in parallelism. In (E) the semi-colon produces a confusing sentence.

29. E. In (A) the comma produces a comma splice. In (B) <u>they</u> and <u>their</u> have no specific antecedents. In (C) the two parts of the sentence (before and after the semi-colon) do not function together logically. In (D) <u>and</u> creates an error in parallelism.

30. D. (A), (B), and (E) are wordy. (C) implies a condition that may not be true.

31. B. All other choices are wordy and ambiguous. (A) is redundant; <u>consensus</u> means the opinion of a group.

32. A. All other choices are wordy or ambiguous.

33. C. (C) is the only choice which produces a clear, logical, unambiguous sentence.

34. C. All other choices are words which would be illogical in the sentence.

35. E. All the other choices would create wordy or ambiguous sentences.

36. D. (A) seems to compare <u>results</u> with <u>physicists</u>. (B) seems to compare <u>products</u> with <u>physicists</u>. (C) and (E) are wordy.

37. D. (C) is wordy. (A), (B), and (E) contain poor word choices, the first word in each phrase.

38. A. In (B) <u>just about</u> is a vague phrase. In (C) <u>worthy</u> is a poor word choice. (D) is wordy, and (E) is ambiguous.

39. A. <u>unique</u> and <u>perfect</u> in (C) and (E) are adjectives which logically cannot be preceded by <u>most</u>. (B) uses <u>delighting</u> incorrectly. (D) uses <u>thoughtful</u> illogically.

40. C. Insomnia, especially if long standing, is one of the most troublesome of man's afflictions as well as one . . . .

41. A. Communists have permitted few Americans to visit mainland China since Chiang fled to Formosa in 1948.

42. E. Everyone finds it incomprehensible that I can eat and . . . .

43. B. Some unstable women whose marriages fail and who are bereft of a husband at a fairly early age suffer irreversible traumas.

44. C. With the doleful sound of the funeral bell reverberating through the village, we could see the dismal cortege winding . . . .

45. D. Java, one of the most densely populated areas in the world with more than twelve hundred people per square mile, does not need an increasing birth rate.

46. A. Hard cash pleases me more than the mere satisfaction of a job well done, in spite of what old timers say.

47. D. The sun's rays illuminating each small piece of colored glass and radiating glorious hues throughout the cathedral create a really spectacular effect.

48. E. An enemy could quite easily conquer the United States, if its population ever becomes predominantly submissive and passive.

49. B. Paul McCartney has had as much influence upon contemporary popular music as, if not more than, almost any other composer with the possible exception of Johann Sebastian Bach.

50. C. If a man constantly represses his feelings and sublimates his desires, psychiatrists say that his real personality can become distorted.

51. A. Some beautiful gypsum deposits on the walls of Kentucky's Mammoth Cave have resulted from the slow evaporation of underground waters.

52. C. Some traditional ideas about the possibility of teaching a deaf child to speak have been altered by the advent of new techniques for identifying deafness in babies.

53. D. The hiker, weary after his twenty-mile walk, rested for half an hour; then he picked up his pack and walked off into the west again.

54. A. There are some doctors who say that about half of their patients' problems are psychosomatic in origin rather than caused by any actual diseases.

55. B. If an author expects a literary critic to praise a novel, he must provide some new twists on a traditional plot and writing that is free of clichés.

56. A. A good recipe lists each ingredient of a dish as well as the exact amount of each the cook should use.

57. E. Minimal brain dysfunction causes certain learning difficulties in about five per cent of all American school children.

58. D. That ghetto children of pre-kindergarten age learn rapidly but soon regress if nothing is done to improve their home situations was one startling conclusion drawn by researchers from data accumulated during the Head Start program.

59. C. The president announced that labor leaders had given him a tacit commitment not to demand exorbitant wage increases upon the expiration of current union contracts.

60. E. As a black, James Baldwin met bigotry and intolerance wherever he went in the United States; therefore, he fled to Europe as a young man.

61. B. In (A) the phrase beginning according is a misplaced modifier; it should be at the beginning of the sentence. The word overpraise in (C) may overstate the critic's opinion. In (D) them has no specific antecedent. (E) is wordy, especially the phrase the reason why.

62. D. In (A) they has no specific antecedent. (B) states a condition which does not exist; the Supreme Court is not a censor. In (C), the introductory phrase is a dangling modifier. In (E) without is illogical.

63. C. In (A) rapidly is a squinting modifier. In (B) and (D) rapidly is a misplaced modifier. (E) is illogical—how can a corner be rapid?

64. E. In (A) better cannot be preceded by more. (B), (C), and (D) are awkward sentences.

65. D. In (A) the phrase beginning When is a dangling modifier. In (B) the phrase beginning at is also a dangling modifier. (C) is wordy and ambiguous. In (E) the phrase beginning at is a dangling modifier.

Part II

66. B. Choice (A) is an illogical response to the statement. (C) and (D) use facts not in the original statement. (E) is an illogical inference from the statement.

67. A. (B) and (D) go beyond the facts in the statement. (C) and (E) are illogical inferences from the statement.

68. E. (A), (C), and (D) are illogical inferences from the statement. (B) seems to contradict the original statement.

69. C. (A), (B), (D), and (E) contain inferences which cannot logically be drawn from the statement.
70. D. (A), (C), and (E) go beyond the facts in the statement. (B) is incorrect because the district attorney had information about only four.
71. C. (A), (B), (D), and (E) cannot logically be inferred from the original statement.
72. A. (B), (C), (D), and (E) cannot logically be inferred from the statement.
73. E. Conclusions in (A), (B), (C), and (D) require facts which are not in the original statement.
74. B. (A), (C), (D), and (E) are illogical inferences from the statement.
75. E. (A) is wrong because the writing is not especially vivid. (B), (C), and (D) are incorrect because they are illogical inferences.
76. C. (A), (B), (D), and (E) are unwarranted conclusions from the statement.
77. A. It is clear that the speaker is using a pun on the word strike; therefore (B), (C), (D), and (E) cannot be correct.
78. A. (B) is incorrect because the statement gives a good reason for the increase in prices. (C) is incorrect because the statement does not say that government regulations are confusing but that there are too many forms to be filled out. There are no facts in the statement to support conclusions (D) and (E).
79. C. (A) is wrong because better tells a buyer very little about the quality of the car. (B) and (E) are unwarranted conclusions from the facts given. (D) is incorrect; the statement provides nothing specific.
80. B. The conclusions in (A), (C), and (E) have no facts in the statement to support them.
81. E. Conclusions (A), (B), (C), and (D) are based on inadequate evidence.
82. D. (A) is incorrect because we do not know what facts the speaker used. (B) is incorrect because many words and phrases are clearly anti-Communist. (C) is an unwarranted inference. (E) is a gross overstatement.
83. E. (E) is the only possible correct answer.
84. D. The conclusions in (A), (C), and (E) cannot be supported by the facts in the statement. (B) contradicts the original statement.
85. E. The conclusions drawn in (A), (B), (C) and (D) go beyond the facts in the statement.
86. B. The conclusions in (A), (C), and (D) are not supported by the facts in the statement. (E) states a ridiculous basis for choosing an architect.
87. B. The conclusions in (A), (C), and (D) cannot be supported by the facts in the statement. We do not know enough to judge the conclusion in (E).
88. C. (A) shows an attitude toward Bob's car. (B) shows an attitude toward his hair style. (D) shows her attitude toward his clothes. (E) shows the mother's attitude, not Sandy's.
89. B. The other choices tell the reader something about the quality of the product or restaurant.
90. A. (C) and (E) are also negative but not as negative as (A). (B) and (D) may or may not be negative.
91. C. (C) is the only choice which has something specific about quality; the others are vaguely phrased slogans.
92. B. (A) tells us about school officials, not Paul. (C) does not tell us much about Paul's attitude. (D) and (E) focus on the opinions of people other than Paul.
93. E. (A), (B), (C), and (D) may be true, but there is no evidence that Carl's leadership caused these results.
94. E. (A) and (C) say nothing about Jill's ability as a cook. (B) and (D) show only two characteristics of a good cook and do not make a complete evaluation.
95. A. All of the statements are negative, but (A) is the most negative.
96. C. (A), (B), and (D) say nothing about Shaun's singing. (E) says something about his poor selection of material, not about his abilities as a singer.
97. C. (A), (B), and (D) say nothing about the contents of the novel. (E) is ambiguous because the statement could be positive or negative. Note the word tedious in (C).

98. D. (A), (B), (C), and (E) are incorrect.
99. D. (A), (B), (C), and (E) are unwarranted conclusions.
100. B. (A), (C), (D), and (E) cannot be supported by the facts in the statement.
101. B. (A) is incorrect because no two things are being compared. (C) is incorrect because sentence 2 does not state a cause. (D) is incorrect because sentence 2 does not illustrate. (E) is wrong because it does not make an exception.
102. A. (A) is the only possible correct answer.
103. A. (B), (C), (D), and (E) are unwarranted conclusions from the facts.
104. E. The location of the people in the car is the only possible answer. (A) is incorrect, because the people in the front seat may have no blood relationship to the people in the back seat.
105. A. Not one of the other choices is applicable.
106. D. (A) is incorrect because the sentences say nothing about the amount of each check. (B), (C), and (E) are unwarranted conclusions.
107. E. (A), (B), (C), and (D) are unwarranted conclusions.
108. C. Sentence 2 defines at least one concept of Christianity. The other choices are incorrect.
109. B. (A) is incorrect—the sentences say nothing about passenger comfort. (C) is incorrect because there is no contrast between the plane makers; they are merely different companies. (D) is wrong because no conclusion is drawn. (E) is incorrect because there is no definition here.
110. D. (A) is incorrect; there is no comparison of varieties. (B) is wrong; there is no conclusion. (C) is incorrect; there is no recommendation. (E) is incorrect; there is no generalization.
111. E. The source of the fruits and vegetables (Michigan) is the only basis of organization.
112. A. (B) is wrong; there is no generalization. (C) is wrong; shapes are not mentioned. (D) is wrong; no two things are being compared. (E) reverses the correct answer.
113. B. (B) is the only possible correct answer.
114. C. A comparison between Yves St. Laurent and Calvin Klein is implied; no other answer is correct.
115. B. (A) and (D) are incorrect because there is no comparison or contrast here. (C) is incorrect; no concept is defined. (E) is incorrect; no exception is made.
116. E. No other answer supports the facts given in the two sentences.
117. B. All other responses are false inferences which cannot logically be made.
118. C. Sentence 2 defines the generalization in sentence one. The other choices are incorrect.
119. A. (B) contradicts the original sentence. (C) is a sentence fragment. (D) and (E) are incorrect; Mr. Rockefeller was not defeated.
120. C. Sentence 4 seems to introduce a conclusion to a longer editorial or news story, and a new paragraph might well begin here.
121. B. Sentences 2 and 4 say almost the same thing, and there is no need for the repetition.
122. C. Sentence 4 adds an editorial word (crackpots) which destroys the factual quality of the rest of the paragraph.
123. E. The other choices would create a nonsense sentence.
124. D. Sentences 1 and 2 ask questions. Sentence 3 is a generalization which could well begin a paragraph. Sentence 5 is what may be the beginning of a review of the book.
125. B. Sentence 6 begins the author's exploration of issues raised in sentences 1, 2, and 3.
126. B. The period between sentences 7 and 8 could be easily replaced with a comma with no other changes being necessary in either sentence.
127. A. The whole paragraph demands this sentence as a conclusion; any other choice would distort what the writer has said.
128. D. Sentence 2 is out of place just after sentence 1, and the paragraph is more coherent if sentence 2 immediately follows sentence 4.
129. C. The last part of sentence 5 is out of place in the paragraph and should be omitted.
130. E. All the other choices would create awkward or ambiguous sentences.

CHAPTER

4 Background and Practice Questions

Note: The College-Level Examination Program (CLEP) has three different examinations which cover the material a student is supposed to master in an English composition course:

1. The English composition examination in the General Examinations battery for which this chapter is a guide
2. A CLEP subject examination named *College Composition*
3. A CLEP subject examination named *Freshman English*

BE SURE YOU KNOW WHICH OF THE THREE EXAMINATIONS THE INSTITUTION TO WHICH YOU WILL SEND YOUR SCORES WILL ACCEPT, AND TAKE THE PROPER EXAMINATION. Barron's has also published a guide to the two subject examinations which you might want to consult once you know the specific examination the college requires you to submit scores for.

The English Composition Examination of the General Examinations battery is offered in two forms:

1. An all multiple-choice test consisting of 120–130 multiple-choice questions divided into two separately timed 45-minute sections. This is the form of the trial test given in the last chapter and of the three sample exams given later.
2. A combination of multiple-choice and essay test consisting of Section I (60–65 multiple-choice items requiring 45 minutes) and Section II (a written composition on an assigned topic which also requires 45 minutes). This version of the test is not available each time a CLEP test is administered by a national testing center. Therefore, you will need to check with your college to be sure you are taking the version it accepts and with the test center to be sure when that version is being offered.

As you probably noticed while taking the trial test the questions deal with logical and structural relationships within sentences, between sentences, and between paragraphs. Part I of both versions of the examination deals with logical and structural relationships within sentences. The following abilities are tested in Part I:

- Ability to reword sentences to change emphasis or phrasing or to improve clarity (about 75–80% of the questions)
- Ability to choose the word or phrase that best conveys an intended meaning (about 15–20% of the questions)
- Ability to recognize ambiguity and confusing inexactness of communication (about 5–10% of the questions)

Part II of both versions of the examination focuses on logical and structural relationships between the sentences and within and between paragraphs. Questions in Part II of the all-multiple-choice version require the following abilities:

- Ability to recognize writing that is illogical or uses poorly supported generalization (about 33% of the questions)
- Ability to recognize underlying assumptions and particular attitudes conveyed through tone and implication rather than through the literal meaning of the words (about 15–20% of the questions)
- Ability to determine the relationships between sentences, such as cause and effect, comparison and contrast, example and supporting generalization, chronological organization (about 33% of the questions)
- Ability to determine the logical order of sentences in a paragraph, to identify irrelevant sentences, to improve the connection between ideas, and to designate where the introduction of new ideas calls for a new paragraph (about 15–20% of the questions)

Candidates taking Part II of the version with essay are expected to demonstrate that they have the abilities listed above for Part II of the all-multiple-choice version and that they can write an effective essay which addresses a given topic and uses the structures and conventions of standard written English.

All multiple-choice items are based upon the generally accepted conventions of standard written English, not conversational English. This means that many expressions, constructions, and sentence patterns that may be acceptable in spoken English are not accepted as standard usage in written form. If you would like to review the conventions of standard written English forms, consult any handbook of English published by many major publishing companies or one of the texts listed below.

Axelrod, R.B., and Charles R. Cooper. *The St. Martin's Guide to Writing*. New York: St. Martin's Press, 1985

Chaffee, John. *Thinking Critically*. Boston: Houghton-Mifflin, 1985

Dornan, Edward A., and Charles W. Dawes. *The Brief English Handbook*. Boston: Little, Brown and Co., 1985

Gale, C., and M. Bromberg. *Building an Effective Vocabulary*. Woodbury, N.Y.: Barron's Educational Series, Inc., 1979

Guth, Hans P. *New Concise Handbook*. Belmont, CA: Wadsworth, Publishing Co., 1985

Hodges, John C., and Mary E. Whitten. *Harbrace College Handbook*. 10th Edition. New York: Harcourt Brace Jovanovich, 1985

Hopper, V.F., C. Gale, and R.C. Foote. *Essentials of English*. 3rd Edition. Woodbury, N.Y.: Barron's Educational Series, Inc., 1982

Hopper, V.F., and C. Gale. Revised by B. W. Griffith. *Essentials of Writing*. 3rd Edition. Woodbury, NY: Barron's Educational Series, Inc., 1983

Marius, Richard, and Harvey S. Weiner. *The McGraw-Hill Handbook*. New York: McGraw-Hill Book Co., 1985

McCrimmon, James M. *Writing with a Purpose*. 8th Edition. Boston: Houghton-Mifflin, 1985

Moore, W. Edgar. *Creative and Critical Thinking*. Boston: Houghton-Mifflin Co., 1967

Nordquist, Richard. *Writing Exercises: Building, Combining, and Revising*. New York: Macmillan Publishing Co., 1985

Strunk, William, and E.B. White. *The Elements of Style*. 3rd Edition. New York: Macmillan Publishing Co., 1979

Waddell, M.L., R. Walker, and R. Esch. *The Art of Styling Sentences*. 2nd Edition. Woodbury, N.Y.: Barron's Educational Series, Inc., 1983

This chapter is organized around the eight different types of test items which you will encounter on Parts I and II of an actual CLEP examination, plus some material on the essay version of Part II. In the introductory matter, each type of item will be illustrated and some explanations will be given so that you will know how to arrive at the appropriate answer in each case. Answers and answer explanations for all questions will be provided. In the next chapter, you will find three sample CLEP English Composition Examinations based on Parts I and II, set up exactly as you will find them in an actual testing situation. We can only offer general guidance on the essay version of Part II, because each writing sample will be read and rated by English teachers, and there is no accurate way we can predict how different individuals will react to specific compositions.

Study these eight types of items to which we have attached a name, work through the illustrations of each one; and then try your hand at a complete simulated examination in the next chapter.

Part I (to be taken by all students)

Type 1: The Sentence Variety Item: about 45% of items in Part I

Directions: For each of these questions, you are to choose the version of the underlined sentences or part of the sentence that not only has the same or nearly the same meaning as the original but follows the requirements of standard written English. That is, in selecting the version that matches the underlined part in meaning, pay attention to grammar, choice of words, sentence structure, and punctuation. The answer you select should, when inserted in the original sentence, produce an effective sentence – clear and exact, without awkwardness or ambiguity.

1. Whomever we select to represent us at the national convention will have <u>her costs defrayed from</u> the funds of the local organization.   1. Ⓐ Ⓑ Ⓒ Ⓓ Ⓔ
    (A) received an expense-free trip from
    (B) not one penny to pay out of her own pocket but from
    (C) a prepaid ticket and eating money from among
    (D) enjoyed a free trip at the expense of
    (E) her expenses paid from

    The correct answer is (E).

    Explanation: (A) is not correct because *expense-free* does not mean the same thing as the phrase in the original sentence.
    (B) is ineffective because it uses too many words to make the point.
    (C) is wrong because the word *among* confuses the sense of the sentence.
    (D) is ineffective because this version is ambiguous (not clear).

2. In these times of social change, we can now see that our past <u>was not as</u> <u>great</u> as we thought it was.
   (A) has not always been as nearly perfect   (D) was not the ideal state
   (B) was not the state of perfectable bliss   (E) has not been as near ideal
   (C) has not ever been so delightful

2.   Ⓐ Ⓑ Ⓒ Ⓓ Ⓔ

The correct answer is (A).

Explanation: (B) is incorrect because the phrase *perfectable bliss* is ambiguous and does not mean the same thing as the phrase in the original sentence.
(C) is incorrect because *so* sets up an incorrect parallellism with *as*.
(D) is incorrect because it does not mean the same thing as the original phrase.
(E) is incorrect because *near* must be an adverb form — *nearly*.

3. The minister disappointed his congregation <u>in the course of his initial</u> sermon in which he asked for larger contributions.
   (A) by his initial first   (D) by his first sample
   (B) during his first   (E) by his opening introductory
   (C) with his inaugural beginning

3.   Ⓐ Ⓑ Ⓒ Ⓓ Ⓔ

The correct answer is (B).

Explanation: (A), (C), and (E) are incorrect because each contains two words which mean the same thing.
(D) is incorrect because the meaning is not the same.

4. <u>It is a sad characteristic of today's world that we do not have the precious</u> <u>gift of laughing at ourselves.</u>
   (A) Laughing at ourselves is a sad characteristic of today's world which we do not have.
   (B) The precious gift of laughing at ourselves is a human characteristic missing from today's world.
   (C) In today's contemporary modern civilization, we have lost that not so precious gift of laughing at ourselves.
   (D) Laughing at ourselves is something he has lost as he grew up in today's world.
   (E) Laughing at ourselves, a precious gift is something they do not have in today's world.

4.   Ⓐ Ⓑ Ⓒ Ⓓ Ⓔ

The correct answer is (B).

Explanation: (A) is incorrect because the clause beginning *which* is a misplaced modifier.
(C) is incorrect because the phrase beginning *In* has three words which mean the same thing and because the meaning of the original sentence has been changed.
(D) is incorrect because *he* cannot logically refer to the plural *ourselves*; the person of the pronoun has also been shifted from first to third.
(E) is wrong because there should be a comma after *gift* and because *they* has no antecedent.

5. Americans have the right to change their form of government whenever they are unhappy about it.

    (A) Whenever Americans become unhappy with their form of government, they has the right to change it.

    (B) Americans becoming unhappy with their form of government, they have the right to change it.

    (C) Americans can change their form of government as often as it fails to satisfy them.

    (D) Americans who have the right to change their form of government are unhappy with it.

    (E) Americans have the right to change their form of government, they are unhappy with it.

The correct answer is (C).

Explanation: (A) is incorrect because *they has* is an improper agreement of subject and verb.

                  (B) is incorrect because the phrase beginning *Americans* is an ambiguous modifier.

                  (D) is incorrect because the meaning of the original sentence has been changed too much.

                  (E) is incorrect because the comma is a comma splice.

6. After the confusion in the park was over, the city council passed an ordinance prohibiting rock concerts in any public park.

    (A) in prohibiting forever rock concerts

    (B) to imply discouragement upon rock concerts

    (C) which makes it impossible for rock concerts to be held

    (D) for making illegal rock concerts

    (E) to ban completely rock concerts

The correct answer is (E).

Explanation: (A) is incorrect because the word *in* confuses the meaning.

                  (B) is incorrect because the meaning is unclear.

                  (C) is incorrect because to be held is a needless shift from active to passive voice.

                  (D) is incorrect because the phrase is not clear.

Now that you see how this type of item works, let's try several more.

1. The candidate eagerly sought out voters, rushing from speech to speech in his own airplane.

    (A) campaigned hard for voters

    (B) beat the ever-increasing bushes

    (C) dashed madly about the state for voters

    (D) practiced little finesse in looking for voters

    (E) stumped the state in wild-eyed enthusiasm

2. Suburbanites who are accustomed to commuting into a city by train know not to get upset if schedules cannot be maintained exactly.

2. Ⓐ Ⓑ Ⓒ Ⓓ Ⓔ

   (A) Suburbanites, commuting to a city by train, knows that schedules cannot always be maintained exactly.
   (B) If schedules cannot be maintained exactly, they know enough not to rave and rant and froth at the mouth.
   (C) Commuting suburbanites are not usually angry if trains do not run exactly on time.
   (D) Suburbanites have discovered the secret of impatience when their trains do not run on time.
   (E) Trains that do not run according to schedule upset the patience of suburbanites.

3. When I think of men travelling to the moon in a spaceship, my mind pays great tribute to the achievements of modern science.

3. Ⓐ Ⓑ Ⓒ Ⓓ Ⓔ

   (A) boggles and stammers at   (D) is filled with respect for
   (B) delights and is pleased about   (E) breaks out into a cold sweat for
   (C) is dazed and bewildered about

4. Any student may quarrel with a college's regulations, provided he allows everyone else the same privilege.

4. Ⓐ Ⓑ Ⓒ Ⓓ Ⓔ

   (A) If a student is willing to accept the reponsibility for his actions, quarreling with a college's regulations.
   (B) Any student can worry the college administration into a tizzy about college regulation's when he does not permit everyone else the same privilege.
   (C) If a student expresses an objection to a college's rules, he must allow all other students the same right.
   (D) Any student, demonstrating nonviolently against a college, they should accept violent demonstrations as well.
   (E) All demonstrations against a college's rules are of equal value, they are meant to be protested against.

5. John Browing showed his stupidity because he did not save money for his old age.

5. Ⓐ Ⓑ Ⓒ Ⓓ Ⓔ

   (A) cooked his own goose
   (B) killed the fatted calf too often
   (C) illustrated his extremely foolish notions
   (D) worked too hard to be wealthy
   (E) was very foolish

6. No single man can fight the forces of evil which might corrupt his young children.

6. Ⓐ Ⓑ Ⓒ Ⓓ Ⓔ

   (A) Corrupting young children should be the goal of every single man.
   (B) Community action is required if the evils that harm juveniles are to be battled.
   (C) No single, solitary man, all by himself, can save young children from the evils of the world.
   (D) If young children are to be saved from the world, we will all have to engage in the evils which surround us.
   (E) Today's children do not want to be saved from the world; single men tell us so.

7. People who live in Los Angeles have learned <u>to cope with</u> the effects of smog which clouds the city frequently.

    (A) to daily live with   (D) with becoming accustomed to
    (B) to adjust to   (E) to be relieved by
    (C) in getting used to

7. Ⓐ Ⓑ Ⓒ Ⓓ Ⓔ

8. Jonathan's father was born in Hawaii, <u>the male child</u> of a native princess and a sugar-cane worker.

    (A) the son   (D) being produced
    (B) being the only male   (E) the only male son
    (C) having been sired

8. Ⓐ Ⓑ Ⓒ Ⓓ Ⓔ

9. An expert secretary keeps complete notes on all meetings he attends so that his minutes <u>will reproduce completely</u> all important decisions.

    (A) will record with moderate accuracy
    (B) will make passing mention of
    (C) will record accurately
    (D) will be a fulsome list of
    (E) will begin with accurate honesty

9. Ⓐ Ⓑ Ⓒ Ⓓ Ⓔ

10. <u>Above all her other desires, Virginia wanted to succeed either as a nurse or as a teacher.</u>

    (A) Almost to the height of her abilities, as a nurse or as a teacher, Virginia wanted to progress.
    (B) Her ambition as a nurse nor a teacher in question, Virginia desired her success.
    (C) Along with Virginia's usual desires, she also had an ambition to study nurse and teacher.
    (D) More than anything else, Virginia wished to achieve eminence as a nurse or as a teacher.
    (E) No matter whatever else she might want to do; Virginia felt that she should become a successful teacher and nurse.

10. Ⓐ Ⓑ Ⓒ Ⓓ Ⓔ

11. The judges of the Miss Universe contest had eliminated all but five of the original contestants, and now their only problem was choosing the winner <u>from among the remaining women.</u>

    (A) between the finalists
    (B) within the finalists
    (C) from between the finalists
    (D) for about the finalists
    (E) from the finalists

11. Ⓐ Ⓑ Ⓒ Ⓓ Ⓔ

12. Motorists who cross the California desert <u>are constantly told to</u> take plenty of water for their car radiators.

    (A) have ever been cautioned to
    (B) are always advised to
    (C) should always be wary and
    (D) would be wise to beware and
    (E) cannot but be warned to

12. Ⓐ Ⓑ Ⓒ Ⓓ Ⓔ

13. It is difficult for the average person who works hard at a boring job to understand that some kinds of work <u>can provide some personal and monetary rewards.</u>

13. Ⓐ Ⓑ Ⓒ Ⓓ Ⓔ

   (A) has to award a person intellectual and financial returns
   (B) could hardly be both intellectual ánd financial
   (C) wishes to reward an intellectual as well as a financial person
   (D) can be both intellectually and financially rewarding
   (E) must be intellectual as well as financial

14. <u>A. Conan Doyle's Sherlock Holmes almost always used the principles of deductive reasoning to figure out who committed a crime.</u>

14. Ⓐ Ⓑ Ⓒ Ⓓ Ⓔ

   (A) When solving a crime, A. Conan Doyle's Sherlock Holmes usually used deductive reasoning.
   (B) To figure out the guilty party, A. Conan Doyle's Sherlock Holmes deducted the facts from all the evidence.
   (C) Committing a crime was difficult for anyone when they ran into the deductive powers of A. Conan Doyle's Sherlock Holmes.
   (D) A. Conan Doyle's Sherlock Holmes almost never used his inductive sensibilities when he was solving a crime.
   (E) Solving a crime was easy for A. Conan Doyle's Sherlock Holmes, he simply put his deducing powers to work.

15. George Washington knew how to submit an expense account; he was careful to list and explain small items <u>but was ambiguous about</u> large expenditures.

15. Ⓐ Ⓑ Ⓒ Ⓓ Ⓔ

   (A) , but he did not keep careful records from
   (B) , but he was rather incomplete about
   (C) but was rather helpless with
   (D) but was vague about
   (E) although he did not mention

16. <u>Napoleon's retreat from Moscow was made through the snow and cold which are dominant characteristics of a Russian winter.</u>

16. Ⓐ Ⓑ Ⓒ Ⓓ Ⓔ

   (A) Moscow's and Russia's winters are filled with snow and cold, thus Napoleon's retreat was hampered.
   (B) Napoleon's retreat from Moscow was not a success due to the fact that they had lots of cold and snow.
   (C) The reason Napoleon's retreat from Moscow was not successful was because of the winter's snow and cold.
   (D) Napoleon failed to get his army out of Russia successfully; they suffered from too much cold and snow.
   (E) When Napoleon made his retreat from Moscow, his efforts were struck by Russia's snow and cold.

17. In the South, dogwood and azaleas announce the arrival of spring <u>when they display their blooms</u> in every garden.

17. Ⓐ Ⓑ Ⓒ Ⓓ Ⓔ

   (A) with their busting into bloom
   (B) after they have exploded into bloom
   (C) by bursting into bloom
   (D) when they force their buds into bloom
   (E) because they burst into bloom

18. Since the invitation was addressed to both of us, you <u>should not have been so angry</u> when I opened the envelope.
    (A) could not have been more wrong
    (B) should not have been upset
    (C) would not have been so angry
    (D) should not have tizzied so easily
    (E) would not have become so undelighted

18. Ⓐ Ⓑ Ⓒ Ⓓ Ⓔ

19. <u>Resisting temptation is usually impossible for most people, because they have insufficient strength of character.</u>
    (A) Because they have insufficient characteristics, most people cannot resist temptation.
    (B) People's strength of character is the reason they cannot resist temptation.
    (C) People discover their weak characters, which gives them the strength to resist temptation.
    (D) Working hard to overcome temptation, most people find that they have the strength of character.
    (E) People lack willpower; therefore, they find it hard to avoid doing what temptation entices them into.

19. Ⓐ Ⓑ Ⓒ Ⓓ Ⓔ

20. Without being invited, the <u>attractive, youthful</u> woman took a seat at our table and ordered champagne.
    (A) pretty and lovely
    (B) beauteous and attractive
    (C) young and beautiful
    (D) beautiful young
    (E) beauty who was also young

20. Ⓐ Ⓑ Ⓒ Ⓓ Ⓔ

ANSWERS AND EXPLANATIONS

1. A. (B) and (D) are incorrect because the phrases are ambiguous when placed in the original sentence. (C) and (E) are incorrect because they are over-statements of the original.

2. C. (A) contains an error in agreement of subject and verb. (B) contains the vague pronoun <u>they</u> without a specific antecedent. (D) and (E) do not mean the same thing as the original sentence.

3. D. The other choices do not mean the same thing as the original sentence or omit a key preposition.

4. C. (A) is a sentence fragment. (B) is wordy and contains an error in the use of the apostrophe. (D) is an incomplete sentence. (E) contains a comma splice.

5. E. (A), (B), and (C) are wordy and use clichés. (D) contradicts the original sentence.

6. B. (A) contradicts the original sentence. (C) is wordy and contains needless repetition. (D) makes no sense. (E) does not have the meaning of the original sentence.

7. B. (A) is awkward. (C) and (D) create nonsense sentences, and (E) contradicts the original sentence.

8. A. (B) <u>only</u> changes the meaning of the original phrase. (C) and (D) create ambiguous sentences. (E) is redundant—male, son.

9. C. (A), (B) and (D) change the meaning of the original sentence, and (E) creates a nonsense sentence.

10. D. (A) and (B) create nonsense sentences. (C) says that Virginia wanted to study <u>nurse</u> and <u>teacher</u>, which are not the correct words for the professions. In (E) the semi-colon is misused.

11. E. (A) and (C) misuse the word <u>between</u>. (B) and (D) create nonsense sentences.

12. B. (A) is wordy. (C), (D), and (E) are wordy and contain ambiguous or incorrect word choices.

13. D. (A) creates an error in agreement of subject and verb. (B) and (E) create incomplete sentences; the idea is not finished. (C) is an ambiguous completion of the sentence.

14. A. (B) is incorrect because the word <u>deducted</u> is confused with <u>deduced</u>. (C) is incorrect because of the error in agreement between <u>anyone</u> and <u>they</u>. (D) contradicts the original sentence. (E) contains a comma splice.

15. D. (A) contradicts the original sentence. (B) creates a confused sentence. (C) is incorrect because <u>helpless</u> and <u>ambiguous</u> are not synonyms.

16. E. (A) is incorrect; it contains a comma splice. (B) is ambiguous because <u>they</u> has no clear antecedent. (C) is incorrect because <u>The reason ... was because</u> is wordy and redundant. (D) <u>they</u> has no clear antecedent.

17. C. (A) is incorrect because <u>busting</u> is an incorrect form of the verb <u>burst</u>. (B) The word <u>after</u> changes the time sequence of the original sentence. (D) creates an illogical sentence because plants cannot <u>force</u> buds. (E) <u>because</u> is illogical here.

18. B. (A) changes the meaning of the original sentence. (C) <u>would have been</u> is incorrect tense sequence. (D) <u>tizzied</u> is a poor choice of words. (E) contains a double negative.

19. E. (A) and (D) are nonsense sentences. (B) contradicts the meaning of the original sentence. (C) the two parts of this sentence have opposite meanings.

20. D. (A) is a poor choice because <u>pretty</u> and <u>lovely</u> mean almost the same thing. (B) <u>beauteous</u> and <u>attractive</u> are not synonyms. (C) <u>young</u> does not mean the same thing as <u>youthful</u>. (E) is wordy and thus less effective.

Type 2: The Sentence Completion Item: about 15%–20% of Part I

Type 2 questions ask you to select the one of five choices which best completes a sentence. Almost all of the choices will fit the sense of the sentence, but only one is grammatically correct, clear, concise, and conventional written English. Be careful about confused figures of speech, wordiness, and idioms which may not be standard written English phrases.

Directions: For each of these sentences, select the answer that, when inserted in the blank in the original sentence, produces the best sentence. Pay attention to meaning and to choice of words.

1. His theory seems incredible, especially since he obviously knows _____ about the skeleton of the Gila monster.
    (A) nothing whatever
    (B) simply very little
    (C) absolutely nothing whatsoever
    (D) more than nothing
    (E) almost nothing that is of little consequence.

    1. Ⓐ Ⓑ Ⓒ Ⓓ Ⓔ

The correct answer is (A). All of the other choices are wordy or vague.

2. The club's membership could only _____ the president's reasons for shifting the annual social from July to October.
   (A) come to some confused conclusions about
   (B) speculate about
   (C) expect
   (D) be all up in the air in confusion about
   (E) eliminate

2. Ⓐ Ⓑ Ⓒ Ⓓ Ⓔ

The correct answer is (B). All the other answers are wordy, vague, or lacking in good sense.

3. Hotel and motel managers usually _____ from guests who have no luggage.
   (A) require payment in advance
   (B) insist upon an advanced payment
   (C) demand cash or credit card reimbursement
   (D) ask for some advancing deposit
   (E) seek an advance deposit for reimbursement

3. Ⓐ Ⓑ Ⓒ Ⓓ Ⓔ

The correct answer is (A). All of the other answers are wordy or ambiguous.

Now, try your hand at several of these questions:

1. The teacher carefully instructed each child to go straight home after school without _____.
   (A) his being unusually late in arriving there
   (B) anyone stopping to waste time in dawdling
   (C) his having wasted any time in getting there
   (D) dawdling along the way
   (E) the time spent getting there being too long

1. Ⓐ Ⓑ Ⓒ Ⓓ Ⓔ

2. No English grammar ever published _____ every English teacher.
   (A) has ever brought total satisfaction with
   (B) has been satisfactory to a small minority of
   (C) completely satisfies
   (D) ever makes it satisfactory
   (E) can hope to provide absolute satisfaction to

2. Ⓐ Ⓑ Ⓒ Ⓓ Ⓔ

3. Simple answers are often not _____ for complex questions.
   (A) the least efficient ones
   (B) the best ones
   (C) the least effective ones
   (D) the most inefficient ones
   (E) the most ineffective ones

3. Ⓐ Ⓑ Ⓒ Ⓓ Ⓔ

4. Many recent college graduates have discovered that there are more teachers _____ employment opportunities.
   (A) moreso because there are few
   (B) so that there are not many
   (C) due to the fact that there are
   (D) because of the reason why there are few
   (E) than there are

4. Ⓐ Ⓑ Ⓒ Ⓓ Ⓔ

5. The high volume setting that children use for their record players could lead to _____.
   (A) their having a gradual deafening effect
   (B) their ears becoming more and more hard of hearing
   (C) their hearing becoming rather somewhat impaired
   (D) their developing a hearing loss
   (E) impairing their hearing loss

5. Ⓐ Ⓑ Ⓒ Ⓓ Ⓔ

6. No matter how hard I try to succeed, I find myself _____ in life.
   (A) getting further and further behind myself
   (B) getting nowhere
   (C) running down the tubes
   (D) reaching a downward trend
   (E) furthering my dislike

6. Ⓐ Ⓑ Ⓒ Ⓓ Ⓔ

7. Without leaving her bed, the sick old lady managed to terrorize her children and forced them to _____.
   (A) wait on her hand and foot
   (B) give in for her every whim
   (C) serve her like they were slaves
   (D) slavishly do their duty
   (E) obey her commands without question.

7. Ⓐ Ⓑ Ⓒ Ⓓ Ⓔ

8. Henry Thoreau would not recognize Walden Pond if _____ and see its condition today.
   (A) Henry Thoreau could arise from his tomb
   (B) he could appear from the long ago dead
   (C) he could return from the grave
   (D) he could look from wherever he is
   (E) he could visit the cemetery

8. Ⓐ Ⓑ Ⓒ Ⓓ Ⓔ

9. No one should discuss defense secrets except in a room which has been _____.
   (A) screened assiduously by eavesdropping equipment
   (B) most very cleverly secured
   (C) rated clear by a secure master spy
   (D) spied upon by someone in the security force
   (E) carefully checked for bugging devices

9. Ⓐ Ⓑ Ⓒ Ⓓ Ⓔ

10. Working hard for one's _____ is often not fun, but everyone has to do it.
   (A) daily bread
   (B) half a loaf of dry whole wheat
   (C) individual daily sustenance every day
   (D) worthwhile everyday food
   (E) salt as we used to say in the olden by-gone days

10. Ⓐ Ⓑ Ⓒ Ⓓ Ⓔ

ANSWERS AND EXPLANATIONS

1. **D.** All other choices are wordy or create ambiguous sentences.
2. **C.** All other choices are wordy or create ambiguous sentences.
3. **B.** All other choices are incorrect; they use a double negative.
4. **E.** All the other choices are wordy and thus less effective.
5. **D.** (A) has <u>their</u> without a specific antecedent. (B) creates a nonsense sentence. (C) <u>rather somewhat</u> is redundant. (E) creates a nonsense sentence.
6. **B.** (A) needlessly repeats <u>myself</u>. (C) is too informal; besides, the metaphor (<u>running down the tubes</u>) makes no sense. (D) is mere jargon. (E) is a nonsense sentence.
7. **E.** (A) <u>wait in</u> is an incorrect idiom. (B) <u>give in for</u> is also a poor idiom. (C) Many grammarians still object to <u>like</u> as a conjunction. (D) <u>Duty</u> seems to destroy the meaning of the sentence.
8. **C.** (A) repeats <u>Henry Thoreau</u> needlessly. (B) <u>long ago dead</u> is a meaningless phrase. (D) adds an idea which might not fit with Thoreau's philosophy. (E) Walden Pond is not a cemetery.
9. **E.** (A) contains too much jargon to communicate effectively. (B) <u>most . . . secured</u> is at least wordy and redundant. (C) is vague. (D) contradicts <u>No</u> at the beginning of the sentence.
10. **A.** All other choices contain needless repetition of words or ideas.

Type 3: The Construction Shift Item: about 33% of Part I

Type 3 questions ask you to reconstruct a perfectly correct sentence so that it says the same thing as the original sentence. The original sentence is followed by directions for the change or changes which you should make; therefore, the real problem is your finding alternative constructions which produce the same sentence meaning as that of the original sentence. For instance, if you must change one part of the sentence, you have to be sure that any pronouns in a later part of the sentence are also changed, if necessary; that subjects and verbs agree in person and number; that needless repetition is eliminated; and that a good sentence results from your changes. Pay careful attention to possible ambiguity and other problems which may develop if you do not make all the changes consistent.

Try a few examples:

Directions: Revise each of the following sentences according to the directions which follow it. Rephrase the sentence mentally to save time, making notes in your book if you wish. Although the directions may at times require you to change the relationship between parts of the sentence or to make slight changes in other ways, *make only those changes that the directions require.*

Below each sentence and its directions are listed words or phrases that may occur in your revised sentence. When you have thought out a good sentence, look at the choices A through E for the word or entire phrase that is included in your revised sentence.

Of course, a number of different sentences can be obtained if the sentence is revised according to directions, and not all of these possibilities can be included in only five choices. If you should find that you have thought of a sentence that contains none of the words listed in the choices, rephrase the sentence again to include a word or phrase that *is* listed.

1. *Sentence:*   In the tenth inning, Reggie Jackson knocked the ball into the
   left-field stands for a home run.
   Directions: Change <u>knocked</u> to <u>was knocked.</u>
   (A) from   (B) at which   (C) under
   (D) with   (E) by

1. Ⓐ Ⓑ Ⓒ Ⓓ Ⓔ

Your new sentence probably reads:
In the tenth inning, the ball was knocked by Reggie Jackson into the left-field
stands for a home run.

The sentence contains the correct answer (E). Any sentence which includes any of
the other choices would not be as good a sentence.

2. *Sentence:*   Looking up, we saw four of the new 747s, flying in perfect
   formation.
   Directions: Begin with <u>While we were.</u>
   (A) looking   (B) being looked   (C) having looked
   (D) looked   (E) having been looked

2. Ⓐ Ⓑ Ⓒ Ⓓ Ⓔ

Your new sentence should read:
While we were looking up, we saw four of the new 747s flying in perfect
formation.

Choice (A) <u>looking</u> is contained within the new sentence, and that is the correct
answer.

3. *Sentence:*   Unless a criminal charge can be proved in court, a defendant
   will not be punished.
   Directions: Change <u>can</u> to <u>could.</u>
   (A) should   (B) shall   (C) will
   (D) would   (E) must

3. Ⓐ Ⓑ Ⓒ Ⓓ Ⓔ

Your new sentence should read:
Unless a criminal charge could be proved in court, a defendant would not be
punished.

Answer (D) <u>would</u> is the only possible choice, for the conventions of written
English require <u>would</u> following a dependent clause containing <u>could.</u>

4. *Sentence:*   The young man walked to the door; he wanted to see who had
   rung the bell.
   Directions: Begin with <u>Because he wanted.</u>
   (A) bell so   (B) bell;   (C) bell and
   (D) bell for   (E) bell,

4. Ⓐ Ⓑ Ⓒ Ⓓ Ⓔ

Your new sentence should read:
Because he wanted to see who had rung the bell, the young man walked to the
door.

Choice (E) <u>bell,</u> is the only possible choice.

5. *Sentence:*   That man is a vertebrate animal has been affirmed by many
   scientific experiments.
   Directions: Begin with <u>Many scientific experiments.</u>
   (A) has   (B) have   (C) would
   (D) been   (E) was

5. Ⓐ Ⓑ Ⓒ Ⓓ Ⓔ

Your new sentence should read:

Many scientific experiments have affirmed that man is a vertebrate animal.

Choice (B) have is the only possible answer.

6. *Sentence:* Not only was he a great fan of Humphrey Bogart, but he had also seen every film directed by Alfred Hitchcock.

    Directions: Eliminate but.

        (A) so   (B) either   (C) just

        (D) and   (E) however

6. Ⓐ Ⓑ Ⓒ Ⓓ Ⓔ

Your new sentence should read:

He was a great fan of Humphrey Bogart and had seen every film directed by Alfred Hitchcock.

Choice (D) and is the only possible choice.

7. *Sentence:* James Smithers settled in Virginia in the early eighteenth century after the King in London had rewarded with a large tract of free land his faithful service to the throne.

    Directions: Begin with After James Smithers was rewarded.

        (A) by   (B) from   (C) on

        (D) of   (E) into

7. Ⓐ Ⓑ Ⓒ Ⓓ Ⓔ

Your new sentence should read:

After James Smithers was rewarded with a large tract of free land by the King in London, he settled in Virginia in the early eighteenth century.

Choice (A) by is the only possible answer.

8. *Sentence:* As landmarks immediately recognized by everyone, Paris has its Eiffel Tower, Rome its Trevi Fountain, London its Buckingham Palace, and New York its Empire State Building.

    Directions: Begin with As immediately.

        (A) landmarks recognized   (B) recognizable landmarks

        (C) identified landmarks   (D) recognized landmarks

        (E) recognized by everyone landmarks

8. Ⓐ Ⓑ Ⓒ Ⓓ Ⓔ

Your new sentence should read:

As immediately recognizable landmarks, Paris has its . . .

Choice (B) recognizable landmarks is the answer.

9. *Sentence:* Some teachers declare vociferously that they are in the classroom to teach students, but their every glance or attitude contradicts what they say.

    Directions: Begin with Some teachers who.

        (A) contradicts what they say by

        (B) contradict what they say for

        (C) contradicts what they say from

        (D) contradict what they say with

        (E) contradicts what they say into

9. Ⓐ Ⓑ Ⓒ Ⓓ Ⓔ

Your new sentence should read:

Some teachers who declare vociferously that they are in the classroom to teach students contradict what they say with their every glance and attitude.

Choice (D) contradict what they say with is the correct answer.

10. *Sentence:*   Women who take meticulous care of their bodies in their youth are usually rewarded in old age with skin which does not wrinkle and hair that does not turn gray.

10. Ⓐ Ⓑ Ⓒ Ⓓ Ⓔ

Directions: Begin with <u>Skin which does not wrinkle.</u>

    (A) is the reward sought
    (B) reward women in old age
    (C) rewards those women who
    (D) are awarded to women in old age
    (E) are the rewards sought

Your new sentence should read:

Skin which does not wrinkle and hair that does not turn gray are the rewards sought by women who take meticulous care of their bodies in their youth.

Choice (E) <u>are the rewards sought</u> is the correct answer.

Now, try the following ten items.

1. Certain specialized drugs have been used with remarkable success by doctors treating some mental disorders, particularly the manic-depressive syndrome, that thirty years ago would have required the patient to be hospitalized indefinitely.

1. Ⓐ Ⓑ Ⓒ Ⓓ Ⓔ

Begin with <u>Thirty years ago some mental.</u>

(A) patient, now these disorders
(B) patient, and now these disorders
(C) patient, for these disorders
(D) patient, with these disorders
(E) patient; now these disorders

2. He was trapped into a loveless marriage by an overly anxious girl; therefore, he was already weary of her chattering before a month had passed.

2. Ⓐ Ⓑ Ⓒ Ⓓ Ⓔ

Begin with <u>Trapped into.</u>

(A) girl, he   (B) girl; he   (C) girl, therefore, he
(D) girl, so he   (E) girl; therefore, he

3. Members of that loose coalition of groups calling themselves "The New Left" believe that the only solution for the nation's problems is the overthrow, through violence if necessary, of both corrupt capitalism and a corrupt governmental system.

3. Ⓐ Ⓑ Ⓒ Ⓓ Ⓔ

Substitute <u>advocate</u> for <u>believe.</u>

(A) system for the only   (B) system through the only
(C) system as well as the only   (D) system as the only
(E) system by the only

4. Anyone's first flight is always a unique experience, no matter how many times he has seen pictures of planes flying or heard tales about the first flights of others.

4. Ⓐ Ⓑ Ⓒ Ⓓ Ⓔ

Begin with <u>No matter</u> and substitute <u>anyone</u> for <u>he.</u>

(A) anyone's own   (B) a person's own   (C) his own
(D) their own   (E) theirs

5. The truck driver, tired after forty hours on the highway without rest, took a pep pill; he knew that just one would keep him awake and alert for about three hours.

Begin with The truck driver knew.

(A) hours; so tired   (B) hours; therefore, tired
(C) hours; moreover, tired   (D) hours, tired
(E) hours, therefore, tired

5. Ⓐ Ⓑ Ⓒ Ⓓ Ⓔ

6. The average laborer with no income except his monthly wages is frequently hard pressed for immediate cash to pay his personal bills.

Substitute whose only for with.

(A) no income except his   (B) income except his
(C) income accepts his   (D) income is his   (E) no income but

6. Ⓐ Ⓑ Ⓒ Ⓓ Ⓔ

7. Radical blacks angrily charge that a corporation which hires minority group workers and then lays them off during a recession is actually intensifying the frustrations of black workers rather than helping them.

Substitute a corporation's for a corporation.

(A) actually intensifying   (B) intensifies minority workers
(C) actually intensifies   (D) must actually intensify
(E) actually brings on

7. Ⓐ Ⓑ Ⓒ Ⓓ Ⓔ

8. According to an American Medical Association report, psychiatrists should be aware that certain types of female patients will attempt to seduce them.

Begin with An American Medical Association.

(A) bewares psychiatrists   (B) arouses psychiatrists
(C) defends psychiatrists   (D) declares psychiatrists
(E) warns psychiatrists

8. Ⓐ Ⓑ Ⓒ Ⓓ Ⓔ

9. No depression in American history has ever lasted as long as the one which began in 1929; it is ironic that only the beginning of World War II in Europe brought prosperity to the United States.

Begin with It is ironic, and substitute ended for brought.
(A) the lasting depression
(B) the longest depression
(C) the 1929 beginning depression
(D) no prosperity in the United States
(E) no depression in American history

9. Ⓐ Ⓑ Ⓒ Ⓓ Ⓔ

10. In their support of rising minority group aspirations, large corporations are not only evidencing true altruism in improving the lot of minorities but also producing social changes within the communities in which their plants are located.

Substitute both for not only.
(A) and   (B) but   (C) and so   (D) as much as   (E) for

10. Ⓐ Ⓑ Ⓒ Ⓓ Ⓔ

ANSWERS AND EXPLANATIONS

1. E. Thirty years ago, some mental disorders would have required the indefinite hospitalization of the patient; now these disorders respond to treatment by certain specialized drugs.

2. A. Trapped into a loveless marriage by an overly anxious girl, he was already weary of her chattering before a month had passed.

3. D. Members of that loose coalition of groups calling themselves "The New Left" advocate the overthrow, through violence if necessary, of both corrupt capitalism and a corrupt governmental system as the only solution for the nation's problems.

4. B. No matter how many times anyone has seen pictures of planes flying or heard tales about the first flights of others, a person's own first flight is always a unique experience.

5. B. The truck driver knew that one pep pill would keep him awake and alert for about three hours; therefore, tired after forty hours on the highway without rest, he took one.

6. D. The average laborer whose only income is his monthly wages is often hard pressed for immediate cash to pay his personal bills.

7. C. Radical blacks angrily charge that a corporation's hiring minority group workers and then laying them off during a recession actually intensifies the frustration of black workers rather than helps them.

8. E. An American Medical Association report warns psychiatrists that certain types of female patients will attempt to seduce them.

9. B. It is ironic that only the outbreak of World War II ended the longest depression in American history and brought prosperity to the United States.

10. A. In their support of rising minority group aspirations, large corporations are both evidencing true altruism in improving the lot of minorities and producing social changes within the communities in which their plants are located.

Now that you have the knack of doing this kind of test item, try ten more exactly like those which you have just finished. The same directions apply.

1. The young girl, untrained and inexperienced but willing to learn, arrived in New York seeking a role on the Broadway stage.

   Substitute New York with for New York.
   (A) neither training or experience   (B) neither training nor experience
   (C) both no training and no experience   (D) either no training or no experience
   (E) neither training as well as experience

   1. Ⓐ Ⓑ Ⓒ Ⓓ Ⓔ

2. Just before her death, the old woman had one lucid moment during which she blessed her children.

   Substitute spent her last for had one.
   (A) to bless her children   (B) she blessed her children
   (C) after blessing her children   (D) blessing her children
   (E) to blessing her children

   2. Ⓐ Ⓑ Ⓒ Ⓓ Ⓔ

3. Authorities on alcohol control agree that chronic alcoholism is more likely to occur among those whose families are total abstainers than among those whose families serve alcoholic beverages in moderation.

   Substitute families who are total abstainers for chronic alcoholism is more likely.
   (A) produce fewer chronic alcoholic offspring
   (B) chronic alcoholics among their children
   (C) prohibit alcoholic beverages even in moderation
   (D) produce no more chronic alcoholic offspring
   (E) produce more chronic alcoholic offspring

   3. Ⓐ Ⓑ Ⓒ Ⓓ Ⓔ

4. We all observe the simple phenomena of nature, but most of us could not explain what causes a breeze or how a cloud is formed.

4. Ⓐ Ⓑ Ⓒ Ⓓ Ⓔ

Substitute <u>what causes</u> for <u>but most of</u>.

(A) Unless we all observe   (B) How we all observe

(C) Although we all observe   (D) As we all observe

(E) Until we all observe

5. The incidence of paralytic polio has been dramatically reduced since 1955 when the Salk vaccine became generally available; in fact, some authorities say that an epidemic of poliomyelitis is probably a thing of the past.

5. Ⓐ Ⓑ Ⓒ Ⓓ Ⓔ

Begin with <u>Since 1955, the Salk vaccine has so</u>.

(A) dramatically reduced the incidence

(B) crippled polio that

(C) generally become available that

(D) successfully changed crippling polio that

(E) completely availed itself that

6. To receive critical plaudits for playing Hedda Gabler would fulfill the dream of almost every actress in the theater today because it is one of the most difficult roles ever written.

6. Ⓐ Ⓑ Ⓒ Ⓓ Ⓔ

Eliminate <u>because it is</u>.

(A) plaudits for one   (B) dream of one   (C) Hedda Gabler, one

(D) actress for one   (E) fulfilling one

7. American ballet companies cannot survive unless foundations or wealthy patrons subsidize their performances of both the classical and the modern repertories.

7. Ⓐ Ⓑ Ⓒ Ⓓ Ⓔ

Substitute <u>without</u> for <u>unless</u>.

(A) subsidy for   (B) subsidize their

(C) become subsidiary to   (D) offer to subsidize

(E) performing both

8. Within the past decade, many popular magazines like *The Saturday Evening Post* did not respond to America's changing reading habits and were forced to suspend publication.

8. Ⓐ Ⓑ Ⓒ Ⓓ Ⓔ

Substitute <u>were forced</u> for <u>did not respond</u>.

(A) although they did respond

(C) without responding

(E) because they did not respond

9. Comedians who appear frequently on television complain that they use more material than they did when they were performing exclusively in nightclubs.

9. Ⓐ Ⓑ Ⓒ Ⓓ Ⓔ

Begin with <u>Comedians complain</u>.

(A) about frequent television appearances

(B) that frequent television appearances expend more

(C) about their nightclub performances

(D) that their nightclub performances expend more

(E) more material than frequent television appearances

10. Isometric exercises, once recommended by doctors for sedentary patients, are now suspected of creating additional health problems for those who have high blood pressure or damaged heart valves.

Begin with <u>Doctors who once recommended</u>.

(A) should not suspect such exercises
(B) should create such exercises
(C) should have such exercises
(D) should avoid such exercises
(E) should damage such exercises

10. Ⓐ Ⓑ Ⓒ Ⓓ Ⓔ

ANSWERS AND EXPLANATIONS

1. B. The young girl arrived in New York with neither training nor experience, seeking a role on the Broadway stage.

2. D. Just before her death, the old woman spent her last lucid moment blessing her children.

3. E. Authorities on alcohol control agree that families who are total abstainers are more likely to produce chronic alcoholic offspring than are families who serve alcoholic beverages in moderation.

4. C. Although we all observe the simple phenomena of nature, what causes a breeze or how a cloud forms is still a mystery to most of us.

5. A. Since 1955, the Salk vaccine has so dramatically reduced the incidence of paralytic polio that some authorities say that an epidemic of poliomyelitis is probably a thing of the past.

6. C. The dream of almost every actress in the theater today is to receive plaudits for playing Hedda Gabler, one of the most difficult roles ever written.

7. A. American ballet companies cannot survive without subsidy for their performances of both the classical and the modern repertories from foundations or wealthy patrons.

8. E. Within the past decade many popular magazines like *The Saturday Evening Post* were forced to suspend publication because they did not respond to America's changing reading habits.

9. B. Comedians complain that frequent television appearances expend more material than performances in nightclubs.

10. D. Doctors who once recommended isometric exercises for sedentary patients now suspect that those who have high blood pressure or damaged heart valves should avoid such exercises.

Type 4: The Ambiguous Sentence Item: about 5%–10% of Part I

The fourth type of item in Part I asks you to recognize sentences which do not make sense, that is, which are ambiguous. Each question will give five statements, only one of which is clear, and you are asked to select the answer which avoids awkwardness and lack of clarity. Sometimes, there will be a modifier that is misplaced, sometimes a pronoun that has no clear antecedent, sometimes comparisons that are vague. Sometimes, there will be words or phrases that are vague or not clear. Read each of the five choices carefully so that you can be sure you have selected the one good, clear sentence from the others.

Directions: For each of the following, choose the one phrasing that makes the intended meaning clear; that is, the one that avoids ambiguity, that does not leave the actual meaning open to question or that does not leave the reader guessing about what is intended.

1. (A) An automobile worker's tiresome job is rewarded with good pay, but the union's members are still not satisfied and demand more money.
    (B) The automobile worker's tiresome job is rewarded with good pay, but they are unsatisfied and demand higher wages.
    (C) The automobile worker's union is demanding more wages, which is too much to ask since they are already well paid.
    (D) The wages paid to an automobile worker are good, but they are asking for more compensation for their tiresome jobs.
    (E) Whatever wages automobile workers receive for their tiresome jobs is good, but the union wants more pay for it.

    The correct answer is (A). All of the other choices are not clear.

1. Ⓐ Ⓑ Ⓒ Ⓓ Ⓔ

2. (A) The principal did not hear the truth about the teacher's attack by him.
    (B) No angry student had attacked the teacher; she had not told the principal the truth.
    (C) The teacher did not tell the principal the truth about having been attacked by an angry student.
    (D) The principal could not have heard the truth from the teacher about her attack by a student.
    (E) No attack by an angry student occurred to the teacher when she lied to the principal.

    The correct answer is (C); all the other choices are ambiguous.

2. Ⓐ Ⓑ Ⓒ Ⓓ Ⓔ

3. (A) Diamonds are as valuable if not more valuable than gold.
    (B) Gold is just as if not more valuable than diamonds.
    (C) Between gold and diamonds, you cannot decide which is the most valuable.
    (D) Gold and diamonds are almost equal in value; they cannot decide which is more valuable.
    (E) Diamonds are as valuable as, if not more valuable than, gold.

    The correct answer is (E); all of the others are ambiguous or contain an error in grammar.

3. Ⓐ Ⓑ Ⓒ Ⓓ Ⓔ

4. (A) Fortunately, you and I understand each other so completely that there is no need for elaborate explanations between us.
    (B) Each understands the other completely; therefore, you do not need to explain anything.
    (C) If we did not need elaborate explanations, you can understand me completely.
    (D) Our understanding each other so completely eliminates the need for elaborate explanations between them.
    (E) When two people understand each other as completely as we do, he doesn't need elaborate explanations.

    The correct answer is (A); all the other choices are ambiguous.

4. Ⓐ Ⓑ Ⓒ Ⓓ Ⓔ

5. (A) Recent high school graduates have greater experience with advanced courses in science and mathematics than thirty years ago.
   (B) Thirty years ago, recent high school graduates have had more advanced courses in science and mathematics.
   (C) More advanced courses in science and mathematics is the result of high school graduation thirty years ago.
   (D) More recent high school graduates than thirty years ago have had greater experience with advanced science and mathematics courses.
   (E) Recent high school graduates have greater experience with advanced courses in science and mathematics than those who completed the twelfth grade thirty years ago.

5. Ⓐ Ⓑ Ⓒ Ⓓ Ⓔ

The correct answer is (E); all of the other choices are ambiguous.

Now try a series of questions like these:

1. (A) I do not like Susie because she always steals my boy friends.
   (B) Susie's stealing my boyfriends causes me not to like them very much.
   (C) The more Susie steals my boyfriends, the less use I have for him.
   (D) The reason I do not like Susie is because she steals my boyfriends.
   (E) My boyfriends are always stolen by Susie, which is a bad thing to do.

1. Ⓐ Ⓑ Ⓒ Ⓓ Ⓔ

2. (A) There are rules in any sport which both an amateur and a professional should study before he plays with him.
   (B) In any sport, there are rules which an amateur should study before he plays with a professional.
   (C) His studying the rules of any sport is necessary before an amateur played with a professional.
   (D) An amateur should never play with a professional unless he studies the rules of the sport.
   (E) Without his studying the rules of the sport, an amateur should never play with a professional.

2. Ⓐ Ⓑ Ⓒ Ⓓ Ⓔ

3. (A) In the gold fields of a century ago, they could not replace the donkey with as hardworking an animal.
   (B) Another animal which would work as hard as the donkey could not be found in the gold fields a century ago, so he was used.
   (C) The gold fields of a century ago required a hardworking animal; therefore, they used the donkey.
   (D) A century ago, the donkey was used in the gold fields because no one could find another animal that would work as hard.
   (E) The donkey, a hardworking animal, was their choice in the gold fields of a century ago.

3. Ⓐ Ⓑ Ⓒ Ⓓ Ⓔ

4. (A) Emily Post's books will help you act well in formal situations if he has studied them well.
   (B) Conforming with certain rules of behavior in formal situations is difficult for anyone unless that person has studied Emily Post's books.
   (C) The modes of behavior in formal situations are set forth in the books of Emily Post in which they are clear.
   (D) Advice on anyone's behavior in formal situations is contained in Emily Post's books, and they should study them thoroughly.
   (E) A thorough study of Emily Post's books is necessary to understand how they should behave in social situations.

4. Ⓐ Ⓑ Ⓒ Ⓓ Ⓔ

5. (A) What we sincerely believe affects our ability to choose wisely among alternative courses of action.
   (B) What we believe sincerely affects our ability to choose wisely among alternative courses of action.
   (C) Among alternative courses of action, that which we believe in completely influences our choices.
   (D) Our choices are frequently determined by our ability to wisely distinguish among alternatives.
   (E) If we choose wisely among alternatives, you must know what you sincerely believe.

5. Ⓐ Ⓑ Ⓒ Ⓓ Ⓔ

6. (A) Anyone telling me that he has no selfish bone in their body proves that they do not understand human psychology.
   (B) Human psychology is poorly understood by anyone who denies having a selfish bone in their body.
   (C) If someone tells me that there is no selfish bone in his body, I realize right away that he does not understand human psychology.
   (D) Their denial of selfishness demonstrates that someone does not understand human psychology.
   (E) Selfishness is present in all of us, if you understand human psychology properly.

6. Ⓐ Ⓑ Ⓒ Ⓓ Ⓔ

7. (A) Joan Sutherland enjoys more singing the roles by Mozart than Wagner.
   (B) Singing the roles written by Mozart are preferred by Joan Sutherland to Wagner.
   (C) Joan Sutherland enjoys singing the roles written by Mozart more than she enjoys the roles written by Wagner.
   (D) Between the singing roles written by Mozart and those by Wagner, Joan Sutherland prefers Mozart.
   (E) Both Wagner and Mozart wrote singing roles, and Joan Sutherland prefers one over the other.

7. Ⓐ Ⓑ Ⓒ Ⓓ Ⓔ

8. (A) Bill was angry with Robert because he had to wait for two hours while he fought heavy traffic.
   (B) Robert made Bill angry, being two hours late while he was driving his car through heavy traffic.
   (C) Bill's anger at Robert which caused his being two hours late was serious to him.
   (D) Bill was angry with Robert because Robert was two hours late, having been delayed in heavy traffic.
   (E) Robert made Bill angry driving two hours late through heavy traffic.

8. Ⓐ Ⓑ Ⓒ Ⓓ Ⓔ

9. (A) Tennessee state parks are toured each year by the president and garden club members, which is a delightful experience.
   (B) Both the president and every member of the garden clubs tour Tennessee's state parks each year, a remarkable event.
   (C) Along with every member of the garden clubs, Tennessee state parks are toured by the president each year.
   (D) Tennessee state parks have annually been enjoyed by the president and every member of the garden clubs.
   (E) The president along with every member of the garden clubs tours the Tennessee state parks each year.

9. Ⓐ Ⓑ Ⓒ Ⓓ Ⓔ

10. (A) Income tax time approaching fast, a savings account was started by Jack.
    (B) When Jack realized that income tax time was approaching fast, a savings account was started by him.
    (C) Even with income tax time approaching fast, Jack started a savings account.
    (D) Income tax time approaching fast, Jack started saving his money.
    (E) Making income tax time come fast, Jack started a savings account.

10. Ⓐ Ⓑ Ⓒ Ⓓ Ⓔ

ANSWERS AND EXPLANATIONS

1. A. (B)—them has no clear antecedent as well as shifting the dislike from Susie to the boy friends. In (C), him and boy friends create an error in agreement of pronoun and antecedent. In (D), The reason is . . . because construction is redundant. In (E), the clause beginning with which is a dangling modifier.
2. B. (A) contains vague references of the pronouns he and him. In (C) the past tense verb played violates the appropriate tense sequence. (D) is ambiguous; he could refer to amateur or professional. (E) is wordy.
3. D. In (A) and (C), they is too vague. In (B), he is vague. In (E), their is also vague.
4. B. In (A), you and he are second and third person pronouns, respectively; the words should be the same person. (C) contains two problems: the vague they and the clause beginning in which is a dangling modifier. In (D) and (E), they is ambiguous.
5. A. In (B), sincerely may function with believes or affects; it is a "squinting" modifier. In (C), the phrase beginning with Among is a dangling modifier. (D) and (E) have misplaced modifiers.
6. C. In (A), anyone, he, and they should all be singular or plural. (B) is wordy as well as containing an unnecessary shift to the passive voice. (D) is simply ambiguous and unclear. In (E), you makes no sense.
7. C. In (A), more could function with enjoys or singing. In (B) the phrase beginning with by is unclear. (D) does not clarify what the second use of Mozart refers to. In (E) the reader cannot tell which singing roles the artist prefers.
8. D. All the other choices are vague and ambiguous.
9. E. In (A), there are two problems: the use of the weak passive voice are toured and the dangling modifier beginning with which. In (B) a remarkable event is a dangling modifier. (C) sounds as if the parks as well as members of the garden club are toured. In (D) annually is a misplaced modifier.
10. D. In (A) the phrase beginning Income tax is a dangling modifier. In (B), there is a poor shift from the active voice (realized) to the passive voice (was started). In (C) the two parts of the sentence do not relate logically. In (E) the phrase beginning with Making is a dangling modifier.

Note: THIS CONCLUDES THE TYPES OF ITEMS YOU WILL FIND ON PART I OF AN ACTUAL CLEP ENGLISH COMPOSITION EXAMINATION. REMEMBER, THAT THE CLEP EXAMINATION OFFERS TWO OPTIONS FOR PART II: ANOTHER MULTIPLE CHOICE EXAMINATION OR AN ESSAY ON AN ASSIGNED TOPIC WHICH YOU WILL HAVE FORTY-FIVE MINUTES TO COMPLETE. SEE PAGES 94-97 OF THIS BOOK FOR INFORMATION ABOUT THE ESSAY OPTION. BE SURE THAT YOU KNOW WHICH OPTION YOU ARE REQUIRED TO TAKE BY THE COLLEGE TO WHICH YOU WILL HAVE CREDITS SENT. SOME COLLEGES ARE NOW REQUIRING BOTH MULTIPLE CHOICE SECTIONS OF CLEP AND ARE GIVING A LOCALLY DEVELOPED AND GRADED WRITTEN ESSAY. KNOW IN ADVANCE WHAT WILL BE REQUIRED OF YOU.

Part II   (of the all-multiple-choice version)

Almost all of the items within Part II of the examination require you to use the principles of formal logic as well as the vocabulary associated with that course. We urge that you review a logic textbook before you start this section of the book, especially W. Edgar Moore's *Creative and Critical Thinking,* recommended in the bibliography at the beginning of this chapter as well as John Chaffee's *Thinking Critically,* also listed there.

Type 1:   The Illogical Statement Item: about 33% of Part II

Each of these items consists of a statement which may contain an illogical argument, a poorly supported generalization, or a logical flaw because the prejudice of the speaker relies upon emotion rather than reason for a conclusion. You are to determine among the five choices what that logical flaw is or what conclusion must be reached if the speaker's assumption is accepted by a reader or hearer. You will need to be careful with this type of question, because almost every word in English has two types of meanings: its *denotation* (the literal meaning that can be found in any dictionary) and its *connotation* (the meaning or meanings which are suggested by the word). Some people confuse these two types of meaning and make statements that are illogical or nonsensical. Study each of the sample questions below before you select your answers. Logic seems tricky, but clear and accurate thinking will enable you to select the correct choice. Remember, you *must* use *only* the facts given in the statement and not project a possible meaning for the statement which is not there. Be wary, think, and you should be all right.

Directions: These questions are each based on a short passage. Read the passage and then select the one best answer to the questions that follow the passage, using the information provided by or suggested in the passage.

1.   "Every apple in that basket is sour. I tasted four, and I know."   1. Ⓐ Ⓑ Ⓒ Ⓓ Ⓔ

   The speaker

   (A) ignores the fact that the apples are in a basket
   (B) has tasted all the apples in the basket
   (C) has eaten many apples in his lifetime
   (D) cannot distinguish between sweet and sour apples
   (E) assumes all the apples in the basket are alike

   The correct answer is (E). Answers (A) and (B) are incorrect because they do not fit the "facts" given in the statement. (C) is incorrect because the reader does not have enough information to come to this conclusion, and (D) is incorrect for the same reason.

Questions 2 and 3 are based on this statement.

   "Tell me how many automobiles a home has in its driveway, and I can tell you how much money that family makes each year."

2.   The writer represents a person who   2. Ⓐ Ⓑ Ⓒ Ⓓ Ⓔ
   (A) can form logical conclusions from sufficient evidence

(B) forms opinions on the basis of possibly inadequate evidence

(C) makes reasonable choices among alternatives based on his keen eyesight

(D) does not form opinions until all the evidence has been considered

(E) considers that some people may be illogical

The correct answer is (B).

3. From the statement, a reader might conclude that the writer   3. Ⓐ Ⓑ Ⓒ Ⓓ Ⓔ

(A) loves all kinds of automobiles

(B) works on an automobile assembly line

(C) is objecting to the high prices of certain automobiles

(D) rejects the notion that there is some connection between the number of automobiles a person owns and his social class

(E) knows the prices of automobiles from practical experience or from study.

The correct answer is (E). Choices (A), (B), and (C) assume information not in the original statement, and choice (D) brings in social class which is not in the statement.

4. Betty said, "The summer heat always makes me perspire."   4. Ⓐ Ⓑ Ⓒ Ⓓ Ⓔ

From this statement, anyone can conclude

(A) nothing except that Betty sweats in the summertime

(B) that Betty hates the heat of the summer

(C) that Betty likes to ski in the winter

(D) that Betty works for a travel agency

(E) that Betty enjoys sweating in the summertime

The correct answer is (A); all other choices include facts not covered in the original statement.

5. "President Reagan should keep his children in California all the time." Whoever made that statement

(A) obviously did not support President Reagan in 1984

(B) says more about Reagan's family than about Reagan himself

(C) is neutral towards the President's family

(D) resents Ronald Reagan being in the White House

(E) finds all political families unworthy of respect

The correct answer is (B), the only choice which can be concluded logically from the statement.

6. "When I was a child, fresh vegetables had more flavor than they do now.   6. Ⓐ Ⓑ Ⓒ Ⓓ Ⓔ
Someone has done something to the spinach we eat today."

In this statement, the speaker

(A) forgets that a person's taste buds change over the years

(B) accepts the idea that the change in taste could be a natural result of changing growing methods

(C) places the proper cause and effect together

(D) reasons correctly from observed effects

(E) has arrived at an obvious conclusion

The correct answer is (A), the only choice which is a logical conclusion.

Now try a group of these items:

Questions 1 and 2 are based on the following statement:

The American Civil Liberties Union (ACLU) has defended in court the right of neo-Nazis to march in Skokie, Illinois, which has a large Jewish population. The ACLU should not involve itself in anti-Jewish demonstrations.

1. This statement means that
   (A) the ACLU is an anti-Jewish organization
   (B) no one should defend the neo-Nazi's right to march in Skokie
   (C) all Jews are opposed to neo-Nazi marchers
   (D) Skokie, Illinois, is anti-Jewish
   (E) the ACLU should not defend the neo-Nazis

1. Ⓐ Ⓑ Ⓒ Ⓓ Ⓔ

2. From the statement, a reader might conclude that
   (A) neo-Nazis are a threat to the United States
   (B) the march of the neo-Nazis in Skokie would be considered an anti-Jewish demonstration.
   (C) Skokie, Illinois, is prejudiced against the ACLU
   (D) demonstrating in Skokie, Illinois, is a chore for anyone
   (E) the ACLU is a radical organization

2. Ⓐ Ⓑ Ⓒ Ⓓ Ⓔ

3. "My neighbor voted against Margaret Smith who was running for mayor; therefore, he thinks women cannot assume positions of political leadership."

   The speaker of that sentence

   (A) considers that Margaret Smith would be an excellent mayor
   (B) does not enjoy living next door to his neighbor
   (C) jumps to a conclusion which is valid
   (D) uses a specific action as evidence to support what may be an invalid generalization
   (E) believes that all women are superior to men

3. Ⓐ Ⓑ Ⓒ Ⓓ Ⓔ

Questions 4 and 5 are based on the following:

"When they need to relax, some people go outside and work in their gardens. I prefer to go into the kitchen and bake bread."

4. The speaker
   (A) has admiration for those who work in their gardens
   (B) must bake many loaves of bread
   (C) says that people find their own ways to relieve their tensions
   (D) does not care for gardening under any circumstances
   (E) believes baking bread more creative than gardening

4. Ⓐ Ⓑ Ⓒ Ⓓ Ⓔ

5. What conclusion about relaxation must we accept if we believe this statement?
   (A) There are only two acceptable ways for anyone to relax.
   (B) Relaxation is not really necessary for anyone.

5. Ⓐ Ⓑ Ⓒ Ⓓ Ⓔ

(C) Laziness and relaxation are equal in his mind.

(D) Anyone who gardens is working, not relaxing.

(E) The speaker is a person who finds baking bread more relaxing than working in a garden.

6. In at least one of Hemingway's novels, the heroine dies in childbirth. From that novel, a reader might assume that Hemingway

    6. Ⓐ Ⓑ Ⓒ Ⓓ Ⓔ

(A) hates children

(B) used any plot device which seemed appropriate to the story

(C) dislikes any act associated with the birth of children

(D) always wrote novels with unhappy endings

(E) would have opposed passage of the Equal Rights Amendment

7. The bedroom in which Burt Reynolds sleeps has a mirrored ceiling. That fact demonstrates conclusively that

    7. Ⓐ Ⓑ Ⓒ Ⓓ Ⓔ

(A) Reynolds' bedroom has a mirrored ceiling

(B) Reynolds is a very conceited person

(C) Reynolds can afford to satisfy his desires

(D) Reynolds enjoys looking at his body

(E) Reynolds does some strange things in his bed

Questions 8 and 9 are based on the following:

"The United States Supreme Court, under Chief Justice Warren Burger, has been changing decisions that the court made under Chief Justice Earl Warren. The court should not be allowed to change laws that way."

8. The speaker assumes that the Supreme Court

    8. Ⓐ Ⓑ Ⓒ Ⓓ Ⓔ

(A) has few reasons for revising decisions

(B) should not change decisions already made

(C) has become corrupt under Warren Burger

(D) should still have Earl Warren as Chief Justice

(E) is inefficient in rendering decisions

9. What attitude toward the Supreme Court is the speaker expressing in the statement?

    9. Ⓐ Ⓑ Ⓒ Ⓓ Ⓔ

(A) Earl Warren was a better Chief Justice than Warren Burger is.

(B) Warren Burger is a better Chief Justice than Earl Warren was.

(C) The decisions of the Supreme Court are made by the Chief Justice.

(D) No other Supreme Court Justice matches the abilities of Earl Warren and Warren Burger.

(E) The Chief Justice may have some influence on decisions made by members of the Supreme Court.

10. "Everybody is going to the ball game tonight. Why do you have to stay home and study?"

    10. Ⓐ Ⓑ Ⓒ Ⓓ Ⓔ

The asker of that question

(A) says that studying may be more important than attending a ball game

(B) enjoys staying home to study

(C) says that attending ball games is more important than studying

(D) makes poor grades in school

(E) finds studying rather boring and monotonous

Questions 11 and 12 are based on the following:

"Many children watch television several hours each day. The medium has become an excellent baby-sitter."

11. This statement 11. Ⓐ Ⓑ Ⓒ Ⓓ Ⓔ
    (A) is negative about the quality of television programs
    (B) says nothing about the quality of television programs
    (C) is positive about the quality of television programs
    (D) says children watch too much television each day
    (E) means that the speaker does not like children

12. The phrase "an excellent baby sitter" in the statement could imply that the writer 12. Ⓐ Ⓑ Ⓒ Ⓓ Ⓔ
    (A) would be opposed to hiring a baby-sitter for his children
    (B) enjoys watching television with the children
    (C) believes that television programs are too simple to appeal to adults
    (D) believes that many television programs have been written primarily for children
    (E) cannot watch many television programs without feeling guilty

13. "Many men and women enjoy cooking nowadays. That's the reason so many people are overweight." 13. Ⓐ Ⓑ Ⓒ Ⓓ Ⓔ

    The writer of these sentences assumes that

    (A) fewer people should cook to prevent their becoming overweight
    (B) all cooks eat every dish which they prepare
    (C) there are some meals which are not fattening
    (D) cooks prepare food which causes them to be underweight
    (E) there is some kind of inverse relationship between cooking and eating

14. In *Saturday Night Fever*, John Travolta played the role of a young Italian who found complete happiness only while dancing at a disco. What does this tell us about John Travolta? 14. Ⓐ Ⓑ Ⓒ Ⓓ Ⓔ
    (A) He always dresses in skin-tight pants and goes dancing every night.
    (B) His only complete satisfaction comes from performing on the dance floor.
    (C) John Travolta is an actor and plays a role which the script of the film requires.
    (D) John Travolta's private and professional lives cannot be separated.
    (E) John Travolta is a very wealthy young man.

Questions 15 and 16 are based on the following:

Dean Martin is over sixty years old and still attracts crowds to his performances in Las Vegas and Reno, Nevada, which permit legalized gambling. Martin is famous as a heavy drinker of alcoholic beverages.

15. These sentences might lead a reader to conclude that Dean Martin 15. Ⓐ Ⓑ Ⓒ Ⓓ Ⓔ
    (A) is unsuccessful in attracting crowds except in Reno and Las Vegas
    (B) should join Alcoholics Anonymous
    (C) can provide customers with entertainment in Las Vegas and Reno

(D) gambles when he appears in Reno and Las Vegas

(E) is too old to be successful anywhere except Reno and Las Vegas

16. The statement also assumes that Dean Martin's alleged heavy drinking of alcoholic beverages

(A) has ruined his career in Las Vegas and Reno

(B) interferes with his abilities as a gambler

(C) guarantees an audience for him in Reno and Las Vegas

(D) makes him more popular with women than with men in Las Vegas and Reno

(E) has had no effect upon his ability as an entertainer in Reno and Las Vegas

ANSWERS AND EXPLANATIONS

1. E. The other choices cannot be supported by the facts in the statement.
2. B. The other choices cannot be concluded from the facts given.
3. D. No other choice would be valid.
4. C. The other choices contain generalizations for which there is no evidence in the statement.
5. E. The other choices cannot be concluded by the facts given.
6. B. There is no evidence to support the other choices.
7. A. The other choices are hasty generalizations based on insufficient evidence.
8. B. All other choices cannot be concluded from the original statement.
9. E. Note the word may in (E). All the others are invalid.
10. C. No other valid conclusion could be drawn.
11. B. The other choices cannot be supported by the statement.
12. D. Note the words could imply in the statement; (D), then, is the only valid response.
13. B. (B) is the only valid choice.
14. C. The other choices are illogical.
15. C. The other choices are invalid conclusions from the facts.
16. E. No other choice is valid.

Type 2: The Attitude Discerning Item: about 15%–20% of Part II

Again, in this section of the CLEP examination you will be concerned with logical conclusions, this time from the connotations of words and the tone of a statement rather than what the words mean on a literal level. For instance, someone might say, "I *like* her," with a smile on his face, emphasizing the word *like*. Someone else might also say "I like *her*," emphasizing the word *her*. Even though the words are exactly the same, the meaning conveyed is entirely different. Look carefully at the question which precedes each set of five sentences, and study carefully the choices which are provided. Remember, also, that words may say more than their literal meanings and that you should be aware of both the denotations and connotations of words.

Directions: In the following questions, you are to compare various statements in the light of the questions posed. Pay attention to the tone, emphasis, and implications of each of the statements as you select the one response that is best in each case.

1. Which of the following statements is the most negative about John's abilities as a football player?

    (A) John has scored only four touchdowns this year.

    (B) The team did not elect John captain this year.

    (C) None of the coaches believe John can become a professional.

    (D) None of the female cheerleaders think John is handsome.

    (E) John is unable to run through a defensive line if the opponents are too heavy for him.

1. Ⓐ Ⓑ Ⓒ Ⓓ Ⓔ

The answer is (E). (B) and (C) are also negative about John's football playing ability; (D) is also negative but does not deal with John's football playing ability; and (A) may or may not be negative. (E) is the most negative.

2. Which of the following statements is the most positive about Sarah's abilities as a graduate student?

    (A) Sarah always hands in her papers ahead of the deadline.

    (B) Sarah can track down the most obscure reference and discover the source of the information.

    (C) Sarah listens to music while she is writing her papers.

    (D) Sarah's professors believe she will become a successful teacher.

    (E) Sarah keeps the library staff on their toes finding material for her.

2. Ⓐ Ⓑ Ⓒ Ⓓ Ⓔ

The correct answer is (B). All of the other statements are positive about Sarah, but none of the others have anything to do with her abilities as a graduate student.

3. Which of the following statements is the most negative about Sarah's abilities as a graduate student?

    (A) Sarah never hands in her papers ahead of the deadline.

    (B) Sarah listens to loud music while she is writing her papers.

    (C) Sarah can seldom find what she is looking for in the library; thus, her research is inadequate.

    (D) Sarah's professors do not believe that she can become a successful teacher.

    (E) Sarah does not go to the library very often.

3. Ⓐ Ⓑ Ⓒ Ⓓ Ⓔ

The correct answer is (C). All of the other choices are negative, but (C) is the most negative.

4. Which of the following statements can be proven true or false by specific pieces of concrete evidence?

    (A) There is a god in heaven.

    (B) John Jones is guilty of murder.

    (C) Love makes the world go round.

    (D) Susie Smith is an attractive young woman.

    (E) The world is going to hell in a handbasket.

4. Ⓐ Ⓑ Ⓒ Ⓓ Ⓔ

The correct answer is (B). All of the other choices could not be proved because each statement represents a personal reaction to an idea or subject.

Now, try several items of this type.

1. Which of the following statements is the most positive about Jeanne as a dress designer?
   (A) Jeanne's evening gowns are suitable for every woman, no matter what her age or size.
   (B) Jeanne buys good fabrics from the most expensive weavers of fine silks and satins.
   (C) Jeanne's clothing designs are based on those that were popular during the 1920s.
   (D) Jeanne employs many women to work in her clothing manufacturing department.
   (E) Jeanne became a famous fashion designer after many years of working with more famous designers.

1. Ⓐ Ⓑ Ⓒ Ⓓ Ⓔ

2. Which of the following statements is the most negative about Jeanne as a dress designer?
   (A) Jeanne's evening gowns have many pleats and ribbons.
   (B) Jeanne's fabrics reflect her taste for silks and satins.
   (C) Jeanne's clothing designs are too much like those popular during the 1920s.
   (D) Jeanne worked for many years as an assistant to a famous Paris clothes designer.
   (E) Jeanne's clothing designs are not suitable for young women.

2. Ⓐ Ⓑ Ⓒ Ⓓ Ⓔ

3. Which of the following statements best expresses the speaker's attitude toward a minority group?
   (A) If my grandfather could make it in this country, so can they.
   (B) Most of that group are on welfare; they are too lazy to work.
   (C) That group should all go back where they came from.
   (D) The members of that group certainly do not look after their children.
   (E) They don't even know English and should be forced to learn the language.

3. Ⓐ Ⓑ Ⓒ Ⓓ Ⓔ

4. Which of the following statements is the most complimentary of Jacques' ability as a cook?
   (A) His sauces are seldom too thick or too rich with butter.
   (B) He buys the most expensive cut of meat for his beef stew.
   (C) He can always find something in the refrigerator to eat.
   (D) He can take a few simple ingredients and produce a fine meal.
   (E) He can follow a recipe with few problems.

4. Ⓐ Ⓑ Ⓒ Ⓓ Ⓔ

5. Which of the following statements expresses the most negative attitude toward the federal income tax form?
   (A) The paper on which the form is printed is too large to go into my typewriter.
   (B) I can hardly read the fine print on the second page of the form.
   (C) The directions for filling out the form are in such long sentences that I cannot understand what information is required.
   (D) The calculations are so complex that I have to use an adding machine.
   (E) There is not enough space on the form for me to answer questions completely.

5. Ⓐ Ⓑ Ⓒ Ⓓ Ⓔ

6. Most magazines are edited and published with a specific audience in mind. Which of the following statements most clearly indicates the expected audience for the magazine?
   (A) *The New Yorker* has many advertisements for luxury automobiles and expensive clothes.
   (B) *New York* publishes reviews of books, plays, films, and classical recordings.
   (C) *Time* contains at least one long essay each week on a current news figure or topic.
   (D) *Good Housekeeping* publishes recipes for dishes which are inexpensive to prepare and which would appeal to young homemakers.
   (E) *Mother Jones* is a publication which emphasizes news and articles that might not be published in other magazines.

   6. Ⓐ Ⓑ Ⓒ Ⓓ Ⓔ

7. Which of the following suggests that the speaker has no definite opinion about marijuana smoking?
   (A) Many young people these days smoke marijuana.
   (B) Smoking too much marijuana could be damaging to your health.
   (C) At least, marijuana is not as dangerous as alcohol.
   (D) There is no organization called Marijuana Anonymous.
   (E) People who smoke marijuana always wind up shooting heroin.

   7. Ⓐ Ⓑ Ⓒ Ⓓ Ⓔ

8. Which of the following suggests that John does not have the support of his community?
   (A) John always speaks up at town council meetings.
   (B) The town council never approves what John proposes.
   (C) John always trades with home-town merchants.
   (D) With John, you can never tell what his real motives are.
   (E) John scheduled a speech in the town hall, and no one showed up.

   8. Ⓐ Ⓑ Ⓒ Ⓓ Ⓔ

9. Which of the following is the most positive opinion of the film *Star Wars*?
   (A) George Lucas, the director, combined features from the old-fashioned western with space gimmicks.
   (B) Everyone who worked on the film caught the magic flavor that the director wanted to convey.
   (C) The costumes that the cast wore were elegant.
   (D) Harrison Ford and Carrie Fisher made a delightful team.
   (E) The special effects were extraordinary.

   9. Ⓐ Ⓑ Ⓒ Ⓓ Ⓔ

10. Which of the following statements is the most negative about the film *Beverly Hills Cop*?
    (A) Eddie Murphy is not a very good actor.
    (B) The plot, such as there was, was too unbelievable.
    (C) The director lost control of the film about half way through, and from that point on, there was too much violence.
    (D) There was not one single attractive actress on the screen.
    (E) The film was obviously filmed with fake settings, because they did not look realistic.

    10. Ⓐ Ⓑ Ⓒ Ⓓ Ⓔ

ANSWERS AND EXPLANATIONS

1. A.   (B), (D), and (E) say nothing about Jeanne's ability as a designer of clothes. (C) refers to only one characteristic of Jeanne's designs.
2. C.   (E) is also negative but not as negative as (C). (A), (B), and (D) are not necessarily negative.
3. B.   All of the choices are negative about the minority group, but (B) is the most negative.
4. D.   The other choices comment on only one characteristic of a good cook.
5. C.   All of the choices are negative about the income tax form, but (C) is the most negative.
6. D.   The other choices do not say very much about the audience for the magazines whose names are given; they make statements about certain features which the magazines contain.
7. A.   (A) makes a statement which the speaker believes to be true, but it expresses no opinion about marijuana smoking.
8. E.   (A) and (C) say nothing about John's support from the community. (B) speaks only of the town council, not the community as a whole, and (D) implies that John does not reveal his motives, a characteristic which may be bad or good.
9. B.   (B) is the only choice which considers the film as a whole; the others select certain isolated features of the film.
10. C.   (C) is the only choice which considers the film as a whole, rather than individual aspects of the movie.

Type 3:   The Sentence Relationship Item: about 33% of Part II

Type 3 questions require you to figure out the relationship between two sentences. In order to do well on this section of the test you need to know what certain words mean and how to apply those meanings to specific sentences; therefore, be sure to check such words as *generalization, exception, comparison, contrast, cause, effect, definition, conclusion* (the definition from formal logic), *affirms* (also from formal logic), *example,* and a few other words you will run across in the sample questions below.

Directions: In this group of questions, two underlined sentences are followed by a question or incomplete statement about them. Read each group of sentences and then choose the best answer to the question or the best completion of the statement.

1.   The Cuisinart Food Processor is an expensive kitchen appliance.
     It can be used to make delicious salad dressings.

     Sentence two

     (A) compares the cost of the Cuisinart with its usefulness
     (B) provides an exception to the cost of the Cuisinart
     (C) draws a conclusion about the function of the Cuisinart
     (D) implies that the Cuisinart is not worth its cost
     (E) gives an example of the Cuisinart's function

     The correct answer is (E). The other choices are incorrect.

1.   Ⓐ Ⓑ Ⓒ Ⓓ Ⓔ

2. Next to the window was an old chair with a red cushion on its seat. Across the room there was a sofa with ten blue pillows on it.

In these two sentences, the objects are organized according to

(A) their size and shape
(B) the colors of the pillows and cushion
(C) the age of the two pieces of furniture
(D) their location in the room
(E) their uses as furniture

The correct answer is (D), the only choice which states the one thing the two sentences have in common—the location of the furniture.

3. The Art Deco style of interior decoration uses aluminum and white as major colors. The Radio City Music Hall in New York is in the Art Deco style.

Sentence two

(A) makes an exception
(B) provides an illustration
(C) draws a conclusion
(D) makes a comparison
(E) defines Art Deco

The correct answer is (B). The other choices are incorrect.

4. John Travolta is a better dancer than is Olivia Newton-John. Olivia Newton-John is a better singer than is John Travolta.

What can the reader conclude from these two sentences?

(A) Both John Travolta and Olivia Newton-John are talented, but their talents are different.
(B) The contrast between the two performers is not valid.
(C) John Travolta is more popular than is Olivia Newton-John.
(D) Olivia Newton-John is more popular than is John Travolta.
(E) Singing and dancing represent different aspects of the same talent.

The correct answer is (A). Note: In arriving at your choice for an answer, do not go beyond the facts actually stated in the two sentences. For example, (C) and (D) are incorrect, because the sentences say nothing about the popularity of either celebrity.

5. Jim works hard every day at his job. He reports for duty at 7:30 and does not leave until 6:00.

Sentence two

(A) provides a cause for the statement in sentence one
(B) contrasts Jim with other employees
(C) says that Jim is different from other employees
(D) introduces an idea which has nothing to do with sentence one
(E) implies a confirmation of the generalization in sentence one

The correct answer is (E). The other choices go beyond the facts given in the two sentences.

Now try a group of these items:

1. The politicans in city hall are interested only in staying in office.
   The mayor campaigns for reelection all year long.

   Sentence two

   (A) compares the mayor to the average voter
   (B) contrasts the mayor with other politicians
   (C) defines the generalization in sentence one
   (D) is an example to support the generalization in sentence one
   (E) gives an exception to the generalization in sentence one

   1. Ⓐ Ⓑ Ⓒ Ⓓ Ⓔ

2. There is no wind tonight.
   The water of the lake is calm.

   Sentence two

   (A) states the cause of the facts in sentence one
   (B) generalizes upon the facts in sentence one
   (C) is a contrast to what happens in sentence one
   (D) defines what is stated in sentence one
   (E) shows the effect of the cause stated in sentence one

   2. Ⓐ Ⓑ Ⓒ Ⓓ Ⓔ

3. The front of the old house faces a small lake.
   Behind the house, there are many large trees.

   The relationship established by these two sentences is one based on

   (A) the shape of objects
   (B) the age of the objects
   (C) the size of the objects
   (D) the usefulness of the objects
   (E) the location of objects

   3. Ⓐ Ⓑ Ⓒ Ⓓ Ⓔ

4. *Grease* is a film about high school students in the 1950s.
   American Graffiti, a film made earlier, is set in the same period.

   What is happening in these two sentences?

   (A) A contrast is developed on the basis of the quality of the films.
   (B) A comparison is made on the basis of the decade in which the films are set.
   (C) A conclusion is drawn about the times during which the films were actually made.
   (D) A generalization is made about high school students in the 1950s.
   (E) Each sentence is an example which supports an earlier generalization.

   4. Ⓐ Ⓑ Ⓒ Ⓓ Ⓔ

5. Mary is a very neat person.
   She can never find anything in her pocketbook.

   What is the effect of sentence two?

   (A) It gives an example.
   (B) It makes a comparison to the first sentence.
   (C) It is an illustration.
   (D) It makes an exception.
   (E) It is a generalization.

   5. Ⓐ Ⓑ Ⓒ Ⓓ Ⓔ

6. The teacher's table is in the front of the room.
    The students' desks are in a circle around the walls.

    Which of the following sentences best describes what the two sentences tell
    us about the organization of the classroom?

    (A) The teacher's table is not remote from the students' desks.
    (B) The students' desks are arranged awkwardly.
    (C) The room arrangement separates students from teacher.
    (D) The room may be too large for the class and teacher.
    (E) The teacher's table must be square and the student's desks round.

6. Ⓐ Ⓑ Ⓒ Ⓓ Ⓔ

7. In the picture, there are two trees in the background.
    In the foreground, the painted lady smiles sweetly.

    The objects in these two sentences are related according to

    (A) where they are in the picture
    (B) who painted the picture
    (C) how the colors blend into each other
    (D) the appearance of the painting from the right side
    (E) which were painted first

7. Ⓐ Ⓑ Ⓒ Ⓓ Ⓔ

8. Too many french fries at dinner always make me thirsty.
    I was up all night drinking water.

    The two sentences illustrate

    (A) a comparison between two unlike ideas
    (B) a contrast between two similar ideas
    (C) a possible cause-effect relationship
    (D) generalization with an illustration
    (E) two totally unrelated ideas

8. Ⓐ Ⓑ Ⓒ Ⓓ Ⓔ

9. All young people today listen to loud music.
    The Bee Gees compose and play loud music.

    Sentence two seems to imply that

    (A) loud music may not be popular with the Bee Gees
    (B) all young people listen to the Bee Gees
    (C) the Bee Gees are popular only with young people
    (D) the Bee Gees may be an exception to the rule
    (E) young people today have no musical taste

9. Ⓐ Ⓑ Ⓒ Ⓓ Ⓔ

10. "Disaster" films were very popular during the 1970s.
    One of the best of this type is *Jaws*.

    Sentence two
    (A) says nothing about the quality of *Jaws*
    (B) defines the "disaster" type of film
    (C) implies that *Jaws* is a popular film
    (D) considers *Jaws* an unimportant film
    (E) states that *Jaws* was not very popular

10. Ⓐ Ⓑ Ⓒ Ⓓ Ⓔ

11. More expensive cuts of beef are usually more tender.
A filet mignon can be very expensive.

What does sentence two do here?

(A) It draws a conclusion about one cut of beef.
(B) It compares two cuts of beef.
(C) It makes an exception.
(D) It gives a possible example.
(E) It contrasts filet mignon with other cuts of beef.

11. Ⓐ Ⓑ Ⓒ Ⓓ Ⓔ

12. Many antique chairs are pleasant to look at but uncomfortable to sit in.
I like to sit in my old Morris chair.

Sentence two

(A) makes an exception
(B) implies that the Morris chair is not an antique
(C) compares chairs on the basis of their age
(D) contrasts two kinds of chairs
(E) draws a conclusion about antique chairs

12. Ⓐ Ⓑ Ⓒ Ⓓ Ⓔ

13. Many small foreign automobiles have seats for two people.
Large American cars provide seating for at least five people.

What is happening in these sentences?

(A) A contrast is made on the basis of comfort and capacity.
(B) A conclusion is drawn on the basis of size.
(C) A comparison is made on the basis of size and capacity.
(D) A relationship is developed between the origins of the automobiles.
(E) A comparison is made on the basis of size and cost.

13. Ⓐ Ⓑ Ⓒ Ⓓ Ⓔ

14. All men are yellow.
John is a man.

What does the second sentence do?

(A) It states a generalization.
(B) It gives an example.
(C) It makes an exception.
(D) It gives the effect from the cause in the first sentence.
(E) It supports the concrete generalization of sentence one.

14. Ⓐ Ⓑ Ⓒ Ⓓ Ⓔ

15. John lives on the lake nine months of each year.
The other three months he lives in town.
What does the second sentence do?
(A) It completes the time sequence begun in sentence one.
(B) It gives an example.
(C) It is a vague generalization.
(D) It provides an exception.
(E) It introduces a new idea.

ANSWERS AND EXPLANATIONS

1. **D.** (A) and (B) are incorrect because the two sentences neither compare nor contrast anything. (C) is incorrect because sentence 2 is not a definition. (E) is incorrect because no exception is stated.

2. **E.** (A) is wrong because sentence 2 is an effect, not a cause. Choice (B) is a specific fact, not a generalization. (C) is incorrect because two things are not being contrasted. (D) is incorrect because sentence 2 is not a definition.

3. **E.** (E) is the only choice which relates trees and the lake by reference to the house. Shape, age, size, and usefulness of the objects are not mentioned in the two sentences.

4. **B.** (A) is incorrect because there is no contrast. (C) is incorrect because no conclusion can be drawn from the statement of the two facts. (D) and (E) are incorrect because no generalization is stated.

5. **D.** (A) says the two sentences are complementary; they are contradictory. (B) is incorrect, because the two sentences are almost contrasting in meaning. (C) is incorrect, because sentence 2 does not illustrate sentence 1. (E) is incorrect because sentence 2 is not a generalization.

6. **C.** There are no facts in the sentences which would support choices (A), (B), (D) or (E); they represent incorrect inferences from the facts.

7. **A.** The other choices cannot be supported by the facts given in the two sentences.

8. **C.** The other choices are illogical; there is no evidence for a contrast, a comparison, or a generalization. (E) is also incorrect because the two sentences are related in some way.

9. **B.** (A) is incorrect because we do not know what kind of music the Bee Gees like. (C) and (D) go beyond the facts in the two sentences. (E) is an unwarranted conclusion which the facts cannot support.

10. **C.** (A) contradicts sentence 2. (B) is incorrect because sentence 2 is not a definition. (D) and (E) are inferences which cannot be supported by the facts in the two sentences.

11. **D.** The other choices cannot be correct, because sentence 2 draws no conclusion, makes no comparison, makes no exception, or makes no contrast.

12. **A.** The other choices cannot be supported by the facts in the sentences.

13. **C.** (C) is the only one which considers both the size (small, large) and the seating capacity (two, five) of the two kinds of automobiles. The others consider other characteristics.

14. **B.** The other choices are illogical inferences from the facts given.

15. **A.** The other choices say nothing about the time sequence developed in the two sentences.

Type 4: The Paragraph Organization Item: about 15%–20% of Part II

To do well on this type of question, you need to be aware that most paragraphs have a logical organization — a beginning, a middle, and a conclusion. They begin with a topic sentence — the sentence which announces what the paragraph will concern, and then a writer supports that topic sentence (often in the form of a generalization) with specific details, illustrations, examples, or some other means of development. In these items, you will be asked to read a passage which may be more than one paragraph. You may be asked to shift the order of sentences so that the logical organization of the paragraph may be maintained. You may also be asked to divide the passage into two or more paragraphs at the appropriate point in the passage. You may be asked to omit certain sentences so that details which do not apply to the topic sentence may be eliminated. You may also be asked to revise certain sentences and connect them with others in the passage to improve the coherence of the passage. Study any of the books listed in the bibliography at the beginning of this chapter, especially any chapters on rhetoric, and you will receive some valuable tips on how to handle this type of item.

Let's try one example:

Directions: Each of the questions or incomplete statements in the following questions is followed by five suggested answers or completions. Select the one that is best in each case, paying attention to grammar, usage, diction, idiom, and tone.

Questions 1-3 are based on the following passage:

[1]Congress seems to have quite a few disciples of Paddy Bauer, the late 43rd Ward alderman who declared that "Chicago ain't ready for reform." [2]In their view, civil service ain't ready for reform either, and they are out to keep President Carter from reforming it. [3]The House Post Office and Civil Service Committee recently got hold of Mr. Carter's proposal to streamline hiring and dismissal procedures for federal employees — the program he called the keystone to his efforts to make government more efficient. [4]The bill it finally approved, 18 to 7, was not only useless as a reform measure, it attacked the whole purpose of civil service. [5]The Committee's bill would allow government employees to engage in partisan political activities, meaning that they would be subject to political pressures from their superiors. [6]That is exactly the practice from which civil service was intended to protect them, and which in any event is strictly forbidden by the Hatch Act. [7]The series of hearings show clearly that Congress is protecting those employees who owe their jobs to the political clout of their political sponsors.

1. What should be done with sentence 4?
   (A) It should be moved to the end of the passage.
   (B) It should be placed after sentence 1.
   (C) It should be left where it is.
   (D) It should be omitted.
   (E) It should be placed just after sentence 6.

1. Ⓐ Ⓑ Ⓒ Ⓓ Ⓔ

2. Sentence 7
   (A) is a logical conclusion to the passage
   (B) introduces material which is not really relevant to the rest of the passage
   (C) should be the first sentence in the passage
   (D) should begin with *While* and be connected to sentence 6
   (E) should immediately precede sentence 3

2. Ⓐ Ⓑ Ⓒ Ⓓ Ⓔ

3. If you were to divide the passage into two paragraphs, the second paragraph would logically begin with
   (A) sentence 6
   (B) sentence 4
   (C) sentence 2
   (D) sentence 3
   (E) sentence 5

3. Ⓐ Ⓑ Ⓒ Ⓓ Ⓔ

ANSWERS AND EXPLANATIONS

1. **C.** Any change in the position of the sentence would disrupt the coherence of the paragraph.
2. **A.** (B) is not true; no new ideas being introduced here. The other choices are also incorrect.
3. **D.** Sentence 3 gets to the specifics of the whole paragraph after the historical review in sentences 1 and 2. None of the other sentences would be acceptable as topic sentences for a new paragraph.

Now try another passage:

Questions 1-3 are based on the following passage:

¹My basement is designed to be a family room, although we do not usually use it that way. ²My desk is down here where it is cool, quiet, and away from the noise of the street outside the house. ³My living room has three large windows which look out on my neighbors' driveway; thus, I can keep up with their comings and goings all hours of the day. ⁴In my basement, I have my typewriter, all the files I need to do my writing, and a radio which I keep tuned to a good FM station. ⁵I can get more work done if I have some "white noise" to block out the interference of other noises in the house. ⁶When I withdraw to the basement to read papers or write, my wife knows that she is not to disturb me except in case of an extreme emergency like the house catching on fire or something like that. ⁷I also have my library stored down here so that I can reach for a book that I might need to refer to when I read or write. ⁸There is also a bed; sometimes I get tired of typing and want to stretch out for a few minutes to rest my weary back and fingers.

1. What should be done with sentence 3?
   (A) It should begin the passage.
   (B) It should be omitted.
   (C) It should come after sentence 5.
   (D) It should come after sentence 8.
   (E) It should be combined with sentence 4.

   1. Ⓐ Ⓑ Ⓒ Ⓓ Ⓔ

2. Sentence 5
   (A) should be omitted
   (B) should be reduced to a clause, beginning *if*, and joined to sentence 7
   (C) should begin with *and* and be joined to sentence 8
   (D) should come at the beginning of the passage
   (E) should begin with *because* and be joined to sentence 4

   2. Ⓐ Ⓑ Ⓒ Ⓓ Ⓔ

3. A logical concluding sentence for this passage would be which of the following?
   (A) My library is the most important thing in my life.
   (B) I spend many happy hours in my living room, watching my neighbors.
   (C) My basement is the center of my professional life; without it, I would be forced to write less than I do.
   (D) My basement is furnished with early American antiques.
   (E) My FM radio provides me with many hours of amusement.

   3. Ⓐ Ⓑ Ⓒ Ⓓ Ⓔ

ANSWERS AND EXPLANATIONS

1. **B.** (B) shifts from the basement to the living room, and the whole paragraph is about the basement; thus, sentence 3 is irrelevant to the paragraph.
2. **E.** (A) is incorrect, because sentence 5 adds important information. (B) and (C) would create illogical sentences. (D) is incorrect, because sentence 5 would not be a good topic sentence for the whole paragraph.
3. **C.** All of the other choices focus on minor points in the paragraph; only (C) summarizes the paragraph effectively.

Now try several passages:

Questions 1-3 are based on the following passage:

¹Since it's four days before the final day to register to vote, I'll say it once: register. ²On February 21, just go to your precinct from 8 AM to 9 AM. ³If you don't register, then don't read the rest of this column. ⁴It's directed toward people who care about what's happening. ⁵The rest of you can slide along on the efforts of the people who care. ⁶But don't gripe about the state of affairs.⁷As a nonregistered voter, you give up your most prized possession, the ability to say and demand that the government operate for your benefit, not for the benefit of a handful of machine politicians and their flunkies. ⁸March 21 will be significant for two reasons. ⁹It's the first day of spring, traditionally the day when nature renews herself. ¹⁰The animals come out of hibernation (or out of the bars depending on the animals you know), the flowers start blooming, the grass grows green, and the birds leave their mark on your new spring outfit. ¹¹But whether these events actually take place on March 21 or not is out of your control. ¹²You can't legislate the laws of nature but on March 21 you can legislate the laws of man, assuming, of course, that we choose the right man to represent us.

From *GayLife*, Feb. 17, 1978. Reprinted by permission.

1. Sentence 4 should begin

    1. Ⓐ Ⓑ Ⓒ Ⓓ Ⓔ

    (A) *Not registering,*
    (B) *Because you did not register,*
    (C) *That you don't register,*
    (D) the way it does now
    (E) *Not reading the rest of this column,*

2. A more logical replacement for sentence 1 would be which of the following?

    2. Ⓐ Ⓑ Ⓒ Ⓓ Ⓔ

    (A) I have a feeling that many people will not register to vote as they should.
    (B) Voting is a prime responsibility of every American, but if you do not register, you cannot vote.
    (C) What are you doing on February 21?
    (D) If you do not vote, you should not gripe about what happens to you.
    (E) Registering to vote is a complicated procedure; therefore, you should start preparing to register several days in advance.

3. If you were to divide the passage into two paragraphs, the logical sentence to begin paragraph 2 would be

    3. Ⓐ Ⓑ Ⓒ Ⓓ Ⓔ

    (A) sentence 2
    (B) sentence 6
    (C) sentence 12
    (D) sentence 4
    (E) sentence 8

Questions 4-6 are based on the following passage:

[1]*Sgt. Pepper's Lonely Hearts Club Band* is a mountainous project that has turned into a real molehill of a movie. [2]This is movie-making by committee, its subject matter and stars picked according to their affiliations with the producer-managers. [3]Looming behind it all is Robert Stigwood, the pop entrepreneur who successfully packaged *Saturday Night Fever* and whose past experiences with *Tommy* and *Jesus Christ Superstar* led him to this attempt to create a new rock opera out of some two dozen songs by John Lennon, Paul McCartney, and George Harrison. [4]The result, for all the money spent, is a movie that has no real reason for being, except the merchandising opportunities it offers in spinoffs of books, records, T-shirts, and other paraphenalia. [5]It is ironic indeed that a film so obviously fabricated for commercial purposes is based on a story about innocence corrupted by greedy big business. [6]The fable constructed by Henry Edwards, a former pop music critic, concerns Billy Shears (Peter Frampton), a grandson of the original Sgt. Pepper, and his three pals, the Henderson boys (Barry, Robin, and Maurice, the Brothers Gibb) who leave their idyllic hometown of Heartland to pursue a career in a wicked world with Big Deal Records. [7]Meanwhile, back in Heartland, the precious instruments of the original Lonely Hearts Club Band are stolen and the town is turned into punk decadence by the venal real estate dealer, Mean Mr. Mustard (English comedian Frankie Howord). [8]Racing home to save Heartland, the four boys retrieve the instruments from various villains, but in so doing, they lose the life of Strawberry Fields (Sandy Farina), Billy's best girl. [9]Only when a weather vane of Sgt. Pepper comes to life (in the person of the frenetic Billy Preston) does the story end happily.

Reprinted from the *Chicago Tribune*. Courtesy of the *Chicago Tribune*.

4. Sentence 5 should begin
   (A) The way it begins now
   (B) *Moreover, while it is ironic*
   (C) *Therefore, it is ironic*
   (D) *As well as being ironic*
   (E) *Indeed, being ironic*

4. Ⓐ Ⓑ Ⓒ Ⓓ Ⓔ

5. What should be done with sentence 3?
   (A) The part after *and whose past* should be omitted.
   (B) It should begin with *Having been loomed*.
   (C) It should be left as it is.
   (D) It should be omitted completely.
   (E) It should be placed after sentence 9.

5. Ⓐ Ⓑ Ⓒ Ⓓ Ⓔ

6. A logical conclusion for the passage would be which of the following sentences?
   (A) The film deserves to be very popular with Beatle music fans.
   (B) I got up and walked out on the film after the first fifty minutes.
   (C) The film is not very good, because too much money was spent creating a monumental bore.
   (D) Robert Stigwood, the producer, is famous in Hollywood for producing previously successful films.
   (E) Peter Frampton who plays Billy Spears seems miscast in his role.

6. Ⓐ Ⓑ Ⓒ Ⓓ Ⓔ

Questions 7-9 are based on the following passage:

¹In jazz, there are musicmakers and stylemakers. ²While it's not true that never the twain shall meet, the differences between the two types can be obvious — especially when it comes to pianists. ³Ahmad Jamal, who plays through Sunday at the Jazz Showcase, is a classic example of a stylemaker. ⁴Or at least he used to be. ⁵When his trio made it big in 1958, Jamal's music was all patterns. ⁶With the light swing of Vernell Fournier's cymbals and the deep throb of Israel Crosby's bass, it served as a background for the pianist's carefully calculated alternations between kittenish delicacy and hammered-out crescendos. ⁷As someone once said of the old Jamal, his real instrument was the audience, not the piano. ⁸Well, Jamal circa 1978 is close to being something else altogether — although as he progressed Wednesday night, the links to his former manner became apparent. ⁹The first piece in a generously long set of original compositions, all unidentified by the leader, must have left oldtime Jamal fans in the audience wondering whether they had walked in by mistake on McCoy Tyner. ¹⁰Instead of the familiar cute melodies separated by acres of silence, there was a continuous flow of sound — harmonically dense, beautifully articulated modal lines that build powerfully in the fashion of the mid-1960s John Coltrane rhythm section, in which Tyner was paired with Jimmy Garrison and Elvin Jones. ¹¹It made for nervous music at first, but it was a good kind of nervousness. ¹²And when Taylor and Crossley got into the groove, the tension in the band become entirely positive.

Adapted from the *Chicago Tribune*. Courtesy of the *Chicago Tribune*.

7. What should be done with sentence 6?
   (A) It should be left as it is.
   (B) It should begin with *With the light swinging*.
   (C) Eliminate *With* and , *it*, and let the rest of the sentence stand as it is.
   (D) Eliminate everything after *Israel Crosby's bass*.
   (E) It should be reduced in length.

7. Ⓐ Ⓑ Ⓒ Ⓓ Ⓔ

8. A better version of sentence 7 is which of the following?
   (A) Someone once said of the old Jamal that his real instrument was the audience, not the piano.
   (B) The piano, not the audience, has always been Jamal's best audience.
   (C) Jamal has always played his audiences as if they were better than the piano.
   (D) Working hard on his piano, Jamal played it as if it were his real audience.
   (E) Jamal's use of his piano has always been better than his uses of his audience.

8. Ⓐ Ⓑ Ⓒ Ⓓ Ⓔ

9. Sentence one
   (A) is an unsatisfactory topic sentence for the passage
   (B) establishes the point that the reviewer makes in his review of Jamal's concert
   (C) should be changed to include Jamal's name
   (D) is too short to be a topic sentence for this passage
   (E) states a contrast that is explained in the passage

9. Ⓐ Ⓑ Ⓒ Ⓓ Ⓔ

ANSWERS AND EXPLANATIONS

1. **D.** (D) is the only choice which keeps the paragraph coherent. Any other change would create a nonsense sentence.
2. **B.** (B) is the only logical restatement of sentence 1. (A) is weak. (C) omits the importance of registering to vote, not merely voting. (D) also omits the matter of registering to vote. (E) is wordy and not a good opening sentence.
3. **E.** Since the rest of the passage concerns some events which occur on March 21, sentence 8 would make a good introduction to a new paragraph.
4. **A.** (B), (D), and (E) would produce sentence fragments. In (C) therefore adds little to the meaning of the sentence.
5. **C.** (A) would omit some significant information about Robert Stigwood. The other choices would also create ineffective sentences.
6. **C.** (A) is incorrect, because that sentence (maybe positive about the film) contradicts the negative tone of the whole review. (B) is not a summary of the passage. (D) and (E) select what may be minor points in the review to emphasize in the conclusion.
7. **C.** (A) is incorrect, because the sentence contains it, a vague pronoun. (C) corrects that problem. The other choices would not create effective sentences.
8. **A.** The other choices would create confused or ambiguous sentences.
9. **B.** (B) is the only correct response, because the whole passage emphasizes Jamal as a piano player for whom style is most important.

Part II (essay version)

This section asks you to use forty-five minutes to write an essay on a given topic. You will find below specific directions, one sample topic, and three sample essays written in response to the topic.

In scoring essays, readers look for logical development of the argument, appropriate use of specific examples, unity in the composition, and clarity and effectiveness of expression, as well as use of the conventions of standard written English. They recognize that some errors are the result of haste rather than of ignorance and do not allow such errors to influence their rating of the quality of the total essay. You may wish to rate the sample essays below high, medium, or low using these guidelines.

Directions: You will have 45 minutes to plan and write an essay on the topic specified. Read the topic carefully. You are expected to spend a few minutes considering the topic and organizing your thoughts before you begin writing. *Do not write on a topic other than the one specified. (An essay on a topic of your own choice is not acceptable.)*

The essay is being assigned to give you an opportunity to demonstrate your ability to write effectively. You should, therefore, take care to express your thoughts on a topic clearly and exactly and to make them interesting. Be specific, using supporting examples whenever appropriate. How well you write is much more important than how much you write.

Assignment: Some people feel that studying "traditional" subjects such as history, sciences, and literature does not have much importance today. They believe that education should be directed toward a career and that the most significant studies in college are those which will help one earn a living in today's society. As examples, they point to accounting courses, secretarial studies, electronics courses, and data processing courses.

Write an essay in which you support or refute this argument for career-oriented education. Be sure to give reasons for your opinion and to support those reasons with specific examples from your reading or experience.

Essay A

Traditional subjects such as history, science, and literature have just as important place in our society, today as they did years ago. A person uses these subjects everyday of their life. These subjects are the basis of all career oriented subjects. English, science and history each play an important role in a person's life.

In carrying out a normal life, the knowledge that we use can all be traced back to either history, science or literature. History plays an important role in our everyday lives such as on election day. On election day one uses what had been learned in a history class to help one make decisions on who to vote for or what governmental practices one wants. When one awakes in the morning and is trying to decide what to have for breakfast, then one is using knowledge learned in a science related course. The science that is learned in one's education is constantly being used. While one is eating breakfast, one may, also, read the morning paper. To read and fully comprehend the newspaper, one must have had some type of education in literature.

The traditional subjects are the basis of the career oriented subjects. If one is to be master of a certain career, then that one must have a strong background in the traditional subjects as well. How can one be a good secretary without having had a strong literature background. A secretary needs to know how to compose letters correctly, how to write comprehensively, and how to read with understanding. An electronics course could not be taught to someone unless they have been exposed to a solid science background. The same is true for someone who wants to go into a politically oriented profession. They must have a lot of knowledge in the field of history.

A person's career is very important but a career does not take up every minute of a person's life. One should take courses that will prepare him or her for a career but just as many courses should be taken that will help prepare him or her for the functions of everyday life. Education's sole purpose is not to prepare a person for a career. Education is to prepare a person for life.

The most significant studies in college and anywhere's else, are those which not only help a person with their career but, also, with their life.

Essay B

As technology has become more sophisticated and important in today's society, education has adapted itself to offer more programs that train people to perform certain technological functions. Computer programming offers a good example of an educational "discipline" that has appeared within the last thirty years. People can go to school solely for the purpose of learning how to run a computer. After they have finished all of the training required, they are able to quite easily find a job running computers. Unfortunately, the only thing people who have gone through this type of training program can do is operate a computer. If suddenly they realize they are tired of watching computers whirl and twirl and buzz all day, they are stuck: they have no other marketable skill. If they had followed a liberal arts program in college, chances are they would have some background which would enable them to go back to school for a little while, and then change careers. Unfortunately, society is deemphasizing the liberal arts education in favor of career education. The Renaissance Man is going down the drain.

Ever since the early seventeenth century in Europe, the man who could converse on the most subjects with a high degree of intelligence, the man who could write well and appreciate the arts has been most admired. A liberal arts education is the extension of this ideal. A diversified education encourages students to explore many disciplines to find things that interest them. As a result of this exploration, the student becomes well versed in many areas.

A liberal arts education also provides the base for learning. A computer programmer learns how to operate a computer, but he does not understand why he is doing what he is, or the theories behind how a computer works. It's like building a house from the second floor up, forgetting about the basement and first floor.

A career oriented program tends to eliminate thinking. This is a major and serious fault. The world is facing many problems such as energy shortages, arms races and food crises that are going to have to be dealt with in the years to come. The solution to these problems will be found only through experimentation. Experimentation is based on theory: a scientist usually does not haphazardly add to things together to see what he gets, he researches and forms a hypothesis. All of his experimentation is based on theory and the basic principles of science.

The reward of obtaining a liberal arts education is that of flexibility. The student has the opportunity of pursuing a career in several different fields. He can also continue his education is he so desires.

It seems that the greatest danger of encouraging career education, is the intellectual loss the career trained people suffer. They will be able to understand only one thing—the career for which they were trained. They will lose the appreciation of literature and theatre: the things in life that are so enjoyable.

Essay C

While in some of my classes, this question about, if "traditional" subjects such as history, sciences, and literature should be part of the schools curriculum comes up once in a while. Many people feel that the sensible courses that should be taught are courses teaching techniques that one may use in today's society, such as accounting, secretarial studies, electronics and data processing courses. However I feel that the "traditional" courses should still be taught.

First of all these "traditional" courses may lead one to a future career. At first one may not enjoy studying English; then they have a great English teacher and they decide to major in English at college. As a career they may choose teaching, researching for books or many other fields.

One of the main reasons I feel these "traditional" courses are important in a persons education is because it gives one a background of interesting events and at the same time adds to ones culture. An example of one such subject is history. While taking a history course many interesting events such as Wars, peace treaties, time periods, people and eras are taught. At the same time students may see the mistakes made in the past and also see how improvements were made in the world and how problems were solved. These facts may help stop the same mistakes and help make new improvements in future years. Another "traditional" subject that has many positive values is English. Through English students learn many things about novels, short stories, plays and authors. They also learn how to write creatively and intelligently. Through reading and writing people may enjoy themselves and express their beliefs, opinions and creativeness. If English was excluded we would lose many of the talented and brilliant writers and novelists. The third "traditional" subject which shouldn't be omitted from a curriculum is Science courses. Students learn about their surrounding environment through Sciences. They also learn about many of nature's laws and facts about the atmosphere. After learning these facts one may be able to enjoy, become aware and not take our environment for granted.

Through these 'traditional" subjects many people learn about different people and parts of the world. If such technical courses as I mentioned before were only taught then students would only associate with machines, and numbers not information about their environment and ancestors. Appreciation would also be lost in our world if the only thing were taught is how to run a machine and how to make money. Finally, how would anyone be taught any culture if the only objects one related to were machines.

Essay A — middle
Essay B — high
Essay C — low

You may want to practice writing an essay of your own. Here is a topic for you to write on.

The School Board has proposed to alleviate a serious budget problem for next year by eliminating certain extra-curricular activities; the Board has so far proposed eliminating football trips outside the immediate vicinity and eliminating the marching band entirely.

Next year, in the event of continued tight budgets, the Board will eliminate student newspapers and courses in drama, music, and art.

As a thoughtful and concerned citizen, write an essay setting forth your ideas on this subject. You may either support the budget cuts or oppose them. Draw upon your own educational experiences, if you wish to do so. You need not know the details of school finance. For purposes of your essay you may invent some statistics and situations related to the school system which are appropriate to your argument.

Conclusion

After you have worked through the sample questions in this chapter, you should be prepared for a whole CLEP Examination in English Composition. Three such examinations are given in the next chapter, models of those which you may encounter on an actual CLEP test. Again, we must caution you to ask the college to which your scores will be sent which version of the examination you are required to take—the version *with* the written composition or the version *without* the written composition. Remember, the version *with* the written composition will be given only twice a year, therefore timing is important to you. Good luck on this examination!

CHAPTER

Sample Examinations

This chapter includes three sample examinations, each with an answer key, scoring chart, and answer explanations. Take the first exam, check your answers, determine your raw score, and record it on the Progress Chart provided on page 14. Then, as you gain familiarity with the test, take the other two examinations and see your scores climb.

SAMPLE EXAMINATION I

Part I

Number of Items: 65
Time: 45 minutes

Directions: For each of these questions, you are to choose the version of the underlined sentence or part of the sentence that not only has the same or nearly the same meaning as the original but follows the requirements of standard written English. That is, in selecting the version that matches the underlined part in meaning, pay attention to grammar, choice of words, sentence structure, and punctuation. The answer you select should, when inserted in the original sentence, produce an effective sentence—clear and exact, without awkwardness or ambiguity.

1. Rising up above the top of a very high mountain, the sun made its way slowly to its zenith at noon.
   (A) ; the sun made its way
   (B) , the sun making its way
   (C) , the sun approached
   (D) , and the sun approached
   (E) , to which the sun made its way

   1. Ⓐ Ⓑ Ⓒ Ⓓ Ⓔ

2. No matter how hard I try to finish an assignment, I cannot do it if there is anything lying around I can play with.
   (A) Regardless of my efforts
   (B) That I try hard
   (C) If I try hard
   (D) Even though I try hard
   (E) Without my trying

   2. Ⓐ Ⓑ Ⓒ Ⓓ Ⓔ

3. Charles Johnson, one of the smartest lawyers in the United States, has often told me that almost all criminals really want to be kept in jail.

    (A) That Charles Johnson is one of the smartest lawyers in the United States

    (B) Charles Johnson and who is one of the smartest lawyers in the United States

    (C) In the United States, one of the smartest lawyers is Charles Johnson,

    (D) Among the smartest lawyers in the United States is Charles Johnson,

    (E) Charles Johnson, who is one of the smartest lawyers in the United States,

3. Ⓐ Ⓑ Ⓒ Ⓓ Ⓔ

4. I will neither give you money to waste on that junk nor offer any further advice if you do not follow my orders.

    (A) Giving you money to waste on that junk is out of the question, nor will I give you further advice if you do not follow my orders.

    (B) Any further advice from me is impossible because you insist on wasting money on junk against my orders.

    (C) My orders are irrevocable: either you stop wasting money on junk or get no more advice.

    (D) Ignoring my orders causes you to lose the money I might have given you as well as any further advice I could give you.

    (E) I will both give you money to waste on junk and give you further advice, despite your ignoring my orders.

4. Ⓐ Ⓑ Ⓒ Ⓓ Ⓔ

5. As a result of her efforts to promote Black pride, Maya Angelou was refused a chance to direct a film for television.

    (A) Directing a film for television was refused to Maya Angelou because she promoted Black pride.

    (B) Maya Angelou declined to accept a chance to direct a film for television because she advocated Black pride.

    (C) Her advocacy of Black pride cost Maya Angelou an opportunity to direct a film for television.

    (D) A film for television could not be directed by Maya Angelou because of her insistence on her Black pride.

    (E) The Black pride caused producers of a television movie to refuse Maya Angelou an opportunity to direct.

5. Ⓐ Ⓑ Ⓒ Ⓓ Ⓔ

6. Because we insist on our rights as citizens, some organizations say that we are un-American.

    (A) Seeing as how we are called un-American because we insist upon our rights as citizens.

    (B) Some organizations label us un-American because we insist upon our rights as citizens.

    (C) We are called un-American, being that we insist upon our rights as citizens.

    (D) Despite the fact that we insist upon our rights as citizens, we are called un-American.

    (E) Having been called un-American, we maintain our rights as citizens.

6. Ⓐ Ⓑ Ⓒ Ⓓ Ⓔ

7. Ely Culbertson, a famous professional player, said that thirteen cards of a single suit was the only unique bridge hand he had ever seen.

    (A) suit was the only poor

7. Ⓐ Ⓑ Ⓒ Ⓓ Ⓔ

(B) suit was the only completely novel
(C) suit was the uniquest
(D) suit was the one
(E) suit was the only

8. President Carter implied that opposition to his foreign policy could come only from those who had not voted for him in 1976.
    (A) President Carter implied, that opposition to his foreign policy
    (B) That President Carter's foreign policy is opposed
    (C) President Carter made a speech, he inferred that opposition to his foreign policy
    (D) President Carter's press conference said that opposition to his foreign policy
    (E) Negative reactions to his foreign policy, President Carter hinted,

8. Ⓐ Ⓑ Ⓒ Ⓓ Ⓔ

9. The more Chinese food I eat, the greater my satisfaction.
    (A) the more satisfied I become
    (B) I am satisfied to completion
    (C) the more satisfactorily I felt
    (D) invariably I feel satisfactorily
    (E) the more intense is my repletion

9. Ⓐ Ⓑ Ⓒ Ⓓ Ⓔ

10. Bill and John started on their hike this morning; we hope they can walk the twenty miles without stopping.
    (A) Starting on their hike this morning, we hope Bill and John can walk the twenty miles without stopping.
    (B) Bill's and John's hike this morning is twenty miles long, without stopping they should make it.
    (C) A twenty-mile hike without stopping is a difficult feat for them to accomplish this morning.
    (D) When Bill and John started their twenty-mile hike this morning, we wished they could make it without stopping.
    (E) A non-stop twenty-mile hike is difficult so that we hope Bill and John can make it.

10. Ⓐ Ⓑ Ⓒ Ⓓ Ⓔ

11. After many repetitions of the manual of arms, a raw recruit becomes used to going through the drill without thinking too hard about what he is doing.
    (A) not considering too hardly his actions
    (B) bothering his subconscious mind very little
    (C) reacting to outside stimulation very difficulty
    (D) choosing to react to orders indifferently
    (E) almost unconscious of his movements

11. Ⓐ Ⓑ Ⓒ Ⓓ Ⓔ

12. Apple pie or ice cream—which has more calories? Even the best diet books give no clear answer.
    (A) No diet books state clearly the comparative calorie content of apple pie and ice cream.
    (B) Neither apple pie nor ice cream have more calories than the other, most diet books say.
    (C) Without a good book, a dieter can never know whether apple pie or ice cream has the most calories.

12. Ⓐ Ⓑ Ⓒ Ⓓ Ⓔ

(D) No clear answer to the question about which has the most calories—ice cream or apple pie—is given in good diet books.

(E) Which has more calories—apple pie or ice cream? Some diet book may give an answer to that question.

13. According to the lawyers' code of ethics, no lawyer should take any action, within or outside the courtroom, which might damage a client's rights to a fair trial.

13. Ⓐ Ⓑ Ⓒ Ⓓ Ⓔ

(A) action; inside or outside the courtroom, they might damage
(B) action either inside or outside the courtroom which might interfere with
(C) action neither within or outside the courtroom which might damage
(D) action, whether inside and outside the courtroom which might damage
(E) activity that they thought it might be nonbeneficial to

14. John Travolta is a current phenomenon: he played a role in a successful television series and became a star in *Saturday Night Fever* and *Grease*.

14. Ⓐ Ⓑ Ⓒ Ⓓ Ⓔ

(A) *Saturday Night Fever* and *Grease* made John Travolta a star even though he had appeared in a television series.
(B) A current phenomenon, he had a role in a television series and became a star in two motion pictures.
(C) John Travolta is a current phenomenon in *Saturday Night Fever* and *Grease*, he has also appeared in a television series.
(D) *Saturday Night Fever* and *Grease* brought stardom to John Travolta after his appearance in a television series.
(E) Working hard at being a current phenomenon, *Saturday Night Fever* and *Grease* made John Travolta a star.

15. If the State Department would only reveal the facts about our involvement in Angola, the American people would have more complete information upon which to base opinions.

15. Ⓐ Ⓑ Ⓒ Ⓓ Ⓔ

(A) tell the whole truth
(B) reveal the untrue facts
(C) reveal our misapprehensions
(D) reveal the true facts
(E) disclose the slanted information

16. That Nixon covered up the facts about Watergate has been positively proven by several investigations.

16. Ⓐ Ⓑ Ⓒ Ⓓ Ⓔ

(A) Several investigations have demonstrated that Watergate facts were covered up, which was why Nixon resigned.
(B) Investigations of the Watergate break-in were started by Nixon's refusal to admit this cover up of the facts.
(C) Covering up the facts about Watergate, Nixon triggered several investigations of his part in the situation.
(D) Nixon covered up facts about Watergate, therefore, investigations proved him wrong.
(E) Several investigations have proven Nixon's cover-up of facts about the Watergate break-in.

17. Because of the cold which seemed to develop suddenly, Dorothy decided not to go to work on Tuesday.
    (A) The reason Dorothy stayed home on Tuesday was due to the fact that her cold developed suddenly.
    (B) Due to the fact that her cold developed caused Dorothy to stay home from work Tuesday.
    (C) When she suddenly developed a cold, Dorothy stayed home from work Tuesday.
    (D) Dorothy's cold having developed suddenly kept her from going to work Tuesday.
    (E) On Tuesday, Dorothy developed a cold, therefore, she decided to stay at home.

17.   A B C D E

18. The chairman of the board of directors announced today that the company would neither accede to the monetary demands of the strikers nor accept any further delays by union leaders.
    (A) strikers or accept any further delays by union leaders
    (B) strikers, and they resisted additional postponements of negotiations
    (C) strikers nor agree that union leaders could postpone negotiations any longer
    (D) strikers without accepting any further delays by union leaders
    (E) strikers, agreeing to further delays by union leaders

18.   A B C D E

19. If all materials are delivered by the deadlines the architect has established, we should occupy our new building no later than November 15.
    (A) Our new building should be ready for a November 15 occupancy; the architect says that all materials will be delivered to meet his deadlines.
    (B) The delivery of all materials meeting the architect's deadlines will establish November 15 as the occupancy date of our new building.
    (C) Assuming all materials being delivered by the architect's deadlines, November 15 is the occupancy date of our new building.
    (D) The delivery deadlines of the materials having been established, the architect promises November 15 as the occupancy date of our new building.
    (E) Meeting delivery dates for materials will determine the architect's occupancy of our new building.

19.   A B C D E

20. The more Willie Mays practiced baseball, the greater his success.
    (A) the more successful he became
    (B) he more successfully played
    (C) he became more successfully
    (D) he succeeded more favorably
    (E) the more greatly he succeeded

20.   A B C D E

21. As a result of his efforts to expose Stalin as evil, Solzhenitsyn was taken to a concentration camp.
    (A) detained, having been taken
    (B) detained; they had flown him
    (C) detained and moved to
    (D) detained and being flown
    (E) detained, and he had been taken by them

21.   A B C D E

22. Use any set of criteria you want, but you will not convince me that Beethoven is as good a composer as J. S. Bach.

    (A) J. S. Bach is an inferior composer to Beethoven

    (B) Beethoven is a better composer than J. S. Bach

    (C) J. S. Bach is a superior composer to Beethoven

    (D) Beethoven and J. S. Bach are equal composers

    (E) Beethoven is a lesser composer than J. S. Bach

22. Ⓐ Ⓑ Ⓒ Ⓓ Ⓔ

23. The Pulitzer Prize Committee awarded $1,000 to Bill Mauldin; the group voted his drawings in a Chicago newspaper the best editorial cartoons published in the nation that year.

    (A) , whenever the group voted

    (B) ; which the group had voted

    (C) , being as how the group voted

    (D) , the result of the group's voting

    (E) , and the group voted

23. Ⓐ Ⓑ Ⓒ Ⓓ Ⓔ

24. Anyone who insists on saving every piece of string that comes into the house collects many bits that are not useful to anyone.

    (A) Some people insist on saving every piece of string that comes into the house which collect many bits not useful to anyone.

    (B) That some bits of string, not useful to anyone, are collected by someone leads to a pile of useless bits.

    (C) No one likes to find many bits of string, useful to no one, have been saved up by those who collect it.

    (D) When anyone collects every piece of string that comes into the house, they usually wind up with bits useful to no one.

    (E) Those people who save every bit of string that comes into the house collect many pieces useful to no one.

24. Ⓐ Ⓑ Ⓒ Ⓓ Ⓔ

25. Some insecure corporation vice presidents engage in many maneuvers to protect their positions from those climbing the corporate status ladder.

    (A) The corporate status ladder is climbed by many who threaten the many maneuvers of corporation vice presidents.

    (B) Those climbing the corporate status ladder should be wary of the many maneuvers insecure vice presidents use to protect their positions.

    (C) Many maneuvers are engaged in by those climbing the corporate status ladder against some insecure vice presidents.

    (D) That some insecure corporation vice presidents connive against those climbing the corporate status ladder is untrue.

    (E) Climbing the corporate status ladder is such a chore that only insecure vice presidents engage in the task.

25. Ⓐ Ⓑ Ⓒ Ⓓ Ⓔ

26. All of the students' talents were exercised to their fullest extent by the long, complicated, and somewhat ambiguous assignment.

    (A) Each of the student's talents were exercised to their fullest extent by the long, complicated, and such ambiguous assignment.

    (B) The long, complicated, and rather confusing assignment thoroughly tested the students' talents.

    (C) Since the students' talents were tested, the long assignment was complicated and ambiguous.

26. Ⓐ Ⓑ Ⓒ Ⓓ Ⓔ

(D) No students like to have their talents tested by long, complicated, and ambiguous assignments.

(E) The long, complicated, and somewhat ambiguous assignment tested the students' talents to an indifferent degree.

27. If a local arrangements committee can reserve hotel rooms at a reasonable rate, the board of directors plans to have the 1986 stockholders' meeting in Cleveland.

    27. Ⓐ Ⓑ Ⓒ Ⓓ Ⓔ

(A) the board of directors have held
(B) the board of directors plans on having
(C) the board of directors planned to have
(D) the board of directors was held
(E) the board of directors will hold

28. Our new computer has more memory cells than our old one; therefore, data can be recorded and almost instantaneously retrieved.

    28. Ⓐ Ⓑ Ⓒ Ⓓ Ⓔ

(A) data which can be recorded and almost instantaneously retrieved is unlimited
(B) although data can be recorded and retrieved almost instantaneously
(C) our new computer is somewhat more complete than our old one
(D) it can record and retrieve data almost instantly
(E) we can record and retrieve data at the same time

29. No serious effort to consider all the facts can be expected from someone who announces at the beginning of an investigation that he has already formed an opinion.

    29. Ⓐ Ⓑ Ⓒ Ⓓ Ⓔ

(A) Anyone who has already formed an opinion before hearing all the facts cannot be trusted to be impartial.
(B) An opinion should not be formed by anyone who does not have all the essential information.
(C) You cannot trust anyone who announces their mind is made up before all the evidence has been presented.
(D) An investigation should reveal all of the facts; therefore, no one should make their mind up in advance.
(E) Facts are often misinterpreted by those who make up their minds before hearing them.

Directions: For each of these sentences, select the answer that, when inserted in the blank in the original sentence, produces the best sentence. Pay attention to meaning and to choice of words.

30. Russia is larger in land area than _____ country in the world.

    30. Ⓐ Ⓑ Ⓒ Ⓓ Ⓔ

(A) any   (B) almost any   (C) any other
(D) most any   (E) most other

31. When all the evidence the prosecutor had so carefully gathered was _____ by the jury, he almost wept from frustration.

    31. Ⓐ Ⓑ Ⓒ Ⓓ Ⓔ

(A) passed by without a thought
(B) prohibited
(C) ignored

(D) simply devoured

(E) banned

32. If no one can find a _____ explanation for the strange events taking place in the world today, do not be surprised.

32. Ⓐ Ⓑ Ⓒ Ⓓ Ⓔ

(A) reasonable   (B) completely illogical   (C) convincingly

(D) masterful   (E) marvelously complex

33. After working on a project for a number of hours, any employee likes to hear _____.

33. Ⓐ Ⓑ Ⓒ Ⓓ Ⓔ

(A) encomiums of praise

(B) more than a bare modicum of thanksgiving

(C) whole hosts of glowing adjectives

(D) a few sincere words of appreciation

(E) a simple pat on the back

34. The young woman _____ her education at a famed college for females in New England.

34. Ⓐ Ⓑ Ⓒ Ⓓ Ⓔ

(A) farthered   (B) completed   (C) complicated

(D) restricted   (E) condensed

35. Many amateur investors assume they can increase their capital by _____ stocks and bonds.

35. Ⓐ Ⓑ Ⓒ Ⓓ Ⓔ

(A) having a fling at

(B) buying

(C) rather heavily dabbling in

(D) hoarding money in

(E) relaxing in

36. As centuries passed and the world changed, civilization evolved from the age of dinosaurs to _____.

36. Ⓐ Ⓑ Ⓒ Ⓓ Ⓔ

(A) this point in time

(B) the elevated state of the world today

(C) the contemporary civilization of today

(D) today's advanced culture

(E) today's supreme achievements

37. Our superior was always urging us to use _____ when we worked with our class of deaf children.

37. Ⓐ Ⓑ Ⓒ Ⓓ Ⓔ

(A) new innovations

(B) modern methods of today

(C) materials beyond our scope

(D) contemporary procedures

(E) appropriate methods

38. Population control experts have urged couples _____ having a child of their own and to adopt one already born.

38. Ⓐ Ⓑ Ⓒ Ⓓ Ⓔ

(A) to forego   (B) to prevent   (C) to simulate

(D) not   (E) to resent

39. Only one of _____ who threw rocks at the officers was arrested because all the others escaped.

    (A) the large mass of people

    (B) a crowded host of people

    (C) the group

    (D) a small amount of people

    (E) the majority of persons

39. Ⓐ Ⓑ Ⓒ Ⓓ Ⓔ

Directions: Revise each of the following sentences according to the directions which follow it. Rephrase the sentence mentally to save time, making notes in your book if you wish. Although the directions may at times require you to change the relationship between parts of the sentence or to make slight changes in other ways, *make only those changes that the directions require.*

Below each sentence and its directions are listed words or phrases that may occur in your revised sentence. When you have thought out a good sentence, look at the choices A through E for the word or entire phrase that is included in your revised sentence.

Of course, a number of different sentences can be obtained if the sentence is revised according to the directions, and not all of these possibilities can be included in only five choices. If you should find that you have thought of a sentence that contains none of the words listed in the choices, rephrase the sentence again to include a word or phrase that *is* listed.

40. Once the pastor had started his sermon, he was annoyed at being interrupted by late arriving parishioners.

    Begin with Parishioners arriving once.

    (A) from their interruption

    (B) with their interruption

    (C) without their interruption

    (D) out of their interruption

    (E) between their interruption

40. Ⓐ Ⓑ Ⓒ Ⓓ Ⓔ

41. The chief along with fifteen Indians attacks the heavily defended fort at least once each day.

    Change along with to and.

    (A) attacks   (B) is attacking   (C) attack

    (D) has attacked   (E) has been attacking

41. Ⓐ Ⓑ Ⓒ Ⓓ Ⓔ

42. The millionaire became cynical and hardhearted because so many people tried for so long to swindle him out of his money with foolish proposals.

    Begin with The many attempts.

    (A) tried him to become   (B) caused him to become

    (C) caused him to try   (D) caused him to make

    (E) caused him cynicism

42. Ⓐ Ⓑ Ⓒ Ⓓ Ⓔ

43. Migrant workers, whether Blacks or Hispanics, deserve better pay, better housing, and more services from the communities which they serve.

43. Ⓐ Ⓑ Ⓒ Ⓓ Ⓔ

Begin with The communities which they serve.

(A) deserve   (B) owed   (C) deserved

(D) owe   (E) will deserve

44. The publisher was astounded by the sales of Bill Jones' first novel; therefore, he offered a much higher royalty arrangement for the second.

    44. Ⓐ Ⓑ Ⓒ Ⓓ Ⓔ

Begin with Astounded by.

(A) novel, he   (B) novel, so the publisher

(C) novel, the publisher   (D) novel; so he

(E) novel; the publisher

45. The new electronic ovens which employ high frequency sound waves rather than heat as a means of cooking food use a clock instead of a thermostat as a control device.

    45. Ⓐ Ⓑ Ⓒ Ⓓ Ⓔ

Begin with A thermostat is useless in.

(A) because high frequency sound waves employ

(B) because heat employs

(C) because a control device employs

(D) because clocks employ

(E) because they employ

46. Orphans are considered adoptable until they reach the age of seven; if no family has taken them by then, the welfare agency must be willing to keep the children until they finish high school.

    46. Ⓐ Ⓑ Ⓒ Ⓓ Ⓔ

Begin with Orphans are not considered adoptable.

(A) after they become seven years old

(B) until they reach the age of seven

(C) since they became seven years old

(D) because they become seven years old

(E) as they reach the age of seven

47. Any success that attends my efforts to write the great American novel will be completely due to the lessons I learned from my tenth grade English teacher.

    47. Ⓐ Ⓑ Ⓒ Ⓓ Ⓔ

Substitute If I succeed for Any success.

(A) is completely due   (B) is completely attentive

(C) is completely learned   (D) is completely responsible

(E) is completely effortless

48. Because Amanda Wingfield had a number of gentleman callers in her youth, she assumed that the number of a girl's suitors was a measure of her popularity.

    48. Ⓐ Ⓑ Ⓒ Ⓓ Ⓔ

Eliminate because.

(A) youth, therefore,   (B) youth; therefore,

(C) youth, therefore;   (D) youth, so therefore,

(E) youth; so thus

49. Some pain relievers claim to be nonaddictive, no matter how many tablets a user takes, but others warn against anyone's taking more than four every twenty-four hours.

49. Ⓐ Ⓑ Ⓒ Ⓓ Ⓔ

Begin with Users may take an unlimited.

(A) to become addicted   (B) for becoming addicted
(C) from becoming addicted   (D) with becoming addicted
(E) without becoming addicted

50. When a politician prepares a speech for delivery to a woman's organization, he is sure to include some ringing phrases praising motherhood and home cooking.

50. Ⓐ Ⓑ Ⓒ Ⓓ Ⓔ

Change is sure to include to surely includes.

(A) When a politician prepared
(B) Often when a politician prepares
(C) A politician preparing
(D) A politician praising
(E) A politician cooking

51. Many Americans buy foreign-made automobiles like the Volkswagen or the Datsun because these cars have a reputation for high gas mileage.

51. Ⓐ Ⓑ Ⓒ Ⓓ Ⓔ

Begin with The Volkswagen and the Datsun attract.

(A) because of their reputation
(B) because American buyers
(C) because all foreign cars
(D) because American cars
(E) because of lower prices

52. Chefs consider their own recipes more valuable than gold, for a cook's reputation and salary may well depend upon the uniqueness of his sauces.

52. Ⓐ Ⓑ Ⓒ Ⓓ Ⓔ

Begin with Since the uniqueness of a chef's sauces.

(A) may well depend upon
(B) may well be determined by
(C) may well be dependent upon
(D) may well determine
(E) may well constitute a determination of

53. Our scoutmaster called the three of us to the front of the auditorium and announced that each of us had won five merit badges within a month.

53. Ⓐ Ⓑ Ⓒ Ⓓ Ⓔ

Begin with We three boys.

(A) it was announced by our scoutmaster
(B) and announced by our scoutmaster
(C) our scoutmaster announced
(D) announcing by our scoutmaster
(E) our scoutmaster was called

54. In Illinois, the season for locally grown fresh vegetables lasts about two months; frosts in September usually kill the plants that provide us with tomatoes and beans.

54. Ⓐ Ⓑ Ⓒ Ⓓ Ⓔ

Begin with For about two months, we in Illinois.

(A) grow locally produced
(B) locally produced are grown
(C) has locally grown
(D) used to have locally grown
(E) have locally grown

55. Georgia was among the thirteen original colonies as well as one of the states which seceded from the Union in 1861.

Change was among to one of.

(A) was as well as   (B) was both   (C) was also
(D) was and   (E) was therefore

56. Several social psychologists have offered a number of explanations for the rising rate of venereal disease infection among today's teenagers, but none completely satisfies the doctor who must treat these cases.

Begin with No explanation, which is completely satisfactory.

(A) has been treated by doctors
(B) has been offered by social psychologists
(C) has been satisfied by statistics
(D) has been offered by doctors
(E) has been provided by today's teenagers

57. Most electric wrist watches are powered by a small battery which most manufacturers guarantee for one year.

Change are powered to powers.

(A) Most electric wrist watches   (B) A guarantee of one year
(C) For one year   (D) A small battery
(E) Most manufacturers

58. Researchers know that different kinds of cancer respond to different kinds of treatment; surgical eradication is effective in some cases, but in others, drugs seem to arrest the spread of cancerous cells.

Change different kinds of cancer to either surgery or certain drugs effectively.

(A) eradicate or arrest
(B) eradicating or arresting
(C) the eradication or the arresting
(D) to eradicate or to arrest
(E) having eradicated or having arrested

59. Snowfalls in Chicago average forty inches a year, but in 1979, January alone produced more than that average.

Begin with January, 1979.

(A) more snow than
(B) into a forty inch average
(C) no more snow than
(D) no less snow than
(E) a lot less snow

60. John Travolta and Lily Tomlin, separately, had made successful films; their co-starring movie, however, was severely attacked by critics.

    Eliminate the semi-colon so that the new sentence begins with

    (A) But . . . also
    (B) Even though
    (C) Whenever
    (D) Because
    (E) Why

60. Ⓐ Ⓑ Ⓒ Ⓓ Ⓔ

Directions: For each of the following, choose the one phrasing that makes the intended meaning clear; that is, the one that avoids ambiguity, that does not leave the actual meaning open to question or that does not leave the reader guessing about what is intended.

61. (A) The jeweler guaranteed that he had placed a genuine diamond in the sponsor's pendant.
    (B) The pendant we gave the sponsor was guaranteed by them to contain a genuine diamond.
    (C) A genuine diamond was contained in the pendant by the jeweler we gave our sponsor.
    (D) The sponsor's pendant contained a genuine diamond which we had bought for the sponsor.
    (E) We bought the sponsor containing a guaranteed genuine diamond from a jeweler.

61. Ⓐ Ⓑ Ⓒ Ⓓ Ⓔ

62. (A) The family had a large amount of children, with the percent of boys larger than the number of girls.
    (B) Within the large family, they had more boys than girls.
    (C) In the large family, the percentage of boys exceeded the girls.
    (D) The number of boys was greater than the percent of girls in the large family.
    (E) The family had many children; the number of boys was greater than the number of girls.

62. Ⓐ Ⓑ Ⓒ Ⓓ Ⓔ

63. (A) Some one took the five-dollar bill Mother put in the desk drawer, and Father punished George for it.
    (B) Father punished George for lying about who had taken the five-dollar bill Mother had put in the desk drawer.
    (C) George was punished for lying to Father about who had taken the five-dollar bill she had put in the desk drawer.
    (D) Mother put a five-dollar bill in the desk drawer, he took it, and Father punished him for lying about it.
    (E) George took the five-dollar bill which Mother put into the desk drawer and was punished for lying by Father.

63. Ⓐ Ⓑ Ⓒ Ⓓ Ⓔ

64. (A) It says in the paper that California local government lost revenue when its citizens approved Proposition 13.
    (B) The newspaper article concerns the loss of tax money to local governments when the people of California approved Proposition 13.

64. Ⓐ Ⓑ Ⓒ Ⓓ Ⓔ

(C) California's citizens approved Proposition 13 because the newspaper said tax money would be reduced to them.

(D) Proposition 13 having been approved by California, they lost tax money, according to the newspaper.

(E) According to the newspaper, Proposition 13 was passed in California, and they lost local tax revenue as a result.

65. (A) People who attend baseball games do not know enough about the fine points of offense and defense to enjoy them.

(B) People who attend enough baseball games always appreciate the fine points of defense and offense by them.

(C) People who frequently attend baseball games do not know enough about the fine points of offensive and defensive strategy.

(D) The fine points of offense and defense are often not well understood by people who attend enough baseball games.

(E) People who attend baseball games often enough do not understand the fine point of offense and defense.

65. Ⓐ Ⓑ Ⓒ Ⓓ Ⓔ

Part II

Number of Items: 65
Time: 45 minutes

Directions: Questions 66–87 are each based on a short passage. Read the passage and then select the one best answer to the questions that follow the passage, using the information provided by or suggested in the passage.

66. A member of a company's board of directors said, "The company hasn't made a profit for the past five years. I think it's time to fire the president and bring in a new man."

The speaker believes that

(A) he knows the markets which the company is seeking
(B) he will not accept any idea at face value
(C) he has spent hours of thought before arriving at his decision
(D) there is only one reason for the company's lack of profits
(E) he is a very illogical thinker

66. Ⓐ Ⓑ Ⓒ Ⓓ Ⓔ

67. My mother said to my sister, "Always wear clean underwear when you leave the house. You never know—you might be in an accident and have to go to the hospital, and I'd be embarrassed if my daughter were found wearing soiled underwear."

My mother always

(A) is a pessimist
(B) is an optimist
(C) is not a very sensitive woman
(D) washes Sister's clothes every day
(E) keeps the house spotlessly clean

67. Ⓐ Ⓑ Ⓒ Ⓓ Ⓔ

68. The old lady said, "My religion is much better than yours. I have much more faith in Jesus Christ than you have in Allah."

The old lady

(A) does not know anything about Allah

68. Ⓐ Ⓑ Ⓒ Ⓓ Ⓔ

(B) establishes her own faith as the only possible criterion by which all other faiths must be measured

(C) has had few opportunities to judge other religions

(D) is one of the pillars of her church

(E) reads her Bible at least an hour each day

69. The accountant said, "I can't please my boss. I'm at my office desk at 7:30 AM and do not leave until after 6:30 PM. Yet, he has passed me over for promotion four times."

The accountant

(A) is insane to work so long for so little reward

(B) must live close to the office if he can get there so early

(C) does not realize that long hours at a desk are not the only method of evaluation the boss knows about

(D) works hard because he is supporting two ex-wives and five children

(E) cannot understand that his efforts really are appreciated by his boss

69. Ⓐ Ⓑ Ⓒ Ⓓ Ⓔ

70. A union organizer said, "I stopped four people outside the plant this morning, and they all favored my union. Management must accept the fact that the union will be approved."

The union organizer

(A) has no problem with carefully thought out proposals

(B) can be sure that his unionizing activities will be successful

(C) speaks with authority when he refers to company management

(D) is interested in raising the workers' pay and increasing their fringe benefits

(E) doesn't say that the four people even worked for the company

70. Ⓐ Ⓑ Ⓒ Ⓓ Ⓔ

71. My mother said, "My mother and grandmother used this recipe for making biscuits, and I'm not going to change one ingredient when I make mine."

My mother

(A) is not a very good cook

(B) does not make biscuits very often

(C) is too lazy to develop her own biscuit recipe

(D) does not believe that anything can be better than it used to be

(E) makes biscuits every day

71. Ⓐ Ⓑ Ⓒ Ⓓ Ⓔ

Questions 72-73 are based on the following dialogue:

Beggar: "Brother, can you spare a dollar? I have five hungry children at home."

Passerby: "Why don't you go to work to support them?"

Beggar: "What and lose my place on this corner where begging is so profitable?"

72. The beggar

(A) attempts to appeal to the sympathy of the passerby

(B) is too proud to accept welfare

(C) enjoys being a beggar

72. Ⓐ Ⓑ Ⓒ Ⓓ Ⓔ

(D) is unable to work because of a bad back

(E) does not really have five children at home

73. The statement that the beggar is making is:
(A) It's better to beg for a dollar than work for fifty cents
(B) Who steals my purse steals trash
(C) Everything comes to those who stand and wait
(D) A bird in the hand is worth two in the bush
(E) No one person can know everything about anything

74. Harriet Simmons, a renowned scholar and writer in the field of biology, could not understand why no automobile company asked her to endorse the latest European import with low gasoline mileage. It is clear that no automobile company
(A) had a new European import for sale
(B) would trust Simmons to endorse a car—she does not have a driver's license
(C) would trust a biology scholar to endorse an automobile
(D) wanted to associate its automobile with biological matters
(E) could afford to pay the fee her agent demanded

75. "If I am elected this fall, I will advocate spending more money for education, highways, rapid transit systems, and welfare. Beside all that, I promise to reduce your taxes by at least 25%."

The candidate who makes such a statement

(A) knows that he is lying to prospective voters
(B) is assured of an overwhelming victory
(C) bases his appeal primarily on voters over 70
(D) could not answer the question, "Where is the money coming from for these improvements?"
(E) probably has not filed an income tax return for five years

Questions 76-77 are based on the following statement:

The farmer said, "I won't hire any more minority people as bean pickers. The last one I hired wrecked my truck, and I had no insurance. You can't trust any of those people."

76. The farmer
(A) is a member of the American Farm Bureau
(B) has had a series of unfortunate experiences with members of minority groups
(C) never carried insurance on his truck
(D) does not need bean pickers this year because he planted corn
(E) extends one unfortunate instance to apply to a number of possible instances

77. If a reader accepts the statement, the person must also accept which of the following?
(A) All minority workers wreck trucks.
(B) No farmer carries insurance on his trucks.

(C) All bean pickers are untrustworthy.

(D) All farmers dislike minority workers.

(E) Some farmers dislike some minority workers.

78. The engineer stated, "It's a waste of time for any engineering major to study the fine arts or literature. He should be cramming mathematics, physics, and computer technology."

    78. Ⓐ Ⓑ Ⓒ Ⓓ Ⓔ

    The engineer

    (A) reads at least one poem a week

    (B) wants specialists who may have a very narrow education

    (C) attends the opera regularly

    (D) has an advanced degree in engineering

    (E) works an eighteen-hour day to solve engineering problems

79. A Republican governor said, "If Gerald Ford had been elected president in 1976, the United States would have already solved its problems with inflation and unemployment."

    79. Ⓐ Ⓑ Ⓒ Ⓓ Ⓔ

    The governor

    (A) indulges in wishful thinking because Ford was not elected

    (B) does not support Carter's anti-inflation policies

    (C) has voted against Carter's energy proposals

    (D) is still a supporter of Richard Nixon

    (E) wants to become president himself

80. Early Greek philosophers believed the world to be flat, supported by a large tortoise at each of its four corners. They also believed that the sun and moon were pulled across the sky by chariots. These philosophers committed these errors because

    80. Ⓐ Ⓑ Ⓒ Ⓓ Ⓔ

    (A) they did not study geography and astronomy

    (B) they were concerned with ideas, not facts

    (C) they were ignorant

    (D) they were stupid

    (E) they were too prejudiced to learn the facts

Questions 81-82 are based on the following dialogue:

    Son: "May I use the car tonight?"
    Father: "No. Your mother and I are going out."
    Son: "What kind of gas should I put in the tank?"
    Father: "Unleaded, of course; that's what the manufacturer calls for."

81. The son

    81. Ⓐ Ⓑ Ⓒ Ⓓ Ⓔ

    (A) is a nuisance to the whole family

    (B) has made an unreasonable request

    (C) can buy gasoline for the car with his own money

    (D) knows how to get an implied "yes" answer instead of a flat "no"

    (E) appeals to his mother to overrule his father's "no"

82. The father

    82. Ⓐ Ⓑ Ⓒ Ⓓ Ⓔ

    (A) does not trust his son to drive carefully

(B) does not carry his son on the car's insurance policy

(C) cannot afford to buy his own gasoline

(D) is unreasonable in his refusal to lend the car

(E) is trapped into an implied "yes" by the son's second question

83. "Every flower in the garden is beautiful. Give me one of each, and I am sure I will have a beautiful bouquet when I stick them in a vase."

The writer

(A) is a professional florist

(B) cannot separate individuals from a crowd of the same objects

(C) has worked hard in a difficult field—botany

(D) does not consider a whole greater than the sum of its parts

(E) assumes that sticking beautiful flowers into a vase will produce a beautiful bouquet

83. Ⓐ Ⓑ Ⓒ Ⓓ Ⓔ

84. A pastor states, "I know that the Bible is the word from God. I can find no errors anywhere in Holy Writ."

The pastor

(A) is a victim of hallucinations

(B) uses the phrase *I know* when someone else would use the phrase *I have faith*

(C) in his thinking, cannot separate knowledge from doubt about his convictions

(D) is convinced that the Bible may be true

(E) preaches five sermons on Sunday morning

84. Ⓐ Ⓑ Ⓒ Ⓓ Ⓔ

85. I have been offered a promotion which means an increase in my salary and responsibilities as well as a move to a new city. Yet I have lived in this community for so long that I do not want to leave.

The writer shows that she

(A) really wants to move to a new community

(B) may not be able to decide between the alternatives without advice from a disinterested person

(C) does not want the additional salary because her taxes would be increased

(D) would change jobs even though that would mean a salary reduction

(E) thinks money is more important than her pleasures in a new job

85. Ⓐ Ⓑ Ⓒ Ⓓ Ⓔ

86. Joe Namath, a famous professional football player, has made television commercials for panty hose, boots, and reclining chairs. Anyone who buys these products solely on the basis of Namath's recommendations is

(A) in love with Joe Namath

(B) stupid for believing anything Namath says

(C) convinced that Namath would not endorse an inferior product

(D) a fan of professional football

(E) looking for an excuse to buy panty hose

86. Ⓐ Ⓑ Ⓒ Ⓓ Ⓔ

87. The new vice president said, "The more I read the policy manual of the company, the more confused I become. There seems to be a company policy to cover every possible employee action, but I cannot learn all those policies very quickly."

87. Ⓐ Ⓑ Ⓒ Ⓓ Ⓔ

The new vice president is actually expressing

(A) the usual reaction anyone has to a new job
(B) his admiration for the red tape involved in his new position
(C) his anxiety about being vice president rather than president
(D) his emotional responses to his new position
(E) his concern that his superiors will promote him too slowly

Directions: In questions 88–97, you are to compare various statements in the light of the questions posed. Pay attention to the tone, emphasis, and implications of each of the statements as you select the one response that is best in each case.

88. Which of the following most strongly implies the speaker's attitude toward Jack's financial operations?
(A) Jack's wife has a closet full of beautiful clothes.
(B) Jack has more money than his brother has.
(C) Jack's business has been good for the past year.
(D) Jack can make money faster than he can spend it.
(E) Jack's children graduated from Harvard and Yale.

88. Ⓐ Ⓑ Ⓒ Ⓓ Ⓔ

89. Which of the following is the most negative about all professional baseball players?
(A) They make more money than President Reagan.
(B) They have barred female reporters from the locker room after games.
(C) They are more interested in endorsing various products than in playing baseball.
(D) They do not give autographs to fans after a game.
(E) They get their uniforms dirty during a game.

89. Ⓐ Ⓑ Ⓒ Ⓓ Ⓔ

90. Which of the following statements reveals most clearly the speaker's feelings about his grandchildren?
(A) I have just made reservations to fly my grandchildren home to their mother.
(B) I love my grandchildren except when they need a spanking.
(C) I wish my grandchildren would not be so noisy when they play.
(D) My grandchildren don't bother me very much.
(E) Having grandchildren, for some people, is one of the joys of growing old.

90. Ⓐ Ⓑ Ⓒ Ⓓ Ⓔ

91. Which of the following statements says most clearly that Vivian is not a good actress?
(A) Vivian knew all of her lines opening night.
(B) Vivian moved about the stage awkwardly.
(C) Vivian reacted too strongly to the director's advice.
(D) Vivian was somewhat shorter than her leading man.
(E) Vivian could not convince the audience that she was an old woman.

91. Ⓐ Ⓑ Ⓒ Ⓓ Ⓔ

92. Which of the following speakers demonstrates the greatest faith?
(A) *Faith* is a five letter word.
(B) My faith in God is unarguable.
(C) My faith in my god is complete, most of the time.
(D) My faith in my god is a sometime thing.
(E) Faith in some higher power is necessary for everyone.

92. Ⓐ Ⓑ Ⓒ Ⓓ Ⓔ

93. Which of the following sentences shows how the speaker really feels about his wife?
93. Ⓐ Ⓑ Ⓒ Ⓓ Ⓔ
   (A) All of my children really love their mother.
   (B) My wife helps everyone in her family all the time.
   (C) My wife is a great kid.
   (D) No one has ever said an unkind word about my wife.
   (E) My wife and I have been married for thirty years.

94. Which of the following sentences expresses the worker's real attitude toward her job?
94. Ⓐ Ⓑ Ⓒ Ⓓ Ⓔ
   (A) All of my co-workers like their jobs very much.
   (B) The cafeteria at my place of work serves excellent food.
   (C) My superior just recommended that I get a raise this month.
   (D) I could do my job very well if I were allowed to.
   (E) My parking space at the plant has my name on it.

95. Which of the following sentences makes the most positive reference to Joan?
95. Ⓐ Ⓑ Ⓒ Ⓓ Ⓔ
   (A) Joan could appear intelligent if she wanted to.
   (B) With Joan, I feel comfortable and relaxed some of the time.
   (C) Joan always wears clothes in the latest fashion.
   (D) Without Joan, I would have no one to tease.
   (E) Joan always speaks to me when she sees me.

96. Which of the following sentences expresses the most negative feelings toward Joan?
96. Ⓐ Ⓑ Ⓒ Ⓓ Ⓔ
   (A) Most of the time, Joan serves her family good meals.
   (B) Joan spoils her loving husband outrageously.
   (C) Joan does not care about going to a disco every weekend.
   (D) With Joan, her children always know how far they can go in bending rules.
   (E) Joan speaks to all her friends in exactly the same way.

97. Which of the following statements reveals the speaker's reaction to political corruption?
97. Ⓐ Ⓑ Ⓒ Ⓓ Ⓔ
   (A) All politicians are crooks—everyone knows that.
   (B) Newspapers recently have had several stories about political corruption in our city.
   (C) Political corruption has always been with us; why get upset about it?
   (D) The politicians in city hall are all ignorant and do nothing for the good of the community.
   (E) My tax money should not be spent buying a fancy car for the mayor who gets a commission on the sale.

Directions: In this group of questions, two or three underlined sentences are followed by a question or incomplete statement about them. Read each group of sentences and then choose the best answer to the question or the best completion of the statement.

98. A careful shopper will get several estimates for a remodeling job on her house.
98. Ⓐ Ⓑ Ⓒ Ⓓ Ⓔ

Jennie consulted several contractors before deciding upon the one to do the work.

Sentence two

(A) makes a comparison
(B) implies a conclusion
(C) makes an exception
(D) illustrates a false cause-effect argument
(E) is a contrast

99. Every woman admires a handsome man.
Sylvester Stallone is a handsome man.
What is the only logical conclusion that can be drawn from these two statements?
(A) Every woman admires Sylvester Stallone.
(B) Sylvester Stallone is an excellent actor.
(C) Some women do not like Sylvester Stallone.
(D) Sylvester Stallone's films make money.
(E) Sylvester Stallone is an admirable person.

99. Ⓐ Ⓑ Ⓒ Ⓓ Ⓔ

100. Mowing the grass is a tedious chore for most home owners.
Apartment dwellers do not have to mow grass.

What is happening in these two sentences?

(A) A comparison is implied.
(B) A generalization is established.
(C) A contrast is being made.
(D) An illustration is given.
(E) An exception is being made.

100. Ⓐ Ⓑ Ⓒ Ⓓ Ⓔ

101. Many products are made from oil imported from the Middle East.
Nylon is made from oil.

Sentence two

(A) implies a comparison
(B) provides an example
(C) contradicts sentence one
(D) contrasts two ideas
(E) draws a conclusion

101. Ⓐ Ⓑ Ⓒ Ⓓ Ⓔ

102. Eric is a very methodical person.
He cannot remember to take his car into the shop for regular servicing.

Sentence two

(A) affirms the idea in sentence one
(B) introduces an abstract idea
(C) makes a comparison
(D) is emotional rather than realistic
(E) is an exception

102. Ⓐ Ⓑ Ⓒ Ⓓ Ⓔ

103. Fear can be expressed in many ways.
Some people break into a cold sweat when they are afraid.

103. Ⓐ Ⓑ Ⓒ Ⓓ Ⓔ

Sentence two

(A) is a comparison
(B) contrasts two ideas
(C) draws a conclusion
(D) illustrates an abstract concept
(E) generalizes upon an idea

104. Nelson Rockefeller is a multimillionaire.
He can buy anything he wants.

104. Ⓐ Ⓑ Ⓒ Ⓓ Ⓔ

Sentence two

(A) compares Rockefeller with other millionaires
(B) makes an exception
(C) makes an untrue assumption
(D) is a vague generalization
(E) affirms sentence one

105. Real estate agents show buyers homes for sale.
Automobile salesmen demonstrate the features of new cars.

105. Ⓐ Ⓑ Ⓒ Ⓓ Ⓔ

In these two sentences, persons are classified according

(A) to the duties their jobs involve
(B) how much money they make
(C) where they work, inside or outside a building
(D) how old they are
(E) their self-concepts

106. My grandmother was a real Southern lady.
She had to ignore many things her husband did.

106. Ⓐ Ⓑ Ⓒ Ⓓ Ⓔ

What is happening in these two sentences?

(A) A comparison is being made.
(B) A contrast is being established.
(C) An idea is being illustrated.
(D) An exception is stated.
(E) Two vague generalizations are provided.

107. Barbara Walters is being paid almost one million dollars a year as a
television newsperson.
She developed her talents on *Today*, a long-running television program.

107. Ⓐ Ⓑ Ⓒ Ⓓ Ⓔ

Sentence two

(A) makes a comparison
(B) draws a conclusion
(C) provides a cause
(D) defines an idea
(E) makes an exception

108. Smallpox has been eliminated from the world.
Almost everyone has been innoculated with antibodies which effectively
prevent the disease.

108. Ⓐ Ⓑ Ⓒ Ⓓ Ⓔ

Sentence two

(A) states a cause
(B) provides an effect

(C) makes a comparison
(D) is a generalization
(E) is a contrasting statement

109. All men are green.
Socrates is a man.

Which of the following is the only logical conclusion to be drawn from these statements?

(A) Socrates may or may not be green.
(B) Socrates is Greek.
(C) Socrates is a philosopher.
(D) Socrates is green.
(E) The color of Socrates is unknown.

109. Ⓐ Ⓑ Ⓒ Ⓓ Ⓔ

110. My wife's dress for the wedding was a bright salmon color.
The groom's mother wore a light-blue gown.

The objects in the sentences are categorized

(A) on the basis of their function
(B) according to the materials from which they were made
(C) on the basis of their cost
(D) in comparison with their styles
(E) according to their colors

110. Ⓐ Ⓑ Ⓒ Ⓓ Ⓔ

111. No one born in Alaska has ever been elected president of the United States.
Ohio and Virginia produced several United States presidents.

In these sentences, the objects are organized

(A) according to their age
(B) according to their quality
(C) geographically
(D) by their religions
(E) according to their political persuasion

111. Ⓐ Ⓑ Ⓒ Ⓓ Ⓔ

112. The roast in my oven burned to a crisp.
I had the temperature set too high.

Sentence two is

(A) a cause
(B) a conclusion
(C) a generalization
(D) an effect
(E) an exception

112. Ⓐ Ⓑ Ⓒ Ⓓ Ⓔ

113. Dentists will do almost anything to avoid pulling a tooth.
Dr. Hoffman filled two deep cavities for me yesterday.

Sentence two is

(A) an exception
(B) an example
(C) a comparison
(D) a contrast
(E) a cause

113. Ⓐ Ⓑ Ⓒ Ⓓ Ⓔ

114. The cost of mailing a letter has gone from three cents to twenty-two cents.
The cost of pork chops has risen from eighty-nine cents to $1.26 a pound.

The objects in these sentences

(A) are contrasted on the basis of their function
(B) are contrasted according to their quality
(C) are compared according to how they are used
(D) are compared on the basis of their cost
(E) have no relationship to each other

114. Ⓐ Ⓑ Ⓒ Ⓓ Ⓔ

115. Many organizations have attacked certain television programs because they feature excessive sex and violence.
These same groups have praised *Sesame Street*.

A conclusion that could be drawn from these sentences is that *Sesame Street*

(A) is an ineffective program, not worthy of being attacked
(B) is a program for children only
(C) does not please many adults
(D) is too simple for most children
(E) contains no excessive sex or violence

115. Ⓐ Ⓑ Ⓒ Ⓓ Ⓔ

116. Federal government regulations provide that all new cars must use unleaded gasoline only.
Unleaded gasoline costs more than leaded gasoline.

A conclusion that could be drawn from these two sentences is that

(A) the government should not have made the regulation
(B) new cars will be more expensive to operate
(C) new cars will be much more efficient
(D) old cars are less expensive to buy
(E) new cars are less powerful

116. Ⓐ Ⓑ Ⓒ Ⓓ Ⓔ

117. When the cost of manufacturing something rises, the price of that product also rises.
The cost of gasoline almost doubled within three years.

Sentence two

(A) gives an exception
(B) provides an example
(C) implies a contrast
(D) makes a comparison
(E) is a logical deduction

117. Ⓐ Ⓑ Ⓒ Ⓓ Ⓔ

118. Food prices went up at least 25% in 1978.
Coffee is cheaper in 1978 than it was in 1977.

Sentence two

(A) provides an exception
(B) gives a cause
(C) demonstrates an effect
(D) makes a comparison
(E) gives an effect

118. Ⓐ Ⓑ Ⓒ Ⓓ Ⓔ

Directions: Each of the questions or incomplete statements in questions 119–130 is followed by five suggested answers or completions. Select the one that is best in each case, paying attention to grammar, usage, diction, idiom, and tone.

Questions 119–121 are based on the following passage:

¹For several years, films like *Grease, Star Wars, Saturday Night Fever,* and *Jaws* have made millions of dollars for their producers. ²Other films imitating these massive films have also been made, producers hoping that their efforts will also strike box office gold. ³With all of this activity, the stocks of various motion picture companies have risen dramatically in price. ⁴When stock market analysts note such a trend, they recommend that their clients purchase these stock immediately, thus driving the prices even higher. ⁵Many small investors have seen dividend increases and are satisfied with the results of their investments, although many of them have not seen the films which created their increased income. ⁶Where the whole thing will end, no one knows for sure, but some producers are laughing all the way to the bank.

119. What should be done with sentence 2?
(A) It should be joined with sentence 1 with, *and*.
(B) It should be the opening sentence of the passage.
(C) It should be placed after sentence 5.
(D) It should be omitted.
(E) The words *Other films* should be omitted, and it should be joined to sentence 1 with *however*.

119. Ⓐ Ⓑ Ⓒ Ⓓ Ⓔ

120. In sentence 4, the last part of the sentence beginning *immediately, thus* could be rewritten. Which of the following is the correct new version of the sentence?
(A) immediately, thus drive the prices even higher
(B) immediately, and the prices are driven even higher.
(C) immediately; therefore driving the prices even higher.
(D) immediately, and therefore driving the prices even higher.
(E) immediately. Thus driving the prices even higher.

120. Ⓐ Ⓑ Ⓒ Ⓓ Ⓔ

121. What should be done with sentence 6?
(A) It should be left as it is.
(B) It should be placed after sentence 2.
(C) It should be placed before sentence 4.
(D) It should be placed after sentence 1.
(E) It should be replaced with another sentence which would provide a more logical conclusion for the paragraph.

121. Ⓐ Ⓑ Ⓒ Ⓓ Ⓔ

Questions 122–124 are based on the following passage:

¹Closeup photography can produce strikingly beautiful art, but equipping your camera with a closeup or macro lens is no guarantee of success. ²Many newcomers to closeup photography frequently are disappointed with the results. ³Even shots that are technically perfect—well composed, in sharp focus, properly exposed—often turn out little better than blah. ⁴There are several possible reasons, but the most likely is insufficient light. ⁵Insufficient light means poor contrast (the difference in brightness between the lightest and darkest shades). ⁶And, with rare exception, poor contrast means dull photos. ⁷What can be done with poor lighting on a

cloudy day or deep in the woods where direct sunlight rarely falls? [8]Perhaps more than you'd think.

Reprinted from the *Chicago Tribune*, July 19, 1978. Courtesy of the *Chicago Tribune*.

122. If you wanted to divide the passage into three paragraphs, logical beginnings for paragraphs two and three would be, respectively,
    (A) sentences 2 and 4
    (B) sentences 2 and 5
    (C) sentences 4 and 5
    (D) sentences 4 and 7
    (E) sentences 4 and 8

122. Ⓐ Ⓑ Ⓒ Ⓓ Ⓔ

123. The nature of the material which the passage covers indicates that it is
    (A) an introduction to a longer essay
    (B) a conclusion to a shorter essay
    (C) the answer to a question about photography that is complete
    (D) a comparison of two types of cameras
    (E) a contrast between two types of lighting effects

123. Ⓐ Ⓑ Ⓒ Ⓓ Ⓔ

124. Sentence 3 contains
    (A) an incorrect intrusion of an insignificant idea
    (B) a parenthetical remark that is irrelevant
    (C) a parenthetical series of words which define the idea in the first part of the sentence
    (D) some incorrect grammar
    (E) correct sentence structure that is, however, illogical

124. Ⓐ Ⓑ Ⓒ Ⓓ Ⓔ

Questions 125-127 are based on the following passage:

[1]A sixth charactertistic of language is that it is symbolic in its vocabulary. [2]Sometimes this process of association is conscious, and sometimes it is unconscious. [3]The sound of a word triggers some part of a person's brain and suggests to him/her all kinds of associations and feelings. [4]Take the word *fire*, for example. [5]To one person, the word suggests a blaze on a hearth or out in the open, a sizzling steak, a songfest, a picnic, or the like. [6]In another person, the word might strike terror, because of serious burns received in a burning building. [7]These reactions will differ from person to person, depending upon the context with which the person associates the word. [8]The symbol-making power of words is tremendous, and wars have been fought over the precise meaning of a certain word. [9]Words can also bestow status on an individual: we no longer employ *janitors*—we hire *custodians;* we no longer have *morons*—we have *exceptional children;* we no longer have *garbage collectors*—we have *sanitary engineers.* [10]The second word or phrase in each of these pairs conveys more *tone* than does the first; the first word lies in the discard pile in connection with the individuals named by the word.

125. What should be done with sentence 2?
    (A) It should be placed after sentence 6.
    (B) It should be placed before sentence 10.
    (C) It should begin the passage.
    (D) It should be omitted.
    (E) It should be placed just after sentence 3.

125. Ⓐ Ⓑ Ⓒ Ⓓ Ⓔ

126. Sentence 9

(A) should begin with some kind of transition phrase

(B) should be left as it is

(C) should be changed so that it is shorter

(D) should be made longer to include more examples

(E) is really a conclusion to the passage

126. A B C D E

127. A logical conclusion to the passage would be which of the following?

(A) The science of word meanings, discussed here, is called *semantics*, a word coined by linguists about a century ago.

(B) A student of language does not need to concern himself/herself with the minor points of word meanings.

(C) Many books about semantics have been written, and none of them is very clear.

(D) A dictionary is a very valuable aid to anyone who wishes to know more about language.

(E) Working with language can be a fascinating field of activity.

127. A B C D E

Questions 128-130 are based on the following passage:

¹The English language is primarily Germanic in structure. ²By this we mean that the order in which words are arranged in a sentence gives meaning to that sentence, in many cases. ³Often, a word in isolation means nothing. ⁴For instance, if the word *bear* appeared on a sheet of paper without any other word to give you a clue to its meaning, you might wonder whether the writer is talking about the animal with that name or about the verb which means *to carry*. ⁵If someone spoke the word all by itself, you might wonder if a third meaning—*nude*—might not be possible. ⁶Thus, it is important to study words in interrelationships, to see how sentences are put together, and to learn why certain types of words function in certain ways and in those ways only. ⁷It is important to learn that the function of a word is frequently determined by its placement in a sentence, and vice versa—sometimes the placement of a word determines its function in that sentence.

128. Sentence 7 could be combined with sentence 6. The correct form of the combination is

(A) ways only, it is important

(B) ways only, and therefore, however, it is important

(C) ways only; is important

(D) ways only; it is important

(E) ways only: it is important

128. A B C D E

129. Sentence 3

(A) should be combined with sentence 2

(B) should be placed after sentence 5

(C) should be placed after sentence 7

(D) should be left as it is

(E) should be moved to the beginning of the passage

129. A B C D E

130. Sentence 6
    (A) should be shortened to eliminate unnecessary words
    (B) should be left as it is
    (C) should be lengthened to include more examples
    (D) should be eliminated
    (E) should be moved to the end of the passage

130.   Ⓐ Ⓑ Ⓒ Ⓓ Ⓔ

ANSWER KEY—SAMPLE EXAMINATION 1

Part I

1. C	12. A	23. D	34. B	45. E	56. B
2. A	13. B	24. E	35. B	46. A	57. D
3. E	14. D	25. B	36. D	47. D	58. A
4. D	15. A	26. B	37. E	48. B	59. A
5. C	16. E	27. E	38. A	49. E	60. B
6. B	17. C	28. D	39. C	50. C	61. A
7. B	18. C	29. A	40. B	51. A	62. E
8. E	19. D	30. C	41. C	52. D	63. B
9. A	20. A	31. C	42. B	53. C	64. B
10. D	21. C	32. A	43. D	54. E	65. C
11. E	22. C	33. D	44. C	55. C	

Part II

66. D	77. E	88. D	99. A	110. E	121. E
67. A	78. B	89. C	100. C	111. C	122. D
68. B	79. A	90. A	101. B	112. A	123. A
69. C	80. C	91. E	102. E	113. B	124. C
70. E	81. D	92. B	103. D	114. D	125. E
71. D	82. E	93. C	104. E	115. E	126. B
72. A	83. E	94. D	105. A	116. B	127. A
73. A	84. B	95. A	106. C	117. B	128. D
74. C	85. B	96. E	107. C	118. A	129. D
75. D	86. C	97. C	108. A	119. D	130. B
76. E	87. D	98. B	109. D	120. B	

SCORING CHART—SAMPLE EXAMINATION 1

After you have scored your Sample Examination 1, enter the results in the chart below; then transfer your Raw Score to the Progress Chart on page 14.

Total Test	Number Right	Number Wrong	Number Omitted	Raw Score
Part I:				
Part II:				
Total:				

ANSWER EXPLANATIONS—SAMPLE EXAMINATION 1

Part I

1. **C.** In (A) a semi-colon is incorrect because what precedes that mark is an incomplete sentence. (B) and (E) are sentence fragments, thus also incorrect. In (D) <u>and</u> is incorrect, because the structure of the two parts of the sentence is <u>not</u> the same—an incomplete sentence and a complete sentence.

2. **A.** (B) creates an illogical sentence. (C), (D), and (E) are also illogical as well as changing the meaning of the original sentence.

3. **E.** (A) has an introductory noun clause which changes the meaning of the original sentence. In (B) <u>and</u> is incorrect, because it joins two non-parallel sentence parts. (C) and (D) are incorrect because <u>has told</u> would have no logical subject.

4. **D.** (A) is incorrect because <u>nor</u> creates a sentence which makes no sense. (B) changes the meaning of the original as well as being awkwardly constructed. (C) changes the meaning of the original. (E) contradicts the meaning of the original: a shift from <u>neither-nor</u> to <u>both-and</u>.

5. **C.** In (A) the phrase beginning <u>Directing</u> is not a logical subject for <u>was refused</u>. (B) changes the meaning of the original; Maya Angelou did not refuse anything. (D) is an awkward, wordy sentence and uses a weak passive voice verb, <u>could be directed</u>. (E) changes the meaning of the sentence.

6. **B.** In (A) <u>seeing as how</u> is redundant; in addition, (A) is a sentence fragment. In (C) <u>being that</u> is an incorrect idiom in American English. In (D) the phrase <u>Despite the fact</u> reverses the meaning of the original sentence. In (E) the introductory phrase (Having . . . an American) is a dangling modifier.

7. **B.** (A) is incorrect because <u>unique</u> and <u>poor</u> are not synonyms. (C) is incorrect because <u>uniquest</u> does not exist as a correct word in the English language. (D) and (E) and incorrect because they change the meaning of the original sentence.

8. **E.** (A) is incorrect because the comma is unnecessary. (B) is a sentence fragment, thus incorrect. In (C) the comma creates a comma splice. (D) is illogical, because the press conference itself could make no statement; only President Carter could.

9. **A.** (B) is incorrect because the sentence is an illogical completion of the idea. (C) is incorrect because <u>satisfactorily</u> is an adverb, and the sentence sense requires the adjective <u>satisfactory</u>. (D) and (E) are incorrect because of poor word choices and phrase construction: <u>satisfactorily</u> and <u>intense in my repletion</u>.

10. **D.** (A) is incorrect because the phrase beginning <u>Starting</u> is a dangling modifier. (B) is incorrect because the sentence contains a comma splice. (C) is incorrect because <u>them</u> has no specific antecedent. (E) is incorrect because <u>so that</u> is a poor choice of conjunctions.

11. **E.** (A) is incorrect because <u>hardly</u> is an incorrect choice of words. Choices (B), (C), and (D) would create nonsense sentences and thus are also incorrect.

12. **A.** Choices (B) and (C) change the meaning of the original sentence. (D) is incorrect, because <u>most</u> cannot be used when only two items are being compared. (E) contradicts the meaning of the original sentence.

13. **B.** In (A) the semi-colon is used incorrectly; the second part of the sentence is illogical. (C) is incorrect because <u>neither</u> requires <u>nor</u> rather than <u>or</u>. (D) is incorrect because a comma after <u>action</u> also requires a comma after <u>courtroom</u> to set off the interrupting phrase. (E) is wordy and confusing.

14. **D.** (A) is incorrect, because <u>even though</u> implies a contrast which the original sentence does not have. (B) is incorrect, because too much information is omitted from the sentence. In (C) the comma produces a comma splice. (E) is incorrect because the phrase beginning <u>Working</u> is a dangling modifier.

15. **A.** (B) is wrong, because <u>facts</u> cannot logically be <u>untrue</u>, a contradictory phrase. (C) is also incorrect because <u>misapprehensions</u> is a poor word choice. (D) is incorrect because <u>true facts</u> is redundant; by definition facts

must be true. (E) is incorrect because it adds an idea (<u>slanted information</u>) not included in the original sentence.

16. E.   (A) is incorrect because the clause beginning <u>which</u> is a dangling modifier. (B) is wordy and contains <u>this</u> which has no specific antecedent. The first comma in (D) creates a comma splice.

17. C.   (A) is wordy; <u>reason</u> followed by <u>due to the fact that</u>. (B) is incorrect because <u>caused</u> has no logical subject. (D) is incorrect because there is no logical subject for <u>kept</u>. (E) is incorrect because the first comma creates a comma splice.

18. C.   (A) is incorrect because <u>neither</u> requires <u>nor</u> rather than <u>or</u> as the completion of the correlative. (B) is incorrect because <u>they</u> has no specific antecedent. (D) is incorrect because the phrase beginning <u>without</u> would produce a confusing sentence. (E) is incorrect because the phrase beginning <u>agreeing</u> is a dangling modifier.

19. D.   (A) is incorrect because the comma creates a comma splice. (B) is a confused sentence that does not make sense. (C) is incorrect because the phrase beginning <u>Assuming</u> is a dangling modifier. (E) changes the meaning of the original sentence.

20. A.   (B) is incorrect because the two parts of the sentence (before and after the comma) do not function logically together. (C) is incorrect because <u>successfully</u> (an adverb) should be <u>successful</u> (an adjective). (D) would create a sentence that does not make much sense. (E) is incorrect, because <u>greatly</u> (an adverb) should be <u>greater</u> (an adjective); however, that version of the sentence seems awkward.

21. C.   (A) is incorrect because the phrase beginning <u>having</u> is a dangling modifier. (B) is incorrect because <u>they</u> has no specific antecedent. (D) is incorrect because the phrase <u>being flown</u> is not parallel with was taken (a verb). (E) is wordy; too, <u>had been taken</u> is the weak passive voice and <u>them</u> has no specific antecedent.

22. C.   The other choices are incorrect because they change the meaning of the original sentence. In order to arrive at a correct response, you must be sure what each of the choices says and then compare that statement with the original sentence.

23. D.   (A) is incorrect because <u>whenever</u> distorts the meaning of the sentence. In (B) the semi-colon is incorrect because what follows is not a complete sentence. (C) is wrong because <u>being as how</u> is an incorrect idiom in English. (E) is incorrect because <u>and</u> distorts the meaning of the original sentence.

24. E.   (A) is incorrect because the dependent clause beginning <u>which</u> does not function logically with the rest of the sentence. (B) and (C) are awkward, rather complicated sentences and therefore incorrect. (D) is incorrect because <u>anyone</u> and <u>they</u> represent an error in agreement between a pronoun and its antecedent.

25. B.   (A) is incorrect because <u>is climbed</u> is a weak passive verb. (C) is incorrect because the phrase beginning <u>against</u> is misplaced; it should be placed closer to <u>maneuvers</u>. (D) and (E) contradict the original meaning of the sentence.

26. B.   (A) is incorrect; <u>each</u> is singular, and <u>were</u> is plural; therefore, there is faulty agreement of subject and verb. (C) is incorrect because the two parts of the sentence, before and after the comma, establish a cause-effect relationship not in the original sentence. (D) and (E) change the meaning of the original sentence.

27. E.   (A) and (C) are incorrect because <u>have held</u> and <u>planned</u> are past tense verbs; the verb in the original is in the present tense. (B) is wrong because <u>plans on having</u> is an incorrect English idiom; <u>plans to have</u> would be correct. (D) is incorrect because it changes the meaning of the original sentence.

28. D.   (A) is an awkward sentence, therefore wrong. (B) is incorrect because <u>although</u> changes the meaning of the original sentence. (C) is incorrect because the phrase <u>somewhat more complete</u> is vague. (E) makes a statement that is not present in the original.

29. A. (B) is incorrect because should be . . . formed is a weak passive verb. (C) is incorrect because anyone and their do not agree; both words should be singular or plural. (D) also contains an error in agreement: no one and their. (E) is incorrect because them has no specific antecedent.

30. C. All of the other choices would produce an illogical statement.

31. C. ignored is the only word among the choices which fits the sentence.

32. A. reasonable is the only adjective which fits the contexts, completely illogical (B) changes the meaning, convincingly (C) is an adverb, masterful (D) would be used incorrectly, and marvelously complex (E) distorts the meaning.

33. D. (A) is too "high flown" as a choice of words. (B) is incorrect because modicum does not fit the context. (C) is wordy. (E) is illogical: how could anyone hear a pat on the back?

34. B. All the other choices represent very poor word selections.

35. B. None of the other choices fit the context as well.

36. D. In (A) this point in time is wordy for now. (B) is too wordy. In (C) contemporary and today needlessly repeat the same idea. (E) is too vague.

37. E. (A) and (B) contain redundant phrases. (C) and (D) are vague.

38. A. The other choices are illogical.

39. C. All the other choices are too wordy.

40. B. Parishioners arriving once the pastor had started his sermon annoyed him with their interruption.

41. C. The chief and fifteen Indians attack the heavily defended fort at least once a day.

42. B. The many attempts of so many people to swindle the millionaire out of his money with foolish proposals caused him to become cynical and hardhearted.

43. D. The communities which they serve owe better pay, better housing, and more services to migrant workers, whether Blacks or Hispanics.

44. C. Astounded by the sales of Bill Jones' first novel, the publisher offered a much higher royalty arrangement for the second.

45. E. A thermostat is useless in the new electronic ovens because they employ sound waves rather than heat as a means of cooking and a clock as a control device.

46. A. Orphans are not considered adoptable after they become seven years old; if no family. . . .

47. D. If I succeed in my efforts to write the great American novel, my tenth grade English teacher is completely responsible.

48. B. Amanda Wingfield had a number of gentleman callers in her youth; therefore, she assumed that. . . .

49. E. Users may take an unlimited number of tablets of some pain relievers without becoming addicted, but others warn against anyone's. . . .

50. C. A politician preparing a speech for delivery to a women's organization surely includes some ringing phrases. . . .

51. A. The Volkswagen and the Datsun attract many American buyers of foreign-made automobiles because of their reputation for high gas mileage.

52. D. Since the uniqueness of a chef's sauces may well determine his reputation and salary, he considers his recipes more valuable than gold.

53. C. We three boys were called to the front of the auditorium, and our scoutmaster announced that each of us had won three merit badges within a month.

54. E. For about two months, we in Illinois have locally grown fresh vegetables; frosts in September usually. . . .

55. C. Georgia was one of the thirteen original colonies and was also one of the states which seceded from the Union in 1861.

56. B. No explanation, which is completely satisfactory to doctors who must treat the venereal disease cases among today's teenagers, has been offered by social psychologists for the rising rate of infection.

57. D. A small battery which most manufacturers guarantee for one year powers most electric wrist watches.

58. A. Researchers know that either surgery or certain drugs effectively eradicate or arrest the spread of cancerous cells.

59. A. January, 1979, brought Chicago more snow than the annual forty inch average.

60. B. Even though John Travolta and Lily Tomlin had made successful movies separately, their co-starring film was severely attacked by critics.

61. A. (B) is incorrect because them has no specific antecedent. (C) is illogical because the phrase by the jeweler is a misplaced modifier. (D) is illogical and omits information. (E) is also illogical because it says that we bought the sponsor.

62. E. (A) is wrong because percent is used incorrectly. (B) is wrong because they has no specific antecedent. (C) is illogical, paralleling percentage with girls. (D) is wordy.

63. B. (A) is incorrect because it has no specific antecedent. (C) is incorrect because she has no specific antecedent. (D) is incorrect because he and him have no specific antecedent. (E) is incorrect because by Father is a misplaced modifier.

64. B. In (A) It has no specific antecedent. (C) is wrong because them is vague. (D) and (E) are also incorrect because they is vague.

65. C. (A) is incorrect because to enjoy them is a misplaced phrase; we do not know what is to be enjoyed. (B) is wrong because them may have one of several antecedents. (D) is wrong, because enough is illogical. (E) is incorrect because point should be plural.

Part II

66. D. All of the other choices are illogical or not supported by the facts in the statement.

67. A. (B) is wrong because optimist is incorrectly used. (C), (D) and (E) are hasty generalizations from insufficient evidence.

68. B. The other choices are subjective rather than objective reactions to the statement.

69. C. The other choices cannot be supported by the facts in the statement.

70. E. The other choices cannot logically be deduced from the statement.

71. D. Again, the facts in the statement do not support the other choices.

72. A. A represents the only logical conclusion a reader can draw.

73. A. The other proverbs do not fit as a response to the statement.

74. C. The other conclusions cannot be logically inferred.

75. D. The other inferences are illogical, based on insufficient evidence.

76. E. The reader does not have enough information to conclude (A), (B), (C), or (D).

77. E. (A), (C), and (D) are wrong because of the word all. (B) cannot be a logical conclusion, because nothing in the statement implies anything about insurance.

78. B. Inadequate evidence for the conclusions invalidate (A), (C), (D), and (E).

79. A. (B) is incorrect because it omits any consideration of unemployment problems. (C) is incorrect because there is nothing in the statement about energy proposals. The reader does not have enough information to make (D) and (E) valid conclusions.

80. C. The word ignorant in (C) is the key; here, the word has no negative connotations. All the other choices are incorrect: (A) because they did study geography and astronomy but not the information which we now have available; (B) because facts may imply eternal truths, but we know that facts change as discoveries are made; (D) because stupid has negative connotations; (E) because, again, facts change as discoveries are made—they knew the facts of their time.

81. D. (A) and (E) cannot be valid conclusions from the facts given. (B) is incorrect because unreasonable may be merely the reader's reaction. We do not know enough to conclude (C). In (D), note the word implied, for Son is clever enough to attempt to manipulate Father.

82. E. (A), (B), and (C) may be valid, but we do not have sufficient information to be sure. (D) is wrong because his reason for refusing seems reasonable. Again, <u>implied</u> is the key word which makes (E) correct.

83. E. (A) and (C) generalize from insufficient information. (B) and (D) are invalid, because the reactions are subjective rather than objective.

84. B. (A) is a subjective reaction. (C) is incorrect because the pastor expresses no doubt in his assertion. (D) is incorrect, because the word <u>may</u> implies a doubt which is not contained in the statement. (E) is incorrect because it is an unwarranted assumption.

85. B. (A) and (D) seem to contradict the statement. (C) is incorrect because the statement says nothing about taxes. (E) is an unwarranted assumption.

86. C. (A) and (E) are not logical conclusions from the facts. (B) and (D) are illogical assumptions.

87. D. (A) is too broad a statement. (B) contradicts the statement, a protest against the many company policies. (C) and (E) are too subjective.

88. D. (A) is incorrect because Jack's wife's clothes may have nothing to do with Jack's financial operations; perhaps she has a job and buys her own clothes. (B) is invalid because it establishes an illogical comparison. (C) and (E) say nothing about Jack's financial operations.

89. C. (A) and (B) make a statement of a fact which is neither positive nor negative. (D) and (E) are negative but not as strongly negative as (C).

90. A. (B) and (C) are mildly negative statements of facts but imply no strong feelings. (D) is a neutral statement. (E) states a positive feeling but not one of the speaker's.

91. E. (A) and (D) are facts, but they have nothing to do with her ability as an actress. (B) indicates that she may not be a good actress, but (E) is a much stronger statement about her failings. (C) shows no evidence of her acting ability; it gives evidence of her personal relations with others.

92. B. (A) is a statement of fact. (C) and (D) express some reservations about faith in some god. (E) asserts a condition which may or may not be true.

93. C. (A) and (D) express the feelings of people other than the speaker. (B) and (E) are statements of fact and imply no feelings at all.

94. D. (A), (C), and (E) are statements of fact which could be verified objectively. (B) is a value judgment about food, not about the job.

95. A. The phrase <u>some of the time</u> in (B) implies that Joan changes her personality. (C) and (E) are verifiable statements. (D) says more about the speaker than about Joan; Joan may dislike the teasing.

96. E. (A), (C), and (D) could be verified and facts discovered to prove or disprove the conclusions. (B) is a value judgment. (E) implies that Joan makes no distinctions among her friends and that characteristic may denote insincerity.

97. C. In (A) <u>All politicians are crooks</u> is an assertion which the second part of the statement does not support. (B) is a verifiable statement, neither positive nor negative. (D) is also an unsupported assertion. (E) is a subjective reaction, but the mayor's commission is not necessarily an example of political corruption.

98. B. The implied conclusion is that Jennie is a careful shopper; therefore, none of the other choices is valid.

99. A. The two statements are the major and minor premises of a classic syllogism; thus (A) is the only possible response. (B), (D), and (E) are incorrect because the two sentences do not mention his acting ability, the profitability of his films, or his qualities as a person. (C) is incorrect because it denies the major premise.

100. C. (A), (B), (D), and (E) are incorrect, because the two statements do not compare two things, do not make a generalization (although sentence 1 does), do not illustrate a generalization, and do not make an exception to a generalization.

101. B. (A) is incorrect because no comparison is implied. (C) does not contradict sentence 1. (D) is incorrect because there is no contrast. (E) is incorrect because no conclusion is drawn.

102. **E.** (A) is incorrect because an affirming statement cannot contain <u>not</u> unless the first sentence also contains <u>not</u>. (B) is incorrect because the idea expressed is concrete, not abstract. (C) is wrong because no comparison is implied. (D) is wrong because it contains nothing emotional.

103. **D.** (A) is incorrect because there is no comparison. (B) is wrong because the two statements are not contrasted. (C) is wrong because no conclusion is drawn. (E) is wrong because sentence 2 is specific, not general.

104. **E.** (A), (B), and (D) are incorrect, because sentence 2 is not a comparison, an exception, or a generalization. (C) is incorrect because the word <u>untrue</u> contradicts sentence 2.

105. **A.** (B) is incorrect because how much money is made is not mentioned in either statement. (C) is incorrect because there is no indication in the two sentences of the place of employment. (D) is incorrect because the word <u>age</u> appears in neither sentence. (E) is wrong; we know nothing about the self-concepts of the agents or salesmen.

106. **C.** (A), (B), (D), and (E) are incorrect because the terms from formal logic (<u>comparison</u>, <u>contrast</u>, <u>exception</u>, <u>generalization</u>) are not relevant to the two sentences.

107. **C.** (C) is correct because the effect (sentence 1) is the result of the cause (sentence 2). None of the other answers state the correct relationship between the two sentences.

108. **A.** Sentence 2 states the cause from which sentence 1 is the effect; therefore (A) is the only correct answer. (B) is incorrect because it reverses the relationship between the two sentences. (C), (D), and (E) do not state a correct relationship and are wrong.

109. **D.** Sentences 1 and 2 are the major and minor premises of a classic syllogism; thus, the only logical conclusion is (D). (B) is incorrect because there is no indication in the sentences of Socrates' nationality. (C) is incorrect because Socrates' interests are not mentioned in either sentence. (A) and (E) are invalid conclusions.

110. **E.** (A) is incorrect because sentence 2 does not clearly state the possible use of the gown. (B), (C), and (D) are incorrect because the three characteristics (materials, cost, styles) are not mentioned in either sentence.

111. **C.** The only common feature which the two sentences have is the name of the state. (C) is the only correct response because the characteristics in (A), (B), (D), and (E) are not mentioned in the two sentences.

112. **A.** Sentence 2 is the cause which produced the effect stated in sentence 1. (A) is correct. (D) is wrong because it reverses the actual relationship between the two sentences. (B), (C), and (E) are also wrong because the terms from logic do not apply.

113. **B.** Since sentence 2 provides an example to support the generalization of sentence 1. The terms in (A), (C), (D), and (E) do not apply to the two sentences; thus, these choices are incorrect.

114. **D.** The cost of the two commodities is the only common idea in the two sentences. (E) is incorrect, because there is a relationship between the two sentences. (A), (B), and (C) are wrong because the phrases suggest comparison or contrast based on characteristics which are not stated in the two sentences.

115. **E.** The conclusion in (E) is the only correct one. (A) is incorrect because sentence 2 says nothing specific about the quality of *Sesame Street*. (B), (C), and (D) are incorrect because there is no evidence in the two sentences to support these inferences.

116. **B.** (A) is incorrect because the two sentences imply no negative attitude toward the government regulations. (C) is incorrect because the two sentences say nothing about the efficiency of new cars. (D) is an illogical conclusion from the two sentences. (E) is an unwarranted assumption.

117. **B.** (A), (C), and (D) are incorrect because the terms from logic are not applicable to the two sentences. (E) is incorrect because the deduction is not logical.

118. A. Read the two sentences carefully. Sentence 1 is a generalization; sentence 2 is an example which refutes the generalization. (A) is the only correct answer. In (B), (C), (D), and (E), the terms from logic are not applicable.

119. D. (D) seems to introduce an idea which does not fit after the thesis statement in sentence 1; therefore, it should be omitted from the paragraph. (B) is wrong because other films would be too vague to be in the thesis statement. Choice (C) is wrong because sentence 2 would be even more out of place following sentence 5. (E) is incorrect because the change with however implies a contrast which would distort the meaning of the paragraph.

120. B. (A) is incorrect because drive would have no subject. In (C) the semi-colon is used incorrectly. (D) contains and therefore, a redundant phrase. In (E), the period makes what follows that mark a sentence fragment.

121. E. Sentence 6 should be replaced with a more complete conclusion, because the sentence shifts from a discussion of stock trading and profits to film producers. (E) is correct and the other choices are incorrect.

122. D. Sentence 4 introduces an idea (several reasons) which is followed by explanations. Sentences 7 and 8 are a logical conclusion for the paragraph. Thus (D) is the only correct choice; the other possibilities would make illogical divisions of the material.

123. A. Sentence 8 implies that further discussion will follow so that the problem of poor lighting can be solved. Thus, (A) is correct. (B) is incorrect, because sentence 8 as a conclusion would leave the reader up in the air. (C) is wrong, because a question is posed in sentence 7, but that question is not completely answered. (D) and (E) are incorrect, because they offer information which is not included in the paragraph.

124. C. The words between the two dashes define a technically perfect photograph; thus (C) is correct. (A) is wrong because the idea is necessary to provide the definition. (B) is wrong because the remark is relevant to the discussion. (D) is incorrect because the grammar of the sentence is correct. (E) is wrong because the sentence structure is logical.

125. E. Reversing sentences 2 and 3 provides a more logical development of the idea in the paragraph; therefore (E) is correct. (D) is incorrect because sentence 2 expands the idea contained in sentence 3; sentence 2 should not be omitted, but its position needs to be changed. (A), (B), and (C) are incorrect, because these changes would be even more illogical than the version provided in the book.

126. B. Any choice other than (B) would make the whole sentence unclear and the passage too short (C) so that examples would be omitted, or too long (D) with more examples than necessary to support the generalization in sentence 8. There is no need for a transition phrase (A), and the sentence is not a conclusion (E).

127. A. The passage leads logically to the word semantics; thus, (A) is the only correct choice. (B) is incorrect because it obviously contradicts the implications of the paragraph. (C) is incorrect; it is too vague to be a conclusion. (D) is wrong because there is no discussion of dictionaries in the passage. (E) is too vague and general to be a conclusion.

128. D. (A) is incorrect because it would create a comma splice. (B) is incorrect because and therefore, however, is wordy and contradictory. (C) is incorrect because there is no logical subject for is. (E) is incorrect because the colon is incorrectly used.

129. D. (A) is incorrect because such a combination would weaken both sentences. (B) is incorrect because such a placement would be illogical. (C) is incorrect because sentence 3 would not be a logical conclusion for the paragraph. (E) is incorrect because sentence 3 would not be logical as an introduction to the paragraph.

130. B. (A) is incorrect because any shortening might eliminate an important idea. (C) is incorrect because any additional ideas would complicate the sentence. (D) is incorrect because, if the sentence were eliminated, important ideas would be omitted. (E) is incorrect because sentence 6 would not be a good conclusion for the paragraph.

SAMPLE EXAMINATION 2

Part I

Number of Items: 65
Time: 45 minutes

Directions: For each of these questions, you are to choose the version of the underlined sentence or part of the sentence that not only has the same or nearly the same meaning as the original but follows the requirements of standard written English. That is, in selecting the version that matches the underlined part in meaning, pay attention to grammar, choice of words, sentence structure, and punctuation. The answer you select should, when inserted in the original sentence, produce an effective sentence—clear and exact, without awkwardness or ambiguity.

1. Good writing can frequently be identified by its clarity, its brevity, its ability to please, <u>and its freedom from grammatical errors.</u>
   - (A) ; therefore, it should be free of grammatical errors
   - (B) , and it should be free of grammatical errors
   - (C) , to be free of grammatical errors
   - (D) ; moreover, there should be no grammatical errors
   - (E) , and the absence of grammatical errors

   1. Ⓐ Ⓑ Ⓒ Ⓓ Ⓔ

2. Luckily, the arsonist <u>was arrested</u> before he could set any more serious fires.
   - (A) was caught
   - (B) having been arrested
   - (C) shall have been caught
   - (D) being caught
   - (E) having been arrested

   2. Ⓐ Ⓑ Ⓒ Ⓓ Ⓔ

3. <u>Geography can teach anyone more about the small planet on which he lives than just the physical boundary lines between any two countries.</u>
   - (A) Anyone who studies geography should learn more about the world than they can memorize from studying a map.
   - (B) Learning the boundary lines between two countries should be of secondary interest for anyone studying geography.
   - (C) More than the physical boundary lines between countries can have been learned in a geography course.
   - (D) The earth has more to teach us in geography than about where two countries come together.
   - (E) Boundary lines between countries should be the prime lessons to be learned from geography.

   3. Ⓐ Ⓑ Ⓒ Ⓓ Ⓔ

4. Twenty years from now, <u>the Boeing 747 will be as obsolete as the Douglas DC-3 is</u> today, but millions of passengers will remember how they used to marvel at the size of the jumbo jet.
   - (A) will be so obsolete as is the Douglas DC-3
   - (B) should have been as obsolete as is the Douglas DC-3
   - (C) will be even more outmoded than the Douglas DC-3 is
   - (D) will be out-of-date just as is the Douglas DC-3
   - (E) will be just as outmoded as is the Douglas DC-3

   4. Ⓐ Ⓑ Ⓒ Ⓓ Ⓔ

5. Raising her hand for permission to leave the room, Joan asked the teacher if she could be gone for fifteen minutes without missing anything.

  (A) Having raised her hand for permission to leave the room, the teacher told Joan she would not miss anything in fifteen minutes.
  (B) Without missing anything for fifteen minutes, Joan raised her hand for permission to leave the room.
  (C) Joan asked permission to leave the room; she also asked if she would miss anything if she were gone for fifteen minutes.
  (D) Leaving the room without missing anything for fifteen minutes, the teacher gave Joan permission to go.
  (E) Joan's hand having been raised for permission to leave the room, she said she would be gone for fifteen minutes.

5. Ⓐ Ⓑ Ⓒ Ⓓ Ⓔ

6. *Jaws* was such a popular movie that the producers made plans to film *Jaws 2*.

  (A) When *Jaws* became so popular, the producers planned *Jaws 2*.
  (B) *Jaws* was a popular movie; therefore, they planned to film *Jaws 2*.
  (C) Because *Jaws* was such a popular movie, they planned to film *Jaws 2*.
  (D) *Jaws 2* was made when *Jaws* having been such a popular movie.
  (E) *Jaws 2* was the result of *Jaws* having been made such a popular movie.

6. Ⓐ Ⓑ Ⓒ Ⓓ Ⓔ

7. To avert a population explosion, young couples might consider adopting children already born instead of bringing more into the world.

  (A) To invert a population explosion,
  (B) Having inverted excess population,
  (C) A population explosion having been prevented,
  (D) To prevent excess population,
  (E) Averting excessive population,

7. Ⓐ Ⓑ Ⓒ Ⓓ Ⓔ

8. Even after breaking every speed limit on the expressway, I still missed my plane.

  (A) Having broken every speed limit on the expressway, my plane left without me.
  (B) I broke every speed limit on the expressway but still missed my plane.
  (C) My plane was gone when I reached the airport; they let it leave on schedule.
  (D) Notwithstanding the fact that I broke all the speed limits on the expressway, my plane could not help leaving me at the gate.
  (E) I missed my plane due to the fact that I broke all expressway speed limits.

8. Ⓐ Ⓑ Ⓒ Ⓓ Ⓔ

9. Everyone judges himself with a harsher yardstick than he uses to measure the performance of others.

  (A) than they use to evaluate others' performances
  (B) than the one used for other people
  (C) whether the performance of other people can measure up
  (D) or than the one he uses on other people
  (E) , than he decides would best measure the performance of others

9. Ⓐ Ⓑ Ⓒ Ⓓ Ⓔ

10. The minister walked up to the front of the church to begin the morning service, and he was ten minutes late as usual.

    10. Ⓐ Ⓑ Ⓒ Ⓓ Ⓔ

(A) , ten minutes late as usual
(B) , so as usual he had been ten minutes late
(C) and that he was ten minutes late as usual
(D) and ten minutes late as usual
(E) , too late by more than ten minutes

11. No one dared to dream that President Reagan himself would present the medal to the retiring crossing guard.

    11. Ⓐ Ⓑ Ⓒ Ⓓ Ⓔ

(A) The presentation of the retiring crossing guard's medal by President Reagan had not been expected which is why we dreamed it.
(B) Presenting the medal to the retiring crossing guard, President Reagan dared to dream about the whole affair.
(C) The retiring crossing guard received her medal from President Reagan and which surprised us all.
(D) We did not dare dream that the retiring crossing guard had received her medal from President Reagan.
(E) President Reagan's presenting the medal to the retiring crossing guard surprised us all.

12. No one who sees well at night has any reason to complain about the dim street lights on our block.

    12. Ⓐ Ⓑ Ⓒ Ⓓ Ⓔ

(A) If anyone sees well at night complains about the dim street lights on our block.
(B) The street lights on our block are dim; therefore, we all see well at night.
(C) Having dim street lights is the reason why we all complain about night blindness.
(D) That we have dim street lights is the source of our complaints.
(E) Those on our block who see well at night do not complain about the dim street lights.

13. When we reached the wreck, we found the driver pinned between the steering wheel and the dashboard, unconscious and bleeding profusely.

    13. Ⓐ Ⓑ Ⓒ Ⓓ Ⓔ

(A) dashboard, and that was the reason he was
(B) and that he was
(C) dashboard which was
(D) dashboard; he was
(E) dashboard, having been

14. Many Amish barns are decorated with strange symbols to ward off evil and with weather vanes in the shape of roosters.

    14. Ⓐ Ⓑ Ⓒ Ⓓ Ⓔ

(A) to protect them from disaster and with weather vanes
(B) that ward off evil and that with weather vanes
(C) that result in the protection of evil and with weather vanes
(D) to ward off evil and that the weather vanes
(E) which are shaped like weather vanes to ward off evil

15. Grandfather's hearing has been gradually degenerating, but no one in the family can persuade him to buy an electronic aid.

    (A) Grandfather's hearing having been gradually degenerating,

    (B) Because Grandfather's hearing has been gradually getting worse,

    (C) Even though Grandfather's hearing has been gradually getting poorer,

    (D) Grandfather's hearing, gradually degenerating, but

    (E) Gradually getting poorer, Grandfather's hearing, but

15. Ⓐ Ⓑ Ⓒ Ⓓ Ⓔ

16. By the time the average person is twenty, he has completed high school and is attending college or has chosen some sort of occupation which he may or may not continue for the rest of his life.

    (A) but he is attending college

    (B) ; he is attending college or

    (C) neither is attending college nor

    (D) or is attending college or

    (E) , and is attending college,

16. Ⓐ Ⓑ Ⓒ Ⓓ Ⓔ

17. Johnny Carson asked Joan Rivers to substitute for him on *The Tonight Show*; Ms. Rivers had hosted the show before and had done a creditable job.

    (A) before Ms. Rivers had hosted the show, she had done a creditable job

    (B) when Ms. Rivers had hosted previously she had done an excellent job

    (C) with Ms. Rivers as host, she had done an incredible job

    (D) Ms. Rivers was an incredible host which was the reason why Carson invited her again

    (E) Ms. Rivers had been pleased by Carson into doing a credible job before

17. Ⓐ Ⓑ Ⓒ Ⓓ Ⓔ

18. Arriving home after a long afternoon of sailing on Lake Michigan, we stored the boat in the shed next to the garage.

    (A) The shed next to the garage housed our boat after it had sailed Lake Michigan all afternoon.

    (B) Arriving home after a long afternoon sailing on Lake Michigan, the boat was stored in its shed next to the garage.

    (C) When we returned home after sailing all afternoon on Lake Michigan, the shed next to the garage housed our boat.

    (D) We put the boat into its shed next to the garage after we finished sailing on Lake Michigan all afternoon.

    (E) Having been sailed all afternoon on Lake Michigan, we put our boat into the shed next to the garage.

18. Ⓐ Ⓑ Ⓒ Ⓓ Ⓔ

19. A professional dressmaker can alter a dress so cleverly that the wearer is not conscious that it did not fit perfectly the first time she put it on.

    (A) so well that the lady believes it

    (B) with such agility that the wearer's conscience is unaware it did not

    (C) so easily that her consciousness thought it

    (D) that, with such ease, it

    (E) with such dexterity that it did

19. Ⓐ Ⓑ Ⓒ Ⓓ Ⓔ

20. Because the official tabulation showed John Jones winning by only five votes, the teller ordered all ballot boxes sealed, pending another tally of the results.

20. Ⓐ Ⓑ Ⓒ Ⓓ Ⓔ

(A) John Jones' winning by only five votes
(B) Winning by five votes, John Jones was the official tabulation
(C) The official tabulation showed John Jones winning by only five votes,
(D) By five votes, the official tabulation showing John Jones the winner,
(E) John Jones won the election by only five votes, and

21. The team's trainer had to make a quick decision about the first baseman's legs, for the star could neither walk around without intense pain nor move his toes because of a severe swelling of the joints.

21. Ⓐ Ⓑ Ⓒ Ⓓ Ⓔ

(A) either had severe pain or move his toes because of large joint swellings
(B) not have severe swelling of his joints or intense pain without being effective
(C) not move his toes nor walk, caused by a severe swelling of his joints
(D) neither because of severe swelling of the joints nor the inability to move his toes
(E) not walk around or move his toes without pain because of a severe swelling of his joints

22. I shall rely on my ability to speak French fluently when I travel to Paris this year.

22. Ⓐ Ⓑ Ⓒ Ⓓ Ⓔ

(A) I shall rely on my ability to fluently speak French when I travel to Paris this year.
(B) When I travel to Paris this year, my ability to speak French fluently will be relied on by me.
(C) I will travel to Paris this year; my fluent French will be a definite asset.
(D) My ability to speak French fluently could hardly be an asset when I travel to Paris this year.
(E) Because I am travelling to Paris this year, my ability to speak French fluently will be something of an asset.

23. Each time I moved my hand across the top of my desk, I had the feeling I was removing some dust from its surface.

23. Ⓐ Ⓑ Ⓒ Ⓓ Ⓔ

(A) The top of my desk is susceptible to moving my hand,
(B) I move my hand across the top of my desk,
(C) Whenever I brushed the top of my desk with my hand,
(D) My hand moved across the top of my desk and
(E) Although I moved my hand across the top of my desk,

24. With all of the prosecution of gangsters for income tax evasion, it would seem that they would have good tax lawyers to keep them clear.

24. Ⓐ Ⓑ Ⓒ Ⓓ Ⓔ

(A) that good tax lawyers have kept them clear
(B) that each one would have a good tax lawyer to keep him clear
(C) that it takes a tax lawyer to keep him clear
(D) that a good tax lawyer is the reason because gangsters are not punished for income tax evasion
(E) that no gangster cannot afford to be without a good tax lawyer

25. Our instructor urged us not to feel bad if we did not understand his assignment because he had not made the directions clear.
    (A) Our instructor urged us not to feel badly if we did not understand
    (B) That we did not understand, our instructor urged us to feel badly
    (C) Just because we did not understand his assignment, our instructor said, was
    (D) To feel bad that we did not understand the assignment was nonsense, our instructor said,
    (E) When our instructor said we should have understood his assignment,

25. Ⓐ Ⓑ Ⓒ Ⓓ Ⓔ

26. Alarmed by the possibility of an Indian attack, the settlers gathered in the stockade and began loading muskets.
    (A) Alarmed by the possibility of an Indian attack, the stockade was opened by the settlers, and their muskets were loaded by them.
    (B) Alarmed by the possibility of an Indian attack, the settlers gather in the stockade and began to load their muskets.
    (C) Because they were alarmed by a possible Indian attack, the settlers gathered in the stockade, and muskets began to be loaded.
    (D) When an Indian attack seemed possible, the settlers came together in the stockade and loaded their muskets.
    (E) The reason the settlers gathered in the stockade and began to load muskets was because of the eminent Indian attack.

26. Ⓐ Ⓑ Ⓒ Ⓓ Ⓔ

27. At no time can there be a machine which uses the principle of perpetual motion.
    (A) They can never invent a perpetual motion machine.
    (B) A machine which uses the principle of perpetual motion is definitely possible.
    (C) Perpetual motion machines are not real possible because they cannot invent them.
    (D) What with the perpetual motion machine, man can use certain principles.
    (E) For a long time, a perpetual motion machine has been considered scientifically impossible.

27. Ⓐ Ⓑ Ⓒ Ⓓ Ⓔ

28. It's too bad that rain spoiled our summer vacation plans, and we can only hope that next year's weather will be different.
    (A) plans; we can only
    (B) plans, therefore, we
    (C) plans, in which we
    (D) plans, and we cannot but only
    (E) plans, what with our

28. Ⓐ Ⓑ Ⓒ Ⓓ Ⓔ

29. *E.T.* has made more money than any other motion picture in history, surpassing *Star Wars* and *Gone With the Wind* within the first year of its release.
    (A) *E.T.* has made more money than any motion picture in history,
    (B) Box office grosses for *E.T.* are the highest in motion picture history,
    (C) *E.T.*, making more money at the box office,

29. Ⓐ Ⓑ Ⓒ Ⓓ Ⓔ

(D) With the release of *E.T.*, motion picture box office grosses had to be rewritten

(E) No motion picture in history grossed the most money than *E.T.*

Directions: For each of these sentences, select the answer that, when inserted in the blank in the original sentence, produces the best sentence. Pay attention to meaning and to choice of words.

30. Within twelve months, the number of aircraft hijackings was reduced to zero after _____ at US airports.

    (A) the installation of special security devices
    (B) building vast numbers of X-ray scanners
    (C) the increase in the appropriate number of police
    (D) the resistance of air passengers
    (E) checking all those boarded flights

    30. Ⓐ Ⓑ Ⓒ Ⓓ Ⓔ

31. When you reach your desk this morning, please _____ our correspondence, for I do not want to repeat my order.

    (A) refer back to
    (B) reread again
    (C) review
    (D) make a brief reference to
    (E) consult our previously written

    31. Ⓐ Ⓑ Ⓒ Ⓓ Ⓔ

32. Dissatisfied with conditions in our society, many Americans have _____ Australia which has opened its doors to skilled workers.

    (A) become nonresident aliens in
    (B) decided to enlist in
    (C) emigrated to
    (D) gone the whole route to
    (E) travelled as tourists to

    32. Ⓐ Ⓑ Ⓒ Ⓓ Ⓔ

33. Do nothing _____ he makes a decision, if he can ever make up his mind.

    (A) unless and until
    (B) without
    (C) because
    (D) insofar as
    (E) until

    33. Ⓐ Ⓑ Ⓒ Ⓓ Ⓔ

34. The old engine _____ push the leaky boat's speed above five knots.

    (A) could not but
    (B) could not hardly
    (C) could, with its total maximum effort,
    (D) could barely
    (E) had consistently been able to not

    34. Ⓐ Ⓑ Ⓒ Ⓓ Ⓔ

35. In order for John and his friends to see *Witness*, they had to find an adult _____ a parent or guardian.
    (A) to make out like he was
    (B) to pretend to be
    (C) to pose as a stand-in for a possible
    (D) to play like he was
    (E) to happen to come along to be

35. Ⓐ Ⓑ Ⓒ Ⓓ Ⓔ

36. Mary was not permitted to buy the new dress _____ already having clothes she had not worn in months.
    (A) because of her
    (B) due to her
    (C) unless she could show her
    (D) without her
    (E) instead of her

36. Ⓐ Ⓑ Ⓒ Ⓓ Ⓔ

37. When all else failed, he _____ singing folk music for a country and music radio station.
    (A) tried his hand at
    (B) worked his way around to
    (C) had given up and turned to
    (D) elevated his morale
    (E) applied for a job

37. Ⓐ Ⓑ Ⓒ Ⓓ Ⓔ

38. While still a child, Joan suffered _____ that she had been adopted and that her biological parents were dead.
    (A) from the constantly re-occurring daydream
    (B) with the true factual knowledge
    (C) from the illusion
    (D) from the real problem
    (E) under the completely false notion

38. Ⓐ Ⓑ Ⓒ Ⓓ Ⓔ

39. Upon _____, I saw that the cookie contained grains of pepper and that it looked good.
    (A) explicit inspection
    (B) minute and detailed examination
    (C) watching with my eyes
    (D) careful visual viewing
    (E) closer near inspection

39. Ⓐ Ⓑ Ⓒ Ⓓ Ⓔ

Directions: Revise each of the following sentences according to the directions which follow it. Rephrase the sentence mentally to save time, making notes in your book if you wish. Although the directions may at times require you to change the relationship between parts of the sentence or to make slight changes in other ways, *make only those changes that the directions require.*

Below each sentence and its directions are listed words or phrases that may occur in your revised sentence. When you have thought out a good sentence, look at the choices A through E for the word or entire phrase that is included in your revised sentence.

Of course, a number of different sentences can be obtained if the sentence is revised according to the directions, and not all of these possibilities can be included in only five choices. If you should find that you have thought of a sentence that contains none of the words listed in the choices, rephrase the sentence again to include a word or phrase that *is* listed.

40. Coney Island, a beach in New York City, is famed for its roller coaster and its many hot dog stands.

   Begin with Coney Island, famed.

   (A) is   (B) was   (C) will be
   (D) has been   (E) had been

   40. Ⓐ Ⓑ Ⓒ Ⓓ Ⓔ

41. A woman can seldom force a reluctant husband to attend a concert, an opera, or the opening of a new art gallery unless she resorts to tears or other purely feminine wiles.

   Change unless to if.

   (A) does   (B) do   (C) does not
   (D) do not   (E) should not

   41. Ⓐ Ⓑ Ⓒ Ⓓ Ⓔ

42. The proper amount of iron is often just as important in a woman's daily diet as the proper number of units of vitamins A and C.

   Substitute more for just as.

   (A) only   (B) than   (C) also   (D) both   (E) as

   42. Ⓐ Ⓑ Ⓒ Ⓓ Ⓔ

43. To eliminate confusion and uncertainty for motorists, Congress should pass a law establishing a nationally uniform code of traffic laws, for, now, every state has its own peculiar rules and regulations.

   Begin with Motorists would be spared.

   (A) if Congress must pass
   (B) if Congress ought to pass
   (C) if Congress should not pass
   (D) if Congress must establish
   (E) if Congress would pass

   43. Ⓐ Ⓑ Ⓒ Ⓓ Ⓔ

44. No contemporary man can afford to retreat, as Thoreau did to Walden Pond, unless he has a few benevolent acquaintances who will provide him with the necessities of life.

   Begin with When Thoreau retreated to.

   (A) just so   (B) thus   (C) so   (D) also   (E) too

   44. Ⓐ Ⓑ Ⓒ Ⓓ Ⓔ

45. The recent collapse of prices on the New York Stock Exchange has been both a welcome sign that the inflationary spiral is slowing and a signal for large stockholders to begin purchasing large blocks of shares at bargain rates.

   Substitute but also for and.

   (A) as well as   (B) as much as   (C) as
   (D) too   (E) not only

   45. Ⓐ Ⓑ Ⓒ Ⓓ Ⓔ

46. Following the ceremony, there will be a small reception in the parish hall only for those who were mailed individual invitations.

Begin with A small reception.

(A) preceding   (B) precede   (C) follow
(D) following   (E) followed

47. Any professional golfer who plays on the tournament circuit year after year may eventually attain his goal of winning the Masters or the National Open.

Delete who.

(A) having played   (B) being played   (C) having been played
(D) having playing   (E) playing

48. After the judge had pronounced sentence upon the convicted bank robber, the spectators in the courtroom applauded because the wretch received ten years in the state penitentiary.

Begin with The convicted bank robber's sentence.

(A) from   (B) to   (C) into
(D) by means of   (E) after

49. A careful reader can often infer a newspaper editor's opinions by noting the amount of space a story is given as well as the page on which the account is printed.

Begin with The amount of space and change as well as to and.

(A) infers   (B) indicate   (C) inferred
(D) indicated   (E) infer

50. Today's newspaper reporters have access to more sources of information within the administration than their predecessors did a century ago.

Begin with More sources of information.

(A) is available
(B) will have been available
(C) having been available
(D) are available
(E) being available

51. The sacrifices which parents make so that their children may enjoy some of life's luxuries are often unappreciated by the ungrateful progeny.

Begin with Ungrateful progeny.

(A) none   (B) not   (C) no
(D) some   (E) any

52. Hester Prynne, the heroine of Hawthorne's *The Scarlet Letter*, was found guilty of adultery and sentenced by colonial magistrates to wear a red A for the rest of her life.

Begin with Colonial magistrates.

(A) finds   (B) has found   (C) found
(D) has been found   (E) was found

53. Mary as well as twenty of her classmates attends the theater every Saturday morning when special matinee prices are in effect at the box office.

Change as well as to and.

(A) attends the theater
(B) has been attending the theater
(C) have been attended at the theater
(D) shall have attended by the theater
(E) attend the theater

53. Ⓐ Ⓑ Ⓒ Ⓓ Ⓔ

54. China and the Soviet Union share a long, almost unprotectable boundary across almost all of Asia, and within recent years disputes over the exact location of that boundary have brought tensions between the two nations.

Begin with Not only.

(A) do   (B) does   (C) did   (D) have shared   (E) will share

54. Ⓐ Ⓑ Ⓒ Ⓓ Ⓔ

55. Nowadays, not many of those voters eligible to cast a ballot bother to exercise their franchise on election day.

Change not many to not one.

(A) their   (B) him   (C) his   (D) himself   (E) theirs

55. Ⓐ Ⓑ Ⓒ Ⓓ Ⓔ

56. Among the effects of the deceased railroad president was a solid gold watch which he had been awarded after twenty-five years of faithful service to the company.

Begin with The company awarded.

(A) until his death   (B) from his death   (C) for his death
(D) after his death   (E) with his death

56. Ⓐ Ⓑ Ⓒ Ⓓ Ⓔ

57. Whether the young man is stupid or ignorant is difficult to determine, but we do know that he made a fool of himself at the party last night.

Begin with Whether through and change stupid and ignorant to nouns.

(A) his   (B) the young man   (C) who   (D) he   (E) him

57. Ⓐ Ⓑ Ⓒ Ⓓ Ⓔ

58. Marshall McLuhan, a Canadian scholar whose studies of television's effects upon the human personality have revolutionized our thinking about the mass media, has been the target not only of praise but also of severe criticism for his theories.

Begin with Marshall McLuhan is.

(A) ; he   (B) , but he   (C) , for he
(D) ; however, he   (E) , although he

58. Ⓐ Ⓑ Ⓒ Ⓓ Ⓔ

59. A good assistant can relieve an administrator of much of the paperwork that must be handled within any large organization to expedite its day-to-day operations.

Substitute generates for must be handled.

(A) within any large organization generates
(B) an administrator generates

59. Ⓐ Ⓑ Ⓒ Ⓓ Ⓔ

(C) its operation generates

(D) a good assistant generates

(E) any large organization generates

60. Young grandchildren can be a great comfort to grandparents, but sometimes the older folks give them too much attention and spoil them outrageously.

Begin with <u>Young grandchildren who</u>.

(A) is   (B) are   (C) was

(D) were   (E) have been

60. Ⓐ Ⓑ Ⓒ Ⓓ Ⓔ

Directions: For each of the following, choose the one phrasing that makes the intended meaning clear; that is, the one that avoids ambiguity, that does not leave the actual meaning open to question or that does not leave the reader guessing what is intended.

61. (A) Selling spoiled banana splits caused our neighborhood ice-cream vendor to have his license revoked by them.

(B) As a result of his selling banana splits to customers which were spoiled, our neighborhood ice-cream vendor was refused a license.

(C) They refused our neighborhood ice-cream vendor a license when they caught him selling spoiled banana splits.

(D) Our neighborhood ice-cream vendor was refused a license because he sold spoiled banana splits.

(E) Customers to whom he had sold spoiled banana splits protested their giving our neighborhood ice-cream vendor a license.

61. Ⓐ Ⓑ Ⓒ Ⓓ Ⓔ

62. (A) The dissidents created a noisy disturbance when the speaker announced that he did not favor their proposals in the rear of the hall.

(B) The proposals in the rear of the hall were not approved by the speaker to the noisy dissidents.

(C) The speaker did not approve their proposals in the rear of the hall when the dissidents created a noisy disturbance.

(D) The noisy dissidents did not let the speaker approve their proposal in the rear of the hall.

(E) The dissidents in the rear of the hall created a noisy disturbance when the speaker did not approve their proposals.

62. Ⓐ Ⓑ Ⓒ Ⓓ Ⓔ

63. (A) After landing the Boeing 747 safely, we greeted the tourists who deplaned through the narrow passageway that connected plane and terminal.

(B) The Boeing 747, having landed safely, was connected to the terminal with a narrow passageway through which they thronged.

(C) The Boeing 747 having landed safely, we greeted the tourists who thronged through the narrow passageway which connected plane and terminal.

(D) A narrow passageway connected the Boeing 747 and the terminal; we greeted the tourists who thronged through it.

63. Ⓐ Ⓑ Ⓒ Ⓓ Ⓔ

(E) When the Boeing 747 landed safely, a narrow passageway was thronged with tourists whom we greeted that connected plane and terminal.

64. (A) Before I was a student in her class, I heard that Ms. Singleton was a hard teacher.
(B) Ms. Singleton is a hard teacher; moreover, I entered her class anyhow.
(C) As a student in her class, Ms. Singleton is a hard teacher.
(D) Ms. Singleton allowed me to enter her class, a hard teacher.
(E) Hearing that Ms. Singleton is a hard teacher, my entry was into her class.

64. Ⓐ Ⓑ Ⓒ Ⓓ Ⓔ

65. (A) I had to leave my car, its front axle broken and its radiator leaking, on a dark side street.
(B) My car, since it had a broken front axle and a leaking radiator, was left by me in a dark side street.
(C) With its broken front axle and its leaking radiator, I had to leave it on a dark side street.
(D) On a dark side street with a broken front axle and a leaking radiator, I had to leave my car.
(E) Its front axle broken and its radiator leaking, on a dark side street, I had to leave my car.

65. Ⓐ Ⓑ Ⓒ Ⓓ Ⓔ

Part II

Number of Items: 65
Time: 45 minutes

Directions: Questions 66–89 are each based on a short passage. Read the passage and then select the one best answer to the questions that follow the passage, using the information provided by or suggested in the passage.

66. The senior said, "Watching television or attending a movie always relaxes me the night before an examination. After a night enjoying these pleasures, I don't care whether I pass or fail."

With this statement, the senior demonstrates that

(A) he finds television and movies a poor substitute for studying
(B) he is not really interested in succeeding in school
(C) he wants to work hard in school
(D) he finds studying a relief from television and the movies
(E) he wishes he could be more motivated to study harder

66. Ⓐ Ⓑ Ⓒ Ⓓ Ⓔ

67. A wife said, "My husband was unfaithful to me once, and I forgave him. Why do I feel so insecure when he tells me he loves me? I know he never sees the other woman anymore."

In this statement, the wife illustrates the old saying

(A) "a bird in the hand is worth two in the bush"
(B) "you can lead a horse to water, but you can't make him drink"
(C) "you can forgive, but you can't forget"
(D) "you should never knock a good thing"
(E) "a leopard never changes its spots"

67. Ⓐ Ⓑ Ⓒ Ⓓ Ⓔ

68. A student said, "My father never attended college. I would be much more satisfied if I had a full-time job, but I will try college even though I hate the idea."

The student demonstrates

(A) he is probably a poor student
(B) he cannot compromise with what he believes wrong
(C) he has very good study habits
(D) he can do only what he finds satisfying
(E) he is controlled by his father, not by his own wishes

Questions 69-70 are based on the following dialogue:

Daughter: "Don't blame me for not keeping my room clean.
When I was a child, you came in drunk every Friday night."
Father: "If you don't clean your room, you cannot have the car tomorrow."
Daughter: "That's not right."

69. In the dialogue, Daughter
(A) is convinced that her father is an alcoholic
(B) indicates that she will not clean up her room
(C) relies on a poor excuse for her room not being clean
(D) seems to waste time arguing
(E) tries to make her own duties more important than her father's

70. In the dialogue, Father
(A) implies that his drinking has affected his daughter
(B) issues an ultimatum which Daughter must abide by
(C) says that he does not respect his daughter
(D) says he has tried to show Daughter the right way to clean up her room
(E) implies that he is responsible for the cleanliness of Daughter's room

71. Kathy said, "Joe never asks me to go out for dinner. I'd rather stay at home to study anyhow."

From these statements, it is obvious that

(A) Kathy is an honor student
(B) Kathy would rather go out with Bill
(C) Kathy wants to get married
(D) Kathy wishes that she were a beautiful woman
(E) Kathy is unhappy that Joe has not asked her to go out

72. "I know I am correct in my conclusions. Anyone who dares disagree with me is prejudiced and a liar."

The speaker believes

(A) no one should disagree with him
(B) a liar might well disagree with him
(C) a prejudiced person could not be an evil person
(D) prejudiced people are all liars
(E) liars could have a few redeeming characteristics

73. "Have you ever seen anything like the large number of Middle East oil millionaires who have descended upon London? I must admit that I have never seen anything like this."

The writer subtly discloses that

(A) he is neutral toward Middle East oil millionaires
(B) he is working to become a Middle East oil millionaire
(C) he likes Middle East oil millionaires
(D) he is concerned that oil millionaires will take over the world
(E) he does not trust Middle East oil millionaires

73. Ⓐ Ⓑ Ⓒ Ⓓ Ⓔ

74. A bumper sticker reads, "If guns are outlawed, only outlaws will have guns."

The sticker

(A) is very careful to use words with exact meanings
(B) obviously supports some sort of gun control legislation
(C) was placed on the bumper by a member of a radical group urging the overthrow of the government
(D) uses *outlaw* twice with different meanings
(E) was purchased by someone not concerned about legislation to prohibit the sale of rifles

74. Ⓐ Ⓑ Ⓒ Ⓓ Ⓔ

75. A politician said, "Everyone should have the best possible education. No one would argue against that point. I also believe that those who are most capable financially should contribute to the cost of educating everyone."

If the politician were asked to vote for increasing taxes on his own property 20% to support education, how would he vote?

(A) He would favor the increase.
(B) He would not favor the increase.
(C) He would vote for a smaller increase.
(D) A reader cannot decide.
(E) He would vote for a decrease.

75. Ⓐ Ⓑ Ⓒ Ⓓ Ⓔ

76. "My instructor always gives me bad grades, no matter how hard I study. I am convinced he does not like me."

The student Jane has concluded that

(A) her personality may be more important than the quality of her work
(B) she is being discriminated against for some reason
(C) she can often make mistakes in her work
(D) all instructors are unfair in their grading standards
(E) she cannot do well with any assignment

76. Ⓐ Ⓑ Ⓒ Ⓓ Ⓔ

77. The laboratory test showed a new drug helped three people overcome a common cold. There were only three people who took the drug. The manufacturer said in his advertisement, "100% of those tested were cured after they took Coldgone."

The manufacturer's claims

(A) should be accepted as conclusive proof that Coldgone will cure colds
(B) show that curing the common cold is not easy

77. Ⓐ Ⓑ Ⓒ Ⓓ Ⓔ

(C) may not be supported by a larger test sample

(D) are not worth further investigation

(E) are inaccurate because the experiments were not completed

Questions 78-79 are based on the following dialogue:

Student: "My grade point average is 1.9, and I have been placed on probation. That's not fair."

Dean: "But you must have a grade point average of 2.0 to remain off probation."

Student: "But for a lousy .1—that's not fair."

78. The dean   78. Ⓐ Ⓑ Ⓒ Ⓓ Ⓔ
    (A) is being unfair
    (B) believes in holding to exact school standards
    (C) is using his influence to ruin the student
    (D) is going against school policies
    (E) is helping the student pass a course

79. The student   79. Ⓐ Ⓑ Ⓒ Ⓓ Ⓔ
    (A) is substituting reason for emotion
    (B) has not been studying
    (C) has a full-time job
    (D) has had severe personal problems
    (E) is asking for an exception

80. "I am right in doing whatever I want to do. Thus, I have the right to eat nine full meals a day."   80. Ⓐ Ⓑ Ⓒ Ⓓ Ⓔ

    The speaker has

    (A) used the same word with two different meanings
    (B) given a reason for his not gaining twenty pounds
    (C) provided a logical excuse for his suffering a heart attack
    (D) made a modified declaration of independence against all laws and regulations
    (E) argued against his joining Weight Watchers

81. A young man said, "I love my mother, my car, my girlfriend, apple pie, Wendy's hamburgers, and a cold bottle of beer when I am hot."   81. Ⓐ Ⓑ Ⓒ Ⓓ Ⓔ

    The young man is clearly

    (A) too young to know what *love* means
    (B) using *love* to denote different attitudes
    (C) a highly emotional person who loves everything
    (D) very careful to choose words that communicate his feeling precisely
    (E) saying that he likes beer better than he loves his mother

Questions 82-83 are based on the following:

"Golfing is good exercise. There is nothing like playing nine holes on a hot summer afternoon to iron out all the kinks in a man's mind."

82. The speaker indicates that
   (A) not everyone can become a fan of golf
   (B) hot summer afternoons are pleasant
   (C) nine holes of golf are the ideal number for a golf course
   (D) he enjoys playing golf
   (E) the game of golf can be played easily

82. Ⓐ Ⓑ Ⓒ Ⓓ Ⓔ

83. What generalization about golf must the reader believe if the speaker's statement is believable?
   (A) Every man would profit from belonging to a golf club.
   (B) Golfing is the perfect exercise.
   (C) All men have kinks in their minds.
   (D) Everyone can resist the attractions of a golf course.
   (E) All men play golf on hot summer afternoons.

83. Ⓐ Ⓑ Ⓒ Ⓓ Ⓔ

84. A senator said, "The United States must develop the neutron bomb. The Russians are far ahead of us in the building of atomic-powered submarines."

   The senator appears to believe that

   (A) some military weapons cannot be overpowered
   (B) the United States is the equal of the Russians in certain armaments
   (C) Russia's nuclear-powered submarines can win any future war
   (D) there is no real difference between the neutron bomb and the nuclear-powered submarine
   (E) the neutron bomb might be used to overwhelm nuclear-powered submarines

84. Ⓐ Ⓑ Ⓒ Ⓓ Ⓔ

85. "If I don't do anything, my problems will solve themselves."
   The speaker is really saying

   (A) "My problems have no solution"
   (B) "Some one should step in to solve my problems"
   (C) "Problems like mine are really difficult to solve"
   (D) "No action is better than some wrong action'
   (E) "Help—I need help"

85. Ⓐ Ⓑ Ⓒ Ⓓ Ⓔ

Questions 86-87 are based on the following:

"Jimmy Carter was born and brought up in South Georgia where many people are opposed to Blacks' having voting privileges."

86. In this statement, the writer
   (A) is opposing Blacks voting in general elections
   (B) seems to indicate his membership in many anti-Black organizations
   (C) may imply that Jimmy Carter is also opposed to Blacks having the privilege of voting
   (D) opposes all of Jimmy Carter's foreign policies
   (E) says that he wants a government office which Jimmy Carter has refused to offer him

86. Ⓐ Ⓑ Ⓒ Ⓓ Ⓔ

87. The statement also indicates that the writer
   (A) always accepts the majority's opinion about any controversial issue
   (B) does not express an opinion about Blacks' voting privileges
   (C) would not contribute one penny to any group supporting Blacks' voting rights
   (D) believes that Jimmy Carter has been a very poor president
   (E) feels that Jimmy Carter should go back to Georgia and raise peanuts

87. Ⓐ Ⓑ Ⓒ Ⓓ Ⓔ

88. "No one should try to change my mind by giving me any information that shows I might be wrong. I have made up my mind and will not change."

   In this statement, the speaker
   (A) displays his stubbornness
   (B) makes up his mind too quickly
   (C) demands only facts before making up his mind
   (D) is obviously a person who has considered all the information on an issue
   (E) has many prejudices which may not be changed

88. Ⓐ Ⓑ Ⓒ Ⓓ Ⓔ

89. "Hard work is good for everyone. As a young person, I worked hard, and look at what I have accomplished."

   In this statement the speaker is saying
   (A) she has done something, but the hearer cannot be sure what she has done
   (B) she has made a fortune
   (C) she has risen above a youth of poverty
   (D) people who work hard will accomplish little
   (E) her hard work has kept her from enjoying life

89. Ⓐ Ⓑ Ⓒ Ⓓ Ⓔ

Directions: In questions 90–97, you are to compare various statements in the light of the questions posed. Pay attention to the tone, emphasis, and implications of each of the statements as you select the one response that is best in each case.

90. Which of the following possible advertising slogans tells most about the good qualities of the product?
   (A) "The Mercedes is the best engineered car ever produced."
   (B) "The new Toyota gives you that carefree feeling as you drive."
   (C) "Buy a Buick—ask the man who owns one."
   (D) "Get a Jeep with genuine Levi denim upholstery."
   (E) "The Volkswagen Rabbit goes thirty miles on a gallon of gas."

90. Ⓐ Ⓑ Ⓒ Ⓓ Ⓔ

91. Which of the following statements would be the most insulting to a high government official?
   (A) The cabinet official spent too much money redecorating an office.
   (B) The press secretary concealed some of the official's movements.
   (C) The Secretary of State may be involved in secret negotiations with the Russians.
   (D) The Attorney General approved illegal wire taps.
   (E) The Supreme Court Justice was having an affair with his secretary.

91. Ⓐ Ⓑ Ⓒ Ⓓ Ⓔ

92. Which of the following statements would be most flattering to Joan?
   (A) Everyone in the club has some kind of reaction to Joan.
   (B) Joan's husband always has a clean shirt to wear.

92. Ⓐ Ⓑ Ⓒ Ⓓ Ⓔ

(C) Joan's children wash the dishes every day.

(D) Joan's taste in movies are those of a famous magazine critic.

(E) Joan knows how to dress well without spending too much money.

93. Which of the following is the most complimentary of John's fiancee?

(A) She is not the most beautiful woman I have ever seen.

(B) She has a somewhat bland personality.

(C) Her personality always fits the mood John is in.

(D) Her hair is always neatly combed.

(E) She seems to follow John's wishes too much.

93. Ⓐ Ⓑ Ⓒ Ⓓ Ⓔ

94. Which of the following political slogans would most likely appeal to someone who consistently votes against any tax increases on his personal property?

(A) "Throw the rascals out."

(B) "Elect anyone to Congress."

(C) "Replace the incumbents."

(D) "No taxation without representation."

(E) "Balance the budget."

94. Ⓐ Ⓑ Ⓒ Ⓓ Ⓔ

95. Which one of the following sentences shows the writer's opinion about a book she has read recently?

(A) "The author has written a story that covers the life of a ghetto family in New York."

(B) "The characters in the story all seemed to be real people."

(C) "The print was easy to read, and the publisher used a paper of high quality."

(D) "The author uses long paragraphs to tell the reader what is happening in the story."

(E) "The author uses much dialogue to dramatize the events of the story."

95. Ⓐ Ⓑ Ⓒ Ⓓ Ⓔ

96. Which of the following statements reveals what the speaker believes about possible law violators?

(A) When I suspect someone of a crime, I want to hear all of the evidence before deciding upon that person's guilt or innocence.

(B) If everyone would only obey the law, we would be able to close our prisons.

(C) All criminals should suffer for their crimes—an eye for an eye, a tooth for a tooth.

(D) Congress passed some laws which are supposed to be violated.

(E) No one should cry when convicted law violators are held in prison.

96. Ⓐ Ⓑ Ⓒ Ⓓ Ⓔ

97. Which of the following statements most clearly reveals the speaker's opinion about professional football players?

(A) Too many nuts go to ball games on Sunday afternoons.

(B) Those sports writers pick a favorite and ignore every other player on the team.

(C) The good old boys in football uniforms are an OK bunch.

(D) Those guys on the gridiron don't have to work too hard.

(E) Those muscle-bound jocks get too much loot.

97. Ⓐ Ⓑ Ⓒ Ⓓ Ⓔ

Directions: In this group of questions, two underlined sentences are followed by a question or incomplete statement about them. Read each group of sentences and then choose the best answer to the question or the best completion of the statement.

98. <u>My house is warm in winter and cool in summer.</u>
    <u>I installed a new heating and cooling system in 1977.</u>

    Sentence two

    (A) names an effect
    (B) makes a contrast
    (C) affirms a generalization
    (D) gives a cause
    (E) introduces a new idea

    98. Ⓐ Ⓑ Ⓒ Ⓓ Ⓔ

99. <u>The box of tissues on my desk is green and brown.</u>
    <u>The tissues inside are green and white.</u>

    The objects in the size of the sentences are categorized according to their

    (A) cost   (B) size   (C) shape
    (D) quality   (E) colors

    99. Ⓐ Ⓑ Ⓒ Ⓓ Ⓔ

100. <u>Many of today's high school students smoke marijuana.</u>
     <u>My grandson keeps some in his drawer all the time.</u>

     Sentence two

     (A) illustrates a generalization
     (B) states a cause
     (C) provides a contrast
     (D) brings up a different issue
     (E) makes an exception

     100. Ⓐ Ⓑ Ⓒ Ⓓ Ⓔ

101. <u>All but one of the students passed the examination.</u>
     <u>Hannah was the only one who failed.</u>

     Sentence two

     (A) contradicts sentence one
     (B) provides an exception
     (C) affirms sentence one
     (D) makes a generalization
     (E) provides a comparison

     101. Ⓐ Ⓑ Ⓒ Ⓓ Ⓔ

102. <u>*Annie Hall* won several Academy Awards for Woody Allen.</u>
     <u>He wrote, directed, and starred in the film.</u>

     Sentence two

     (A) demonstrates an effect
     (B) provides a cause
     (C) defines an idea
     (D) gives an example
     (E) makes a comparison clear

     102. Ⓐ Ⓑ Ⓒ Ⓓ Ⓔ

103. <u>My daughter's house has pine wood floors.</u>
     <u>I do not like floors of pine wood.</u>

     103. Ⓐ Ⓑ Ⓒ Ⓓ Ⓔ

The conclusion which could be drawn from these two sentences is that

(A) I prefer a house with concrete floors
(B) I do not like my daughter's house
(C) my daughter's house builder used cheap materials
(D) my daughter's house was inexpensive
(E) I like my daughter's house

104. All people who live in Miami enjoy fresh orange juice daily.
Abner has tomato juice for his breakfast.

104. Ⓐ Ⓑ Ⓒ Ⓓ Ⓔ

Sentence two demonstrates that Abner

(A) may not live in Miami
(B) does not like orange juice
(C) is allergic to orange juice
(D) works for a company that produces tomato juice
(E) is a peculiar person

105. The large bottle holds eight ounces of shampoo.
The small bottle holds three ounces of shampoo.

105. Ⓐ Ⓑ Ⓒ Ⓓ Ⓔ

What is happening in these two sentences?

(A) A comparison is made according to quality and capacity.
(B) A conclusion is drawn about quality and cost.
(C) Two examples of size and quantity are provided.
(D) Two exceptions to cost and size are given.
(E) Two examples of size and quality are provided.

106. Justice for all Americans is guaranteed by the United States Constitution.
All persons accused of crimes are entitled to a lawyer to advise them.

106. Ⓐ Ⓑ Ⓒ Ⓓ Ⓔ

Sentence two

(A) makes an exception
(B) defines the concept *justice*
(C) supports a generalization through a comparison
(D) provides an example
(E) implies a contrast

107. Countries have different customs for celebrating Christmas.
The idea of Santa Claus bringing toys developed only recently in the
United States.

107. Ⓐ Ⓑ Ⓒ Ⓓ Ⓔ

What is happening in these two sentences?

(A) Sentence two is a generalization, sentence one an example.
(B) Both sentences are generalizations.
(C) Both sentences are illustrations.
(D) Sentence one is a generalization, sentence two an illustration.
(E) Neither sentence is a generalization.

108. The brown house is on lot 22.
The green house is on lot 23.

108. Ⓐ Ⓑ Ⓒ Ⓓ Ⓔ

In these sentences, the objects are organized according to

(A) their location   (B) their size   (C) their cost
(D) their comfort   (E) their color

109. In recent years, George Burns has acted roles as an old vaudeville comedian and God.
He is a versatile actor.

Sentence two

(A) illustrates an idea
(B) defines a concept
(C) denies sentence one
(D) is an example
(E) draws a conclusion

109. Ⓐ Ⓑ Ⓒ Ⓓ Ⓔ

110. *Saturday Night Fever* provided an Academy Award nomination for John Travolta.
His price for acting in a film more than doubled.

Sentence two

(A) states a cause
(B) makes a comparison
(C) implies a contrast
(D) cites an example
(E) gives an effect

110. Ⓐ Ⓑ Ⓒ Ⓓ Ⓔ

111. All generalizations are false.
Sentence one is false.

What is happening in these two sentences?

(A) Sentence two affirms sentence one.
(B) Sentence two denies sentence one.
(C) Both sentences are generalizations.
(D) Sentence two is an example.
(E) Both sentences are conclusions.

111. Ⓐ Ⓑ Ⓒ Ⓓ Ⓔ

112. Federal architecture is characterized by an equal number of windows of the same size and shape on each side of the front door.
The White House in Washington is a Federal-style building.

The second sentence

(A) defines Federal-style architecture
(B) gives an example
(C) compares the White House to other buildings
(D) draws a conclusion
(E) provides an exception

112. Ⓐ Ⓑ Ⓒ Ⓓ Ⓔ

113. Many migratory birds fly south in the fall.
Some geese spend the winter near open lakes in the north.

Sentence two

(A) affirms sentence one
(B) makes a comparison
(C) draws a conclusion
(D) provides an exception
(E) is a vague generalization

113. Ⓐ Ⓑ Ⓒ Ⓓ Ⓔ

114. The salad bowl has developed a rich color from years of use.
The bottom is a darker brown than the sides.

In these two sentences, only one characteristic of the bowl is emphasized—

(A) its size   (B) its shape   (C) its shade
(D) its age   (E) its value

114. Ⓐ Ⓑ Ⓒ Ⓓ Ⓔ

115. In the shop, there is an antique sofa that is beautiful.
The proprietor also owns an old table which is ugly.

In these sentences, the objects are classified according to

(A) their age   (B) their cost   (C) their appearance
(D) their style   (E) their location

115. Ⓐ Ⓑ Ⓒ Ⓓ Ⓔ

116. Some Pennsylvania Dutch farmers have hex signs on their barns.
John Dostert does not have a hex sign on his barn.

Which of the following is the only logical conclusion to be drawn from these two statements?

(A) John Dostert is a Pennsylvania Dutch farmer.
(B) John Dostert may or may not be a Pennsylvania Dutch farmer.
(C) John Dostert does not like hex signs.
(D) John Dostert is not a Pennsylvania Dutch farmer.
(E) John Dostert's wife likes hex signs.

116. Ⓐ Ⓑ Ⓒ Ⓓ Ⓔ

117. Many trees shed their leaves in the fall.
Some oak trees are bare all winter long.

Sentence two

(A) draws a conclusion
(B) affirms the first sentence
(C) makes a comparison
(D) gives an example
(E) is a definition of an abstract idea

117. Ⓐ Ⓑ Ⓒ Ⓓ Ⓔ

118. The oak tree is twenty feet to the left of the hickory tree.
The red maple tree is forty feet to the right of the hickory tree.

The trees in these sentences are related according to their

(A) size   (B) leaf color   (C) location
(D) blooming season   (E) leaf shape

118. Ⓐ Ⓑ Ⓒ Ⓓ Ⓔ

Directions: Each of the questions or incomplete statements in questions 119–130 is followed by five suggested answers or completions. Select the one that is best in each case, paying attention to grammar, usage, diction, idiom, and tone.

Questions 119-121 are based on the following passage:

¹*Sesame Street* and *The Electric Company* revolutionized the whole idea of television programing for children. ²Until these programs were produced and aired by the Public Broadcasting System, parents had no real options for children's television viewing except *Captain Kangaroo,* violent and

crude cartoons on Saturday morning, and a few locally originated programs. [3]But *Sesame Street* and *The Electric Company* are different. [4]Not only do they provide entertainment for viewers but they also provide educational opportunities for children under about age ten. [5]The Sesame Street Generation, as some teachers are calling the group of children now in the primary grades, know their numbers and the letters of the alphabet as well as many other facts about life. [6]Perhaps the most important lessons taught by these two programs derive from their interracial casts; both of these programs demonstrate that people of all races can live and play together without racially-based friction. [7]Whatever these programs have cost has been money well spent.

119. Sentences 2 and 3 might be combined. Which of the following is the correct form of the combination?
(A) originated programs, *Sesame Street*
(B) originated programs, however, *Sesame Street*
(C) originated programs, but *Sesame Street*
(D) originated programs, and *Sesame Street*
(E) originated programs with the exception that *Sesame Street*

119. Ⓐ Ⓑ Ⓒ Ⓓ Ⓔ

120. What should be done with sentence 5?
(A) It should be left as it is.
(B) It should be omitted.
(C) It should be placed after sentence 7.
(D) It should be combined with sentence 2.
(E) It should be after sentence 1.

120. Ⓐ Ⓑ Ⓒ Ⓓ Ⓔ

121. Which of the following might better replace sentence 7 as a conclusion to the passage?
(A) *Sesame Street* and *The Electric Company* have revolutionized children's television.
(B) *Sesame Street* and *The Electric Company* are excellent television programs.
(C) The Sesame Street Generation will take over the world when it grows up.
(D) The Public Broadcasting System should be congratulated for providing such excellent television programs as *Sesame Street* and *The Electric Company*.
(E) The money which the Public Broadcasting System has spent on these two programs may have some questionable returns.

121. Ⓐ Ⓑ Ⓒ Ⓓ Ⓔ

Questions 122-124 are based on the following passage:

[1]If you're a rib fancier, you'll be happy to know that just minutes away there's a relatively new restaurant that features these meaty specialities. [2]The Branding Iron in Downers Grove has built its reputation on these outstanding ribs. [3]The Branding Iron starts with lean, baby back ribs, slowly smokes them for hours, drizzles them with an enticing sauce and serves them smoky pink. [4]Forego your best table manners . . . use your fingers. [5]One bite will tell you why these ribs are so popular: over 10,000 pounds are served each month. [6]Another house speciality at the Branding

Iron that's gaining in popularity is the Toasted Polynesian Shrimp. [7]They're served with sweet and sour sauce and a pungent mustard sauce. [8]The Polynesian Shrimp are a true delicacy, yet filling and satisfying. [9]Next time, you'll want to order the complete dinner.

Reprinted from the *Chicago Tribune*, July 19, 1978. Courtesy of the *Chicago Tribune*.

122. Sentence 3
  (A) should be omitted
  (B) should be combined with the second part of sentence 1
  (C) should be left as it is
  (D) should begin with Starting with lean, baby back ribs, they
  (E) should be placed after sentence 8

122. Ⓐ Ⓑ Ⓒ Ⓓ Ⓔ

123. If you divided this passage into two paragraphs, the obvious sentence with which paragraph two would begin is
  (A) sentence 2
  (B) sentence 5
  (C) sentence 8
  (D) sentence 7
  (E) sentence 6

123. Ⓐ Ⓑ Ⓒ Ⓓ Ⓔ

124. Which of the following provides a more logical conclusion to the passage?
  (A) The Branding Iron is located in Downers Grove, Illinois.
  (B) The Branding Iron features barbequed ribs and Polynesian Shrimp, both of which you should try the next time you eat out.
  (C) Their prices are in the moderate to expensive range.
  (D) If you don't like barbequed ribs, stay away from The Branding Iron.
  (E) Polynesian Shrimp is just one of the delicacies on the menu at The Branding Iron.

124. Ⓐ Ⓑ Ⓒ Ⓓ Ⓔ

Questions 125-127 are based on the following passage:

[1]My daughter's wedding was very inexpensive. [2]We did not have a dinner at the reception. [3]Flowers were few and simple. [4]The bridal gown was on sale for half price. [5]The groom and ushers wore tuxedoes which had been rented, not purchased. [6]There was no champagne for the toast because the church does not permit alcoholic beverages in its parlor. [7]Still, the wedding was beautiful, and the more than one hundred guests seemed to enjoy the festivities. [8]Debbie and Steve are living in Decatur where Steve is selling insurance for one of the large companies which specialize in life and health insurance programs.

125. What should be done with sentence 7?
  (A) It should be left as it is.
  (B) The word *Still* should be omitted, and the sentence placed before sentence 1.
  (C) The words *In the spring* should be added before *Still*.
  (D) The word *Still* should be omitted and the sentence joined with sentence 5.
  (E) It should be joined to sentence 6: *in its parlor; however, the*

125. Ⓐ Ⓑ Ⓒ Ⓓ Ⓔ

126. Sentence 8

(A) should be moved to the beginning of the passage

(B) should begin a second paragraph

(C) should be shorter and less detailed

(D) should come immediately after sentence 1

(E) should be combined with sentence 2

127. Sentences 1 through 6 could be combined by

(A) substituting commas for all of the periods

(B) substituting colons for all of the periods

(C) changing the period at the end of sentence 1 to a semicolon and leaving the rest as it is

(D) changing the period at the end of sentence 1 to a colon and the periods at the end of sentences 2, 3, 4, and 5 to semicolons.

(E) eliminating sentence 2 and making sentences 4 and 5 parts of sentence 1

Questions 128-130 are based on the following passage:

¹In fact, this play has piled up more continuous performances in the same theater than any other play in American theatrical history, and the end of the run is not in sight. ²*The Fantasticks*, a musical, has been running at a small off-Broadway theater for more than twenty years. ³Many actors and actresses made their debuts in this simple musical comedy and have moved on to starring roles in Broadway productions, on television, and in Hollywood. ⁴Why this play, which was ignored by sophisticated critics when it opened, has established such a record is a mystery to many people. ⁵The story line is a kind of fairy story, the music is not very distinctive, and the lyrics are full of clichés. ⁶But the musical continues to attract an audience, and as long as the producers sell tickets and make money, the play will continue.

128. Sentence 2

(A) should be at the beginning of the passage

(B) should be at the end of the passage

(C) should be placed after sentence 4

(D) should be omitted completely

(E) should be left as it is

129. Sentence 6 should begin

(A) with *The musical continues to, however, attract*

(B) with *Therefore, the musical continues to attract*

(C) with *As a result, the musical continues to attract*

(D) with *On the other hand, the musical continues to attract*

(E) the way it begins now

130. Sentence 4 should

(A) come immediately after sentence 1

(B) come where it is now

(C) be changed so that the first word is *That*

(D) have the word *not* inserted before *established*

(E) come immediately before sentence 6

ANSWER KEY—SAMPLE EXAMINATION 2

Part I

1. E	12. E	23. C	34. D	45. E	56. D
2. A	13. D	24. B	35. B	46. C	57. B
3. B	14. A	25. D	36. A	47. E	58. A
4. E	15. C	26. D	37. E	48. A	59. E
5. C	16. B	27. E	38. C	49. B	60. B
6. A	17. B	28. A	39. A	50. D	61. D
7. D	18. D	29. B	40. A	51. B	62. E
8. B	19. A	30. A	41. C	52. C	63. C
9. B	20. E	31. C	42. B	53. E	64. A
10. A	21. E	32. C	43. E	54. A	65. A
11. E	22. C	33. E	44. C	55. C	

Part II

66. B	77. C	88. A	99. E	110. E	121. D
67. C	78. B	89. A	100. A	111. A	122. C
68. E	79. E	90. A	101. C	112. B	123. E
69. C	80. A	91. D	102. B	113. D	124. B
70. B	81. B	92. E	103. B	114. C	125. A
71. E	82. D	93. D	104. A	115. A	126. B
72. A	83. A	94. E	105. C	116. B	127. D
73. E	84. E	95. B	106. D	117. D	128. A
74. D	85. D	96. C	107. D	118. C	129. E
75. D	86. C	97. E	108. A	119. C	130. B
76. B	87. B	98. D	109. E	120. A	

SCORING CHART—SAMPLE EXAMINATION 2

After you have scored your Sample Examination 2, enter the results in the chart below; then transfer your Raw Score to the Progress Chart on page 14.

Total Test		Number Right	Number Wrong	Number Omitted	Raw Score
Part I:	65				
Part II:	65				
Total:	130				

Part I

1. **E.** (A) and (D) are incorrect because what follows the semi-colon is a complete sentence, thus destroying the parallelism with the other three members of the series (after <u>by</u>). (B) is wrong for the same reason. In (C) the shift to the infinitive <u>to be</u> is awkward.

2. **A.** (B), (D), and (E) are incorrect because the substitution would produce a sentence fragment in each case. (C) is incorrect because the shift to the weak passive voice is poor and that choice would also destroy the correct sequence of tenses.

3. **B.** (A) is incorrect because <u>anyone</u> and <u>they</u> do not agree; both words have to be singular or plural. (C) is incorrect because the verb phrase <u>can have been learned</u> is awkward as well as a weak passive verb. In (D) <u>than about</u> creates a vague and ambiguous sentence. (E) is incorrect because the sense of the sentence contradicts the original.

4. **E.** (A) is incorrect because the conjunction <u>so—as</u> is awkward. (B) is incorrect because the verb phrase <u>should have been</u> destroys the correct sequence of tenses. (C) is incorrect because the phrase <u>will—than</u> is not an accurate restatement of the original sentence. (D) is incorrect because <u>just as</u> produces a weaker sentence than the correct version in (E).

5. **C.** (A) is incorrect because the phrase beginning <u>Having</u> down to the comma is dangling modifier. In (B) the phrase beginning <u>Without</u> down to the comma is both awkward and a dangling modifier. (D) is incorrect because the phrase beginning <u>Leaving</u> down to the comma is a dangling modifier as well as awkward. (E) is incorrect because <u>having been raised</u> is a poor passive participle.

6. **A.** (B) and (C) are incorrect because of the vague <u>they</u> in both choices. (D) is incorrect because the dependent clause beginning <u>when</u> does not have a verb but a verbal phrase—<u>having been</u>. (E) is incorrect because it is an awkward restatement of the original sentence.

7. **D.** (A) and (B) are incorrect, because <u>invert</u> and <u>inverted</u> are not synonyms for <u>avert</u>—incorrect word choice. (C) would be an illogical introductory phrase for the sentence. (E) is incorrect because it uses <u>averting</u> (a verbal form) for the more specific <u>to avert</u> in the original sentence.

8. **B.** (A) is incorrect because it says the plane broke every speed limit on the expressway—an illogical modifier. (C) would be an illogical sentence, because <u>they</u> has no specific antecedent. (D) is incorrect; the negative words and phrase (<u>notwithstanding</u>, <u>could not help</u>) cannot logically function in the same sentence. (E) misstates the original by reversing the actual cause-effect relationship.

9. **B.** (A) is incorrect because of the vague <u>they</u>. (D) is incorrect because the conjunction <u>or than</u> is an illogical choice of words. (E) is incorrect because what follows <u>than</u> is an ambiguous contrast with what precedes <u>than</u>.

10. **A.** (B) is incorrect because <u>so</u> is an incorrectly chosen conjunction here. (C) is incorrect; <u>that</u> introduces a dependent clause and <u>and</u> parallels an independent clause with a dependent clause. (D) is incorrect because <u>and</u> is unnecessary to the sense of the sentence. (E) is incorrect, because it misstates the original sentence.

11. **E.** (E) is the correct answer because correct grammar requires the possessive form <u>Reagan's</u> before a gerund, a verbal form used as a noun. (A) is incorrect, because the clause beginning <u>which</u> is an illogical modifier; (A) is also wordy. (B) is correct grammatically, but it misstates the original sentence. (C) is incorrect because <u>and which</u> creates an illogical modifier. In (D) the resulting sentence is ambiguous.

12. **E.** (A) is incorrect because it is a sentence fragment. (B) is a misstatement of the original sentence. (C) is incorrect because of the phrase <u>the reason why</u> which should be <u>the reason that</u>. (D) is incorrect because it is an incomplete version of the original sentence.

13. D. (A) is incorrect because the phrase <u>that was the reason</u> is wordy and ambiguous. (B) is incorrect because <u>and that</u> is also ambiguous. (C) misstates the original sentence because it <u>says that the dashboard was bleeding</u>. In (E), the participial phrase creating by <u>having been</u> is an illogical modifier.

14. A. (B) is incorrect because the second <u>that</u> is ambiguous. (C) is wrong because it incorrectly states the original sentence—evil is protected in this choice. (D) is incorrect because the structures before and after <u>that</u> are not parallel in structure. (E) is incorrect because it confuses the original sentence.

15. C. (A) is wrong because the participial form <u>having been degenerating</u> is incorrect in form. (B) states an incorrect cause-effect relationship. In (D) the two commas and <u>but</u> are incorrect. In (E) the commas are also incorrect; also, there is no verb to function with <u>hearing</u>.

16. B. (A) is wrong because <u>but</u> creates an illogical contrast of ideas in the sentence. (C) is incorrect because <u>neither-nor</u> reverses the meaning of the original sentence. (D) is incorrect because the second <u>or</u> is unnecessary, therefore wordy. (E) is incorrect because the comma is unnecessary.

17. B. (A) is incorrect because <u>before</u> changes the chronology of the original sentence. (C) is wrong because <u>incredible</u> is an incorrect word choice. (D) is wrong because <u>incredible</u> is wrong and the clause beginning <u>which</u> is a dangling modifier. (E) is incorrect because the sentence does not make sense.

18. D. (A) is incorrect because the sentence is illogical; it seems to say that the boat sailed itself. In (B), the phrase beginning <u>Arriving</u> is a dangling modifier. (C) is incorrect because the whole sentence seems to present some confused ideas. In (E) <u>Having been sailed</u> cannot function logically as a modifier of <u>we</u>.

19. A. (B) is wrong because the word <u>conscience</u> is incorrectly chosen. (C) is also wrong because the word <u>consciousness</u> is incorrect in the context. (D) and (E) change the meaning of the original sentence.

20. E. (A) is incorrect because it would be an illogical dangling modifier. (B) is a nonsense sentence because John Jones could not be the tabulation. (C) is incorrect because the comma would produce a comma splice. (D) is confused in structure and therefore incorrect.

21. E. In (A) the use of <u>either-or</u> as correlatives is incorrect. (B) is wrong because the meaning of the sentence is not clear. In (C) the word <u>caused</u> creates an ambiguous cause-effect relationship in the sentence. (D) is incorrect because the phrase after <u>neither</u> and after <u>nor</u> are not parallel in structure.

22. C. In (A) <u>fluently</u> is a misplaced modifier. (Note: the phrase <u>to fluently speak</u> is a split infinitive, but such a construction is no longer considered incorrect unless the phrase is illogical as it is here.) (B) is incorrect because of the weak passive voice verb. (D) is incorrect because it reverses the meaning of the original sentence. (E) is incorrect because the phrase <u>something of an asset</u> softens the meaning of the original sentence.

23. C. (A) is incorrect for two reasons: (1) the phrase implies that the desk might move the hand; (2) the comma creates a comma splice. (B) is incorrect for two reasons: (1) the verb <u>move</u> is the incorrect tense with <u>had</u> in the second part of the sentence; (2) without a semi-colon or period after <u>desk</u>, there is a run together sentence. (D) is incorrect because there should be a comma after <u>desk</u>. (E) is incorrect because <u>Although</u> implies a contrast of some kind, and there is none in the sentence.

24. B. (A) is incorrect because <u>have kept</u> is not the correct tense sequence with <u>would seem</u>. (C) is incorrect because <u>him</u> does not agree with <u>gangsters</u>, a plural form. (D) is incorrect; <u>the reasons is because</u> is a redundant phrase. (E) is incorrect because <u>no</u> and <u>cannot</u> constitute an illogical double negative.

25. D. (A) is incorrect because <u>badly</u> (an adverb) should be <u>bad</u> (an adjective). (B) is incorrect because the word order seems confused. (C) is also incorrect because of the confused word order. (E) is incorrect, because it seems to contradict the meaning of the original sentence.

26. D. (A) is incorrect because the passive voice verbs (was opened, were loaded) are weaker than the active voice verbs in the original sentence. (B) is also incorrect because gather (a present tense verb) and began (a past tense verb) for an illogical sequence of tenses. (C) is incorrect because of the shift to the passive voice verb: began to be loaded. (E) is incorrect because The reason . . . was because construction is redundant and wordy.

27. E. (A) is incorrect because they has no specific antecedent. (B) is incorrect because it contradicts the meaning of the original sentence. (C) is wrong for two reasons: (1) the adjective real should be an adverb really; (2) they and them have no specific antecedents. (D) is incorrect because the phrase what with would make the second part of the sentence illogical.

28. A. (B) is incorrect because the first comma creates a comma splice. (C) is incorrect because the phrase in which would make the last part of the sentence an illogical modifier. (D) is incorrect because cannot but only would be a double negative. (E) is incorrect because the phrase what with would make the second part of the sentence illogical.

29. B. (A) is incorrect because there is an illogical comparison; any motion picture would also have to include E.T. (C) is incorrect, because the change would produce a sentence fragment. (D) is incorrect because it is wordy. (E) is wrong because of the incorrect and illogical comparison in the phrase the most money than.

30. A. (B) is incorrect because this choice would create a dangling modifier. (C) is incorrect because it is wordy and vague—what would be an appropriate number of police? (D) is incorrect because the phrase is ambiguous. (E) is also incorrect because of vagueness—who was checking all those boarded planes?

31. C. (A) is incorrect because refer back is redundant. (B) is also redundant; reread again implies that the person would have to read something for the third time at least. (D) and (E) are incorrect, because they are wordy.

32. C. (A) is illogical because non-residents could hardly live in Australia. (B) is wrong because enlist implies someone's joining a branch of the armed services. (D) is incorrect because the whole route is a vague slang phrase. (E) is incorrect because the sentence implies that people who went to Australia were more than tourists.

33. E. (A) is incorrect because the two words seem redundant. (B) is incorrect because without is not a conjunction. (C) is wrong for because is an incorrect choice of conjunctions. (D) also represents an incorrect conjunction choice with insofar as.

34. D. (A) is incorrect, because could not but is a double negative as is could not hardly in (B). (C) and (E) are incorrect because of wordiness.

35. B. (A), (C), (D), and (E) are all incorrect because of wordiness.

36. A. (B) is wrong because due to is an inaccurate choice of prepositions. (C), (D), and (E) are wrong because the phrases are wordy or contain incorrectly chosen prepositions.

37. E. (A) is incorrect because tried his hand at could hardly be logical with singing. (B), (C), and (D) are incorrect because these choices are wordy or redundant.

38. C. The other choices contain wordy or redundant phrases.

39. A. The other choices are all wordy or redundant.

40. A. Coney Island, famed for its roller coaster and its many hot dog stands, is a beach in New York City.

41. C. A woman . . . art gallery if she does not resort to tears. . . .

42. B. The proper amount of iron is often more important in a woman's daily diet than the proper number. . . .

43. E. Motorists would be spared confusion and uncertainty, if Congress would pass a law establishing a nationally. . . .

44. C. When Thoreau retreated to Walden Pond, he had a few benevolent acquaintances to provide his necessities of life; no contemporary man can so retreat without the same kind of help.

45. E. The recent collapse of prices on the New York Stock Exchange has been not only a welcome sign that the inflationary spiral is slowing down but also a signal for large stockholders to begin purchasing large blocks of shares at bargain prices.

46. C. A small reception in the parish hall will follow the ceremony but only for those who were mailed individual invitations.

47. E. Any professional golfer playing on the tournament circuit year after year may eventually attain. . . .

48. A. The convicted bank robber's sentence of ten years in the state penitentiary, which the wretch received from the judge, brought applause from the spectators in the courtroom.

49. B. The amount of space a story is given and the page it is printed on indicate to a careful reader a newspaper editor's opinions.

50. D. More sources of information within the administration are available to today's newspaper reporters than to their predecessors a century ago.

51. B. Ungrateful progeny do not appreciate the sacrifices which parents make so that their children may enjoy some of life's luxuries.

52. C. Colonial magistrates found Hester Prynne, the heroine of Hawthorne's *The Scarlet Letter*, guilty of adultery and sentenced her to wear a red A.

53. E. Mary and twenty of her classmates attend the theater. . . .

54. A. Not only do China and the Soviet Union share a long, almost unprotectable boundary across almost all of Asia, but within recent years disputes over the exact. . . .

55. C. Nowadays, not one of those voters eligible to cast a ballot bothers to exercise his franchise on election day.

56. D. The company awarded the railroad president a solid gold watch which was found among his effects after his death.

57. B. Whether through stupidity or ignorance is difficult to determine, but we do know that the young man made a fool of himself at the party last night.

58. A. Marshall McLuhan is a Canadian scholar whose studies of television's effects upon the human personality have revolutionized our thinking about the mass media; he has been the target. . . .

59. E. A good assistant can relieve an administrator of much of the paperwork that any large organization generates to expedite its day-to-day operations.

60. B. Young grandchildren who can be given too much attention and spoiled outrageously by grandparents are often a great comfort to them.

61. D. (A) is incorrect because <u>them</u> has no specific antecedent. (B) is wrong because the clause <u>which were spoiled</u> is a misplaced modifier. (C) is incorrect because <u>they</u> has no specific antecedent. (E) is incorrect because <u>their</u> has no specific antecedent.

62. E. (A) is incorrect because <u>in the rear of the hall</u> is a misplaced modifier. (B) is an ambiguous sentence. (D) is also wrong, because the sentence might imply that the dissidents might have approved the speaker's proposals if he had not made them in the back of the hall.

63. C. (A) is incorrect because the sentence says that <u>we</u> landed the plane. (B) is incorrect because <u>they</u> has no specific antecedent. (D) is incorrect, because <u>connected</u> and <u>greeted</u> are past tense while <u>throng</u> is present tense; thus, there is an illogical tense sequence. (E) is incorrect, because the phrase <u>with . . . greeted</u> is a misplaced modifier.

64. A. (B) is incorrect because <u>moreover</u> confuses the sense of the sentence. In (C), the phrase <u>As . . . class</u> is a dangling modifier. (D) is wrong, because <u>a hard teacher</u> is a misplaced appositive phrase. (E) is wrong because the phrase <u>Hearing . . . teacher</u> is a dangling modifier.

65. A. (B) is incorrect because the passive verb <u>was left</u> is weak and vague. In (C) the phrase beginning <u>With</u> is a dangling modifier. (D) is illogical and ambiguous. (E) is ambiguous and confusing.

Part II

66. **B.** (A) and (C) are incorrect because they contradict the meaning of the statement. From the statement (D) and (E) would not be logical conclusions.

67. **C.** None of the other choices would be logical. (E) is a possibility, but the last sentence in the statement makes that choice incorrect.

68. **E.** (A) and (C) are incorrect because there is no evidence in the statement which would permit these conclusions. (B) and (D) are also incorrect because they seem to contradict the implications of the statement.

69. **C.** (A) and (B) are incorrect; we have insufficient evidence in the dialogue to draw these conclusions. (D) and (E) are incorrect for the same reason.

70. **B.** There is insufficient evidence in the dialogue to make the other choices logical conclusions.

71. **E.** There is insufficient evidence in the statement to make the other choices logical conclusions.

72. **A.** (B) is incorrect because the word <u>liar</u> seems to have shifted its referent slightly. (C), (D), and (E) are incorrect, because there is not enough information in the statement to permit them to be logical or valid conclusions. These statements may or may not be true, however.

73. **D.** A reader must consider the implications of the statement. (D) is the only valid choice, because the writer is obviously not neutral (A), and it is not valid to say that he likes Middle East millionaires. (C), then, is incorrect. There is inadequate information in the statement to permit (B) and (E) to be valid conclusions.

74. **D.** Choice (D), correct, demonstrates that (A) is incorrect; they are contradictory. (B) is incorrect because the implications indicate that the sticker does not support gun control. (C) is incorrect because there is insufficient evidence to make the conclusion valid. (E) is incorrect because the sticker obviously opposes gun control legislation.

75. **D.** (D) is the only valid answer. The statement has no information about the politician's ability to pay increased taxes nor does the reader know much about his voting record on increasing or decreasing taxes to support education.

76. **B.** (A) is incorrect because the statement says nothing about Jane's personality. (C) is incorrect because the word <u>can</u> is ambiguous; it implies that she may or may not make mistakes. (D) is incorrect because the statement is about <u>one</u> instructor, and a generalization to <u>all</u> instructors would be illogical. (E) is also incorrect because it extends the meaning of the statement to <u>all</u> assignments, not just those from one instructor.

77. **C.** (C) is the only valid answer. (A) is incorrect because three instances are not sufficient cases to support such a generalization. (B) is incorrect, because the reader does not have enough information to make the conclusion valid. (D) is incorrect because the statement may be untrue. (E) is incorrect because the test may be complete even though the number of subjects was limited.

78. **B.** (A) is incorrect because there is no evidence that the dean is being unfair. (C) and (E) are also incorrect for the same reason. (D) is incorrect because it contradicts (B), the only correct answer.

79. **E.** (A) is incorrect, because the student is not using reason. We do not have enough information to make (B), (C), and (D) valid conclusions; therefore, these choices are also incorrect.

80. **A.** (B) is wrong because the word <u>not</u> seems to reverse what may be the actual case; the speaker has probably gained weight. (C) is incorrect because of insufficient evidence in the statement. (D) is incorrect because it is an overstatement. (E) is incorrect because <u>against</u> seems wrong.

81. **B.** (A) is wrong because we do not know what age <u>young</u> denotes or connotes. (C) is incorrect because there may be many things which the young man does not <u>love</u>. (D) is obviously incorrect because the speaker's original statement demonstrates the falsity of the choice. There is no evidence to make (E) correct.

82. **D.** (D) is the only valid conclusion which can logically be drawn from the very subjective statements.

83. **A.** (B) is incorrect because the word perfect is an overstatement as is the word All in (E); therefore, (E) is also wrong. The reader does not have sufficient information to make (C) or (D) valid conclusions.

84. **E.** (A) and (C) are incorrect as overstatements. (B) may or may not be true; therefore, (B) is incorrect. (D) is incorrect because the senator implies that there is a difference.

85. **D.** None of the other choices is a valid interpretation of what the speaker is implying in his statement.

86. **C.** (A), (B), (D), and (E) are incorrect, because there is not enough information provided to make these conclusions valid. may imply is the key phrase which makes (C) correct.

87. **B.** No opinion of the speaker is stated or implied in the statement; therefore, (B) is the only correct choice. The other choices are all false assumptions.

88. **A.** (B) and (E) are incorrect because of insufficient evidence. (C) and (D) are incorrect because both choices are contradicted by the original statement.

89. **A.** (A) is the only valid choice. (D) is incorrect, because it contradicts the original statement. (B) and (C) are incorrect because they are hasty assumptions based on insufficient evidence.

90. **A.** The phrase best engineered makes (A) the only correct response. (E) gives the reader a positive statement about the Rabbit, but it says little about the quality of the car. (B), (C), and (D) are incorrect because quality is not mentioned in either of the choices.

91. **D.** All of the statements could be considered insulting, but (D) is the most insulting. (C) is incorrect because the phrase may be states a situation which may be untrue.

92. **E.** (A) is incorrect because the reactions of the club members may be positive or negative and therefore not flattering. (B) and (C) say something about Joan's husband and children, but the reader cannot be sure that Joan had anything to do with either. (D) is incorrect, because it might be demonstrated that Joan has no ideas of her own.

93. **D.** Choice (D) is the only complimentary statement of the five choices. The others are all negative, although they differ in the degree of their negativeness.

94. **E.** (E) is the only possible correct statement, because none of the others even imply anything about how someone might feel about tax increases.

95. **B.** (B) is the only statement which is an opinion; all of the others can be proved correct or incorrect by anyone who could examine the physical evidence in the book itself.

96. **C.** (B) and (D) are incorrect because they are not real opinions. (A) and (E) may be opinions, but neither says anything specific about possible law violators.

97. **E.** (A) and (B) are incorrect, because neither concerns professional football players. (C) is an opinion but not a very strong one. (D) may say more about the game than about the players and is incorrect.

98. **D.** Sentence 2 is a cause from which sentence 1 is the effect. No other completion of the sentence is valid.

99. **E.** (E) is the only correct response, because neither of the sentences says anything about cost, size, shape, or quality of the tissue.

100. **A.** Choice (A) is the only logical and correct answer; the other four state no cause, no contrast, no distractor, no exception.

101. **C.** Choice (C) is the specific which supports sentence 1; the other terms from logic do not apply.

102. **B.** Sentence 1 is an effect; sentence 2 provides the cause for that effect. No other choice is applicable.

103. **B.** Choice (B) is the only correct response. Choices (A), (C), and (D) cannot be conclusions from the facts in the statement. (E) is incorrect because it contradicts the only correct response.

104. B. Choices (A), (C), (D), and (E) may or may not be true, but the reader does not have enough information to discriminate among them.

105. C. (A), (B), (D), and (E) are incorrect, because the statement says nothing about quality or cost of the shampoo; therefore, only choice (C) is correct.

106. D. Choice (A) is incorrect; sentence 2 is not an exception, (B) is incorrect; sentence 2 is not a definition of justice, (C) is incorrect; sentence 2 is not a comparison, and (E) is incorrect; sentence 2 does not imply a contrast.

107. D. Choice (D) is the only valid, correct answer. The other choices illustrate inapplicable terms from logic.

108. A. The location (next to each other, perhaps) is the only characteristic which the houses have in common. The other choices are incorrect.

109. E. Choice (E) is an inference drawn from the two sentences. Not one of the other choices draws a valid inference.

110. E. The Academy Award nomination caused John Travolta's salary for a film to more than double, an effect. The other choices are incorrect.

111. A. Sentence 2 does affirm that sentence 1 is true; therefore, choice (A) is the only possible answer. (Note: With items like these and others, you should be sure that you understand terms from formal logic.) All other choices are incorrect.

112. B. (A) is incorrect because sentence 1, not sentence 2, is a definition. Choice (C) is incorrect because the White House is not compared to any other building. (D) and (E) are incorrect because no conclusion is drawn and no exception is given.

113. D. (A) is incorrect because sentence 2 does not affirm sentence 1. (E) is incorrect, because sentence 2 is not a vague generalization. (B) and (C) are incorrect because there is no comparison or conclusion.

114. C. (C) is the only correct answer, because the two sentences make no reference to the size, shape, age, or value of the salad bowl.

115. A. (A) is correct because the age of the sofa and table is the only characteristic which they share.

116. B. (B) is the only correct choice. (A) cannot be correct; note the word some in sentence 1. There is insufficient information to make (C), (D), or (E) valid conclusions.

117. D. (A) is incorrect because sentence 2 is not a conclusion. (B) is incorrect because sentence 2 gives an example, not an affirmation. (C) and (E) are incorrect because there is no comparison or definition.

118. C. Location (C) is the only basis for the relationship between the two trees. All other choices are incorrect.

119. C. (A) and (B) would create comma splices (the first comma in B) and would be incorrect sentence structure. In (D), and would change the meaning of the original sentence. (E) contradicts the original sentence, because no exception is being stated.

120. A. (B) is incorrect, because the omission of this sentence would eliminate a key idea. Placing the sentence anywhere else in the paragraph would damage the logic of the passage; thus, (C), (D), and (E) are incorrect.

121. D. (A) is incorrect because it merely restates sentence 1. (B) is too weak as a conclusion and therefore is incorrect. (C) may be an overstatement of what the paragraph contains and is therefore incorrect. (E) is incorrect because of the word questionable.

122. C. (A) is incorrect because sentence 3 describes in detail the production of the succulent ribs. (B) is incorrect because the relocation of the sentence would damage the coherence of the paragraph. (D) is incorrect because sentence 3 would be out of place in this position.

123. E. Sentence 6 shifts the focus from ribs to shrimp and would be a logical introduction for a new paragraph. All of the other choices are incorrect, because they are not logical sentences with which to begin a new paragraph.

124. B. Choice (B) is the only one of the five which mentions both house specialties, ribs and shrimp. Choice (A) is incorrect, because it merely repeats sentence 2. (C) is too vague to be a conclusion. (D) is also an inadequate conclusion

because it seems to be negative. (E) is incorrect because it mentions only shrimp.

125. **A.** (B) is incorrect because the sentence, even without <u>Still</u>, would not be a good topic sentence for the paragraph. (C) is incorrect for <u>In the spring</u> adds nothing to the paragraph. (D) is incorrect because the change would damage the coherence of the paragraph. (E) is incorrect because extraneous words would be added.

126. **B.** (A) is incorrect because in front of sentence 1, sentence 8 would be out of place. (C) is incorrect because shortening the sentence would eliminate some necessary details. (D) and (E) are incorrect because changing the position of sentence 8 would confuse the paragraph.

127. **D.** (A) is incorrect because such a change would create a series of comma splices. (B) is wrong, because such punctuation would be illogical. (C) is incorrect because a semi-colon would signal a closer connection between the sentences than actually exists from the sense of the sentences. (E) is incorrect because sentence 2 is another illustration of the inexpensiveness of the wedding.

128. **A.** Sentence 2 is a logical introductory sentence for the paragraph; therefore, (A) is correct. All the other choices would affect the coherence of the paragraph, and (E) would omit the topic sentence of the paragraph. Thus, the other choices are incorrect.

129. **E.** (A) is incorrect because <u>however</u> would be a misplaced modifier. (B) is incorrect because <u>but</u> and <u>therefore</u> are not synonyms. (C) is incorrect because <u>As a result</u> implies an effect, but no cause is given which would produce that effect. (D) is incorrect because <u>On the other hand</u> implies a contrast, and no two things are being contrasted.

130. **B.** (B) is the only correct answer; any changes would affect the coherence of the paragraph.

SAMPLE EXAMINATION 3

Part I

Number of Items: 65
Time: 45 minutes

Directions: For each of these questions, you are to choose the version of the underlined sentence or part of the sentence that not only has the same or nearly the same meaning as the original but follows the requirements of standard written English. That is, in selecting the version that matches the underlined part in meaning, pay attention to grammar, choice of words, sentence structure, and punctuation. The answer you select should, when inserted in the original sentence, produce an effective sentence—clear and exact, without awkwardness or ambiguity.

1. In the foreword, the editor explains how the book is organized and how the material is arranged.

   1. Ⓐ Ⓑ Ⓒ Ⓓ Ⓔ

   (A) In the foreword, the editor explains how the book is organized and how she had arranged the material.
   (B) How the book is organized and how the material is arranged are explained by the editor in the foreword.
   (C) At the beginning of the book and in her foreword, she explains how her book is organized and how the material is arranged.
   (D) Being as how in the foreword the editor explains the organization and arrangement of the book.
   (E) The book's foreword explains how she organized the book and also how the material is arranged.

2. The concept of eternity is so abstract that most dictionaries do not supply any synonyms for the word.
   (A) That dictionaries do not provide a synonym for *eternity* show how abstract the word is.
   (B) No dictionary has provided an exact synonym for *eternity*, seeing as how the whole concept is so abstract.
   (C) The concept of eternity is such an abstract idea that few dictionaries have provided a synonym for the word.
   (D) Most dictionaries do not provide a synonym for the word *eternity* because the concept denoted by that word is so abstract.
   (E) What with the concept being so abstract, most dictionaries do not provide a synonym for *eternity*.

2. Ⓐ Ⓑ Ⓒ Ⓓ Ⓔ

Whenever students talk about their best teachers in college, they recall those who were hard but fair, understanding yet firm.
   (A) he recalls those who were hard but fair, understanding yet firm
   (B) those who were hard but firm, understanding yet fair, are recalled by them
   (C) understanding yet firm, hard but fair, teachers are those whom they recall
   (D) she believes that those who are hard but fair, understanding yet firm, are the best
   (E) they remember those who required work but who were fair, who were stern but sympathetic

3. Ⓐ Ⓑ Ⓒ Ⓓ Ⓔ

4. Nobody tells me anything any more; if my father's business failed or if my brother and I were suddenly orphaned, I would know nothing about it.
   (A) if my father's business failed and if my brother and me
   (B) both my father's business failed and my brother and I
   (C) whether my father's business failed or whether my brother and I
   (D) if either my father's business failed or my brother and me
   (E) without knowing whether my father's business failed or if we

4. Ⓐ Ⓑ Ⓒ Ⓓ Ⓔ

5. Some British citizens acknowledge that performing groups like the Culture Club have provided England with much needed foreign exchange through tours and the sale of records.
   (A) England with muchly needed foreign exchange as a result of their tours and the sale of their records
   (B) England with a source of foreign exchange: tours and the sale of records
   (C) England with their tours and sales of records, foreign exchange having been needed
   (D) England which has needed foreign exchange and their tours and the sales of records
   (E) England, but they have needed foreign exchange from tours and record sales

5. Ⓐ Ⓑ Ⓒ Ⓓ Ⓔ

6. The cook had only enough cake to provide a few crumbs and a bit of icing for those campers who arrived late for dinner.
   (A) Some campers were late for dinner; the cook had only enough cake left to give them crumbs and a bit of icing.

6. Ⓐ Ⓑ Ⓒ Ⓓ Ⓔ

(B) Late for dinner, the cook could provide those campers with only a few crumbs and a bit of icing from the cake.

(C) Those campers who arrived late for dinner have to be provided with a few crumbs and a bit of icing from the cook's cake.

(D) When the cook was late for dinner, he could give the campers only a few crumbs and a bit of icing from the cake.

(E) The campers, having been late for dinner, could expect no more than a few crumbs and a bit of icing from the cook's cake.

7. His brow was furrowed from care, each wrinkle bearing permanent witness to his host of worries.　　　　　　　　　7. Ⓐ Ⓑ Ⓒ Ⓓ Ⓔ

(A) Having a host of worries, his brow was permanently furrowed.

(B) The host of worries were permanent furrows in the wrinkles of his brow.

(C) His host of worries having been permanent, his brow was continually wrinkled.

(D) Bearing permanent witness to his worries, he had his brow furrowed with care.

(E) He had many concerns, and his brow had permanent wrinkles.

8. She is likely to be arrested for indecent exposure, if she insists on running around town in nothing but her underwear.　　　　　　8. Ⓐ Ⓑ Ⓒ Ⓓ Ⓔ

(A) Her appearing in nothing but underwear is liable to get her arrested for indecent exposure.

(B) When she appears in nothing but her underwear, her arrest for indecent exposure is apt.

(C) If she insists on running around town in nothing but her underwear, she would most probably be arrested for indecent exposure.

(D) Her running around town in nothing but her underwear could result in her being arrested for indecent exposure.

(E) Running around town in underwear can be the cause for her having been arrested for indecent exposure.

9. The boy who we thought would be the best swimmer could not participate in today's contest because he fell and broke his leg last night.　　9. Ⓐ Ⓑ Ⓒ Ⓓ Ⓔ

(A) The boy whom we thought would be the best swimmer

(B) The boy we thought would be the best swimmer

(C) The boy, who we thought would be the best swimmer,

(D) The boy, whom we thought, would be the best swimmer

(E) The boy that we thought could have been the best swimmer

10. Going up the stairs, Bill dropped Jack's typewriter, and Jack was furious.　10. Ⓐ Ⓑ Ⓒ Ⓓ Ⓔ

(A) When Bill dropped Jack's typewriter on his way to his room, he was furious.

(B) Jack's typewriter was dropped on the stairs by Bill; he was furious.

(C) Bill's dropping Jack's typewriter on the stairs made Jack furious.

(D) Jack became furious when he dropped his typewriter on the stairs.

(E) Bill's dropping his typewriter on the stairs made Jack furious.

11. The group's opinion was changed radically by the speech of its president, but they elected him to serve another term anyhow.

    11. Ⓐ Ⓑ Ⓒ Ⓓ Ⓔ

    (A) president; which they elected him to serve another term
    (B) president; they elected him to serve another term anyhow
    (C) president, irregardless of which they elected him to serve another term anyhow
    (D) president, even though they elected him to serve another term anyhow
    (E) president, just as they had elected him to serve another term anyhow

12. Everybody knows that *Close Encounters of the Third Kind* was nominated for several Academy Awards in 1978, but few people know that Steve Spielberg directed the film.

    12. Ⓐ Ⓑ Ⓒ Ⓓ Ⓔ

    (A) in 1978, but Steve Spielberg directed the film, few people do not know
    (B) in 1978; which Steve Spielberg directed, few people know
    (C) in 1978; however, not many people know that Steve Spielberg directed the film
    (D) in 1978, and that was directed by Steve Spielberg
    (E) in 1978, moreover, that Steve Spielberg directed the film

13. Duke Ellington's death was not the shock that George Gershwin's was, because Ellington was seventy-five and Gershwin was only in his late thirties.

    13. Ⓐ Ⓑ Ⓒ Ⓓ Ⓔ

    (A) the reason was because Ellington was seventy-five and that Gershwin was only in his late thirties
    (B) despite the fact that Ellington was seventy-five and Gershwin was in his late thirties
    (C) what with Ellington being seventy-five and that Gershwin only in his late thirties
    (D) caused by Ellington's being seventy-five and Gershwin's being only in his late thirties
    (E) for Ellington was seventy-five and Gershwin was only in his late thirties

14. We liked our philosophy instructor because in his lectures he always provided illustrations from literature, but our sociology teacher never referred to any source except the textbook.

    14. Ⓐ Ⓑ Ⓒ Ⓓ Ⓔ

    (A) We liked our sociology teacher who referred only to the textbook less than our philosophy teacher who provided illustrations from literature.
    (B) Our philosophy teacher was better liked by us because of his literary illustrations than our sociology teacher with his sticking to the textbook.
    (C) Not liking our sociology teacher because he used only the textbook, we enjoyed our philosophy teacher's literary illustrations.
    (D) Our philosophy teacher's literary references were liked by us more than the sociology teacher who relied on the textbook.
    (E) Our sociology teacher used only his textbook while our philosophy teacher made many literary allusions, which pleased us more.

15. A home owner who sells his house had better be sure the purchaser has enough cash for a down payment and sufficient salary to support the mortgage.

15. Ⓐ Ⓑ Ⓒ Ⓓ Ⓔ

    (A) about the purchaser to have enough cash for the down payment and salary
    (B) with a purchaser who offers a salary for a down payment and a mortgage
    (C) to settle on a buyer who has enough cash for the down payment and which sufficient salary
    (D) of the buyer's sufficient cash for the down payment and a salary to support the mortgage.
    (E) to sell to a buyer's large enough down payment and a sufficient salary

16. When the doctor gave me the prescription, he advised me about possible side effects of the drug.

16. Ⓐ Ⓑ Ⓒ Ⓓ Ⓔ

    (A) provided me with some ineffective information
    (B) made me unconsciously aware
    (C) warned me
    (D) prohibited me
    (E) did not emphasize to me

17. A knitter who does not buy all the wool she needs at the same time may find it difficult to get additional hanks which are the same as the color she chose.

17. Ⓐ Ⓑ Ⓒ Ⓓ Ⓔ

    (A) correspond exactly in every way with
    (B) are harmonious with
    (C) do not deviate in some small shaded tone from
    (D) agree completely with
    (E) exactly match

18. Some service men are paid extra for service in areas which are considered places of high risk.

18. Ⓐ Ⓑ Ⓒ Ⓓ Ⓔ

    (A) without some small degree of danger   (B) dangerous
    (C) filled with the possibilities of danger   (D) remotely distant from harm
    (E) harmfully dangerous to life and limb

19. The Chicago premiere of the film *Grease* attracted a large audience to see Olivia Newton-John.

19. Ⓐ Ⓑ Ⓒ Ⓓ Ⓔ

    (A) an enormous horde of hundreds of persons
    (B) hundreds of people
    (C) an exciting mob of folks
    (D) a massive crowd of several hundred people
    (E) persons by the hundreds in a tremendous horde

20. Young people are often tempted to disobey their parents, especially when something that may not be right is concerned.

20. Ⓐ Ⓑ Ⓒ Ⓓ Ⓔ

    (A) something which cops and others might possibly say is against the law
    (B) anything which could be reasonably called a law violation
    (C) an activity which some pig has set them up for
    (D) some possibly illegal activity
    (E) an illegal activity called upon

21. When we rang the bell hanging on the post, the old ferryman set aside his pipe and cranked up the ferry.

    (A) started the ferry's motor
    (B) made as if to start the ferry's motor
    (C) acted as though he was about to think about starting the ferry's motor
    (D) raced over to start the ferry's motor
    (E) played like he was about to start the ferry's motor

21. Ⓐ Ⓑ Ⓒ Ⓓ Ⓔ

22. Eleanor had to be treated by a doctor when she was not admitted to Smith.

    (A) her admittance to Smith was declined
    (B) her application to Smith was turned down
    (C) her admission and application to Smith was refused
    (D) her coming enrollment to Smith was exacerbated
    (E) her application for recent admission to Smith was rejected

22. Ⓐ Ⓑ Ⓒ Ⓓ Ⓔ

23. The committee worked for five hours and tried to assure everyone that no one would be harmed by the administrative changes.

    (A) would be adversely affected
    (B) could be injured in a fatal fashion
    (C) can be possibly hurt in a negative way
    (D) would have his position altered too seriously
    (E) might be injuriously affected

23. Ⓐ Ⓑ Ⓒ Ⓓ Ⓔ

24. William ate the roast beef on his plate, ignoring the beans, carrots, and potatoes.

    (A) although he could not stomach   (B) and in addition he did not eat
    (C) and therefore he would not eat   (D) and also he could not finish up
    (E) but he would not touch

24. Ⓐ Ⓑ Ⓒ Ⓓ Ⓔ

25. Old rivals, Woodbridge and Oakland High Schools play one game each year in a stadium halfway between the two towns.

    (A) the annual football game they play every year
    (B) their competitive game of football
    (C) the game of football every year
    (D) an annual competition of the game of football
    (E) their annual football game

25. Ⓐ Ⓑ Ⓒ Ⓓ Ⓔ

26. Even though Jovan produces many popular men's colognes, most men would rather not smell like a flower in spring or a dirty saddle in a tack room.

    (A) do not enjoy it's fragrance or the smell
    (B) have a decided aversion against smelling
    (C) make their strong wishes known that they wish to smell
    (D) still prefer not to smell
    (E) wish that they could often smell

26. Ⓐ Ⓑ Ⓒ Ⓓ Ⓔ

27. Some of the pie is still left in the bottom of the refrigerator if you are hungry before you go to bed.

    (A) feel the need for a delicious repast
    (B) want a snack

27. Ⓐ Ⓑ Ⓒ Ⓓ Ⓔ

(C) can devour even another bite

(D) must have still more than the dinner you consumed

(E) break out in a rash at the thought of food

28. Convinced that there must be some kind of drug that insures sexual potency, many deluded men and women have bought ineffective aphrodisiacs.

    28. Ⓐ Ⓑ Ⓒ Ⓓ Ⓔ

    (A) buy alleged powders and pills which are phoney

    (B) have wasted their money upon being

    (C) have purchased useless

    (D) have spent their money foolishly to pursue

    (E) have been bought by

29. When he spoke, the dean urged all the students to become active in their home communities.

    29. Ⓐ Ⓑ Ⓒ Ⓓ Ⓔ

    (A) own   (B) native home

    (C) resident   (D) friendly home town neighborhood

    (E) town of birth

Directions: For each of these sentences, select the answer that, when inserted in the blank in the original sentence, produces the best sentence. Pay attention to meaning and choice of words.

30. The United States Public Health Service declares that wearing a copper bracelet will _____ anyone's arthritis.

    30. Ⓐ Ⓑ Ⓒ Ⓓ Ⓔ

    (A) have not one single, solitary effect upon curing

    (B) do nothing to cure

    (C) be most ineffective in the process of curing

    (D) provide no possibility of curing

    (E) bring about nothing that will help to cure

31. Tourists who are not careful when they dispose of garbage create _____ of litter.

    31. Ⓐ Ⓑ Ⓒ Ⓓ Ⓔ

    (A) great whole piles

    (B) increased piles

    (C) massive numbers

    (D) increasingly piling up amounts

    (E) large amounts

32. People who are not so old recall the penny licorice stick, the five-cent candy bar, _____ the nickel bottle of soda pop.

    32. Ⓐ Ⓑ Ⓒ Ⓓ Ⓔ

    (A) as well as   (B) in addition to

    (C) moreover insofar as   (D) and

    (E) therefore, and so

33. If you insist on violating the school's rules against smoking on campus, you will have _____.

    33. Ⓐ Ⓑ Ⓒ Ⓓ Ⓔ

    (A) no alternative but to accept whatever follows

    (B) to adjust to the regulations

    (C) to suffer the consequences

(D) to reject whatever happens
(E) to project your behavior upon someone else

34. If all's well that ends well, the completion of this examination is
_____.
(A) a cause for great celebration
(B) a reason for overwhelming joy
(C) a marvelous moment of delightful pleasure
(D) an intense attitude of contentment
(E) to be welcomed with the highest extreme pleasure

34. Ⓐ Ⓑ Ⓒ Ⓓ Ⓔ

35. Western Union has always functioned as a public utility and has been
_____ state utility commissions.
(A) superintended by
(B) under the careful watchfulness of
(C) closely under the watch of
(D) regulated by
(E) supervised for

35. Ⓐ Ⓑ Ⓒ Ⓓ Ⓔ

36. Investigations of any kind often reveal some information which someone
would _____.
(A) prefer not to openly discuss
(B) like to keep secret
(C) allow to remain unknown
(D) draw some fair conclusions about
(E) dissuade others from knowing about

36. Ⓐ Ⓑ Ⓒ Ⓓ Ⓔ

37. An unconventional sex education program in the public schools _____
because it refrains from preaching and provides the facts about human
reproduction.
(A) has many sincere people of two minds
(B) resulted in becoming controversial
(C) has, by its very content, become of two minds
(D) has become tremendously controversial in nature
(E) has created controversy

37. Ⓐ Ⓑ Ⓒ Ⓓ Ⓔ

38. Airlines began an immediate advertising campaign to convince everyone
that _____ an automobile.
(A) an airplane is safer than
(B) flying is much more dependable than riding in
(C) flight is more safety cautious than
(D) it is much safer than
(E) an airplane is much more safer than

38. Ⓐ Ⓑ Ⓒ Ⓓ Ⓔ

39. The depositors in a Chicago savings and loan association _____ when
it declared bankruptcy last month.
(A) prevented their loss of many millions of dollars
(B) lost whole scads of millions of dollars
(C) were deprived of whole lots of dollars
(D) had bunches of dollars taken away from them
(E) lost millions of dollars

39. Ⓐ Ⓑ Ⓒ Ⓓ Ⓔ

Directions: Revise each of the following sentences according to the directions which follow it. Rephrase the sentence mentally to save time, making notes in your book if you wish. Although the directions may at times require you to change the relationship between parts of the sentence or to make slight changes in other ways, *make only those changes that the directions require.*

Below each sentence and its directions are listed words or phrases that may occur in your revised sentence. When you have thought out a good sentence, look at the choices A through E for the word or entire phrase that is included in your revised sentence.

Of course, a number of different sentences can be obtained if the sentence is revised according to the directions, and not all of these possibilities can be included in only five choices. If you should find that you have thought of a sentence that contains none of the words listed in the choices, rephrase the sentence again to include a word or phrase that *is* listed.

40. Unfortunately, you have incorrectly inferred from my speech criticizing the college administration that I am unalterably opposed to the regime of President Banks.

    Begin with My speech criticizing.

    (A) no inference   (B) no reference   (C) no allegation
    (D) no implication   (E) no desire

    40. Ⓐ Ⓑ Ⓒ Ⓓ Ⓔ

41. In any role Helen Hayes undertakes, she is always sheer magic and plays to the gallery as much as to front row patrons.

    Begin with Fans in the gallery as well as.

    (A) enjoy the sheer magic of Helen Hayes
    (B) undertake the sheer magic of Helen Hayes
    (C) plays the sheer magic of Helen Hayes
    (D) always radiates sheer magic
    (E) act with sheer magic

    41. Ⓐ Ⓑ Ⓒ Ⓓ Ⓔ

42. Some historians insist that Columbus did not discover America but that he was preceded on these shores by both Eric the Red and a Mediterranean Semitic people, among others.

    Change was preceded to preceded.

    (A) Columbus on these shores
    (B) Eric the Red on these shores
    (C) him on these shores
    (D) a Mediterranean Semitic people on these shores
    (E) historians on these shores

    42. Ⓐ Ⓑ Ⓒ Ⓓ Ⓔ

43. If all species have some innate desire to reproduce, there is evidence that all living things have one thing in common at least.

    Change If all species have to All species having.

    (A) there was   (B) was   (C) is there   (D) there is
    (E) is

    43. Ⓐ Ⓑ Ⓒ Ⓓ Ⓔ

44. A prudent man should consider all the possibilities before investing money in any plan which seems to promise unlimited profits almost immediately.

Begin with Before a prudent man.

(A) him (B) it (C) his (D) its (E) he

44. Ⓐ Ⓑ Ⓒ Ⓓ Ⓔ

45. Neither the president of the class nor any of its members will be permitted to attend the rally in the park this afternoon.

Substitute Either for Neither.

(A) and any (B) for any (C) or any (D) with any
(E) nor any

45. Ⓐ Ⓑ Ⓒ Ⓓ Ⓔ

46. Won't Christine's parents object if you don't take her home by midnight?

Change the question to a statement.

(A) shall object (B) will object (C) will not object
(D) shall not object (E) had not objected

46. Ⓐ Ⓑ Ⓒ Ⓓ Ⓔ

47. Some people are so immature that they cannot accept any frustration without indulging in violent temper tantrums.

Begin with Some very immature people indulge.

(A) they are frustrated (B) any frustrations
(C) he is frustrated (D) they frustrate
(E) he frustrates

47. Ⓐ Ⓑ Ⓒ Ⓓ Ⓔ

48. Without the slightest shred of evidence to support the allegation, the prosecutor charged the hostile witness with perjury and demanded his arrest.

Change the prosecutor charged to the prosecutor demanded.

(A) the hostile witness' allegation for perjury
(B) the hostile witness' charged with perjury
(C) the hostile witness' alleged perjury
(D) the hostile witness' arrested for perjury
(E) the hostile witness' arrest for perjury

48. Ⓐ Ⓑ Ⓒ Ⓓ Ⓔ

49. The undertow was so strong that the lifeguard warned all bathers to return to the beach and not risk being pulled out to sea.

Begin with All bathers.

(A) although (B) how (C) as much as (D) because
(E) where

49. Ⓐ Ⓑ Ⓒ Ⓓ Ⓔ

50. Thoroughly spoiled children are so obnoxious that even their parents become disgusted with their atrocious behavior.

Begin with Thoroughly spoiled children behave so.

(A) atrociously (B) atrocious (C) disgustedly
(D) behaviorally (E) behavioral

50. Ⓐ Ⓑ Ⓒ Ⓓ Ⓔ

51. Conservative bankers do not agree that providing low interest rates for home loans is the best method of fighting inflation.

51. Ⓐ Ⓑ Ⓒ Ⓓ Ⓔ

Begin with <u>No conservative banker</u>.

(A) does not agree   (B) do agree   (C) agrees

(D) has been agreed   (E) will have agreed

52. As head of the copy editing department, Matthew earned a high salary from the nationally distributed news magazine.

    52. Ⓐ Ⓑ Ⓒ Ⓓ Ⓔ

Change <u>earned</u> to <u>was paid</u>.

(A) from the nationally   (B) by the nationally

(C) with the nationally   (D) to the nationally

(E) at the nationally

53. Since the chairman was not really congenial with other committee members, he did not solicit their opinions before announcing decisions to the press.

    53. Ⓐ Ⓑ Ⓒ Ⓓ Ⓔ

Begin with <u>Not really</u>.

(A) members, the chairman   (B) members, he

(C) members the chairman   (D) members; thus the chairman

(E) members, and so the chairman

54. Owing to his skill as a football player, John Johns had many offers of athletic scholarships from colleges all over the nation.

    54. Ⓐ Ⓑ Ⓒ Ⓓ Ⓔ

Begin with <u>Colleges all over the nation offered</u>.

(A) so   (B) therefore   (C) because

(D) and   (E) while

55. The American Medical Association's canon of ethics declares that no doctor shall participate in a mercy death even if the patient and his family request euthanasia.

    55. Ⓐ Ⓑ Ⓒ Ⓓ Ⓔ

Change <u>declares that no doctor</u> to <u>prohibits a doctor's</u>.

(A) with participating   (B) having any participation

(C) for participating   (D) from participating

(E) participation

56. When Boris Pasternak won the Nobel Prize for Literature, the Soviet government refused to grant him permission to attend the awards dinner in Stockholm.

    56. Ⓐ Ⓑ Ⓒ Ⓓ Ⓔ

Begin with <u>Boris Pasternak was refused</u>.

(A) would have given   (B) would have attended

(C) would be received   (D) would have received

(E) would be given

57. Colleges and universities now offer students more than a traditional basic education, for their registrants are demanding that all subjects be more relevant to contemporary life.

    57. Ⓐ Ⓑ Ⓒ Ⓓ Ⓔ

Change <u>more than a traditional</u> to <u>not only a traditional</u>

(A) but also more relevant

(B) but also subjects more relevant

(C) but also contemporary life

(D) but also more life

(E) but also more tradition

58. Any teenager receiving an allowance from his parents at least owes them some thanks for the money which they provide.

58. Ⓐ Ⓑ Ⓒ Ⓓ Ⓔ

Change receiving to being given.

(A) by his parents   (B) from his parents
(C) through his parents   (D) like his parents
(E) for his parents

59. Hunting for the elusive wild deer and fishing for the fighting mountain trout are two of his favorite sports.

59. Ⓐ Ⓑ Ⓒ Ⓓ Ⓔ

Substitute to fish for fishing.

(A) To be hunting   (B) To hunting   (C) To have hunted
(D) To hunt   (E) To be hunted

60. In their conflicts with militant demonstrators, hard-hat construction workers are merely defending those social values and attitudes which they learned from their parents' and their own work ethic.

60. Ⓐ Ⓑ Ⓒ Ⓓ Ⓔ

Begin with Their parents' and their own work ethic are the sources.

(A) within their conflicts with   (B) in their conflicts with
(C) by their conflicts with   (D) from their conflicts with
(E) against their conflicts with

Directions: For each of the following, choose the one phrasing that makes the intended meaning clear; that is, the one that avoids ambiguity, that does not leave the actual meaning open to question or that does not leave the reader guessing about what is intended.

61. (A) The secretary's advice was rejected by the senator which was often correct in his judgment.

61. Ⓐ Ⓑ Ⓒ Ⓓ Ⓔ

(B) The secretary's judgment was often correct, but the senator declined to consider him sound.

(C) The senator refused to accept the secretary's advice which he had often been correct in.

(D) Even though the senator's secretary had been often correct in his advice, the senator refused to accept the employee's judgment.

(E) The judgment of the secretary of the senator was often correct; his advice was good.

62. (A) When repairing an electric motor, it should be disconnected from the power source.

62. Ⓐ Ⓑ Ⓒ Ⓓ Ⓔ

(B) They should always disconnect an electric motor from its power source before repairing it.

(C) Anyone repairing an electric motor should disconnect it from its power source.

(D) Before repairing an electric motor, the power source should be disconnected.

(E) When repairing an electric motor, they should always disconnect the power source.

63. (A) With her job, Jane likes it better than her fellow workers.
    (B) Jane likes her job better than she likes her fellow workers.
    (C) Her fellow workers are less liked by Jane than her job.
    (D) Jane likes her job better than her fellow workers.
    (E) Her jobs' fellow workers are not too well liked by Jane.

64. (A) The first five cars of the CTA train derailed and injured many people because the motorman who was driving the train carelessly turned the curve too fast.
    (B) Carelessly turning the curve too fast, the CTA motorman derailed the train and injured many people.
    (C) Many people were injured when the CTA motorman who was driving the train carelessly turned the curve too fast, and five cars were derailed.
    (D) Five cars were derailed, injuring many people, when the CTA train was derailed by the careless motorman who was turning a curve.
    (E) When the CTA motorman who was carelessly driving the train turned a curve too fast, the first five cars derailed, and people were injured.

65. (A) The jury found both the office manager and the clerk guilty of the large embezzlement.
    (B) The jury found both the office manager as well as the clerk equally guilty of the large embezzlement.
    (C) The jury decided that the office manager and the clerk were just as guilty of the large embezzlement.
    (D) The jury found that the office manager and the clerk were both guilty of his embezzlement.
    (E) The manager of the office was just as guilty of the large embezzlement as the clerk was, the jury found.

Part II

Number of Items: 65
Time: 45 minutes

Directions: Questions 66–90 are each based on a short passage. Read the passage and then select the one best answer to the questions that follow the passage, using the information provided by or suggested in the passage.

66. "Our students are too involved in extracurricular clubs and organizations; therefore, if we reduce the number of these organizations, our students will study harder.

    The speaker believes that participation in extracurricular activities

    (A) is a complete waste of the student's time
    (B) encourages students to do better work
    (C) should be prohibited completely
    (D) prevent students from studying
    (E) should be encouraged so that students can show their school spirit

67. "Wage earners pay too many taxes. I could buy a new home if I could reduce my tax bill."

One conclusion a reader could draw from this statement is that "I"

(A) never votes for tax increases for schools
(B) is on welfare or a social security pension
(C) works hard for his pay
(D) writes his congressman about taxes
(E) is a wage earner

Questions 68-69 are based on the following:

"Our children today are not being taught basic skills. Since my son cannot spell, I know that he cannot write well."

68. The speaker has drawn the conclusion that

68. Ⓐ Ⓑ Ⓒ Ⓓ Ⓔ

(A) there is a direct connection between poor spelling and written communication
(B) teachers are not paid salaries that are high enough
(C) all students are not like the speaker's son
(D) one of the "basic skills" is not necessarily spelling
(E) teaching should insulate students from the basic skills

69. From the statement, a listener might conclude that the speaker

69. Ⓐ Ⓑ Ⓒ Ⓓ Ⓔ

(A) voted to increase his taxes to support education
(B) has not defined what the term "basic skills" means
(C) has a good opinion of today's educational system
(D) would agree that there should be increased educational opportunities for all children
(E) must have had good teachers when he/she was in school

Questions 70-71 are based on the following:

Laura, a young research chemist, develops a new detergent which is less expensive to manufacture than her company's older detergent. Her role in the development of the new product is not announced by the company.

70. One possible conclusion a reader might have about the company is that

70. Ⓐ Ⓑ Ⓒ Ⓓ Ⓔ

(A) Laura has been denied recognition solely because she is female
(B) Laura was insulted when the company omitted her name from the announcement of the new product
(C) Laura's experiments were not that important to the company
(D) the company's products have not been selling well in the past
(E) the company may have a policy against recognizing any employee publicly by name

71. From the situation described, a reader

71. Ⓐ Ⓑ Ⓒ Ⓓ Ⓔ

(A) should agree that the company thought little of Laura's talents
(B) would be correct in saying that Laura was mistreated
(C) could conclude that a cheaper detergent is of no importance to the company
(D) can really conclude nothing about the company's personnel policies
(E) should join Laura in suing the company for discriminating against her

72. "Today's students cannot read or write well. Those in the future will surely be no better."

The speaker assumes

(A) future students will be different from today's students
(B) all students are exactly alike
(C) student abilities will not change as time passes
(D) student abilities are not measurable
(E) good reading and writing abilities are the only basis anyone needs in order to judge a student's abilities

72. Ⓐ Ⓑ Ⓒ Ⓓ Ⓔ

73. "Mary Smith should be elected president of her sorority. Her mother and grandmother both had that position when they were in college."

The speaker

(A) assumes that Mary's qualifications for the job are not so good
(B) rejects the idea that Mary is not a qualified person for the job
(C) implies that Mary is just as qualified as her mother and grandmother were for the position
(D) complicates the whole matter of the presidential election
(E) has worked hard to elect Mary president

73. Ⓐ Ⓑ Ⓒ Ⓓ Ⓔ

Questions 74-75 are based on the following:

Everyone responds to a certain situation with emotions or with reason.

74. Which of the following statements represents an emotional response to a young man's murder?
(A) I cried all night when I heard that John had been murdered.
(B) The senior class has lost a handsome young man.
(C) John's mother will have no one to pay the rent now that he has been murdered.
(D) John was capable of good work; it's too bad he was murdered.
(E) With John's murder, the high school will not seem the same.

74. Ⓐ Ⓑ Ⓒ Ⓓ Ⓔ

75. Which of the statements in question 74 represents a response based on reason?
(A) C   (B) E   (C) B   (D) D   (E) A

75. Ⓐ Ⓑ Ⓒ Ⓓ Ⓔ

76. "I don't think that students who have to drive a great distance to a campus should attend college. They waste too much time commuting."

The speaker assumes that commuting students

(A) are too lazy to study
(B) can think while they are commuting
(C) are too stupid to study
(D) will not have enough time to study because they commute
(E) cannot study after the commuting time is over

76. Ⓐ Ⓑ Ⓒ Ⓓ Ⓔ

77. "Having a beer or two with friends in a tavern is a good way to unwind after a hard day's work. Four or five beers never hurt anyone."

The speaker implies that everyone

(A) can unwind in the same way

77. Ⓐ Ⓑ Ⓒ Ⓓ Ⓔ

(B) needs to unwind after working hard
(C) cannot consume the same amount of beer
(D) is an alcoholic
(E) works hard every day

78. "Why should I pay any attention to Ronald Reagan's arguments against our turning over the Panama Canal to the Panamanians? I never saw one of his movie performances without walking out of the theater."

78. Ⓐ Ⓑ Ⓒ Ⓓ Ⓔ

The writer assumes that Ronald Reagan's film career

(A) is over
(B) makes him an expert on Panama
(C) is more important than his political career
(D) works against his political career
(E) affects his political views

Questions 79-80 are based on the following:

Son: "How do you like my new Bearcat with a 400 cc. engine, four carburetors, four exhausts, heavy duty springs, and oversize radial tires and wheels?"

Father: "If you drive that car to church, you are no son of mine."

79. The father is concerned that

79. Ⓐ Ⓑ Ⓒ Ⓓ Ⓔ

(A) his son will drive the car too fast
(B) his neighbors will be afraid of his son's car
(C) his son is a sinner
(D) his son's car is too expensive to operate on Sunday
(E) his son's car will upset some members of the church

80. The father makes which of the following assumptions about his son and the car?

80. Ⓐ Ⓑ Ⓒ Ⓓ Ⓔ

(A) A sporty car will be accepted by church members.
(B) There is a connection between his son's car and his religious practices.
(C) The church's pastor will preach a sermon against sinful youth.
(D) The reality of a situation is more important than the appearance.
(E) The car alone can have little effect upon his son's religious activities.

81. "I knew that Jim would wind up in jail. Just look at how poor his parents are and how they have lived on welfare for ten years."

81. Ⓐ Ⓑ Ⓒ Ⓓ Ⓔ

The writer implies

(A) all welfare families should be poor
(B) Jim could have avoided jail if he had had an expensive attorney
(C) Jim was not guilty of the crime for which he was convicted
(D) poor people who must accept welfare cannot raise children who will not get into trouble
(E) that poor families encourage their children to go to jail

82. The documentary film showed drunks passed out in doorways, prostitutes openly soliciting business on 42nd Street, and advertisements for

82. Ⓐ Ⓑ Ⓒ Ⓓ Ⓔ

pornographic films in theaters on Eighth Avenue. The title of the film is *The Real New York City.*

The makers of the film assumed that

(A) the word *real* could apply to nothing but what was ugly or sexually oriented
(B) New York City could save itself from bankruptcy if it legalized prostitution
(C) St. Patrick's Cathedral is a part of New York City
(D) residents of New York City are all law-abiding citizens
(E) the word *real* always connotes something beautiful

83. "Only readers with some kind of perversion buy magazines like *Playboy, Playgirl, Hustler,* and *Penthouse.* No person should have those publications in his home."

        83. Ⓐ Ⓑ Ⓒ Ⓓ Ⓔ

A conclusion that could be drawn from these statements is that

(A) the publications are not popular magazines
(B) only strange people read these publications
(C) people who read these magazines outside their homes are safe from negative criticism
(D) all of these magazines feature overt sex acts
(E) the publications should be banned from newsstands

84. "The new 55 mile-per-hour speed limit is ridiculous. My 1949 Chevrolet can't go that fast without rattling and being hard to steer."

        84. Ⓐ Ⓑ Ⓒ Ⓓ Ⓔ

The speaker implies

(A) no one should be concerned about wasted energy
(B) fast drivers are dangerous drivers
(C) slow drivers are good drivers
(D) automobiles should be banned from expressways
(E) all cars are like his 1949 Chevrolet

85. "Sure, I sell lottery tickets to poor people who can barely afford to buy food. Why shouldn't I? Think of the thousands of dollars someone will win eventually when a certain number is drawn."

        85. Ⓐ Ⓑ Ⓒ Ⓓ Ⓔ

The speaker has concluded that

(A) the winning of thousands of dollars should be uppermost in the minds of every seller of lottery tickets
(B) the selling of lottery tickets to the poor should be limited
(C) all poor people should buy lottery tickets so that they can get off welfare with their winnings
(D) his profits from the sale of lottery tickets outweigh his feelings about poor people
(E) every lottery ticket has a winning number

Questions 86-87 are based on the following:

"All of today's movies feature explicit scenes of sex and violence. No one should attend a movie theater except to see *Gone With the Wind.*"

86. The speaker implies that
(A) she has seen every movie produced within the past year
(B) scenes of sex and violence arouse her interest
(C) today's movie audiences have the same attitudes that she does
(D) film producers and theater owners are not permissive enough
(E) movie theaters do not employ enough custodians

87. If we accept the conclusion implied by the speaker, we must also accept the conclusion that
(A) no one should see an explicitly sexual film
(B) film producers are all sex maniacs
(C) violent films may be as good as *Gone With the Wind*
(D) Gone With the Wind is the greatest film ever made
(E) she has seen *Gone With the Wind*

88. "Jenny Fields supported the Equal Rights Amendment as did a number of female homosexuals." From this statement, a reader should draw the obvious conclusion that
(A) Jenny Fields is a female homosexual
(B) Jenny Fields agreed with a number of female homosexuals in supporting the Equal Rights Amendment
(C) all female homosexuals supported the Equal Rights Amendment
(D) Jenny Fields had the support of all female homosexuals
(E) the Equal Rights Amendment was not worthy of female homosexual support

89. A Chinese worker is visiting the United States for the first time. Which of the following sentences most clearly expresses his attitude about his experiences in this country?
(A) You Americans waste too much of everything.
(B) I never saw such tall buildings in my life.
(C) You Americans should spend more money on mass transportation and less on automobiles.
(D) The department stores in the United States sell many expensive kitchen utensils.
(E) American young people seem to be respectful to older people.

90. The bumper sticker, "America—Love It or Leave It", makes a statement that
(A) is the highest form of patriotism
(B) waves the American flag for everyone to see
(C) expresses the feelings of all Americans who think right
(D) acts upon the American peoples' reason rather than their emotions
(E) sets up two courses of action, neither of which may apply to the person reading the bumper sticker

Directions: In questions 91–97, you are to compare various statements in the light of the questions posed. Pay attention to the tone, emphasis, and implications of each of the statements as you select the one response that is best in each case.

91. Which of the following statements reveals how the writer feels about the new movie?
(A) The film broke box office records in Chicago last weekend.

(B) Some people have already suggested that the starring actress be nominated for an Academy Award.

(C) Only the most childlike members of the audience could possibly applaud the film.

(D) The leading actor looked handsome in his unbuttoned shirt.

(E) The music thundered from the sound track throughout the film.

92. Which of the following statements expresses the speaker's real feeling about being a farmer?
92. Ⓐ Ⓑ Ⓒ Ⓓ Ⓔ

(A) My father's farm consisted of five hundred acres of poor soil which required too much hard work to produce good crops.

(B) My father was a farmer all of his life, and I could only follow his example.

(C) My father died and left me his farm, complete with all the equipment I needed.

(D) Even though my farm has no mortgage, I have to work hard to earn enough to pay the taxes.

(E) At least, from my father's farm, we have enough food to feed the animals through the winter.

93. Which of the following is the most positive statement about John's ability as a football player?
93. Ⓐ Ⓑ Ⓒ Ⓓ Ⓔ

(A) John has scored fourteen touchdowns this year.

(B) The team elected John captain two years in a row.

(C) The coaches think that John will play better next year.

(D) John can run and break through the strongest defensive line other teams have been able to produce.

(E) The female cheerleaders think John is very handsome.

94. Which of the following statements is the most negative about *Jaws 2*, the sequel to the successful film *Jaws*?
94. Ⓐ Ⓑ Ⓒ Ⓓ Ⓔ

(A) The ocean has been photographed with its colors intact.

(B) The sequel enlarges some of the mistakes of the original film.

(C) The mechanical sharks in both films seem too phoney.

(D) The actors in the sequel are just about as good as those in the original.

(E) Of the two films, I enjoyed *Jaws* more than *Jaws 2*.

95. Which of the following statements expresses most clearly a student's opinion about a teacher, Mr. Brown?
95. Ⓐ Ⓑ Ⓒ Ⓓ Ⓔ

(A) Mr. Brown was always in class at least one minute before the bell rang.

(B) Mr. Brown usually wore blue jeans and a gold neck chain to class.

(C) Mr. Brown selected the textbooks for his class, choosing inexpensive ones when he could.

(D) Mr. Brown was popular with the other teachers at Hinsdale Central High School.

(E) I always found Mr. Brown willing to listen to my problems and to help me solve them.

96. Which of the following statements is the most negative about Dave who has a reputation as an excellent cook?
96. Ⓐ Ⓑ Ⓒ Ⓓ Ⓔ

(A) Dave studied cooking with Julia Child, who serves excellent meals.

(B) We eat anything which Dave serves, and we wonder what ingredients he uses.

    (C) Dave's reputation as a good cook is deserved because he follows recipes exactly.

    (D) We had dinner at Dave's house last night and could not identify any dish he served us.

    (E) Dave's dinner last night was a combination of fair dishes which should have had more salt.

97. Which of the following statements reveals what the speaker believes about the achievements of most members of Congress?

    (A) Most members of Congress are out of touch with the people they represent.

    (B) Most Congressmen are lawyers, and you know how lawyers behave.

    (C) Most members of Congress vote according to their own beliefs about controversial issues.

    (D) Most Congressmen depend upon their assistants and aides to gather information.

    (E) Most members of Congress do not behave well when they drink too much.

97. Ⓐ Ⓑ Ⓒ Ⓓ Ⓔ

Directions: In this group of questions, two underlined sentences are followed by a question or incomplete statement about them. Read each group of sentences and then choose the best answer to the question or the best completion of the statement.

98. Dogs will usually eat anything.
My dog Martin will not touch dry dog food.

Sentence 2

    (A) makes a generalization
    (B) supports the generalization of sentence 1
    (C) confirms the first sentence
    (D) provides an exception
    (E) illustrates that my dog is crazy

98. Ⓐ Ⓑ Ⓒ Ⓓ Ⓔ

99. The word *hate* labels an abstract concept.
The Nazis had nothing but hate for Jews and homosexuals.

Sentence two

    (A) provides an example
    (B) produces a strong contrast
    (C) makes a generalization
    (D) compares two unlike things
    (E) introduces a new generalization

99. Ⓐ Ⓑ Ⓒ Ⓓ Ⓔ

100. Bill's jeans feature embroidery on the back pockets.
Phil's jeans have no back pockets.

These two sentences

    (A) compare two articles on the basis of several characteristics
    (B) conclude that Bill's jeans are better than Phil's
    (C) contrast two articles on the basis of one characteristic
    (D) define two different kinds of jeans
    (E) imply that Phil's jeans are more stylish than Bill's

100. Ⓐ Ⓑ Ⓒ Ⓓ Ⓔ

101. A television commercial reader states, "Use Gemmo to clean your pots and
     pans."
     On the screen, this sentence appears, "Read and follow label directions."

     The second quotation indicates that

     (A) Gemmo should not be used on fine china
     (B) Gemmo may be used to clean anything in the kitchen
     (C) Gemmo has a new cleaning ingredient
     (D) Gemmo should be used under certain conditions
     (E) Gemmo should be banned by the Federal Trade Commission

     101. Ⓐ Ⓑ Ⓒ Ⓓ Ⓔ

102. All banks pay interest on savings deposit accounts.
     A checking account is not a savings deposit account.

     What do these sentences do?

     (A) They make a comparison between two types of bank accounts.
     (B) They present a cause-effect relationship.
     (C) They draw a conclusion about certain bank accounts.
     (D) They give a generalization and provide an example.
     (E) They make a generalization and state a contrast.

     102. Ⓐ Ⓑ Ⓒ Ⓓ Ⓔ

103. Lola was a show girl at the Copacabana.
     She dressed in yellow and danced in the chorus.

     Sentence 2

     (A) makes all show girls seem cheap
     (B) lists two of Lola's job requirements
     (C) draws a conclusion about Lola
     (D) makes a comparison
     (E) combines description and contrast

     103. Ⓐ Ⓑ Ⓒ Ⓓ Ⓔ

104. Julia Child is famous for her television series which features gourmet
     cooking.
     One program was devoted to her cooking a duck in orange sauce.

     Sentence two

     (A) implies that Julia Child is a good cook
     (B) illustrates the term "gourmet cooking"
     (C) compares Julia Child's recipe for duck in orange sauce with that of
         another gourmet cook
     (D) says that Julia Child's duck in orange sauce is a delicious dish
     (E) makes an exception

     104. Ⓐ Ⓑ Ⓒ Ⓓ Ⓔ

105. Morris is a very famous cat.
     He makes television commercials for a cat food.
     Sentence two

     (A) gives a cause
     (B) presents an effect
     (C) makes a comparison
     (D) draws a conclusion
     (E) makes a generalization

     105. Ⓐ Ⓑ Ⓒ Ⓓ Ⓔ

106. Jeanette hates getting up early in the morning.
She is a very lazy woman.

Sentence two

(A) provides a specific example
(B) gives an exception
(C) provides an effect
(D) presents an illustration
(E) makes a generalization

106. Ⓐ Ⓑ Ⓒ Ⓓ Ⓔ

107. The Mercedes-Benz is an expensive automobile
Anyone who drives that car must be very wealthy.

Sentence two

(A) gives an example
(B) makes an exception
(C) defines an idea
(D) draws a conclusion
(E) illustrates a generalization

107. Ⓐ Ⓑ Ⓒ Ⓓ Ⓔ

108. Jones is considered an amusing fellow.
He has a joke for every occasion.

Sentence two

(A) presents a generalization
(B) provides a cause
(C) gives an exception
(D) draws a conclusion
(E) makes an irrelevant observation

108. Ⓐ Ⓑ Ⓒ Ⓓ Ⓔ

109. The black Labrador is a large dog.
The Mexican hairless is a small dog.

What is happening in these sentences?

(A) Two dogs are being classified according to their country of origin.
(B) Two dogs are being compared according to their cost.
(C) Two dogs are being classified according to their size.
(D) Two dogs are being rated according to their value.
(E) Two dogs are being contrasted according to their shapes.

109. Ⓐ Ⓑ Ⓒ Ⓓ Ⓔ

110. The oak chair and table are in the store window.
On the table is a blue pepper mill.

The objects in these sentences are organized according to

(A) their cost
(B) their style
(C) their colors
(D) their construction methods
(E) their location

110. Ⓐ Ⓑ Ⓒ Ⓓ Ⓔ

111. Most men today take care to dress well.
Jim always wears scuffed and unpolished shoes.

Sentence two

(A) supports a generalization with an example

111. Ⓐ Ⓑ Ⓒ Ⓓ Ⓔ

(B) illustrates the connection between Jim and most men
(C) makes an exception to a generalization
(D) defines an abstract idea
(E) makes a concrete idea an abstraction

112. *Love* is an abstract word.   112. Ⓐ Ⓑ Ⓒ Ⓓ Ⓔ
The feeling that a mother has for her child could be called one kind of love.

Sentence two

(A) states an exception to a generalization
(B) defines an abstract concept
(C) compares two different kinds of love
(D) gives a specific illustration of an abstract concept
(E) requires additional explanation before a reader can understand it

113. Passing a test is often difficult.   113. Ⓐ Ⓑ Ⓒ Ⓓ Ⓔ
It is also hard to make up test questions.

These two sentences

(A) make a comparison
(B) define an idea
(C) illustrate an abstraction
(D) draw a conclusion
(E) present a contrast

114. Farm fresh vegetables are rather expensive.   114. Ⓐ Ⓑ Ⓒ Ⓓ Ⓔ
They also have a better flavor than those shipped across the country.

Sentence two

(A) generalizes upon vegetables shipped across the country
(B) implies that farm fresh vegetables are worth the extra cost
(C) contrasts the two types of vegetables on the basis of their cost
(D) draws a conclusion about farm fresh vegetables on the basis of their
size
(E) says the cost of vegetables shipped across the country is high

115. Madonna and John Denver make records which sell millions of copies.   115. Ⓐ Ⓑ Ⓒ Ⓓ Ⓔ
They usually record different kinds of songs.

What happens in these two sentences?

(A) A comparison is made on the basis of quality.
(B) A preference is stated for one singer over the other.
(C) A contrast is made on the basis of the number of records each singer
sells.
(D) A conclusion is drawn on the basis of types of songs each records.
(E) They illustrate that different types of singers can make popular
records.

116. President Reagan has recommended a large tax cut for middle-income   116. Ⓐ Ⓑ Ⓒ Ⓓ Ⓔ
individuals.

This group will have more money to spend on themselves if the proposal is approved by Congress.

These two sentences

(A) make a comparison
(B) draw a conclusion from limited evidence
(C) state a cause-effect relationship
(D) define a tax cut
(E) establish a contrast

117. Mildred Jones is a very meticulous person.
All the spices in her cabinet are arranged alphabetically.

117. Ⓐ Ⓑ Ⓒ Ⓓ Ⓔ

Sentence two

(A) makes an implied comparison
(B) draws a conclusion
(C) makes an exception
(D) provides an illustration
(E) defines an abstract word

118. The long, narrow theater holds 600 people.
The square theater holds 800 people.

118. Ⓐ Ⓑ Ⓒ Ⓓ Ⓔ

What do these sentences do?

(A) They compare the two theaters on the basis of their shape and capacity.
(B) They contrast the two theaters on the basis of comfort.
(C) They recommend one of the two theaters.
(D) They compare two theaters on the basis of their shape and cost.
(E) They make a generalization about all theaters.

Directions: At the end of each passage there are questions or incomplete statements, followed by five suggested answers or completions. Select the one that is best in each case, paying attention to grammar, usage, diction, idiom, and tone.

Questions 119-121 are based on the following passage:

¹In 1972, Congress approved the Equal Rights Amendment (ERA) and decreed that it would become part of the United States Constitution if thirty-nine state legislatures agreed by 1979. ²Within the first year or two, a number of these legislative bodies did approve, and it seemed that the amendment would become a part of the basic law of the land without difficulty. ³Yet, a year away from the deadline, three states are still needed, and proponents and opponents are locked in a bitter battle. ⁴In Illinois, one of the states in which ERA has not been approved, political maneuverings in the State House in Springfield had some of the qualities of the backstage in-fighting which characterize nominations for president. ⁵Those favoring ERA are now attempting to pressure Congress to extend the deadline so that they can work further in certain states where approval seems possible. ⁶Those opposed to ERA are crying "foul," saying that such an extension is against all the precedents followed by all other amendment approval

processes. [7]Because many organizations are refusing to hold national meetings in those states which have not passed ERA, those states have suffered economic losses. [8]Whether Congress will approve the extension of time so that passage of ERA will be given another chance is uncertain, and the fight continues on both the state and the national level.

119. What should be done with sentence 7?
    (A) It should be left as it is.
    (B) *Because* should be changed to *instead of*, and the sentence connected to sentence 3.
    (C) It should follow sentence 8.
    (D) It should be omitted.
    (E) *Because* should be changed to *For the reason that*, and the sentence connected to sentence 4.

119. Ⓐ Ⓑ Ⓒ Ⓓ Ⓔ

120. The passage could be divided into two paragraphs. If this were done, the second paragraph should begin with
    (A) sentence 5
    (B) sentence 2
    (C) sentence 7
    (D) sentence 6
    (E) sentence 4

120. Ⓐ Ⓑ Ⓒ Ⓓ Ⓔ

121. Sentence 8 might be revised in one of the following ways. Which is the correct choice?
    (A) Change *Whether Congress* to *If Congress*.
    (B) Eliminate *Whether* and *is uncertain;* add *perhaps* after *Congress*.
    (C) Change *continues on* to *just adds to*.
    (D) Change *uncertain, and ine fight* to *uncertain, therefore the fight*.
    (E) Change *the extension of time so that* to *the extension of time such that*.

121. Ⓐ Ⓑ Ⓒ Ⓓ Ⓔ

Questions 122-124 are based on the following passage:

[1]The "Filthy Words" case (Federal Communications Commission——FCC—vs. Pacifica Foundation et al) was and will remain a close call. [2]Close—and we believe, wrong. [3]A father, driving with his young son, tuned in to an afternoon radio broadcast that moved him to complain to the FCC. [4]The FCC investigated, sided with the complainant, and put notice of that fact in the station's file, to be considered with other material at license renewal time. [5]By a 2 to 1 vote, a Court of Appeals reversed the FCC. [6]Now, by a 5 to 4 vote, the Supreme Court has reversed the Appellate Court. [7]Close. [8]Justice John Paul Stevens, writing for the majority, began by saying, "This case requires that we decide whether the FCC has any power to regulate a radio broadcast that is indecent but not obscene." [9]All the justices agree that the broadcast in question lacked the appeal to prurient interest essential in obscenity. [10]The "satiric humorist" in question, George Carlin, had a respectable point—that prevailing attitudes toward "filthy words" are silly. [11]But in making his point he repeatedly used words that are generally taboo. [12]But there are other and better ways to

chide poor taste on the part of a radio station's management than for the FCC to take disciplinary action. [13]The marketplace of speech and thought should feel the heavy hand of government as little as possible.

Reprinted from the *Chicago Tribune*, July 10, 1978. Courtesy of the *Chicago Tribune*.

122. Sentence 11 should read

    122. Ⓐ Ⓑ Ⓒ Ⓓ Ⓔ

(A) *Words that are generally taboo were repeatedly used by George Carlin who was making a point*
(B) *George Carlin, using repeatedly taboo words, made his point*
(C) the way it does now
(D) *They are generally taboo as repeatedly used by George Carlin*
(E) *Using taboo words repeatedly, his point was made by George Carlin*

123. What should be done with sentence 7?

    123. Ⓐ Ⓑ Ⓒ Ⓓ Ⓔ

(A) It should be eliminated.
(B) It should be expanded so that it is a complete sentence.
(C) It should be left as it is.
(D) It should be joined to sentence 6, preceded by , *and*.
(E) It should be placed at the beginning of sentence 9.

124. A new paragraph could start with

    124. Ⓐ Ⓑ Ⓒ Ⓓ Ⓔ

(A) sentence 2
(B) sentence 4
(C) sentence 13
(D) sentence 11
(E) sentence 3

Questions 125-127 are based on the following passage:

[1]For Bobby Murcer and Mike Krukow, the All-Star break is like taking away the dice from a crapshooter who's on a string of passes. [2]For Bruce Sutter, it's a chance to prove to the other league what's accepted as gospel in the National League: that he's the best relief pitcher in baseball. [3]Murcer's sizzling bat and Krukow's smoking fastball made things too hot for the Mets in muggy Shea Stadium Sunday afternoon. [4]Then Sutter's icy calm and torrid split-finger fastball chilled a seventh-inning rally, preserving a 4-1 triumph for Krukow and the Cubs. [5]It brought them to the traditional midsummer night's dream game 4½ lengths behind Philadelphia, the team that supposedly left the Cubs for dead in the NL East race not long ago. [6]Instead, they took their walking wounded on tour and got well with a 5-2 trip that didn't hurt their mental health, either. [7]"Everybody on this team believes we can beat Philadelphia," said Murcer, whose two-run homer off loser Pat Zachry was the key hit. [8]"We're fortunate to be in this position with our heads above water. [9]Now I'm starting to hit a little bit, and that's got to help us in the second half." [10]Actually, Murcer is hitting a lot these days. [11]Sunday's home run, his fifth, and a single boosted the outfielder's average to .273 and stretched his hitting streak to 13 games.

Reprinted from the *Chicago Tribune*, July 10, 1978. Courtesy of the *Chicago Tribune*.

125. In sentence 2, the section after the colon should be revised to read
    (A) he's the best relief pitcher in baseball
    (B) the best relief pitcher he is in baseball
    (C) in baseball's relief pitcher, he is the best
    (D) he is the best pitcher in baseball's relief
    (E) as baseball's relief pitcher, he is the best

126. Sentence 11 should begin
    (A) The outfielder's average was boosted to .273
    (B) His fifth Sunday's home run
    (C) Stretching his hitting streak to 13 games
    (D) Sunday's home run, his fifth,
    (E) A single boosted his batting average

127. An effective conclusion to this passage is which of the following?
    (A) The Chicago Cub players are getting their act together and will win the World Series in 1978.
    (B) After being called the poorest team in baseball, the Cubs have a small chance of redeeming themselves this year.
    (C) If all Cub players were as effective as Murcer, Sutter, and Krukow, the team might stand a chance of winning its division race this year.
    (D) Krukow's pitching can do nothing but improve in August.
    (E) Bobby Murcer is the best hitter on the 1978 Cub team.

Questions 128-130 are based on the following passage:

[1]Some of the herbs and plants available in health food stores are potentially dangerous and may even cause death, according to a researcher from Washington University in St. Louis. [2]Most people believe that goods bought from retail stores have been tested and approved for human use, Dr. Walter H. Lewis said. [3]"However, many newly available plant products have not been tested; their effects on the body are not fully understood, or their effects simply are unknown to the majority of casual purchasers," Lewis reports in the current issue of the *Journal of the American Medical Association.* [4]For example, chamomile, one of the most popular herbal teas made from flower heads, may cause severe shock or an allergy reaction in persons sensitive to ragweed pollen, he said. [5]Senna leaves, also used in herbal teas, can cause serious diarrhea, he said. [6]Deaths associated with overdoses of senna have been reported in Africa. [7]Other herbs are also suspected of carrying poisonous residues from spraying with DDT and other weed and pest controlling substances, for, often, "natural" or "health" food stores do not wash any of the leaves before packaging them for sale.

      Adapted from the *Chicago Tribune*, July 11, 1978. Courtesy of the *Chicago Tribune*.

128. Sentence 1 should begin
    (A) In health food stores,
    (B) A researcher from Washington University has announced that
    (C) All herbs and plants available in health food stores
    (D) Causing death, some herbs and plants
    (E) Washington University is in St. Louis, and

129. What should be done with sentence 5?
   (A) It should begin <u>therefore</u> and joined to sentence 4.
   (B) It should come immediately after sentence 4.
   (C) It should come immediately after sentence 7.
   (D) It should begin <u>And senna leaves</u>.
   (E) It should be left as it is.

130. An appropriate conclusion for the passage is which of the following?
   (A) No thinking person would set foot in a health food store
   (B) All "health" foods are contaminated by foreign substances
   (C) Dr. Walter H. Lewis is a world-renowned authority on health food stores
   (D) A cautious individual will be careful not to drink anything prepared from certain leaves available in health food stores
   (E) Senna leaves are the most dangerous plant product available in health food stores

ANSWER KEY—SAMPLE EXAMINATION 3

Part I

1.	B	12.	C	23.	A	34.	A	45.	C	56.	D
2.	D	13.	E	24.	E	35.	D	46.	B	57.	B
3.	E	14.	A	25.	E	36.	B	47.	A	58.	A
4.	C	15.	D	26.	D	37.	E	48.	E	59.	D
5.	B	16.	C	27.	B	38.	A	49.	D	60.	B
6.	A	17.	E	28.	C	39.	E	50.	A	61.	D
7.	E	18.	B	29.	A	40.	D	51.	C	62.	C
8.	D	19.	B	30.	B	41.	A	52.	B	63.	B
9.	B	20.	D	31.	E	42.	A	53.	A	64.	E
10.	C	21.	A	32.	D	43.	E	54.	C	65.	A
11.	B	22.	B	33.	C	44.	E	55.	E		

Part II

66.	D	77.	B	88.	B	99.	A	110.	E	121.	B
67.	E	78.	E	89.	A	100.	C	111.	C	122.	C
68.	A	79.	E	90.	E	101.	D	112.	E	123.	C
69.	B	80.	B	91.	C	102.	E	113.	A	124.	E
70.	E	81.	D	92.	A	103.	B	114.	B	125.	A
71.	D	82.	A	93.	D	104.	B	115.	E	126.	D
72.	C	83.	C	94.	B	105.	A	116.	C	127.	C
73.	C	84.	E	95.	E	106.	E	117.	D	128.	B
74.	A	85.	D	96.	E	107.	D	118.	A	129.	E
75.	A	86.	A	97.	A	108.	B	119.	D	130.	D
76.	D	87.	E	98.	D	109.	C	120.	A		

SCORING CHART—SAMPLE EXAMINATION 3

After you have scored your Sample Examination 3, enter the results in the chart below; then transfer your Raw Score to the Progress Chart on page 14.

Total Test		Number Right	Number Wrong	Number Omitted	Raw Score
Part I:	65				
Part II:	65				
Total:	130				

ANSWER EXPLANATIONS—SAMPLE EXAMINATION 3

Part I

1. **B.** (A) is incorrect because the verbs in the noun clauses (is organized, had arranged) are incorrect tense sequence. (C) is incorrect because the author would not have explained these things in two different places. (D) is incorrect because Being as how is a poor English idiom. (E) is incorrect because she has no specific antecedent.

2. **D.** (A) is incorrect because show must be a singular verb; the noun clause is the subject. (B) is wrong because seeing as how is an incorrect English idiom. (C) is incorrect because it confuses a concept with the word which names the concept—eternity. (E) is wrong because the introductory phrase, beginning What, is wordy and ambiguous.

3. **E.** (A) is incorrect because he (singular) refers to students (plural); both of these words must be singular or plural. (B) is incorrect because the verb are recalled is the weak passive voice. (C) is incorrect because the word order is confusing and the placement of the modifiers is poor. (D) is incorrect because she is singular and refers to the plural word students; also, the use of the present tense verb are seems to destroy the proper sequence of tenses.

4. **C.** (A) is incorrect because me (objective case form) should be I (nominative case form) as subject of a verb. (B) is wrong because the shift from or to both is confusing. (D) is incorrect for two reasons: (1) the poor placement of either; (2) me should be I. (E) is incorrect because it is unnecessarily wordy.

5. **B.** (A) is incorrect because muchly (an adverb form) should be much (an adjective form). (C) is incorrect because the phrase after the comma is a misplaced modifier. (D) is incorrect because and implies a parallel structure and the same meaning of two words or phrases, and in D the phrases are not parallel. (E) is incorrect because they has no specific antecedent.

6. **A.** (B) is incorrect because the phrase beginning Late cannot function logically as a modifier of cook. (C) is incorrect, because the verb have does not maintain a logical sequence of tenses with arrived. (D) is incorrect because the introductory clause beginning When changes the meaning of the original sentence. (E) is incorrect because expect (present tense) violates the appropriate tense sequence after having been.

7. E. (A) is incorrect because it is illogical; it says his brow had a host of worries. (B) is incorrect because it changes the meaning of the original sentence. (C) is incorrect because the word permanent is misplaced from the original sentence. (D) is incorrect because the introductory phrase beginning Bearing is a dangling modifier.

8. D. (A) is wrong because the word liable is an incorrect choice of words. (B) is wrong because the clause beginning When cannot logically function as a modifier of arrest. (C) is wrong because the sequence of tenses (insists, would be arrested) is incorrect. (E) is wrong because it changes the meaning of the original sentence.

9. B. (A) is incorrect because whom (objective case) should be who (nominative case) as subject of the verb would be. (C) is wrong because the two commas set off a restrictive adjective clause incorrectly. (D) is also incorrect because the commas are incorrect and illogically break up the sentence. (E) is incorrect because it changes the meaning of the original.

10. C. (A) is incorrect because his and his are squinting modifiers; each could refer to Bill or Jack, and he could also refer to either male. (B) is also incorrect because he could refer to either Jack or Bill. (D) is incorrect because only Jack is mentioned, and we know from the original that Jack did not drop the typewriter. (E) is also incorrect because his has no specific antecedent.

11. B. (A) is wrong because the semi-colon is used incorrectly and the clause beginning which is a dangling modifier. (C) is incorrect because there is no such word as irregardless in the English language. (D) is incorrect because the conjunction even though changes the meaning of the original sentence. (E) is wrong because just as is an inappropriate conjunction.

12. C. (A) is incorrect because the commas are incorrect, and the words after the second comma are misplaced. (B) is wrong because the use of the semi-colon is incorrect, and this choice would produce a confused sentence. (D) is wrong because and connects a dependent clause to a complete sentence. (E) is wrong because the commas are incorrect and the dependent clause beginning that does not express the idea of the original sentence.

13. E. (A) is incorrect because the reason was because is incorrect English grammar and sentence structure. (B) is incorrect because the phrase despite the fact changes the meaning of the original sentence. (C) is incorrect because the phrase what with and the word that produce an ambiguous sentence. (D) is illogical because the choice says that Ellington's death was caused by his age.

14. A. (B) is incorrect because the verb was liked is the weak passive voice. (C) is incorrect because the introductory phrase beginning Not is poorly constructed and ambiguous. (D) is incorrect for two reasons: (1) the weak passive verb were liked; the choice compares literary references to sociology teachers, an illogical comparison. (E) is incorrect because the clause beginning which is a dangling modifier.

15. D. (A) is incorrect because the resulting sentence would be confusing and ambiguous. (B) is incorrect because the meaning of the original sentence is changed. (C) is incorrect because which sufficient salary would be ambiguous. (E) is incorrect because it is illogical; large enough is also a misplaced modifier.

16. C. (A) is incorrect because ineffective adds an idea not in the original sentence. (B) is incorrect because unconsciously aware is a poor choice of words. (D) is wrong because prohibited is an incorrect choice of words. (E) is wrong because it reverses the meaning of the original sentence.

17. E. (A) is incorrect because the extra words create a very wordy sentence. (B) is incorrect because harmonious and same are not synonyms. (C) is also wordy. (D) is incorrect because agree represents a poor word choice.

18. B. The other choices are incorrect because they are wordy or change the meaning of the original sentence too much.

19. B. All of the other choices are incorrect because they are wordy.

20. D.   (A) is incorrect because the sentence is wordy and introduces <u>cops and others</u>, persons not mentioned in the original sentence. The other possibilities are too wordy and therefore incorrect.

21. A.   (B) is incorrect because <u>made as if</u> is awkward. (C) and (D) are also wordy and incorrect. (E) uses <u>played like</u> an unacceptable slang term in formal written English.

22. B.   (A) is wrong because <u>admittance</u> is an incorrect word choice. (C) is incorrect because there is a <u>compound</u> subject (<u>admission and application</u>) with a singular verb <u>was</u>; the verb must be plural (<u>were</u>). (D) is wrong because <u>exacerbated</u> is an incorrect word choice. (E) is incorrect because the phrase <u>for recent admission</u> damages the logical chronology of the original sentence.

23. A.   (B) is incorrect because <u>injured in a fatal way</u> is an illogical phrase. (C) is also illogical (the placement of <u>possibly</u>) as well as wordy. (D) and (E) are wordy and therefore incorrect choices.

24. E.   All of the other choices are incorrect because they change the meaning of the original sentence.

25. E.   (A) is incorrect because <u>annual</u> and <u>every year</u> are redundant. (B) is wrong because <u>competitive</u> repeats an idea implied by the rest of the sentence. (C) is incorrect because <u>the</u> instead of <u>one</u> weakens the resulting sentence. (D) is wordy and therefore incorrect.

26. D.   (A) is incorrect, because <u>it's</u> means <u>it is</u>; the correct possessive form is <u>its</u> (no apostrophe). (B) is wordy and uses an incorrect idiom <u>aversion against</u>. (C) is incorrect because that choice is wordy as well as reversing the original's meaning. (E) reverses the meaning of the original sentence.

27. B.   All of the other choices are too wordy and therefore incorrect.

28. C.   (A) is incorrect because the word <u>alleged</u> is a poor choice. (B) is incorrect because <u>upon being</u> would introduce a nonsense phrase. (D) is incorrect because <u>to pursue aphrodisiacs</u> is illogical. (E) is wrong because the verb shifts to the weak passive.

29. A.   (B) is incorrect because <u>native home</u> may be redundant. (C) is incorrect because a student may be a resident of a strange community; the word is ambiguous. (D) and (E) are unnecessarily wordy.

30. B.   The other choices are wordy.

31. E.   All of the other choices are very wordy.

32. D.   All of the other choices would destroy the parallelism of the series of three similarly constructed phrases. In choices (A) and (B), the first comma would have to be eliminated and <u>and</u> used before <u>the</u>. (C) and (E) are too wordy and would create ambiguity.

33. C.   (A) is incorrect because of its wordiness. (B) is wrong because <u>to adjust</u> changes the meaning of the original. (D) is also incorrect because <u>to reject</u> also changes the meaning. (E) is incorrect because <u>to project</u> alters the meaning of the original sentence.

34. A.   (B) might be correct but <u>overwhelming joy</u> is an overstatement. (C), (D), and (E) are wordy.

35. D.   Correct word choice is tested in this item; <u>superintended</u> (A) and <u>supervised for</u> (E) are not as precise as <u>regulated by</u> (D). Choices (B) and (C) are wordy.

36. B.   Again, a reader's deciding on the <u>best</u> choice is tested in this item. Choice (A) is poor because <u>openly</u> is perhaps a misplaced modifier as well as weak. Choice (C) is also weaker than (B). Choices (D) and (E) are wordy.

37. E.   All of the other choices are too wordy.

38. A.   (B) is incorrect because the word <u>dependable</u> seems ambiguous. (C) contains the redundant <u>safety cautions</u> and is incorrect. (D) is incorrect because <u>it</u> has no specific antecedent. (E) is wrong because <u>more safer</u> is incorrect; <u>more safe</u> would be correct.

39. E.   All of the other choices are wordy.

40. D.   My speech criticizing the college administration contained no implication that I am unalterably opposed to the regime of President Banks.

41. A. Fans in the gallery as well as front row patrons enjoy the sheer magic of Helen Hayes, playing any role she undertakes.

42. A. Some historians insist that both Eric the Red and a Mediterranean Semitic people preceded Columbus on these shores; therefore, the claim that Columbus discovered America may be false.

43. E. All species having some innate desire to reproduce is one piece of evidence that all living things have one thing in common at least.

44. E. Before a prudent man invests money in any plan which seems to promise unlimited profits at once, he should investigate all the possibilities.

45. C. Either the president of the class or any of its members will not be permitted to attend the rally in the park this afternoon.

46. B. Christine's parents will object if you don't take her home by midnight.

47. A. Some very immature people indulge in violent temper tantrums whenever they are frustrated.

48. E. Without the slightest shred of evidence to support the allegation, the prosecutor demanded the hostile witness' arrest for perjury.

49. D. All bathers were warned by the lifeguard to return to the beach because of the dangerous undertow which might pull them out to sea.

50. A. Thoroughly spoiled children behave so atrociously that even their parents are disgusted with their obnoxious behavior.

51. C. No conservative banker agrees that providing low interest rates for home loans is the best method of fighting inflation.

52. B. As head of the copy editing department, Matthew was paid a high salary by the nationally distributed news magazine.

53. A. Not really congenial with the other committee members, the chairman did not solicit their opinions before announcing decisions to the press.

54. C. Colleges all over the nation offered John Johns athletic scholarships because of his skills as a football player.

55. E. The American Medical Association's canon of ethics prohibits a doctor's participation in a mercy death even if the patient and his family request euthanasia.

56. D. Boris Pasternak was refused permission by the Soviet government to attend the Nobel awards dinner in Stockholm, where he would have received the prize for literature.

57. B. Colleges and universities now offer students not only a traditional basic education but also subjects more relevant to contemporary life.

58. A. Any teenager being given an allowance by his parents at least owes them some thanks for the money which they provide.

59. D. To hunt for the elusive wild deer and to fish for the fighting mountain trout are two of his favorite sports.

60. B. Their parents' and their own work ethic are the sources of hard-hat construction workers' defenses in their conflicts with militant demonstrators.

61. D. (A) is wrong because which should be who, the correct relative pronoun used to refer to a person (senator). (B) is incorrect because the sentence implies an illogical comparison between the secretary's judgment and the secretary. (C) is incorrect because the clause beginning which has no specific word to modify. (Note, also about (C): the sentence ends with a preposition; that construction is no longer considered incorrect if the sentence is logical otherwise.) (E) equates judgment and advice and is incorrect.

62. C. (A) is incorrect because the phrase beginning when is a dangling modifier. (B) is incorrect because they has no specific antecedent. (D) is incorrect because the phrase beginning Before is a dangling modifier. (E) is incorrect because they has no specific antecedent.

63. B. (A) is ambiguous and therefore incorrect. (C) is incorrect because of the weak passive voice construction are less liked by. (D) is ambiguous because the verb do is probably understood after workers. (E) is an awkward sentence.

64. E. (A) is ambiguous because carelessly might indicate how the motorman was driving the train or how the train turned the corner. (B) is incorrect because it implies that the motorman deliberately derailed the train. (C) is

also incorrect because of the ambiguous placement of <u>carelessly</u>. (D) is wordy and seems to say that the motorman and perhaps not the train turned a corner.

65. A. (B) is incorrect because <u>both</u> and <u>as well as</u> cannot function as correct correlative conjunctions. (C) is ambiguous; <u>just as</u> confuses the sentence. (D) is incorrect, because <u>his</u> could refer to either the office manager or to the clerk. (E) is incorrect because the phrase <u>the jury found</u> is misplaced.

Part II

66. D. (A) and (B) are incorrect because they are conclusions not justified by the facts given. (C) is incorrect because the statement says nothing about a prohibition of extracurricular activities. (E) is also incorrect because no facts in the statement support it.

67. E. (E) is the only correct answer. The other choices cannot be correct because they are assumptions not supported by facts.

68. A. (B) is incorrect because the statement neither says nor implies anything about teacher salaries (C) is incorrect because no comparison is implied between the speaker's son and other children. (D) is incorrect because <u>not</u> seems to deny the implication of the second sentence. (E) is incorrect because <u>insulate</u> also denies the implications of the statement.

69. B. All of the other choices are unjustified assertions based on insufficient evidence.

70. E. (A) is incorrect because there is no evidence to support it. (B) is incorrect because the reader does not know anything about Laura's reaction. (C) is incorrect for it may or may not be true; thus, the sentence is ambiguous. (D) is an unwarranted assumption or conclusion, not based on facts.

71. D. None of the other choices fits the facts in the statement and each would be an invalid conclusion.

72. C. (A) is incorrect because the sentence contradicts the statement. (B) is incorrect as an unwarranted assumption. (D) is incorrect because the reader does not have sufficient information. (E) is incorrect because <u>only</u> makes the sentence a hasty generalization and therefore incorrect.

73. C. (A) and (B) are incorrect because the statement makes no specific reference to Mary's qualifications to be president. (D) and (E) are incorrect as unwarranted assumptions.

74. A. Choice (A) is the only one of the five which even implies an emotional response to the young man's murder—<u>I cried</u>. (B), (C), (D), and (E) state facts which might be verified through investigation or are purely subjective responses.

75. A. Choice (C) (from item 74) is the most reasonable of the four remaining choices.

76. D. (A) is incorrect because the statement says nothing about student laziness. (C) is also incorrect; there is nothing about student intelligence. Neither (B) nor (E) is correct; both are unwarranted assumptions.

77. B. (A) is incorrect because it seems to equate unwinding with the amount of beer consumed. (C) is incorrect, an unwarranted assumption. (D) and (E) are incorrect, because the reader does not have enough evidence to make them valid conclusions.

78. E. The speaker has incorrectly equated Ronald Reagan's film performances with his performance as president when there may be no logical connection between the two kinds of performance. Thus, only (E) is correct.

79. E. Only (E) can be correct. Not one of the other choices is valid to express the father's concern, because there is insufficient information in the statement.

80. B. (B) is the only correct response. (D) reverses two words (<u>reality, appearance</u>) to express a conclusion that most logicians would not agree with from the statement.

81. D. The speaker states an invalid cause-effect relationship as well as a hasty generalization. (D) is the only choice which restates the illogical implications.

82. A. Choice (A) is the correct answer. (B), (C), and (D) are unwarranted assumptions which the facts do not support, although (C) is factually accurate. (E) is a subjective reaction which many people would not accept.

83. C. (A) is incorrect because there is insufficient evidence to make the conclusion valid or invalid. (B) is incorrect because a strange person is not necessarily a pervert. (D) is also incorrect because there is insufficient evidence. (E) is incorrect as a subjective value judgment.

84. E. This item may seem tricky, but analyze the responses. In the statement ridiculous is ambiguous, because the reader does not know what the word applies to. Certainly, not to energy conservation—thus, (A) is incorrect. (B) and (C) are incorrect because the speaker may imply that either going too fast or going too slow is ridiculous. (D) is an unwarranted assumption. Therefore, by process of elimination, (E) is the only correct response.

85. D. (A) is incorrect because this choice shifts the emphasis from the seller of lottery tickets to the buyers. (B) is obviously incorrect. (C) is an unwarranted assumption. (E) is obviously incorrect factually.

86. A. (B) and (C) are incorrect as hasty conclusions based on insufficient evidence. (D) is incorrect because the word permissive seems to contradict the statement. (E) is incorrect as totally irrelevant to the statement.

87. E. (A), (B), and (D) are unwarranted assumptions and therefore incorrect. (C) cannot be supported by the facts in the statement.

88. B. (A), (C), (D), and (E) are incorrect because they cannot be supported by the facts in the statement.

89. A. Choices (B), (C), (D), and (E) are verifiable facts; choice (A) is the only one which expresses an attitude or opinion.

90. E. (A) is incorrect because many people who do not love everything about America would not want to leave it. In formal logic, this statement on the bumper sticker has two names: the either-or-fallacy or the black-or-white fallacy. Neither extreme position may be true or accurate; thus, both extremes are invalid. Otherwise, (B) is illogical—how could a bumper sticker literally wave a flag? (C) is incorrect, because the word right is ambiguous—does it mean correctly, or does it refer to a political position, right vs. left? (D) is obviously incorrect because the statement on the sticker is entirely emotional.

91. C. (A), (B), (D), and (E) are verifiable facts except for the word handsome in (D), which is a value judgment about the actor, not the film. (C) is the only opinion about the film.

92. A. (B), (C), (D), and (E) may be true; only (A) expresses an attitude toward farming.

93. D. (A) and (B) are incorrect; they are facts which may have nothing to do with John's ability as a football player. (C) is incorrect, because it may be negative about his current ability to play football. (E) is incorrect as irrelevant to John's ability as a football player.

94. B. (A) and (D) are mildly affirmative statements about *Jaws 2* and thus incorrect. (C) is negative about only feature of the film. (E) is I's subjective opinion about *Jaws* and *Jaws 2* and not very negative.

95. E. (A), (B), and (C) say more about Mr. Brown than about his abilities as a teacher. (D) gives the opinion of other teachers, maybe based on factors which have nothing to do with Brown's teaching.

96. E. (A), (B), and (C) are incorrect because none states an opinion. (D) is also incorrect because the reader does not know whether the comment is positive or negative.

97. A. Only (A) expresses anything about the achievements of Congressmen. All of the other choices are about the behavior of these people which may have nothing to do with their achievements.

98. D. All of the others are incorrect.

99. A. All of the others are incorrect.

100.	C.	All of the others are incorrect.
101.	D.	(A), (B), and (C) are incorrect because of the statement in sentence 2. (E) may be true, but no evidence is provided to support it.
102.	E.	All of the other choices are incorrect.
103.	B.	(A) and (C) are incorrect because neither sentence expresses an opinion about Lola. (D) and (E) are incorrect because there is no comparison or contrast implied or stated in the two sentences.
104.	B.	Choice (B) is an illustration of sentence 1. Each of the other choices is incorrect.
105.	A.	Sentence 1 is the effect for which sentence 2 provides a cause. (C), (D), and (E) are thus incorrect as is (B).
106.	E.	(A) is incorrect because sentence 2 is not a specific example; it is a generalization. (B), (C), and (D) are incorrect because no exception, effect, or illustration is given.
107.	D.	Sentence 1 is a fact as well as a generalization. Thus only (D) [a conclusion from a generalization] is correct.
108.	B.	Sentence 1 is a conclusion or example for which sentence 2 provides an illustration or cause. All other choices are incorrect.
109.	C.	(A) is incorrect because Labrador is not a country. (B), (D), and (E) are incorrect because cost, value, and shape are not mentioned in the sentences. The size (C) is the only basis for the classification of the two dogs.
110.	E.	Since the location is the only basis of the organization of the objects, choice (E) is the only correct answer.
111.	C.	Sentence 2 is an exception to the generalization in sentence 1; therefore, choice (C) is the correct response.
112.	E.	This item may seem tricky, because the reader is asked to discriminate among (B), (D), and (E) to find the correct response; (A) and (C) can be eliminated almost immediately. (B) is incorrect because could be called in sentence two is vague and indefinite and thus not a definition. (D) is incorrect because the word feeling is ambiguous. Thus, by process of elimination, (E) is the correct choice.
113.	A.	The only relationship between the sentences is the comparison between preparing and taking a test; both procedures are difficult. Choice (A) is correct, and the other choices are incorrect.
114.	B.	The implication in choice (B) is valid; all other choices are incorrect.
115.	E.	Sentence 1 is a statement of fact; sentence 2 is a follow-up sentence. (E) is the correct response.
116.	C.	Sentence 1 is a cause for which sentence 2 is the effect. Choice (C) is the correct response.
117.	D.	The key to this item is the word meticulous; thus, choice (D), an illustration, is the correct answer.
118.	A.	The shape and capacity of the two theaters are the only facts given in the sentence; thus, choice (A) is the correct response.
119.	D.	The sentence should be omitted, because it brings up an issue which is unconnected with the political maneuverings surrounding the passage of ERA. Since the sentence is irrelevant in the paragraph, the other choices are obviously incorrect.
120.	A.	Sentence 5 seems to shift from one idea to one that is slightly different; therefore, choice (A) is correct. Any other choices would make the two paragraphs incoherent.
121.	B.	(A) is incorrect because whether and if are not synonyms. (C) is incorrect because adds to would create a nonsense sentence. (D) is incorrect because the comma would create a comma splice. (E) is incorrect because such that is an incorrect English idiom.
122.	C.	(A) is wordy and therefore incorrect. (B) has a misplaced modifier repeatedly and is incorrect. (D) is incorrect because they would have no specific antecedent. (E) is incorrect because the introductory phrase is a dangling modifier.
123.	C.	The one word—close—is effective and should be left as is. Any other change would produce a less effective sentence and paragraph.

124. **E.** Sentence 3 could be an effective sentence with which to begin a new paragraph, because it introduces the specific case which brought on the FCC action discussed in sentences 1 and 2. Any other paragraph shift would be illogical and break up the effective organization of the material.

125. **A.** Eliminating <u>that</u> would not affect the style of the passage. (B) is incorrect because <u>he is</u> is out of place. (C) is incorrect because the phrase beginning <u>in</u> makes no sense. (D) is wrong because the phrase beginning <u>in</u> is also nonsense. (E) is incorrect because the resulting sentence is illogical.

126. **D.** Choice (D), the way the sentence appears in the paragraph, is the correct choice. Any of the changes suggested in (A), (B), (C), and (E) would omit important information or create a sentence which does not make sense.

127. **C.** (A) is incorrect as a possible overstatement. (B) is incorrect, because it seems to contradict what the whole paragraph says. (D) and (E) are incorrect because they mention only Krukow and Bobby Mercer, not Bruce Sutter whose feats are highlighted in the paragraph.

128. **B.** Placing the material in choice (B) at the beginning of the sentence would be effective. (A) is incorrect because the sentence would imply that the herbs and plants would be dangerous inside the health food stores and nowhere else. (C) is incorrect because of the substitution of <u>all</u> for <u>some</u> in the original sentence. (D) is incorrect because <u>causing</u> death is an overstatement of the original idea. (E) is incorrect because this beginning would create a very weak sentence.

129. **E.** Any change in the wording or placement of the sentence would be incorrect.

130. **D.** (A) is incorrect as an overstatement. (B) is incorrect because it is an assertion not supported by the information in the paragraph. (C) and (E) are incorrect because they would use a minor point at the end of the paragraph.

PART TWO

THE HUMANITIES EXAMINATION

Trial Test

The Humanities examination measures your knowledge of literature, the visual arts, music, the performing arts, and architecture. The examination is divided into two parts, each containing 75 questions. On the CLEP examination you are given 45 minutes for each part.

Take the Trial Test and check your answers, thus finding out how you would score before you review any material or practice the type of questions asked.

Part I

Directions: Each of the questions or incomplete statements below is followed by five suggested answers or completions. Select the one that is best in each case.

Number of Questions: 75
Time: 45 minutes

1. Expressionism in art has most to do with
   (A) the intellect   (B) the emotions   (C) the dreamworld
   (D) geometric forfms   (E) decorative line

   1. Ⓐ Ⓑ Ⓒ Ⓓ Ⓔ

2. The Impressionists were least concerned with
   (A) the effects of light   (B) informal treatment of subject matter
   (C) painting out-of-doors   (D) interpenetration of forms
   (E) broken application of color

   2. Ⓐ Ⓑ Ⓒ Ⓓ Ⓔ

3. The length of a vibrating string or a column of air and the pitch either produces was the beginning of the science of
   (A) logarithms   (B) rhythms   (C) acoustics   (D) theory   (E) fuguery

   3. Ⓐ Ⓑ Ⓒ Ⓓ Ⓔ

4. The man who, practically single-handedly, unified the ballet and founded French opera was
   (A) Lully   (B) Glinka   (C) Gluck   (D) Massenet   (E) Offenbach

   4. Ⓐ Ⓑ Ⓒ Ⓓ Ⓔ

5. An important architect of the Romantic period was
   (A) Walter Gropius   (B) Christopher Wren   (C) James Wyatt
   (D) Joseph Paxton   (E) Henri Labrouste

   5. Ⓐ Ⓑ Ⓒ Ⓓ Ⓔ

6. Ibsen did not write
   (A) plays about contemporary people (B) plays with realistic settings
   (C) plays employing well-made structure   (D) comedies of manners
   (E) thesis plays

   6. Ⓐ Ⓑ Ⓒ Ⓓ Ⓔ

7. The release of emotions and the attaining of tranquility therefrom in the theater is called
   (A) pyramidal plot structure
   (B) the author's use of hubris
   (C) the audience escaping dull lives by identifying with kings, aristocrats, and famous people
   (D) empathy
   (E) catharsis

   7. Ⓐ Ⓑ Ⓒ Ⓓ Ⓔ

8. One of the most characteristic types of 18th-century literature was the
   (A) novella   (B) epic   (C) nature poem
   (D) periodical essay   (E) thesis play

   8. Ⓐ Ⓑ Ⓒ Ⓓ Ⓔ

9. Harriet Beecher Stowe unwittingly became a pioneer in her "propaganda novel" when she wrote
   (A) *Erewhon*   (B) *A Man's Woman*   (C) *The Female Quixote*
   (D) *Uncle Tom's Cabin*   (E) *The Mysterious Stranger*

   9. Ⓐ Ⓑ Ⓒ Ⓓ Ⓔ

10. "Bring in my bow of burning gold" is an example of
    (A) dissonance   (B) alliteration   (C) assonance
    (D) masculine rhyme   (E) feminine rhyme

    10. Ⓐ Ⓑ Ⓒ Ⓓ Ⓔ

11. Stravinsky's "Rite of Spring"
    (A) is a Baroque-style program piece
    (B) was called the destruction of music
    (C) is representative of the Classical styles
    (D) is in sonata-allegro form
    (E) is a symphony

    11. Ⓐ Ⓑ Ⓒ Ⓓ Ⓔ

12. An instrumental form usually associated with opera is
    (A) the overture   (B) the symphony   (C) the suite
    (D) the tone poem   (E) the cadenza

    12. Ⓐ Ⓑ Ⓒ Ⓓ Ⓔ

13. Prehistoric cave art was
    (A) executed at about the time of the pyramids
    (B) contemporary with archaic Greek art
    (C) contemporary with the discovery of metals
    (D) accomplished 15,000 to 20,000 years ago
    (E) accomplished from about 900 to 1,000 A.D.

    13. Ⓐ Ⓑ Ⓒ Ⓓ Ⓔ

14. Paintings which reflect an interest in the fantastic, dream associations, and the impossible are most likely to be executed by
    (A) Cezanne, van Gogh, Toulouse-Lautrec
    (B) Gris, Braque, Picasso
    (C) Dali, Miro, de Chirico
    (D) Pollack, Motherwell, Mondrian
    (E) Renoir, Degas, Seurat

    14. Ⓐ Ⓑ Ⓒ Ⓓ Ⓔ

15. Samuel Langhorne Clemens was the real name of writer
    (A) William Faulkner   (B) O. Henry   (C) Henry James
    (D) T. S. Eliot   (E) Mark Twain

    15. Ⓐ Ⓑ Ⓒ Ⓓ Ⓔ

Questions 16 and 17 are based on this quotation:

"O mother, mother, make my bed,
O make it soft and narrow:
Since my love died for me today,
I'll die for him tomorrow."

16. Which of the following describes these lines? 16. Ⓐ Ⓑ Ⓒ Ⓓ Ⓔ
    (A) a couplet   (B) a triolet   (C) a quatrain   (D) a tercet
    (E) a sestet

17. The lines are from the ballad 17. Ⓐ Ⓑ Ⓒ Ⓓ Ⓔ
    (A) "Sir Patrick Spens"   (B) "Barbara Allen"   (C) "Lord Randall"
    (D) "The Three Ravens"   (E) "Robin Hood and the Three Squires"

18. Pop art refers to 18. Ⓐ Ⓑ Ⓒ Ⓓ Ⓔ
    (A) musical themes
    (B) abstract expressionism
    (C) contemporary materialism and commercialism
    (D) the religious revival in contemporary art
    (E) a return to classicism

19. The first to dedicate their art to the beauty of life were the 19. Ⓐ Ⓑ Ⓒ Ⓓ Ⓔ
    (A) Egyptians   (B) Renaissance artists   (C) Romans
    (D) Greeks   (E) French impressionists

20. Frank Lloyd Wright's basic role in architecture was 20. Ⓐ Ⓑ Ⓒ Ⓓ Ⓔ
    (A) to build a structure that was inexpensive
    (B) to use a minimum of materials
    (C) to build a structure in harmony with the past
    (D) to build a structure as if it grew out of the ground
    (E) to build a structure that overpowers man and nature

21. The creator of the essay as a genre was 21. Ⓐ Ⓑ Ⓒ Ⓓ Ⓔ
    (A) Voltaire   (B) Johnson   (C) Addison   (D) Defoe
    (E) Montaigne

22. One of the greatest of the Middle High German epics is 22. Ⓐ Ⓑ Ⓒ Ⓓ Ⓔ
    (A) *The Nibelungenlied*   (B) *The Story of Sigurd the Volsung*
    (C) *Beowulf*   (D) *The Vikings at Helgeland*   (E) *The Valkyrie*

23. A famous overture often associated with graduation exercises was 23. Ⓐ Ⓑ Ⓒ Ⓓ Ⓔ
    written by
    (A) Brahms   (B) Condon   (C) Gluck   (D) Palestrina   (E) Haydn

24. A famous jazz guitarist of the 1940s was 24. Ⓐ Ⓑ Ⓒ Ⓓ Ⓔ
    (A) F. Waller   (B) B. Davidson   (C) E. Condon
    (D) J. Teagarden   (E) M. Feld

25. Shakespeare was noted for all but one of the following: 25. Ⓐ Ⓑ Ⓒ Ⓓ Ⓔ
    (A) comedies   (B) tragedies   (C) bourgeois dramas
    (D) histories   (E) tragi-comedies

26. Chekhov's plays are noted for 26. Ⓐ Ⓑ Ⓒ Ⓓ Ⓔ
    (A) exaggerated elocution
    (B) florid gesturing

    (C) upper-class problems and characters

    (D) a lack of strong plotting to reproduce a "slice of life"

    (E) elaborate costumes

27. The "father" of Greek tragedy was   27. A B C D E

    (A) Aristotle   (B) Sophocles   (C) Euripides

    (D) Aeschylus   (E) Aristophanes

28. All but one of the following are parts of the Greek theater: 28. A B C D E

    (A) eccyclema   (B) skene   (C) deus ex machina

    (D) orchestra   (E) movable panels

29. To musicians, the theme of "The Lone Ranger" is better known as   29. A B C D E

    (A) Rossini's "William Tell Overture"

    (B) Beethoven's "Fifth Symphony"

    (C) Bach's "Variations on a Fugue in D Minor"

    (D) Handel's "Messiah"

    (E) Tchaikovsky's "Swan Lake"

30. "Western" man or civilization refers to   30. A B C D E

    (A) the Western hemisphere

    (B) our present cultural tradition going back about 4,000 years

    (C) a force of history which always moves to the west

    (D) Europe

    (E) Europe and the United States, exclusive of Russia

31. Richard Strauss is best known for his   31. A B C D E

    (A) fugues   (B) motets   (C) waltzes   (D) madrigals

    (E) tone poems

32. Albert Camus, French existentialist writer, believed that the only real   32. A B C D E
    philosophical problem was that of suicide. What Shakespearean
    character expresses this same thought?

    (A) Iago   (B) Cleopatra   (C) Hamlet   (D) Caliban

    (E) Julius Caesar

33. Cubism is indebted to the pioneering work of   33. A B C D E

    (A) Pollack   (B) Cezanne   (C) van Gogh   (D) Munch   (E) Hals

34. One of the following is not a stylistic (formal) element of Cubism: 34. A B C D E

    (A) compressed or "flat" space

    (B) multiple perspective

    (C) atmospheric perspective

    (D) interpenetration of line, color, and shape

    (E) an equal stress on negative and positive areas

35. Ishmael is the narrator of   35. A B C D E

    (A) *The Return of the Native* (B) *Moby Dick* (C) *Wuthering Heights*

    (D) *The Mayor of Casterbridge*   (E) *Jane Eyre*

36. All of the following short stories were written by Edgar Allan Poe   36. A B C D E
    except

    (A) "The Fall of the House of Usher"

(B) "The Murders in the Rue Morgue"
(C) "Rappaccini's Daughter"
(D) "The Purloined Letter"
(E) "The Cask of Amontillado"

37. Sculpture is the art of   37. Ⓐ Ⓑ Ⓒ Ⓓ Ⓔ
   (A) making life-like figures   (B) making statues of heroes
   (C) making memorials to heroes   (D) cutting stone and marble
   (E) composing in mass and space

38. *Poor Richard's Almanac* was written by   38. Ⓐ Ⓑ Ⓒ Ⓓ Ⓔ
   (A) Walt Whitman   (B) Benjamin Franklin
   (C) Jonathan Edwards   (D) E. A. Robinson   (E) Thomas Paine

39. The beginning of the Renaissance may be traced to the city of   39. Ⓐ Ⓑ Ⓒ Ⓓ Ⓔ
   (A) Rome   (B) San Miniate   (C) Venice   (D) Florence
   (E) Hackensack

40. The "School of Lyon" was   40. Ⓐ Ⓑ Ⓒ Ⓓ Ⓔ
   (A) a 16th-century group of Neo-Platonist and Petrarchan poets
   (B) an 18th-century artistic movement
   (C) the college attended by Hugo and de Maupassant
   (D) a chamber music society founded by Massenet
   (E) an attempt to establish a classical spirit in French painting

41. The first most completely American naturalistic novel, *Maggie: A*   41. Ⓐ Ⓑ Ⓒ Ⓓ Ⓔ
Girl of the Streets, was written by
   (A) Anderson   (B) Garland   (C) Norris   (D) Crane
   (E) Robinson

42. The painters Renoir, Monet, and Pissaro were   42. Ⓐ Ⓑ Ⓒ Ⓓ Ⓔ
   (A) Expressionists   (B) Cubists   (C) Mannerists
   (D) Impressionists   (E) Surrealists

43. The Romans made special use of   43. Ⓐ Ⓑ Ⓒ Ⓓ Ⓔ
   (A) post and lintel construction
   (B) friezes carved over temple doorways
   (C) the rounded arch   (D) the pointed arch   (E) tempera painting

44. In music, a smooth transition from key to key is known as   44. Ⓐ Ⓑ Ⓒ Ⓓ Ⓔ
   (A) modulation   (B) constructioning   (C) harmony
   (D) invention   (E) translation

45. All of the following deal with the Trojan War or the men who fought   45. Ⓐ Ⓑ Ⓒ Ⓓ Ⓔ
in that war except
   (A) *The Odyssey*   (B) *Agamemnon*   (C) *The Iliad*
   (D) *Oedipus the King*   (E) *The Aeneid*

46. The following are periods in art history. Which group is not in chrono-   46. Ⓐ Ⓑ Ⓒ Ⓓ Ⓔ
logical order?
   (A) Baroque, French Romanticism, Impressionism
   (B) Abstract Expressionism, Pop Art, Op Art
   (C) Gothic, Baroque, Renaissance
   (D) Egyptian, Greek, Roman
   (E) prehistoric, Egyptian, Greek

47. The first major American author to be born west of the Mississippi was
   (A) William Dean Howells   (B) Walt Whitman
   (C) Carl Sandburg   (D) Mark Twain   (E) Ellen Glasgow

47. Ⓐ Ⓑ Ⓒ Ⓓ Ⓔ

48. "Twas brillig, and the slithy toves, Did gyre and gimble in the wabe," is an example of
   (A) *vers de société*   (D) shaped verse
   (B) nonsense verse   (E) Goliardic verse
   (C) a limerick

48. Ⓐ Ⓑ Ⓒ Ⓓ Ⓔ

49. Farcical interludes in dramas
   (A) developed during the Middle Ages
   (B) dealt with sin
   (C) were essentially romantic comedies
   (D) developed during the Renaissance
   (E) adhered to the unities of time, place, and action

49. Ⓐ Ⓑ Ⓒ Ⓓ Ⓔ

50. *The Decameron*, like *The Canterbury Tales*, has a specific dramatic framework. However, instead of pilgrims journeying to Canterbury, *The Decameron* has seven women and three men withdrawing from their native city for what purpose?
   (A) To seek the Holy Grail
   (B) To visit the Pope
   (C) To see Charles the Great
   (D) To make a pilgrimage to the tomb of Abelard
   (E) To escape the Black Death

50. Ⓐ Ⓑ Ⓒ Ⓓ Ⓔ

51. "All pigs are equal, but some pigs are more equal than others" is reminiscent of what novel?
   (A) *Lassie, Come Home*   (B) *The Red Pony*
   (C) *Federico and his Falcon*   (D) *Animal Farm*
   (E) *A Day at the Zoo*

51. Ⓐ Ⓑ Ⓒ Ⓓ Ⓔ

52. The "New World Symphony" was composed by
   (A) Anton Dvořák   (B) George M. Cohan
   (C) Edward McDowell   (D) Aaron Copeland   (E) Ferde Grofe

52. Ⓐ Ⓑ Ⓒ Ⓓ Ⓔ

53. "The Grand Canyon Suite" was composed by
   (A) Anton Dvořák   (B) George M. Cohan
   (C) Edward McDowell   (D) Aaron Copeland   (E) Ferde Grofe

53. Ⓐ Ⓑ Ⓒ Ⓓ Ⓔ

54. The medieval architect symbolized God's presence in the cathedral by
   (A) creating great areas of interior space
   (B) embellishing the surface with great columns and lacy decorations
   (C) the creation of the choir and high altar areas
   (D) combining the arts of painting and freestanding sculpture
   (E) placing gargoyles atop the roof to ward off evil spirits

54. Ⓐ Ⓑ Ⓒ Ⓓ Ⓔ

55. "The lost generation" refers to those who lived during the period
   (A) 1900-1915   (B) 1920-1940   (C) 1940-1950
   (D) 1950-1960   (E) 1960-1970

55. Ⓐ Ⓑ Ⓒ Ⓓ Ⓔ

56. A leader of the "beat generation" was
   (A) Ernest Hemingway   (B) John Steinbeck
   (C) Jack Kerouac   (D) Ring Lardner
   (E) Flannery O'Connor

56. Ⓐ Ⓑ Ⓒ Ⓓ Ⓔ

57. A short narrative from which a moral can be drawn is
   (A) a parable   (B) an anecdote   (C) an abstraction
   (D) an aphorism   (E) a frame story

57. Ⓐ Ⓑ Ⓒ Ⓓ Ⓔ

58. Lascaux and Altamira are
   (A) the names of two French Gothic cathedrals
   (B) two painters working in a surrealistic style
   (C) caves in which prehistoric paintings have been found
   (D) mythological subjects used by Pierre Cott in "The Tempest"
   (E) leaders in the Fauve movement

58. Ⓐ Ⓑ Ⓒ Ⓓ Ⓔ

59. A feeling of unrest and tension in a painting can be achieved by a powerful emphasis upon
   (A) horizontal line   (B) vertical line   (C) parallel line
   (D) diagonal line   (E) linear grid pattern

59. Ⓐ Ⓑ Ⓒ Ⓓ Ⓔ

60. The way in which we perceive abstractly is largely determined by
   (A) cultural conditioning   (B) memory learning
   (C) individual genes   (D) intellectual association
   (E) abstract behavior patterns

60. Ⓐ Ⓑ Ⓒ Ⓓ Ⓔ

61. One of the first American "troubadors" and minstrels was
   (A) Vachel Lindsay   (B) Edward McDowell
   (C) John Knowles Pain   (D) Aaron Copeland
   (E) Stephen Foster

61. Ⓐ Ⓑ Ⓒ Ⓓ Ⓔ

62. An early American statesman, writer, inventor, and foreign correspondent, also known as the first American music critic, was
   (A) Paul Revere   (B) Cotton Mather   (C) Benjamin Franklin
   (D) Thomas Jefferson   (E) Patrick Henry

62. Ⓐ Ⓑ Ⓒ Ⓓ Ⓔ

63. "I have measured out my life with coffee spoons," said
   (A) Benjamin Compson   (B) Lady Brett Ashley
   (C) Scarlet O'Hara   (D) Phillip Jordan
   (E) J. Alfred Prufrock

63. Ⓐ Ⓑ Ⓒ Ⓓ Ⓔ

64. A " mystery cycle " may best be described as
   (A) based upon scriptures
   (B) basically religious
   (C) short biblical plays produced outside the church
   (D) performed by the guilds
   (E) all of the above

64. Ⓐ Ⓑ Ⓒ Ⓓ Ⓔ

65. A writer who brought about many social reforms in 19th-century England through his passionate writings was
   (A) Hobbes   (B) Pater   (C) Hardy   (D) Dickens
   (E) Wilde

65. Ⓐ Ⓑ Ⓒ Ⓓ Ⓔ

66. A satire on the medieval chivalric code is
    (A) *Don Quixote*   (B) *Gulliver's Travels*   (C) *Candide*
    (D) *Idylls of the King*   (E) *Erewhon*

66. Ⓐ Ⓑ Ⓒ Ⓓ Ⓔ

67. One of the most popular English painters of the 18th century, noted
    for his society portraits, was
    (A) John Singleton Copley   (D) John Constable
    (B) Sir Edward Burne-Jones   (E) William Blake
    (C) Thomas Gainsborough

67. Ⓐ Ⓑ Ⓒ Ⓓ Ⓔ

68. Included among Johann Sebastian Bach's great works is
    (A) "The Well-Tempered Clavier"   (B) "The Pathetique Sonata"
    (C) *The Student Prince*   (D) "The Unfinished Symphony"
    (E) *Der Rosenkavalier*

68. Ⓐ Ⓑ Ⓒ Ⓓ Ⓔ

69. Included among Beethoven's great works is
    (A) "The Symphonie Espagnole"   (D) *The Messiah*
    (B) "The Moonlight Sonata"   (E) "The Minute Waltz"
    (C) "The Mass in B Minor"

69. Ⓐ Ⓑ Ⓒ Ⓓ Ⓔ

70. Nicknamed "Red," the man who became famous for his novels about
    "main street" America was
    (A) Ernest Hemingway   (B) John Steinbeck
    (C) Sinclair Lewis   (D) Upton Sinclair
    (E) Booth Tarkington

70. Ⓐ Ⓑ Ⓒ Ⓓ Ⓔ

71. The creative process is
    (A) limited to art   (D) limited to the arts and sciences
    (B) limited to art and music   (E) not limited
    (C) limited to the humanities

71. Ⓐ Ⓑ Ⓒ Ⓓ Ⓔ

72. Of the Greek playwrights, Euripides is considered the most "modern"
    because he
    (A) usually disregards the unities
    (B) concentrates on message rather than moments
    (C) does not use women as protagonists
    (D) stresses his belief in reform
    (E) is most psychological in his treatment of conflict

72. Ⓐ Ⓑ Ⓒ Ⓓ Ⓔ

73. Nearly every character in his plays is at one time or another the hero
    of a tiny "microscosmic" drama that has a beginning, middle, and an
    end in itself, but does not become the basis for the total plot. He is
    (A) George Bernard Shaw   (D) Anton Chekhov
    (B) Henrik Ibsen   (E) Oscar Wilde
    (C) Arthur Miller

73. Ⓐ Ⓑ Ⓒ Ⓓ Ⓔ

74. The opera *I Pagliacci* was written by
    (A) Puccini   (B) Leoncavallo   (C) Mascagni
    (D) Verdi   (E) Mozart

74. Ⓐ Ⓑ Ⓒ Ⓓ Ⓔ

75. Beethoven's *Eroica* is his Symphony Number
    (A) One   (B) Three   (C) Five   (D) Seven   (E) Nine

75. Ⓐ Ⓑ Ⓒ Ⓓ Ⓔ

Part II

Number of Questions: 75
Time: 45 minutes

76. The photograph is

(A) Nike of Samothrace
(B) Venus de Milo
(C) Mercury
(D) Apollo Belvedere
(E) Dionysius

76. A B C D E

Hirmer Fotoarchiv Munchen

77. The audiences who attended Shakespeare's plays were

(A) aristocrats who enjoyed occasionally letting their hair down
(B) commoners who had aristocratic taste in poetry
(C) primarily drawn from the middle classes
(D) a mixture of all classes
(E) the most tightly knit "in group" in the history of the theater

77. A B C D E

78. All of the following represent serious barriers to critical perception of plays and films except

(A) failing to remember that a drama is not reality
(B) viewing the drama in terms of a particular occupation with which the viewer is familiar
(C) reacting to the characterization of an ethnic type
(D) accepting the drama on its own terms without any bias
(E) entering the theater with the expectation of seeing one's moral values upheld

78. A B C D E

79. All of the following painters were called by critics "Fauve" or "wild beasts" except

(A) Matisse   (B) Dufy   (C) Vlaminck   (D) Rouault
(E) Gauguin

79. A B C D E

80. The chief exponent of pointillism was

(A) Cezanne   (B) Monet   (C) de Chirico   (D) Courbet
(E) Seurat

80. A B C D E

81. A leading rock group of the late 1960s took its name from the title of a novel by a German author who died in 1962 and whose works have recently won a new following. The book and the author are
(A) *Steppenwolf* by Herman Hesse
(B) *Death in Venice* by Thomas Mann
(C) *The Weavers* by Gerhart Hauptmanr
(D) *Siddhartha* by Herman Hesse
(E) *The Castle* by Franz Kafka

81. Ⓐ Ⓑ Ⓒ Ⓓ Ⓔ

82. A chromatic scale is
(A) all half steps played in order
(B) every other half step played in order
(C) no half steps played
(D) only half steps played
(E) all full steps played in order

82. Ⓐ Ⓑ Ⓒ Ⓓ Ⓔ

83. The text of one of Haydn's greatest cantatas comes from Genesis and Milton's *Paradise Lost.* Its title is
(A) *Jesus and Lucifer*
(B) *Exodus*
(C) *The Victory of Jeremiah*
(D) *The Creation*
(E) *The Three Temptations*

83. Ⓐ Ⓑ Ⓒ Ⓓ Ⓔ

84. The world's first free-lance composer was
(A) Franz Liszt   (B) Franco Pizzicato   (C) Giacomo Puccini
(D) Sidney Bechet   (E) Wolfgang Amadeus Mozart

84. Ⓐ Ⓑ Ⓒ Ⓓ Ⓔ

85. All except one of the following 20th-century American authors have used materials from their Jewish backgrounds. The one exception is
(A) Phillip Roth   (B) Saul Bellow   (C) John Updike
(D) Paul Goodman   (E) Bernard Malamud

85. Ⓐ Ⓑ Ⓒ Ⓓ Ⓔ

86. Most basic to a fundamental appreciation of art are
(A) seeing and feeling
(B) words and descriptions
(C) knowing the life of the artist and understanding his ethnic background
(D) understanding the theories of art and their corollaries
(E) courses in art history

86. Ⓐ Ⓑ Ⓒ Ⓓ Ⓔ

87. "Comfort ye, comfort ye, my people," saith your God. "Speak ye comfortably to Jerusalem, and cry unto her, that her warfare is accomplished, that her iniquity is pardoned."
The quotation is a portion of the libretto of Handel's *The Messiah* and was taken directly from the Bible. The source was
(A) Amos   (B) Misab   (C) Isaiah   (D) Ezekiel
(E) Hosea

87. Ⓐ Ⓑ Ⓒ Ⓓ Ⓔ

Questions 88–90 refer to the following groups of people.

(A) John Williams, Bert Bacharach, Henry Mancini
(B) Sir George Solti, Andre Previn, Leonard Bernstein
(C) Pearl Buck, William Faulkner, Sinclair Lewis
(D) Andy Warhol, Joan Miro, Claes Oldenburg
(E) Twyla Tharp, Michael Bennett, Gower Champion

88. Which is a group of contemporary symphony conductors?

88. Ⓐ Ⓑ Ⓒ Ⓓ Ⓔ

89. Which is a group of novelists who won the Nobel Prize for Literature?

89. Ⓐ Ⓑ Ⓒ Ⓓ Ⓔ

90. Which is a group of choreographers for Broadway musicals of the 1970s and 1980s?

90. Ⓐ Ⓑ Ⓒ Ⓓ Ⓔ

91. *The Great Gatsby* was written by
(A) Emerson   (B) Lewis   (C) Dreiser
(D) Dos Passos   (E) Fitzgerald

91. Ⓐ Ⓑ Ⓒ Ⓓ Ⓔ

92. All of the following are children in *Oedipus the King* except
(A) Antigone   (B) Ismene   (C) Polynices   (D) Eteocles
(E) Theseus

92. Ⓐ Ⓑ Ⓒ Ⓓ Ⓔ

93. *Kiss Me Kate* is based upon William Shakespeare's play
(A) *Romeo and Juliet*   (B) *The Winter's Tale*
(C) *A Midsummer Night's Dream*   (D) *The Tempest*
(E) *The Taming of the Shrew*

93. Ⓐ Ⓑ Ⓒ Ⓓ Ⓔ

94. The artist van Gogh wrote that he
(A) did his best not to put in detail
(B) avoided using black altogether
(C) could only paint when he was nervous
(D) became an artist in order to travel and see the world
(E) became an artist in order to prove he was sane

94. Ⓐ Ⓑ Ⓒ Ⓓ Ⓔ

95. The musical notation 𝄞 indicates
(A) the bass clef   (B) crescendo   (C) pianissimo
(D) the treble clef   (E) 1/2 time

95. Ⓐ Ⓑ Ⓒ Ⓓ Ⓔ

96. A term used to describe choral music without instrumental accompaniment is
(A) cantilena   (B) a cappella   (C) enharmonic
(D) appoggiatura   (E) oratorio

96. Ⓐ Ⓑ Ⓒ Ⓓ Ⓔ

97. All of the following are part of Wagner's cycle of operas *Der Ring des Nibelungen* except
(A) *Das Rheingold*
(B) *Die Walkure*
(C) *Die Meistersinger von Nurnberg*
(D) *Siegfried*
(E) *Die Gotterdammerung*

97. Ⓐ Ⓑ Ⓒ Ⓓ Ⓔ

98. The name Phidias belongs with
   (A) the Romantic period
   (B) the Renaissance
   (C) the Middle Ages
   (D) the marble statues of the Greek Parthenon
   (E) Roman portrait painting

98. Ⓐ Ⓑ Ⓒ Ⓓ Ⓔ

99. Baroque architecture is characterized by
   (A) severe simplicity
   (B) ornamentation and curved lines
   (C) post and lintel construction
   (D) steel and re-enforced concrete
   (E) low, heavy domes

99. Ⓐ Ⓑ Ⓒ Ⓓ Ⓔ

100. A good definition of art is
   (A) significant form
   (B) a production or procession of images expressing the personality of the artist
   (C) a reflection in visual form of the philosophy and culture of the period
   (D) nature seen through the emotion and intellect of man
   (E) all of the above

100. Ⓐ Ⓑ Ⓒ Ⓓ Ⓔ

101. The first spoken line by Hamlet in the play is an aside: "A little more than kin, and less than kind." By this line, he indicates that
   (A) he already suspects Claudius of some sort of duplicity
   (B) he already knows that Claudius has killed his father
   (C) he already has designs on the throne
   (D) he is already plotting revenge
   (E) since he is not related by blood to Claudius, he intends his remark to be interpreted as madness

101. Ⓐ Ⓑ Ⓒ Ⓓ Ⓔ

102. The Connecticut Wits
   (A) were devoted to the modernization of the Yale curriculum and the declaration of independence of American letters from British influences
   (B) favored Unitarianism and Transcendentalism
   (C) included Timothy Dwight, John Trumbull, and Joel Barlow
   (D) all of the above
   (E) A and C above

102. Ⓐ Ⓑ Ⓒ Ⓓ Ⓔ

103. Phaedra lusted for her stepson
   (A) Oedipus   (B) Theseus   (C) Orestes
   (D) Hippolytus   (E) Jason

103. Ⓐ Ⓑ Ⓒ Ⓓ Ⓔ

104. The creator of Charlie Brown is
   (A) Bud Blake   (B) Al Capp   (C) Charles Schulz
   (D) Alex Kotsby   (E) Fred Lasswell

104. Ⓐ Ⓑ Ⓒ Ⓓ Ⓔ

105. "Each narrow cell in which we dwell" provides an example of
   (A) alliteration   (B) internal rhyme   (C) sprung rhythm
   (D) end rhyme   (E) spondaic trimeter

105. Ⓐ Ⓑ Ⓒ Ⓓ Ⓔ

106. A playwright who wrote a modern comic-psychological version of *Antigone* is
    (A) Arthur Miller   (B) Jean Anouilh   (C) Edward Albee
    (D) Jean-Paul Sartre   (E) Georges Clemenceau

106. Ⓐ Ⓑ Ⓒ Ⓓ Ⓔ

107. This is an example of
    (A) Mesopotamian sculpture
    (B) Egyptian sculpture
    (C) Indian sculpture
    (D) prehistoric sculpture
    (E) modern sculpture

107. Ⓐ Ⓑ Ⓒ Ⓓ Ⓔ

Estate of David Smith, courtesy of Marlborough
Gallery, New York

108. Molière's audiences were predominantly
    (A) peasants
    (B) a great cross-section of the population
    (C) people pretending to a higher station in life
    (D) aristocrats
    (E) middle class only

108. Ⓐ Ⓑ Ⓒ Ⓓ Ⓔ

109. Edgar Allan Poe believed a short story should
    (A) be sufficiently short to permit the reader to finish the work in a single sitting
    (B) have a surprise ending
    (C) delight and instruct the reader
    (D) have complicated characters
    (E) be realistic

109. Ⓐ Ⓑ Ⓒ Ⓓ Ⓔ

110. The term *genre* is a French word meaning
    (A) plot   (B) category   (C) climax   (D) story
    (E) introduction

110. Ⓐ Ⓑ Ⓒ Ⓓ Ⓔ

111. What Renaissance writer do you associate with the Abbey of Theleme?
    (A) Castiglione   (B) Shakespeare   (C) Ariosto
    (D) Rabelais   (E) Cervantes

111. Ⓐ Ⓑ Ⓒ Ⓓ Ⓔ

112. Niccolo Machiavelli is primarily known for *The Prince* and *Discourses*. However, he was also a playwright. A classic of Italian dramatic literature is his comedy
    (A) *The Betrothed*
    (B) *Cesare Borgia*
    (C) *Mandragola*
    (D) *The Princess of Mantua*
    (E) *Bitter Rice*

112. Ⓐ Ⓑ Ⓒ Ⓓ Ⓔ

113. A 19th-century novelist who anticipated many 20th-century discoveries and inventions was
(A) T. H. Huxley   (B) Mary Shelley   (C) Thomas Hardy
(D) Jules Verne   (E) Bram Stoker

113. Ⓐ Ⓑ Ⓒ Ⓓ Ⓔ

114. According to tradition, who wrote *The Odyssey* and *The Iliad?*
(A) Achilles   (B) Tacitus   (C) Homer   (D) Vergil
(E) Thucydides

114. Ⓐ Ⓑ Ⓒ Ⓓ Ⓔ

115. A form of music drama without stage action, of which Handel became a master, is the
(A) oratorio   (B) opera   (C) cantata   (D) castrati
(E) duet

115. Ⓐ Ⓑ Ⓒ Ⓓ Ⓔ

116. To play a musical composition, each musician must have a copy of the notes. The conductor has a similar copy, called the
(A) score   (B) libretto   (C) manuscript   (D) theme
(E) thesis

116. Ⓐ Ⓑ Ⓒ Ⓓ Ⓔ

117. The theme of John Steinbeck's *In Dubious Battle* is
(A) the exodus of the Okies from Oklahoma
(B) the growth of labor unions in America
(C) what modern America is like
(D) the Negro's fight for freedom
(E) World War II

117. Ⓐ Ⓑ Ⓒ Ⓓ Ⓔ

118. An Aeschylean dramatic pattern made possible the first true plays because it introduced
(A) villainy   (B) humanism   (C) plausibility
(D) conflict between two characters   (E) the family theme

118. Ⓐ Ⓑ Ⓒ Ⓓ Ⓔ

119. The portrait was painted by
(A) da Vinci
(B) Delacroix
(C) van Gogh
(D) Michelangelo
(E) Dali

Roger Viollet

119. Ⓐ Ⓑ Ⓒ Ⓓ Ⓔ

120. In the play *Medea*, what was the name of Jason's ship?
(A) *Tiki*   (B) *Pelias*   (C) *Dreadnaught*   (D) *Medea*
(E) *Argo*

120. Ⓐ Ⓑ Ⓒ Ⓓ Ⓔ

121. Why did Jason set sail on his fateful voyage?
(A) To search for the Golden Fleece
(B) To make war on Sparta
(C) To destroy the port of Colchis
(D) In search of the Holy Grail
(E) To put a stop to pirateering

121. Ⓐ Ⓑ Ⓒ Ⓓ Ⓔ

122. The first permanent stringed orchestra in Europe, introduced during the reign of Louis XIV, was called the
(A) Chapelle   (B) Twenty-four Viols   (C) Grand Ecurie
(D) Chambre   (E) Academy

122. Ⓐ Ⓑ Ⓒ Ⓓ Ⓔ

123. The architect associated with St. Paul's Cathedral is
(A) Inigo Jones   (B) Christopher Wren   (C) Le Corbusier
(D) Frank Lloyd Wright   (E) Walter Gropius

123. Ⓐ Ⓑ Ⓒ Ⓓ Ⓔ

124. The opening scene of Shakespeare's *Henry IV, Part I* establishes for the audience that
(A) all is well in England
(B) a pilgrimage to the Holy Land is in progress
(C) it is raining
(D) the king has two major problems confronting him
(E) the king is dead

124. Ⓐ Ⓑ Ⓒ Ⓓ Ⓔ

125. Byzantine art was a major contribution to the world because of its
(A) sculpture   (B) portraits   (C) armor   (D) mosaics
(E) glassware

125. Ⓐ Ⓑ Ⓒ Ⓓ Ⓔ

126. The variety of styles in modern art is a reflection of
(A) the complexity of modern life
(B) a lack of purpose
(C) a loss of values
(D) foreign influence
(E) our susceptibility to sensationalism and fads

126. Ⓐ Ⓑ Ⓒ Ⓓ Ⓔ

127. The top notes of a yodel are sung in
(A) bel canto   (B) vibrato   (C) contralto   (D) falsetto
(E) absolute pitch

127. Ⓐ Ⓑ Ⓒ Ⓓ Ⓔ

128. The poem "Trees" was written by
(A) E. E. Cummings   (B) Edna St. Vincent Millay
(C) Joyce Kilmer   (D) Lawrence Ferlinghetti
(E) John Frederick Nims

128. Ⓐ Ⓑ Ⓒ Ⓓ Ⓔ

129. Voltaire's Candide journeyed from continent to continent to find his elusive Cunegonde, whose chief virtue was
(A) beauty   (B) physical indestructibility   (C) piety
(D) faithfulness   (E) mental alertness

129. Ⓐ Ⓑ Ⓒ Ⓓ Ⓔ

130. *The Tales of Hoffman* were written by
(A) De Maistre   (B) Bierce   (C) Poe   (D) Hoffman
(E) Irving

130. Ⓐ Ⓑ Ⓒ Ⓓ Ⓔ

131. The operatic setting for *The Tales of Hoffman* was written by   131. Ⓐ Ⓑ Ⓒ Ⓓ Ⓔ
  (A) Offenbach   (B) Adam   (C) Rimsky-Korsakoff
  (D) Schubert   (E) Schumann

132. When the Christian Church came into power after the fall of the   132. Ⓐ Ⓑ Ⓒ Ⓓ Ⓔ
  Roman Empire, it
  (A) used professional actors to perform plays
  (B) urged the wealthy to sponsor acting groups
  (C) emphasized the "here" rather than the "hereafter"
  (D) abolished all theatrical activities
  (E) began putting on plays in the church itself

133. The death of Seneca in 65 A.D. marks the   133. Ⓐ Ⓑ Ⓒ Ⓓ Ⓔ
  (A) end of the Roman Empire
  (B) beginning of creative playwrighting
  (C) end of creative playwrighting until the Middle Ages
  (D) beginning of the Middle Ages
  (E) birth of comedy

134. Which of the following, written during the Revolutionary period, is   134. Ⓐ Ⓑ Ⓒ Ⓓ Ⓔ
  often considered the first American novel?
  (A) *McTeague*   (B) *Moby Dick*   (C) *Huckleberry Finn*
  (D) *Golden Wedding*   (E) *The Power of Sympathy*

135. The Artful Dodger is a character in the novel   135. Ⓐ Ⓑ Ⓒ Ⓓ Ⓔ
  (A) *Oliver Twist*   (B) *The Little Prince*   (C) *Hard Times*
  (D) *David Copperfield*   (E) *Vanity Fair*

136. The musical sign #   136. Ⓐ Ⓑ Ⓒ Ⓓ Ⓔ
  (A) precedes a note to be raised a half step
  (B) lowers the pitch of a note a half step
  (C) indicates tempo   (D) indicates key   (E) indicates pitch

137. John Milton in *Paradise Lost* attempted to   137. Ⓐ Ⓑ Ⓒ Ⓓ Ⓔ
  (A) justify the ways of men to God
  (B) justify the ways of God to men
  (C) explain evil
  (D) show that Satan and God have equal powers
  (E) explain why good and evil are necessary

138. The two great Italian writers of the 14th century were   138. Ⓐ Ⓑ Ⓒ Ⓓ Ⓔ
  (A) Petrarch and Pirandello   (D) Boccaccio and Silone
  (B) Petrarch and Boccaccio   (E) Machiavelli and Borgia
  (C) Dante and Fellini

139. The ghost advises Hamlet, concerning his mother, to   139. Ⓐ Ⓑ Ⓒ Ⓓ Ⓔ
  (A) make certain that she does not escape death
  (B) bring her to public trial and let the people of Denmark decide
      her fate
  (C) wash her incestuous sheets
  (D) allow heaven to decide her fate
  (E) deny her Christian burial so that her soul will wander forever,
      as his is doomed to do

140. A sonata is a musical composition for instrument. A cantata is
(A) a slow symphony   (B) an aria   (C) a slow madrigal
(D) a choral work   (E) a round

140. Ⓐ Ⓑ Ⓒ Ⓓ Ⓔ

141. "But I will start afresh and make dark things plain. In doing right by Laius, I protect myself . . ." said
(A) Phoebus   (B) Oedipus   (C) Ismene   (D) Creon
(E) Jocasta

141. Ⓐ Ⓑ Ⓒ Ⓓ Ⓔ

Jerry Frank

142. The above photograph pictures
(A) an Egyptian temple   (B) an Etruscan temple   (C) a Mayan temple
(D) a Greek temple   (E) a Roman temple

142. Ⓐ Ⓑ Ⓒ Ⓓ Ⓔ

143. Goethe's friend and amanuensis was
(A) Eckermann   (B) Wagner   (C) Holderlin
(D) Fichte   (E) Schelling

143. Ⓐ Ⓑ Ⓒ Ⓓ Ⓔ

144. The rhyme scheme of Dante's *Divine Comedy* in its original Italian is
(A) sestina   (B) terza rima   (C) sonnet   (D) ballade
(E) rondeau

144. Ⓐ Ⓑ Ⓒ Ⓓ Ⓔ

145. The magnificent achievements of Gothic art are found especially in
(A) the buildings of the great cathedrals
(B) the carving of statues on the porches of these cathedrals
(C) the beauty of stained glass
(D) the invention of the flying buttress
(E) all of the above

145. Ⓐ Ⓑ Ⓒ Ⓓ Ⓔ

146. All of the following Americans *except one* were awarded the Nobel Prize for Literature:
(A) Pearl S. Buck   (B) William Faulkner   (C) Robert Frost
(D) Ernest Hemingway   (E) Sinclair Lewis

146. Ⓐ Ⓑ Ⓒ Ⓓ Ⓔ

147. A *soliloquy* is 147. Ⓐ Ⓑ Ⓒ Ⓓ Ⓔ
   (A) a short speech delivered to the audience while other characters
       are on stage
   (B) a few moments of pantomime by the main character in a play
   (C) a speech of some length spoken directly to the audience while the
       character speaking is alone on stage
   (D) a verbal exchange between two characters on stage
   (E) a short, comic speech by the protagonist

148. Which of the following painters produced a number of canvasses of 148. Ⓐ Ⓑ Ⓒ Ⓓ Ⓔ
   jungle plants and animals?
   (A) Henri Rousseau   (B) Paul Cezanne   (C) Jackson Pollock
   (D) Mary Cassatt   (E) Andy Warhol

149. Which of the following conductors began with opera and for many 149. Ⓐ Ⓑ Ⓒ Ⓓ Ⓔ
   years headed the New York Philarmonic?
   (A) George Szell   (B) Sir John Barbarolli
   (C) Herbert van Karajan   (D) Arturo Toscanini
   (E) André Previn

150. A handkerchief plays a key role in which of the following tragedies? 150. Ⓐ Ⓑ Ⓒ Ⓓ Ⓔ
   (A) *All for Love*   (B) *Othello*   (C) *King Lear*
   (D) *Anthony and Cleopatra*   (E) *Macbeth*

ANSWER KEY—TRIAL TEST

Part I

1.	B	14.	C	27.	D	40.	A	52.	A	64.	E
2.	D	15.	E	28.	E	41.	D	53.	E	65.	D
3.	C	16.	C	29.	A	42.	D	54.	A	66.	A
4.	A	17.	B	30.	B	43.	C	55.	B	67.	C
5.	C	18.	C	31.	E	44.	A	56.	C	68.	A
6.	D	19.	D	32.	C	45.	D	57.	A	69.	B
7.	E	20.	D	33.	B	46.	C	58.	C	70.	C
8.	D	21.	E	34.	C	47.	D	59.	D	71.	E
9.	D	22.	A	35.	B	48.	B	60.	A	72.	E
10.	B	23.	A	36.	C	49.	A	61.	E	73.	D
11.	B	24.	E	37.	E	50.	E	62.	C	74.	B
12.	A	25.	C	38.	B	51.	D	63.	E	75.	B
13.	D	26.	D	39.	D						

Part II

76.	A	89.	C	102.	E	115.	A	127.	D	139.	D
77.	D	90.	E	103.	D	116.	A	128.	C	140.	D
78.	D	91.	E	104.	C	117.	B	129.	B	141.	B
79.	E	92.	E	105.	C	118.	D	130.	D	142.	C
80.	E	93.	E	106.	B	119.	A	131.	A	143.	A
81.	A	94.	E	107.	E	120.	E	132.	D	144.	B
82.	A	95.	D	108.	D	121.	A	133.	C	145.	E
83.	D	96.	B	109.	A	122.	B	134.	E	146.	C
84.	E	97.	C	110.	B	123.	B	135.	A	147.	C
85.	C	98.	D	111.	D	124.	D	136.	A	148.	A
86.	A	99.	B	112.	C	125.	D	137.	B	149.	D
87.	C	100.	E	113.	D	126.	A	138.	B	150.	B
88.	B	101.	A	114.	C						

SCORING CHART—TRIAL TEST

After you have scored your Trial Test, enter the results in the chart below (the Raw Score computation is explained on page 14); then transfer your Raw Score to the Progress Chart on page 14. As you complete the Sample Examinations later in this part of the book, you should be able to achieve increasingly higher Raw Scores.

Total Test		Number Right	Number Wrong	Number Omitted	Raw Score
Part I:	75				
Part II:	75				
Total:	150				

ANSWER EXPLANATIONS—TRIAL TEST

Part I

1. **B.** Expressionism in the arts was a movement during the latter part of the 19th and early part of the 20th centuries that emphasized the objective expression of inner experience through conventional characters and symbols.
2. **D.** The Impressionists were a group of late 19th century painters who created a general impression of a scene or object by the use of unmixed primary colors and small strokes to simulate actual reflected light.
3. **C.** Acoustics is the study of sound.
4. **A.** Jean Baptiste Lully (c. 1633–1687) was an Italian operatic composer who has been called "the father of French opera." In 1653 he was made court composer by Louis XIV, for whom he composed many ballets.
5. **C.** James Wyatt (1746–1813) restored English Gothic cathedrals at Lincoln and Salisbury and built several buildings at Magdelen College, Oxford.
6. **D.** A "comedy of manners" is a type of social farce. Ibsen wrote plays of a more serious nature.
7. **E.** Aristotle stated that the primary purpose of tragedy is to create a catharsis, or purgation, of the emotions.
8. **D.** The best known essayists of this period were Joseph Addison and Richard Steele, who contributed to both *The Tattler* and *The Spectator*.
9. **D.** *Uncle Tom's Cabin* ran as a serial in the *National Era*, an abolitionist paper, from June 1851 to April 1852, and was later published as a book.
10. **B.** Alliteration is the occurrence in a phrase, or line of a speech or writing of two or more words of the same initial sound, as in the "b" sound in "bring," "bow," and "burning."
11. **B.** The ballet "The Rite of Spring" was first produced by Diaghileff's Ballets Russes in Paris in 1913. It raised a storm of protest and was given only six times.
12. **A.** An overture is an instrumental introduction to an opera.
13. **D.** The other periods are not considered "prehistoric."
14. **C.** Dali, Miro, and de Chirico are three artists noted for their surrealist paintings.
15. **E.** Clemens, who once worked on a Mississippi riverboat, derived his name from the call of the leadsman on riverboats when a depth of two fathoms was sounded.

16. C. A quatrain is a stanza or poem of four lines.
17. B. "Barbara Allen" is an ancient British folk ballad.
18. C. Pop art frequently depicts such things as Campbell's soup cans, flashy cars, and movie stars.
19. D. The Greeks are noted for their graceful statues depicting the human body.
20. D. Wright believed that a building should be built of the materials native to the area and should blend in with its particular surroundings.
21. E. The first two volumes of Montaigne's *Essays*, appearing in 1580, ushered in a new form of literature.
22. A. The *Nibelungenlied*, of unknown origin, was probably composed between the 12th and 14th centuries.
23. A. This is the famous "Pomp and Circumstance" overture.
24. E. None of the others were jazz guitarists.
25. C. Shakespeare never wrote dramas about the middle class.
26. D. Chekhov was a Russian realist who presented life "as it is," without imaginative embellishments.
27. D. Aeschylus, the Athenian tragic poet, is the first of the three great tragedians, the others being Sophocles and Euripides.
28. E. No scenery or props were employed by the Greeks in their open, outdoor theater.
29. A. "The Lone Ranger" was a popular radio program and film serial of the 1930's; its theme was the "William Tell Overture."
30. B. This is a standard definition of "Western man or civilization."
31. E. A tone poem is an elaborate orchestral composition, usually in one movement, having no fixed form and based upon some non-musical, poetic or descriptive theme. Strauss' best known tone poem is "Thus Spake Zarathustra."
32. C. Hamlet's famous "to be or not to be" soliloquy addresses this problem.
33. B. Paul Cezanne (1839–1906) was a French post-impressionist painter. He was noted for the use of very vivid colors, and for a striving for depth in place of flatness, which he achieved by very dark shadows and outlines.
34. C. Cubism is a school of modern art characterized by the use of cubes and other abstract geometric forms rather than by a realistic representation of nature.
35. B. Melville's novel *Moby Dick* opens with the narrator stating that his name is Ishmael.
36. C. "Rappaccini's Daughter" is a short story written by Nathaniel Hawthorne.
37. E. Not all sculpture is a realistic portrayal of the human being; stone and marble can be cut for flooring and may be functional, but not necessarily artistic.
38. B. Franklin was an 18th century American statesman, scientist, inventor, and writer. *Poor Richard's Almanac* contains a collection of well-known proverbs, many of which became household sayings in America.
39. D. Florence is a city in Tuscany, Italy. Among the artists who have added luster to its name are Michelangelo, Dante, and Boccaccio.
40. A. The principle members of the School of Lyon, headed by Maurice Scève, were Antoine Heroet, Pernette de Guillet, and Louise Labé, all poets.
41. D. Stephen Crane (1871–1900) was an American novelist, poet, and journalist. His *Red Badge of Courage* is a well-known tale of the American Civil War.
42. D. Renoir, Monet, and Pissaro were 19th century painters who attempted to create a general impression of a scene or object by the use of unmixed primary colors and small strokes to simulate actual reflected light.
43. C. This is noticeable in Roman roads and aqueducts as well as in buildings.
44. A. Modulation, in music, is defined as a shifting from one key to another by the transitional use of a chord common to both.
45. D. *Oedipus the King*, a play written by Sophocles, concerns Oedipus, who killed his father and married his mother.
46. C. The order should be Gothic, Renaissance, Baroque.

47. D. Mark Twain, the pseudonym of Samuel L. Clemens, was born in Florida, Missouri, in 1835, and spent his childhood in Hannibal, Missouri.
48. B. This example of nonsense verse is from the poem "Jabberwocky," by Lewis Carroll, and is to be found in *Through the Looking Glass*.
49. A. With the fall of the Roman Empire, Christian forces had succeeded in driving the actors out of Rome. Modern drama, including farcical interludes, had its origins in the Middle Ages.
50. E. The Black Death was an epidemic of Plague in the 14th century.
51. D. *Animal Farm* is a political satire by George Orwell.
52. A. Anton Dvořák (1841–1904) was a Bohemian composer. In 1892–95 he visited the United States, where he gathered impressions for his "New World Symphony," the most popular of his seven symphonies.
53. E. Ferde Grofé was an American composer and arranger who became famous when he orchestrated Gershwin's *Rhapsody in Blue* in 1924. He also wrote other music describing the American scene, including "The Grand Canyon Suite."
54. A. The great areas of interior space created the feeling of man's insignificance and God's infinite and all-powerful presence.
55. B. Some authors pictured the effects of the Great Depression and laborers brutalized by machines.
56. C. Kerouac's novel *On The Road* began a new movement in American literature.
57. A. A parable is sometimes a religious lesson as well.
58. C. Altamira is in northern Spain, and Lascaux is in south-central France.
59. D. This is a basic principle of art.
60. A. Modern psychologists and sociologists have demonstrated that cultural conditioning determines the way we perceive.
61. E. Foster was the composer of "Old Folks at Home," "Oh Susannah," "My Old Kentucky Home," and many other songs.
62. C. Benjamin Franklin (1706–1790) was one of the most versatile of the early American fathers.
63. E. The line comes from T. S. Eliot's poem, "The Love Song of J. Alfred Prufrock."
64. E. The mystery plays were the forerunner of modern drama.
65. D. Charles Dickens (1812–1870) wrote *David Copperfield, Oliver Twist, A Christmas Carol,* and many other novels championing the individual against the institution and, particularly, championing the child as a victim of society.
66. A. *Don Quixote*, the best known work of Miguel de Cervantes, is a satire.
67. C. Among Gainsborough's best known works are "Mrs. Siddons" and "The Blue Boy."
68. A. "The Well-Tempered Clavier," sometimes called "The Well-Tempered Clavichord," consists of forty-eight preludes and fugues.
69. B. None of the other works was written by Beethoven.
70. C. Among Lewis' best known novels are *Main Street* and *Babbitt.*
71. E. All people have unlimited abilities.
72. E. Aeschylus and Sophocles were more conservative and traditional in their approach.
73. D. Chekhov is noted for presenting small "slices of life" in his plays.
74. B. Leoncavallo wrote several operas, but only *I Pagliacci* was successful.
75. B. Beethoven wrote nine symphonies in all.

Part II

76. A. This famous Greek statue is presently to be seen in the Louvre in Paris.
77. D. Shakespeare's plays contain elements such as song, dance, and ghostly apparitions because it was necessary for him to appeal to a diverse audience.

78. D. In other words, the viewer must enter the theater with an open mind.
79. E. Paul Gauguin was a French landscape and figure painter best known for his paintings of Tahitian subjects.
80. E. Pointillism is characterized by the application of paint in small dots and brush strokes so as to create an effect of blending and luminosity.
81. A. Hermann Hesse was a Swiss author who wrote *Siddhartha, Demian* and *A Journey to the East,* as well as many other novels.
82. A. This answer is true by definition.
83. D. This story comes from the Judeo-Christian tradition.
84. E. Mozart had a sponsor, but he also wrote operas for the popular theaters of his day.
85. C. Updike's best known works are *Rabbit, Run* and *Rabbit Redux.*
86. A. The appreciation of art is basically an emotional, sensory experience.
87. C. Isaiah was one of the greatest of the Hebrew prophets.
88. B. The other groups consist of those who are not symphony conductors.
89. C. The others are not writers.
90. E. The others are not choreographers.
91. E. F. Scott Fitzgerald is probably the best known writer of the "roaring 20s."
92. E. Theseus was a mythical Greek hero who conquered the Minotaur.
93. E. Kate is the name of the female lead in Shakespeare's play.
94. E. Van Gogh became an artist, but he did not prove his point.
95. D. This is a traditional musical notation.
96. B. This is a definition of a cappella.
97. C. *Die Meistersinger* is not part of the Germanic myth cycle.
98. D. Phidias was a Greek sculptor.
99. B. This ornate style in art and architecture developed in Europe about 1550 to 1700.
100. E. "Art" is an abstract concept, and therefore may have many definitions.
101. A. Hamlet's mother, Gertrude, is married to Claudius, but Hamlet mistrusts him.
102. E. This group, also called the Hartford Wits, flourished in the late 18th and early 19th centuries.
103. D. In Greek mythology, Phaedra was the daughter of Minos and Pasiphae; she was married to Theseus.
104. C. Shultz is the creator of *Peanuts.*
105. C. Sprung rhythm is a forcefully accentual verse rhythm in which a stressed syllable is followed by an irregular number of unstressed or slack syllables to form a foot having a metrical value equal to that of the other feet in the line.
106. B. Anouilh's play is also entitled *Antigone.*
107. E. Metal is a popular medium for modern sculptors.
108. D. Môlière's attacks on bourgeois morality greatly appealed to his aristocratic audience.
109. A. Poe, one of the first great American short story writers, coined this definition.
110. B. This is a translation from the French.
111. D. Francois Rabelais (1494–1553) entered a convent but later abandoned monasticism. His best known works are *Gargantua* and *Pantagruel.*
112. C. The play is rarely performed outside Italy, however.
113. D. Perhaps Verne's best known work is *20,000 Leagues Under the Sea,* in which he anticipated the invention of the submarine.
114. C. There is no proof, but tradition does hold that Homer was the author.
115. A. Handel's most famous oratorios are on biblical subjects, such as *Esther, Deborah,* and *Samson.*
116. A. The score is the written form of a musical composition. The conductor's copy is complete.
117. B. This book shows how labor was oppressed by management in the early days of unionization.
118. D. These characters were termed the protagonist and the antagonist. Without conflict, there can be no drama.

119. A. The painting is of La Gioconda, popularly known as the *Mona Lisa*.
120. E. His men were called Argonauts, after the ship, *Argo*.
121. A. Jason stole the Golden Fleece from Aeetes, with the help of Aeete's daughter, Medea.
122. B. Louis XIV, the "Sun-King," indulged his taste for luxury and elegance to the full. The arts flourished during his reign in France.
123. B. Sir Christopher Wren (1632–1723) was one of the foremost architects of his day. All of his buildings exhibit elegance, vigor, and dignity.
124. D. The king had learned of uprisings in both Scotland and Wales.
125. D. A mosaic is a decorative design or picture made by setting small colored pieces, such as tile, in mortar.
126. A. All the answers to the above are true, but only partial explanations. "A," "the complexity of modern life," encompasses all of them and more.
127. D. Falsetto is a typically male singing voice when artificially producing tones in an upper register beyond its normal range.
128. C. Kilmer's "Trees" is often recited on Arbor Day.
129. B. Cunegonde's many experiences would have killed a weaker individual.
130. D. Ernst Hoffmann (1776–1822) was a German musician, artist, and Romantic writer, who is one of the masters in the field of fantastic prose.
131. A. Jacques Offenbach (1819–1880), a French composer of light operas, is best known for his adaptation of Hoffmann's stories.
132. D. The Roman Church abolished all "immoral activities," theater among them.
133. C. There was no theater under the Roman Church during the Dark Ages in Europe.
134. E. This is the only work mentioned written during the Revolutionary period.
135. A. *Oliver Twist,* written by Charles Dickens in 1838.
136. A. This is a standard musical notation—the "sharp."
137. B. Milton states this in *Paradise Lost.*
138. B. The others are Italian, but not all 14th century writers.
139. D. Hamlet had been contemplating murder, but he listened to the Ghost.
140. D. A cantata is a vocal and instrumental composition comprising choruses, solos, and recitatives.
141. B. Laius, King of Thebes, was the father of Oedipus, who killed him.
142. C. Mayan architecture is to be found in sections of Mexico and Central America.
143. A. Johann Eckermann was a German scholar and author who assisted Goethe in various literary endeavors.
144. B. Terza rima is composed of tercets which are not separate stanzas, because each is joined to the one preceding and the one following by a common rhyme: aba, bcb, cdc, ded, etc.
145. E. All of the above are to be found in Gothic cathedrals.
146. C. Robert Frost, one of America's most beloved poets, never received the Nobel Prize.
147. C. This is the answer by definition of "soliloquy."
148. A. Henri Rousseau was a French primitive painter best known for his "Sleeping Gypsy" and "The Jungle."
149. D. The others either did not begin with opera, did not head the New York Philharmonic, or did neither.
150. B. It is Desdemona's handkerchief that spurs Othello to such jealousy that he kills her.

7 | Background and Practice Questions

The Humanities Examination measures your general knowledge of literature and the fine arts. There are two sections to the examination, each consisting of approximately 75 questions and each requiring 45 minutes to complete. See the following chart for approximate percentages of examination items:

Literature (50%)		Fine Arts (50%)	
10%	Drama	20%	Visual arts (painting, sculpture, etc.)
15–20%	Poetry	15%	Music
10–15%	Fiction	10%	Performing arts (film, dance, etc.)
10%	Nonfiction	5%	Architecture

Questions on these topics are interspersed randomly throughout the test. The questions cover all periods from the classical to the contemporary and include aspects of the humanities not necessarily covered in courses in school. In addition to your course work, then, you should have a general interest in the arts. Attending the movies, the theater, and concerts; visiting museums; watching television; and reading widely should provide you with sufficient background. You might also consult any one of a number of excellent histories of the theater, literature, music, the film, and the other fine arts which are available in every public library.

The questions require factual answers, not answers which depend upon your emotional responses or aesthetic tastes. Some questions cover material with which you should be familiar from course work. For other questions, the correct answer can be derived from your ability to analyze artistic creations, to recognize certain basic artistic techniques, and to make analogies between two works of art. You will be expected to identify literary passages and authors. In some cases, you will be presented with pictures of art works which you will be expected to identify by artist, period, or in some other way.

A knowledge of foreign languages is not required. All literary works included are readily available in English translations. It is not necessary to read music to answer any of the questions about music. Though a few questions may appear rather technical, remember that no one is expected to have complete mastery of all fields of the humanities.

If you would like to review some of the information which you may already have studied or fill in some gaps in your formal education, we recommend the following as excellent sources:

ART

The Larousse series. New York: Prometheus Press, various dates. There are several books in this series which cover many aspects of art: painting, music, sculpture, architecture, etc.

MUSIC

Apel, Willi. *Harvard Dictionary of Music*, 2nd ed. Cambridge, MA: Harvard University Press, 1969.

Grout, Donald. *A History of Western Music*, 3rd ed. New York: W.W. Norton and Co., Inc., 1980.

LITERATURE

Benet, William Rose. *Readers' Encyclopedia*, 2nd ed. New York: Thomas Y. Crowell, 1965.

Brooks, Cleanth et al., eds. *American Literature: The Makers and the Making*, 4 volumes. New York: St. Martin's Press, Inc., 1974.

Heiney, D.W. and Downs, L.H. *Contemporary*

Literature of the Western World, 4 volumes. Woodbury, N.Y.: Barron's Educational Series, Inc., 1974.

Magill, Frank, ed. *Masterpieces of World Literature*. Third Series. New York: Harper and Row, 1968.

In addition to these specific works, you might consult the excellent series of dictionaries to the various art forms published by Oxford University Press in New York. For very recent information, you might consult the music, art and book reviews and film criticisms which appear regularly in such publications as *Playboy, Esquire, Saturday Review, The National Review, The New Republic, The New York Times, The New York Review of Books, The New Yorker, The Film Quarterly*, and other periodicals.

For practice, we will now give you some sample questions in each of the areas which the CLEP Humanities examination will cover; these questions should be considered typical.

PRACTICE QUESTIONS ON THE HUMANITIES

Questions about Literature

Directions: Each of the questions or incomplete statements below is followed by five suggested answers or completions. Select the one that is best in each case.

1. What 17th-century poet attempted to "justify the ways of God to man"?
   (A) John Bunyan   (B) Samuel Johnson   (C) John Dryden
   (D) John Milton   (E) John Donne

2. A Greek historian who wrote *The History of the Peloponnesian War* was
   (A) Sophocles   (B) Euripides   (C) Thucydides
   (D) Tacitus   (E) Socrates

3. A Japanese poem of seventeen syllables is the
   (A) kyogen   (B) haiku   (C) sentyu   (D) tanka
   (E) renka

4. The Greek theater contained all but one of the following:
   (A) masks   (B) boots   (C) proscenium
   (D) movable props   (E) song and dance

5. A well-known 19th-century symbolist poem is "Afternoon of a Faun." This poem was written by
   (A) Baudelaire   (B) Rimbaud   (C) Valéry
   (D) Mallarmé   (E) Claudel

6. A pastoral elegy, bewailing the death of Edward King, is

6. Ⓐ Ⓑ Ⓒ Ⓓ Ⓔ

   (A) "In Memoriam" (B) "Lycidas" (C) "Thyrsis"
   (D) "Il Penseroso"   (E) "Adonais"

7. An example of an Old English folk epic is

7. Ⓐ Ⓑ Ⓒ Ⓓ Ⓔ

   (A) *The Canterbury Tales*   (B) *The Iliad*   (C) *Beowulf*
   (D) *A Midsummer Night's Dream*   (E) *Paradise Lost*

8. The essence of comedy is

8. Ⓐ Ⓑ Ⓒ Ⓓ Ⓔ

   (A) satire   (B) surprise   (C) mistaken identity
   (D) disguise   (E) incongruity

9. The Greek word for "overweening pride" is

9. Ⓐ Ⓑ Ⓒ Ⓓ Ⓔ

   (A) hamartia   (B) catharsis   (C) anagnorisis
   (D) peripety   (E) hubris

10. The word *utopia* comes from a 16th-century book by

10. Ⓐ Ⓑ Ⓒ Ⓓ Ⓔ

    (A) Sir Thomas More   (B) Thomas à Becket
    (C) Samuel Beckett   (D) William Shakespeare
    (E) Ben Jonson

11. A famous contemporary of John Dryden was

11. Ⓐ Ⓑ Ⓒ Ⓓ Ⓔ

    (A) Alexander Pope   (B) Ben Jonson   (C) Thomas Macaulay
    (D) Leigh Hunt   (E) John Milton

12. According to Aristotle, tragedy evokes pity and fear and produces a

12. Ⓐ Ⓑ Ⓒ Ⓓ Ⓔ

    (A) catharsis   (B) dénouement   (C) climax
    (D) recognition   (E) kothurnos

13. A Japanese play which exists as a harmony of all theatrical elements —poetry, music, dance, costume, mask, setting, and the interaction of performance—is the

13. Ⓐ Ⓑ Ⓒ Ⓓ Ⓔ

    (A) kabuki   (B) shinto   (C) hari kiri
    (D) nō   (E) joruri

14. The 16th century believed the main purpose of poetry was to

14. Ⓐ Ⓑ Ⓒ Ⓓ Ⓔ

    (A) relieve the emotions   (B) make science bearable
    (C) enliven life   (D) delight and instruct   (E) philosophize

15. Shakespeare's best known comic character is

15. Ⓐ Ⓑ Ⓒ Ⓓ Ⓔ

    (A) Titania   (B) Falstaff   (C) Henry VIII
    (D) Ariel   (E) Friar Lawrence

16. A collection of medieval stories concerning a group of people on a pilgrimage is

16. Ⓐ Ⓑ Ⓒ Ⓓ Ⓔ

    (A) *The Decameron*   (B) *The Canterbury Tales*
    (C) *Sir Gawain and the Green Knight*   (D) *Morte d'Arthur*
    (E) *Idylls of the King*

17. A playwright noted for his "thesis" plays is

17. Ⓐ Ⓑ Ⓒ Ⓓ Ⓔ

    (A) Shaw   (B) Goethe   (C) Arthur Miller
    (D) Edward Albee   (E) Sophocles

18. "All are but parts of one stupendous whole,/Whose body Nature is, and God the soul" was written by
(A) Matthew Arnold   (B) Alexander Pope
(C) Percy B. Shelley   (D) John Milton   (E) Robert Browning

18. Ⓐ Ⓑ Ⓒ Ⓓ Ⓔ

19. Dr. Samuel Johnson's amanuensis was
(A) Dryden   (B) Swift   (C) Pope   (D) Milton
(E) Boswell

19. Ⓐ Ⓑ Ⓒ Ⓓ Ⓔ

20. John Donne and his followers are known to literary historians as the
(A) metaphysical poets   (B) Molly Maguires
(C) cavalier poets   (D) graveyard school   (E) Sons of Ben

20. Ⓐ Ⓑ Ⓒ Ⓓ Ⓔ

21. The "hero" of Milton's *Paradise Lost* is
(A) Satan   (B) man   (C) God   (D) Adam   (E) Jesus

21. Ⓐ Ⓑ Ⓒ Ⓓ Ⓔ

22. A convention in drama wherein a character speaks his innermost thoughts aloud while alone on stage is the
(A) aside   (B) prologue   (C) soliloquy
(D) epilogue   (E) proscenium

22. Ⓐ Ⓑ Ⓒ Ⓓ Ⓔ

23. A fire-breathing monster, part lion, part goat, and part serpent, slain by Bellerophon, was the
(A) medusa   (B) chimera   (C) phoenix
(D) minotaur   (E) hydra

23. Ⓐ Ⓑ Ⓒ Ⓓ Ⓔ

24. The French poet Arthur Rimbaud was a forerunner of the
(A) Pre-Raphaelites   (B) absurdists   (C) realists
(D) naturalists   (E) symbolists

24. Ⓐ Ⓑ Ⓒ Ⓓ Ⓔ

25. One of the great Sanskrit epics of Western India is
(A) *The Mahabharata*   (B) *Siddhartha*   (C) *The Tripitaka*
(D) *The Analects*   (E) *The Rubáiyát*

25. Ⓐ Ⓑ Ⓒ Ⓓ Ⓔ

26. A well-known contemporary of William Shakespeare was
(A) John Milton   (B) Dante Alighieri   (C) Geoffrey Chaucer
(D) Christopher Marlowe   (E) John Dryden

26. Ⓐ Ⓑ Ⓒ Ⓓ Ⓔ

27. A 20th-century novel which made the public aware of the plight of migrant laborers is
(A) *East of Eden*   (B) *To a God Unknown*   (C) *Cannery Row*
(D) *The Grapes of Wrath*   (E) *Tortilla Flat*

27. Ⓐ Ⓑ Ⓒ Ⓓ Ⓔ

28. A poet who writes of ordinary people and of nature is considered a
(A) naturalist   (B) realist   (C) romanticist
(D) medievalist   (E) Victorian

28. Ⓐ Ⓑ Ⓒ Ⓓ Ⓔ

29. The "comedy of manners" was most popular during the
(A) 16th century   (B) 17th century   (C) 18th century
(D) 19th century   (E) 20th century

29. Ⓐ Ⓑ Ⓒ Ⓓ Ⓔ

30. One of the first American short story writers was
(A) Washington Irving   (B) Edgar Allan Poe
(C) Ambrose Bierce   (D) Stephen Crane   (E) O. Henry

30. Ⓐ Ⓑ Ⓒ Ⓓ Ⓔ

31. A Greek divinity who punished crimes, particularly those of impiety and hubris, was
(A) Artemis   (B) Mercury   (C) Clio
(D) Clytaemnestra   (E) Nemesis

31. Ⓐ Ⓑ Ⓒ Ⓓ Ⓔ

32. The greatest lyric poet in German before Goethe was a minnesinger:
(A) Heinrich Heine   (B) Gerhart Hauptmann
(C) Walter von der Vogelweide   (D) Gottfried von Strassburg
(E) Friedrich Schiller

32. Ⓐ Ⓑ Ⓒ Ⓓ Ⓔ

33. The author of three very popular 18th-century French plays, which form a trilogy—*The Barber of Seville, The Marriage of Figaro,* and *The Guilty Mother*—was
(A) Molière   (B) Beaumarchais   (C) Diderot
(D) Racine   (E) Marivaux

33. Ⓐ Ⓑ Ⓒ Ⓓ Ⓔ

34. Empathy involves which of the following responses on the part of the play-going audience?
(A) alienation   (B) projection   (C) nostalgia
(D) intensification   (E) escape

34. Ⓐ Ⓑ Ⓒ Ⓓ Ⓔ

35. A 20th-century writer who refused the Nobel Prize for Literature was
(A) Faulkner   (B) Sartre   (C) Camus
(D) Lewis   (E) Hemingway

35. Ⓐ Ⓑ Ⓒ Ⓓ Ⓔ

Questions 36–38 refer to the following poem "The Eagle" by Alfred, Lord Tennyson.

> He clasps the crag with crooked hands;
> Close to the sun in lonely lands,
> Ringed with the azure world, he stands.
>
> The wrinkled sea beneath him crawls;
> He watches from his mountain walls,
> And like a thunderbolt he falls.

36. Which line contains a metaphor?
(A) line 2   (B) line 4   (C) line 5   (D) line 6
(E) all of these lines

36. Ⓐ Ⓑ Ⓒ Ⓓ Ⓔ

37. Which line contains a simile?
(A) line 1   (B) line 2   (C) line 3   (D) line 5   (E) line 6

37. Ⓐ Ⓑ Ⓒ Ⓓ Ⓔ

38. Which line contains an example of alliteration?
(A) line 1   (B) line 3   (C) line 4   (D) line 5   (E) line 6

38. Ⓐ Ⓑ Ⓒ Ⓓ Ⓔ

ANSWERS TO QUESTIONS ABOUT LITERATURE

1. D	6. B	11. E	16. B	21. B	26. D	31. E	36. B
2. C	7. C	12. A	17. A	22. C	27. D	32. C	37. E
3. B	8. E	13. D	18. B	23. B	28. C	33. B	38. A
4. D	9. E	14. D	19. E	24. E	29. C	34. B	
5. D	10. A	15. B	20. A	25. A	30. A	35. B	

Questions about Music

Directions: Each of the questions or incomplete statements below is followed by five suggested answers or completions. Select the one that is best in each case.

1. The assistant conductor or concertmaster of the orchestra is
   (A) the first chair violinist   (B) the second chair violinist
   (C) a pianist   (D) a harpist
   (E) standing in the wings ready to take over

   1. A B C D E

2. The instrument with the stablest pitch and therefore the one asked to "sound your A" for all other players is the
   (A) piano   (B) first violin   (C) first oboe   (D) clarinet
   (E) trumpet

   2. A B C D E

3. The tone poem from "Afternoon of a Faun" was composed by
   (A) Debussy   (B) Liszt   (C) Bizet
   (D) Rimsky-Korsakoff   (E) Poulenc

   3. A B C D E

4. The first American music comes from the American Indian and, with its emphasis on single rhythms, American Indian music is primarily
   (A) emotional   (B) formal   (C) heterophonic
   (D) polyphonic   (E) choral

   4. A B C D E

5. The difference between the kettle drums and other forms of timpani is that
   (A) they can be used to store small instruments
   (B) they can be tuned   (C) they augment strings
   (D) they keep the beat   (E) they add a marching effect

   5. A B C D E

6. The "licorice stick" reached the peak of its popularity with band leader Benny Goodman. The "licorice stick" is a
   (A) piccolo   (B) flute   (C) trombone   (D) trumpet
   (E) clarinet

   6. A B C D E

7. The development of early church music and plainsong is attributed to
   (A) Marlo v   (B) Paul   (C) Caniauis   (D) Lucifer
   (E) Gregory the Great

   7. A B C D E

8. In music, one tone used against another tone is called
   (A) abstraction   (B) a chord   (C) a staff
   (D) counterpoint   (E) alteration

   8. A B C D E

9. Scarlatti is known chiefly for his work with which of the following instruments?
   (A) oboe   (B) harpsichord   (C) harp   (D) cymbal
   (E) French horn

   9. A B C D E

10. One of America's most popular operas, composed by George and Ira Gershwin, is
    (A) *The Medium*   (B) *The Black Crook*   (C) *Porgy and Bess*
    (D) *The Little Tycoon*   (E) *Amahl and the Night Visitor*

    10. A B C D E

11. Running through music literature is a persistent thread that has affected, positively or negatively, the work of every composer from Bach to our 20th-century modernists. This thread is

    (A) melody   (B) sonata   (C) tone-poem
    (D) counterpart   (E) atonality

    11. Ⓐ Ⓑ Ⓒ Ⓓ Ⓔ

12. The "Unfinished Symphony" was written by

    (A) Mendelssohn   (B) Schubert   (C) Brahms
    (D) Tchaikovsky   (E) Chopin

    12. Ⓐ Ⓑ Ⓒ Ⓓ Ⓔ

13. The opera *The Barber of Seville* had music by

    (A) Puccini   (B) Verdi   (C) Mendelssohn
    (D) Rossini   (E) Poulenc

    13. Ⓐ Ⓑ Ⓒ Ⓓ Ⓔ

14. The opera *The Marriage of Figaro* had music by

    (A) Mozart   (B) Haydn   (C) Verdi   (D) Rossini
    (E) Puccini

    14. Ⓐ Ⓑ Ⓒ Ⓓ Ⓔ

15. Greek music was organized into an order of harmonious proportions, purposeful numbers. The discoverer of this principle was

    (A) Pythagoras   (B) Socrates   (C) Aristotle
    (D) Democritus   (E) Crito

    15. Ⓐ Ⓑ Ⓒ Ⓓ Ⓔ

16. We get the word *octave* from a Latin word meaning

    (A) two   (B) four   (C) six   (D) eight   (E) nine

    16. Ⓐ Ⓑ Ⓒ Ⓓ Ⓔ

17. The direct ancestor of the symphony is the

    (A) concerto   (B) sonata   (C) motet   (D) aria
    (E) overture

    17. Ⓐ Ⓑ Ⓒ Ⓓ Ⓔ

18. The method of four voices singing different tunes at the same time, yet linked by strict rules, is called a

    (A) motet   (B) combo   (C) chorus   (D) fugue
    (E) baroque

    18. Ⓐ Ⓑ Ⓒ Ⓓ Ⓔ

19. Beethoven is best known for his

    (A) tone poems   (B) operas   (C) symphonies
    (D) waltzes   (E) fugues

    19. Ⓐ Ⓑ Ⓒ Ⓓ Ⓔ

20. Many musicians agree that the greatest choral work ever written is
    (A) Beethoven's "Moonlight Sonata"
    (B) Bach's "Mass in B Minor"
    (C) Schubert's "Second Symphony"
    (D) Chopin's "Polonaise Militaire"
    (E) Bizet's *Carmen*

    20. Ⓐ Ⓑ Ⓒ Ⓓ Ⓔ

ANSWERS TO QUESTIONS ABOUT MUSIC

1.	A	8.	D	15.	A
2.	C	9.	B	16.	D
3.	A	10.	C	17.	E
4.	D	11.	E	18.	A
5.	B	12.	B	19.	C
6.	E	13.	D	20.	B
7.	E	14.	A		

Directions: Each of the questions or incomplete statements below is followed by five suggested answers or completions. Select the one that is best in each case.

1. In painting, *chiaroscuro* refers to
   (A) a light-and-dark technique   (B) brilliant colors
   (C) monochromes   (D) perspective
   (E) a single stroke technique

   1. A B C D E

2. All of the following were Renaissance painters *except*
   (A) Masaccio   (B) Rembrandt   (C) Botticelli
   (D) van Eyck   (E) Michelangelo

   2. A B C D E

3. A painter who was also knowledgeable about mathematics, geology, music, and engineering was
   (A) Michelangelo   (B) Cellini   (C) Titian   (D) da Vinci
   (E) Tintoretto

   3. A B C D E

4. One of the most famous modern ballet choreographers was
   (A) George Balanchine   (B) Nicholas Sergeyev
   (C) Marius Petipa   (D) Phillippe Taglioni
   (E) Rudolf von Laban

   4. A B C D E

5. The artist famous for his painting on the ceiling of the Sistine Chapel is
   (A) Raphael   (B) da Vinci   (C) Michelangelo
   (D) Rembrandt   (E) Delacroix

   5. A B C D E

6. A painter noted for his madonnas is
   (A) Botticelli   (B) van Gogh   (C) Raphael   (D) Picasso
   (E) Goya

   6. A B C D E

7. The art of painting on freshly spread moist lime plaster with pigments suspended in a water vehicle is called
   (A) collage   (B) pointillism   (C) surrealism
   (D) primitivism   (E) fresco

   7. A B C D E

8. Ballet, as we know it today, had its origins in
   (A) Italy   (B) Germany   (C) France   (D) Russia
   (E) England

   8. A B C D E

9. An artistic composition of fragments of printed matter and other materials pasted on a picture surface is called
   (A) dadaism   (B) a fresco   (C) art nouveau
   (D) a collage   (E) pop art

   9. A B C D E

10. Perhaps the outstanding master of the engraving and the woodcut was
    (A) Pieter Brueghel   (B) Albrecht Dürer   (C) William Blake
    (D) Leonardo da Vinci   (E) Honoré Daumier

    10. A B C D E

11. An American painter noted for his social realism is
    (A) Ben Shahn   (B) Jackson Pollock   (C) Mary Cassatt
    (D) John Singer Sargent   (E) Benjamin West

    11. A B C D E

12. A "Spanish" painter noted for his thin-faced, elongated individuals was
    (A) Goya   (B) Velásquez   (C) El Greco   (D) Picasso
    (E) Orozco

12. Ⓐ Ⓑ Ⓒ Ⓓ Ⓔ

13. A mode of sculpture in which forms and figures are distinguished from a surrounding plane surface is called a
    (A) frieze   (B) collage   (C) fresco   (D) relief
    (E) plaque

13. Ⓐ Ⓑ Ⓒ Ⓓ Ⓔ

14. All of the following are famous male ballet dancers *except*
    (A) Andre Eglevsky   (B) Feodor Chaliapin
    (C) Vaslav Nijinsky   (D) Kurt Joos   (E) Robert Helpmann

14. Ⓐ Ⓑ Ⓒ Ⓓ Ⓔ

15. Inigo Jones was a
    (A) 17th-century architect and set designer
    (B) clarinetist with Bunk Johnson's orchestra
    (C) Restoration playwright
    (D) leading tenor with the La Scala Opera
    (E) 19th-century impressionist painter

15. Ⓐ Ⓑ Ⓒ Ⓓ Ⓔ

16. All of the following painted in the Rococo tradition *except*
    (A) Boucher   (B) Watteau   (C) Fragonard
    (D) Chardin   (E) Cezanne

16. Ⓐ Ⓑ Ⓒ Ⓓ Ⓔ

17. Perspective, as a unified system for representing space, was brought to perfection during the
    (A) Golden Age of Greece   (B) Roman Republic
    (C) Byzantine period   (D) Renaissance
    (E) nineteenth century

17. Ⓐ Ⓑ Ⓒ Ⓓ Ⓔ

18. The Temple of Athena at Athens is called the
    (A) Pallas Athene   (B) Pantheon   (C) Parthenon
    (D) Forum   (E) Coliseum

18. Ⓐ Ⓑ Ⓒ Ⓓ Ⓔ

19. A Flemish painter noted for his feeling for the fantastic as well as his manual techniques was
    (A) Jan van Eyck   (B) Hans Holbein
    (C) Rogier van der Weyden   (D) Pieter Brueghel
    (E) Hugo van der Goes

19. Ⓐ Ⓑ Ⓒ Ⓓ Ⓔ

20. The technique of portraying "a scientifically accurate, detached picture of life, including everything and selecting nothing" is called
    (A) Romanticism   (B) Realism   (C) Naturalism
    (D) Primitivism   (E) Sentimentalism

20. Ⓐ Ⓑ Ⓒ Ⓓ Ⓔ

ANSWERS TO QUESTIONS ABOUT THE FINE ARTS

1. A	6. C	11. A	16. E
2. B	7. E	12. C	17. D
3. D	8. A	13. D	18. C
4. A	9. D	14. B	19. D
5. C	10. B	15. A	20. C

Sample Examinations

This chapter contains three sample Humanities examinations, each with an answer key, scoring chart, and answer explanations. Calculate and record your scores and see your improvement on the Progress Chart on page 14.

SAMPLE EXAMINATION 1
Part I

Number of Questions: 75
Time: 45 minutes

Directions: Each of the questions or incomplete statements below is followed by five suggested answers or completions. Select the one that is best in each case.

1. Beethoven's only opera is
   (A) *Fidelio*   (B) *Eroica*   (C) *Peleas and Melisande*
   (D) *Egmont*   (E) *Prometheus*

   1. Ⓐ Ⓑ Ⓒ Ⓓ Ⓔ

2. Renaissance art is characterized by
   (A) a growing appreciation for the pleasures and satisfaction of this life
   (B) a reflection of the increasing wealth and luxury of the cities of Italy
   (C) an emphasis on human values and the philosophy of Humanism
   (D) the combination of Christian legend with a rediscovery of pagan art and Greek myths
   (E) all of the above

   2. Ⓐ Ⓑ Ⓒ Ⓓ Ⓔ

3. The Latin Secretary to Emperor Hadrian and author of the biographical work called *The Lives of the Twelve Caesars* was
   (A) Maximus (B) Crispus (C) Suetonius (D) Claudius (E) Augustus

   3. Ⓐ Ⓑ Ⓒ Ⓓ Ⓔ

4. The meter of a musical composition
   (A) has to do with regularly recurring accents (B) determines tempo
   (C) indicates texture (D) determines dynamics
   (E) is the same as rhythm

   4. Ⓐ Ⓑ Ⓒ Ⓓ Ⓔ

5. Spenser intended *The Faerie Queene* to be all of the following except
   (A) praise for Queen Elizabeth I   (B) a political allegory
   (C) a religious allegory   (D) contained within twelve books
   (E) a true picture of Elizabethan England

   5. Ⓐ Ⓑ Ⓒ Ⓓ Ⓔ

6. Michelangelo's greatest paintings appear in the
   (A) Brancusi Chapel   (B) St. Mark's Cathedral
   (C) Cathedral of Pisa   (D) Sistine Chapel
   (E) St. Patrick's Cathedral

   6. Ⓐ Ⓑ Ⓒ Ⓓ Ⓔ

7. Structural elements or architecture such as the pointed arch and the flying buttress were extensively used in the period known as
   (A) Byzantine   (B) Gothic   (C) Renaissance
   (D) Baroque   (E) Victorian

        7. Ⓐ Ⓑ Ⓒ Ⓓ Ⓔ

8. The most intrinsically American and most durable of all motion picture genres is
   (A) romantic comedy   (B) black comedy   (C) musical comedy
   (D) the western   (E) tragedy

        8. Ⓐ Ⓑ Ⓒ Ⓓ Ⓔ

9. "I have found that all the bronze my furnace contained had been exhausted in the head of this figure [of the statue of Perseus]. . . . It was a miracle . . . I seemed to see in this head the head of God. . . ." This statement was made by
   (A) Grangousier   (B) Cellini   (C) Machiavelli
   (D) Michelangelo   (E) Praxiteles

        9. Ⓐ Ⓑ Ⓒ Ⓓ Ⓔ

10. One of the following plays was not written by Shakespeare:
    (A) *Titus Andronicus*   (B) *Dr. Faustus*
    (C) *Love's Labour's Lost*   (D) *The Tempest*   (E) *Coriolanus*

       10. Ⓐ Ⓑ Ⓒ Ⓓ Ⓔ

11. The monarch known as the "Sun King" was
    (A) Charles II of England   (B) Edward I of England
    (C) George VI of England   (D) Henry IV of France
    (E) Louis XIV of France

       11. Ⓐ Ⓑ Ⓒ Ⓓ Ⓔ

12. The difference between sonata and sonata-allegro is
    (A) the sonata is more contrapuntal
    (B) the sonata is more homophonic
    (C) one is faster than the other
    (D) the sonata is a broad form which may contain movements in the sonata-allegro form
    (E) the sonata-allegro form preceded the sonata

       12. Ⓐ Ⓑ Ⓒ Ⓓ Ⓔ

13. Impressionism in music originated in France under the leadership of
    (A) Debussy and Ravel   (B) Poulenc and Hindemith
    (C) Stravinsky and Bartok   (D) Debussy and Chopin
    (E) Sessions and Varese

       13. Ⓐ Ⓑ Ⓒ Ⓓ Ⓔ

14. Leonardo da Vinci was one of the greatest artists of the period known as
    (A) Baroque   (B) the early Renaissance
    (C) the high Renaissance   (D) Gothic   (E) Byzantine

       14. Ⓐ Ⓑ Ⓒ Ⓓ Ⓔ

15. The biographer of Charlemagne was
    (A) Eginhard (B) Tacitus (C) Hilderich (D) Pippin (E) Carloman

       15. Ⓐ Ⓑ Ⓒ Ⓓ Ⓔ

16. The play which shows the downfall of a man as a result of biological urges or his social environment is called
    (A) epic theater   (B) neorealism   (C) romantic tragedy
    (D) deterministic tragedy   (E) Ibsenian irony

       16. Ⓐ Ⓑ Ⓒ Ⓓ Ⓔ

17. The unresolved or "open" ending is one of the trademarks of
    (A) Greek tragedy   (B) Restoration comedy
    (C) Shakespearean comedy   (D) Roman tragedy
    (E) modern plays and cinema

       17. Ⓐ Ⓑ Ⓒ Ⓓ Ⓔ

18. Dante's *Divine Comedy* contains how many cantos?

    (A) 3   (B) 4   (C) 33   (D) 99   (E) 100

18. Ⓐ Ⓑ Ⓒ Ⓓ Ⓔ

19. The origins of baroque architecture can be traced to Sansovino, Palladio, and

    (A) Bellini   (B) Michelangelo   (C) Giotto

    (D) da Vinci   (E) Lorenzo

19. Ⓐ Ⓑ Ⓒ Ⓓ Ⓔ

20. The poem "Richard Cory" was written by

    (A) Edward Arlington Robinson   (B) Robert Frost

    (C) Erskine Caldwell   (D) T. S. Eliot   (E) Walt Whitman

20. Ⓐ Ⓑ Ⓒ Ⓓ Ⓔ

21. The greatest ballet dancer of the beginning of the 20th century and prima ballerina of the Maryinsky Theater was

    (A) Tamara Karsavina   (B) Galina Ulanova   (C) Anna Pavlova

    (D) Tamara Toumanova   (E) Alexandra Danilova

21. Ⓐ Ⓑ Ⓒ Ⓓ Ⓔ

22. James Branch Cabell's novel that infused medieval romance with obvious sexual symbolism is entitled

    (A) *The Harbor*   (B) *Jurgen*   (C) *The Brass Check*

    (D) *The Jungle*   (E) *Winesburg, Ohio*

22. Ⓐ Ⓑ Ⓒ Ⓓ Ⓔ

23. Polyphonic texture is

    (A) chordal texture   (B) unaccompanied melody

    (C) accompanied melody   (D) a combination of melodies

    (E) common to all forms

23. Ⓐ Ⓑ Ⓒ Ⓓ Ⓔ

24. *The Tempest* is a play of airy fancy and romantic charm, but it cannot be mistaken for a young man's work because

    (A) its comic situations are in reality serious

    (B) its conclusion offers no hope for mankind

    (C) it contains the kind of crowd-pleasing devices that can only come with experience

    (D) it abounds in wise reflections on human nature and human existence

    (E) we know that it was the last play that Shakespeare ever wrote

24. Ⓐ Ⓑ Ⓒ Ⓓ Ⓔ

25. One of the most popular films of the late 1960s concerned a young man who has an affair with his future wife's mother. The name of the film is

    (A) *Hello, Dolly*   (B) *Joe*   (C) *Midnight Cowboy*

    (D) *Easy Rider*   (E) *The Graduate*

25. Ⓐ Ⓑ Ⓒ Ⓓ Ⓔ

26. A well-known Spanish court painter of the 18th century was

    (A) Velasquez   (B) Ribera   (C) Pisarro

    (D) Goya   (E) Pisano

26. Ⓐ Ⓑ Ⓒ Ⓓ Ⓔ

27. The Greek playwright who introduced the third actor into tragedy was

    (A) Agamemnon   (B) Euripides   (C) Socrates

    (D) Thespis   (E) Clytaemnestra

27. Ⓐ Ⓑ Ⓒ Ⓓ Ⓔ

28. The Romantic Period of literature gave birth to a special kind of horror story, the

    (A) pastoral romance   (B) epic   (C) vignette

    (D) Gothic novel   (E) dramatic monologue

28. Ⓐ Ⓑ Ⓒ Ⓓ Ⓔ

29. The story of the founding of Rome by the mythical Aeneas was written by   29. Ⓐ Ⓑ Ⓒ Ⓓ Ⓔ
   (A) Augustus   (B) Vergil   (C) Homer   (D) Sibyl
   (E) Romulus

30. Wagner's last opera concerning the search for the Holy Grail is   30. Ⓐ Ⓑ Ⓒ Ⓓ Ⓔ
   (A) *Festspielhaus*   (B) *Cosima*   (C) *Siegfried*
   (D) *Parsifal*   (E) *Wahnfried*

31. Rome contributed *all but one* of the following to architecture: 31. Ⓐ Ⓑ Ⓒ Ⓓ Ⓔ
   (A) an emphasis on verticality
   (B) design of significant interiors
   (C) buildings for use
   (D) the arch and vault as a building principle
   (E) the flying buttress

32. A Post-Impressionist painter best known for his South Seas subjects was   32. Ⓐ Ⓑ Ⓒ Ⓓ Ⓔ
   (A) Paul Gauguin   (B) Vincent van Gogh
   (C) Toulouse-Lautrec   (D) Paul Cezanne
   (E) Georges Seurat

33. A modern playwright who believes in "aesthetic distancing" is   33. Ⓐ Ⓑ Ⓒ Ⓓ Ⓔ
   (A) Arthur Miller   (B) Eugene O'Neill
   (C) Jean Paul Sartre   (D) Stanley Kubrick
   (E) Bertolt Brecht

34. The central figure in the Bayeux tapestry is   34. Ⓐ Ⓑ Ⓒ Ⓓ Ⓔ
   (A) Alexander the Great
   (B) William the Conqueror
   (C) Edward the Confessor
   (D) Gregory the Great
   (E) Charlemagne

35. During the Hellenic Period, the great center of Greek culture was located at   35. Ⓐ Ⓑ Ⓒ Ⓓ Ⓔ
   (A) Alexandria   (B) Antioch   (C) Athens
   (D) Rhodes   (E) Pergamon

Questions 36–38 refer to the following groups of people.

   (A) Paul Klee, Marc Chagall, Pablo Picasso
   (B) Samuel Barber, Alban Berg, George Gershwin
   (C) Paul Johnson, Mies van der Rohe, Louis Sullivan
   (D) Anne Jackson, Anne Tyler, Anne Bradstreet
   (E) Amy Lowell, May Swenson, Nikki Giovanni

36. Which is a group of twentieth century painters?   36. Ⓐ Ⓑ Ⓒ Ⓓ Ⓔ

37. Which is a group of twentieth century American poets?   37. Ⓐ Ⓑ Ⓒ Ⓓ Ⓔ

38. Which is a group of twentieth century composers of opera?   38. Ⓐ Ⓑ Ⓒ Ⓓ Ⓔ

39. All of the following are of the House of Atreus *except*
    (A) Agamemnon   (B) Menelaus   (C) Orestes
    (D) Iphigenia   (E) Aphrodite

    39. Ⓐ Ⓑ Ⓒ Ⓓ Ⓔ

40. Willy Loman is one of the most famous characters in the modern American theater. He appears in
    (A) *Cat on a Hot Tin Roof*   (B) *Murder in the Cathedral*
    (C) *The Sand Box*   (D) *Oklahoma!*   (E) *Death of a Salesman*

    40. Ⓐ Ⓑ Ⓒ Ⓓ Ⓔ

41. A playwright who anticipated the contemporary "Theater of the Absurd," author of *Six Characters in Search of an Author*, was
    (A) Lorca   (B) Brecht   (C) Gilbert   (D) O'Neill
    (E) Pirandello

    41. Ⓐ Ⓑ Ⓒ Ⓓ Ⓔ

42. Though a Greek slave of Rome, this historian became very interested in the imperial expansion of Rome and wrote much about it. He was
    (A) Caesar   (B) Polybius   (C) Plautus   (D) Seneca
    (E) Pompey

    42. Ⓐ Ⓑ Ⓒ Ⓓ Ⓔ

43. A painter noted for his scenes of the American West was
    (A) Thomas Hart Benton   (B) Frederick Remington
    (C) Grant Wood   (D) Edward Hopper   (E) John Marin

    43. Ⓐ Ⓑ Ⓒ Ⓓ Ⓔ

44. "Capriccio Espagnol" and "Scheherezade" were written by
    (A) Glinka   (B) Moussorgsky   (C) Tchaikovsky
    (D) Borodin   (E) Rimsky-Korsakov

    44. Ⓐ Ⓑ Ⓒ Ⓓ Ⓔ

45. Which of the following composers served as a bridge between the Romantic and Classical periods?
    (A) Bruckner   (B) Wagner   (C) Tchaikovsky
    (D) Beethoven   (E) Berlioz

    45. Ⓐ Ⓑ Ⓒ Ⓓ Ⓔ

46. John Steinbeck traveled America and reported on the people he met, the things he saw. His constant companion on one trip was his dog.
    (A) Mitzi   (B) Rocinante   (C) Charlie   (D) Joseph
    (E) Willie

    46. Ⓐ Ⓑ Ⓒ Ⓓ Ⓔ

47. The creator of the character L'il Abner is
    (A) Mort Walker   (B) Hank Ketcham   (C) Charles Schulz
    (D) Chester Gould   (E) Al Capp

    47. Ⓐ Ⓑ Ⓒ Ⓓ Ⓔ

48. All of the following operas were written by Mozart *except*
    (A) *Don Giovanni*   (B) *The Marriage of Figaro*
    (C) *Orpheus and Eurydice*   (D) *The Magic Flute*
    (E) *Cosi fan tutte*

    48. Ⓐ Ⓑ Ⓒ Ⓓ Ⓔ

49. The American poet who wrote such works as "Abraham Lincoln Walks at Midnight" and "The Santa Fe Trail" was
    (A) Vachel Lindsay   (B) William Carlos Williams
    (C) Walt Whitman   (D) Carl Sandburg   (E) Van Wyck Brooks

    49. Ⓐ Ⓑ Ⓒ Ⓓ Ⓔ

50. The medieval liturgical drama   50. Ⓐ Ⓑ Ⓒ Ⓓ Ⓔ
  (A) was an outgrowth of the Roman theater
  (B) was an outgrowth of the Greek theater
  (C) sprang up independently of Roman and Greek theaters
  (D) was based upon pagan rites and rituals
  (E) owed much to such writers as Ben Jonson and William Shakespeare

51. The best known of the medieval morality plays is   51. Ⓐ Ⓑ Ⓒ Ⓓ Ⓔ
  (A) *Quem Quaeritis Trope*   (B) *The Castell of Perseverance*
  (C) *The Life of Christ*   (D) *Hamlet*   (E) *Everyman*

52. The first collected edition of Shakespeare's plays is known as   52. Ⓐ Ⓑ Ⓒ Ⓓ Ⓔ
  (A) *The Collected Works of William Shakespeare*
  (B) *The First Quarto*
  (C) *The First Folio*
  (D) *"Othello" and Other Plays by William Shakespeare*
  (E) *Shakespeare's Plays: 1623*

53. An American author who vigorously attacked the "genteel tradition"   53. Ⓐ Ⓑ Ⓒ Ⓓ Ⓔ
  and who took an active interest in American social problems was
  (A) Stephen Crane   (B) Edward Arlington Robinson
  (C) Edgar Lee Masters   (D) Theodore Dreiser
  (E) Thomas Wolfe

54. Two composers from the Baroque period are   54. Ⓐ Ⓑ Ⓒ Ⓓ Ⓔ
  (A) Brahms and Berlioz   (B) Stravinsky and Piston
  (C) Bach and Handel   (D) Mozart and Haydn
  (E) Verdi and Puccini

55. Most jazz has a standard form of   55. Ⓐ Ⓑ Ⓒ Ⓓ Ⓔ
  (A) sonata-allegro   (B) rondo   (C) theme and variation
  (D) fugue   (E) canon

56. Surrealist art is associated with   56. Ⓐ Ⓑ Ⓒ Ⓓ Ⓔ
  (A) frottage, the subconscious, paradox
  (B) anxiety, silence, the metaphysical
  (C) timelessness, literary origins, loneliness
  (D) fantasy, Freud, free association
  (E) all of these

57. Unlike most of the later troubadors, the *jongleurs* of the 11th century   57. Ⓐ Ⓑ Ⓒ Ⓓ Ⓔ
  were
  (A) not of noble birth
  (B) accompanied by a small orchestra
  (C) able to sing the *chanson de geste*
  (D) more sophisticated
  (E) accompanied by two men

58. "The Russian Five" included   58. Ⓐ Ⓑ Ⓒ Ⓓ Ⓔ
  (A) Pushkin and Tchaikovsky   (B) Borodin and Balakirev
  (C) Stravinsky and Glinka   (D) Tolstoy and Dostoevsky
  (E) Turgenev and Moussorgsky

59. Two composers of the Italian Renaissance were
    (A) Ockeghem and Paderewski   (D) Josquin and Cellini
    (B) Monteverdi and Bellini   (E) Parmagianino and Cavalli
    (C) Palestrina and Josquin

59. Ⓐ Ⓑ Ⓒ Ⓓ Ⓔ

60. Which of the following is not found in the ninth circle of Dante's Hell?
    (A) Cania   (B) Antenora   (C) Ptolomea   (D) Judecca   (E) Dis

60. Ⓐ Ⓑ Ⓒ Ⓓ Ⓔ

61. The convention by which an actor, "unnoticed" by others on the stage,
    makes a brief comment to the audience, is the
    (A) soliloquy   (B) perspective   (C) aside
    (D) periphery   (E) denouement

61. Ⓐ Ⓑ Ⓒ Ⓓ Ⓔ

62. The Globe Theater
    (A) was closed on all sides but open on top
    (B) had a stage which extended into the audience area
    (C) depended upon natural lighting
    (D) was built in 1599
    (E) all of these

62. Ⓐ Ⓑ Ⓒ Ⓓ Ⓔ

63. "One that lov'd not wisely but too well," describes
    (A) Hamlet   (B) Romeo   (C) Cleopatra   (D) Othello   (E) Desdemona

63. Ⓐ Ⓑ Ⓒ Ⓓ Ⓔ

64. Chaconne and passacaglia are both
    (A) sonata-allegro   (B) rondo form   (C) scherzo and trio
    (D) vocal forms   (E) theme and variations

64. Ⓐ Ⓑ Ⓒ Ⓓ Ⓔ

65. Canon and fugue are musical forms characterized by
    (A) sonata-allegro form   (B) repeated entrance of a theme
    (C) augmentation   (D) atonality   (E) dynamic contrast

65. Ⓐ Ⓑ Ⓒ Ⓓ Ⓔ

66. The above is an example of the architecture of
    (A) Christopher Wren   (B) Inigo Jones
    (C) Frank Lloyd Wright   (D) Joseph Paxton
    (E) Gustave Eiffel

66. Ⓐ Ⓑ Ⓒ Ⓓ Ⓔ

67. Artists rediscovered man, glorified him as part of the world, and
    scientists discovered the world around man in the time of
    (A) the Roman Empire   (B) the Middle Ages
    (C) the late 19th century   (D) the Greek period
    (E) the Renaissance

68. All of the following were written by Ernest Hemingway *except*
    (A) *For Whom the Bell Tolls*   (B) *The Old Lions*
    (C) *The Old Man and the Sea*   (D) *Death in the Afternoon*
    (E) *The Sun Also Rises*

69. The Renaissance Italian author who, writing in the vernacular, op-
    posed the extension of the Pope's secular power was
    (A) Cellini   (B) Machiavelli   (C) Dante   (D) Scotti
    (E) Manzoni

70. John Steinbeck once undertook a study of tide pools with Dr. Ed
    Ricketts, a noted marine biologist. The trip is recorded in Steinbeck's
    (A) *Two Years Before the Mast*
    (B) *Tide Pools and Sea Urchins*
    (C) *Log of the Sea of Cortez*
    (D) *The Dory*
    (E) *Innocents Abroad*

71. In Shakespeare's plays,
    (A) all the female roles were played by boys when the plays were
        first produced
    (B) highly stylized language was a convention of the theater
    (C) the "tragic hero" was always of noble birth
    (D) the dialogue was written in poetic forms
    (E) all of the above

72. A Roman writer of comedy was
    (A) Menander   (B) Hrosvitha   (C) Plautus
    (D) Seneca   (E) Sodomaeus

73. The American author who gave the English language the word "bab-
    bitry" was
    (A) Sinclair Lewis   (B) Robinson Jeffers   (C) Willa Cather
    (D) Edward Arlington Robinson   (E) John Steinbeck

74. The author of *Robinson Crusoe* was
    (A) Alexander Pope   (B) Jean Jacques Rousseau
    (C) Daniel Defoe   (D) Jonathan Swift   (E) Jean Corneille

75. Rubens was one of the most influential of the Baroque painters. One
    of his most typical paintings is
    (A) "The Death of the Virgin"   (B) "Guernica"
    (C) "Portrait of Philip of Spain"
    (D) "The Descent from the Cross"   (E) "The Forge"

Part II

Directions: Each of the questions or incomplete statements below is followed by five suggested answers or completions. Select the one that is best in each case.

Number of Questions: 75
Time: 45 minutes

76. The photograph above is an example of a style of painting popular during which century?

    (A) 15th   (B) 17th   (C) 18th   (D) 19th   (E) 20th

76. Ⓐ Ⓑ Ⓒ Ⓓ Ⓔ

77. When the ghost in *Hamlet* appeared, most people in Shakespeare's audience would have

    (A) laughed, because the supernatural was considered ridiculous
    (B) recognized the figure as a dramatic symbol
    (C) been unimpressed, since the device had been over-used
    (D) reacted in a manner which we are unable to guess
    (E) believed in the actuality of ghosts appearing on stage

77. Ⓐ Ⓑ Ⓒ Ⓓ Ⓔ

78. The architect who designed the Crystal Palace was
    (A) Charles Percier   (B) P. F. L. Fontaine
    (C) Joseph Paxton   (D) James Wyatt
    (E) Georges-Eugene Haussmann

78. Ⓐ Ⓑ Ⓒ Ⓓ Ⓔ

79. Agamemnon's wife was
    (A) Jocasta   (B) Clytaemnestra   (C) Cassandra
    (D) Iphigenia   (E) Antigone

79. Ⓐ Ⓑ Ⓒ Ⓓ Ⓔ

80. *The Screw Tape Letters* was written by
    (A) T. S. Eliot   (B) Goethe   (C) Mephistopheles
    (D) C. S. Lewis   (E) H. L. Mencken

80. Ⓐ Ⓑ Ⓒ Ⓓ Ⓔ

81. The "green ey'd monster which doth mock the meat it feeds on" is
    (A) revenge   (B) jealousy   (C) pride   (D) hatred
    (E) lust

81. Ⓐ Ⓑ Ⓒ Ⓓ Ⓔ

82. Molière wrote during the reign of
    (A) Charles III   (B) James II   (C) Henry IV
    (D) Louis XIV   (E) Elizabeth I

82. Ⓐ Ⓑ Ⓒ Ⓓ Ⓔ

83. The Greek chorus did not
    (A) foretell the future   (B) explain past actions
    (C) serve as an additional character in the play
    (D) philosophize   (E) help to move scenery

83. Ⓐ Ⓑ Ⓒ Ⓓ Ⓔ

84. Creon repents and goes to free Antigone, but she has already hanged
    herself. This is an example of
    (A) denouement   (B) proscenium   (C) deus ex machina
    (D) irony   (E) *in medias res*

84. Ⓐ Ⓑ Ⓒ Ⓓ Ⓔ

85. The modern meaning of *deus ex machina* is
    (A) a wheeled platform used as part of the scenery
    (B) a god from a machine
    (C) a mechanical device for staging elaborate effects
    (D) the catastrophic event at the climax
    (E) an unsatisfactory resolution to problems of plot by means of an
        event for which the audience has not been prepared

85. Ⓐ Ⓑ Ⓒ Ⓓ Ⓔ

86. Vincent van Gogh
    (A) faithfully followed the Impressionist techniques
    (B) felt that Impressionism did not allow the artist enough freedom
        to express his inner feelings
    (C) believed the artist must paint only what he could see, not what
        appeared, in the mind
    (D) founded the movement in art called "abstract art"
    (E) led seventeenth-century art back to natural forms of realism

86. Ⓐ Ⓑ Ⓒ Ⓓ Ⓔ

87. A single melody with subordinate harmony demonstrates
    (A) polyphonic texture   (B) homophonic texture
    (C) monophonic texture   (D) bitonality   (E) rondo form

87. Ⓐ Ⓑ Ⓒ Ⓓ Ⓔ

88. The musical terms consonance and dissonance are most properly used
    in a discussion of
    (A) texture   (B) tone color   (C) melody   (D) rhythm
    (E) harmony

88. Ⓐ Ⓑ Ⓒ Ⓓ Ⓔ

89. Gregorian chants are examples of which textures?
    (A) monophonic   (B) contrapuntal   (C) polyphonic
    (D) homophonic   (E) modern

89. Ⓐ Ⓑ Ⓒ Ⓓ Ⓔ

90. Which of the following is not characteristic of the Gregorian chant?
    (A) meter   (B) use of Latin   (C) use of eight church modes
    (D) male choir   (E) a capella

90. Ⓐ Ⓑ Ⓒ Ⓓ Ⓔ

91. A school of art known as *Surrealism* developed in the 1920s. A fore-runner of the Surrealist school and painter of "I and My Village" was
(A) Picasso   (B) Chagall   (C) Klee   (D) Kandinsky
(E) Beckman

91. A B C D E

92. Sometimes called a western realist, this author wrote many tales of the American West and its mining towns. He is
(A) A. P. Oakhurst
(B) Ambrose Bierce
(C) Stephen Crane
(D) Bret Harte
(E) M. Shipton

92. A B C D E

93. The book *The Satyricon* was written by
(A) Federico Fellini
(B) Hylette
(C) Encolpius
(D) Trimalchio
(E) Petronius

93. A B C D E

94. "The Rhapsody in Blue" was composed by
(A) Paul Whiteman
(B) Oscar Levant
(C) Leonard Bernstein
(D) Antheil Carpenter
(E) George Gershwin

94. A B C D E

95. The first "King of Jazz" was a New Orleans barber named
(A) Al Hirt
(B) Bix Beiderbecke
(C) Sidney Bechet
(D) Charles Bolden
(E) Papa Celestine

95. A B C D E

96. Almost every country in Europe has a national hero who has been enshrined in epic poems and myths. The national hero of Italy is
(A) El Cid   (B) Orlando Furioso   (C) Beowulf
(D) Roland   (E) Giovanni Magnifioso

96. A B C D E

97. "The Canticle of the Sun" was written by
(A) Dante   (B) Chaucer   (C) St. Francis of Assisi
(D) Caedmon   (E) The Venerable Bede

97. A B C D E

98. The 20th-century composer who first used the twelve-tone scale was
(A) Arnold Schoenberg   (B) Leonard Bernstein
(C) John Cage   (D) George Gershwin
(E) Richard Rodgers

98. A B C D E

99. Which of the following statements is *false?*
    (A) Satire is a means of showing dissatisfaction with an established institution or principle.
    (B) Satire is most easily accepted by an audience holding various beliefs or beliefs different from those of the playwright.
    (C) Satire was an early form of comedy.
    (D) *Lysistrata* is a classic example of satire.
    (E) Modern satire does not run the risk of being offensive.

100. LADY BRACKNELL: "Do you smoke?"
     JACK: "Well, yes, I must admit I smoke."
     LADY BRACKNELL: "I am glad to hear it. A man should always have an occupation of some sort."

    The dialogue from Oscar Wilde's *The Importance of Being Earnest* illustrates
    (A) sympathy
    (B) empathy
    (C) corn
    (D) comic pathos
    (E) linguistic wit

101. Probably the most famous conductor today, especially noted for his Young Peoples Concert with the New York Philharmonic, is
    (A) Leonard Bernstein   (B) Leopold Stokowski
    (C) Sir Thomas Beecham   (D) Rudolf Serkin
    (E) Elliot Mordkin

102. Which American author, grandchild of a president, wrote a famous book about his own education?
    (A) Henry Adams   (B) Robert Jackson   (C) Jonathan Tyler
    (D) Elliot Roosevelt   (E) Howard Taft

103. Shakespeare did not invent any of his plots, but adapted material from other sources, including a history of the British Isles. One of his plays tells of the efforts of a Scots nobleman to become king through murder and blackmail; this play is
    (A) *Richard the III*
    (B) *Henry the IV, Part I*
    (C) *Macbeth*
    (D) *As You Like It*
    (E) *A Comedy of Errors*

104. That Alfred, Lord Tennyson was poet laureate of England's Victorian Age was fitting because he
    (A) pleased his queen only
    (B) only felt as the English felt
    (C) only thought as Englishmen thought
    (D) raised both his feeling and his thought to the realm of the universal
    (E) pleased the landed gentry

105. The composer who wrote the musical portions of Molière's plays was
(A) Purcell   (B) Cavalli   (C) Liszt   (D) Quinalt
(E) Lully

106. "I saw the sky descending black and white" is an example of
(A) iambic pentameter
(B) anapestic dimeter
(C) spondaic hexameter
(D) dactylic pentameter
(E) iambic tetrameter

107. Which of the following statements concerning courtly love is *false?*
(A) The idea was born in Provence in the 11th century.
(B) It was limited to the nobility.
(C) True love was considered impossible between husband and wife.
(D) Christian behavior was shunned.
(E) It glorified adultery.

108. The site of Apollo's great oracle was
(A) Parnassus   (B) Olympus   (C) Athens   (D) Crete
(E) Delphi

109. The "Age of Faith" is a term which best applies to the
(A) classical Greek period   (B) Baroque period
(C) Gothic period   (D) Renaissance   (E) 18th century

110. Good design is primarily
(A) ornamental and decorative
(B) functional and aesthetically pleasing
(C) expressive of the personality of the designer
(D) a reflection of the philosophical attitudes of the day
(E) religious

111. The man who engineered the Eiffel Tower was
(A) Joseph Paxton   (B) Henri Labrouste   (C) James Wyatt
(D) Charles Percier   (E) Gustave Eiffel

112. With substantial truth, it may be said that French literature begins with
(A) *The Conquests of Charlemagne*
(B) *The Song of Roland*
(C) *The Romance of the Rose*
(D) *Ganelon's Victory*
(E) *Gargantua and Pantagruel*

113. One of the most charming literary works of the Middle Ages, an alternation between prose and verse, is
(A) "Stabat Mater"
(B) "Our Lady's Tumbler"
(C) "Romans d'Aventure"
(D) "Garin de Beaucaire"
(E) "Aucassin and Nicolette"

114. Giotto is noted for
   (A) writing a poem on a Grecian urn
   (B) discovering the principle of the flying buttress
   (C) the beginning of realistic painting in Western art, about 1300
   (D) impressionistic painting since 1900
   (E) inventing a secret process, now lost, for turning jewels into
       stained glass

114. A B C D E

British Crown Copyright —
reproduced with the permission of
the Controller of Her Britannic
Majesty's Stationery office.

115. The above is a photograph of
   (A) the Parthenon   (B) the Coliseum   (C) Stonehenge
   (D) the Temple at Karnak   (E) the Lighthouse at Knossos

115. A B C D E

116. In 1814 Franz Schubert became the assistant headmaster at his
   father's school. He did not really wish to take the job but did so
   because
   (A) it provided him with a meager salary
   (B) it kept him out of the draft
   (C) it gave him much needed experience
   (D) his voice had changed
   (E) his mother wanted him to take the position

116. A B C D E

117. Deucalion is
   (A) the Greek Noah
   (B) the 10th book of the Bible
   (C) one of the daughters of Danaus
   (D) a whirlpool Odysseus encountered on his voyage
   (E) the hero of the Trojan War

117. A B C D E

118. "Ding, dong, bell;
   Pussy's in the well.
   Who put her in?
   Little Johnny Thin."
   This is an example of
   (A) slant rhyme   (B) a run-on line   (C) sprung rhythm
   (D) hidden alliteration   (E) ottava rima

118. A B C D E

250   The Humanities

119. One of the greatest "heroines" of the Middle Ages and the subject of
innumerable paintings, musical compositions, stained glass windows,
and poems was
(A) St. Elizabeth (B) Mary Magdalene (C) St. Monica
(D) St. Agnes (E) St. Bernadette

119. Ⓐ Ⓑ Ⓒ Ⓓ Ⓔ

120. The musical sign ♭
(A) indicates false notes: falsetto
(B) lowers the pitch of a note by a full step
(C) precedes a note to be raised a full step
(D) precedes a note to be raised by a half step
(E) lowers the pitch of a note by a half step

120. Ⓐ Ⓑ Ⓒ Ⓓ Ⓔ

121. Songs that are not as unreal as operatic arias but much more sophis-
ticated than folk songs are called
(A) natural (B) erotic (C) lieder
(D) appassionata (E) nova

121. Ⓐ Ⓑ Ⓒ Ⓓ Ⓔ

122. As Candide journeyed from continent to continent, he searched for
(A) Dr. Pangloss (B) the Oreillons (C) Providence
(D) Cacambo (E) Cunegonde

122. Ⓐ Ⓑ Ⓒ Ⓓ Ⓔ

123. The photograph is a bust of
(A) Queen Elizabeth I
(B) Queen Nefertiti
(C) the goddess Athena
(D) Buddha
(E) an unknown African
warrior

123. Ⓐ Ⓑ Ⓒ Ⓓ Ⓔ

Hirmer Fotoarchiv Munchen

124.   "Whereas in silks my Julia goes
Then, then (methinks) how sweetly flows
That liquefaction of her clothes."
is an example of a
(A) sestet (B) sonnet (C) quatrain (D) triplet (E) couplet

124. Ⓐ Ⓑ Ⓒ Ⓓ Ⓔ

125. Most important to the success of a 19th-century drama was
(A) realism (B) kitchenism (C) contrast
(D) melodrama (E) gentle humor

125. Ⓐ Ⓑ Ⓒ Ⓓ Ⓔ

126. Even though there are relatively few ballads of the American city, perhaps the classic example is "Frankie and Johnny," the main theme of which is
    (A) the love of a man for his wife
    (B) a woman's love that leads her to destroy her lover
    (C) the love of Peddler Frank for his sway-backed horse
    (D) the love of a boy for his dog
    (E) the love of a man for a woman above his situation in life

127. Two principle forms of irony in tragedy are
    (A) Euripidean and Sophoclean   (B) Aeschylean and Euripidean
    (C) Ibsenian and Shavian   (D) Sophoclean and Aeschylean
    (E) comic and tragic

128. Leitmotif means
    (A) a note that is sung only once
    (B) a note or theme that is repeated
    (C) the leading motive
    (D) an aria
    (E) the first violinist is to take over leading the orchestra

129. Which of the following is not a convention of the Elizabethan theater?
    (A) Women's roles acted by young boys
    (B) Setting established by dialogue
    (C) A chorus of elders
    (D) Poetic language
    (E) The soliloquy

130. Rembrandt is an artist noted for the skill he shows in
    (A) use of light and shadow
    (B) the realistic inner feeling of his portraits
    (C) paintings and etchings of Biblical scenes
    (D) using the same model as he or she gradually changes and grows older
    (E) all of the above

131. In Greek mythology, the greatest of all musicians was
    (A) Dionysius
    (B) Musicus
    (C) Pan
    (D) Apollo
    (E) Orpheus

132. Odysseus' old nurse, who recognizes him from a scar on his leg, was named
    (A) Argus   (B) Euryclea   (C) Menelaus
    (D) Calliope   (E) Nausicaa

133. This Florentine autobiographer, goldsmith, and sculptor was a child of will rather than of reason and the quintessential Renaissance man:
    (A) Cellini   (B) Lucagnolo   (C) Urbrino
    (D) Francesco   (E) Machiavelli

126. Ⓐ Ⓑ Ⓒ Ⓓ Ⓔ

127. Ⓐ Ⓑ Ⓒ Ⓓ Ⓔ

128. Ⓐ Ⓑ Ⓒ Ⓓ Ⓔ

129. Ⓐ Ⓑ Ⓒ Ⓓ Ⓔ

130. Ⓐ Ⓑ Ⓒ Ⓓ Ⓔ

131. Ⓐ Ⓑ Ⓒ Ⓓ Ⓔ

132. Ⓐ Ⓑ Ⓒ Ⓓ Ⓔ

133. Ⓐ Ⓑ Ⓒ Ⓓ Ⓔ

134. *Libretto* means the
    (A) rhythm of a musical composition
    (B) words of a musical composition, especially an opera
    (C) tempo of a musical composition
    (D) directions to the conductor
    (E) full orchestra is to play

134. Ⓐ Ⓑ Ⓒ Ⓓ Ⓔ

135. A 20th-century poet who left America, went to England, and became one of England's most famous citizens was
    (A) Ezra Pound   (B) Robinson Jeffers
    (C) Archibald MacLeish   (D) Thomas Wolfe   (E) T. S. Eliot

135. Ⓐ Ⓑ Ⓒ Ⓓ Ⓔ

136. In the tale "Sir Gawain and the Green Knight," who was Gringolet? Gawain's
    (A) faithful hound   (B) horse   (C) sweetheart
    (D) page   (E) trusty sword

136. Ⓐ Ⓑ Ⓒ Ⓓ Ⓔ

137. The rebirth of the drama in the Middle Ages can be traced to
    (A) the Church   (B) strolling players   (C) Hroswitha
    (D) rich merchants   (E) professional acting guilds

137. Ⓐ Ⓑ Ⓒ Ⓓ Ⓔ

138. A versatile artist, the representative sculptor of his period, and immediate artistic ancestor of Michelangelo was
    (A) Donatello   (B) Cimabue   (C) Giotto
    (D) da Vinci   (E) Ghiberti

138. Ⓐ Ⓑ Ⓒ Ⓓ Ⓔ

139. All of the following operas were written by Puccini *except*
    (A) *Norma*   (B) *Madama Butterfly*   (C) *La Boheme*
    (D) *Gianni Schicchi*   (E) *Tosca*

139. Ⓐ Ⓑ Ⓒ Ⓓ Ⓔ

140. The Romantic poets were
    (A) uninterested in personal liberty
    (B) individualistic
    (C) conformists
    (D) appreciative of formal gardens
    (E) all drug addicts

140. Ⓐ Ⓑ Ⓒ Ⓓ Ⓔ

141. The first woman to earn her living as a novelist was
    (A) George Eliot   (B) Aphra Behn
    (C) Harriet Beecher Stowe   (D) George Sand
    (E) Anna Mowatt Richie

141. Ⓐ Ⓑ Ⓒ Ⓓ Ⓔ

142. Toulouse-Lautrec died from
    (A) absinthe poisoning
    (B) a fall from a cliff
    (C) strychnine, administered by his mistress
    (D) a knife wound, administered by a robber
    (E) a kick in the head from a horse

142. Ⓐ Ⓑ Ⓒ Ⓓ Ⓔ

143. Coleridge wrote all of the following except
    (A) poetry   (B) novels   (C) dramas
    (D) criticism   (E) essays

143. Ⓐ Ⓑ Ⓒ Ⓓ Ⓔ

144. This art is an example of
- (A) expressionism
- (B) impressionism
- (C) Greek art
- (D) Byzantine art
- (E) primitive art

144. [A] [B] [C] [D] [E]

145. The author of the one-act plays *The Toilet* and *Dutchman* is
- (A) Thomas Wolfe   (B) James Baldwin
- (C) Lorraine Hansbury   (D) LeRoi Jones (Imamu Baraka)
- (E) Countee Cullen

145. [A] [B] [C] [D] [E]

146. A contemporary British composer of the opera *Billy Budd* as well as other major works for orchestra and chorus is
- (A) Benjamin Britten   (B) John Lennon
- (C) Sir Thomas Beecham   (D) Floyd Carlisle
- (E) Richard Rodgers

146. [A] [B] [C] [D] [E]

147. The author of the classics of American humor *My World — And Welcome to It* and *Fables for our Time* was
- (A) Don Marquis   (B) Goodman Ace   (C) Abe Burrows
- (D) E. B. White   (E) James Thurber

147. [A] [B] [C] [D] [E]

148. The composer of *The Seven Last Words* was
- (A) Weber
- (B) Bach
- (C) Schubert
- (D) Haydn
- (E) Handel

148. [A] [B] [C] [D] [E]

149. A cathedral noted for its famous rose windows is located at
- (A) Canterbury
- (B) Rome
- (C) London
- (D) Chartres
- (E) Istanbul

149. [A] [B] [C] [D] [E]

150. Laocoön was
- (A) a priest of Poseidon, who died for trying to warn the Trojans against the Wooden Horse
- (B) a caterpillar who turned into a moth
- (C) the Roman God of Laughter
- (D) an Egyptian Pharaoh
- (E) a six-armed monster in Greek mythology

150. [A] [B] [C] [D] [E]

ANSWER KEY—SAMPLE EXAMINATION 1

Part I

1. A	14. C	27. B	40. E	52. C	64. E
2. E	15. A	28. D	41. E	53. D	65. B
3. C	16. D	29. B	42. B	54. C	66. C*
4. A	17. E	30. D	43. B	55. C	67. E
5. E	18. E	31. E	44. E	56. E	68. B
6. D	19. B	32. A	45. D	57. A	69. C
7. B	20. A	33. E	46. C	58. B	70. C
8. D	21. C	34. B	47. E	59. C	71. E
9. B	22. B	35. C	48. C	60. E	72. C
10. B	23. D	36. A	49. A	61. C	73. A
11. E	24. E	37. E	50. C	62. E	74. C
12. D	25. E	38. B	51. E	63. D	75. D
13. A	26. D	39. E			

Part II

76. D**	89. A	102. A	115. C	127. A	139. A
77. B	90. A	103. C	116. B	128. B	140. B
78. C	91. B	104. D	117. A	129. C	141. B
79. B	92. D	105. E	118. C	130. E	142. A
80. D	93. E	106. A	119. B	131. E	143. B
81. B	94. E	107. D	120. E	132. B	144. D***
82. D	95. D	108. E	121. C	133. A	145. D
83. E	96. B	109. C	122. E	134. B	146. A
84. D	97. C	110. B	123. B	135. E	147. E
85. E	98. A	111. E	124. D	136. B	148. D
86. B	99. E	112. B	125. D	137. A	149. D
87. B	100. E	113. E	126. B	138. A	150. A
88. E	101. A	114. C			

*The Solomon R. Guggenheim Museum.

**Van Gogh, *The Starry Night*, 1889, Oil on Canvas, 29″ x 36¼″, Collection, the Museum of Modern Art, New York. Acquired through the Lillie B. Bliss Bequest.

***Enthroned Madonna and Child, Byzantine School, National Gallery of Art, Washington, D.C., Andrew Mellon Collection.

SCORING CHART—SAMPLE EXAMINATION 1

After you have scored your Sample Examination 1, enter the results in the chart below; then transfer your Raw Score to the Progress Chart on page 14.

Total Test		Number Right	Number Wrong	Number Omitted	Raw Score
Part I:	75				
Part II:	75				
Total:	150				

ANSWER EXPLANATIONS—SAMPLE EXAMINATION 1
Part I

1. **A.** The other works are either not operas or were not written by Beethoven.
2. **E.** The Renaissance "rediscovered" all of the glories of the Hellenistic world, including its art, literature, and philosophy.
3. **C.** Suetonius wrote this series of biographies of Roman emperors from Julius Caesar to Domitian. This work had a great influence on the writing of biography in ancient times and in the Middle Ages.
4. **A.** A meter means a division of music into measures or bars.
5. **E.** *The Faerie Queene* is a social, political, and religious allegory, and is not to be taken as a factual representation of life.
6. **D.** The ceiling of the Sistine Chapel is one of Italy's greatest art treasures.
7. **B.** "Gothic" pertains to an architectural style prevalent in western Europe from the 12th through the 15th centuries.
8. **D.** Other countries have attempted to make westerns, but none has been successful.
9. **B.** Benvenuto Cellini (1500–1571) was an Italian sculptor, metal-worker, and author.
10. **B.** *Dr. Faustus* was written by Christopher Marlowe.
11. **E.** Louis XIV (1638–1715) was King of France from 1643 to 1715.
12. **D.** This is true by definition.
13. **A.** Impressionism was a late 19th century movement. The other composers listed are either not French, not Impressionist composers, or not both.
14. **C.** The Renaissance originated in Italy in the 14th century, and later spread through Europe. Leonardo da Vinci (1452–1519) lived during the peak of the Italian Renaissance.
15. **A.** Eginhard was a Frankish historian. His biography of Charlemagne is an important contemporary source on Charlemagne's reign.
16. **D.** The point is that man is "determined" by heredity and/or environment.
17. **E.** During other periods in time, all plays had a beginning, a middle, and an end.
18. **E.** The poem is divided into three canticles, each made up of thirty-three cantos, plus the first canto iñ "Inferno," which serves as an introduction to the entire poem.
19. **B.** Michelangelo was the famous painter of the Sistine Chapel.
20. **A.** E.A. Robinson (1869–1935) was an American poet who won the Pulitzer Prize three times.
21. **C.** Pavlova was promoted to prima ballerina in 1906, after a performance of *Swan Lake*.
22. **B.** The other works were not written by Cabell.
23. **D.** This is true by definition.
24. **E.** It is believed *The Tempest* was written between 1611 and 1616. It was first published in the First Folio.
25. **E.** Mrs. Robinson is the name of the woman, played by Anne Bancroft. Dustin Hoffman starred as the young man.
26. **D.** Goya was the leading painter, etcher, and designer of his day.
27. **B.** None of the others were Greek playwrights.
28. **D.** One of the most enduring popular examples of this genre is Mary Shelley's *Frankenstein*.
29. **B.** The work is *The Aeneid*.
30. **D.** *Parsifal* was first presented in 1882 in Bayreuth.
31. **E.** The flying buttress was a development in Gothic architecture.
32. **A.** Gauguin spent many years in Tahiti, painting native subjects.
33. **E.** Brecht has even written plays within plays within plays so that the audience is always aware it is attending a play, and not experiencing reality.
34. **B.** The Bayreux Tapestry depicts the Norman Conquest of England and the events leading up to it.
35. **C.** Athens was the home of the arts, mathematics, philosophy, etc.
36. **A.** The others are not 20th century painters.

37.	E.	The others are not 20th century poets.
38.	B.	The others are not 20th century composers of opera.
39.	E.	Aphrodite was the Greek goddess of love.
40.	E.	The play was written by Arthur Miller, and it ushered in a new concept of tragedy.
41.	E.	The others were playwrights, but they did not write *Six Characters in Search of an Author.*
42.	B.	Polybius is the only Greek slave in the group.
43.	B.	Remington is especially noted for his cowboys, Indians, and soldiers.
44.	E.	Rimsky-Korsakov (1844–1908) was a Russian composer.
45.	D.	Ludwig van Beethoven (1770–1827) studied with Mozart and Haydn and influenced the later Romantic composers.
46.	C.	The book Steinbeck wrote was entitled *Travels with Charlie.*
47.	E.	The others are cartoonists, but it was Al Capp who created L'il Abner, Daisy Mae, and the other inhabitants of Dogpatch.
48.	C.	*Orpheus and Eurydice* was written by Gluck.
49.	A.	Vachel Lindsay (1897–1931) was an American poet noted for his individualistic style, characterized by jazz-like rhythm.
50.	C.	The medieval liturgical drama developed during the celebration of the mass.
51.	E.	*Everyman* is a 15th century allegorical play. Everyman, the hero, is summoned by Death to appear before God. Of all his friends and virtues, only Good Deeds may accompany him.
52.	C.	The First Folio was printed in 1623.
53.	D.	Two of his best known novels are *An American Tragedy* and *Sister Carrie.*
54.	C.	The other composers are not both from the Baroque period.
55.	C.	Each time a musician plays a jazz work, he or she interprets the piece. Jazz is notoriously individualistic and variable.
56.	E.	To select but one of the other answers would be to only partially explain surrealism.
57.	A.	These early medieval minstrels came from the lower classes. They usually accompanied themselves on a simple musical instrument, such as a lute.
58.	B.	The Russian Five consisted of Borodin, Balakirev, Cui, Mussorgsky, and Rimsky-Korsakov. These men came to represent Russian music to the world in the mid-19th century.
59.	C.	This is the only example of two composers, both Italian and of the Renaissance period.
60.	E.	Dis is to be found in the fifth circle of Hell.
61.	C.	This is true by definition. It differs from the soliloquy in that, in the latter, the character reveals his thoughts in the form of a monologue, without addressing a listener.
62.	E.	To ignore any of the above would be to give an incomplete answer.
63.	D.	This line is spoken after the death of Othello, and refers to his intense passion for Desdemona, which led to his murdering her in a fit of jealousy.
64.	E.	This is true by definition.
65.	B.	This is true by definition.
66.	C.	Wright was a modern architect who believed in functional buildings, made of materials native to the region.
67.	E.	The clue is in the word "rediscovered." Renaissance means rebirth or revival of interest in learning.
68.	B.	Hemingway was a famous 20th century American writer who won the Nobel Prize for literature.
69.	C.	Dante's best known work is *The Divine Comedy.*
70.	C.	The Sea of Cortez, located in Mexico, sometimes called the Gulf of California, separates Baja California from Sonora.
71.	E.	The others are true, but only partial answers.
72.	C.	Plautus and Terence were the great Roman writers of comedy.
73.	A.	The word was coined from the title of Lewis' novel, *Babbitt.*
74.	C.	Defoe's second best known novel is *Moll Flanders.*
75.	D.	The other paintings were not done by Rubens.

Part II

76.	D.	The painting is "The Starry Night," by Van Gogh.

76. D.   The painting is "The Starry Night," by Van Gogh.

77. B.   Ghosts often appeared in Elizabethan plays as dramatic symbols. The audience was accustomed to the dramatic use of the ghost.

78. C.   Paxton first designed a similar but larger structure for the London Exhibition of 1851. In 1853 and 1854 he supervised the building of the Crystal Palace at Sydenham.

79. B.   Agamemnon was the leader of the Greeks in the Trojan War. Upon his return from the war Clytaemnestra and Aegisthus, her lover, murdered Agamemnon in his bath.

80. D.   Lewis' writings generally contain strong religious overtones.

81. B.   This line is from Shakespeare's *Othello*.

82. D.   Louis XIV ruled France from 1643 to 1715.

83. E.   The Greeks did not use scenery in their plays.

84. D.   Dramatic irony occurs when the audience understands the incongruity between a situation and the accompanying speeches, while the characters in the play remain unaware of the incongruity.

85. E.   The modern meaning is that of a contrived or improbable conclusion.

86. B.   Van Gogh is generally considered a Post-Impressionist.

87. B.   This is true by definition.

88. E.   Harmony, in music, refers to the structure of a musical composition from the point of view of its chordal characteristics and relationships.

89. A.   Gregorian chants contain a single melodic line.

90. A.   Gregorian chant is the monodic liturgical plainsong of the Roman Catholic Church.

91. B.   Chagall is also well known for his stained glass windows which adorn churches and synagogues throughout Europe and Israel.

92. D.   Two of Harte's best known short stories are "The Outcasts of Poker Flat" and "The Luck of Roaring Camp."

93. E.   Petronius, a Roman satirist, died circa 66 A.D.

94. E.   Gershwin was also the composer of the folk opera Porgy and Bess, as well as many popular songs.

95. D.   The others are jazz figures, but none were barbers.

96. B.   Ariosto's "Orlando Furioso" is the best known poem on the subject.

97. C.   Francis of Assisi was the founder of the Franciscan Order and one of the greatest of Christian saints.

98. A.   His twelve-tone system has become perhaps the most controversial musical development of the 20th century.

99. E.   Modern satire is often intentionally offensive.

100. E.   Wilde was noted for his linguistic wit.

101. A.   Bernstein is also a composer of merit. His best known Broadway show is the now-classic *West Side Story*.

102. A.   The book is entitled *The Education of Henry Adams*.

103. C.   The plots of the other plays mentioned are far different.

104. D.   The Victorian Era was one of England's greatest periods. It was an era of artistic achievement, industrialization, and colonization.

105. E.   Jean Baptiste Lully was an Italian operatic composer who lived mostly in France, and was court composer for Louis XIV.

106. A.   The iamb is a metrical foot consisting of a short syllable followed by a long or an unstressed syllable followed by a stressed. "Pentameter" means "five meters", or feet, and so iambic pentameter equals five iambs to the line.

107. D.   Under the rules of courtly love, the true knight was expected to be the epitome of the Christian man.

108. E.   Delphi is located near Mount Parnassus in ancient Greece. The legendary founder of the oracle was the goddess Gaea.

109. C.   The Gothic Period approximates the Middle Ages. It was during this period that the Roman Catholic Church had its greatest hold on the populace.

110. B. Good design may also be ornamental, decorative, and expressive of the personality of the designer, but primarily it is functional and aesthetically pleasing.

111. E. Eiffel was a French engineer, constructor of bridges and viaducts. The Eiffel Tower was erected in 1889 for the Paris Exposition.

112. B. "The Song of Roland" was an 11th century poem which immortalized the great French hero, Charlemagne.

113. E. "Aucassin and Nicolette," a love story partly in prose and partly in verse, was composed in the late 12th or early 13th century.

114. C. Giotto (c.1266–c.1337), Florentine painter and architect, was a perfector of form and movement. His faces and gestures are graceful and lifelike.

115. C. Stonehenge, a prehistoric structure, is located on Salisbury Plain, in England.

116. B. Schubert was a composer who was interested in music, not politics nor the military. Because of his position as assistant headmaster, he became draft exempt.

117. A. Deucalion and his wife, Pyrrha, are the principal figures in the Greek flood story.

118. C. Sprung rhythm is a term for a mixed meter in which the foot consists of a stressed syllable which may stand alone, or be combined with from one to three more unstressed syllables.

119. B. Mary Magdalene was a faithful follower of Jesus who stood at the cross when he was crucified.

120. E. This is a standard musical notation, a flat.

121. C. The other words have nothing to do with songs.

122. E. Cunegonde was the woman with whom Candide was in love.

123. B. Nefertiti was an ancient Egyptian queen, wife of Akhenaton, a pharoah who ruled from 1367 to 1350 B.C.

124. D. A triplet is three lines of poetry.

125. D. Melodrama is sometimes said to bear the same relation to tragedy that farce does to comedy. The protagonists are ultra-pure, the antagonists ultra-evil, and the credibility of both character and action is sacrificed for violent effect and emotional opportunism.

126. B. Frankie kills Johnny because he had been unfaithful to her.

127. A. In Sophoclean irony the characters are symbols of tragic human fate. In Euripidean tragedy, the irony lies in the inner psyche of humans, who no longer struggle with fate, but fight with the demons of their own souls; each man is responsible for his actions.

128. B. This is true by definition.

129. C. The Elizabethan theater, unlike the Greek, did not make use of a chorus.

130. E. All of the others are just partial answers.

131. E. Orpheus was so skilled in singing and in playing the lyre that he could enchant not only men and animals, but even trees and stones.

132. B. She appears in the story "The Odyssey."

133. A. None of the others mentioned was as knowledgeable and talented in so many areas as Cellini.

134. B. This is true by definition.

135. E. T.S. Eliot is known as the author of "The Wasteland," "The Love Song of J. Alfred Prufrock," the play *Murder in the Cathedral*, and a large number of other works.

136. B. Gringolet was to Gawain as Rociñante was to Don Quixote.

137. A. The beginnings of the modern drama can be traced to the Quem Quaeritis Trope.

138. A. Donatello (c. 1386–1466) was an Italian sculptor of the Italian Renaissance.

139. A. *Norma* was written by Vincenzo Bellini.

140. B. All of the other answers are completely untrue. The Romantic poets were concerned with individual liberty, were nonconformists, liked wild, informal gardens, with a hermit ensconced in the property, if possible, and, only a few were drug addicts.

141. B. Aphra Behn (1640–1689) was an English poet, dramatist, and novelist.

142. A. Absinthe is a green liqueur having a bitter licorice flavor and a high alcohol content.

143. B. Coleridge was a versatile writer of prose and poetry, but he never worked in the genre of the novel.

144. D. Byzantine refers to the style developed in Byzantium from the 5th century A.D. It is characterized by formality of design, frontal, stylized presentation of figures, rich use of color, especially gold, and generally religious subject matter.

145. D. The contemporary American author LeRoi Jones changed his name to Imamu Baraka when he adopted the Muslim faith.

146. A. Britten had become popular with children through his *Young Person's Guide to the Orchestra.*

147. E. Thurber often wrote concerning the battle between the sexes, with meek, mild-mannered man pitted against loud, aggressive woman. He frequently illustrated his works.

148. D. The Austrian composer Haydn, sometimes called the Father of the Symphony, is also famous as a developer of the sonata form and as a composer of oratorios.

149. D. The Gothic cathedral of Chartres is located in northern France.

150. A. As Laocoön warned the Trojans of the trick, two huge serpents swam in from the sea, seized Laocoön and his two sons, and killed them.

SAMPLE EXAMINATION 2

Part I

Directions: Each of the questions or incomplete statements below is followed by five suggested answers or completions. Select the one that is best in each case.

Number of Questions: 75
Time: 45 minutes

1. The French legend that dates from the time of Charlemagne is
   (A) *The Song of Ganelon*   (B) *The Song of Roland*
   (C) *The Song of Charlemagne*   (D) *Heloise and Abelard*
   (E) *The Decameron*

   1. Ⓐ Ⓑ Ⓒ Ⓓ Ⓔ

2. A playwright often called the "father of the thesis play" is
   (A) Oscar Wilde   (B) Jean Racine   (C) William D'Avenant
   (D) Henrik Ibsen   (E) Hermann Hesse

   2. Ⓐ Ⓑ Ⓒ Ⓓ Ⓔ

3. The Greek tragedies *Oedipus the King* and *Oedipus at Colonnus* were written by
   (A) Aeschylus   (B) Aristophanes   (C) Sophocles
   (D) Aristotle   (E) Euripides

   3. Ⓐ Ⓑ Ⓒ Ⓓ Ⓔ

4. The most popular meter in English poetry is
   (A) trochaic trimeter
   (B) anapestic dimeter
   (C) the alexandrine
   (D) iambic hexameter
   (E) iambic pentameter

   4. Ⓐ Ⓑ Ⓒ Ⓓ Ⓔ

5. In music, the notation $<$ indicates
   (A) diminuendo
   (B) crescendo
   (C) sharp
   (D) flat
   (E) natural

   5. Ⓐ Ⓑ Ⓒ Ⓓ Ⓔ

6. In art, *fresco* is
   (A) a form of sculpture
   (B) diverse materials pasted on a picture surface
   (C) a technique of dotting a surface with color
   (D) a light-and-dark technique
   (E) painting on moist plaster

   6. Ⓐ Ⓑ Ⓒ Ⓓ Ⓔ

7. What is commonly called the "song book" of the Bible?
   (A) Proverbs   (B) Song of Deborah   (C) Ecclesiastes
   (D) The Psalms   (E) Daniel

   7. Ⓐ Ⓑ Ⓒ Ⓓ Ⓔ

8. *Lysistrata* is considered a great classical satire because
   (A) the protagonist is a good comedian
   (B) it was written about war
   (C) the author has been dead 2,000 years
   (D) it continues to be relevant
   (E) it deals with sex

   8. Ⓐ Ⓑ Ⓒ Ⓓ Ⓔ

9. Menotti wrote all of the following operas *except*
(A) *The Medium*
(B) *The Telephone*
(C) *The Rake's Progress*
(D) *The Consul*
(E) *Amahl and the Night Visitor*

10. The photograph (right) is an example of
(A) neolithic art
(B) Corinthian art
(C) Greek art
(D) Renaissance art
(E) Egyptian art

Hirmer Fotoarchiv Munchen

11. A modern musical based on the novel *Don Quixote* is
(A) *Man of La Mancha*
(B) *West Side Story*　(C) *Hair*
(D) *Carousel*　(E) *Oklahoma!*

12. The conclusion of *Candide* is that
(A) "whatever is, is right"
(B) "love conquers all"
(C) "do unto others as you would have others do unto you"
(D) "we must cultivate our gardens"
(E) "the end justifies the means"

13. The prefix "ur" (as in *Ur-Faust, Ur-Hamlet*) means
(A) early or primitive　(B) alternate　(C) pirated
(D) last known　(E) composite

14. All of the following are 19th-century Russian writers *except*
(A) Chekhov　(B) Nabokov　(C) Tolstoy
(D) Turgenev　(E) Dostoevsky

15. The term *chamber music* can be applied to all of the following *except*
(A) quartets　(B) quintets　(C) trios
(D) symphonies　(E) duo sonatas

16. An outside wall of a room or building carried above an adjoining roof and pierced with windows is called a
    (A) transept   (B) clerestory   (C) pilaster
    (D) transverse arch   (E) atrium

17. A contemporary of E. A. Robinson, Edgar Lee Masters, Stephen Crane, and Theodore Dreiser, this poet holds a permanent place in American literature. His poetry was not only highly original, but it also stressed the problems of his age. He is
    (A) Robert Morse Lovett   (B) Walt Whitman
    (C) Vachel Lindsay   (D) Robinson Jeffers
    (E) William Vaughn Moody

18. This female satirist is known especially for her novel *Ethan Frome*. She was influenced by Henry James, and her interests were centered mainly in the changing society of New York City. She is
    (A) Edith Wharton   (B) Lily Bart   (C) Zelda Fitzgerald
    (D) Dorothy Parker   (E) Willa Cather

19. The blind seer who appears in several Greek tragedies is
    (A) Tiresias   (B) Homer   (C) Clytaemnestra
    (D) Oedipus   (E) Agamemnon

20. A large composition for voices and orchestra, usually based on a religious text, is
    (A) an aria   (B) an oratorio   (C) a capella
    (D) a madrigal   (E) a mass

21. France's two greatest writers of classical tragedy were
    (A) Molière and Rostand
    (B) Corneille and Racine
    (C) Jarry and Racine
    (D) Molière and Corneille
    (E) Balzac and Hugo

22. The above painting is
    (A) Whistler's "Arrangement in Gray and Black"
    (B) Klee's "Around the Fish"
    (C) Picasso's "Guernica"
    (D) Dürer's "Four Horsemen of the Apocalypse"
    (E) Poussin's "Triumph of Neptune and Amphitrite"

23. The author of *The Flies* and *The Clouds* was
    - (A) Beckett
    - (B) Sartre
    - (C) Menander
    - (D) Aristophanes
    - (E) Molière

24. Of the following statements concerning a literary work read in translation, which is true?
    - (A) It cannot escape the linguistic characteristics of the language into which it is turned.
    - (B) Often one loses the *shade* of meaning when translating from an ancient language.
    - (C) The translated work reflects the individuality of the age in which it is done.
    - (D) Both A and B
    - (E) All of the above

25. The opera *Boris Godunov* was based on a play by
    - (A) Chekhov
    - (B) Tolstoy
    - (C) Turgenev
    - (D) Gorki
    - (E) Pushkin

26. The musical notation 𝄢 : is
    - (A) the bass clef
    - (B) the treble clef
    - (C) sharp
    - (D) flat
    - (E) diminuendo

27. The prologue of *Oedipus the King* contains which of the following?
    - (A) the riddle of the Sphinx
    - (B) the chorus' request for Oedipus to rid the city of a plague
    - (C) the revelation that Polybus had died a natural death
    - (D) the birth of the protagonist
    - (E) a classic example of Euripidean irony

28. In the theater, the exploitation of "tender" emotions for their own sake—that is, whether motivated by the action or not—is called
    - (A) virtue
    - (B) temperamentality
    - (C) melodrama
    - (D) drama
    - (E) sentimentality

29. If you raise a musical note from G to G sharp, or lower a note from E to E flat, you are practicing
    - (A) staffing
    - (B) writing musical shorthand
    - (C) lengthening the composition
    - (D) harmonizing
    - (E) alteration

30. When the fingers of the hand that holds the bow are used to pluck the strings of an instrument, we call this
    - (A) fortissimo
    - (B) dissonance
    - (C) pizzicato
    - (D) diminuendo
    - (E) espressivo

31. Perhaps the "perfect courtier" of the Renaissance was
(A) Castiglione   (B) Shakespeare   (C) Maddox of Leicester
(D) Henry VIII   (E) Andrew the Chaplain

31. Ⓐ Ⓑ Ⓒ Ⓓ Ⓔ

32. The beaker in the photograph (right) is
(A) Egyptian
(B) Peruvian
(C) Byzantine
(D) Roman
(E) Greek

32. Ⓐ Ⓑ Ⓒ Ⓓ Ⓔ

The Metropolitan Museum of Art, Rogers Fund, 1917.

Questions 33, 34, and 35 are based on the following quotation:
"All nature is but Art, unknown to thee;
All Chance, Direction, which thou canst not see;
All Discord, Harmony not understood;
All partial Evil, universal Good:
And, spite of Pride, in erring Reason's spite,
One truth is clear, *Whatever is, is Right.*"

33. The preceding lines are from
(A) Yeats' "Sailing to Byzantium"
(B) Tennyson's "In Memoriam"
(C) Whitman's "Song of Myself"
(D) Wordsworth's "Ode on Intimations of Immortality"
(E) Pope's "Essay on Man"

33. Ⓐ Ⓑ Ⓒ Ⓓ Ⓔ

34. The verse form is the
(A) sestina   (B) ballad   (C) heroic couplet
(D) sonnet   (E) haiku

34. Ⓐ Ⓑ Ⓒ Ⓓ Ⓔ

35. The meter is
(A) iambic pentameter   (B) trochaic dimeter
(C) anapestic tetrameter   (D) iambic tetrameter
(E) trochaic pentameter

35. Ⓐ Ⓑ Ⓒ Ⓓ Ⓔ

36. Aeneas was supposedly the son of
(A) Helen   (B) Aphrodite   (C) Dido
(D) Minerva   (E) Ganymede

36. Ⓐ Ⓑ Ⓒ Ⓓ Ⓔ

37. Two 20th–century composers of atonal music are
(A) Bartok and Schoenberg   (B) Stravinsky and Debussy
(C) Ives and Wagner   (D) Prokofiev and Poulenc
(E) Rimsky-Korsakoff and Rachmaninoff

37. Ⓐ Ⓑ Ⓒ Ⓓ Ⓔ

38. The novels of Honoré de Balzac are known collectively as
    (A) *"Pere Goriot" and Other Stories*
    (B) *The Collected Works of Honore de Balzac*
    (C) *The Human Tragedy*
    (D) *The Human Comedy*
    (E) *Tales of the Tatras*

39. Only one of the following was a Renaissance painter:
    (A) Degas
    (B) Picasso
    (C) Michelangelo
    (D) Goya
    (E) Gainsborough

40. "To be, or not to be," is the beginning of a famous soliloquy from
    (A) *Dr. Faustus*   (B) *Romeo and Juliet*   (C) *Tamburlaine*
    (D) *Othello*   (E) *Hamlet*

41. Just as Aristophanes used satire and humor to attack the existing
    society in early Athens, so did this American author use these media
    to express the discrepancy between American expectations and the
    very disturbing reality of his times:
    (A) Charles Brockden Brown   (B) Augustus Longstreet
    (C) Robert Frost   (D) Edwin Arlington Robinson
    (E) Mark Twain

42. A period of enthusiasm for the classics in art, architecture, literature,
    drama, etc., is known as
    (A) the Age of Enlightenment   (B) the Neo-Classic Age
    (C) Romantic Age   (D) the Classical Age
    (E) the Renaissance

43. The painter who became interested in politics and who, under
    Napoleon, became First Painter of the Empire was:
    (A) Goya   (B) Gros   (C) Géricault   (D) Ingres
    (E) David

44. The early 14th century innovated what is called *ars nova* or a *faster
    time,* which has, to each measure,
    (A) 3 beats   (B) 4 beats   (C) 5 beats   (D) 6 beats
    (E) 8 beats

45. After the Dark Ages, the first professional people to make songs
    popular were called
    (A) troubadors   (B) barbershop quartets   (C) castrati
    (D) church choirs   (E) motets

46. In a Greek drama, the protagonist's tragic flaw is frequently pride;
    in a Greek comedy, it is often
    (A) anguish   (B) single-mindedness   (C) open-mindedness
    (D) lust   (E) super-intellectualism

47. Stimulated by the Cubist style, the Italian artists who introduced the additional concept of movement in "space-time" were the
    (A) Expressionists   (B) Impressionists   (C) Non-objectivists
    (D) Futurists   (E) Romanticists

47. Ⓐ Ⓑ Ⓒ Ⓓ Ⓔ

48. Henri Matisse is to Fauvism what Edvard Munch is to
    (A) Impressionism   (B) Surrealism   (C) Cubism
    (D) German Expressionism   (E) *Die Brucke*

48. Ⓐ Ⓑ Ⓒ Ⓓ Ⓔ

49. Franz Liszt
    (A) used classical forms in his music
    (B) experimented with atonal music
    (C) used romantic forms such as the tone poem
    (D) was a virtuoso performer on the violin
    (E) rejected the ideals of romanticism

49. Ⓐ Ⓑ Ⓒ Ⓓ Ⓔ

50. Oedipus married his mother
    (A) Helen   (B) Ismene   (C) Jocasta   (D) Tiresias   (E) Aphrodite

50. Ⓐ Ⓑ Ⓒ Ⓓ Ⓔ

51. Johann Strauss is best known for his
    (A) waltzes   (B) tone poems   (C) fugues   (D) sonatas
    (E) symphonies

51. Ⓐ Ⓑ Ⓒ Ⓓ Ⓔ

52. Often considered the "showpiece of French realism" is
    (A) Flaubert's *Madame Bovary*   (B) Balzac's *Eugénie Grandet*
    (C) Hugo's *Les Misérables*   (D) Zola's *Nana*
    (E) Voltaire's *The Huron*

52. Ⓐ Ⓑ Ⓒ Ⓓ Ⓔ

53. In an orthodox sense, Arabic literature begins with
    (A) *The Rubáiyát*   (B) *The Koran*   (C) *The Book of the Dead*
    (D) *The Ramayana*   (E) *The Mahabharata*

53. Ⓐ Ⓑ Ⓒ Ⓓ Ⓔ

Questions 54–55 refer to the photograph below.

54. The work pictured is
    (A) Michelangelo's "David"
    (B) Michelangelo's "Pietá"
    (C) "The Nike of Samothrace"
    (D) Brancusi's "Father and Son"
    (E) Praxiteles' "Hermes"

54. Ⓐ Ⓑ Ⓒ Ⓓ Ⓔ

Hirmer Fotoarchiv Munchen

55. If you wanted to see sculpture of this type, you would visit
    (A) Paris   (B) Washington, D.C.   (C) Rome   (D) Greece   (E) Munich

55. Ⓐ Ⓑ Ⓒ Ⓓ Ⓔ

56. Satan and God were talking about a certain pious man who had many blessings. Satan claimed that, if the man's blessings were taken away, and he were made to suffer, he would curse God, rather than love Him. God doubted this but, nevertheless, gave Satan permission to try. This saintly man was
(A) Joseph   (B) Bildad   (C) Job   (D) Eliphaz
(E) Zophar

56. Ⓐ Ⓑ Ⓒ Ⓓ Ⓔ

57. According to legend, what was the cause of the Trojan War?
(A) Argos needed more land
(B) the sacrifice of Iphigenia
(C) the adultery of Clytaemnestra
(D) the murder of Aegisthus
(E) the kidnapping of Helen by Paris

57. Ⓐ Ⓑ Ⓒ Ⓓ Ⓔ

58. "The Executions of May Third, 1808" was painted by
(A) Goya   (B) Canova   (C) Vignon   (D) Ingres
(E) David

58. Ⓐ Ⓑ Ⓒ Ⓓ Ⓔ

59. A writer who exerted a profound influence on the development of the American short story was William Sidney Porter, better known as
(A) Artemus Ward
(B) Josh Billings
(C) Edgar Allan Poe
(D) Mark Twain
(E) O. Henry

59. Ⓐ Ⓑ Ⓒ Ⓓ Ⓔ

60. An American author best known for his depictions of the old French Quarter of New Orleans, ante-bellum plantations, and the survival of the chivalric code in the South was
(A) Rhett Butler   (B) George Washington Cable
(C) Joel Chandler Harris   (D) William Faulkner
(E) Joseph Lee

60. Ⓐ Ⓑ Ⓒ Ⓓ Ⓔ

61. The most sensitively expressive of all musical instruments made by the family of Stradivari is the
(A) drum   (B) violin   (C) cymbal   (D) oboe
(E) piano

61. Ⓐ Ⓑ Ⓒ Ⓓ Ⓔ

62. A contemporary of Johann Sebastian Bach, though not as great an innovator, nevertheless one of the most successful of the world's serious composers, was
(A) Beethoven   (B) Mendelssohn   (C) Handel
(D) Silbermann   (E) Schmidt

62. Ⓐ Ⓑ Ⓒ Ⓓ Ⓔ

63. The one-eyed giant whom Odysseus met on his voyage was named
(A) Dryope   (B) Polyphemus   (C) Aeolus
(D) Circe   (E) Medea

63. Ⓐ Ⓑ Ⓒ Ⓓ Ⓔ

64. The proximity of the audience to the players influenced some of the theatrical devices used by Shakespeare. This proximity made feasible
(A) the soliloquy   (B) the appearance of boys in feminine roles
(C) the use of special effects   (D) music with dance sequences
(E) pantomime

64. Ⓐ Ⓑ Ⓒ Ⓓ Ⓔ

65. The three hideous sisters of Greek mythology, one of whom (Medusa) was killed by Perseus, were called
    (A) Gorgons   (B) Sphinxes   (C) Furies   (D) Sirens
    (E) Charities

65. A B C D E

66. The music Beethoven wrote for the theater was all of the following *except* one:
    (A) based on a theme of the quest for individual liberty
    (B) based on the cause of popular freedom
    (C) reflective of high moral purpose
    (D) religious in nature
    (E) based on an ideal of human creativity

66. A B C D E

67. In poetry, the omission of one or more final unstressed syllables is called
    (A) anacrusis   (B) catalexis   (C) feminine rhyme
    (D) masculine rhyme   (E) caesura

67. A B C D E

68. Penelope's chief suitor was named
    (A) Telemachus   (B) Oedipus   (C) Creon
    (D) Telegonus   (E) Antinous

68. A B C D E

69. Because of his innovations of style, his free hand with form, and his use of extra-musical devices, the man often called the first Romantic composer is
    (A) Liszt   (B) Beethoven   (C) Haydn   (D) Mozart
    (E) von Weber

69. A B C D E

70. The great French tragic dramatist of the Neo-Classic period was
    (A) Racine   (B) Pascal   (C) Molière
    (D) La Fontaine   (E) Sainte-Beuve

70. A B C D E

71. A stale phrase used where a fresh one is needed is
    (A) parallelism   (B) a cliché   (C) denouement
    (D) poetic license   (E) a pun

71. A B C D E

72. An impromptu folk contest wherein two contenders heap abuse on one another is called
    (A) a fytte   (B) flyting   (C) an epigram
    (D) an epithet   (E) a joust

72. A B C D E

73. Shelley's elegy on the death of John Keats is
    (A) "In Memoriam"   (B) "Adonais"   (C) "Thyrsis"
    (D) "Lycidas"   (E) "Stanzas Written in Dejection near Naples"

73. A B C D E

74. Thomas Henry Huxley was
    (A) primarily a man of letters
    (B) author of *Brave New World*
    (C) devoted to the popularization of science
    (D) noted for his florid, romantic style
    (E) the founder of *The Spectator*

74. A B C D E

75. A florid, ornate portion of prose or poetry, which stands out by its rhythm, diction, or figurative language, is called

    (A) pure poetry   (B) a purple passage

    (C) quantitative verse   (D) prosody   (E) poetic license

75. Ⓐ Ⓑ Ⓒ Ⓓ Ⓔ

Part II

Directions: Each of the questions or incomplete statements below is followed by five suggested answers or completions. Select the one that is best in each case.

Number of Questions: 75
Time: 45 minutes

Photo Alinari

76. The above painting is

    (A) Donatello's "Annunciation"

    (B) Correggio's "Holy Night"

    (C) Raphael's "Sistine Madonna"

    (D) Botticelli's "Birth of Venus"

    (E) Rogier van der Weyden's "Nativity"

76. Ⓐ Ⓑ Ⓒ Ⓓ Ⓔ

77. A well-known sonneteer of the 14th century was

    (A) Petrarch   (B) Dante   (C) Shakespeare

    (D) Shelley   (E) Boccaccio

77. Ⓐ Ⓑ Ⓒ Ⓓ Ⓔ

78. Today's audiences would find strange the theater for which Shakespeare wrote because they

    (A) prefer to attend matinees

    (B) are not accustomed to intermissions

    (C) prefer simple sets and costumes

    (D) are not used to listening to such complex language

    (E) are less well educated

78. Ⓐ Ⓑ Ⓒ Ⓓ Ⓔ

79. The literal meaning of the word "Renaissance" is

    (A) rebirth   (B) clarification   (C) analysis

    (D) enlightenment   (E) question

79. Ⓐ Ⓑ Ⓒ Ⓓ Ⓔ

80. Canio is the famous clown from the opera

    (A) *I Pagliacci*   (B) *Rigoletto*   (C) *Cavalleria Rusticana*

    (D) *Gianni Schicchi*   (E) *Così fan tutte*

80. Ⓐ Ⓑ Ⓒ Ⓓ Ⓔ

81. The English language is most closely related to which of the following   81.   Ⓐ Ⓑ Ⓒ Ⓓ Ⓔ
    in the structure of its sentences?
    (A) Latin   (B) German   (C) French   (D) Bulgarian
    (E) Italian

82. The period in English literature called the "Restoration" is commonly   82.   Ⓐ Ⓑ Ⓒ Ⓓ Ⓔ
    regarded as running from
    (A) 1300 to 1450   (B) 1500 to 1550   (C) 1660 to 1700
    (D) 1798 to 1848   (E) 1848 to 1900

83. The above is a photograph of   83.   Ⓐ Ⓑ Ⓒ Ⓓ Ⓔ
    (A) a Greek temple   (B) a Roman temple
    (C) an Egyptian temple   (D) the University of South Florida
    (E) the University of Mexico

84. Walter Pater believed that one should   84.   Ⓐ Ⓑ Ⓒ Ⓓ Ⓔ
    (A) "cultivate one's own garden"
    (B) "justify the ways of God to man"
    (C) "follow the sun"
    (D) "burn with a hard, gem-like flame"
    (E) "contemplate the Absolute"

85. The expressive combination of re-enforced concrete material, canti-   85.   Ⓐ Ⓑ Ⓒ Ⓓ Ⓔ
    levered construction, and a dramatic site are characteristic of the
    modern architect
    (A) J. J. P. Oud   (B) Walter Gropius   (C) Louis Sullivan
    (D) Frank Lloyd Wright   (E) Le Corbusier

86. The "Theater of the Absurd" is basically   86.   Ⓐ Ⓑ Ⓒ Ⓓ Ⓔ
    (A) ridiculous   (B) emotional   (C) comic   (D) tragic
    (E) intellectual

87. John Dryden wrote perhaps the first great English opera libretto, *Dido and Aeneas*, set to music by

    (A) Lully   (B) Purcell   (C) Tate   (D) Mozart

    (E) Poulenc

87. Ⓐ Ⓑ Ⓒ Ⓓ Ⓔ

88. Don Quixote's horse was named

    (A) Escudero   (B) Rocinante   (C) Sancho Panza

    (D) Dulcinea   (E) Gringolet

88. Ⓐ Ⓑ Ⓒ Ⓓ Ⓔ

89. All of the following books were written by Jean Jacques Rousseau except

    (A) *Confessions*   (B) *The Social Contract*

    (C) *The New Heloise*   (D) *Emile*   (E) *Germinal*

89. Ⓐ Ⓑ Ⓒ Ⓓ Ⓔ

90. *The Tempest*, it is commonly believed, was the last play Shakespeare wrote. If such is the case, we might say that Shakespeare ended his writing career

    (A) in a pessimistic vein

    (B) with high hopes for the human race

    (C) in full knowledge of human weakness and evil but disposed to be forgiving

    (D) by deciding that God must certainly exist

    (E) in the belief that one must derive as much pleasure as possible from life since it was a meaningless joke that might cease at any moment

90. Ⓐ Ⓑ Ⓒ Ⓓ Ⓔ

91. The institution of the villain in drama goes back to

    (A) the Greek epics

    (B) the medieval romance

    (C) Christianity and the writings of Machiavelli

    (D) the Protestant attack on corrupt clergy

    (E) an ancient source, probably a ritual

91. Ⓐ Ⓑ Ⓒ Ⓓ Ⓔ

92. The slogan of the 19th-century Aesthetic Movement was

    (A) "Art is the opiate of the masses"

    (B) "Art is life"

    (C) "Art for art's sake"

    (D) "What is art, that it should have a sake?"

    (E) "Burn with a hard, gem-like flame"

92. Ⓐ Ⓑ Ⓒ Ⓓ Ⓔ

93. The most famous medieval tapestry is the

    (A) Bayeux   (B) Byzantine   (C) Canterbury

    (D) Hastings   (E) Norman

93. Ⓐ Ⓑ Ⓒ Ⓓ Ⓔ

94. The main difference between the Pantheon (in Italy) and the Parthenon (in Greece) is that

    (A) the Parthenon was constructed of raw concrete

    (B) the Pantheon used red bricks and mortar

    (C) the Pantheon is topped with a dome, while the roof of the Parthenon is triangular

    (D) the Parthenon used plain pillars without any ornamentation, while those in the Pantheon are elaborately decorated

    (E) the floor space in the Parthenon is about four times larger

94. Ⓐ Ⓑ Ⓒ Ⓓ Ⓔ

95. The Greek tragedy *Antigone* was written by

    (A) Socrates   (B) Plato   (C) Aristotle

    (D) Sophocles   (E) Agamemnon

95. Ⓐ Ⓑ Ⓒ Ⓓ Ⓔ

96. A modern musical based on Shakespeare's *Twelfth Night* is

    (A) *A Funny Thing Happened on the Way to the Forum*

    (B) *Fiddler on the Roof*

    (C) *Finian's Rainbow*

    (D) *Your Own Thing*

    (E) *The Fantasticks*

96. Ⓐ Ⓑ Ⓒ Ⓓ Ⓔ

97. Which of the following Hindu holy books especially influenced the so-called "beat generation" of poets and novelists?

    (A) *The Bhagavad-Gita*

    (B) *Upanishads*

    (C) *Carmina Burana*

    (D) *Jaina Sutras*

    (E) *Mahabharata*

97. Ⓐ Ⓑ Ⓒ Ⓓ Ⓔ

98. When people began to sing different tunes together, which of the following had its beginnings?

    (A) Monophony   (B) Jazz   (C) Polyphony

    (D) A capella   (E) Homophony

98. Ⓐ Ⓑ Ⓒ Ⓓ Ⓔ

99. During the Renaissance, composers attempting to express a line of poetry in music developed the

    (A) madrigal   (B) symphony   (C) motet

    (D) harmony   (E) sonata

99. Ⓐ Ⓑ Ⓒ Ⓓ Ⓔ

100. *The Charterhouse of Parma* was written by

    (A) Hoffman

    (B) Balzac

    (C) Dumas

    (D) Stendhal

    (E) Pushkin

100. Ⓐ Ⓑ Ⓒ Ⓓ Ⓔ

101. *Waverly, Ivanhoe,* and *Quentin Durward* were written by

    (A) Sir Thomas Hardy   (B) Sir Walter Scott

    (C) Henry Makepeace Thackeray   (D) Charlotte Brontë

    (E) Emily Brontë

101. Ⓐ Ⓑ Ⓒ Ⓓ Ⓔ

102. The medieval poem "Piers Plowman" belongs to the literature of

    (A) chivalry   (B) social protest   (C) mythology

    (D) social satire   (E) pastoral philosophy

102. Ⓐ Ⓑ Ⓒ Ⓓ Ⓔ

103. The greatest Spanish painter of the 17th century, who lived and worked almost exclusively with portraits of the nobility and court figures, was

    (A) Velásquez   (B) Murillo   (C) Goya   (D) Utrillo

    (E) El Greco

103. Ⓐ Ⓑ Ⓒ Ⓓ Ⓔ

104. A contemporary (1972) cellist and conductor, a self-exile from Franco's Spain, is
  (A) Luis Flamenco   (B) Pablo Picasso   (C) Vincente Gomez
  (D) Luis Arroyo   (E) Pablo Casals

104. Ⓐ Ⓑ Ⓒ Ⓓ Ⓔ

105. In music, gradual decrease of tempo is called
  (A) retardando   (B) accelerando   (C) moderato
  (D) presto   (E) allegro

105. Ⓐ Ⓑ Ⓒ Ⓓ Ⓔ

106. The Greek architect-engineer who built the Forum of Trajan was
  (A) Polyclitus   (B) Apollodorus   (C) Boethius
  (D) Myron   (E) Laocoon

106. Ⓐ Ⓑ Ⓒ Ⓓ Ⓔ

107. This is an example of
  (A) Hindu art
  (B) Chinese art
  (C) Egyptian art
  (D) primitive art
  (E) Etruscan art

107. Ⓐ Ⓑ Ⓒ Ⓓ Ⓔ

108. The Russian writer thought to have coined the word "nihilist" was
  (A) Chekhov   (B) Dostoevsky   (C) Pushkin
  (D) Tolstoy   (E) Turgenev

108. Ⓐ Ⓑ Ⓒ Ⓓ Ⓔ

109. Most critics agree that one of the following is the greatest novel which has ever been written:
  (A) *War and Peace*
  (B) *The Brothers Karamazov*
  (C) *The Forsyte Saga*
  (D) *The Sound and the Fury*
  (E) *Pride and Prejudice*

109. Ⓐ Ⓑ Ⓒ Ⓓ Ⓔ

110. How many muses were there in Greek mythology?
  (A) 3   (B) 4   (C) 7   (D) 9   (E) 11

110. Ⓐ Ⓑ Ⓒ Ⓓ Ⓔ

111. In three novels, called collectively *U.S.A.*, this author employed interludes he dubbed "The Camera Eye" and "Newsreels." The author is
  (A) John Dos Passos   (B) James Jones   (C) John Steinbeck
  (D) Truman Capote   (E) John P. Marquand

111. Ⓐ Ⓑ Ⓒ Ⓓ Ⓔ

112. The "Father of the Irish Renaissance" was

    (A) George Moore   (B) George Russell   (C) J. M. Synge

    (D) W. B. Yeats   (E) G. B. Shaw

112. Ⓐ Ⓑ Ⓒ Ⓓ Ⓔ

113. Josiah Wedgwood began making pottery in England during which period?

    (A) Medieval   (B) Renaissance   (C) Neo-Classic

    (D) Romantic   (E) Victorian

113. Ⓐ Ⓑ Ⓒ Ⓓ Ⓔ

114. A contemporary choreographer whose ballets include "Fancy Free" and the dances in *West Side Story* is

    (A) Michael Kidd   (B) Agnes de Mille   (C) Jerome Robbins

    (D) John Cranko   (E) Gene Kelly

114. Ⓐ Ⓑ Ⓒ Ⓓ Ⓔ

115. All but one of the following are Italian film directors who have achieved world-wide fame since 1945:

    (A) Roberto Rossellini

    (B) Michaelangelo Antonioni

    (C) Michelangelo Buonarroti

    (D) Federico Fellini

    (E) Vittorio de Sica

115. Ⓐ Ⓑ Ⓒ Ⓓ Ⓔ

116. All of the following were considered medieval knightly virtues except

    (A) chastity   (B) honesty   (C) fortitude

    (D) faithfulness   (E) duplicity

116. Ⓐ Ⓑ Ⓒ Ⓓ Ⓔ

117. Chaucer wrote in the dialect of

    (A) Mercia   (B) Wessex   (C) Kent   (D) Northumbria

    (E) London

117. Ⓐ Ⓑ Ⓒ Ⓓ Ⓔ

Questions 118–120 are based on the following quotation:

"Ring out the old, ring in the new;
Ring, happy bells, across the snow:
The year is going, let him go;
Ring out the false, ring in the true."

118. The lines are quoted from

    (A) Tennyson's "In Memoriam"

    (B) Milton's "Lycidas"

    (C) Browning's "Pippa Passes"

    (D) Anonymous: "Christmas Bells"

    (E) Poe's "The Bells"

118. Ⓐ Ⓑ Ⓒ Ⓓ Ⓔ

119. The verse form is a

    (A) sonnet   (B) quatrain   (C) couplet   (D) tercet

    (E) cinquaine

119. Ⓐ Ⓑ Ⓒ Ⓓ Ⓔ

120. The rhyme scheme is

    (A) a b a b   (B) a b c d   (C) a b b c   (D) a b b a

    (E) a b c b

120. Ⓐ Ⓑ Ⓒ Ⓓ Ⓔ

121. Impressionism found its most frequent expression in painting and
    music, but there was at least one sculptor who utilized the principles
    of Impressionism in his work:
    (A) Gustave Moreau   (B) Odilon Redon
    (C) Giovanni Segantini   (D) P. W. Steer
    (E) Auguste Rodin

121. Ⓐ Ⓑ Ⓒ Ⓓ Ⓔ

122. A contemporary Russian novelist recently in political difficulties with
    Soviet authorities because of his criticisms of Stalin and communism is
    (A) Ivan Denisovich   (B) Konstantin Fedin
    (C) Pavel Antokolsky   (D) Aleksandr Solzhenitsyn
    (E) Alexander Bek

122. Ⓐ Ⓑ Ⓒ Ⓓ Ⓔ

123. Instrumental music which stands on its own merits and has no in-
    trinsic association with extra-musical ideas is called
    (A) absolute music   (B) national music
    (C) extra-musical music   (D) liturgical music
    (E) program music

123. Ⓐ Ⓑ Ⓒ Ⓓ Ⓔ

124. The first Gothic novel was written in 1764 by Horace Walpole. It was
    (A) *The Castle of Otranto*   (B) *Frankenstein*
    (C) *Caleb Williams*   (D) *Northanger Abbey*   (E) *Dracula*

124. Ⓐ Ⓑ Ⓒ Ⓓ Ⓔ

125. When an author selects a title for a novel, he may quote another
    author. When Ernest Hemingway chose *For Whom the Bell Tolls* as
    the title for his novel about the Spanish Civil War, he was referring
    to
    (A) a poem by Andrew Marvell   (B) a satire by Juvenal
    (C) a meditation by John Donne   (D) a tragedy by John Ford
    (E) an essay by William Hazlitt

125. Ⓐ Ⓑ Ⓒ Ⓓ Ⓔ

126. W. S. Gilbert was the librettist for
    (A) Boito   (B) Verdi   (C) Sullivan   (D) Scarlatti
    (E) Gluck

126. Ⓐ Ⓑ Ⓒ Ⓓ Ⓔ

127. Samuel Johnson attached the label "Metaphysical Poets" to which of
    the following groups?
    (A) Donne, Marvel, Crashaw, and Herbert
    (B) Dryden, Pope, and Young
    (C) Greene, Jonson, and Herrick
    (D) Shakespeare, Milton, and Pope
    (E) Wordsworth, Keats, Shelley, and Byron

127. Ⓐ Ⓑ Ⓒ Ⓓ Ⓔ

128. Since his beginning as an improvisational comedian with a female
    partner, this American has achieved great success as a director of
    Broadway plays and Hollywood films:
    (A) Gore Vidal   (B) Stanley Kramer   (C) Robert Wise
    (D) Jerome Robbins   (E) Mike Nichols

128. Ⓐ Ⓑ Ⓒ Ⓓ Ⓔ

129. Which of the following lists of musical periods is arranged in the
    correct chronological sequence?
    (A) Renaissance, Classical, Baroque

129. Ⓐ Ⓑ Ⓒ Ⓓ Ⓔ

(B) Classical, Medieval, Romantic
(C) Renaissance, Baroque, Romantic
(D) Romantic, Renaissance, Baroque
(E) Medieval, Baroque, Renaissance

130. The artist usually considered the father of modern abstract sculpture is
   (A) Brancusi   (B) Maillol   (C) Rodin
   (D) Lehmbruck   (E) Archipenko

130. Ⓐ Ⓑ Ⓒ Ⓓ Ⓔ

131. Most readers consider *Frankenstein* only a horror story about a fabricated monster. Few realize it has a social theme of
   (A) racial prejudice
   (B) class bigotry
   (C) the rejection by society of an individual who differs from the norm
   (D) sexual immorality
   (E) an individual's dependence upon drugs

131. Ⓐ Ⓑ Ⓒ Ⓓ Ⓔ

132. *Frankenstein* was written in 1817 by
   (A) Sir Walter Scott
   (B) Horace Walpole
   (C) William Godwin
   (D) Mary Godwin
   (E) Mary Wollstonecraft Shelley

132. Ⓐ Ⓑ Ⓒ Ⓓ Ⓔ

Questions 133–135 are based on the following quotation:

"It is an ancient Mariner
And he stoppeth one of three.
'By thy long gray beard and glittering eye,
Now wherefore stopp'st thou me?"

133. The lines were written by
   (A) Keats   (B) Eliot   (C) Coleridge   (D) Tennyson
   (E) Shelley

133. Ⓐ Ⓑ Ⓒ Ⓓ Ⓔ

134. The form is a
   (A) tercet   (B) quatrain   (C) rondelay   (D) haiku
   (E) sestina

134. Ⓐ Ⓑ Ⓒ Ⓓ Ⓔ

135. The form of the whole poem is
   (A) a ballade
   (B) a dramatic monologue
   (C) a traditional ballad
   (D) a literary ballad
   (E) an unconventional form which the author invented for this poem and never used again

135. Ⓐ Ⓑ Ⓒ Ⓓ Ⓔ

136. The contemporary American author of *The Fire Next Time* and *Tell Me How Long the Train's Been Gone* is

136. Ⓐ Ⓑ Ⓒ Ⓓ Ⓔ

(A) James Baldwin   (D) Frederick Douglass
(B) Margaret Walker   (E) John Williams
(C) LeRoi Jones (Imamu Baraka)

137. The immediate intention of the comic theater is to   137. Ⓐ Ⓑ Ⓒ Ⓓ Ⓔ
    (A) show the absurdity of life
    (B) make us feel better
    (C) drive a group of people into hysterical laughter
    (D) act as an emotional tranquilizer
    (E) convert the audience into giggling optimists

138. In the beginning, conductors performed their task from   138. Ⓐ Ⓑ Ⓒ Ⓓ Ⓔ
    (A) a podium
    (B) the right side of the stage
    (C) the left side of the stage
    (D) an instrument, usually a clavier
    (E) a pit hidden from the audience

139. A contemporary conductor who "graduated" from arranging and   139. Ⓐ Ⓑ Ⓒ Ⓓ Ⓔ
conducting scores for films to the leadership of major symphony
orchestras is
    (A) John Green   (B) André Previn   (C) Johnny Williams
    (D) Burt Bacharach   (E) Hugo Montenegro

140. While David extolled the virtues and nobility of the conqueror   140. Ⓐ Ⓑ Ⓒ Ⓓ Ⓔ
Napoleon in his paintings, another artist depicted the sufferings of
a subjugated people. He was
    (A) Rodin   (B) Gros   (C) Géricault   (D) Goya
    (E) Ingres

141. All of the following were essayists of the English Romantic Move-   141. Ⓐ Ⓑ Ⓒ Ⓓ Ⓔ
ment except
    (A) De Quincey   (B) Lamb   (C) Addison   (D) Hazlitt
    (E) Hunt

142. A contemporary Greek author who wrote a sequel to *The Odyssey*   142. Ⓐ Ⓑ Ⓒ Ⓓ Ⓔ
and *Zorba the Greek* was
    (A) Gunther Grass   (B) Ivo Andric   (C) Aristotle Onassis
    (D) Stavros Livornos   (E) Niklos Kazantzakis

143. The first composer to use hammering repetition as a dramatic device   143. Ⓐ Ⓑ Ⓒ Ⓓ Ⓔ
was
    (A) Schmoll   (B) Beethoven   (C) Oberon   (D) Offenbach
    (E) Stravinsky

144. A 19th-century writer noted for his short stories about life in India,   144. Ⓐ Ⓑ Ⓒ Ⓓ Ⓔ
his novels, poems, and children's stories was
    (A) George Orwell   (B) Thomas Hardy   (C) John Masefield
    (D) Joseph Conrad   (E) Rudyard Kipling

145. In the lines, "Hail to thee, blithe Spirit! Bird thou never wert," the   145. Ⓐ Ⓑ Ⓒ Ⓓ Ⓔ
bird referred to is a
    (A) sparrow   (B) nightingale   (C) robin   (D) skylark
    (E) mockingbird

146. **A defector from the Soviet Union and a British Dame formed one of the greatest ballet teams of all time. They are**
    (A) Mikhail Baryshnikov and Cyd Charisse
    (B) Vaslav Nijinsky and Isadora Duncan
    (C) Boris Chaliapin and Martha Graham
    (D) Rudolf Nureyev and Margot Fonteyn
    (E) Jacques d'Amboise and Maria Tallchief

146. Ⓐ Ⓑ Ⓒ Ⓓ Ⓔ

147. Jane Austen's novels *Pride and Prejudice* and *Emma* deal with
    (A) the English lower middle-class
    (B) the English working class
    (C) getting married
    (D) child labor laws
    (E) the plight of coal miners in Wales

147. Ⓐ Ⓑ Ⓒ Ⓓ Ⓔ

148. Robert Browning is especially noted for his
    (A) short stories   (B) dramatic monologues   (C) sonnets
    (D) ballads   (E) dirges

148. Ⓐ Ⓑ Ⓒ Ⓓ Ⓔ

149. An American poet who was also an obstetrician in Paterson, New Jersey, was
    (A) Wallace Stevens   (B) Howard Nemerov
    (C) James Dickey   (D) William Carlos Williams
    (E) Gertrude Stein

149. Ⓐ Ⓑ Ⓒ Ⓓ Ⓔ

150. In scansion of poetry, the symbol / indicates
    (A) a slight pause within a line   (B) a foot
    (C) read more slowly   (D) read faster   (E) stress the syllable

150. Ⓐ Ⓑ Ⓒ Ⓓ Ⓔ

ANSWER KEY—SAMPLE EXAMINATION 2

Part I

1.	B	14.	B	27.	B	40.	E	52.	A	64.	A
2.	D	15.	D	28.	E	41.	E	53.	B	65.	A
3.	C	16.	B	29.	E	42.	B	54.	E	66.	D
4.	E	17.	E	30.	C	43.	E	55.	D	67.	B
5.	B	18.	A	31.	A	44.	B	56.	C	68.	E
6.	E	19.	A	32.	E	45.	A	57.	E	69.	E
7.	D	20.	B	33.	E	46.	B	58.	A	70.	A
8.	D	21.	B	34.	C	47.	D	59.	E	71.	B
9.	C	22.	C*	35.	A	48.	D	60.	B	72.	B
10.	E	23.	D	36.	B	49.	C	61.	B	73.	B
11.	A	24.	E	37.	A	50.	C	62.	C	74.	C
12.	D	25.	E	38.	D	51.	A	63.	B	75.	B
13.	A	26.	A	39.	C						

Part II

76. D	89. E	102. B	115. C	127. A	139. B
77. A	90. C	103. A	116. E	128. E	140. D
78. D	91. C	104. E	117. E	129. B	141. C
79. A	92. C	105. A	118. A	130. A	142. E
80. A	93. A	106. B	119. B	131. C	143. B
81. B	94. C	107. D***	120. D	132. E	144. E
82. C	95. D	108. E	121. E	133. C	145. D
83. E**	96. D	109. A	122. D	134. B	146. D
84. D	97. A	110. D	123. A	135. D	147. C
85. D	98. C	111. A	124. A	136. A	148. B
86. E	99. A	112. D	125. C	137. B	149. D
87. B	100. D	113. C	126. C	138. D	150. E
88. B	101. B	114. C			

*Picasso, *Guernica*, 1937, Oil on Canvas, 11' 5½" x 25' 5¾". On extended loan to the Museum of Modern Art, New York, from the artist.

**Mexican National Tourist Council.

***Courtesy of the Museum of Primitive Art, New York.

SCORING CHART—SAMPLE EXAMINATION 2

After you have scored your Sample Examination 2, enter the results in the chart below; then transfer your Raw Score to the Progress Chart on page 14.

Total Test		Number Right	Number Wrong	Number Omitted	Raw Score
Part I:	75				
Part II:	75				
Total:	150				

ANSWER EXPLANATIONS—SAMPLE EXAMINATION 2

Part I

1. B. Charlemagne is the hero of "The Song of Roland."
2. D. Ibsen was a Norwegian poet and dramatist. He was noted for his realistic social dramas.
3. C. The others were Greek playwrights, but they did not write *Oedipus the King* and *Oedipus at Colonnus*.
4. E. The iambic foot contains an unstressed followed by a stressed syllable. Pentameter means five meters, or beats. Iambic pentameter, therefore, means five units of unstressed/stressed syllables in a line.
5. B. This is a standard musical notation.
6. E. This is true by definition.
7. D. The Psalms contain 150 hymns. (In the Septuagint canons, 151.)
8. D. *Lysistrata* deals with war, sex, and women's liberation.
9. C. *The Rake's Progress* is a ballet by Gavin-Gordon.

10.	E.	The statue is of Queen Nefertiti.
11.	A.	*Man of La Mancha* is the only musical listed based on the story of Don Quixote.
12.	D.	These lines appear in the final chapter of Voltaire's novel.
13.	A.	This is true by definition.
14.	B.	Nabokov is a 20th century writer.
15.	D.	A large symphony orchestra is composed of string, wind, and percussion sections. The other answers refer to two to four instruments.
16.	B.	This is true by definition.
17.	E.	None of the other poets has all of the qualifications listed.
18.	A.	Edith Wharton (1862–1937) was an American poet, short story writer, and novelist.
19.	A.	Tiresias is important in many of the stories of Thebes. He is consulted also, in the underworld, by Odysseus.
20.	B.	This is true by definition.
21.	B.	Pierre Corneille (1606–1684) was the first of the great tragic writers of the era. Jean Racine (1639–1699) is generally described as France's greatest writer of tragedy.
22.	C.	"Guernica" depicts the ravaging of a small town by that name in Spain during the Revolution.
23.	D.	Aristophanes was the great Greek writer of comedy.
24.	E.	To limit the answer to only one of the other statements would be to make an inadequate statement.
25.	E.	Alexander Pushkin (1799–1837) was one of Russia's greatest writers and the first major Russian to become widely known outside his own country.
26.	A.	This is a standard musical notation.
27.	B.	None of the other examples is to be found in the prologue.
28.	E.	This is true by definition.
29.	E.	This answer is true by definition.
30.	C.	This answer is true by definition.
31.	A.	Baldassare Castiglione (1478–1529) wrote a handbook of manners, *The Courtier*, which was a guidebook for elegant deportment.
32.	E.	The artistic style and decorations of the Greeks is far different from any of the others mentioned.
33.	E.	The philosophy expressed is typical of the Neo-Classic period.
34.	C.	Couplets are lines of poetry rhyming in pairs. The most widely used couplet form is the iambic pentameter, known as the heroic couplet.
35.	A.	Iambic pentameter is five feet of unstressed/stressed syllables to the line.
36.	B.	Aphrodite is the Roman goddess of love.
37.	A.	The others are either not 20th century composers, not composers of atonal music, or both.
38.	D.	Honoré de Balzac (1799–1850) wrote *The Human Comedy*. The chief novels in this group are *Père Goriot* and *Eugénie Grandet*.
39.	C.	Michelangelo (1475–1564) was the most famous artist of the Renaissance period.
40.	E.	In his famous soliloquy, Hamlet is pondering whether or not to commit suicide.
41.	E.	Perhaps Twain's most famous satire on contemporary society is *Huckleberry Finn*.
42.	B.	The late 18th century and early 19th century are known as the Neo-Classic Age.
43.	E.	Jacques Louis David (1748–1825) was one of the most famous painters of his day.
44.	B.	This is true by definition.
45.	A.	The troubadours were lyric poets of the 12th and 13th centuries attached to the courts of Provence and northern Italy.
46.	B.	A character with one over-riding purpose or opinion is often hilarious.
47.	D.	Futurism, an artistic movement that originated in Italy about 1910, attempted to depict the dynamic quality of contemporary life influenced by the force and motion of modern machinery.

48. D. Edvard Munch (1863–1944) was a Norwegian painter and printmaker who used intense colors and body attitudes to show love, sickness, anxiety, and death. He greatly influenced the German Expressionist movement of the early 1900s.
49. C. Liszt wrote twelve tone poems, the form of which he invented.
50. C. According to legend, Oedipus killed his father, Laius, and married his mother, Jocasta.
51. A. Johann Strauss was a composer of comic operas, but his reputation rests on some 400 waltzes.
52. A. Flaubert's *Madame Bovary*, published in 1859, was the first of the works which made him a model for later writers of the realistic school.
53. B. *The Koran* is the sacred book of Islam, purportedly revealed by God to the Prophet Mohammed.
54. E. Praxiteles was the most famous of the Attic sculptors.
55. D. Praxiteles was from Athens, Greece.
56. C. The Book of Job is the 18th book of the Old Testament.
57. E. Paris kidnapped Helen, wife of Menelaus, King of Sparta, and brought her back to Troy. The Greek leaders rallied to aid Menelaus, and thus began the Trojan War.
58. A. Goya (1746–1828) was a Spanish painter, etcher, and designer.
59. E. O. Henry is noted for his surprise endings. One of his best known short stories is "The Gift of the Magi." The other writers did not use the pseudonym "O. Henry."
60. B. The others were not writers of ante-bellum New Orleans chivalric literature.
61. B. The Stradivarius is also perhaps the most famous and most expensive violin in the world.
62. C. George Friedrich Handel (1685–1759) is perhaps best known as the composer of "The Messiah."
63. B. Polyphemus is the only cyclops Odysseus met.
64. A. In the soliloquy, the actor could speak his innermost thoughts aloud.
65. A. The others are mythological creatures, but no other fits the description.
66. D. Beethoven was a prolific composer of symphonies, sonatas, opera, but he did not write religious music.
67. B. This is true by definition.
68. E. The other characters were not suitors of Penelope.
69. E. von Weber (1786–1826) was a German who composed his first opera at age thirteen.
70. A. The others were not tragic dramatists of the Neo-Classic period.
71. B. This is true by definition.
72. B. This is true by definition.
73. B. John Keats, English Romantic poet, was a friend of Shelley.
74. C. Huxley was a 19th century evolutionist and social reformer who was instrumental in popularizing science. He was the grandfather of Aldous Huxley, author of *Brave New World*.
75. B. This is true by literary definition.

Part II

76. D. Sandro Botticelli (1444–1510), a Florentine, was one of the great painters of the Renaissance; "The Birth of Venus" is one of his most famous paintings.
77. A. Petrarch's sonnets, mostly inspired by Laura, from one of the most splendid bodies of verse in literature. Petrarch's sonnets were first imitated in England by Sir Thomas Wyatt; the form was later used by Milton, Wordsworth, and other sonneteers.
78. D. The Elizabethan audience insisted upon inflated, poetic language.
79. A. This answer is true by definition.
80. A. *I Pagliacci* is an opera in two acts by Leoncavallo.
81. B. English is considered a Germanic language. Old English and German are similar in many respects.

82. C. In English literature, Restoration generally refers to the period from the accession of Charles II to the throne in 1660 to the death of Dryden in 1770. This period is sometimes called "The Age of Dryden."

83. E. Brilliantly colored mosaics are typical of the art and architecture of the University of Mexico.

84. D. Pater was an important Victorian essayist and literary critic.

85. D. Wright's immensely functional, yet artistic, buildings always blend in with the environment.

86. E. One must be able to intellectualize the absurdity of life in order to enjoy this type of theater.

87. B. Purcell was an English composer who wrote incidental music to dramatic poems by Dryden and others.

88. B. Rocinante was a run-down nag Don Quixote rode into his famous, or infamous, battles.

89. E. *Germinal* was written by Emile Zola.

90. C. This is often characteristic of the older individual who, in preparation for meeting his Maker, hopes his weaknesses will be forgiven.

91. C. In Christianity, the Devil is evil incarnate. In Machiavelli's *The Prince*, his greatest work, evil is permissible, if necessary.

92. C. The "art for art's sake" movement was an attempt to break away from all theories and traditions of the past.

93. A. This tapestry depicts scenes of the Norman Conquest of England and the events leading up to it.

94. C. Other than this distinction, the two buildings are architecturally similar in many respects.

95. D. Sophocles is the only playwright in this group.

96. D. The original *Twelfth Night* has proved much more popular, however.

97. A. Allen Ginsberg, one of the most popular "beat" poets, was greatly influenced by Hindu philosophy and incorporated Hindu chants into some of his poetry.

98. C. Polyphony means the simultaneous combination of two or more independent melodic parts, especially when in close harmonic relationship.

99. A. A madrigal, in Renaissance Italy, was a lyric poem with a pastoral, idyllic, or amatory subject. It may also be further defined as an unaccompanied vocal composition for two or three voices in simple harmony, following a strict poetic form.

100. D. Stendhal, the pseudonym of Marie Henri Beyle, was a French novelist of the late 18th-early 19th century.

101. B. Sir Walter Scott (1771–1832) was a British novelist and poet.

102. B. "Piers Plowman" is a 14th century English allegorical poem satirizing and attacking the clergy and exalting the simple and truthful life.

103. A. Diego Velázquez (1599–1660) was perhaps the most naturalistic and objective of all the court painters.

104. E. None of the others listed is a cellist.

105. A. This is true by definition.

106. B. Apollodorus of Damascus also constructed a bridge over the Danube for the Roman emperor Trajan.

107. D. One should notice the lack of sophistication in the sculpture.

108. E. *Fathers and Sons* is the most famous nihilist novel by Turgenev.

109. A. This monumental work was written by the Russian writer Tolstoy.

110. D. The Muses, the nine daughters of Zeus and Mnemosyne, were originally the patronesses of literature.

111. A. This trilogy is Dos Passos' most famous work.

112. D. W.B. Yeats (1865–1939) was influenced by Irish folklore and mythology and the French Symbolists. He brought to the Irish literary movement a sophistication of technique it had previously lacked.

113. C. "Neo-Classic" refers to the 17th and 18th centuries in Europe.

114. C. The others are well known figures in the field, but Robbins' dances in *West Side Story* have become classics.

115. C. Michelagnolo Buonarroti is another name for Michelangelo, the famous Italian Renaissance artist.

116.	E.	Duplicity is not a virtue.
117.	E.	Most of the educated people in England lived in London, and Chaucer spent most of his life there.
118.	A.	Tennyson wrote this poem to commemorate the death of his very dear friend, Arthur Hallam.
119.	B.	Quatrain means four lines of verse.
120.	D.	The rhyme scheme is determined by listening to the vowel sounds of the last word of each line, and lettering alphabetically; therefore, new = a; snow = b; go (which has the same vowel sound as "snow") = b, and true (which has the same vowel sound as "new") = a.
121.	E.	Auguste Rodin (1840–1917) was a French sculptor and perhaps the strongest influence on 20th century art.
122.	D.	Nobel Prize winner Solzhenitsyn has written *Gulag Archipelago, Cancer Ward*, and *One Day in the Life of Ivan Denisovich*.
123.	A.	This is true by definition.
124.	A.	The others were not written by Walpole.
125.	C.	John Donne was an English poet and preacher. The meditation referred to is his 17th.
126.	C.	Gilbert and Sullivan combined talents to create some of the world's greatest operettas.
127.	A.	The most conspicuous characteristics of this group of 17th century poets are the use of conceits, harshness of versification, and a combination of different types of emotions.
128.	E.	Nichols, who began his career with partner Elaine May, is the only director in the group who originally was a comedian.
129.	B.	Classic: pertaining to the ancient Greek or Roman period; Medieval: pertaining to the Middle Ages; Romantic: pertaining to the late 18th and early 19th century.
130.	A.	Constantin Brancusi (1876–1957) was a Rumanian abstract sculptor.
131.	C.	Mary Shelley intended the monster to arouse the sympathy of her readers.
132.	E.	Mary Shelley published her novel *Frankenstein* in 1818.
133.	C.	The poem is "The Ancient Mariner."
134.	B.	Quatrain means four lines of verse.
135.	D.	A literary ballad is written in deliberate imitation of the form and spirit of a folk ballad. The ballad stanza is usually a quatrain in alternate 4-end 3-stress lines, rhyming abcb.
136.	A.	Baldwin is one of America's best known contemporary Black writers.
137.	B.	A good laugh is the best cure for many ills.
138.	D.	A clavier is a stringed keyboard instrument, such as a harpsichord.
139.	B.	Previn is the only one of the group who fulfills all of the requirements of the answer.
140.	D.	Goya (1746–1828) was a Spanish painter, etcher, and designer, and a leading representative of the Spanish school of his day.
141.	C.	Addison was the leading prose stylist of the early 18th century.
142.	E.	Kazantzakis' *Zorba the Greek* was so popular it was made into both a successful movie and a successful stage play.
143.	B.	Beethoven's Fifth Symphony is the most obvious example of the use of this technique.
144.	E.	Kipling is well known for such works as *Gunga Din, Kim*, and *The Jungle Book*.
145.	D.	The lines are from the poem "To a Skylark," by Shelley.
146.	D.	Nureyev is the only one of the group to defect from the Soviet Union; Fonteyn is the only British Dame listed.
147.	C.	Getting married was of prime consideration to a woman in Victorian England.
148.	B.	Browning's "My Last Duchess" is perhaps his best known dramatic monologue.
149.	D.	Williams is noted for using standard American speech patterns in his poetry.
150.	E.	This is a standard accent mark used when scanning poetry.

SAMPLE EXAMINATION 3

Part I

Number of Questions: 75
Time: 45 minutes

Directions: Each of the questions or incomplete statements below is followed by five suggested answers or completions. Select the one that is best in each case.

1. A study of the development of American literature is not complete without the reading of *The Leather-Stocking Tales*. The author of this series of novels was
   (A) Herman Melville (B) Nathaniel Hawthorne (C) Mark Twain
   (D) James Fenimore Cooper (E) Henry Miller

   1. Ⓐ Ⓑ Ⓒ Ⓓ Ⓔ

2. The hero of *The Leather-Stocking Tales* is
   (A) a sado-masochistic pervert in New York
   (B) a brave white man on the American frontier
   (C) a lesbian who holds weird parties in a Chicago penthouse
   (D) a cool black who revolts against Southern intolerance
   (E) a Puritan minister who seduced an innocent young woman

   2. Ⓐ Ⓑ Ⓒ Ⓓ Ⓔ

3. One of the best-selling novels of the late 1960s is a dramatic monologue in form, delivered from a psychiatrist's couch. The title of this book is
   (A) *No More Brave Men* (B) *Been Down So Long Looks Like Up to Me*
   (C) *Portnoy's Complaint* (D) *Lolita* (E) *Naked Lunch*

   3. Ⓐ Ⓑ Ⓒ Ⓓ Ⓔ

4. The author of *Portnoy's Complaint* is
   (A) Philip Roth (B) William Burroughs (C) Richard Farina
   (D) Vladimir Nabokov (E) Norman Mailer

   4. Ⓐ Ⓑ Ⓒ Ⓓ Ⓔ

5. The painting is
   (A) primordial
   (B) Etruscan
   (C) Egyptian
   (D) African primitive
   (E) modern

   5. Ⓐ Ⓑ Ⓒ Ⓓ Ⓔ

The Solomon R. Guggenheim Museum, New York

6. The Brothers Grimm wrote many fairy tales. Among these is the story of *Hansel and Gretel*, set to music as an opera by
   (A) Michael Glinka (B) Richard Strauss (C) Giacomo Puccini
   (D) Engelbert Humperdinck (E) Guiseppe Verdi

   6. Ⓐ Ⓑ Ⓒ Ⓓ Ⓔ

7. Rabelais is noted for his
   (A) prodigious vocabulary (B) shifting point of view
   (C) satire (D) obscenities (E) all of the above

   7. Ⓐ Ⓑ Ⓒ Ⓓ Ⓔ

8. The hit musical by Stephen Sondheim and Leonard Bernstein called *West Side Story* was based, loosely, on
   (A) Dryden's *All for Love* (B) Marlowe's *Dr. Faustus*
   (C) Shakespeare's *Romeo and Juliet* (D) Hawthorne's *The Scarlet Letter*
   (E) Whitman's *Leaves of Grass*

   8. Ⓐ Ⓑ Ⓒ Ⓓ Ⓔ

9. Perhaps the greatest novel written about American soldiers in World War II is

    (A) John Dos Passos' *Three Soldiers*
    (B) Erich Maria Remarque's *All Quiet on the Western Front*
    (C) E. E. Cummings' *The Enormous Room*
    (D) Norman Mailer's *The Naked and the Dead*
    (E) James Michener's *The Bridges of Toko-Ri*

9. Ⓐ Ⓑ Ⓒ Ⓓ Ⓔ

Photo Alinari

Questions 10–11 refer to the above work of art.

10. The work was painted by

    (A) Michelangelo   (B) Botticelli   (C) da Vinci
    (D) van Gogh   (E) Picasso

10. Ⓐ Ⓑ Ⓒ Ⓓ Ⓔ

11. The work is an example of

    (A) an engraving   (B) a watercolor on paper   (C) oil paint on canvas   (D) baked enamel on wood   (E) a fresco

11. Ⓐ Ⓑ Ⓒ Ⓓ Ⓔ

12. *All but one* of the following are characters in *King Lear*:

    (A) Oswald   (B) Cordelia   (C) Ophelia   (D) Goneril   (E) Regan

12. Ⓐ Ⓑ Ⓒ Ⓓ Ⓔ

13. Picasso is noted for painting in which of the following styles?

    (A) Realist   (B) Classic   (C) Abstract   (D) Cubist
    (E) All of the above

13. Ⓐ Ⓑ Ⓒ Ⓓ Ⓔ

Questions 14 and 15 are based on the following quotation: "Fear not, for behold I bring you good tidings of great joy, which shall be to all people. For unto you is born this day in the City of David a Saviour, which is Christ the Lord."

14. The above quotation is from the Book of

    (A) Peter   (B) Mark   (C) John   (D) Luke   (E) Revelations

14. Ⓐ Ⓑ Ⓒ Ⓓ Ⓔ

15. Many years later, the quotation was used in a great oratorio, composed by
    (A) Handel   (B) Haydn   (C) Bach   (D) Mendelssohn   (E) Liszt

16. Which of the following would be most characteristic of a naturalistic play?
    (A) The belief that the world is moving toward a recognizable goal
    (B) The position that nature, including society, is indifferent to human needs
    (C) Dialogue as a key to character
    (D) Pyramidal or classical structure
    (E) A protagonist of noble birth

17. "Tragedy, then, is an imitation of an action that is serious, complete, and of a certain magnitude . . . effecting the proper purgation of the emotions." These are the words of the first drama critic:
    (A) Socrates   (B) Thespis   (C) Plato   (D) Crito   (E) Aristotle

18. The life of decadent Europe is contrasted unfavorably with life on an unspoiled, Eden-like island. This is indicative of an Age called
    (A) Romantic   (B) Neo-Classic   (C) Classic
    (D) Elizabethan   (E) Victorian

19. The author of *The Catcher in the Rye* is
    (A) John Barth   (B) John Updike   (C) John Phillips
    (D) J. D. Salinger   (E) John Galsworthy

20. During the late 1960s, this American playwright had four hit plays running in Broadway theaters simultaneously, a possibly unprecedented feat:
    (A) David Merrick   (B) Neil Simon   (C) Arthur Miller
    (D) Joe Orton   (E) Jerry Herman

21. A contemporary "pop" artist who has produced and sold pictures of larger-than-life-size Brillo boxes and Campbell's Soup labels:
    (A) Claes Oldenburg   (B) Jackson Pollock   (C) Andy Warhol
    (D) Michael Chaplin   (E) Norman Rockwell

22. Byron's great poetic satire is
    (A) "Childe Harold's Pilgrimage"   (B) "Hours of Idleness"
    (C) "Don Juan"   (D) "Maid of Athens, Ere We Part"
    (E) "The Destruction of Sennacherib"

23.   "Beauty is truth, truth beauty,—that is all
          Ye know on earth, and all ye need to know.
    The above lines are from
    (A) Keat's "Ode on a Grecian Urn"
    (B) Keat's "Ode to a Nightingale"
    (C) Shelley's "To a Skylark"
    (D) Shelley's "Ode to the West Wind"
    (E) Wordsworth's "My Heart Leaps Up"

24. Odysseus' home was in
    (A) Troy   (B) Athens   (C) Ithaca   (D) Ogygia   (E) Scheria

25. The architect whom Napoleon commissioned to change the Church of La Madelaine into a Temple of Glory was
(A) Chalgrin   (B) Fontaine   (C) Vignon   (D) Percier
(E) Goya

26. Bertolt Brecht is famous for a theory which asserts that the aim of drama is to entertain by arousing the intellect, not the emotions. The effect sought by this theory is that of
(A) catharsis   (B) alienation   (C) exposition
(D) symbolism   (E) professionalism

27. King Alfred the Great of England (849-901) is noted for all of the following except
(A) translating Boethius' *Consolations of Philosophy*
(B) translating Bede's *Ecclesiastical History of the English People* into English
(C) the consolidation and continuation of *The Anglo-Saxon Chronicles*
(D) establishing English prose literature at a time when most of the other European countries were just producing their first works in verse
(E) establishing English poetic literature at a time when most of the other European countries were just producing their first works in prose

28. The first great composer whose income was derived more often from commissions and the proceeds of his published compositions than from service to the nobility was
(A) Mendelssohn   (B) Schumann   (C) Mozart
(D) Beethoven   (E) Bach

29. *Wuthering Heights* was written by
(A) Aphra Behn   (B) Charlotte Brontë   (C) Jane Austen
(D) Emily Brontë   (E) Mary Wollstonecraft

30. The most famous French Neo-Classic playwright was
(A) Molière   (B) Corneille   (C) Racine   (D) Cocteau
(E) Rostand

31. The Greek playwright noted for his use of "dramatic irony" was
(A) Aristophanes   (B) Persephone   (C) Antigone
(D) Sophocles   (E) Iphigenia

32. An American poet who found inspiration in the familiar objects and characters of New England ("The Wood Pile," "Birches," "The Death of the Hired Man") was
(A) Emily Dickinson   (B) Carl Sandburg   (C) Robert Frost
(D) Edgar Lee Masters   (E) Vachel Lindsay

33. The sculptor who utilizes heavy, monumental forms which are perforated or bored through and who said, "A sculptor is interested in the shape of things" is
(A) Hepworth   (B) Moore   (C) Armitage   (D) Butler
(E) Hofman

34. The Greek moralist who wrote biographies of both Greeks and Romans was
    (A) Parmenides   (B) Epictetus   (C) Heraclitus
    (D) Plotinus   (E) Plutarch

35. The Roman historian who wrote about the customs and manners of the Germans was
    (A) Suetonius   (B) Caesar   (C) Aurelius   (D) Tacitus
    (E) Quintas

36. The American theater of 1919-1922 saw the development of a new spiritual symbolism. The leading playwright of this period was
    (A) Eugene O'Neill   (B) Robinson Jeffers
    (C) Archibald MacLeish   (D) Edward Albee
    (E) Tennessee Williams

37. The author of the plays *The Death of Bessie Smith, The Zoo Story,* and *The Sand Box* is
    (A) Edward Albee   (B) Samuel Beckett   (C) Eugene O'Neill
    (D) Jack Richardson   (E) Neil Simon

38. *My Fair Lady* is a musical version of a play by
    (A) Neil Simon   (B) George Bernard Shaw
    (C) Arthur Wing Pinero   (D) Oscar Wilde
    (E) Thornton Wilder

39. The modern author who was interested in Africa and the plight of both the English and Dutch, as well as native tribesmen, was
    (A) Donald Wiedner   (B) Richard Wright   (C) Robert Ruark
    (D) Edgar Rice Burroughs   (E) Herbert Wendt

40. Two well-known works by Robert Ruark are
    (A) *Black Man in White Africa* and *Mau Mau*
    (B) *Born Free* and *Living Free*
    (C) *The English and the Dutch* and *Mau Mau*
    (D) *Uhuru* and *Something of Value*
    (E) *Tarzan* and *Black Man in White Africa*

41. John Steinbeck was the author of *Cannery Row.* The title of the sequel to *Cannery Row* is
    (A) *To a God Unknown*   (B) *The Grapes of Wrath*
    (C) *In Dubious Battle*   (D) *The Red Pony*
    (E) *Sweet Thursday*

42. Rachmaninoff was a pianist-composer of the
    (A) 16th century   (B) 17th century   (C) 18th century
    (D) 19th century   (E) 20th century

43. Which of the following artists was still alive in 1970?
    (A) Picasso   (B) Pissaro   (D) van Gogh   (D) Goya
    (E) Manet

44. Who was largely responsible for writing the Declaration of Independence?

(A) Benjamin Franklin   (B) Thomas Jefferson
(C) George Washington   (D) Samuel Johnson
(E) John Adams

45. The author of *The Mucker* and the Tarzan series was
    (A) John Steinbeck   (B) Edgar Rice Burroughs
    (C) Luke Short   (D) Michael Crichton   (E) William Burroughs

45. Ⓐ Ⓑ Ⓒ Ⓓ Ⓔ

46. The most famous pupil of Haydn, "that great mogul," was
    (A) Beethoven   (B) Liszt   (C) Chopin   (D) Debussy
    (E) Moussorgsky

46. Ⓐ Ⓑ Ⓒ Ⓓ Ⓔ

47. A collection of medieval tales, supposedly told by a group of people attempting to escape a plague, is
    (A) *Beowulf*   (B) *The Decameron*   (C) *The Canterbury Tales*
    (D) *The Heptameron*   (E) *Piers Plowman*

47. Ⓐ Ⓑ Ⓒ Ⓓ Ⓔ

48. A modern artist whose paintings have served as designs for linoleum is
    (A) Braque   (B) Miro   (C) Dali   (D) Gris   (E) Mondrian

48. Ⓐ Ⓑ Ⓒ Ⓓ Ⓔ

49. A well-known architect and set designer of the 17th century was
    (A) Marc Chagall   (B) Paul Klee   (C) Igor Stravinsky
    (D) Inigo Jones   (E) Norman bel Geddes

49. Ⓐ Ⓑ Ⓒ Ⓓ Ⓔ

50. Goldsmith's "Deserted Village" is known for its
    (A) description of 18th-century funeral customs
    (B) musical sound and poetic beauty
    (C) minute detail   (D) ghoulish overtones   (E) slovenly language

50. Ⓐ Ⓑ Ⓒ Ⓓ Ⓔ

51. In his later plays, Shakespeare became interested in
    (A) pyramidal plot structure
    (B) obeying the unities of time, place, and action
    (C) character delineation
    (D) flattering Queen Elizabeth I
    (E) the hero's struggle with external forces

51. Ⓐ Ⓑ Ⓒ Ⓓ Ⓔ

52. A *leitmotif* is
    (A) a short, characteristic musical pattern symbolizing an idea or a person   (B) another name for "aria"   (C) a tremolo
    (D) bel canto   (E) a vibrato

52. Ⓐ Ⓑ Ⓒ Ⓓ Ⓔ

53. The term *catharsis*, which Aristotle thought was the main purpose of tragedy, may be defined as
    (A) the excitation of the emotions during a performance
    (B) the arousal of the killer instinct
    (C) the tragic flaw of the classical protagonist
    (D) the purging of the emotions leading to a restoration of equilibrium after the tragedy
    (E) the point at which the intensification begins

53. Ⓐ Ⓑ Ⓒ Ⓓ Ⓔ

54. Stanislavsky was led away from traditional methods of staging 19th-century plays by his attempt to produce

54. Ⓐ Ⓑ Ⓒ Ⓓ Ⓔ

(A) Ibsen's *Master Builder*
(B) Chekhov's *The Seagull*
(C) Miller's *Death of a Salesman*
(D) Wilde's *The Importance of Being Earnest*
(E) Williams' *The Glass Menagerie*

55. The author of *Portrait of a Lady, Daisy Miller*, and *The Turn of the Screw* was
    (A) James Fenimore Cooper   (B) Jack London
    (C) William Dean Howells   (D) Upton Sinclair
    (E) Henry James

55. Ⓐ Ⓑ Ⓒ Ⓓ Ⓔ

56. Many of our national airs are considered American in origin; yet the basic melody may come from "the old country," possibly England or Scotland. Which one of the following is truly American?
    (A) "Hail, Columbia"   (B) "Yankee Doodle"
    (C) "The Star-Spangled Banner"
    (D) "The Glass Harmonica"
    (E) "God Save America"

56. Ⓐ Ⓑ Ⓒ Ⓓ Ⓔ

57. "Phlebas the Phoenician, a fortnight dead, Forgot the cry of gulls, and the deep sea swell And the profit and loss." This passage was written in the
    (A) 8th century   (B) 15th century   (C) 17th century
    (D) 18th century   (E) 20th century

57. Ⓐ Ⓑ Ⓒ Ⓓ Ⓔ

58. Witty dialogue introduced for its own sake characterized
    (A) Neo-Classic tragedy
    (B) sentimental drama of the 19th century
    (C) comedy of manners   (D) theater of cruelty
    (E) Elizabethan chronicle plays

58. Ⓐ Ⓑ Ⓒ Ⓓ Ⓔ

59. A surrealist painter whose subjects come from psychoanalytic literature is
    (A) Picasso   (B) Miro   (C) Dali   (D) Klee
    (E) Duchamp

59. Ⓐ Ⓑ Ⓒ Ⓓ Ⓔ

60. All of the following are 20th-century architects *except*
    (A) Alexander Archipenko   (B) Frank Lloyd Wright
    (C) Le Corbusier   (D) Mies van der Rohe   (E) Walter Gropius

60. Ⓐ Ⓑ Ⓒ Ⓓ Ⓔ

61. "You don't know about me, without you have read a book by the name of *The Adventures of Tom Sawyer*, but that ain't no matter. That book was made by Mr. Mark Twain, and he told the truth, mainly," are the opening sentences to
    (A) *The Prince and the Pauper*
    (B) *A Connecticut Yankee in King Arthur's Court*
    (C) *The Innocents Abroad*
    (D) *Huckleberry Finn*   (E) *The Adventures of Tom Sawyer*

61. Ⓐ Ⓑ Ⓒ Ⓓ Ⓔ

62. Prosper Merimée's short story "Carmen" was the subject of an opera by

62. Ⓐ Ⓑ Ⓒ Ⓓ Ⓔ

(A) Puccini   (B) Verdi   (C) Mozart   (D) Bizet
(E) Menotti

63. The "Wheel of Fortune" as an image of human experience is particularly associated with the work of
(A) Euripides   (B) Molière   (C) Chekhov   (D) Ibsen
(E) Shakespeare

63. Ⓐ Ⓑ Ⓒ Ⓓ Ⓔ

64. Two Roman satiric poets were
(A) Horace and Juvenal   (B) Plautus and Terence
(C) Menander and Marcus Aurelius   (D) Lucretius and Suetonius
(E) Cicero and Petronius

64. Ⓐ Ⓑ Ⓒ Ⓓ Ⓔ

65. The man who made possible the emergence of the modern ballet as a concrete organization was
(A) Vaslav Nijinsky   (B) Serge Diaghileff
(C) Mikhail Mordkin   (D) Michel Fokine   (E) Leonide Massine

65. Ⓐ Ⓑ Ⓒ Ⓓ Ⓔ

66. Painting that has no content in the literal or narrative sense is called
(A) Impressionism   (B) Surrealism   (C) Non-objective art
(D) Pop art   (E) Social Realism

66. Ⓐ Ⓑ Ⓒ Ⓓ Ⓔ

67. Longfellow and Whittier were writers belonging to the
(A) gilded age   (B) mauve decade   (C) local-colorist school
(D) Transcendental movement   (E) genteel tradition

67. Ⓐ Ⓑ Ⓒ Ⓓ Ⓔ

68. The Romantic Movement in English literature was ushered in by the publication of
(A) "The Seasons" (B) *Lyrical Ballads* (C) "Ode to the West Wind"
(D) *Childe Harold's Pilgrimage*   (E) "The Eve of St. Agnes"

68. Ⓐ Ⓑ Ⓒ Ⓓ Ⓔ

69. A Scotch poet who wrote about his own experience and emotions was
(A) Rudyard Kipling   (B) John Keats   (C) Robert Burns
(D) William Blake   (E) Robert Browning

69. Ⓐ Ⓑ Ⓒ Ⓓ Ⓔ

70. The additive method of sculpturing is primarily concerned with
(A) modeling   (B) carving   (C) mobility
(D) decreasing mass   (E) visual qualities

70. Ⓐ Ⓑ Ⓒ Ⓓ Ⓔ

71. A member of the Fauve group who used color in new and daring ways was
(A) Goya (B) Michelangelo (C) da Vinci (D) El Greco (E) Matisse

71. Ⓐ Ⓑ Ⓒ Ⓓ Ⓔ

72. According to *The Iliad,* a great Greek warrior sulked in his tent after a quarrel over a woman and did not rejoin the battle unil a friend was killed. This warrior was
(A) Aeneas   (B) Ajax   (C) Anchises   (D) Achilles
(E) Aphrodite

72. Ⓐ Ⓑ Ⓒ Ⓓ Ⓔ

73. The *Synoptic Gospels* are
(A) Matthew, Mark, and Luke   (B) Matthew, Luke, and John
(C) Mark, Luke, and John   (D) Luke, Mark, and Romans
(E) Matthew, Mark, and John

73. Ⓐ Ⓑ Ⓒ Ⓓ Ⓔ

74. In Elizabeth Barrett Browning's "Sonnets from the Portuguese," she   **74.** Ⓐ Ⓑ Ⓒ Ⓓ Ⓔ
   (A) asks her husband to love her for her beauty
   (B) says she shall love him only until her death
   (C) says she and her lover are equals
   (D) contrasts her poetry with that of her husband
   (E) says she feels as young as her husband

Photo Alinari

75. The above is an example of   **75.** Ⓐ Ⓑ Ⓒ Ⓓ Ⓔ
   (A) Byzantine art   (B) Greek art   (C) Roman art
   (D) Egyptian art   (E) American primitive art

Part II   **Directions:**   Each of the questions or incomplete statements below is followed
by five suggested answers or completions. Select the one that is best in each case.

Number of Questions: 75
Time: 45 minutes

76. Musical tone consists of all of the following except   **76.** Ⓐ Ⓑ Ⓒ Ⓓ Ⓔ
   (A) pitch   (B) duration   (C) intensity   (D) quality   (E) tempo

77. Laurence Olivier has produced and starred in all but one of the fol-   **77.** Ⓐ Ⓑ Ⓒ Ⓓ Ⓔ
lowing film versions of Shakespeare's plays:
   (A) *Othello*   (B) *Hamlet*   (C) *Henry V*   (D) Mercutio
   (E) *Richard III*

78. All of the following were labors of Hercules except
    (A) killing the Nemean lion
    (B) killing the Hydra
    (C) bringing back the Golden Fleece
    (D) cleaning the Augean Stables
    (E) bringing the Erymanthian Boar back alive to Eurytheus

79. The mighty Beowulf fought the monster
    (A) Hrothgar   (B) Hygelac   (C) Gringolet
    (D) Grendel   (E) Wealtheow

80. Go and catch a falling star;
    Get with child a mandrake root;
    Tell me where all lost years are,
    Or who cleft the devil's foot."

    The author of these lines was
    (A) George Herbert
    (B) John Donne
    (C) Ben Jonson
    (D) The Earl of Rochester
    (E) Queen Elizabeth I

81. This example is
    (A) Greek
    (B) Roman
    (C) Egyptian
    (D) Mesopotamian
    (E) Mayan

Hirmer Fotoarchiv Munchen

82. Beethoven was known for his
    (A) ordered forms of Classicism   (B) atonality
    (C) humanism   (D) sentimentality
    (E) thematic development

The Metropolitan Museum of Art, Purchase, 1890, Levi Hale Willard Bequest.

83. The above is a photograph of the

    (A) Coliseum   (B) Forum   (C) Parthenon

    (D) palace at Knossos   (E) Pentagon

83. A B C D E

84. The Romantic poets were, as a whole,

    (A) objective

    (B) unemotional

    (C) unconcerned with nature

    (D) influenced by medieval and classical themes

    (E) influenced by the Renaissance

84. A B C D E

85. A Neo-Classic French writer noted for his fables was

    (A) Voltaire   (B) Montaigne   (C) La Rouchefoucauld

    (D) La Fontaine   (E) Pascal

85. A B C D E

86. Odysseus' wife was named

    (A) Eumaneus   (B) Euryclea   (C) Antinous

    (D) Penelope   (E) Telemachus

86. A B C D E

87. The musical notation < > means

    (A) stop playing after four beats   (B) crescendo-diminuendo

    (C) play together   (D) slow the tempo   (E) both B and C

87. A B C D E

88. All of the following operas were written by Richard Wagner *except*

    (A) *Tannhauser*   (B) *Salome*   (C) *Tristan und Isolde*

    (D) *Lohengrin*   (E) *Die Meistersinger von Nurnberg*

88. A B C D E

89. The greatest French satiric dramatist of the Neo-Classic Period was

    (A) Pascal   (B) Racine   (C) Sainte-Beuve

    (D) Molière   (E) Montaigne

89. A B C D E

90. *Beowulf* is an example of a

    (A) chanson de geste   (B) folk epic   (C) long short story

    (D) medieval metrical romance   (E) literary epic

90. A B C D E

91. Hermann Hesse wrote all but which of the following novels?

    (A) *Journey to the West*   (B) *Demian*   (C) *Steppenwolf*

    (D) *Siddhartha*   (E) *Magister Ludi or The Glass Bead Game*

91. A B C D E

92. One of the outstanding science fiction writers of today who also first advanced 92. Ⓐ Ⓑ Ⓒ Ⓓ Ⓔ
    the theory of communications satellites is
    (A) Asimov   (B) Clarke   (C) Heinlein   (D) Pohl
    (E) Bradbury

93. The voice of the Beat Generation, author of *On the Road*, was   93. Ⓐ Ⓑ Ⓒ Ⓓ Ⓔ
    (A) Ginsberg   (B) Kesey   (C) Ferlinghetti   (D) Kerouac
    (E) Wolfe

94. *The Martian Chronicles* is a collection of stories by   94. Ⓐ Ⓑ Ⓒ Ⓓ Ⓔ
    (A) Ellison   (B) Heinlein   (C) Bradbury   (D) Steinbeck
    (E) Wells

95. Noted for their civil war stories are   95. Ⓐ Ⓑ Ⓒ Ⓓ Ⓔ
    (A) Thoreau and Richardson   (B) Crane and Twain   (C) Harte
    and London   (D) Emerson and Hawthorne   (E) Bierce and Crane

96. *The Mental Radio* was written by   96. Ⓐ Ⓑ Ⓒ Ⓓ Ⓔ
    (A) Sinclair Lewis   (B) H. G. Wells   (C) George Orwell
    (D) Upton Sinclair   (E) D.H. Lawrence

97. The *Bhagavad-Gita* is one of the holy books of which major religion?   97. Ⓐ Ⓑ Ⓒ Ⓓ Ⓔ
    (A) Buddhism   (B) Hinduism   (C) Taoism   (D) Islam
    (E) Confucianism

98. A *suite* is   98. Ⓐ Ⓑ Ⓒ Ⓓ Ⓔ
    (A) a synonym for *symphony*
    (B) the second movement of a concerto
    (C) a collection of dance tunes
    (D) very similar to a fugue
    (E) a religious vocal form

99. One of the most noted Americans of the 20th century, composer of   99. Ⓐ Ⓑ Ⓒ Ⓓ Ⓔ
    "Appalachian Spring," is
    (A) Aaron Copland   (B) George Gershwin
    (C) Tommy Dorsey   (D) Vernon Duke   (E) Leonard Bernstein

100. A great illustrator and creator of the modern poster was   100. Ⓐ Ⓑ Ⓒ Ⓓ Ⓔ
    (A) van Gogh   (B) Norman Rockwell   (C) Toulouse-Lautrec
    (D) Braque   (E) Grant Wood

101. A sculptured or richly ornamented band (as on a building) is called a   101. Ⓐ Ⓑ Ⓒ Ⓓ Ⓔ
    (A) frieze   (B) bartizan   (C) fresco   (D) flying buttress
    (E) batik

102. Plot and character are among the six ingredients of a play, according   102. Ⓐ Ⓑ Ⓒ Ⓓ Ⓔ
    to Aristotle. So are all of the following *except*
    (A) music   (B) alienation   (C) thought   (D) diction
    (E) spectacle

103. The Portuguese poet, famous for his national epic *The Lusiads*, was   103. Ⓐ Ⓑ Ⓒ Ⓓ Ⓔ
    (A) Lazarillo de Tormes   (B) Miguel de Cervantes
    (C) Lope de Vega   (D) Luis vaz de Camoens
    (E) Guillen de Castro

104. The enchantress who changed Odysseus' sailors into swine was

    (A) Scylla   (B) Phaedra   (C) Nausicaa   (D) Circe

    (E) Calypso

104. Ⓐ Ⓑ Ⓒ Ⓓ Ⓔ

105. One of the most famous members of the Fabian Society was

    (A) Thomas Carlyle   (B) Ezra Pound   (C) John Ruskin

    (D) William Butler Yeats   (E) George Bernard Shaw

105. Ⓐ Ⓑ Ⓒ Ⓓ Ⓔ

106. The time lapse between Sophocles and Shakespeare is about

    (A) 500 years   (B) 1,000 years   (C) 1,500 years

    (D) 2,000 years   (E) 3,000 years

106. Ⓐ Ⓑ Ⓒ Ⓓ Ⓔ

107. One of the most famous American paintings "Arrangement in Gray and Black" was painted by

    (A) James McNeill Whistler   (B) John Singer Sargent

    (C) Thomas Eakins   (D) Asher B. Durand

    (E) Winslow Homer

107. Ⓐ Ⓑ Ⓒ Ⓓ Ⓔ

108. One of the best known Greek sculptors of the 4th century B.C. was

    (A) Lysistrata   (B) Praxiteles   (C) Constantine

    (D) Scorpios   (E) Euphronius

108. Ⓐ Ⓑ Ⓒ Ⓓ Ⓔ

109. The omission of a part of a word, as in "o'er" ("over") is called

    (A) elision   (B) enjambment   (C) poetic diction

    (D) stichomythia   (E) threnody

109. Ⓐ Ⓑ Ⓒ Ⓓ Ⓔ

110. Which of the following is *not* a simile?

    (A) I wandered lonely as a cloud

    (B) Busy old fool, unruly Sun

    (C) My love is like a red, red rose

    (D) Her eyes are lovely as the stars

    (E) My heart is like a singing bird

110. Ⓐ Ⓑ Ⓒ Ⓓ Ⓔ

111. Dramatic comedy employing stock characters, performed by professional Italian actors, who improvised while they performed, is called

    (A) kabuki   (B) mise en scene   (C) commedia dell'arte

    (D) deus ex machina   (E) Einfuhlung

111. Ⓐ Ⓑ Ⓒ Ⓓ Ⓔ

112. A *libretto* is

    (A) an instrumental form

    (B) a small music library

    (C) part of a concerto

    (D) an unaccompanied solo passage

    (E) the text of an opera

112. Ⓐ Ⓑ Ⓒ Ⓓ Ⓔ

113. Puccini wrote an opera based on Belasco's play

    (A) *Madame Butterfly*   (B) *Rigoletto*   (C) *Manon*

    (D) *La Bohème*   (E) *The Consul*

113. Ⓐ Ⓑ Ⓒ Ⓓ Ⓔ

114. Peter Weiss' *Marat/Sade* belongs to the school of contemporary drama known as

    (A) naturalism   (B) verisimilitude   (C) comedy of manners

    (D) expressionism   (E) theater of cruelty

114. Ⓐ Ⓑ Ⓒ Ⓓ Ⓔ

115. One of the masterpieces of what the French call the "literature of passion," is

    (A) *Manon Lescaut*   (B) *The Count of Monte Cristo*

    (C) *Candide*   (D) *Aucassin and Nicolette*   (E) *Les Misérables*

    115. Ⓐ Ⓑ Ⓒ Ⓓ Ⓔ

116. Which of the following was *not* written by Dostoevsky?

    (A) *The Idiot*   (B) *Crime and Punishment*

    (C) *The Brothers Karamazov*   (D) *War and Peace*

    (E) *Notes from the Underground*

    116. Ⓐ Ⓑ Ⓒ Ⓓ Ⓔ

117. A 14-line poem with the rhyme scheme A B A B C D C D E F E F G G is called a

    (A) sestina   (B) Petrarchan sonnet   (C) Rondeau

    (D) Rondelay   (E) Shakespearean sonnet

    117. Ⓐ Ⓑ Ⓒ Ⓓ Ⓔ

118. In the Middle Ages, art

    (A) declined in importance

    (B) grew in importance

    (C) reflected the prevailing thought

    (D) became more realistic

    (E) became decadent

    118. Ⓐ Ⓑ Ⓒ Ⓓ Ⓔ

119. A dance by two people is called a(n)

    (A) pas de quatre   (B) entrechat   (C) pirouette

    (D) pas de deux   (E) raccourci

    119. Ⓐ Ⓑ Ⓒ Ⓓ Ⓔ

120. A painter famous for his scenes of the American West is

    (A) Stuart Davis   (B) George Catlin   (C) William Gropper

    (D) John Marin   (E) James McNeill Whistler

    120. Ⓐ Ⓑ Ⓒ Ⓓ Ⓔ

121. An undecorated stage which presents actions occurring in both England and France during the course of a single play might be expected by the audience in

    (A) the 4th century B.C.

    (B) the Elizabethan era

    (C) Neo-Classic France

    (D) an avant-garde play about two tramps in a park

    (E) the early 20th century when verisimilitude was the rage

    121. Ⓐ Ⓑ Ⓒ Ⓓ Ⓔ

122. When Jocasta describes her late husband, the former king, as a tall man who resembled Oedipus, we have a good example of

    (A) Sophoclean irony   (B) exposition

    (C) Aristotelian recognition   (D) alienation   (E) hubris

    122. Ⓐ Ⓑ Ⓒ Ⓓ Ⓔ

123. Which of the following can a drama *not* do without?

    (A) verisimilitude   (B) denouement   (C) audience empathy

    (D) conflict   (E) elaborate sets

    123. Ⓐ Ⓑ Ⓒ Ⓓ Ⓔ

124. An example of a strict canon is

    (A) "Jailhouse Blues"

    (B) "Rock, Rock, Rock Around the Clock"

    (C) Beethoven's "Fidelio"

    (D) Handel's "Messiah"

    (E) "Row, Row, Row Your Boat"

    124. Ⓐ Ⓑ Ⓒ Ⓓ Ⓔ

125. Which of the following terms relates to *tempo?*
125. Ⓐ Ⓑ Ⓒ Ⓓ Ⓔ
(A) timbre   (B) monophonic   (C) crescendo
(D) triad   (E) allegro

Questions 126 and 127 are based on this quotation from Alexander Pope:

"Go, wiser thou! and, in thy scale of sense,
Weigh thy opinion against Providence . . .
Snatch from His hand the balance of the rod,
Re-judge His Justice, be the God of God."

126. The above is an example of
126. Ⓐ Ⓑ Ⓒ Ⓓ Ⓔ
(A) satire   (B) imagery   (C) melodrama   (D) euphony
(E) verbal irony

127. The verse form is the
127. Ⓐ Ⓑ Ⓒ Ⓓ Ⓔ
(A) quatrain   (B) ballade   (C) heroic couplet
(D) rondeau   (E) rhyme royal

128. A musical instrument that is tuned with sand paper is
128. Ⓐ Ⓑ Ⓒ Ⓓ Ⓔ
(A) a lute   (B) a harpsichord   (C) a ukelele   (D) a harp
(E) an oboe

129. The Greek drama is said to have developed from
129. Ⓐ Ⓑ Ⓒ Ⓓ Ⓔ
(A) Lenaean rites of spring
(B) city activities during the winter solstice
(C) political action
(D) Dionysian dithyrambs associated with regeneration and spring
(E) Aristotle's *Poetics*

130. An American author noted for folk tales in which the animals of the woods and fields reflect the comedy of mankind is
130. Ⓐ Ⓑ Ⓒ Ⓓ Ⓔ
(A) Joel Chandler Harris   (B) George Washington Cable
(C) Mary Wilkins Freeman   (D) Henry James
(E) William Dean Howells

131. Though his best known work is *The Rise of Silas Lapham,* this author is also known for his biography of the Republican presidential candidate Abraham Lincoln.
131. Ⓐ Ⓑ Ⓒ Ⓓ Ⓔ
(A) Edwin H. Cady   (B) Theodore Dreiser
(C) Nathaniel Hawthorne   (D) Carl Sandburg
(E) William Dean Howells

132. The practice or technique of applying dots of color to a surface so that from a distance they blend together is called
132. Ⓐ Ⓑ Ⓒ Ⓓ Ⓔ
(A) cubism   (B) primitivism   (C) chiaroscuro
(D) pointillism   (E) rococo

133. All of the following are considered post-Impressionist painters *except*
133. Ⓐ Ⓑ Ⓒ Ⓓ Ⓔ
(A) David   (B) Cezanne   (C) Gauguin   (D) von Gogh
(E) Seurat

134. Egyptian wall painting demonstrates
134. Ⓐ Ⓑ Ⓒ Ⓓ Ⓔ

(A) a fear of death
(B) what the artist knew rather than what he saw
(C) on overriding concern with factual appearances
(D) the style of the individual artist
(E) a knowledge of anatomy

135. All of the following are characteristic of the epic *except*   135. Ⓐ Ⓑ Ⓒ Ⓓ Ⓔ
    (A) it is a long narrative poem
    (B) the setting is usually the past
    (C) it contains figurative language that gives it cosmic significance
    (D) there is always a trip to the underworld
    (E) it is written, always, in the vernacular of the people

136. Dante's greatest work was called a "comedy" because   136. Ⓐ Ⓑ Ⓒ Ⓓ Ⓔ
    (A) it was written in the vulgar language of the people
    (B) no one dies during the course of the poem
    (C) it begins in misery and ends in happiness
    (D) there are many amusing scenes in the poem
    (E) the subject matter was not serious enough for the people of his day

137. In Greek tragedy, the "tragic flaw" within a character which precipitates his fall is called   137. Ⓐ Ⓑ Ⓒ Ⓓ Ⓔ
    (A) nemesis   (B) deus ex machina   (C) antistrophe
    (D) hubris   (E) hamartia

138. A composer noted principally for his piano compositions is   138. Ⓐ Ⓑ Ⓒ Ⓓ Ⓔ
    (A) Chopin (B) Haydn
    (C) Brahms (D) Tchaikovsky
    (E) Mozart

139. *Oratorios* are   139. Ⓐ Ⓑ Ⓒ Ⓓ Ⓔ
    (A) large compositions for orchestra
    (B) short compositions for solo voice
    (C) a part of a religious service
    (D) secular compositions for voice and orchestra
    (E) large compositions for voice and orchestra usually based on religious texts

140. The founders of Cubism were   140. Ⓐ Ⓑ Ⓒ Ⓓ Ⓔ
    (A) Dali and Klee   (B) Miro and Gris
    (C) Chagall and Cezanne   (D) Picasso and Braque
    (E) Mondrian and Gauguin

141. Mystic and poet, illustrator and engraver of the Bible, Dante, Milton, and Shakespeare, was   141. Ⓐ Ⓑ Ⓒ Ⓓ Ⓔ
    (A) Albrecht Dürer   (B) William Blake   (C) Hieronymus Bosch
    (D) Eugène Delacroix   (E) Dante Gabriel Rossetti

142. "The Pleiade" is all of the following *except*   142. Ⓐ Ⓑ Ⓒ Ⓓ Ⓔ
    (A) a heavenly constellation
    (B) an organized attempt to establish a classical spirit in French writing

(C) a movement begun about 1547 at Paris

(D) a literary group led by Pierre de Ronsard

(E) an opera by Massenet

143. A 19th-century poet famous for his dramatic monologues was   143. Ⓐ Ⓑ Ⓒ Ⓓ Ⓔ
(A) Ruskin   (B) Browning   (C) Pater   (D) Arnold
(E) Tennyson

144. The theory that "this is the best of all possible worlds" was satirized in   144. Ⓐ Ⓑ Ⓒ Ⓓ Ⓔ
(A) Congreve's *Way of the World*
(B) Dostoevsky's *Crime and Punishment*
(C) Zola's *Germinal*
(D) Voltaire's *Candide*
(E) Swift's *Gulliver's Travels*

145. A *motet* is   145. Ⓐ Ⓑ Ⓒ Ⓓ Ⓔ
(A) an instrumental form   (B) monophonic
(C) usually secular   (D) a choral composition
(E) a 20th-century musical form

146. A *recitative* would most likely be found in   146. Ⓐ Ⓑ Ⓒ Ⓓ Ⓔ
(A) a symphony   (B) an opera   (C) a sonata
(D) a concerto   (E) a quartet

147. All of the following are conventions of the Elizabethan theater *except*   147. Ⓐ Ⓑ Ⓒ Ⓓ Ⓔ
(A) women's roles enacted by young boys
(B) setting established by dialogue
(C) poetic language
(D) a chorus of elders
(E) the soliloquy

148. Literature intended to be enjoyed for its own sake rather than to convey   148. Ⓐ Ⓑ Ⓒ Ⓓ Ⓔ
information or serve some immediate practical purpose is called
(A) macaronic   (B) belles-lettres   (C) paradoxical
(D) georgic   (E) Bildungsroman

149 Which of the following lists of vocal registers moves properly from high   149. Ⓐ Ⓑ Ⓒ Ⓓ Ⓔ
to low?
(A) bass, baritone, tenor, alto, soprano, mezzo soprano
(B) alto, tenor, mezzo soprano, bass, baritone, soprano
(C) tenor, bass, baritone, soprano, mezzo soprano
(D) soprano, mezzo soprano, alto, tenor, baritone, bass
(E) alto, soprano, mezzo soprano, tenor, baritone, bass

150. *The Betrothed* is the masterpiece of   150. Ⓐ Ⓑ Ⓒ Ⓓ Ⓔ
(A) Alessandro Manzoni   (B) Michelangelo
(C) Leonardo da Vinci   (D) Boccaccio
(E) Gabriele D'Annunzio

ANSWER KEY—SAMPLE EXAMINATION 3

Part I

1.	D	14.	D	27.	E	40.	D	52.	A	64.	A
2.	B	15.	A	28.	E	41.	E	53.	D	65.	B
3.	C	16.	B	29.	D	42.	E	54.	B	66.	C
4.	A	17.	E	30.	A	43.	A	55.	E	67.	E
5.	E	18.	A	31.	D	44.	E	56.	A	68.	B
6.	D	19.	D	32.	C	45.	B	57.	E	69.	C
7.	E	20.	B	33.	B	46.	A	58.	C	70.	A
8.	C	21.	C	34.	E	47.	B	59.	C	71.	E
9.	D	22.	C	35.	D	48.	E	60.	A	72.	D
10.	C	23.	A	36.	A	49.	D	61.	D	73.	A
11.	E	24.	C	37.	A	50.	C	62.	D	74.	D
12.	C	25.	C	38.	B	51.	C	63.	A	75.	A
13.	E	26.	E	39.	C						

Part II

76.	E	89.	D	102.	B	115.	A	127.	C	139.	E
77.	D	90.	B	103.	D	116.	D	128.	B	140.	D
78.	C	91.	A	104.	D	117.	E	129.	D	141.	B
79.	D	92.	B	105.	E	118.	C	130.	A	142.	E
80.	B	93.	D	106.	D	119.	D	131.	E	143.	B
81.	B	94.	C	107.	A	120.	B	132.	D	144.	D
82.	E	95.	E	108.	B	121.	B	133.	A	145.	D
83.	C	96.	D	109.	A	122.	A	134.	B	146.	B
84.	D	97.	B	110.	B	123.	D	135.	E	147.	D
85.	D	98.	C	111.	C	124.	E	136.	C	148.	B
86.	D	99.	A	112.	E	125.	E	137.	E	149.	D
87.	B	100.	C	113.	A	126.	E	138.	A	150.	A
88.	B	101.	A	114.	E						

SCORING CHART—SAMPLE EXAMINATION 3

After you have scored your Sample Examination 3, enter the results in the chart below; then transfer your Raw Score to the Progress Chart on page 14.

Total Test		Number Right	Number Wrong	Number Omitted	Raw Score
Part I:	75				
Part II:	75				
Total:	150				

ANSWER EXPLANATIONS—SAMPLE EXAMINATION 3

Part I

1. **D.** The best known of the *Leather Stocking Tales* is *The Last of the Mohicans*.
2. **B.** Leatherstocking is scout, hunter, and trapper.
3. **C.** None of the others fits the description.
4. **A.** Roth is a rather controversial 20th century American writer.
5. **E.** The abstract techniques employed could not be anything but modern.
6. **D.** Engelbert Humperdinck (1854–1921) was a German operatic composer. His second most famous opera is *Die Königskinder*.
7. **E.** Any other answer would be incomplete.
8. **C.** In the modern version, the play takes place in New York's Spanish Harlem.
9. **D.** The other works were not written about American soldiers in World War II.
10. **C.** The picture is of the fresco known as "The Last Supper."
11. **E.** Fresco is the art of painting on fresh plaster.
12. **C.** Ophelia is a character in Shakespeare's *Hamlet*.
13. **E.** Picasso was a virtuoso who mastered a variety of styles in painting. He also was a great sculptor.
14. **D.** Luke was the third of the evangelists, author of the Gospel bearing his name, and of the Book of Acts. "The Gospel According to Luke" is the third book of *The New Testament*.
15. **A.** Handel's great work was *The Messiah*.
16. **B.** This is an adequate definition of literary naturalism.
17. **E.** Aristotle, in "On the Nature of Tragedy, " made this statement.
18. **A.** The Romantic Age originated in Europe toward the end of the 18th century. It asserted the validity of subjective experience.
19. **D.** Salinger is one of America's most reclusive writers. The *Catcher in the Rye* has become a classic with students.
20. **B.** Simon today is one of Broadway's most prolific playwrights.
21. **C.** The others are not considered "pop" artists.
22. **C.** The other works are by Byron, but are not satires.
23. **A.** These are some of the most famous lines of English Romantic poetry.
24. **C.** Ithaca is one of the Ionian Islands, between Cephalonca and the mainland of Greece.
25. **C.** Vignon produced the imposing building with its surrounding Corinthian colonnade.
26. **E.** Brecht believed that theater was contrived. He wanted the audience to examine the work of art as a work of art, not as a game, a childish performance.
27. **E.** King Alfred's works were in prose.
28. **E.** Johann Sebastian Bach (1685–1750) was generally unrecognized until the 1800s when Mendelssohn became one of his most zealous champions.
29. **D.** Emily and her sister Charlotte, author of *Jane Eyre,* originally published their works under assumed names.
30. **A.** None of the others is a French Neo-Classic playwright.
31. **D.** The only other person named who was a playwright was Aristophanes, and he was a writer of comedy, not tragedy.
32. **C.** Frost, one of America's most beloved poets, spent much of his adult life in New England and is most noted for his nature poems of the region.
33. **B.** Henry Moore is perhaps the outstanding contemporary sculptor. His concept of art is to treat space as volume instead of emptiness.
34. **E.** Plutarch lived from about 46 to 120. Although his history is not always trustworthy, his biographical technique is excellent.
35. **D.** Tacitus, the celebrated Roman historian, is the only one of this group who wrote about the customs and manners of the Germans.
36. **A.** O'Neill is the only author mentioned who wrote during the period 1919–1922.
37. **A.** Albee, an American playwright, deals with ordinary people in commonplace settings. Some plays, like *Who's Afraid of Virginia Woolf?*, are noted for their realism and grim humor.

38. B.   *My Fair Lady* is based upon Shaw's *Pygmalion*.
39. C.   Ruark is perhaps best known for *Uhuru* and *Something of Value*.
40. D.   Ruark specializes in novels concerning Africa, especially the problems facing the inhabitants of South Africa.
41. E.   Many of the same characters appear in both novels.
42. E.   Rachmaninoff was one of the greatest 20th century pianist-composers.
43. A.   Picasso, the only 20th century artist mentioned, has since died.
44. E.   John Adams (1735–1826), second President of the United States, was on the committee which drafted the Declaration of Independence, and, in Jefferson's words, "was the pillar of its support on the floor of Congress."
45. B.   Edgar Rice Burroughs (1875–1950), an American author, created Tarzan, one of the most famous characters in fiction.
46. A.   Beethoven, the great German composer, has been called "the Shakespeare of music."
47. B.   Boccaccio's *Decameron* is the only work mentioned that was supposedly told by a group of people attempting to escape a plague.
48. E.   Piet Mondrian (1872–1944) was a Dutch Abstractionist.
49. D.   Jones, influenced by Italian architecture, erected the royal Banqueting House in Whitehall, London, the earliest portion of Greenwich Hospital, and Covent Garden.
50. C.   Goldsmith, who had a degree in medicine, may have been influenced by his medical studies to develop the acute attention to detail found in his works.
51. C.   As Shakespeare matured, so did his characters.
52. A.   This is true by definition.
53. D.   Aristotle discusses this point in his essay *On the Nature of Tragedy*.
54. B.   Chekhov's "slice of life" technique was, in itself, an innovation. Stanislavski's method was to force each actor to "feel" the role he was playing.
55. E.   Henry James (1843–1916) was a novelist and essayist, and brother of William James, the noted psychologist.
56. A.   "Hail, Columbia" is an American patriotic song with words written in 1798 by Joseph Hopkinson. The tune was probably written by Philip Phile, although claims are also made for Johannes Roth.
57. E.   These lines are from T.S. Eliot's poem "The Wasteland."
58. C.   The comedy of manners is a type of play that satirizes the extremes of fashion and manners of a highly sophisticated society. The English Restoration Period is especially noted for this type of play.
59. C.   In drawing on the Freudian theory of psychoanalysis, Dali tried to bring elements of the subconscious to the surface, expressing them in symbolic forms. In Dali's "Persistence of Memory," he suggests that, by the artist's created work, he defeats time and achieves immortality.
60. A.   Archipenko was a sculptor and painter who specialized in female nudes.
61. D.   In these lines, Huck mentions that he was a character in an earlier work by Twain, *The Adventures of Tom Sawyer*.
62. D.   Georges Bizet's *Carmen,* his greatest success, was first produced in 1875.
63. A.   In Euripidean tragedy, the "Wheel of Fortune" or "Fate" plays a great role.
64. A.   The others are Romans, but not satiric playwrights.
65. B.   The Diaghileff ballet played in London, Paris, Berlin, Vienna, and Budapest, as well as Moscow, and was headed by such stars as Michel Fokine, Anna Pavlova, and Vaslav Nijinsky.
66. C.   "Non-objective" designates a style of graphic art that does not represent objects.
67. E.   Writers of the genteel tradition upheld middle-class manners and morality.
68. B.   The joint publication in 1798 of *Lyrical Ballads* by William Wordsworth and Samuel Taylor Coleridge is considered the beginning of the English Romantic Movement.
69. C.   Burns is the only Scottish poet in the group.
70. A.   In this sense "modeling" means to make by shaping a plastic substance.
71. E.   The Fauve or "wild beasts" were organized in 1905 under the leadership of Matisse and included Derain, Vlaminck, Rouault, and Dufy.

72. D. Achilles was famous for his invincibility. The only place he could be injured was in his heel.
73. A. These are the first three *Gospels*.
74. D. Robert Browning was one of the major poets of the Victorian Era.
75. A. Byzantine art employed, with true Eastern impulse, materials of opulence and rich coloring, though the plastic forms themselves maintained a general simplicity.

Part II

76. E. Tempo is the relative speed at which a composition is to be played.
77. D. Mercutio is a character in *Romeo and Juliet*, not the title of a play.
78. C. Jason was the mythical hero who went in search of the Golden Fleece.
79. D. Grendel is the name of the monster in the Anglo-Saxon epic *Beowulf*.
80. B. The lines are from Donne's poem "Go and Catch a Falling Star," titled after the opening line.
81. B. The border design, plus the physiognomy of the man and the lion, should indicate that the urn is Roman.
82. E. None of the other answers applies to Beethoven's music. He was, however, noted for development, and repetition, of a theme.
83. C. The Parthenon, on the Acropolis at Athens, is the temple sacred to the goddess Athena.
84. D. The Romantic poets were subjective, emotional, and concerned with nature. They were fascinated by the cultures of ancient Greece and Rome and by the chivalric code of the Middle Ages.
85. D. Jean de La Fontaine (1621–1695) was a French poet and fabulist. His fables, written in verse, are models of delicate satire on the society of the period.
86. D. The other characters also appear in *The Odyssey*, but Penelope was the name of Odysseus' faithful wife.
87. B. This is a standard musical notation.
88. B. The music for *Salome* was written by Richard Strauss.
89. D. Mólière was the great French playwright noted for his satiric comedies. None of the others mentioned wrote comedies.
90. B. The epic is a long, narrative poem on a serious subject, centered about a heroic figure on whose actions depends to some degree the fate of a nation or race. The folk epic is traditional in nature, and not written by a sophisticated craftsman, as is the literary epic.
91. A. Hesse's novel is entitled *Journey to the East*, not *Journey to the West*.
92. B. The others are also science-fiction writers, but Arthur C. Clarke is the one credited with first advancing the theory of communications satellites. His short story on the subject, "I Remember Babylon," has become a science-fiction classic.
93. D. Jack Kerouac's *On the Road* began a new era in American literature.
94. C. Ray Bradbury is one of the foremost science fiction writers of today.
95. E. Ambrose Bierce's collection of short stories *Tales of Soldiers and Civilians* and Stephen Crane's novel *The Red Badge of Courage* are classics of this period.
96. D. Upton Sinclair, American novelist and socialist, is probably best known for his novel *The Jungle,* an expose of conditions in Chicago stockyards.
97. B. *The Bhagavad-Gita* is a Sanskrit philosophical poem incorporated in the great Hindu epic, the *Mahabharata*.
98. C. This is true by definition.
99. A. Copland won the Pulitzer Prize and the New York Music Critics' Award for "Appalachian Spring."
100. C. Henri de Toulouse-Lautrec (1864–1901) was a French lithographer and illustrator, noted for his lithographs of Montmartre and the music halls of Paris.
101. A. This is true by definition.
102. B. "Alienation" means a state of isolation. Aristotle believed the theater audience, through empathy, would suffer a catharsis of the emotions.

103. D. "The Lusiads, " considered one of the great poems of the world, celebrates the adventures of Vasco da Gama and the splendors of Portuguese heroism and history.

104. D. Circe, a celebrated enchantress of Greek mythology, lived on the island of Aeaea.

105. E. Shaw was one of the greatest playwrights of the English language. Among his best known plays are *Candida, Mrs. Warren's Profession, Pygmalion, Caesar and Cleopatra,* and *Man and Superman.*

106. D. Sophocles, the great Greek tragic poet, was born circa 496 B.C. and died circa 406 B.C. Shakespeare, the great English poet and dramatist, was born in 1564 and died in 1616.

107. A. This painting is more popularly known as "Whistler's Mother."

108. B. None of the others was a sculptor.

109. A. This is true by definition.

110. B. A "simile" is a comparison using "like" or "as."

111. C. "Commedia dell'arte", a type of comedy derived from ancient Greek and Roman models and presented by groups of strolling players in Italy, reached its height in the 16th century and spread through the Continent to England, greatly influencing literature and drama.

112. E. This is true by definition.

113. A. The play was first performed in New York in 1900. Puccini's opera was first performed in 1904.

114. E. The play, set in a lunatic asylum, ends with the cast "escaping" and attacking the audience.

115. A. *Manon Lescaut,* a novel by the Abbé Prévost, was written in 1731, and is the subject of three operas by Auber, Puccini, and Massenet, and a ballet by Halévy.

116. D. *War and Peace* was written by Tolstoy.

117. E. The Shakespearean sonnet contains three quatrains and a concluding couplet.

118. C. Most medieval art centered on legends of great heroes or religion.

119. D. This is a translation from the French meaning "step of two."

120. B. The others are well-known American painters, but they did not paint Western scenes.

121. B. These are characteristics of Shakespeare's era.

122. A. The irony is that Oedipus is in reality the son of Laius, her former husband.

123. D. This is one of the basic tenets of drama.

124. E. This may be defined as a composition or passage in which the same melody is repeated by one or more voices, overlapping in time in the same or a related key.

125. E. Allegro means a rapid tempo.

126. E. In this passage, Pope is telling man to play God, if he dare.

127. C. The heroic couplet consists of two lines of verse, rhyming in pairs, in iambic pentameter.

128. B. None of the other instruments is tuned in this fashion.

129. D. The Greek god Dionysus, god of wine, is the patron of music and the arts.

130. A. Harris is famous for his "Uncle Remus" stories.

131. E. William Dean Howells (1837–1920) was an American novelist, playwright, editor, and critic.

132. D. This is true by definition.

133. A. Jacques Louis David was a French painter who was born in 1748 and died in 1825. The post-Impressionists were late 19th century painters.

134. B. Egyptian wall paintings are highly stylized and anatomically unrealistic.

135. E. The vernacular, or language of the people, rarely contains figurative language that gives it cosmic significance. The tone of the epic was always lofty, and therefore did not approximate ordinary speech.

136. C. During the Renaissance, a story that ended happily or, at least, did not end miserably, was considered a "comedy."

137. E. This is a translation from the Greek.

138. A. The other composers may have written compositions for the piano, but Chopin is the best known of the group in this area.
139. E. This is true by definition.
140. D. In Cubism, the portrayals of natural forms are geometric. This school was founded circa 1910.
141. B. William Blake (1757–1827) is especially known for his *Songs of Innocence* and *Songs of Experience*.
142. E. Jules Massenet, a French operatic composer, never wrote an opera by this name.
143. B. Robert Browning's best known dramatic monologues are "My Last Duchess," "Fra Lippo Lippi," and "Andrea del Sarto."
144. D. Voltaire's *Candide* satirized the optimistic philosophy of the German Leibnitz.
145. D. This is true by definition.
146. B. A recitative is a musical style in which the text is declaimed in the rhythm of natural speech with slight melodic variation.
147. D. The chorus of elders is a convention of the Greek theater.
148. B. This is true by definition.
149. D. This is the only answer in which the order is correct.
150. A. Manzoni (1785–1873) was an Italian novelist and poet. *The Betrothed* is considered one of the world's great romances and has been translated into many languages.

PART THREE

THE MATHEMATICS EXAMINATION

Trial Test

9

The trial Mathematics test will show you what an actual examination is like and help you decide which areas of mathematics you may need to review.

The examination consists of two separately timed sections. Part I (Basic Skills and Concepts) has 40 questions to be answered in 30 minutes. It tests skills that are generally taught in high school and that are frequently used in college courses other than mathematics—arithmetic, algebra, geometry, and data interpretation. Part II (Content) has 50 questions to be answered in 60 minutes. It covers material that is studied at the college level—sets, logic, the real number system, functions, and probability and statistics.

Part I   Basic Skills and Concepts

Directions for questions 1–25: Each of these questions consists of two quantities, one in Column A and one in Column B. You are to compare the two quantities and in the answer column blacken space

A   if the quantity in Column A is greater;

B   if the quantity in Column B is greater;

C   if the two quantities are equal;

D   if the relationship cannot be determined from the information given.

Notes:
1. In certain questions, information concerning one or both of the quantities to be compared is centered above the two columns.
2. A symbol that appears in both columns represents the same thing in Column A as it does in Column B.
3. Letters such as x, n, and k stand for real numbers.

QUESTIONS	COLUMN A	COLUMN B		
1.	$3 - 5 + 6 - 8 - 4 + 7$	-2	**1.**	Ⓐ Ⓑ Ⓒ Ⓓ

Ice cream sells for $0.55 a pint.

2.	the cost of $2\frac{1}{2}$ quarts of ice cream	$2.75	**2.**	Ⓐ Ⓑ Ⓒ Ⓓ

Everything in a store is marked down 15% in a sale.

3.	sale price of a $95 minicomputer	$80	**3.**	Ⓐ Ⓑ Ⓒ Ⓓ

The sides of two squares are in the ratio $\sqrt{2} : 1$. Their diagonals are in the ratio $y : \sqrt{2}$

4.	y	2	**4.**	Ⓐ Ⓑ Ⓒ Ⓓ

A 2¼-lb. package of meat costs $3.04.

5.	the cost of one ounce of meat	8¢	**5.**	Ⓐ Ⓑ Ⓒ Ⓓ
6.	one square yard	1600 square inches	**6.**	Ⓐ Ⓑ Ⓒ Ⓓ
7.	the number of cents in d dimes and q quarters	$35q$	**7.**	Ⓐ Ⓑ Ⓒ Ⓓ
8.	$5 - [6 - 2(1 + 3)]$	7	**8.**	Ⓐ Ⓑ Ⓒ Ⓓ
9.	$\dfrac{|x - y|}{y - x}$	1	**9.**	Ⓐ Ⓑ Ⓒ Ⓓ

Mike takes 3 hours to mow a lawn; his younger brother Cary takes 4 hours.

10.	time it takes both boys working together to mow the lawn	$1\frac{1}{2}$ hours	**10.**	Ⓐ Ⓑ Ⓒ Ⓓ
11.	$(1.1)^{-1}$	1	**11.**	Ⓐ Ⓑ Ⓒ Ⓓ

12.	$L'M'$	LN	**12.**	Ⓐ Ⓑ Ⓒ Ⓓ

The top of a 25-foot pole is leaning against a building. The bottom is on the ground 7 feet away from the building.

13.	the distance of the top of the pole from the ground	24	**13.**	Ⓐ Ⓑ Ⓒ Ⓓ

$MN \parallel QP$ in circle O.

	COLUMN A	COLUMN B		
14.	measure of $\overparen{MRN}$	96°	14.	A B C D

	COLUMN A	COLUMN B		
15.	$m(\angle M)$	80°	15.	A B C D

radius $OB = 2''$
$BC = 3''$

	COLUMN A	COLUMN B		
16.	AC	OB	16.	A B C D

The hypotenuse of an isosceles right triangle is 2".

	COLUMN A	COLUMN B		
17.	length of one leg of the triangle	1"	17.	A B C D

$$2x - y = 2$$
$$x + 2y = 6$$

	COLUMN A	COLUMN B		
18.	x	y	18.	A B C D

∠*MNQ* is a right angle

| 19. | x | y | 19. | A B C D |

A rectangular flower garden 20 ft. by 4 ft. is surrounded by a walk that is 4 ft. wide.

| 20. | area, in sq. ft., of the walk | 256 | 20. | A B C D |

Use this pictograph for questions 21 and 22.

THE TEN LARGEST COUNTRIES: 1969

	Percent of world land area	Population (in millions)
Mainland China	7.0	740
India	2.4	537
USSR	16.5	241
USA	6.9	203
Indonesia	1.1	116
Pakistan	0.7	112
Japan	0.3	102
Brazil	6.3	91
Nigeria	0.7	64
Germany (Fed. Rep.)	0.2	61

TOTAL WORLD LAND AREA   TOTAL WORLD POPULATION
52,420,000 SQ. MI.   3,552,000,000

Source: Data, inside front cover.

QUESTIONS	COLUMN A	COLUMN B	
21.	population, in millions, of Pakistan in 1969	116	21. A B C D
22.	difference, in millions, between populations of USSR and USA in 1969	38	22. A B C D

Use this bar graph for question 23.

ECONOMIC GROWTH RATES

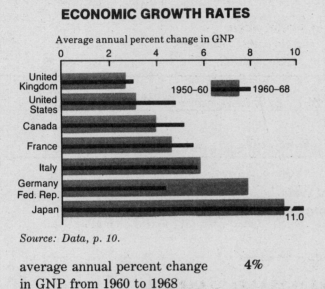

Average annual percent change in GNP

Source: Data, p. 10.

23.	average annual percent change in GNP from 1960 to 1968 in the USA	4%	23. A B C D

Use this figure for questions 24 and 25.

INTERCITY FREIGHT TRAFFIC

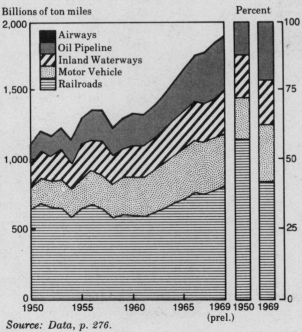

Source: Data, p. 276.

24.	percent of intercity freight traffic carried by motor vehicles in 1969	30	24. Ⓐ Ⓑ Ⓒ Ⓓ

Percent of total intercity freight traffic carried by railroads

25. Ⓐ Ⓑ Ⓒ Ⓓ

25.	1950	1969

Directions for questions 26–40: For these questions, indicate the correct answer in the appropriate space on the answer sheet.

Note: Figures that accompany the following problems are intended to provide information useful in answering the questions. The figures are drawn as accurately as possible *except* when it is stated in a specific question that the figure is not drawn to scale. All figures lie in a plane unless otherwise stated.

Use this table for questions 26 and 27.

EXPECTATION OF LIFE AT VARIOUS AGES IN THE UNITED STATES 1971

(Years)

	WHITE			ALL OTHER			TOTAL		
YEAR	Male	Female	Total	Male	Female	Total	Male	Female	Total
1900	46.6	48.7	47.6	32.5	33.5	33.0	46.3	48.3	47.3
1910	48.6	52.0	50.3	33.8	37.5	35.6	48.4	51.8	50.0
1920	54.4	55.6	54.9	45.5	45.2	45.3	53.6	54.6	54.1
1930	59.7	63.5	61.4	47.3	49.2	48.1	58.1	61.6	59.7
1940	62.1	66.6	64.2	51.5	54.9	53.1	60.8	65.2	62.9
1950	66.5	72.2	69.1	59.1	62.9	60.8	65.6	71.1	68.2
1960	67.4	74.1	70.6	61.1	66.3	63.6	66.6	73.1	69.7
1961	67.8	74.5	71.0	61.9	67.0	64.4	67.0	73.6	70.2
1962	67.6	74.4	70.9	61.5	66.8	64.1	66.8	73.4	70.0
1963	67.5	74.4	70.8	60.9	66.5	63.6	66.6	73.4	69.9
1964	67.7	74.6	71.0	61.1	67.2	64.1	66.9	73.7	70.2
1965	67.6	74.7	71.0	61.1	67.4	64.1	66.8	73.7	70.2
1966	67.6	74.7	71.0	60.7	67.4	64.0	66.7	73.8	70.1
1967	67.8	75.1	71.3	61.1	68.2	64.6	67.0	74.2	70.5
1968	67.5	74.9	71.1	60.1	67.5	63.7	66.6	74.0	70.2
1969	67.8	75.1	71.3	60.5	68.4	64.3	66.8	74.3	70.4
1970	68.1	75.4	71.7	60.5	68.9	64.6	67.1	74.6	70.8
1971	68.3	75.7	71.9	61.3	69.4	65.2	67.4	74.9	71.1

Source: Fact, p. 93.

26. The life expectancy of a white male born in 1971 is
    (A) 61.3 yrs.   (B) 67.4 yrs.   (C) 68.3 yrs.   (D) 71.1 yrs.

26. Ⓐ Ⓑ Ⓒ Ⓓ

27. If p is the percent of increase in the life expectancy of a nonwhite female from 1900 to 1971, then
(A) $p \approx 35$ (B) $p > 100$ (C) $125 < p < 150$ (D) $p \approx 200$

27. Ⓐ Ⓑ Ⓒ Ⓓ

28. The wavelength of the shortest ultraviolet light is 7.6×10^{-9} meters. If this is written as 7.6×10^n centimeters, then n equals
(A) -11 (B) -10 (C) -8 (D) -7

28. Ⓐ Ⓑ Ⓒ Ⓓ

29. If $m \neq 0$, then $\dfrac{4^0 m^4 n^0}{4m^4} =$
(A) $\dfrac{1}{4}$ (B) $\dfrac{n}{4}$ (C) 1 (D) n

29. Ⓐ Ⓑ Ⓒ Ⓓ

30. The smallest integer that satisfies the inequality $5x + 9 > 1$ is
(A) -2 (B) -1 (C) 0 (D) 1

30. Ⓐ Ⓑ Ⓒ Ⓓ

31. If $x > y$ and $x > z$, which of the following must be true for all real x, y, z?
(A) $y > z$ (B) $(x - y)(x - z) > 0$
(C) $x^2 > xy$ (D) $x > 0$

31. Ⓐ Ⓑ Ⓒ Ⓓ

32. $^{13}/_4 =$
(A) 3.25% (B) $3.33^1/_3\%$ (C) 320% (D) 325%

32. Ⓐ Ⓑ Ⓒ Ⓓ

33. If $a:b = 2:3$ and $a = 7$, then $b =$
(A) $^2/_{21}$ (B) $4^2/_3$ (C) 14 (D) $10^1/_2$

33. Ⓐ Ⓑ Ⓒ Ⓓ

34. Which equation is not satisfied by $x = -3$?
(A) $x^2 - 9 = 0$ (B) $x^2 + 3x = 0$
(C) $x^2 + 9 = 0$ (D) $x^2 + x - 6 = 0$

34. Ⓐ Ⓑ Ⓒ Ⓓ

35. 20 is 125% of what number?
(A) 12 (B) 16 (C) 18 (D) 25

35. Ⓐ Ⓑ Ⓒ Ⓓ

36. Which of the following lines is parallel to the line $4x + 3y - 12 = 0$?
(A) $x + 3y - 12 = 0$ (B) $y = {}^4/_3 x + 2$
(C) $y = -{}^4/_3 x + 4$ (D) $y = -{}^3/_4 x + 2$

36. Ⓐ Ⓑ Ⓒ Ⓓ

37. The reciprocal of a real number other than zero is also called its
(A) additive identity   (B) additive inverse
(C) multiplicative identity   (D) multiplicative inverse

37. Ⓐ Ⓑ Ⓒ Ⓓ

38. If x is different from 0 and 1, then $\dfrac{x^2 - x}{x(x^2 - 1)} =$
(A) $\dfrac{1}{x + 1}$ (B) $\dfrac{1}{x - 1}$ (C) $\dfrac{1}{x(x + 1)}$ (D) $\dfrac{1}{x}$

38. Ⓐ Ⓑ Ⓒ Ⓓ

39. What does x equal if the average of x, 5, 8, and 13 is 8?
(A) 6 (B) 7 (C) 8 (D) 10

39. Ⓐ Ⓑ Ⓒ Ⓓ

40. $3^0 + 3^1 + 3^2 =$
(A) 9 (B) 12 (C) 13 (D) 27

40. Ⓐ Ⓑ Ⓒ Ⓓ

Part II   Content

Directions: For each of the following problems, indicate the correct answer in the appropriate space in the answer column.

Note: Figures that accompany problems in this part are intended to provide information useful in solving the problems. They are drawn as accurately as possible *except* when it is stated in a specific problem that the figure is not drawn to scale. All figures lie in a plane unless otherwise stated.

41. If $R = \{a,b\}$, $S = \{a,c,d\}$, and $T = \{b,c\}$, then $R \cap (S \cup T)$ equals
    (A) $\{a\}$ (B) $\{b\}$ (C) $\{a,b\}$ (D) $\{a,b,c,d\}$

    41.   Ⓐ Ⓑ Ⓒ Ⓓ

42. If S has 3 elements, then the number of ordered triples in $S \times S \times S$ is
    (A) 3   (B) 9   (C) 27   (D) 81

    42.   Ⓐ Ⓑ Ⓒ Ⓓ

43. If $R = \{6\}$, $S = \{3,6\}$, $T = \{1,2,3\}$, and $W = \{2,3,6\}$, then it is false that
    (A) $R \cup S = W$ (B) $R \cap T = \emptyset$ (C) $R \subset S \subset W$ (D) $(R \cap S) \subset W$

    43.   Ⓐ Ⓑ Ⓒ Ⓓ

44. $R - S = \{x : x \in R, x \notin S\}$. The Venn diagram for $R - S$ is

    44.   Ⓐ Ⓑ Ⓒ Ⓓ

45. If R^+ is the set of positive real numbers and Z is the set of integers, then $R^+ \cap Z$ equals
    (A) the set of positive integers   (B) $\{x : x$ is an integer, $x \geq 0\}$
    (C) Z (D) R^+

    45.   Ⓐ Ⓑ Ⓒ Ⓓ

46. Which statement is *not* equivalent to "If a korb chools, then it stibbles"?
    (A) If a korb does not stibble, then it does not chool.
    (B) A necessary condition for a korb to stibble is that it chool.
    (C) A korb chools only if it stibbles.
    (D) For a korb to stibble it suffices that it chool.

    46.   Ⓐ Ⓑ Ⓒ Ⓓ

47. If the statements $p \rightarrow q$ and $q \rightarrow \sim r$ are true, then a valid conclusion is
    (A) $p \rightarrow r$ (B) $\sim p \rightarrow r$ (C) $r \rightarrow p$ (D) $r \rightarrow \sim p$

    47.   Ⓐ Ⓑ Ⓒ Ⓓ

48. $\sim(p \lor \sim q)$ is true whenever

    (A) p is false and q is true   (B) p is true
    (C) q is true   (D) p and q are both false

48.   A B C D

49. Let x be an integer. A proof of the claim that "if x^2 is odd, then x is odd" may proceed as follows:
    (A) Take an example, say $x = 5$. Note that x^2 is odd and so is x.
    (B) Show that if x^2 is even, then so is x.
    (C) Show that if x is odd, then so is x^2.
    (D) Show that if x is even, then so is x^2.

49.   A B C D

50. Suppose $a < b$ (a, b real). Then it always follows that
    (A) $-a > -b$ (B) $-a < -b$ (C) $-a < b$ (D) none of the preceding

50.   A B C D

51. $(3^2 + 4^2)^{-1/2} =$
    (A) $\frac{1}{49}$ (B) $\frac{1}{25}$ (C) $\frac{1}{7}$ (D) $\frac{1}{5}$

51.   A B C D

52. Which number is irrational?
    (A) 0 (B) x such that $x^2 = 8$ (C) $\frac{1}{6}$ (D) $\sqrt{121}$

52.   A B C D

53. If a, b, c, d are integers and $bd \neq 0$, then it is false that
    (A) $\frac{a}{b} \div \frac{c}{d} = \frac{ad}{bc}$ (B) $\frac{-a}{b} = \frac{a}{-b}$

    (C) $\frac{b}{b + d} = \frac{1}{1 + d}$ (D) $\frac{b + d}{d} = 1 + \frac{b}{d}$

53.   A B C D

54. The set of odd integers is closed under
    (A) multiplication   (B) addition
    (C) division   (D) subtraction and multiplication

54.   A B C D

55. The function whose graph is shown is
    (A) $y = x(x^2 + 4)$
    (B) $y = x(4 - x^2)$
    (C) $y = x(x^2 - 4)$
    (D) $y = x(x^2 + 2)$

55.   A B C D

56. If $f(x) = \dfrac{1}{x + 2}$ and $g(x) = \dfrac{1}{x} - 2$, then $f(g(x)) =$

    (A) $\dfrac{1}{x + 2} - 2$ (B) $x + 2$ (C) $\dfrac{1}{x}$ (D) x

56.   A B C D

57. Which pair of integers (m,n) does not satisfy the inequality $3m - 2n \leq 4$?
    (A) $(-4,-9)$ (B) $(-1,2)$ (C) $(2,1)$ (D) $(0,-2)$

57.   A B C D

58. Which diagram does not define a function from $X(x_1,x_2,x_3,x_4)$ into $Y(y_1,y_2,y_3)$?

58. Ⓐ Ⓑ Ⓒ Ⓓ

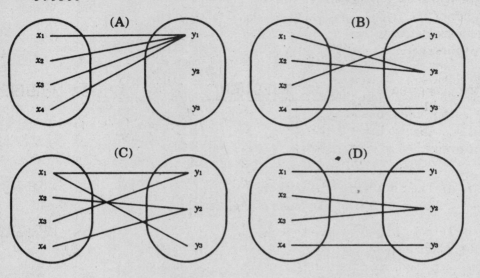

(A) (B)

(C) (D)

59. Let m and n be integers greater than 1. Which definition of $*$ is for a commutative operation?
(A) $m * n = m - n + 1$
(B) $m * n =$ the least common multiple of m and n
(C) $m * n =$ the remainder obtained when m is divided by n
(D) $m * n = m^n$

59. Ⓐ Ⓑ Ⓒ Ⓓ

60. The odds that the Panthers will beat the Lynxes in a game are 3 to 2. The probability that the Lynxes will win is
(A) $^2/_3$ (B) 0.6   (C) $^3/_5$ (D) 0.4

60. Ⓐ Ⓑ Ⓒ Ⓓ

61. Two balls are drawn at the same time from a box of 5 of which 1 is red, 1 is blue, and 3 are black. The probability that both are black is
(A) $^6/_{25}$ (B) $^3/_{10}$ (C) $^2/_5$ (D) $^3/_5$

61. Ⓐ Ⓑ Ⓒ Ⓓ

62. A student is allowed to choose 5 out of 7 questions on an examination. The number of ways it can be done is
(A) 21   (B) 35   (C) 42   (D) 2520

62. Ⓐ Ⓑ Ⓒ Ⓓ

63. Box 1 contains 2 red and 5 black marbles; box 2 contains 4 green and 2 black marbles. If 1 marble is drawn from each box the probability that they will be of different colors is
(A) $^{20}/_{147}$ (B) $^5/_{21}$ (C) $^4/_7$ (D) $^{16}/_{21}$

63. Ⓐ Ⓑ Ⓒ Ⓓ

64. Which of the following numbers is the largest?
(A) 224_{FIVE} (B) 332_{FOUR} (C) 2102_{THREE} (D) 111111_{TWO}

64. Ⓐ Ⓑ Ⓒ Ⓓ

65. If the domain of the function $f(x) = 4x^2 + 12x + 9$ is the set of reals, then
(A) $f(x)$ is always positive
(B) $f(x)$ is nonnegative
(C) the graph of $f(x)$ does not intersect the x-axis
(D) the equation $f(x) = 0$ has two distinct roots

65. Ⓐ Ⓑ Ⓒ Ⓓ

66. Which set is not closed under multiplication?
    (A) The set of squares of positive integers.
    (B) The set of multiples of 7.
    (C) The set of integers greater than 1.
    (D) The set of negative integers.

66. Ⓐ Ⓑ Ⓒ Ⓓ

67. The median age for the data given is
    (A) 19   (B) 20   (C) 21   (D) 22

AGE	FREQUENCY
15	6
18	2
20	9
22	2
30	8
31	1

67. Ⓐ Ⓑ Ⓒ Ⓓ

68. The converse of "If she is thin, then she is beautiful" is
    (A) She is beautiful but not thin.
    (B) If she is beautiful, then she is thin.
    (C) If she is not beautiful, then she is not thin.
    (D) If she is not thin, then she is not beautiful.

68. Ⓐ Ⓑ Ⓒ Ⓓ

69. Which of the following is not a function on the set of real numbers?
    (A) $f(x) = x^2$ (B) $f(x) = 3x + 1$
    (C) $f(x) = \sqrt{x}$ (D) $f(x) = 1$

69. Ⓐ Ⓑ Ⓒ Ⓓ

70. For which real numbers is the function $f(x) = \dfrac{x}{x^2 - 9}$ not defined?
    (A) only $x = 0$ (B) only $x = 3$ (C) $x = 0$ or 3 (D) $x = 3$ or -3

70. Ⓐ Ⓑ Ⓒ Ⓓ

71. The set $\{x : x$ is an integer and $|x - 1| < 2\}$ equals
    (A) $\{1, 2\}$ (B) $\{-2, -1, 1, 2\}$
    (C) $\{-2, -1, 0, 1, 2\}$ (D) $\{0, 1, 2\}$

71. Ⓐ Ⓑ Ⓒ Ⓓ

72. If n is divisible both by 6 and by 10, then it must also be divisible by
    (A) 12   (B) 20   (C) 30   (D) 60

72. Ⓐ Ⓑ Ⓒ Ⓓ

73. If $f(x) = x^2 + bx + c$, if $f(0) = 1$ and $f(1) = 2$, then $f(x) =$
    (A) $x^2 + 1$ (B) $x^2 + x + 1$
    (C) $x^2 - x + 1$ (D) $x^2 + 2x + 1$

73. Ⓐ Ⓑ Ⓒ Ⓓ

74. If a, b, and c are real numbers and $a > b > c$, then which of the following could be false?
    (A) $b - a > 0$ (B) $ab > ac$ (C) $-a < -b$ (D) $c - a < 0$

74. Ⓐ Ⓑ Ⓒ Ⓓ

75. If m and n are positive integers, m even and n odd, which of the following numbers is odd?
    (A) $mn + 2$ (B) m^n (C) $5n + 1$ (D) n^m

75. Ⓐ Ⓑ Ⓒ Ⓓ

76. If p is false and q is true, then which of the following is false?
    (A) $\sim p \to \sim q$ (B) $p \to q$ (C) $\sim p \to q$ (D) $p \to \sim q$

76. Ⓐ Ⓑ Ⓒ Ⓓ

77. If $f(x) = ax + b$, $f(0) = 2$, and $f(1) = -1$, then

    (A) $a = 3$, $b = 2$ (B) $a = 3$, $b = -2$

    (C) $a = -3$, $b = 2$ (D) $a = -3$, $b = -2$

77. Ⓐ Ⓑ Ⓒ Ⓓ

78. If m and n are real numbers, which of the following statements is false?

    (A) $2^m \cdot 2^n = 2^{mn}$ (B) $(2^m)^n = 2^{mn}$

    (C) $2^m \div 2^n = 2^{m-n}$ (D) $2^m \cdot 2^n = 2^{m+n}$

78. Ⓐ Ⓑ Ⓒ Ⓓ

79. $\log_4 8 =$

    (A) $1/2$ (B) $2/3$ (C) $3/2$ (D) 2

79. Ⓐ Ⓑ Ⓒ Ⓓ

80. If $\log_{10} m = 0.1$, then $\log_{10} m^3 =$

    (A) 0.001   (B) 0.3   (C) 3.1   (D) 3.3

80. Ⓐ Ⓑ Ⓒ Ⓓ

81. If $m * n = m^2 - 2n$, then $3 * (2 * 1) =$

    (A) 23   (B) 9   (C) 7   (D) 5

81. Ⓐ Ⓑ Ⓒ Ⓓ

82. If $i = \sqrt{-1}$, then $i^{19} =$

    (A) 1   (B) -1 (C) i (D) $-i$

82. Ⓐ Ⓑ Ⓒ Ⓓ

83. If a die is tossed, what is the probability that the top face will not show a 1 or a 2?

    (A) $1/36$ (B) $1/6$ (C) $1/3$ (D) $2/3$

83. Ⓐ Ⓑ Ⓒ Ⓓ

84. If $f(x) = x^3 + k$ and $f(x)$ is divisible by the factor $(x + 2)$, then $k =$

    (A) -8 (B) -2 (C) 0   (D) 8

84. Ⓐ Ⓑ Ⓒ Ⓓ

85. The set satisfying the inequality $|x| < 2$ is

    (A) $\{x : -2 < x < 2\}$ (B) $\{x : -2 \leq x \leq 2\}$

    (C) $\{x : x < -2 \text{ or } x > 2\}$ (D) $\{x : 0 < x < 2\}$

85. Ⓐ Ⓑ Ⓒ Ⓓ

86. For what value of k do the equations

$$\begin{cases} 2x - y = 4 \\ 4x + ky = 3 \end{cases} \quad \text{have no solution?}$$

    (A) -8 (B) -2 (C) 2   (D) 8

86. Ⓐ Ⓑ Ⓒ Ⓓ

87. If $x^2 - x > 0$, then which of the following statements is false?

    (A) $x < 0$ (B) $x > 1$ (C) $0 < x < 1$ (D) $x < 0 \text{ or } x > 1$

87. Ⓐ Ⓑ Ⓒ Ⓓ

88. Which function has a graph symmetric to the origin?

    (A) $y = x^2$ (B) $y = \dfrac{1}{x^2}$ (C) $y = x + 3$ (D) $y = \dfrac{1}{x}$

88. Ⓐ Ⓑ Ⓒ Ⓓ

89. The difference between the mean and the median (mean minus median) for the set $\{35, 41, 52, 33, 49\}$ is

    (A) 0   (B) 1   (C) 2   (D) 3

89. Ⓐ Ⓑ Ⓒ Ⓓ

90. The inverse of the function $y = 2^x$ is

    (A) $y = \log_2 x$ (B) $y = -2^x$ (C) $y = 2^{-x}$ (D) $y = x^2$

90. Ⓐ Ⓑ Ⓒ Ⓓ

ANSWER KEY AND REFERENCE CHART—
TRIAL TEST

Each answer in the key below is followed by a reference* to the section of the book in which the topic of the question is reviewed. (Explanations of the answers follow the answer key.) The topics covered on the Mathematics examination are listed below with their reference code and the page on which review of the topic begins.

Topic	Reference	Page
Arithmetic	A1	335
Algebra	A2	339
Geometry	A3	342
Data Interpretation	A4	348
Sets	B1	364
Logic	B2	368
Real Number System	B3	372
Functions and their Graphs	B4	375
Probability and Statistics	B5	380
Miscellaneous Topics	B6	357 & 387

*A question in mathematics is often on material from two or more topics. The reference given for each question lists the principal topic covered.

Part I

1.	A (A1)	11.	B (A2)	21.	B (A4)	31.	B (A2)
2.	C (A1)	12.	A (A3)	22.	C (A4)	32.	D (A1)
3.	A (A1)	13.	C (A3)	23.	A (A4)	33.	D (A1)
4.	C (A3)	14.	C (A3)	24.	B (A4)	34.	C (A2)
5.	A (A1)	15.	B (A3)	25.	A (A4)	35.	B (A1)
6.	B (A1)	16.	A (A3)	26.	C (A4)	36.	C (A3)
7.	D (A2)	17.	A (A3)	27.	B (A4)	37.	D (A1)
8.	C (A2)	18.	C (A2)	28.	D (A1)	38.	A (A2)
9.	D (A2)	19.	A (A3)	29.	A (A2)	39.	A (A2)
10.	A (A2)	20.	C (A3)	30.	B (A2)	40.	C (A2)

Part II

41.	C (B1)	51.	D (B3)	61.	B (B5)	71.	D (B3)	81.	D (B6)
42.	C (B1)	52.	B (B3)	62.	A (B5)	72.	C (B3)	82.	D (B6)
43.	A (B1)	53.	C (B3)	63.	D (B5)	73.	A (B4)	83.	D (B5)
44.	B (B1)	54.	A (B3)	64.	C (B6)	74.	B (B3)	84.	D (B4)
45.	A (B1)	55.	B (B4)	65.	B (B4)	75.	D (B3)	85.	A (B3)
46.	B (B2)	56.	D (B4)	66.	D (B3)	76.	A (B2)	86.	B (B3)
47.	D (B2)	57.	A (B3)	67.	B (B5)	77.	C (B4)	87.	C (B3)
48.	A (B2)	58.	C (B4)	68.	B (B2)	78.	A (B3)	88.	D (B4)
49.	D (B2)	59.	B (B6)	69.	C (B4)	79.	C (B6)	89.	B (B5)
50.	A (B3)	60.	D (B5)	70.	D (B4)	80.	B (B6)	90.	A (B6)

SCORING CHART—TRIAL TEST

After you have scored your Trial Test, enter the results in the chart below (the Raw Score computation is explained on page 14); then transfer your Raw Score to the Progress Chart on page 14. As you complete the Sample Examinations later in this part of the book, you should be able to achieve increasingly higher Raw Scores.

Total Test		Number Right	Number Wrong	Number Omitted	Raw Score
Part I	40				
Part II	50				
Total:	90				

ANSWER EXPLANATIONS—TRIAL TEST

Part I

1. **A.** $3 - 5 + 6 - 8 - 4 + 7 = 3 + 6 + 7 - (5 + 8 + 4) = 16 - 17 = -1$.
2. **C.** $2\frac{1}{2}$ qts. $= 5$ pts.; $5(0.55) = 2.75$.
3. **A.** $0.15(95) < 0.15(100) = 15$; therefore $95 - 0.15(95) > 80$.
4. **C.** The diagonals are in the ratio $2x : \sqrt{2}x$ or $2 : \sqrt{2}$.

5. **A.** There are 36 oz. in $2\frac{1}{4}$ lbs.; $304 \div 36 > 8$.
6. **B.** 1 sq. yd. $= 36 \times 36 < 40 \times 40$ sq. in.
7. **D.** There are $10d + 25q$ cents, but this cannot be compared with $35q$ without information on d and q.
8. **C.** $5 - [6 - 2(1 + 3)] = 5 - (6 - 8) = 5 - (-2) = 7$.
9. **D.** If $x = y$, $\dfrac{|x - y|}{y - x}$ is not defined. If $x - y > 0$, $\dfrac{|x - y|}{y - x} = -1$; if $y - x > 0$, $\dfrac{|x - y|}{y - x} = 1$.
10. **A.** Since Mike takes 3 hours to mow the lawn alone it would have to take Cary only 3 hours alone for them to do it together in $1\frac{1}{2}$ hours. Since Cary takes 4 hrs alone, it takes more than $1\frac{1}{2}$ hours if both boys mow.
11. **B.** $(1.1)^{-1} = \dfrac{1}{1.1} < \dfrac{1}{1} = 1$.
12. **A.** $\dfrac{LN}{10} = \dfrac{2.4}{4}$, so $LN = 6$. But $L'M'$ must be greater than 6 for the sum of the lengths of two sides of the triangle to exceed the third.

13. C. Use the Pythagorean theorem; we
     have a 7-24-25 triangle.

25′

7′

14. C. $\widehat{MQ} = \widehat{NP} = 2(21°) = 42°.$ $\widehat{MRN} = 180° - 84° = 96°.$

15. B. $\angle M = 3x°$ and $3x + x = 104$. Therefore $x = 26$ and $3x = 78$.

16. A. $\angle C$ is a right angle; $AC = \sqrt{4^2 - 3^2} = \sqrt{7} > 2$.

17. A. If $x =$ the length of one leg of the isosceles right triangle. then $x^2 + x^2 = 4$
     and $x = \sqrt{2}$.

18. C. $\begin{array}{r} 2x - y = 2 \\ x + 2y = 6 \end{array} \rightarrow \begin{array}{r} 4x - 2y = 4 \\ \underline{x + 2y = 6} \\ 5x \quad\quad = 10, x = 2. \end{array}$

     By substitution in either equation, $y = 2$.

19. A. $x = 47°$ since $\angle MNS$ is supplementary to $\angle PNM$; $y = 43°$.

20. C. The area of the walk is $(28 \times 12) - (20 \times 4) = 336 - 80 = 256$.

21. B. Pakistan's population in 1969 was 112 million.

22. C. The difference is $241 - 203$ or 38 million.

23. A. The change for 1960–1968 is the narrower of the two bars. It is almost 5% for
     the U.S.

24. B. Use the rightmost bar. The percent carried by motor vehicles is just over 20.

25. A. The two vertical bars show that the *percent* of traffic via railroads was
     greater in 1950 than in 1969.

26. C. The last entry in the male column under "white" is the correct one.

27. B. $p = \dfrac{69.4 - 33.5}{33.5} \approx \dfrac{36}{33} = 100^\cdot$.

28. D. Since 1 m = 100 cm, (7.6×10^{-9})m $= (7.6 \times 10^{-9} \cdot 10^2)$cm $= (7.6 \times 10^{-7})$cm.

29. A. $\dfrac{4^0 m^4 n^0}{4m^4} = \dfrac{1 \cdot m^4 \cdot 1}{4 \cdot m^4} = \dfrac{1}{4}$ if $m \neq 0$.

30. B. $(5x + 9) > 1 \rightarrow 5x > -8 \rightarrow x > -1\tfrac{3}{5}$. If x is an integer, then x may be
     $-1, 0, 1, 2, \ldots$.

31. B. Note that $x - y$ and $x - z$ are both positive. Find counterexamples for (A),
     (C), and (D).

32. D. $\dfrac{13}{4} = 3\tfrac{1}{4} = 3.25 = 325\%$.

33. D. $\dfrac{7}{b} = \dfrac{2}{3} \rightarrow 2b = 21 \rightarrow b = 10\tfrac{1}{2}$.

34. C. When $x = -3, x^2 + 9 = (-3)^2 + 9 = 9 + 9 = 18 \neq 0$.

35. B. $20 = (1.25) \times x \rightarrow x = \dfrac{20}{1.25} = \dfrac{2000}{125} = 16$.

36. C. Rewriting $4x + 3y - 12 = 0$ in the form $y = -\tfrac{4}{3}x + 4$ shows that its slope is
     $-\tfrac{4}{3}$.

37. D. If x is a nonzero real number, the reciprocal or multiplicative inverse is $\dfrac{1}{x}$. The
     product of a number and its multiplicative inverse is equal to 1.

38. A. $\dfrac{x^2 - x}{x(x^2 - 1)} = \dfrac{x(x - 1)}{x(x - 1)(x + 1)} = \dfrac{1}{x + 1)}$ if $x \neq 0, 1$.

39. A. $\dfrac{x + 5 + 8 + 13}{4} = 8 \rightarrow \dfrac{x + 26}{4} = 8 \rightarrow x = 6$.

40. C. $3^0 + 3^1 + 3^2 = 1 + 3 + 9 = 13$.

Part II

41.   C. $S \cup T = \{a,b,c,d\}$; $R \cap (S \cup T) = \{a,b\}$.

42.   C. $S \times S$ has (3×3) or 9 elements, and $S \times S \times S$ has (9×3) elements.

43.   A.   If $R = \{6\}$ and $S = \{3,6\}$, then $R \cup S = \{3,6\}$.

44.   B.   The set $R - S$ contains all the elements of R that are not in S. The shaded region in (B) is $R - S$.

45.   A. $R^+ \cap Z$ is the set of elements in both R^+ and Z; that is, the set of positive integers.

46.   B.   "If p, then q" is equivalent to "if not q, then not p," "p only if q," "p is sufficient for q," and "q is necessary for p."

47.   D. $p \to q$ and $q \to r$ are equivalent respectively to $\sim q \to \sim p$ and $r \to \sim q$, from which it follows that $r \to \sim p$.

48.   A.   Here is the truth table:

$\sim$	$(p$	$\vee$	$\sim$	$q)$
F	T	T	F	T
F	T	T	T	F
$\boxed{\text{T}}$	F	F	F	T
F	F	T	T	F
(5)	(1)	(4)	(3)	(2)

49.   D.   This proof uses the contrapositive of the given statement.

50.   A. $a < b$ implies that $(b - a) > 0$, so $-a > -b$.

51.   D. $(3^2 + 4^2)^{-1/2} = \dfrac{1}{\sqrt{3^2 + 4^2}} = \dfrac{1}{5}$.

52.   B.   Note that $\sqrt{121} = 11$, a rational number.

53.   C.   Note that although b is a factor of the numerator in (C) it is not a factor of the denominator $b + d$. It therefore cannot be canceled.

54.   A.   A set S is closed under an operation, say $*$, if for every pair of elements a and b in S, $a * b$ is also in S. Note, if a and b are odd integers, that so is $a \times b$.

55.   B.   The intercepts can be read from the graph: they are 0, 2, -2. So only (B) and (C) are possible. But from the graph $f(1) > 0$ while for (C) $f(1) < 0$; so (C) is eliminated.

56.   D. $f(g(x)) = \dfrac{1}{\dfrac{1}{x} - 2 + 2} = x$.

57.   A.   Substitute the first number in the ordered pair for m, the second for n. Only for (A) is $3m - 2n$ greater than 4.

58.   C.   Note, in (C), that x_1 maps into both y_1 and y_2.

59.   B.   Only in (B) does $m * n = n * m$.

60.   D.   The probability that the Lynxes will win is $2 \div (3 + 2)$, which equals $\dfrac{2}{5}$ or 0.4.

61.   B.   The probability is $_3C_2/_5C_2$, or $(3 \cdot 2)/(5 \cdot 4)$.

62.   A.   The answer is the number of combinations of 7 elements taken 5 at a time, or $_7C_5$. Since $_7C_5 = {}_7C_2$, we get $(7 \cdot 6)/(1 \cdot 2)$, or 21.

63.   D.   Compute the probability of obtaining two marbles of the same color and subtract from 1. The probability of getting two blacks is $(5/7) \cdot (2/6)$, or $5/21$. The required probability is $1 - 5/21 = 16/21$.

64.   C. $224_{\text{FIVE}} = 2(5)^2 + 2(5) + 4 = 64_{\text{TEN}}$
            $332_{\text{FOUR}} = 3(4)^2 + 3(4) + 2 = 62_{\text{TEN}}$
            $2102_{\text{THREE}} = 2(3)^3 + 1(3)^2 + 2 = 65_{\text{TEN}}$
            $111111_{\text{TWO}} = 2^5 + 2^4 + 2^3 + 2^2 + 2^1 + 2^0 = 63_{\text{TEN}}$

65.   B. $f(x) = (2x + 3)^2$, which is zero if $x = -3/2$; otherwise $f(x) > 0$.

66.   D.   The product of two negative integers is positive.

67.   B. The total number reported on (the sum of the frequencies) is 28; the middle one (14th or 15th) has age 20.

68.   B. The converse of "If p, then q" is "If q, then p."

69.   C. $f(x) = \sqrt{x}$ is a function but its domain is the set of nonnegative numbers.

70.   D. Division by zero is excluded.

71.   D. If $|x - 1| < 2$, then x is within 2 units of 1; that is, $-1 < x < 3$.

72.   C. Since $6 = 2 \cdot 3$ and $10 = 2 \cdot 5$, n must be divisible by 2, 3, and 5.

73.   A. $f(0) = c = 1$ and $f(1) = 1 + b + c = 1 + b + 1 = 2$, so $b = 0$.

74.   B. If $a < 0$, $ab < ac$.

75.   D. Let $m = 2$, $n = 3$. Note that (A), (B), (C) are all even.

76.   A. $\sim p$ is T, $\sim q$ is F. So $\sim p \rightarrow \sim q$ is F.

77.   C. $f(0) = b = 2$; $f(1) = a + b = -1$; so $a + 2 = -1$ and $a = -3$.

78.   A. $2^m \cdot 2^n = 2^{m+n}$ as in (D).

79.   C. If $\log_4 8 = x$, then $4^x = 8$ or $2^{2x} = 2^3$.

80.   B. $\log_{10} m = 3 \log_{10} m = 3(0.1)$.

81.   D. $3 * (2 * 1) = 3 * (2^2 - 2 \cdot 1) = 3 * 2 = 3^2 - 2 \cdot 2 = 5$.

82.   D. $i^{19} = i^{16} \cdot i^3 = 1 \cdot (-i)$. Note that $i^2 = -1$; $i^3 = i(i^2) = i(-1) = -i$; $i^4 = (i^2)^2 = (-1)^2 = 1$; and so on.

83.   D. The die shows 3, 4, 5, or 6 in 4 out of 6 outcomes. So the answer is $1 - \frac{4}{6}$.

84.   D. $f(-2) = 0 = (-2)^3 + k \rightarrow k = 8$.

85.   A. $|x| < a$ is equivalent to $-a < x < a$.

86.   B. The coefficients of y must be in the same ratio as those of x: $k : -1 = 4 : 2 \rightarrow 2k = -4 \rightarrow k = -2$.

87.   C. $x^2 - x = x(x - 1)$; the product is positive if $x > 1$ or if $x < 0$.

88.   D. A graph of $y = f(x)$ is symmetric to the origin if $(-x, -y)$ lies on the graph, that is, if it satisfies the equation. Note that $(-y) = \dfrac{1}{(-x)}$ is equivalent to $y = \dfrac{1}{x}$.

89.   B. The mean is the average, or 42; the median is 41.

90.   A. To find the inverse of a function, interchange x and y, then solve for y. For $y = 2^x$, we write $x = 2^y$, which yields, after taking the log of each side to base 2, $\log_2 x = y$.

Background, Review, and Practice Questions

10

The General Examination in Mathematics measures your knowledge of fundamental principles and concepts of mathematics. It covers material that is generally taught in a college course for nonmathematics majors. The examination consists of two separately timed sections. Part I (Basic Skills and Concepts) has approximately 40 questions to be answered in 30 minutes. It tests skills that are generally taught in high school and that are frequently used in college courses besides mathematics—arithmetic, algebra, geometry, and data interpretation. Part II (Content) has approximately 50 questions to be answered in 60 minutes. It covers material that is studied at the college level—sets, logic, the real number system, functions, and probability and statistics.

DESCRIPTION OF THE GENERAL EXAMINATION IN MATHEMATICS

Part I. Basic Skills and Concepts.

Approximately 40 questions; time allowed 30 minutes.

Subject Area	Approximate percentage of questions	Approximate number of questions
Arithmetic	30%	12
Algebra	35%	14
Geometry	15–20%	6–8
Data Interpretation	15–20%	6–8

Part II.   Content.

Approximately 50 questions; time allowed 60 minutes.

Subject Area	Approximate percentage of questions	Approximate number of questions
Sets	10%	5
Logic	10%	5
Real Number System	30%	15
Functions and their Graphs	20%	10
Probability and Statistics	15%	7–8
Miscellaneous Topics	15%	7–8

SCORING; PENALTY FOR GUESSING

Each correct answer on the mathematics examination earns you one point, but you lose one-third of a point for each incorrect answer. Because of this penalty, we advise against wild or blind guessing, which is likely to lower your score. Educated guesses, however, are recommended. If you can eliminate as wrong one or more of the choices listed for a question, then your chance of guessing the correct answer from among the remaining ones is increased. Omitted answers are not counted in the score.

Both a subscore for each section and a total score are reported. Since Part II is allowed twice as much time as Part I, it counts twice as much as Part I in determining the total score. This reflects the greater emphasis given college-level material, which is tested in Part II.

CALCULATORS PROHIBITED

According to the CLEP brochure, calculators or other computing devices are *not* permitted on the examination. It is noted that questions were not designed for the use of calculators and that little emphasis is placed on arithmetical computations.

COMMON MATHEMATICAL SYMBOLS AND FORMULAS

Symbols used in arithmetic, algebra, geometry, and so forth.

$a = b$	a equals b
$a \neq b$	a does not equal b
$a \approx b$	a is approximately equal to b
$a > b$	a is greater than b
$a \geq b$	a is greater than or equal to b
$a < b$	a is less than b
$a \leq b$	a is less than or equal to b
$\lvert x \rvert$	the absolute value, or magnitude, of x
$\sqrt{q}$	the square root of q
$\sqrt[3]{q}, \sqrt[4]{q}, \sqrt[n]{q}$	the cube root of q, the fourth root of q, the nth root of q
$a : b$	the ratio of a to b, "a is to b"
$A \cong B$	A is congruent to B
$A \sim B$	A is similar to B
$\angle PRQ$	angle PRQ
$l \perp m$	l is perpendicular to m
$l \parallel m$	l is parallel to m
$\overparen{AB}$	arc AB (of a circle)
π	the constant pi (the ratio of the circumference of a circle to its diameter; approximately 22/7 or 3.14)

Symbols used in set theory: †

$a \in S$	a is an element of set S
$a \notin S$	a is not an element of set S
$\{a, b, c\}$	the set containing the elements a, b, and c
$\emptyset$	the null or empty set
U	the universal set
$\overline{R}$ (or R' or $\widetilde{R}$)	the complement of set R: the set of all elements that are not in set R
$A \cup B$	the union of sets A and B
$A \cap B$	the intersection of sets A and B
$A \times B$	the Cartesian product of A and B: the set of all ordered pairs whose first element is in A and whose second element is in B
$A \subset B$	A is a subset of B.
	(Some authors use "$A \subset B$" to mean A is a proper subset of B and "$A \subseteq B$" to mean A is a subset, proper or improper, of B.)

Symbols used in logic. †

$\sim p$	not p (the negation of p)
$p \wedge q$	p and q (conjunction)
$p \vee q$	p or q (disjunction: p or q or both)
$p \rightarrow q$	if p then q; or p implies q
$p \leftrightarrow q$	p if and only if q, or p is equivalent to q
$\exists_x$	there exists an x; for some x
$\forall_x$	for all x; for each x

Other symbols.

$n!$	n factorial
e.g., $5! = 5 \cdot 4 \cdot 3 \cdot 2 \cdot 1$	
i	the imaginary unit in complex numbers; $i = \sqrt{-1}$
$a * b$	"$*$" stands for some algebraic operation; thus $a * b$ is the element obtained by applying this operation to the ordered pair of elements (a,b). For example, if $*$ is ordinary subtraction on the set of integers, then $3 * 7 = 3 - 7 = -4$.

† Most of these symbols are defined or illustrated when they first occur in the chapter.

$P(n,r)$ the *permutation* (or ordered arrangement) of n elements taken r at a time:

$$P(n,r) = \frac{n!}{(n-r)!}$$

$C(n,r)$ the *combination* (a selection where order does not count) of n objects taken r at a time:

$$C(n,r) = \frac{P(n,r)}{r!} = \frac{n!}{r!(n-r)!}$$

COMMON GEOMETRIC FORMULAS

Sum of the angles of a triangle. The sum is 180°.

$\angle A + \angle B + \angle C = 180°$

Pythagorean Theorem.
In a right triangle, the square of the length of the hypotenuse equals the sum of the squares of the other two sides:
$$c^2 = a^2 + b^2$$

		Areas	**Perimeters**
RECTANGLE		$A = lw$	$P = 2l + 2w$
SQUARE		$A = s^2$	$P = 4s$
PARALLELOGRAM		$A = bh$	
TRIANGLE		$A = \frac{1}{2} bh$	$P = a + b + c$
TRAPEZOID		$A = \frac{1}{2}(b + b^1)\, h$	
CIRCLE		$A = \pi r^2$	

Volumes

PRISM		$V = lwh$
CYLINDER		$V = \pi r^2 h$
CONE		$V = \frac{1}{3}\pi r^2 h$
PYRAMID		$V = \frac{1}{3}Bh$
SPHERE		$V = \frac{4}{3}\pi r^3$

Surface Areas

PRISM		$A = 2(lw + wh + lh)$
CYLINDER		lateral area $= 2\pi rh$ total area $= 2\pi rh + 2\pi r^2$

ORGANIZATION OF THE CHAPTER

In this chapter we present, through practice questions and explanations, a review of the skills and content tested on the CLEP General Examination in Mathematics.

Part A contains sets of practice questions, followed by answers and explanations, on each of the topics included in Part I of the Examination: arithmetic, algebra, geometry, and data interpretation.

Part B has sets of practice questions, followed by answers and explanations, on each of the topics tested in Part II of the Examination: sets, logic, the real number system, functions and their graphs, probability and statistics, and miscellaneous topics.

Throughout this chapter, we will encourage you to develop a systematic approach to problem-solving, suggesting specific techniques and offering hints on taking the test. You may find it helpful for your review to refer to one or more of the books listed below. These books, or others covering similar material, are available in public and school libraries.

Allendoerfer & Oakley, *Principles of Mathematics*. Third Edition. New York: McGraw-Hill, 1969.

Benice, Daniel D., *Arithmetic and Algebra*. Englewood Cliffs NJ: Prentice-Hall, 1985.

Blau, Barbara Lee, *Forgotten Algebra: A Refresher Course*. Woodbury NY: Barron's Educational Series, Inc., 1983.

Dressler, Isidore, and Edward P. Keenan, *Integrated Mathematics*. New York: Amsco School Publications, 1980.

Hockett, Shirley O., Barron's *Developing Skills for the High School Equivalency Examination in Mathematics*. Second revised edition. Woodbury NY: Barron's Educational Series, Inc., 1978.

Hockett, Shirley O., *Basic Mathematics: What Every College Student Should Know*. Englewood Cliffs NJ: Prentice-Hall, 1977.

Lipschutz, S., *Finite Mathematics*. New York: Schaum Outline Series, 1966.

McWaters, Marcus, and You-Fong Lin, *Intermediate Algebra*. Lexington MA: D. C. Heath & Company, 1985.

Peters, M., *College Algebra*. Woodbury NY: Barron's Educational Series, Inc., 1982.

Prindle, Anthony, *Math the Easy Way*. Woodbury NY: Barron's Educational Series, Inc., 1982.

Rich, Barnett. *Review of Elementary Mathematics*. New York: Schaum Outline Series, 1977.

PART A

Practice Questions for Part I

The 40 questions in Part I of the examination are of two types: quantitative-comparison type and regular multiple-choice type. To provide plenty of practice with the quantitative-comparison type, we will use questions of this type to review the various topics in Part I. We will follow this by a set of supplementary questions on Part I topics, but these will be of the multiple-choice type.

The directions for quantitative comparison are as follows:

Directions: Each question consists of two quantities, one in Column A and one in Column B. You are to compare the two quantities and in the answer column blacken space

    A if the quantity in Column A is greater;
    B if the quantity in Column B is greater;
    C if the two quantities are equal;
    D if the relationship cannot be determined from the information given.

Notes: 1. In certain questions, information concerning one or both of the quantities to be compared is centered above the two columns.

          2. A symbol that appears in both columns represents the same thing in Column A as it does in Column B.

          3. Letters such as x, n, and k stand for real numbers.

We begin with seven illustrative examples with answers indicated at the right and explanations given in parentheses.

EXAMPLES	COLUMN A	COLUMN B	ANSWERS
1.	$3 + 5$	3×5	**1.** A ■ C D

($3 + 5 = 8$, $3 \times 5 = 15$. Since $15 > 8$, we have marked choice B. Note that you can always immediately eliminate D as the answer to a question such as this which involves only straightforward computation with numbers. The relationship *can* be determined from the information given.)

Example 2 refers to $\triangle ABC$.

$AB = AC$

Note: Figure is not drawn to scale.

---

2. (answer) A B C ■

2.	x	z

(Since $AB = AC$, the triangle is isosceles and $x = y$; but since the figure is not drawn to scale, we cannot determine how x and z compare.)

3.	an odd number whose square is between 14 and 47	5

3. A B ■ D

(The squares between 14 and 47 are $16 = 4^2$, $25 = 5^2$, and $36 = 6^2$. Only 5 is odd.)

4.	m	$2m$

4. A B C ■

(Be careful! $2m > m$ if m is positive, as for $m = 3$, *but* if $m = 0$ then $2m = m$. Further, if $m = -3$, then $2m < m$ since $2(-3) = -6$ and $-6 < -3$. In a question involving unknowns, try not to overlook zero and the negative numbers. It is often very helpful, also, in comparing signed numbers to visualize the number line:

Of two numbers, the one represented by the point to the right is the larger. So, zero is greater than any negative number, $-2 > -5$, $-1 > -2$, every positive number is greater than every negative number, etc.)

5.	$(13)(\frac{1}{7})(\frac{3}{8})$	$(\frac{3}{7})(13)(\frac{1}{10})$

5. ■ B C D

(Instead of computing either of the items we can mentally rearrange the entry in Column B as $(13)(\frac{3}{7})(\frac{1}{10})$ or $(13)(\frac{1}{7})(\frac{3}{10})$ so that it most resembles Column A, or vice versa. Then we eliminate the common factors 13, $\frac{1}{7}$, and 3. Now we need compare only $\frac{1}{8}$ and $\frac{1}{10}$, and since $\frac{1}{8} > \frac{1}{10}$, the answer is A. Common factors should always be eliminated from the quantities given in the two columns to simplify the comparison. Also, avoid using pencil and paper wherever possible, to save time.)

Example 6 refers to this figure.

$w + y = 70$

6.	x	150	**6.** [A] ■ [C] [D]

(Since vertical angles are equal, $x = z$ and also $y = w$. Therefore $2w = 70$ and $w = 35$. Then $x = 180 - 35 = 145$.)

Example 7 refers to this chart.

DOW-JONES INDUSTRIAL AVERAGES

7.	the high Dow-Jones industrial average for 1967	the closing Dow-Jones average in 1968	**7.** ■ [B] [C] [D]

(This question is on data interpretation. The key at the right indicates how to use the graph. Since the high for 1967 is to the right of the closing indicator for 1968, A is the correct answer.)

We now give a set of practice questions of the quantitative-comparison type on each topic covered by Part I. Each set begins with a few illustrative examples. Reread the test directions given on page 333 if necessary.

A1. Arithmetic

The subtopics are whole numbers; fractions; decimals; percent; powers and roots; ratio and proportion.

Here are a few introductory examples, with answers and explanations.

EXAMPLES	COLUMN A	COLUMN B	ANSWERS
1.	6×1	$6 \div 1$	**1.** [A] [B] ■ [D]

(Since $6 \times 1 = 6$ and $6 \div 1 = 6$, the quantities are equal. We've therefore marked C.)

---

2.   price per ounce of detergent if   2.1¢   **2.** ■ Ⓑ Ⓒ Ⓓ
a 40-ounce box costs $0.85

($85 \div 40 = 2.125$, which is greater than 2.1. Note, however, that we need carry out the first computation only far enough to see that the answer *exceeds* 2.1.)

3. 8.1×0.04 0.32   **3.** ■ Ⓑ Ⓒ Ⓓ

($8.1 \times 0.04 = 0.324$, but even this computation is unnecessary. Since $8.1 \times 0.04 > 8 \times 0.04 = 0.32$, A is obviously the answer.)

4.   a prime factor of 6   3   **4.** Ⓐ Ⓑ Ⓒ ■

(6 has two prime factors, 2 and 3. The relationship cannot be determined from the information given.)

PRACTICE QUESTIONS ON ARITHMETIC

Follow the directions on this set of Part I questions on arithmetic. First, try to answer the questions. Then check with the answers, which follow. It will also be beneficial to study the explanations carefully.

QUESTIONS	COLUMN A	COLUMN B	
1.	$8 \div 4$	$8 \times \frac{1}{4}$	**1.** Ⓐ Ⓑ Ⓒ Ⓓ
2.	0.16	$\frac{1}{6}$	**2.** Ⓐ Ⓑ Ⓒ Ⓓ
3.	6	$\sqrt{35}$	**3.** Ⓐ Ⓑ Ⓒ Ⓓ
4.	$\dfrac{1}{0.004}$	250	**4.** Ⓐ Ⓑ Ⓒ Ⓓ
5.	$3 + 5 \cdot 2$	$(3 + 5) \cdot 2$	**5.** Ⓐ Ⓑ Ⓒ Ⓓ
6.	$\frac{1}{2} + \frac{1}{3} + \frac{1}{6}$	$\frac{11}{12}$	**6.** Ⓐ Ⓑ Ⓒ Ⓓ
7.	$5 - 0.31$	4.7	**7.** Ⓐ Ⓑ Ⓒ Ⓓ
8.	a number between 0.3 and $\frac{1}{3}$	0.32	**8.** Ⓐ Ⓑ Ⓒ Ⓓ

A compact car gets 25 miles to the gallon on the open road.

9.	number of gallons of gas needed for a 550-mile trip	23	**9.** Ⓐ Ⓑ Ⓒ Ⓓ
10.	62,364 rounded off to the nearest hundred	62,300	**10.** Ⓐ Ⓑ Ⓒ Ⓓ
11.	$\dfrac{100.52}{100}$	1	**11.** Ⓐ Ⓑ Ⓒ Ⓓ
12.	the simple interest on $350 after 2 years	$42	**12.** Ⓐ Ⓑ Ⓒ Ⓓ

QUESTIONS	COLUMN A	COLUMN B	
13.	$\lvert 2-4 \rvert$	$\lvert 4-2 \rvert$	13. Ⓐ Ⓑ Ⓒ Ⓓ
14.	the average of 20, 29, 35, and 37	the average of 19, 29, 34, and 37	14. Ⓐ Ⓑ Ⓒ Ⓓ
15.	$2900 - 1900.1$	1000.1	15. Ⓐ Ⓑ Ⓒ Ⓓ
16.	$\tfrac{7}{25}$	0.26	16. Ⓐ Ⓑ Ⓒ Ⓓ
17.	4% of 4805	190	17. Ⓐ Ⓑ Ⓒ Ⓓ

18. A TV set can be bought on time for $25 down and twelve monthly payments of $30 each.

	the total cost of the TV set bought on time	$385	18. Ⓐ Ⓑ Ⓒ Ⓓ

19. Bruce borrows $960 at 5½% for 3 months.

	the total amount Bruce must repay	$974	19. Ⓐ Ⓑ Ⓒ Ⓓ

20.	the cost of automobile insurance for 15 years if each annual premium is $110	$1600	20. Ⓐ Ⓑ Ⓒ Ⓓ

Mr. King buys a man-made fur coat marked down 10% in a pre-Christmas sale, and a pair of shoes costing $15. He pays $60 for both items.

QUESTIONS	COLUMN A	COLUMN B	
21.	the original price of the coat	$50	21. Ⓐ Ⓑ Ⓒ Ⓓ
22.	$5\tfrac{1}{3}$ yards	190 inches	22. Ⓐ Ⓑ Ⓒ Ⓓ
23.	the additive inverse of 2	the multiplicative inverse of 2	23. Ⓐ Ⓑ Ⓒ Ⓓ
24.	the time it takes to fly 300 miles if the plane covers one mile in ten seconds	50 minutes	24. Ⓐ Ⓑ Ⓒ Ⓓ
25.	the number of ounces in a can of fruit juice	46 oz.	25. Ⓐ Ⓑ Ⓒ Ⓓ
26.	$\lvert 5-3 \rvert$	$\lvert (-5)-3 \rvert$	26. Ⓐ Ⓑ Ⓒ Ⓓ
27.	the fifth term of the sequence 2, 6, 18, 54, . . .	the fourth term of the sequence 21, 42, 84, . . .	27. Ⓐ Ⓑ Ⓒ Ⓓ
28.	the fraction obtained if both the numerator and the denominator of $\tfrac{3}{4}$ are increased by 1	0.8	28. Ⓐ Ⓑ Ⓒ Ⓓ
29.	the reciprocal of $\tfrac{3}{2}$	0.6	29. Ⓐ Ⓑ Ⓒ Ⓓ
30.	the least common multiple of 4 and 6	24	30. Ⓐ Ⓑ Ⓒ Ⓓ

ANSWERS AND EXPLANATIONS
to practice Part I questions on arithmetic.

1.   C. $8 \div 4 = 2$; $8 \times \frac{1}{4} = 2$.
2.   B. $\frac{1}{6} = 0.1666 \ldots = 0.16\frac{2}{3}$.
3.   A. $6^2 = 36 > 35$.
4.   C. $\frac{1}{0.004} = \frac{1000}{4} = 250$.
5.   B. $3 + 5 \cdot 2 = 3 + 10 = 13$; $(3 + 5) \cdot 2 = 8 \cdot 2 = 16$.
6.   A. $\frac{1}{2} + \frac{1}{3} + \frac{1}{6} = \frac{3}{6} + \frac{2}{6} + \frac{1}{6} = \frac{6}{6} = 1$.
7.   B. $5 - 0.31 = 4.69$.
8.   D. There are an infinite number of numbers between 0.3 and 0.333 . . .; some are less than 0.32, some are greater, and exactly one equals 0.32.
9.   B. $550 \div 25 = 22$.
10.   A. 62,364 rounded off to the nearest hundred equals 62,400, since the digit in the tens place is 5 or more.
11.   A. $\frac{100.52}{100} = 1.0052$. To divide by 100 we simply move the decimal point two places to the left.
12.   D. The rate of interest is not given.
13.   C. $|2 - 4| = |-2| = 2$; $|4 - 2| = |2| = 2$.
14.   A. The average or arithmetic mean of a set of four numbers is their sum divided by 4. Since 29 and 37 are in both sets, we need only *compare* the other numbers. Since 20 and 35 (in the A column) are greater respectively than 19 and 34 (in the B column), the average in Column A is greater than the average in Column B.
15.   B. $2900 - 1900.1 = 999.9$. Since $(2900 - 1900.1) < (2900 - 1900) = 1000$, the correct answer can be selected quickly.
16.   A. $\frac{7}{25} = \frac{28}{100} = 0.28$.
17.   A. 4% of $4805 = 0.04 \times 4805 = 192.20$. But note that $0.04 \times 4800 = 192$, which is greater than 190.
18.   C. Cost on time $= \$25 + 12(\$30) = \$385$.
19.   B. The interest equals $\$960 \times \frac{11}{200} \times \frac{1}{4} = \$13.20$. The amount equals $\$960 + \$13.20 = \$973.20$.
20.   A. $15 \times \$110 = \$1650$.
21.   C. The sale price of the coat is $45. $45 = \frac{9}{10}$ of 50.
22.   A. $\frac{16}{3} \times 36 = 16 \times 12 = 192$.
23.   B. The additive inverse of 2 is -2; the multiplicative inverse of 2 is $\frac{1}{2}$; $\frac{1}{2} > -2$.
24.   C. Since 300×10 seconds $= 3000$ seconds, the number of minutes required is $\frac{3000}{60}$ or 50; or, since one mile in 10 seconds means 6 miles a minute, we can divide 300 by 6, again getting 50 minutes.
25.   D. Information is lacking on the size or liquid measure of the can.
26.   B. $|5 - 3| = 2$; $|(-5) - 3| = |-8| = 8$.
27.   B. The fifth term of the sequence 2, 6, 18, 54, . . . is 162 (each term is 3 times the preceding one). The fourth term of 21, 42, 84, . . . is 168 (the ratio here is 2).
28.   C. $\frac{3 + 1}{4 + 1} = \frac{4}{5} = 0.8$.
29.   A. The reciprocal of $\frac{3}{2}$ is $\frac{2}{3}$ or $0.66 \cdots$, which is greater than 0.6.
30.   B. The smallest number having both 4 and 6 as factors is 12.

A2. Algebra

The subtopics are signed numbers; algebraic expressions, laws and operations; polynomials; equations; inequalities; special products; factoring; algebraic fractions; and word problems.

Be sure you are familiar with the test directions given on page 333.

Here are a few introductory examples, with answers and explanations.

EXAMPLES	COLUMN A	COLUMN B	ANSWERS
1.	the solution of the equation $x - 1 = 0$	2	1. Ⓐ ■ Ⓒ Ⓓ

(The solution of the equation is $x = 1$.)

$$y \geq 5$$

| 2. | y | 5 | 2. Ⓐ Ⓑ Ⓒ ■ |

(Since the solution set of the inequality $y \geq 5$ is the set of real numbers 5 or larger, the relationship cannot be determined.)

$$x = 2, y = 3, z = 1$$

| 3. | $x - y + z$ | $(x - y + z)^2$ | 3. Ⓐ Ⓑ ■ Ⓓ |

$(x - y + z = 0; 0^2 = 0 \cdot 0 = 0.)$

| 4. | Twice a number diminished by 7 equals -1. the number | -3 | 4. ■ Ⓑ Ⓒ Ⓓ |

(The equation, if x is the number, is $2x - 7 = -1$, yielding $x = 3$; $3 > -3$.)

PRACTICE QUESTIONS ON ELEMENTARY ALGEBRA

Follow the directions given on page 333. First, try to answer the questions. Then check with the answers, which follow, studying the explanations carefully.

QUESTIONS	COLUMN A	COLUMN B	
	$x = 3$ and $y = -4$		
1.	$x - y$	7	1. Ⓐ Ⓑ Ⓒ Ⓓ
2.	the root of the equation $3x - 1 = 4$	$1\frac{1}{3}$	2. Ⓐ Ⓑ Ⓒ Ⓓ
3.	$x + y$	$x - y$	3. Ⓐ Ⓑ Ⓒ Ⓓ
4.	the number of solutions of the equation $x^2 = 4$	1	4. Ⓐ Ⓑ Ⓒ Ⓓ
	$n > d$		
5.	the number of cents in n nickels	the number of cents in d dimes	5. Ⓐ Ⓑ Ⓒ Ⓓ
6.	the coefficient of xy in the product $(2x + y)(3x - 2y)$	1	6. Ⓐ Ⓑ Ⓒ Ⓓ

	Column A	Column B	
	$y \neq 0$		
7.	$3(x + y^2)$	$3x + y^2$	7. Ⓐ Ⓑ Ⓒ Ⓓ
	$y = 3$		
8.	$y^2 + 7y + 12$	$(y + 3)(y + 4)$	8. Ⓐ Ⓑ Ⓒ Ⓓ
	$x^2 - x - 2 = 0$		
9.	the smaller root of the equation	the negative of the larger root of the equation	9. Ⓐ Ⓑ Ⓒ Ⓓ
	$z = -1$		
10.	$(z - 2)(z + 2)$	$z^2 - 4z$	10. Ⓐ Ⓑ Ⓒ Ⓓ

On a map, 1″ represents 80 miles. Two cities are 2½″ apart on the map.

	Column A	Column B	
11.	the actual distance, in miles, between the two cities	220	11. Ⓐ Ⓑ Ⓒ Ⓓ
	$x < 1$		
12.	x^2	1	12. Ⓐ Ⓑ Ⓒ Ⓓ
13.	the exponent of x in the quotient x^2/x^3	1	13. Ⓐ Ⓑ Ⓒ Ⓓ
14.	$(1 - \sqrt{2})(1 + \sqrt{2})$	1	14. Ⓐ Ⓑ Ⓒ Ⓓ
	$y - z = 2$ $2y + z = 7$		
15.	z	1	15. Ⓐ Ⓑ Ⓒ Ⓓ
16.	the product of the roots of the equation $x^2 + x + 1 = 0$	-1	16. Ⓐ Ⓑ Ⓒ Ⓓ
	$x \neq 2$		
17.	$\dfrac{x^2 - 4}{x - 2}$	$x + 3$	17. Ⓐ Ⓑ Ⓒ Ⓓ
18.	$|x - 1|$	$x - 1$	18. Ⓐ Ⓑ Ⓒ Ⓓ
	$\dfrac{a}{b} = \dfrac{b}{c}$ $bc \neq 0$		
19.	b^2	ac	19. Ⓐ Ⓑ Ⓒ Ⓓ
20.	the number of real roots of the equation $x^3 - 4x = 0$	2	20. Ⓐ Ⓑ Ⓒ Ⓓ
	$u : v = 2 : 3$ and $u : u + v = 2 : z$		
21.	z	6	21. Ⓐ Ⓑ Ⓒ Ⓓ
22.	the slope of the line $y = 2x - 1$	the slope of the line $2y = x - 1$	22. Ⓐ Ⓑ Ⓒ Ⓓ
	$a = 2, \ b = -1$		
23.	$2a + 3b$	$-a - 3b$	23. Ⓐ Ⓑ Ⓒ Ⓓ

QUESTIONS	COLUMN A	COLUMN B	
	$x = -1$		
24.	the value of $(4x)^3$	the value of $\left(\dfrac{4}{x}\right)^3$	24. Ⓐ Ⓑ Ⓒ Ⓓ
25.	the reciprocal of $(\frac{1}{4} + \frac{1}{5})$	2.2	25. Ⓐ Ⓑ Ⓒ Ⓓ
26.	the root of the equation $2x - 3 = 3 - x$	3	26. Ⓐ Ⓑ Ⓒ Ⓓ

Robert walks a distance of 6 miles from A to B in two hours, but takes 3 hours to return.

27.	Robert's average rate, in miles per hour, for the round trip	2.5	27. Ⓐ Ⓑ Ⓒ Ⓓ
	$y > x + 1$		
28.	x	y	28. Ⓐ Ⓑ Ⓒ Ⓓ
	$\dfrac{1}{x} = \dfrac{y}{1}$		
29.	x	y	29. Ⓐ Ⓑ Ⓒ Ⓓ

Three numbers whose sum is 310 are in the ratio $2 : 3 : 5$.

30.	the smallest of the three numbers	62	30. Ⓐ Ⓑ Ⓒ Ⓓ

ANSWERS AND EXPLANATIONS

to practice Part I questions on algebra.

1. C. $3 - (-4) = 7$.
2. A. If $3x - 1 = 4$, $3x = 5$ and $x = 1\frac{2}{3}$.
3. D. The relationship cannot be determined unless values for x and y are given. Note that

$$x + y > x + y \quad \text{if } y > 0$$
$$x + y = x - y \quad \text{if } y = 0$$
$$x + y < x - y \quad \text{if } y < 0.$$

Don't forget zero and negative numbers in a question involving unknowns.
4. A. If $x^2 = 4$, then $x^2 - 4 = 0$ and $(x - 2)(x + 2) = 0$. There are *two* solutions, $x = -2$ and $x = 2$.
5. D. If $n < 2d$, $5n < 10d$; if $n = 2d$, $5n = 10d$; if $n > 2d$, $5n > 10d$.
6. B. $(2x + y)(3x - 2y) = 6x^2 + (3 - 4)xy - 2y^2 = 6x^2 - xy - 2y^2$. The coefficient of xy is -1.
7. A. If $y \neq 0$, $3y^2 > y^2 > 0$. Note that $3(x + y^2) = 3x + 3y^2$.
8. C. $y^2 + 7y + 12 = (y + 3)(y + 4)$ for *all* y.
9. A. $x^2 - x - 2 = 0$ yields $(x - 2)(x + 1) = 0$ with roots $x = 2$, $x = -1$. The smaller root is -1; the negative of the larger root is -2. And $-1 > -2$.
10. B. $(z - 2)(z + 2) = z^2 - 4$. When $z = -1$, this equals -3, while $z^2 - 4z = (-1)^2 - 4(-1) = 1 + 4 = 5$.
11. B. If $x =$ the actual distance, in miles, then

$$\frac{x}{80} = \frac{2\frac{1}{2}}{1} \quad \text{or} \quad x = 80 \times \frac{5}{2} = 200.$$

12. D. If $0 < x < 1$, then $x^2 < 1$, but if $x < -1$, then $-x > 1$ and $x^2 > 1$.
13. B. $x^2 \div x^3 = x^{2-3} = x^{-1}$.

14. B. $(1 - \sqrt{2})(1 + \sqrt{2}) = 1 \cdot 1 - (\sqrt{2})(\sqrt{2}) = 1 - 2 = -1.$

15. C. Add the equations. Then $3y = 9$ and $y = 3$. Substituting in either equation yields $z = 1$.

16. A. For the quadratic equation $ax^2 + bx + c = 0$, the product of the roots is c/a. For the given equation, this is $(+1)/1$ or 1.

17. B. If $x = 2$, $\dfrac{x^2 - 4}{x - 2} = x + 2$. Regardless of the value of x, $x + 3 > x + 2$.

18. D. $|x - 1| = x - 1$ if $x \geqq 1$
   $\qquad\qquad = 1 - x$ if $x < 1$.
   Information about the value of x is needed.

19. C. The product of the means in a proportion, equals the product of the extremes. Multiply both sides of the given equation by bc.

20. A. If $x^3 - 4x = 0$, then $x(x - 2)(x + 2) = 0$ and the roots are 0, 2, and -2.

21. B. $\dfrac{u}{v} = \dfrac{2}{3}$ implies that $v = \tfrac{3}{2}u$. So

$$\frac{u}{u + v} = \frac{u}{u + \frac{3}{2}u} = \frac{u}{\frac{5}{2}u} = \frac{1}{\frac{5}{2}} = \frac{2}{5} = \frac{2}{z}. \text{ So } z = 5.$$

22. A. If the equation of a line is written in the form $y = mx + b$, then its slope is m. So $y = 2x - 1$ has slope 2. Since $2y = x - 2$ can be written $y = \frac{1}{2}x - 1$, its slope is $\frac{1}{2}$.

23. C. $2a + 3b = 2(2) + 3(-1) = 4 - 3 = 1$;
   $-a - 3b = -2 - 3(-1) = -2 + 3 = 1$.

24. C. $(4x)^3 = 4x \cdot 4x \cdot 4x$; here it's $(-4)(-4)(-4) = -64$.

$$\left\{\frac{4}{x}\right\}^3 \text{ here is } \left\{\frac{4}{-1}\right\}^3 = -64.$$

25. A. $\frac{1}{4} + \frac{1}{5} = \frac{5}{20} + \frac{4}{20} = \frac{9}{20}$; the reciprocal is $\frac{20}{9} = 2.22\ldots$ or $2\frac{2}{9}$; $2.2 = 2\frac{2}{10}$.

26. B. $2x - 3 = 3 - x \rightarrow 3x = 6 \rightarrow x = 2.$

27. B. His average rate is $\dfrac{6 + 6}{2 + 3} = \frac{12}{5} = 2\frac{2}{5}$, or 2.4 mph.

28. B. Visualize points x and y on the number line such that $y > x + 1$. The point y is to the right of $x + 1$ and therefore to the right of x.

29. D. It follows from the equation that $xy = 1$, but the relative sizes of x and y cannot be determined.

30. C. Let x be the common ratio. Then $2x + 3x + 5x = 310$ and $x = 31$. The smallest number is $2(31)$ or 62.

A3. Geometry

The subtopics are angles and lines; triangles; polygons and circles; perimeter, area and volume; analytic geometry including the Cartesian plane, distance between points, midpoints, equations, and graphs of lines; and properties of the 30°-60°-90° triangle.

Be sure you are familiar with the test directions given on page 333.

Here are a few introductory examples, with answers and explanations.

EXAMPLES	COLUMN A	COLUMN B	ANSWERS

The vertex angle of an isosceles triangle measures 80°.

1. 　　the number of degrees in each　　50　　　　　　**1.** Ⓐ Ⓑ ■ Ⓓ
　　　base angle of the triangle

(The sum of the angles of the triangle is 180°.)

EXAMPLES	COLUMN A	COLUMN B	ANSWERS
2.	the number of degrees in one angle of a hexagon	the number of degrees in a base angle of an isosceles triangle	2. Ⓐ Ⓑ Ⓒ ■

(Different isosceles triangles have base angles of different sizes.)

| 3. | number of square tiles, one foot on a side, needed to cover a floor 12 feet by 8½ feet | 100 | 3. ■ Ⓑ Ⓒ Ⓓ |

(The number of square feet in the floor is $12 \times 8\frac{1}{2} = (12 \times 8) + (12 \times \frac{1}{2}) = 96 + 6 = 102$. Since each tile has area one square foot, 102 tiles are needed.)

| 4. | the hypotenuse, in feet, of a right triangle whose legs are 3.09 feet and 4.02 feet | 5 | 4. ■ Ⓑ Ⓒ Ⓓ |

(By the Pythagorean theorem, the length of the hypotenuse is $\sqrt{(3.09)^2 + (4.02)^2}$ feet; but no computation is necessary if you recall the 3-4-5 right triangle. The hypotenuse of the given triangle must exceed 5.)

PRACTICE QUESTIONS ON GEOMETRY

Follow the directions given on page 333. First, try to answer the questions. Then check with the answers, which follow, studying the explanations carefully.

QUESTIONS	COLUMN A	COLUMN B	
1.	the number of degrees in the largest angle of an obtuse triangle	90	1. Ⓐ Ⓑ Ⓒ Ⓓ
2.	the supplement of 55°40′18″	125°	2. Ⓐ Ⓑ Ⓒ Ⓓ

Two angles are complementary and one is 11° larger than twice the other.

| 3. | number of degrees in the smaller of the two angles | 26 | 3. Ⓐ Ⓑ Ⓒ Ⓓ |

Note: Figure is not drawn to scale.

| 4. | x | 65 | 4. Ⓐ Ⓑ Ⓒ Ⓓ |

5.   number of inches in the perimeter of the above triangle   13   **5.** Ⓐ Ⓑ Ⓒ Ⓓ

This figure is for questions 6-10.

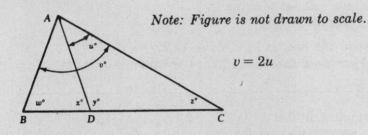

Note: Figure is not drawn to scale.

$v = 2u$

#	Column A	Column B	
6.	x	$u + z$	**6.** Ⓐ Ⓑ Ⓒ Ⓓ
7.	$\frac{1}{2}v$	x	**7.** Ⓐ Ⓑ Ⓒ Ⓓ
8.	y	$u + w$	**8.** Ⓐ Ⓑ Ⓒ Ⓓ
9.	x	y	**9.** Ⓐ Ⓑ Ⓒ Ⓓ
10.	BD	DC	**10.** Ⓐ Ⓑ Ⓒ Ⓓ

Two angles of a triangle measure 63° and 81°.

11.   number of degrees in third angle   46   **11.** Ⓐ Ⓑ Ⓒ Ⓓ

$\angle CBD = 90°$

$x° = 10°29'$

12. y $79\frac{1}{2}$ **12.** Ⓐ Ⓑ Ⓒ Ⓓ

This figure is for questions 13 and 14.

$AB\|CD$

13.   length, in inches, of AC 8   **13.** Ⓐ Ⓑ Ⓒ Ⓓ

14. AC BD **14.** Ⓐ Ⓑ Ⓒ Ⓓ

15.   number of degrees in the sum of two angles of an acute triangle   90   **15.** Ⓐ Ⓑ Ⓒ Ⓓ

QUESTIONS	COLUMN A	COLUMN B	
16.	circumference, in inches, of a circle whose diameter is 7.1″ (use $\pi = 3.1$)	22	16. Ⓐ Ⓑ Ⓒ Ⓓ
17.	the area, in square inches, of a rectangle 6 inches by 3 feet	218	17. Ⓐ Ⓑ Ⓒ Ⓓ

18.	the area, in square inches, of the shaded ring	three times the area, in square inches, of the smaller circle	18. Ⓐ Ⓑ Ⓒ Ⓓ
19.	the perimeter of a square whose edge is 1 unit	the circumference of a circle whose diameter is 1 unit	19. Ⓐ Ⓑ Ⓒ Ⓓ

The sum of the complement and supplement of an angle equals 184°.

20.	the angle	its complement	20. Ⓐ Ⓑ Ⓒ Ⓓ

The diameter of a wheel measures 35″.

21.	number of complete turns of the wheel if it travels 550 feet (use $\pi = {}^{22}/_{7}$)	55	21. Ⓐ Ⓑ Ⓒ Ⓓ
22.	volume of a sphere of radius 3	volume of a cylinder of radius 3 and height 4	22. Ⓐ Ⓑ Ⓒ Ⓓ

Bathroom tiles, one half inch on a side, are available in sheets of 10 by 12 tiles.

23.	number of sheets needed to cover a wall $5' \times 8'$	200	23. Ⓐ Ⓑ Ⓒ Ⓓ

This figure is for questions 24 and 25.

This square has quarter-circles of radius 2″ at each vertex. The shaded part has area (in square inches) $16 - k\pi$

24.	k	4	24. Ⓐ Ⓑ Ⓒ Ⓓ
25.	area of the shaded portion	area of one quarter-circle	25. Ⓐ Ⓑ Ⓒ Ⓓ

A cone and a cylinder of equal volumes have equal heights.

26.	the radius of the cylinder	the radius of the cone	26. Ⓐ Ⓑ Ⓒ Ⓓ

measure of ∠A = measure of ∠A'

measure of ∠B = measure of ∠B'

27.   A'C'   6   27. Ⓐ Ⓑ Ⓒ Ⓓ

This figure is for questions 28 and 29.

$l \| m$

$m \perp n$

$b = 50$

28. a 125   28. Ⓐ Ⓑ Ⓒ Ⓓ

29. c 40   29. Ⓐ Ⓑ Ⓒ Ⓓ

$AB = AC$

30.   measure of ∠A   measure of supple-   30. Ⓐ Ⓑ Ⓒ Ⓓ

                                            ment of 2∠B

ANSWERS AND EXPLANATIONS

to practice Part I questions on geometry.

1.   A. An obtuse triangle has one obtuse angle—an angle larger than 90°.

2.   B. $180° - 55°40'18'' = 179°59'60'' - 55°40'18'' = 124°19'42''$. But this computation is unnecessary, since $180 - 55 = 125 > 180 - 55^+$.

3.   A. If x is the number of degrees in the smaller angle, then $x + 2x + 11 = 90$ and $x = 26\frac{1}{3}$.

4.   D. We cannot assume the triangle is isosceles.

5.   A. The perimeter in inches $= 3\frac{1}{2} + 4\frac{1}{5} + 5\frac{1}{3} = 12\frac{31}{30} = 13\frac{1}{30}$.

6.   C. ∠ADB, the exterior angle of △ADC, equals the sum of the two opposite interior angles. So $x = u + z$.

7.   B. From question 6, we know that $x > u$. Since $u = \frac{1}{2}v$, $x > \frac{1}{2}v$.

8.   C. $y = \frac{1}{2}v + w$ (see answer to 6).

9.   D. It appears from the figure that $x < y$, but figures can be drawn with $v = 2u$ where $x > y$ or $x = y$.

10.   D. Draw figures in which BD is less than, equal to, or greater than DC.

11.   B. $180 - (63 + 81) = 36$.

12.   A. Since AE is a straight line, $\angle DBE = 90° - 10°29' = 79°31' > 79\frac{1}{2}°$.

13.   C.

Draw $AH \perp CD$. In a $30°-60°-90°$ triangle the hypotenuse is twice the leg opposite the $30°$ angle. So $AC = 8''$.

14.   B. Draw $BP \perp CD$, and $BS = AC$. Now $\angle BSP = 30°$ and $BD > BS$. So $BD > AC$.

15.   A. If the sum of any two angles of the triangle *were* less than or equal to $90°$, the third angle would have to measure at least $90°$. Therefore the sum must exceed $90°$.

16.   A. The circumference, C, of a circle of diameter d is πd. $7.1 \times 3.1 = 22.01$.

17.   B. The area, in square inches, equals $6 \times 36 = 216$.

18.   C. The shaded ring has area $2^2\pi - 1^2\pi$ or 3π square inches. Three times the area of the smaller circle is $3 \times \pi$, or 3π square inches.

19.   A. The perimeter of the square is $4 \cdot 1$ or 4 units. The circle has circumference $2\pi \cdot \frac{1}{2}$ or π units; $\pi \approx 3.1$.

20.   B. If x denotes the number of degrees in the angle, then $90 - x + 180 - x = 184$ and $x = 43$. Its complement $= 47°$.

21.   A. Divide the distance travelled, in inches, by the circumference of the wheel in inches:
$$\frac{550 \times 12}{35 \times ^{22}\!/_7} = 60.$$
The wheel makes 60 complete turns.

22.   C. Volume of a sphere of radius r is $\frac{4}{3}\pi r^3$; volume of a cylinder of radius r and height h is $\pi r^2 h$.
$$V_{\text{sphere}} = \frac{4}{3}\pi \cdot 3^3 = 36\pi;$$
$$V_{\text{cylinder}} = \pi \cdot 3^2 \cdot 4 = 36\pi.$$

23.   B. We divide the area of the wall, in square inches, by the area of a sheet of tiles, in inches:
$$\frac{5 \times 12 \times 8 \times 12}{10 \times \frac{1}{2} \times 12 \times \frac{1}{2}} = 192 \text{ sheets.}$$

24.   C. The area of one quarter-circle is $\frac{1}{4} \cdot \pi \cdot 2^2 = \pi$. The shaded part has area $4^2 - 4 \cdot \pi = 16 - 4\pi$.

25.   A. $16 - 4\pi = 16 - 4(3.1) \approx 3.6 > \pi$.

26.   B. Let the radii of the cylinder and cone be R and r respectively, and let h denote the common height. $V_{\text{cyl}} = \pi R^2 h$; $V_{\text{cone}} = \frac{1}{3}\pi r^2 h$. Since $\pi R^2 h = \frac{1}{3}\pi r^2 h$, therefore $r^2 = 3R^2$ and $r = R\sqrt{3}$. So $r > R$.

27.   C. Since the triangles are similar, $A'C':AC = A'B':AB$; so $A'C':4 = 3:2$ and $A'C' = 6$.

28.   A. Since $l \parallel m$, the corresponding angles are equal. Therefore $d = b$ and a and b are supplementary: $a = 130$.

29. C. Since $m \perp n$, $c = 90 - d = 90 - b = 90 - 50 = 40$.

30. C. $\angle B = \angle C$ and $\angle A + \angle B + \angle C = 180°$. Therefore $\angle A = 180° - 2\angle B$.

A4. Data Interpretation

This topic includes tables, charts, graphs (bar, line, circle, or pie), and pictographs.

Be sure you are familiar with the test directions given on page 333.

Here are a few introductory examples, with answers and explanations.

Examples 1-4 refer to the following table.

ENROLLMENTS IN COLLEGES IN 1970 (IN THOUSANDS) BY SEX AND RESIDENCE				
	TOTAL ENROLLMENT	2-YR COLLEGES	4-YR COLLEGES 1 and 2 yrs	3 and 4 yrs
Sex				
male	3,627	1,001	1,206	1,319
female	2,646	691	1,038	814
total (ages 16-34)	6,274	1,692	2,244	2,133
Residence				
metropolitan areas	4,401	1,220	1,507	1,525
nonmetropolitan areas	1,873	472	737	608

(Figures listed do not add up to total enrollments because some enrolled did not give information requested.)

EXAMPLES	COLUMN A	COLUMN B	ANSWERS
			1. ■ B C D

1. number of male enrollees who did not report on type of college attended — 100,000

(The total enrollment of males minus those listed for 2-year and 4-year colleges equals 101,000.)

2. A ■ C D

2. percent of total enrolled in metropolitan areas — 75%

(Since $^3/_4 \times 6274 > 4500 > 4401$, choice B is correct.)

3. A B C ■

3. ratio of men in college to men not in college — ratio of women in college to women not in college

(Since figures are not given for those *not* enrolled in college, the question cannot be answered.)

4. A B ■ D

4. number, to the nearest million, of those aged 16 to 34 from metropolitan areas — 4,000,000

(The numbers given are in thousands; the total enrollment from metropolitan areas is 4,401,000, which rounds to 4,000,000.)

PRACTICE QUESTIONS ON DATA INTERPRETATION

We begin with some specific tips on answering questions involving data interpretation.

(1) Decide what sort of information is given by a graph, chart, or table before trying to answer a question about it.

(2) Note the scale on a graph, the key on a chart, or the units (thousands, millions, or the like) in a table.

(3) Use a straightedge (your pencil will do) to follow across a row of figures in a table.

(4) In using a table or chart, be certain that you correctly locate the entry referred to (that is, that you are in the right row *and* in the right column).

(5) To compare distances on a graph, or to estimate a particular distance, use your pencil or other straightedge.

(6) To find a percent or to calculate a ratio, it is often convenient to round off numbers that are given. However, be careful about the units and round off similarly in both numerator and denominator to obtain an equivalent answer.

Follow the directions given on page 333. After you answer the questions, check your answers against those which follow immediately. The explanations that accompany the answers will show how the above tips are used.

QUESTIONS	COLUMN A	COLUMN B	

Questions 1-4 refer to the table on enrollments in colleges in 1970, given on page 272.

1.	number, to the nearest million, of women enrolled in 4-yr colleges	2,000,000	1. Ⓐ Ⓑ Ⓒ Ⓓ
2.	percent of total enrolled in college from nonmetropolitan areas	40	2. Ⓐ Ⓑ Ⓒ Ⓓ
3.	ratio of women enrolled in college to men enrolled	1 : 2	3. Ⓐ Ⓑ Ⓒ Ⓓ
4.	percent of males enrolled who did not report on whether they attended 2-yr. or 4-yr. college	3	4. Ⓐ Ⓑ Ⓒ Ⓓ

Questions 5-7 refer to the pictograph of population given below; each house represents 10,000 people.

City A

City B

City C

Source: Developing Skills, p. 212*.

	Column A	Column B	
5.	difference in population, in thousands, between largest and smallest cities	55	**5.** Ⓐ Ⓑ Ⓒ Ⓓ
6.	ratio of population of city C to that of city B	ratio of population of city B to that of city A	**6.** Ⓐ Ⓑ Ⓒ Ⓓ
7.	total population, in thousands, of the five cities	245	**7.** Ⓐ Ⓑ Ⓒ Ⓓ

Questions 8-10 refer to the bar graph given below.*

HOW THE COLLINS FAMILY BUDGETED EACH DOLLAR OF INCOME

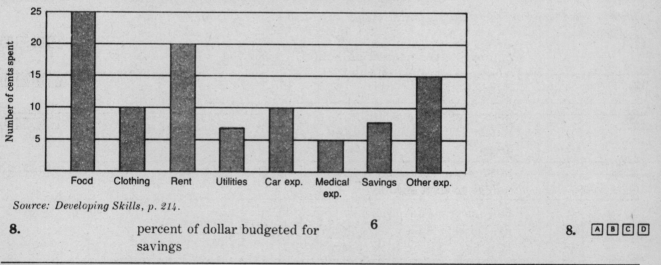

Source: Developing Skills, p. 214.

	Column A	Column B	
8.	percent of dollar budgeted for savings	6	**8.** Ⓐ Ⓑ Ⓒ Ⓓ

---

* The source of a chart, graph, or table presented as the basis of a problem is indicated briefly under the figure. The full references are as follows:

Data: Pocket Data Book, USA 1971 (Washington, D.C.: U.S. Department of Commerce, Bureau of the Census, 1971).

Developing Skills: Shirley O. Hockett, *Barron's Developing Skills for the High School Equivalency Examination in Mathematics.* Woodbury, N.Y.: Barron's Educational Series, Inc., 1978

Fact: Life Insurance Fact Book 1973 (New York: Institute of Life Insurance, 1973).

Social Security Bulletin. issued monthly by the Social Security Administration, Washington, D.C.

The Collins's income, in 1971, was $14,500.

9.	amount allowed for food, rent, and medical expenses in 1971	$7500	9.	Ⓐ Ⓑ Ⓒ Ⓓ
10.	amount budgeted in 1971 for electricity and gas	$1000	10.	Ⓐ Ⓑ Ⓒ Ⓓ

Questions 11-13 refer to the following table.

EMPLOYMENT AND UNEMPLOYMENT IN THE UNITED STATES (IN THOUSANDS) CIVILIAN LABOR FORCE, AGED 16 OR OVER

	CIVILIAN LABOR FORCE	EMPLOYED	UNEMPLOYED
1968	78,737	75,920	2,817
1969	80,733	77,902	2,831
1970	82,715	78,627	4,088
1971	84,113	79,120	4,993
(1972	85,615	80,524	5,090)
first-half			
average)			

Source: U.S. Bureau of Labor Statistics.

11.	percent unemployed for the year 1972	percent unemployed for 1971	11.	Ⓐ Ⓑ Ⓒ Ⓓ
12.	ratio of employed to unemployed in 1971	15 : 1	12.	Ⓐ Ⓑ Ⓒ Ⓓ
13.	percent of civilian labor force unemployed based on the first-half average 1972	6½	13.	Ⓐ Ⓑ Ⓒ Ⓓ

Questions 14-16 refer to the table below.

AVERAGE PRICES RECEIVED BY U.S. FARMERS (DOLLARS PER 100 LBS.)

	hogs	beef cattle	lambs
1968	18.50	23.40	24.40
1969	22.20	26.20	27.20
1970	22.70	27.10	26.40
1971	17.50	29.00	25.90

Source: U.S. Department of Agriculture.

14.	average price for beef cattle in 1970	average price for lambs in 1969	14.	Ⓐ Ⓑ Ⓒ Ⓓ

15. percent of increase in price of hogs from 1968 to 1970 | percent of increase in price of beef cattle from 1968 to 1970 | **15.** Ⓐ Ⓑ Ⓒ Ⓓ

16. percentage decrease in price of hogs from 1970 to 1971 | 20 | **16.** Ⓐ Ⓑ Ⓒ Ⓓ

Questions 17-19 refer to the line graph below.

MEDICAL EXPENSES OF SUTTON FAMILY FROM 1960-1971

Source: Developing Skills, p. 215.

17. the Sutton family's medical expenses in 1963 | the Sutton family's medical expenses in 1968 | **17.** Ⓐ Ⓑ Ⓒ Ⓓ

18. percent of increase in medical expenses from 1961 to 1971 | 300 | **18.** Ⓐ Ⓑ Ⓒ Ⓓ

19. difference in medical expenses between 1966 and 1967 | difference in medical expenses between 1970 and 1971 | **19.** Ⓐ Ⓑ Ⓒ Ⓓ

Use these graphs for questions 20-22.

Percentage distribution of expenditures for personal health care, by source of funds and age group, fiscal years 1966 and 1972

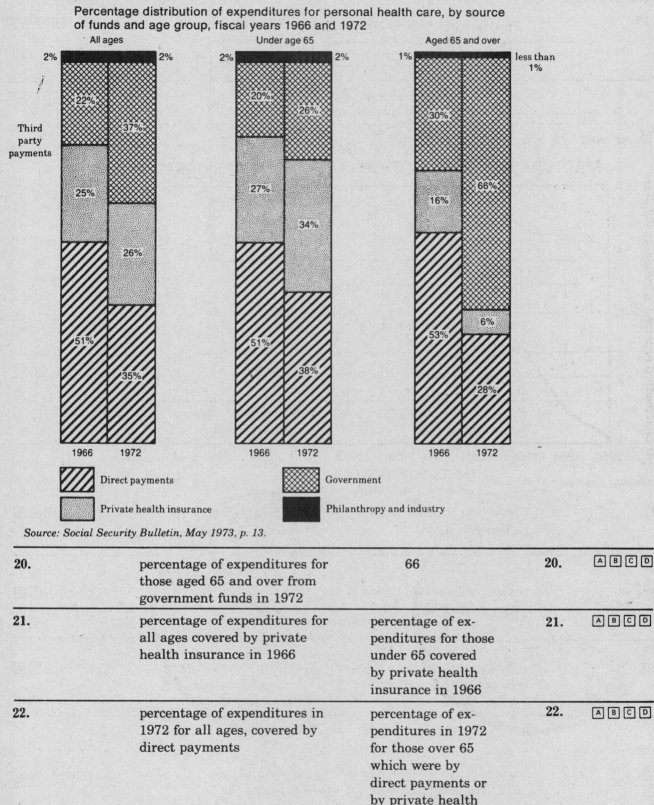

Source: *Social Security Bulletin, May 1973, p. 13.*

20.	percentage of expenditures for those aged 65 and over from government funds in 1972	66	**20.** ⒶⒷⒸⒹ
21.	percentage of expenditures for all ages covered by private health insurance in 1966	percentage of expenditures for those under 65 covered by private health insurance in 1966	**21.** ⒶⒷⒸⒹ
22.	percentage of expenditures in 1972 for all ages, covered by direct payments	percentage of expenditures in 1972 for those over 65 which were by direct payments or by private health insurance	**22.** ⒶⒷⒸⒹ

Questions 23-25 refer to the figure below.

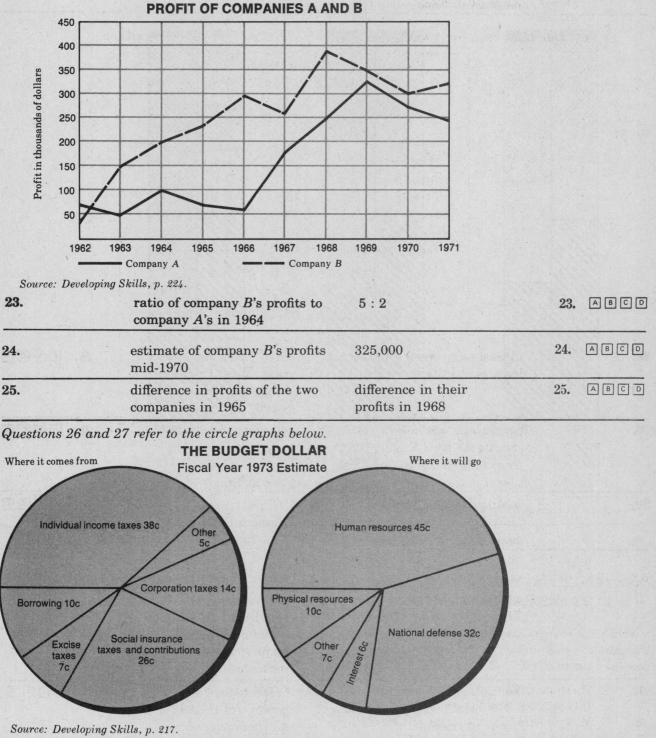

PROFIT OF COMPANIES A AND B

Company A ———   Company B — — —

Source: Developing Skills, p. 224.

	COLUMN A	COLUMN B	
23.	ratio of company *B*'s profits to company *A*'s in 1964	5 : 2	23. Ⓐ Ⓑ Ⓒ Ⓓ
24.	estimate of company *B*'s profits mid-1970	325,000	24. Ⓐ Ⓑ Ⓒ Ⓓ
25.	difference in profits of the two companies in 1965	difference in their profits in 1968	25. Ⓐ Ⓑ Ⓒ Ⓓ

Questions 26 and 27 refer to the circle graphs below.

THE BUDGET DOLLAR
Fiscal Year 1973 Estimate

Where it comes from

Individual income taxes 38c
Other 5c
Corporation taxes 14c
Borrowing 10c
Excise taxes 7c
Social insurance taxes and contributions 26c

Where it will go

Human resources 45c
Physical resources 10c
Other 7c
Interest 6c
National defense 32c

Source: Developing Skills, p. 217.

	COLUMN A	COLUMN B	
26.	percent of income expected in 1973 from individual income taxes	percent of dollar estimated for expenditures on national defense and interest	26. Ⓐ Ⓑ Ⓒ Ⓓ

Questions	COLUMN A	COLUMN B	
27.	ratio of expected expenditure for human resources to that for national defense	5 : 4	27. Ⓐ Ⓑ Ⓒ Ⓓ

Questions 28-30 refer to the following table.

PER CAPITA PERSONAL INCOME, BY REGIONS OF THE U.S.

Region	Per capita income (in dollars)		
	1969	1970	1971
New England	4,012	4,259	4,454
Mideast	4,182	4,453	4,697
Great Lakes	3,956	4,098	4,348
Plains	3,509	3,741	3,958
Southeast	2,978	3,214	3,442
Southwest	3,257	3,514	3,688
Rocky Mountain	3,277	3,557	3,809
Far West	4,122	4,327	4,522
United States	3,708	3,933	4,156

Source: U.S. Department of Commerce.

	COLUMN A	COLUMN B	
28.	difference between greatest and least per capita income in 1971	difference between greatest and least per capita income in 1969	28. Ⓐ Ⓑ Ⓒ Ⓓ
29.	percentage increase in per capita income for New England region from 1969 to 1971	percentage increase in per capita income for the U.S. from 1969 to 1971	29. Ⓐ Ⓑ Ⓒ Ⓓ
30.	median per capita income in 1971 for the eight regions of the country	U.S. per capita income in 1971	30. Ⓐ Ⓑ Ⓒ Ⓓ

ANSWERS AND EXPLANATIONS
to practice Part I questions on data interpretation.

Note: For many of these questions, only an estimate is needed in order to compare the quantities given in Columns A and B. Valuable time can be saved by avoiding unnecessary computations. This will be demonstrated in the explanations that follow.

1. C. There are (1038 + 814) or 1852 *thousand* women; this rounds up to 2 million. It is sufficient here to note that there are *about* 1,800 thousand women.
2. B. Multiply 6274 by 0.4, or (approximately) 6000 by 0.4.   2400 > 1873.
3. A. Instead of dividing 2646 by 3627, we estimate: 2600 ÷ 3600. It is clearly greater than $\frac{1}{2}$.
4. B. In example 1, we noted that 101 thousand males did not report. 1 divided by 36 (instead of 101 divided by 3627) is less than 0.03.

5.   C. $80 - 25 = 55$.

6.   A. $6 \div 4\frac{1}{2} = 6 \times \frac{2}{9} = \frac{4}{3} = 1.3^{+}$.

      $4\frac{1}{2} \div 3\frac{1}{2} = \frac{9}{2} \times \frac{2}{7} = 1.3^{-}$.

      $1.3^{+} > 1.3^{-}$.

7.   C. There are 3 half-houses, plus, from top to bottom $(3 + 4 + 6 + 2 + 8)$ whole houses for a total of $24\frac{1}{2}$ houses or 245,000 people.

8.   A. The top of the bar above "Savings" is midway between the 5¢ and 10¢ horizontal line; savings, therefore, were allowed about $7\frac{1}{2}\%$ of the family's dollar.

9.   B. Total allowed is $(25 + 20 + 5)$ cents, or 50¢. Half of 14,500 is 7,250.

10.   D. Utilities may include more than electricity and gas; e.g., water or telephone.

11.   D. It cannot be assumed that the first-half average will apply for the entire year.

12.   A. $79 \div 5$ (instead of $79,120 \div 4,993$) $> 15 : 1$. (Note that we've rounded both to thousands, and that we've both decreased the numerator *and* increased the denominator; the exact ratio is therefore even greater than $79 : 5$.)

13.   B. Is $0.06\frac{1}{2} \times 80,524$ greater than, less than, or equal to 5090? We approximate: $6\frac{1}{2} \times 800 = 5100$.

14.   B. The average price for beef cattle in 1970 was $27.10 (per 100 lbs); the average price for lambs in 1969 was $27.20.

15.   A. $(420 \div 1850) > (370 \div 2340)$ since $(42 \div 19) > 2$ while $(37 \div 23) < 2$.

16.   A. Percentage decrease $= \dfrac{22.70 - 17.50}{22.7} > \dfrac{5}{23} > 0.2 = 20\%$.

17.   A. The point on the graph above 1963 is higher than that for 1968.

18.   B. Percentage increase $\approx \dfrac{450 - 150}{150} \approx 200\%$.

19.   A. The difference in medical expenses between 1966 and 1967 > 150; between 1970 and 1971, the difference < 150.

20.   C. Use the rightmost bar.

21.   B. The Column A percentage is 25; the Column B percentage is 27.

22.   A. The answer for Column A is 35%; for Column B $(28 + 6)\%$.

23.   B. The ratio in 1964 $\approx 2 : 1$.

24.   D. In a graph of this sort, the points representing profits for 2 successive years are connected by a line segment. We cannot interpolate here because we cannot assume that the profits during the year are linear.

25.   A. The solid and dotted graphs are farther apart in 1965 than they are in 1968.

26.   C. 38%.

27.   A. $45 : 32 > 45 : 36 = 5 : 4$.

28.   A. $(4697 - 3442) > (4182 - 2978)$.

29.   B. For New England, the increase equals $\dfrac{4454 - 4012}{4012} = \dfrac{442}{4012}$; for the U.S. it is $\dfrac{4156 - 3708}{3708} = \dfrac{448}{3708}$. The latter is clearly the greater.

30.   B. If an odd set of numbers is arranged in order of size, the middle number is the *median*. If there are an even number of numbers in the set, the average of the two middle numbers is the median. Here the median is $(4348 + 3958) \div 2$, or 4153.

Quantitative Comparison Questions: Tips

Here are tips on solving questions involving quantitative comparison:
(1) Be certain you understand the directions given on page 333.
    space A   if the quantity in Column A is greater;
    space B   if the quantity in Column B is greater;

space C if the two quantities are equal;

space D if the relationship cannot be determined from the information given.

(2) Study any illustrative example given and note how the answer is obtained by following the directions.

(3) For each quantitative-comparison question given, see if any information is furnished. If it is, it is centered above the two columns. This information will help you choose the correct answer.

(4) Avoid excessive computation. Estimate where possible.

(5) Don't use pencil and paper unless you must.

(6) When comparing expressions involving only numerals (no variables), choice D is *never* correct. You can always determine the relation between the quantities in Columns A and B.

(7) Remember that you're *comparing* two items. Since it matters only which is the larger, or if they're equal, don't evaluate unless you must. The questions involving quantitative comparison are not intended to require tedious arithmetic calculations.

(8) A symbol that appears in both columns represents the same thing in Column A as it does in Column B.

(9) When quantities involve variables $(x, y, p, q, \ldots)$, don't forget fractions, negative numbers, and zero. Visualizing the number line may help.

(10) When a figure is furnished, make sure you understand what information is given about it. If a note says that the figure is *not* drawn to scale, do not make false assumptions on the basis of the picture.

(11) Follow the tips given on page 349 on doing questions on data interpretation.

A5. Miscellaneous: Multiple-Choice Questions on Part I Topics

In this subsection we include practice questions on topics that have already been covered in Part A (A1 through A4), as well as on other mathematical topics. Since some of the questions on Part I of the CLEP mathematics examination are of the regular multiple-choice type, the questions that follow are also of this type. Even though the answer column may have five answer boxes, labeled A, B, C, D, and E, you are to choose the *one* correct answer from among A, B, C, and D. Do not make any marks whatever in column E.

Example:
0. 4 − (6 − 1) =
    (A) −9   (B) −3   (C) −1   (D) 1

Explanation
Since $4 - (6 - 1) = 4 - 5 = -1$, we fill in the box for choice C.

Answers and explanations follow this set of questions. Note especially the test directions for these questions, which are as follows:

Directions: For each of the following problems, indicate the correct answer in the appropriate space in the answer column.

Note: Figures that accompany problems are intended to provide information useful in solving the problems. They are drawn as accurately as possible *except* when it is stated in a specific problem that the figure is not drawn to scale. All figures lie in a plane unless otherwise indicated.

1. $5 - [8 - (3 - 1)] =$
    (A) 11   (B) 1   (C) -1 (D) -7

    1. Ⓐ Ⓑ Ⓒ Ⓓ

2. $(2x + 3)(x - 1) =$
    (A) $2x^2 - x - 3$ (B) $2x^2 + x + 3$
    (C) $2x^2 + 2x - 3$ (D) $2x^2 + x - 3$

    2. Ⓐ Ⓑ Ⓒ Ⓓ

3. The point with coordinates $(-3,2)$ is in quadrant
    (A) I   (B) II   (C) III   (D) IV

    3. Ⓐ Ⓑ Ⓒ Ⓓ

4. The value of y that satisfies the pair of equations
    $$\begin{cases} x + 2y = a \\ x - 2y = a \end{cases} \text{ is}$$
    (A) 0   (B) $\frac{a}{2}$ (C) $\frac{a}{4}$ (D) $-\frac{a}{4}$

    4. Ⓐ Ⓑ Ⓒ Ⓓ

5. If x is 150% of 10, then x equals
    (A) 1.5   (B) $6\frac{2}{3}$ (C) 15   (D) 150

    5. Ⓐ Ⓑ Ⓒ Ⓓ

6. The number of zeros in $(2 \times 10^3)^2 \times 5$ is
    (A) 6   (B) 7   (C) 9   (D) 10

    6. Ⓐ Ⓑ Ⓒ Ⓓ

7. It takes 3 men 8 days to build a wall. How long does it take 2 men working at the same rate to build the wall?
    (A) $5\frac{1}{3}$ days   (B) 10 days
    (C) 12 days   (D) none of these

    7. Ⓐ Ⓑ Ⓒ Ⓓ

8. If an alloy contains 60% silver by weight, how much does the silver in a 270-gram sample weigh?
    (A) 16 grams   (B) 16.2 grams   (C) 162 grams   (D) 180 grams

    8. Ⓐ Ⓑ Ⓒ Ⓓ

9. If $4x + 3y + 24 = 0$, then when $y = 0$, $x =$
    (A) -8 (B) -6 (C) 6   (D) 8

    9. Ⓐ Ⓑ Ⓒ Ⓓ

10. The area, in square feet, of a circle is π^2. The length, in feet, of its radius is
    (A) π (B) $\sqrt{\pi}$ (C) $\frac{\pi}{2}$ (D) 1

    10. Ⓐ Ⓑ Ⓒ Ⓓ

11. $3^2 + 3^0 + 3^{-1} =$
    (A) 3   (B) 9   (C) $9\frac{1}{3}$ (D) $10\frac{1}{3}$

    11. Ⓐ Ⓑ Ⓒ Ⓓ

12. If a 12-oz. bottle of beer is 3.5% alcohol, then the amount of alcohol in the bottle is about
    (A) 0.4 oz.   (B) 0.5 oz.   (C) 3 oz.   (D) 4 oz.

    12. Ⓐ Ⓑ Ⓒ Ⓓ

13. In scientific notation 0.12 parts of a substance per million is written "1.2 × 10^k." What does k equal?

13. Ⓐ Ⓑ Ⓒ Ⓓ

   (A) −7   (B) −6   (C) 6   (D) 7

14. The area of the shaded region is

14. Ⓐ Ⓑ Ⓒ Ⓓ

   (A) 37 cm²   (B) 40 cm²   (C) 42 cm²   (D) 52 cm²

15. If $x \neq 0$, then $\dfrac{2x + 4}{2x} =$

15. Ⓐ Ⓑ Ⓒ Ⓓ

   (A) 5   (B) $1 + \dfrac{1}{x}$ (C) $1 + 2x$ (D) $1 + \dfrac{2}{x}$

16. The linear relationship defined by the table is

x	−1	0	1
y	3	1	−1

16. Ⓐ Ⓑ Ⓒ Ⓓ

   (A) $y = x + 2$ (B) $y = 2x + 1$
   (C) $y = 2x + 1$ (D) $y = -2x + 1$

17. The length, to the nearest inch, of the hypotenuse of a right triangle whose legs are 8″ and 10″ is

17. Ⓐ Ⓑ Ⓒ Ⓓ

   (A) 11″   (B) 12″   (C) 13″   (D) 14″

18. The slope of the line $3y = x - 3$ is

18. Ⓐ Ⓑ Ⓒ Ⓓ

   (A) −1   (B) ⅓   (C) 1   (D) 3

19. If $0.25x + 0.41 = 0.75x - 2.59$, then $x =$

19. Ⓐ Ⓑ Ⓒ Ⓓ

   (A) 6   (B) 3   (C) 0.6   (D) −6

20. Suppose $z = \dfrac{v^3}{w}$. If v is doubled and w is multiplied by 4, then the ratio of the new value of z to the old is

20. Ⓐ Ⓑ Ⓒ Ⓓ

   (A) 1:2   (B) 1:1   (C) 2:1   (D) 4:1

The pie graph is for questions 21 and 22.

21. When the family's annual income is $22,000, the amount budgeted for mortgage and utilities is
    (A) $8800   (B) $8000   (C) $7700   (D) $880

21. Ⓐ Ⓑ Ⓒ Ⓓ

22. The ratio of the amount budgeted for food to that for savings and travel combined is
    (A) 7:2   (B) 7:3   (C) 2:1   (D) 7:4

22. Ⓐ Ⓑ Ⓒ Ⓓ

23. If $3x - 4 < x + 2$, then
    (A) $x > 3$ (B) $x < 3$ (C) $x < 1$ (D) $x < -3$

23. Ⓐ Ⓑ Ⓒ Ⓓ

24. If $(½)^x = 0.25$, then $x =$
    (A) 3   (B) 2   (C) -2 (D) -3

24. Ⓐ Ⓑ Ⓒ Ⓓ

25. If $\dfrac{1}{z} = \dfrac{1}{x} + \dfrac{1}{y}$, then when $x = 15$ and $y = 30$, $z =$
    (A) $\dfrac{1}{45}$ (B) $\dfrac{1}{10}$ (C) 10   (D) 45

25. Ⓐ Ⓑ Ⓒ Ⓓ

26. The sun is 93 million miles from earth and the speed of light is 186,000 mi./sec. How many minutes, approximately, does it take sunlight to reach the earth?
    (A) 1   (B) 8   (C) 10   (D) 12

26. Ⓐ Ⓑ Ⓒ Ⓓ

27. The correct complete factorization of the expression $2t^3 - 8t$ is
    (A) $2t(t - 2)(t + 2)$ (B) $2(t - 2)(t^2 + 2t + 4)$
    (C) $2t(t^2 + 4)$ (D) $2t(t^2 - 8)$

27. Ⓐ Ⓑ Ⓒ Ⓓ

The figure at the right is for questions 28 and 29; it is NOT drawn to scale.

28. The complement of $\angle BAC$ measures   28. Ⓐ Ⓑ Ⓒ Ⓓ
    (A) 15°   (B) 20°   (C) 25°   (D) 35°

29. The measure of $\angle DBC$ is   29. Ⓐ Ⓑ Ⓒ Ⓓ
    (A) 110°   (B) 115°   (C) 125°   (D) 135°

The graph and table below are for questions 30-32.

USE OF LIFE INSURANCE BENEFITS UNDER SUPPLEMENTARY CONTRACTS IN THE UNITED STATES

BILLIONS OF DOLLARS

PAYMENTS FROM ACCUMULATED FUNDS
BENEFITS SET ASIDE

1957   1962   1967   1972

USE OF LIFE INSURANCE BENEFITS UNDER SUPPLEMENTARY CONTRACTS IN THE UNITED STATES

(000,000 Omitted)

Year	Benefits Set Aside	Payments From Accumulated Funds
1945.........	$540	$ 295
1950.........	680	520
1955.........	780	720
1960.........	760	970
1965.........	920	1,110
1966.........	920	1,180
1967.........	940	1,190
1968.........	890	1,240
1969.........	840	1,310
1970.........	790	1,290
1971.........	870	1,220
1972.........	870	1,210

Source: Fact, p. 52.

30. The difference between payments from accumulated funds and benefits set aside was least in   30. Ⓐ Ⓑ Ⓒ Ⓓ
    (A) 1957   (B) 1958   (C) 1970   (D) 1971

31. The difference noted in question 30 was greatest in   31. Ⓐ Ⓑ Ⓒ Ⓓ
    (A) 1960   (B) 1969   (C) 1970   (D) 1971

32. The percent of increase in benefits set aside from 1969 to 1972 was approximately   32. Ⓐ Ⓑ Ⓒ Ⓓ
    (A) 0.04%   (B) 0.4%   (C) 4%   (D) 40%

33. $\left(\dfrac{5ab}{2u}\right)\left(\dfrac{6u^2}{10a^2b}\right) =$ 33. Ⓐ Ⓑ Ⓒ Ⓓ
    (A) $\dfrac{3u}{2ab}$ (B) $\dfrac{6au}{4b}$ (C) $\dfrac{3u}{2}$ (D) $\dfrac{3u}{2a}$

34. How much change should you get from a check for $25.58 if your purchases are as follows: meat for $4.67, oranges for 89¢, and eggs for 95¢?   34. Ⓐ Ⓑ Ⓒ Ⓓ
    (A) $19.07   (B) $19.17   (C) $19.87   (D) $20.07

35. The solutions of the quadratic equation $x^2 - 5x + 6 = 0$ are

(A) 1 and 6   (B) 1 and -6

(C) -1 and -6 (D) none of these

35. Ⓐ Ⓑ Ⓒ Ⓓ

The table below is for questions 36 and 37.

PERCENTAGE DISTRIBUTION OF ORDINARY
POLICYHOLDER DEATHS BY CAUSE
U.S. LIFE INSURANCE COMPANIES

Cause of Death	1945	1950	1955	1960	1965	1971	1972
Natural Causes							
Cardiovascular-renal	49.3%	57.0%	57.2%	55.7%	53.9%	51.7%	51.2%
Cancer	14.8	17.3	18.6	18.7	19.2	20.0	20.4
Pneumonia and Influenza ...	3.1	1.9	2.0	3.2	3.1	3.0	3.0
Tuberculosis (all forms)	2.8	1.3	.5	.3	.2	.1	.1
Diabetes	1.5	1.3	.9	1.0	1.1	.9	1.0
Other Diseases²	18.2	12.0	12.3	13.1	13.6	15.5	15.4
Total	89.7	90.8	91.5	92.0	91.1	91.2	91.1
External Causes							
Motor Vehicle Accidents	2.3	3.1	3.1	2.9	3.6	3.5	3.5
Other Accidents	5.9	3.6	3.2	3.1	3.2	3.0	3.1
Suicide	1.9	2.2	2.0	1.8	1.8	1.7	1.6
Homicide	.2	.3	.2	.2	.3	.6	.7
Total	10.3	9.2	8.5	8.0	8.9	8.8	8.9
Total All Causes	100.0%	100.0%	100.0%	100.0%	100.0%	100.0%	100.0%

Source: Fact, p. 104.

36. The cause of death with the largest *relative* increase from 1945 to 1972 was

(A) cardiovascular-renal   (B) cancer

(C) motor vehicle accidents   (D) homicide

36. Ⓐ Ⓑ Ⓒ Ⓓ

37. Which cause of death increased by the most percentage points from 1945 to 1972?

(A) cardiovascular-renal   (B) cancer

(C) motor vehicle accidents   (D) homicide

37. Ⓐ Ⓑ Ⓒ Ⓓ

38. Which of the following statements is incorrect?

(A) $\sqrt{9} + \sqrt{16} = 5$ (B) $\sqrt{4} \cdot \sqrt{9} = 6$

(C) $\dfrac{\sqrt{25} + \sqrt{9}}{\sqrt{4}} = 4$ (D) $\dfrac{\sqrt{9} + \sqrt{4}}{\sqrt{4}} = 1\frac{2}{3}$

38. Ⓐ Ⓑ Ⓒ Ⓓ

39. The product of the roots of the equation $x^2 + 5x - 66 = 0$ is

(A) 66   (B) 5   (C) -5 (D) -66

39. Ⓐ Ⓑ Ⓒ Ⓓ

40. If the average of the set of numbers $\{3,5,6,11,x\}$ is 6, then $x =$

(A) 5   (B) $5\frac{1}{2}$

(C) 6   (D) none of these

40. Ⓐ Ⓑ Ⓒ Ⓓ

ANSWERS AND EXPLANATIONS

to practice Part I questions on miscellaneous topics.

1.   C. $5 - [8 - (3 - 1)] = 5 - [8 - 2] = 5 - 6 = -1$.
2.   D. $(2x + 3)(x - 1) = (2x)(x) + (2x)(-1) + (3)(x) + (3)(-1) = 2x^2 + x - 3$.
3.   B. The signs of a point (x,y) determine the quadrant as follows: $(+,+)$ in quadrant I; $(-,+)$ in II; $(-,-)$ in III; $(+,-)$ in IV.
4.   A. Adding the equations yields $2x = 2a$; so $x = a$. Then, using the first equation, we get $a + 2y = a$, $y = 0$.
5.   C. Since $150\% = 1.5$, $x = (1.5)(10) = 15$.
6.   B. $(2 \times 10^3)^2 \times 5 = 2^2 \times 10^6 \times 5 = 20 \times 10^6 = 2 \times 10^7$.
7.   C. Since 3 men take 8 days, 1 man takes 24 days. So 2 men require 12 days.
8.   C. $60\% = 0.60$; $0.6 \times 270 = 162$.
9.   B. $4x + 3(0) + 24 = 0 \to 4x = -24 \to x = -6$.
10.   B. Since the area of a circle equals πr^2, we have $\pi^2 = \pi r^2$, $\pi = r^2$, and $r = \sqrt{\pi}$.
11.   D. $3^2 + 3^0 + 3^{-1} = 9 + 1 + \frac{1}{3} = 10\frac{1}{3}$.
12.   A. Since $3.5\% = 0.035$, we find 0.035×12, which equals 0.42.
13.   A. $0.12 \div 1,000,000 = 0.00000012 = 1.2 \times 10^{-7}$.
14.   C. The rectangle has area $(10)(8) = 80$ cm²; the unshaded triangle at the top has area $\frac{1}{2}(10)(7) = 35$ cm²; the unshaded triangle in the right corner has area $\frac{1}{2}(6)(1) = 3$ cm². $80 - (35 + 3) = 42$.
15.   D. $\frac{2x + 4}{2x} = \frac{2x}{2x} + \frac{4}{2x} = 1 + \frac{2}{x}$.
16.   D. Perhaps the fastest approach here is to test the points given. In fact, the first one, $(-1,3)$, does not satisfy (A), (B), or (C).
17.   C. $\sqrt{8^2 + 10^2} = \sqrt{64 + 100} = \sqrt{164} \approx 13$.
18.   B. Rewrite the equation in the form $y = mx + b$, getting $y = \frac{1}{3}x - 1$. The slope, m, is $\frac{1}{3}$.
19.   A. $0.25x + 0.41 = 0.75x - 2.59$

$$2.59 + 0.41 = 0.75x - 0.25x$$

$$3 = 0.5x \to x = \frac{3}{0.5} = \frac{30}{5} = 6.$$

20.   C. If z' is the new z, then

$$z' = \frac{(2v)^3}{4w} = \frac{8v^3}{4w} = 2\left(\frac{v^3}{w}\right) = 2z.$$

21.   A. $40\% = 0.4$; $0.4 \times 22,000 = \$8800$.
22.   D. Savings and travel together come to 20%; $35:20 = 7:4$.
23.   B. $3x - 4 < x + 2 \to 2x < 6 \to x < 3$.
24.   B. $\left(\frac{1}{2}\right)^x = 0.25 \to \left(\frac{1}{2}\right)^x = \frac{1}{4} \to x = 2$.
25.   C. $\frac{1}{z} = \frac{1}{x} + \frac{1}{y}$ yields $\frac{1}{z} = \frac{1}{15} + \frac{1}{30} = \frac{2}{30} + \frac{1}{30} = \frac{3}{30} = \frac{1}{10}$ So $z = 10$.
26.   B. $\frac{93,000,000}{186,000} = 500$ sec. $= \frac{500}{60}$ min. $= 8\frac{1}{3}$ min.
27.   A. $2t^3 - 8t = 2t(t^2 - 4) = 2t(t - 2)(t + 2)$.
28.   D. Since the triangle is isosceles, $x = y$. So $2x + 70 = 180$ and $x = 55$; the complement of $\angle BAC$ measures $90 - 55 = 35$ degrees.
29.   C. $\angle DBC$ is the supplement of $\angle ABC$; its measure is $180 - 55 = 125$ degrees.
30.   B. The graphs are closest together in 1958.
31.   C. The graphs are farthest apart in 1970.
32.   C. $(30 \div 840) = (3 \div 84) \approx 0.035 \approx 4\%$.
33.   D. $\left(\frac{5ab}{2u}\right)\left(\frac{6u^2}{10a^2b}\right) = \left(\frac{5 \cdot 6}{2 \cdot 10}\right)\left(\frac{a}{a^2}\right)\left(\frac{b}{b}\right)\left(\frac{u^2}{u}\right) = \frac{3u}{2a}$.
34.   A. $25.58 - (4.67 + 0.89 + 0.95) = 25.58 - 6.51 = \$19.07$.

35. D. $x^2 - 5x + 6 = (x - 2)(x - 3)$, which equals zero if $x = 2$ or 3.

36. D. Note that the percent of increase in homicide deaths from 1945 to 1972 is

$$\frac{0.7 - 0.2}{0.2} = \frac{0.5}{0.2} = 2.5 = 250\%$$

No other cause approaches this in *relative* increase.

37. B. The largest difference between 1945 and 1972 is in cancer (20.4 − 14.8, or 6%).

38. A. $\sqrt{9} + \sqrt{16} = 3 + 4 = 7 \neq 5$.

39. D. The product of the roots of the equation $ax^2 + bx + c = 0$ is c/a. For $x^2 + 5x - 66 = 0$, $a = 1$, $b = 5$, and $c = -66$.

40. A. $(3 + 5 + 6 + 11 + x) \div 5 = 6 \rightarrow (25 + x) \div 5 = 6 \rightarrow 25 + x = 30 \rightarrow x = 5$.

PART B — Practice Questions for Part II, Content

Part II of the CLEP mathematics examination is the Content portion. It measures the body of mathematical knowledge that is usually taught in a college course designed for nonmathematics majors. The topics tested are frequently covered in survey courses in mathematics, courses in mathematics offered to meet general education requirements, or courses in the structure of mathematics designed for majors in elementary education.

You will be expected to understand conventional symbols and notation, especially as used for the topics of sets, logic, and functions. Contemporary mathematical terminology and symbolism will generally be used here to familiarize you with it, or afford review of it, as may be necessary.

In the material to follow, practice questions are given separately for each topic covered in Part II: sets, logic, the real number system, functions and graphs, and probability and statistics. The last group of practice questions is on miscellaneous topics.

As noted earlier, you will be allowed 60 minutes for the 50 questions in Part II. All the questions in this section are of the regular multiple-choice type. Even though the answer sheet on the examination may have five answer boxes, labeled A, B, C, D, and E, remember that you are to choose the *one* correct answer from among A, B, C, and D. Do not make any marks whatever in column E.

The following instructions apply both to the Content part of the CLEP examination and to the practice questions below:

Directions: For each of the following problems, indicate the correct answer in the appropriate space in the answer column.

Note: Figures that accompany problems in this part are intended to provide information useful in solving the problems. They are drawn as accurately as possible EXCEPT when it is stated in a specific problem that the figure is not drawn to scale. All figures lie in a plane unless otherwise indicated.

B1. Sets

The subtopics are: union and intersection; subsets; Venn diagrams; and Cartesian product.

We begin with illustrative examples accompanied by answers and explanations.

1. If $R = \{0,1\}$ and $S = \{2,3,4\}$, then $R \cup S$ equals   1. [A][B][C]■
   (A) $\{0\}$ (B) $\{2,3,4\}$ (C) $\{1,2,3,4\}$ (D) $\{0,1,2,3,4\}$

($R \cup S$ denotes the *union* of sets R and S; it consists of *all* the elements in set R or in set S or in both.)

2. The Venn diagram above is for the set   2. [A]■[C][D]
   (A) $R \cap (S \cup T)$ (B) $(R \cap S) \cup T$
   (C) $(R \cup S) \cap T$ (D) $R \cap S \cap T$

(The shaded area consists of elements that are either in both R and S, i.e., in $R \cap S$, or in T.)

PRACTICE QUESTIONS ON SETS

Follow the directions given above for this group of practice questions on sets. If you can eliminate one or more choices, then guess among the remaining ones. The correct answers and explanations will be found following the group of questions.

1. If $R = \{0,2,4\}$ and $S = \{0\}$, then $R \cap S =$ 1. [A][B][C][D][E]
   (A) $\{0,2,4\}$ (B) $\{2,4\}$ (C) $\{0\}$ (D) 0

2. If $R = \{a,b\}$, $S = \{b,c\}$, and $T = \{a,c\}$, then $R \cup (S \cap T)$ equals   2. [A][B][C][D][E]
   (A) 0 (B) $\{a,b,c\}$ (C) $\{a,b\}$ (D) $\{c\}$

3. Which of the following is not a subset of $\{p,q,s,v,w\}$?   3. [A][B][C][D][E]
   (A) $\{p,q,s,v,w\}$ (B) $\emptyset$ (C) $\{p\}$ (D) $\{p,q,t\}$

4. If $\overline{P}$ denotes the complement of set P, then the shaded region in the diagram is   4. [A][B][C][D][E]
   (A) $\overline{R \cup S}$
   (B) $\overline{R} \cup \overline{S}$
   (C) $\overline{R} \cup S$
   (D) $R \cap \overline{S}$

5. If $U = \{a,b,c\}$ and $V = \{d\}$, then $U \times V =$ 5. [A][B][C][D][E]
   (A) $\{a,b,c,d\}$ (B) 0
   (C) $\{(a,d)(b,d)(c,d)\}$ (D) $\{(d,a)(d,b)(d,c)\}$

6. If $R = \{x : 1 < x < 5\}$, then the number of integers in R is

    (A) 2   (B) 3   (C) 4   (D) 5

6. Ⓐ Ⓑ Ⓒ Ⓓ

7. $R = \{x : x \geqslant 0\}$ and $S = \{x : x \leqslant 3\}$. The number of integers in $R \cup S$ is

    (A) none   (B) 2   (C) 4   (D) infinite

7. Ⓐ Ⓑ Ⓒ Ⓓ

8. Which of the following is a Venn diagram for $(R \cup S) \cap T$?

8. Ⓐ Ⓑ Ⓒ Ⓓ

9. $V = \{a,b,c,d\}$ and $W = \{b,d,f\}$. Which of the following statements is true?

    (A) $W \subset V$ (B) $\{b,f\}$ is a subset of $V \cap W$

    (C) $\{a,c\}$ belongs to $V \times W$.   (D) $\{a,c,f\}$ is a subset of $V \cup W$.

9. Ⓐ Ⓑ Ⓒ Ⓓ

10. If $R = \{x : x > 1\}$ and $S = \{x : x \leqq 2\}$, then which of the following is false?

    (A) $R \cap S$ contains two integers   (B) $1 \notin R$

    (C) $R \cap S = \{x : 1 < x \leqq 2\}$ (D) $1 \epsilon S$

10. Ⓐ Ⓑ Ⓒ Ⓓ

11. If $R = \{a,b\}$ and $S = \{a,c\}$, then the number of ordered pairs in $R \times S$ is

    (A) 2   (B) 3   (C) 4   (D) 5

11. Ⓐ Ⓑ Ⓒ Ⓓ

12. The number of subsets of $\{a,b,c\}$ is

    (A) 8   (B) 6   (C) 5   (D) 3

12. Ⓐ Ⓑ Ⓒ Ⓓ

13. $R \cap (S \cup T)$ equals

    (A) $(R \cap S) \cup T$ (B) $(R \cap S) \cup (R \cap T)$

    (C) $(R \cup S) \cap (R \cup T)$ (D) $(R \cup S) \cap T$

13. Ⓐ Ⓑ Ⓒ Ⓓ

14. Which of the following is a false statement about the Venn diagram?

    (A) $S \subset R$ (B) $R \cap S = S$

    (C) $(R \cap S) \subset R$ (D) $R \cap S = \emptyset$

14. Ⓐ Ⓑ Ⓒ Ⓓ

15. $S - T$ is the set of elements in S but not in T. If S is the set $\{a,b,c,d,e\}$ and $T = \{a,c,f,g\}$, then $S - T$ equals

    (A) $\{b,d\}$ (B) $\{b,d,e,f,g\}$ (C) $\{b,d,e\}$ (D) $\{f,g\}$

15. Ⓐ Ⓑ Ⓒ Ⓓ

ANSWERS AND EXPLANATIONS

to practice Part II questions on sets.

1.   C. $R \cap S$ is the *intersection* of sets R and S; it consists of the elements that are in both R and S.
2.   B. $S \cap T = \{c\}$; $R \cup (S \cap T) = \{a,b,c\}$.
3.   D. Each element in a subset of a set must be an element of the set.
4.   A. $\overline{T}$ denotes the complement of T; i.e., the elements not in T. $\overline{R \cup S}$ consists of elements in the universal set which are not in $R \cup S$.
5.   C. $U \times V$ is the set of ordered pairs whose first element is an element of U and whose second is an element of V. $U \times V$ is called the *Cartesian product* of U and V.
6.   B. The integers are 2, 3, 4.
7.   D. Think of a number line:

     $R \cup S$ is the whole number line.

8.   B. Often it helps to label the disjoint, exhaustive sets as shown:

     R consists of regions 2, 4, 5, 6
     S consists of regions 3, 4, 5, 7
     T consists of regions 5, 6, 7, 8
     $(R \cup S) \cap T$ consists of $(2, 3, 4, 5, 6, 7) \cap (5, 6, 7, 8) = 5, 6, 7$.

9.   D. Note that $V \cap W = \{b,d\}$, that $\{a,c\} \notin V \times W$, that $V \cup W = \{a,b,c,d,f\}$.

10.   A.

     (Note that "ϵ" denotes "is an element of," "$\notin$" denotes "is not an element of," some specified set.)

11.   C. $R \times S = \{(a,a), (a,c), (b,a), (b,c)\}$.
12.   A. The subsets of $\{a,b,c\}$ are 0, $\{a\}$, $\{b\}$, $\{c\}$, $\{a,b\}$, $\{a,c\}$, $\{b,c\}$, and $\{a,b,c\}$.
     (0 is the null or empty set with no elements at all; it is a subset of every set.)
13.   B. A Venn diagram helps.

The crosshatched region is $R \cap (S \cup T)$ or $(R \cap S) \cup (R \cap T)$. See also the explanation to question 8 above. Note that $R \cap (S \cup T)$ includes regions 4, 5, 6.

14.   D. Note that $R \cap S = S$, and that $S \neq \emptyset$.

15.   C. $S - T$ is the set S with all elements in T that are also in S removed from S.

B2. Logic

The subtopics are: truth tables; conjunctions and disjunctions; negations; conditional statements; necessary and sufficient conditions; converse, inverse, and contrapositive; implications, conclusions, and counterexample.

Here are two illustrative examples, with answers and explanations.

ANSWERS

1.   The converse of the statement $p \to q$ is

     (A) $p \to \sim q$ (B) $q \to p$ (C) $\sim q \to \sim p$ (D) $\sim p \to \sim q$

   ($p \to q$ denotes "if p then q"; its converse is "if q then p," i.e., $q \to p$.)

1. A ■ C D

2.   Which of the following is false?

     (A) If p is false, then $p \to q$ is true.

     (B) If p and q are both false, then $p \longleftrightarrow q$ is true.

     (C) If q is true, then $p \wedge q$ is true.

     (D) If p is true, then $p \vee q$ is true.

2. A B ■ D

(Here are the truth tables for the most common logical connectives:

p	$\wedge$	q		p	$\vee$	q		p	$\to$	q		p	$\leftrightarrow$	q
T	T	T		T	T	T		T	T	T		T	T	T
T	F	F		T	T	F		T	F	F		T	F	F
F	F	T		F	T	T		F	T	T		F	F	T
F	F	F		F	F	F		F	T	F		F	T	F

Use the tables to verify (A), (B), and (D). Note that for $p \wedge q$ to be true, *both* p and q must be true.)

PRACTICE QUESTIONS ON LOGIC

Follow the directions given on page 364. The correct answers and explanations follow the set of questions.

1.   If p denotes "He is a professor" and q denotes "He is absent-minded," then the statement "It is not true that he is an absent-minded professor" can be written symbolically

     (A) $p \wedge \sim q$ (B) $\sim (p \vee q)$.   (C) $\sim p \wedge q$ (D) $\sim (p \wedge q)$

1. A B C D

2. Let p be "Mary is smart" and q be "Mary is conscientious." Then $p \to q$ may be translated

    (A) If Mary is conscientious, then she is smart.

    (B) If Mary is smart, then she is conscientious.

    (C) Mary is smart but not conscientious.

    (D) Mary is both smart and conscientious.

2. Ⓐ Ⓑ Ⓒ Ⓓ

3. $\sim(p \vee q)$ is equivalent to

    (A) $\sim p \vee \sim q$ (B) $\sim p \wedge q$ (C) $\sim p \wedge \sim q$ (D) $p \wedge \sim q$

3. Ⓐ Ⓑ Ⓒ Ⓓ

4. Given the hypotheses:

        if cats laugh, then $3 < 5$,

        either dogs dance or gas will be rationed,

select a valid conclusion.

    (A) Cats do not laugh.

    (B) If dogs do not dance, then gas will be rationed.

    (C) Dogs do not dance.

    (D) Gas will be rationed.

4. Ⓐ Ⓑ Ⓒ Ⓓ

5. Which of the following is the truth table for $p \wedge \sim q$?

p	q	(A)	(B)	(C)	(D)
T	T	T	F	F	F
T	F	F	T	F	F
F	T	F	F	F	T
F	F	F	F	T	F

5. Ⓐ Ⓑ Ⓒ Ⓓ

6. The statement $\sim p \vee q$ is false only when

    (A) p is true, q is false   (B) p and q are both true

    (B) p is false, q is true   (D) p and q are both false

6. Ⓐ Ⓑ Ⓒ Ⓓ

7. $p \vee (q \wedge r)$ is equivalent to

    (A) $(p \vee q) \wedge r$ (B) $(p \vee q) \wedge (p \vee r)$

    (C) $(p \wedge q) \vee (p \wedge r)$ (D) $(p \vee q) \wedge (p \wedge r)$

7. Ⓐ Ⓑ Ⓒ Ⓓ

8. Which of the following statements is not equivalent to "All oriental men are clever"?

    (A) If a man is oriental, then he's clever.

    (B) If a man is not clever, then he's not oriental.

    (C) If a man is clever, then he's an oriental.

    (D) A man is oriental only if he is clever.

8. Ⓐ Ⓑ Ⓒ Ⓓ

9. The negation of the statement "If stock prices are rising, then food prices are high" is

    (A) If stocks are not rising, then food prices are not high.

    (B) If food prices are not high, then stocks are not rising.

    (C) If stocks are falling, then food prices are low.

    (D) Stocks are rising but prices are not high.

9. Ⓐ Ⓑ Ⓒ Ⓓ

10. Let p be "A triangle is isosceles" and q be "A triangle is equilateral." Symbolically, the statement "In order for a triangle to be equilateral it must be isosceles" is

    (A) $p \leftrightarrow q$ (B) $p \to q$

    (C) $q \leftrightarrow p$ (D) $q \to p$

10. Ⓐ Ⓑ Ⓒ Ⓓ

11. $q \to p$ may be translated
    (A) q is sufficient for p (B) p only if q
    (C) p implies q (D) q is necessary for p

12. Which of the following is false?
    (A) $2 + 1 = 4$ if and only if $(-1)^2 = -1$.
    (B) $3 + 2 = 5$ if and only if $(-x)^2 = x^2$.
    (C) $\sqrt{9} = 3$ if and only if $\sqrt{9} = -3$.
    (D) $x^2 = 4$ if and only if $x = 2$ or $x = -2$.

13. If a statement is true so is its
    (A) converse   (B) contrapositive
    (C) inverse   (D) negation

14. Given the statement $p \to q$, its contrapositive is
    (A) $\sim q \to \sim p$ (B) $q \to p$
    (C) $\sim p \to \sim q$ (D) $p \to \sim q$

15. Consider the set of true implications: "If Carl enjoys a subject, then he studies it. If he studies a subject, then he does not fail it." Which of the following is a valid conclusion?
    (A) Since Carl failed history he did not enjoy it.
    (B) If Carl does not enjoy history, then he fails it.
    (C) If Carl does not study a subject, then he does not pass it.
    (D) Carl did not fail mathematics; therefore he enjoyed it.

16. The converse of the statement "If dentists have no cavities, then they use Screen toothpaste" is
    (A) If dentists have cavities, then they do not use Screen.
    (B) If dentists do not use Screen, then they have cavities.
    (C) If dentists use Screen, then they have no cavities.
    (D) Dentists must use Screen if they are to have no cavities.

17. The negation of the statement "Some students have part-time jobs" is
    (A) All students have part-time jobs.
    (B) Some students do not have part-time jobs.
    (C) Only one student has a part-time job.
    (D) No student has a part-time job.

18. To disprove the statement $x^2 > 0$ for all real x, the following may be offered as a counterexample
    (A) $x = -2$ (B) $x = -1$
    (C) $x = 0$ (D) $x = 1$

19. A statement equivalent to "Some teenagers are poor drivers" is
    (A) At least one teenager is a poor driver.
    (B) Not all teenagers are poor drivers.
    (C) At least one teenager is not a poor driver.
    (D) Good drivers are not teenagers.

20. Given the true implications $p \to q$ and $q \to r$, which of the following is true?
    (A) $r \to p$ (B) $\sim q \to \sim r$
    (C) $\sim r \to \sim p$ (D) $\sim p \to \sim r$

ANSWERS AND EXPLANATIONS
to practice Part II questions on logic.

1. D. $p \wedge q$ denotes "He is an absent-minded professor."
2. B. A translation of $p \to q$ is "if p then q."
3. C. By one of DeMorgan's laws, $\sim(p \vee q) \equiv \sim p \wedge \sim q$.
4. B. Note that $p \vee q$ is equivalent to $\sim p \to q$. (Verify with truth tables.)
5. B. The truth table is:

p	q	$\sim q$	$p \wedge \sim q$
T	T	F	F
T	F	T	T
F	T	F	F
F	F	T	F

6. A. Look at the truth table:

p	$\sim p$	$\vee$	q
T	F	T	T
T	F	F	F
F	T	T	T
F	T	T	F

7. B. One of the distributive laws applies here.
8. C. If x is an element of the set of men,
    p_x denotes "He is oriental,"
    q_x denotes "He is clever,"
    then the original statement is $\forall_x(p_x \to q_x)$. (C) is $\forall_x(q_x \to p_x)$, which is the (nonequivalent) converse.
9. D. If p denotes "Stock prices are rising" and q denotes "Food prices are high," then we want $\sim(p \to q)$. This is equivalent to $\sim(\sim p \vee q)$ or $p \wedge \sim q$.
10. D. A restatement is "If a triangle is equilateral, then it is isosceles."
11. A. $q \to p$ may be translated "If q then p," "p only if q," "q is sufficient for p," "p is necessary for q," or "q implies p."
12. C. The biconditional or equivalence $p \leftrightarrow q$ is true if p and q are both true or both false; $p \leftrightarrow q$ is false if p and q have opposite truth values. $\sqrt{a^2} = |a|$ by definition; i.e., $\sqrt{a^2} \geq 0$ always.
13. B. A statement and its contrapositive are equivalent.
14. A. The contrapositive of "if r then s" is "if not s then not r."
15. A. Let p be "Carl enjoys a subject,"
          q be "Carl studies a subject,"
    and r be "Carl fails a subject."
    Then it is true that $p \to q$ and $q \to \sim r$. (A) can be written symbolically: $r \to \sim p$. Since $q \to \sim r$ is equivalent to $r \to \sim q$ and $p \to q$ is equivalent to $\sim q \to \sim p$, it follows that $r \to \sim p$ (syllogism). None of the others is a valid conclusion.
16. C. The converse of "if r then s" is "if s then r."
17. D. If x denotes "students" and p_x "a student has a part-time job" then we have, symbolically, $\exists_x p_x$. $\sim(\exists_x p_x)$ is equivalent to $\forall_x \sim p_x$, i.e., "no student has a part-time job."
18. C. If $x \neq 0$, then $x^2 > 0$. But if $x = 0$ then $x^2 = 0$.
19. A. "Some" means "at least one."
20. C. $p \to q$ is equivalent to $\sim q \to \sim p$. $q \to r$ is equivalent to $\sim r \to \sim q$. So $p \to q \wedge q \to r$ is equivalent to $\sim r \to \sim p$ (syllogism).

B3. Real Number System

The subtopics are: prime and composite numbers; odd and even numbers; factors and divisibility; rational and irrational numbers; absolute value and order.

Here are introductory examples, with answers and explanations.

1. If a and b are real numbers, then $(a)[b + (-b)] = (ab) + (a)(-b)$ because
   (A) addition is commutative
   (B) multiplication is commutative
   (C) the real numbers are closed under multiplication
   (D) multiplication is distributive over addition
   (This is referred to briefly as the *distributive property*.)

   1. Ⓐ Ⓑ Ⓒ ■

2. If $a > b > 0$, then

   (A) $\frac{1}{a} > \frac{1}{b}$ (B) $\frac{1}{a} < \frac{1}{b}$

   (C) $\frac{1}{a} = \frac{1}{b}$ (D) $-a > -b$

   (Since $a - b > 0$ and $ab > 0$, it follows that

   $$\frac{a - b}{ab} > 0 \quad \text{or} \quad \frac{1}{b} - \frac{1}{a} > 0.$$

   $$\text{So } \frac{1}{b} > \frac{1}{a}.)$$

   2. Ⓐ ■ Ⓒ Ⓓ

PRACTICE QUESTIONS ON THE REAL NUMBER SYSTEM

Follow the directions given on page 364. If you can eliminate one or more choices, then guess among the remaining ones. The correct answers and explanations follow the set of questions.

1. Which of the following is not a prime number?
   (A) 2   (B) 17   (C) 27   (D) 37

   1. Ⓐ Ⓑ Ⓒ Ⓓ

2. Which of the following statements is false?
   (A) If $ab > 0$, then a and b are both positive.
   (B) $a < 0 \rightarrow -a > 0$.
   (C) If $a > b$, then $-a < -b$.
   (D) If $0 < a < 1$, then $a^2 < a$.

   2. Ⓐ Ⓑ Ⓒ Ⓓ

3. Which of the following provides a counterexample to the false statement "If $a > b$, then $a^2 > b^2$"?
   (A) $a = 2, b = 1$ (B) $a = 1, b = 0$
   (C) $a = -2, b = -1$ (D) $a = 1, b = -1$

   3. Ⓐ Ⓑ Ⓒ Ⓓ

4. If $ac < bc$, which of the following is impossible?
   (A) $a > b$ (B) $a < b$
   (C) $c = 0$ (D) $c < 0$

   4. Ⓐ Ⓑ Ⓒ Ⓓ

5. Suppose $a < 0 < b$. Which of the following must hold? **5.** Ⓐ Ⓑ Ⓒ Ⓓ
    (A) $|a| < |b|$ (B) $|b| < |a|$
    (C) $|b - a| = b + a$ (D) $|b - a| = b - a$

6. Which of the following statements about the real number system is false? **6.** Ⓐ Ⓑ Ⓒ Ⓓ
    (A) The real numbers are closed under addition and multiplication.
    (B) Subtraction of reals is commutative.
    (C) Every number except 0 has a multiplicative inverse.
    (D) The square of every nonzero number is positive.

7. If none of the denominators below is zero, which of the following is true? **7.** Ⓐ Ⓑ Ⓒ Ⓓ
    (A) $\dfrac{2p + 4q}{p + 2q} = 2$ (B) $\dfrac{2m + p}{2q} = \dfrac{m + p}{q}$

    (C) $\dfrac{q}{q + p} = \dfrac{1}{p}$ (D) $\dfrac{3m}{3q + p} = \dfrac{m}{q + p}$

8. If $|a - 2| = a - 2$, then it is false that **8.** Ⓐ Ⓑ Ⓒ Ⓓ
    (A) $a > 0$ (B) $a = 2$ (C) $a > 2$ (D) $a < 2$

9. Which of the following numbers is rational? **9.** Ⓐ Ⓑ Ⓒ Ⓓ
    (A) $\sqrt{2}$ (B) $\sqrt{3}$ (C) $\sqrt{4}$ (D) $\sqrt{5}$

10. The prime factorization of 300 is **10.** Ⓐ Ⓑ Ⓒ Ⓓ
    (A) $3^2 \cdot 10^2$ (B) $2 \cdot 3^2 \cdot 5^2$ (C) $2 \cdot 3 \cdot 5^2$ (D) $2^2 \cdot 3 \cdot 5^2$

11. Which of the following is meaningless? **11.** Ⓐ Ⓑ Ⓒ Ⓓ
    (A) $0 \cdot 1$ (B) $0/_1$ (C) 1^0 (D) $1/_0$

12. Which statement is false? **12.** Ⓐ Ⓑ Ⓒ Ⓓ
    (A) There is a rational number between every pair of rationals.
    (B) There is an irrational between every pair of rationals.
    (C) There is a rational number between every pair of irrationals.
    (D) The sum of two irrational numbers is always irrational.

13. The repeating decimal $0.444 \cdots$ equals **13.** Ⓐ Ⓑ Ⓒ Ⓓ
    (A) $^4/_{10}$ (B) $^3/_7$ (C) $^4/_9$ (D) $^5/_{11}$

14. If $R = \{x : x \text{ is an integer}\}$ and $S = \{x : x \text{ is a positive real number}\}$, then **14.** Ⓐ Ⓑ Ⓒ Ⓓ
    $R \cap S$ equals
    (A) $\{x : x \text{ is a positive integer}\}$
    (B) the empty set
    (C) R
    (D) S

15. If $a - b = b - a$, then **15.** Ⓐ Ⓑ Ⓒ Ⓓ
    (A) $a = b$
    (B) $|a - b| = |a + b|$
    (C) a and b have opposite signs
    (D) a and b must both equal 0

16. If a and b are positive integers with a odd and b even, then which of the **16.** Ⓐ Ⓑ Ⓒ Ⓓ
    following is odd?
    (A) $2a + b$ (B) $a^2 + 3b$ (C) $ab + 2a$ (D) b^a

17. The repeating part of the decimal expansion for a rational number whose **17.** Ⓐ Ⓑ Ⓒ Ⓓ
    denominator is 7 has at most
    (A) 4 digits   (B) 5 digits   (C) 6 digits   (D) 7 digits

This number line with points q and t as shown is for questions 18 and 19.

18. Which statement is false?   18. Ⓐ Ⓑ Ⓒ Ⓓ
     (A) $q + t > 0$ (B) $q - t > 0$ (C) $q^2 > 1$ (D) $t > -t$

19. Which number is largest?   19. Ⓐ Ⓑ Ⓒ Ⓓ
     (A) $q + t$ (B) $q - t$ (C) $t - q$ (D) qt

20. Which set is not empty?   20. Ⓐ Ⓑ Ⓒ Ⓓ
     (A) $\{x : x + 2 = 2\}$
     (B) $\{x : |x| = -1\}$
     (C) $\{x : x$ is real and $x^2 + 1 = 0\}$
     (D) $\{x : x \neq x\}$

21. The set of different factors of 135 is   21. Ⓐ Ⓑ Ⓒ Ⓓ
     (A) $\{3, 5\}$ (B) $\{3, 7\}$ (C) $\{5, 7\}$ (D) $\{7, 9\}$

22. If $m + n$ is divisible by 6 and m is even, then it is necessarily true that .   22. Ⓐ Ⓑ Ⓒ Ⓓ
     (A) n is divisible by 3
     (B) m is divisible by 3
     (C) n is even
     (D) m and n are both divisible by 6

23. If p denotes "$x \leqslant 1$" and q denotes "$x > -2$," then the set that satisfies   23. Ⓐ Ⓑ Ⓒ Ⓓ
     $p \wedge q$ is
     (A) $-2 < x \leqslant 1$
     (B) $1 \leqslant x$ or $x > -2$
     (C) $x < -2$ and $x \geqslant 1$
     (D) $-2 \leqslant x < 1$

24. To disprove the statement "If x is irrational, then x^2 is rational," choose   24. Ⓐ Ⓑ Ⓒ Ⓓ
     x to be

     (A) $\sqrt{2}$ (B) $3\sqrt{2}$ (C) π (D) $\dfrac{1}{\sqrt{2}}$

25. If p is divisible by 2 and q is divisible by 5 which of the following must be   25. Ⓐ Ⓑ Ⓒ Ⓓ
     divisible by 10?
     (A) $pq + 15$ (B) $5p + 2q$ (C) $5(p + q)$ (D) $p + q + 10$

ANSWERS AND EXPLANATIONS
   to practice Part II questions on the real number system.

1.   C. A prime number has only itself and 1 as factors.
2.   A. If a and b are both negative, then ab is positive. Verify the truth of (B), (C), and (D).
3.   D. $1 > -1$, but $(1)^2 \not> (-1)^2$. (C) is not a counterexample because $-2 \not> -1$.
4.   C. Verify that (A), (B), and (D) are possible.
5.   D. If $a < 0 < b$, then $b - a$ is a positive number; by definition of absolute value, $|x| = x$ if $x > 0$.
6.   B. A counterexample to statement (B): $5 - 3 \neq 3 - 5$.

7. A. $\dfrac{2p + 4q}{p + 2q} = \dfrac{2(p + 2q)}{p + 2q} = 2$ if $(p + 2q) \neq 0$.

8. D. $|a - 2| = a - 2$ if $a - 2 \geqslant 0$, i.e., if $a > 2$ or $a = 2$. If $a \geqslant 2$, certainly $a > 0$.

9. C. $\sqrt{4} = 2$.

10. D. No other product given even equals 300!

11. D. Division by 0 is impossible.

12. D. $\sqrt{2} + (3 - \sqrt{2}) = 3$ is a counterexample to statement (D). (A), (B), and (C) are true.

13. C. Let $r = 0.444 \cdots$ (where the three dots indicate an infinite number of 4's). Then

$$10r = 4.44 \cdots$$
$$9r = 4$$

and $r = \text{4/9}$.

14. A. The intersection of two sets contains those elements that are in both sets.

15. A. $a - b = b - a$ yields $2a = 2b$ or $a = b$.

16. B. Convince yourself that the other choices are all even integers.

17. C. When dividing by 7, only one of the remainders 1, 2, 3, 4, 5, or 6 can be obtained. If a particular remainder recurs, the decimal must repeat.

18. D. In (D), note that $t < 0$, so that $-t > 0$.

19. B. The numbers in (C) and (D) are negative. Since $t < 0$, $q - t > q$, whereas $q + t < q$.

20. A. $\{x : x + 2 = 2\} = \{0\}$. None of the other sets contain any elements.

21. A. Note that $135 = 3 \cdot 45 = 3 \cdot 3 \cdot 15 = 3 \cdot 3 \cdot 3 \cdot 5$ or $3^3 \cdot 5$.

22. C. Find examples to show that (A), (B), and (D) may be false.

23. A. $(x \leqslant 1) \wedge (x > -2)$ is true when both inequalities are satisfied. Thus, x must both exceed -2 and be less than or equal to 1.

24. C. π is irrational, but so is π^2.

25. B. Find p and q that satisfy the given conditions but for which the expressions in (A), (C), and (D) are not divisible by 10.

B4. Functions and Their Graphs

The subtopics are: domain and range; linear, polynomial, composite, and inverse functions.

Here are introductory examples, with answers and explanations.

1. If $f(x) = x^3 - x - 1$, then $f(-1) =$
    (A) -3 (B) -1 (C) 0   (D) 1

    $(f(-1) = (-1)^3 - (-1) - 1 = -1 + 1 - 1 = -1.)$

1. Ⓐ ∎ Ⓒ Ⓓ

2. If $R = \{1,2,3\}$, which of the following is a function from R into R?
    (A) $\{(1,3), (2,1)\}$ (B) $\{(3,1), (2,3), (1,5)\}$
    (C) $\{(1,2), (2,2), (3,2)\}$ (D) $\{(1,2), (2,3), (3,1), (3,3)\}$

    (A function from R into R may be defined as a set of ordered pairs in which each element of R must be a first element of exactly one pair, and the second element of that pair, its image, must belong to R. (A) is not a function because although $3 \in R$, it has no image; in (B), the image of 1 is 5, which is not in R; and in (D) the element 3 has *two* images.)

2. Ⓐ Ⓑ ∎ Ⓓ

3. Which of the following is the graph of a function $y = f(x)$?

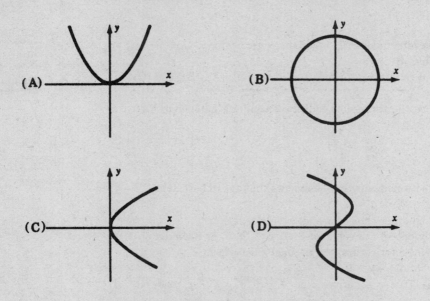

(If $y = f(x)$ is a function, then for each x in the domain there is a *unique* y. A vertical line can cut the graph of a function only once.)

PRACTICE QUESTIONS ON FUNCTIONS AND THEIR GRAPHS

Follow the directions given on page 364. If you can eliminate one or more choices, then guess among the remaining ones. The correct answers and explanations follow the set of questions.

1. If $g(x) = x^2 - 2x + 1$, then $g(-x) =$
    (A) $x^2 - 2x + 1$ (B) $-x^2 + 2x + 1$
    (C) $x^2 + 2x + 1$ (D) $x^2 + 2x - 1$

2. Which of the following is the graph of $x + 2y = 2$?

3. If $f(x) = x^2 - x + 3$, then $f(2) =$

   (A) 0   (B) 3   (C) 5   (D) 9

   3. Ⓐ Ⓑ Ⓒ Ⓓ

4. If $f(x) = \dfrac{x + 1}{(x - 1)^3}$, then $f(0)$ equals

   (A) -1 (B) 0   (C) 1   (D) none of these

   4. Ⓐ Ⓑ Ⓒ Ⓓ

5. If $f(x) = x^2 + 1$, then the domain of f is

   (A) $\{x : x > 0\{$ (B) $\{x : -\infty < x < \infty\}$
   (C) $\{x : x \geq 0\}$ (D) $\{x : x \geq 1\}$

   5. Ⓐ Ⓑ Ⓒ Ⓓ

6. The range of the function of question 5 is
   (A) all real numbers
   (B) all positive numbers
   (C) all numbers greater than one
   (D) all numbers y such that $y \geq 1$

   6. Ⓐ Ⓑ Ⓒ Ⓓ

7. Let $g(x) = \dfrac{x + 1}{x^2 - x}$. Then the set of real numbers excluded from the domain

   of g is:

   (A) $\{-1, 0, 1\}$ (B) $\{0, 1\}$ (C) $\{1\}$ (D) $\{-1, 1\}$

   7. Ⓐ Ⓑ Ⓒ Ⓓ

8. A function $y = f(x)$ is *even* if $f(-x) = f(x)$. Which of the following functions
   is even?

   (A) $f(x) = 2x + 4$ (B) $f(x) = x^2 + 2x$
   (C) $f(x) = 3x^2 + 5$ (D) $f(x) = 4x$

   8. Ⓐ Ⓑ Ⓒ Ⓓ

9. **The graph to the right is for the function**

   (A) $2y = x^2 - 4$

   (B) $y = x^2 - 2$

   (C) $2y = x^2$

   (D) $y = x^2 - 4$

   9. Ⓐ Ⓑ Ⓒ Ⓓ

10. Which of the following points lies on the line $2x - 3y = 6$?
    (A) (3,2)   (B) (0,2)   (C) (−3,0)   (D) (−3,−4)

    10. Ⓐ Ⓑ Ⓒ Ⓓ

11. $f(x) = x(x - 2)$ and $g(x) = x + 1$. Then $f(g(0)) =$
    (A) 1   (B) 0   (C) −1   (D) −2

    11. Ⓐ Ⓑ Ⓒ Ⓓ

12. With f and g defined as in question 5, $g(f(0)) =$
    (A) 1   (B) 0   (C) −1   (D) −2

    12. Ⓐ Ⓑ Ⓒ Ⓓ

13. If $f(x) = x^2 - 2x + c$ and $f(0) = 1$, then $c =$
    (A) −1   (B) 0   (C) 1   (D) 2

    13. Ⓐ Ⓑ Ⓒ Ⓓ

14. The graph of $y = x^2 - 3$ is obtained from that of $y = x^2$ by translating the latter

    (A) to the right 3 units   (B) to the left 3 units

    (C) up three units   (D) down 3 units

14. Ⓐ Ⓑ Ⓒ Ⓓ

15. Which of the following is a polynomial function?

    (A) $y = 2^x$ (B) $y = \dfrac{1}{x}$ (C) $y = \log_2 x$ (D) $y = \dfrac{1}{3}x^2$

15. Ⓐ Ⓑ Ⓒ Ⓓ

16. Which of the following diagrams does not define a function from $\{a,b,c\}$ into $\{d,e,f\}$?

16. Ⓐ Ⓑ Ⓒ Ⓓ

17. Let $f(x) = \begin{cases} x - 1 & \text{if } x < 2 \\ x^2 - 3 & \text{if } x \geqslant 2 \end{cases}$ The graph of f is

17. Ⓐ Ⓑ Ⓒ Ⓓ

18. If $f(x) = 3x + 2$ and $g(x) = x^2 - 3$, then $f(g(x))$ equals

    (A) $9x^2 + 12x + 1$ (B) $3x^2 - 7$

    (C) $3x^2 - 1$ (D) $9x^2 + 6x + 1$

18. Ⓐ Ⓑ Ⓒ Ⓓ

19. If $g(x) = 3x + k$ and $g(1) = -2$, then $g(2) =$

    (A) -1 (B) 1   (C) 7   (D) 11

19. Ⓐ Ⓑ Ⓒ Ⓓ

20.

The graph above is for the set
(A) $\{x : -2 < x < 1\}$ (B) $\{x : x < -2, x = 1\}$
(C) $\{x : x > 1, x \neq -2\}$ (D) $\{x : x < -2 \text{ or } x > 1\}$

21. The graphs of inverse functions are symmetric
(A) to the x-axis (B) to the y-axis
(C) to the line $y = x$ (D) to the origin

22. The points in the interior, but not on the boundary, of the triangle in the figure satisfy
(A) $y < 2 - x, y > 0, x > 0$
(B) $y > 2 - x, y > 0, x > 0$
(C) $y \leqslant 2 - x, y \geqslant 0, x \geqslant 0$
(D) $y < x - 2, y > 0, x > 0$

23. If $[x]$ denotes the greatest integer less than or equal to x, then $[-1.2]$ equals
(A) -2 (B) -1 (C) 0 (D) 1

24. Which of the equations below defines exactly one function $y = f(x)$ from the reals into the reals?
(A) $y^2 = x^2 + 1$ (B) $x^3 - y = 4$
(C) $x - 4y^2 = 2$ (D) $4x^2 + 9y^2 = 36$

25. Which of the following is the graph of a function $y = f(x)$?

(A) (B) (C) (D)

ANSWERS AND EXPLANATIONS
to practice Part II questions on functions and their graphs.

1. C. $g(-x) = (-x)^2 - 2(-x) + 1 = x^2 + 2x + 1$.
2. D. Checking the intercepts of the line is fastest. Here, they are $x = 2$ and $y = 1$. Only (D) qualifies.
3. C. $f(2) = 2^2 - 2 + 3 = 4 - 2 + 3 = 5$.
4. A. $f(0) = \dfrac{0 + 1}{(0 - 1)^3} = \dfrac{1}{-1} = -1$.
5. B. } A sketch of the graph may help
6. D. } for these two questions.

7. B. Set the denominator of g equal to zero. $x^2 - x = x(x - 1) = 0$ when $x = 0$ or $x = 1$.
8. C. Note that (A), (B), and (D) are not even.
9. A. Check intercepts first. From the graph we see that $x = \pm 2$ and $y = -2$. Only $2y = x^2 - 4$ has these intercepts.
10. D. Substitute 3 for x and 2 for y. The left-hand side must equal 6.
11. C. $g(0) = 0 + 1 = 1$, and $f(g(0)) = f(1) = 1(1 - 2) = 1 \cdot -1 = -1$.
12. A. $f(0) = 0(0 - 2) = 0 \cdot -2 = 0$, and $g(f(0)) = g(0) = 0 + 1 = 1$.
13. C. $f(0) = 0^2 - 2(0) + c = 1 \rightarrow c = 1$.
14. D. For a given x, each y-value of $y = x^2 - 3$ is 3 *less* than that of $y = x^2$.
15. D. A polynomial in x is an expression of the form
$$a_0 x^n + a_1 x^{n-1} + a_2 x^{n-2} + \ldots + a_{n-1} x + a_n$$
where the a's are real numbers and n is a positive integer. The variable never appears in the denominator and the exponents of the variable are always positive integers.
16. A. Note in (A) that the element c has two images, d and f.
17. C. The graph consists of part of a straight line ($y = x - 1$ if $x < 2$) and part of a parabola ($y = x^2 - 3$ if $x \geq 2$). Checking intercepts helps.
18. B. $f(g(x)) = 3(x^2 + 3) + 2 = 3x^2 - 9 + 2 = 3x^2 - 7$.
19. B. Since $g(1) = 3(1) + k = -2$, $k = -5$. So $g(2) = 3(2) + (-5) = 1$.
20. D. The x-axis has been darkened to the left of $x = -2$ and to the right of $x = 1$. The hollow circles tell us to exclude these two points.
21. C. If point (a,b) is on the graph of $y = f(x)$, then (b,a) lies on the graph of its inverse.
22. A. Since the line goes through the points $(0,2)$ and $(2,0)$, it has slope -1. Its equation is $y = 2 - x$. The coordinates (x,y) of each point in the interior of the triangle satisfy the inequalities $x > 0, y > 0, y < 2 - x$.
23. A. The greatest integer less than or equal to -1.2 is -2. Verify this with a number line if necessary.
24. B. If the exponent of y is even, then there is more than one value of y for any x in the domain.
25. C. The graphs in (A), (B), and (D) do *not* pass the vertical-line test (p. 376).

B5. Probability and Statistics

The subtopics are: counting problems, including permutations and combinations; computation of probabilities of simple and compound events; simple conditional probability; the mean and median.

Here are introductory examples, with answers and explanations.

1. How many ways can an 8-member council elect a chairman, a vice-chairman, and a secretary if no member may hold more than one office?

   (A) $\dfrac{8!}{3!}$ (B) $\dfrac{8!}{5!}$ (C) $\dfrac{8!}{3!5!}$ (D) 8^3

(The chairman can be elected in 8 ways, after which the vice-chairman can be elected in 7 different ways; following this, the secretary can be chosen from among 6 different people. There are then $8 \cdot 7 \cdot 6$ different ways the officers can be elected. For this question the *order* matters. An ordered arrangement of n objects taken r at a time is called a *permutation*, and is denoted by $P(n,r)$, or by $_nP_r$, $P_{n,r}$, or P_r^n. Note that

$$P(n,r) = \frac{n!}{(n-r)!}.$$

If common factors are eliminated from numerator and denominator, a product of exactly r factors remains. Thus

$$\frac{8!}{5!} = \frac{8 \cdot 7 \cdot 6 \cdot 5 \cdot 4 \cdot 3 \cdot 2 \cdot 1}{5 \cdot 4 \cdot 3 \cdot 2 \cdot 1} = 8 \cdot 7 \cdot 6.)$$

2. How many different 3-member committees can be selected from a group of 5 people?

   (A) 60   (B) 20   (C) 10   (D) 5

(This question calls for a *combination* of 5 objects taken 3 at a time; i.e., a selection where order does *not* count. A combination of n objects taken r at a time is just the number of different r-element subsets that an n-element set has. We'll use the notation $C(n,r)$; others used are $_nC_r$, $C_{n,r}$, and $\binom{n}{r}$. Since there are $r!$ permutations of each r-element set, we find $C(n,r)$ by dividing $P(n,r)$ by $r!$. Here the answer is $C(5,3)$ or

$$\frac{5!}{2!3!} = \frac{5 \cdot 4 \cdot 3 \cdot 2 \cdot 1}{2 \cdot 1 \cdot 3 \cdot 2 \cdot 1} = 10.$$

For computation, it's easiest to remember $C(5,3)$ as

$$\frac{5 \cdot 4 \cdot 3}{1 \cdot 2 \cdot 3},$$

where you have the same number of factors in the numerator as in the denominator. Also, $C(n,r) = C(n,n-r)$. So, for example, to compute $C(9,7)$ we use instead $C(9,2)$. Recalling that $P(9,2) = 9 \cdot 8$, we have $C(9,2) =$

$$\frac{9 \cdot 8}{1 \cdot 2}.)$$

3. A box contains 4 black and 3 white chips. Two chips are selected at random. The probability that one is black and one is white is

   (A) $^2/_7$ (B) $^3/_7$ (C) $^4/_7$ (D) $^7/_{12}$

(The probability of an event is the ratio

$$\frac{\text{number of ways the event can occur}}{\text{total number of possible outcomes}}$$

There are $4 \cdot 3$ or 12 ways of selecting 1 black chip and 1 white chip. There are $C(7,2)$ or $(7 \cdot 6)/(1 \cdot 2)$ ways of choosing 2 chips from 7. The answer is $^{12}/_{21}$ or $^4/_7$.)

Use the following mortality table to answer questions 4 and 5.

4. At age 25, the probability that death will occur within one year is

    (A) 0.00193   (B) 0.0193   (C) 0.193   (D) 1.93

4. ■ Ⓑ Ⓒ Ⓓ

(1.93 ÷ 1000 = 0.00193. Note that (D) is impossible since no probability can exceed 1, which implies certainty of occurrence. Life insurance companies usually refer to the *annual death rate* (per thousand) at a certain age rather than to the probability of death.)

5. The probability, to the nearest tenth, that a 65-year-old person will live at least to age 70 is

    (A) 0.6   (B) 0.7   (C) 0.8   (D) 0.9

5. Ⓐ Ⓑ ■ Ⓓ

(The answer is $\dfrac{\text{number living at age 70}}{\text{number living at age 65}}$.

It is approximately $^{56}/_{68}$, or about 0.82.)

TABLE OF MORTALITY
Commissioners 1958 Standard Ordinary

Age	Number Living	Deaths Each Year	Deaths Per 1,000	Age	Number Living	Deaths Each Year	Deaths Per 1,000	Age	Number Living	Deaths Each Year	Deaths Per 1,000
0	10,000,000	70,800	7.08	34	9,396,358	22,551	2.40	67	6,355,865	241,777	38.04
1	9,929,200	17,475	1.76					68	6,114,088	254,835	41.68
2	9,911,725	15,066	1.52	35	9,373,807	23,528	2.51	69	5,859,253	267,241	45.61
3	9,896,659	14,449	1.46	36	9,350,279	24,685	2.64				
4	9,882,210	13,835	1.40	37	9,325,594	26,112	2.80	70	5,592,012	278,426	49.79
				38	9,299,482	27,991	3.01	71	5,313,586	287,731	54.15
5	9,868,375	13,322	1.35	39	9,271,491	30,132	3.25	72	5,025,855	294,766	58.65
6	9,855,053	12,812	1.30					73	4,731,089	299,289	63.26
7	9,842,241	12,401	1.26	40	9,241,359	32,622	3.53	74	4,431,800	301,894	68.12
8	9,829,840	12,091	1.23	41	9,208,737	35,362	3.84				
9	9,817,749	11,879	1.21	42	9,173,375	38,253	4.17	75	4,129,906	303,011	73.37
				43	9,135,122	41,382	4.53	76	3,826,895	303,014	79.18
10	9,805,870	11,865	1.21	44	9,093,740	44,741	4.92	77	3,523,881	301,997	85.70
11	9,794,005	12,047	1.23					78	3,221,884	299,829	93.06
12	9,781,958	12,325	1.26	45	9,048,999	48,412	5.35	79	2,922,055	295,683	101.19
13	9,769,633	12,896	1.32	46	9,000,587	52,473	5.83				
14	9,756,737	13,562	1.39	47	8,948,114	56,910	6.36	80	2,626,372	288,848	109.98
				48	8,891,204	61,794	6.95	81	2,337,524	278,983	119.35
15	9,743,175	14,225	1.46	49	8,829,410	67,104	7.60	82	2,058,541	265,902	129.17
16	9,728,950	14,983	1.54					83	1,792,639	249,858	139.38
17	9,713,967	15,737	1.62	50	8,762,306	72,902	8.32	84	1,542,781	231,433	150.01
18	9,698,230	16,390	1.69	51	8,689,404	79,160	9.11				
19	9,681,840	16,846	1.74	52	8,610,244	85,758	9.96	85	1,311,348	211,311	161.14
				53	8,524,486	92,832	10.89	86	1,100,037	190,108	172.82
20	9,664,994	17,300	1.79	54	8,431,654	100,337	11.90	87	909,929	168,455	185.13
21	9,647,694	17,655	1.83					88	741,474	146,997	198.25
22	9,630,039	17,912	1.86	55	8,331,317	108,307	13.00	89	594,477	126,303	212.46
23	9,612,127	18,167	1.89	56	8,223,010	116,849	14.21				
24	9,593,960	18,324	1.91	57	8,106,161	125,970	15.54	90	468,174	106,809	228.14
				58	7,980,191	135,663	17.00	91	361,365	88,813	245.77
25	9,575,636	18,481	1.93	59	7,844,528	145,830	18.59	92	272,552	72,480	265.93
26	9,557,155	18,732	1.96					93	200,072	57,881	289.30
27	9,538,423	18,981	1.99	60	7,698,698	156,592	20.34	94	142,191	45,026	316.66
28	9,519,442	19,324	2.03	61	7,542,106	167,736	22.24				
29	9,500,118	19,760	2.08	62	7,374,370	179,271	24.31	95	97,165	34,128	351.24
				63	7,195,099	191,174	26.57	96	63,037	25,250	400.56
30	9,480,358	20,193	2.13	64	7,003,925	203,394	29.04	97	37,787	18,456	488.42
31	9,460,165	20,718	2.19					98	19,331	12,916	668.15
32	9,439,447	21,239	2.25	65	6,800,531	215,917	31.75	99	6,415	6,415	1000.00
33	9,418,208	21,850	2.32	66	6,584,614	228,749	34.74				

Source: Institute of Life Insurance.

PRACTICE QUESTIONS ON PROBABILITY AND STATISTICS

Follow the directions given on page 364. If you can eliminate one or more choices, then guess among the remaining ones. The correct answers and explanations follow the set of questions.

1. The number of different license plates that start with one letter followed by three different digits selected from the set {0,1,2,3,4,5,6,7,8,9} is
   (A) $26 \cdot 10 \cdot 10 \cdot 10$ (B) $26 \cdot 9 \cdot 9 \cdot 9$
   (C) $26 \cdot 10 \cdot 9 \cdot 8$ (D) $16 \cdot 9 \cdot 8 \cdot 7$

   1. Ⓐ Ⓑ Ⓒ Ⓓ

2. The number of different license plates beginning with two different letters followed by two digits either of which may be any digit other than zero is
   (A) $26^2 \cdot 8^2$ (B) $26 \cdot 25 \cdot 9 \cdot 9$
   (C) $26^2 \cdot 9 \cdot 8$ (D) $26^2 \cdot 9^2$

   2. Ⓐ Ⓑ Ⓒ Ⓓ

3. A box contains 6 green pens and 5 red pens. The number of ways of drawing 4 pens if they must all be green is
   (A) 5   (B) 6   (C) 10   (D) 15

   3. Ⓐ Ⓑ Ⓒ Ⓓ

4. How many committees consisting of 3 girls and 2 boys may be selected from a club of 5 girls and 4 boys?
   (A) 6   (B) 20   (C) 60   (D) 72

   4. Ⓐ Ⓑ Ⓒ Ⓓ

5. In how many ways can 2 or more bonus books be selected from a set of 5 offered by a book club?
   (A) 32   (B) 26   (C) 20   (D) 10

   5. Ⓐ Ⓑ Ⓒ Ⓓ

6. The number of different ways a student can answer a 10-question true-false test is
   (A) 2   (B) 20   (C) 10^2 (D) 2^{10}

   6. Ⓐ Ⓑ Ⓒ Ⓓ

7. The probability of obtaining a 5 when an ordinary die is cast is *
   (A) $\frac{1}{3}$ (B) $\frac{1}{4}$ (C) $\frac{1}{5}$ (D) $\frac{1}{6}$

   7. Ⓐ Ⓑ Ⓒ Ⓓ

8. If a penny is tossed 3 times, then the number of different possible outcomes is
   (A) 9   (B) 8   (C) 6   (D) 3

   8. Ⓐ Ⓑ Ⓒ Ⓓ

9. If a penny and a die are tossed, then the probability that the penny shows heads and the die an even number is
   (A) $\frac{1}{4}$ (B) $\frac{1}{3}$ (C) $\frac{1}{2}$ (D) $\frac{2}{3}$

   9. Ⓐ Ⓑ Ⓒ Ⓓ

10. The probability that at least one head shows in a toss of three coins is
    (A) $\frac{1}{8}$ (B) $\frac{3}{8}$ (C) $\frac{1}{2}$ (D) $\frac{7}{8}$

    10. Ⓐ Ⓑ Ⓒ Ⓓ

11. A college that administered two tests to 100 freshmen got the following results: 14 failed both exams; 28 failed the mathematics exam; 33 failed the English exam. The number of students who passed both exams is
    (A) 53   (B) 67   (C) 72   (D) 86

    11. Ⓐ Ⓑ Ⓒ Ⓓ

12. If a letter is chosen at random from the word MISSISSIPPI, the probability that it occurs four times in the word is
    (A) $\frac{4}{11}$ (B) $\frac{1}{2}$ (C) $\frac{8}{11}$ (D) $\frac{10}{11}$

    12. Ⓐ Ⓑ Ⓒ Ⓓ

---

* *In any question on probability in this book, you may assume that a die or coin is fair; that is, that the outcomes (a particular face showing on the die, or head versus tail on the coin) are equally probable.*

13. According to polls, candidates X, Y, and Z have a 0.5, 0.3, and 0.2 chance respectively of winning an election. If candidate Z withdraws, then Y's chance of winning is

(A) 0.375   (B) 0.4   (C) 0.475   (D) 0.5

13. Ⓐ Ⓑ Ⓒ Ⓓ

Use this table on the numbers of Americans living at various ages to answer questions 14 and 15.

AGE	NUMBER LIVING	AGE	NUMBER LIVING
0	100,000	45	91,785
1	98,090	50	89,223
5	97,778	55	85,477
10	97,582	60	80,165
15	97,384	65	72,464
20	96,860	70	52,512
25	96,158	75	49,958
30	95,472	80	35,814
35	94,649	85 and up	21,972
40	93,514		

14. The probability, to the nearest tenth, that a person aged 10 will be alive at 65 is

(A) 0.6   (B) 0.7   (C) 0.8   (D) 0.9

14. Ⓐ Ⓑ Ⓒ Ⓓ

15. The probability, to the nearest tenth, that a person aged 40 will die before he is 80 is

(A) 0.4   (B) 0.5   (C) 0.6   (D) 0.7

15. Ⓐ Ⓑ Ⓒ Ⓓ

16. Based on a sample of 500,000 people, the American Cancer Society estimated that 750 persons would die of cancer in 1973. The probability of death from cancer in 1973 for this sample was

(A) 0.17   (B) 0.015   (C) 0.0017   (D) 0.0015

16. Ⓐ Ⓑ Ⓒ Ⓓ

17. If two cards are drawn from an ordinary deck of cards, the probability that they will both be clubs is

(A) $\frac{1}{18}$ (B) $\frac{1}{17}$ (C) $\frac{1}{16}$ (D) $\frac{1}{15}$

17. Ⓐ Ⓑ Ⓒ Ⓓ

18. The number of distinguishable permutations of letters in the word CANAL is

(A) 31   (B) 4!   (C) 60   (D) 5!

18. Ⓐ Ⓑ Ⓒ Ⓓ

19. The eye-color of students in a class is given by the chart. The probability that a person selected at random is a male or has blue eyes is

	MALES	FEMALES
BROWN EYES	6	4
BLUE EYES	3	7

(A) $\frac{3}{4}$ (B) $\frac{4}{5}$ (C) $\frac{9}{10}$ (D) $\frac{19}{20}$

19. Ⓐ Ⓑ Ⓒ Ⓓ

20. One bag contains 5 black and 3 green marbles. A second bag has 4 black and 2 green marbles. If one marble is chosen from each bag at random, the probability that they are both green is

(A) $\frac{1}{8}$ (B) $\frac{1}{4}$ (C) $\frac{1}{3}$ (D) $\frac{5}{14}$

20. Ⓐ Ⓑ Ⓒ Ⓓ

21. If a pair of dice are cast, then the probability that the sum is greater than 9 is

(A) $\frac{1}{18}$ (B) $\frac{1}{12}$ (C) $\frac{1}{9}$ (D) $\frac{1}{6}$

21. Ⓐ Ⓑ Ⓒ Ⓓ

22. Assume that the probability that it will rain on a day to be selected at random for a picnic is 10%. The probability that a Tuesday will be chosen and that that Tuesday will be dry is

(A) $\frac{10}{9}$ (B) $\frac{9}{10}$ (C) $\frac{9}{70}$ (D) $\frac{1}{70}$

22. Ⓐ Ⓑ Ⓒ Ⓓ

Use the following for questions 23 and 24.

> A college registrar reports the following statistics on 360 students:
> 200 take politics   70 take politics and biology
> 150 take biology   50 take biology and mathematics
> 75 take mathematics   10 take politics and mathematics
>   5 take all three subjects

23. How many students in the report do not take politics, biology, or mathematics?

(A) 0   (B) 30   (C) 60   (D) 100

23. Ⓐ Ⓑ Ⓒ Ⓓ

24. If a student in the report is chosen at random, what is the probability that he studies mathematics but neither politics nor biology?

(A) $1/24$ (B) $1/18$ (C) $1/6$ (D) $5/24$

24. Ⓐ Ⓑ Ⓒ Ⓓ

25. If the average of the set of numbers $\{3, 5, 6, 11, x\}$ is 7, then the median is

(A) 5   (B) $5\frac{1}{2}$ (C) 6   (D) 7

25. Ⓐ Ⓑ Ⓒ Ⓓ

ANSWERS AND EXPLANATIONS

to practice Part II questions on probability and statistics.

1.   C. We can show how to fill the four "slots" in the license plate schematically by

$$26 \times 10 \times 9 \times 8$$
$$\square \quad \square \quad \square \quad \square$$

where the number above a position indicates how many ways it may be filled. Note that a digit may *not* be repeated.

2.   B. Here we have

$$26 \times 25 \times 9 \times 9$$
$$\square \quad \square \quad \square \quad \square$$

The letter may not be repeated, but any of the 9 nonzero digits may be.

3.   D. $C(6,4)$ or its equal, $C(6,2)$, which is $(6 \cdot 5)/(1 \cdot 2)$.

4.   C. $C(5,3) \times C(4,2)$, or $(5 \cdot 4)/(1 \cdot 2) \times (4 \cdot 3)/(1 \cdot 2)$ since $C(5,3) = C(5,2)$.

5.   B. $C(5,2) + C(5,3) + C(5,4) + C(5,5)$.

6.   D. The first may be answered in 2 ways, after which the second may be answered in 2 ways, after which the third and so on. This yields $2 \times 2 \times 2 \ldots \times 2$, where there are 10 twos, or 2^{10}. Note for just 3 T-F questions that there are 8 different ways of answering them.

7.   D. There are six possible outcomes, of which obtaining 5 is one outcome.

8. **B.** A tree diagram may be useful:

There are 8 possible outcomes. Note that the answer is obtainable immediately from

$$2 \times 2 \times 2$$
□ □ □

where there are 2 outcomes on the first toss, then 2 on the second, then 2 on the third.

9. **A.** The probability that the penny shows heads is $\frac{1}{2}$ and that the die shows an even number is $\frac{1}{2}$. The answer is the product since the events are independent.

10. **D.** The tree in the answer to question 8 shows that at least one H occurs in 7 of 8 possible outcomes. Or note that the probability of getting all (3) tails is $\frac{1}{2} \times \frac{1}{2} \times \frac{1}{2}$, or $\frac{1}{8}$; so the answer is $1 - \frac{1}{8}$.

11. **A.** Draw a Venn diagram. Since $14 + 14 + 19$, or 47, students failed one or both exams, it follows that $100 - 47$ passed both.

failed math   failed English

14   14   19

12. **C.** There are 11 letters in MISSISSIPPI; 8 of them are I or S.

13. **A.** Assuming that the chances for X and Y are increased proportionately when Z withdraws, then Y's chances become

$$\frac{0.3}{0.5 + 0.3}$$

14. **B.** $\dfrac{72,464}{97,582} \approx \dfrac{72}{98} \approx 0.7.$

15. **C.** $\dfrac{93,514 - 35,814}{93,514} \approx \dfrac{58}{94} \approx 0.6.$

16. **D.** $\dfrac{750}{500,000} = 0.0015.$

17. **B.** $\dfrac{_{13}C_2}{_{52}C_2} = \dfrac{13 \cdot 12}{1 \cdot 2} \div \dfrac{52 \cdot 51}{1 \cdot 2} = \dfrac{13 \cdot 12}{52 \cdot 51} = \dfrac{1}{17}.$

18. **C.** If the two A's were distinguishable (perhaps subscripted), there would be 5! permutations. We divide by 2 to eliminate identical pairs of permutations.

19. **B.** If M is the set of males and B the set of blue-eyed people, then we want

$$\frac{P(M \cup B)}{\text{number in the class}} = \frac{6 + 3 + 7}{20} = \frac{4}{5}.$$

20. **A.** $\dfrac{C(3,1)}{8} \times \dfrac{C(2,1)}{6} = \dfrac{3}{8} \times \dfrac{1}{3} = \dfrac{1}{8}.$

21.　D. There are 6 × 6 or 36 possible outcomes when the pair of dice is cast. A sum that exceeds 9 can be obtained in the following six ways:

DIE I	DIE II
4	6
5	6
5	5
6	6
6	5
6	4

Therefore the probability of the event is $^6/_{36}$.

22.　C. The two events, day of the week selected and whether it rains, are independent. The desired product is $^1/_7 × ^9/_{10}$.

23.　C. A Venn diagram helps.

24.　B. Since 20 students out of 360 take mathematics but neither politics nor biology, the answer is $^{20}/_{360}$, or $^1/_{18}$.

25.　C. $(3 + 5 + 6 + 11 + x) ÷ 5 = 7 → (25 + x) ÷ 5 = 7 → x = 10$. The median of the set {3, 5, 6, 10, 11} is the middle number, 6.

B6.　Miscellaneous Topics

The subtopics are: complex numbers; number bases; logarithms and exponentials; newly defined binary operations; identity, and inverse elements.
Here are some illustrative examples.

ANSWERS

1.　If for all elements p, q, r in a mathematical system, $p(q + r) = pq + pr$, then the system satisfies
(A) the commutative law for addition
(B) the commutative law for multiplication
(C) a distributive law
(D) an associative law

1.　Ⓐ Ⓑ ■ Ⓓ

2. If $i = \sqrt{-1}$, then $i^7 =$

2. Ⓐ Ⓑ Ⓒ ■

   (A) 1   (B) -1 (C) i (D) $-i$

(Note that $i^2 = -1$ and $i^4 = (-1)(-1) = 1$; thus $i^7 = i^4 \cdot i^2 \cdot i = (1)(-1)(i) = -i$.)

3. 1001_2 equals what numeral base 10?

3. Ⓐ ■ Ⓒ Ⓓ

   (A) 17   (B) 9   (C) 5   (D) 2

$(1001_2 = 1 \times 2^3 + 0 \times 2^2 + 0 \times 2^1 + 1 \times 2^0 = 8 + 0 + 0 + 1 = 9.)$

4. If $\log_b 2 = r$ and $\log_b 3 = s$, then $\log_b 18 =$

4. ■ Ⓑ Ⓒ Ⓓ

   (A) $r + 2s$ (B) $2r + s$ (C) $2rs$ (D) r^2s

(Since $18 = 2 \cdot 3^2$, $\log_b 18 = \log_b 2 + \log_b 3^2 = \log_b 2 + 2\log_b 3 = r + 2s.$)

PRACTICE QUESTIONS ON MISCELLANEOUS TOPICS

Follow the directions given on page 364. If you can eliminate one or more choices, then guess among the remaining ones. The correct answers and explanations follow the set of questions.

1. If the product of every pair of elements in a set is an element of the set, then

1. Ⓐ Ⓑ Ⓒ Ⓓ

   (A) the operation is commutative   (B) the set is closed
   (C) the set is a group   (D) the operation is associative

Use this multiplication table for questions 2 through 4.

+	p	q	r	s
p	p	q	r	s
q	q	r	s	p
r	r	s	p	q
s	s	p	q	r

2. The sum $(r + s)$ equals

2. Ⓐ Ⓑ Ⓒ Ⓓ

   (A) p (B) q (C) r (D) s

3. The identity element is

3. Ⓐ Ⓑ Ⓒ Ⓓ

   (A) p (B) q (C) r (D) s

4. The additive inverse of q is

4. Ⓐ Ⓑ Ⓒ Ⓓ

   (A) p (B) q (C) r (D) s

Use this multiplication table for questions 5–8.

×	0	1	2	3
0	0	0	0	0
1	0	1	2	3
2	0	2	0	2
3	0	3	2	1

5. According to the table, $(2 \times 3) \times 2$ equals

   (A) 0   (B) 1   (C) 2   (D) 3

5. A B C D

6. The multiplicative identity is

   (A) 0   (B) 1   (C) 2   (D) 3

6. A B C D

7. The inverse of 3 is

   (A) 0   (B) 1   (C) 2   (D) 3

7. A B C D

8. Which of the following is false?

   (A) The operation is commutative.

   (B) The set is closed.

   (C) The operation is associative.

   (D) Every element has a multiplicative inverse in the set.

8. A B C D

9. The roots of the equation $x^2 + 2 = 0$ are

   (A) $\pm\sqrt{2}$ (B) $+2i$ (where $i = \sqrt{-1}$)

   (C) $\pm i\sqrt{2}$ (D) $\pm\sqrt{2i}$

9. A B C D

10. If $\log_a 2 = p$ and $\log_a 3 = s$, then $\log_a \dfrac{9}{2} =$

   (A) $\dfrac{2s}{p}$ (B) $2s - p$ (C) $\dfrac{s^2}{p}$ (D) $2s + \dfrac{1}{p}$

10. A B C D

11. $(a^x)^y =$

   (A) a^{x+y} (B) $a^x \cdot a^y$ (C) a^{xy} (D) ya^x

11. A B C D

12. $(2 + i)(3 - i)$, where $i = \sqrt{-1}$, equals

   (A) 7   (B) 5   (C) $5 + i$ (D) $7 + i$

12. A B C D

13. If the roots of $x^2 + 2x + d = 0$ are real, then d *cannot* equal

   (A) 2   (B) 1   (C) 0   (D) -1

13. A B C D

14. If $p * q = p + pq - 1$, then $a * -1$ equals

   (A) $a + 1$ (B) $-a + 1$ (C) $-a - 1$ (D) -1

14. A B C D

15. If $f(x) = ax^3 + bx^2 + cx + d$ and $f(-1) = 0$, then f must be divisible by

   (A) x (B) $x - 1$ (C) $x + 1$ (D) $x^2 - 1$

15. A B C D

16. $1001_2 + 11_2 =$

   (A) 1010_2 (B) 1100_2 (C) 1110_2 (D) 1111_2

16. A B C D

17. $\dfrac{2^p}{2^{p+q}} =$

   (A) 2^q (B) 2^{2p-q} (C) 2^{-q} (D) $\dfrac{1}{q}$

17. A B C D

18. If $\log_3 p = m$ and $\log_3 q = 2m$, then $\log_3 pq =$

   (A) $2m$ (B) $3m$ (C) $6m$ (D) $3m^2$

18. A B C D

19. Which set is not closed under ordinary multiplication?

   (A) $\{0, 1\}$ (B) $\{-1, 1\}$ (C) $\{1, 2\}$ (D) $\{-1, 0, 1\}$

19. A B C D

20. If $3^{x+1} = 3$, then $x =$
(A) 0   (B) 1   (C) 2   (D) −1

21. Which of the following is the graph of $y = \log_2 x$?

22. 10110_2 corresponds to the base-ten number
(A) 14   (B) 20   (C) 22   (D) 28

23. Let $f(x) = x^3 - 2x^2 - x + d$. If $f(1) = 0$, then the roots of $f(x) = 0$ are
(A) 1, 2, and −2   (B) 1, −1, and −2
(C) −1, 2, and −2   (D) 1, −1, and 2

24. $\sqrt{3} \cdot \sqrt{-27} =$
(A) −9   (B) $-9i$ (where $i = \sqrt{-1}$)
(C) $9i$ (D) 9

25. Which equation does *not* have real roots?
(A) $x^2 + 1 = 0$ (B) $x^2 - 2 = 0$
(C) $x^2 + x - 1 = 0$ (D) $x^2 + 4x = 0$

ANSWERS AND EXPLANATIONS
to practice Part II questions on miscellaneous topics.

1.   B. A set S is closed under an operation $\times$ if, for every pair of elements a, b in S, the "product" $a \times b$ is in S.
2.   B. To find the sum of r and s we move across the r row until we come to the column headed s.
3.   A. If e is the identity of a set of elements S under an operation $*$ and x is *any* element of S, then $x * e = e * x = x$. To find e from a table, look for the row which is identical with the row across the top of the table; the element to the left of this row is the identity.

4. D. The inverse element for q is the one such that q "plus" it yields the identity. Since p is the identity for this table, and $q + s = p$, s is the inverse of q. (Note, also, that $s + q = p$.)

5. A. $(2 \times 3) \times 2 = 2 \times 2 = 0$.

6. B. If e denotes the multiplicative identity and a is any element in the set, then $a \times e = e \times a = a$. Look for a column (or row) that is the same as the lead column (or row).

7. D. Since 1 is the identity and $3 \times 3 = 1$, 3 is its own inverse.

8. D. Neither 0 nor 2 has an inverse. Note that there is no element such that the product of 2 with it yields 1.

9. C. $x^2 = -2 \rightarrow x = \pm\sqrt{-2} = \pm\sqrt{2}i$ or $\pm i\sqrt{2}$.

10. B. $\log_a \frac{9}{2} = \log_a 9 - \log_a 2 = \log_a 3^2 - \log_a 2 = 2\log_a 3 - \log_a 2 = 2s - p$.

11. C. Note if x and y are integers that $(a^x)^y$ indicates a product of y factors, each equal to a^x.

$$(a^x)^y = \underbrace{a^x \cdot a^x \cdots a^x}_{y \text{ factors}} = \underbrace{a^{x+x+\cdots+x}}_{y \text{ addends}} = a^{xy}$$

12. D. $(2 + i)(3 - i) = (2)(3) + (2)(-i) + (i)(3) + (i)(-i)$
    $= 6 + i - i^2 = 6 + i - (-1) = 7 + i$.

13. A. If the roots of $ax^2 + bx + c = 0$ are real, then $b^2 - 4ac \geq 0$. Here $a = 1$, $b = 2$, $c = d$, so $b^2 - 4ac = 4 - 4d$, which is greater than zero if $d \leq 1$.

14. D. With $p = a$, $q = -1$, we get $a * -1 = a + a(-1) - 1 = -1$.

15. C. If $f(x)$ is a polynomial and $f(r) = 0$, then $f(x)$ is divisible by $(x - r)$. The converse is also true. These follow from the so-called *factor* and *remainder theorems* of algebra.

16. B. Note how we add in base 2:

$$
\begin{array}{r}
\text{eights} \; \text{fours} \; \text{twos} \; \text{units} \\
1 \; 1 \quad\quad \\
1 \; 0 \; 0 \; 1 \\
+ \quad\quad 1 \; 1 \\
\hline
1 \; 1 \; 0 \; 0
\end{array}
$$

Here we replaced $1 + 1$ (or 2) in the units column by 10, $1 + 1$ in the twos column by 100.

17. C. $\frac{2^p}{2^{p+q}} = 2^{p-(p+q)} = 2^{p-p-q} = 2^{-q}$.

18. B. $\log_3 pq = \log_3 p + \log_3 q = m + 2m = 3m$.

19. C. Note for the set $\{1, 2\}$ that $2 \cdot 2 = 4$, which is not in the set. Verify that the other sets are all closed under ordinary multiplication.

20. A. $3^{x+1} = 3 = 3^1 \rightarrow x + 1 = 1 \rightarrow x = 0$.

21. C. Some of the properties of the graph of $y = \log_2 x$ are: $\log_2 1 = 0$, the domain is $\{x : x > 0\}$. Only the graph in (C) satisfies these.

22. C. $10110_2 = 1 \times 2^4 + 0 \times 2^3 + 1 \times 2^2 + 1 \times 2^1 + 0 \times 2^0$
    $= \quad 2^4 + \quad 0 + \quad 2^2 + \quad 2^1 + \quad 0$
    $= 22$.

23. D. $f(1) = 1^3 - 2(1)^2 - 1 + d = d - 2$.
    Since $f(1) = 0$, $d = 2$ and $f(x) = x^3 - 2x^2 - x + 2$.
    Since $f(1) = 0$, $x - 1$ is a factor of $f(x)$.
    Indeed, $x^3 - 2x^2 - x + 2 = (x - 1)(x + 1)(x - 2)$.

24. C. $\sqrt{3} \cdot \sqrt{-27} = \sqrt{3} \cdot \sqrt{27} \cdot \sqrt{-1} = \sqrt{81} \cdot i = 9i$.

25. A. The roots in (A) are $\pm i$; verify that the roots of the others are all real. Remember, the roots of $ax^2 + bx + c = 0$ are

$$x = \frac{-b \pm \sqrt{b^2 - 4ac}}{2a};$$

the roots are real only if $b^2 - 4ac \geq 0$.

Sample Examinations

This chapter has three sample CLEP mathematics examinations. Each examination is followed by an answer key and reference chart, a scoring chart, and answer explanations. The mathematics examination consists both of Part I on Basic Skills and Concepts and Part II on Content. As noted earlier, Part I contains 40 questions, some of the quantitative-comparison type and some of the regular multiple-choice type; Part II has 50 questions, all of the regular multiple-choice type.

Remember that the examination is timed with 90 minutes allowed *altogether* for both parts. However, you will be allowed to *work only on the first part during the first 30 minutes* and *only on the second part during the last 60 minutes*. If you finish Part I before time is called, do *not* go on to Part II; instead, check over your answers in Part I. If you finish Part II before time is called, do *not* go back to Part I; instead, check over Part II. It is recommended that you observe this timing when taking each of the four sample tests in this book.

It is very important that you do not spend too much time on any one question. It is best to answer first those questions that you are pretty sure about, returning after you've gone through the entire examination to those questions that need more thought or work. Keep track of the time so you can pace yourself, remembering that it is not expected that anyone taking the test will answer every question.

For a reminder about the major topics that are covered in each part and the approximate number of questions for each topic, see page 328. The scoring of the examination and whether or not to guess are discussed on page 329.

It will probably be helpful at this point to reread the tips on answering questions involving data interpretation (page 349) and on handling questions of the quantitative-comparison type (pages 356-57). Here are some further reminders and tips:

(1) Read the test directions carefully and study any illustrative examples.

(2) Pay attention to any notes about figures. In Part II, figures are intended to provide information useful in answering the questions and are drawn as accurately as possible *except* when specifically noted otherwise.

(3) Answer the easy questions first, putting a check by, or encircling, the number of any question you skip. Go back to the latter if you have time.

(4) Skip any question on a topic with which you are not familiar.

(5) Guess intelligently; avoid wild guessing.

(6) When practicing it is often worthwhile to verify that choices not selected are truly incorrect. However, when taking the actual examination it would be needlessly time-consuming (and therefore foolish) to do that. When you decide on the answer to a particular question, mark it in the proper box and move on immediately to the next question.

(7) Work steadily, trying not to be careless.

(8) Pace yourself but try to take a breather or two in each part.

(9) Keep cool. Remember that practically no one answers every question.

(10) Even though the answer column may have five answer boxes for each question, labeled A, B, C, D, and E, you are to choose the *one* correct answer from among A, B, C, and D. Do not make any marks whatever in column E.

SAMPLE EXAMINATION 1

Part I: Basic Skills and Concepts

Directions for questions 1–25: Each question consists of two quantities, one in Column A and one in Column B. You are to compare the two quantities and in the answer column blacken space

    A if the quantity in Column A is greater;
    B if the quantity in Column B is greater;
    C if the two quantities are equal;
    D if the relationship cannot be determined from the information given.

Notes:
1. In certain questions, information concerning one or both of the quantities to be compared is centered above the two columns.
2. A symbol that appears in both columns represents the same thing in Column A as it does in Column B.
3. Letters such as x, n, and k stand for real numbers.

QUESTIONS	COLUMN A	COLUMN B	
1.	3^2	2^3	1. Ⓐ Ⓑ Ⓒ Ⓓ
2.	$3/4 \div 3$	0.25	2. Ⓐ Ⓑ Ⓒ Ⓓ
3.	a fraction between $1/3$ and $1/5$	$1/4$	3. Ⓐ Ⓑ Ⓒ Ⓓ
4.	$(1 - 0.01)(1 + 0.1)(1/10)$	$(0.1)(1.1)(0.99)$	4. Ⓐ Ⓑ Ⓒ Ⓓ
5.	Angles X and Y are supplementary; $m(\angle X) = 109°10'$.		5. Ⓐ Ⓑ Ⓒ Ⓓ
	number of degrees in $\angle Y$	70	

6.	y	$2x$	6. Ⓐ Ⓑ Ⓒ Ⓓ

Use this chart for questions 7 and 8.

DOW-JONES AVERAGE OF 30 INDUSTRIALS: YEARLY RANGES

QUESTIONS	COLUMN A	COLUMN B	
7.	the number of points difference in the high and low Dow-Jones averages for the year when that difference was greatest	225	**7.** A B C D
8.	the low Dow-Jones average in 1972	the high Dow-Jones average for 1970	**8.** A B C D
9.	the cost of 4 candy bars if a dozen bars cost 35¢	14¢	**9.** A B C D
10.	2.9×10^{-4}	0.000029	**10.** A B C D
11.	The average of Paul's test grades is 76.		**11.** A B C C
	grade Paul must get on next test to average 80	88	
12.	$2^{3}/_{10}$ expressed as a percent	203%	**12.** A B C D
13.	$\sqrt{4} + \sqrt{9}$	$\sqrt{13}$	**13.** A B C D
14.	$r = -1, s = 1, t = 3$		**14.** A B C D
	$2s - (r + t)$	0	
15.	$|x|$	x	**15.** A B C D
16.	the product of the roots of $x^2 + 2x - 3 = 0$	the sum of the roots of $x^2 + 2x - 3 = 0$	**16.** A B C D
17.	$3 \times (2 + 8)$	$3 \times 2 + 8$	**17.** A B C D
18.	$\frac{x^r}{x^s}$ is written as x^q, and $q = 0$.		**18.** A B C D
	r	s	
	$\begin{cases} 5x - y = 11 \\ \quad x = y + 3 \end{cases}$		
19.	y	1	**19.** A B C D

A bag contains red, green, blue, and white marbles. The ratio of green marbles to red is 1 : 2.

20.	ratio of green marbles to the total number	1 : 2	**20.** A B C D

$VT \perp ST$

$VR \perp RS$

21.	$m + n$	180	**21.** A B C D

A central angle of a circle measures 24° and intercepts an arc *MN*.

22.   ratio of arc *MN* to the cir-   1 : 16   22. Ⓐ Ⓑ Ⓒ Ⓓ
         cumference of the circle

Use this chart for questions 23, 24, and 25.

Average annual percentage increase in the consumer price index, all services and medical care services for selected periods

Source: *Consumer Price Index, Bureau of Labor Statistics. Social Security Bulletin, July 1967, p. 17.*

23.   average annual increase in CPI   average annual in-   23. Ⓐ Ⓑ Ⓒ Ⓓ
         as a whole for the period   crease in CPI as a
         1946-1960   whole for the period
                                           1965-1966

24.   average annual percentage   5.4   24. Ⓐ Ⓑ Ⓒ Ⓓ
         increase for medical services for
         the year 1966

QUESTIONS	COLUMN A	COLUMN B	
25.	decrease in average annual percentage increase for all services from that for the period 1946-60 to that for the period 1960-65	1.9	25. Ⓐ Ⓑ Ⓒ Ⓓ

Directions for questions 26–40: For these questions, indicate the correct answer in the appropriate space in the answer column.

Note: Figures that accompany the following problems are intended to provide information useful in answering the questions. The figures are drawn as accurately as possible *except* when it is stated in a specific question that the figure is not drawn to scale. All figures lie in a plane unless otherwise stated.

26. $4.05 =$
    (A) $9/2$ (B) $21/5$ (C) $81/20$ (D) $81/25$

26. Ⓐ Ⓑ Ⓒ Ⓓ

27. $(y^2 - 3y + 2) - (2y^2 + 3y - 2) =$
    (A) $3y^2$ (B) $-y^2 - 6y + 4$ (C) $-y^2$ (D) $-y^2 + 4$

27. Ⓐ Ⓑ Ⓒ Ⓓ

28. If two positive numbers are in the ratio 6 to 11 and differ by 15, then the smaller number is
    (A) 3   (B) 6   (C) 12   (D) 18

28. Ⓐ Ⓑ Ⓒ Ⓓ

29. If $0.0328 = 3.28 \times 10^k$, then $k =$
    (A) -4 (B) -3 (C) -2 (D) 2

29. Ⓐ Ⓑ Ⓒ Ⓓ

30.   *Note: Figure is not drawn to scale.*

30. Ⓐ Ⓑ Ⓒ Ⓓ

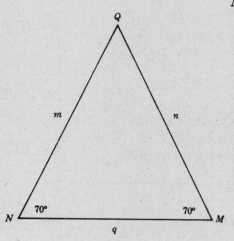

Which of the following statements is false?
(A) $m = n$ (B) $q > n$ (C) $m > q$ (D) $n > q$

Use this figure for questions 31 and 32.

TELEPHONES AND MAIL

Phones (per 1,000 population)
1950   281
1960   408
1965   478
1969   563

Average daily calls (in millions)
1950   176
1960   285
1965   367
1969   462

First Class and Airmail (pieces per capita)
1950   168
1960   193
1965   205
1969   238

Source: Pocket Data Book, USA 1971, Figure 65, p. 292

31. Approximately how many million average daily calls does one telephone dial represent?
 (A) 25   (B) 35   (C) 50   (D) 176

31. Ⓐ Ⓑ Ⓒ Ⓓ

32. By approximately what percentage did phones (per 1000 population) increase from 1950 to 1969?
 (A) 100   (B) 200   (C) 281   (D) 282

32. Ⓐ Ⓑ Ⓒ Ⓓ

33. $(5x + 3)(2x - 3) =$
 (A) $10x^2 - 9x$ (B) $10x^2 + 9x - 9$
 (C) $10x^2 - 2x - 9$ (D) $10x^2 - 9x - 9$

33. Ⓐ Ⓑ Ⓒ Ⓓ

34. The y-intercept of the line $2x - 3y + 9 = 0$ is
 (A) 3   (B) -3 (C) $-4\frac{1}{2}$ (D) -9

34. Ⓐ Ⓑ Ⓒ Ⓓ

35. If the dimensions of a box are all doubled, then the ratio of the volume of the larger to that of the smaller is
 (A) $2:1$ (B) $4:1$ (C) $6:1$ (D) $8:1$

35. Ⓐ Ⓑ Ⓒ Ⓓ

36. The area of a circle is 4π square inches. Its circumference equals
 (A) π (B) 2π (C) 4π (D) 8π

36. Ⓐ Ⓑ Ⓒ Ⓓ

37. $3^2 - 3^0 - 3^{-2} =$
 (A) -1 (B) $7\frac{1}{9}$ (C) $7\frac{8}{9}$ (D) $8\frac{1}{9}$

37. Ⓐ Ⓑ Ⓒ Ⓓ

38. $(0.02) \times (0.004) =$

    (A) 0.000008   (B) 0.00008   (C) 0.0008   (D) 0.008

38. Ⓐ Ⓑ Ⓒ Ⓓ

39.

Which point above has coordinates $(2, -1)$?

    (A) P (B) Q (C) R (D) S

39. Ⓐ Ⓑ Ⓒ Ⓓ

40. A car travels a scenic route of 15 miles in 30 minutes and the 60-mile balance of a trip in one hour. Its average speed for the trip is

    (A) 40 mph   (B) 45 mph   (C) 50 mph   (D) 55 mph

40. Ⓐ Ⓑ Ⓒ Ⓓ

Part II: Content

Directions: For each of the following problems, indicate the correct answer in the appropriate space in the answer column.

Note: Figures that accompany problems in this part are intended to provide information useful in solving the problems. They are drawn as accurately as possible *except* when it is stated in a specific problem that the figure is not drawn to scale. All figures lie in a plane unless otherwise indicated.

41. If $R = \{a,b,c,w\}$ and $S = \{a,c,d,w\}$, then $R \cap S$ equals

    (A) $\{a,b,c,d,w\}$ (B) $\{a\}$

    (C) $\{a,c\}$ (D) $\{a,c,w\}$

41. Ⓐ Ⓑ Ⓒ Ⓓ

42. The solution set of $\{x : x$ is a real number and $x^3 - x^2 - 2x = 0\}$ is

    (A) $\{0,1,2\}$ (B) $\{0,-1,2\}$

    (C) $\{-1,2\}$ (D) $\{0,1,-2\}$

42. Ⓐ Ⓑ Ⓒ Ⓓ

43. Let Z, Q, R denote respectively the sets of integers, of rationals, and of reals. Then it is false that

    (A) $(3, 5) \in Z \times Z$ (B) $Z \times Z \subset Q \times Q$

    (C) $(1, 1) \in Q \times Q$ (D) $Q \subset R \times R$

43. Ⓐ Ⓑ Ⓒ Ⓓ

44. Which of the following sets is not infinite?

    (A) the set of multiples of 3

    (B) the set of prime numbers

    (C) the set of subsets of the set $\{1,2,3, \ldots , 100\}$

    (D) the set of integers less than -100

44. Ⓐ Ⓑ Ⓒ Ⓓ

45. Let p denote "Warren wears braces" and let q denote "Warren wears glasses." Then the statement "Warren wears neither braces nor glasses" is written symbolically as

(A) $\sim(p \wedge q)$ (B) $\sim p \vee q$ (C) $\sim p \wedge \sim q$ (D) $\sim p \wedge q$

45. Ⓐ Ⓑ Ⓒ Ⓓ

46. If $\log_2 2^x = 3$, then $x =$

(A) 8   (B) 6   (C) 3   (D) 2

46. Ⓐ Ⓑ Ⓒ Ⓓ

47. To prove that there is a rational number between every pair of rational numbers,

(A) take a pair, such as $\frac{1}{2}$ and $\frac{1}{3}$, and find a rational number between them

(B) show that the statement is true for several different pairs of rational numbers

(C) consider in order every pair of rational numbers and show in each case that there is a rational number between them

(D) let p and q denote any pair of rational numbers, and show that $(p + q)/2$ is a rational number between p and q

47. Ⓐ Ⓑ Ⓒ Ⓓ

48. The negation of "every college graduate has studied geometry" is

(A) some college graduates have not studied geometry

(B) no college graduate has studied geometry

(C) geometry is not necessary for graduation from college

(D) if a person has studied geometry then he is not a college graduate

48. Ⓐ Ⓑ Ⓒ Ⓓ

49. The truth table of $p \rightarrow q$ is

49. Ⓐ Ⓑ Ⓒ Ⓓ

p	q	(A)	(B)	(C)	(D)
T	T	T	T	T	T
T	F	F	F	F	F
F	T	T	F	F	T
F	F	F	F	T	T

50. A counterexample to the claim that $(a^2 > b^2) \rightarrow (a > b)$ is

(A) $a = 3, b = 2$ (B) $a = -2, b = -1$

(C) $a = 1, b = 0$ (D) $a = \frac{1}{2}, b = \frac{1}{3}$

50. Ⓐ Ⓑ Ⓒ Ⓓ

51. $|b - 1| =$

(A) $b - 1$ (B) $1 - b$ (C) $b + 1$ (D) none of the preceding

51. Ⓐ Ⓑ Ⓒ Ⓓ

52. Which of the following fractions cannot be written as a terminating decimal?

(A) $\frac{2}{7}$ (B) $\frac{5}{16}$ (C) $\frac{17}{40}$ (D) $\frac{19}{25}$

52. Ⓐ Ⓑ Ⓒ Ⓓ

53. Which of the laws below holds for real numbers?

(A) division is commutative

(B) subtraction is associative

(C) $(a + b) \div c = (a \div c) + (b \div c)$

(D) $a - b = b - a$

53. Ⓐ Ⓑ Ⓒ Ⓓ

54. Which of the following cannot be a rational number?   54. Ⓐ Ⓑ Ⓒ Ⓓ
   (A) the sum of two irrational numbers
   (B) the product of two irrational numbers
   (C) the sum of a rational number and an irrational number
   (D) the quotient of two irrational numbers

55. If $f(x) = 2x^2 - 3x + 2$, then $f(-x) =$ 55. Ⓐ Ⓑ Ⓒ Ⓓ
   (A) $2x^2 + 3x + 2$ (B) $-2x^2 + 3x - 2$
   (C) $-2x^2 + 3x + 2$ (D) $-f(x)$

56. Which of the following equations has a graph that is symmetric to the   56. Ⓐ Ⓑ Ⓒ Ⓓ
   x-axis?
   (A) $y = x$ (B) $y = x^2 + 3$ (C) $y^2 = x$ (D) $y = x^3 - x$

57. If $f(x) = x + \dfrac{4}{x}$ and $g(x) = \sqrt{x + 4}$, then $f(g(0))$ is   57. Ⓐ Ⓑ Ⓒ Ⓓ
   (A) 2   (B) 3   (C) 4   (D) undefined

58.   The graph of $\begin{cases} y \geqq 1 - x \\ x^2 + y^2 \leqq 4 \\ x \geqq 0, y \geqq 0 \end{cases}$ is   58. Ⓐ Ⓑ Ⓒ Ⓓ

59. Which graph of points, shown below, is not that of a function of x?   59. Ⓐ Ⓑ Ⓒ Ⓓ

60. If $f(x) = x^2 - 3x - 1$, then $f(1 + h) - f(1)$ equals

    (A) $h^2 - h - 3$ (B) $h^2 - h - 6$ (C) $h^2 + 5h$ (D) $h^2 - h$

60. Ⓐ Ⓑ Ⓒ Ⓓ

Use this table for questions 61, 62, and 63.

*	r	s	t	u
r	r	r	r	r
s	r	s	t	u
t	r	t	r	t
u	r	u	t	s

61. $(t * t) * t$ equals

    (A) r (B) s (C) t (D) u

61. Ⓐ Ⓑ Ⓒ Ⓓ

62. The inverse of u is

    (A) r (B) s (C) t (D) u

62. Ⓐ Ⓑ Ⓒ Ⓓ

63. Which of the statements below is not true?

    (A) The set has an identity.

    (B) The operation is commutative.

    (C) Every element has an inverse.

    (D) The set is closed under $*$.

63. Ⓐ Ⓑ Ⓒ Ⓓ

64. The number of different 2-digit numerals that can be formed if the digits 2, 4, 6, 7, and 9 are used, and repetitions are permitted, is

    (A) 10   (B) 20   (C) 25   (D) 32

64. Ⓐ Ⓑ Ⓒ Ⓓ

65. If the probability that an egg will hatch is 0.20, then the odds in favor of its hatching are

    (A) $\frac{1}{5}$ (B) 1 to 5   (C) $\frac{1}{4}$ (D) 1 to 4

65. Ⓐ Ⓑ Ⓒ Ⓓ

66. If a die is tossed twice the probability of getting a 4 on both tosses is

    (A) $\frac{1}{36}$ (B) $\frac{1}{12}$ (C) $\frac{1}{6}$ (D) $\frac{1}{4}$

66. Ⓐ Ⓑ Ⓒ Ⓓ

67. Two machine parts are chosen in sequence from a set of 10 of which 3 are known to be defective. The probability that both will be okay is

    (A) $\frac{21}{50}$ (B) $\frac{7}{15}$ (C) $\frac{4}{15}$ (D) $\frac{1}{15}$

67. Ⓐ Ⓑ Ⓒ Ⓓ

68. The largest value of the function $f(x) = -2(x + 1)^2 + 3$ is

    (A) 3   (B) 2   (C) 1   (D) -1

68. Ⓐ Ⓑ Ⓒ Ⓓ

69. A simple closed curve is one that starts and stops at the same point without passing through any point twice. Which of the following is a simple closed curve?

69. Ⓐ Ⓑ Ⓒ Ⓓ

    (A)   (B)   (C)   (D)

70. Suppose $q < 0$ in the equation $x^2 + px + q = 0$. Then
   (A) the equation has no real roots
   (B) the equation has one real root
   (C) the equation has two real unequal roots
   (D) the roots must both be positive

71. Which statement about real numbers is false?
   (A) If $\frac{a}{b} = \frac{c}{d}$ $(bd \neq 0)$, then $a = c$ and $b = d$.
   (B) If $ab \neq 0$, then neither a nor b can equal 0.
   (C) If $\frac{a}{b} = c$ and $b \neq 0$, then $a = bc$.
   (D) $1 \div (ab) = (1 \div a)(1 \div b)$ if $ab \neq 0$.

72. The graph is for the function
   $y = f(x) =$
   (A) 2^x
   (B) 2^{-x}
   (C) $\log_2 x$
   (D) 3^{-x}

73. A test shows that 10 out of 100 bulbs are defective. If a random sample of 2 bulbs is chosen, then the probability that both are defective is
   (A) $^1/_{110}$ (B) 0.01   (C) 0.02   (D) $^1/_{10}$

74. If the length of one leg of an isosceles right triangle is an integer x, then which statement is false?
   (A) The hypotenuse has length $x\sqrt{2}$.
   (B) The altitude to the hypotenuse equals one half the hypotenuse.
   (C) The length of the hypotenuse is a rational number for appropriate values of x.
   (D) The area of the triangle equals $\frac{x^2}{2}$.

75. If $23_{\text{TEN}} = n_{\text{TWO}}$, then n equals
   (A) 10101   (B) 10111   (C) 11001   (D) 11011

76. The largest prime factor of 1040 is
   (A) 2   (B) 5   (C) 13   (D) 17

77. Which of the following statements is false?
   (A) The intersection of the sets of irrational and rational real numbers is empty.
   (B) The set of natural numbers is not a subset of the set of rational numbers.
   (C) The set of real numbers is a proper subset of the set of complex numbers.
   (D) 0 is an integer.

78. Two cards are simultaneously drawn from an ordinary deck of 52 cards. The probability that they are not both of the same suit is

(A) $\frac{4}{17}$ (B) $\frac{5}{17}$ (C) $\frac{12}{17}$ (D) $\frac{13}{17}$

78. Ⓐ Ⓑ Ⓒ Ⓓ

79. Which one of the following tables defines a function $y = f(x)$?

79. Ⓐ Ⓑ Ⓒ Ⓓ

(A)

x	1	1	2
y	3	4	5

(B)

x	0	0	1
y	−1	1	2

(C)

x	−1	0	1	1
y	0	1	2	3

(D)

x	1	2	3	4
y	2	2	2	2

80. Which number is prime?
(A) 4   (B) 5   (C) 25   (D) 39

80. Ⓐ Ⓑ Ⓒ Ⓓ

81. The prime factors of 96 are
(A) 2 and 3   (B) 6 and 8   (C) 2, 3, and 4   (D) 8 and 12

81. Ⓐ Ⓑ Ⓒ Ⓓ

82. If $y > 0 > x$, then which of the following is necessarily positive?
(A) $y + x$ (B) $y - x$ (C) $y^2 + x$ (D) $x^2 - 1$

82. Ⓐ Ⓑ Ⓒ Ⓓ

83. If $(x + 1)$ is a factor of $f(x) = x^3 - 2x^2 + 3x + d$, then $d =$
(A) −2   (B) −1   (C) 2   (D) 6

83. Ⓐ Ⓑ Ⓒ Ⓓ

84. Let $f(x) = x + 2$ and $g(x) = x^2$; let p and q be the statements that the point (x,y) lies on the graph of f and on that of g, respectively. If $(x,y) = (1,3)$, which of the following is false?
(A) $\sim q$ (B) $p \vee q$ (C) $p \wedge q$ (D) $p \wedge \sim q$

84. Ⓐ Ⓑ Ⓒ Ⓓ

85. For what value of k is the line $3y - kx = 6$ parallel to the line $y + 3x = 9$?
(A) 9   (B) 3   (C) −3   (D) −9

85. Ⓐ Ⓑ Ⓒ Ⓓ

86. If $\overline{P}$ denotes the complement of Set P, then the shaded set in the Venn diagram is
(A) $\overline{V \cup W}$
(B) $\overline{V \cap W}$
(C) $\overline{V} \cap \overline{W}$
(D) $\overline{V} \cup W$

86. Ⓐ Ⓑ Ⓒ Ⓓ

87. If the domain of $f(x) = \dfrac{1}{x^2}$ is $\{x : x \text{ is a real number}, x \neq 0\}$, then the range of f is
(A) all positive numbers
(B) all real numbers
(C) all numbers other than 0
(D) all numbers greater than or equal to 0

87. Ⓐ Ⓑ Ⓒ Ⓓ

88. Let the operation ϕ be defined on the real numbers by $m \phi n = mn - n$. Then $1 \phi -1 =$
(A) −2   (B) −1   (C) 0   (D) 1

88. Ⓐ Ⓑ Ⓒ Ⓓ

89. $(4 + i)(4 - i)$, where $i = \sqrt{-1}$, equals

(A) 17   (B) 15   (C) $16 + 8i$ (D) $8i$

90. $(x - 1)(3 - x)^2 > 0$ if and only if

(A) $x > 1$ (B) $1 < x < 3$ (C) $x < 1$ (D) $x > 1, x \neq 3$

89. Ⓐ Ⓑ Ⓒ Ⓓ

90. Ⓐ Ⓑ Ⓒ Ⓓ

ANSWER KEY AND REFERENCE CHART—SAMPLE EXAMINATION 1

Each answer in the key below is followed by a reference to the section of the book in which the topic of the question is reviewed. The topics covered on the examination are listed again below, with their reference codes and the page on which review of the topic begins. Refer to this reference-topic guide when using the answer keys for all of the sample examinations.

Topic	Reference	Page
Arithmetic	A1	335
Algebra	A2	339
Geometry	A3	342
Data Interpretation	A4	348
Sets	B1	364
Logic	B2	368
Real Number System	B3	372
Functions and their Graphs	B4	375
Probability and Statistics	B5	380
Miscellaneous Topics	B6	357 & 387

Part I

1.	A (A1)	11.	D (A1)	21.	C (A3)	31.	B (A4)
2.	C (A1)	12.	A (A1)	22.	A (A3)	32.	A (A4)
3.	D (A1)	13.	A (A1)	23.	A (A4)	33.	D (A2)
4.	C (A1)	14.	C (A2)	24.	D (A4)	34.	A (A2)
5.	A (A3)	15.	D (A2)	25.	C (A4)	35.	D (A3)
6.	B (A3)	16.	B (A2)	26.	C (A1)	36.	C (A3)
7.	A (A4)	17.	A (A2)	27.	B (A2)	37.	C (A2)
8.	A (A4)	18.	C (A2)	28.	D (A2)	38.	B (A1)
9.	B (A1)	19.	B (A2)	29.	C (A2)	39.	B (A3)
10.	A (A1)	20.	B (A2)	30.	B (A3)	40.	C (A2)

Part II

41.	D (B1)	51.	D (B3)	61.	A (B6)	71.	A (B3)	81.	A (B3)
42.	B (B1)	52.	A (B3)	62.	D (B6)	72.	B (B4)	82.	B (B3)
43.	D (B1)	53.	C (B3)	63.	C (B6)	73.	A (B5)	83.	D (B3)
44.	C (B1)	54.	C (B3)	64.	C (B5)	74.	C (B3)	84.	C (B4)
45.	C (B2)	55.	A (B4)	65.	D (B5)	75.	B (B6)	85.	D (B4)
46.	C (B6)	56.	C (B4)	66.	A (B5)	76.	C (B3)	86.	B (B1)
47.	D (B2)	57.	D (B4)	67.	B (B5)	77.	B (B3)	87.	A (B4)
48.	A (B2)	58.	D (B4)	68.	A (B4)	78.	D (B5)	88.	C (B6)
49.	D (B2)	59.	B (B4)	69.	C (B3)	79.	D (B4)	89.	A (B6)
50.	B (B2)	60.	D (B4)	70.	C (B3)	80.	B (B3)	90.	D (B3)

SCORING CHART—SAMPLE EXAMINATION I

After you have scored your Sample Examination 1, enter the results in the chart below; then transfer your Raw Score to the Progress Chart on page 14.

Total Test	Number Right	Number Wrong	Number Omitted	Raw Score
Part I: 40				
Part II: 50				
Total: 90				

ANSWER EXPLANATIONS—SAMPLE EXAMINATION 1

Part I

1. **A.** $3^2 = 3 \cdot 3 = 9$; $2^3 = 2 \cdot 2 \cdot 2 = 8$.
2. **C.** $^3/_4 \div 3 = {}^3/_4 \times {}^1/_3 = {}^1/_4 = 0.25$.
3. **D.** There are an infinite number of fractions between $^1/_3$ and $^1/_5$; one of them is $^1/_4$.
4. **C.** Rewrite the quantity in Column A as $(0.99)(1.1)(0.1)$.
5. **A.** $m(\angle Y) > 180° - 110°$ (or $70°$).
6. **B.** $y = x\sqrt{3} \approx 1.7x < 2x$.
7. **A.** The range was greatest in 1966 and appears to be at least 250 points.
8. **A.** The low Dow-Jones average was approximately 880 in 1972; the high for 1970 was approximately 850.
9. **B.** $^1/_3$ of $35 \approx 12$.
10. **A.** $2.9 \times 10^{-4} = 0.00029 > 0.000029$. The negative exponent tells us to move the decimal point 4 places to the left.
11. **D.** Information is needed about the *number* of tests that averaged to 76.
12. **A.** $2^3/_{10} = 2.3 = 230\%$.
13. **A.** $\sqrt{4} + \sqrt{9} = 2 + 3 = 5$; $\sqrt{13} < \sqrt{16} = 4$.
14. **C.** $2s - (r + t) = 2(1) - (-1 + 3) = 2 - 2 = 0$.
15. **D.** If $x \geq 0$, then $|x| = x$; otherwise $|x| = -x$. Test this with $x = 3$, then with $x = -3$.
16. **B.** $x^2 + 2x - 3 = (x + 3)(x - 1) = 0$ for $x = -3$ and $x = 1$. The sum of the roots is -2; the product is -3.
17. **A.** $3 \times (2 + 8) = 3 \times 10 = 30$; $3 \times 2 + 8 = (3 \times 2) + 8 = 6 + 8 = 14$.
18. **C.** $\frac{x^r}{x^s} = x^{r-s}$, which equals x^0 if $r = s$.
19. **B.** Substitute $x = y + 3$ in the first equation. If $5(y + 3) - y = 11$, then $4y = -4$ and $y = -1$.
20. **B.** The ratio of green marbles to the total number is $1:n$, where $n > 2$. Therefore
$$\frac{1}{2} > \frac{1}{n}$$
21. **C.** The sum of the interior angles is $360°$.
22. **A.** $24:360 = 1:15 > 1:16$.
23. **A.** For the period 1946-1960, the average annual percentage increase in the CPI was 3.0; for 1965-1966, it was 2.9.
24. **D.** No information is given about the index for the year 1966.
25. **C.** The average annual percentage increase for all services decreased from 3.9 for 1946-1960 to 2.0 for 1960-1965.
26. **C.** $4.05 = 4^5/_{100} = 4^1/_{20} = {}^{81}/_{20}$.

27.   B. $(y^2 - 3y + 2) - (2y^2 + 3y - 2) = y^2 - 3y + 2 - 2y^2 - 3y + 2$
$$= -y^2 - 6y + 4.$$

28.   D. Let the numbers be $6x$ and $11x$. Then $11x - 6x$ or $5x = 15$, and $x = 3$. So the smaller number is $6(3)$, or 18.

29.   C. To get 0.0328 from 3.28 we must move the decimal point *two* places to the *left*. So $k = -2$.

30.   B. Since the triangle is isosceles, $m = n$. Also, $m(\angle Q) = 180 - 2(70)$, or $40°$. Therefore m and n both exceed q.

31.   B. $176 \div 5 \approx 35$.

32.   A. $\dfrac{563 - 281}{281} = \dfrac{282}{281} \approx 1$; the answer is 100%.

33.   D. $(5x + 3)(2x - 3) = (5x)(2x) + (5x)(-3) + (3)(2x) + (3)(-3)$
$$= 10x^2 - 9x - 9.$$

34.   A. In the form $y = mx + b$ (where m is the slope and b the y-intercept), we get
$$y = \frac{2}{3}x + 3.$$

35.   D. If the dimensions of the original box are l, w, h, then the ratio of the volumes (larger to smaller) is $(2l)(2w)(2h):lwh = 8:1$.

36.   C. If r is the radius, the formulas are $A = \pi r^2$ and $C = 2\pi r$. Since $\pi r^2 = 4\pi$, $r = 2$ and $C = 2\pi(2) = 4\pi$.

37.   C. $3^2 - 3^0 - 3^{-2} = 9 - 1 - \dfrac{1}{9} = 8 - \dfrac{1}{9} = 7\dfrac{8}{9}$.

38.   B. $(0.02) \times (0.004) = 0.00008$, where we counted off as many decimal places in the answer as in the factors combined.

39.   B. The point $(2, -1)$ is 2 units to the right of the y-axis and one unit below the x-axis.

40.   C. The average speed equals total distance divided by total time.
$$(15 + 60) \div (\tfrac{1}{2} + 1) = 75 \div \tfrac{3}{2} = 75 \times \tfrac{2}{3} = 50 \text{ mph.}$$

Part II

41.   D. $R \cap S$ contains elements both in R and in S.
42.   B. $x^3 - x^2 - 2x = x(x^2 - x - 2) = x(x + 1)(x - 2)$
43.   D. $R \times R$, the Cartesian product, consists only of ordered pairs. Note that (A), (B), (C) are all true.
44.   C. $\{1,2,3,\dots,100\}$ has 2^{100} subsets, a large but finite number.
45.   C. A restatement is "He does not wear braces and he does not wear glasses."
46.   C. $\log_2 2^x = x \log_2 2 = x \cdot 1 = x$.
47.   D. With (A) or (B) we would verify the statement for only some pairs of rational numbers; (D) is impossible to do since the set of rationals is infinite.
48.   A. $\sim(\forall_x, p_x) = \exists_x, \sim p_x$.
49.   D. The conditional $p \to q$ is defined as true whenever p is false.
50.   B. A counterexample cites values of a and b that satisfy the hypothesis but not the conclusion. Although $(-2)^2 > (-1)^2$, $-2 \not> -1$.
51.   D. $|b - 1| = \begin{cases} b - 1 & \text{if } b \geq 1 \\ 1 - b & \text{if } b < 1 \end{cases}$
52.   A. Every fraction whose denominator contains only the factors 2 or 5 can be written as a terminating (nonrepeating) decimal.
53.   C. (A), (B), and (D) are all false statements.
54.   C. If the irrational numbers are $\sqrt{2}$ and $-\sqrt{2}$, for instance, then their sum, product, and quotient are all rational.
55.   A. $f(-x) = 2(-x)^2 - 3(-x) + 2 = 2x^2 + 3x + 2$.

56. C. Here are the graphs

$y = x$ $y = x^2 + 3$ $y^2 = x$ $y = x^3 - x$

57. D. Since $g(0) = \sqrt{4} = 2$, $f(g(0)) = f(2) = 2 + \frac{4}{2} = 4$.

58. D. The inequalities $x \geq 0$, $y \geq 0$ restrict the graph to the first quadrant.

59. B. For each x in the domain of a function, there must be a *unique* y.

60. D. $f(1) = 1^2 - 3 - 1 = -3$. $f(1 + h) - f(1) = (1 + h)^2 - 3(1 + h) - 1 - (-3)$
$$= 1 + 2h + h^2 - 3 - 3h - 1 + 3$$
$$= h^2 - h.$$

61. A. $(t * t) * t = r * t = r$.

62. D. s is the identity element and $u * u = s$.

63. C. t has no inverse under $*$.

64. C. The first digit may be one of five and for each of these so may the second be one of five, yielding $5 \cdot 5$.

65. D. If the probability of an event is p, the odds in its favor are the ratio of p to $(1 - p)$. Here it is 0.2 to 0.8, or 1 to 4.

66. A. The probability equals $\frac{1}{6} \times \frac{1}{6}$.

67. B. The probability is $_7C_2 / _{10}C_2$ or $\binom{7}{2} / \binom{10}{2}$, or $\dfrac{7 \cdot 6}{10 \cdot 9}$, which equals $\frac{7}{15}$.

68. A. Note that the largest value of $-2(x + 1)^2$ is $-2(-1 + 1)^2$, or 0. Any value of x other than -1 yields an f which is less than 3. The graph of $f(x)$ is shown here.

69. C. (A) starts and stops at different points. Each curve in (B) and (D) goes through one point twice.

70. C. If $q < 0$, then the discriminant $p^2 - 4q > 0$; therefore the roots are real. Note also that $q < 0$ implies that the roots have opposite signs.

71. A. To show that (A) is false, let $\frac{a}{b}$ be $\frac{2}{3}$ and $\frac{c}{d}$ be $\frac{4}{6}$.

72. B. Check out some "easy" points: $(0,1)$, $(1, \frac{1}{2})$, $(-1, 2)$. All three lie only on $y = 2^{-x}$.

73. A. The probability that the first bulb is defective is $\frac{10}{100}$, that the next one is defective is $\frac{9}{99}$. Multiply these.

74. C. Here is a sketch:

75. B. $23_{\text{TEN}} = 16 + 4 + 2 + 1 = 2^4 + 2^2 + 2^1 + 2^0 = 10111_{\text{TWO}}$.

76. C. $1040 = 16 \cdot 65 = 2^4 \cdot 5 \cdot 13$.

77. B. (A), (C), and (D) are all true statements.

78. D. One of the cards may be any of 52 (selected from 52 cards); the other (selected from the remaining 51 cards) can be one of 39. The answer is $\dfrac{52}{52} \cdot \dfrac{39}{51} = \dfrac{13}{17}$

79. D. Remember that if f is a function from a set X into a set Y, each element of X must correspond to a *unique* element in Y. In (A), (B), and (C) there are *two* different images of a single element in the domain.

80. B. A prime number has only 1 and itself as factors. Since $4 = 2 \cdot 2$, $25 = 5 \cdot 5$, and $39 = 3 \cdot 13$, 4, 25, and 39 are composite numbers.

81. A. $96 = 32 \times 3 = 2^5 \cdot 3$; the prime factors are 2 and 3.

82. B. Since $x < 0$, $-x > 0$. Each of the numbers in (A), (B), (D) *can*, for appropriate choices of x and y, be negative or zero.

83. D. Since $(x + 1)$ is a factor of $f(x)$, $f(-1) = 0$. So $(-1)^3 - 2(-1)^2 + 3(-1) + d = 0$ and $d = 6$.

84. C. The point $(1,3)$ lies on the graph of f but not on the graph of g. So p is true, q false. Only $p \wedge q$ is false.

85. D. The slope of $y + 3x = 9$ or $y = -3x + 9$ is -3. Therefore $\dfrac{k}{3}$ must equal -3.

86. B. The unshaded region is $V \cap W$. The complement is the shaded region.

87. A. $\dfrac{1}{x^2} > 0$ for all real $x \neq 0$.

88. C. $1 \, \phi \, -1 = 1(-1) - (-1) = -1 + 1 = 0$.

89. A. $(4 + i)(4 - i) = 16 - i^2 = 16 - (-1) = 16 + 1 = 17$.

90. D. $(x - 1)(3 - x)^2 > 0$ if and only if $x - 1 > 0$ and $3 - x \neq 0$; i.e., if and only if $x > 1$, $x \neq 3$.

SAMPLE EXAMINATION 2

Part I: Basic Skills and Concepts

Directions to questions 1–25: Each of these questions consists of two quantities, one in Column A and one in Column B. You are to compare the two quantities and in the answer column blacken space

A if the quantity in Column A is greater;

B if the quantity in Column B is greater;

C if the two quantities are equal;

D if the relationship cannot be determined from the information given

Notes:

1. In certain questions, information concerning one or both of the quantities to be compared is centered above the two columns.

2. A symbol that appears in both columns represents the same thing in Column A as it does in Column B.

3. Letters such as x, n, and k stand for real numbers.

QUESTIONS	COLUMN A	COLUMN B	
1.	simple interest on $150 at $4\frac{1}{2}\%$ for 2 years	$13.50	1. Ⓐ Ⓑ Ⓒ Ⓓ
2.	the reciprocal of $2\frac{1}{3}$	0.5	2. Ⓐ Ⓑ Ⓒ Ⓓ

An average of 50 on a battery of 5 objective tests, with range 0 to 80, is considered passing. Carly's average on 4 tests is 44.

3.	score Carly must get on fifth test to pass the battery	72	3. Ⓐ Ⓑ Ⓒ Ⓓ
4.	cost per pound of peaches if 3 pounds cost 55¢	18¢	4. Ⓐ Ⓑ Ⓒ Ⓓ

An airline allows 44 pounds of luggage. One kilogram (kg) ≈ 2.2 pounds.

5.	the weight limit	21 kg	5. Ⓐ Ⓑ Ⓒ Ⓓ

There are three landmarks, A, B, and C, in a big city. A and B are 3 miles apart, and B and C are 4 miles apart.

6.	distance between A and C	5.1 miles	6. Ⓐ Ⓑ Ⓒ Ⓓ

A 12-foot board is cut into two pieces in the ratio 7 : 3.

7.	length of the smaller piece	3 ft. 6 in.	7. Ⓐ Ⓑ Ⓒ Ⓓ

$$m = 3, n = -2$$

8.	$(m + n)^2$	$(2n + m)^2$	8. Ⓐ Ⓑ Ⓒ Ⓓ

$$xy \neq 0$$

9.	$|x + y|$	$|x| + |y|$	9. Ⓐ Ⓑ Ⓒ Ⓓ
10.	y	y^2	10. Ⓐ Ⓑ Ⓒ Ⓓ
11.	$2^0 + 2^{1/2} + 2^{-1}$	3	11. Ⓐ Ⓑ Ⓒ Ⓓ
12.	$(2m - 1)(2m + 1)$	$m^4 - 1$	12. Ⓐ Ⓑ Ⓒ Ⓓ

$$\begin{cases} 3x + 2y = 4 \\ 9x + 6y = 12 \end{cases}$$

13.	x	y	13. Ⓐ Ⓑ Ⓒ Ⓓ

$\angle A \cong \angle A'$
$\angle C \cong \angle C'$

14.	$A'C'$	7.4	14. Ⓐ Ⓑ Ⓒ Ⓓ

$x = y = 2z$

15.	v	$1.5x$	15. Ⓐ Ⓑ Ⓒ Ⓓ

The measures of two complementary angles are in the ratio 5 : 3.

16.	the smaller angle	35°	16. Ⓐ Ⓑ Ⓒ Ⓓ

The figure shown is
a rectangle.

17.   area of unshaded region   48 cm²   17. Ⓐ Ⓑ Ⓒ Ⓓ

The radius of a circle is doubled.

18.   ratio of circumference of new   2 : 1   18. Ⓐ Ⓑ Ⓒ Ⓓ
           circle to that of old

$l \parallel m$

19. $x + y + z$ 360   19. Ⓐ Ⓑ Ⓒ Ⓓ

1¼ inches on a map = 18 miles; 3¾ inches on the map = k miles.

20. k 54   20. Ⓐ Ⓑ Ⓒ Ⓓ

Use this bar graph for questions 21 and 22.

AVERAGE MONTHLY RAINFALL FOR 6 MONTHS

Source: Developing Skills

21.   average monthly rainfall for   3.7   21. Ⓐ Ⓑ Ⓒ Ⓓ
           the six-month period

QUESTIONS	COLUMN A	COLUMN B	
22.	difference, in inches, of average monthly rainfall between least and greatest monthly rainfalls	0.7	22. Ⓐ Ⓑ Ⓒ Ⓓ

Use these circle graphs for questions 23, 24, and 25.

1972 MERCHANDISE TRADE BY COMMODITY GROUPS
Sources of New York State's Projected Income for 1973-74

Exports $48,300,000,000   Imports $55,600,000,000

23.	raw materials exported	raw materials imported	23. Ⓐ Ⓑ Ⓒ Ⓓ
24.	manufactured goods exported, in billions of dollars	33	24. Ⓐ Ⓑ Ⓒ Ⓓ
25.	foods, beverages, tobacco imported, in billions of dollars	8	25. Ⓐ Ⓑ Ⓒ Ⓓ

Directions for questions 26–40: For these questions, indicate the correct answer in the appropriate space on the answer sheet.

Note: Figures that accompany the following problems are intended to provide information useful in answering them. The figures are drawn as accurately as possible *except* when it is stated in a specific question that the figure is not drawn to scale. All figures lie in a plane unless otherwise stated.

Use this graph for questions 26 and 27.

AVERAGE SIZE ORDINARY LIFE INSURANCE POLICY PURCHASED IN THE UNITED STATES

Source: Fact, p. 19.

26. The average size of an ordinary life insurance policy purchased in the United States in 1971 was approximately
    (A) $6000   (B) $9000   (C) $10,000   (D) $12,000

    26. Ⓐ Ⓑ Ⓒ Ⓓ

27. The ratio of the average size of an ordinary life insurance policy purchased in the U.S. in 1962 to that purchased in 1972 is approximately equal to
    (A) 1:3   (B) 1:2   (C) 2:3   (D) 2:1

    27. Ⓐ Ⓑ Ⓒ Ⓓ

28. $1\frac{1}{5} =$
    (A) 1.2%   (B) 102%   (C) 120%   (D) 125%

    28. Ⓐ Ⓑ Ⓒ Ⓓ

29. What percent profit was made on a motorcycle that was bought for $200 and sold for $210?
    (A) 5   (B) 7½   (C) 10   (D) 20

    29. Ⓐ Ⓑ Ⓒ Ⓓ

30. The area of a square is 100. The length of its diagonal is approximately
    (A) 10   (B) 12   (C) 14   (D) 20

    30. Ⓐ Ⓑ Ⓒ Ⓓ

31. $(3.2) \times (0.01) =$
    (A) 0.0032   (B) 0.032   (C) 0.32   (D) 320

    31. Ⓐ Ⓑ Ⓒ Ⓓ

32. 8 is what percent of 6?
    (A) 1.25   (B) 75   (C) 125   (D) 133⅓

    32. Ⓐ Ⓑ Ⓒ Ⓓ

33. Which number is biggest?
    (A) |3 − 1| (B) |−3| + 1   (C) |−3| (D) 1 − |3|

    33. Ⓐ Ⓑ Ⓒ Ⓓ

34. $2^{-3} =$

(A) -8 (B) -6 (C) $-\dfrac{1}{8}$ (D) $\dfrac{1}{8}$

34. Ⓐ Ⓑ Ⓒ Ⓓ

35. The line $3x + 4y - 6 = 0$ cuts the x-axis at $x =$

(A) -2 (B) $-1\dfrac{1}{2}$ (C) 2 (D) 3

35. Ⓐ Ⓑ Ⓒ Ⓓ

36. The factors of $3x^2 + 5x - 2$ are

(A) $(3x + 1)$ and $(x + 2)$ (B) $(3x - 1)$ and $(x + 2)$

(C) $(3x + 1)$ and $(x - 2)$ (D) $(3x - 1)$ and $(x - 2)$

36. Ⓐ Ⓑ Ⓒ Ⓓ

37. $(2 + \sqrt{3})(3 - \sqrt{3}) =$

(A) 3 (B) $6 + \sqrt{3}$ (C) $3 - \sqrt{3}$ (D) $3 + \sqrt{3}$

37. Ⓐ Ⓑ Ⓒ Ⓓ

38. If $x + 1 < 3x + 5$, then

(A) $x > -2$ (B) $x < -2$ (C) $x < 2$ (D) $x > 2$

38. Ⓐ Ⓑ Ⓒ Ⓓ

39. If $x \neq -3$, then $\dfrac{1}{x + 3} - \dfrac{1}{3} =$

39. Ⓐ Ⓑ Ⓒ Ⓓ

40. The product of the roots of the equation $x^2 - x - 30 = 0$ is

(A) -1 (B) -30 (C) 1 (D) 30

40. Ⓐ Ⓑ Ⓒ Ⓓ

Part II: Content

Directions: For each of the following problems, indicate the correct answer in the appropriate space in the answer column.

Note: Figures that accompany problems in this part are intended to provide information useful in solving the problems. They are drawn as accurately as possible *except* when it is stated in a specific problem that the figure is not drawn to scale. All figures lie in a plane unless otherwise stated.

41. The shaded region in the Venn diagram is for the set

(A) $R \cup (S \cap T)$

(B) $R \cap (S \cup T)$

(C) $(R \cup S) \cap T$

(D) $R \cup (S \cup T)$

41. Ⓐ Ⓑ Ⓒ Ⓓ

42. If Z, Q, R denote respectively the sets of integers, of rationals, and of reals, then each point of the Cartesian plane corresponds to an element of

(A) $R \times R$ (B) $Q \times Q$ (C) $Z \times Z$ (D) R

42. Ⓐ Ⓑ Ⓒ Ⓓ

43. Which of the sets below is not a subset of Q, where $Q = \{x \mid x$ is a prime number$\}$?   43. Ⓐ Ⓑ Ⓒ Ⓓ
    (A) {2}   (B) {2,3,51}   (C) {5,7,11,47}   (D) {2,3,97}

44. If $P = \{x : x^2 - 2x - 3 = 0\}$ and $Q = \{x \mid x^2 + x = 0\}$, then $P \cap Q$ equals   44. Ⓐ Ⓑ Ⓒ Ⓓ
    (A) $\emptyset$ (B) {0,−1,3}   (C) {1}   (D) {−1}

45. A statement with the truth table shown on the right is: 45. Ⓐ Ⓑ Ⓒ Ⓓ
    (A) $\sim(p \wedge q)$ (B) $p \vee \sim q$
    (C) $\sim q$ (D) $\sim(p \vee q)$

p	q	
T	T	F
T	F	T
F	T	F
F	F	T

46. The negation of $s \rightarrow t$ is   46. Ⓐ Ⓑ Ⓒ Ⓓ
    (A) $s \wedge \sim t$ (B) $\sim s \rightarrow t$ (C) $\sim s \wedge \sim t$ (D) $t \rightarrow \sim s$

47. Let s be "Sam is conscientious" and let t be "Sam is bright." Then symbolically the statement "Sam is bright but not conscientious" is   47. Ⓐ Ⓑ Ⓒ Ⓓ
    (A) $\sim s \vee t$ (B) $\sim s \wedge t$ (C) $s \vee \sim t$ (D) $\sim(s \wedge t)$

48. A statement equivalent to "If a snuggy is groobly, then it is flissy" is   48. Ⓐ Ⓑ Ⓒ Ⓓ
    (A) If a snuggy is not groobly, then it is not flissy
    (B) If a snuggy is not flissy, then it is not groobly
    (C) If a snuggy is flissy, then it is groobly
    (D) A snuggy is groobly if and only if it is flissy

49. If $a, b,$ and c in the equation $ax^2 + bx + c = 0$ are all positive real numbers, then which statement below is true of every such equation?   49. Ⓐ Ⓑ Ⓒ Ⓓ
    (A) $b^2 - 4ac$ is negative.
    (B) The equation has no real roots.
    (C) The equation has no positive root.
    (D) $b^2 - 4ac$ equals zero.

50. Consider the sequence of fractions   50. Ⓐ Ⓑ Ⓒ Ⓓ
    $$\tfrac{1}{2},\; \tfrac{2}{3},\; \tfrac{3}{5},\; \tfrac{5}{8},\; \tfrac{8}{13},\; \ldots$$
    If a term in the sequence is denoted by $\dfrac{p}{q}$, then the next term is
    (A) $\dfrac{p+n}{q+n}$ (B) $\dfrac{p+3}{q+5}$ (C) $\dfrac{p+q}{p+2q}$ (D) $\dfrac{q}{p+q}$

51. Which statement about real numbers is false?   51. Ⓐ Ⓑ Ⓒ Ⓓ
    (A) If $a \neq 0$, then $a^2 > 0$.   (B) If $a > 0$, then $\dfrac{1}{a} > 0$.
    (C) If $a^2 > b^2$ then $|a| > |b|$.   (D) If $a < b$, then $a^2 < b^2$.

52. A rational number between the rational numbers p and q, for all p and q, is   52. Ⓐ Ⓑ Ⓒ Ⓓ
    (A) $\dfrac{p-q}{2}$ (B) $\dfrac{p+q}{2}$ (C) $\dfrac{q-p}{2}$ (D) $\dfrac{p}{2}$

53. Which of the numbers below cannot be represented by a repeating decimal?   53. Ⓐ Ⓑ Ⓒ Ⓓ
    (A) $^{11}/_9$ (B) $^{23}/_7$ (C) $\sqrt{3}$ (D) $4^1/_3$

54. Points in the region enclosed by the parabola and line, shown in the diagram, satisfy the inequalities

(A) $y < 1 + x, y < x^2$
(B) $y > x^2, y < x + 1$
(C) $y > 1 + x, y < x^2$
(D) $y > x^2, y > 1 + x$

[The dotted line segment and dotted curve indicate that the boundaries of the region are excluded.]

55. Which equation has no real root?

(A) $x^3 + x^2 = 0$ (B) $4x^4 + 1 = 0$
(C) $2x^4 - 1 = 0$ (D) $\dfrac{1}{x} + 1 = 0$

56. The inverse of the function $y = x + 3$ is

(A) $y = 3 - x$ (B) $y = \dfrac{1}{x + 3}$
(C) $y = 3x$ (D) $y = x - 3$

57. Which statement about the intersection of a cubic curve and a line is false?

(A) They need have no intersection.
(B) They intersect at least once.
(C) They may intersect twice.
(D) They cannot intersect more than three times.

58. If "$m \equiv n \bmod 5$" means that $(m - n)$ is divisible by 5, which statement below is false?

(A) $19 \equiv 12 \bmod 5$ (B) $13 \equiv 3 \bmod 5$
(C) $17 \equiv 2 \bmod 5$ (D) $3 \equiv 3 \bmod 5$

59. If a die is tossed, the probability that it shows a number greater than or equal to 2 is

(A) ⅓   (B) ½   (C) ⅔   (D) ⅚

60. Suppose 3 of a dozen apples are bruised and 2 are chosen at random from the dozen. The probability that both are bruised is

(A) $\frac{1}{22}$ (B) $\frac{1}{11}$ (C) $\frac{1}{6}$ (D) $\frac{1}{4}$

61. For the data 3, 3, 7, 11, 11, 13, 15 the difference (median minus mean) is

(A) 0   (B) 2   (C) 3   (D) 5

62. $\{x : -1 \leq x \leq 3\} \cap \{x : 0 \leq x \leq 5\}$ equals

(A) $\{x : -1 < x \leq 5\}$ (B) $\{x : 0 < x \leq 5\}$
(C) $\{x : 0 \leq x \leq 3\}$ (D) the empty set

63. You have randomly drawn 4 cards from a shuffled deck (of 52 cards—no jokers): an ace, a king, a seven, and a three. The probability that the next card you draw will give you a pair is

(A) $\frac{1}{16}$ (B) $\frac{3}{13}$ (C) $\frac{1}{4}$ (D) $\frac{1}{3}$

64. The reason the multiplication 13×42 is to be performed

as $\begin{array}{r} 13 \\ 42 \\ \hline 26 \\ 52 \\ \hline 546 \end{array}$ and not as $\begin{array}{r} 13 \\ 42 \\ \hline 26 \\ 52 \\ \hline 78 \end{array}$ is

    (A) $13 \times 42 = (10 + 3) \times 42$
    (B) $13 \times 42 = 13 \times (40 + 2)$
    (C) the commutative law
    (D) the associativity of multiplication

64. Ⓐ Ⓑ Ⓒ Ⓓ

65. Which set is not closed under the binary operation $*$, if $m * n = m^n$?
    (A) the set of positive integers
    (B) the set of even positive integers
    (C) the set of odd positive integers
    (D) the set of nonzero integers

65. Ⓐ Ⓑ Ⓒ Ⓓ

66. If $f(x) = 2x + 1$ and $g(x) = x^2 - 3$, then $g(f(x)) =$
    (A) $4x^2 + 4x - 2$ (B) $2x^2 - 5$
    (C) $4x^2 + 2x - 2$ (D) $2x^2 - 2$

66. Ⓐ Ⓑ Ⓒ Ⓓ

67. The probability of obtaining all heads or tails when three coins are tossed simultaneously is
    (A) $1/6$ (B) $1/8$ (C) $1/4$ (D) $1/2$

67. Ⓐ Ⓑ Ⓒ Ⓓ

68. Which equation has no rational root?
    (A) $x^2 - 1 = 0$ (B) $x^2 - 2 = 0$
    (C) $x^2 - 4x + 4 = 0$ (D) $x^2 - x - 2 = 0$

68. Ⓐ Ⓑ Ⓒ Ⓓ

69.

The graph above represents which set?
    (A) $\{x : x < 0 \text{ or } x > 3\}$ (B) $\{x : 0 < x < 3\}$
    (C) $\{x : x \leq 0 \text{ or } x \geq 3\}$ (D) $\{x : 0 > x > 3\}$

69. Ⓐ Ⓑ Ⓒ Ⓓ

70. If $f(x) = \log_2 x$ and $g(x) = 2^x$, then their graphs are symmetric to the
    (A) origin   (B) x-axis   (C) y-axis   (D) line $y = x$

70. Ⓐ Ⓑ Ⓒ Ⓓ

71. If $p * q = p^2 - q^2$ for all real p, q, then it is *not* true that
    (A) $p * q = q * p$ (B) $p * (-p) = p * p$
    (C) $p * 0 = -(0 * p)$ (D) $p * q = (-p) * (-q)$

71. Ⓐ Ⓑ Ⓒ Ⓓ

72. If $a > 0$ and $a^x = 0.6$, then $a^{-2x} =$

    (A) -1.2 (B) -0.36 (C) $-\dfrac{1}{0.36}$ (D) $\dfrac{1}{0.36}$

72. Ⓐ Ⓑ Ⓒ Ⓓ

73. If Z is the set of integers, Q the set of rationals, and R the set of reals, then
    (A) $Q \subset Z \subset R$ (B) $R \subset Q \subset Z$
    (C) $Z \subset Q \subset R$ (D) $Z \subset R \subset Q$

73. Ⓐ Ⓑ Ⓒ Ⓓ

74. If $i = \sqrt{-1}$, then $5\sqrt{-1} + \sqrt{-4} - \sqrt{-9} =$

74. Ⓐ Ⓑ Ⓒ Ⓓ

(A) 10   (B) $4i$ (C) 0   (D) $-6i$

75. $111_2 + 1_2 =$

75. Ⓐ Ⓑ Ⓒ Ⓓ

(A) 1110_2 (B) 1010_2 (C) 1100_2 (D) 1000_2

76. If $V = \{0, 1, 3\}$, $W = \{1, 2\}$, and $Z = \{0, 1, 4\}$, then $(V \cup W) \cap Z =$

76. Ⓐ Ⓑ Ⓒ Ⓓ

(A) $\{0, 1, 2, 3, 4\}$ (B) $\{0, 1\}$

(C) $\{1\}$ (D) 0

77. The domain of the function $f(x) = \dfrac{x^2}{x^2 - 4}$ is the set of all reals except

77. Ⓐ Ⓑ Ⓒ Ⓓ

(A) 0   (B) 2   (C) 2 and -2 (D) 0, 2, and -2

78. A counterexample to the statement "If $ax^2 + bx + c = 0$ has two real unequal roots, then $b^2 - 4ac > 3$" is

78. Ⓐ Ⓑ Ⓒ Ⓓ

(A) $x^2 - 3x + 2 = 0$ (B) $x^2 - x + 1 = 0$

(C) $x^2 - 2x + 1 = 0$ (D) $x^2 - 4x + 3 = 0$

79. Which graph below is not that of a function $y = f(x)$?

79. Ⓐ Ⓑ Ⓒ Ⓓ

(A)

(B)

(C)

(D)

80. Which statement about primes is false?

80. Ⓐ Ⓑ Ⓒ Ⓓ

(A) Every odd prime is of the form $2^n - 1$, where n is an integer.

(B) If a product mn of 2 positive integers is divisible by a prime p, then either m or n is divisible by p.

(C) Every positive integer can be uniquely expressed as a product of primes, except perhaps for the order in which the factors occur.

(D) There are an infinite number of primes.

81. If a divided by 4 leaves a remainder of 2, and b divided by 4 leaves a remainder of 3, then when $a + b$ is divided by 4 the remainder is
   (A) 0   (B) 1   (C) 2   (D) 3

81. Ⓐ Ⓑ Ⓒ Ⓓ

82. Which number is not a prime factor of 84?
   (A) 2   (B) 3   (C) 6   (D) 7

82. Ⓐ Ⓑ Ⓒ Ⓓ

83. If p and q are each divisible by 3, which of the following is *not* necessarily divisible by 3?
   (A) $2q + 3$ (B) $4p + q$ (C) $pq + 2$ (D) $p^2 + q$

83. Ⓐ Ⓑ Ⓒ Ⓓ

84. If $g(x) = \dfrac{\sqrt{x - 3}}{x}$, then $g(4) =$

   (A) $\dfrac{1}{2}$ (B) $\dfrac{1}{4}$ (C) $-\dfrac{1}{4}$ (D) $\pm\dfrac{1}{4}$

84. Ⓐ Ⓑ Ⓒ Ⓓ

Use the table at the right for questions 85 and 86.

*	a	b	c	d
a	a	a	a	a
b	a	b	c	d
c	a	c	a	c
d	a	d	c	b

85. $(b * c) * d =$
   (A) a (B) b (C) c (D) d

85. Ⓐ Ⓑ Ⓒ Ⓓ

86. The identity element for the operation * is
   (A) a (B) c (C) d (D) none of the preceding

86. Ⓐ Ⓑ Ⓒ Ⓓ

87. If 60% of a population reads the *Journal*, 45% reads the *Moon*, and 30% reads both papers, what percent of the population reads neither paper?
   (A) 40   (B) 25   (C) 15   (D) 10

87. Ⓐ Ⓑ Ⓒ Ⓓ

88. How many two-person committees can be formed from a group of 8 volunteers?
   (A) 8   (B) 16   (C) 28   (D) 56

88. Ⓐ Ⓑ Ⓒ Ⓓ

89. Which function has a graph symmetric to the y-axis?
   (A) $y = |x|$ (B) $y = 2x$ (C) $y = \dfrac{1}{x}$ (D) $y = x^2 + x$

89. Ⓐ Ⓑ Ⓒ Ⓓ

90. If $R = \{x : x > 2\}$ and $S = \{x : x < 13\}$, then the number of primes in $R \cap S$ is
   (A) 3   (B) 4   (C) 5   (D) infinite

90. Ⓐ Ⓑ Ⓒ Ⓓ

ANSWER KEY AND REFERENCE CHART—SAMPLE EXAMINATION 2

See page 323 for an explanation of the reference code given in parentheses after each answer.

Part I

1.	C (A1)	11.	B (A2)	21.	B (A4)	31.	B (A1)
2.	B (A1)	12.	D (A2)	22.	A (A4)	32.	D (A1)
3.	A (A1)	13.	D (A2)	23.	B (A4)	33.	B (A2)
4.	A (A1)	14.	A (A3)	24.	A (A4)	34.	D (A2)
5.	B (A1)	15.	C (A3)	25.	B (A4)	35.	A (A2)
6.	D (A3)	16.	B (A3)	26.	D (A4)	36.	B (A2)
7.	A (A1)	17.	C (A3)	27.	B (A4)	37.	D (A2)
8.	C (A2)	18.	C (A3)	28.	C (A1)	38.	A (A2)
9.	B (A2)	19.	C (A3)	29.	A (A1)	39.	B (A2)
10.	D (A2)	20.	C (A1)	30.	C (A3)	40.	B (A2)

Part II

41.	A (B1)	51.	D (B3)	61.	B (B5)	71.	A (B6)	81.	B (B3)
42.	A (B1)	52.	B (B3)	62.	C (B1)	72.	D (B6)	82.	C (B3)
43.	B (B1)	53.	C (B3)	63.	C (B5)	73.	C (B3)	83.	C (B3)
44.	D (B1)	54.	B (B4)	64.	B (B3)	74.	B (B6)	84.	B (B4)
45.	C (B2)	55.	B (B4)	65.	D (B6)	75.	D (B6)	85.	C (B6)
46.	A (B2)	56.	D (B4)	66.	A (B4)	76.	B (B1)	86.	D (B6)
47.	B (B2)	57.	A (B4)	67.	C (B5)	77.	C (B4)	87.	B (B5)
48.	B (B2)	58.	A (B6)	68.	B (B3)	78.	A (B2)	88.	C (B5)
49.	C (B3)	59.	D (B5)	69.	A (B3)	79.	D (B4)	89.	A (B4)
50.	D (B3)	60.	A (B5)	70.	D (B6)	80.	A (B3)	90.	B (B3)

SCORING CHART—SAMPLE EXAMINATION 2

After you have scored your Sample Examination 2, enter the results in the chart below; then transfer your Raw Score to the Progress Chart on page 14.

Total Test	Number Right	Number Wrong	Number Omitted	Raw Score
Part I: 40				
Part II: 50				
Total: 90				

ANSWER EXPLANATIONS—SAMPLE EXAMINATION 2

1.   C. $150 \times 2 = 300$, and $300 \times 4\frac{1}{2} = 300 \times 4 + 300 \times \frac{1}{2} = 1200 + 150$. The answer is \$13.50.

2.   B. $2\frac{1}{3} = \frac{7}{3}$; its reciprocal is $\frac{3}{7}$, which is less than $\frac{1}{2}$.

3.   A. Let $x =$ required score on the fifth test. Then $\dfrac{4 \cdot 44 + x}{5}$ must equal 50.

   $176 + x = 250$, and $x = 74$.

4. A. $55 \div 3 > 18$.
5. B. $44 \div 2.2 = 20$.
6. D. Don't assume that $\triangle ABC$ is a right triangle!
7. A. Solving $7x + 3x = 12$ yields $x = 1.2$, and $3x = 3.6$, which is greater than 3.5 (3 ft. 6 in.).
8. C. $(m + n)^2 = (3 - 2)^2 = 1$; $(2n + m)^2 = (-4 + 3)^2 = 1$.
9. B. In all cases $|x| + |y| > |x + y|$ if neither x nor y is zero.
10. D. Don't forget that y may be negative. zero, or a fraction. If, for example. $y = 0$, then $y = y^2$; if $y = -1$, then $y < y^2$; if, however, $y = \frac{1}{2}$, then $y > y^2$.
11. B. $2^0 \alpha\, 2^{\frac{1}{2}} + 2^{-1} = 1 + \sqrt{2} + \frac{1}{2} < 1 + 1.42 + 0.5 < 3.$ ($\sqrt{2} \approx 1.414$.)
12. D. $(2m - 1)(2m + 1) = 4m^2 - 1$. The relationship between $4m^2$ and m^4 cannot be determined without information about m.
13. D. $\begin{cases} 3x + 2y = 4 \\ 9x + 6y = 12 \end{cases} \longrightarrow \begin{cases} 9x + 6y = 12 \\ 9x + 6y = 12 \end{cases}$
    There are an infinite number of solutions for this pair of equations.
14. A. If $A'C' = x$, $\frac{2}{3} = \frac{5}{x}$ since the triangles are similar, and $x = 7.5$.
15. C. $v = y + z = x + \frac{1}{2}x = 1.5x$.
16. B. $5x + 3x = 90$ yields $x = 45/4$, and $3x = 135/4$, which is less than 35.
17. C. Area in cm^2 of unshaded region $= (8 \times 10) - \frac{1}{2}(8 \times 8) = 80 - 32 = 48$.
18. C. $\dfrac{\text{circumference of new circle}}{\text{circumference of old circle}} = \dfrac{2\pi(2r)}{2\pi r} = \dfrac{2}{1}.$
19. C.

$a + b = x;\ c + d = y$
$a + c + z = 180$
$b + d = 180$ (since $l \parallel m$)
$\therefore x + y + z = 360.$

20. C. Mental arithmetic shows that $54 = 3 \times 18$, and that $(3 \times 1\frac{1}{4}) = 3\frac{3}{4}$.
21. B. Use a straightedge, if necessary, to pinpoint number of inches of rainfall for each month. Here the rainfall is *less* than 3.7 during four of the six months. The six-month average is also less.
22. A. Use a straightedge! It's about 3.9 inches in June, about 3.1 in February. The difference is about 0.8 inches.
23. B. Raw materials are 16% of imports, but only 15% of exports, and total imports exceed exports.
24. A. 70% of $48 = 33.6$; this is less than 70% of 48.3 billion.
25. B. 13% of $56 = 7.28$, which exceeds the actual amount (13% of 55.6 billion).
26. D. The fourth dot on the graph to the right of the one for 1967 is for 1971. It is just below the horizontal $12,000 line.
27. B. In 1962 the average policy was approximately $6000, in 1972 $12,000.
28. C. $1\frac{1}{5} = 1\frac{20}{100} = 1.20 = 120\%$.
29. A. $(210 - 200) \div 200 = 10 \div 200 = 1 \div 20 = 0.05 = 5\%$.
30. C. If the diagonal has length x, then x^2 Qa5h 100 + 100 235h 200 and $x \approx 14$.
31. B. Multiply 32 by 1, then mark off 3 decimal places to the left.
32. D. $8 = 6x \rightarrow x = 8 \div 6 = 1\frac{1}{3} = 1.33\frac{1}{3} = 133\frac{1}{3}\%$.
33. B. $|3 - 1| = |2| = 2$; $|-3| + 1 = 3 + 1 = 4$; $|-3| = 3$; $1 - |-3| = 1 - 3 = -2$.
34. D. $2^{-3} = \dfrac{1}{2^3} = \dfrac{1}{8}$.

35.   A. A line cuts the x-axis when $y = 0$: $3x + 4(0) + 6 = 0 \rightarrow x = -2$.

36.   B. Consider *only* (B) and (C) since the product of the second terms of their factors is -2. Then check the cross-products; the sum of these must be $-5x$.

37.   D. $(2 + \sqrt{3})(3 - \sqrt{3}) = (2)(3) + (2)(-\sqrt{3}) + (3)(\sqrt{3}) + (\sqrt{3})(-\sqrt{3})$
$$= 6 + \sqrt{3} - 3 = 3 + \sqrt{3}.$$

38.   A. $x + 1 < 3x + 5 \rightarrow -4 < 2x \rightarrow -2 < x$.

39.   B. $\dfrac{1}{x+3} - \dfrac{1}{3} = \dfrac{3 - (x+3)}{3(x+3)} = \dfrac{-x}{3(x+3)}$.

40.   B. Since $x^2 - x - 30 = (x - 6)(x + 5)$, and therefore is zero if $x = 6$ or -5, the product of the roots is $(6)(-5)$, or -30.

Part II

41.   A. The shaded region consists of elements in R or in the intersection of S and T. Verification is also possible by assigning numbers to the exhaustive disjoint sets, as indicated:

$R \cup (S \cap T) =$
$(1,2,4,5) \cup (2,3,5,6 \cap 4,5,6,7) =$
$(1,2,4,5) \cup (5,6) = 1,2,4,5,6$
which is the shaded region.

42.   A. If R is the set of reals, then each point in the plane is of the form (x,y) where $(x,y) \in R \times R$.

43.   B. $51 = 3 \times 17$; therefore 51 is not prime.

44.   D. $P = \{3, -1\}$; $Q = \{0, -1\}$.

45.   C. Note that the statement is true precisely when q is false.

46.   A. $s \rightarrow t$ is equivalent to $\sim s \vee t$. $\sim(\sim s \vee t) = s \wedge \sim t$.

47.   B. A translation of $\sim s \wedge t$ is "Sam is not conscientious and Sam is bright."

48.   B. (B) is the contrapositive of the given statement.

49.   C. If $x > 0$, then $ax^2 + bx + c > 0$. Thus the equation never equals zero for a positive number.

50.   D. Note that the numerator of a term is equal to the denominator of the preceding one; a term's denominator equals the sum of the numerator and denominator of the preceding term.

51.   D. Note that if $a = -2$, $b = -1$, then $a < b$ but $a^2 > b^2$.

52.   B. Let $p = 1$, $q = 2$ to show that the numbers in (A), (C), (D) do not lie between p and q.

53.   C. $\sqrt{3}$ is not a rational number; a number can be represented by a repeating or terminating decimal if and only if it is rational.

54.   B. The area enclosed by the dotted line segment and dotted arc of the parabola is both above the parabola (that is, $y > x^2$) and below the line (that is, $y < 1 + x$).

55.   B. $4x^4 + 1 = 0$ is equivalent to $4x^4 = -1$. No real x satisfies this equation, since $4x^4 \geq 0$ for all real x.

56.   D. If $g(x)$ is the inverse of the function $f(x)$, then $g(x)$ is also a function such that $g(f(x)) = f(g(x)) = x$.

57.   A. Every cubic curve and every line intersect at least once and at most three times.

58.   A. $19 - 12 = 7$ and 7 is not divisible by 5.

59. D. There are 5 out of 6 ways to get a 2 or more when tossing a die.

60. A. The probability is

$$\frac{_3C_2}{_{12}C_2} = \frac{3 \cdot 2}{2 \cdot 1} \div \frac{12 \cdot 11}{2 \cdot 1} \text{ or just } \frac{3 \cdot 2}{12 \cdot 11}.$$

61. B. The median or middle number is 11; the mean is

$$\frac{3 + 3 + 7 + 11 + 11 + 13 + 15}{7} = \frac{63}{7} = 9.$$

62. C. The intersection contains elements in both sets. Use a number line:

63. C. You have 48 choices. To get a pair, your card must be an ace, king, seven, or three. There are 12 of these left in the deck; therefore the probability is $^{12}/_{48}$.

64. B. $13 \times 42 = 13 \times (40 + 2) = (13 \times 40) + (13 \times 2)$
$= (13 \times 2) + (13 \times 40) = 26 + 520 = 546.$

65. D. If $m = 3$ and $n = -2$, for example, then $m * n = 3^{-2} = ^1/_9$, which is not an integer.

66. A. $g(f(x)) = (2x^2 + 1) - 3 = 4x^2 + 4x + 1 - 3 = 4x^2 + 4x - 2.$

67. C. See the tree diagram in answer 8 on page 310. Of a total of 8 outcomes, one is all heads, one all tails. The probability of both is the sum $\frac{1}{8} + \frac{1}{8}$.

68. B. $x^2 - 2 = 0$ has roots $\pm \sqrt{2}$. Both roots are irrational.

69. A. The hollow circles at -1 and 3 signify *exclusion* of these points.

70. D. The functions are inverses. Graphs of inverses are symmetric to the line $y = x$.

71. A. $p * q = p^2 - q^2$, but $q * p = q^2 - p^2$. Verify that (B), (C), and (D) are true.

72. D. $a^{-2x} = \frac{1}{a^{2x}} = \frac{1}{(a^x)^2} = \frac{1}{(0.6)^2} = \frac{1}{0.36}.$

73. C. Every integer is a rational number; every rational number is a real number.

74. B. $5\sqrt{-1} + \sqrt{-4} - \sqrt{-9} = 5i + 2i - 3i = 4i.$

75. D. See the answer to 16 on page 315 for information on adding numbers in base 2.

76. B. $V \cup W = \{0, 1, 2, 3\}$. Only the elements 0 and 1 are common to $V \cup W$ and Z.

77. C. Division by zero is prohibited.

78. A. $x^2 - 3x + 2 = (x - 1)(x - 2)$, which is zero for $x = 1, 2$. But $b^2 - 4ac = (-3)^2 - 4(2) = 1.$

79. D. For some x's there are two y's in the graph in (D).

80. A. 5 is a prime, for example, but there is no positive integer n such that $5 = 2^n - 1.$

81. B. Since there are integers p and q such that $a = 4p + 2$ and $b = 4q + 3$, $a + b = 4(p + q) + 5 = 4(p + q + 1) + 1 = 4m + 1$, where m is an integer.

82. C. Since $84 = 4 \cdot 21 = 2^2 \cdot 3 \cdot 7$, the prime factors are 2, 3, and 7; 6 is not a prime number.

83. C. To show this, let $p = q = 3$, for example.

84. B. $g(4) = \frac{\sqrt{4 - 3}}{4} = \frac{\sqrt{1}}{4} = \frac{1}{4}.$ The square root of a positive number is positive, by definition.

85. C. $(b * c) = c$; so $(b * c) * d = c * d = c.$

86. D. The identity element is b.

87. B. Use a Venn diagram to show
         the percentages of people who
         read the papers.

88. C. $C(8,2) = \dfrac{8 \cdot 7}{1 \cdot 2} = 28.$

89. A. Remember that $|x|$ is positive
         or zero for all x. Its graph is
         at the right.

90. B. $R \cap S = \{x : 2 < x < 13\}$. The primes in this set are 3, 5, 7, 11.

SAMPLE EXAMINATION 3

Part I: Basic Skills and Concepts

Directions for questions 1–25: Each question consists of two quantities, one in Column A and one in Column B. You are to compare the two quantities and in the answer column blacken space

  A if the quantity in Column A is greater;
  B if the quantity in Column B is greater;
  C if the two quantities are equal;
  D if the relationship cannot be determined from the information given.

Notes:
1. In certain questions, information concerning one or both of the quantities to be compared is centered above the two columns.
2. A symbol that appears in both columns represents the same thing in Column A as it does in Column B.
3. Letters such as x, n, and k stand for real numbers.

QUESTIONS	COLUMN A	COLUMN B	
1.	$3 \times 5 - 5$	0	1. Ⓐ Ⓑ Ⓒ Ⓓ
2.	$\sqrt{\dfrac{1}{16}}$	$\dfrac{0.3}{1.2}$	2. Ⓐ Ⓑ Ⓒ Ⓓ
3.	The average of seven numbers is 13. the sum of the seven numbers 90		3. Ⓐ Ⓑ Ⓒ Ⓓ
4.	Carpeting costs $9.50 per square yard. cost of 122 square yards of carpet	$1220	4. Ⓐ Ⓑ Ⓒ Ⓓ

QUESTIONS	COLUMN A	COLUMN B	
5.	the cost per ounce of cheese if 12 oz. cost 70¢	the cost per ounce if 1 pound costs 98¢	5. A B C D

The sum of x and a number is zero.

6.	x	0	6. A B C D
7.	$20 \times \frac{6}{17} \times 31$	$62 \times \frac{2}{17} \times 30$	7. A B C D

An open field, in the shape of a rectangle, is 10 yards by 20 yards.

8.	the distance, to the nearest yard, between opposite corners of the field	25	8. A B C D

A one-foot square vinyl tile costs 20¢. A kitchen floor has the shape shown:

9.	the cost of covering the kitchen floor with vinyl tiles	$30	9. A B C D

Andy takes an hour to bike to his friend's house 8 miles away but takes only 40 minutes to return.

10.	Andy's average speed on the trip	9 mph	10. A B C D
11.	the thousands digit in 40,010	the hundreds digit in 3.01×10^3	11. A B C D

x is an integer such that $-1 \leqq 2x + 1 < 2$

12.	x	0	12. A B C D

$$\frac{a}{b} > \frac{c}{d}, \; bd > 0$$

13.	ad	bc	13. A B C D

$$5(3x - 1) - x = 5$$

14.	x	$\frac{7}{5}$	14. A B C D
15.	the numerical coefficient if $(3x)(8x^{11})(x^{12})$ is simplified	the exponent of x in the final product	15. A B C D

$$\frac{8}{x} + \frac{1}{2} = \frac{11}{x}$$

16.	x	$\frac{3}{2}$	16. A B C D

QUESTIONS	COLUMN A	COLUMN B	

A registry has names of doctors from cities X, Y, and Z. The ratio of the number of doctors from city Y to the number from city Z is 3 : 1.

17. ratio of the total number of doctors to the number from city Z | 3 : 1 | 17. Ⓐ Ⓑ Ⓒ Ⓓ

$m = n$ Note: figure is not drawn to scale.

18. length of RS | length of ST | 18. Ⓐ Ⓑ Ⓒ Ⓓ

A right triangle has sides of lengths 3 in., 4 in., and 5 in.

19. the length of the altitude to the 5-inch side | 2.4 in. | 19. Ⓐ Ⓑ Ⓒ Ⓓ

$$\frac{m(\overarc{QTR})}{m(\overarc{NSP})} = \frac{2}{1}$$

O is the center of the circle.

20. $\dfrac{m(\angle QOR)}{m(\angle NMP)}$ | 4 : 1 | 20. Ⓐ Ⓑ Ⓒ Ⓓ

21. y | 72 | 21. Ⓐ Ⓑ Ⓒ Ⓓ

Area of rectangle $RSTU$ = 8 times area of triangle QRS.

| 22. | QU | $3RQ$ | 22. Ⓐ Ⓑ Ⓒ Ⓓ |

Use this bar graph of employee-benefit plans for questions 23, 24, and 25.

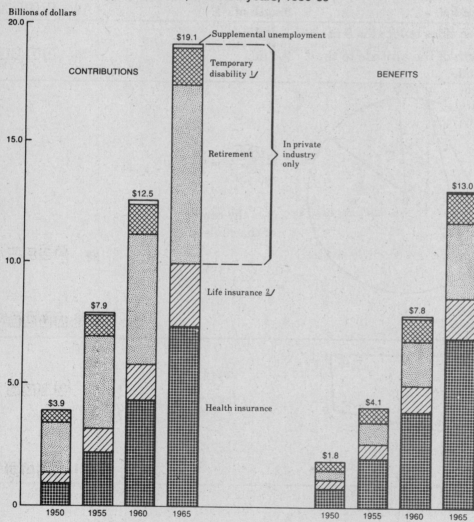

Contributions and benefits under employee-benefit plans, by type of benefit, selected years, 1950-65

1. Including sick leave.   2. Including accidental death and dismemberment insurance.

Source: Social Security Bulletin, April 1967, p. 16.

QUESTIONS	COLUMN A	COLUMN B	
23.	total contributions in 1950 to the nearest billion	4 billion	23. Ⓐ Ⓑ Ⓒ Ⓓ
24.	percentage increase overall in contributions from 1950 to 1965	500	24. Ⓐ Ⓑ Ⓒ Ⓓ
25.	ratio of contributions in 1965 for health insurance to total contributions	ratio of benefits in 1965 from health insurance to total benefits	25. Ⓐ Ⓑ Ⓒ Ⓓ

Directions for questions 26–40: For these questions, indicate the correct answer in the appropriate space in the answer column.

Note: Figures that accompany the following problems are intended to provide information useful in answering the questions. The figures are drawn as accurately as possible *except* when it is stated in a specific question that the figure is not drawn to scale. All figures lie in a plane unless otherwise stated.

Four equal circles are drawn tangent to the sides of the square and to each other, as shown. The radius of each circle is r.

26. The area of the square not within the circles equals   26. Ⓐ Ⓑ Ⓒ Ⓓ
   (A) $12r^2$ (B) $4\pi r^2$ (C) $(16 - 4\pi)r^2$ (D) $16 - 4\pi r^2$

27. $(5 - \sqrt{2})(5 + \sqrt{2}) =$ 27. Ⓐ Ⓑ Ⓒ Ⓓ
   (A) 21   (B) 23   (C) 27   (D) 29

28. Which line does not contain the point $(3, -1)$?   28. Ⓐ Ⓑ Ⓒ Ⓓ
   (A) $x + y = 2$ (B) $x + 3y = 0$
   (C) $y - 2x + 5 = 0$ (D) $y = -3x + 8$

29. $1 \div 0.02 =$ 29. Ⓐ Ⓑ Ⓒ Ⓓ
   (A) 0.05   (B) 0.5   (C) 5   (D) 50

Use this figure for questions 30 and 31.

HOUSEHOLDS HAVING CARS, TV, AND TELEPHONES

Source: *Pocket Data Book, USA 1971, Figure 13, p. 15.*

30. The percentage of households with one or more cars in 1960 was approximately
    (A) 20　　　(B) 30　　　(C) 75　　　(D) 80

    30. Ⓐ Ⓑ Ⓒ Ⓓ

31. The ratio, 1970 to 1960, of households with two or more cars was approximately
    (A) 2:1　　　(B) 3:2　　　(C) 2:3　　　(D) 1:2

    31. Ⓐ Ⓑ Ⓒ Ⓓ

32. $\sqrt{75} - \sqrt{27} - \sqrt{12} =$
    (A) 0　　　(B) $\sqrt{3}$　　　(C) $-\sqrt{3}$　　　(D) $5 - 5\sqrt{3}$

    32. Ⓐ Ⓑ Ⓒ Ⓓ

33. How much does 5 yards of material cost at 50¢ a foot if it is marked down 10%?
    (A) $2.25　　　(B) $6.50　　　(C) $6.75　　　(D) $7.00

    33. Ⓐ Ⓑ Ⓒ Ⓓ

34. If 3 is to x as 5 is to 8, then $x =$
    (A) 4.4　　　(B) 4.8　　　(C) 6　　　(D) 7

    34. Ⓐ Ⓑ Ⓒ Ⓓ

35. If $1.06 \times 10^k = 106{,}000$, then $k =$
    (A) −5　　　(B) 3　　　(C) 4　　　(D) 5

    35. Ⓐ Ⓑ Ⓒ Ⓓ

36. $^{7}/_{4} =$
    (A) 1.75%　　　(B) 17.5%　　　(C) $17^{3}/_{4}$%　　　(D) 175%

    36. Ⓐ Ⓑ Ⓒ Ⓓ

37. $\dfrac{x^2 - x}{x(x^2 + 1)} = \dfrac{x - 1}{x^2 + 1}$ for
    (A) all real x　　　　　　(B) $x \neq 0$
    (C) $x \neq 1$　　　　　　(D) $x \neq \pm 1$

    37. Ⓐ Ⓑ Ⓒ Ⓓ

38. The solution of the system of equations
    $\begin{cases} x + 2y = 1 \\ x - 3y = 6 \end{cases}$ is
    (A) $x = 1, y = 0$　　　　　　(B) $x = -1, y = 1$
    (C) $x = 3, y = -1$　　　　　　(D) $x = -1, y = 2$

    38. Ⓐ Ⓑ Ⓒ Ⓓ

428　Mathematics

Use this table for questions 39 and 40.

Table 6.--Community hospital utilization and expenses, by age group, fiscal years 1969-72

Item	Fiscal year amounts				Percentage change from preceding year		
	1969	1970	1971	1972	1970	1971	1972
Number of admissions (in thousands)......	28,027	29,247	30,312	30,706	4.4	3.6	1.3
Under age 65...........................	22,122	23,110	23,966	24,071	4.5	3.7	0.4
Aged 65 and over.......................	5,904	6,137	6,346	6,635	3.9	3.4	4.6
Number of patient days (in thousands)....	227,633	231,643	234,413	232,892	1.8	1.2	-0.6
Under age 65...........................	149,585	153,070	155,475	153,587	2.3	1.6	-1.2
Aged 65 and over.......................	78,048	78,573	78,938	79,305	0.7	0.5	0.5
Average length of stay (days)...........	8.12	7.92	7.73	7.58	-2.4	-2.4	-2.0
Under age 65...........................	6.76	6.62	6.49	6.38	-2.1	-2.0	-1.7
Aged 65 and over.......................	13.22	12.80	12.44	11.95	-3.2	-2.8	-3.9
Total expenses (in millions)............	$15,965	$18,693	$21,418	$23,925	17.1	14.6	11.7
Expenses per patient day................	$70.13	$80.70	$91.37	$102.73	15.1	13.2	12.4

Source: Social Security Bulletin, May 1973, p. 12.

39. The percentage increase in expenses per patient day from 1970 to 1971 was   39. Ⓐ Ⓑ Ⓒ Ⓓ
(A) over 15%   (B) less than 12%
(C) between 13 and 14%   (D) between 12 and 13%

40. Of the following, which percentage decrease from the preceding year on the average length of stay was greatest?   40. Ⓐ Ⓑ Ⓒ Ⓓ
(A) aged 65 and over in 1972   (B) aged 65 and over in 1970
(C) under age 65 in 1972   (D) under age 65 in 1970

SECTION II: CONTENT

Directions: For each of the following questions, indicate the correct answer in the appropriate space in the answer column.

Note: Figures that accompany problems in this part are intended to provide information useful in solving the problems. They are drawn as accurately as possible *except* when it is stated in a specific problem that the figure is not drawn to scale. All figures lie in a plane unless otherwise stated.

41. Which set is infinite?   41. Ⓐ Ⓑ Ⓒ Ⓓ
(A) the set of blades of grass in a lawn
(B) the set of grains of sand on Waikiki
(C) the set of points on a 1-inch line segment.
(D) the set of natural numbers less than 10^{10}

42. A Venn diagram for $\overline{R \cup S}$ (where $\overline{T}$ denotes the complement of T) is

42. Ⓐ Ⓑ Ⓒ Ⓓ

(A)

(B)

(C)

(D)

43. If $G = \{\, x : x$ is a prime number$\}$ and $H = \{x : x < 11\}$, then the number of elements in $G \cup H$ is

43. Ⓐ Ⓑ Ⓒ Ⓓ

(A) 4   (B) 5   (C) 6   (D) infinite

44. If $r \to s$ is true, then so is

44. Ⓐ Ⓑ Ⓒ Ⓓ

(A) $s \to r$ (B) $\sim s \to \sim r$ (C) $\sim r \to \sim s$ (D) $\sim s \to r$

45. The negation of the statement "Some people cheat on their tax returns" is

45. Ⓐ Ⓑ Ⓒ Ⓓ

(A) Some people do not cheat on their tax returns.
(B) No one cheats on his tax return.
(C) All people cheat on their tax returns.
(D) At least one person cheats on his tax return.

46. The truth table of $p \vee \sim(p \wedge q)$ is

46. Ⓐ Ⓑ Ⓒ Ⓓ

p	q	(A)	(B)	(C)	(D)
T	T	T	T	T	T
T	F	T	T	T	F
F	T	T	F	T	T
F	F	F	F	T	T

47. Assume the truth of the statements: (1) If women astronauts are used, then the space program will be improved; (2) If the space program is improved, then it will cost less. A valid conclusion is

47. Ⓐ Ⓑ Ⓒ Ⓓ

(A) If the space program does not cost less, then women astronauts are not being used.
(B) If women astronauts are not used, then the space program will cost more.
(C) If the space program costs less, then women astronauts are used.
(D) If only men are used as astronauts, then the space program will not be improved.

48. Let r be "Tony will pass the CLEP mathematics exam" and let s be "Tony is ill." Then the statement "If Tony is not ill, then he will pass the CLEP mathematics exam" may be written symbolically

48. Ⓐ Ⓑ Ⓒ Ⓓ

(A) $s \to \sim r$ (B) $\sim r \to \sim s$ (C) $r \to \sim s$ (D) $\sim s \to r$

49. A Pythagorean triple is a set of 3 numbers (x,y,z) that satisfies the equation $x^2 + y^2 = z^2$. A counterexample to the claim that the elements of Pythagorean triples are integers is the triple
(A) (3,4,5)　　(B) (1,2,3)　　(C) $(1,1,\sqrt{2})$　　(D) $(2,3,\sqrt{10})$

49. Ⓐ Ⓑ Ⓒ Ⓓ

50. The number of different real values of x for which $x^3 - 4x^2 = 0$ is
(A) 0　　(B) 1　　(C) 2　　(D) 3

50. Ⓐ Ⓑ Ⓒ Ⓓ

51. Which statement below about real numbers is false?
(A) If $a < b$, then $(a + c) < (b + c)$
(B) Every real number has an additive inverse.
(C) Every real number has a multiplicative inverse.
(D) If $a < 0$ and $b > c$, then $ab < ac$.

51. Ⓐ Ⓑ Ⓒ Ⓓ

52. Which of the following is not a real number?

(A) $\dfrac{0}{1/2}$　　(B) $\dfrac{3}{0}$　　(C) $\dfrac{\sqrt{3}}{\sqrt{3}}$　　(D) π

52. Ⓐ Ⓑ Ⓒ Ⓓ

53. If $4^{x-2} = 64$, then x equals
(A) 6　　(B) 5　　(C) 4　　(D) 3

53. Ⓐ Ⓑ Ⓒ Ⓓ

54. If the domain of $f(x) = 2x^2 + 1$ is the set of all integers, then the range of f is
(A) all integers
(B) all nonnegative integers
(C) a subset of the positive integers
(D) all integers greater than or equal to 1

54. Ⓐ Ⓑ Ⓒ Ⓓ

55. If $f(x) = 2x + 3$, then $f(f(x)) =$
(A) $4x + 9$　　(B) $2x + 6$　　(C) $4x + 6$　　(D) $4x + 3$

55. Ⓐ Ⓑ Ⓒ Ⓓ

56. If the graph at the right is of the function $y = f(x)$, then the graph of $y = -f(x)$ is

56. Ⓐ Ⓑ Ⓒ Ⓓ

(A)

(B)

(C)

(D)

57. Which of the following describes a function with domain the set of real numbers?

(A) $f(x) = \begin{cases} x & \text{if } x \leq 1 \\ x+1 & \text{if } x \geq 1 \end{cases}$ (B) $f(x) = |x|$ if $x \geq 0$

(C) $f(x) = \dfrac{1}{x}$ (D) $f(x) = \begin{cases} 0 & \text{if } x \text{ is rational} \\ 1 & \text{if } x \text{ is irrational} \end{cases}$

58. If for all elements x, y, z in a mathematical system $x \times (y+z) = x \times (z+y)$, then the system satisfies

(A) an associative law
(B) a distributive law
(C) the commutative law for addition
(D) the commutative law for multiplication

59. If $m * n$ denotes the least common multiple of the integers m and n, then which set below is closed under $*$?

(A) {1,2,3}   (B) {1,2,3,4,6}
(C) {1,2,3,4}   (D) {1,2,3,4,6,12}

60. Which of the binary operations $*$ defined below on the set of positive integers is not commutative?

(A) $m * n = m^n$ (B) $m * n = mn + 3$
(C) $m * n = mn + m + n$ (D) $m * n = 2^{mn}$

61. If a restaurant offers 5 different fillings for sandwiches on 3 different kinds of bread, with mayonnaise, butter, neither, or both, then the number of different kinds of sandwiches available is

(A) 120   (B) 60   (C) 45   (D) 30

62. If a penny is tossed three times, then the probability of 2 heads and 1 tail is

(A) $\frac{1}{8}$ (B) $\frac{1}{4}$ (C) $\frac{3}{8}$ (D) $\frac{1}{2}$

63. Which statement about the probability of an event is false?

(A) It may equal zero.
(B) It may exceed one.
(C) If it equals p, then $0 \leq p \leq 1$.
(D) It may equal one.

64. The number of different ways one may answer a 5-item true-false test is

(A) 2   (B) 5   (C) 25   (D) 32

65. The probability that Mrs. Corn watches certain TV shows is as follows:

The Lovers	0.29
The Killers	0.34
The Ticklers	0.12

If they are all shown at the same time, then the probability that she watches none of these shows is

(A) $(1 - 0.29) + (1 - 0.34) + (1 - 0.12)$
(B) $1 - (0.29)(0.34)(0.12)$
(C) $1 - (0.29 + 0.34 + 0.12)$
(D) $1 - 0.29 + 0.34 + 0.12$

66. Which pair of points shown is on the parabola $y = x^2 + 2$?
(A) M and N (B) N and Q
(C) M and P (D) P and Q

66. Ⓐ Ⓑ Ⓒ Ⓓ

$N(-1,3)$ ● ┼ 3 ● $M(1,3)$
┼ 2
┼ 1
-3 -2 -1 ┼ 1 2 3 x
-1
-2
$Q(-1,-3)$ ● ┼ ● $P(1,-3)$

67. Which of the following is a nonnegative integer?
(A) $3 \div 0$ (B) $2 - 4$ (C) $5 \div 2$ (D) $0 \div 1$

67. Ⓐ Ⓑ Ⓒ Ⓓ

68. The number of divisors of 3^{10} which are greater than one but less than 3^{10} is
(A) 8   (B) 9   (C) 10   (D) 36

68. Ⓐ Ⓑ Ⓒ Ⓓ

69. Which line is perpendicular to $5x - y = 1$?
(A) $x + 5y = 9$ (B) $5x - y = 1$
(C) $5x + y = 1$ (D) $5x + y = -1$

69. Ⓐ Ⓑ Ⓒ Ⓓ

70. The largest base-ten number that is a three-digit number base five is
(A) 124   (B) 444   (C) 720   (D) 999

70. Ⓐ Ⓑ Ⓒ Ⓓ

71. If $\log_a x = p$, then $\log_a x^4 =$
(A) 4   (B) $4p$ (C) p^4 (D) $p + 4$

71. Ⓐ Ⓑ Ⓒ Ⓓ

72. If, for real p and q, $p * q = \dfrac{p + q}{p + q - 1}$, then the only pair among the following for which $p * q$ is defined is
(A) $p = 0, q = 0$ (B) $p = 0, q = 1$
(C) $p = 1, q = 0$ (D) $p = -1, q = 2$

72. Ⓐ Ⓑ Ⓒ Ⓓ

73. If $i = \sqrt{-1}$, then $(1 + i)(1 - i) =$
(A) 0   (B) 2   (C) $2i$ (D) $-2i$

73. Ⓐ Ⓑ Ⓒ Ⓓ

74. 2012_3 equals what number base 10?
(A) 59   (B) 32   (C) 15   (D) 14

74. Ⓐ Ⓑ Ⓒ Ⓓ

75. If $x * y$ is defined to be $x + y - xy$, where x and y are real numbers, which of the following statements is false?
(A) $2 * 3 = 0$ (B) $4 * -1 = 7$
(C) $*$ is commutative   (D) 0 is the identity element

75. Ⓐ Ⓑ Ⓒ Ⓓ

76. The roots of the equation $3v^2 + 5v - 1 = 0$ are
(A) not real   (B) real, irrational, unequal
(C) real, rational, equal   (D) real, rational, unequal

76. Ⓐ Ⓑ Ⓒ Ⓓ

Use this addition table for questions 77 and 78.

+	p	q	r
p	r	p	q
q	p	q	r
r	q	r	p

77. The identity element is

    (A) p (B) q (C) r (D) none of the preceding

77.   A B C D

78. The additive inverse of r is

    (A) p (B) q (C) r (D) none of the preceding

78.   A B C D

79. If $T = \{x : x$ is an integer and $1 < x < 7\}$, then the number of subsets of T is

    (A) 6   (B) 12   (C) 16   (D) 32

79.   A B C D

80. A counterexample to the claim "If n is an odd prime, then so is $n^2 + 4$" is

    (A) 11   (B) 7   (C) 2   (D) 1

80.   A B C D

81. Which of the following is a real number?

    (A) $\dfrac{1}{0}$ (B) $\dfrac{0}{0}$ (C) $\dfrac{0}{-2}$ (D) 0^0

81.   A B C D

82. If $f(x) = x^2 - 5$ and $g(x) = 2^{-x}$, then $f(g(-1)) =$

    (A) $-4\frac{1}{4}$ (B) -3 (C) -1 (D) $\frac{1}{16}$

82.   A B C D

83. Each of the 3-digit numbers that can be formed from the set $\{2,5,7,9\}$, allowing repetitions, is written on a piece of paper. One slip is then chosen at random. The probability that the number chosen begins with a 7 is

    (A) $\frac{1}{4}$ (B) $\frac{3}{10}$

    (C) $\frac{1}{3}$ (D) none of the preceding

83.   A B C D

84. The median of the set $\{4,10,7,15,9,10,7,10\}$ is

    (A) 8   (B) 9   (C) 9.5   (D) 10

84.   A B C D

85. The negation of the statement "Every cat meows" is

    (A) No cat meows.   (B) Some cats meow.

    (C) Most cats do not meow.   (D) Some cat does not meow.

85.   A B C D

86. $\log_2 \frac{1}{2} =$

    (A) -1 (B) $\frac{1}{4}$ (C) 1   (D) $\sqrt{2}$

86.   A B C D

87. The graph of $y = (x - 3)^2$ has a minimum at the point

    (A) $(0,3)$ (B) $(0,-3)$ (C) $(3,0)$ (D) $(-3,0)$

87.   A B C D

88. The additive inverse of $a - b$ is

    (A) $-a - b$ (B) $a + b$ (C) $b - a$ (D) $-(a + b)$

88.   A B C D

89. A function $f(x)$ is even if $f(-x) = f(x)$. Which of the following functions is *not* even?

    (A) $f(x) = x^2 + 3$ (B) $f(x) = (x + 1)^2$

    (C) $f(x) = \dfrac{3}{x^2}$ (D) $f(x) = 1 - x^2$

89.   A B C D

90. For what number a does $a^{-1/2}$ equal 2?

    (A) $\frac{1}{4}$ (B) $\frac{1}{2}$ (C) 2   (D) 4

90.   A B C D

ANSWER KEY AND REFERENCE CHART—SAMPLE EXAMINATION 3

See page 323 for an explanation of the reference code given in parentheses after each answer.

Part I

1. A (A1)	11. C (A1)	21. A (A3)	31. A (A4)
2. C (A1)	12. D (A2)	22. C (A3)	32. A (A2)
3. A (A1)	13. A (A2)	23. C (A4)	33. C (A1)
4. B (A1)	14. B (A2)	24. B (A4)	34. B (A2)
5. B (A1)	15. C (A2)	25. B (A5)	35. D (A1)
6. D (A2)	16. A (A2)	26. C (A3)	36. D (A1)
7. C (A1)	17. A (A2)	27. B (A2)	37. B (A2)
8. B (A3)	18. D (A3)	28. C (A2)	38. C (A2)
9. B (A3)	19. C (A3)	29. D (A1)	39. C (A4)
10. A (A1)	20. C (A3)	30. C (A4)	40. A (A4)

Part II

41. C (B1)	51. C (B3)	61. B (B5)	71. B (B6)	81. C (B3)
42. A (B1)	52. B (B3)	62. C (B5)	72. A (B3)	82. C (B4)
43. D (B1)	53. B (B3)	63. B (B6)	73. B (B6)	83. A (B5)
44. B (B2)	54. C (B4)	64. D (B5)	74. A (B6)	84. C (B5)
45. B (B2)	55. A (B4)	65. C (B5)	75. A (B6)	85. D (B2)
46. C (B2)	56. A (B4)	66. A (B4)	76. B (B2)	86. A (B6)
47. A (B2)	57. D (B4)	67. D (B3)	77. B (B6)	87. C (B4)
48. D (B2)	58. C (B3)	68. B (B3)	78. A (B6)	88. C (B6)
49. C (B2)	59. D (B6)	69. A (B4)	79. D (B1)	89. B (B4)
50. C (B3)	60. A (B6)	70. A (B6)	80. A (B2)	90. A (B3)

SCORING CHART—SAMPLE EXAMINATION 3

After you have scored your Sample Examination 3, enter the results in the chart below; then transfer your Raw Score to the Progress Chart on page 14.

Total Test	Number Right	Number Wrong	Number Omitted	Raw Score
Part I: 40				
Part II: 50				
Total: 90				

ANSWER EXPLANATIONS—SAMPLE EXAMINATION 3

Part I

1. A. $3 \times 5 - 5 = (3 \times 5) - 5 = 15 - 5 = 10$

2. C. $\sqrt{1/16} = 1/4$; $\dfrac{0.3}{1.2} = 3/12 = 1/4$.

3. A. If the average of 7 numbers is 13, then their sum divided by 7 equals 13; therefore their sum must be 7×13, or 91.

4.   B. If the carpet costs $10 a square yard, the total cost of 122 yards would be $1220.

5.   B. $(70 \div 12) < 6$; $(98 \div 16) > 6$.

6.   D. x may be negative, positive, or even zero.

7.   C. We can rearrange (mentally) the Column B entry, with an eye on Column A, as follows

$$62 \times \tfrac{2}{17} \times 30 = (31 \times 2) \times \tfrac{2}{17} \times (3 \times 10)$$
$$= 2 \times 10 \times 3 \times \tfrac{2}{17} \times 31$$
$$= 20 \times \tfrac{6}{17} \times 31$$

8.   B.

$$x^2 = 100 + 400 = 500$$

$$x = 10\sqrt{5} < 10(2.5) = 25$$

9.   B. The area is $(12 \times 12) - (2 \times 2)$, or 140 square feet; $140 \times 0.20 = \$28$.

10. A. Be careful. The average speed is

$$\frac{8+8}{1+\tfrac{2}{3}} = \frac{16}{\tfrac{5}{3}} = 16 \times \tfrac{3}{5} = \tfrac{48}{5} > 9.$$

11. C. The thousands digit in 40,0<u>1</u>0, which is underlined, is 0. $3.01 \times 10^3 = 3010$, and the (underlined) hundreds digit is also 0.

12. D. If $-1 \le 2x + 1 < 2$, then $-1 - 1 \le 2x < 2 - 1$, $-2 \le 2x < 1$, and $-1 \le x < \tfrac{1}{2}$. So if x must be an integer, it may be either -1 or 0.

13. A. If $bd > 0$, then the inequality is preserved when we multiply by bd. Thus, $ad > bc$.

14. B. If $5(3x - 1) - x = 5$, then $15x - 5 - x = 5$, $14x = 10$, and $x = \tfrac{5}{7}$.

15. C. $(3x)(8x^{11})(x^{12}) = 24x^{24}$.

16. A. If $\dfrac{8}{x} + \dfrac{1}{2} = \dfrac{11}{x}$, then $\dfrac{1}{2} = \dfrac{3}{x}$ and $x = 6$.

17. A. The ratio of the total number of doctors to the number from city $Z = n : 1$, where $n > 3$.

18. D. Don't assume that the segments are of equal length. A counterexample is shown at the right.

19. C. In this right triangle, $\tfrac{5}{3} = \tfrac{3}{x}$, so $x = \tfrac{9}{5}$. Then $h^2 = 9 - (\tfrac{9}{5})^2 = \tfrac{144}{25}$, yielding $h = \tfrac{12}{5} = 2.4$.

20. C. $m(\angle QOR) = m(QTR)$, since $\angle QOR$ is a central angle; $m(\angle NMP) = \tfrac{1}{2}m(NSP)$, since $\angle NMP$ is inscribed. Then

$$\frac{m(\angle QOR)}{m(\angle NMP)} = \frac{m(QTR)}{\tfrac{1}{2}m(NSP)} = \frac{1}{\tfrac{1}{2}} \cdot \frac{2}{1} = \frac{4}{1} = 4:1.$$

21. A. The interior angles of the quadrilateral sum to 360°; therefore $y = 82$.

22. C. Area $RSTU = 4(x + y) =$
8(area $\triangle QRS$) $= 8 \cdot {}^{1}/_{2} \cdot 4x$.
$4x + 4y = 16x$; $4y = 12x$,
and $y = 3x$.

23. C. Contributions under employee-benefit plans in 1950 were \$3.9 billion.

24. B. Percentage increase $= \dfrac{19.1 - 3.9}{3.9} = \dfrac{15.2}{3.9}$ $<500\%$

25. B .Ratio described is clearly less for contributions, since the amounts shown for health insurance are roughly equal but total contributions are much greater than total benefits.

26. C. The area of the square is $(4r)^2 = 16r^2$; the area of the four circles is $4\pi r^2$.

27. B. $(5 - \sqrt{2})(5 + \sqrt{2}) = 25 - 2 = 23$.

28. C. Replace x by 3 and y by -1 in each equation. The left side in (C) does not equal the right.

29. D. $\dfrac{1}{0.02} = \dfrac{100}{2} = 50$.

30. C. Use the top unshaded bar.

31. A. The black bar is about twice the length of the unshaded one.

32. A. $\sqrt{75} - \sqrt{27} - \sqrt{12} = \sqrt{25 \cdot 3} - \sqrt{9 \cdot 3} - \sqrt{4 \cdot 3}$
$$= 5\sqrt{3} - 3\sqrt{3} - 2\sqrt{3} = 0.$$

33. C. 5 yd. = 15 ft.; $15 \times 0.50 = 7.50$; $7.50 - {}^{1}/_{10}(7.50) = 7.50 - 0.75 = \$6.75$.

34. B. $3:x = 5:8 \rightarrow 5x = 24 \rightarrow x = 4.8$.

35. D. The decimal point in 1.06 is moved 5 places to the right to yield 106,000.

36. D. $\dfrac{7}{4} = 1\dfrac{3}{4} = 1.75 = 175\%$.

37. B. The fraction at the left is divided by $\dfrac{x}{x}$. To avoid dividing by zero, x cannot equal zero.

38. C. Subtracting the lower equation from the upper yields $5y = -5$, so $y = -1$; substituting in either equation yields $x = 3$. Or, check the pairs given to see which one satisfies *both* equations.

39. C. It's 13.2%.

40. A. The table tells us that (A) is -3.9%, (B) is -3.2%, (C) is -1.7%, and (D) is -2.1%.

Part II

41. C. Although each set in (A), (B), and (D) is large, it is finite; that is, the elements can (theoretically) be counted.

42. A. Note that $\overline{R \cup S} = \overline{R} \cap \overline{S}$.

43. D. Remember that $G \cup H$ contains elements in G *or* in H and note that G is infinite.

44. B. A statement and its contrapositive are equivalent.

45. B. The negation of $\exists_x, p_x$ is $\forall_x, \sim p_x$.

46. C. Here it is worked out: the numbers at the bottoms of the columns indicate the order in which the columns were filled:

p	$\lor$	$\sim$	(p	$\land$	q)
T	T	F	T	T	T
T	T	T	T	F	F
F	T	T	F	F	T
F	T	T	F	F	F
(1)	(5)	(4)	(1)	(3)	(2)

47.   A. If w denotes "women astronauts are used," s "the space program will be improved," and c "the space program will cost less," then we have $w \rightarrow s$ and $s \rightarrow c$. One valid conclusion is $\sim c \rightarrow \sim s$ and $\sim s \rightarrow \sim w$ or $\sim c \rightarrow \sim w$. No other choice is valid.

48.   D. The statement is equivalent to "If not s, then r."

49.   C. $(2, 3\sqrt{10})$ is *not* a Pythagorean triple.

50.   C. $x^3 - 4x^2 = x^2(x - 4) = 0$ if $x = 0, 4$.

51.   C. 0 has no multiplicative inverse.

52.   B. Division by zero is not permitted.

53.   B. $4^{x-2} = 64 \rightarrow 4^{x-2} = 4^3$; so $x = 5$.

54.   C. $f(x) \geqslant 1$ but the range consists of only some integers, e.g., $f(1) = 3$, $f(2) = 9$, $f(3) = 19$, and so forth.

55.   A. $f(f(x)) = 2(2x + 3) + 3 = 4x + 6 + 3 = 4x + 9$.

56.   A. $-f(x)$ is the reflection of $f(x)$ in the x-axis.

57.   D. In (A), $f(1) = 1$ and 2; (B) is not defined for $x < 0$; and in (C) $f(0)$ is not defined.

58.   C. The commutative law for addition specifies for any pair of elements a and b that $a + b = b + a$.

59.   D. The lcm for (A) is 6, for (B) 12, for (C) 12, and for (D) 12. Note that 6 is not in (A) and that 12 is only in (D).

60.   A. $m * n = m^n \neq n * m = n^m$.

61.   B. $5 \times 3 \times 4 = 60$.

62.   C. A tree may be most helpful here. There are 3 ways, out of a total of 8 outcomes, of obtaining 2 heads and 1 tail.

63.   B. If p is the probability of an event, then $0 \leqslant p \leqslant 1$; p cannot exceed 1.

64.   D. Each of the five items may be answered in two ways, yielding 2^5.

65.   C. Let L, K, T denote her watching *The Lovers, Killers,* or *Ticklers* respectively. Then $p(L \text{ or } K \text{ or } T) = p(L) + p(K) + p(T) = 0.29 + 0.34 + 0.12$ (since the events are mutually exclusive). The probability that she watches none of these is $1 - [p(L) + p(K) + p(T)]$.

66.   A. The graph of $y = x^2 + 2$ is symmetric to the y-axis since $y(-x) = y(x)$.

67.   D. $0 \div 1 = 0$. The set of nonnegative integers consists of all the positive integers and zero.

68.   B. Since 3 is prime, the divisors of 3^{10} (greater than 1 and less than 3^{10}) are 3^1, $3^2, 3^3, 3^4, 3^5, 3^6, 3^7, 3^8$, and 3^9.

69.   A. The slope of $5x - y = 1$ is 5 (write the equation in the form $y = 5x - 1$). The slope of a line perpendicular to it is the negative reciprocal of 5, i.e., $-\frac{1}{5}$.

70.   A. The largest three-digit number base 5 is 444_{five}, which equals, base 10, $4 \cdot 5^2 + 4 \cdot 5 + 4$.

71.   B. $\log_a x^4 = 4 \log_a x = 4p$.

72.   A. The denominator equals 0 except for choice (A).

73.   B. $(1 + i)(1 - i) = 1 - i^2 = 1 - (-1) = 2$.

74. A. $2012_3 = 2 \times 3^3 + 0 \times 3^2 + 1 \times 3^1 + 2 \times 3^0 = 54 + 3 + 2 = 59$.

75. A. $2 * 3 = 2 + 3 - 2 \times 3 = 5 - 6 = -1$. Verify the truth of (B), (C), (D).

76. B. The discriminant equals $5^2 - 4(3)(-1) = 37$.

77. B. Note that if s is any one of the elements in the set, then $s + q = q + s = s$. To find the identity element, look for a column (or a row) identical with the lead column (or row).

78. A. Note that q is the identity and that $r + p = q$.

79. D. Since there are 5 integers in T, T has 2^5 subsets.

80. A. 11 is an odd prime, but $11^2 + 4 = 125$ is not prime.

81. C. Division by zero is prohibited. The numeral "0^0" is not defined.

82. C. $g(-1) = 2^{-(-1)} = 2$, and $f(2) = 2^2 - 5 = -1$.

83. A. There are 4^3 or 64 slips of which 4^2 begin with 7.

84. C. The median is the average of the two "middle" numbers in the arranged set $\{4, 7, 7, 9, 10, 10, 10, 15\}$.

85. D. The negation of $\forall_x, p_x$ is $\exists_x, \sim p_x$.

86. A. Since $2^{-1} = \frac{1}{2}$, $\log_{1/2} 2 = -1$.

87. C. It is the graph of $y = x^2$ translated 3 units to the right.

88. C. The additive inverse of the real number x is $-x$; $-(a - b) = -a + b = b - a$.

89. B. Note that if $f(x) = (x + 1)^2$, $f(-x) = (-x + 1)^2 \neq f(x)$.

90. A. $a^{-1/2} = 2 \rightarrow \dfrac{1}{a^{1/2}} = 2 \rightarrow \dfrac{1}{\sqrt{a}} = 2$. So $\dfrac{1}{a} = 4$ and $a = \dfrac{1}{4}$.

PART FOUR

THE NATURAL SCIENCES EXAMINATION

Trial Test $\boxed{12}$

The trial Natural Sciences test in this chapter will give you an idea of what the actual exam is like. Take the test, determine your score, and find out which areas of the natural sciences you may need to review.

The test is made up of two parts, one with 60 multiple-choice questions covering the biological sciences, the other with 60 multiple-choice questions covering the physical sciences.

Part I Biological Sciences

Number of Questions: 60
Time: 45 minutes

Directions: Each of the questions or incomplete statements below is followed by five suggested answers or completions. Select the one that is best in each case.

1. Malaria, amoebic dysentery, and African sleeping sickness have in common the fact that

   (A) all are found in Africa only
   (B) they are caused by protozoans
   (C) each constitutes a serious disease of the central nervous system
   (D) they are of little significance to man
   (E) they are all transmitted by direct contact

   1. Ⓐ Ⓑ Ⓒ Ⓓ Ⓔ

2. Cellular structures responsible for oxidizing food and converting energy to adenosine triphosphate are called
   (A) the golgi apparatus   (B) ribosomes   (C) chromoplasts
   (D) mitochondria   (E) the endoplasmic reticulum

   2. Ⓐ Ⓑ Ⓒ Ⓓ Ⓔ

3. According to Weismann's theory of the continuity of the germ plasm,
   (A) embryos recapitulate embryonic forms of their ancestors
   (B) germ plasm remains unaffected by the somaplasm
   (C) germ plasm can only be influenced by the somaplasm

   3. Ⓐ Ⓑ Ⓒ Ⓓ Ⓔ

(D) genes exist in pairs

(E) genes are in linear order along chromosomes

4. The ribosomes associated with the endoplasmic reticulum consist of 　　4. Ⓐ Ⓑ Ⓒ Ⓓ Ⓔ

(A) secretory nodes which control metabolism

(B) deoxyribose nucleic acid which synthesizes chromatin

(C) granular bodies associated with cell division

(D) ribonucleic acid which synthesizes protein

(E) various nucleic acids, each of which is self-perpetuating

5. If a living cell is placed in a hypotonic solution,　　5. Ⓐ Ⓑ Ⓒ Ⓓ Ⓔ

(A) turgor pressure decreases

(B) osmotic pressure increases

(C) osmotic pressure decreases

(D) turgor pressure is not affected

(E) turgor pressure increases

6. In typical ecosystems, the producers are　　6. Ⓐ Ⓑ Ⓒ Ⓓ Ⓔ

(A) heterotrophic　　(B) parasitic　　(C) chemotrophic

(D) photosynthetic　　(E) saprophytic

7. The light reactions of photosynthesis are those in which　　7. Ⓐ Ⓑ Ⓒ Ⓓ Ⓔ

(A) radiant energy is synthesized into organic materials

(B) radiant energy is stored

(C) carbon dioxide is absorbed

(D) radiant energy is changed to chemical energy

(E) sugar is formed and oxygen is released

8. The principal water-absorbing structure of a typical root is the　　8. Ⓐ Ⓑ Ⓒ Ⓓ Ⓔ

(A) hair root　　(B) root cap　　(C) endodermis

(D) root hair cell　　(E) cortex

9. A photosynthetic organism is one which　　9. Ⓐ Ⓑ Ⓒ Ⓓ Ⓔ

(A) obtains energy by the oxidation of inorganic materials

(B) utilizes solid materials after eating and digesting them

(C) obtains its nourishment from decaying organic materials

(D) lives at the expense of other organisms

(E) uses radiant energy in food synthesis

10. A growth response to the stimulus of light is a　　10. Ⓐ Ⓑ Ⓒ Ⓓ Ⓔ

(A) geotropism　　(B) phototropism　　(C) thigmotropism

(D) photoperiodism　　(E) hydrotropism

11. The growing of plants under soil-less conditions is called　　11. Ⓐ Ⓑ Ⓒ Ⓓ Ⓔ

(A) aquatics　　(B) hydrology　　(C) hydrotropism

(D) hydroponics　　(E) hydrotaxis

12. When you eat asparagus, you are mainly eating　　12. Ⓐ Ⓑ Ⓒ Ⓓ Ⓔ

(A) roots　　(B) stems　　(C) leaves　　(D) flowers

(E) fruit

13. The enzyme-controlled breakdown of carbohydrates under anaerobic conditions is called　　13. Ⓐ Ⓑ Ⓒ Ⓓ Ⓔ

(A) autolysis　　(B) putrefaction　　(C) bacteriophage

(D) fermentation　　(E) interferon

14. In plant reproduction, selected cells of the diploid, spore-producing generation undergo
    (A) diploidization   (B) oogenesis   (C) spermatogenesis
    (D) meiosis   (E) mitosis

14. A B C D E

15. Structures which are similar because of function are said to be
    (A) analogous   (B) homosporous   (C) monoecious
    (D) homologous   (E) dioecious

15. A B C D E

16. In blood transfusions, individuals referred to as universal receivers may receive blood from
    (A) group AB   (B) groups A, AB   (C) groups B, AB
    (D) group O only   (E) groups O, A, B, AB

16. A B C D E

17. Many plants produce an orange pigment called carotene which animals convert to
    (A) ATP   (B) hemoglobin   (C) vitamin A
    (D) phytol   (E) vitamin C

17. A B C D E

18. The semicircular canals are innervated by the
    (A) auditory nerve   (B) facial nerve   (C) trochlear nerve
    (D) spinal accessory nerve   (E) optic nerve

18. A B C D E

19. The hormone that controls the rate of food conversion to energy is
    (A) insulin   (B) thyroxin   (C) adrenalin
    (D) cortisone   (E) secretin

19. A B C D E

20. Stimulation by the sympathetic nervous system would result in
    (A) constricted pupils   (B) dilated arteries
    (C) accelerated heart beat   (D) increased peristalsis
    (E) lower blood pressure

20. A B C D E

21. Progesterone
    (A) constricts blood vessels
    (B) regulates the menstrual cycle
    (C) stimulates production of thyroxin
    (D) regulates rate of basal metabolism
    (E) regulates sodium metabolism

21. A B C D E

22. The significance of mitosis is that there is
    (A) a quantitative division of the cell
    (B) precise distribution of all cell content to the daughter cells
    (C) a qualitative division of all cell components
    (D) a reduction of chromosome number
    (E) precise distribution of DNA to each daughter cell

22. A B C D E

23. Transfer of genetic information from one generation to the next is accomplished by
    (A) RNA   (B) messenger RNA   (C) codon
    (D) translation   (E) DNA

23. A B C D E

24. The inherited variations which are so essential to the concept of natural selection have their source in
    (A) acquired characteristics   (B) chance variations

24. A B C D E

(C) mutation   (D) the environment   (E) special creation

25. Preformationists who were advocates of the theory of embryo development from structures within the sperm were called   25. Ⓐ Ⓑ Ⓒ Ⓓ Ⓔ
(A) ovists   (B) animalculists   (C) epigenesists
(D) pangenesists   (E) phylogenists

26. A cultured, Greek-educated, Roman poet who spent most of his life writing *De Rerum Natura (On The Nature of Things)* was   26. Ⓐ Ⓑ Ⓒ Ⓓ Ⓔ
(A) Dioscorides   (B) Isidore   (C) Pliny   (D) Galen
(E) Lucretius

27. You would expect to observe caribou and lichens in   27. Ⓐ Ⓑ Ⓒ Ⓓ Ⓔ
(A) a tropical rain forest   (B) the arctic tundra
(C) a desert   (D) a deciduous forest   (E) a coniferous forest

28. Plankton includes marine organisms which   28. Ⓐ Ⓑ Ⓒ Ⓓ Ⓔ
(A) exist below low tide and on the continental shelf
(B) exist only in darkness
(C) exist to a depth of 5,000 feet
(D) float on the surface
(E) exist in the deepest ocean trenches

29. Marine organisms characteristic of the abyssal zone would be found   29. Ⓐ Ⓑ Ⓒ Ⓓ Ⓔ
(A) in the inter-tidal zone
(B) on the continental shelf to a depth of 500-600 feet
(C) in light
(D) in the deepest ocean trenches
(E) to a depth of 5,000 feet

30. A biologist specializing in the study of insects is called   30. Ⓐ Ⓑ Ⓒ Ⓓ Ⓔ
(A) an herpetologist   (B) a paleontologist
(C) an entomologist   (D) an ornithologist
(E) an ichthyologist

31. Interrelationships between organisms are termed commensalism when   31. Ⓐ Ⓑ Ⓒ Ⓓ Ⓔ
(A) both organisms are benefited
(B) mates are defended
(C) one organism benefits at the expense of the other
(D) territories are defended
(E) one organism benefits and the other is not harmed

32. The Cenozoic era is best described as the age of   32. Ⓐ Ⓑ Ⓒ Ⓓ Ⓔ
(A) reptiles   (B) seed ferns   (C) seed plants and mammals
(D) primitive fishes   (E) amphibians

33. In the human circulatory system, blood returns to the heart from the lungs through the   33. Ⓐ Ⓑ Ⓒ Ⓓ Ⓔ
(A) superior vena cava   (B) pulmonary veins
(C) inferior vena cava   (D) pulmonary artery
(E) descending aorta

34. Blood is supplied to the muscle wall of the heart by the   34. Ⓐ Ⓑ Ⓒ Ⓓ Ⓔ
(A) hepatic portal vein   (B) coronary arteries
(C) auricular artery   (D) mesenteric artery
(E) coronary veins

35. Hookworm larvae gain access to the body
    (A) by penetrating unbroken skin
    (B) incidental to insect bites
    (C) through the mouth in contaminated food
    (D) in improperly cooked pork
    (E) in improperly cooked fish

36. A disease of man transmitted by the bite of certain ticks is
    (A) tularemia   (B) Rocky Mountain spotted fever
    (C) sleeping sickness   (D) psittacosis   (E) amebiasis

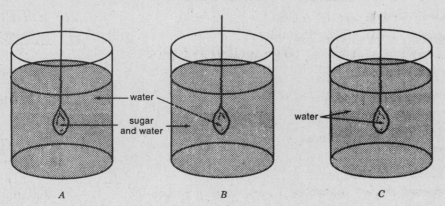

NOTE: In the diagrams above, water and sugar solutions are separated by cellophane membranes, as indicated. These cellophane membranes are permeable to water molecules and impermeable to sugar molecules. Assume that temperatures are constant and that the cellophane bags are filled equally.

37. In diagram A
    (A) the bag will shrink
    (B) the addition of sugar to the water in the container will cause the turgidity of the bag to increase
    (C) diffusion does not occur
    (D) water molecules diffuse into the bag because there is a greater concentration of water outside than inside of the bag
    (E) there is a net movement of water molecules out of the cellophane bag

38. In diagram B
    (A) the bag will shrink
    (B) the bag will swell
    (C) there will be a net movement of water molecules into the bag
    (D) there will be a net movement of sugar molecules into the bag
    (E) sugar draws water out of the bag

39. In diagram C
   (A) water will diffuse into the bag causing it to swell
   (B) water will diffuse out of the bag causing it to shrink
   (C) there is a state of equilibrium in respect to water molecules
   (D) osmosis occurs in the system
   (E) the addition of glass marbles to the container will cause the bag to shrink

40. An organism which obtains energy from the oxidation of inorganic substances is
   (A) chemosynthetic   (B) photosynthetic   (C) parasitic
   (D) saprophytic   (E) holozoic

41. In a typical lake, the important producers are
   (A) commmensals   (B) zooplankton   (C) nekton
   (D) phytoplankton   (E) benthos

42. Photosynthesis
   (A) results in a decrease in dry weight
   (B) is continuous in both light and darkness
   (C) produces carbon dioxide and water
   (D) results in an increase in dry weight
   (E) uses oxygen and glucose as raw materials

43. Photosynthesis
   (A) occurs in all living cells
   (B) occurs only in the presence of radiant energy
   (C) produces carbon dioxide and water
   (D) decreases dry weight
   (E) occurs in either light or darkness

44. Xylem is the principal constituent of a plant product called
   (A) wood   (B) bark   (C) latex   (D) pith   (E) resin

45. One side effect that may be produced by the antigen-antibody reaction of the body is
   (A) allergy   (B) dehydration   (C) convulsions
   (D) infection   (E) pain

46. The body responds to an invasion of viruses by producing
   (A) antibodies   (B) vaccine   (C) antibiotics
   (D) antigens   (E) immune serum

47. The active substance which appears in a virus-infected cell and which prevents infection by a second virus is called
   (A) autolysis   (B) interferon   (C) lysozyme
   (D) bacteriophage   (E) rickettsias

48. It is unfortunate for humans that
   (A) red blood cells are constantly being formed
   (B) blood pressure decreases in the capillaries
   (C) the heart beat is a regular rhythmic cycle
   (D) the lymphatic system returns fluid to the circulatory system
   (E) hemoglobin bonds more firmly to carbon monoxide than to oxygen

49. The Rh factor is fundamentally

49. A B C D E

    (A) a hormonal reaction   (B) an antigen-antibody reaction
    (C) a form of anemia   (D) phagocytosis
    (E) a vitamin deficiency

50. A deficiency of vitamin K may result in

50. A B C D E

    (A) soft, weak bones   (B) sterility   (C) scurvy
    (D) beriberi   (E) hemorrhage following surgery

51. Roughage is important in the human diet because it

51. A B C D E

    (A) contains vitamins
    (B) speeds up digestion
    (C) stimulates the walls of the large intestine
    (D) slows digestion
    (E) stimulates the production of antibodies

52. "Animal starch," a nutrient stored in various types of animal cells is correctly called

52. A B C D E

    (A) angstrom   (B) antigen   (C) myosin
    (D) glycogen   (E) actin

53. When the thyroid gland produces insufficient amounts of thyroxine,

53. A B C D E

    (A) tetany occurs   (B) the basal metabolism rate increases
    (C) irregularities in sodium metabolism develop
    (D) acromegaly develops
    (E) the basal metabolism rate decreases

54. Among the contributions of the ancient Greek scholars

54. A B C D E

    (A) was the law of independent assortment
    (B) was the concept of biogenesis
    (C) was the concept of recapitulation
    (D) were elements of the theory that living organisms have evolved
    (E) was the preformation theory

55. The physical basis for heredity was established by T. H. Morgan when he demonstrated his

55. A B C D E

    (A) mutation theory   (B) principle of eugenics
    (C) gene theory   (D) theory of recapitulation
    (E) chromosome theory of inheritance

56. Paul Ehrlich is best known for his discoveries in

56. A B C D E

    (A) immunization   (B) attenuation   (C) chemotherapy
    (D) antibiosis   (E) phytopathology

57. A famous anatomist during the Renaissance was

57. A B C D E

    (A) Bacon   (B) Linnaeus   (C) Pliny   (D) Vesalius
    (E) Galen

58. In general, short food chains are more efficient than long food chains because in short food chains

58. A B C D E

    (A) there can be no carnivores   (B) there is more energy loss
    (C) there are fewer producers   (D) there is less energy loss
    (E) there are more producers

59. A population displaying a great number of homologous structures is considered to be

(A) an order   (B) a class   (C) a family   (D) a genus   (E) a species

59. Ⓐ Ⓑ Ⓒ Ⓓ Ⓔ

60. Under the conditions of unilateral lighting imposed upon the plant in the diagram above, the plant bends towards the light because

(A) the plant needs more light in order to carry on photosynthesis

(B) the plant grows away from darkness

(C) this is a growth response caused by the unequal distribution of growth-promoting substances in the plant stem

(D) the plant is attracted to light

(E) this is a growth response in an attempt to overcome the growth-repressing effects of darkness

60. Ⓐ Ⓑ Ⓒ Ⓓ Ⓔ

Part II: Physical Sciences

Number of Questions: 60
Time: 45 minutes

Directions: Each of the questions or incomplete statements below is followed by five suggested answers or completions. Select the one that is best in each case.

1. If you are standing at 90 degrees north latitude, you would be at the

(A) equator   (B) Tropic of Cancer   (C) Tropic of Capricorn

(D) North Pole   (E) international dateline

1. Ⓐ Ⓑ Ⓒ Ⓓ Ⓔ

2. We credit Pythagoras with the theory which bears his name; but he also discovered

(A) that planets revolve from west to east

(B) that planets revolve from east to west

(C) that big rocks fall faster than little rocks

(D) the nature of eclipses

(E) the cause of earthquakes

2. Ⓐ Ⓑ Ⓒ Ⓓ Ⓔ

3. The basic energy-producing reaction in the sun is the conversion of

(A) mass to energy due to pressure

(B) helium to hydrogen

(C) fuels to heat

(D) heavy elements into lighter elements

(E) hydrogen into helium

3. Ⓐ Ⓑ Ⓒ Ⓓ Ⓔ

4. A term to describe the solar system when the earth is presumably in the center is
   (A) rotation   (B) parallax   (C) geocentric
   (D) heliocentric   (E) ecliptic

   4. Ⓐ Ⓑ Ⓒ Ⓓ Ⓔ

5. The milky way galaxy is best described as
   (A) a spherical grouping of about fifty million stars spread over approximately 2,000 light-years
   (B) the solar system together with its moons and asteroids
   (C) a disk-shaped grouping of billions of stars which spreads over approximately 100,000 light-years
   (D) a galactic system comprising all the constellations
   (E) a spherical grouping of over a billion stars

   5. Ⓐ Ⓑ Ⓒ Ⓓ Ⓔ

6. An eastbound traveler crossing the international dateline should
   (A) set his watch back one hour
   (B) set his watch ahead one hour
   (C) wait until he reaches the midnight meridian
   (D) subtract a day
   (E) add a day

   6. Ⓐ Ⓑ Ⓒ Ⓓ Ⓔ

7. When an astronomer detects a shift towards the red end of the spectrum, he correctly infers
   (A) the chemical composition of a star
   (B) the age of a star
   (C) that a star is receding
   (D) the speed-up of the star
   (E) that a star is approaching

   7. Ⓐ Ⓑ Ⓒ Ⓓ Ⓔ

8. One example of geological crosscutting is
   (A) a fault   (B) an oxbow   (C) a moraine
   (D) a flood plain   (E) a stalagmite

   8. Ⓐ Ⓑ Ⓒ Ⓓ Ⓔ

9. Fossilized resin from ancient coniferous trees is called
   (A) amber   (B) basalt   (C) chert   (D) dolomite
   (E) halite

   9. Ⓐ Ⓑ Ⓒ Ⓓ Ⓔ

10. One outstanding and distinguishing feature of sedimentary rocks is
    (A) their complete lack of fossils
    (B) that they are formed exclusively of precipitates
    (C) that they are formed exclusively of crystals
    (D) the presence of different layers
    (E) that they are formed by the cooling of magma

    10. Ⓐ Ⓑ Ⓒ Ⓓ Ⓔ

11. During the radioactive decay of a given element,
    (A) X-rays are emitted
    (B) alpha and beta rays and X-rays are emitted
    (C) alpha and gamma rays and X-rays are emitted
    (D) beta and gamma rays are emitted
    (E) alpha, beta, and gamma rays are emitted

    11. Ⓐ Ⓑ Ⓒ Ⓓ Ⓔ

12. As a result of nuclear fission
    (A) there is an increase in mass   (B) light atomic nuclei fuse
    (C) X-rays are emitted   (D) much energy is consumed
    (E) a chain reaction may occur

    12. Ⓐ Ⓑ Ⓒ Ⓓ Ⓔ

13. Color aberrations encountered when using lenses are corrected by   13. Ⓐ Ⓑ Ⓒ Ⓓ Ⓔ
    (A) use of convex lenses
    (B) use of concave lenses
    (C) use of achromatic lenses
    (D) reducing the field or the aperture
    (E) proper focusing

14. When a body is immersed in a liquid, its weight is determined by   14. Ⓐ Ⓑ Ⓒ Ⓓ Ⓔ
    (A) the sum of the external pressures on it
    (B) the force per unit area
    (C) the depth at which point the weights are equal
    (D) the weight of the liquid displaced
    (E) the volume of the liquid displaced

15. The three ways by which heat is transferred from a warm to a cold region are   15. Ⓐ Ⓑ Ⓒ Ⓓ Ⓔ
    (A) absorption, adsorption and radiation
    (B) conduction, convection and infusion
    (C) absorption, adsorption and convection
    (D) conduction, infusion and vaporization
    (E) conduction, convection and radiation

16. One basic function of a transistor is   16. Ⓐ Ⓑ Ⓒ Ⓓ Ⓔ
    (A) rectification
    (B) to form an electrical connection with any electron-receptive object
    (C) to provide high voltage from direct current
    (D) to transfer an electric signal across a resistor
    (E) to counteract the Edison effect

17. For every known subatomic particle, there is believed to exist   17. Ⓐ Ⓑ Ⓒ Ⓒ Ⓔ
    (A) an isotope   (B) an ionized equivalent
    (C) an anti-particle or anti-matter   (D) coherent radiation
    (E) a thermoelectric effect

18. The science of acoustics is concerned chiefly with   18. Ⓐ Ⓑ Ⓒ Ⓓ Ⓔ
    (A) wavelengths   (B) loudness   (C) frequencies
    (D) reverberations   (E) amplitude

19. The distance between the crests of any two adjacent waves is called   19. Ⓐ Ⓑ Ⓒ Ⓓ Ⓔ
    (A) velocity   (B) wavelength   (C) amplitude
    (D) impulse   (E) frequency

20. The continual change in the plane in which a Foucault pendulum   20. Ⓐ Ⓑ Ⓒ Ⓓ Ⓔ
    swings is evidence that
    (A) the earth rotates
    (B) the moon revolves around the earth
    (C) the earth revolves around the sun
    (D) the sun is the center of the solar system
    (E) the earth is round

21. When a glass rod is rubbed with a silk cloth   21. Ⓐ Ⓑ Ⓒ Ⓓ Ⓔ
    (A) the glass rod gains electrons and becomes negatively charged
    (B) the glass rod gains electrons and becomes positively charged
    (C) the glass rod remains neutral
    (D) the glass rod loses electrons and becomes negatively charged
    (E) the glass rod loses electrons and becomes positively charged

22. Devices used to change the voltage of alternating current are

22. Ⓐ Ⓑ Ⓒ Ⓓ Ⓔ

(A) transformers   (B) solenoids   (C) commutators

(D) dynamos   (E) magnetos

23. The speed of molecular activity is dependent upon

23. Ⓐ Ⓑ Ⓒ Ⓓ Ⓔ

(A) sulfornation   (B) temperature   (C) defloration

(D) offset   (E) saturation

24. Work is accomplished when

24. Ⓐ Ⓑ Ⓒ Ⓓ Ⓔ

(A) direction is imposed upon a moving object

(B) energy output equals energy input

(C) a machine operates without expending energy

(D) force is exerted upon an object causing it to move

(E) a weight is held stationary at a certain height

25. How much effort is required to push the 90 pound barrel up the inclined plane?

25. Ⓐ Ⓑ Ⓒ Ⓓ Ⓔ

(A) 45 pounds effort

(B) 30 pounds effort

(C) 15 pounds effort

(D) 10 pounds effort

(E) 5 pounds effort

26. A two-scale ruler is about 15.2 centimeters long. What is its length in inches?

26. Ⓐ Ⓑ Ⓒ Ⓓ Ⓔ

(A) 4.2   (B) 6

(C) 7.6   (D) 10.6

(E) 12.5

27. The body of any free falling object in motion continues to accelerate until

27. Ⓐ Ⓑ Ⓒ Ⓓ Ⓔ

(A) the law of gravity takes over

(B) its velocity equals the speed of light

(C) air resistance becomes a factor

(D) the law of inertia takes over

(E) it is influenced by the Doppler effect

28. According to Newton's third law, there must be a reaction to the force which propels a bullet from the barrel of a rifle. This force is in the

28. Ⓐ Ⓑ Ⓒ Ⓓ Ⓔ

(A) recoil

(B) friction of the bullet in the barrel

(C) pressure used to squeeze the trigger

(D) shoulder of the person firing the rifle

(E) inertia of the bullet

29. Fusion reactions for the peaceful production of power have been un-successful because
  (A) they are too powerful
  (B) they are too rapid
  (C) there is no practical way to control the rate of the fusion reaction
  (D) of the extremely high cost
  (E) radioactive electricity is too dangerous

29. Ⓐ Ⓑ Ⓒ Ⓓ Ⓔ

NOTE: The symbols illustrated below are commonly found on weather maps.

30. The symbol which indicates a clear day with easterly breezes of 1–4 miles per hour is
  (A) A
  (B) B
  (C) C
  (D) D
  (E) E

30. Ⓐ Ⓑ Ⓒ Ⓓ Ⓔ

31. The symbol indicating 25 mile per hour wind from the southwest is
  (A) A
  (B) B
  (C) C
  (D) D
  (E) E

31. Ⓐ Ⓑ Ⓒ Ⓓ Ⓔ

32. High altitude satellites will some day fall to earth due to
  (A) drag caused by cosmic radiation
  (B) drag caused by infrared radiation
  (C) centrifugal force
  (D) centrifugal force and the moon's gravity
  (E) drag caused by air and particles

32. Ⓐ Ⓑ Ⓒ Ⓓ Ⓔ

33. According to Einstein's theory of relativity, as the speed of a spaceship approaches 186,000 mi/sec,
  (A) mass and metabolism increase
  (B) mass and metabolism decrease
  (C) mass and metabolism remain constant
  (D) aging, relative to earth, would speed up
  (E) aging, relative to earth, would slow down

33. Ⓐ Ⓑ Ⓒ Ⓓ Ⓔ

34. When an object is transferred from the moon to earth, its mass
  (A) increases   (B) decreases   (C) remains constant
  (D) and weight increase on earth
  (E) and weight decrease on earth

34. Ⓐ Ⓑ Ⓒ Ⓓ Ⓔ

35. The thermodynamic measure of disorder is called
    (A) entropy   (B) spontaneity   (C) momentum
    (D) redundancy   (E) valence

    35. Ⓐ Ⓑ Ⓒ Ⓓ Ⓔ

36. Through a microscope, minute particles are observed to be in an almost constant state of random movement, a phenomenon called
    (A) surface tension   (B) capillarity   (C) osmosis
    (D) diffusion   (E) Brownian movement

    36. Ⓐ Ⓑ Ⓒ Ⓓ Ⓔ

37. The force causing a liquid to rise inside a tube of very small diameter is
    (A) surface tension   (B) kinetic energy
    (C) potential energy   (D) adhesion   (E) cohesion

    37. Ⓐ Ⓑ Ⓒ Ⓓ Ⓔ

38. The atomic number of an element refers to
    (A) the total number of electrons and protons it possesses
    (B) the number of neutrons it possesses
    (C) the number of protons it possesses
    (D) its sequential number in the atomic scale
    (E) the total number of neutrons and protons it possesses

    38. Ⓐ Ⓑ Ⓒ Ⓓ Ⓔ

39. A dispersion in which the particles eventually settle out is an example of
    (A) an emulsion   (B) a solution   (C) a mixture
    (D) a colloid   (E) a suspension

    39. Ⓐ Ⓑ Ⓒ Ⓓ Ⓔ

40. The alkali metal family of chemical elements includes potassium and
    (A) calcium   (B) iron   (C) nickel
    (D) sodium   (E) aluminum

    40. Ⓐ Ⓑ Ⓒ Ⓓ Ⓔ

41. In reduction reactions of organic chemistry
    (A) oxygen acts as a catalyst
    (B) oxygen is a dephlogisticant
    (C) ionic oxygen is consumed
    (D) oxygen is removed from a compound
    (E) oxygen combines chemically with another substance

    41. Ⓐ Ⓑ Ⓒ Ⓓ Ⓔ

42. The primary concern of alchemy was
    (A) sublimation   (B) vaporization   (C) solidification
    (D) liquefaction   (E) transmutation

    42. Ⓐ Ⓑ Ⓒ Ⓓ Ⓔ

43. In any given process
    (A) energy may be created
    (B) energy may be destroyed
    (C) energy may neither be created nor destroyed
    (D) the energies of the reactants and products are variable
    (E) energy and work are totally unrelated

    43. Ⓐ Ⓑ Ⓒ Ⓓ Ⓔ

44. In accordance with Einstein's theory of relativity, as a body gains speed
    (A) its mass decreases proportionately
    (B) its mass increases proportionately
    (C) only electrons in the outer shells of its atoms are affected
    (D) mass and energy are not related
    (E) only energy is lost

    44. Ⓐ Ⓑ Ⓒ Ⓓ Ⓔ

45. Substances which form ions in solution and which can conduct an electric current are called

(A) reactors (B) dispersions (C) substrates

(D) electrolytes (E) conductors

46. When different atoms of an element have different weights, we call them

(A) ions (B) isotopes (C) molecules (D) electrons (E) nuclei

47. Gamma radiation is frequently used successfully to treat tumors and cancer tissue because

(A) such tissues are immune to radiation

(B) such tissues are more sensitive to radiation than are healthy tissues

(C) it acts faster than surgery without the risks of surgery

(D) the induced rate of radioactive decay is indicative of the extent of cure

(E) gamma radiation is low energy radiation

48. During the process called nuclear fission,

(A) neutrons are emitted (B) light atomic nuclei fuse

(C) alpha particles are emitted (D) much energy is consumed

(E) there is an increase in mass

49. A vibrating string on a musical instrument will produce a high pitch if it is

(A) long, loose, and of small diameter

(B) short, stretched, and of large diameter

(C) short, stretched, and of small diameter

(D) short, loose, and of small diameter

(E) long, stretched, and of small diameter

50. By mixing all of the colors of the visible spectrum we produce

(A) infrared light (B) black light (C) purple light

(D) green light (E) white light

51. The change of certain substances from solid to gaseous states without passing through the liquid state is called

(A) sublimation (B) fusion (C) convergence

(D) thermal coefficient (E) reciprocation

Humidity is an expression of the water-holding capacity of the atmosphere and may be expressed in terms of the number of grams of water vapor held per cubic meter of air.

Water Vapor (grams per M³)

52. According to the illustration above, one may conclude that
    (A) humidity increases at lower temperatures
    (B) humidity decreases at lower temperatures
    (C) temperature does not affect humidity
    (D) higher temperatures decrease humidity
    (E) above 20° C humidity remains constant

52. Ⓐ Ⓑ Ⓒ Ⓓ Ⓔ

53. Based upon study of the illustration above, one may also conclude that
    (A) if the humidity increases the temperature will rise
    (B) if the humidity decreases the temperature will rise
    (C) humidity increases uniformly as temperature increases
    (D) saturated air cannot retain its water if the temperature is lowered
    (E) saturated air can hold additional water if the temperature is lowered

53. Ⓐ Ⓑ Ⓒ Ⓓ Ⓔ

54. Although ahead of his time, Roger Bacon contributed to science by stating that intuition or reason is insufficient to justify scientific theory and that to give certainty to science, there must be
    (A) research   (B) data   (C) facts   (D) observation
    (E) experimentation

54. Ⓐ Ⓑ Ⓒ Ⓓ Ⓔ

55. Electromagnetic waves of extremely high frequency are called
    (A) photons   (B) matter waves   (C) gamma rays
    (D) X-rays   (E) Beta rays

55. Ⓐ Ⓑ Ⓒ Ⓓ Ⓔ

Directions: Each group of questions below consists of five lettered choices followed by a list of numbered phrases or sentences. For each numbered phrase or sentence select the one choice that is most closely related to it. Each choice may be used once, more than once, or not at all in each group.

Questions 56–58

   (A) Distillation
   (B) Evaporation
   (C) Radiolysis
   (D) Sublimation
   (E) Transmutation

56. The conversion of one element to another

56. Ⓐ Ⓑ Ⓒ Ⓓ Ⓔ

57. The radioactive disintegration of radium to radon

57. Ⓐ Ⓑ Ⓒ Ⓓ Ⓔ

58. The direct conversion of a solid to a vapor

58. Ⓐ Ⓑ Ⓒ Ⓓ Ⓔ

Questions 59–60

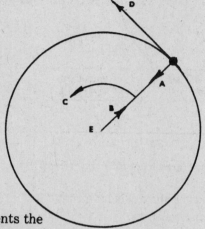

The diagram above represents the circular path of a moving weight tied to the end of a string.

59. Which letter indicates the velocity of the weight?

59. Ⓐ Ⓑ Ⓒ Ⓓ Ⓔ

60. Which letter indicates centrifugal force on the moving weight?

60. Ⓐ Ⓑ Ⓒ Ⓓ Ⓔ

ANSWER KEY—TRIAL TEST

Part I Biological Sciences

1. B	11. D	21. B	31. E	41. D	51. C
2. D	12. B	22. E	32. C	42. D	52. D
3. B	13. D	23. E	33. B	43. B	53. E
4. D	14. D	24. C	34. B	44. A	54. D
5. E	15. A	25. B	35. A	45. A	55. C
6. D	16. E	26. E	36. B	46. A	56. C
7. D	17. C	27. B	37. D	47. B	57. D
8. D	18. A	28. D	38. A	48. E	58. D
9. E	19. B	29. D	39. C	49. B	59. E
10. B	20. C	30. C	40. A	50. E	60. C

Part II Physical Sciences

1. D	11. E	21. E	31. A	41. D	51. A
2. A	12. E	22. A	32. E	42. E	52. B
3. E	13. C	23. B	33. E	43. C	53. D
4. C	14. D	24. D	34. C	44. B	54. E
5. C	15. E	25. B	35. A	45. D	55. B
6. D	16. D	26. B	36. E	46. B	56. E
7. D	17. C	27. C	37. D	47. B	57. E
8. A	18. D	28. A	38. C	48. A	58. D
9. A	19. B	29. C	39. E	49. C	59. D
10. D	20. A	30. B	40. D	50. E	60. B

SCORING CHART—TRIAL TEST

After you have scored your Trial Examination, enter the results in the chart below (the Raw Score computation is explained on page 14); then transfer your Raw Score to the Progress Chart on page 14. As you complete the Sample Examinations later in this part of the book, you should be able to achieve increasingly higher Raw Scores.

Total Test	Number Right	Number Wrong	Number Omitted	Raw Score
Part I: 60				
Part II: 60				
Total: 120				

ANSWER EXPLANATIONS—TRIAL TEST

Part I   Biological Sciences

1. **B.** Protozoans include some 30,000 single-celled usually nongreen organisms, some of which cause these serious human diseases.
2. **D.** Mitochondria are the sites where energy is transferred from molecules of carbohydrate to those of ATP.
3. **B.** Reproduction is accomplished not by somaplasm, but by germ plasm, which is transmitted essentially unchanged from generation to generation.
4. **D.** Ribosomes are found scattered in the cytoplasms of living cells and in association with the endoplasmic reticulum. They are composed of ribonucleic acid and protein and function in the synthesis of proteins and enzymes.
5. **E.** A living cell placed in a hypotonic solution, i.e., hypotonic to the cell sap, will increase in turgidity.
6. **D.** Basic food production for most of the biological world is accomplished by photosynthetic producers.
7. **D.** Photosynthesis is an energy-storing biochemical reaction in which the radiant energy of sunlight is stored in simple sugars in the form of chemical bonds.
8. **D.** Root hair cells are hairlike extensions of the epidermal cells of most kinds of plant roots. These provide greatly increased surfaces for water absorption.
9. **E.** A photosynthetic organism possesses chlorophyll and, in the presence of radiant energy, synthesizes glucose from carbon dioxide and water and stores energy.
10. **B.** Growth responses of plants are called tropisms. The growth response of plants to light is called phototropism.
11. **D.** Hydroponics is the growing of plants in a liquid or moist environment (without soil) to which essential mineral nutrients are added.
12. **B.** The familiar asparagus stalk is stem tissue; leaves are the small triangular scalelike structures scattered along the stem.

13. D. Fermentation is the anaerobic decomposition of carbohydrates by the enzymes produced by living microorganisms such as yeasts.

14. D. In plants, diploid spore-mother cells undergo meiosis to produce haploid spores.

15. A. Analogous structures are similar because of functions; the wing of a bird and the wing of a bee are analogous structures.

16. E. Persons with AB type blood are designated as universal receivers. They can receive blood from any other person, regardless of blood type since they have both antigen A and antigen B.

17. C. Carotene is a precursor of vitamin A.

18. A. The semicircular canals are associated with the inner ear and function to keep the body aware of its position with respect to gravity and motion.

19. B. Thyroxin controls the rate of metabolism by controlling the cellular respiration of food.

20. C. The sympathetic nervous system responds to perceived emotional situations such as anger or fear. One body response to anger or fear is accelerated heart beat.

21. B. The corpus luteum secretes progesterone which regulates the menstrual cycle and prepares the body for pregnancy.

22. E. Mitosis is both a quantitative and qualitative division of the nucleus of a cell which results in precise and equal distribution of chromatin and, therefore, DNA to each daughter cell.

23. E. Deoxyribonucleic acid (DNA) is the only substance transmitted qualitatively and quantitatively from one generation to the next.

24. C. A mutation is a gene change. Mutations, therefore, are sources of variations and they continue to be handed down to future generations until they mutate again.

25. B. Animalculists were preformationists who believed in a preformation of the individual within the sperm.

26. E. Lucretius spent most of his life writing a single poem entitled "De rerum natura," which was unfinished at the time of his death.

27. B. The arctic tundra is treeless and the home of caribou and numerous lichens. It is also the summer breeding ground for numerous migratory birds.

28. D. Plankton consists of free-floating, usually microscopic, plants and animals in a body of water.

29. D. The abyssal zones of the oceans are the deepest ocean trenches.

30. C. The word entomologist is from the Greek entomon, meaning insect.

31. E. Commensalism is a relationship between two species in which one benefits from the other without harming it or giving benefit to it.

32. C. The Cenozoic Era is the last of the great periods of geologic time and is characterized by the advent of mammals and seed plants.

33. B. Pulmonary veins return oxygenated blood from the lungs to the left atrium of the heart.

34. B. Coronary arteries branch from the aorta and carry blood to the heart muscle.

35. A. Hookworm larvae on the ground penetrate unbroken skin, commonly the feet of barefoot children in warm climates.

36. B. Rocky Mountain spotted fever is caused by a rickettsia transmitted to humans through the bite of a tick.

37. D. Sugar molecules inside the bag lower the concentration of water molecules in comparison to the water outside. Therefore, water molecules diffuse into the bag.

38. A. The bag, containing only water, has a higher concentration of water molecules than the surrounding water which also contains sugar molecules. Water will, therefore, diffuse out of the bag and the bag will shrink.

39. C. A state of equilibrium exists and there will be no net diffusion of water either into or out of the bag.

40. A. Some bacteria, such as iron and sulfur bacteria, obtain energy through the oxidation of iron and sulfur compounds respectively.

41. D. Phytoplankton are photosynthetic organisms and because they are so numerous, they are important producers.
42. D. Photosynthesis produces the carbohydrate glucose and therefore increases the dry weight of the plant.
43. B. By definition, photosynthesis means putting together by means of light; hence light is necessary.
44. A. Wood is the tree tissue inside the vascular cambium and is a term synonymous with xylem.
45. A. A single injection of a foreign protein into the body may hyper-sensitize an individual so that future exposure to the same protein results in an allergic reaction.
46. A. A virus invading the body is an antigen. The body's immune system responds by producing antibodies.
47. B. Interferon is produced by body cells into which the foreign nucleic acid of a virus has entered and it renders uninfected cells immune to the virus.
48. E. Carbon monoxide is a major concern since it has a high affinity for hemoglobin.
49. B. Rh negative individuals develop antibodies to the Rh antigen and these destroy Rh-positive cells.
50. E. Vitamin K is essential for prothrombin synthesis, a step in blood clotting.
51. C. Roughage, such as total grain cereals, is important to the diet because it stimulates the large intestine.
52. D. In humans and other animals, excess glucose is converted into a starch called glycogen, which is stored in muscles and in the liver where it is readily available.
53. E. Thyroxine deficiency in humans leads to cretinism in early childhood and to a lowered metabolic rate in adults.
54. D. Anaximander, a Greek philosopher (611–547 B.C.), proposed an explanation of evolution based upon observation and reasoning.
55. C. T. H. Morgan first stated the gene theory of inheritance in 1910.
56. C. Ehrlich studied the effects of chemicals upon body tissues and discovered salvarsan, a chemical used to treat syphilis. He was the first to use a systematic approach to treat chemotherapeutic investigations.
57. D. Vesalius was the greatest anatomist of the 16th century and was noted for performing his own dissections.
58. D. At each level in a food chain there is a loss of energy and, for this reason, shorter food chains with fewer energy transfers are more efficient.
59. E. One definition identifies a species on the basis of its number of shared homologous structures.
60. C. Unilateral light is responsible for the unequal distribution of growth-promoting substances in the stem, thus causing uneven stem elongation.

Part II Physical Sciences

1. D. Ninety degrees north latitude is as far north as one can travel and is everywhere equidistant from the equator—hence, the north pole.
2. A. Pythagoras believed that the earth was spherical and that the sun, moon, and planets had movements of their own.
3. E. Hydrogen atoms in the sun undergo fusion. Four atoms of hydrogen fuse to form one atom of helium with a minute quantity of mass left over. This mass is converted into energy.
4. C. Geocentric describes a concept pertaining to the solar system which supposes that the earth is the center of the system.
5. C. The Milky Way is a large spiral galaxy shaped like a disk and is approximately 5,000 light-years thick and 100,000 light years in diameter.
6. D. When crossing the international dateline in an easterly direction, a traveler loses a day. If, for example, the traveler crosses the international dateline on a Monday, he or she finds that it is now Sunday east of the line.

7. D. The observed frequency of a light wave will decrease (shift) if the source is traveling away from the observer. This is the Doppler effect.

8. A. A fault is a fracture of the earth's crust accompanied by a shift of one side with respect to the other.

9. A. Amber is fossilized resin.

10. D. Probably the most distinguishing feature of sedimentary rock is the fact that it is a layered structure.

11. E. During radioactive decay alpha, beta, and gamma rays are emitted.

12. E. A chain reaction proceeds in a series of steps, each being made possible by the preceeding. If the fission is initiated by neutrons, neutrons are released to continue the reaction.

13. C. Color or chromatic aberration is the failure of the different colors contained in white light to meet in a common point, called the focal point, after they pass through a convex lens. It may be reduced by use of an achromatic lens.

14. D. An object in water displaces an amount of water equal to its own weight.

15. E. Heat may be transferred by conduction, convection, and radiation.

16. D. A transistor is a semiconductor used in modern amplifier and switching circuits.

17. C. In certain situations, such as pair annihilation, an electron and a positron interact and disappear. The positron in this situation is the so-called antiparticle of the electron.

18. D. Sound reverberations are reflections of sound waves, i.e., echoes.

19. B. Wavelength is defined as the measured distance between two successive wave crests.

20. A. A Foucault pendulum is so constructed that it always swings in the same plane. The rotation of the earth makes the pendulum appear to change the plane in which it swings.

21. E. Static electricity can be produced by rubbing a glass rod with a piece of silk, during which the silk takes up electrons to become negatively charged. The glass rod gives up electrons to become positively charged.

22. A. Transformers are used to increase or decrease the voltage of alternating current.

23. B. The speed of molecules is directly proportional to their temperature.

24. D. Work is defined as the force exerted upon an object multiplied by the distance the object is moved.

25. B. The ratio of the height of the inclined plane to its hypotenuse determines the effort required to move the barrel up the inclined plane.

26. B. One centimeter equals 2.54 inches.

27. C. The acceleration of a falling body is expressed as 32.16 feet per second per second, subject to the air resistance on a particular falling body.

28. A. According to Newton's third law, to each and every action, there is an equal and opposite reaction.

29. C. To date, no useful fusion reactor has been designed.

30. B. } On weather maps, "wind feathers" show wind speed and direction. The end
31. A. } of the arrow with the "feathers" points out the direction from which the wind is blowing. The number and design of the "feather" indicates the wind speed.

32. E. All earth satellites will eventually fall back to earth because of drag which is caused by air molecules (even though sparse) and particulate matter in space.

33. E. At speeds approaching 186,000 miles per second, if the speed of the observer on earth is not equal to the speed of the space ship as observed by that passenger, differing rates of time and therefore, aging would occur.

34. C. Mass always remains constant. However, on the moon, due to a lower gravity, an object would appear to be lighter.

35. A. Entropy is the thermodynamic measure of disorder and always increases during any spontaneous process.

36. E. Brownian movement is the result of molecular activity. Under the microscope, visible particles appear to be in a state of erratic motion because

they are continually being bombarded (bumped) from all sides by molecules in motion.

37. D. A liquid rises in a tube of small diameter due to the attraction between the liquid and the solid, i.e., adhesion.

38. C. The number of protons in an atomic nucleus is the atomic number.

39. E. Muddy water is a suspension, i.e., it is a dispersion in which the particles eventually settle out.

40. D. The alkali metal family includes sodium, potassium, lithium, cesium, etc.

41. D. In a basic sense, the oxidation/reduction reactions of organic chemistry are concerned with the addition or removal of oxygen.

42. E. In medieval times, alchemy was an endeavor to change base metals into gold, i.e., transmutation.

43. C. The First Law of Thermodynamics states that energy may be neither created nor destroyed.

44. B. Mass and velocity are proportional; as speed approaches the velocity of light, mass approaches infinity.

45. D. Certain molecules ionize (example: NaCl ionizes to Na^+ Cl^- ions) when placed in liquids and are able to conduct an electric current.

46. B. Isotopes are atoms of the same element that have different mass numbers, that is, varying numbers of neutrons in their nuclei.

47. B. Tumor cells are more sensitive to radiation generally than are healthy cells. Therefore, radiation therapy is often a successful tumor therapy.

48. A. Nuclear fission results in the splitting of atomic nuclei accompanied by the release of neutrons.

49. C. When a vibrating string of a musical instrument is of small diameter and stretched tightly, it will produce tones of higher pitch than a string of greater diameter which is not stretched as tightly.

50. E. Visible light is white and includes wavelengths from red to violet with orange, yellow, green, and blue in between.

51. A. The direct change from the solid state to the gaseous state is called sublimation. An example is the sublimation of ice or snow when air flows over it at below freezing temperatures.

52. B. The ability of the air to hold moisture in vapor form is inversely propor-
53. D. tional to the temperature.

54. E. Roger Bacon is credited with the introduction of the experimental method of science.

55. B. At certain speeds, all matter exhibits wavelengths of extremely high frequency and these have been observed to affect spaces between atoms in crystals.

56. E. Transmutation in the historic sense, is the conversion of base metals to gold or silver and was a medieval philosophy that never materialized.

57. E. Radioactive decay of certain elements accounts for one form of transmutation which was unknown before its discovery by Becquerel.

58. D. Under certain conditions, solids may be changed directly into gases or vapors by sublimation.

59. D. ⎫ The weight tied to the end of the string tends to move in a straight line but
60. B. ⎬ is held in circular orbit by the string. Centrifugal force acts in the direction away from the axis or center.

Background and Practice Questions

13

The Natural Sciences Examination tests your knowledge, understanding, and utilization of principles, concepts, and ideas in the biological and physical sciences. Its achievement level is that attained by the *average*, non-science major after satisfying a distribution or general education requirement in science. Your ability to answer certain questions will depend upon the extent of your reading science articles and science-based materials in magazines, newspapers, and other periodicals, all written for the non-scientist.

The examination consists of 120 multiple-choice questions from the traditional areas of the natural sciences. The examination is given in two separately timed 45-minute sections, one covering biological science and the other covering physical science. The content of the examination and the approximate percent of questions in each of the content areas is as follows:

Biological Science (50%)

10% Origin and evolution of life, classification of organisms

10% Cell organization, cell division, chemical nature of the gene, bioenergetics, biosynthesis

20% Structure, function, and development in organisms; patterns of heredity

10% Concepts of population biology with emphasis on ecology

Physical Science (50%)

7% Atomic and nuclear structure and properties, elementary particles, nuclear reactions

10% Chemical elements, compounds and reactions; molecular structure and bonding

12% Heat, thermodynamics, and states of matter; classical mechanics; relativity

4% Electricity and magnetism, waves, light and sound

7% The universe: galaxies, stars, the solar system

10% The Earth: atmosphere, hydrosphere, structure, properties, surface features, geological processes, history

For additional review, you might consult the following books which exemplify a variety of the type of concepts pertinent to a general understanding of the sciences:

HISTORY AND PHILOSOPHY OF SCIENCE

Asimov, Isaac. *Asimov's Guide to Science*. Rev. ed. New York: Basic Books, 1972.

Bonner, John T. *The Scale of Nature*. New York: Harper and Row, 1969.

Collis, John Stewart. *The Vision of Glory: The Extraordinary Nature of the Ordinary*. New York: George Braziller, Inc., 1973.

Dampier, Sir William C. *A History of Science* (with a postscript by I. Bernard Cohen). 4th ed. New York: Cambridge University Press, 1965.

Dietz, David. *The New Outline of Science*. New York: Dodd, Mead and Company, 1972.

Guest, John, ed. *The Earth and Its Satellites*. New York: David McKay Co., 1971.

Jastrow, Robert. *Red Giants and White Dwarfs*. New York: Warner Books, 1980.

Lepp, Henry. *Dynamic Earth*. New York: McGraw-Hill Book Co., 1973.

Lounsbury, John F. *Earth Science*. 3rd ed. New York: Harper and Row, 1979.

Tarbuck, Edward J., and Frederick K. Lutgens. *Earth Science*. 3rd ed. Columbus Ohio: Merrill Publishing Co., 1982.

ASTRONOMY AND THE UNIVERSE

Abell, George. *Exploration of the Universe* (updated brief edition). New York: Holt, Rinehart and Winston, 1973.

Botkin, David B., and Edward A. Keller. *Environmental Studies*. Columbus, Ohio: Merrill Publishing Co., 1982.

Brown, F. Martin, and Wayne Bailey. *Earth Science*. Glenview, Ill.: Scott-Foresman, 1978.

Eardley, A. J. *Science of the Earth*. New York: Harper and Row, 1972.

Flint, Richard F. *The Earth and Its History*. New York: W. W. Norton and Company, 1973.

LIFE SCIENCE

Asimov, Isaac. *The Human Body*. Boston: Houghton Mifflin Co., 1963.

Camp, Pamela S., and Karen Arms. *Exploring Biology*. Philadelphia: Saunders College Publishing Co., 1981.

Gillie, Oliver. *The Living Cell*. New York: Funk and Wagnalls, 1971.

Goldsby, Richard A. *Basic Biology*. New York: Harper and Row, 1976.

Keeten, William T. and Carol Hardy McFadden. *Elements of Biological Science*, 3rd Ed. W. W. Norton and Company, 1983.

Luria, Salvador E., Stephen Jay Gould and Sam Singer. *A View of Life*. The Benjamin/Cummings Publishing Company, Inc., 1981.

Memmler, Ruth L., and Dena L. Wood. *The Human Body in Health and Disease*. 4th ed. Philadelphia: J. B. Lippincott Co., 1977.

Tippo, Oswald, and William L. Stern. *Humanistic Botany*. New York: W. W. Norton and Company, 1977.

PHYSICAL SCIENCE

Beiser, Arthur. *Physical Science* (Schaum's Outline Series). New York: McGraw-Hill, Inc., 1974.

Stine, William R. *Chemistry for the Consumer*. Boston, Mass.: Allyn and Bacon, Inc., 1978.

Turk, Jonathan, and Amos Turk. *Physical Science*. 2nd ed. Philadelphia: Saunders College Publishing Co., 1981.

Young, Jay A. *Chemistry: A Human Concern*. New York: Macmillan Publishing Co., Inc., 1978.

THE KINDS OF QUESTIONS THAT APPEAR ON THE EXAMINATION

Now, look at the two following diagrams which are like some which you will find on a CLEP examination.

In the diagrams above, aquatic photosynthetic plants are placed under inverted test tubes which are filled with water. Except for light, all environmental and genetic factors are constant and the same for each. After exposing "A" to several hours of sunlight, while "B" is maintained in darkness, it may correctly be concluded that:

1. In respect to gas production,
    (A) plant "A" carried on photosynthesis
    (B) plant "A" carried on both photosynthesis and respiration
    (C) darkness inhibits respiration
    (D) sunlight is necessary for gas production
    (E) sunlight inhibits respiration

1. Ⓐ 🅱 Ⓒ Ⓓ Ⓔ

2. When a glowing wood splint is introduced into the tube of gas and subsequently bursts into flame, the gas is
    (A) hydrogen   (B) methane   (C) oxygen   (D) helium
    (E) carbon dioxide

2. Ⓐ Ⓑ Ⓒ Ⓓ Ⓔ

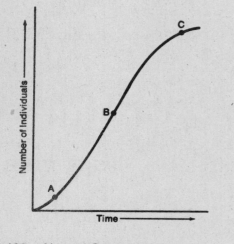

KEY
(A) limiting factors of the environment
(B) high mortality rate
(C) high reproductive rate
(D) short length of time
(E) small number of individuals

NOTE: Base your answers to the following questions on the graph and key.

3. The growth rate at position A on the curve is limited by _____ 3. Ⓐ Ⓑ Ⓒ Ⓓ Ⓔ

4. The growth rate at position B on the curve is affected by _____ 4. Ⓐ Ⓑ Ⓒ Ⓓ Ⓔ

5. The growth rate at position C on the curve is limited by _____ 5. Ⓐ Ⓑ Ⓒ Ⓓ Ⓔ

ANSWERS AND EXPLANATIONS

1. **D.** Plants A and B are exposed to identical conditions except for sunlight/darkness. There is no evidence that photosynthesis or respiration are occurring. An unidentified gas produced by A is the only observable outcome of this experiment.

2. **C.** A standard laboratory test for oxygen production is that a glowing wood splint bursts into flame in the presence of oxygen.

3. **E.** ⎫ The graph represents a standard growth (sigmoid) curve. Over a period of
4. **C.** ⎬ time a small number of individuals existing under normal conditions will
5. **A.** ⎭ increase in number while food, space, etc., are ample, but, as the numbers of individuals increase, competition for food, space, etc., increases and the accumulation of metabolic wastes at the same time slows growth.

PRACTICE QUESTIONS ON THE NATURAL SCIENCES

Now, let's look at some of the specific science areas with some sample questions covering each:

Questions about Biology

Directions: Each of the questions or incomplete statements below is followed by five suggested answers or completions. Select the one that is best in each case.

1. At the tissue level of organization 1. Ⓐ Ⓑ Ⓒ Ⓓ Ⓔ
   (A) cells retain their separate functional identity
   (B) dissimilar cells are associated to conduct a variety of functions
   (C) cells are completely independent
   (D) similar cells are associated in the performance of a particular function
   (E) there is no cellular specialization

2. A scientist specializing in the study of the transmission of inherited 2. Ⓐ Ⓑ Ⓒ Ⓓ Ⓔ
   traits from one generation to another is called a
   (A) physiologist   (B) taxonomist   (C) parasitologist
   (D) cytologist   (E) geneticist

3. All cellular metabolism is controlled by organic catalysts called
   (A) hormones   (B) vitamins   (C) auxin   (D) phlogistons
   (E) enzymes

3. Ⓐ Ⓑ Ⓒ Ⓓ Ⓔ

A   B

Pasteur placed a nutrient broth in each of two flasks similar to those illustrated above. Both flasks were open to air, but flask B was open only through its curved neck. The broth in both flasks was boiled initially to kill their contained organisms and then they were left standing. Living organisms soon reappeared in flask A but no life appeared in flask B.

4. Since flask B remained free of life indefinitely, it can be concluded that
   (A) life does not arise spontaneously from the nutrient broth
   (B) flask A permits microorganisms to enter readily
   (C) the curved neck of flask B apparently prevents microorganisms from entering the flask
   (D) none of the above
   (E) all of the above, except D

4. Ⓐ Ⓑ Ⓒ Ⓓ Ⓔ

5. The evidence generated by this experiment supports
   (A) Koch's postulates
   (B) The Hardy-Weinberg Law
   (C) the Germ Theory of disease
   (D) Virchow's theory of biogenesis
   (E) the Cell Theory

5. Ⓐ Ⓑ Ⓒ Ⓓ Ⓔ

6. An organism which utilizes radiant energy in food synthesis is
   (A) holozoic   (B) parasitic   (C) chemosynthetic
   (D) saprophytic   (E) photosynthetic

6. Ⓐ Ⓑ Ⓒ Ⓓ Ⓔ

7. The typical consumers in an ecosystem are
   (A) saprophytic   (B) photosynthetic   (C) parasitic
   (D) chemosynthetic   (E) holozoic

7. Ⓐ Ⓑ Ⓒ Ⓓ Ⓔ

8. In the "dark reactions" of photosynthesis   8. Ⓐ Ⓑ Ⓒ Ⓓ Ⓔ
   (A) chemical energy is changed to radiant energy
   (B) organic synthesis occurs
   (C) carbon dioxide is absorbed
   (D) radiant energy is released
   (E) radiant energy is changed to chemical energy

9. Photosynthesis   9. Ⓐ Ⓑ Ⓒ Ⓓ Ⓔ
   (A) produces oxygen and inorganic compounds
   (B) produces carbon dioxide and water
   (C) produces carbon dioxide and organic compounds
   (D) produces oxygen and organic compounds
   (E) produces oxygen and water

10. A process which results, in part, in the production of carbon dioxide   10. Ⓐ Ⓑ Ⓒ Ⓓ Ⓔ
    and water is
    (A) respiration   (B) photosynthesis   (C) secretion
    (D) osmosis   (E) phosphorylation

11. An orientation movement by plants in response to a stimulus is a   11. Ⓐ Ⓑ Ⓒ Ⓓ Ⓔ
    (A) tropism   (B) synergism   (C) polymorphism
    (D) cyclosis   (E) taxis

12. The photoperiodic response for "long-day" plants to short days is   12. Ⓐ Ⓑ Ⓒ Ⓓ Ⓔ
    (A) flowering   (B) phototropism   (C) flower inhibition
    (D) parthenocarpy   (E) photosynthesis

13. The primary substance of wood is a plant tissue called   13. Ⓐ Ⓑ Ⓒ Ⓓ Ⓔ
    (A) xylem   (B) epidermis   (C) cortex   (D) endodermis
    (E) phloem

14. When you eat a celery "stalk," you are eating   14. Ⓐ Ⓑ Ⓒ Ⓓ Ⓔ
    (A) root tissue   (B) stem tissue   (C) leaf tissue
    (D) fruit   (E) seed

15. Water loss from plants by transpiration would be increased by   15. Ⓐ Ⓑ Ⓒ Ⓓ Ⓔ
    (A) increased air circulation
    (B) darkness
    (C) increased humidity
    (D) lowering the temperature
    (E) decreased air circulation

16. The enzyme-controlled breakdown of proteins under anaerobic con-   16. Ⓐ Ⓑ Ⓒ Ⓓ Ⓔ
    ditions is called
    (A) autolysis   (B) putrefaction   (C) bacteriophage
    (D) fermentation   (E) interferon

17. In plants, selected cells of the haploid, gamete-producing generation   17. Ⓐ Ⓑ Ⓒ Ⓓ Ⓔ
    (A) become or produce spores
    (B) undergo meiosis
    (C) undergo cleavage
    (D) become or produce eggs or sperm
    (E) are polyploid

18. Structures which are similar because of anatomy and development   18. Ⓐ Ⓑ Ⓒ Ⓓ Ⓔ
    are said to be
    (A) analogous   (B) dioecious   (C) monoecious
    (D) homologous   (E) homosporous

19. The Rh factor assumes serious proportions when
    (A) an Rh negative mother carries an Rh positive fetus in a first pregnancy
    (B) an Rh negative mother carries an Rh negative fetus in a second pregnancy
    (C) an Rh positive mother carries an Rh negative fetus
    (D) an Rh positive mother carries an Rh positive fetus
    (E) an Rh negative mother carries an Rh positive fetus in a second pregnancy

19. A B C D E

20. Carotene functions in maintaining
    (A) night vision   (B) normal blood clotting
    (C) normal nerves   (D) fertility
    (E) normal tooth and bone development

20. A B C D E

21. In the United States today, the most serious dietary problem is
    (A) mineral deficiency   (B) dental cavities   (C) obesity
    (D) high cholesterol   (E) vitamin deficiency

21. A B C D E

22. Impairment of the spinal accessory nerves would affect
    (A) muscles of the shoulder   (B) facial muscles
    (C) the parotid gland   (D) swallowing   (E) muscles of the tongue

22. A B C D E

23. Teeth are innervated by the
    (A) oculomotor nerve   (B) facial nerve   (C) vagus nerve
    (D) trochlear nerve   (E) trigeminal nerve

23. A B C D E

24. Stimulation by the parasympathetic nervous system would result in
    (A) weaker heart beat   (B) erection of hair   (C) dilated pupils
    (D) higher blood pressure   (E) increased sweat secretion

24. A B C D E

25. Pathologic conditions caused by defects in hormonal action are called
    (A) atrophy   (B) pheromones   (C) infectious diseases
    (D) deficiency diseases   (E) functional diseases

25. A B C D E

26. Oxytocin
    (A) stimulates basal metabolism
    (B) regulates calcium metabolism
    (C) constricts blood vessels
    (D) regulates phosphorus metabolism
    (E) stimulates lactation

26. A B C D E

27. *All but one* of the following may occur during synapsis in meiosis:
    (A) crossing over   (B) transduction   (C) inversion
    (D) translocation   (E) duplication

27. A B C D E

28. The appearance of variations in a population may be attributed to either genetic change or to
    (A) genetic drift   (B) changed environmental factors
    (C) non-random mating   (D) parthenogenesis
    (E) adaptive radiation

28. A B C D E

29. One of the following is *not* a type of RNA:
    (A) template RNA   (B) ribosomal RNA   (C) messenger RNA
    (D) gametic RNA   (E) transfer RNA

29. A B C D E

30. The concept that all eggs have existed since the creation of the world
is entailed in the beliefs of
(A) pangenesists   (B) animaculists   (C) epigenesists
(D) ovists   (E) parthenogenesists

30. Ⓐ Ⓑ Ⓒ Ⓓ Ⓔ

31. The ovary of a flower matures into
(A) a seed   (B) an embryo   (C) a fruit
(D) the endosperm   (E) the receptacle

31. Ⓐ Ⓑ Ⓒ Ⓓ Ⓔ

32. You would expect to observe moose and spruce in the
(A) alpine tundra   (B) coniferous forest
(C) tropical rain forest   (D) grasslands
(E) deciduous forest

32. Ⓐ Ⓑ Ⓒ Ⓓ Ⓔ

33. Nekton includes marine organisms which
(A) exist only in darkness
(B) swim by their own propulsion
(C) exist to a depth of 5,000 feet
(D) exist in the deepest ocean trenches
(E) float on the surface

33. Ⓐ Ⓑ Ⓒ Ⓓ Ⓔ

34. A student of cytogenetics would be concerned with the
(A) physiology of the liver
(B) cellular basis of inheritance
(C) prenatal development
(D) muscle physiology
(E) digestion and assimilation

34. Ⓐ Ⓑ Ⓒ Ⓓ Ⓔ

35. A paleontologist is a biologist concerned primarily with studying
(A) birds   (B) snakes   (C) rocks   (D) insects
(E) fossils

35. Ⓐ Ⓑ Ⓒ Ⓓ Ⓔ

36. An interrelationship between two organisms in which one receives all
of the benefits at the expense of the other is called
(A) parasitism   (B) commensalism   (C) mutualism
(D) symbiosis   (E) saprophytism

36. Ⓐ Ⓑ Ⓒ Ⓓ Ⓔ

37. In the human circulatory system, leakage of blood back into the heart
is prevented by the
(A) tricuspid valve   (B) aortic valve   (C) ventricular valves
(D) semilunar valves   (E) bicuspid valve

37. Ⓐ Ⓑ Ⓒ Ⓓ Ⓔ

38. Blood leaves the human liver through the hepatic vein and returns to
the heart through the
(A) hepatic portal system (B) anterior vena cava (C) azygous vein
(D) inferior mesenteric artery   (E) inferior vena cava

38. Ⓐ Ⓑ Ⓒ Ⓓ Ⓔ

39. The Schick test is used to determine whether or not individuals need
immunization or whether or not immunization procedures have been
effective against
(A) small pox   (B) yellow fever   (C) polio
(D) scarlet fever   (E) diphtheria

39. Ⓐ Ⓑ Ⓒ Ⓓ Ⓔ

40. The greatest significance of sexual reproduction is that it   40. Ⓐ Ⓑ Ⓒ Ⓓ Ⓔ
  (A) insures invariable genetic lines
  (B) permits new combinations of genes
  (C) insures that traits are never lost
  (D) eliminates the need for meiosis
  (E) stimulates mating

41. The probability that any one child will be a boy is   41. Ⓐ Ⓑ Ⓒ Ⓓ Ⓔ
  (A) 1/16   (B) 1/8   (C) 1/4   (D) 1/2   (E) 3/4

42. In an individual with genotype "AaBb," the probability of producing   42. Ⓐ Ⓑ Ⓒ Ⓓ Ⓔ
  gametes with dominant genes ("AB") is
  (A) unpredictable   (B) 1/16   (C) 1/8   (D) 1/4   (E) 1/2

43. Based on biochemical analysis of normal and sickle-cell hemoglobin,   43. Ⓐ Ⓑ Ⓒ Ⓓ Ⓔ
  the difference between the two is based on
  (A) sex chromosomes   (B) transformation   (C) amino acids
  (D) different antigens   (E) agglutination

44. An ecological niche   44. Ⓐ Ⓑ Ⓒ Ⓓ Ⓔ
  (A) is a micro-habitat
  (B) is really non-distinguishable
  (C) may be occupied by only one species
  (D) may be occupied by any number of species
  (E) may be occupied by only one individual

45. An organism which exhibits bilateral symmetry   45. Ⓐ Ⓑ Ⓒ Ⓓ Ⓔ
  (A) always has a right and left leg
  (B) always has a right side and a left side
  (C) exhibits universal symmetry internally
  (D) could never possess an anterior or posterior end
  (E) would give birth to living young

46. The biological speciality called anatomy is concerned with the study of   46. Ⓐ Ⓑ Ⓒ Ⓓ Ⓔ
  (A) structure   (B) tissues   (C) inheritance   (D) function
  (E) development

47. Amino acids contain a carboxyl group (-COOH) and an amino group   47. Ⓐ Ⓑ Ⓒ Ⓓ Ⓔ
  (A) HOH   (B) CH_3 (C) CH_2 (D) H_3C (E) ($-NH_2$)

48. When a living cell is placed in a fluid and there is net movement of   48. Ⓐ Ⓑ Ⓒ Ⓓ Ⓔ
  water molecules out of the cell, the fluid is said to be
  (A) isotonic   (B) hypotonic   (C) plasmolyzed
  (D) hypertonic   (E) hydrolyzed

49. An organism capable of synthesizing its own food is described as   49. Ⓐ Ⓑ Ⓒ Ⓓ Ⓔ
  (A) holozoic   (B) heterotrophic   (C) autotrophic
  (D) parasitic   (E) saprophytic

50. Heterotrophic organisms relying upon decomposing organic materials   50. Ⓐ Ⓑ Ⓒ Ⓓ Ⓔ
  for nutrition are
  (A) parasitic   (B) autotrophic   (C) holozoic
  (D) saprophytic   (E) chemotrophic

51. In 1772, Joseph Priestly demonstrated that green plants   51. Ⓐ Ⓑ Ⓒ Ⓓ Ⓔ
    (A) carry on photosynthesis   (B) absorb water from the soil
    (C) give off carbon dioxide   (D) absorb minerals from the soil
    (E) give off oxygen

52. An enzyme-regulated process in living cells resulting in the transfer   52. Ⓐ Ⓑ Ⓒ Ⓓ Ⓔ
    of energy to ATP is
    (A) reduction   (B) assimilation   (C) osmosis
    (D) absorption   (E) respiration

53. Cellular organelles called ribosomes are the sites of   53. Ⓐ Ⓑ Ⓒ Ⓓ Ⓔ
    (A) enzyme storage   (B) protein synthesis
    (C) chromosomal replication   (D) cellular respiration
    (E) photosynthesis in plants

54. The principal absorbing structure of typical roots is the   54. Ⓐ Ⓑ Ⓒ Ⓓ Ⓔ
    (A) root cap   (B) root hair cell   (C) endodermis
    (D) hair roots   (E) xylem

55. The loss of water by transpiration is the result of   55. Ⓐ Ⓑ Ⓒ Ⓓ Ⓔ
    (A) capillarity   (B) diffusion   (C) mass movement
    (D) cohesive forces   (E) adhesive forces

56. The classification of bacteria is determined chiefly by their   56. Ⓐ Ⓑ Ⓒ Ⓓ Ⓔ
    (A) cell membranes and capsules   (B) movements and environments
    (C) morphological characteristics   (D) anatomical characteristics
    (E) physiological characteristics

57. The union of a sperm and an egg is called   57. Ⓐ Ⓑ Ⓒ Ⓓ Ⓔ
    (A) germination   (B) homospory   (C) fertilization
    (D) reduction   (E) meiosis

58. The most significant benefit of flowering to humans is   58. Ⓐ Ⓑ Ⓒ Ⓓ Ⓔ
    (A) double fertilization   (B) the production of fruit and seeds
    (C) pollination   (D) alternation of generations   (E) aesthetic

59. Antigens are foreign proteins which stimulate the production of   59. Ⓐ Ⓑ Ⓒ Ⓓ Ⓔ
    (A) fibrin   (B) globulins   (C) cytochrome
    (D) antibodies   (E) lymphocytes

60. A deficiency of vitamin D may cause   60. Ⓐ Ⓑ Ⓒ Ⓓ Ⓔ
    (A) muscular cramps   (B) stunted growth   (C) xerophthalmia
    (D) retardation of bone and tooth formation   (E) paralysis

61. To overcome a thiamine deficiency, you should enrich your diet with   61. Ⓐ Ⓑ Ⓒ Ⓓ Ⓔ
    (A) fresh vegetables   (B) eggs and dairy products
    (C) citrus fruit   (D) red meats   (E) whole grain cereals

62. Scientific research on the human cerebral cortex reveals that   62. Ⓐ Ⓑ Ⓒ Ⓓ Ⓔ
    (A) the parasympathetic system is centered here
    (B) it controls smooth muscle
    (C) it controls endocrine secretions
    (D) it controls subconscious muscle coordination
    (E) specific areas control particular functions

63. The phases of mitosis occur in the following sequence: 63. Ⓐ Ⓑ Ⓒ Ⓓ Ⓔ
    (A) prophase, anaphase, metaphase, telophase, and interphase
    (B) interphase, telophase, prophase, anaphase, and metaphase
    (C) interphase, prophase, metaphase, telophase, and anaphase
    (D) interphase, telophase, prophase, anaphase, and metaphase
    (E) prophase, metaphase, anaphase, telophase, and interphase

64. The constancy of linkage groups may be altered by   64. Ⓐ Ⓑ Ⓒ Ⓓ Ⓔ
    (A) transduction   (B) crossing over   (C) recombination
    (D) synapsis   (E) assimilation

65. The "dark" reactions of photosynthesis take place in portions of the   65. Ⓐ Ⓑ Ⓒ Ⓓ Ⓔ
    chloroplast called
    (A) grana (B) stomata (C) carotene (D) chlorophyll (E) stroma

66. Cytoplasmic streaming within living cells is called   66. Ⓐ Ⓑ Ⓒ Ⓓ Ⓔ
    (A) translocation   (B) transpiration   (C) helicotropism
    (D) helicotaxis   (E) cyclosis

67. Cellular respiration in mitochondria may   67. Ⓐ Ⓑ Ⓒ Ⓓ Ⓔ
    (A) result in further energy storage
    (B) form ATP, an energy-yielding molecule
    (C) form ADP, an energy-related substance
    (D) release sugar molecules
    (E) release a variety of cellular hormones

68. Fibrinogen is   68. Ⓐ Ⓑ Ⓒ Ⓓ Ⓔ
    (A) a constituent of serum   (D) a source of globulin
    (B) formed from fibrin during clotting   (E) a reservoir of antibodies
    (C) involved with blood clotting

69. Systolic pressure is
    (A) the lowest pressure of the blood, between heartbeats
    (B) the result of a leak in a heart valve
    (C) the blood pressure in veins
    (D) the pressure on the blood as the ventricles contract
    (E) the blood pressure in arteries

70. A toothache involves nerve impulses along the   70. Ⓐ Ⓑ Ⓒ Ⓓ Ⓔ
    (A) trochlear nerve   (B) facial nerve   (C) abducens nerve
    (D) trigeminal nerve   (E) glossopharyngeal nerve

71. In the prophase of mitosis,   71. Ⓐ Ⓑ Ⓒ Ⓓ Ⓔ
    (A) homologous chromosomes become paired
    (B) the centriole reappears
    (C) chromosomes are doubled and the duplicate chromatids may be
        observed
    (D) tetrads of chromatids appear
    (E) synapsis takes place

72. Ⓐ Ⓑ Ⓒ Ⓓ Ⓔ

72. Marine organisms which move by drifting are referred to as
    (A) plankton   (B) neritic   (C) littoral   (D) sessile   (E) nekton

73. Genes, the material which controls inheritance, are composed of the chemical

73. Ⓐ Ⓑ Ⓒ Ⓓ Ⓔ

   (A) adenosine triphosphate   (B) ribonucleic acid
   (C) adenosine diphosphate   (D) deoxyribonucleic acid
   (E) acetylcholine

74. Nephrons

74. Ⓐ Ⓑ Ⓒ Ⓓ Ⓔ

   (A) are functional units of the pancreas
   (B) excrete only water
   (C) are functional units of the spleen
   (D) regulate body temperature
   (E) filter the blood and resorb useful substances

In the diagrams shown above, figure A illustrates a simple mercury barometer, a column of mercury in a sealed glass tube, the open end of which is immersed in a container of mercury which is exposed to atmospheric pressure at sea level. Figure B illustrates a living plant stem with leaves which is sealed in water in the upper end of the glass tubing, which is likewise filled with mercury.

75. The mercury in figure A rises to a height of 76 centimeters due to

75. Ⓐ Ⓑ Ⓒ Ⓓ Ⓔ

   (A) adhesive forces
   (B) cohesive forces
   (C) sunlight heating the mercury, which expands
   (D) atmospheric pressure on the mercury in the dish
   (E) the vacuum above the mercury in the glass tube

76. The mercury in figure B rises above 76 centimeters because

76. Ⓐ Ⓑ Ⓒ Ⓓ Ⓔ

   (A) the plant stem absorbs mercury, pulling the mercury up the tube
   (B) plants grow better at sea level
   (C) of external and internal forces, including transpirational pull
   (D) the top of the glass tube is not sealed, thus destroying the vacuum
   (E) atmospheric pressure is highest at sea level

77. When a living cell is placed in a fluid and there is a net movement of water molecules into the cell, the fluid is said to be
(A) hypertonic   (B) hydrolyzed   (C) hypotonic
(D) plasmolyzed   (E) isotonic

78. Recent experiments using labeled carbon as a tracer have demonstrated that all living cells
(A) require radiant energy   (B) are dependent upon photosynthesis
(C) carry out chemosynthesis (D) are able to assimilate carbon compounds
(E) produce organic substances and release oxygen

79. Etiolation in plants is the result of
(A) synergism   (B) insufficient light   (C) photoperiodism
(D) parthenocarpy   (E) taxis

80. Eutrophication of a lake may occur
(A) when essential nutrients are insufficient
(B) as a result of too many fish
(C) during prolonged high temperatures
(D) when there is insufficient phosphorus
(E) when there is excess phosphorus

81. When you eat peanuts, you are eating
(A) fruits and seeds   (B) leaf tissue   (C) roots
(D) stem tissue   (E) seeds only

82. That each organism develops from the undifferentiated material of the fertilized egg is the premise of
(A) pangenesis   (B) regeneration   (C) special creation
(D) fertilization   (E) epigenesis

83. Muscles used in chewing are innervated by the
(A) facial nerve   (B) glossopharyngeal nerve
(C) abducens nerve   (D) trigeminal nerve (E) hypoglossal nerve

84. Blood leaves the right ventricle of the human heart through the
(A) bicuspid valve   (B) pulmonary vein
(C) pulmonary artery   (D) aorta   (E) tricuspid valve

85. When one population cannot survive without the benefits received from another population, the relationship is called
(A) coordination   (B) mutualism   (C) neutralism
(D) aggregation   (E) commensalism

86. Sulphur is important in an ecosystem because it is
(A) important in nerve impulse transmission
(B) important for salt balance in vertebrate blood
(C) essential in photosynthesis
(D) essential for many proteins and certain enzymes
(E) essential in respiration

87. Botanically, potato "seed" is
(A) stem tissue (B) root tissue (C) leaf tissue (D) fruit (E) seed

88. Those viruses which attack and parasitize bacteria are called
    (A) interferon   (B) synergids   (C) rickettsias
    (D) lysozymes   (E) bacteriophages

88. [A] [B] [C] [D] [E]

89. When no oxygen is available to cells, they may produce ATP by
    (A) glycolysis   (B) anaerobic respiration   (C) use of the TCA cycle
    (D) cytochrome interaction   (E) the citric acid cycle

89. [A] [B] [C] [D] [E]

90. Niacin functions in maintaining
    (A) normal bone formation   (B) normal nerve functioning
    (C) normal blood clotting   (D) normal cellular oxidations
    (E) night vision

90. [A] [B] [C] [D] [E]

91. Impairment of the vagus nerves would affect
    (A) muscles of the tongue   (B) some of the internal organs
    (C) facial muscles   (D) shoulder muscles   (E) swallowing

91. [A] [B] [C] [D] [E]

92. In the farsighted eye,
    (A) light rays converge in front of the retina   (B) the cornea is defective
    (C) light rays converge in the fovea   (D) vision is not blurred
    (E) light rays converge behind the retina

92. [A] [B] [C] [D] [E]

93. Based on the Watson and Crick model of DNA, the bases are paired as follows:
    (A) adenine-thymine and cytosine-guanine
    (B) adenine-uracil and cytosine-guanine
    (C) adenine-cytosine and guanine-thymine
    (D) adenine-guanine and cytosine-thymine
    (E) adenine-thymine and guanine-uracil

93. [A] [B] [C] [D] [E]

94. The flower part which matures into a fruit is the
    (A) ovule   (B) calyx   (C) receptacle   (D) corolla   (E) ovary

94. [A] [B] [C] [D] [E]

95. The probability that a couple's two children will be one boy and one girl is
    (A) 1/16   (B) 1/8   (C) 1/4   (D) 1/2   (E) 3/4

95. [A] [B] [C] [D] [E]

96. Fats, like carbohydrates, are composed of carbon, hydrogen, and oxygen, but differ from them by having
    (A) proportionally more oxygen   (B) little stored energy
    (C) twice as much hydrogen as oxygen   (D) an excess of carbon
    (E) proportionally less oxygen

96. [A] [B] [C] [D] [E]

97. Isolation of a population over a long period of time produces
    (A) adaptive radiation   (B) hybridization   (C) inbreeding
    (D) interspecific competition   (E) parallel evolution

97. [A] [B] [C] [D] [E]

98. As a result of photosynthesis
    (A) CO_2 is stored in carbohydrates
    (B) light energy is converted into stored chemical energy
    (C) entropy is neutralized
    (D) energy is released
    (E) ATP is energized

98. [A] [B] [C] [D] [E]

99. A deficiency of folic acid could result in
   (A) a type of anemia   (B) sterility   (C) beriberi
   (D) gray hair   (E) hemorrhage following surgery

99. Ⓐ Ⓑ Ⓒ Ⓓ Ⓔ

100. You would expect to observe buffalo grass and bison in the
   (A) desert   (B) tropical rain forest   (C) deciduous forest
   (D) arctic tundra   (E) grasslands

100. Ⓐ Ⓑ Ⓒ Ⓓ Ⓔ

101. Blood leaving the left atrium of the human heart enters the
   (A) left ventricle   (B) pulmonary artery   (C) aorta
   (D) pulmonary vein   (E) superior vena cava

101. Ⓐ Ⓑ Ⓒ Ⓓ Ⓔ

102. An association of species in which neither is able to survive without the other is called
   (A) mutualism   (B) neutralism   (C) competition
   (D) amensalism   (E) commensalism

102. Ⓐ Ⓑ Ⓒ Ⓓ Ⓔ

103. One of the reasons that Mendel was successful when others before him failed was that
   (A) he studied the inheritance of single contrasting characters
   (B) he understood mutations
   (C) he was able to verify his results by making chromosome studies
   (D) he concerned himself with genes, not with how they expressed themselves
   (E) he was lucky

103. Ⓐ Ⓑ Ⓒ Ⓓ Ⓔ

104. Straight-line evolutionary trends lacking the usual side branches are called
   (A) orthogenesis   (B) convergent evolution
   (C) divergent evolution   (D) adaptive radiation
   (E) polymorphism

104. Ⓐ Ⓑ Ⓒ Ⓓ Ⓔ

105. If a couple has a child which is a girl, the probability that the second child will be a boy is
   (A) 1/16   (B) 1/8   (C) 1/4
   (D) 1/2   (E) 3/4

105. Ⓐ Ⓑ Ⓒ Ⓓ Ⓔ

106. A process which results in a decrease in dry weight is
   (A) osmosis   (B) photosynthesis   (C) diffusion
   (D) respiration   (E) reduction

106. Ⓐ Ⓑ Ⓒ Ⓓ Ⓔ

107. During the blood clotting process, the action of thromboplastin and thrombin is similar to that of
   (A) hormones   (B) phagocytosis   (C) enzymes
   (D) antigens   (E) vitamins

107. Ⓐ Ⓑ Ⓒ Ⓓ Ⓔ

108. Conversion of molecular nitrogen to ammonia or nitrate is carried out only by
   (A) certain bacteria and photosynthesis
   (B) bacteria and fungi
   (C) earthworms and soil bacteria
   (D) lightning, certain bacteria or blue-green algae
   (E) lightning, decomposition and fungi

108. Ⓐ Ⓑ Ⓒ Ⓓ Ⓔ

Directions: The group of questions below consists of five lettered choices followed by a list of numbered phrases or sentences. For each numbered phrase or sentence select the one choice that is most closely related to it. Each choice may be used once, more than once, or not at all.

Questions 109–111

    (A) Adenosine triphosphate
    (B) Deoxyribonucleic acid
    (C) Disaccharide
    (D) Nucleotide
    (E) Phospholipid

109. A chemical compound found in chromosomes that stores hereditary information   109. Ⓐ Ⓑ Ⓒ Ⓓ Ⓔ

110. The immediate source of energy for cellular activities   110. Ⓐ Ⓑ Ⓒ Ⓓ Ⓔ

111. Energy-rich molecules formed in the mitochondrion   111. Ⓐ Ⓑ Ⓒ Ⓓ Ⓔ

ANSWERS AND EXPLANATIONS

1.   D.   By definition, a tissue is a group of similar cells specialized to perform a particular function or functions.
2.   E.   Genetics is that branch of biology concerned with the study of heredity and variation in organisms and with the means by which it takes place.
3.   E.   Enzymes are proteinaceous materials produced by living cells. Enzymes control cellular metabolism.
4.   E.   Flask A permits microorganisms to enter readily and the material broth supports their existence and growth. Flask B severely restricts or prevents the entrance of microorganisms and, due to the lack of microorganisms in its broth, one must conclude that microorganisms do not arise spontaneously.
5.   D.   Biogenesis is the concept that life arises only from preexisting life, a proposal first suggested by Virchow.
6.   E.   Photosynthesis is the biochemical process which occurs in living cells containing chlorophyll; it occurs only when radiant energy is present and results in the production of the basic food glucose.
7.   E.   Typical holozoic organisms obtain nourishment by ingesting (eating) their food.
8.   B.   The dark reactions of photosynthesis include the reduction of CO_2 and its combination into 3-and-6-carbon sugars. This is followed by a series of reactions in which the sugar ribulose is replaced.
9.   D. $6CO_2 + 6H_2O + \text{Radiant Energy} \rightarrow C_6H_{12}O_6 + 6O_2$
10.   A. $C_6H_{12}O_6 + 6O_2 \rightarrow 6CO_2 + 6H_2O + energy$ (respiration)
11.   A.   Tropisms are growth responses of plants to environmental stimuli such as light, water, and gravity.
12.   C.   "Long day" plants require more than a minimum exposure of 13–14 hours of daylight for flowering. Under conditions of fewer than 13–14 hours of daylight, flowering does not occur.
13.   A.   In plants having a cylindrical cambium, all tissues (except the pith) internal to the cambium are designated as xylem, i.e., wood. All tissues external to the cambium are "bark."

14. C. Typically, celery has a short, cushiony stem to which the "stalks" are attached. Celery has a compound leaf, i.e., a leaf consists of a petiole, or "stem," and leaflets.

15. A. Transpiration is the *evaporation* of water from the aerial parts of plants. Any condition which would increase the evaporation of water from an open dish would similarly increase transpiration.

16. B. Putrefaction is the decompensation of organic substances by living organisms in the absence of free oxygen.

17. D. The typical plant life cycle is an "alternation of generations", i.e., the alternation of a diploid, spore-producing generation with a haploid, gamete-producing generation. Following meiosis, haploid spores give rise to the gametophyte generation; haploid gametes, produced by the gametophyte, fuse (fertilization) to produce the zygote, which develops into the diploid sporophyte generation.

18. D. Homologous structures have similarities of structure, embryonic development and relationships.

19. E. An Rh negative mother carrying an Rh positive fetus develops antibodies to the Rh antigen, which, in turn, destroy the Rh-positive red blood cells of the fetus.

20. A. Carotenes are a group of orange to red pigments found in the chromoplastids of certain plant cells. The pigments are converted to vitamin A.

21. C. Overeating and the lack of sufficient, appropriate exercise results in a high percentage of the population being overweight.

22. A. Spinal nerves typically innervate muscles and organs of the body while cranial nerves innervate muscles and organs associated with the head.

23. E. Nerve innervations are specific, i.e., the trigeminal nerve innervates the teeth; the optic nerve innervates the eye.

24. A. The sympathetic nervous system typically responds to situations involving anger, fear, etc., with bodily response that provides greater courage, strength, etc. The parasympathetic nervous system tends to counter these by reducing blood pressure, decreasing heart rate, etc.

25. E. Disease may be caused by invading organisms and their products, such as diphtheria or poliomylitis; by deficiencies of minerals and vitamins, such as scurvy or rickets; or by defects in hormonal production and secretion such as goiter, etc. The latter are called functional diseases.

26. E. Endocrine secretions—hormones—are specific in action. Oxytoxin stimulates lactation, or the release of milk.

27. B. Crossing over, inversion, translocation and duplication are events which frequently happen to chromatin materials during meiosis.

28. B. The total development of any individual is determined by its genetic makeup as affected by its environment. A change in genetic makeup through new gene combinations or by mutation, and/or by changed environmental factors are the only causes of variation in a population.

29. D. No type of RNA is designated "gametic RNA." The RNA of gametes is not so designated.

30. D. Ovists contend that miniature organisms were contained in eggs and that all eggs were created together and have existed since the beginning of the world.

31. C. By definition, a fruit is the matured ovary of a flower.

32. B. The coniferous forest biome, the taiga, is dominated by conifers, especially spruces. It is populated by bears, rodents, birds, and moose.

33. B. Nekton includes large fishes, giant squids, and whales which swim in direct relation to their food supply and independent of wave or current actions.

34. B. Cytogenetics is that branch or division of cytology which emphasizes the behavior of the genetic apparatus, or chromosomes of the cell.

35. E. Paleontology is concerned with a study of life of past geological time periods as revealed by fossil remains.

36. A. A parasite derives its food from the living tissue of other organisms.

37. D. Semilunar valves are found at both the entrance of the pulmonary artery and the aorta.

38. E. The hepatic vein empties into the inferior vena cava.
39. E. The Schick test determines the presence of diphtheria antitoxin in the blood.
40. B. Sexual reproduction is the only reproductive measure which permits new combinations of genes, thus establishing the basis for evolution and adaptation to a constantly changing environment.
41. D. In human sex inheritance, the X and Y chromosome types of sex inheritance is involved. Females are "XX". Males are "XY" and produce sperm carrying either "X" or "Y" chromosomes. Eggs carry only an "X" chromosome. If the fertilized egg contains two "X" chromosomes, the individual will be female. If it contains an "X" and a "Y" chromosome, the individual will be a male.
42. D. The chance of an AB segregation of genes following meiosis in an individual with an "AaBb" genotype is one in four.
43. C. Sickle-cell anemia is due to a mutation and the subsequent substitution of one amino acid for another in the normal hemoglobin protein chain.
44. C. In biotic communities, most populations can be assigned to one of several roles such as a food producer, a first-order consumer, a parasite, a scavenger, etc. Each role is recognized as a niche and only one species occupies a particular and specific niche in a community.
45. B. Animals with bilateral symmetry have right and left sides, a front and back and are active movers.
46. A. Anatomy is the study of structure.
47. E. The amino group is represented as —NH_2.
48. D. A hypertonic solution is one with a higher osmotic pressure than the reference (in this case, the living cell) solution.
49. C. An autotrophic organism is able to manufacture its own food, usually by photosynthesis.
50. D. A saprophytic organism derives its food from nonliving organic matter.
51. E. Priestly discovered the opposing nature of photosynthesis and respiration. Respiration uses oxygen and releases carbon dioxide, while photosynthesis uses carbon dioxide and releases oxygen.
52. E. In respiration the energy of foodstuffs is converted through a series of enzyme-regulated reactions into ATP, adenosine triphosphate, the principal energy storage molecule.
53. B. Ribosomes are RNA-containing organelles that are the sites of the synthesis of proteins.
54. B. Root hair cells increase the absorbing surface of roots.
55. B. Transpiration is the evaporation of water from the aerial part of plants. Evaporation is the result of the molecular activity called diffusion.
56. E. There are over 2,000 species of bacteria. Bacteria have few morphological/anatomical characteristics. Bacteria are distinguished by their growth in selected nutrient media and by such tests as the production of acid, gas, etc.—all of which are physiological traits.
57. C. By definition, fertilization is the union or fusion of an egg and sperm which results in the formation of a fertilized egg, or zygote.
58. B. Flowering plants produce the cereal grains in addition to numerous fruits and seeds , all of which are essential to the nutrition of humans and other animals.
59. D. An antigen is any substance which, when introduced into the body, causes the body to produce antibodies against it.
60. D. The physiological function of vitamin D is the regulation of calcium and phosphorus metabolism, hence, bone and tooth formation.
61. E. The chief sources of thiamine are yeast, wheat germ, corn meal and enriched (whole grain) flower products, i.e, the cereals.
62. E. Billions of nerve cell bodies make up the cerebral cortex. By various means (i.e., disease, surgery, electrical stimulation), it has been shown that specific regions of the cerebral cortex control specific functions such as hearing, movement, balance, memory, etc.
63. E. Mitosis is a process consisting of recognized phases which occur in the order prophase, metaphase, anaphase, telophase, and interphase.

64. B. A linkage group consists of a series of inherited traits which are inherited as a "package" because they are in a linear arrangement along a single chromatid. Crossing over, the exchange of segments between the chromatids of a tetrad may disrupt this inheritance package.

65. E. The dark reactions of photosynthesis use the energy of ATP, which is formed in the light, for their essential process, all of which take place in the clear stroma, which surround the grana of the chloroplast.

66. E. A streaming movement of the cytoplasm (cyclosis) within a cell during periods of photosynthesis apparently presents the contained chloroplastids of each cell to maximum light exposure in sequence.

67. B. Enzymes that control respiration are generally found in the mitochondria and, under suitable conditions, the oxidation of pyruvic acid to carbon dioxide and water with the production of ATP molecules can be demonstrated.

68. C. Under the influence of the enzyme thrombin, fibrinogen is converted into fibrin, which gradually forms a mesh in which blood cells become embedded, thus forming a clot.

69. D. Systole is that phase of the heart's action in which blood is forced out of the ventricles.

70. D. The trigeminal nerve innervates teeth.

71. C. The prophase is recognized as the phase of mitosis in which the chromatids may be observed in the doubled chromosomes.

72. A. Plankton is the myriad of small, microscopic, free-floating aquatic organisms found at or near the surface and subject to tides and currents.

73. D. The genetic material must be able to contain a code and to copy itself exactly. Deoxyribonucleic acid, often abbreviated DNA, has this capability. In addition, it meets the requirements of being able to mutate and undergo crossing-over.

74. E. Nephrons are the functional units of the kidneys that, while secreting quantities of fluid, reabsorb blood sugar and amino acids as well as urea, various ions, and a large amount of water.

75. D. Atmospheric pressure on the surface of the mercury in the sealed tube pushes the mercury to a height of 760 millimeters. This is the basis of the common mercury barometer.

76. C. Atmospheric pressure on the surface of the mercury plus the effects of transpirational pull—the evaporation of water from the stem and leaves of the plant—work together in raising the level of the mercury in figure B above 760 millimeters of mercury.

77. C. In this situation, the living cell is hypertonic and water diffuses into the cell.

78. D. Carbon is an element basic to all organic compounds and is essential to the synthesis of carbohydrates, fats, and proteins.

79. B. Insufficient light stimulates stem elongation, which, when carried to extremes, is known as etiolation.

80. E. Eutrophication occurs when chemical fertilizers containing phosphorus and nitrogen wash into a lake causing photoplankton and bottom vegetation to high productivity. This tremendous growth blocks out light, causing deeper plants to die while certain decomposers use all the oxygen, thus suffocating the fish.

81. E. The peanuts we eat are matured ovules—therefore seeds—of the pea ovary.

82. E. According to epigenesis, the individual arises from the undifferentiated material of the egg.

83. D. The trigeminal nerve innervates the jaw muscles.

84. C. Blood leaving the right ventricle enters the pulmonary artery; blood leaving the left ventricle enters the aorta.

85. B. The distinguishing factor of mutualism is that at least one of the populations cannot survive without the other.

86. D. While carbon, hydrogen and oxygen suffice for all carbohydrates and fats, proteins cannot be synthesized without additional elements including nitrogen and, sometimes, sulfur.

87. A. Potatoes are propagated vegetatively (asexually) by planting pieces of cut-up potato tuber. (Tubers are modified, underground stems.)

88. E. Bacteriophages are viruses that attack and invade bacterial cells converting bacterial DNA to viral DNA.

89. B. Fermentation takes place in yeasts and other cells in the absence of free oxygen and a similar type of reaction takes place in muscle cells. This process produces lactic acid from which the energy-bearing ATP molecule is formed.

90. B. Niacin is usually thought of as the vitamin that prevents pellagra. Persons consuming insufficient niacin may also develop disorders of the digestive system, skin, and the nervous system.

91. B. The vagus nerve innervates the heart, the bronchi, the bladder, and other internal organs, and it is involved with peristaltic movements and secretion.

92. E. In the farsighted eye, the misshapen lens focuses the image behind the retina.

93. A. In the complex DNA molecule, the bases adenine and thymine are always paired as are cytosine and guanine.

94. E. A fruit is a matured flower ovary.

95. D   At the time of fertilization, the probability for a male or a female in humans is one half or 50%.

96. E. In fats, the ratio of hydrogen atoms to oxygen atoms is much higher than 2:1. Tristearin, for example, has the formula $C_{57}H_{110}O_6$.

97. A. Under conditions of isolation, exemplified by Darwin's finches, the production of a number of diverse species from a single ancestral one is referred to as adaptive radiation.

98. B. Photosynthesis results in the conversion of radiant, or light, energy into chemical energy and its storage in the glucose molecule.

99. A. Folic acid is important for normal bone marrow function and a deficiency could result in certain types of anemia.

100. E. Native perennial grasses of the grasslands (prairies) of North America include the so-called buffalo grass and the predominant animal, the bison.

101. A. In the human heart (and 4-chambered hearts in general), blood goes from the left atrium into the left ventricle and from the right atrium into the right ventricle.

102. A. In a mutualistic relationship, at least one partner is unable to survive without the other.

103. A. Prior to Mendel, most students of inheritance attempted to study inheritance patterns involving all or groups of supposedly inheritable traits. The usual result was confusion and chaos.

104. A. Variation in successive generations along a predestined line and which results in evolutionary trends that are independent of external factors is called orthogenesis.

105. D. At the time of fertilization, the probability that a given child will be either a boy or a girl is 50%.

106. D. Respiration is a biochemical process that releases energy and carbon dioxide. Dry weight is lost during respiration because organic compounds are used up.

107. C. During blood clotting, thromboplastin acts on prothrombin to produce thrombin, and thrombin, in turn, acts on fibrinogen to produce fibrin. Both reactions are enzymatic.

108. D. Under natural conditions only lightning, certain bacteria and blue-green algae are able to "fix" nitrogen.

109. B. DNA, deoxyribonucleic acid, is found in chromosomes and stores hereditary information in coded form.

110. A. ⎫ In the mitochondria, during cellular respiration, energy is transformed
111. A. ⎬ from carbohydrate molecules to energy-rich adenosine triphosphate (ATP) for use throughout the cell.

Directions: Each of the questions or incomplete statements below is followed by five suggested answers or completions. Select the one that is best in each case.

1. Retrograde motion is the
   (A) apparent backward motion of a planet
   (B) apparent backward motion of the moon
   (C) seasonal movement between the vernal equinox and the autumnal equinox
   (D) reciprocal movement of the earth's axis
   (E) retreat of a meteorite

   1. Ⓐ Ⓑ Ⓒ Ⓓ Ⓔ

2. Since the same face of the moon is always visible on earth, we must conclude that
   (A) the earth and moon rotate at the same relative rate
   (B) the earth and moon are rotating in opposite directions
   (C) the moon must make one rotation on its axis while revolving once around the earth
   (D) the earth must make one rotation on its axis while revolving around the moon
   (E) their orbits are equal

   2. Ⓐ Ⓑ Ⓒ Ⓓ Ⓔ

3. To say that the solar system is heliocentric means that
   (A) the earth is the center of the solar system
   (B) the sun is the center of the solar system
   (C) the sun is highest in the sky
   (D) the sun is lowest in the sky
   (E) the center reflects the perimeter

   3. Ⓐ Ⓑ Ⓒ Ⓓ Ⓔ

4. A star that increases to a maximum brightness and does not return to its original condition is known as a
   (A) nova   (B) supernova   (C) giant
   (D) supergiant   (E) binary

   4. Ⓐ Ⓑ Ⓒ Ⓓ Ⓔ

5. During a solar eclipse
   (A) the earth's shadow is cast on the moon
   (B) the moon's shadow is cast on the earth
   (C) the earth's shadow falls on the sun
   (D) the earth moves between the sun and moon
   (E) the sun moves between the earth and moon

   5. Ⓐ Ⓑ Ⓒ Ⓓ Ⓔ

6. An early Egyptian achievement, based on a knowledge of astronomy, was the
   (A) recording of eclipses
   (B) recording of earthquakes
   (C) invention of time
   (D) development of a 365-day calendar
   (E) development of a decimal system

   6. Ⓐ Ⓑ Ⓒ Ⓓ Ⓔ

7. Radio waves of broadcasting frequency are reflected by
   (A) ozone in the stratosphere
   (B) an ionized layer of the troposphere
   (C) a non-ionized layer of the troposphere
   (D) the exosphere
   (E) the ionosphere

8. An eclipse of the moon
   (A) occurs when the earth passes into the shadow of the moon
   (B) occurs when the moon passes between the sun and the earth
   (C) occurs every eight years
   (D) can occur only during a new moon
   (E) can occur only during a full moon

9. The Hawaiian Islands are just east of the international dateline while Wake Island is west. When it is July 4 at Pearl Harbor, what is the date at Wake Island?
   (A) July 2   (B) July 3   (C) July 4   (D) July 5
   (E) July 6

10. When a space vehicle is at apogee, it is at
    (A) maximum speed
    (B) minimum speed
    (C) the point farthest away from the sun
    (D) a point in orbit farthest from the earth
    (E) a point in orbit closest to the earth

11. At the time of the summer solstice in the northern hemisphere,
    (A) the sun's rays are tangent to the poles
    (B) the sun's rays are perpendicular to the equator
    (C) days and nights are equal over the entire earth
    (D) the sun is directly overhead at the Tropic of Cancer
    (E) the sun is directly overhead at the Tropic of Capricorn

12. Small celestial bodies whose orbits generally lie between Mars and Jupiter are called
    (A) comets   (B) meteoroids   (C) asteroids
    (D) planets   (E) micrometeorites

13. One evidence of the earth's rotation is
    (A) the solar eclipse
    (B) the lunar eclipse
    (C) the changing phases of the moon
    (D) the tilt of the earth's axis
    (E) the circulation of air as reported on weather maps

14. A lunar eclipse occurs when
    (A) the sun, moon, and earth form a triangle
    (B) the moon's shadow falls on the earth
    (C) the sun moves between the moon and the earth
    (D) the moon comes between the earth and the sun
    (E) the earth travels between the sun and the moon

ANSWERS AND EXPLANATIONS

1. A. Occasionally planets appear to become stationary and then to drift westward for a short time; then the planet resumes its normal eastward motion. This is known as retrograde motion.

2. C. The direction of the moon's rotation is in the same direction as the earth's rotation and it makes only one rotation on its axis during one revolution around the earth. Therefore, the moon keeps the same side directed towards the earth.

3. B. By definition: having the sun as a center.

4. B. A supernova is a star that has collapsed under intense gravitation and then exploded.

5. B. When the moon lies directly between the earth and the sun we witness a solar eclipse.

6. D. The Egyptians were the first to develop a 365-day calendar.

7. E. A layer of the atmosphere characterized by electrical properties and the presence of ionized particles is called the ionosphere. Radio waves from the earth travel upward to these ionized layers and are reflected back to earth.

8. E. In an eclipse, both the sun and the center of the earth lie in the ecliptic plane and so must the moon lie in the ecliptic plane for, if it is too far from the ecliptic plane, it cannot pass into the shadow of the earth to cause a lunar eclipse. When lying in the ecliptic plane, the moon is, by its location, in the "full moon" phase.

9. D. The International Date Line is designated ± 12 hours based on Greenwich time. Points east and west of this line differ in time by 24 hours.

10. D. In an elliptical orbit, a space vehicle at apogee is at the orbit's farthest distance from earth.

11. D. On June 21, the sun is as far north as it will go and is directly over the Tropic of Cancer, 23° 27′ north of the equator. This date and this position of the sun mark the summer solstice.

12. C. Asteroids include thousands of small planets between Mars and Jupiter with diameters of a fraction of a mile to almost 500 miles.

13. E. Winds are deflected to the right of their paths in the Northern Hemisphere and to the left of their paths in the Southern Hemisphere, deviations which are the result of the earth's rotation. This deviation is called the Coriolis effect. The circulation of air as indicated on weather maps, is, therefore, a direct effect of the earth's rotation.

14. E. In a lunar eclipse, the earth's shadow falls on the moon.

Questions about Earth Science

Directions: Each of the questions or incomplete statements below is followed by five suggested answers or completions. Select the one that is best in each case.

1. A contemporary source of support for the theory of sphericity of the earth is
   (A) the Foucault pendulum   (B) photographs taken by astronauts
   (C) computer data   (D) coriolis forces   (E) parallax of stars

   1. Ⓐ Ⓑ Ⓒ Ⓓ Ⓔ

2. Crystalline calcite columns hanging from cave ceilings are called
   (A) stalagmites   (B) anthracite   (C) dolomite
   (D) alabaster   (E) stalactites

   2. Ⓐ Ⓑ Ⓒ Ⓓ Ⓔ

3. Lava, which solidifies in the air and falls to the earth as solid particles, is called
   (A) xenoliths   (B) laccoliths   (C) pyroclastics
   (D) batholiths   (E) pahoehoes

   3. Ⓐ Ⓑ Ⓒ Ⓓ Ⓔ

4. About 99% of the earth's atmosphere consists of
   (A) nitrogen and oxygen   (B) nitrogen   (C) oxygen
   (D) oxygen and carbon dioxide   (E) nitrogen and carbon dioxide

   4. Ⓐ Ⓑ Ⓒ Ⓓ Ⓔ

5. A weathering of rock by a combination of mechanical and chemical forces is
   (A) hydration   (B) crosscutting   (C) lamination
   (D) intrusion   (E) intumescence

   5. Ⓐ Ⓑ Ⓒ Ⓓ Ⓔ

6. A surface separating young rocks from older ones is
   (A) a moraine   (B) a bench   (C) a stack
   (D) an unconformity   (E) a disjunction

   6. Ⓐ Ⓑ Ⓒ Ⓓ Ⓔ

7. An earthquake that follows a larger earthquake and originates at or near the same focus is called
   (A) the epicenter   (B) surface wave   (C) an aftershock
   (D) seismogram   (E) reflected wave

   7. Ⓐ Ⓑ Ⓒ Ⓓ Ⓔ

8. A dark-brown residue formed by the partial decomposition of plants that grow in marshes and other wet places is called
   (A) coal   (B) dolomite   (C) peat   (D) chert   (E) coquins

   8. Ⓐ Ⓑ Ⓒ Ⓓ Ⓔ

9. The time period described as the age of the great coal swamps is called the
   (A) Oligocene epoch   (B) Jurassic period   (C) Pennsylvanian period
   (D) Pleistocene period   (E) Silurian period

   9. Ⓐ Ⓑ Ⓒ Ⓓ Ⓔ

10. Rocks formed by solidification of molten material are called
    (A) sedimentary   (B) igneous   (C) fossiliferous
    (D) metamorphic   (E) monomineralic

    10. Ⓐ Ⓑ Ⓒ Ⓓ Ⓔ

11. The gradual dome-like buildup of calcite mounds or columns on the floors of caves results in formations called
    (A) stalactites   (B) diamonds   (C) gypsum
    (D) dolomite   (E) stalagmites

    11. Ⓐ Ⓑ Ⓒ Ⓓ Ⓔ

12. A fracture line of the earth's crust where one portion has shifted vertically in reference to the other is called

(A) a fault (B) a P wave (C) an L wave
(D) an S wave (E) a tremor

12. Ⓐ Ⓑ Ⓒ Ⓓ Ⓔ

13. Stalagmites are

(A) graphite columns "growing" down from a cave ceiling
(B) calcite mounds or columns built up from cave floors
(C) anthracite deposits in caves
(D) graphite mounds or columns built up from cave floors
(E) calcite columns "growing" down from cave ceilings

13. Ⓐ Ⓑ Ⓒ Ⓓ Ⓔ

ANSWERS AND EXPLANATIONS

1. B. Photographs taken from outer space show the earth to be a sphere.

2. E. Crystalline calcite columns called stalactites are formed over long periods of time by dripping water.

3. C. Pyroclastics are particles of solidified lava which have fallen to earth.

4. A. The earth's atmosphere is 78% nitrogen and 21% oxygen. The remaining 1% consists of carbon dioxide, argon, helium, and other gases.

5. A. Mechanical weathering is the breaking of rock into smaller pieces, each retaining the characteristics of the original material. Chemical weathering results when chemical actions alter the rock by either the removal or addition of elements.

6. D. Breaks in the rock record are called uncomformities. One easily recognized unconformity consists of tilted or folded sedimentary rocks that are overlain by other more flat-lying rock strata.

7. C. Aftershocks are earthquakes of less severity that usually follow the primary earthquake.

8. C. As a layer of sphagnum (peat moss) grows over water, older growth is pressed deeper in the water and into darkness where it dies. Initial decay products contain much tannin and this slows down bacterial decay. This becomes the peat of commerce.

9. C. During the Pennsylvanian period, lush vegetation was so profuse that it was buried under successive layers, which in aging under high pressures eventually became coal.

10. B. Rock formed by the cooling of magma is known as igneous rock.

11. E. The calcite mounds built up on cave floors are called stalagmites.

12. A. When portions of the earth's crust fracture as a result of earthquakes, these fracture lines are called faults.

13. B. Stalagmites are calcite mounds built up on cave floors and are the result of dripping water over long periods of time.

Questions about Physics

Directions: Each of the questions or incomplete statements below is followed by five suggested answers or completions. Select the one that is best in each case.

1. During the process called nuclear fission,
   (A) alpha particles are emitted
   (B) light atomic nuclei fuse
   (C) there is an increase in mass
   (D) radioactive fragments are formed
   (E) much energy is consumed

1. Ⓐ Ⓑ Ⓒ Ⓓ Ⓔ

2. Chromatic aberration may be eliminated by the use of
   (A) a convex lens   (B) a concave lens
   (C) monochromatic light   (D) proper focusing
   (E) a wider lens

2. Ⓐ Ⓑ Ⓒ Ⓓ Ⓔ

3. When a musical note is raised one half step in pitch, it is called
   (A) tremolo   (B) syncopation   (C) sharp   (D) flat
   (E) overtone

3. Ⓐ Ⓑ Ⓒ Ⓓ Ⓔ

4. Pressure in a liquid
   (A) is inversely proportional to depth
   (B) decreases with depth
   (C) is variable at all points at the same level
   (D) is the same at different points at different levels
   (E) is the same at all points at the same level

4. Ⓐ Ⓑ Ⓒ Ⓓ Ⓔ

5. A device in which chemical energy is converted into electrical energy is the
   (A) induction coil   (B) rectifier   (C) vacuum tube
   (D) amplifier   (E) fuel cell

5. Ⓐ Ⓑ Ⓒ Ⓓ Ⓔ

6. The condition created when two wires are connected through such a low resistance that current flow is excessive is called
   (A) a short circuit   (B) induction   (C) rectification
   (D) a circuit breaker   (E) transition

6. Ⓐ Ⓑ Ⓒ Ⓓ Ⓔ

7. Electronics is a field of applied science concerned with
   (A) the flow of electrons along a wire
   (B) the flow of electrons through gases or through a vacuum
   (C) the flow of electrons in liquids
   (D) amplitude modulation
   (E) frequency modulation

7. Ⓐ Ⓑ Ⓒ Ⓓ Ⓔ

8. A prism separates white light because
   (A) parallel rays are reflected
   (B) parallel rays are focused
   (C) the angle of incidence equals the angle of reflection
   (D) the different frequencies are refracted differently
   (E) light rays are absorbed

8. Ⓐ Ⓑ Ⓒ Ⓓ Ⓔ

9. An object traveling at mach 2 is traveling approximately how many mph?
   (A) 750   (B) 1,500   (C) 2,000   (D) 15,000   (E) 20,000

9. Ⓐ Ⓑ Ⓒ Ⓓ Ⓔ

10. A shift in the wave length of light or sound is known as the
    (A) Bernoulian Principle   (B) Compton effect
    (C) Doppler effect   (D) Edison effect   (E) Bell effect

10. Ⓐ Ⓑ Ⓒ Ⓓ Ⓔ

11. Heat is the energy represented by
    (A) friction   (B) molecular motion   (C) thermodynamics
    (D) absolute zero   (E) thermostats

11. Ⓐ Ⓑ Ⓒ Ⓓ Ⓔ

12. Magnetic fields
    (A) are indefinite and variable
    (B) cannot exist in a vacuum
    (C) cannot be demonstrated
    (D) can be explained by Gilbert's Theory
    (E) cannot penetrate non-magnetic materials

12. Ⓐ Ⓑ Ⓒ Ⓓ Ⓔ

13. In reference to electrical circuitry, the ohm represents
    (A) the unit of current   (B) a force between two electric fields
    (C) the difference of potential   (D) the flow of coulombs
    (E) the unit of resistance

13. Ⓐ Ⓑ Ⓒ Ⓓ Ⓔ

14. Work requires that
    (A) direction be changed
    (B) a body is moved by a force
    (C) a definite rate is maintained
    (D) the rate of motion increase
    (E) the rate of motion decrease

14. Ⓐ Ⓑ Ⓒ Ⓓ Ⓔ

15. In using a lever,
    (A) force is gained when the force arm is longer than the weight arm
    (B) force is gained when the force arm is shorter than the weight arm
    (C) force is gained when the force arm and the weight arm are equal
    (D) distance is gained when the force arm is longer than the weight
        arm
    (E) distance is gained when the fulcrum is central

15. Ⓐ Ⓑ Ⓒ Ⓓ Ⓔ

16. Attics should have provision for ventilation so that hot summer air
    may be removed by
    (A) conduction   (B) expansion   (C) convection
    (D) entropy   (E) radiation

16. Ⓐ Ⓑ Ⓒ Ⓓ Ⓔ

17. If you swim one kilometer to an island off-shore, how many miles do
    you swim?
    (A) 0.36 mile   (B) 0.5 mile   (C) 0.84 mile   (D) 0.62 mile
    (E) 1.6 miles

17. Ⓐ Ⓑ Ⓒ Ⓓ Ⓔ

18. Every object remains in its state of rest or in its state of uniform motion unless
    (A) its velocity changes   (B) its acceleration varies
    (C) internal forces change   (D) internal forces remain constant
    (E) external forces change that state

18. Ⓐ Ⓑ Ⓒ Ⓓ Ⓔ

19. According to Newton's third law of motion,
    (A) force is proportional to mass times acceleration
    (B) momentum equals mass times velocity
    (C) the weight of a body is equal to the gravitational attraction exerted upon it by the earth
    (D) the weight of a body is equal to the gravitational attraction exerted upon it by the sun
    (E) to every action, there is an equal and opposite reaction

19. Ⓐ Ⓑ Ⓒ Ⓓ Ⓔ

NOTE: The illustration above applies to the next three questions.

20. A fluid moving through a constriction, as illustrated above, speeds up and at the same time
    (A) its temperature also increases
    (B) its temperature decreases
    (C) its molecules begin to cling together
    (D) the pressure of the fluid within the constriction decreases
    (E) the pressure of the fluid within the constriction increases

20. Ⓐ Ⓑ Ⓒ Ⓓ Ⓔ

21. The phenomenon illustrated above is known as
    (A) the Doppler Effect
    (B) Borelli's Constant
    (C) Bernoulli's Principle
    (D) the Mach Effect
    (E) the Schlieren Process

21. Ⓐ Ⓑ Ⓒ Ⓓ Ⓔ

22. One application of the phenomenon illustrated above is in the
    (A) calculation of barometric pressure
    (B) verification of translational motion
    (C) design of airplane wings
    (D) determination of wave frequency
    (E) design of internal guidance systems

22. Ⓐ Ⓑ Ⓒ Ⓓ Ⓔ

NOTE: The illustration above applies to the next three questions.

In the figures illustrated above, cubes A, B, and C, which have equal dimensions, are shown in containers of water.

23. In respect to the relative densities of the cubes, it may be concluded that
  (A) cube C has the greatest density
  (B) cube C sinks because its density is equal to the density of water
  (C) cube A has the greatest density
  (D) cube B has the greatest density
  (E) water has less buoyant force than cubes A or B

23. Ⓐ Ⓑ Ⓒ Ⓓ Ⓔ

24. Cube C sinks to the bottom because
  (A) cube C has a very low density
  (B) the weight of the displaced water is greater than the weight of cube C
  (C) cube C displaces too much water
  (D) the weight of the displaced water is equal to the weight of cube C
  (E) the weight of the displaced water is less than the weight of cube C

24. Ⓐ Ⓑ Ⓒ Ⓓ Ⓔ

25. The phenomenon illustrated in these figures is best summarized or explained by
  (A) Faraday's Postulates
  (B) Boyle's Law
  (C) Dalton's Theory
  (D) Archimedes' Principle
  (E) Kepler's Laws

25. Ⓐ Ⓑ Ⓒ Ⓓ Ⓔ

26. The energy exerted by a bowling ball as it strikes the pins is
  (A) inertia   (B) mass energy   (C) kinetic energy
  (D) potential energy   (E) transferred energy

26. Ⓐ Ⓑ Ⓒ Ⓓ Ⓔ

27. If a container of ether is unstoppered in a closed room where there are no air currents or air circulation, we soon smell ether because of
  (A) osmosis   (B) diffusion   (C) transpiration
  (D) capillarity   (E) surface tension

27. Ⓐ Ⓑ Ⓒ Ⓓ Ⓔ

28. When electricity flows through a wire wound in the form of a coil, the coil functions as
  (A) a generator   (B) a resistor   (C) an electromagnet
  (D) an electrostatic generator   (E) an electroscope

28. Ⓐ Ⓑ Ⓒ Ⓓ Ⓔ

29. When the nucleus of a radium atom emits an alpha particle,

(A) only its atomic number changes

(B) only its mass changes

(C) neither its mass nor atomic number changes

(D) both its mass and atomic number change

(E) it becomes uranium

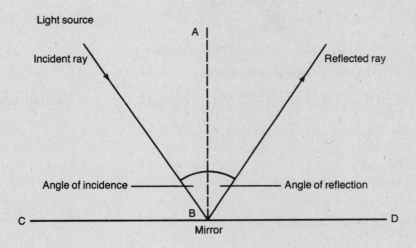

The diagram above illustrates the reflection of a ray of light from a mirror. The imaginary line AB is perpendicular to line CD.

30. The nature of a reflected ray of light is such that

(A) the angle of incidence is greater than the angle of reflection

(B) the angle of reflection always equals the angle of incidence

(C) the angle of reflection is greater than the angle of incidence

(D) the angle of reflection varies and changes

(E) the sum of the angle of incidence and the angle of reflection is a right angle

31. A vibrating string on a musical instrument will produce a low pitch if it is

(A) short, stretched, and of small diameter

(B) long, stretched, and of small diameter

(C) long, loose, and of small diameter

(D) long, loose, and of large diameter

(E) short, stretched, and of large diameter

Effort

50 inches

20 pounds

20 inches

NOTE: The illustration above pertains to the following two questions.

32. The effort required to lift the 20 pound load in the illustration above is   32. Ⓐ Ⓑ Ⓒ Ⓓ Ⓔ
(A) 8 pounds
(B) 10 pounds
(C) 2 pounds
(D) 20 pounds
(E) 40 pounds

33. The mechanical advantage of the lever illustrated above is   33. Ⓐ Ⓑ Ⓒ Ⓓ Ⓔ
(A) 1
(B) 10
(C) 7½
(D) 5
(E) 2½

34. In the transmission of electric power, alternating current is used because   34. Ⓐ Ⓑ Ⓒ Ⓓ Ⓔ
(A) its voltage is readily transformed
(B) it is cheaper
(C) it is readily grounded
(D) it is ready to use in household appliances
(E) it has greater resistance

35. Ultraviolet radiation will cause a metal to emit electrons, an activity called   35. Ⓐ Ⓑ Ⓒ Ⓓ Ⓔ
(A) ionization   (B) facsimile transmission
(C) electron transformation   (D) the Compton effect
(E) the photoelectric effect

36. Materials which transmit no light are referred to as   36. Ⓐ Ⓑ Ⓒ Ⓓ Ⓔ
(A) luminous   (B) opaque   (C) transparent   (D) lucid
(E) translucent

37. Concave lenses cause light rays to diverge by   37. Ⓐ Ⓑ Ⓒ Ⓓ Ⓔ
(A) reflection   (B) absorption   (C) diffraction
(D) dispersion   (E) diffusion

38. The acoustical engineer is chiefly concerned with   38. Ⓐ Ⓑ Ⓒ Ⓓ Ⓔ
(A) amplitude   (B) frequencies   (C) loudness
(D) reverberations   (E) wave length

494   Natural Sciences

39. When a bullet is fired upwards vertically, it gains in
   (A) momentum   (B) speed   (C) kinetic energy
   (D) potential energy   (E) inertia

39. Ⓐ Ⓑ Ⓒ Ⓓ Ⓔ

40. Work is the
   (A) direction of movement
   (B) distance of movement
   (C) rate of movement
   (D) product of the rate of movement multiplied by the distance moved
   (E) product of the force on an object multiplied by the distance it moves

40. Ⓐ Ⓑ Ⓒ Ⓓ Ⓔ

41. When a hard rubber ball is rubbed by wool, it
   (A) gains electrons and becomes positively charged
   (B) gains electrons and becomes negatively charged
   (C) remains neutral
   (D) loses electrons and becomes positively charged
   (E) loses electrons and becomes negatively charged

41. Ⓐ Ⓑ Ⓒ Ⓓ Ⓔ

42. Transformers
   (A) are coils of wire carrying electric current
   (B) change the voltage of alternating current
   (C) have the capacity of storing electric charges
   (D) change the voltage of direct current
   (E) are used to break circuits

42. Ⓐ Ⓑ Ⓒ Ⓓ Ⓔ

43. According to Boyle's Law, when the temperature is constant, the volume of a given quantity of gas is inversely proportional to the
   (A) viscosity   (B) temperature   (C) density
   (D) surface tension   (E) pressure

43. Ⓐ Ⓑ Ⓒ Ⓓ Ⓔ

44. Roger Bacon contributed the
   (A) heliocentric theory
   (B) idea of the rotation of the earth
   (C) experimental approach to science
   (D) concept of buoyancy and density
   (E) idea of the sphericity of the earth

44. Ⓐ Ⓑ Ⓒ Ⓓ Ⓔ

45. The usual unit of measure used to express the dimensions of living cells is the micron, which is equivalent to
   (A) 0.001 kilogram   (B) 0.001 meter   (C) 0.01 centimeter
   (D) 0.000,001 meter   (E) 0.000,001 kilometer

45. Ⓐ Ⓑ Ⓒ Ⓓ Ⓔ

46. The inward force that is necessary to keep an object in circular motion is called
   (A) centrifugal force   (B) inertia   (C) centripetal force
   (D) net force   (E) weightlessness

46. Ⓐ Ⓑ Ⓒ Ⓓ Ⓔ

47. When an object exhibits inertia, it
   (A) resists being set in motion
   (B) resists friction and slowing down
   (C) responds directly to friction forces
   (D) exhibits velocity in a specified direction
   (E) possesses direction and magnitude

47. Ⓐ Ⓑ Ⓒ Ⓓ Ⓔ

48. The difference between an induced fusion reaction and a thermo-nuclear reaction is that, in a thermonuclear reaction, nuclei of
(A) heavy atoms are split   (B) heavy atoms are fused
(C) light atoms are split   (D) light atoms are fused
(E) either heavy or light atoms are split

49. The phenomenon called interference is produced when
(A) light waves are bent
(B) light waves are parallel
(C) two or more waves of the same frequency are superposed
(D) the velocities of sound in air are identical
(E) the frequencies of wave vibrations are equal

50. Which of the following illustrates the phenomenon of "double-bonding"?

51. At the higher altitudes, the existence of a satellite is limited because of drag caused by
(A) cosmic rays from the sun
(B) air and other particles in space
(C) infrared radiation from the sun
(D) centrifugal force
(E) both cosmic rays and centrifugal force

52. According to Einstein's theory of relativity, as the speed of a space ship approaches the speed of light,
(A) metabolism and mass increase
(B) metabolism and mass decrease
(C) metabolism and mass remain constant
(D) aging, relative to earth, would slow down
(E) aging, relative to earth, would speed up

53. When a tractor applies a horizontal force of 400 pounds and pushes an object 20 feet across a loading platform, the work accomplished is equal to
(A) 200 foot-pounds   (B) 400 foot-pounds
(C) 2,000 foot-pounds   (D) 4,000 foot-pounds
(E) 8,000 foot-pounds

54. When a gas is compressed by pressure,

   (A) its component molecules are compressed

   (B) space between its molecules decreases

   (C) its volume increases

   (D) its molecules speed up

   (E) its molecules slow down

54. Ⓐ Ⓑ Ⓒ Ⓓ Ⓔ

55. The tendency of all molecules to be in continuous motion is a physical phenomenon called

   (A) diffusion   (B) capillarity   (C) surface tension

   (D) transpiration   (E) osmosis

55. Ⓐ Ⓑ Ⓒ Ⓓ Ⓔ

56. The velocity of an object is a description of

   (A) distance and time   (D) its mass and weight

   (B) its acceleration   (E) its speed and direction

   (C) its resistance to inertia

56. Ⓐ Ⓑ Ⓒ Ⓓ Ⓔ

30 pounds

90 pounds

57. The mechanical advantage of the block and tackle illustrated above is

   (A) 1

   (B) 2

   (C) 3

   (D) 6

   (E) 9

57. Ⓐ Ⓑ Ⓒ Ⓓ Ⓔ

58. The conversion of alternating current to direct current is called
    (A) amplification   (B) modulation   (C) transistorization
    (D) induction   (E) rectification

58. [A] [B] [C] [D] [E]

59. That property of matter which tends to maintain any motionless body at rest is called
    (A) friction   (B) mass   (C) inertia   (D) force
    (E) velocity

59. [A] [B] [C] [D] [E]

60. Electric current in which the direction of flow is reversed at regular intervals is called
    (A) effective current   (B) alternating current
    (C) direct current   (D) induced current   (E) universal current

60. [A] [B] [C] [D] [E]

61. In connection with nuclear reactions, that mass which is just sufficient to make the reaction self-sustaining is called
    (A) a fusion reaction   (B) a fission reaction
    (C) a critical mass   (D) deuterium   (E) plutonium

61. [A] [B] [C] [D] [E]

62. Echoes are
    (A) decibels   (B) reflected sound waves
    (C) interference   (D) reinforcement
    (E) diffracted sound waves

62. [A] [B] [C] [D] [E]

63. Heat energy is expressed in
    (A) calories   (B) ergs   (C) joules   (D) watts   (E) kilowatts

63. [A] [B] [C] [D] [E]

NOTE: The next four questions refer to the diagrams on the preceding page.

The three diagrams illustrate a sequence in which ball A is moving towards stationary ball B in diagram I; strikes ball B in diagram II; and both balls are moving after ball A strikes ball B in diagram III.

64. In diagram I, the moving ball (ball A)   64. Ⓐ Ⓑ Ⓒ Ⓓ Ⓔ
    (A) has a momentum equal to that of ball B
    (B) accelerates in direct proportion to its mass
    (C) accelerates in indirect proportion to its mass
    (D) has zero momentum
    (E) has a momentum equal to its mass times its velocity

65. When ball A collides with ball B   65. Ⓐ Ⓑ Ⓒ Ⓓ Ⓔ
    (A) ball A's momentum will increase
    (B) ball A will retain its initial velocity
    (C) ball A's momentum will remain constant
    (D) ball A will slow down
    (E) the force of the collision represents a gain in momentum

66. After the collision of ball A with ball B   66. Ⓐ Ⓑ Ⓒ Ⓓ Ⓔ
    (A) both ball A and ball B will be moving
    (B) ball A will have slowed down and changed direction
    (C) ball A will have lost momentum; ball B will have gained momentum
    (D) the total initial and final velocities of balls A and B will be equal
    (E) all of the above

67. Based upon study and observation of the three diagrams, one may con-   67. Ⓐ Ⓑ Ⓒ Ⓓ Ⓔ
    clude that in accord with Newton's Second Law,
    (A) momentum decreases mass
    (B) momentum increases mass
    (C) velocity is constant
    (D) a force is necessary for acceleration
    (E) energy is gained following the collision

68. One of the following is not an acceptable statement in respect to magnetic   68. Ⓐ Ⓑ Ⓒ Ⓓ Ⓔ
    fields:
    (A) They require the presence of matter.
    (B) Lines of force are changeable.
    (C) They can penetrate glass and wood.
    (D) They can penetrate thin sheets of copper.
    (E) They may exist in a vacuum.

69. A footcandle is a unit of illumination received at a distance of one foot
from a source of one
(A) volt   (B) roentgen   (C) erg   (D) candlepower
(E) watt

69. Ⓐ Ⓑ Ⓒ Ⓓ Ⓔ

70. Which of the following is not an example of luminescence?
(A) Electroluminescence   (B) Fluorescence
(C) Phosphorescence   (D) Bioluminescence   (E) Incandescence

70. Ⓐ Ⓑ Ⓒ Ⓓ Ⓔ

71. When white light is directed through a glass prism, a spectrum is formed
by its
(A) absorption   (B) dispersion   (C) reflection
(D) refraction   (E) diffusion

71. Ⓐ Ⓑ Ⓒ Ⓓ Ⓔ

72. Ⓐ Ⓑ Ⓒ Ⓓ Ⓔ

72. When light is reflected, the angle of incidence equals the angle of
(A) convergence   (B) divergence   (C) reflection
(D) refraction   (E) dispersion

73. A unit of measure for the flow of light equal to the amount of flow
from a uniform point source of one candle power is
(A) one kilowatt   (B) a lumen   (C) a footcandle
(D) 10 footcandles   (E) an erg

73. Ⓐ Ⓑ Ⓒ Ⓓ Ⓔ

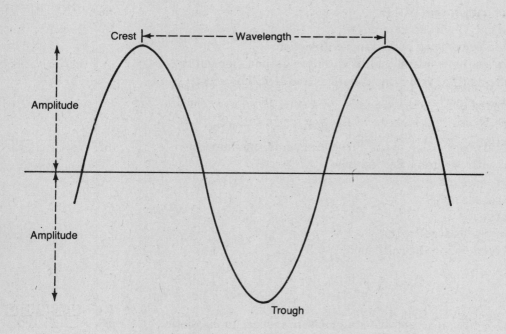

NOTE: The diagram above illustrates the basic characteristics of waves and
applies to the following two questions.

74. Amplitude may be thought of as
    74. Ⓐ Ⓑ Ⓒ Ⓓ Ⓔ
    (A) an interaction between two different waves
    (B) the number of crests passing a given point per second
    (C) the distance between two adjacent crests
    (D) a complete cycle, from crest to trough
    (E) one-half of the vertical distance between crests and troughs

75. Interference is
    75. Ⓐ Ⓑ Ⓒ Ⓓ Ⓔ
    (A) the simultaneous arrival of two different waves at a single point in space
    (B) the combining of two different waves at some point in space
    (C) the interaction of two or more waves
    (D) "in phase" if two interacting waves are of the same frequency and shape and if they meet crest to crest and trough to trough
    (E) all of the above

76. Pressures exerted by the water over a submerged object such as a submarine
    76. Ⓐ Ⓑ Ⓒ Ⓓ Ⓔ
    (A) are equal to the area divided by the force
    (B) are dependent upon direction
    (C) are not affected by rate of flow
    (D) are lower nearest the bottom
    (E) are equal to the weight of a column of water above it

77. In order to accomplish 800 foot-pounds of work, an 80-pound object must be lifted
    77. Ⓐ Ⓑ Ⓒ Ⓓ Ⓔ
    (A) 1/8 foot   (B) 8 feet   (C) 10 feet   (D) 80 feet
    (E) 100 feet

Directions: The group of questions below consists of five lettered choices followed by a list of numbered phrases or sentences. For each numbered phrase or sentence select the one choice that is most closely related to it. Each choice may be used once, more than once, or not at all.

Questions 78–80

    (A) Alpha particle
    (B) Beta particle
    (C) Meson
    (D) Neutron
    (E) Proton

78. A fundamental atomic particle that is electrically neutral
    78. Ⓐ Ⓑ Ⓒ Ⓓ Ⓔ

79. The nucleus of a helium atom
    79. Ⓐ Ⓑ Ⓒ Ⓓ Ⓔ

80. A particle in the nucleus of an atom having about the same mass as the proton
    80. Ⓐ Ⓑ Ⓒ Ⓓ Ⓔ

ANSWERS AND EXPLANATIONS

1. **D.** When an atom undergoes fission, it splits into two smaller atoms which are called fission fragments and these are usually radioactive.

2. **C.** Chromatic aberration is the failure of different colors (wavelengths) of light to meet at the focal point after passing through a convex lens. This can be corrected by combining two or more lenses to ensure that the various colors of light meet at the focal point. The use of monochromatic light (light of one or a few nearly similar wavelengths) also eliminates the condition.

3. **C.** In music, sharps are notes that are raised one-half step in pitch.

4. **E.** Pressure is exerted equally in all directions at a given level.

5. **E.** In a fuel cell, gaseous hydrocarbons are the oxidizable material and air supplies oxygen.

6. **A.** A "short" is an electrical circuit with a very low resistance.

7. **B.** Electronics is that branch of physics that studies the emission behavior and effects of electrons in vacuums and in gases.

8. **D.** When white light passes through a prism it is broken up into an array of colors called a spectrum. The shortest rays of light bend the most and are the violet end of the spectrum. The longest rays bend the least and are the red end of the spectrum. All other colors fall in between, i.e., orange, yellow, green and blue.

9. **B.** The speed of sound in air at sea level at 0°C is about 741 miles per hour. This rate of speed is rated as Mach 1.

10. **C.** When the source of a light wave or a sound wave is moving relative to the observer, a change in the frequency of light or sound occurs and this change or shift is called the Doppler effect.

11. **B.** All molecules tend to be in constant motion. The more rapidly molecules move, the more frequent will be their collisions and, therefore, the higher will be the temperature.

12. **A.** When an alternating current is carried in a wire, a changing magnetic field is produced which, in turn, generates a varying electric field.

13. **E.** The ohm is the unit of electrical resistance in a given circuit.

14. **B.** Work is performed when an effort or a force causes a body to move.

15. **A.** A lever is in balance when the effort and load are in balance, i.e., effort × length of force arm = load × length of weight arm. If other factors remain constant, increasing the length of the force arm gives a gain in force.

16. **C.** Convection currents transfer heat energy in air by a circulatory motion due to variation in density and the forces of gravity.

17. **D.** A kilometer is 1000 meters or 0.62 miles.

18. **E.** Inertia is that property of every object that causes it to remain at rest, or, if in motion, to remain at a constant velocity unless made to change by external forces.

19. **E.** Whenever something is lifted, pulled, or pushed, it pushes down or resists in return.

20. **D.** The pressure of a moving fluid (including gases) changes with and is inversely proportional to its speed of motion.

21. **C.** According to Bernoulli's principle, when a fluid flows through a constriction, it speeds up and its pressure, therefore, decreases.

22. **C.** An airplane wing is so shaped that air molecules moving over the top surface have farther to travel and, in so doing, they must speed up. This creates a lower air pressure on the top of the wing and the result is lift.

23. **A.** } All matter consists of atoms. The density of a substance depends on the
24. **E.** } masses of its atoms and the closeness by which its atoms are packed. A given object, when placed in water, displaces a volume of water equal to its weight.

25. **D.** According to Archimedes' principle, a floating object displaces an amount of water equal to its own weight.

26. **C.** Kinetic energy is the energy possessed by a moving object.

27. **B.** All molecules, except when at absolute zero temperature, tend to remain

in constant motion and to spread out throughout all space available to them. This is diffusion.

28.   C.   The magnetic field around any long straight wire is circular when an electric current passes through the wire. If an electric current is passed through a coil of wire, the strength of the magnetic field is equal to the number of coils of wire and the amount of current in the coil.

29.   D.   Radium emits charged helium atoms which are called alpha particles and these are very heavy. This results in a loss of mass. Radium ($_{88}$Ra) has an atomic number of 88, the 88 representing 88 protons or alpha particles. Since helium is $_2$He and comes from the radium atom, the loss of two from the radium to the helium means that the atom is now $_{86}$R, which is another element—radon.

30.   B.   When a ray of light strikes an object at a specific angle and is reflected, it bounces off the reflecting surface at the same angle at which it approached.

31.   D.   Small-diametered musical strings produce a high pitch if stretched tightly and large diametered strings produce a low pitch if strung loosely.

32.   A.   Effort multiplied by the length of the effort arm equals the load multiplied by the length of the load arm.

33.   E.   Mechanical advantage is calculated either by dividing the load by the effort or by dividing the length of the effort arm by the length of the load arm.

34.   A.   Electric power transmission is normally transmitted efficiently at higher voltages. Alternating current is easier to transmit and its voltage is readily transformed.

35.   E.   The outermost electrons of certain metals are not held strongly by the nucleus. Light of certain frequencies can dislodge surface electrons and this movement of electrons constitutes an electric current which is called the photoelectric effect.

36.   B.   Opaque substances do not permit light penetration.

37.   C.   Parallel rays of light passing through a concave lens bend outward or spread apart and this is called diffraction.

38.   D.   Reverberations are sound echoes which distort vocal and musical sounds.

39.   D.   Potential energy is the energy possessed by a body because of its position. A bullet fired into the air has potential energy because it will fall back to earth due to gravity.

40.   E.   Work is determined by multiplying the force of an object by the distance it is moved.

41.   B.   The atoms in the wool lose electrons, becoming positively charged; the atoms in the rubber ball gain electrons, becoming negatively charged.

42.   B.   Transformers are used to increase or decrease the voltage of alternating current.

43.   E.   At a constant temperature, the volume of a gas is inversely proportional to the pressure.

44.   C.   Roger Bacon opposed the scholastic method of education and advocated the values derived from observation and experimentation.

45.   D.   One meter equals one million microns.

46.   C.   Centripetal force is the inward force that holds an object, such as a satellite, in circular motion in its orbit.

47.   A.   Inertia is the tendency of a body in motion to remain in motion or the tendency of a body at rest to remain at rest.

48.   D.   The light atoms of hydrogen isotopes are fused in a thermonuclear reaction.

49.   C.   When two different sound waves reach a single point simultaneously they combine in a process called interference.

50.   E.   The double chemical bond occurs when two electron pairs are shared by bonded atoms.

51.   B.   Any body anywhere in space is subject to drag caused by the air molecules and other particles found throughout space.

52.   D.   Speed and time as measured by an observer on a rocket traveling at a speed near the speed of light are different from the speed and time measured by an observer on earth. To the space traveler, light from earth is catching up to the spaceship at one speed; to the observer on earth, light is catching up

to the spaceship at a different speed. Both observers are correct.

53. E. Work is defined as weight times distance moved. One foot pound equals a one pound weight being moved one foot.

54. B. In a sense, the same number of molecules occupy less space when a gas is compressed.

55. A. Diffusion is the tendency of molecules to spread out throughout all space available to them.

56. E. Velocity is linear motion in a specific direction.

57. C. Mechanical advantage, in a pulley system, is determined by the number of ropes that support the weight.

58. E. A rectifier is a device used to convert alternating current to direct current.

59. C. That property of any object that keeps it at rest or at a constant velocity unless it is forced to change by external forces is called inertia.

60. B. In alternating current, the direction of current flow is reversed at regular intervals.

61. C. In a nuclear reaction, the minimum mass required to support a self-sustaining chain reaction is called the critical mass.

62. B. Echoes are reflected sound waves.

63. C. The older unit of heat is the calorie, the newer is the joule. One calorie equals 4.184 joules (4.184J).

64. E. The momentum of any moving body is the product of its mass times its velocity.

65. D. ⎤ When two bodies collide, total momentum after the collision equals total
66. E. ⎦ momentum before the collision. Speed and direction may change because the original momentum is redistributed during the collision.

67. D. The acceleration of a body is directly proportional to the force acting on it and inversely proportional to it mass.

68. A. Magnetic fields exist in vacuums and can also penetrate most kinds of matter.

69. D. A footcandle is a unit of luminescence on a surface of one square foot that is everywhere equidistant from a unit of light identified as one candle.

70. E. Incandescence is the emission of radiation by a hot body which makes the body visible.

71. D. When a ray of light moves from one medium to another, such as air through glass, the ray bends. This is refraction. The different wavelengths of white light are, therefore, separated into the visible spectrum since each has its own refractive index.

72. D. When light is reflected from a surface, the angle of reflection equals the angle of incidence.

73. B. A lumen is the amount of light emitted by a point source of one candle.

74. E. Amplitude is measured from a zero point and is one half the vertical distance between the crest of a wave and its trough.

75. E. Interference is the combining of two different waves which meet at a point in space. If they meet crest to crest, trough to trough, they are in phase. If they combine out of phase, they cancel out. If waves of different frequencies combine, they reinforce each other part of the time and cancel each other part of the time.

76. E. Pressures in fluids increase with depth and are higher as depth increases due to the effects of gravity and the weight of the column of water above an object at any given depth.

77. C. Work is the force exerted on an object multiplied by the distance the object is moved.

78. D. Neutrons are fundamental atomic particles that are electrically neutral.

79. A. The nucleus of a helium atom is an alpha particle.

80. D. Neutrons have the same mass as protons.

Questions about Chemistry

Directions: Each of the questions or incomplete statements below is followed by five suggested answers or completions. Select the one that is best in each case.

1. When referring to the half-life of a radioactive element, we mean
   (A) an interval of time during which half of its atoms will undergo radioactive decay
   (B) half of the interval of time during which half of its atoms will undergo radioactive decay
   (C) an interval of time in which a specific atom of the element decays one half
   (D) an interval of time during which a random atom of the element decays one half
   (E) an interval of time during which all atoms of the element undergo one half radioactive decay

1. A B C D E

2. In a process called electrolysis,
   (A) there is an interaction between electric currents and magnets
   (B) the motions of electrons in magnetic fields are studied
   (C) chemical compounds are synthesized
   (D) chemical compounds are decomposed by means of electric current
   (E) ionizing radiation may be measured

2. A B C D E

3. That the volume of a gas is inversely proportional to the pressure is known as
   (A) Kepler's law   (B) Boyle's law
   (C) the first law of thermodynamics   (D) Charles' law
   (E) Aristotle's theory

3. A B C D E

4. Elements included in the alkali metal family are unique in that they
   (A) are all heavy metals
   (B) have varying combining qualities
   (C) are difficult to obtain and keep in pure form
   (D) all combine in the same ratio with other elements
   (E) have two valence electrons

4. A B C D E

Nucleus ----------- O   O ---------- Electron

NOTE: The illustration above pertains to the next two questions.

5. The two joined hydrogen atoms shown above illustrate
   (A) surface tension
   (B) ionization
   (C) mass number
   (D) hydrogen bonding
   (E) covalent bonding

5. A B C D E

6. In the hydrogen molecule, H_2, illustrated above
   (A) each atom shares its electron with the other atom
   (B) two hydrogen isotopes are attracted to each other
   (C) positively charged electrons neutralize each other
   (D) the atomic number of each of its hydrogen atoms is four
   (E) hydrogen molecules are held together by surface tension

6. Ⓐ Ⓑ Ⓒ Ⓓ Ⓔ

7. The amino acids in proteins are connected by substances called
   (A) carboxyl groups   (B) peptide linkages   (C) polymers
   (D) alkyl groups   (E) esters

7. Ⓐ Ⓑ Ⓒ Ⓓ Ⓔ

8. When mercuric oxide is heated, it forms metallic mercury and gaseous oxygen, a type of reaction called
   (A) synthesis   (B) distillation   (C) neutralization
   (D) rearrangement   (E) decomposition

8. Ⓐ Ⓑ Ⓒ Ⓓ Ⓔ

9. The chemical property called acidity is always identified with
   (A) turning phenolphthalein pink   (B) turning litmus blue
   (C) hydroxide ions   (D) bitter or soapy taste
   (E) the hydrogen atom

9. Ⓐ Ⓑ Ⓒ Ⓓ Ⓔ

10. Different forms of a chemical element are called
   (A) anions   (B) allotrophs   (C) ketones   (D) buffers
   (E) cations

10. Ⓐ Ⓑ Ⓒ Ⓓ Ⓔ

11. Which of the following would give you the least concern?
   (A) Carcinogens in soft drinks
   (B) Strontium 90 in dairy products
   (C) DDT in fresh vegetables
   (D) Riboflavin and niacin in bread
   (E) Herbicidal residues in vegetables

11. Ⓐ Ⓑ Ⓒ Ⓓ Ⓔ

12. Atoms having the same atomic number but having different masses
   (A) have the same number of protons and neutrons
   (B) have the same number of electrons and neutrons
   (C) are called isotopes
   (D) are artificially made by man and do not occur naturally
   (E) cannot be made artificially and occur naturally only

12. Ⓐ Ⓑ Ⓒ Ⓓ Ⓔ

13. A solution can be exemplified by
   (A) a scattering of fine particles in water
   (B) a dispersion of sugar molecules in water
   (C) a dispersion of particles which are larger than molecules but too small to be microscopic
   (D) a dispersion in which the suspended particles eventually settle out
   (E) the immiscibility of the dispersed substances

13. Ⓐ Ⓑ Ⓒ Ⓓ Ⓔ

14. The alkali metal family of chemical elements includes sodium and
   (A) aluminum   (B) lithium   (C) calcium
   (D) phosphorus   (E) potassium

14. Ⓐ Ⓑ Ⓒ Ⓓ Ⓔ

15. The energy liberated or consumed in exothermic and endothermic chemical processes is primarily that of
(A) vaporization   (B) compression   (C) chemical bonds
(D) catalysts   (D) enzymes

15. Ⓐ Ⓑ Ⓒ Ⓓ Ⓔ

16. In general, the rate of chemical reactions is directly proportional to
(A) the temperature and concentration of the reacting substances
(B) the exothermic quotient
(C) the endothermic quotient
(D) the availability of ions
(E) the availability of cations

16. Ⓐ Ⓑ Ⓒ Ⓓ Ⓔ

17. A substance consisting of two or more ingredients which are not in chemical combination is called
(A) an ion   (B) a mixture   (C) a molecule   (D) an oxide
(E) a compound

17. Ⓐ Ⓑ Ⓒ Ⓓ Ⓔ

18. The atoms of non-metals tend to gain electrons, resulting in the creacion of negatively charged atoms called
(A) cations   (B) acid-base pairs   (C) base pairs
(D) anions   (E) ions

18. Ⓐ Ⓑ Ⓒ Ⓓ Ⓔ

19. The chemical properties of elements are determined primarily by
(A) electrons   (B) ions   (C) neutrons   (D) mesons
(E) protons

19. Ⓐ Ⓑ Ⓒ Ⓓ Ⓔ

20. Mass number represents
(A) atomic weight expressed in grams
(B) the number of atoms in one gram atomic weight
(C) atomic mass
(D) the sum of the protons and neutrons
(E) atomic weight

20. Ⓐ Ⓑ Ⓒ Ⓓ Ⓔ

21. According to the Celsius scale,
(A) water boils at 212 degrees   (B) water boils at 100 degrees
(C) water freezes at 32 degrees   (D) ice melts at 32 degrees
(E) water boils at 98.6 degrees

21. Ⓐ Ⓑ Ⓒ Ⓓ Ⓔ

NOTE: The following statement refers to the next two questions.

According to Boyles' Law, the pressure and volume of a confined gas are inversely proportional. As a consequence, the product of the pressure and volume of a gas is constant at a given temperature, i.e., PV = constant.

22. If the pressure of a volume of a gas is halved
(A) its volume is halved
(B) its volume is doubled
(C) its volume remains constant
(D) its volume decreases according to a geometric progression
(E) its volume increases according to a geometric progression

22. Ⓐ Ⓑ Ⓒ Ⓓ Ⓔ

23. Which of the following illustrates the pressure-volume relationship for a gas?
(P = pressure and V = volume)

23. Ⓐ Ⓑ Ⓒ Ⓓ Ⓔ

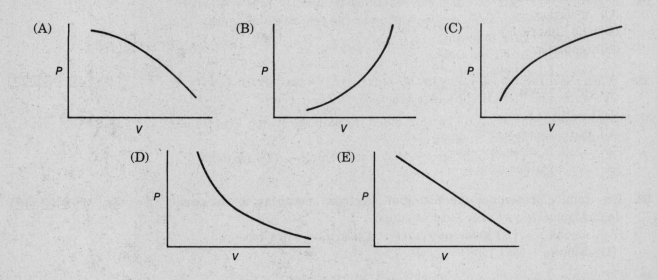

24. The family of chemical elements commonly referred to as the noble gases is characterized chiefly by the fact that its members

24. Ⓐ Ⓑ Ⓒ Ⓓ Ⓔ

(A) form salts when they combine with metals
(B) react violently with water
(C) are not very active chemically
(D) are light, active metals
(E) are heavy, active metals

25. Substances with identical chemical formulas but with various physical and chemical properties are called

25. Ⓐ Ⓑ Ⓒ Ⓓ Ⓔ

(A) ethers   (B) ions   (C) polymers   (D) esters
(E) isomers

26. The chemical element which is found in all proteins is

26. Ⓐ Ⓑ Ⓒ Ⓓ Ⓔ

(A) sulfur   (B) potassium   (C) phosphorus
(D) manganese   (E) nitrogen

27. The atomic number of an element means

27. Ⓐ Ⓑ Ⓒ Ⓓ Ⓔ

(A) the number of electrons in its nucleus
(B) the number of neutrons in its nucleus
(C) the sum of its electrons and neutrons
(D) the number of protons in its nucleus
(E) the number of protons in its orbits

28. In the chemical reaction

$$2C_6H_{12}O_6 \rightarrow C_{12}H_{22}O_{11} + H_2O$$

a disaccharide sugar is formed. This kind of reaction is called
(A) condensation
(B) the dark reaction
(C) oxidation
(D) the light reaction
(E) reduction

28. Ⓐ Ⓑ Ⓒ Ⓓ Ⓔ

29. When the disaccharide sugar in the equation above undergoes digestion
(A) water and CO_2 are the end products
(B) energy is stored
(C) water is consumed
(D) water is the end product
(E) condensation occurs

29. Ⓐ Ⓑ Ⓒ Ⓓ Ⓔ

30. The family of nonmetallic chemical elements known as the halogens includes
(A) silicon   (B) fluorine   (C) nitrogen   (D) oxygen
(E) lithium

30. Ⓐ Ⓑ Ⓒ Ⓓ Ⓔ

31. The chemistry of plastics could well be called the chemistry of
(A) synergy   (B) the halogen family   (C) detergents
(D) polymers   (E) biodegradability

31. Ⓐ Ⓑ Ⓒ Ⓓ Ⓔ

32. The smallest existing particle of any chemically pure substance is the
(A) electron   (B) proton   (C) nucleus   (D) ion   (E) molecule

32. Ⓐ Ⓑ Ⓒ Ⓓ Ⓔ

33. The changing of one atom into another is called
(A) ionization   (B) radiography   (C) nuclear fusion
(D) transmutation   (E) transduction

33. Ⓐ Ⓑ Ⓒ Ⓓ Ⓔ

34. The chemical bonds which result when two atoms share a pair of electrons are called
(A) double bonds   (B) covalent bonds   (C) hybridizations
(D) ionic-coordinates   (E) double-coordinates

34. Ⓐ Ⓑ Ⓒ Ⓓ Ⓔ

35. Two or more different forms of the same chemical element are called
(A) salts   (B) ions   (C) esters   (D) conformations
(E) allotrophs

35. Ⓐ Ⓑ Ⓒ Ⓓ Ⓔ

36. An element's atomic weight is
(A) the total weight of its electrons
(B) dependent upon uniform temperatures
(C) its weight relative to that of the hydrogen atom
(D) determined by the number of protons in its nucleus
(E) expressed in grams

36. Ⓐ Ⓑ Ⓒ Ⓓ Ⓔ

ANSWERS AND EXPLANATIONS

1. A. Half-life is the time in which half of the atoms of a radioactive material will decay.

2. D. In electrolysis, an electric current is passed through a liquid causing a chemical reaction. In industry, sodium may be produced (purified) by the electrolysis of liquid sodium chloride.

3. B. According to Boyles' Law, the volume of a gas is inversely proportional to the pressure.

4. C. Alkali metals are very reactive, readily giving up one electron to form ions.

5. E. } A covalent bond occurs when two atoms share electrons.
6. A. }

7. B. Proteins are composed of amino acids which are united or held together by the C—N—C linkage, commonly called the peptide linkage.

8. E. Heat causes mercuric oxide bonds to break down, thereby, permitting the component elements to separate without entering into other compounds— literally, a decomposing of the molecule due to heat.

9. E. Acids are substances whose water solutions contain an excess of hydrogen ions.

10. B. Chemical elements often exist in different forms and these are called allotrophs.

11. D. Riboflavin and niacin are vitamins; all of the other substances listed are hazardous to health.

12. C. Atoms of any element that differ in the number of neutrons in their nucleus are different in mass and are called isotopes.

13. B. Homogenous mixtures have the same composition at the microscopic level throughout. When the dispersed particles are on a molecular scale the mixture is referred to as a solution.

14. E. Sodium and potassium are among the members of the alkali metals family.

15. C. Energy transformations in chemical reactions are concerned with the energy of chemical bonds. Energy loss may be due to the formation of chemical bonds, or energy may be added to break the chemical bonds.

16. A. The rates of chemical reactions are controlled by only a few factors, the most common being the concentrations of the reactants, the temperature, the nature of the reactants, and catalysts.

17. B. A mixture is any portion of matter consisting of two or more substances which can be separated from each other by physical means, i.e., without reacting to form new substances.

18. D. An ion is an atom or a group of atoms functioning as a unit and carrying an electrical charge. Those with positive charges are called cations, those with negative charges anions.

19. A. The chemical properties of elements are an expression of their attraction to or their repulsion from other elements, based primarily on circumstances pertaining to their electrons.

20. D. Mass number is the total number of neutrons and protons in the atom's nucleus.

21. B. The Celsius scale (formerly the Centigrade scale) divides the range of temperatures between the freezing and boiling points of water into 100 units, or degrees, each of which is called 1°C.

22. B. } According to Boyles' Law, the pressure and the volume of a confined gas
23. D. } are inversely proportional.

24. C. Noble gases are extremely stable and undergo reaction only under rigorous conditions. The first noble gas compound was not prepared until 1962, and, prior to this, it was thought that noble gases were chemically inert.

25. E. Isomers are chemical compounds that have the same number of atoms of the same elements, but differ in structural arrangements and properties.

26. E. Nitrogen is found in amino acids and hence, in proteins.

27. D. The atomic number of an element is the number of protons in its nucleus.

28. A. Disaccharides form by the joining of two monosaccharide units in a condensation reaction in which a molecule of water is split out.

29. C. Disaccharides can react with water in the presence of a catalyst to form monosaccharides. This is digestion and a water-consuming reaction.
30. B. Halogens include fluorine, chlorine, bromine, etc.
31. D. Polymers are molecules composed of two or more small and repeated units that are chemically bonded together. They may be linear, branched or three-dimensional. Plastic materials are polymers.
32. E. The molecule cannot be further broken down without destroying it and changing its characteristics.
33. D. The concepts that atoms (elements) may be changed from one to another is called transmutation.
34. B. A chemical bond represented by a pair of electrons in orbits that are part of both atoms is a covalent bond.
35. E. Allotrophs are the different forms of a given element in the same state of matter.
36. C. An atom's weight is a characteristic of a particular element and the atoms of each element have their own specific atomic weight. Hydrogen has arbitrarily been assigned an atomic weight of 1; the atoms of all the other elements are assigned atomic weights relative to the atomic weight of hydrogen.

Questions about History of Science

Directions: Each of the questions or incomplete statements below is followed by five suggested answers or completions. Select the one that is best in each case.

1. The philosopher from Thrace famous for his atomic theory was
   (A) Aristotle   (B) Democritus   (C) Thales
   (D) Theophrastus   (E) Empedocles

   1. A B C D E

2. That living organisms have evolved was first theorized by
   (A) Lamarck
   (B) ancient Greek philosophers
   (C) Darwin and Wallace
   (D) Romans in the first century B.C.
   (E) the geologist, Charles Lyell

   2. A B C D E

3. A famous anatomist during the Renaissance was
   (A) Linnaeus   (B) Michelangelo   (C) Pliny   (D) Bacon
   (E) Galen

   3. A B C D E

4. A Roman naturalist, literary man, and government worker who composed an encyclopedia called "Historia Naturalis" ("Natural History") was
   (A) Lucretius   (B) Galen   (C) Celsus
   (D) Pliny the Elder   (E) Dioscorides

   4. A B C D E

5. A pupil of Thales, one of the earliest Greek scholars to be concerned with the evolution of man, and one who believed in transmutations as a cause of diversity was
   (A) Anaximander   (B) Galen   (C) Heraclitus
   (D) Pliny   (E) Empedocles

   5. A B C D E

6. A stimulus which influenced the thinking of both Darwin and Wallace was
   (A) Lyell's *Principles of Geology*
   (B) Malthus' writing on population

   6. A B C D E

(C) Lucretius' poem "De Rerum Natura"

(D) Lamarck's *Philosophie Zooligique*

(E) the writings of Aristotle

7. The ancient Greek scholar who became the "father of medicine" was   7. Ⓐ Ⓑ Ⓒ Ⓓ Ⓔ
   (A) Aristotle   (B) Theophrastus   (C) Alcmaeon
   (D) Hippocrates   (E) Empedocles

8. The 365-day calendar was first proposed by   8. Ⓐ Ⓑ Ⓒ Ⓓ Ⓔ
   (A) Pythagoras   (B) Archimedes   (C) the Babylonians
   (D) the Egyptians   (E) the Greeks

9. The field of immunization had its beginning with the work of   9. Ⓐ Ⓑ Ⓒ Ⓓ Ⓔ
   (A) Lister   (B) Jenner   (C) Koch   (D) Pasteur   (E) Ehrlich

10. According to Ptolemy,   10. Ⓐ Ⓑ Ⓒ Ⓓ Ⓔ
    (A) the sun is the center of the solar system
    (B) the earth is round, with a circumference of 24,000 miles
    (C) the universe is infinite
    (D) the earth is a flat, floating disc
    (E) the earth is the center of the solar system

11. The concept advocating the particulate or atomic structure of matter   11. Ⓐ Ⓑ Ⓒ Ⓓ Ⓔ
    was first proposed by
    (A) Theophrastus   (B) Democritus   (C) Pliny
    (D) Aristotle   (E) Plato

12. The most significant contribution of Isaac Newton was his   12. Ⓐ Ⓑ Ⓒ Ⓓ Ⓔ
    (A) heliocentric theory   (B) universal law of gravitation
    (C) concept of the atom   (D) photon theory of light energy
    (E) phlogiston theory

13. The earliest of the Greek scholars to hold that the entire universe is   13. Ⓐ Ⓑ Ⓒ Ⓓ Ⓔ
    subject to natural law was
    (A) Aristotle   (B) Thales   (C) Anaximander
    (D) Theophrastus   (E) Empedocles

14. The recording of eclipses was first undertaken by the   14. Ⓐ Ⓑ Ⓒ Ⓓ Ⓔ
    (A) Babylonians   (B) Egyptians   (C) Greeks
    (D) Chinese   (E) Romans

15. Sterile and antiseptic surgical procedures were introduced by   15. Ⓐ Ⓑ Ⓒ Ⓓ Ⓔ
    (A) Fleming   (B) Semmelweis   (C) Banting
    (D) Lister   (E) Gorgas

16. First to propose the concept of the atomic structure of matter was   16. Ⓐ Ⓑ Ⓒ Ⓓ Ⓔ
    (A) Boyle   (B) Kepler   (C) Einstein   (D) Aristotle
    (E) Democritus

17. An early Greek physician whose writings considered medical ethics   17. Ⓐ Ⓑ Ⓒ Ⓓ Ⓔ
    was
    (A) Galen   (B) Hippocrates   (C) Anaximander
    (D) Aristotle   (E) Theophrastus

18. A Greek scholar who was the first to relate fossils to living plants
and animals was

    (A) Anaximander   (B) Theophrastus   (C) Empedocles

    (D) Xenophanes   (E) Aristotle

18. Ⓐ Ⓑ Ⓒ Ⓓ Ⓔ

ANSWERS AND EXPLANATIONS

1. **B.** Democritus was one of the first Greeks to advocate the atomic theory.
2. **B.** The early Greek philosophers Anaximander and Xerrophanes formulated ideas concerning the origins of life and evolution.
3. **B.** Michelangelo made dissections of human internal structures so as to represent the features accurately and in proper relation to each other. His statues give evidence of his knowledge of human anatomy.
4. **D.** Pliny the Elder (23–79 A.D.) compiled a comprehensive encyclopedia called "Natural History".
5. **A.** Anaximander proposed that humans evolved.
6. **B.** Malthus' writing on population presented the theme that humans multiply more rapidly than does food supply, thereby creating conditions for the competition for existence.
7. **D.** The "Hippocratic Oath" honors Hippocrates as the "father of medicine".
8. **D.** The Egyptians first proposed the 365-day calendar.
9. **B.** Jenner was not the first to use vaccinations, but he developed its practicality and usefulness.
10. **E.** Ptolemy developed a model of the universe that accounted for the movements of the planets in circular orbits around a motionless earth.
11. **B.** Democritus' greatest contribution was his atomic theory which held that the universe consists of atoms moving in space with all physical change dependent upon the union and separation of atoms.
12. **B.** Newton was the first person to recognize gravity as a universal force relative to both "the falling apple" and the orbits of the planets.
13. **B.** Thales supported both the concept of rational inquiry into nature and the school of thought that presumed that the entire universe is controlled by natural law.
14. **A.** Earliest written records, found in Babylonia and Mesopotamia, describe eclipses and other astronomical events inscribed in the clay and stone tablets of the time.
15. **D.** Prior to Lister, most surgical procedures were complicated by infection. Lister devised methods of sterilizing the operating room and its equipment by spraying carbolic acid over the hands of the surgeons and the immediate surroundings while the surgery was in progress.
16. **E.** Democritus first proposed the atomic structure of matter.
17. **B.** Hippocrates is called the "father of medicine".
18. **D.** Xenophanes was the first Greek scholar to compare fossils to living organisms.

Sample Examinations

14

This chapter has three sample CLEP natural sciences examinations. Each examination is followed by an answer key, scoring chart, and answer explanations.

SAMPLE EXAMINATION 1

Part I: Biological Sciences

Number of Questions: 60
Time: 45 minutes

Directions: Each of the questions or incomplete statements below is followed by five suggested answers or completions. Select the one that is best in each case.

1. The smallest and least complex unit of living matter is the
    (A) electron   (B) atom   (C) ion   (D) cell   (E) molecule

1. Ⓐ Ⓑ Ⓒ Ⓓ Ⓔ

2. A physiologist is concerned with the
    (A) classification of organisms
    (B) structure of organisms
    (C) functioning of organisms
    (D) interrelationships of organisms
    (E) development of organisms

2. Ⓐ Ⓑ Ⓒ Ⓓ Ⓔ

3. If a living cell is placed in an isotonic fluid, there will be
    (A) a net movement of water molecules into the cell
    (B) an increase in turgidity
    (C) no net movement of water molecules into or out of the cell
    (D) a decrease in cell turgidity
    (E) a net movement of water molecules out of the cell

3. Ⓐ Ⓑ Ⓒ Ⓓ Ⓔ

4. One of the following factors does not influence enzyme activity:
    (A) temperature   (B) pH   (C) humidity
    (D) enzyme   poisons   (E) concentration

4. Ⓐ Ⓑ Ⓒ Ⓓ Ⓔ

5. Heterotrophs
    (A) utilize radiant energy
    (B) cannot synthesize organic materials from inorganic substances
    (C) are food synthesizers
    (D) oxidize inorganic materials
    (E) synthesize organic materials from inorganic substances

5. Ⓐ Ⓑ Ⓒ Ⓓ Ⓔ

6. A relationship between two organisms in which one is benefited while the second is neither benefited nor harmed is called
    (A) neutralism   (B) amensalism   (C) mutualism
    (D) competition   (E) commensalism

6. Ⓐ Ⓑ Ⓒ Ⓓ Ⓔ

7. A niacin deficiency may best be relieved by enriching the diet with
   (A) eggs and dairy products   (B) fresh green vegetables
   (C) whole grain cereals   (D) animal products
   (E) citrus fruits

7. Ⓐ Ⓑ Ⓒ Ⓓ Ⓔ

8. Cellular respiration
   (A) stores energy
   (B) uses oxygen and organic compounds as raw materials
   (C) increases dry weight
   (D) occurs only in the presence of radiant energy
   (E) uses carbon dioxide and water as raw materials

8. Ⓐ Ⓑ Ⓒ Ⓓ Ⓔ

9. A process which increases dry weight is
   (A) phosphorylation
   (B) osmosis
   (C) diffusion
   (D) respiration
   (E) photosynthesis

9. Ⓐ Ⓑ Ⓒ Ⓓ Ⓔ

10. Plants grown in the dark become
    (A) plasmolyzed   (B) asphixiated   (C) synergistic
    (D) etiolated   (E) parthenocarpic

10. Ⓐ Ⓑ Ⓒ Ⓓ Ⓔ

11. In plants, water is normally conducted upward by a tissue called the
    (A) phloem   (B) cortex   (C) cuticle   (D) pith
    (E) xylem

11. Ⓐ Ⓑ Ⓒ Ⓓ Ⓔ

12. The edible part of the sweet potato is
    (A) stem tissue   (B) root tissue   (C) leaf tissue
    (D) fruit   (E) seed

12. Ⓐ Ⓑ Ⓒ Ⓓ Ⓔ

13. Primitive plants having neither vascular tissues nor multicellular embryos
    are called
    (A) bryophytes   (B) thallophytes   (C) pteridophytes
    (D) spermatophytes   (E) xerophytes

13. Ⓐ Ⓑ Ⓒ Ⓓ Ⓔ

14. Plants basic in many food chains are
    (A) fungi
    (B) bryophytes
    (C) gymnosperms
    (D) pteridophytes
    (E) algae

14. Ⓐ Ⓑ Ⓒ Ⓓ Ⓔ

15. The first step in the formation of a blood clot is the disintegration of
    platelets and the release of
    (A) thrombin   (B) fibrinogen   (C) fibrin
    (D) thromboplastin   (E) prothrombin

15. Ⓐ Ⓑ Ⓒ Ⓓ Ⓔ

16. If you have a type A blood, agglutination tests will reveal that
    (A) type A serum will clump part of the time
    (B) type B serum clumps
    (C) both type A and B sera will clump
    (D) type A serum clumps
    (E) neither type A nor B sera will clump

16. Ⓐ Ⓑ Ⓒ Ⓓ Ⓔ

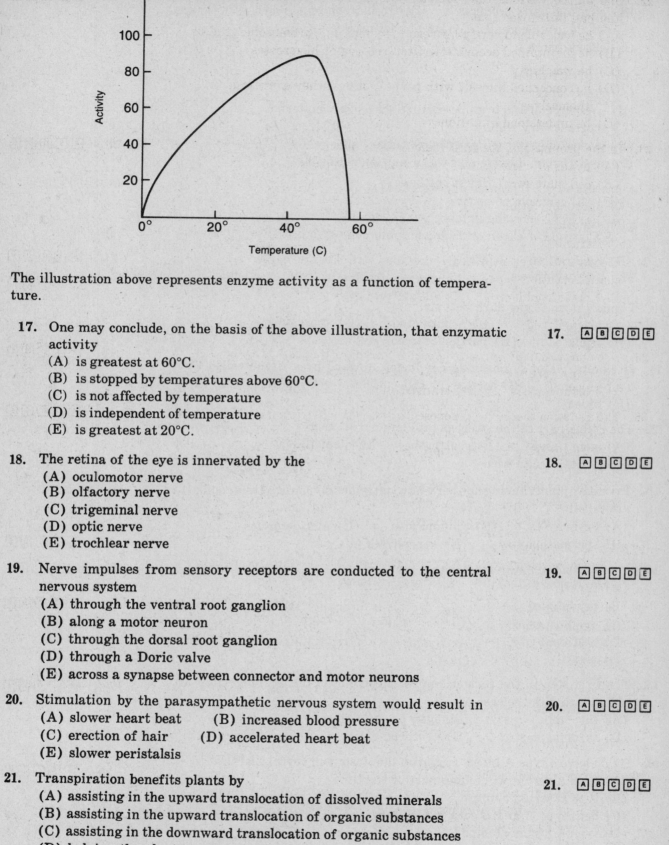

The illustration above represents enzyme activity as a function of temperature.

17. One may conclude, on the basis of the above illustration, that enzymatic activity
    (A) is greatest at 60°C.
    (B) is stopped by temperatures above 60°C.
    (C) is not affected by temperature
    (D) is independent of temperature
    (E) is greatest at 20°C.

17. Ⓐ Ⓑ Ⓒ Ⓓ Ⓔ

18. The retina of the eye is innervated by the
    (A) oculomotor nerve
    (B) olfactory nerve
    (C) trigeminal nerve
    (D) optic nerve
    (E) trochlear nerve

18. Ⓐ Ⓑ Ⓒ Ⓓ Ⓔ

19. Nerve impulses from sensory receptors are conducted to the central nervous system
    (A) through the ventral root ganglion
    (B) along a motor neuron
    (C) through the dorsal root ganglion
    (D) through a Doric valve
    (E) across a synapse between connector and motor neurons

19. Ⓐ Ⓑ Ⓒ Ⓓ Ⓔ

20. Stimulation by the parasympathetic nervous system would result in
    (A) slower heart beat   (B) increased blood pressure
    (C) erection of hair   (D) accelerated heart beat
    (E) slower peristalsis

20. Ⓐ Ⓑ Ⓒ Ⓓ Ⓔ

21. Transpiration benefits plants by
    (A) assisting in the upward translocation of dissolved minerals
    (B) assisting in the upward translocation of organic substances
    (C) assisting in the downward translocation of organic substances
    (D) helping the plant to retain heat
    (E) maintaining a constant root pressure

21. Ⓐ Ⓑ Ⓒ Ⓓ Ⓔ

22. One of the reasons that Mendel was successful when others before
him had failed was that
(A) he was able to verify his results by making chromosome studies
(B) he maintained accurate written records of his crosses
(C) he was lucky
(D) he concerned himself with genes, not how they expressed
themselves
(E) he understood mutations

23. In the prophase of the first meiotic division,
(A) dyads of chromatids appear following synapsis
(B) cell plate formation is initiated
(C) the centriole reappears
(D) the chromosome number is haploid
(E) tetrads of chromatids appear following synapsis

24. Floods and fires repeatedly destroyed all life on earth, but acts of
special creation repopulated the earth: this doctrine was called
(A) catastrophism   (B) adaptation
(C) uniformitarianism   (D) natural selection
(E) Lamarckianism

25. The adaptation of unrelated species to similar habitats is called
(A) polymorphism   (B) divergent evolution
(C) orthogenesis   (D) translocation   (E) convergent evolution

26. The mutation theory was proposed by De Vries to explain abrupt changes
in inheritance patterns which
(A) result from hybridization
(B) breed true
(C) do not breed true in subsequent generations
(D) are environmentally induced
(E) are based on mitotic errors

27. Antiseptic surgery was first performed by
(A) Louis Pasteur   (B) John Tyndall   (C) Lazaro Spallanzani
(D) John Needham   (E) Joseph Lister

28. A Dutch microscope maker who was probably the first to describe
bacteria and protozoa was
(A) Harvey   (B) Leeuwenhoek   (C) Flemming
(D) Galen   (E) Versalius

29. Aristotle's greatest contribution to science has been the
(A) theory of the four humors   (B) scientific method
(C) theory of evolution   (D) study of anatomy and medicine
(E) atomic theory

30. The first to isolate the hormone insulin were
(A) Ascheim and Zondek   (B) Banting and Best
(C) Bromer and du Vigneaud   (D) Absolam and Grendel
(E) Bayliss and Starling

31. Marine organisms found between the limits of high and low tide exist in the
    - (A) neritic zone
    - (B) abyssal zone
    - (C) zone of perpetual darkness
    - (D) bathyal zone
    - (E) littoral zone

31. A B C D E

32. An ichthyologist is a specialist in the study of
    - (A) insects
    - (B) birds
    - (C) reptiles
    - (D) fossils
    - (E) fishes

32. A B C D E

33. When corresponding structures of different species are based on similarities in function only, they are said to be
    - (A) homologous
    - (B) divergent
    - (C) parallel
    - (D) convergent
    - (E) analogous

33. A B C D E

34. An interrelationship between living organisms is called
    - (A) speciation
    - (B) metamorphosis
    - (C) symbiosis
    - (D) epigenesis
    - (E) morphogenesis

34. A B C D E

35. The time period described as the age of reptiles is the
    - (A) Ordovician period
    - (B) Proterozoic era
    - (C) Mesozoic era
    - (D) Cenozoic era
    - (E) Miocene epoch

35. A B C D E

36. In the digestive system of humans, the stomach-produced enzyme rennin splits the
    - (A) ester bond of fats
    - (B) phosphate esters of DNA
    - (C) peptide bonds of trypsinogen
    - (D) phosphate esters of RNA
    - (E) peptide bonds in casein

36. A B C D E

37. Rodent control is necessary to prevent outbreaks of the following bacterial disease:
    - (A) psitticosis
    - (B) amebiasis
    - (C) plague
    - (D) typhoid fever
    - (E) polio

37. A B C D E

38. If a couple has a child which is a boy, the probability that the second child will be a girl is
    - (A) 1/16
    - (B) 1/8
    - (C) 1/4
    - (D) 1/2
    - (E) 3/4

38. A B C D E

39. In matings involving individuals which are heterozygous for "A", the genotypes produced would be
    - (A) 1/8 AA, 3/4 Aa, 1/8 aa
    - (B) 3/8 AA, 1/4 Aa, 3/8 aa
    - (C) 1/3 AA, 1/3 Aa, 1/3 aa
    - (D) 1/4 AA, 1/2 Aa, 1/4 aa
    - (E) impossible to predict

39. A B C D E

40. The frequency of crossing over between two linked genes is
   (A) controlled by sex chromosomes
   (B) controlled by the law of independent assortment
   (C) controlled by the Hardy-Weinberg law
   (D) inversely proportional to the distance separating them
   (E) directly proportional to the distance separating them

41. An antigen stimulates the production of
   (A) blood groups
   (B) platelets
   (C) toxins
   (D) an antibody
   (E) Rh

42. The roots of biology go back to 3000 B.C. in China where the first principles identified
   (A) were the medicinal values of plants
   (B) related to the theory of the four humors
   (C) reflected early concepts about evolution
   (D) were about atomic theory
   (E) were taxonomy and classification

Questions 43-46 refer to the following diagram.

Fresh water   Salt water

The plant cells diagrammed above are located in fresh water and in salt water, as indicated.

43. Water has moved out of the cell in salt water by a process called
   (A) diffusion (B) imbibition (C) capillarity
   (D) adhesion (E) plasmolysis

44. The cell in fresh water is "plump" with water, a condition referred to as
   (A) rigid (B) plasmolyzed (C) saturated
   (D) hydrolyzed (E) turgid

45. The condition of the cell in the salt water is a result of   45.   Ⓐ Ⓑ Ⓒ Ⓓ Ⓔ
- (A) the flow of water out of the cell
- (B) a net movement of water out of the cell
- (C) salt pulling the water out of the cell
- (D) the forces of imbibition
- (E) the force called cohesion

46. In the case of the cell in fresh water   46.   Ⓐ Ⓑ Ⓒ Ⓓ Ⓔ
- (A) nothing is able to move into the cell
- (B) adhesive forces hold water in the vacuoles
- (C) the vacuoles continue to lose and to take in water by diffusion
- (D) the cell walls are impermeable to water
- (E) the cell walls are impermeable to salt

47. The light-sensitive pigment called phytochrome appears to influence   47.   Ⓐ Ⓑ Ⓒ Ⓓ Ⓔ
- (A) phototropism   (B) parthenocarpy   (C) photosynthesis
- (D) synergistic responses   (E) photoperiodism

48. Stems increase in diameter mainly because of cell division by the   48.   Ⓐ Ⓑ Ⓒ Ⓓ Ⓔ
- (A) cork cambium   (B) endodermis   (C) medullary rays
- (D) cortex   (E) vascular cambium

49. The evaporation of water from the aerial surfaces of plants is called   49.   Ⓐ Ⓑ Ⓒ Ⓓ Ⓔ
- (A) translocation   (B) hydrotropism   (C) hydroponics
- (D) aquaculture   (E) transpiration

50. Adrenalin   50.   Ⓐ Ⓑ Ⓒ Ⓓ Ⓔ
- (A) regulates potassium metabolism
- (B) constricts blood vessels
- (C) controls bone growth
- (D) regulates thyroxine production
- (E) regulates the pulse rate and muscle tone

51. The primary significance of mitosis is the fact that   51.   Ⓐ Ⓑ Ⓒ Ⓓ Ⓔ
- (A) it is quantitative   (B) the chromosome number is increased
- (C) it results in the production of either eggs or sperm
- (D) the chromosome number is reduced   (E) it is qualitative

52. The area in the retina of the human eye lacking both rods and cones is called the   52.   Ⓐ Ⓑ Ⓒ Ⓓ Ⓔ
- (A) alveolus   (B) fundibulum   (C) fovea
- (D) blind spot   (E) cornea

53. During the initial stages of blood clot formation, blood platelets require   53.   Ⓐ Ⓑ Ⓒ Ⓓ Ⓔ
- (A) calcium ions   (B) the antihemophilic factor
- (C) thrombin   (D) prothrombin   (E) cytochrome

54. Simple sugars are stored in the liver as   54.   Ⓐ Ⓑ Ⓒ Ⓓ Ⓔ
- (A) glycerol   (B) maltose   (C) nucleotides   (D) glycogen
- (E) casein

Directions: Each group of questions below consists of five lettered choices followed by a list of numbered phrases or sentences. For each numbered phrase or sentence select the one choice that is most closely related to it. Each choice may be used once, more than once, or not at all in each group.

Questions 55–57

    (A) Cuvier
    (B) Darwin
    (C) Lamarck
    (D) Lyell
    (E) Tyson

55. Proposed the doctrine of Catastrophism   55. Ⓐ Ⓑ Ⓒ Ⓓ Ⓔ

56. Suggested that the events in the geologic history of the earth were the product of the same natural forces that are active today   56. Ⓐ Ⓑ Ⓒ Ⓓ Ⓔ

57. Proposed the doctrine of Uniformitarianism   57. Ⓐ Ⓑ Ⓒ Ⓓ Ⓔ

Questions 58–60

    (A) Cambrian period
    (B) Devonian period
    (C) Jurassic period
    (D) Carboniferous period
    (E) Tertiary period

58. A period of psilopsids, lycopsids and seed ferns   58. Ⓐ Ⓑ Ⓒ Ⓓ Ⓔ

59. The period of modern mammals and herbacious angiosperms   59. Ⓐ Ⓑ Ⓒ Ⓓ Ⓔ

60. The age of the great coal swamps   60. Ⓐ Ⓑ Ⓒ Ⓓ Ⓔ

Part II: Physical Sciences

Number of Questions: 60
Time: 45 minutes

Directions: Each of the questions or incomplete statements below is followed by five suggested answers or completions. Select the one that is best in each case.

1. Insofar as the earth's atmosphere is concerned, without supplemental oxygen man is restricted to the   1. Ⓐ Ⓑ Ⓒ Ⓓ Ⓔ
    (A) ionosphere   (B) exosphere   (C) troposphere
    (D) stratopause   (E) stratosphere

2. The same side of the moon is **always** observed from the earth because the

    (A) moon does not rotate

    (B) moon's orbit is an ellipse

    (C) moon's orbit is inclined

    (D) moon's period of rotation equals its period of revolution

    (E) moon's period of rotation is greater than its period of revolution

2. Ⓐ Ⓑ Ⓒ Ⓓ Ⓔ

3. When a space vehicle is at perigee, it is at

    (A) maximum speed

    (B) minimum speed

    (C) the point farthest from the sun

    (D) a point in orbit farthest from the earth

    (E) a point in orbit closest to the earth

3. Ⓐ Ⓑ Ⓒ Ⓓ Ⓔ

4. There are always two calendar days in effect except

    (A) during the summer solstice

    (B) the instant it is noon at Greenwich, England

    (C) the instant it is noon at longitude 180°

    (D) on February 29th

    (E) the instant of crossing the international dateline

4. Ⓐ Ⓑ Ⓒ Ⓓ Ⓔ

5. The accumulated sediment deposited outward from the mouth of a stream forms

    (A) a sand bar   (B) a flood plain   (C) a delta

    (D) an alluvial fan   (E) an oxbow

5. Ⓐ Ⓑ Ⓒ Ⓓ Ⓔ

6. The theory that land masses wander over the surface of the globe is called

    (A) catastrophism   (B) plate tectonics   (C) sedimentation

    (D) fossilization   (E) discontinuity

6. Ⓐ Ⓑ Ⓒ Ⓓ Ⓔ

7. Anhydrous chemicals are completely

    (A) combustible

    (B) without water

    (C) hydrated

    (D) inactive

    (E) pure

7. Ⓐ Ⓑ Ⓒ Ⓓ Ⓔ

8. Stalactites are

    (A) crystalline calcite columns hanging from cave ceilings

    (B) anthracite deposits in caves

    (C) calcite columns built up from cave floors

    (D) graphite columns hanging from cave ceilings

    (E) graphite columns built up from cave floors

8. Ⓐ Ⓑ Ⓒ Ⓓ Ⓔ

9. How much effort is required to lift the 18 pound weight illustrated in the diagram above, when the weight arm is 2 feet long and the effort arm is 9 feet long?

    (A) $\frac{1}{2}$ pound
    (B) 1 pound
    (C) 2 pounds
    (D) 3 pounds
    (E) 4 pounds

9. Ⓐ Ⓑ Ⓒ Ⓓ Ⓔ

10. The advantage of the lever (above) would be increased by
    (A) lengthening the weight arm
    (B) lengthening the effort arm
    (C) increasing the weight
    (D) shortening the effort arm
    (E) increasing the length of both arms

10. Ⓐ Ⓑ Ⓒ Ⓓ Ⓔ

11. Electron microscopes have a greater resolving power than light microscopes because
    (A) there is a laser effect
    (B) electrons travel faster than photons
    (C) their magnifications are greater
    (D) electrons possess less resolving power
    (E) electrons possess greater resolving power

11. Ⓐ Ⓑ Ⓒ Ⓓ Ⓔ

12. When light is thrown back from any surface, it is said to be
    (A) refracted   (B) diffused   (C) absorbed
    (D) reflected   (E) diffracted

12. Ⓐ Ⓑ Ⓒ Ⓓ Ⓔ

13. Interference is a wave phenomenon created when
    (A) there is interaction between two waves which arrive simultaneously at a given point
    (B) waves bend around corners
    (C) wavelength and frequency are equal
    (D) wavelength is greater than frequency
    (E) frequency is greater than wavelength

13. Ⓐ Ⓑ Ⓒ Ⓓ Ⓔ

14. The frequency of sound vibrations is called
    (A) resonance   (B) key   (C) tone   (D) pitch
    (E) overtone

14. Ⓐ Ⓑ Ⓒ Ⓓ Ⓔ

15. Which of the following is an acid?
    (A) NaCl   (B) NH_3 (C) $NaNO_3$
    (D) H_3PO_4 (E) NaOH

15. Ⓐ Ⓑ Ⓒ Ⓓ Ⓔ

16. One of the following is not an acceptable statement in respect to magnetic fields:
    (A) lines of force are unchanging
    (B) they do not require the presence of matter
    (C) they can penetrate wood
    (D) they may exist in a vacuum
    (E) they can penetrate glass

16. Ⓐ Ⓑ Ⓒ Ⓓ Ⓔ

17. The unit of measurement of electric current is the
    (A) ohm   (B) volt   (C) ampere   (D) coulomb
    (E) watt

17. Ⓐ Ⓑ Ⓒ Ⓓ Ⓔ

18. A device which produces electricity as a result of rotating a coil between the poles of a magnet is
    (A) an electric motor   (B) a commutator   (C) a transformer
    (D) an induction coil   (E) a generator

18. Ⓐ Ⓑ Ⓒ Ⓓ Ⓔ

19. The part of the atom involved in all instances of radioactive change is the
    (A) orbit   (B) electron   (C) electrical charge
    (D) half-life   (E) nucleus

19. Ⓐ Ⓑ Ⓒ Ⓓ Ⓔ

20. The unusable heat energy "lost" to the environment in converting heat to work is known as
    (A) latent heat of fusion   (B) specific heat
    (C) latent heat of vaporization   (D) temperature
    (E) entropy

20. Ⓐ Ⓑ Ⓒ Ⓓ Ⓔ

21. Which of the following is a metric unit of length?
    (A) milligram   (B) kilometer   (C) kilogram   (D) liter
    (E) gram

21. Ⓐ Ⓑ Ⓒ Ⓓ Ⓔ

22. Adoption of which one of the following as standard made the original platinum-iridium standard meter rod useless?
    (A) Use of the cesium atom
    (B) Substitution of the nickel meter rod
    (C) Use of the xenon atom
    (D) Orange light emitted by krypton-86
    (E) Use of the infrared spectrum

22. Ⓐ Ⓑ Ⓒ Ⓓ Ⓔ

23. In order to apply a force to one object, one must be able to
    (A) push against another object
    (B) use centrifugal force
    (C) use centripetal force
    (D) overcome gravity
    (E) maintain a constant velocity

23. Ⓐ Ⓑ Ⓒ Ⓓ Ⓔ

24. Energy is defined as the
    (A) rate of doing work   (B) rate of supply of energy
    (C) capacity to accelerate   (D) capacity to resist acceleration
    (E) capacity to do work

24. Ⓐ Ⓑ Ⓒ Ⓓ Ⓔ

25. A fundamental particle of negative electricity is   25. Ⓐ Ⓑ Ⓒ Ⓓ Ⓔ
    (A) a proton   (B) an electron   (C) a neutron
    (D) a meson   (E) an ion

26. In reference to light or sound waves, the Doppler effect occurs when   26. Ⓐ Ⓑ Ⓒ Ⓓ Ⓔ
    (A) the source and receiver are in motion relative to one another
    (B) waves are of unequal length
    (C) waves are parallel
    (D) the source and the receiver are stationary
    (E) temperature increases

27. A self-sustaining reaction in which the first atoms to react trigger   27. Ⓐ Ⓑ Ⓒ Ⓓ Ⓔ
    more reactions is called
    (A) a photochemical reaction   (B) a chain reaction
    (C) an accelerator reaction   (D) an electrical reaction
    (E) a biophysical reaction

28. According to Einstein's theory of relativity, as a spaceship approaches   28. Ⓐ Ⓑ Ⓒ Ⓓ Ⓔ
    the speed of light
    (A) everything aboard increases in mass
    (B) everything aboard decreases in mass
    (C) mass remains constant
    (D) mass and metabolism decrease
    (E) mass and metabolism increase

29. The true weight of an object is defined as the   29. Ⓐ Ⓑ Ⓒ Ⓓ Ⓔ
    (A) gravitational attraction of the sun on that object
    (B) gravitational attraction of the earth on that object
    (C) force of repulsion by the earth on that object
    (D) combined gravitational attraction of the sun and moon on that
        object
    (E) total mass of that object

30. For every force there is a force of reaction which is   30. Ⓐ Ⓑ Ⓒ Ⓓ Ⓔ
    (A) equal and parallel   (B) unequal and transverse
    (C) equal and transverse   (D) equal and oppositive
    (E) unequal and opposite

31. Electricity produced by a nuclear power plant   31. Ⓐ Ⓑ Ⓒ Ⓓ Ⓔ
    (A) has higher voltage   (B) has lower voltage
    (C) is radioactive   (D) is the same as any other electricity
    (E) is D.C. only

32. One degree on the Celsius scale equals how many Fahrenheit degrees?   32. Ⓐ Ⓑ Ⓒ Ⓓ Ⓔ
    (A) $5/9°$ F.
    (B) $9/5°$ F.
    (C) $1°$ F.
    (D) $-5/9°$ F.
    (E) $-9/5°$ F.

33. Which of the following is not consistent with Dalton's atomic theory?   33. Ⓐ Ⓑ Ⓒ Ⓓ Ⓔ
    (A) All matter consists of minute particles called atoms.
    (B) Atoms of a given element are alike.
    (C) Atoms are neither created nor destroyed in chemical reactions.

(D) Atoms of different elements have the same weight but different electrical charges.

(E) Typically, atoms combine in small numbers to form chemical compounds.

34. The efficiency of machines is always reduced by
    (A) temperature   (B) sublimation   (C) momentum
    (D) friction   (E) refraction

    34. Ⓐ Ⓑ Ⓒ Ⓓ Ⓔ

35. Valence is
    (A) a bundle or quantum of energy
    (B) a measure of acidity
    (C) a measure of alkalinity
    (D) the combining capacity of an element
    (E) the energy used in doing work

    35. Ⓐ Ⓑ Ⓒ Ⓓ Ⓔ

36. Chemical elements classifield in the halogen family are commonly referred to as
    (A) noble gases   (B) inert gases   (C) alkaline earths
    (D) salt formers   (E) heavy metals

    36. Ⓐ Ⓑ Ⓒ Ⓓ Ⓔ

37. Substances which sometimes change the rate of chemical reactions are called
    (A) ions   (B) isotopes   (C) catalysts   (D) neutralizers
    (E) bases

    37. Ⓐ Ⓑ Ⓒ Ⓓ Ⓔ

38. A special branch of chemistry which has developed around the study of carbon compounds is called
    (A) physical chemistry   (B) organic chemistry
    (C) inorganic chemistry   (D) colloidal chemistry
    (E) biochemistry

    38. Ⓐ Ⓑ Ⓒ Ⓓ Ⓔ

39. Separation of the components in liquid solution by distillation is dependent upon
    (A) varying solubilities   (B) heat of solidification
    (C) adsorption   (D) differences in volatility   (E) absorption

    39. Ⓐ Ⓑ Ⓒ Ⓓ Ⓔ

40. Chemical decomposition accomplished by means of an electric current is called
    (A) electrography   (B) electromagnetism   (C) electrophoresis
    (D) electrovalency   (E) electrolysis

    40. Ⓐ Ⓑ Ⓒ Ⓓ Ⓔ

41. Chemical formulas enable us to determine the kind and number of atoms in a compound, each element's percentage, and
    (A) the number and kinds of isotopes   (B) its physical properties
    (C) its nuclear reactions   (D) its half-life
    (E) its molecular weight

    41. Ⓐ Ⓑ Ⓒ Ⓓ Ⓔ

42. Thermosetting plastics polymerize irreversibly under conditions of
    (A) freezing   (B) bonding   (C) volitilization
    (D) heat or pressure   (E) crystallization

    42. Ⓐ Ⓑ Ⓒ Ⓓ Ⓔ

43. By 1000 A.D., when Western Europe was beginning to emerge from the Dark Ages, intellectual development was hindered because
    (A) most Arabic and Greek knowledge had been lost
    (B) man hesitated to experiment

    43. Ⓐ Ⓑ Ⓒ Ⓓ Ⓔ

(C) alchemy was supreme

(D) there were formal centers of learning

(E) the Christian Church advocated Aristotle's logic

44. Naturally radioactive elements change to other elements subsequent to their emission of

(A) gamma rays   (B) X-rays

(C) alpha particles   (D) beta rays   (E) gamma rays

44. Ⓐ Ⓑ Ⓒ Ⓓ Ⓔ

45. Parallel light rays are made divergent by

(A) an achromatic lens   (B) monochromatic light

(C) a convex lens   (D) a plano-concave lens

(E) a concave lens

45. Ⓐ Ⓑ Ⓒ Ⓓ Ⓔ

46. Amplitude and frequency determine

(A) tempo   (B) loudness   (C) rhythm   (D) meter   (E) resonance

46. Ⓐ Ⓑ Ⓒ Ⓓ Ⓔ

47. In referring to wave phenomena, the term wavelength means

(A) the bending of the direction of wave motion

(B) the interaction of waves arriving simultaneously at the same point

(C) the distance between crests

(D) one half of the distance in height between a crest and a trough

(E) the number of crests passing a point in a given time

47. Ⓐ Ⓑ Ⓒ Ⓓ Ⓔ

48. The height of transverse sound waves is expressed as

(A) frequency   (B) wavelength   (C) rarefaction

(D) modulation   (E) amplitude

48. Ⓐ Ⓑ Ⓒ Ⓓ Ⓔ

49. A mechanism that proves the earth's rotation is a

(A) barometer   (B) compass   (C) Foucault pendulum

(D) seismograph   (E) calorimeter

49. Ⓐ Ⓑ Ⓒ Ⓓ Ⓔ

50. In reference to electrical circuitry, the ampere is

(A) the unit of resistance

(B) an induced static charge

(C) a force between two electric fields

(D) the unit of current

(E) the difference of potential

50. Ⓐ Ⓑ Ⓒ Ⓓ Ⓔ

51. Electron emission by certain heated metals is

(A) the photoelectric effect   (B) electromagnetic induction

(C) commutation   (D) the thermionic effect

(E) transformation

51. Ⓐ Ⓑ Ⓒ Ⓓ Ⓔ

52. A lever with a great mechanical advantage for gaining distance would have

(A) a short force arm and a short weight arm

(B) a terminal fulcrum

(C) a long force arm and long weight arm

(D) a long force arm and short weight arm

(E) a short force arm and long weight arm

52. Ⓐ Ⓑ Ⓒ Ⓓ Ⓔ

Question 53 refers to the following diagram.

Lithium atom   Sodium atom

53. The chemical and physical properties of lithium and sodium are simi-
lar because
(A) both possess an uneven number of protons
(B) both have a single electron in their outermost shell
(C) both possess an uneven number of electrons
(D) of coincidence
(E) these atoms do not have similar chemical properties

53. Ⓐ Ⓑ Ⓒ Ⓓ Ⓔ

54. Christian theology and Aristotelian philosophy were reconciled in
Summa Theologica written by
(A) Francis Bacon   (B) Albertus Magnus   (C) Roger Bacon
(D) Thomas Aquinas   (E) Pope Paul III

54. Ⓐ Ⓑ Ⓒ Ⓓ Ⓔ

55. If the corner of a cube of sugar is placed in contact with iodine solu-
tion, the entire cube quickly becomes the color of iodine due to
(A) capillarity   (B) surface tension   (C) kinetic energy
(D) potential energy   (E) convection

55. Ⓐ Ⓑ Ⓒ Ⓓ Ⓔ

56. If one side of a solid is warmer than the other, the faster-moving
warm molecules collide with the cooler ones, transferring some of
their energy to the slower ones. The transfer of heat energy is called
(A) convection   (B) radiation   (C) adhesion
(D) conduction   (E) concussion

56. Ⓐ Ⓑ Ⓒ Ⓓ Ⓔ

57. According to the concept of the conservation of mass, when two or
more elements react chemically,
(A) the sum of their masses equals the mass of the compound formed
(B) the sum of their masses is less than the mass of the compound
formed
(C) the sum of their masses is greater than the mass of the compound
formed
(D) atoms may be created, modified, or destroyed
(E) atoms may be changed from one kind to another

57. Ⓐ Ⓑ Ⓒ Ⓓ Ⓔ

58. The process by which substances are separated by utilization of differences in the degree to which they are absorbed to the surface of any inert material is

(A) fractional distillation
(B) chromatography
(C) filtration
(D) neutralization
(E) isomerism

58. Ⓐ Ⓑ Ⓒ Ⓓ Ⓔ

59. The maintenance of acid-base balance is accomplished by chemical substances called

(A) ionizers   (B) polarizers   (C) buffers   (D) neutralizers
(E) catalysts

59. Ⓐ Ⓑ Ⓒ Ⓓ Ⓔ

60. The equation $Cu(OH)_2 + H_2SO_4 \rightarrow CuSO_4 + 2H_2O$ is an example of a reaction called

(A) oxidation   (B) salt formation
(C) an exothermic reaction   (D) a chain reaction   (E) reduction

60. Ⓐ Ⓑ Ⓒ Ⓓ Ⓔ

ANSWER KEY—SAMPLE EXAMINATION 1

Part I Biological Sciences

1. D	11. E	21. A	31. E	41. D	51. E
2. C	12. B	22. B	32. E	42. A	52. D
3. C	13. B	23. E	33. E	43. A	53. B
4. C	14. E	24. A	34. C	44. E	54. D
5. B	15. D	25. E	35. C	45. B	55. A
6. E	16. B	26. B	36. E	46. C	56. D
7. B	17. B	27. E	37. C	47. E	57. D
8. B	18. D	28. B	38. D	48. E	58. B
9. E	19. C	29. B	39. D	49. E	59. E
10. D	20. A	30. B	40. E	50. E	60. D

Part II Physical Sciences

1. C	11. E	21. B	31. D	41. E	51. D
2. D	12. D	22. D	32. B	42. D	52. E
3. E	13. A	23. A	33. D	43. E	53. B
4. B	14. D	24. E	34. D	44. C	54. D
5. C	15. D	25. B	35. D	45. E	55. A
6. B	16. A	26. A	36. D	46. B	56. D
7. B	17. C	27. B	37. C	47. C	57. A
8. A	18. E	28. A	38. B	48. E	58. B
9. E	19. E	29. B	39. D	49. C	59. C
10. B	20. E	30. D	40. E	50. D	60. B

SCORING CHART—SAMPLE EXAMINATION 1

After you have scored your Sample Examination 1, enter the results in the chart below; then transfer your Raw Score to the Progress Chart on page 14.

Total Test	Number Right	Number Wrong	Number Omitted	Raw Score
Part I: 60				
Part II: 60				
Total: 120				

ANSWER EXPLANATIONS—SAMPLE EXAMINATION 1

Part I   Biological Sciences

1. D.   Of the choices given, the cell is the smallest and least complex unit of living matter. (If one accepts viruses as units of living matter, then these are smaller and less complex.)

2. C.   A physiologist is concerned with the study of function in living organisms.

3. C.   An isotonic solution is one with an osmotic pressure equal to the reference solution—in this case, the living cell.

4. C.   Humidity has no effect on enzyme activity.

5. B.   Heterotrophic organisms require organic compounds as food.

6. E.   Commensalism occurs when a smaller, unprotected animal is associated with another, usually for protection.

7. B.   Among the chief sources of niacin are yeast, green vegetables, and wheat germ.

8. B.   Cellular respiration combines oxygen and organic compounds to release energy, carbon dioxide, and water.

9. E.   Photosynthesis produces glucose which increases, or adds to, the dry weight of the plant.

10. D.   The absence of light stimulates stem elongation in plants and results in the failure of chlorophyll synthesis. This is etiolation.

11. E.   In plants xylem functions chiefly in the upward conduction of water and dissolved minerals and in the support or strengthening of stems.

12. B.   The edible portions of the sweet potato plant are the roots which become enlarged due to the accumulation of stored foods.

13. B.   Thallophytes, or thallus plants, lack xylem and phloem, the conducting tissues, and they also do not develop multicellular embryos.

14. E.   Under normal favorable conditions in the seas and in freshwater lakes and streams, algae are so prolific that they constitute the basic food in many established food chains.

15. D.   In blood clotting, in the presence of the antihemophilic factor, blood platelets stick to torn tissue and release thromboplastin and serotonin.

16. B.   Type A blood cells contain antigen A and its serum contains antibody B; type B blood cells contain antigen B and its serum contains anitbody A. Type B serum will cause type A blood to clump.

17. B.   As indicated on the graph, at temperatures approaching 60°C, enzyme activity stops.

18. D.   All nerve impulses initiated in and by the rods and cones of the retina are carried to the brain via the optic nerve.

19. C. All nerve impulses from sensory receptors are conducted to the central nervous system through a dorsal root ganglion.

20. A. The parasympathetic nervous system in a general sense functions to counter the sympathetic nervous system. When the sympathetic nervous system increases the rate of heart beat, the parasympathetic system tends to slow it, etc.

21. A. Transpiration is the evaporation of water from the aerial parts of plants. It has the beneficial effect of transporting dissolved minerals upward from the roots to the stem and leaves.

22. B. Mendel maintained meticulous records of his crosses with peas. These were most beneficial when he analyzed his results and formulated his conclusions.

23. E. During the first meiotic division, chromosome reduction has not yet occurred. Hence, the chromatids of any pair of chromosomes are still in groups of four or tetrads.

24. A. According to *catastrophism* sudden and violent events changed the earth's surface and destroyed all life and subsequent acts of special creation repopulated the earth.

25. E. Convergent evolution is the development of similar traits, including adaptation to certain habitats, by unrelated or distantly related species.

26. B. Mutations are abrupt and unexpected changes in inheritance patterns that breed true.

27. E. Joseph Lister initiated the era of antiseptic surgery when he began spraying the surgical scene with carbolic acid.

28. B. Leeuwenhoek made sketches of bacteria and other microorganisms from the plaque around his teeth and from hay infusions.

29. B. Among Aristotle's most noted contributions was the concept of the scientific method.

30. B. In 1920, Banting and Best isolated insulin from pancreatic tissue.

31. E. The littoral zone exists from the high tide level to the area 200 meters deep.

32. E. Ichthyology is the study of fish.

33. E. The key to analogous structures is the word function. The wing of a bird and the wing of a bee are similar in only one category, function. Structurally, they are unrelated.

34. C. The term symbiosis is a general term meaning "living together," often with mutual benefits.

35. C. The giant reptiles flourished in the geologic time period called the Mesozoic era.

36. E. Rennin is a digestive enzyme secreted by the stomach which is partially responsible for casein digestion.

37. C. Plague still exists in certain parts of the world and, since it is associated with rodents and their fleas, rodent control is a necessary control measure.

38. D. In each instance of sex determination in humans, the probability that any one individual will be male or female is one-half at the time of conception.

39. D. When both parents are heterozygous, segregation results in gamete types *A* and *a* for both parents. Random fertilization produces three mating types in a ratio of 1:2:1, with one-half being heterozygous for *Aa*.

40. E. Since the probability of crossing-over between two linked genes on a pair of chromosomes is directly proportional to the distance separating them, crossing-over frequencies are greatest in widely separated genes.

41. D. An antigen is any substance, which when introduced into the body, causes the body to produce antibodies.

42. A. In general, the interest of ancient peoples in biology was limited to the medicinal values of plants.

43. A. Diffusion in this instance is the movement of water molecules from an area of high concentration of water molecules to or towards an area of low or lower concentration of water molecules.

44. E. Turgid or turgor pressure is a positive pressure developed within living

plant cells, and therefore in stems and leaves, as a result of internal water pressure.

45. B. The cell in the salt water has lost water by diffusion, the net movement of water molecules out of the cell.

46. C. Diffusion is the movement of water molecules as a result of their molecular activity. In the case of the cell in fresh water, as in the case of the cell in salt water also, water molecules move freely into and out of the cell.

47. E. Phytochrome appears to be necessary for the formation of the hypothetical hormone florigen, which supposedly controls floral initiation.

48. E. Cell division by the vascular cambium produces xylem internally and phloem externally, thus adding to the diameter of the stem.

49. E. Water which moistens the cell walls of leaf mesophyll cells evaporates since

50. E. The effects of adrenalin are body wide, affecting pulse, muscle tone, and the rate of nerve conduction.

51. E. Mitosis is a qualitative distribution of chromatin to each of two different daughter cells. Its primary significance is that each daughter cell receives identical chromatin materials.

52. D. The point where the optic nerve enters the eyeball has neither rods nor cones and, therefore, has no sight capability. It is called the blind spot.

53. B. The antihemophilic factor causes blood platelets to swell into spherical masses and these tend to prevent the loss of other blood components.

54. D. Humans and other animals store simple sugars in the form of glycogen in muscles and in the liver.

55. A. Cuvier suggested that there must have been many floods (catastrophes) that killed most of the organisms living at the time, followed by repeated special creations to repopulate the earth. This idea was called *catastrophism*.

56. D. ⎱ Lyell opposed catastrophism and special creation. He stated that events in
57. D. ⎰ the geological history of the earth were the products of the same natural forces active today, i.e, erosion, sedimentation, etc. This doctrine was called *uniformitarianism*.

58. B. The Devonian period was the beginning of true land plants with stomata, vascular tissues and multicellular embryos.

59. E. During the Tertiary, early modern mammals assumed dominance, together with the flowering (seed) plants.

60. D. During the Carboniferous, giant ferns, clubmosses, and horsetails grew in widespread low and swampy regions of the earth. These later formed layers of dead vegetation which did not decompose. This plant material became coal.

Part II Physical Sciences

1. C. The trophosphere is the layer of the earth's atmosphere closest to the earth's surface and only the lower half of the trophosphere will support life without supplemental oxygen.

2. D. The periods of rotation and revolution of the moon are the same, 27⅓ days. Because of this, the same "face" of the moon is always turned towards the earth.

3. E. Perigee is that point in the orbit of a satellite that is nearest to the earth.

4. B. When it is noon at Greenwich, England, it is 12:00 P.M./00:00 A.M. at the International Date Line. At this instant, only one calendar day is in effect, worldwide.

5. C. A delta is a triangle-shaped deposition of sediments at the mouth of a river.

6. B. Plate tectonics is the concept that continents drift in relation to one another on the earth's surface.

7. B. The term anhydrous means free from or without water, especially the water of crystallization.

8. A. Stalactites are calcite columns hanging from cave ceilings. They are formed over long periods of time when water leaking through the cave ceiling evaporates leaving calcite deposits.

9. E. } In determining effort when using a lever and fulcrum, the effort multiplied
10. B. } by its distance from the fulcrum equals the weight multiplied by its distance from the fulcrum.

11. E. The wavelength beam of electrons is very short and, therefore, permits a higher degree of resolution than with a light microscope.

12. D. When electromagnetic waves bounce back from an object, they are said to be reflected.

13. A. Interference is the combining of two or more waves when they reach a given point simultaneously.

14. D. Pitch is a determination of how rapidly an object vibrates; the higher the frequency, the higher the pitch.

15. D. Svante Arrhenius proposed that acids form H^+ ions in water solutions. When H_3PO_4 is added to water, H^+ ions are formed.

16. A. Magnetic fields vary according to their source, the position of their source, and the intensity of their source.

17. C. Electrical current is measured in amperes, one ampere being equal to one coulomb of change past a point in one second.

18. E. When a coil of wire is rotated between the poles of a magnet an electric current is generated.

19. E. In radioactive decomposition as well as in other radioactive changes, the nucleus of the atom is involved exclusively.

20. E. Entropy is a thermodynamic measure of disorder; entropy of any undisturbed system always increases.

21. B. The kilometer is the standard metric unit for measuring longer distances, i.e., distances comparable to miles.

22. D. The standard meter is based on the wavelength of light emitted by the krypton atom.

23. A. For every force in one direction, there is an equal force in the opposite direction.

24. E. By definition, energy is the capacity to do work.

25. B. By definition, an electron is a fundamental particle of negative electricity.

26. A. The Doppler effect is the apparent change in the pitch of sounds produced by moving objects when an observer is stationary or moving at a different speed than the producer of the sound.

27. B. In a chain nuclear reaction, neutrons strike other atoms which, in turn, release neutrons, which strike additional atoms. When a chain reaction can be sustained, the number or amount of fissionable material is described as a critical mass.

28. A. According to relativity the mass of an object increases with its velocity.

29. B. Weight is the force of gravity acting upon an object.

30. D. For every force in one direction, there is an equal force in the opposite direction.

31. D. The nature of electricity is not affected by the source of its production—hydroelectric power plants, nuclear power plants, or plants that burn fossil fuels.

32. B. Celsius temperatures may be converted to Fahrenheit by multiplying the Celsius temperature by 1.8 and adding 32 degrees.

33. D. Dalton's atomic theory holds that atoms are the unit particles of matter and cannot be subdivided, that atoms of a given element are alike and have the same weight, that atoms of different elements have different weights, that in chemical reactions it is atoms that combine and that the relative weights of the atoms that combine are directly related to the weights of the atoms themselves.

34. D. Friction is a force that opposes motion when two objects in contact with each other attempt to move relative to each other. Friction uses energy and, therefore, reduces mechanical efficiency.

35. D. Valence is the combining capacity of an element—specifically, the number of hydrogen atoms that combine with one atom of that element.

36. D. Elements placed in the halogen family of chemical elements associate readily with other elements and are often referred to as salt formers.

37. C. A catalyst is a substance that initiates or speeds up a chemical reaction without participating in the reaction process.

38. B. The field of organic chemistry deals primarily with the compounds of carbon.

39. D. Distillation is a process of boiling a liquid and condensing its vapor. Two or more liquids will usually have different boiling points so they may be separated by first boiling off the vapor of one liquid and condensing it and then boiling-off the vapor of the second liquid and condensing it.

40. E. Electrolysis effects chemical change by passing an electrical current through a substance—for example, a salt (NaCl) solution. In the case of a NaCl solution, the result is the separation of the Na^+ and Cl^- ions with the Na^+ ions moving to the cathode and the Cl^- ions moving to the anode.

41. E. A chemical formula is a description, using chemical symbols, of the ratio of atoms in a chemical compound. If the weight ratio and the atomic weight of the elements of a compound are known, the molecular weight of the compound can be calculated.

42. D. The family of plastics referred to as "thermosetting" consists of substances that polymerize irreversibly under heat or pressure forming a hard mass.

43. E. Albertus Magnus and Saint Thomas Aquinas endeavored to harmonize the teachings of Aristotle with church doctrine. Roger Bacon, in opposition, demonstrated the values of observation and experimentation and argued against the age-old scholastic method of education.

44. C. When an atomic nucleus decomposes by emitting alpha or beta particles, it is said to be radioactive. An example would be the loss of an alpha particle by uranium-238 and its subsequent change to thorium-234.

45. E. Parallel light rays passing through a concave lens bend outward so that they spread apart.

46. B. The intensity and loudness of sound are determined by the amplitude of vibration and number of vibrations (frequency) per second.

47. C. Wavelength is the measure of distance between two adjacent crests.

48. E. Amplitude of a sound vibration is the distance that a vibrating object moves as it vibrates.

49. C. A Foucault pendulum always swings in the same plane unless changed by an outside force. During a 24-hour day, the swing of the pendulum appears to change position, but in actuality, the earth beneath it is rotating.

50. D. The ampere is defined as a measure of electrical current and equals one coulomb of change per second past a given point in a wire.

51. D. When certain metals are heated, they emit electrons, a phenomenon called the thermionic effect.

52. E. Since the effort multiplied by its distance from the fulcrum equals the weight multiplied by its diameter from the fulcrum, a lever with a short force arm and a long weight arm would provide advantage for gaining distance.

53. B. In general, the chemical and physical properties of lithium and sodium are similar because the outer orbit of each atom contains a single electron.

54. D. Thomas Aquinas taught that there is no conflict between faith and reason.

55. A. The forces of adhesion between a solid and a liquid based on the relative attraction of the molecules of the liquid in each other and for the solid is called capillarity.

56. D. Conduction is the process whereby heat energy is transmitted directly through materials.

57. A. The law of conservation of mass holds that there is no detectable gain or loss of mass in or as a result of chemical change.

58. B. Various substances may be separated by using the degree to which they are absorbed onto an inert material. If the inert material is paper, the process is called paper chromatography.

59. C. A buffer is any substance capable of neutralizing acids and bases to maintain a given hydrogen ion concentration.

60. B. In a chemical reaction between an acid and a base (in this case, H_2SO_4 and $Cu(OH)_2$, respectively), a salt, $CuSO_4$, is formed.

SAMPLE EXAMINATION 2

Part I: Biological Sciences

Number of Questions: 60
Time: 45 minutes

Directions: Each of the questions or incomplete statements below is followed by five suggested answers or completions. Select the one that is best in each case.

1. The term most appropriate to the passage of molecules across cellular membranes is
   (A) selective permeability   (B) porosity
   (C) mass movement   (D) capillarity   (E) imbibition

   1. Ⓐ Ⓑ Ⓒ Ⓓ Ⓔ

2. According to the principle of biogenesis,
   (A) organic evolution is a reality
   (B) life comes from life
   (C) genetics is the study of heredity
   (D) life arose as the result of special creation
   (E) life arises directly from non-living matter

   2. Ⓐ Ⓑ Ⓒ Ⓓ Ⓔ

3. The study of cellular and organismal functioning is a biological specialty called
   (A) anatomy   (B) physiology   (C) genetics
   (D) parasitology   (E) cytology

   3. Ⓐ Ⓑ Ⓒ Ⓓ Ⓔ

4. When a living cell is placed in a hypertonic fluid, there will be
   (A) a net movement of water molecules into the cell
   (B) no net movement of water molecules into or out of the cell
   (C) an increase in cell turgidity
   (D) an increase in Brownian movement
   (E) a net movement of water molecules out of the cell

   4. Ⓐ Ⓑ Ⓒ Ⓓ Ⓔ

5. When an organism is incapable of synthesizing its food from inorganic materials, it is described as
   (A) chemosynthetic   (B) autotrophic   (C) autophobic
   (D) heterotrophic   (E) photosynthetic

   5. Ⓐ Ⓑ Ⓒ Ⓓ Ⓔ

6. Carotene of plants can be considered a precursor of
   (A) vitamin C   (B) phytol   (C) chlorophyll
   (D) hemoglobin   (E) vitamin A

   6. Ⓐ Ⓑ Ⓒ Ⓓ Ⓔ

7. As a result of the process called cellular respiration,
   (A) dry weight increases
   (B) oxygen and organic compounds are produced
   (C) water and carbon dioxide are consumed
   (D) dry weight decreases
   (E) water and organic compounds are produced

   7. Ⓐ Ⓑ Ⓒ Ⓓ Ⓔ

8. An energy-releasing process occurring continuously in all living cells is
   (A) respiration   (B) osmosis   (C) absorption
   (D) diffusion   (E) photosynthesis

   8. Ⓐ Ⓑ Ⓒ Ⓓ Ⓔ

9. The chemical compounds called gibberelins   9. A B C D E
   (A) result in chemosynthesis   (B) cause unusual cell elongation in plant cells
   (C) cause etiolation in plants   (D) are inactivated by fungal enzymes
   (E) act as intracellular parasites in plants

10. The total amount of organic matter in a population is referred to as   10. A B C D E
   (A) alluvium   (B) humus   (C) laterite
   (D) schist   (E) biomass

11. In plants one of the functions of the xylem is to   11. A B C C E
   (A) manufacture organic substances from carbon dioxide and water
   (B) reduce transpiration
   (C) increase stem diameter by continued cell division
   (D) conduct water upwards   (E) conduct food substances

12. A grain of wheat is   12. A B C C E
   (A) a fruit   (B) a seed   (C) an embryo
   (D) a cotyledon   (E) an hypocotyl

13. Water loss from plants by transpiration would be decreased by   13. A B C D E
   (A) light   (B) increased air circulation
   (C) increased temperature   (D) increased humidity
   (E) decreased humidity

14. A type of nuclear division in which the chromosome number in the   14. A B C D E
   daughter nuclei is reduced is called
   (A) karyokinesis   (B) mitosis   (C) amitosis
   (D) meiosis   (E) cytokinesis

15. In plants, fertilization   15. A B C D E
   (A) gives rise to the gametophyte
   (B) precedes spore formation
   (C) precedes gamete formation
   (D) restores the diploid condition
   (E) may take place between two spores

16. During the initial stages of blood clot formation, thromboplastin is   16. A B C D E
   released by
   (A) antibodies   (B) neutrophils   (C) red cells
   (D) basophils   (E) platelets

17. Blood leaving the right ventricle of the human heart is pumped into   17. A B C D E
   the
   (A) pulmonary artery   (B) pulmonary veins
   (C) aorta   (D) sinus venosus   (E) coronary artery

18. To overcome a deficiency of vitamin C, you would include in your diet   18. A B C D E
   (A) fish liver oils
   (B) citrus fruits
   (C) whole grain cereals
   (D) nuts
   (E) red meats

19. Impairment of the olfactory nerves would affect
   (A) chewing
   (B) muscles which move the eyeballs
   (C) swallowing
   (D) vision
   (E) the sense of smell

19. Ⓐ Ⓑ Ⓒ Ⓓ Ⓔ

20. Nerve impulses along motor nerves leave the central nervous system
   (A) along a dorsal root axon
   (B) along a ventral root axon
   (C) after passing through a dorsal root ganglion
   (D) along a connector dendrite
   (E) along dendrites of sensory neurons

20. Ⓐ Ⓑ Ⓒ Ⓓ Ⓔ

21. The capability of focusing both eyes on the same object is
   (A) stigmatism   (B) binocular vision   (C) glaucoma
   (D) hypermetropia   (E) myopia

21. Ⓐ Ⓑ Ⓒ Ⓓ Ⓔ

22. Parathormone
   (A) dilates blood vessels   (B) stimulates lactation
   (C) regulates sodium metabolism   (D) controls blood sugar
   (E) regulates calcium metabolism

22. Ⓐ Ⓑ Ⓒ Ⓓ Ⓔ

23. The mutual exchange of chromosome fragments, which is called crossing over, occurs during
   (A) interphase   (B) fertilization   (C) transduction
   (D) synapsis   (E) cell plate formation

23. Ⓐ Ⓑ Ⓒ Ⓓ Ⓔ

24. The theory proposing the inheritance of acquired characteristics was proposed by
   (A) Alfred R. Wallace   (B) Charles Darwin
   (C) Jean Baptiste de Lamarck   (D) Sir Charles Lyell
   (E) Thomas Hunt Morgan

24. Ⓐ Ⓑ Ⓒ Ⓓ Ⓔ

25. The mutation theory was eventually shown to strengthen Darwin's theory of natural selection because it provided
   (A) an explanation for genetic coding
   (B) for cytoplasmic inheritance
   (C) an explanation for pangenesis
   (D) a source of inheritable variations
   (E) the bridge between biometrics and the Mendelean ratios

25. Ⓐ Ⓑ Ⓒ Ⓓ Ⓔ

26. A disease transmitted by an arthropod vector is
   (A) smallpox   (B) malaria   (C) tuberculosis   (D) polio
   (E) lockjaw

26. Ⓐ Ⓑ Ⓒ Ⓓ Ⓔ

27. The first to use the word *cell* after studying plant tissue with his microscope was
   (A) Brown   (B) Leonardo da Vinci   (C) Hooke
   (D) Grew   (E) Schleiden and Schwann

27. Ⓐ Ⓑ Ⓒ Ⓓ Ⓔ

28. An ancient Greek scholar and one of the first to consider water basic to both the physical and biological worlds was
    (A) Theophrastus   (B) Anaximander   (C) Thales
    (D) Empedocles   (E) Aristotle

29. Harvey was the first to verify experimentally
    (A) chemical oxidation   (B) cell reproduction
    (C) the biogenetic hypothesis   (D) the nerve impulse
    (E) circulation of the blood

30. You would expect to encounter numerous epiphytes and a variety of arboreal mammals in
    (A) a tropical rain forest   (B) a deciduous forest
    (C) a coniferous forest   (D) an alpine tundra   (E) a taiga

31. Marine organisms found on the continental shelf live in the
    (A) zone of perpetual darkness   (B) neritic zone
    (C) littoral zone   (D) abyssal zone   (E) bathyal zone

32. An ornithologist is a specialist in the study of
    (A) worms   (B) insects   (C) birds   (D) reptiles
    (E) mammals

33. Homologous structures are indicative of
    (A) common ancestry   (B) convergence   (C) parallel evolution
    (D) divergence   (E) similar function

34. An organism which obtains its food from non-living organic materials is called a
    (A) symbiont   (B) saprophyte   (C) commensal
    (D) parasite   (E) buffer

35. The time period described as the age of glaciers is called the
    (A) Eocene epoch   (B) Late Mesozoic   (C) Triassic period
    (D) Early Mesozoic   (E) Pleistocene epoch

36. Blood enters the left ventricle of the human heart through the
    (A) inferior vena cava   (B) tricuspid valve
    (C) semilunar valves   (D) bicuspid valve   (E) aorta

37. Inclusion of sea foods in the human diet normally prevents an insufficiency of thyroxin and the development of
    (A) muscular spasms   (B) anemia   (C) many enzymes
    (D) goiter   (E) hemoglobin

38. Pasteurization of milk ensures almost complete protection from the bacterial disease called
    (A) measles   (B) plague   (C) smallpox   (D) polio
    (E) undulant fever

39. In reference to a trait designated as "A", the genotype(s) resulting from a mating between a male parent homozygeous for "A" and a heterozygous female parent would be
    (A) ½ AA, ½ Aa   (B) ¼ AA, ½ Aa, ¼ aa   (C) ¾ Aa, ¼ aa
    (D) ¼ Aa, ¾ aa   (E) impossible to predict

40. Enzymes are specific with reference to   40. Ⓐ Ⓑ Ⓒ Ⓓ Ⓔ
    (A) the units of energy released (B) the units of energy absorbed
    (C) the high temperatures required for their activation
    (D) the low temperatures required for their activation (E) the raw materials worked on

41. In single-celled organisms such as Amoeba, pinocytic vesicles function by   41. Ⓐ Ⓑ Ⓒ Ⓓ Ⓔ
    (A) bringing some solid particles into the cell
    (B) discharging needle-like barbs containing poison
    (C) propelling the organism   (D) reacting to environmental stimuli
    (E) excreting waste substances from the cell

42. Amino acid analysis of proteins has been advanced by   42. Ⓐ Ⓑ Ⓒ Ⓓ Ⓔ
    (A) study of hydrolysis reactions
    (B) better understanding of anabolic reactions
    (C) a technique called paper chromatography
    (D) production and study of autoradiographs
    (E) study of condensation reactions

43. Saprophytes   43. Ⓐ Ⓑ Ⓒ Ⓓ Ⓔ
    (A) utilize radiant energy
    (B) rely upon the absorption of nutrients from decomposing organic
        materials
    (C) eat, digest, and assimilate food materials
    (D) oxidize inorganic materials
    (E) exist at the expense of living organisms

44. As a result of the process called cellular respiration   44. Ⓐ Ⓑ Ⓒ Ⓓ Ⓔ
    (A) dry weight increases
    (B) oxygen and organic compounds are produced
    (C) water and carbon dioxide are consumed
    (D) dry weight decreases
    (E) water and organic compounds are produced

Questions 45-46 refer to the following diagram.

% Full Sunlight

The graph represents the relationship between the rate of photosynthesis
(expressed as milligrams of carbon dioxide absorbed per 0.5 square meters
of leaf area per hour) and light intensity (expressed as percentages of full
sunlight) for woodland ferns.

45. Under the conditions noted above, one may conclude that 45. Ⓐ Ⓑ Ⓒ Ⓓ Ⓔ
    (A) ferns use the most sunlight at 100% full sunlight
    (B) photosynthesis decreases dry weight
    (C) optimum light intensity for ferns is 30-40% full sunlight
    (D) photosynthesis increases dry weight
    (E) equal increases in light intensity throughout the range of 0-100% of
        full sunlight bring about equal increases in the rate of photosynthesis
        for ferns

46. One may also infer that 46. Ⓐ Ⓑ Ⓒ Ⓓ Ⓔ
    (A) ferns prefer shade
    (B) absorbed carbon dioxide increases to 4 or more milligrams in ferns when
        exposed to greater than 100% full sunlight
    (C) fern leaves are inefficient when it comes to photosynthesis
    (D) ferns use more carbon dioxide at 10-50% full sunlight than at 60-100%
        full sunlight
    (E) ferns would grow best in 100% full sunlight

47. Which of the following best describes a nerve impulse? 47. Ⓐ Ⓑ Ⓒ Ⓓ Ⓔ
    (A) the transmission of coded signals along a nerve fiber
    (B) a wave of depolarization passing along a nerve fiber
    (C) a flow of electrons along a nerve fiber
    (D) a chemical reaction
    (E) a wave of contraction passing along the myelin sheath

48. Stimulation by the sympathetic nervous system would result in 48. Ⓐ Ⓑ Ⓒ Ⓓ Ⓔ
    (A) slower heart beat   (B) dilated bronchi
    (C) faster peristalsis   (D) dilated arteries   (E) constricted pupils

49. In the myopic eye, the 49. Ⓐ Ⓑ Ⓒ Ⓓ Ⓔ
    (A) light rays converge in front of the retina
    (B) light rays converge in the fovea
    (C) light rays converge behind the retina
    (D) vision is not blurred
    (E) cornea is defective

50. Glucose metabolism is regulated by 50. Ⓐ Ⓑ Ⓒ Ⓓ Ⓔ
    (A) thyrotropin   (B) epinephrine   (C) estradiol
    (D) progesterone   (E) insulin

51. In humans, sex-linked inheritance is concerned with inheritance of 51. Ⓐ Ⓑ Ⓒ Ⓓ Ⓔ
    (A) traits whose genes are located on autosomes
    (B) traits whose genes are located on the X chromosome
    (C) traits whose genes are located on chromosome number 21
    (D) traits whose genes are located on the Y chromosome
    (E) traits whose genes determine sex

52. The inherited variations usually referred to in treatises on natural 52. Ⓐ Ⓑ Ⓒ Ⓓ Ⓔ
    selection and evolution are, in reality,
    (A) merely chance variations   (B) induced by the environment
    (C) special creations   (D) mutations
    (E) acquired characteristics

53. Deoxyribose nucleic acid consists of simple sugars, phosphate units, and four specific nitrogenous bases:
    (A) cytosine, guanine, thymine, and uracil
    (B) adenine, guanine, thymine, and uracil
    (C) adenine, cytosine, guanine, and thymine
    (D) adenine, cytosine, thymine, and uracil
    (E) adenine, cytosine, guanine, and uracil

53. Ⓐ Ⓑ Ⓒ Ⓓ Ⓔ

54. Sugar metabolism is regulated by
    (A) insulin   (B) cortisone and adrenalin
    (C) parathormone   (D) cortisone   (E) thyroxine

54. Ⓐ Ⓑ Ⓒ Ⓓ Ⓔ

55. A Renaissance artist renowned for his knowledge of human musculature was
    (A) Albertus Magnus   (B) Galen   (C) Michelangelo
    (D) Vesalius   (E) De Chauliac

55. Ⓐ Ⓑ Ⓒ Ⓓ Ⓔ

56. The ancient Greek scholar who devoted much study to and wrote much about plant reproduction and seed development, and who is referred to as the "father of botany" is
    (A) Aristotle   (B) Empedocles   (C) Thales
    (D) Anaximander   (E) Theophrastus

56. Ⓐ Ⓑ Ⓒ Ⓓ Ⓔ

57. Growth responses to external stimuli by actively growing plants are called
    (A) plasmolysis   (B) synergisms   (C) auxins
    (D) tropisms   (E) parthenocarpy

57. Ⓐ Ⓑ Ⓒ Ⓓ Ⓔ

58. The primary function of root hair cells is
    (A) anchorage   (B) storage   (C) photosynthesis
    (D) absorption   (E) synergism

58. Ⓐ Ⓑ Ⓒ Ⓓ Ⓔ

59. As a result of photosynthesis, light energy is transformed into
    (A) radiant energy   (B) chemical energy
    (C) kinetic energy   (D) electrical energy   (E) heat energy

59. Ⓐ Ⓑ Ⓒ Ⓓ Ⓔ

60. When environmental conditions become unfavorable, certain species of bacteria
    (A) develop flagella   (B) become aerobic   (C) form spores
    (D) become anaerobic   (E) develop capsules

60. Ⓐ Ⓑ Ⓒ Ⓓ Ⓔ

Part II: Physical Sciences

Number of Questions: 60
Time: 45 minutes

Directions: Each of the questions or incomplete statements below is followed by five suggested answers or completions. Select the one that is best in each case.

1. When certain types of atmospheric particles act as nuclei on which water condensation occurs, these fog-forming nuclei are called
   (A) hydrologic nuclei   (B) condensation nuclei
   (C) hydroscopic nuclei   (D) hygroscopic nuclei   (E) aquifers

   1. Ⓐ Ⓑ Ⓒ Ⓓ Ⓔ

2. The earth's orbit follows a pathway called
   (A) a parabola   (B) a circle   (C) an ellipse
   (D) a hyperbola   (E) a spiral

   2. Ⓐ Ⓑ Ⓒ Ⓓ Ⓔ

3. One significant scientific contribution of the Babylonians was the
   (A) Pythagorean theorem
   (B) combining of mathematics with experimental theory
   (C) recording of eclipses
   (D) science of alchemy
   (E) principle of Archimedes

   3. Ⓐ Ⓑ Ⓒ Ⓓ Ⓔ

4. The most accurate timepiece known to man today is the
   (A) atomic clock using the cesium atom   (B) electric clock
   (C) quartz-crystal clock   (D) pendulum clock
   (E) solar calendar

   4. Ⓐ Ⓑ Ⓒ Ⓓ Ⓔ

5. A star that suddenly increases in brightness and then slowly fades is know as a
   (A) supernova   (B) nova   (C) giant star
   (D) visual binary   (E) white dwarf

   5. Ⓐ Ⓑ Ⓒ Ⓓ Ⓔ

6. One evidence of the earth's rotation is the
   (A) behavior of the Foucault pendulum   (B) lunar eclipse
   (C) solar eclipse   (D) change of seasons
   (E) tilt of the earth's axis

   6. Ⓐ Ⓑ Ⓒ Ⓓ Ⓔ

7. Deposits of glacial till forming various ridge patterns are called
   (A) bergschrunds   (B) moraines   (C) uplifts
   (D) displacements   (E) sediments

   7. Ⓐ Ⓑ Ⓒ Ⓓ Ⓔ

8. An offshore ridge formed by coral is called
   (A) a fjord   (B) a continental shelf   (C) sediment
   (D) a barrier reef   (E) an upwelling

   8. Ⓐ Ⓑ Ⓒ Ⓓ Ⓔ

9. "Atom-smashing" machines are capable of changing one chemical element into another, a change called
   (A) aberration   (B) transmutation   (C) compression
   (D) transduction   (E) assimilation

   9. Ⓐ Ⓑ Ⓒ Ⓓ Ⓔ

10. A concave lens causes
    (A) chromatic aberration   (B) spherical aberration

    10. Ⓐ Ⓑ Ⓒ Ⓓ Ⓔ

(C) parallel light rays to converge

(D) parallel light rays to diverge   (E) spherical convergence

11. Light is made up of tiny particles of packaged energy called   11. Ⓐ Ⓑ Ⓒ Ⓓ Ⓔ
    (A) electrons
    (B) wavelengths
    (C) refractions
    (D) photons
    (E) mesons

12. Color is primarily the property of those wavelengths of light which   12. Ⓐ Ⓑ Ⓒ Ⓓ Ⓔ
    are
    (A) absorbed   (B) reflected   (C) produced
    (D) attracted   (E) adsorbed

13. The scattering of light by colloidal particles is called   13. Ⓐ Ⓑ Ⓒ Ⓓ Ⓔ
    (A) resonance
    (B) radiation
    (C) hydrolysis
    (D) ionization
    (E) the Tyndall effect

14. The flow of electric current may be measured by   14. Ⓐ Ⓑ Ⓒ Ⓓ Ⓔ
    (A) a transistor   (B) a galvanometer   (C) a rectifier
    (D) an induction coil   (E) a conductor

15. A device used to switch electricity on and off and to amplify weak electrical   15. Ⓐ Ⓑ Ⓒ Ⓓ Ⓔ
    currents into strong ones is
    (A) the generator
    (B) the joule
    (C) the transistor
    (D) the moderator
    (E) the transformer

16. When light is reflected from a surface, the ray striking the surface   16. Ⓐ Ⓑ Ⓒ Ⓓ Ⓔ
    is
    (A) absorbed   (B) incident   (C) adsorbed   (D) refracted
    (E) diffused

17. In referring to wave phenomena, the distance between crests is called   17. Ⓐ Ⓑ Ⓒ Ⓓ Ⓔ
    (A) the wavelength   (B) a reverberation   (C) the amplitude
    (D) a trough   (E) the frequency

18. Radio waves and light waves differ in respect to   18. Ⓐ Ⓑ Ⓒ Ⓓ Ⓔ
    (A) amplitude   (B) wavelength   (C) visibility
    (D) velocities   (E) diffraction

19. One of the following is not an acceptable statement in respect to   19. Ⓐ Ⓑ Ⓒ Ⓓ Ⓔ
    magnetic fields:
    (A) they may exist in a vacuum
    (B) lines of force are indefinite and variable
    (C) they can penetrate glass
    (D) they can penetrate thin sheets of copper
    (E) they do not require the presence of matter

20. In electrical circuits, the unit of resistance is called the 20. Ⓐ Ⓑ Ⓒ Ⓒ Ⓔ
    (A) ohm   (B) watt   (C) volt   (D) ampere
    (E) coulomb

21. Commercial and home use of alternating current has been made 21. Ⓐ Ⓑ Ⓒ Ⓓ Ⓔ
    possible by
    (A) commutators   (B) transformers   (C) magnetos
    (D) capacitors   (E) solenoids

22. Simple machines such as levers enable man to 22. Ⓐ Ⓑ Ⓒ Ⓓ Ⓔ
    (A) gain both force and distance
    (B) gain both mechanical advantage and speed
    (C) decrease the force arm and increase the weight arm without
        increasing force
    (D) eliminate friction
    (E) trade force for distance, or vice versa

23. Heat transfer is accomplished by conduction, radiation, and 23. Ⓐ Ⓑ Ⓒ Ⓓ Ⓔ
    (A) vaporization   (B) convection   (C) expansion
    (D) entropy   (E) insulation

24. If you walked five miles, how many kilometers would you walk? 24. Ⓐ Ⓑ Ⓒ Ⓓ Ⓔ
    (A) 12   (B) 8   (C) 6.2   (D) 5   (E) 3

25. A property of matter which tends to make it resist any change in 25. Ⓐ Ⓑ Ⓒ Ⓓ Ⓔ
    motion is called
    (A) gravity   (B) force   (C) mass
    (D) acceleration   (E) inertia

26. Any physical system is said to possess energy if it 26. Ⓐ Ⓑ Ⓒ Ⓓ Ⓔ
    (A) has the capacity to do work   (B) has mass
    (C) is at absolute zero   (D) resists acceleration
    (E) resists gravity

27. A fundamental particle with a positive charge found in the nuclei of 27. Ⓐ Ⓑ Ⓒ Ⓓ Ⓔ
    all heavier atoms is
    (A) an ion   (B) a meson   (C) a proton
    (D) an electron   (E) a neutron

28. The apparent change in frequency and wavelength of light or sound 28. Ⓐ Ⓑ Ⓒ Ⓓ Ⓔ
    occurring when the sound and the observer are moving relative to
    one another is called
    (A) the absorption spectrum   (B) the band spectrum
    (C) the line spectrum   (D) the Doppler effect
    (E) Stefan's Law

29. In a chain reaction, 29. Ⓐ Ⓑ Ⓒ Ⓓ Ⓔ
    (A) electricity serves as the trigger
    (B) light energy stimulates atoms
    (C) light energy stimulates molecules
    (D) neutrons combine with photons
    (E) the first atoms to react trigger additional reactions

30. To state that a football player weighs 220 pounds means that 30. Ⓐ Ⓑ Ⓒ Ⓓ Ⓔ
    (A) his body is attracted by the sun with a force equal to 220 pounds

(B) his body is attracted by the sun and the moon with a combined force equal to 220 pounds

(C) his body is attracted by the earth with a force equal to 220 pounds

(D) he has a negative mass equal to 220 pounds

(E) he has a positive mass equal to 220 pounds

31. Water held behind a dam represents what kind of energy?   31. Ⓐ Ⓑ Ⓒ Ⓓ Ⓔ
    (A) Kinetic   (B) Potential   (C) Mass   (D) Conserved
    (E) Transformed

32. Water will rise inside a glass tube of very small diameter because of   32. Ⓐ Ⓑ Ⓒ Ⓓ Ⓔ
    (A) kinetic energy   (B) potential energy   (C) cohesion
    (D) adhesion   (E) surface tension

33. In the process called evaporation, the faster molecules of a liquid   33. Ⓐ Ⓑ Ⓒ Ⓓ Ⓔ
    are able to escape the attractive forces of their slower neighboring
    molecules. This results in
    (A) an increase in temperature   (B) a decrease in temperature
    (C) adhesion   (D) cohesion   (E) friction

34. Specific gravity is a measure of the relative density of a liquid in   34. Ⓐ Ⓑ Ⓒ Ⓓ Ⓔ
    relation to
    (A) water   (B) air   (C) ice
    (D) mercury   (E) oxygen

35. Which produces hydrogen gas when interacting with metals?   35. Ⓐ Ⓑ Ⓒ Ⓓ Ⓔ
    (A) Salts   (B) Acids   (C) Bases   (D) Oxides
    (E) Hydroxides

36. The halogen family of chemical elements includes fluorine and   36. Ⓐ Ⓑ Ⓒ Ⓓ Ⓔ
    (A) sulfur   (B) potassium   (C) chromium
    (D) bismuth   (E) iodine

37. In the photosynthetic process, one role of chlorophyll is that of   37. Ⓐ Ⓑ Ⓒ Ⓓ Ⓔ
    (A) an ionizer   (B) a polarizer   (C) a neutralizer
    (D) a catalyst   (E) an isotope

38. One class of organic compounds constitutes the building blocks of   38. Ⓐ Ⓑ Ⓒ Ⓓ Ⓔ
    proteins and is characterized by possessing
    (A) a carboxyl group only
    (B) an NH_2 group in addition to a carboxyl group
    (C) hydrocarbons   (D) an alkyl group   (E) esters

39. In any physical change,   39. Ⓐ Ⓑ Ⓒ Ⓓ Ⓔ
    (A) the reactants disappear
    (B) matter does not lose its chemical identity
    (C) new substances with different properties appear
    (D) energy is released
    (E) energy is absorbed

40. In chemical equations, the total molecular weight of the reactants   40. Ⓐ Ⓑ Ⓒ Ⓓ Ⓔ
    (A) equals the total molecular weight of the products
    (B) is less than the total molecular weight of the products

(C) is greater than the total molecular weight of the products
(D) is not relative to the total molecular weight of the products
(E) is determined by the atomic number of the reactant

41. Alkyd resins are the base of polyesters used in boat construction, fishing rods, and other household items because of their
(A) strength, resistance, and durability   (B) thermoplasticity
(C) similarity to foam rubber   (D) insulation capability
(E) tensile coefficient

41. Ⓐ Ⓑ Ⓒ Ⓓ Ⓔ

42. Scholasticism was concerned primarily with
(A) literature and language   (B) social reforms
(C) medicine   (D) Aristotle's works and teachings
(E) astronomy

42. Ⓐ Ⓑ Ⓒ Ⓓ Ⓔ

43. Proteins are complex compounds containing carbon, hydrogen, oxygen, and nitrogen, and usually
(A) sulfur and potassium   (B) sulfur and phosphorus
(C) manganese and phosphorus   (D) manganese and potassium
(E) sulfur and manganese

43. Ⓐ Ⓑ Ⓒ Ⓓ Ⓔ

44. Chemical processes in which electrons are taken away from atoms or molecules are referred to as
(A) recombinations   (B) tropisms   (C) decompositions
(D) oxidations   (E) reductions

44. Ⓐ Ⓑ Ⓒ Ⓓ Ⓔ

45. During radioactive decay, a given radioactive element may emit
(A) beta and gamma rays only   (B) alpha and gamma rays only
(C) alpha, beta and gamma rays
(D) alpha, beta and gamma, and X-rays   (E) X-rays only

45. Ⓐ Ⓑ Ⓒ Ⓓ Ⓔ

Questions 46-47 refer to the following diagram.

46. After study of the illustration above, one may conclude that
(A) water molecules are attracted by the electrodes
(B) sodium ions are attracted to the positive electrode

46. Ⓐ Ⓑ Ⓒ Ⓓ Ⓔ

(C) sodium chloride dissociates when placed in water

(D) chlorine ions are attracted to the negative electrode

(E) current flow causes an increase in water temperature

47. One may also conclude that   47. Ⓐ Ⓑ Ⓒ Ⓓ Ⓔ
    (A) the solution will not conduct current
    (B) only sodium ions conduct current
    (C) only chlorine ions conduct current
    (D) the closed circuit illustrated results in neutrality
    (E) when ions are present they are attracted to electrodes having opposite
        electrical charges

48. Certain metals and alloys, such as nichrome wire, are used in electrical   48. Ⓐ Ⓑ Ⓒ Ⓓ Ⓔ
    heating devices (toasters for example) because of their
    (A) low melting point   (B) high specific resistance
    (C) great current flow   (D) capacity to discharge electrons
    (E) capacity to modify electrons

49. A unique feature of lasers is   49. Ⓐ Ⓑ Ⓒ Ⓓ Ⓔ
    (A) the abrupt spreading of their beam of light
    (B) their production of coherent radiation
    (C) the Peltier effect
    (D) the Seebeck effect
    (E) the very narrow beam of light produced

50. Ultraviolet light   50. Ⓐ Ⓑ Ⓒ Ⓓ Ⓔ
    (A) is more energetic than visual light
    (B) is not harmful
    (C) has longer wavelengths than visible light
    (D) lies in a low energy section of the electromagnetic spectrum
    (E) is the light source used in lasers

51. When an electric current is passed through electrodes immersed in an   51. Ⓐ Ⓑ Ⓒ Ⓓ Ⓔ
    electrolyte, molecules of the electrolyte
    (A) precipitate   (B) dissociate   (C) crystallize
    (D) combine   (E) neutralize

52. According to the law of reflection,   52. Ⓐ Ⓑ Ⓒ Ⓓ Ⓔ
    (A) the angle of incidence is equal to the angle of reflection
    (B) the angle of incidence is less than the angle of reflection
    (C) the angle of incidence is greater than the angle of reflection
    (D) the angle of incidence equals the angle of reflection squared
    (E) the angle of reflection equals the angle of incidence squared

53. Whenever an electric current flows   53. Ⓐ Ⓑ Ⓒ Ⓓ Ⓔ
    (A) charged particles combine
    (B) no effect if detectable in the wire
    (C) a transformer is needed
    (D) power obtained equals current times amperage
    (E) a magnetic field is generated

54. A coil of wire carrying an electric current behaves as   54. Ⓐ Ⓑ Ⓒ Ⓓ Ⓔ
    (A) a stator   (B) a commutator   (C) a transistor
    (D) a bar magnet   (E) a capacitor

Directions: Each group of questions below consists of five lettered choices followed by a list of numbered phrases or sentences. For each numbered phrase or sentence select the one choice that is most closely related to it. Each choice may be used once, more than once, or not at all in each group.

Questions 55–57

    (A) Binary stars
    (B) Black holes
    (C) Dwarfs
    (D) Neutron stars
    (E) Variable stars

55. Stars which fluctuate in brightness

    55. Ⓐ Ⓑ Ⓒ Ⓓ Ⓔ

56. Stars appearing to lie in the same line of sight

    56. Ⓐ Ⓑ Ⓒ Ⓓ Ⓔ

57. Supernovae are their most spectacular examples

    57. Ⓐ Ⓑ Ⓒ Ⓓ Ⓔ

Questions 58–60

    (A) Avogadro's law
    (B) Boyle's law
    (C) Kinetic-molecular theory
    (D) First Law of Thermodynamics
    (E) Uncertainty Principle

58. Energy may neither be created or destroyed

    58. Ⓐ Ⓑ Ⓒ Ⓓ Ⓔ

59. The concept that we cannot know both the position and the energy of an electron at the same time

    59. Ⓐ Ⓑ Ⓒ Ⓓ Ⓔ

60. Assumes that gases consist of independently moving molecules

    60. Ⓐ Ⓑ Ⓒ Ⓓ Ⓔ

ANSWER KEY—SAMPLE EXAMINATION 2

Part I   Biological Sciences

1. A	11. D	21. B	31. B	41. A	51. B
2. B	12. A	22. E	32. C	42. C	52. D
3. B	13. D	23. D	33. A	43. B	53. C
4. E	14. D	24. C	34. B	44. D	54. A
5. D	15. D	25. D	35. E	45. C	55. C
6. E	16. E	26. B	36. D	46. D	56. E
7. D	17. A	27. C	37. D	47. B	57. D
8. A	18. B	28. C	38. E	48. B	58. D
9. B	19. E	29. E	39. A	49. A	59. B
10. E	20. B	30. A	40. E	50. E	60. C

Part II   Physical Sciences

1. B	11. D	21. B	31. B	41. A	51. B
2. C	12. B	22. E	32. D	42. D	52. A
3. C	13. E	23. B	33. B	43. B	53. E
4. A	14. B	24. B	34. A	44. D	54. D
5. B	15. C	25. E	35. B	45. C	55. E
6. A	16. B	26. A	36. E	46. C	56. A
7. B	17. A	27. C	37. D	47. E	57. E
8. D	18. B	28. D	38. B	48. B	58. D
9. B	19. B	29. E	39. B	49. E	59. E
10. D	20. A	30. C	40. A	50. A	60. C

SCORING CHART—SAMPLE EXAMINATION 2

After you have scored your Sample Examination 2, enter the results in the chart below; then transfer your Raw Score to the Progress Chart on page 14.

Total Test	Number Right	Number Wrong	Number Omitted	Raw Score
Part I: 60				
Part II: 60				
Total: 120				

ANSWER EXPLANATIONS—SAMPLE EXAMINATION 2

Part I Biological Sciences

1. A. Cellular membranes are selectively permeable since they permit different kinds of molecules to pass at varying rates or not at all and this permeability may constantly change.
2. B. According to biogenesis, all life comes from pre-existing life.
3. B. Physiology is the study of function.
4. E. A hypertonic solution has a higher osmotic pressure than the protoplasm of the cell in question and, therefore, water will diffuse out of the cell with a consequent decrease in turgor pressure.
5. D. Autotrophic organisms have the ability to synthesize their food from inorganic materials; heterotrophic organisms lack this ability.
6. E. Carotenoid pigments (carotenes) of yellow and leafy vegetables are precursors in vitamin A synthesis.
7. D. In cellular respiration organic substances are broken down to release their stored energy. This results in a decrease in dry weight.
8. A. All living cells carry on cellular respiration which is a process that provides energy for the cell's use.
9. B. Like auxins, gibberellins are growth-promoting substances found in plants which cause stem elongation, promote flowering and play a role in seed germination.
10. E. The total weight of protoplasm in a community is referred to as biomass.
11. D. Xylem is the principal water-conducting tissue in vascular plants.
12. A. A fruit is the matured ovary of a flower. A grain of wheat is a matured ovary of the wheat plant.
13. D. Any factor that affects the evaporation of water from an open container will have a similar effect on transpiration by plants. Transpiration is defined as the evaporation of water from the aerial parts of plants.
14. D. In meiosis, the chromosome number is reduced by one half. Actually, chromosomes exist in pairs and in meiosis, the members of each pair are segregated to the daughter cells resulting in the reduced number of chromosomes.
15. D. The fusion of two haploid (N) gametes in plants restores the diploid ($2N$) chromosome number.
16. E. During the initial stages of blood clotting, blood platelets, in the presence of the antihemophilic factor, release thromboplastin.
17. A. The right side of the heart is concerned with pumping blood to the lungs through the pulmonary artery.
18. B. Citrus fruits and other selected uncooked fruits and vegetables contain vitamin C (ascorbic acid).
19. E. The olfactory nerves connect the olfactory epithelium in the nose to the brain and function in the sense of smell.
20. B. Motor nerve impulses leave the central nervous system along ventral root axons, while sensory impulses move towards the central nervous system along dorsal roots.
21. B. The human visual system is binocular and stereoscopic, i.e., the images of the two eyes fit together to produce roundness and depth.
22. E. Parathormone is necessary for maintaining the proper calcium ion concentration in the blood. Calcium is involved in nerve impulse transmission, blood clotting, bone and teeth formation, and fertilization.
23. D. Synapsis is the pairing of the chromosomes during the prophase and metaphase of the first meiotic division. Since each chromosome consists of two daughter chromatids during this period, a tetrad of four chromatids exists and crossing-over occurs often.
24. C. Lamarck proposed the theory of the inheritance of acquired characteristics, frequently referred to as the theory of "use and disuse".

25. D. The mutation theory proposed by de Vries strengthened Darwin's theory of natural selection because it provided a good explanation for the source of inheritable variations, something Darwin was not able to do.

26. B. The Anopheles mosquito is the vector, or carrier, of the protozoan parasite that causes malaria.

27. C. Robert Hooke was the first to use the term "cell" in describing the microscopic units that comprise the tissues and organs of multicellular plants and animals.

28. C. Thales observed that water was the most abundant material on the earth and that both plants and animals require moisture.

29. E. William Harvey verified experimentally that the blood circulates. He described arteries and veins and predicted the existence of blood capillaries.

30. A. In the tropical rain forest with its excessive rains, the ground level environment is poor. Therefore, many forms of plants and animals are tree dwellers.

31. B. The neritic environment is identified as a region of shallow water adjoining the seacoast and above the continental shelf.

32. C. Ornithology is that branch of zoology concerned with the study of birds.

33. A. Homologous structures are similar from the standpoint of structure, embryonic development, and relationship and thus indicate common ancestry.

34. B. A saprophyte is an heterotrophic plant that obtains its nourishment from nonliving organic matter.

35. E. In the Pleistocene epoch climates cooled dramatically and there were two glacial periods during which the ice advanced twice.

36. D. Blood passes through the bicuspid valve from the left atrium into the left ventricle.

37. D. Seafood contains small quantities of iodine and this element is required for normal thyroid function and the production of thyroxin.

38. E. Protection from undulant fever (brucellosis) can be achieved if all milk is pasteurized and if diseased animals are removed from the herd.

39. A. The male parent produces A-type gametes only, while the female parent produces both A-type and a-type gametes in a 1:1 ratio. During random fertilization, zygotes will be $\frac{1}{2} AA$ and $\frac{1}{2} Aa$.

40. E. Enzymes are always specific with respect to the substrate (raw material) worked on.

41. A. Solid food particles such as bacterial cells may be brought into the cell by pinocytosis and released into the cytoplasm as a food vacuole.

42. C. Paper chromatography permits the separation of amino acids and relies upon the different solubilities of amino acids and on their differential absorption on paper.

43. B. Saprophytes are heterotrophic plants which obtain their nourishment from non-living organic matter.

44. D. Cellular respiration is the oxidation of carbohydrates which results in the release of energy. The loss of the carbohydrate results in a decrease in dry weight.

45. C. Based upon study of the graph, optimum light intensity for the ferns is 30–
46. D. 40%, since this represents the light intensity at which there is greatest absorption of CO_2. Similarly, ferns use more CO_2 at 10–50% of full sunlight than at 60–100%. On the basis of the information given, no other conclusions are valid.

47. B. The resting nerve fiber is polarized, having its outside positively charged and its inside negatively charged. A stimulus causes a wave of depolarization to pass along the fiber, from which it recovers in about 0.001 second.

48. B. The sympathetic nervous system prepares the body for emergencies. Among the changes it brings about are accelerated heart beat, secretion of adrenalin, and dilation of the bronchi.

49. A. In myopia, the eyeball is elongated to the extent that the image falls in front of the retina. This is nearsightedness.

50. E. Insulin is produced in the pancreas and is one of the glucose-regulating hormones.

51. B. Sex-linked inheritance in humans is concerned with the inheritance traits whose genes are located on the X chromosome. (The Y chromosome has only a few genes and for different traits.)

52. D. Mutations are the source of the inherited variations and support the theory of evolution by providing the variations needed for natural selection.

53. C. The specific nitrogenous bases of deoxyribonucleic acid are the amino acids adenine, cytosine, guanine, and thymine.

54. A. Sugar (glucose) metabolism is regulated by the hormone insulin, which is produced by the pancreas.

55. C. Michelangelo Buonarroti was a great student of human anatomy who performed many of his own dissections. Evidence of his vast knowledge of anatomy is found in his paintings.

56. E. Theophrastus' writings on plants have been preserved and represent the extent of the Greeks' knowledge of science. His greatest work was "Historia Plantarum".

57. D. Plants react to external stimuli by a series of growth responses called tropisms. A growth response in reaction to gravity is geotropism, in reaction to light is phototropism, etc.

58. D. Root hair cells increase the absorbing surface of roots and are the principal water-absorbing structures of typical land plant roots.

59. B. Photosynthesis is an energy-storing biochemical reaction in which the energy of sunlight is absorbed and stored in glucose molecules as the energy of chemical bonds.

60. C. Spore formation is a response of certain bacteria to an environment which becomes unfavorable. Bacterial spores have thick, resistant spore walls and the living bacterial cell within is in a state of suspended animation. When conditions become favorable, the bacterial cell converts back to its active way of life.

Part II Physical Sciences

1. B. When the atmosphere is saturated with water vapor, minute bits of particulate matter known as condensation nuclei serve as surfaces for the condensation of water vapor.

2. C. Kepler's greatest discovery was the fact that planetary orbits, including that of the earth, are ellipses.

3. C. Ancient civilizations, including the Babylonian, relied on astrology in predicting the future. Astrological events are tied to the behavior of the sun, moon and planets. It is, therefore, not surprising that early Babylonian writings included references to eclipses.

4. A. Since 1964, the international standard for measuring time has been the vibration rate of cesium atoms. According to this standard, one second of time is equal to 9,192,631,770 vibrations of cesium-133.

5. B. Stars that fluctuate in brightness are called variables. In one type, the eruptive variable, a sudden brightening occurs and this is called a nova.

6. A. The Foucault pendulum swings in a given plane, but due to the earth's rotation, the plane appears to change. In actuality, it is the earth's turning that makes it appear that the plane of the pendulum's swing is changing.

7. B. Glaciers cause the erosion, transportation and deposition of mineral matter and this mass of rock debris deposited as residual matter is referred to as a moraine.

8. D. A barrier reef is a long narrow coral embankment lying offshore.

9. B. Transmutation is the act of changing one element into another. It occurs naturally in the radioactive elements and may be induced in atom-smashing machines by bombarding elements with high speed protons and other sub-atomic particles.

10. D. Concave lenses cause parallel light rays to diverge or move apart.

11. D. Einstein once reasoned that light travels as streams of energy packets which today are called photons.

12. B. Those wavelengths of the visible spectrum which are reflected, blended and perceived by the eye as color.

13. E. Colloidal particles are extremely small, yet they are large enough to scatter light, rendering a cloudy or opaque effect. This is called the Tyndall effect.

14. B. A galvanometer is an instrument used to measure electric current.

15. C. The transistor is a small device requiring little power and which can switch electricity on and off. It may also be used to amplify weak electric currents.

16. B. The angle of incidence is the angle between the light ray and a line drawn perpendicular to the surface.

17. A. Wavelength is defined as the distance between the crests of two adjacent waves.

18. B. Radio waves and light waves are different parts of the electromagnetic spectrum differing primarily in that they have different wavelengths.

19. B. In respect to magnetic fields, lines of force are finite and constant for any condition or set of circumstances.

20. A. The ohm is the unit of electrical resistance in a material.

21. B. A transformer is a device that can be used to increase or decrease the voltage of alternating electrical currents.

22. E. A lever is a machine which can be used to gain force or distance, since the length of the force arm multiplied by the force used equals the length of the weight arm multiplied by the weight.

23. B. Heat energy is transferred within a medium by conduction, radiation and convection.

24. B. To convert miles to kilometers, multiply the number of miles by 1.61.

25. E. Inertia is the tendency of a body at rest to remain at rest or the tendency of a body in motion to remain in motion.

26. A. Energy may be defined as the capacity to perform work.

27. C. Protons are one of the fundamental types of particles found in the nuclei of atoms. Protons have positive charges.

28. D. The Doppler effect is the observed change in the frequency of light or sound waves when the source is moving in relation to the observer.

29. E. If a nuclear fission reaction is initiated by bombardment of atomic nuclei with neutrons and the subsequent fission results in the release of additional neutrons which, in turn, bombard additional atoms, a chain reaction is created.

30. C. Weight is defined as the force of gravity upon an object.

31. B. Potential energy is that energy possessed by an object because of its position.

32. D. Adhesion is the force of attraction between the molecules of two different substances which are in contact.

33. B. The heat of vaporization is the heat energy absorbed by the molecules of an evaporating liquid. The result is cooling or a decrease in temperature.

34. A. The specific gravity of a liquid is the ratio of the density of the liquid to the density of water where both densities are obtained in air.

35. B. Acids are well known for their ability to corrode metals. When an acid solution vigorously attacks a metal, hydrogen gas is evolved.

36. E. The halogen family of chemical elements contain fluorine, chlorine, bromine, iodine and astatine.

37. D. In photosynthesis chlorophyll has a dual role, that of absorbing selective wavelengths of radiant energy and as a catalyst by participating in certain chemical reactions which lead to the production of sugar.

38. B. Proteins are polymers consisting of long chains of amino acids, each unit of which is built from an amino group and a carboxyl group.

39. B. In physical changes, the component building blocks of matter, atoms, do not undergo change. They merely combine and separate in different combinations and arrangements.

40. A. In any chemical reaction, the total molecular weight of the reactants always equals the total molecular weight of the products.

41. A. Both thermoplastic and thermosetting plastics made of synthetic resins are used to manufacture thousands of items because of their strength, resistance and durability in various situations.

42. D. Scholasticism was a philosophical movement during the Middle Ages attempting to combine the teachings of Aristotle and St. Augustine to fixed religious dogma.

43. B. Organic compounds always contain carbon, hydrogen and oxygen. Proteins, in addition, have nitrogen and usually sulfur and potassium.

44. D. By definition, oxidation is the loss of electrons by atoms, ions or molecules.

45. C. By placing a naturally radioactive substance in a block of lead, a thin beam comes out of the lead through the open hole. When this emitted beam is placed in an electric field, it is split into alpha, beta and gamma particles.

46. C. Dissociation is the breaking up of a chemical substance into its ionic constituents. In this instance NaCl dissociates to form Na^+ ions and Cl^- ions when placed in water.

47. E. Ionic behavior responds to the concept that like (electrical) charges repel each other and unlike charges attract each other.

48. B. Metals possessing high specific resistance to the conduction of electric current heat-up since it takes more energy to push current through wires having high resistance and this energy is converted to heat.

49. E. A laser is a device that can focus a beam of light to concentrate a great amount of electromagnetic energy on a very small area.

50. A. Ultraviolet light is more energetic than visual light and can excite electrons in many kinds of molecules causing chemical reactions to occur.

51. B. Molecules of an electrolyte dissociate when it conducts an electric current and simultaneously the newly formed ions migrate with anions moving towards the anode and cations moving towards the cathode.

52. A. When electromagnetic waves strike a surface, they are said to be reflected, and careful measurements will reveal that the angle of incidence is equal to the angle of reflection.

53. E. Whenever an electric current flows, a magnetic field is generated around the wire conducting the current.

54. D. The magnetic field generated in a coil of wire when an electric current passes through it behaves in a manner similar to a bar magnet.

55. E. Stars that fluctuate in brightness are known as variable stars.

56. A. Stars which move about each other and which are attracted by their mutual gravitation are called binary stars.

57. E. When a star increases its brightness several million times it is called a supernova.

58. D. According to the First Law of Thermodynamics, energy may be transformed from one type to another, but may neither be created nor destroyed.

59. E. In attempts to locate an electron, the electron is displaced by the energy transmitted to it by the photon that strikes it. The electron will then be in a different location. Thus, the energy and original position of the electron remain unknown, a phenomenon called the uncertainty principle.

60. C. A theory concerning the nature of gases that assumes that gases consist of independently moving molecules is named the kinetic-molecular theory.

SAMPLE EXAMINATION 3

Part I   Biological Sciences

Number of Questions: 60
Time: 45 minutes   **Directions:**   Each of the questions or incomplete statements below is followed by five suggested answers or completions. Select the one that is best in each case.

1. An organism which has a right and left side exhibits
   (A) asymmetry   (B) radial symmetry
   (C) spherical symmetry   (D) bilateral symmetry
   (E) universal symmetry

   1. Ⓐ Ⓑ Ⓒ Ⓓ Ⓔ

2. Which of the following occurs when water evaporates?
   (A) osmosis   (B) simple diffusion   (C) capillarity
   (D) mass movement   (E) imbibition

   2. Ⓐ Ⓑ Ⓒ Ⓓ Ⓔ

3. A scientist specializing in the study of cell structure and function is called a
   (A) cytologist   (B) physiologist   (C) taxonomist
   (D) parasitologist   (E) morphologist

   3. Ⓐ Ⓑ Ⓒ Ⓓ Ⓔ

4. Amino acids contain an amino group ($-NH_2$) and a carboxyl group
   (A) CH_3 (B) H_3C (C) HOH   (D) $(-COOH)$
   (E) CH_2

   4. Ⓐ Ⓑ Ⓒ Ⓓ Ⓔ

5. When a living cell is placed in a fluid and there is no net movement of water molecules into or out of the cell, the fluid is said to be
   (A) hypotonic   (B) dialyzed   (C) diffused   (D) isotonic
   (E) hypertonic

   5. Ⓐ Ⓑ Ⓒ Ⓓ Ⓔ

6. Autotrophic organisms
   (A) are saprophytic
   (B) are able to synthesize their own food
   (C) always live on decaying organic matter
   (D) exist as parasites
   (E) ingest complex organic foods

   6. Ⓐ Ⓑ Ⓒ Ⓓ Ⓔ

7. Organisms which utilize solid food materials after eating them are referred to as
   (A) chemosynthetic   (B) holozoic   (C) photosynthetic
   (D) autophobic   (E) autotrophic

   7. Ⓐ Ⓑ Ⓒ Ⓓ Ⓔ

8. In 1630, van Helmont concluded that green plants
   (A) absorb large quantities of minerals from the soil
   (B) absorb mainly water from the soil
   (C) synthesize their organic materials by photosynthesis
   (D) release energy in respiration
   (E) use carbon dioxide as the chief source of plant materials

   8. Ⓐ Ⓑ Ⓒ Ⓓ Ⓔ

9. Photosynthesis
   (A) consumes oxygen and organic materials such as glucose
   (B) occurs only in cells containing chlorophyll
   (C) gives off carbon dioxide and water
   (D) releases energy
   (E) occurs in all living cells

9.   Ⓐ Ⓑ Ⓒ Ⓓ Ⓔ

10. Cellular respiration
    (A) stores energy
    (B) increases dry weight
    (C) occurs only in plant cells containing chlorophyll
    (D) produces oxygen and organic compounds
    (E) releases energy

10. Ⓐ Ⓑ Ⓒ Ⓓ Ⓔ

11. Flowering in plants is influenced by the ratio of daylight hours to hours of darkness, a phenomenon called
    (A) phototropism   (B) photophosphorylation   (C) synergism
    (D) parthenocarpy   (E) photoperiodism

11. Ⓐ Ⓑ Ⓒ Ⓓ Ⓔ

12. One primary function of the phloem in vascular plants is the
    (A) reduction of transpiration   (B) conduction of food materials
    (C) support of foliage   (D) absorption of water
    (E) conduction of water

12. Ⓐ Ⓑ Ⓒ Ⓓ Ⓔ

13. The physical processes responsible for transpiration are
    (A) evaporation and capillarity   (B) adhesion and cohesion
    (C) diffusion and evaporation   (D) capillarity and cohesion
    (E) capillarity and diffusion

13. Ⓐ Ⓑ Ⓒ Ⓓ Ⓔ

14. Photoperiodism appears to be influenced by
    (A) gibberellin   (B) phytochrome   (C) kinetin
    (D) synergistic responses   (E) indoleacetic acid

14. Ⓐ Ⓑ Ⓒ Ⓓ Ⓔ

15. The best adjective to describe the occurrence of bacteria is
    (A) terrestrial   (B) aquatic   (C) aerial   (D) universal
    (E) glacial

15. Ⓐ Ⓑ Ⓒ Ⓓ Ⓔ

16. During mitosis,
    (A) the chromosome number remains the same
    (B) the chromosome number becomes polyploid
    (C) the chromosome number is reduced
    (D) either eggs or sperm are produced
    (E) one primary and (usually) two secondary polar bodies are formed

16. Ⓐ Ⓑ Ⓒ Ⓓ Ⓔ

17. Double fertilization
    (A) occurs when two sperm cells unite with one egg
    (B) occurs when asexual spores fuse in pairs
    (C) is found in all plants
    (D) is found only in flowering plants
    (E) occurs when two eggs fuse with one sperm

17. Ⓐ Ⓑ Ⓒ Ⓓ Ⓔ

18. A deficiency of vitamin A may cause

    (A) scurvy   (B) beriberi   (C) night blindness

    (D) hemorrhages following surgery   (E) loss of appetite

18. Ⓐ Ⓑ Ⓒ Ⓓ Ⓔ

19. To overcome a deficiency in vitamin C, you would follow a diet rich in

    (A) red meats   (B) whole grain cereals   (C) animal products

    (D) fresh fruits and vegetables   (E) eggs and dairy products

19. Ⓐ Ⓑ Ⓒ Ⓓ Ⓔ

20. Muscles used in swallowing are innervated by the

    (A) hypoglossal nerve   (B) vagus nerve   (C) abducens nerve

    (D) trochlear nerve   (E) glossopharyngeal nerve

20. Ⓐ Ⓑ Ⓒ Ⓓ Ⓔ

21. Insulin

    (A) constricts blood vessels   (B) increases blood sugar

    (C) stimulates lactation   (D) regulates calcium metabolism

    (E) decreases blood sugar

21. Ⓐ Ⓑ Ⓒ Ⓓ Ⓔ

22. As a result of mitosis,

    (A) each daughter cell receives a randomly selected set of chromosomes

    (B) each daughter cell receives the same kind and number of chromosomes

    (C) four daughter cells are produced

    (D) the chromosome number of the daughter cells is reduced

    (E) the chromosome number remains the same; the number of genes is reduced

22. Ⓐ Ⓑ Ⓒ Ⓓ Ⓔ

23. Experimental evidence obtained in studying crossing-over phenomena indicates that

    (A) the genes of a particular linkage group may lie on two or more chromosomes

    (B) linkage groups are not affected by translocation

    (C) genes are arranged in linear order along chromosomes

    (D) crossing over has no genetic significance

    (E) sex linkage involves the total compliment of chromosomes

23. Ⓐ Ⓑ Ⓒ Ⓓ Ⓔ

24. The proof that the earth is much older than a few thousand years and, therefore, is sufficiently aged to provide time for evolution was demonstrated by

    (A) Lucretius (B) Lyell (C) Thales (D) Wallace (E) Anaximander

24. Ⓐ Ⓑ Ⓒ Ⓓ Ⓔ

25. The "operon" model of Jacob and Monod suggests that

    (A) insulin is not produced continuously

    (B) nerves are in a state of continual "excitement"

    (C) hormone production is continuous

    (D) enzyme production is continuous

    (E) genes may be turned on or off

25. Ⓐ Ⓑ Ⓒ Ⓓ Ⓔ

26. An example of a disease transmitted by an arthropod vector is

    (A) typhoid fever   (B) tuberculosis   (C) polio

    (D) sleeping sickness   (E) smallpox

26. Ⓐ Ⓑ Ⓒ Ⓓ Ⓔ

27. In the ancient world of classical Greek scholars, we find such objective thinkers as Anaximander and Anaximenes who
    (A) advocate the scientific method
    (B) attempt to explain the physical and living world
    (C) develop medicine and surgery
    (D) produce an encyclopedia
    (E) predict the existence of atoms

27. Ⓐ Ⓑ Ⓒ Ⓓ Ⓔ

28. During the ancient days of Babylonia, the Code of Hammurabi was established for
    (A) philosophers and teachers   (B) agriculturalists
    (C) physicians   (D) soldiers   (E) scientists

28. Ⓐ Ⓑ Ⓒ Ⓓ Ⓔ

29. You would expect to observe maple trees and black bears in
    (A) a tropical rain forest   (B) the glasslands
    (C) an alpine tundra   (D) a deciduous forest
    (E) a coniferous forest

29. Ⓐ Ⓑ Ⓒ Ⓓ Ⓔ

30. Bottom-dwelling marine organisms which live along shores in the inter-tidal areas are referred to as inhabiting
    (A) the bathyal zone   (B) a littoral zone
    (C) the brackish zone   (D) the neritic zone
    (E) the abyssal zone

30. Ⓐ Ⓑ Ⓒ Ⓓ Ⓔ

31. A biologist specializing in the study of snakes is called
    (A) an herpetologist   (B) an ornithologist
    (C) an entomologist   (D) an ichthyologist
    (E) an helminthologist

31. Ⓐ Ⓑ Ⓒ Ⓓ Ⓔ

32. Interrelationships between organisms are referred to as mutualism when
    (A) one organism benefits and the other is not harmed
    (B) territories are defended
    (C) both organisms are benefited
    (D) mates are defended
    (E) one organism benefits at the expense of the other

32. Ⓐ Ⓑ Ⓒ Ⓓ Ⓔ

33. The Archeozoic era is best characterized as an
    (A) age of mammals   (B) ancient age of unicellular life
    (C) age of early land plants   (D) age of dinosaurs
    (E) age of primitive fishes

33. Ⓐ Ⓑ Ⓒ Ⓓ Ⓔ

34. In the human circulatory system, blood from the body first enters the heart chamber called the
    (A) left ventricle   (B) left atrium   (C) sinus venosus
    (D) right ventricle   (E) right atrium

34. Ⓐ Ⓑ Ⓒ Ⓓ Ⓔ

35. Blood enters the aorta of the human circulatory system from the
    (A) right ventricle   (B) superior vena cava   (C) left ventricle
    (D) inferior vena cava   (E) left atrium

35. Ⓐ Ⓑ Ⓒ Ⓓ Ⓔ

36. After drinking contaminated water, you might develop symptoms of
    (A) malaria   (B) typhoid fever   (C) trichinosis
    (D) yellow fever   (E) schistosomiasis

36. Ⓐ Ⓑ Ⓒ Ⓓ Ⓔ

37. A virus-caused disease which may be prevented by inoculation with   37. Ⓐ Ⓑ Ⓒ Ⓓ Ⓔ
    a vaccine is
    (A) tularemia   (B) typhoid fever   (C) scarlet fever
    (D) septicemia   (E) smallpox

38. An energy-storing process occurring in certain kinds of living cells is   38. Ⓐ Ⓑ Ⓒ Ⓓ Ⓔ
    (A) respiration   (B) phosphorylation   (C) oxidation
    (D) photosynthesis   (E) reduction

39. The shrinkage of the cytoplasm from the cell wall in plant cells sub-   39. Ⓐ Ⓑ Ⓒ Ⓓ Ⓔ
    jected to a hypertonic solution is called
    (A) plasmolysis   (B) turgidity   (C) diffusion
    (D) secretion   (E) osmosis

40. Stringiness in certain otherwise edible plant materials is caused by the 40. Ⓐ Ⓑ Ⓒ Ⓓ Ⓔ
    (A) pith   (B) cortex   (C) vascular bundles   (D) endodermis
    (E) pericycle

41. Over periods of time, ecosystems undergo patterns of development and   41. Ⓐ Ⓑ Ⓒ Ⓓ Ⓔ
    change, a process called
    (A) mutation   (B) succession   (C) riffling
    (D) inversion   (E) foliation

42. Algae are of greatest importance for their role in   42. Ⓐ Ⓑ Ⓒ Ⓓ Ⓔ
    (A) feeding mankind directly   (B) producing oil deposits
    (C) food chains   (D) soil building   (E) producing oxygen

43. Gamma globulin   43. Ⓐ Ⓑ Ⓒ Ⓓ Ⓔ
    (A) contains antibodies   (B) is involved with blood clotting
    (C) moves by ameboid movement   (L) carries on phagocytosis
    (E) functions as an anticoagulant

44. An example of an antigen-antibody reaction is   44. Ⓐ Ⓑ Ⓒ Ⓓ Ⓔ
    (A) blood clotting   (B) anemia   (C) phagocytosis
    (D) the antihemophilic factor   (E) the Rh factor

45. Gregor Mendel   45. Ⓐ Ⓑ Ⓒ Ⓓ Ⓔ
    (A) discovered chromosomes and studied the details of mitosis
    (B) worked with linkage groups and developed chromosome maps
    (C) studied sex-linkage in garden peas
    (D) demonstrated that inheritance is governed by laws
    (E) was the first to apply the mutation theory of natural selection

46. In the prophase of the first meiotic division   46. Ⓐ Ⓑ Ⓒ Ⓓ Ⓔ
    (A) chromatids do not become visible
    (B) homologous chromosomes pair in synapsis
    (C) the centromeres have already divided
    (D) chromosomes remain long and twisted
    (E) the chromosome number is haploid

47. Among his many contributions, Aristotle included a philosophical   47. Ⓐ Ⓑ Ⓒ Ⓓ Ⓔ
    treatise concerning
    (A) evolution   (B) abiogenesis   (C) recapitulation
    (D) genetics   (E) relativity

48. On the basis of evolution and population genetics, each population is characterized by
    (A) polyploidy   (B) orthogenesis   (C) a gene pool
    (D) balanced polymorphism   (E) translocation

49. Abrupt and unexpected changes in inheritance patterns which seem to have no intermediate forms are called
    (A) chromosonal aberrations   (B) variations   (C) deletions
    (D) mutations   (E) hybridizations

50. Francesco Redi appears to have been the first to challange and disprove the concept of
    (A) epigenesis   (B) biogenesis   (C) spontaneous generation
    (D) preformation   (E) pangenesis

51. Binomial nomenclature was the basis of the system of classification proposed by
    (A) Darwin   (B) Cuvier   (C) Linnaeus   (D) Lamarck
    (E) Dioscorides

52. The Roman author of *On Anatomical Preparations*, a recognized medical text for over 1400 years, was
    (A) Celsus   (B) Lucretius   (C) Dioscorides   (D) Pliny
    (E) Galen

53. Proprioceptive senses are concerned with
    (A) the repetitive motion that leads to motion sickness
    (B) complete relaxation of skeletal muscle
    (C) informing the central nervous system of what muscles are doing
    (D) maintaining rythmic and uniform heartbeat   (E) awareness and the thought process

54. Fungi are of importance to humans for all but one of the following
    (A) they are important decomposers   (B) they cause many plant diseases
    (C) they may cause diseases of man and domestic animals
    (D) they are important sources of carbohydrates   (E) they produce a variety of antibiotics

Directions: Each group of questions below consists of five lettered choices followed by a list of numbered phrases or sentences. For each numbered phrase or sentence select the one choice that is most closely related to it. Each choice may be used once, more than once, or not at all in each group.

Questions 55–57

   (A) Amylase
   (B) Lipase
   (C) Pepsin
   (D) Ribonuclease
   (E) Sucrase

55. Breaks bonds between specific amino acids of protein chains

56. Hydrolyzes proteins producing peptid molecules

57. Involved in the breakdown of disaccharides

Questions 58–60

    (A) Adrenalin
    (B) Auxin
    (C) Colchicine
    (D) Thyrotropin
    (E) Vassopressin

58. Stimulates secretion of thyroid hormones   **58.** Ⓐ Ⓑ Ⓒ Ⓓ Ⓔ

59. causes an increase in blood pressure   **59.** Ⓐ Ⓑ Ⓒ Ⓓ Ⓔ

60. Its hyperactivity causes irritability   **60.** Ⓐ Ⓑ Ⓒ Ⓓ Ⓔ

Part II: Physical Sciences

Number of Questions: 60
Time: 45 minutes

Directions: Each of the questions or incomplete statements below is followed by five suggested answers or completions. Select the one that is best in each case.

1. Orbital velocities of earth satellites are dependent upon the   **1.** Ⓐ Ⓑ Ⓒ Ⓓ Ⓔ
    (A) weight of the satellite   (B) direction of orbit
    (C) distance from the earth   (D) inertia of the satellite
    (E) moon's gravity

2. If you were standing on the equator, as a result of the earth's rota-   **2.** Ⓐ Ⓑ Ⓒ Ⓓ Ⓔ
    tion you would be
    (A) moving westward at about 1,000 mph
    (B) moving eastward at about 1,000 mph
    (C) moving westward at less than 700 mph
    (D) moving eastward at less than 700 mph
    (E) stationary

3. Star temperatures are reliably indicated by color. Which of the fol-   **3.** Ⓐ Ⓑ Ⓒ Ⓓ Ⓔ
    lowing would be the coolest?
    (A) A red star   (B) An orange star   (C) A yellow star
    (D) A white star   (E) A blue-white star

4. An equinox occurs when the   **4.** Ⓐ Ⓑ Ⓒ Ⓓ Ⓔ
    (A) sun is highest in the sky   (B) sun crosses the equator
    (C) sun is lowest in the sky   (D) earth and sun are in line
    (E) earth is central in the solar system

5. One of the small number of very large, reddish stars with a diameter   **5.** Ⓐ Ⓑ Ⓒ Ⓓ Ⓔ
    of more than 100 times that of the sun would be a
    (A) giant star   (B) supergiant star   (C) binary star
    (D) nova   (E) supernova

6. During a lunar eclipse,   **6.** Ⓐ Ⓑ Ⓒ Ⓓ Ⓔ
    (A) the earth's shadow is cast on the moon
    (B) the earth's shadow falls on the sun

(C) the moon's shadow falls on the sun
(D) the moon comes between the earth and the sun
(E) the moon's shadow is cast on the earth

7. Wind circulation around a low pressure area is counterclockwise in the northern hemisphere due to
   (A) the revolution of the earth around the sun
   (B) the spheroidal shape of the earth
   (C) the rotation of the earth
   (D) the tidal effects caused by lunar gravity
   (E) the tilting of the earth's axis

7. Ⓐ Ⓑ Ⓒ Ⓓ Ⓔ

8. Igneous or sedimentary rocks which are changed to new forms as the result of interaction with their environment are called
   (A) pyroclastic rocks   (B) metamorphic rocks
   (C) batholithic rocks   (D) concordant batholiths
   (E) xenolithic rocks

8. Ⓐ Ⓑ Ⓒ Ⓓ Ⓔ

9. Rocks formed by the cooling and solidifying of molten materials are classed as
   (A) igneous rocks   (B) metamorphic rocks
   (C) sedimentary rocks   (D) monomineralic rocks
   (E) organic limestone

9. Ⓐ Ⓑ Ⓒ Ⓓ Ⓔ

10. Water vapor in the atmosphere
    (A) is the source of all condensation and precipitation
    (B) may vary in concentration from 0.01 to over 12 per cent
    (C) has no effect on air temperature
    (D) has no effect on body temperature
    (E) neither reflects nor scatters solar radiation

10. Ⓐ Ⓑ Ⓒ Ⓓ Ⓔ

11. Study of the moon samples brought back to earth by returning Apollo astronauts reveals that
    (A) organic matter is abundant
    (B) moon rocks have mineral compositions similar to igneous rocks on earth
    (C) the age of the moon cannot be more than 1.6 million years
    (D) the moon is 913 million years old
    (E) moon rocks have mineral compositions which are totally different from that of any rocks on earth

11. Ⓐ Ⓑ Ⓒ Ⓓ Ⓔ

12. Einstein's theory of relativity resulted in the thought that mass
    (A) is a distinct and completely independent entity
    (B) remains indestructible
    (C) is another form of energy
    (D) is constant throughout the universe
    (E) is measurable only according to the force necessary to accelerate it

12. Ⓐ Ⓑ Ⓒ Ⓓ Ⓔ

13. Parallel light rays are made convergent by
    (A) monochromatic light   (B) an achromatic lens
    (C) a convex lens   (D) a concave lens   (E) a plano-convex lens

13. Ⓐ Ⓑ Ⓒ Ⓓ Ⓔ

14. The amount of energy in sound waves is known as its   14. Ⓐ Ⓑ Ⓒ Ⓓ Ⓔ
 (A) loudness
 (B) tempo
 (C) rhythm
 (D) amplitude
 (E) intensity

15. That property of water which permits a needle to float and not sink is   15. Ⓐ Ⓑ Ⓒ Ⓓ Ⓔ
 (A) viscosity
 (B) fluidity
 (C) diffusion
 (D) surface tension
 (E) sublimation

16. Polarized light is   16. Ⓐ Ⓑ Ⓒ Ⓓ Ⓔ
 (A) light without shadows   (B) incident light
 (C) vibrating in one plane only   (D) light of low intensity
 (E) light from a "Polaroid" source

17. Early in the era of atomic physics, radioactivity was discovered by   17. Ⓐ Ⓑ Ⓒ Ⓓ Ⓔ
 (A) Bohr   (B) Faraday   (C) Fermi
 (D) Becquerel   (E) Planck

18. When light passes from one medium to another, its direction may be   18. Ⓐ Ⓑ Ⓒ Ⓓ Ⓔ
 changed, a phenomenon called
 (A) diffusion   (B) diffraction   (C) refraction
 (D) reflection   (E) absorption

19. Air temperature is directly affected by the absorption of large   19. Ⓐ Ⓑ Ⓒ Ⓓ Ⓔ
 amounts of solar and terrestrial radiation by atmospheric
 (A) dust particles   (B) nitrogen   (C) water vapor
 (D) oxygen   (E) nitrogen and oxygen

20. According to the Bernoullian Principle, as velocity increases   20. Ⓐ Ⓑ Ⓒ Ⓓ Ⓔ
 (A) the pressure increases proportionally   (B) mass increases
 (C) mass decreases   (D) thrust remains constant
 (E) the pressure decreases

21. Interference may result in   21. Ⓐ Ⓑ Ⓒ Ⓓ Ⓔ
 (A) sound waves reinforcing each other
 (B) sound waves compressing each other
 (C) the bending of sound waves
 (D) a decrease in amplitude
 (E) an increase in amplitude

22. In reference to electrical circuitry, the volt represents   22. Ⓐ Ⓑ Ⓒ Ⓓ Ⓔ
 (A) a measure of potential
 (B) the flow of coulombs
 (C) a force between two electrical fields
 (D) the unit of current
 (E) the unit of resistance

23. A lever with a great mechanical advantage for gaining force would   23. Ⓐ Ⓑ Ⓒ Ⓓ Ⓔ
 have a

(A) terminal fulcrum
(B) long force arm and short weight arm
(C) long force arm and long weight arm
(D) short force arm and short weight arm
(E) short force arm and long weight arm

24. Heat transfer is accomplished by convection, radiation, and   24. Ⓐ Ⓑ Ⓒ Ⓓ Ⓔ
    (A) oxidation   (B) reduction   (C) vaporization
    (D) expansion   (E) conduction

25. If you run 10 kilometers, how many miles do you run?   25. Ⓐ Ⓑ Ⓒ Ⓓ Ⓔ
    (A) ⅔   (B) 5   (C) 6.2   (D) 12.5   (E) 16.1

26. That property of matter which tends to maintain the uniform move-   26. Ⓐ Ⓑ Ⓒ Ⓓ Ⓔ
    ment of a moving body is called
    (A) force   (B) acceleration   (C) velocity   (D) deceleration
    (E) inertia

27. That which tends to change the state of motion of a body is called   27. Ⓐ Ⓑ Ⓒ Ⓓ Ⓔ
    (A) acceleration   (B) equilibrium   (C) velocity
    (D) mass   (E) force

28. An alarming feature of nuclear reactions compared to conventional   28. Ⓐ Ⓑ Ⓒ Ⓓ Ⓔ
    chemical explosions is their emission of
    (A) X-rays   (B) fissionable plutonium   (C) gamma rays
    (D) electrons   (E) protons

29. Alternating current is primarily identified by   29. Ⓐ Ⓑ Ⓒ Ⓓ Ⓔ
    (A) reversal of direction of flow at regular intervals
    (B) reversal of direction of flow at random or chance intervals
    (C) a change of magnetic flux
    (D) regular fluctuation
    (E) its electromagnetic induction

30. The physical damage in a nuclear explosion is caused by   30. Ⓐ Ⓑ Ⓒ Ⓓ Ⓔ
    (A) heat and pressure   (B) X-rays   (C) gamma radiation
    (D) intense light   (E) radioactive fallout

31. In relation to mass and weight,   31. Ⓐ Ⓑ Ⓒ Ⓓ Ⓔ
    (A) weight varies from place to place in the universe
    (B) mass varies from place to place in the universe
    (C) both weight and mass vary from place to place in the universe
    (D) both weight and mass remain constant throughout the universe
    (E) weight and mass are affected only by speed

32. In order to accomplish 600 foot-pounds of vertical work, a 20-pound   32. Ⓐ Ⓑ Ⓒ Ⓓ Ⓔ
    object must be lifted how many feet?
    (A) 3   (B) 12   (C) 30   (D) 300   (E) 600

33. The spreading out of molecules free to do so is called   33. Ⓐ Ⓑ Ⓒ Ⓓ Ⓔ
    (A) transpiration   (B) transportation   (C) diffusion
    (D) capillarity   (E) osmosis

34. The energy exerted by a golf club as it strikes the ball is
    (A) mass energy   (B) inertia   (C) transferred energy
    (D) kinetic energy   (E) potential energy

    34. Ⓐ Ⓑ Ⓒ Ⓓ Ⓔ

35. The unit of electricity upon which our electric bills are based is a(n)
    (A) ampere   (B) volt   (C) millivolt   (D) ohm
    (E) kilowatt hour

    35. Ⓐ Ⓑ Ⓒ Ⓓ Ⓔ

36. The name of the process which utilizes an electric current to decompose chemical compounds is
    (A) electrophoresis   (B) electrolysis   (C) electromagnetism
    (D) electrotherapy   (E) electrodynamics

    36. Ⓐ Ⓑ Ⓒ Ⓓ Ⓔ

37. The "venturi effect" in a carburetor is an application of
    (A) Avagadro's law   (B) Archimedes' principle
    (C) Bernoulli's principle   (D) Pascal's law
    (E) Boyle's law

    37. Ⓐ Ⓑ Ⓒ Ⓓ Ⓔ

38. When the positive ions from a base combine with the negative ions from an acid, the resulting substance is called
    (A) a buffer   (B) a salt   (C) a mole   (D) an alkane
    (E) an ester

    38. Ⓐ Ⓑ Ⓒ Ⓓ Ⓔ

39. Forces which hold chemically united atoms together are called
    (A) ions   (B) chemical bonds   (C) magnetism
    (D) atomic numbers   (E) isotopes

    39. Ⓐ Ⓑ Ⓒ Ⓓ Ⓔ

40. Chemical reactions in which oxygen combines with other substances are called
    (A) enzymatic reactions   (B) catalytic reactions
    (C) dephlogistication reactions   (D) reduction reactions
    (E) oxidation reactions

    40. Ⓐ Ⓑ Ⓒ Ⓓ Ⓔ

41. The connecting substance between the amino acids in all proteins is called
    (A) a polymer   (B) a carboxyl group   (C) a fatty acid
    (D) the peptide linkage   (E) an alkyl group

    41. Ⓐ Ⓑ Ⓒ Ⓓ Ⓔ

42. A basic characteristic common to all chemical changes is that
    (A) the reactants are stable and persistent
    (B) energy is neither released nor absorbed
    (C) the initial reactants disappear
    (D) the properties of the products are identical to those of the reactants
    (E) total mass either increases or decreases

    42. Ⓐ Ⓑ Ⓒ Ⓓ Ⓔ

43. In a fundamental sense, chemical reactions are concerned with
    (A) periodicity   (B) potential energy   (C) nuclear energy
    (D) interatomic bonds   (E) ionic conductivity

    43. Ⓐ Ⓑ Ⓒ Ⓓ Ⓔ

44. The major scientific philosopher of the middle ages was Roger Bacon who
    (A) stressed abstract reasoning
    (B) accepted reasoning and logic alone as justification for science

    44. Ⓐ Ⓑ Ⓒ Ⓓ Ⓔ

(C) advocated deductive instead of inductive reasoning
(D) invented the calendar
(E) advanced mathematics and the experimental method

45. The chemical reaction resulting when an acid solution is combined with a basic solution is called

45. Ⓐ Ⓑ Ⓒ Ⓓ Ⓔ

(A) transformation   (B) conservation   (C) neutralization
(D) reversal   (E) phlogiston

46. The pitch of vibrating musical strings is
(A) directly proportional to the rate of vibration
(B) directly proportional to the length
(C) inversely proportional to the tension
(D) inversely proportional to the rate of vibration
(E) directly proportional to linear density

46. Ⓐ Ⓑ Ⓒ Ⓓ Ⓔ

47. Distinction between colloids, solutions and suspensions is based primarily on

47. Ⓐ Ⓑ Ⓒ Ⓓ Ⓔ

(A) fluidity   (B) saturation   (C) emulsification
(D) particle size   (E) solubility

48. An induction coil will
(A) change alternating to direct current
(B) change direct to alternating current
(C) increase the voltage of an alternating current
(D) increase the voltage of a direct current
(E) decrease the voltage of an alternating current

48. Ⓐ Ⓑ Ⓒ Ⓓ Ⓔ

49. According to the law of conservation of energy, in all energy transformations

49. Ⓐ Ⓑ Ⓒ Ⓓ Ⓔ

(A) the latent beat of vaporization is lost energy
(B) the latent beat of fusion is lost energy
(C) heat energy flows from lower to higher temperature
(D) there is no gain or loss of energy
(E) a certain amount of energy is destroyed

50. In 420 B.C., Democritus introduced the "one-element" theory of matter which proposed that the indestructable particles of which everything is made should be called

50. Ⓐ Ⓑ Ⓒ Ⓓ Ⓔ

(A) ions   (B) atoms   (C) electrons
(D) protons   (E) molecules

51. The problem of transmitting high-frequency television signals over great distances has been solved by the

51. Ⓐ Ⓑ Ⓒ Ⓓ Ⓔ

(A) coaxial cable   (B) kinescope tube   (C) tuning coil
(D) phototube   (E) iconoscope tube

Illustrated above are two falling balls. Ball A is also moving horizontally. The balls are of equal weight.

52. The balls strike the bottom simultaneously because   52. Ⓐ Ⓑ Ⓒ Ⓓ Ⓔ
    (A) ball A's speed increases to make-up the difference
    (B) the horizontal motion of ball A increases the force of gravity
    (C) gravity alone is acting on ball B
    (D) horizontal motion does not affect the speed of the fall of ball A
    (E) the horizontal motion of ball A decreases the force of gravity

53. The velocity of a falling object at the end of the second second of fall would   53. Ⓐ Ⓑ Ⓒ Ⓓ Ⓔ
    be
    (A) about 16 feet per second
    (B) about 32 feet per second
    (C) about 48 feet per second
    (D) about 64 feet per second
    (E) about 1036 feet per second

54. Ion rockets are the theoretical future choice for insterstellar space   54. Ⓐ Ⓑ Ⓒ Ⓓ Ⓔ
    travel because
    (A) they are more economical
    (B) they are simpler to operate
    (C) their fuels add less mass to the rocket
    (D) traditional chemical fuels produce insufficient thrust
    (E) traditional chemical fuels produce excessive thrust

55. Water rises inside the small-diametered glass   55. Ⓐ Ⓑ Ⓒ Ⓓ Ⓔ
    tube due to forces called
    (A) osmosis   (B) gravity
    (C) diffusion   (D) capillarity
    (E) suction

56. The equation $Fe + CuSO_4 \rightarrow Cu + FeSO_4$ 56. Ⓐ Ⓑ Ⓒ Ⓓ Ⓔ
    (A) is unbalanced   (B) is unstable   (C) yields an acid
    (D) represents a replacement reaction   (E) represents an explosion

57. The physical phenomenon called surface tension is really 57. Ⓐ Ⓑ Ⓒ Ⓓ Ⓔ
    (A) the sum total of the repulsive forces acting between the mole-
        cules of two different substances
    (B) an illusion
    (C) the result of membrane formation
    (D) the sum total of the attractive forces between the molecules of
        a substance
    (E) capillarity

58. Which of the following is not consistent with Dalton's atomic theory? 58. Ⓐ Ⓑ Ⓒ Ⓓ Ⓔ
    (A) All matter consists of minute particles called atoms.
    (B) Atoms of a given element vary in both weight and electrical charge.
    (C) Atoms are neither created nor destroyed in chemical reactions.
    (D) Atoms of different elements are of different weights.
    (E) Typically, atoms combine in small numbers to form chemical com-
        pounds.

59. In forming chemical compounds, 59. Ⓐ Ⓑ Ⓒ Ⓓ Ⓔ
    (A) all electrons may be involved
    (B) the electrons involved may be from any orbit
    (C) the electrons involved are in the outermost orbit only
    (D) electrons from inner shells are exceedingly active
    (E) electrons may not be shared

60. The two atoms of a sodium chloride (NaCl) molecule are held together by 60. Ⓐ Ⓑ Ⓒ Ⓓ Ⓔ
    (A) dissociation   (B) an increase in positive valence
    (C) the electrical attraction of ions of opposite charges
    (D) a decrease in positive valence   (E) entropy

ANSWER KEY—SAMPLE EXAMINATION 3

Part I   Biological Sciences

1. D	7. B	13. C	19. D	25. E	31. A	37. E	43. A	49. D	55. C
2. B	8. B	14. B	20. E	26. D	32. C	38. D	44. E	50. C	56. C
3. A	9. B	15. D	21. E	27. B	33. B	39. A	45. D	51. C	57. E
4. D	10. E	16. A	22. B	28. C	34. E	40. C	46. B	52. E	58. D
5. D	11. E	17. D	23. C	29. D	35. C	41. B	47. A	53. C	59. D
6. B	12. B	18. C	24. B	30. B	36. B	42. C	48. C	54. D	60. A

Part II   Physical Sciences

1. C	7. C	13. C	19. C	25. C	31. A	37. C	43. D	49. D	55. D
2. B	8. B	14. E	20. E	26. E	32. C	38. B	44. E	50. B	56. D
3. A	9. A	15. D	21. A	27. E	33. C	39. B	45. C	51. A	57. D
4. B	10. A	16. C	22. A	28. C	34. D	40. E	46. A	52. D	58. B
5. B	11. B	17. D	23. B	29. A	35. E	41. D	47. D	53. D	59. C
6. A	12. C	18. C	24. E	30. A	36. B	42. C	48. D	54. C	60. C

SCORING CHART—SAMPLE EXAMINATION 3

After you have score your Sample Examination 3, enter the results in the chart below; then transfer your Raw Score to the Progress Chart on page 14.

Total Test	Number Right	Number Wrong	Number Omitted	Raw Score
Part I: 60				
Part II: 60				
Total: 120				

ANSWER EXPLANATIONS—SAMPLE EXAMINATION 3

Part I   Biological Sciences

1. D. An organism that exhibits bilateral symmetry has a right and left side and a front and back.
2. B. All molecules tend to remain in continuous motion. When water evaporates, some of its faster-moving molecules break through the surface layer of molecules and escape into the air. Thus, the basic activity of evaporation is simple diffusion.
3. A. Cytology is the study of cell structure and function.
4. D. Proteins are polymers consisting of long chains of amino acids, each of which contains an amino group and a carboxyl (—COOH) group.
5. D. In an isotonic solution, the osmotic pressure is equal to that of the solution being compared.
6. B. Autotrophic organisms are capable of synthesizing their own food from inorganic substances.
7. B. Holozoic organisms ingest and utilize solid particles of food.
8. B. In experiments with plants growing in containers, van Helmont concluded that plants absorb mainly water from the soil. Increases in dry weight, therefore, were attributed to the production of foods by photosynthesis.
9. B. The presence of chlorophyll is a requirement for photosynthesis since it acts both to absorb radiant energy and as a catalyst for certain of the photosynthetic reactions.
10. E. Cellular respiration is a complex biochemical reaction in which foods (usually glucose) are broken down and their stored energy released.
11. E. Flower initiation appears to be controlled, at least in part, by the number of daylight hours to which plants are exposed. Long-day plants require more than 14 hours of daylight to flower, while short-day plants require less. Still other plants are indeterminate insofar as light requirements are concerned.
12. B. The basic function of phloem tissue in plants is the conduction of food materials.
13. C. Transpiration is defined as the evaporation of water from the aerial parts of plants. Evaporation is basically a simple diffusion phenomenon.
14. B. Photoperiodism in plants is only partially understood, but a pigment called phytochrome seems to be related to the responses of plants to light and darkness.
15. D. Bacteria are universal. They are found in the soil, within and on living organisms, from the bottom of the deepest ocean trenches to the tops of snow-covered mountains, to the polar ice caps, in hot springs, etc.

16. A. Mitosis is both a qualitative and quantitative division of chromatin materials and the resulting chromosome number remains unchanged.

17. D. In double fertilization, typically one sperm nucleus fuses with the egg nucleus and the second sperm nucleus fuses with the endosperm nucleus. This occurs only in flowering plants.

18. C. Vitamin A is provided to an individual if the diet contains milk, butter, fish liver oils, carrots and other vegetables. A deficiency of vitamin A may result in night blindness.

19. D. Vitamin C is provided if the diet contains citrus fruits, tomatoes and green peppers.

20. E. The glossopharyngeal nerves make up the ninth pair of cranial nerves; they innervate mainly the pharynx, posterior tongue, and the parotid gland.

21. E. Insulin is an endocrine secretion, or hormone, which controls glucose metabolism. Its deficiency results in the disease diabetes mellitus.

22. B. As a result of mitosis, chromatin materials are qualitatively distributed to the two daughter cells, each of which receives a duplicate of every chromosome.

23. C. Studies involving crossing-over phenomena support the concept that genes are arranged in linear order along chromosomes.

24. B. Lyell's writings support the doctrine of uniformitarianism, the concept that the events in the geologic history of the earth were the product of the same natural forces that are active today—erosion, sedimentation, etc. Lyell's efforts established the foundation for Darwin's theory of Natural Selection.

25. E. The Jacob-Monod hypothesis suggests that the interrelated actions of inducer, repressor, and corepressor molecules control the function of genes. When an inducer molecule is present, the repressor is unable to attach itself, the gene functions, and synthesis takes place. When a corepressor molecule is present, the operon is shut down. In short, it appears that gene action may be turned on or off.

26. D. Sleeping sickness is caused by a trypanosome that is transmitted by the bite of the tsetse fly, an arthropod. The tsetse fly is, therefore, the vector of sleeping sickness.

27. B. Anaximander and Anaximenes attempted to explain the physical phenomena of the universe, including the atmosphere, water, and spontaneous generation of life.

28. C. The Code of Hammurabi was a code for physicians and specified fees for medical practice as well as punishments for malpractice. The principle of "an eye for an eye" was the basis for the code.

29. D. Deciduous trees, including maple, beech, oak and hickory, and such dominant animals as black bears are the primary organisms in the deciduous or temperate forest.

30. B. Littoral species are those living along shorelines between high and low tide marks.

31. A. By definition, herpetology is the study of reptiles and amphibians.

32. C. Mutualism is an interrelationship between the individuals of two different species in which both are benefited.

33. B. The Archeozoic era is the age during which it is presumed life emerged on earth. It is thought of as the time when only primitive, unicellular life existed.

34. E. Blood returning to the heart after circulating around the body enters the heart chamber called the right atrium.

35. C. The left ventricle of the human heart pumps blood into the aorta, which distributes it to arteries that carry it to all parts of the body.

36. B. Typhoid fever is basically a disease of the digestive tract. Sewage-contaminated drinking water is presumed to contain the typhoid bacillus.

37. E. A vaccine is an attenuated form of the causative agent of disease, which, while being incapable of causing the disease, does retain its ability to cause the body to produce antibodies.

38. D. Photosynthesis results in the energy of sunlight being absorbed, converted and stored as the energy of chemical bonds in glucose molecules.

39. A. Plasmolysis is that condition of a plant cell whereby the cytoplasm shrinks away from the cell wall due to a loss of water by the cell. The basic cause of plasmolysis is the fact that a cell is immersed in a hypertonic solution which causes water to diffuse out of the cell.

40. C. Stringiness in certain otherwise edible plant material—green beans, for example—is due to the development of fiber cells and the thickening of cell walls by cells of the xylem and phloem which make up the vascular bundles.

41. B. Ecological succession is the succession of both plants and animal species in a given region which is brought about by species-induced environmental changes.

42. C. Algae are of importance to humans and other parts of the biotic world in many ways, chief among them their role in food chains.

43. A. Gamma globulin is a fraction of the globulin of blood serum with which antibodies are associated.

44. E. The Rh factor is an agglutinogen found in the blood of about 85 percent of Caucasians. The Rh factor is an antigen, stimulating the body to produce antibodies against the Rh factor. It is a concern in both blood transfusions and during pregnancy.

45. D. Gregor Mendel is recognized as the "father of genetics" because his research was the first to demonstrate that inheritance is governed by laws.

46. B. Synapsis is a stage in the first meiotic division in which the homologous chromosomes of each pair come to lie side by side. Since each chromosome at this point consists of two chromatids, it is common to refer to the paired, homologous chromosomes as a tetrad of chromatids.

47. A. While Aristotle recognized no formal system of classification for animals or plants, he did conceive an evolutionary concept to explain their origin.

48. C. A gene pool is the total number of genes in a population.

49. D. A mutation is an unexpected and abrupt heritable change in the offspring of an individual resulting from an alteration of a gene or chromosome or a change in chromosome number.

50. C. Redi was one of the first scientists to question the spontaneous origin of living things. He was able to demonstrate conclusively that flies do not develop spontaneously from putrefying meat, but rather that they come from other flies by means of their eggs.

51. C. Carl von Linnaeus introduced the concept of binomial nomenclature, i.e., the system of naming organisms by giving each species a binomial name, the genus name followed by the species name.

52. E. Galen wrote over 200 treatises dealing with medicine, philosophy, mathematics, grammar, and law, but his greatest was "On Anatomical Preparations".

53. C. Proprioceptive senses inform us about the position of our bodies in relation to the environment that surrounds us by telling us what our muscles are doing.

54. D. Fungi (mushrooms) are of little nutritional value although they may supply certain minerals.

55. C. ⎫ In the digestion of proteins, pepsin breaks amino acid bonds in protein
56. C. ⎬ chains. Pepsin also hydrolyzes protein.

57. E. In the digestion of carbohydrates, the enzyme sucrase is involved with disaccharide breakdown and digestion.

58. D. Thyrotropin is a hormone secreted by the anterior lobe of the pituitary that controls the secretion of thyroxin.

59. A. Vasopressin is a hormone that causes the muscular walls of the arteries and arterioles to contract. This decreases the diameter of these blood vessels and causes the blood pressure to increase.

60. A. Adrenalin, or epinephrin, is produced by the adrenal medulla. In situations where there is hypersecretion, irritability may result.

Part II Physical Sciences

1. **C.** Orbital velocity for a spacecraft is dependent upon the spacecraft's distance from the earth since the orbital velocity must overcome the earth's gravity.

2. **B.** The earth's rotation is in an easterly direction. Since the earth is approximately 25,000 miles in circumference and since it completes one rotation per 24 hour period, a person standing on the equator is moving eastward at about 1,000 mph.

3. **A.** The colors of stars range from red, the coolest, through orange, yellow, and white to blue, the hottest.

4. **B.** An equinox occurs at a time when the vertical rays of the sun strike the equator.

5. **B.** Betelgeuse, a bright red supergiant star, has a radius about 800 times that of the sun. If this star were the center of the solar system, it would reach beyond the orbit of Mars.

6. **A.** A lunar eclipse occurs when the moon crosses through the earth's shadow.

7. **C.** Due to the rotation of the earth, the Coriolis force causes winds in the northern hemisphere to be deflected to the right or to rotate clockwise. Winds in the southern hemisphere are deflected to the right also, and therefore, rotate counterclockwise.

8. **B.** Rocks which have been changed in either physical structure or in chemical composition while in a solid state as a result of the action of heat, pressure, shearing stress, or the infusion of elements, all at great depths, are named metamorphic rocks.

9. **A.** Rocks solidified from a high-temperature molten state or by the cooling of magma are named igneous rock.

10. **A.** Whether moisture in the atmosphere condenses on soil or plants directly or whether atmospheric moisture forms droplets while still in the atmosphere as a result of rapid condensation and coalescence which then falls as rain, it is the atmospheric moisture which is the source of the water vapor.

11. **B.** Chemical analysis of moon rocks revealed that their mineral composition is similar to that of igneous rocks on earth.

12. **C.** According to the theory of relativity, mass and energy are different forms of the same phenomenon. When hydrogen is converted to helium in a nuclear fusion reaction, about 1 percent of the mass of the hydrogen is converted to energy.

13. **C.** When parallel light rays pass through a convex lens, they bend inward so that they converge at a point on the other side.

14. **E.** The intensity of sound is the amount of energy in the sound waves.

15. **D.** Surface tension is that property of a liquid caused by cohesive forces attracting adjacent molecules of the liquid to each other.

16. **C.** Polarized light consists of light waves having a simple orderly arrangement that vibrates in one plane or direction only.

17. **D.** In 1896, the French physicist Becquerel discovered that uranium emits energy in the form of radiation and this emission has come to be called radioactivity.

18. **C.** Refraction is the bending of a wave when it moves from one medium to another and strikes the second at an angle—for example, the apparent bending of a partially immersed boat oar.

19. **C.** Water vapor in the atmosphere plays a major role in absorbing heat energy. When water vapor is lacking, air warms rapidly and a high daily temperature results.

20. **E.** According to the Bernoullian Principle, as a fluid passes through a constriction in a pipe, it speeds up and its pressure decreases.

21. **A.** If two waves reach a point in space simultaneously, they combine in a process called interference. If the two waves are of the same frequency and

shape, and if they meet crest to crest and trough to trough, they will combine and their amplitude will be increased.

22. A. The energy in an electrical circuit is proportional to the electrical potential (volts) × the amount of charge (coulombs).

23. B. Levers work according to the formula: effort times the length of the effort arm (distance from the fulcrum) equals the weight times the length of the weight arm (distance from the fulcrum). A longer effort or force arm or a shorter weight arm will increase mechanical advantage.

24. E. Heat is transferred from one body to another by conduction, convection and radiation.

25. C. One kilometer equals .62 mile. Ten miles equals 6.2 kilometers.

26. E. According to the concept of inertia, a moving body tends to remain in motion and a resting body tends to remain at rest.

27. E. Force is defined as any influence that causes a body to accelerate.

28. C. The alarming feature in connection with gamma rays is their high energies, high frequencies and short wavelengths.

29. A. Alternating current is an electric current that oscillates in a wire (reverses its direction of flow at regular intervals).

30. A. The physical damage caused by a nuclear explosion is similar to that caused by any other explosion and is caused by heat and pressure.

31. A. Mass remains the same throughout the universe, but weight varies from place to place in the universe since it is dependent on gravity.

32. C. Work is defined as the force exerted on a body multiplied by the distance the body is moved.

33. C. Diffusion is the tendency of the molecules of a substance to spread out throughout all available space and this is accomplished because all molecules tend to remain in a state of constant motion due to their own inherent energies.

34. D. Kinetic energy is the energy possessed by a moving object.

35. E. The kilowatt hour is the unit of electricity upon which our electric bills are based.

36. B. Electrolysis is a process whereby an electric current, driven by an external electrical source, brings about chemical change.

37. C. According to Bernoulli's Principle, as the speed of a fluid passing through a constriction increases, the pressure decreases. In a carburetor, this results in the metering of gasoline to the engine.

38. B. In a general sense, a salt is produced when an acid and a base react.

39. B. Chemical bonds are linkages that hold atoms together to form molecules; for example, in a covalent bond, two atoms share electrons.

40. E. Oxidation reactions are chemical reactions in which oxygen combines with other substances. In a more general sense, oxidation is the loss of electrons.

41. D. The peptide linkage is one in which the amino group of one amino acid molecule is united with the carboxyl group of other amino acid molecules.

42. C. In chemical reactions, the initial reactants disappear or are changed to become parts of the products.

43. D. Chemical reactions are concerned with the bonds between atoms in chemical compounds.

44. E. Roger Bacon's major interests were in the physical sciences and he is best remembered for his contributions to mathematics and the development of the scientific method.

45. C. When a solution of an acid is mixed with a solution of a base, neutralization occurs and the end products of the reaction have none of the acid or base properties.

46. A. Pitch is measured by the rate an object vibrates. Frequency is the number of vibrations of the object per second.

47. D. When finely divided mud particles are dispersed in water, they eventually settle out because they are much larger than molecules. The dispersed particles of a solution are molecules—sugar dissolved in water, for example. Between these two is the situation in which the dispersed particles are

larger than molecules but not so large as to settle out. The latter is the realm of the colloid.

48. B. An induction coil is a coil of wire used to produce alternating current of high voltage by the rapid interruption of a direct current.

49. D. The law of conservation of energy holds that energy may neither be created nor destroyed. Energy may be lost through friction, heat, escape, etc.

50. B. The greatest contribution of Democritus was his atomic theory, which held that the universe is made of atoms and that all physical changes are due to the union and separation of atoms.

51. A. The coaxial cable is a special type of long distance telephone cable used to transmit telephone calls and television programs over long distances.

52. D. Falling bodies are not affected by horizontal motion when their fall is caused by gravity.

53. D. A falling body accelerates at a rate expressed as 32.16 feet per second per second.

54. C. The percentage of total weight of a space vehicle that is occupied by fuel is a major problem. Fuels for ion rockets add much less weight to the rocket.

55. D. The tendency of liquids to rise in small tubes is a phenomenon called capillarity. It is dependent upon the surface tension of the liquid and the diameter of the tube.

56. D. In a replacement type chemical reaction, one element is exchanged or substituted for another.

57. D. Liquids tend to occupy the smallest volume possible by reducing their surface areas to a minimum, the result of the intermolecular forces that exist between the molecules of the liquid at its surface.

58. B. The atoms of an element do not vary in weight or electrical charge.

59. C. The electrons involved in the bonding of the atoms of a chemical compound are those in the outer orbit only.

60. C. The ionic bond is a chemical bond formed by the attraction between oppositely charged ions. In this example, there is attraction between the positively charged sodium (Na^+) ion and negatively charged Cl^- ion.

PART FIVE

THE SOCIAL SCIENCES– HISTORY EXAMINATION

Trial Test

15

Take the trial Social Sciences examination in this chapter to learn about the examination and determine how you would do on an actual test. Then review those topics you are weak in and prepare to take the sample examinations given later in this part of the book.

Part I

Number of Questions: 63

Time: 45 minutes

Directions: Each of the questions or incomplete statements below is followed by five suggested answers or completions. Select the one that is best in each case.

1. The distribution of members in the House of Representatives by states is determined on the basis of
   (A) population
   (B) population, but subject to a definite maximum number of members from any one state
   (C) the state as a unit regardless of population
   (D) the number of qualified voters of the state
   (E) the number of people who actually vote

   1. Ⓐ Ⓑ Ⓒ Ⓓ Ⓔ

2. In the 19th century, United States Senators were elected by
   (A) popular election
   (B) the state legislatures
   (C) the electoral college
   (D) state conventions
   (E) officials selected from each county in the state

   2. Ⓐ Ⓑ Ⓒ Ⓓ Ⓔ

3. "Boswash" is a term which is sometimes applied to the
   (A) Irish washerwomen in Boston
   (B) effort to clean up Boston
   (C) "bosh" that goes on in Washington
   (D) WASPs of Boston
   (E) continuous urban area between Boston and Washington

   3. Ⓐ Ⓑ Ⓒ Ⓓ Ⓔ

4. Ten men produce 1,000 bushels of tomatoes on ten acres. If ten additional men are hired, the production on the same acreage rises to 1,700 bushels. This phenomenon relates to which one of the following economic concepts?
   (A) Law of diminishing marginal utility
   (B) Supply and demand
   (C) Marginal propensity to consume
   (D) Gross national product
   (E) Law of diminishing returns

   4. Ⓐ Ⓑ Ⓒ Ⓓ Ⓔ

5. To the Marxist, profits are
   - (A) essential to the health of any economy
   - (B) payments to the businessman for his labor
   - (C) transitory and characteristic of only one state of history
   - (D) the key to a rising standard of living
   - (E) constantly increasing in a capitalist society

6. "Most of population-theory teachers are Protestant parsons . . . — Parson Wallace, Parson Townsend, Parson Malthus and his pupil, the arch-Parson Thomas Chalmers, to say nothing of the lesser Reverend scribblers in this line." This quotation is from
   (A) Ricardo   (B) Marshall   (C) Keynes   (D) Marx   (E) J. S. Mill

7. Apes and other primates cannot be taught to use highly complex language because
   - (A) they are without the biological apparatus of speech
   - (B) they are without the ability to learn from communications directed toward them
   - (C) they have little mental ability to store or transmit highly abstract ideas
   - (D) all of the above
   - (E) none of the above

8. The culture concept in social science implies that
   - (A) the biological evolution of man is the most important reason for his advances in the past few centuries
   - (B) the moral aspects of a thinking, cultured society and people must enlighten its institutions
   - (C) the most important lessons for a man are to be found in the cultured societies of Europe
   - (D) the reason for differences between our own and other societies is that we, as members of our society, learn different things from those which others learn
   - (E) art and music are more important than technology in building cultivated tastes

9. Which of the following doctrines has had the greatest influence on 20th-century American education?
   (A) Catholicism   (B) Puritanism   (C) Socialism
   (D) Pragmatism   (E) Transcendentalism

10. The census which is commonly considered to indicate the closing of the American frontier was taken in
    (A) 1870   (B) 1890   (C) 1910   (D) 1920   (E) 1950

11. Which of the following American political figures was unpopular with the Democratic followers of Jefferson?
    (A) Hamilton Fish   (B) John Jay   (C) John Quincy Adams
    (D) James Madison   (E) Patrick Henry

12. Which countries became unified in the 19th century?
    (A) France and Great Britain   (B) France and Spain
    (C) Czechoslovakia and Finland   (D) Germany and Portugal
    (E) Italy and Germany

5. [A] [B] [C] [D] [E]
6. [A] [B] [C] [D] [E]
7. [A] [B] [C] [D] [E]
8. [A] [B] [C] [D] [E]
9. [A] [B] [C] [D] [E]
10. [A] [B] [C] [D] [E]
11. [A] [B] [C] [D] [E]
12. [A] [B] [C] [D] [E]

13. Germany violated the neutrality of which of the following nations in both the First and Second World Wars?
(A) Netherlands   (B) Norway   (C) Switzerland
(D) Belgium   (E) France

13. Ⓐ Ⓑ Ⓒ Ⓓ Ⓔ

14. The United States Senate does not have the power to
(A) approve treaties
(B) approve appointment of federal judges
(C) impeach public officials
(D) approve appointment of Cabinet members
(E) pass legislation already approved by the House of Representatives

14. Ⓐ Ⓑ Ⓒ Ⓓ Ⓔ

15. A man who lived in a certain country from 1860 to 1960 would have lived through absolute monarchy, constitutional monarchy, imperialist expansion, military dictatorship, foreign occupation, extraordinary economic development, and a democratic political order. The above description best fits which country?
(A) Thailand   (B) China   (C) Japan   (D) Egypt   (E) Brazil

15. Ⓐ Ⓑ Ⓒ Ⓓ Ⓔ

16. Which of the following professional associations carries the most power and control over training, certification, and entry?
(A) American Association of University Professors
(B) American Medical Association
(C) American Association of American Geographers
(D) National Education Association
(E) American Historical Association

16. Ⓐ Ⓑ Ⓒ Ⓓ Ⓔ

17. A key article of the Leninist communist creed is that, under capitalism,
(A) depressions are inevitable
(B) war over foreign markets is inevitable
(C) class warfare is inevitable
(D) none of the above   (E) all of the above

17. Ⓐ Ⓑ Ⓒ Ⓓ Ⓔ

18. A correlation coefficient of minus 0.82 between two phenomena is derived. The relationship between the two phenomena would best be characterized by which of the following?
(A) One thing caused the other.
(B) A third thing caused the two things.
(C) One thing is negative, causing a positive reaction in the other.
(D) It is likely that some relationship exists between the two things.
(E) The two things tend to vary in the same direction.

18. Ⓐ Ⓑ Ⓒ Ⓓ Ⓔ

19. According to decisions handed down by the Supreme Court prior to 1972, one of the following was illegal. Which one?
(A) Refusing for religious reasons to salute the American flag
(B) Using public funds to pay bus transportation for students attending parochial schools
(C) Using public funds to purchase secular textbooks for students attending parochial schools
(D) Sending children to parochial schools
(E) Allowing clergymen to give religious indoctrination in public schools

19. Ⓐ Ⓑ Ⓒ Ⓓ Ⓔ

20. The legal basis for the separation of church and state in the U.S. is found in the   20. Ⓐ Ⓑ Ⓒ Ⓓ Ⓔ
    (A) Sixteenth Amendment
    (B) Declaration of Independence
    (C) Fifth Amendment
    (D) First Amendment
    (E) Tenth Amendment

21. The American economy is   21. Ⓐ Ⓑ Ⓒ Ⓓ Ⓔ
    (A) pure laissez-faire
    (B) more planned than laissez-faire
    (C) more laissez-faire than planned
    (D) centrally directed as under socialism
    (E) dominated by traditional custom

22. Marx spoke of "internal contradictions" within the capitalistic order. Which of the following did he have in mind?   22. Ⓐ Ⓑ Ⓒ Ⓓ Ⓔ
    (A) Elections   (B) Depression   (C) Population growth
    (D) High wages   (E) High profits

23. "The community is a fictitious body . . . the sum of the several members who compose it." This individualist viewpoint is the basic premise of   23. Ⓐ Ⓑ Ⓒ Ⓓ Ⓔ
    (A) François Quesnay   (B) Thomas Aquinas
    (C) William Petty   (D) Jeremy Bentham   (E) August Comte

24. More characteristic of class than caste is   24. Ⓐ Ⓑ Ⓒ Ⓓ Ⓔ
    (A) vertical mobility   (B) endogamy   (C) distinguishing attire
    (D) occupational prohibitions   (E) prestige differences

25. Lenin found it necessary to add a corollary to Karl Marx's analysis. This corollary stated that the hour of revolt had been prolonged by   25. Ⓐ Ⓑ Ⓒ Ⓓ Ⓔ
    (A) extending suffrage to women and to others
    (B) the growth of labor unions
    (C) colonial imperialism
    (D) the false benefits of capitalism
    (E) the graduated income tax and other methods of shifting the tax burden to the rich

26. As people become better off economically, on which of the following do they spend a smaller proportion of their income?   26. Ⓐ Ⓑ Ⓒ Ⓓ Ⓔ
    (A) Books   (B) Entertainment   (C) Transportation
    (D) Food   (E) Sports

27. Concerning money, it is false to say that money   27. Ⓐ Ⓑ Ⓒ Ⓓ Ⓔ
    (A) serves as a standard of deferred payments
    (B) is a medium of exchange
    (C) may have intrinsic value, that is, be useful in itself
    (D) is the difference between a price economy and a planned economy
    (E) is a measure of value

28. Which of the following is not a part of our national wealth?   28. Ⓐ Ⓑ Ⓒ Ⓓ Ⓔ
    (A) Factories   (B) Stored grain   (C) Farm land
    (D) Corporate stock   (E) Post offices

29. According to Karl Marx, "surplus value" arose from the fact that
    (A) capitalists sold goods for a profit
    (B) labor, unlike other commodities, created more value than it cost to reproduce itself
    (C) capitalism was an expanding economy and always needed new markets
    (D) each of the four factors of production were entitled to a share of the whole economic product
    (E) the state connived with capitalists to consciously rob the workers

29. Ⓐ Ⓑ Ⓒ Ⓓ Ⓔ

30. In the case of Prohibition (of the production and distribution of alcoholic beverages), which of the following most effectively prevented enforcement?
    (A) Injunctions
    (B) Judicial review
    (C) Popular nullification
    (D) The refusal of federal officials to enforce the law
    (E) Presidential resistance to enforcement

30. Ⓐ Ⓑ Ⓒ Ⓓ Ⓔ

31. Carthage was established as a colony of the
    (A) Greeks
    (B) Phoenicians
    (C) Romans
    (D) Hittites
    (E) Egyptians

31. Ⓐ Ⓑ Ⓒ Ⓓ Ⓔ

32. In the United States at present, the kinship system
    (A) really does not exist
    (B) is formal, highly elaborated, and closely relevant to all the experiences of the family members
    (C) appears only in times of family crises
    (D) puts strong emphasis on the immediate conjugal family
    (E) emphasizes the role of the patriarch

32. Ⓐ Ⓑ Ⓒ Ⓓ Ⓔ

33. Max Weber pointed out that the bureaucratization of society is usually accompanied by
    (A) raising specific educational standards for office holders
    (B) the decline of the role of "experts"
    (C) greater publicity given to public affairs
    (D) a decline in the role played by intellectuals in public affairs
    (E) a more humane order brought about by efficiency

33. Ⓐ Ⓑ Ⓒ Ⓓ Ⓔ

34. Which of the following developments of the first half of the 20th century seem most clearly to have been forecast in 19th-century Marxian writings?
    (A) The increasing number of persons in advanced societies who consider themselves proletarians
    (B) The spread of ownership through the device of corporate stock
    (C) The spread of Communism among non-industrialized peoples
    (D) The rise of wage standards
    (E) Crises of trade and unemployment

34. Ⓐ Ⓑ Ⓒ Ⓓ Ⓔ

35. The American Federation of Labor, in its first fifty years, was characterized by
    (A) shunning political involvement
    (B) a conservative orientation
    (C) cooperation with the existing economic system
    (D) a "no pie in the sky" ideological orientation
    (E) all of the above

36. The Kentucky and Virginia Resolutions of 1798-9 were invoked in order to prove the
    (A) right of social revolution
    (B) right of a state to secede when it feels wronged
    (C) right of a state to be the judge of constitutionality
    (D) right to refuse the authority of the Bank of the United States
    (E) right to treat Indians with a strong hand

37. If you were to visit the sites of ancient Mesopotamian culture, to which modern country would you go?
    (A) Egypt   (B) Turkey   (C) Pakistan   (D) Iraq
    (E) Libya

38. Which of the following ideas would Edmund Burke have rejected?
    (A) The specific is to be preferred over the abstract.
    (B) Society can be safely based on reason alone.
    (C) Lawless action is generally destructive.
    (D) It is often an easy jump from democracy to tyranny.
    (E) Society and government are best when the role of human wisdom and human custom are given due respect.

39. Socrates was condemned to death because he
    (A) taught young men to question accepted ideas and practices
    (B) was the teacher of Alexander
    (C) accepted a bribe from the Persians
    (D) denied that there were any fixed standards of good
    (E) taught the Greeks that they were inferior

40. The Edict of Nantes
    (A) outlawed Roman Catholicism in France
    (B) outlawed Protestantism in France
    (C) permitted a limited toleration to Protestants in France
    (D) established freedom of religion in France
    (E) established the doctrine of the trinity in France

41. The patriotic Greek of the 5th century B.C. was primarily loyal to
    (A) the Greek nation
    (B) his emperor
    (C) his religion, which was thought to have no connection with political affairs
    (D) his city
    (E) his race

42. Which of the following writers hoped that education would engender prudence, late marriage, and smaller families?
(A) Adam Smith   (B) Karl Marx   (C) Thomas Malthus
(D) Walt Rostow   (E) Ragnar Nurske

42. Ⓐ Ⓑ Ⓒ Ⓓ Ⓔ

43. The chief object of Spartan education was to develop
(A) a cultured and artistic citizenry
(B) good soldiers who were obedient citizens
(C) an able body of tradesmen
(D) a select group of priests
(E) expert technicians

43. Ⓐ Ⓑ Ⓒ Ⓓ Ⓔ

44. "People in the same trade seldom meet together but the conversation ends in a conspiracy against the public, or in some diversion to raise prices." This would most likely be found in the writings of
(A) John Law   (B) Adam Smith   (C) William Petty
(D) Thomas Mun   (E) Emile Durkheim

44. Ⓐ Ⓑ Ⓒ Ⓓ Ⓔ

45. "The interest of the landlord is always opposed to the interest of every other class in the community. His situation is never so prosperous, as when food is scarce and dear; whereas, all other persons are greatly benefited by procuring cheap food." You would expect to read this in the writings of
(A) Adam Smith   (B) François Quesnay   (C) David Ricardo
(D) Thomas Jefferson   (E) John Locke

45. Ⓐ Ⓑ Ⓒ Ⓓ Ⓔ

46. Which idea is not included in the theory of Marx?
(A) Man's religious, ethical, political, and social ideas are determined by economic forces.
(B) Capitalism cannot reform itself.
(C) As capitalism matures, much of its greater material wealth will accrue to the workingman.
(D) Human history is the chronology of the inevitable conflict between two opposing economic classes.
(E) Capitalists, if they wished, still could not reform conditions in their own particular industries.

46. Ⓐ Ⓑ Ⓒ Ⓓ Ⓔ

47. Physicist is to engineer as sociologist is to
(A) psychologist   (B) theologian   (C) social reformer
(D) historian   (E) social philosopher

47. Ⓐ Ⓑ Ⓒ Ⓓ Ⓔ

48. The belief that one's patterns of living are superior to those of other groups is termed
(A) relativism   (B) ostracism   (C) ethnocentrism
(D) all of the above   (E) none of the above

48. Ⓐ Ⓑ Ⓒ Ⓓ Ⓔ

49. As a culture becomes more complex it tends to have within it fewer
(A) alternatives
(B) specialities
(C) universals
(D) exigencies
(E) institutions

49. Ⓐ Ⓑ Ⓒ Ⓓ Ⓔ

50. Malthus tried to prove one of the following arguments. Which one?   50. Ⓐ Ⓑ Ⓒ Ⓓ Ⓔ
   (A) Developments in technology are unlikely to relieve, permanently, the pressure of population on the means of subsistence.
   (B) Poverty is primarily the result of employers' greed.
   (C) Population pressure forces national governments into colonization and imperialistic schemes, which is only proper.
   (D) Intelligent government action, such as subsidies to mothers and taxes on bachelors, can alleviate the effects of the laws of population.
   (E) Poverty is particular to capitalism.

51. Which is the most nearly accurate? The 1978 population of the world   51. Ⓐ Ⓑ Ⓒ Ⓓ Ⓔ
   (in billions) was
   (A) 1.5   (B) 2.0   (C) 4.2   (D) 4.8   (E) 6.2

52. Emile Durkheim described a type of suicide resulting from excessive   52. Ⓐ Ⓑ Ⓒ Ⓓ Ⓔ
   social integration and called it
   (A) egoistic (B) alienative (C) altruistic (D) anomic (E) rational

53. The development of agriculture was important in that it enabled man   53. Ⓐ Ⓑ Ⓒ Ⓓ Ⓔ
   to
   (A) settle in one place
   (B) produce more food than required by those producing it
   (C) specialize
   (D) increase his numbers by reducing malnutrition and famine
   (E) all of these

54. Which of the following usually includes all the others?   54. Ⓐ Ⓑ Ⓒ Ⓓ Ⓔ
   (A) Institutions   (B) Folkways   (C) Laws
   (D) Social symbols   (E) Mores

55. The German Imperial constitution of 1871   55. Ⓐ Ⓑ Ⓒ Ⓓ Ⓔ
   (A) gave Prussia a preferred position in the German union
   (B) was a generally democratic instrument
   (C) declared the equality of all member states
   (D) declared the ruler of Austria to be Emperor
   (E) was similar to the British constitution

56. William I (the Conqueror) of England was a   56. Ⓐ Ⓑ Ⓒ Ⓓ Ⓔ
   (A) Roman   (B) Saxon   (C) Dane   (D) Norman   (E) Vandal

57. In 1635, France intervened in the war in Germany in order to   57. Ⓐ Ⓑ Ⓒ Ⓓ Ⓔ
   (A) help defeat the Protestants
   (B) prevent a Swedish victory
   (C) prevent a Hapsburg victory
   (D) win the Holy Roman crown for the King of France
   (E) weaken the power of the English on the continent

58. The period of the "Roman peace" *(Pax Romana)* was   58. Ⓐ Ⓑ Ⓒ Ⓓ Ⓔ
   (A) during the first two hundred years of the Empire
   (B) between the reign of Diocletian and 476 A.D.
   (C) between the last Punic War and the reign of Diocletian
   (D) between the foundation of the Republic and the first Punic War
   (E) during the reign of Charlemagne

59. The Punic Wars were between Rome and
   (A) Macedonia
   (B) Carthage
   (C) Persia
   (D) Athens
   (E) Israel

59. Ⓐ Ⓑ Ⓒ Ⓓ Ⓔ

60. The Caliphs were
   (A) the political successors of Mohammed
   (B) prophets of Islam through whom further revelation of God's will
       was made known
   (C) peoples from Central Asia who adopted the Islamic faith
   (D) a family of Moslem rulers who lived in Spain
   (E) foot soldiers in the armies of Islam

60. Ⓐ Ⓑ Ⓒ Ⓓ Ⓔ

61. Both Aristotle and Plato considered that growing numbers of people
   in a state (if population is already sufficient)
   (A) must be handled by increasing technique
   (B) must be allowed to grow yet larger in number even if mass pov-
       erty result
   (C) were not the concern of the state since matters pertaining to re-
       production were properly not the business of politics or philoso-
       phers
   (D) were to be stopped by infanticide or other methods (emigration,
       if possible) if the stability and well-being of the state were
       threatened
   (E) were always a sign of the increased glory of the state

61. Ⓐ Ⓑ Ⓒ Ⓓ Ⓔ

62. In the latter part of his life Dante became a Ghibelline. This means
   that he
   (A) was a supporter of the Pope
   (B) hoped the Italian cities would retain their complete independence
   (C) believed that only the Holy Roman Emperor could bring unity
       and peace to Italy
   (D) hoped for the independence of Sicily from the rest of Italy
   (E) saw that the merchants and banking class meant liberty and
       progress for the North Italian cities

62. Ⓐ Ⓑ Ⓒ Ⓓ Ⓔ

63. The enlightened despots of the 18th century were so styled because
   they
   (A) saw how important it was to give important concessions to the
       common people
   (B) were enlightened enough to maintain the monarchic form of gov-
       ernment in an age when the people increasingly demanded rep-
       resentation
   (C) were able to expand their domains
   (D) possessed a high degree of learning and a deep belief in religion
   (E) possessed a desire to improve the lot of their subjects and to im-
       prove their own education

63. Ⓐ Ⓑ Ⓒ Ⓓ Ⓔ

Part II

Number of Questions: 62
Time: 45 minutes

Directions: Each of the questions or incomplete statements below is followed by five suggested answers or completions. Select the one that is best in each case.

64. According to Marx and Lenin, the state, in the high stage of communism, will wither away because   64. Ⓐ Ⓑ Ⓒ Ⓓ Ⓔ
   (A) universal coercion will reign over the earth and make national states unnecessary
   (B) the bourgeoisie and proletariat will be able to live in peace without need for the state to mediate between them
   (C) the Communist Party will have consolidated its position to such an extent and rendered the masses so docile that they will no longer need the state
   (D) when there is only one social class, the state, defined as an instrument of class domination, will no longer serve any function and hence will disappear
   (E) the triumphant dialectical process of history will prove statehood to be only a penultimate truth, hence ultimately false in the presence of the final political form, the super-state

65. The Augustinian system of theology held that "Human nature is hopelessly depraved. . . . Only those mortals can be saved whom God for reasons of His own has predestined to inherit eternal life." Which of the following best represents the attitude of the Protestant leaders of the Reformation?   65. Ⓐ Ⓑ Ⓒ Ⓓ Ⓔ
   (A) They knew nothing of Augustine and were ignorant of this idea.
   (B) They strongly opposed this idea since they believed that it would discourage men from doing good works in the hope of winning salvation.
   (C) The idea became very important in the Protestant position.
   (D) They refused to consider the idea, since they thought that Roman Catholic Church fathers such as St. Augustine had no claim to authority.
   (E) They considered it an idea from pagan Rome and without proper Christian charity.

66. The argument most used to support the congressional committee system is that it   66. Ⓐ Ⓑ Ⓒ Ⓓ Ⓔ
   (A) makes sure that minority groups get a fair hearing
   (B) increases congressional control of the executive department
   (C) reduces the cost of lawmaking
   (D) makes possible more careful consideration of bills
   (E) makes sure that presidential wishes will prevail

67. The "heroic age," "time of troubles," "stability," and "decline" are historical concepts found in   67. Ⓐ Ⓑ Ⓒ Ⓓ Ⓔ
   (A) Marx   (B) Sorokin   (C) Toynbee   (D) Becker   (E) Kant

68. "Sire, you can do everything with bayonets but sit on them." This statement made to Napoleon relates to the problem of political
   (A) strategy   (B) tactics   (C) costs   (D) legitimacy
   (E) formalism

68. Ⓐ Ⓑ Ⓒ Ⓓ Ⓔ

69. Which of the following countries had more of their citizens and soldiers killed in World War II?
   (A) The United States   (B) Great Britain   (C) Italy
   (D) France   (E) USSR

69. Ⓐ Ⓑ Ⓒ Ⓓ Ⓔ

70. Which of the following countries was not in the League of Nations in 1935?
   (A) The United States   (B) USSR   (C) The United Kingdom
   (D) France   (E) Yugoslavia

70. Ⓐ Ⓑ Ⓒ Ⓓ Ⓔ

Harding in "Brooklyn Daily Eagle"

"No bathing beyond the ropes"

Questions 71–73 refer to the above cartoon.

71. The cartoon above was drawn in
   (A) 1912   (B) 1919   (C) 1925   (D) 1933   (E) 1940

71. Ⓐ Ⓑ Ⓒ Ⓓ Ⓔ

72. The cartoon implies that the U.S. at the time was
   (A) still immature
   (B) interested in seapower
   (C) being treated as immature when it was, in fact, a great world power
   (D) not ready to assume world responsibility
   (E) afraid to venture into deeper water

72. Ⓐ Ⓑ Ⓒ Ⓓ Ⓔ

73. The President who would have removed the restrictions on U.S. involvement with the League of Nations (represented in the cartoon as "Lodge Reservations") was
   (A) Theodore Roosevelt   (B) Franklin Roosevelt
   (C) Warren Harding   (D) Woodrow Wilson
   (E) Herbert Hoover

73. Ⓐ Ⓑ Ⓒ Ⓓ Ⓔ

74. "He would have liked to establish a colonial empire, but he knew the British fleet ruled the seas, and so, to prevent this vast region from falling to the British, he sold it to the Americans." What was the region called?

(A) Louisiana (B) Florida (C) Alaska (D) Hawaii (E) California

74. Ⓐ Ⓑ Ⓒ Ⓓ Ⓔ

75. The Erie Canal connected
(A) the Susquehanna and the Potomac
(B) the Hudson and the Delaware
(C) Lake Erie and Niagara
(D) the Hudson and Lake Erie
(E) Lake Huron and the Ohio

75. Ⓐ Ⓑ Ⓒ Ⓓ Ⓔ

76. The political dynasty which began in Louisiana in the 1930s was named after
(A) Long   (B) Talmadge   (C) Bilbo   (D) Crump   (E) Wallace

76. Ⓐ Ⓑ Ⓒ Ⓓ Ⓔ

Questions 77–78 relate to GRAPH A.

GRAPH A

77. The line S₂ S₂ compared to the line S₁ S₁ indicates
(A) an increase in demand
(B) an increase in supply
(C) an increase in monopoly
(D) a decrease in supply
(E) a decrease in demand

77. Ⓐ Ⓑ Ⓒ Ⓓ Ⓔ

78. The shift from line S₁ S₁ to S₂ S₂ in Graph A could have occurred because of a
(A) good year in salt production
(B) bad year, in that few people desired to purchase "old masters"
(C) discovery of a new diamond field in Africa
(D) freeze in the orange groves of Florida
(E) famine reducing the number of subsistence farmers in a small area of the economy

78. Ⓐ Ⓑ Ⓒ Ⓓ Ⓔ

79. Which of the following statements comes closest to the true Malthusian idea?
(A) "Population increases rapidly while agriculture lags behind."
(B) "It is the constant tendency in all animated life to increase beyond the nourishment prepared for it."
(C) "No progress is possible because of the basic sex drive which increases population at a geometric rate."
(D) "Nations which are over-populated must be allowed to expand or send their inhabitants abroad."
(E) "Things can be produced more cheaply if more is produced."

79. Ⓐ Ⓑ Ⓒ Ⓓ Ⓔ

80. Which practice is most compatible with the supposedly rational nature of "the economic man"?

(A) Installment buying at high interest
(B) Borrowing from small loan companies
(C) Reading a consumer research publication
(D) Asking a salesman's advice
(E) Buying more than was on your shopping list

80. Ⓐ Ⓑ Ⓒ Ⓓ Ⓔ

81. For many years, until changed by law in 1943, immigrants who had come to the United States from one of the following countries were not allowed to become naturalized citizens. Which one?

(A) Italy   (B) Mexico   (C) China   (D) Syria   (E) Finland

81. Ⓐ Ⓑ Ⓒ Ⓓ Ⓔ

82. In which of the following cities would the proportion of Lutherans in the total population of the city be highest?

(A) San Francisco, California
(B) Nashville, Tennessee
(C) Atlanta, Georgia
(D) Des Moines, Iowa
(E) Minneapolis, Minnesota

82. Ⓐ Ⓑ Ⓒ Ⓓ Ⓔ

83. Under the British Parliamentary Act of 1911, the House of Lords

(A) lost all power in legislation
(B) could delay enactment of an ordinary bill for only two years
(C) was abolished
(D) was transformed into a house appointed for life terms
(E) became finally dominant over the House of Commons

83. Ⓐ Ⓑ Ⓒ Ⓓ Ⓔ

84. If one divides the races of men into Caucasian, Negroid, and Mongoloid, which of the following countries has a head of state who is *not* Caucasian?

(A) Israel   (B) Iran   (C) India   (D) Egypt
(E) South Korea

84. Ⓐ Ⓑ Ⓒ Ⓓ Ⓔ

85. *Anthropomorphism* is a religious concept meaning

(A) belief in animal gods
(B) belief in a god who died and lived again
(C) rituals in common usage
(D) attribution of human characteristics to a god or gods
(E) holding ancestors worthy of worship

85. Ⓐ Ⓑ Ⓒ Ⓓ Ⓔ

86. The behavior expected of any particular group member is his

(A) role   (B) status   (C) performance   (D) culture
(E) ideology

86. Ⓐ Ⓑ Ⓒ Ⓓ Ⓔ

87. "The productive expenditures are employed in agriculture. . . . The sterile expenses are made upon handicraft products . . . commercial expenses . . . etc." This viewpoint is associated with which school of thought?

(A) Marxism   (B) Platonism   (C) Physiocracy
(D) Technocracy   (E) Mercantilism

87. Ⓐ Ⓑ Ⓒ Ⓓ Ⓔ

88. About fifty percent of the adult population in America belong to no church. What is their attitude, seemingly toward the organized denominations?

(A) Anticlerical

(B) Strongly pro-religious on all controversial issues

(C) Utterly indifferent

(D) Mildly friendly

(E) Militantly atheistic

88. Ⓐ Ⓑ Ⓒ Ⓓ Ⓔ

89. In the 1840s and 1850s a considerable number of the immigrants to the United States came from

(A) Germany   (B) Italy   (C) Greece   (D) Russia

(E) Spain

89. Ⓐ Ⓑ Ⓒ Ⓓ Ⓔ

90. After 1815, Germany

(A) consisted of thirty-eight states loosely joined in the German Confederation

(B) was established as a unified state

(C) existed only as the Holy Roman Empire

(D) was all included within the bounds of Prussia

(E) formed a part of the Austrian Empire

90. Ⓐ Ⓑ Ⓒ Ⓓ Ⓔ

91. Under the British system of government, the monarch normally selects a prime minister who commands the support of the

(A) retiring prime minister

(B) majority party and with the concurrence of the minority party in the House of Commons

(C) majority party in the House of Commons

(D) majority party in the House of Commons and the House of Lords

(E) commonwealth nations

91. Ⓐ Ⓑ Ⓒ Ⓓ Ⓔ

92. Which country was the moving spirit in organizing the various coalitions against Napoleon?

(A) Russia   (B) Austria   (C) Britain   (D) Prussia   (E) Sweden

92. Ⓐ Ⓑ Ⓒ Ⓓ Ⓔ

93. The doctrine of "Manifest Destiny" was most closely associated with which of the following wars involving the U.S.?

(A) Civil War   (B) War of 1812   (C) World War I

(D) World War II   (E) Spanish-American War

93. Ⓐ Ⓑ Ⓒ Ⓓ Ⓔ

94. "Non-slaveholders of the South: farmers, mechanics and working men, we take this occasion to assure you that the slaveholders, the arrogant demagogues whom you have elected to offices of power and profit, have hoodwinked you, trifled with you, and used you as mere tools for the consummation of their wicked designs." These words reflect the viewpoint of

(A) Henry Clay

(B) Stephen A. Douglas

(C) William Lloyd Garrison

(D) George Fitzhugh

(E) John C. Calhoun

94. Ⓐ Ⓑ Ⓒ Ⓓ Ⓔ

95. "The great object of Jacobinism, both in its political and moral revolution, is to destroy every trace of civilization in the world and force mankind back into a savage state." These remarks could have been made by

(A) an American Tory during the Revolution of 1776
(B) a follower of Jefferson in 1805
(C) a New England Federalist in 1794
(D) a member of Lincoln's cabinet in 1862
(E) a New Dealer in the 1930s

95. Ⓐ Ⓑ Ⓒ Ⓓ Ⓔ

96. "Men, consciously or unconsciously, derive their moral ideas in the last resort from the practical relations on which their class position is based—from the economic relations in which they carry on production and exchange." Which of the following said this?

(A) Freud   (B) Goethe   (C) Kant
(D) Engels   (E) Hegel

96. Ⓐ Ⓑ Ⓒ Ⓓ Ⓔ

97. The popular election of U.S. Senators was provided for in the
(A) Constitution
(B) Articles of Confederation
(C) Bill of Rights
(D) Declaration of Independence
(E) Seventeenth Amendment

97. Ⓐ Ⓑ Ⓒ Ⓓ Ⓔ

98. The Syllabus of Errors in the 19th century was
(A) a Marxist attack upon the existing society
(B) a list of what Pope Pius IX said were errors in modern thinking
(C) a work by Thomas Huxley setting forth the errors of the old biology
(D) August Comte's attack upon the errors of traditional social philosophy
(E) a syllabus which recounted the virtues of British colonial rule

98. Ⓐ Ⓑ Ⓒ Ⓓ Ⓔ

99. William G. Sumner thought the "social question" (existence of social problems) to be the result of the fact that
(A) all men are not equally equipped for the onerous struggle against nature
(B) the virtuous are not ordinarily successful
(C) political equality is absent
(D) equality before the law is unattainable
(E) man knows too little about his society

99. Ⓐ Ⓑ Ⓒ Ⓓ Ⓔ

100. It is difficult for an addict to avoid taking drugs after he has been released from treatment because
(A) he generally returns to his old circle of drug-using friends
(B) psycho-physiological dependence on drugs, once established, can never be completely eliminated
(C) people around him generally expect him to become readdicted
(D) both A and C
(E) A, B, and C

100. Ⓐ Ⓑ Ⓒ Ⓓ Ⓔ

101. The term "anticlerical" means hostility toward the
    (A) business class (B) government officials
    (C) white collar workers (D) church (E) retail trade

101. Ⓐ Ⓑ Ⓒ Ⓓ Ⓔ

102. The most significant difference between "caste" in the United States and 19th-century India is that in the United States
    (A) there is a great deal of racial intermarriage
    (B) the social inequality of the Negro is sanctioned neither by the dominant religious precepts nor by dominant political ideology
    (C) all occupational fields are equally open to the Negro
    (D) there is no segregation
    (E) the magical notion of pollution is absent

102. Ⓐ Ⓑ Ⓒ Ⓓ Ⓔ

103. The Supreme Court has been referred to as a continuous constitutional convention. The reason for this may be found in the fact that the Supreme Court
    (A) is in session all the time
    (B) changes and enlarges the Constitution by its practice of interpreting the Constitution through its opinions
    (C) is given the right to sit as a constitutional assembly, and to propose, but not ratify or accept, constitutional amendments
    (D) must rule on any proposed amendment regarding its constitutionality
    (E) convokes conventions of high judges which test the Constitution

103. Ⓐ Ⓑ Ⓒ Ⓓ Ⓔ

104. Japan's economy suffered greatly in the late 1920s and early 1930s because of
    (A) the decline of population
    (B) the decline of foreign trade
    (C) industrialization of China
    (D) the growing power of the USSR in Asia
    (E) the increased competitive power of Britain

104. Ⓐ Ⓑ Ⓒ Ⓓ Ⓔ

105. Confucius and Buddha were contemporaries. In which century of the pre-Christian era did they live?
    (A) 20th (B) 12th (C) 6th (D) 1st (E) 3rd

105. Ⓐ Ⓑ Ⓒ Ⓓ Ⓔ

106. There is an inverse relation between fertility and education among most peoples. Among which group has this relation disappeared?
    (A) Southern Negroes (U.S.) (B) Puerto Rico
    (C) Total U.S. population (D) Taiwan (E) Sweden

106. Ⓐ Ⓑ Ⓒ Ⓓ Ⓔ

107. Modern business
    (A) emphasizes teamwork and cooperation
    (B) frowns upon "cutthroat" price competition
    (C) is an important avenue of social mobility
    (D) all of the above
    (E) none of the above

107. Ⓐ Ⓑ Ⓒ Ⓓ Ⓔ

108. In 1900, the percentage of people in the United States over twenty years of age with a high school diploma was about
    (A) 5% (B) 15% (C) 33% (D) 50% (E) 66%

108. Ⓐ Ⓑ Ⓒ Ⓓ Ⓔ

109. In 1298 A.D., he wrote a book which described Cathay and its people. He mentioned strange customs such as the use of paper money, and, he told of the wars which Kublai Khan fought with the Japanese. His book inspired later explorers such as Christopher Columbus. Who was the author of this travel book?

   (A) Dante
   (B) Aquinas
   (C) Marco Polo
   (D) Roger Bacon
   (E) Cicero

109. A B C D E

110. In 1791, the French Constituent Assembly presented France with its first written constitution. This declared France to be

   (A) a limited constitutional monarchy
   (B) an absolute monarchy
   (C) a democracy
   (D) a republic
   (E) a military dictatorship

110. A B C D E

111. The modern name for what was formerly referred to as Persia is

   (A) Iraq
   (B) Kuwait
   (C) Yemen
   (D) Iran
   (E) Pakistan

111. A B C D E

112. The percent of observations which lie between two standard deviations below and two standard deviations above the mean in a normal distribution is approximately

   (A) 30%
   (B) 40%
   (C) 55%
   (D) 75%
   (E) 95%

112. A B C D E

113. The increasing proportion of American eighteen to twenty-four year olds in higher education has probably increased most the relative numerical significance of which the following student subcultures?

   (A) Collegiate
   (B) Academic
   (C) Vocational
   (D) Non-conformist
   (E) Militaristic

113. A B C D E

114. If a President were to be impeached, the trial would be in the

   (A) Supreme Court
   (B) Senate
   (C) United States Court of Appeals
   (D) United States District Court
   (E) House of Representatives

114. A B C D E

115. Which of the following does not always apply to culture? 115. Ⓐ Ⓑ Ⓒ Ⓓ Ⓔ
    (A) It is static.
    (B) It is learned.
    (C) It is material in part.
    (D) It is non-material in part.
    (E) It includes norms.

116. Today, the tendency of most American families is toward 116. Ⓐ Ⓑ Ⓒ Ⓓ Ⓔ
    (A) matriarchy
    (B) patriarchy
    (C) elaboration in symbolism supporting the authority of extended kin
    (D) equality of power of husband and wife
    (E) emphasis on the traditional

117. A caste system of social stratification is extremely difficult to main- 117. Ⓐ Ⓑ Ⓒ Ⓓ Ⓔ
    tain in
    (A) an urban society
    (B) a village or rural society
    (C) a highly religious society
    (D) an economically poor society
    (E) a paternalistic society

118. Which of the following opinions concerning Communism today is *most 118. Ⓐ Ⓑ Ⓒ Ⓓ Ⓔ
    compatible* with John Stuart Mill's principle of liberty in his essay "On
    Liberty"? The discussion of Communism in our schools
    (A) should not be tolerated; Communism contradicts the American
        way of life
    (B) should be encouraged, for Communists are just as likely to be
        right as we are
    (C) should be tolerated, for no one should ever be inhibited in his
        beliefs and speech
    (D) should be tolerated, for it is highly desirable that we face sincere
        arguments against our own conventional beliefs
    (E) should not be tolerated; Communism is a mistaken belief and
        therefore should not be represented in public

119. The Japanese rulers suppressed Christianity in the 17th century be- 119. Ⓐ Ⓑ Ⓒ Ⓓ Ⓔ
    cause they
    (A) thought it would divide their people and bring them under the
        influence of foreign powers
    (B) feared that the peaceful teaching of Christianity would discour-
        age warlike virtues
    (C) believed that Buddhism was the true faith and all other religions
        necessarily false
    (D) said that it was a "white man's" religion
    (E) believed that only God was divine and no man could be

120. The evidence against instinct as an explanation of marriage and the family includes all of the following except one. Which one?
   (A) Marriage limits as well as permits sexual expression.
   (B) Women's desires for offspring are not constant.
   (C) Women's physiology is unrelated to their behavior.
   (D) Father and mother do not have the same degree of responsibility toward their children in all societies.
   (E) Men do not inevitably experience emotional conflict when they suppress their sexual urges.

120. Ⓐ Ⓑ Ⓒ Ⓓ Ⓔ

121. Upon which one of the following viewpoints would Alexis de Tocqueville and Karl Marx agree?
   (A) The tyranny of the majority was the ominous threat of the future.
   (B) Organized religion is an important factor in the preserving of liberty.
   (C) Religion is a good way to calm an oppressed people.
   (D) Most controversy in modern society would be over property rights.
   (E) Societies with conflicting economic interests can, through compromise and proper institutions, achieve a long life.

121. Ⓐ Ⓑ Ⓒ Ⓓ Ⓔ

122. Studies of Western countries show that
   (A) the most secularized and urbanized countries have the highest suicide rates
   (B) the more technologically backward a country is, the higher its suicide rate tends to be
   (C) secularization and urbanization does not seem to account for the relatively low suicide rates of the United States, Canada, England, and Australia
   (D) the larger the proportion of suburban residents in a country, the higher the suicide rate tends to be
   (E) suicide is an excellent indicator of the total worth of a society

122. Ⓐ Ⓑ Ⓒ Ⓓ Ⓔ

123. In the United States today, which of the following contrasts between middle-class and working-class youths seems most defensible? Middle-class youths
   (A) are usually complacent; working-class youths are usually ambitious.
   (B) see their problem as deciding what to do; working-class youths see their problem as finding a job.
   (C) are concerned primarily with income adequate to maintain a given style of life; working-class youths are concerned with achievement that may lead to mobility.
   (D) are likely to have to depend on their families for guidance; working-class youths are likely to have guidance counselors who will help them with occupational choice.
   (E) are conservative; working-class youth is radical.

123. Ⓐ Ⓑ Ⓒ Ⓓ Ⓔ

124. In the early 19th century (when Great Britain confronted Napoleon), the British position on the rights of neutral countries was nearly the opposite of its position in

124. Ⓐ Ⓑ Ⓒ Ⓓ Ⓔ

(A) 1837

(B) 1854

(C) 1863

(D) 1915

(E) 1943

125. All of the following statements concerning banking are true except

125. Ⓐ Ⓑ Ⓒ Ⓓ Ⓔ

(A) state banks can join the Federal Reserve System

(B) bank failure is reduced by the influence of F.D.I.C.

(C) Federal Reserve member banks count their deposits with the Federal Reserve Bank as assets

(D) When all banks are reducing the cash part of their assets, money supply is increased

(E) the Federal Reserve is under the authority of the U.S. Treasury

ANSWER KEY—TRIAL TEST

Part I

1. A	12. E	23. D	34. E	44. B	54. A
2. B	13. D	24. A	35. E	45. C	55. A
3. E	14. C	25. C	36. C	46. C	56. D
4. E	15. C	26. D	37. D	47. C	57. C
5. C	16. B	27. D	38. B	48. C	58. A
6. D	17. E	28. D	39. A	49. C	59. B
7. C	18. D	29. B	40. C	50. A	60. A
8. D	19. E	30. C	41. D	51. C	61. D
9. D	20. D	31. B	42. C	52. C	62. C
10. B	21. C	32. D	43. B	53. E	63. E
11. B	22. B	33. A			

Part II

64. D	75. D	86. A	96. D	106. E	116. D
65. C	76. A	87. C	97. E	107. D	117. A
66. D	77. D	88. D	98. B	108. A	118. D
67. C	78. D	89. A	99. A	109. C	119. A
68. D	79. B	90. A	100. D	110. A	120. C
69. E	80. C	91. C	101. C	111. D	121. D
70. A	81. C	92. C	102. B	112. E	122. C
71. B	82. E	93. E	103. B	113. C	123. B
72. C	83. B	94. C	104. B	114. B	124. C
73. D	84. E	95. C	105. C	115. A	125. E
74. A	85. D				

SCORING CHART—TRIAL TEST

After you have scored your Trial Examination, enter the results in the chart below (the Raw Score computation is explained on page 14); then transfer your Raw Score to the Progress Chart on page 14. As you complete the Sample Examinations later in this part of the book, you should be able to achieve increasingly higher Raw Scores.

Total Test	Number Right	Number Wrong	Number Omitted	Raw Score
Part I: 63				
Part II: 62				
Total: 125				

ANSWER EXPLANATIONS—TRIAL TEST

Part I

1. **A.** The distribution of members in the House of Representatives is determined on the basis of population. The Constitution in Article I Section 2 Clause 3 provides: "Representatives shall be apportioned among the several states which may be included within this Union according to their respective numbers . . . ."

2. **B.** In the 19th century, United States Senators were elected by the state legislatures. Article I Section 3 Clause 1 of the original Constitution reads: "The Senate of the United States shall be composed of two Senators from each state, chosen by the legislature thereof . . . ." This was changed by the 17th amendment, ratified in 1913.

3. **E.** "Boswash" is a term which is sometimes applied to the continuous urban area between Boston and Washington. The word consists of a combination of the first syllables of Boston and Washington.

4. **E.** The law of diminishing returns states that an input of production (such as labor) and the output it helps to produce tend to diminish as more units of the input factor are applied to the same number of the other factors of production (land and capital).

5. **C.** To the Marxist, profits are transitory and characteristic of only one state of history. Marxism holds that capitalism, the economic system of most of the western world, represents a transitory state of history.

6. **D.** Karl Marx (1818–1883), the father of modern socialism and communism, was a materialist. His philosophy, developed in the 3-volume work *Capital*, regarded religion as a prop of capitalism. He rejected the "work ethic of Protestantism" and other aspects of the religious-oriented teaching of Protestant churches.

7. **C.** Apes and other primates cannot be taught to use highly complex language because they have little mental ability to store or transmit highly abstract ideas. Some higher primates have been shown to possess potential for learning from communications directed toward them.

8. D. The culture concept in social science implies that the reason for differences between our own and other societies is that we, as members of our society, learn different things from those which others learn. This is the sense in which sociologists use the term "culture."

9. D. Pragmatism, as an educational philosophy, was developed by William James (1842–1910) in the 19th century and, more fully, by John Dewey (1859–1952) in the 20th. It has been the most influential educational philosophy in the United States.

10. B. The census of 1890 is commonly considered to indicate the closing of the American frontier. By 1890, ownership, if not occupation, of all American land had been established. The census of 1890 counted 63 million Americans of whom 35 per cent lived in urban areas.

11. B. John Jay was unpopular with the Democratic followers of Jefferson. In 1794, Jay negotiated a treaty with England. The treaty helped keep America out of the war in Europe between France and England. The Jeffersonians felt that the treaty was favorable to England. They favored France in the European war.

12. E. The unification of Italy, called Risorgimento, was achieved under the leadership of Count Camillo Cavour. Victor Emmanuel II was proclaimed king of a united Italy in 1861. German unification was accomplished mainly through the efforts of Otto von Bismarck. King William I of Prussia was proclaimed Emperor of a united Germany in 1871.

13. D. German armies attacked neutral Belgium in 1914 at the beginning of World War I and again in May 1940, early in World War II. Switzerland remained independent in both wars. The neutrality of the Netherlands and of Norway was not violated in World War I. France was aligned against Germany in both wars.

14. C. The Constitution in Article I Section 2 Clause 5 says: "The House of Representatives . . . shall have the sole power of impeachment." (bringing charges). Article I Section 3 Clause 6 says: "The Senate shall have the sole power to try all impeachments."

15. B. At the beginning of this hundred-year period (1860), China was an absolute monarchy ruled by an emperor. After the Revolution of 1912, China became a republic. In the interim, much of Chinese territory was under foreign occupation. In 1948, Chiang Kai-shek became President under a democratic constitution. One year later, communist forces under Mao Tsetung drove his armies off the mainland and established the Communist People's Republic of China.

16. B. Each of these is a professional organization, but only the American Medical Association (AMA) exercises dominant control over training of physicians, certification to practice medicine and its various fields of specialization, and entry into the profession of medicine.

17. E. The Leninist communist creed, as one of its key articles, holds that under the capitalist system, depressions are inevitable, war between capitalist countries over markets is inevitable, and war between the capitalist class and the proletariat (working class) is inevitable.

18. D. A coefficient of correlation between two phenomena establishes the relationship between the two in statistical terms. In the situation here described, the relationship is established as minus 0.82.

19. E. Prior to 1972, the Supreme Court had ruled on each of the five issues. Four were declared to be legal. The fifth, allowing clergymen to give religious indoctrination in public schools, was declared unconstitutional in the case of McCollum v. Board of Education (1948).

20. D. The First Amendment states: "Congress shall make no law respecting an establishment of religion, or prohibiting the free exercise thereof . . . ." This is the legal basis for the separation of church and state in the U.S.

21. C. The American economy is described as a "free enterprise" system. This would be completely laissez-faire except that there is some planning under such agencies as the Federal Reserve System, as well as in committees of Congress and in the various executive departments.

22. B. The economic system under which we live is premised on the idea of economic growth and general welfare. Depressions are regarded as temporary aberrations. Marxism holds that they are inevitable because of "internal contradictions."

23. D. Jeremy Bentham (1748–1832), English social philosopher, was the leader of a group called the Utilitarians. He held that each person guides his or her conduct entirely by self-interest.

24. A. In a class system, movement from one class to another (vertical mobility) is possible. In a caste system, endogamy (marriage restrictions), distinguishing attire, occupational prohibitions, and prestige differences tend to prevail.

25. C. Marx contended that the Industrial Revolution would bring about the successful revolt of the working class. Lenin noted that the exploitation of colonies under imperialism would ameliorate the plight of the working class and postpone the day of revolt.

26. D. The proportion of one's income spent on food is more restricted by the inherent ability to consume than are books, entertainment, transportation, or sports.

27. D. Price is an aspect of both a planned economy and a free, or laissez-faire, economy. Money is correctly described in each of the other choices.

28. D. Corporate stock may represent each of the other forms of national wealth. But they, in themselves, are not national wealth. Indeed, corporate stock may be worthless if the corporation that issues it is a spurious entity.

29. B. Karl Marx contended that labor produced more of the final product than it received in wages. This excess was described by Marx as "surplus value."

30. C. Prohibition became a national law by the 18th Amendment to the Constitution, adopted in 1919. One of the reasons for its repeal in 1933 by the 21st Amendment was that it was widely flouted by the people.

31. B. Carthage was established as a colony in North Africa by the Phoenicians about 875 B.C. it was situated opposite Sicily near present-day Tunis.

32. D. In the United States at present, the kinship system puts strong emphasis on the immediate conjugal family, that is, the family consisting of husband, wife, and children.

33. A. Max Weber (1864–1920), German sociologist, described the ideal type of bureaucratic structure in his *Essays in Sociology*. He noted that raising specific standards for office holders went hand in hand with the bureaucratization of society. To Weber, the bureaucratic society, despite its faults, represented an advance over its predecessors.

34. E. In his writings, particularly in his major work entitled *Capital*, which was published in 3 volumes between 1867 and 1894, Karl Marx predicted the downfall of capitalism because of its inherent contradictions. This included, in his view, both mass unemployment and wars among the capitalist nations for control of resources and trade.

35. E. The American Federation of Labor was founded in 1881. During its first 43 years, its leader was Samuel Gompers. Under his leadership, skilled workers were organized into craft unions. The AFL did not support any political party. It worked within the system to obtain better pay, better working conditions, and shorter hours for its members.

36. C. The Kentucky and Virginia Resolutions of 1798–9 were drafted by Jefferson and Madison. They were passed by the legislatures of Kentucky and Virginia. They declared the Alien and Sedition Acts, passed by Congress in 1798, to be unconstitutional.

37. D. Mesopotamia (from the Greek, meaning "between the rivers") was the name given to the ancient civilization that was located in the region between the Tigris and Euphrates Rivers. Today this comprises the territory of Iraq, whose chief city and capital is Baghdad.

38. B. Edmund Burke (1729–1797), English statesman and political philosopher, would have rejected the idea that society can be safely based on reason alone. Burke emphasized the need for gradual and orderly change and the significance of historical antecedents in sound social and political development.

39. A. Socrates was condemned to death as a threat to Athens because he taught young men to question accepted ideas. The story of his accusation, trial, and conviction is related by Plato in his dialogue *Apology*. The last hours of Socrates' life are described by Plato in the dialogue *Phaedo*.

40. C. The Edict of Nantes was issued by King Henry IV of France in 1598 after a series of bloody wars between Protestants and Catholics. It allowed Protestantism in towns where it was the chief form of worship but barred it from Paris and its surroundings.

41. D. In the 5th century B.C., Greece consisted of a number of city-states, that is, cities and their surroundings. Each citizen was loyal to his city-state such as Athens, Sparta, and Thebes, not to Greece. The cities often fought against each other.

42. C. Thomas Malthus (1766–1834), English economist, studied population. He concluded that because population grows much faster than food supply, people are doomed to hunger. Hence, he urged education to bring about smaller families.

43. B. Sparta was one of the leading city-states in ancient Greece. It was famous for its army. Sons of the ruling class were trained to be soldiers. Only these warriors, called Spartiates, had legal and civil rights.

44. B. Adam Smith (1723–1790) is best known for his classic work *An Inquiry into the Nature and Causes of the Wealth of Nations* (1776). He showed great insight into the operation of economic forces, including the tendency of tradesmen to seek control of the market.

45. C. David Ricardo (1772–1823), classical economist, defended the new capitalism and the manufacturing class. He noted that landlords profit from a scarcity of food (food is produced on land). But higher rents reduce the profits of the new manufacturing class.

46. C. Karl Marx (1818–1883) predicted increasing tension between the capitalist class and the working class. The other four ideas are included in his description of capitalism in his 3-volume work entitled *Capital*.

47. C. The physicist does research and develops the theoretical basis for the science of physics. The engineer makes practical applications of the physicist's findings. The sociologist does research and develops the theoretical basis for the social science of sociology. The social reformer puts the theories of the sociologist into practice.

48. C. "Ethnocentrism" is the attitude or belief that the way of life of one's own group is superior to that of any other group. "Relativism" is the view that ethical truths depend on the group holding them. "Ostracism" means exclusion from the group.

49. C. Primitive cultures are relatively monolithic. Virtually all behavior is prescribed and universally practiced. More complex cultures accommodate numerous variations in behavior. Hence, they tend to have fewer universals.

50. A. Thomas R. Malthus (1766–1834) wrote a famous *Essay on Population* (1798). He opposed an increase in wages, arguing that it only encouraged larger families. His thesis was that population increased much faster than the food supply. This would not be relieved by developments in technology.

51. C. The 1978 population of the world was estimated at 4,200,000,000 people. By 1980, the world's population approached 4½ billion. Demographic estimates indicate that the world's population will easily exceed 5 billion by the year 2000.

52. C. Emile Durkheim (1858–1917), French sociologist, wrote a book entitled *Suicide* in 1897. He analyzed the psychologic bases of social behavior. He used the term "altruistic" to describe a type of suicide resulting from excessive social integration.

53. E. Prior to the neolithic age, which dates from about 15,000 B.C., man was a nomad who lived by hunting and gathering. When he learned to till the soil and grow food, i.e., with the development of agriculture, the first four choices in this question followed.

54. A. In sociology, each of the following are classified as institutions: folkways, laws, social symbols, and mores.

55. A. The German Imperial constitution of 1871 went into effect after the defeat of France in the Franco-Prussian War. Prussia became the dominant state under the Constitution. The King of Prussia became Emperor Wilhelm I of Germany.

56. D. William I (the Conqueror) of England is also known in history as Duke William II of Normandy. His army crossed the English Channel and defeated the English at the Battle of Hastings in 1066 A.D. He ruled England as William I until his death in 1087.

57. C. In 1635, during the last phase of the Thirty Years' War, France united with Sweden to prevent the Hapsburgs (both Austrian and Spanish) from gaining the victory.

58. A. The period of the "Roman Peace" (*Pax Romana*) was during the first two hundred years of the Roman Empire. The Empire lasted for five hundred years, from about 31 B.C. to 476 A.D. All the lands around the Mediterranean were part of the Empire. The power and efficiency of the Roman legions kept peace throughout the Empire.

59. B. The Punic Wars (264 B.C.–146 B.C.) were fought between Rome and Carthage. Carthage was founded, as a colony, by the Phoenicians. The Latin word for Phoenicia is Punicus.

60. A. In the Islamic religion, the Caliph is the religious head of the government as the agent of God. When Mohammed, the Prophet, died, Abu Bakr was chosen as first calif. Later, Islam split, and different califs claimed to be God's agent.

61. D. both the great Greek philosopher Plato (428 B.C.–348 B.C.) and his most famous pupil, Aristotle (384 B.C.–322 B.C.), justified infanticide (the killing of infants) as a means of keeping population under control.

62. C. Dante (Alighieri), 1265–1321, was perhaps the greatest Italian poet. Guelphs and Ghibellines were opposing political factions during Dante's lifetime. Dante was at first a supporter of the Guelphs but, in later life, joined the Ghibellines because they were the party of the Emperor and, as Dante thought, could bring unity and peace to Italy.

63. E. The enlightened despots of the 18th century—Joseph II of Austria, Catherine II of Russia, and Frederick II of Prussia—wished to improve both the lot of their impoverished subjects and their own education.

Part II

64. D. Marxism sees history in terms of class struggle with the state as an instrument of the dominant class. In the current (final) stage the bourgeoisie is destroyed by the proletariat. With only one class in society, the state will have no function and will disappear.

65. C. Augustine (354–430) taught that divine grace, not human effort, was the source of salvation. This doctrine, called predestination, was a key tenet of the theology of John Calvin (1509–1564) and other leaders of the Protestant Reformation.

66. D. Under the committee system, all bills introduced in the Senate or House of Representatives are referred to the committee in that chamber which is charged with consideration of the particular subject of the bill. Members of each committee specialize in that committee's particular area of legislation so that bills receive special analysis before they are reported to the House or Senate.

67. C. Arnold J. Toynbee, English historian, wrote a scholarly 12-volume *A Study of History* (1933–1961). He described twenty-one historic civilizations. In his study he found that each undergoes a "heroic age," a "time of trouble," "a period of stability," and a final "decline."

68. D. Legitimacy played an important part in European politics in the 18th and 19th centuries. Napoleon was a great general (symbolized by the sword), but he came from a family of commoners in Corsica. After his defeat, he was replaced by King Louis XVIII, the "legitimate" king of France. All the nations he fought—England, Austria, Russia, Prussia, and Sweden— were ruled by "legitimate" kings.

69. E. The USSR suffered more than 7 million military deaths in World War II. Vast areas of the Soviet Union were overrun by the German armies. Leningrad survived a terrible siege. In addition to the military losses, the USSR lost 13 million civilians in the war for a total of 20 million, by far the heaviest losses of all nations in the conflict.

70. A. Even though President Woodrow Wilson was the architect of the League, the Senate of the United States refused to approve U.S. membership. So the United States did not join the League of Nations.

71. B. In 1919, Senator Henry Cabot Lodge of Massachusetts presented, in the U.S. Senate, 14 "reservations" to joining the League of Nations. These reservations are shown as a roped-off area keeping the United States out of the water (the League of Nations). On November 19, 1919, the U.S. Senate rejected the treaty that would have made the U.S.A. a member of the League of Nations.

72. C. The cartoon shows the United States as a big overgrown child (with pail and shovel in the sand). The little U.S. Senate, dominated by Senator Lodge, is making the "child" behave.

73. D. Woodrow Wilson was president of the United States in 1919. Wilson refused to accept any of the Lodge Reservations, fearing they would weaken the League. He could not get two-thirds of the Senate to approve U.S. membership in the League without the reservations.

74. A. The region was called Louisiana. This vast territory between the Mississippi River and the Rocky Mountains was sold to the United States in 1803 by Napoleon for $15,000,000. Thirteen states or parts of states were later carved out of this purchase.

75. D. The Erie Canal extended from Albany on the Hudson River westward to Buffalo on Lake Erie. It was formally opened in October, 1825.

76. A. The political dynasty which began in Louisiana in the 1930's was named after Huey Pierce Long (1893–1935). Long, called "Kingfish," became Governor of Louisiana and U.S. Senator from Louisiana. He ruled the state with an iron hand. He was a candidate for President of the U.S. when he was assassinated in 1935.

77. D. In the graph, the line S_1S_1 moves to S_2S_2 because of an additional cost to the producer. This additional cost causes a decrease in supply represented by movement of the supply curve from S_1S_1 to S_2S_2.

78. D. The shift from S_1S_1 to S_2S_2 which represents a decrease in supply (question #77 above) could have been caused by a freeze in the orange groves in Florida. It could also be caused by a voluntary decrease resulting, for example, from the imposition of a new tax on the producer.

79. B. The concept "It is the constant tendency in all animated life to increase beyond the nourishment prepared for it" is the basic premise of *An Essay on the Principles of Population* (1798). Malthus believed that this tendency would be counteracted by war, famine, disease, or birth control which he called "moral restraint."

80. C. If "economic man" were to act according to supposedly rational nature, he might well subscribe to a consumer research publication, but he would definitely not act as described in any of the other four choices.

81. C. The Chinese Exclusion Act of 1882 was extended and made permanent in 1902. Chinese immigration to the United States was prohibited, and Chinese could not become naturalized citizens. The law was changed in 1943 to allow Chinese in the United States to become naturalized citizens.

82. E. Many Lutherans from Scandinavia migrated to the United States during the 19th century. They tended to settle in places like Minnesota, where the climate and farming conditions were similar to those in Scandinavia (especially Sweden and Norway).

83. B. Prime Minister Herbert Asquith forced the House of Lords to give up its veto power by voting for the Parliament Act of 1911. The House of Lords could still hold up an ordinary bill for two years but no longer.

84. E. The South Korean head of state, President Chun Doo Hwan, is a member of the Mongoloid race. The people of the other four countries are classified as Caucasian.

85. D. The word "anthropomorphic" comes from the Greek, meaning human form. Anthropomorphism as a religious concept means giving human form or characteristics to a god or goddess. This was a key aspect of the religion of the ancient Greeks.

86. A. The term "role" is used in sociology to mean the way a person is expected to behave in a particular group, i.e., family, work group, school, church, or club. Roles are more formalized in primitive societies than they are, for example, in Europe and America.

87. C. The physiocrats were a group of 18th-century French economists whose founder, Francois Quesnay, held that all wealth originated with land. According to the physiocrats, agriculture alone had the potential to increase wealth.

88. D. The attitude of the fifty per cent of Americans who do not belong to a church toward organized denominations seems to be mildly friendly. This is evidenced by charitable contributions, voting patterns, and other public activities relating to church interests.

89. A. More than 17 million Americans trace their ancestry to Germany alone. If partial European ancestry is included, the number of German ancestry becomes 51 million. This is larger than any other national origin of present-day Americans. Heavy German immigration dates from the failure of the liberal movement of 1848 in Germany.

90. A. The Congress of Vienna (1814–15) reorganized Europe after the Napoleonic Wars. The Holy Roman Empire ceased to exist. Thirty-eight states were loosely joined in the German Confederation.

91. C. Under the parliamentary system of government developed by the British, the prime minister is the leader of the majority in the House of Commons. The appointment of the prime minister by the monarch is a mere formality.

92. C. Britain was the moving spirit in organizing the various coalitions against Napoleon. The Quadruple Alliance of 1814, consisting of Russia, Prussia, Austria, and Britain, was organized by Viscount Castlereagh, the British foreign minister. Their combined armies, led by the British Duke of Wellington, defeated Napoleon at the Battle of Waterloo in Belgium (1815).

93. E. "Manifest Destiny" was the belief of American expansionists that it was the obvious fate of the United States to spread its system of democracy. The phrase was used to justify the annexation of Texas, the acquisition of the Oregon territory, the purchase of Alaska, and, finally, the involvement in the Spanish-American War.

94. C. William Lloyd Garrison (1805–1879) was a militant abolitionist. He was publisher of the Boston abolitionist newspaper, *The Liberator.* In the first issue (Jan. 1, 1831), he announced his intention to fight against slavery and said: "I will not retreat a single inch—AND I WILL BE HEARD. "

95. C. The Jacobins were a radical political club in France. They came to power at the height of the French Revolution and conducted a "reign of terror" in 1794. The New England Federalists were opponents of the aims and methods of the revolutionary government of France.

96. D. These were the ideas of Friedrich Engels (1820–1895). He was co-author, with Karl Marx, of the *Communist Manifesto* (1848). He collaborated with Marx in the latter's great work, the three-volume *Capital*.

97. E. The Seventeenth Amendment to the U.S. Constitution, adopted in 1913, reads: "The Senate of the United States shall be composed of two Senators from each state, elected by the people thereof . . . . " The words "elected by the people thereof" replaced the words "chosen by the legislature thereof" in the original Constitution.

98. B. In *The Syllabus of Errors* (1864), Pope Pius IX rejected the liberal ideas of the European Revolutions of 1848. He denounced faith in rationalism and science. The *Syllabus* was in the form of a warning to Catholics, not a matter of dogma incumbent upon them to believe.

99. A. The idea that social problems derive from the fact that all men are not equipped for the onerous struggle against nature was developed by the pioneer American sociologist, William Graham Sumner (1840–1910). His classic work, *Folkways*, was published in 1907.

100. D. Addicts usually return to their old circle of friends who expect them to become readdicted, but psycho-physiological dependence on drugs can be completely eliminated as evidenced by the fact that drug treatment centers have on their staffs former drug addicts who have been cured.

101. D. The term "anticlerical" means hostility toward the church. The word "cleric" is derived from the Latin "clericus," meaning a member of the clergy.

102. B. "Caste" in 19th-century India, a rigid class system, with prescribed rights and privileges, was sanctioned by dominant religious precepts and political ideology. In the United States, the social inequality of blacks is sanctioned by neither.

103. B. The U.S. Supreme Court interprets the Constitution in difficult cases. Its decisions are given in the form of "opinions," both majority and dissenting. These opinions often have the effect of changing or enlarging the Constitution. Hence, the court may be considered a continuous constitutional convention.

104. B. In the late 1920's and early 1930's, Japan's economy suffered because of the decline of foreign trade. Japan has limited natural resources, and its economy, in an industrial world, is dependent on foreign trade. In the late 19th and early 20th centuries, the major industrial powers erected trade barriers and other economic blocks to foreign trade.

105. C. Both Confucius (551 B.C.–479 B.C.) and Buddha (563 B.C.–483 B.C.) lived in the 6th century of the pre-Christian era.

106. E. In Sweden, 75% of the population between 5–19 are in school. The national literacy rate is 99%. The annual natural increase in population is less than one-half of one per cent. The relation between education and fertility has reached an equilibrium.

107. D. Modern business is in sharp contrast to what it was early in this century. Today, teamwork and cooperation feature labor-management relations. "Cutthroat" price competition is avoided. It is not uncommon for children of working-class parents to reach the highest rung of corporate management and control.

108. A. The population of the United States in 1900 was 76,000,000. Of these, some 51 million were over 20 years of age. Of these, 2,100,000, or less than 5%, were high school graduates.

109. C. Marco Polo, 13th-century merchant and traveler, was born in Venice. He traveled overland to China and reached Peiping in 1272. He remained there 20 years. On his return to Venice he wrote an account of his travels and of Kublai Khan, China's ruler.

110. A. The first written constitution, presented in France in 1791 by the Constituent Assembly, vested sovereign power in the Legislative Assembly. The king was given only a suspensive veto power by which legislation desired by the Assembly could be postponed.

111. D. The modern name for what was formerly referred to as Persia is Iran. After World War I, Turkey, and to a lesser extent its neighbor Persia, experienced revolutions. In 1935, to emphasize its break with the past, Persia took the name of Iran.

112. E. The standard deviation is a measure of the spread of a set of numerical values around their mean. In a normal distribution, the per cent of observations falling between two standard deviations above and below the mean would be approximately 95%.

113.   C.   Higher education has traditionally been academic in character. During the decades since World War II, the vocational, though not entirely absent in the past, has become numerically more significant. Collegiate is an overall term. Non-conformist and militaristic are numerically much less significant.

114.   B.   If a President were to be impeached, the trial would be in the Senate. Article I, Section 3, Clause 6 provides: "The Senate shall have the sole power to try all impeachments."

115.   A.   No culture is entirely static. Every culture is learned by its members, is partly material and partly non-material, and includes norms of behavior.

116.   D.   American culture is in flux and is moving toward equality of power of husband and wife. It is moving away from emphasis on the traditional, away from patriarchy, but not toward matriarchy.

117.   A.   A caste system of social stratification requires that each individual be easily identified by caste and that he or she remain for life within the caste of birth. In an urban society, individuals tend to become anonymous, intermarry more readily, and thus tend to destroy caste structure.

118.   D.   In his *On Liberty* (1859), John Stuart Mill, English philosopher, described
119.   A.   Christianity had been brought to Japan in 1549 by St. Francis Xavier. For a century, it prospered. Then, in the 17th century, it was violently suppressed. Japan's rulers chose isolation for two centuries. They feared that Christianity, a foreign influence, would be harmful to Japan.

120.   C.   Items A, B, D, and E are essentially true. They constitute evidence against instinct as an explanation of marriage and the family. Item C is irrelevant to the argument.

121.   D.   Alexis de Tocqueville (1805–59), French writer, traveled in America during the 1830's. In his *Democracy in America* (1835) he described, with approval, the political and economic growth he saw. He would agree with the economist Karl Marx that most controversy in modern society would be over property rights, a key tenet of Marxian economics.

122.   C.   Suicide rates in the United States, Canada, England, and Australia are in the middle of brackets, i.e., about 10 to 15 per hundred thousand. Austria, West Germany, Hungary, Japan, Sweden, and Switzerland report rates of over 20 per 100,000, while Italy, the Netherlands, and Spain report under 10 per 100,000. Secularization and urbanization do not seem to be directly related to the incidence of suicide.

123.   B.   In the United States today, the contrast between middle-class youth and working-class youth that seems most defensible is: "Middle-class youths see their problem as deciding what to do; working-class youths see their problem as finding a job."

124.   C.   When Great Britain was at war with Napoleon, the British "orders in council" (1807) required that no neutral ship could enter the continent of Europe without first stopping at a British port. In 1863 when Britain was a neutral in the American Civil War, there was strong protest over the removal by the U.S. of two southern agents from the British ship "Trent."

125.   E.   The Federal Reserve, established by Congress in 1913, is directly responsible to Congress. Its authority and responsibility derive from Congressional legislation and oversight, even though members of its Board of Governors are appointed by the President of the United States for 14-year terms.

Background and Practice Questions

History and the social sciences are treated together in the CLEP General Examinations. The test consists of 125 questions divided into two forty-five minute parts. Historical material relating primarily to American, European, and African/Asian history accounts for over one third of the questions. Most of the remainder of the questions relate to concepts and information from sociology, social psychology, economics, political science, and social science methodology. The approximate percent of examination questions for each area covered on the test is as follows:

History (35%)

10–15%	United States History Requires a general under- standing of historical issues associated with the following periods in United States history: colonial, revolutionary, late eighteenth and early nineteenth centuries, Civil War and Reconstruction, and late nineteenth and twentieth centuries
10–15%	Western Civilization Requires familiarity with three broad historical periods: ancient, medieval, and modern

Social Sciences (65%)

25–30%	Sociology, including topics
	such as
	    Methods and statistics
	    Demography
	    Ecology
	    Social stratification
	    Deviance and criminology
	    Social organization

15–20%	Economics, with emphasis
	on microeconomics topics
	such as
	    Consumer theory
	    Production theory
	    Investment function
	    Fiscal policy
	    Monetary policy
	    Money and banking
	    Business cycles

5-10%   African/Asian Civilizations
    Requires knowledge of
    topics such as colonialism,
    growth of empire and
    trade, political develop-
    ments, the role of Europe
    in Africa, and
    independence

15-20%   Political Science, including
    topics such as
    Constitutional government
    Voting and political
        behavior
    International relations
        and comparative
        government

3-5%   Social Psychology, including
    topics such as
    Aggression
    Socialization
    Conformity
    Methodology
    Group formation
    Performance

If you want to do well on this test, you should have a very clear sense of chronological relations in history, as well as an understanding of the issues and ideas which have been current in different historical eras. You should have some idea of the relative significance of various ideologies, scientific concepts, and historical events. If you have, on your own or during the course work, read widely in history and sociology (including the history of economic and sociological theories), you will be able to answer a large number of the questions without difficulty. Technical concepts and terms from contemporary economics, social psychology, and political science are tested in a large number of questions. However, if you have an acquaintance with the material emphasized in introductions to these subjects, you are well prepared to answer the questions.

There are a number of accomplishments which the questions endeavor to test. Some questions require mere factual recall. Others ask you to go beyond factual recall to the deduction of a correct answer from the information given in the question and from your own knowledge. Still others are designed to test your ability to apply conceptual principles or theories to particular problems. Many of the questions will demand much of you. You will be asked to judge, to weigh, to rank, to discriminate, and to compare and contrast facts and ideas.

For review, you might consult the following books:

ECONOMICS

Heilbroner, Robert. *The Worldly Philosophers.*
    5th ed. New York: Simon and Schuster, 1980.
McConnell, Campbell R. *Economics.* 8th ed.
    New York: McGraw-Hill, 1980.
Wiegand, G. C. *Economics, Its Nature and
    Importance.* Barron's Educational Series, Inc.,
    N.Y. 1976.

SOCIOLOGY

Apsler, Alfred. *An Introduction to Social Science.*
    3rd. ed. New York: Random House, Inc., 1980.
Inkeles, Alex. *What Is Sociology?* Englewood
    Cliffs, N.J.: Prentice-Hall, 1964.

EUROPEAN HISTORY

Brinton, Crane, et al. *A History of Civilization.* 5th ed. Englewood Cliffs, N.J.: Prentice-Hall, 1976.

Klose, N. *Essentials of Modern Western Civilization.* 2 vols. Woodbury, N.Y.: Barron's Educational Series, Inc., 1974.

Palmer, R. R., and Joel Colton. *A History of the Modern World.* 5th ed. New York: Alfred A. Knopf, 1977.

AMERICAN HISTORY

Klose, N. *United States History.* 4th ed. 2 vols. Woodbury, N.Y.: Barron's Educational Series, Inc., N.Y., 1983.

Klose, N. and Midgley, D. *American History At A Glance: A Chronological Chart and Dictionary.* Barron's Educational Series, Inc., N.Y., 1978.

EASTERN·HISTORY

Quale, G. R. *Eastern Civilizations.* 2nd ed. New York: Appleton-Century-Crofts, Inc., 1975.

Rosenfeld, E., and H. Geller. *Afro-Asian Culture Studies.* 4th ed. Woodbury, N.Y.: Barron's Educational Series, Inc., 1979.

SOCIAL PSYCHOLOGY

Engle, T. L., and Louis Snellgrove. *Psychology. Its Principles and Applications.* 5th Edition. Harcourt, Brace, & Jovanovich, 1969.

POLITICAL SCIENCE

Johnson, S. A. *Essentials of Political Science.* Barron's Educational Series, Inc., N.Y., 1975.

THE KINDS OF QUESTIONS THAT APPEAR ON THE EXAMINATION

To give you an idea of the various types of questions you will face, we shall give some examples here and, where necessary, explain the process by which the right answer is derived. Simple recall questions are straightforward and require no explanation. Some examples of simple recall items follow, with the correct square blackened.

When did the British Navy defeat the Spanish Armada? Ⓐ ■ Ⓒ Ⓓ Ⓔ
 (A) 1066   (B) 1588   (C) 1648   (D) 1688   (E) 1750

What was the name of the treaty ending the Thirty Years' War? Ⓐ Ⓑ Ⓒ ■ Ⓔ
 (A) Treaty of Ghent   (B) Treaty of Paris
 (C) Treaty of Burgundy   (D) Treaty of Westphalia
 (E) Treaty of London

Where did General Grant in 1865 accept the surrender of General Lee? Ⓐ Ⓑ Ⓒ ■ Ⓔ
 (A) Richmond   (B) Vicksburg   (C) Gettysburg
 (D) Appomattox   (E) Atlanta

Who was the Prime Minister of Great Britain during the negotiations Ⓐ Ⓑ Ⓒ ■ Ⓔ
leading to the Treaty of Versailles in 1919?
 (A) Winston Churchill   (B) William Pitt   (C) Stanley Baldwin
 (D) Lloyd George   (E) Clement Attlee

A number of questions will test your ability to recall a number of related facts. An example of this type follows:

You are in a small country which now is landlocked. In the 19th century, its major was the capital of an empire with a vast polyglot population. In which of the following countries are you? □A □B □C ■D □E

(A) Bolivia   (B) Switzerland   (C) Paraguay   (D) Austria
(E) France

Explanation: Austria is the answer, but you must know a number of facts to deduce this answer. France's major city was the capital of a vast polyglot empire in the 19th century. But France is not landlocked. Bolivia, Switzerland, and Paraguay are all landlocked, but their major cities were not centers of large empires in the 19th century. Only Austria fits all the conditions. It is now landlocked after losing vast holdings at Versailles. Its capital city, Vienna, was the center of the vast polyglot Austrian Empire during the 19th century.

Another type of question tests your ability to attach major concepts to their original authors. An example follows:

Who held that the division of labor was the key to economic progress and that freedom in trade broadened markets, which in turn led to more division of labor and thus economic progress? □A □B ■C □D □E

(A) Toynbee   (B) Marx   (C) Adam Smith
(D) Thomas Aquinas   (E) Aristotle

Explanation: The interests of all the writers except Adam Smith were centered on issues quite otherwise than the effect of free trade on economic progress. Thus, Adam Smith is the answer.

Another type of question attempts to examine your facility in applying certain social science principles. An example follows:

The marginal propensity to consume in a population is 0.50. Investment expenditures increase by one billion dollars. Everything else being equal, you would expect national income to increase by about how many billion dollars? □A ■B □C □D □E

(A) 1   (B) 2   (C) 5   (D) 50   (E) 500

Explanation: The student who is acquainted with the "multiplier" concept and the fact that it is tied to the marginal propensity to consume by the

formula $M = \dfrac{1}{1-MPC}$ would know that two billion dollars is the answer. He would be applying certain principles from economics to get the answer.

Yet another type of question deals with the central themes which characterize various schools or traditions of thought. An example follows:

History moves in a path which ends only when world-wide stateless communism reigns. The struggle of economic classes is the engine of movement. This viewpoint is characteristic of □A □B □C □D ■E

(A) Transcendentalism   (B) Dialectical Idealism
(C) Freudianism   (D) Scholasticism   (E) Dialectical Materialism

Explanation: The student who knows both that Marxism uses dialectical processes and that Marx thought material conditions the basis of change would see that only the term, Dialectical Materialism, could fit the ideas in the above viewpoint.

Before attempting a whole sample examination over the vast social sciences area, let's look at some other examples, by specific subject. You should become acquainted with the various kinds of information which you will be asked to provide when you take the entire CLEP test. Sometimes it is difficult to decide in which subject area a question belongs, and in some cases we have had to arbitrarily assign a question to a particular discipline.

PRACTICE QUESTIONS ON SOCIAL SCIENCES—HISTORY

Questions about American History

Directions: Each of the questions or incomplete statements below is followed by five suggested answers or completions. Select the one that is best in each case.

1. Two churches native to America are
   (A) Mormon and Baptist
   (B) Salvation Army and Baptist
   (C) Quaker and Mormon
   (D) Adventist and Mormon
   (E) Methodist and Quaker

   1. Ⓐ Ⓑ Ⓒ Ⓓ Ⓔ

2. "He made the American vernacular the medium of a great literary work. The vigor of his prose comes directly from the speech of the great valley of the Far West." This statement refers to which of the following people?
   (A) Frederick Jackson Turner
   (B) James Fenimore Cooper
   (C) Thomas Jefferson
   (D) John Dewey
   (E) Samuel Clemens

   2. Ⓐ Ⓑ Ⓒ Ⓓ Ⓔ

3. Tariffs made up more than 85 percent of the federal government's revenue in which of the following years?
   (A) 1800   (B) 1865   (C) 1915   (D) 1937   (E) 1955

   3. Ⓐ Ⓑ Ⓒ Ⓓ Ⓔ

MAP A

Questions 4–7 pertain to MAP A.

4. Which of the following was the location of the surrender of General Lee to General Grant?
(A) 4   (B) 5   (C) 1   (D) 3   (E) 2

5. Which of the following was the location of a speech by Lincoln after Lee's forces were turned back from their northernmost advance?
(A) 4   (B) 5   (C) 1   (D) 2   (E) 3

6. A fort was fired on in the harbor of this city, and the American Civil War began. Where is it?
(A) 4   (B) 5   (C) 1   (D) 3   (E) 2

7. General Sherman took this city before marching to the sea. Where is it?
(A) 4   (B) 5   (C) 1   (D) 3   (E) 2

8. Which of the following states were formed from the area regulated by the Northwest Ordinance?
(A) Ohio, Indiana, Illinois, Michigan, Wisconsin
(B) Ohio, Kentucky, Illinois, Indiana, Michigan
(C) Ohio, Indiana, Kentucky, Tennessee, Illinois
(D) Ohio, Indiana, Illinois, Iowa, Missouri
(E) Ohio, Indiana, Illinois, Iowa, Nebraska

9. The Jacksonian era was related to
(A) a reduction in the restrictions regarding suffrage
(B) the establishment of the Republican party
(C) legislation creating land grant colleges
(D) legislation regulating rail transport
(E) the regular employment of Negroes in government

10. Which of the following sets was not closely associated with the issue of the federal government's sovereignty within the United States?
(A) Little Rock—Faubus—Eisenhower
(B) South Carolina—Nullification—Jackson
(C) Slavery—First Inaugural—Lincoln
(D) New England—Embargo—Jefferson
(E) New Deal—Supreme Court Packing—F. D. Roosevelt

11. Each of the following countries is paired with a decade during which large numbers of its citizens migrated to the United States. Which pair is incorrect?
(A) Sweden—1880s   (B) Ireland—1840s   (C) Italy—1860s
(D) Germany—1850s   (E) Russia—1890s

12. Which of the following pairs is inconsistent with the rest?
(A) Lincoln—Douglas   (B) Jackson—Biddle
(C) Hamilton—Burr   (D) Wilson—Lodge
(E) Jefferson—Madison

13. "How can an industrialized Northeast, a cotton-growing South, and a small farming West now live side by side in peace in our country?" This question about the U.S. might have been asked in

(A) 1780   (B) 1800   (C) 1815   (D) 1850   (E) 1970

13. A B C D E

14. The geographical distribution of Negroes in the U.S. changed most in which period?

(A) 1840-1860   (B) 1860-1880   (C) 1880-1900
(D) 1920-1940   (E) 1940-1960

14. A B C D E

15. American politicians talk of the "border" states. Which of the following is one?

(A) Kansas   (B) Indiana   (C) Ohio
(D) Mississippi   (E) Tennessee

15. A B C D E

16. The United States' membership in which of the following organizations is most consistent with the Monroe Doctrine?

(A) North Atlantic Treaty Organization
(B) Southeast Asia Treaty Organization
(C) International Monetary Fund
(D) Organization of American States
(E) United Nations Organization

16. A B C D E

17. "Every state should agree before an action is taken by the federal government." This sentiment is similar to the ideas expressed by

(A) Jackson   (B) Webster   (C) Hamilton   (D) Adams
(E) Calhoun

17. A B C D E

18. In which presidential election did traditionally Democratic Georgia, Alabama, and Mississippi go Republican?

(A) 1928   (B) 1932   (C) 1956   (D) 1964   (E) 1968

18. A B C D E

19. In order to avoid involvement in Europe and Asia in the 1930s, the United States relied chiefly upon

(A) collective security   (B) neutrality legislation
(C) the Kellogg-Briand Pact   (D) the League of Nations
(E) the "Good-Neighbor" policy

19. A B C D E

20. "Things are in the saddle and ride mankind." This statement reflects a revolt against materialism by certain thinkers in 19th-century America. Of which tradition are we speaking?

(A) Liberalism   (B) Pragmatism   (C) Transcendentalism
(D) Jacksonian Democracy   (E) Populism

20. A B C D E

21. New York became the most populous American city about the time that the

(A) American Revolution ended
(B) Constitution was ratified
(C) Erie Canal was completed
(D) Civil War was fought
(E) link-up of the Union Pacific and the Central Pacific occurred

21. A B C D E

22. The Supreme Court had ruled that martial law could not legitimately
be enforced where civil courts were open. Republicans denounced the
decision and talked of "packing" the court. The President at this time
in history was

22. Ⓐ Ⓑ Ⓒ Ⓓ Ⓔ

(A) John Kennedy (B) Abraham Lincoln
(C) Andrew Johnson (D) Woodrow Wilson
(E) Franklin Roosevelt

ANSWERS TO QUESTIONS ABOUT AMERICAN HISTORY

1. D	5. D	9. A	13. D	17. E	21. C
2. E	6. B	10. E	14. E	18. D	22. C
3. A	7. A	11. C	15. E	19. B	
4. C	8. A	12. E	16. D	20. C	

Questions about Western Civilization

Directions: Each of the questions or incomplete statements below is followed by
five suggested answers or completions. Select the one that is best in each case.

1. Which of the following was known to man before the Neolithic period?

1. Ⓐ Ⓑ Ⓒ Ⓓ Ⓔ

(A) Use of fire
(B) Domestication of animals
(C) Making pottery
(D) Practice of agriculture
(E) Making glass

2. The center of that civilization which we call Minoan was

2. Ⓐ Ⓑ Ⓒ Ⓓ Ⓔ

(A) in the islands along the Black Sea
(B) on the island of Crete
(C) in the central part of Asia Minor
(D) on the mainland of Greece
(E) on the Italian peninsula

3. The decline of power among the Greek city-states can be explained by

3. Ⓐ Ⓑ Ⓒ Ⓓ Ⓔ

(A) the military power of Persia
(B) soft living
(C) rivalry and civil war among the city-states
(D) the pursuit of philosophy and art to the neglect of political action
(E) inability to deal with sea power

4. Zoroaster believed that

4. Ⓐ Ⓑ Ⓒ Ⓓ Ⓔ

(A) the ruler was the living form of a god
(B) the world was a great struggle between the spirit of good and
the spirit of evil
(C) each part of the world was ruled over by its special spirit
(D) there was no relation between man's behavior and that of a god
(E) ancestors should be worshipped

5. As contrasted with English colonial administration, which of the following is true concerning Spanish colonial administration in the 17th and 18th centuries?
   (A) The authority of the Spanish king declined.
   (B) Spain did not maintain or enforce a mercantilist policy.
   (C) Spain permitted religious dissenters in its colonies.
   (D) Spain allowed less autonomy in its provinces in the New World.
   (E) Spain imposed less of a tax burden upon its colonies.

5. Ⓐ Ⓑ Ⓒ Ⓓ Ⓔ

6. Which of the following would have been a member of the bourgeoisie in France prior to 1789?
   (A) Landed noble (B) Peasant (C) Merchant
   (D) Lower-class workman in Paris (E) Bishop

6. Ⓐ Ⓑ Ⓒ Ⓓ Ⓔ

7. In the 4th century B.C., the Greek city-states which had been unable to unite were forcibly brought together under the rule of
   (A) Macedon (B) Persia (C) Phoenicia (D) Carthage
   (E) Rome

7. Ⓐ Ⓑ Ⓒ Ⓓ Ⓔ

8. The "Donation of Constantine" was a document which supposedly established
   (A) Charlemagne's claim to the throne
   (B) the Pope's right to political power in the West
   (C) Christianity as the legal religion within the Roman Empire
   (D) the capital of the Roman Empire at the city of Constantinople
   (E) legitimized transfer of power to Byzantium

8. Ⓐ Ⓑ Ⓒ Ⓓ Ⓔ

9. In 1870, a certain nation was among the four or five most populous nations on earth, its language widely used outside its borders. By 1970 it was not among the top ten countries in population, and its influence was much reduced. To what country are we referring?
   (A) Netherlands (B) Russia (C) U.S.A. (D) Japan
   (E) France

9. Ⓐ Ⓑ Ⓒ Ⓓ Ⓔ

10. What proportion of the USSR's adult citizens are members of the Communist Party?
    (A) Over 75% (B) Over 50% (C) Over 33% (D) Over 25%
    (E) Under 10%

10. Ⓐ Ⓑ Ⓒ Ⓓ Ⓔ

11. "There are perhaps two nations in this state and great efforts have been made to erase this fact. There is hope these efforts (such as changing the flag design) may succeed." To what country does this statement pertain?
    (A) France (B) Sweden (C) Denmark (D) Switzerland
    (E) Canada

11. Ⓐ Ⓑ Ⓒ Ⓓ Ⓔ

12. In the 16th century, England was under the rule of which family?
    (A) Tudors (B) Stuarts (C) Hapsburgs (D) Valois
    (E) Windsors

12. Ⓐ Ⓑ Ⓒ Ⓓ Ⓔ

13. The peace settlement of 1919 divided East Prussia from the rest of   13.   Ⓐ Ⓑ Ⓒ Ⓓ Ⓔ
Germany by a strip of territory belonging to
   (A) Poland   (B) Hungary   (C) Czechoslovakia
   (D) Lithuania   (E) Estonia

14. The reign of Marcus Aurelius marked the end of what Edward Gibbon   14.   Ⓐ Ⓑ Ⓒ Ⓓ Ⓔ
regarded as the great century of the "Roman Peace." Marcus Aurelius
lived in which century?
   (A) 1st B.C.   (B) 1st A.D.   (C) 2nd A.D.   (D) 4th A.D.
   (E) 2nd B.C.

15. Some historians have said that Alexander the Great was "lucky in his   15.   Ⓐ Ⓑ Ⓒ Ⓓ Ⓔ
death." They mean by this that he
   (A) died gloriously in battle amid his troops
   (B) died before the beginning of the disastrous retreat from the
       Indus
   (C) died before having to govern the huge empire he conquered
   (D) did not live to face defeat at the hands of the conquered peoples
       who were in revolt
   (E) died peacefully of old age

16. Which of these people never invaded the British Isles or established a   16.   Ⓐ Ⓑ Ⓒ Ⓓ Ⓔ
state there?
   (A) Romans   (B) Saxons   (C) Slavs   (D) Danes
   (E) Normans

17. Which of these lands was able to remain independent throughout the   17.   Ⓐ Ⓑ Ⓒ Ⓓ Ⓔ
19th century?
   (A) Burma   (B) Java   (C) The Philippines   (D) Siam
   (E) Ceylon

18. In 1904-5, Japan demonstrated its success in modernizing its armed   18.   Ⓐ Ⓑ Ⓒ Ⓓ Ⓔ
forces by defeating which European power?
   (A) Britain   (B) France   (C) Germany   (D) Spain
   (E) Russia

19. The Huns were   19.   Ⓐ Ⓑ Ⓒ Ⓓ Ⓔ
   (A) one of the German tribes
   (B) Asian invaders of Europe
   (C) Moslem invaders of Europe
   (D) the people led by Theodoric who conquered Italy
   (E) Vikings who conquered Normandy

20. "If God shows you a way in which you may lawfully get more than in   20.   Ⓐ Ⓑ Ⓒ Ⓓ Ⓔ
another way (without wrong to your soul or to any other), if you

refuse this and choose the less gainful way, you cross one of the ends of your callings, and you refuse to be God's steward." This sentiment was most representative of

(A) Scholasticism (B) 16th-century Anglicanism
(C) 17th-century English Puritanism (D) Monastic thought
(E) Christianity in the 1st century A.D.

21. The Austrian foreign minister who played an important role at the Congress of Vienna was

21. Ⓐ Ⓑ Ⓒ Ⓓ Ⓔ

(A) Talleyrand (B) Metternich (C) Castlereagh
(D) Baron Von Stein (E) Hindenburg

22. Which of the following best describes Alexander the Great?

22. Ⓐ Ⓑ Ⓒ Ⓓ Ⓔ

(A) He dreamed of blending the peoples and cultures of his empire into one.
(B) He so greatly admired Greek culture that he was highly intolerant of all others.
(C) He was interested in nothing but military conquest.
(D) He tried to exterminate the peoples he conquered.
(E) He saw the need to implement Plato's conception of a just republic.

23. "As to the speeches which were made either before or during the Peloponnesian War, it is hard for me, and for others who reported them to me, to recollect the exact words. I have therefore put into the mouth of each speaker the sentiments proper to the occasion, expressed as I thought he would be likely to express them." Who said this?

23. Ⓐ Ⓑ Ⓒ Ⓓ Ⓔ

(A) Homer (B) Herodotus (C) Thucydides
(D) Plato (E) Zeno

ANSWERS TO QUESTIONS ABOUT WESTERN CIVILIZATION

1. A	6. C	11. E	16. C	21. B
2. B	7. A	12. A	17. D	22. A
3. C	8. C	13. A	18. E	23. C
4. B	9. E	14. C	19. B	
5. D	10. E	15. C	20. C	

Questions about African/Asian Civilizations

Directions: Each of the questions or incomplete statements below is followed by five suggested answers or completions. Select the one that is best in each case.

1. Chinese culture and influence were most significant in shaping the institutions of which of the following countries?

1. Ⓐ Ⓑ Ⓒ Ⓓ Ⓔ

(A) India, Japan, and Korea
(B) Indonesia, Thailand, and the Philippines
(C) Burma, Pakistan, and Bangladesh
(D) Japan, Korea, and Vietnam
(E) Japan, Korea, and the Philippines

2. The area of the African continent is approximately

2. Ⓐ Ⓑ Ⓒ Ⓓ Ⓔ

   (A) half the area of Western Europe

   (B) three times the area of the continental United States

   (C) the same as the area of the United States east of the Mississippi River

   (D) two times the area of California

   (E) four times the area of South America

3. All of the following have been policies of the government of the People's Republic of China EXCEPT

3. Ⓐ Ⓑ Ⓒ Ⓓ Ⓔ

   (A) advocating equality for women in all aspects of Chinese life

   (B) doing away with private ownership of land by collectivizing agriculture

   (C) reemphasizing the importance of marriage and the family as the major socializing institution

   (D) involving all of the people in the political process

   (E) deemphasizing religion, viewing it as merely superstition

4. Between 1965 and 1974, which of the following was true concerning Nigeria, Uganda, and Ethiopia?

4. Ⓐ Ⓑ Ⓒ Ⓓ Ⓔ

   (A) They came under military rule.

   (B) Democratic governments were organized.

   (C) Apartheid became national policy.

   (D) They joined the European Common market.

   (E) They became independent nations.

5. The samurai were

5. Ⓐ Ⓑ Ⓒ Ⓓ Ⓔ

   (A) Japanese scholars

   (B) a people from Central Asia who invaded Japan

   (C) a Buddhist sect in Japan

   (D) a Japanese warrior class

   (E) Japanese industrialists

ANSWERS TO QUESTIONS ABOUT AFRICAN/ASIAN CIVILIZATIONS

1. D   2. B   3. C   4. A   5. D

Questions about Economics

Directions: Each of the questions or incomplete statements below is followed by five suggested answers or completions. Select the one that is best in each case.

1. The most important factor in creating the world "population explosion" has been

1. Ⓐ Ⓑ Ⓒ Ⓓ Ⓔ

   (A) higher fertility   (B) more multiple births

   (C) fewer wars   (D) more family sentiment

   (E) lower death rates

2. Malthus thought that human population, if unchecked, would tend to grow at

2. Ⓐ Ⓑ Ⓒ Ⓓ Ⓔ

   (A) an arithmetic rate   (B) a geometric rate

   (C) a constantly slow rate   (D) an undetermined rate

   (E) a rate determined by the sex ratio

3. Scarcity of resources in relation to desires or needs occurs

    (A) only under capitalism   (B) only under socialism

    (C) only during wartime   (D) in all societies

    (E) in money-using societies

3. A B C D E

4. The percentage of our work force in agricultural pursuits in 1800 was about

    (A) 20%   (B) 33%   (C) 50%   (D) 75%   (E) 95%

4. A B C D E

5. The main reason for organizing the C.I.O. in the 1930s was to

    (A) organize Negroes and immigrants who seldom belonged to a
        labor union

    (B) organize mass-production workers

    (C) escape the high fees of the A.F. of L.

    (D) organize craft workers

    (E) organize white-collar workers

5. A B C D E

6. In what part of the world is the education of women most retarded as to percentage and quality?

    (A) North America

    (B) Europe

    (C) Australia

    (D) Moslem Middle East

    (E) Japan

6. A B C D E

7. Which of the following countries raises the most sugar cane?

    (A) New Zealand

    (B) Canada

    (C) Italy

    (D) USSR

    (E) Cuba

7. A B C D E

8. One prime weakness in the Ricardian system of economics was thought to be its failure to reconcile interest payment with a labor theory of value. This gap was filled with a new theory in which interest was a payment for abstinence. This theory was supplied by

    (A) Say

    (B) Sismondi

    (C) Senior

    (D) Rodbertus

    (E) Marx

8. A B C D E

9. The practice of profitable trade (for monetary ends) was considered by Aristotle to be in the realm of

    (A) the admirable

    (B) "oikonomik," or useful household management

    (C) the sad but necessary pattern of working to resolve economic
        problems

    (D) the unnatural, or "chrematistik"

    (E) the inevitable

9. A B C D E

10. If anyone can be said to profit from a depression, the group favored would likely be
    (A) people with secure sources of fixed income, such as government bonds
    (B) people who borrowed money before the depression and must re-pay during it
    (C) industrial owners producing consumer goods
    (D) assembly-line workers in automobile plants
    (E) low-level local government workers

10. Ⓐ Ⓑ Ⓒ Ⓓ Ⓔ

11. Statistical evidence shows that the typical American family behaves in which of the following ways with respect to spending out of income?
    (A) An increasing proportion of income is spent on consumption as income increases.
    (B) The same proportion of income is spent on consumption at all except very low income levels.
    (C) The same proportion of income is spent on consumption at all income levels.
    (D) A decreasing proportion of income is spent on consumption as income increases.
    (E) The same proportion of income is spent on consumption at all except very high income levels.

11. Ⓐ Ⓑ Ⓒ Ⓓ Ⓔ

GRAPH A

Questions 12–14 refer to GRAPH A.

12. The thick black line in Graph A represents
    (A) supply   (B) cost   (C) subsidy   (D) demand   (E) interest

12. Ⓐ Ⓑ Ⓒ Ⓓ Ⓔ

13. Graph A would be most descriptive (because of the attitude of the thick black line) of one of the following:
    (A) foreign currency   (B) aspirin   (C) land   (D) razor blades
    (E) plastic toys

13. Ⓐ Ⓑ Ⓒ Ⓓ Ⓔ

14. The thick black line in Graph A would be termed
    (A) elastic   (B) inelastic   (C) in attitudinal   (D) formal
    (E) informal

14. Ⓐ Ⓑ Ⓒ Ⓓ Ⓔ

15. The various editions of John Stuart Mill's *Principles of Political Economy* indicate that he

   (A) became increasingly conservative and anti-socialist as he grew older

   (B) made remarkably few changes in the views which he first held as a young Benthamite

   (C) completely abandoned the socialist views he had held as a young man

   (D) increasingly recognized exceptions to a general policy of a laissez-faire society

   (E) became more convinced that economic justice and political monarchy were tied together

15. Ⓐ Ⓑ Ⓒ Ⓓ Ⓔ

16. In Western Europe during the 11th and 12th centuries, the right to coin money was

   (A) reserved to the Holy Roman Emperor

   (B) held only by kings

   (C) a monopoly of the Church

   (D) held by a number of nobles, kings, and cities

   (E) was in the care of the state banks

16. Ⓐ Ⓑ Ⓒ Ⓓ Ⓔ

17. Which of the following countries has the smallest gross national product?

   (A) Sweden   (B) France   (C) West Germany   (D) Japan

   (E) United Kingdom

17. Ⓐ Ⓑ Ⓒ Ⓓ Ⓔ

18. In Western Europe, debate and philosophical conflict over the social value of the private property concept would have been of most concern in

   (A) 1630   (B) 1690   (C) 1750   (D) 1850   (E) 1970

18. Ⓐ Ⓑ Ⓒ Ⓓ Ⓔ

19. In the U.S., if one's family had an annual income of $55,000 in 1978, it had a larger income than

   (A) 25% of all other families   (B) 75% of all other families

   (C) 80% of all other families   (D) 99% of all other families

   (E) none of the above

19. Ⓐ Ⓑ Ⓒ Ⓓ Ⓔ

20. India's gross national product is about twice that of Sweden. This means

   (A) India is more advanced in technology

   (B) that the average Indian is twice as well-off as the average Swede

   (C) India has sufficient capital

   (D) all of these

   (E) none of these

20. Ⓐ Ⓑ Ⓒ Ⓓ Ⓔ

21. Gross national product in the U.S. in 1978 was about how much greater than the value of all imports into the U.S. in that year?

   (A) 3 times greater

   (B) 5 times greater

   (C) 10 times greater

   (D) 15 times greater

   (E) 100 times greater

21. Ⓐ Ⓑ Ⓒ Ⓓ Ⓔ

22. The transport of goods in the U.S. (in terms of ton-miles) is still primarily by
    (A) motor trucks   (B) canal barges   (C) pipelines
    (D) railroads   (E) airlines

    22. Ⓐ Ⓑ Ⓒ Ⓓ Ⓔ

23. In national income accounting, which of the following is not part of national income but of personal income?
    (A) Social Security contributions
    (B) Corporate income taxes
    (C) Undistributed corporate profits
    (D) Personal consumption expenditures
    (E) Transfer payments

    23. Ⓐ Ⓑ Ⓒ Ⓓ Ⓔ

24. Travel by people between cities in the U.S. is now primarily by
    (A) ship   (B) railroad   (C) motor bus   (D) airplane
    (E) automobile

    24. Ⓐ Ⓑ Ⓒ Ⓓ Ⓔ

25. The flow of money can best be envisaged as
    (A) linear
    (B) vertical
    (C) zigzag
    (D) circular
    (E) waving

    25. Ⓐ Ⓑ Ⓒ Ⓓ Ⓔ

26. All firms, whether competitive or not, will tend to produce to the point where
    (A) average revenue equals marginal revenue
    (B) fixed costs equal variable costs
    (C) marginal costs equal marginal revenue
    (D) fixed costs equal marginal revenue
    (E) variable costs equal price

    26. Ⓐ Ⓑ Ⓒ Ⓓ Ⓔ

27. In 1933 the purpose of the United States government in devaluing the dollar in terms of gold was to
    (A) raise domestic prices and make American goods cheaper abroad
    (B) lower domestic prices and make American goods more expensive abroad
    (C) establish the gold standard
    (D) stop excessive exports of American goods
    (E) reduce the ability of the gold-producing USSR to exchange gold for industrial and military goods

    27. Ⓐ Ⓑ Ⓒ Ⓓ Ⓔ

ANSWERS TO QUESTIONS ABOUT ECONOMICS

1. E	5. B	9. D	13. C	17. A	21. D	25. D
2. B	6. D	10. A	14. B	18. D	22. D	26. C
3. D	7. E	11. D	15. D	19. D	23. E	27. A
4. E	8. C	12. A	16. D	20. E	24. E	

Questions about Sociology and Social Psychology

Directions: Each of the questions or incomplete statements below is followed by five suggested answers or completions. Select the one that is best in each case.

1. Caste and class are
   (A) different in degree (B) different kinds of social phenomena
   (C) identical concepts (D) not found in America
   (E) capitalist characteristics

   1. Ⓐ Ⓑ Ⓒ Ⓓ Ⓔ

2. The marriage of one female to more than one male is called
   (A) monogamy (B) celibacy (C) polyandry
   (D) polygyny (E) endogamy

   2. Ⓐ Ⓑ Ⓒ Ⓓ Ⓔ

3. In the original sense, the term civilization meant
   (A) a humane way of living
   (B) citylike ways of life
   (C) a way of living based on food production rather than food gathering
   (D) better ways of living
   (E) a group of tribes with a common king

   3. Ⓐ Ⓑ Ⓒ Ⓓ Ⓔ

4. In 1940, American Negroes faced formal segregation in
   (A) the armed forces of the United States
   (B) railroad trains in interstate commerce in the South
   (C) colleges and universities in the South
   (D) all of the above
   (E) none of the above

   4. Ⓐ Ⓑ Ⓒ Ⓓ Ⓔ

5. The proportion of people under 15 years of age and over 65 to the number between 15 and 65 is the
   (A) demographic ratio (B) sex ratio (C) population ratio
   (D) natural increase ratio (E) dependency ratio

   5. Ⓐ Ⓑ Ⓒ Ⓓ Ⓔ

6. A political role is
   (A) a personality type (B) a position of high prestige
   (C) a sign of success (D) a collection of rights and duties
   (E) independent of reciprocal relations

   6. Ⓐ Ⓑ Ⓒ Ⓓ Ⓔ

7. Stratification is most closely related to social
   (A) identification (B) differentiation (C) amalgamation
   (D) disorganization (E) assimilation

   7. Ⓐ Ⓑ Ⓒ Ⓓ Ⓔ

8. Which series represents a trend from little to more social mobility?
   (A) Caste, class, estates
   (B) Estates, caste, class
   (C) Caste, estates, class
   (D) Class, caste, estates
   (E) There is an equal amount of social mobility in each.

   8. Ⓐ Ⓑ Ⓒ Ⓓ Ⓔ

9. Which of the following statements is incorrect?
   (A) Adherence to the mores is regarded as necessary to the welfare of society.
   (B) In the mores, "right makes might."
   (C) Conviction based on the mores transcends argument and "rational demonstration."
   (D) Mores include taboos and positive injunctions.
   (E) Form and content of mores are universally identical.

9. Ⓐ Ⓑ Ⓒ Ⓓ Ⓔ

10. Folkways might include
    (A) rules of eating
    (B) forms of greeting
    (D) conduct at parties
    (C) all of the above
    (E) none of the above

10. Ⓐ Ⓑ Ⓒ Ⓓ Ⓔ

11. A sociological term for internal migration is
    (A) marginal utility   (B) miscegenation
    (C) horizontal mobility   (D) vertical mobility
    (E) social dynamics

11. Ⓐ Ⓑ Ⓒ Ⓓ Ⓔ

12. Antagonistic cooperation is another name for
    (A) conflict   (B) accommodation   (C) competition
    (D) assimilation   (E) functionalism

12. Ⓐ Ⓑ Ⓒ Ⓓ Ⓔ

13. The social relationships most prevalent in our society are
    (A) secondary   (B) primary   (C) migratory
    (D) all of these   (E) none of these

13. Ⓐ Ⓑ Ⓒ Ⓓ Ⓔ

14. The Negro fertility rate in the U.S. for the past two decades has been
    (A) the same as the white
    (B) somewhat less than the white
    (C) sometimes less and sometimes more than the white
    (D) about 15% higher than the white
    (E) about 35% higher

14. Ⓐ Ⓑ Ⓒ Ⓓ Ⓔ

15. A caste society is characterized by all but which one of the following?
    (A) Intermarriage is forbidden across caste.
    (B) Most statuses are achieved.
    (C) Taboos define social distance between castes.
    (D) Individual status is hereditary and permanent.
    (E) Occupations are specific to special hereditary groups.

15. Ⓐ Ⓑ Ⓒ Ⓓ Ⓔ

16. A "sect" religion tends to be
    (A) in accord with the values of the society in which it exists
    (B) lenient toward the indifferent
    (C) a reforming element hoping to make the society more livable
    (D) withdrawn from societal norms and extremely pietistic
    (E) the official religion of the state in which it exists

16. Ⓐ Ⓑ Ⓒ Ⓓ Ⓔ

17. A Russian by the name of Pavlov conducted a series of experiments with animals and discovered conditioned reflex. This finding was the basis of which school of thought?
   (A) psychoanalysis   (B) behaviorism   (C) relativism
   (D) the new idealism   (E) Hegelianism

17. Ⓐ Ⓑ Ⓒ Ⓓ Ⓔ

18. If teaching facts is the *sole* aim of a teacher, she will probably do better if she is
   (A) non-directive
   (B) permissive and informal
   (C) directive and authoritarian
   (D) disorganized
   (E) group oriented

18. Ⓐ Ⓑ Ⓒ Ⓓ Ⓔ

19. The idea that upper echelon corporate officials develop nervous disorders more frequently than workers down the line is, of course, false. Its persistence is related to the
   (A) aesthetic ethic
   (B) Puritan ethic
   (C) situational ethic
   (D) melioristic ethic
   (E) pragmatic ethic

19. Ⓐ Ⓑ Ⓒ Ⓓ Ⓔ

20. In *Civilization and its Discontents*, Freud expressed his viewpoint concerning the necessity of controlling the antisocial and aggressive propensities of man. Which of the following authors had the most similar ideas?
   (A) Rousseau
   (B) Locke
   (C) Condorcet
   (D) Hobbes
   (E) John Dewey

20. Ⓐ Ⓑ Ⓒ Ⓓ Ⓔ

21. Opposition which focuses on the opponent, basically, and only secondarily on the reward is most closely associated with social
   (A) accommodation
   (B) stratification
   (C) competition
   (D) conflict
   (E) differentiation

21. Ⓐ Ⓑ Ⓒ Ⓓ Ⓔ

22. Cases where infants were subject to prolonged isolation show that
   (A) human beings can acquire culture without human contact
   (B) human beings cannot become socialized unless they are brought up among human beings
   (C) mental-physical development does not depend upon human contacts
   (D) people are born with most of the traits they exhibit as adults
   (E) language use comes at a certain age, regardless of the social situation

22. Ⓐ Ⓑ Ⓒ Ⓓ Ⓔ

ANSWERS TO QUESTIONS ABOUT SOCIOLOGY AND SOCIAL PSYCHOLOGY

1. A	4. D	7. B	10. D	13. A	16. D	19. B	22. B
2. C	5. E	8. C	11. C	14. E	17. B	20. A	
3. B	6. D	9. E	12. B	15. B	18. C	21. D	

Questions about Political Science

Directions: Each of the questions or incomplete statements below is followed by five suggested answers or completions. Select the one that is best in each case.

1. To which of the following did the U.S. Supreme Court apply the phrase "separate but equal"?   1. Ⓐ Ⓑ Ⓒ Ⓓ Ⓔ
   (A) The formula for racial segregation (1896)
   (B) The nature of federal-state relations (1828)
   (C) The status of Indian tribal governments (1874)
   (D) The relative powers of the Senate and House of Representatives (1810)
   (E) The legal status of men and women (1913)

2. The law that can be considered the most important impetus to trade union organization was the   2. Ⓐ Ⓑ Ⓒ Ⓓ Ⓔ
   (A) Sherman Act of 1890
   (B) Wagner Act of 1935
   (C) Taft-Hartley Act of 1947
   (D) Social Security Act of 1935
   (E) National Recovery Act of 1933

3. The case of *McCulloch* v. *Maryland* is considered one of the most important cases decided by the U.S. Supreme Court. In its decision, the court announced a major Constitutional concept concerning   3. Ⓐ Ⓑ Ⓒ Ⓓ Ⓔ
   (A) separation of church and state   (B) judicial review
   (C) segregation   (D) anti-trust regulation
   (E) implied powers

4. All of the following features of American government were derived from English government *except*   4. Ⓐ Ⓑ Ⓒ Ⓓ Ⓔ
   (A) the common law   (B) bicameralism   (C) federalism
   (D) the county as a unit of government
   (E) civil rights such as jury trial and *habeas corpus*

5. One of the following is a judicially recognized limitation of the power of the President to remove civil officers whom he has appointed.   5. Ⓐ Ⓑ Ⓒ Ⓓ Ⓔ
   (A) The Senate has to approve all such removals.
   (B) The President cannot remove individuals belonging to the opposition party.
   (C) The President cannot remove individuals for political reasons.
   (D) Congress can prescribe the reasons for which members of the independent regulatory commissions may be removed from their positions.
   (E) The House must be informed.

6. The position of the Chief Justice of the United States Supreme Court is filled by
   (A) seniority   (B) promotion   (C) specific appointment
   (D) election   (E) rotation among justices

   6. Ⓐ Ⓑ Ⓒ Ⓓ Ⓔ

7. The principle of implied powers in the Constitution was established in the case of
   (A) *Marbury* v. *Madison*   (B) *McCulloch* v. *Maryland*
   (C) *Fletcher* v. *Peck*   (D) *Missouri* v. *Holland*
   (E) *Zorach* v. *Clauson*

   7. Ⓐ Ⓑ Ⓒ Ⓓ Ⓔ

8. The body of legal rules based upon reason as applied in past cases going far back in English history is known as
   (A) constitutional law   (B) statutory law   (C) common law
   (D) administrative law   (E) international law

   8. Ⓐ Ⓑ Ⓒ Ⓓ Ⓔ

9. Which of the following governmental subdivisions in the state of Louisiana corresponds to the county in other states?
   (A) ward   (B) district   (C) township   (D) parish
   (E) province

   9. Ⓐ Ⓑ Ⓒ Ⓓ Ⓔ

10. Ambassadors are appointed by the
    (A) President without the approval of Congress under a special provision of the Constitution
    (B) President from a list chosen by the merit system
    (C) President with the consent of the Senate
    (D) retiring ambassadors, with the approval of the President, from a list of technically trained individuals
    (E) President from a list of graduates of the Foreign Service Academy

    10. Ⓐ Ⓑ Ⓒ Ⓒ Ⓔ

11. Puerto Rico is an illustration of
    (A) an unincorporated or partially organized territory
    (B) an incorporated territory
    (C) a protectorate
    (D) a commonwealth
    (E) a dominion

    11. Ⓐ Ⓑ Ⓒ Ⓓ Ⓔ

12. In matters of high administration, the armed forces of the U.S. are under the control of
    (A) the Departments of War and of the Navy
    (B) the President   (C) Congress   (D) the General Staff
    (E) the Secretary of Defense

    12. Ⓐ Ⓑ Ⓒ Ⓓ Ⓔ

13. The policy of imperialism in the U.S. from 1890 to 1910 was largely the result of
    (A) the theory of isolation
    (B) a desire to build up a colonial empire
    (C) demands for commercial expansion
    (D) a wide spread desire to become a world power
    (E) missionary zeal

    13. Ⓐ Ⓑ Ⓒ Ⓓ Ⓔ

14. In the Constitution, the states were granted the right to   14. Ⓐ Ⓑ Ⓒ Ⓓ Ⓔ
    (A) exercise only the powers given to them by the Constitution
    (B) settle directly their disputes with Mexico or Canada
    (C) establish their own militia without reference to United States
        Army standards
    (D) exercise all powers not denied by the Constitution
    (E) refuse to permit women the vote

15. The Senate must ratify or reject all   15. Ⓐ Ⓑ Ⓒ Ⓓ Ⓔ
    (A) treaties with other nations, by a two-thirds vote of the Senators
        present
    (B) appointments of the President by a majority vote
    (C) treaties or agreements between two states
    (D) treaties with other nations by a two-thirds vote of the full mem-
        bership of the Senate
    (E) appointments of minor officials by the President

16. The work of the Department of Labor in the President's cabinet is,   16. Ⓐ Ⓑ Ⓒ Ⓓ Ⓔ
    in the main,
    (A) supporting the American Federation of Labor and other labor
        organizations in their activities
    (B) collecting statistics on labor conditions and making recommen-
        dations to the President
    (C) regulating labor conditions in industry by issuing orders modi-
        fying wages or hours, or both
    (D) regulating working conditions of government employees
    (E) providing for binding arbitration in industrial disputes

17. The Prohibition Amendment, ratified in 1919, was   17. Ⓐ Ⓑ Ⓒ Ⓓ Ⓔ
    (A) repealed by the Twenty-first Amendment
    (B) modified but not repealed entirely
    (C) repealed by Congress to meet an economic emergency
    (D) acted upon by popular conventions in each state
    (E) a war measure, not intended to be permanent

18. In some states, voters may originate legislation by   18. Ⓐ Ⓑ Ⓒ Ⓓ Ⓔ
    (A) common consent   (B) initiative petition
    (C) letters to the legislature   (D) ordinance   (E) church rules

19. When the government (state or national) takes possession and owner-   19. Ⓐ Ⓑ Ⓒ Ⓓ Ⓔ
    ship of private property for public use, it is exercising the right of
    (A) public ownership   (B) eminent domain
    (C) state confiscation   (D) public domain   (E) *ad hoc* rule

20. An American male in 1983 is white, 50 years old, lives in Topeka, Kansas,   20. Ⓐ Ⓑ Ⓒ Ⓓ Ⓔ
    makes $30,000 a year as an owner of a small business. You would, on the
    basis of probability, expect him to vote
    (A) Democratic
    (B) Socialist
    (C) States Rights or American Independent
    (D) Republican
    (E) Socialist Labor

21. Which of the following do most historians agree is most significant for the continuance of democracy?   **21.** Ⓐ Ⓑ Ⓒ Ⓓ Ⓔ
    (A) A written constitution
    (B) Control of finances by legislatures
    (C) Separation of powers
    (D) A large number of political parties
    (E) Protection of civil liberties for all citizens

22. Which of the following metropolitan areas gave George Wallace a plurality in 1968?   **22.** Ⓐ Ⓑ Ⓒ Ⓓ Ⓔ
    (A) San Francisco   (B) Syracuse   (C) Denver
    (D) Dallas   (E) Nashville

23. "The right of citizens of the United States to vote in any primary or other election for President or Vice-President, for electors for elections for President or Vice-President, or for Senator or Representative in Congress shall not be denied or abridged by the United States or any state by reason of failure to pay any poll tax or other tax." The above statement is taken from which of the following amendments to the United States Constitution?   **23.** Ⓐ Ⓑ Ⓒ Ⓓ Ⓔ
    (A) Fifth   (B) Fifteenth   (C) Twentieth
    (D) Twenty-third   (E) Twenty-fourth

24. The largest absolute vote in American history received by a candidate for president *not* of the Republican or Democratic Parties was achieved by   **24.** Ⓐ Ⓑ Ⓒ Ⓓ Ⓔ
    (A) Weaver in 1892   (B) Roosevelt in 1912
    (C) LaFollette in 1924   (D) Thomas in 1932
    (E) Wallace in 1968

25. The Republican party dominated the presidency from 1860 to 1912. A single Democrat was elected to the presidency in that period. He was   **25.** Ⓐ Ⓑ Ⓒ Ⓓ Ⓔ
    (A) Grover Cleveland   (B) Horace Greeley
    (C) William Howard Taft   (D) William McKinley
    (E) Ulysses S. Grant

26. Sovereignty can be defined as   **26.** Ⓐ Ⓑ Ⓒ Ⓓ Ⓔ
    (A) freedom
    (B) the power to command and control
    (C) government with the consent of the governed
    (D) rule by kings
    (E) a tyranny of the many over the few

ANSWERS TO QUESTIONS ABOUT POLITICAL SCIENCE

1. A	6. C	11. D	16. B	21. E	26. B
2. B	7. B	12. B	17. A	22. E	
3. E	8. C	13. C	18. B	23. E	
4. C	9. D	14. D	19. B	24. E	
5. D	10. C	15. A	20. D	25. A	

Sample Examinations

This chapter contains three sample Social Sciences examinations, each followed by an answer key, scoring chart, and answer explanations. After you complete each exam, determine your score and mark it on the Progress Chart on page 14. You will see your score climb as you work through each test and become more familiar with the type of questions asked.

SAMPLE EXAMINATION 1

Part I

Number of Questions: 63
Time: 45 minutes

Directions: Each of the questions or incomplete statements below is followed by five suggested answers or completions. Select the one that is best in each case.

1. Which of the following were periods of inflation in U.S. history?
   (A) 1919-21   (B) 1946-48   (C) 1951-52
   (D) 1973-78   (E) All of these

   1. Ⓐ Ⓑ Ⓒ Ⓓ Ⓔ

2. Which of the following migrations involved most people?
   (A) Norsemen into Britain in the 9th and 10th centuries
   (B) English into North America in the 17th century
   (C) Blacks from Africa into the Western Hemisphere in the 17th and 18th centuries
   (D) Spaniards into Mexico in the 16th century
   (E) Asiatics into Hawaii in the 19th century

   2. Ⓐ Ⓑ Ⓒ Ⓓ Ⓔ

3. Which of the following countries is not a federation in form?
   (A) Canada   (B) United States   (C) Australia
   (D) USSR   (E) France

   3. Ⓐ Ⓑ Ⓒ Ⓓ Ⓔ

4. Governmental control of the air (for aircraft, radio, and television) exists in which of the following countries? I. The Soviet Union, II. The United States, III. Great Britain.
   (A) I only   (B) II only   (C) III only
   (D) I and III only   (E) I, II, and III

   4. Ⓐ Ⓑ Ⓒ Ⓓ Ⓔ

5. Adam Smith contended that
   (A) government should run the economy
   (B) governments which encourage particular industries with various aids increase real wealth
   (C) governments should not interfere in the natural circulation of labor and capital
   (D) government must do something direct about labor's poverty
   (E) government must redirect the activities of most men

   5. Ⓐ Ⓑ Ⓒ Ⓓ Ⓔ

6. If the present rate (1978) of natural increase and net in-migration

   6. Ⓐ Ⓑ Ⓒ Ⓓ Ⓔ

in America is maintained, the population of the country in the year 2000 A.D. will be approximately

(A) 100,000,000   (B) 180,000,000   (C) 200,000,000
(D) 280,000,000   (E) 500,000,000

7. The proportion of females in the U.S. public school elementary teaching force is about

(A) 95%   (B) 70%   (C) 60%   (D) 50%   (E) 30%

7. A B C D E

8. Which of the following movements has most in common with Calvin's idea of predestination?

(A) Populism   (B) Transcendentalism   (C) Pragmatism
(D) Puritanism   (E) Technocratism

8. A B C D E

9. "It is a symbol of status. It has altered courting patterns. It has contributed to the increase in obesity and heart disease. It has contributed to a host of services and industries. It has helped the growth of suburbs. It has helped to alter state-federal governmental relations." The problematical "it" in the statement is the

(A) automobile   (B) elevator   (C) refrigerator
(D) subway   (E) railroad

9. A B C D E

10. The Supreme Court declared state action unconstitutional in all of the following instances *except*

(A) *Dartmouth College* v. *Woodward*   (B) *Baker* v. *Carr*
(C) *Lochner* v. *New York*   (D) *Gibbons* v. *Ogden*
(E) *Marbury* v. *Madison*

10. A B C D E

11. The Dred Scott decision, in effect, ruled which of the following unconstitutional?

(A) Agricultural Adjustment Act   (B) Sherman Act
(C) Pure Food and Drug Act   (D) Compromise of 1850
(E) The Second Bank of the United States

11. A B C D E

12. The formula for the investment multiplier in Keynesian macroeconomics is

(A) 1/MPC   (B) 1/MPS   (C) 1/1-MPS
(D) MPS/1   (E) MPC/1

12. A B C D E

13. One of the following countries which had been sending large numbers of immigrants to the United States (in the period from 1890 to the mid-1920s) was given a relatively low quota of immigrants by legislation passed in 1924 in the United States. Which one?

(A) Great Britain
(B) China
(C) Japan
(D) Germany
(E) Italy

13. A B C D E

14. During the nineteenth century, which of the following European countries held no colonies?

(A) France and Switzerland   (B) Germany and Finland
(C) Italy and Spain   (D) Sweden and Denmark
(E) Sweden and Switzerland

14. A B C D E

15. Which of the following countries lost territory because of a meeting at Munich in 1938?

    (A) Switzerland   (B) Poland   (C) France

    (D) Hungary   (E) Czechoslovakia

15. Ⓐ Ⓑ Ⓒ Ⓓ Ⓔ

16. Which of the following assertions influenced Darwin in his formulation of the theory of natural selection?

    (A) "Population decreases while agriculture forges ahead?"

    (B) "It is the constant tendency in all animated life to increase beyond the nourishment prepared for it."

    (C) "No progress is possible because of the basic sex drive which increases population at a geometric rate."

    (D) "Nations which are over-populated must be allowed to expand their inhabitants abroad."

    (E) "Selection of the race which is most military is inevitable."

16. Ⓐ Ⓑ Ⓒ Ⓓ Ⓔ

17. Which best describes the attitude of Mazzini?

    (A) He strongly believed in the racial superiority of the Italians since they had given the world so much.

    (B) He believed that Italian unity could best be attained under the leadership of a patriotic monarch.

    (C) He believed that each nation had a special mission to perform to contribute to the welfare of humanity in general.

    (D) He firmly believed in the cosmopolitan ideal of the 18th century, that all men were citizens of the world rather than of a single nation.

    (E) He thought that true leadership in Italy would have to come from within the Roman Catholic Church.

17. Ⓐ Ⓑ Ⓒ Ⓓ Ⓔ

A   B

18. If each dot in A represents five hundred refrigerators in a county and each dot in B one drug store in the same county, which of the following statements are likely to be correct? I. There may be a factor underlying the spatial distribution of refrigerators that also underlies the spatial distribution of drug stores. II. Refrigerators and drug stores are similarly distributed in the county, but refrigerators are in greater quantity. III. There are at least four population concentrations in the county. IV. The county is mountainous.

    (A) I and III only   (B) II and IV only

    (C) I, II, and III only   (D) II, III, and IV only   (E) I only

18. Ⓐ Ⓑ Ⓒ Ⓓ Ⓔ

19. Which of the following belongs in a different category from the others?

    (A) Wagner Act   (B) Norris-LaGuardia Act   (C) Taft-Hartley Act

    (D) National Industrial Recovery Act   (E) Hawley-Smoot Act

19. Ⓐ Ⓑ Ⓒ Ⓓ Ⓔ

20. To declare a law unconstitutional, the decision of the Supreme Court must be
   (A) unanimous
   (B) by a simple majority
   (C) by a two-thirds majority of the court
   (D) by the vote of seven out of nine justices
   (E) eight out of nine

21. The Hundred Years' War was important in military history because it
   (A) demonstrated that foot troops could not withstand a mounted feudal cavalry
   (B) showed the need for heavily armored troops
   (C) increased the importance of the feudal noble in warfare
   (D) proved the effectiveness of foot soldiers armd with longbows
   (E) showed that seapower was tied to the firepower of ships

22. In year B, total spending was 20% greater than in year A. Given this information alone about the United States economy, we
   (A) know that prices were 20% greater in year B
   (B) know that prices were 10% greater in year B
   (C) know that prices were 15% greater in year A
   (D) can tell little about comparative price levels in the two years
   (E) can be sure that more goods were produced in year B

23. The germ theory of disease was primarily the work of
   (A) Galileo   (B) Weismann   (C) Pasteur   (D) Swann
   (E) Mendel

24. Which of these ideas best represents the position of the Medieval Church upon economic affairs?
   (A) Economics belongs to the world; the Church is concerned only with matters of the spirit.
   (B) Profits on a loan are justified when it is a capital investment.
   (C) A just price is whatever people are willing to pay.
   (D) The whole of man's life and activities is governed by Christian law.
   (E) All Christians should share God's material gifts equally.

25. The production possibility curve indicates
   (A) the maximum output series of any two products
   (B) the minimum output series of any two products
   (C) the gains that can be made by mass production in one product area
   (D) the gains in profit from wider markets
   (E) the gains in profit from controlling prices

26. The best definition of the cost of a resource is
   (A) money spent
   (B) the effort put forth in a given time period
   (C) effort times money
   (D) the amount of labor it takes to create the resource
   (E) the value of alternative uses of the resource

27. Which of the following = NNP?

27. Ⓐ Ⓑ Ⓒ Ⓓ Ⓔ

   (A) GNP − direct taxes   (B) GNP − depreciation

   (C) GNP − indirect taxes   (D) GNP − defense costs

   (E) GNP − interest

28. The writer to which Malthus most objected (because of what Malthus considered his shallow optimism concerning population) was

28. Ⓐ Ⓑ Ⓒ Ⓓ Ⓔ

   (A) Adam Smith   (B) David Ricard   (C) John Stuart Mill

   (D) William Godwin   (E) Jeremy Bentham

29. The birth rate in the U.S. over the last 175 years has

29. Ⓐ Ⓑ Ⓒ Ⓓ Ⓔ

   (A) remained fairly static

   (B) increased greatly

   (C) decreased greatly

   (D) tended to fluctuate wildly around a stable average

   (E) declined in depressed economy periods only

30. The best definition for "nation" is a group of people who

30. Ⓐ Ⓑ Ⓒ Ⓓ Ⓔ

   (A) live within the same state

   (B) speak the same language

   (C) simply feel themselves to be a nation

   (D) are of the same racial origin

   (E) have the same religious faith

31. Among the following, the best example of a society which used its educational system mainly to train an avocational "gentlemanly" elite was

31. Ⓐ Ⓑ Ⓒ Ⓓ Ⓔ

   (A) Ancient Sparta   (B) Old China   (C) the Soviet Union

   (D) the United States today   (E) England in the 18th century

32. Which of the following is usually less disapproved of than the others? Illegitimacy resulting from

32. Ⓐ Ⓑ Ⓒ Ⓓ Ⓔ

   (A) adultery

   (B) incest

   (C) cross-caste union

   (D) union before marriage (parents marrying at a later date)

   (E) union between people sworn to religious celibacy

33. The period of the most massive immigration into the United States was between

33. Ⓐ Ⓑ Ⓒ Ⓓ Ⓔ

   (A) 1840 and 1865   (B) 1880 and 1896   (C) 1900 and 1914

   (D) 1920 and 1930   (E) 1940 and 1965

34. The American Declaration of Independence states that "men are endowed by their creator with certain inalienable rights." The same idea is also very clearly expressed in the writings of

34. Ⓐ Ⓑ Ⓒ Ⓓ Ⓔ

   (A) Bossuet   (B) Duke of Sully   (C) Machiavelli

   (D) John Locke   (E) Montaigne

35. Which of the following writers spoke of the potential "despotism of the many" in the United States?

35. Ⓐ Ⓑ Ⓒ Ⓓ Ⓔ

   (A) Marx   (B) Gaitskell   (C) de Tocqueville

   (D) Kluckhohn   (E) Hook

36. "The value of a commodity is, in itself, of no interest to the capitalist. What alone interests him is the surplus value that dwells in it and is realisable by sale." In which of the following works would this statement occur?
   (A) *Wealth of Nations*
   (B) *Essay on Population*
   (C) *The Protestant Ethic and the Spirit of Capitalism*
   (D) *Theory of the Leisure Class*
   (E) *Capital*

   36. Ⓐ Ⓑ Ⓒ Ⓓ Ⓔ

37. The Boers of South Africa were the descendants of settlers who had come to that land from
   (A) England   (B) the Netherlands   (C) Germany
   (D) Portugal   (E) Ireland

   37. Ⓐ Ⓑ Ⓒ Ⓓ Ⓔ

38. Which of these English kings was executed by a revolutionary government?
   (A) James I   (B) Charles I   (C) Charles II   (D) James II
   (E) Henry VIII

   38. Ⓐ Ⓑ Ⓒ Ⓓ Ⓔ

39. Which of the following held that the qualities of pleasure were roughly equal, or that "push-pin was as good as poetry"?
   (A) John Stuart Mill   (B) Wordsworth   (C) William Godwin
   (D) Jeremy Bentham   (E) William Morris

   39. Ⓐ Ⓑ Ⓒ Ⓓ Ⓔ

40. Which of the following peoples were especially influenced by Byzantine civilization and the Byzantine form of Christianity?
   (A) Turks   (B) Germans   (C) Slavs   (D) Celts   (E) Iberians

   40. Ⓐ Ⓑ Ⓒ Ⓓ Ⓔ

41. In the 18th century scientific thought considered "nature" most commonly in terms of
   (A) growth and development   (B) mechanics   (C) pure idea
   (D) essence and vital soul   (E) categorization

   41. Ⓐ Ⓑ Ⓒ Ⓓ Ⓔ

42. The Boxer Rebellion in China was
   (A) an effort to overthrow the rule of the Manchu emperor
   (B) a revolt against the Japanese rule in Korea
   (C) an attack upon foreigners in China
   (D) the revolution which established the Chinese Republic
   (E) a fight to establish Confucianism

   42. Ⓐ Ⓑ Ⓒ Ⓓ Ⓔ

43. If you wanted to visit the oldest sites of the civilization of the Incas, you would go to
   (A) Mexico   (B) Guatemala   (C) Cuba   (D) Peru   (E) Venezuela

   43. Ⓐ Ⓑ Ⓒ Ⓓ Ⓔ

44. Which best describes the following 18th-century rulers: Catherine II of Russia, Frederick II of Prussia, and Joseph II of Austria?
   (A) Made mock of the "divine right" idea of kingship.
   (B) Went to considerable length to avoid war.
   (C) Wished to introduce various reforms which were supposed to contribute to the welfare of their subjects.
   (D) Constitutional monarchs.
   (E) Wished to expand their holdings in South America.

   44. Ⓐ Ⓑ Ⓒ Ⓓ Ⓔ

45. The "Great Trek" refers to
  (A) the expansion of Canada to the west
  (B) the migration of Europeans to New Zealand
  (C) the movement of Dutch-speaking Boers out of Cape Colony
  (D) the great sheep drives in Australia
  (E) General Custer's march into Montana

45. Ⓐ Ⓑ Ⓒ Ⓓ Ⓔ

MAP C

46. Which area, long in Prussian hands, did the USSR annex in 1945?
  (A) 2   (B) 10   (C) 4   (D) 5   (E) 14

46. Ⓐ Ⓑ Ⓒ Ⓓ Ⓔ

47. Bonn is the capital of which country?
  (A) 2   (B) 1   (C) 10   (D) 16   (E) 21

47. Ⓐ Ⓑ Ⓒ Ⓓ Ⓔ

48. Which area is Turkish, in Europe, and dominates the Dardanelles?
  (A) 17   (B) 7   (C) 13   (D) 12   (E) 8

48. Ⓐ Ⓑ Ⓒ Ⓓ Ⓔ

49. The ultimate social aim of all economic activity is to
  (A) insure adequate profits to business
  (B) give material means to government servants
  (C) keep everybody working hard
  (D) make private property secure
  (E) produce goods for final consumption

49. Ⓐ Ⓑ Ⓒ Ⓓ Ⓔ

50. The best way in economics to define "saving" is to call it 50. Ⓐ Ⓑ Ⓒ Ⓓ Ⓔ
    (A) a time deposit (B) an investment
    (C) an act of prudence (D) refraining from consumption
    (E) the building of national solvency

51. "Marginal utility" is associated with the idea that a high price for a 51. Ⓐ Ⓑ Ⓒ Ⓓ Ⓔ
    commodity results from
    (A) much labor being required to produce it
    (B) its relative rarity in relation to demand
    (C) its great usefulness to people
    (D) its association with an exploitive capitalist system
    (E) its not being mass-produced

52. In the U.S., increasing food and fiber production in this century 52. Ⓐ Ⓑ Ⓒ Ⓓ Ⓔ
    cannot be attributed to
    (A) a larger farm work force
    (B) more machinery
    (C) better seeds and fertilizer
    (D) more efficient management
    (E) better agricultural education programs

53. Since people interacting take one another into account and modify their 53. Ⓐ Ⓑ Ⓒ Ⓓ Ⓔ
    behaviors, interaction is
    (A) secondary
    (B) formal
    (C) cohesive
    (D) reciprocal
    (E) marginal

54. Which of these rights from the UN Declaration of Human Rights 54. Ⓐ Ⓑ Ⓒ Ⓓ Ⓔ
    would most likely have *not* been accepted as a right by early 19th-
    century classic liberals?
    (A) Everyone has the right to recognition as a person before the law.
    (B) No one shall be subjected to torture or to cruel, inhuman, or de-
        grading treatment or punishment.
    (C) No one shall be arbitrarily deprived of his property.
    (D) Everyone who works has a right to favorable remuneration,
        which ensures human dignity for his family and provides him
        with social security.
    (E) No one shall be subject to arbitrary arrest.

55. In which state of the U.S. is the rate of college attendance among 55. Ⓐ Ⓑ Ⓒ Ⓓ Ⓔ
    18 to 24 year olds the highest?
    (A) West Virginia (B) Georgia (C) Pennsylvania
    (D) Massachusetts (E) Utah

56. In soliciting funds for volunteer health or community programs, 56. Ⓐ Ⓑ Ⓒ Ⓓ Ⓔ
    motivational researchers have discovered the most efficient tech-
    nique is to utilize
    (A) sex (B) shame and comparison with others
    (C) patriotism (D) charm (E) community welfare

57. The sociologist who was concerned to analyze what he called "mechanical" vs. "organic" solidarity was
(A) Emile Durkheim
(B) C. Wright Mills
(C) Robert Merton
(D) Louis Wirth
(E) Pitirim Sorokin

57. Ⓐ Ⓑ Ⓒ Ⓓ Ⓔ

58. The most common way to secure a wife in most simple patrilocal African societies was by
(A) sororate rules   (B) purchase   (C) royal dispensation
(D) stealing   (E) capture

58. Ⓐ Ⓑ Ⓒ Ⓓ Ⓔ

59. War is utilized in Orwell's *1984* society for all of the following purposes *except*
(A) limiting the relative power of each state through repeated military realignments
(B) assuring the loyalty of party members and the solidarity of the citizenry
(C) gaining permanent control of the uncommitted areas, their resources, and populations
(D) as a means for subjugating the population and destroying the excess products resulting from advanced technology
(E) perpetuating the existent power structure

59. Ⓐ Ⓑ Ⓒ Ⓓ Ⓔ

60. "The young Kaiser William II was jealous of the aged minister who had domineered over Germany so long." Who was the minister?
(A) Tirpitz   (B) Dollfuss   (C) Stein
(D) Bethman-Hollweg   (E) Bismarck

60. Ⓐ Ⓑ Ⓒ Ⓓ Ⓔ

61. In European Medieval agriculture, the three-field system was a
(A) means of dividing agricultural land among the three main social classes
(B) method of rotating crops on the manor
(C) plan in which both the king and the church received part of the product of the land
(D) plan to divide manors among various owners
(E) system of irrigating three or more farms with one canal system

61. Ⓐ Ⓑ Ⓒ Ⓓ Ⓔ

62. When the founding fathers established the electoral college system, they expected that
(A) mass education would improve the electorate and make direct popular election reasonable
(B) partisan conflict over the election of a President could be avoided
(C) a democratic system would evolve whereby the people would select the President according to a weighted formula which equates the popular and electoral votes
(D) a democratic party system would develop, thus making selection of the President a popular decision
(E) Washington would serve two terms, after which an amendment would require the election of a President by the House of Representatives

62. Ⓐ Ⓑ Ⓒ Ⓓ Ⓔ

63. Which of the following is not one of the so-called "Cow Colleges" created under the Morrill Act passed during the Civil War? The University of

(A) Nebraska (B) Tennessee (C) Missouri
(D) Kansas (E) Pennsylvania

Part II

Number of Questions: 62
Time: 45 minutes

Directions: Each of the questions or incomplete statements below is followed by five suggested answers or completions. Select the one that is best in each case.

64. "According to the materialist conception of history the determining element in history is ultimately the production and reproduction in real life. More than this neither Marx nor I have ever asserted." The colleague of Marx who said this was

(A) Lenin (B) Stalin (C) Engels (D) Marshall
(E) Bismarck

65. In the 10th century the ruler of which capital would have called himself "Emperor of the Romans"?

(A) Baghdad (B) Cairo (C) Kiev (D) Constantinople
(E) London

66. Who changed the coins of France so that the old inscription "Liberté, Egalité, Fraternité," was replaced by "Patrie, Travail, Famille"?

(A) DeGaulle
(B) Petain
(C) Mendes-France
(D) Clemenceau
(E) Briand

67. "If an ambitious young man wanted to get into the House of Commons, the quickest way was to pay a large sum to the man whose influence controlled the few votes in some country village that sent members to Parliament." In what year did a reform bill largely end this situation?

(A) 1797 (B) 1832 (C) 1867 (D) 1884 (E) 1929

68. "Forced by the prospect of having to fight both the British and American fleet as well as the Latin American rebels the 'Concert' broke down and Spanish American colonies were allowed to remain republics." This statement refers to the decade starting in

(A) 1790 (B) 1820 (C) 1850 (D) 1870 (E) 1940

69. If greatly diluted amounts of the infection were given in slowly increasing doses, resistance to the disease developed. In 1885, the treatment was tried on a nine-year-old boy bitten by a mad dog. He was cured. Who administered the cure?

(A) Lister (B) Freud (C) Pasteur (D) Spock (E) Koch

70. The animal physiologist whose discovery of the conditioned reflex showed the exclusion of conscious processes from basic behavior patterns was
(A) Darwin (B) Rousseau (C) Freud (D) Pavlov (E) Watson

70. Ⓐ Ⓑ Ⓒ Ⓓ Ⓔ

71. What is the median income of seven families earning the following incomes: (1) $8,000 (2) $10,000 (3) $12,000 (4) $6,000 (5) $15,000 (6) $30,000 (7) $20,000?
(A) $6,000   (B) $12,000   (C) $10,000   (D) $15,000
(E) $16,000

71. Ⓐ Ⓑ Ⓒ Ⓓ Ⓔ

72. Which of the following is not contemporary with the others?
(A) Expansion of U.S. holdings in the Pacific
(B) Heavy immigration into the U.S. from Southern Europe
(C) A tendency to feel that the American frontier had finally vanished
(D) A strong movement to end "Jim Crowism" in the U.S.
(E) Growing sentiment against trusts and monopoly

72. Ⓐ Ⓑ Ⓒ Ⓓ Ⓔ

73. Which of the following is a procedural, rather than a substantive, civil right?
(A) Freedom of religion   (B) Freedom of speech
(C) Freedom of assembly   (D) The right to vote
(E) The right to trial by jury

73. Ⓐ Ⓑ Ⓒ Ⓓ Ⓔ

74. The political boundaries of states in Africa came about mainly because of
(A) geographic and economic ties between tribes
(B) racial antagonisms
(C) tribal organization and power
(D) 19th century European power politics
(E) nationalist sentiments in African populations at the end of the 19th century

74. Ⓐ Ⓑ Ⓒ Ⓓ Ⓔ

75. The Medieval European intellectual class was drawn almost entirely from
(A) lawyers   (B) the clergy
(C) members of the landed aristocracy   (D) guildsmen
(E) royalty

75. Ⓐ Ⓑ Ⓒ Ⓓ Ⓔ

76. One attribute of money which is imperative is
(A) gold backing   (B) scarcity   (C) heavy weight
(D) permanent physical form   (E) none of the above

76. Ⓐ Ⓑ Ⓒ Ⓓ Ⓔ

77. If one said that in a certain year the naval strength of the great powers was in the following order: (1) Great Britain, (2) Germany, (3) United States, (4) France, that year would be
(A) 1802   (B) 1840   (C) 1922   (D) 1932   (E) 1913

77. Ⓐ Ⓑ Ⓒ Ⓓ Ⓔ

78. Although religious freedom was granted to all in England by the 18th century, people of which religion could not be members of Parliament?
(A) Anglican   (B) Methodist   (C) Presbyterian
(D) Quaker   (E) Roman Catholic

78. Ⓐ Ⓑ Ⓒ Ⓓ Ⓔ

79. Which prime minister had most to do with a sizeable extension of suffrage in Great Britain in 1867?
(A) Gladstone   (B) Pitt   (C) Grey   (D) Disraeli   (E) Baldwin

80. The man responsible for gaining independence for Vietnam from French colonial domination was
(A) Mao Tse-tung   (B) Mahatma Gandhi   (C) Ho Chi Minh
(D) Bao Dai   (E) Richard Nixon

81. "It was a grand time for debtors, especially those in debt for land; they could pay off a mortgage on the farm by selling a single load of apples. But thousands of people on pensions, rigid salaries, or on interest found themselves paupers." This statement would describe
(A) the U.S. in 1873
(B) Germany in 1923
(C) the U.S. in 1925
(D) the U.S. in 1933
(E) Great Britain in 1935

82. The civil liberties guaranteed in the Bill of Rights and the Fourteenth and Fifteenth Amendments to the Constitution were of special concern to the Supreme Court whose Chief Justice was
(A) Charles Evans Hughes   (B) William Howard Taft
(C) Roger Taney   (D) Earl Warren   (E) John Marshall

83. Which of the following books, cited in the 1954 school segregation case, was authored by Gunnar Myrdal?
(A) *The American Commonwealth*
(B) *America as a Civilization*
(C) *An American Dilemma*
(D) *The Promise of American Life*
(E) *America's Sixty Families*

84. President Hoover's statement in the early 1930s, "Prosperity is just around the corner," is most in accord with the thought of
(A) Malthus   (B) Ricardo   (C) Keynes   (D) Marx   (E) Veblen

85. American marriage and divorce laws
(A) are outlined in the Constitution
(B) vary from state to state
(C) are uniform for the nation
(D) have no effect on marriage and divorces
(E) all of the above

86. Which group might benefit from inflationary trends?
(A) Old-age pensioners   (B) Bondholders
(C) Land speculators   (D) Salaried workers
(E) Educators

87. Which of the following is *not* one of the component factors which make possible the flow of production?
(A) Land   (B) Labor   (C) Capital   (D) Capitalism
(E) Organization

88. The federal government's efforts to restrict the growth of monopoly are based on
    (A) the Sherman Act   (B) the Clayton Act
    (C) the Federal Trade Commission Act   (D) all of these
    (E) none of these

88. Ⓐ Ⓑ Ⓒ Ⓓ Ⓔ

89. The American family is typically
    (A) matrilocal   (B) patrilocal   (C) neolocal
    (D) paleolocal   (E) rurolocal

89. Ⓐ Ⓑ Ⓒ Ⓓ Ⓔ

90. From a sociological standpoint, the "sacredness" of an object or idea lies in the
    (A) object or idea itself
    (B) spirit which dwells in the object or idea
    (C) type of object or idea
    (D) kind of people who believe in it
    (E) attitude of the observer

90. Ⓐ Ⓑ Ⓒ Ⓓ Ⓔ

91. Max Weber said that this man's ideas about Christianity contributed in an indirect way to the rise of capitalism. He was
    (A) John Calvin   (B) Durkheim   (C) Thomas Aquinas
    (D) Henry VIII   (E) Augustine

91. Ⓐ Ⓑ Ⓒ Ⓓ Ⓔ

92. Which can be defined as any formal ceremony prescribed by the group as having symbolic significance?
    (A) Mores   (B) Folkways   (C) Ritual
    (D) All of the above   (E) None of the above

92. Ⓐ Ⓑ Ⓒ Ⓓ Ⓔ

93. "All persons held as slaves within any State or designated part of a State, the people whereof shall then be in rebellion against the United States shall be then, thenceforward, and forever free." The above statement is taken from the
    (A) Abolitionist papers
    (B) Fifteenth Amendment to the Constitution
    (C) Freedmen's Bureau Act
    (D) Thirteenth Amendment to the Constitution
    (E) Emancipation Proclamation

93. Ⓐ Ⓑ Ⓒ Ⓓ Ⓔ

94. Dialectical materialism (Marxism) bases a theory of social change on
    (A) the struggle of ideas
    (B) free will in history
    (C) the struggle of economic classes
    (D) the cooperation of worker and owner
    (E) the religious impulse to communal spirit

94. Ⓐ Ⓑ Ⓒ Ⓓ Ⓔ

95. Traditional French liberalism included all but one of the following:
    (A) anti-clericalism
    (B) opposition to the aristocracy
    (C) anti-Socialism
    (D) religious education
    (E) protest against big government

95. Ⓐ Ⓑ Ⓒ Ⓓ Ⓔ

96. We sometimes hear a peace described as "Carthaginian." Judging from what you know of the conclusion of the Third Punic War, this term means
    (A) a soft and lenient peace
    (B) an armistice or temporary cessation of the hostilities
    (C) a peace so severe that it means virtual destruction of the enemy
    (D) a peace which leaves both sides exhausted
    (E) the evolution of a group of allies who stand off a common enemy

96. Ⓐ Ⓑ Ⓒ Ⓓ Ⓔ

97. "I proposed never to accept anything for true which I did not clearly know to be such." Who said this?
    (A) Pascal   (B) Descartes   (C) Bayle   (D) Locke   (E) Hobbes

97. Ⓐ Ⓑ Ⓒ Ⓓ Ⓔ

98. "The marginal propensity to consume" refers to the
    (A) level of income at which consumer spending just equals income
    (B) inclination on the part of some to "keep up with the Joneses" in their consumer spending
    (C) fraction of extra income that will be spent on consumption
    (D) amount a family (or community) will spend on consumption at different levels of income
    (E) fact that, at low incomes, families spend more on consumption than the amount of their incomes

98. Ⓐ Ⓑ Ⓒ Ⓓ Ⓔ

99. In the effort to counteract a depression or recession, Federal Reserve Banks might:
    (A) increase the reserve requirement
    (B) decrease the interest rate charged commercial banks
    (C) sell government securities to individuals
    (D) raise the interest rate charged commercial banks
    (E) raise margin requirements on stock purchases

99. Ⓐ Ⓑ Ⓒ Ⓓ Ⓔ

100. The Mullahs are
    (A) a Moslem sect
    (B) teachers of Islamic law and dogma
    (C) political leaders of the Moslems
    (D) a ruling dynasty of Baghdad
    (E) followers of Islam who are black

100. Ⓐ Ⓑ Ⓒ Ⓓ Ⓔ

101. A grand jury is
    (A) an organization of outstanding civic leaders
    (B) a group of citizens whose function is to determine the facts in a civil or criminal trial
    (C) the jury used in appellate courts
    (D) a group of citizens responsible for bringing formal charges against a person accused of a serious crime
    (E) a jury that is called in major cases

101. Ⓐ Ⓑ Ⓒ Ⓓ Ⓔ

102. Justices of the Supreme Court who disagree with a decision may prepare a
    (A) concurring opinion   (B) advisory opinion
    (C) dissenting opinion   (D) declaratory judgment
    (E) *per curiam* decision

102. Ⓐ Ⓑ Ⓒ Ⓓ Ⓔ

103. Which statement is incorrect about the United States Supreme Court?   103. Ⓐ Ⓑ Ⓒ Ⓓ Ⓔ
   (A) The court passes on the constitutionality of all acts of Congress.
   (B) The court has jurisdiction in disputes between states.
   (C) It may overrule a precedent.
   (D) Justices are appointed by the President with the consent of the Senate.
   (E) The court makes decisions on the basis of simple majority.

104. The first significant example of colonial unity in America was the   104. Ⓐ Ⓑ Ⓒ Ⓓ Ⓔ
   (A) First Continental Congress
   (B) Albany Congress
   (C) Second Continental Congress
   (D) Stamp Act Congress
   (E) Articles of Confederation

105. President Roosevelt announced a policy of aid to the opponents of Germany   105. Ⓐ Ⓑ Ⓒ Ⓓ Ⓔ
   (A) soon after Hitler became Chancellor of Germany
   (B) in a message vetoing the Neutrality Act of 1935
   (C) in defining the American attitude toward the Spanish Civil War
   (D) after he won the presidential election in November 1940
   (E) after a series of German victories had occurred in western and northern Europe

106. Which of the following writers felt that the frontier loosened the bonds of custom, offered new experiences, and had a permanent effect on American institutions?   106. Ⓐ Ⓑ Ⓒ Ⓓ Ⓔ
   (A) Henry George   (B) Thorstein Veblen
   (C) Charles A. Beard   (D) Allen Nevins
   (E) Frederick Jackson Turner

107. The Meiji Restoration in Japan (1867-68) was   107. Ⓐ Ⓑ Ⓒ Ⓓ Ⓔ
   (A) an effort to cut all ties with the West and go back to ancient Japanese ways
   (B) the beginning of Japan's modernization
   (C) the capture of Formosa by Japan
   (D) the overthrow of the Japanese Emperor
   (E) the reestablishment of the power of the shogunate

108. "Inconvenience, suffering, and death are the penalties attached by nature to ignorance, as well as to incompetence. . . . It is impossible in any degree to suspend this discipline by stepping in between ignorance and its consequences, without, to a corresponding degree, suspending the progress. If to be ignorant were as safe as to be wise, no one would become wise." This quotation came from   108. Ⓐ Ⓑ Ⓒ Ⓓ Ⓔ
   (A) Nikolai Lenin   (B) Jean Jacques Rousseau
   (C) Cardinal Newman   (D) Herbert Spencer   (E) John Locke

109. Which of the following pairs are examples of ascribed status?   109. Ⓐ Ⓑ Ⓒ Ⓓ Ⓔ
   (A) Age and kinship   (B) Sex and kinship   (C) Age and sex
   (D) All of the above   (E) None of the above

110. Those ideas, habits, and conditioned responses common to the members of a society are
(A) alternatives
(B) specialties
(C) individual peculiarities
(D) universals
(E) all of the above

110. Ⓐ Ⓑ Ⓒ Ⓓ Ⓔ

111. In which of the following years has the dependency ratio (proportion of those under fifteen years of age or sixty-five and above to the rest of the population) been highest in the U.S.?
(A) 1900   (B) 1920   (C) 1940   (D) 1950   (E) 1975

111. Ⓐ Ⓑ Ⓒ Ⓓ Ⓔ

112. The concept of anomie refers to
(A) folk society
(B) a highly normative situation
(C) a condition marked by normlessness
(D) a highly dense population
(E) a warring state armed with atomic weapons

112. Ⓐ Ⓑ Ⓒ Ⓓ Ⓔ

113. If members of two mutually hostile juvenile gangs start taking heavy doses of "downer" drugs, gang fights between them
(A) become more frequent
(B) are more violent in nature
(C) result in more destruction to their neighborhood
(D) become less frequent
(E) are conducted in middle-class neighborhoods

113. Ⓐ Ⓑ Ⓒ Ⓓ Ⓔ

114. The Congo territory was developed and exploited during the last half of the 19th century by a private company which was organized by the king of
(A) Germany
(B) Italy
(C) Portugal
(D) Belgium
(E) Sweden

114. Ⓐ Ⓑ Ⓒ Ⓓ Ⓔ

115. Genghis Khan was the leader of
(A) a nomadic people of Central Asia
(B) the Chinese
(C) a nation of Asian Moslems
(D) a sea-going people of southeast Asia
(E) tribes from northern Japan

115. Ⓐ Ⓑ Ⓒ Ⓓ Ⓔ

116. Thomas Jefferson maintained that
(A) only educated men could know the truth
(B) until the masses were educated aristocratic government was more likely to be just than was republican government
(C) education would make all men equal in ability
(D) by means of education, republican societies should train the ablest minds for leadership
(E) the greatest enemies of liberty were the over-educated

116. Ⓐ Ⓑ Ⓒ Ⓓ Ⓔ

Assume that firm A in a highly competitive industry has the following cost-price situation:

UNITS PRODUCED	PRICE PER UNIT	TOTAL COSTS PER UNIT	MARGINAL COST PER UNIT	TOTAL REVENUE PER UNIT	MARGINAL REVENUE PER UNIT
10,000	$6.00	$17.00	$ 4.00	$6.00	$6.00
30,000	6.00	8.33	4.00	6.00	6.00
50,000	6.00	7.40	6.00	6.00	6.00
60,000	6.00	7.25	6.50	6.00	6.00
70,000	6.00	8.00	12.50	6.00	6.00

117. Firm A will produce a number of units closer to which of the following figures?
   (A) 10,000　　(B) 30,000　　(C) 50,000　　(D) 60,000
   (E) 70,000

118. Firm A is, at a price of $6.00, in a
   (A) slightly profitable situation
   (B) highly profitable situation
   (C) loss situation
   (D) undetermined situation
   (E) up and down situation

119. If firm A were in a monopolistic situation, or a partly monopolistic situation, the figures for
   (A) marginal costs per unit would change
   (B) total costs per unit would change
   (C) all columns would stay the same
   (D) price per unit would change and thus the revenue figures
   (E) the number of units produced would increase

120. Which of the following men would least likely agree with the other four concerning man's basic nature?
   (A) Thomas Hobbes　　(B) Machiavelli　　(C) Condorcet
   (D) Augustine　　(E) St. Paul

121. Which of the following did not occur during the 1760-1826 period in American history?
   (A) A doctrine was formulated concerning American attitudes toward European intervention in the Western Hemisphere.
   (B) Political parties appeared in the U.S. for the first time.
   (C) The first National Bank was established.
   (D) Texas became part of the United States.
   (E) Two wars against the British were conducted.

122. "It is difficult to believe in the dreadful but quiet war of organic beings going on in the peaceful woods and smiling fields." Who would have expressed this idea?
   (A) Karl Marx　　(B) John Locke　　(C) Adam Smith
   (D) Charles Darwin　　(E) Robert Owen

123. "That my life has no aim is evident even from the accidental nature of its origin; that I can posit an aim for myself is another matter." Who said this?

(A) Nickolai Lenin   (B) Friedrich Nietzsche   (C) Pascal
(D) John Stuart Mill   (E) Isaac Newton

123. Ⓐ Ⓑ Ⓒ Ⓓ Ⓔ

124. You are visiting a rural area. Income per family is less than $1,000 per year; housing is mostly shacks with no electricity or running water; mothers average ten live births during their fertile years. In which of the following states would you probably be?

(A) Delaware   (B) Connecticut   (C) Ohio
(D) Rhode Island   (E) South Carolina

124. Ⓐ Ⓑ Ⓒ Ⓓ Ⓔ

125. Human sexual behavior is expressed and controlled primarily by
(A) instinct
(B) drives
(C) internalized learning
(D) rational calculation
(E) laws

125. Ⓐ Ⓑ Ⓒ Ⓓ Ⓔ

ANSWER KEY—SAMPLE EXAMINATION 1

Part I

1. E	12. B	23. C	34. D	44. C	54. D
2. C	13. E	24. D	35. C	45. C	55. E
3. E	14. E	25. A	36. E	46. E	56. B
4. E	15. E	26. E	37. B	47. E	57. A
5. C	16. B	27. B	38. B	48. E	58. B
6. D	17. C	28. D	39. D	49. E	59. C
7. A	18. C	29. C	40. C	50. D	60. E
8. D	19. E	30. C	41. B	51. B	61. B
9. A	20. B	31. E	42. C	52. A	62. B
10. E	21. D	32. D	43. D	53. D	63. E
11. D	22. D	33. C			

Part II

64. C	75. B	86. C	96. C	106. E	116. D
65. D	76. B	87. D	97. B	107. B	117. C
66. B	77. E	88. D	98. C	108. D	118. C
67. B	78. E	89. C	99. B	109. D	119. D
68. B	79. D	90. E	100. B	110. D	120. C
69. C	80. C	91. A	101. D	111. A	121. D
70. D	81. B	92. C	102. C	112. C	122. D
71. B	82. D	93. E	103. A	113. D	123. B
72. D	83. C	94. C	104. B	114. D	124. E
73. E	84. B	95. D	105. E	115. A	125. C
74. D	85. B				

SCORING CHART—SAMPLE EXAMINATION 1

After you have scored your Sample Examination 1, enter the results in the chart below; then transfer your Raw Score to the Progress Chart on page 14.

Total Test	Number Right	Number Wrong	Number Omitted	Raw Score
Part I: 63				
Part II: 62				
Total: 125				

ANSWER EXPLANATIONS—SAMPLE EXAMINATION 1

Part I

1. E.   The following periods in U.S. history were all periods of inflation: 1919–21, 1946–48, 1951–52, and 1973–78. The period 1919–21 followed our participation in World War I; 1946–48 followed World War II: 1951–52 followed the period of major fighting in the Korean War; and 1973–78 followed the Vietnam War.

2. C.   During the 17th and 18th centuries a world wide slave trade centered in Africa, where blacks were kidnaped by slavers and shipped to the Western Hemisphere, particularly the United States, where they were sold as slaves. Some 2 million persons were involved in this forced migration.

3. E.   France is centrally governed from Paris. The districts (called departments) have relatively little autonomy. The other countries are made up of states (the U.S. and Australia), provinces (Canada), or republics (the U.S.S.R.) which, at least in theory, share power with the central government.

4. E.   All the major powers assert control of the air (airspace) over their territory for aircraft, radio, and television.

5. C.   Adam Smith (1723–1790), a Scottish economist, wrote *An Inquiry into the Nature and Causes of the Wealth of Nations*, an extremely influential book. In it he developed the theory, usually referred to as "laissez faire" (let do), that economic forces should be allowed to operate without government interference.

6. D.   The population of the United States in 1985 is estimated at 235 million. The rate of natural increase (births minus deaths) and net in-migration (immigration minus emigration) is estimated at more than 2½ million annually. This would give us a population of 280,000,000 by the year 2000.

7. A.   In the United States, public school elementary teaching has traditionally been a female occupation especially in the elementary schools. About 95% of all teachers in the U.S. public elementary schools are females.

8. D.   Calvin believed that the fate of the individual was determined by God before birth. This doctrine is called predestination. The Puritans were followers of Calvin. They left England because they did not accept the doctrines of the Church of England.

9. A.   The automobile has altered courting patterns, contributed to obesity and heart disease, produced major industries. helped the growth of suburbs and helped to alter state-federal governmental relations. It is also a status symbol. None of the others fit this description.

10. **E.** In *Marbury v. Madison* (1803) the Supreme Court declared part of the Judiciary Act, passed by Congress in 1789, unconstitutional. In the other cases the Court declared state action unconstitutional. In the Dartmouth College case it was New Hampshire, in Lochner and Gibbons it was New York, and in Baker *v.* Carr, it was Tennessee.

11. **D.** The Compromise of 1850 prohibited slavery in the territories north of 36°30′ except Missouri. Dred Scott, a slave, was taken into free territory and claimed his freedom. The Supreme Court ruled that Dred Scott remained a slave even in free territory. Thus, in effect the Court ruled the Missouri Compromise unconstitutional.

12. **B.** The formula for the investment multiplier in Keynesian macroeconomics is 1/MPS, MPS being the Marginal Propensity to Save. The MPS is the fraction of each extra dollar that goes to saving instead of consumption.

13. **E.** The immigration law of 1924 limited immigration to the United States from any country to 2 per cent of the persons of that nationality residing in the United States in 1890. This drastically reduced the numbers admitted from Eastern Europe and Southern Europe (Italy).

14. **E.** Sweden and Switzerland had no colonies during the nineteenth century. France had colonies in Africa and Asia; Germany had colonies in Africa; Denmark ruled Greenland and two of the Virgin Islands; Spain retained control over the Philippines.

15. **E.** Czechoslovakia was forced to yield to Hitler's claim that the Sudetenland should be ceded to Germany because it contained a majority of ethnic Germans. Neville Chamberlain, Prime Minister of Great Britain, returned from Munich saying "I bring you peace in our time."

16. **B.** In his formulation of the theory of natural selection, Darwin was influenced by the assertion, "It is the constant tendency in all animated life to increase beyond the nourishment prepared for it. " Darwin's work, *On the Origin of Species*, was published in 1859.

17. **C.** Mazzini was called "the soul of Italian unification." His belief that each nation had a special mission to perform to contribute to the welfare of humanity in general inspired the Italian people and caused them to fight for Italian unification.

18. **C.** Statements I, II, and III may reasonably be deduced from the diagram. But there is no way of telling whether the country is mountainous or not.

19. **E.** The Hawley-Smoot Act of 1930 was a tariff act. The others related to labor.

20. **B.** Decisions of the United States Supreme Court are by a simple majority. Since 1869, the Court has consisted of nine judges. If all nine judges participate in a decision, a vote of 5 or more for or against the appellant determines the case.

21. **D.** The Hundred Years War 1337–1453 was fought between England and France. At the Battle of Crecy (1346) the English footsoldiers, armed with longbows, routed the French.

22. **D.** Many factors account for the level of total spending. These include total income, taxation, people's perception of the future state of the economy, position on the business cycle, war and peace, stock market trends, interest rates and inflation. Hence the level of spending in any two years tells us little about comparative price levels in the two years or the amount of goods produced in the two years.

23. **C.** Pasteur developed the germ theory of disease and showed that innoculation could prevent anthrax and tetanus.

24. **D.** The Medieval Church taught that the whole of man's life and activities is governed by Christian law. This, of course, included economic affairs.

25. **A.** The production possibility curve indicates the maximum output series of any two products. The two products often used as illustrations in economics are guns and butter. The curve shows the maximum output of either.

26. **E.** The best definition of the cost of a resource is the value of alternative uses of the resource. Of possible alternative uses, the one that has the highest value (in economic terms) determines the cost.

27. **B.** Net National Product equals Gross National Product minus depreciation.

28. **D.** William Godwin (1756–1836) English political philosopher wrote *An Enquiry Concerning Political Justice.* His doctrine that man would improve when coercive institutions were removed was naive according to Malthus.

29. **C.** The factors responsible for the great decrease in the birth rate in the United States during the past 175 years include (1) decrease in the death rate particularly in childhood (2) decline in the farm population and (3) widespread adoption of family planning.

30. **C.** A nation exists only when people feel themselves to be a nation. People who live within the same state, or who speak the same language, or who are of the same racial origin, or who have the same religious faith are often at war with each other.

31. **E.** England in the 18th century reserved its educational system mainly for sons of wealthy families who learned to behave as "gentlemen" and to consider themselves better than members of the lower class.

32. **D.** With the increasing acceptance of cohabitation before marriage, illegitimacy resulting from this union (parents marrying at a later date) has gained a degree of approval. This is partly an outcome of the women's liberation movement.

33. **C.** During the period 1900–1914 more than 13 million immigrants were admitted into the United States. This was the greatest migration of people in world history. It was sparked by the fear of war, a fear which was realized with the outbreak of World War I in 1914.

34. **D.** John Locke (1632–1704) English philosopher expressed this idea in his *Two Treatises on Government* (1689). Jefferson had read Locke and may have gotten the idea from him but did not copy it directly when he wrote the Declaration of Independence.

35. **C.** Alexis de Tocqueville (1805–59) French political scientist traveled in America in 1831 on a mission from his government. When he returned, he described what he had seen in a classic work entitled *Democracy in America.*

36. **E.** Karl Marx (1818–1883) the father of socialism and communism, developed his ideas fully in his major work, *Das Kapital* (Capital). One of the ideas is that workers receive in wages only part of what they produce. The rest he called "surplus value."

37. **B.** The first European settlers in South Africa were farmers from the Netherlands. They were called Boers from the Dutch word "boer" which means farmer.

38. **B.** Charles I was King of England from 1625 to 1649. His army was defeated by the Puritan forces led by Oliver Cromwell. Charles I was beheaded and Cromwell took the titleof Lord Protector.

39. **D.** Jeremy Bentham (1748–1832) English philosopher, taught that the goal of society is to achieve the greatest good (pleasure) for the greatest number.

40. **C.** The Byzantine form of Christianity was centered in Byzantium (Constantinople). Here the East Roman Empire continued to exist for 1,000 years (5th to 15th centuries). The Slavs of Southern and Eastern Europe were especially influenced by the culture and religion (Orthodox Christianity) of Byzantium.

41. **B.** In the 18th century scientific thought considered "nature" most commonly in terms of mechanics. The 18th century is often described as "the age of reason." Scientists concentrated on mechanics. It was the forerunner of the Industrial Revolution.

42. **C.** In the spring of 1900, a secret society which Westerners called "The Boxers," started a rebellion in China against foreigners who were occupying their country. More than 300 nationals of England, France, the United States and other countries were killed.

43. **D.** The pre-Columbian Inca empire had a population of 6,000,000 and territory extending over 650,000 square miles. It was centered in Cuzco, Peru.

44. **C.** The 18th-century rulers Catherine II of Russia, Frederick II of Prussia, and Joseph II of Austria were inspired by the ideas of the 18th-century

Enlightenment. They wished to introduce various reforms, such as liberal land laws, for the welfare of their subjects.

45. C. After the defeat of the Dutch-speaking Boers in South Africa by the British in 1902 the Dutch Boers (farmers) left Cape Colony and made a "Great Trek" north into the interior of the country where they established new settlements and farms.

46. E. After World War II the U.S.S.R. annexed part of East Prussia directly and provided for the annexation of another part of East Prussia to Poland.

47. E. Bonn is the capital of the German Federal Republic (West Germany).

48. E. The area around Instanbul (Constantinople) in Europe is separated from the major part of Turkey in Asia Minor. The Sea of Marmara and the Dardanelles separate European Turkey from Turkey in Asia.

49. E. The ultimate social aim of all economic activity is to produce goods for final consumption. Both capitalism (private enterprise) and Marxism (socialism or communism) agree on this aim. They differ on the means of attaining it.

50. D. The best way in economics to define "saving" is to call it "refraining from consumption." It is in contrast to consuming all that is produced.

51. E. "Marginal utility" in economics refers to the relation between supply and demand in determining the price of a commodity. High price implies big demand and small supply.

52. A. In the U.S., food and fiber production in the 20th century has increased while the farm work force has steadily declined. This is attributed largely to the other four choices in this question.

53. D. When people interact they tend to take one another into account and modify their behavior accordingly. This interaction is said to be reciprocal. Efforts to achieve behavior modification has attained importance in contemporary psychology.

54. D. The 20th-century goals of favorable remuneration, human dignity and particularly social security as rights would have been rejected by early 19th-century classical liberals.

55. E. The rate of college attendance among 18 to 24 year olds in the United States in 1983 was 32.5 per cent. For Utah the rate was 79.9 per cent.

56. B. In soliciting funds for volunteer health and community programs, motivational researchers have found that potential contributors are most likely to respond to appeals based on shame and comparison to others.

57. A. The French sociologist Emile Durkheim (1858–1917) used statistics to support his theories. He analyzed "mechanical" vs. "organic" solidarity. He held that religion and morality originate in the collective mind of society.

58. B. In most patrilocal African societies, the most simple way to secure a wife was by purchase. This was widely accepted. It had no pejorative aspect.

59. C. In Orwell's 1984 the dominant group uses war primarily as a means of strengthening and perpetuating its absolute control over the citizenry.

60. E. Otto von Bismarck (1815–1898) was premier of Prussia from 1862 to 1890 and Chancellor of Germany from 1871 to 1890. He was called the "Iron Chancellor." The young Kaiser William II was jealous of him and dismissed him in 1890.

61. B. In European Medieval agriculture, the three field system was a method of rotating crops on the manor. In the absence of artificial fertilizers one of the three fields would lie fallow. The other two would be planted in crops different from the previous year. Exhaustion of the soil was avoided in this way.

62. B. The founding fathers established the electoral college system for choosing a president and vice-president. They provided that the electors be chosen separately in each state and that no Senator or Representative or other United States officer could be an elector. They expected that partisan conflict over the election of a President would thus be avoided.

63. E. The Morrill Act passed in 1862 and signed into law by President Lincoln provided for the establishment of new colleges in the states to promote

agriculture. The University of Pennsylvania was chartered as Franklin's Academy in 1754 and became the University of Pennsylvania in 1791.

Part II

64. **C.** Friedrich Engels (1820–1895) was a colleague and collaborator of Karl Marx. Together they wrote the *Communist Manifesto* (1848).

65. **D.** The "Roman Empire" in the east continued to exist with its capital in Constantinople for more than ten centuries (5th to 15th centuries) after the decline and fall of Rome.

66. **B.** Henri Philippe Petain (1856–1951) was placed in charge of the French government at Vichy by the Nazis after the German army conquered France in World War II. The motto of France, "Liberty, Equality, Fraternity" adopted during the French Revolution of 1789, was changed to "Patrie, Travail, Famille" (country, work, family).

67. **B.** The reform bill of 1832 in England enfranchised a large number of middle class males who had previously been denied the vote. This made it more difficult for any one man to control enough votes to elect a member to the House of Commons.

68. **B.** In the decade starting in 1820 there was a a movement on the part of the monarchs of continental Europe (the Concert of Europe) to intervene in Latin America against the newly established republics that had broken away from Spain. This failed because of the Monroe Doctrine and the support the U.S. got from Great Britain.

69. **C.** The cure was administered by Louis Pasteur (1882–1895) the French bacteriologist. He had developed a vaccine which, in accordance with his theory, could conquer the dread disease, hydrophobia (rabies).

70. **D.** Ivan Petrovich Pavlov (1849–1936), the Russian physiologist, demonstrated the working of the conditioned reflex by an experiment on his dog. He rang a bell just before feeding his dog daily. Soon the dog would salivate when the bell rang and prior to (or regardless of) the feeding.

71. **B.** The median is determined by arranging the series in order, that is, 6,000, 8,000, etc. to 30,000 and then selecting the middle number, which, in the case of 7 numbers is the fourth (from top or bottom). In this series the median income is $12,000.

72. **D.** A strong movement to end "Jim Crowism" in the U.S. (unequal treatment of blacks) dates from World War II. The other events occurred during the last decade of the 19th century or first decade of the 20th century.

73. **E.** The right to trial by jury is a procedure whereby substantive rights (freedom of speech, press, religion, etc.) may be protected.

74. **D.** During the 19th century, European powers carved out colonies in Africa by asserting their military power against the Africans and against each other. Most of these colonies gained their independence after World War II.

75. **B.** The clergy of Medieval Europe had to read and interpret the Bible (often available only in Hebrew, Greek and Aramaic). They also read the commentators (Aquinas) in Latin or in the newly emerging national languages. Thus, as students of religion, philosophy, and literature they were the intellectuals of their time.

76. **B.** If printing presses continue to turn out money in endless quantities, it becomes debased until it loses all value. This happened to German and Russian money toward the end of World War I.

77. **E.** On the eve of World War I (1913) Great Britain was the greatest naval power in the world. Germany had been building a fleet trying to catch up. The United States was becoming a naval power and had surpassed all but the top two.

78. **E.** Roman Catholics could not be members of Parliament because it was contrary to their faith to take the required Oath of Supremacy.

79. **D.** Benjamin Disraeli, leader of the Conservative Party, became Prime Min-

ister of Great Britain in 1867. His Reform Bill of 1867 enfranchised nearly 2,000,000 men:

80. C. Ho Chi Minh led Vietnam in its fight for independence against France. At the Battle of Dien Bien Phu the French army was defeated and driven from Indo China.

81. B. After World War I the German government printed so many marks that by 1923 they were practically worthless. Debtors could easily pay off their debts. People on pensions received money that would buy little or nothing.

82. D. Earl Warren was appointed Chief Justice of the United States Supreme Court in 1953 by President Eisenhower. Under his leadership the Court showed special concern for the civil liberties guaranteed by the Bill of Rights and the Fourteenth Amendment.

83. C. *An American Dilemma*, written by the Swedish sociologist Gunnar Myrdal, was based on a study of the American Negro. It proved that the blacks in America were receiving inferior education and were victims of injustice.

84. B. David Ricardo (1772–1823) British economist wrote *Principles of Political Economy and Taxation*. It said that economic forces would work their way to correct imbalance in the economy.

85. B. American marriage and divorce laws vary from state to state. Under the Constitution, laws about marriage and divorce are left up to the states not to the Federal government.

86. C. Inflationary trends cause land values to rise rapidly. People on pensions or salaries, or holders of bonds with fixed interest rates, find that their income buys less because of inflation.

87. D. Capitalism is the name given to the economic system. Land, labor, capital, and organization are factors of production under capitalism.

88. D. The Sherman Antitrust Act of 1890, the Clayton Antitrust Act of 1914, and the Federal Trade Commission Act of 1914 were all part of the federal government's efforts to restrict the growth of monopoly.

89. C. The American family is regarded by sociologists as a new and developing form. Its distinguishing aspect is neither mother, father, ancient nor rural.

90. E. The attitude of the observer, which is conditioned by the social group to which he or she belongs determines the "sacredness" of an object or idea. This is the sociological approach to "sacredness."

91. A. In his *Protestant Ethic and the Spirit of Capitalism* (1920) Max Weber, the German sociologist, developed the idea that John Calvin's teaching about self-denial as a measure of spiritual discipline is closely related to the rise of capitalism.

92. C. Ritual is a formal ceremony prescribed by a group. The form and content of the ceremony are followed exactly on each occasion. The symbolic significance (whether religious or political) is recognized by all members of the participating group.

93. E. These were the words of the Emancipation Proclamation issued by President Abraham Lincoln September 22, 1862 to take effect January 1, 1863.

94. C. Marxism bases social change on the dialectic (opposing interplay or struggle) of economic classes. Economic materialism is the reality. The final outcome, according to Marx, will be the victory of the proleteriat (working class).

95. D. Traditional French liberalism opposed clericalism (church power), aristocracy, Socialism, and big government. It did not favor religious education.

96. C. At the conclusion of the Third Punic War 146 B.C., Rome defeated the traditional rival, Carthage, in North Africa. The victor razed Carthage to the ground. This gave rise to the term "a Carthaginian peace."

97. B. René Descartes (1596–1650), French philosopher, mathematician, and scientist said: "I proposed never to accept anything for true which I do not clearly know to be such." He is best known for his saying: "I think, therefore I am."

98. C. "The marginal propensity to consume" refers, in economics, to the extra amount that people will want to spend on consumption if given an extra dollar of income.

99. B. In an effort to counteract a depression or recession, Federal Reserve Banks might decrease the interest rate charged commercial banks. This would make it easier for banks to lend money to business. This, in turn, would help business to continue to function.

100. B. The Mullahs are Muslim religious teachers trained in traditional Islamic law and doctrine.

101. D. A grand jury is a group of citizens that examines the evidence against a person accused of a serious crime. If the evidence warrants, the grand jury brings formal charges. Then the accused must stand trial.

102. C. Justices of the Supreme Court who disagree with the majority of the Court may prepare a dissenting opinion. In the dissent, the justice states his reason for disagreement.

103. A. The court passes on the constitutionality of an act of Congress only when a case involving the act is brought before the court. Even then, the court may, if it chooses, refuse to hear the case.

104. B. The Albany Congress met in 1754. The Stamp Act Congress met in 1765, the First Continental Congress in 1774, and the Second Continental Congress in 1775. The Articles of Confederation were drawn up in 1778.

105. E. In the spring of 1940, Nazi Germany occupied Belgium and Holland, prepared the attack on France, and drove the British off the continent at Dunkirk. At this point President Roosevelt announced a policy of aid to the opponents of Germany.

106. E. The American historian Frederick Jackson Turner (1861–1932) published *The Significance of the Frontier in American History* in 1893. He showed that the frontier exercised the greatest influence on American institutions.

107. B. The Meiji Restoration in Japan (1867–68) was the beginning of Japan's modernization. The Emperor regained power after the Shogunate was overthrown. Then Japan proceeded with modernization along western lines.

108. D. Herbert Spencer 1820–1903, British sociologist made this statement. He applied the idea of biological evolution to social institutions.

109. D. Age and kinship, sex and kinship, and age and sex are examples of ascribed status. These pairs are useful in sociological analyses of cultures.

110. D. Those ideas, habits, and conditioned responses common to the members of a society are described as universals. Universals are means of identifying membership in a society and contrasting social groups with respect to universals that apply to one or another.

111. A. The dependency ratio has declined as the size of the nuclear family has declined. Fewer children per family means fewer dependents at one end. Social security has reduced dependency at the other.

112. C. The concept of anomie is used to describe our society where norms of conduct and belief have been weakened or have actually broken down.

113. D. "Downer" drugs are depressants. When members of juvenile gangs take heavy doses of "downers" they are less likely to engage in gang fights.

114. D. The Congo territory was explored and exploited under the leadership of King Leopold II of Belgium. The Congo, located in south central Africa, was known as the Belgian Congo until it gained its independence in 1960.

115. A. Genghis Khan was the leader of a nomadic people of Central Asia. Under Genghis Khan's leadership, the Mongols invaded Europe during the 13th century and caused havoc in Poland, Hungary, and much of Russia.

116. D. Thomas Jefferson, a strong advocate of education, was the founder of the University of Virginia. He prepared a plan for public elementary and secondary schools also but did not live to see it come to pass. It was part of his plan to train the ablest minds for leadership in the republic.

117. C. Equalizing firm A's marginal cost to marginal revenue gives firm A's maximum profit per units produced. A plotted curve based on the figures in the table shows the number of units produced to be 50,000.

118. C. In the case of firm A, based on the table cited in #117 above, the result is the smallest loss rather than a profit.

119. D. If firm A were in a monopolistic situation, or a partly monopolistic situa-

tion, the figures for price per unit would be lowered (because of firm A's more advantageous position) and a profit would result.

120. C. The Marquis de Cordorcet (1743–1794) believed in the indefinite perfectability of man. He was an optimist so far as man's future was concerned.

121. D. Texas became part of the United States in 1845. The other events did occur during the period 1760–1826. The latest of the other four was the Monroe Doctrine issued in 1823.

122. D. Charles Darwin (1809–82), English naturalist could have expressed this idea in his book *The Origin of Species* published in 1859.

123. B. Friedrich Nietzsche (1844–1900), German philosopher, preached the superiority of the aristocrat (master). He looked forward to the creation of a superman beyond good and evil.

124. E. In per capita personal income, South Carolina ranks 49th (just above Mississippi) of the 50 states.

125. C. While each of the other four play a part, human sexual behavior is expressed and controlled primarily by internalized learning.

SAMPLE EXAMINATION 2

Part I

Number of Questions: 63
Time: 45 minutes

Directions: Each of the questions or incomplete statements below is followed by five suggested answers or completions. Select the one that is best in each case.

MAP A

Questions 1–3 refer to MAP A.

1. In which country did the activists of a Nazi sympathizer give the world the term "Quisling"?
   (A) 21   (B) 15   (C) 24   (D) 23   (E) 20

   1. Ⓐ Ⓑ Ⓒ Ⓓ Ⓔ

2. Which former area of Rumania was taken by the USSR in 1940?
   (A) 13   (B) 14   (C) 19   (D) 4   (E) 12

   2. Ⓐ Ⓑ Ⓒ Ⓓ Ⓔ

3. Which two countries were at war on Albanian soil in 1941?
   (A) 7 and 8   (B) 25 and 9   (C) 13 and 10   (D) 17 and 22
   (E) 17 and 23

   3. Ⓐ Ⓑ Ⓒ Ⓓ Ⓔ

4. Malthus' "principle of population" is an instance of the
   - (A) law of increasing returns
   - (B) law of diminishing returns
   - (C) observation that fertility is greater in the tropical than temperate zones
   - (D) observation that fertility is greater among the lowest class
   - (E) law of diminishing sexual energy

   4. Ⓐ Ⓑ Ⓒ Ⓓ Ⓔ

5. The holding company is possible only because
   - (A) many stockholders do not permit proxies
   - (B) some securities do not have voting rights
   - (C) corporations are permitted to hold stock in other corporations
   - (D) courts do not enforce the law
   - (E) stocks can be bought on margin

   5. Ⓐ Ⓑ Ⓒ Ⓓ Ⓔ

6. The Securities and Exchange Commission is designed to regulate the securities business for the benfit of
   - (A) small business   (B) the consumer   (C) the investor
   - (D) labor   (E) the banking system

   6. Ⓐ Ⓑ Ⓒ Ⓓ Ⓔ

7. Youth-parent tensions in American society today may be explained by
   - (A) rapid change in our society
   - (B) smaller numbers of children per family during the past two decades
   - (C) the increasing patriarchal nature of the family
   - (D) development of a youth subculture and confusion as to the exact time for attaining "adult" status
   - (E) A and D primarily

   7. Ⓐ Ⓑ Ⓒ Ⓓ Ⓔ

8. The term "secular power" in Medieval European history would be used to describe the powers of a
   - (A) king or emperor
   - (B) pope
   - (C) bishop
   - (D) church council
   - (E) cardinal

   8. Ⓐ Ⓑ Ⓒ Ⓓ Ⓔ

9. A campaign speech was made containing a reference to "two chickens in every pot." What event occurred shortly after the speech which made this reference seem ironic?
   - (A) Pullman transportation strike in 1894
   - (B) Defeat of the Populists in 1896
   - (C) Election of Alfred E. Smith in 1928
   - (D) Stock market crash in 1929
   - (E) Rationing of gasoline after 1941

   9. Ⓐ Ⓑ Ⓒ Ⓓ Ⓔ

10. The size of the population of the United States in 1790 was about the same as the 1970 population of which of the following states?
    - (A) New York   (B) California   (C) Illinois   (D) Nevada
    - (E) Tennessee

    10. Ⓐ Ⓑ Ⓒ Ⓓ Ⓔ

11. "Now that the Democrats have captured the liberal imagination of the nation, it is forgotten how much of the architecture of America's liberal society was drafted by the Republicans, who are today regarded as the party of the right." To support his point the author might cite all of the following except the

11. Ⓐ Ⓑ Ⓒ Ⓓ Ⓔ

    (A) abolition of slavery   (B) Pendleton Act
    (C) Social Security Act   (D) Morrill Act for education
    (E) Pure Food and Drug Act

12. Which of these ancient empires was the largest in geographic extent?

12. Ⓐ Ⓑ Ⓒ Ⓓ Ⓔ

    (A) Egyptian   (B) Persian   (C) Assyrian   (D) Chaldean
    (E) Hittite

13. Which of the following is not an Indo-European language?

13. Ⓐ Ⓑ Ⓒ Ⓓ Ⓔ

    (A) Arabic   (B) Sanskrit   (C) Greek   (D) Hittite   (E) Latin

14. Monetary policy in the U.S. is administered by

14. Ⓐ Ⓑ Ⓒ Ⓓ Ⓔ

    (A) Congress
    (B) the President
    (C) the Federal Reserve Board of Governors
    (D) the Department of Commerce
    (E) the Council of Economic Advisors

15. Most of the major rivers in Soviet Asia flow from

15. Ⓐ Ⓑ Ⓒ Ⓓ Ⓔ

    (A) west to east
    (B) east to west
    (C) north to south
    (D) south to north
    (E) north to southeast

16. The belief in reincarnation is an important part of

16. Ⓐ Ⓑ Ⓒ Ⓓ Ⓔ

    (A) Judaism
    (B) Confucius' teachings
    (C) Hinduism
    (D) Zoroastrianism
    (E) Islam

17. The total value (in dollars) of goods and services produced in the American economy during the year is called the

17. Ⓐ Ⓑ Ⓒ Ⓓ Ⓔ

    (A) net national income
    (B) gross private domestic investment
    (C) gross national product
    (D) net producers domestic gain
    (E) net national product

18. In sociology and psychology, "drives" are

18. Ⓐ Ⓑ Ⓒ Ⓓ Ⓔ

    (A) behavior that must always be suppressed
    (B) factors which incite behavior in the individual
    (C) glands which secrete endocrines
    (D) mysterious forces which induce people to commit crimes
    (E) none of the above

MAP B
SOUTHERN
ASIA

Questions 19–21 pertain to this map.

19. Which area was ruled by the Dutch for a number of centuries?   19. Ⓐ Ⓑ Ⓒ Ⓓ Ⓔ
    (A) 2   (B) 3   (C) 5   (D) 7   (E) 6

20. Which country was ruled until 1959 by a Buddhist religious leader   20. Ⓐ Ⓑ Ⓒ Ⓓ Ⓔ
    called the "Dalai Lama"
    (A) 2   (B) 4   (C) 5   (D) 7   (E) 9

21. Which area was split into four states in the 1950s?   21. Ⓐ Ⓑ Ⓒ Ⓓ Ⓔ
    (A) 2   (B) 3   (C) 5   (D) 7   (E) 10

22. In the 1950s and '60s the Supreme Court inclined toward "judicial   22. Ⓐ Ⓑ Ⓒ Ⓓ Ⓔ
    activism" in all of the following areas *except*
    (A) civil rights
    (B) legislative reapportionment
    (C) presidential control over foreign policy
    (D) unlawful search and seizure
    (E) indigent defendants

23. "The bureaucratization of capitalism . . . carries such examinations all   23. Ⓐ Ⓑ Ⓒ Ⓓ Ⓔ
    over the world. . . . Today, the certificate of education becomes what
    the test for ancestors has been in the past." Who said that?
    (A) Karl Marx
    (B) David Ricardo
    (C) Max Weber
    (D) Adam Smith
    (E) John Maynard Keynes

24. At the time when it achieved recognition as an independent state, in which of the following did a substantial migration in or out of the country take place?
   I. Israel, II. India, III. Pakistan, IV. Mexico, V. Yugoslavia.
   (A) II only   (B) I and IV only   (C) I, II, and III only
   (D) II, III, and IV only   (E) I, II, III, IV, and V

   24. Ⓐ Ⓑ Ⓒ Ⓓ Ⓔ

25. In a market economy, price tends to fall whenever
   (A) the quantity supplied increases more rapidly than the quantity demanded
   (B) the quantity demanded increases more rapidly than the quantity supplied
   (C) supply and demand are equal
   (D) both supply and demand increase
   (E) more of a commodity is produced in a mass production technology

   25. Ⓐ Ⓑ Ⓒ Ⓓ Ⓔ

26. The birth rate in country X is 14.0; the death rate, 10.8; the infant mortality rate 9.6; and the per capita income over $8,000.00 per year. The country is
   (A) Brazil   (B) Egypt   (C) Albania   (D) Sweden
   (E) Union of South Africa

   26. Ⓐ Ⓑ Ⓒ Ⓓ Ⓔ

27. The agricultural revolution in the U.S. is related to
   (A) the growth of the use of tractors
   (B) an increase in the use of electric power
   (C) the decline in farm production
   (D) all of the above
   (E) A and B, but not C

   27. Ⓐ Ⓑ Ⓒ Ⓓ Ⓔ

28. The English Reform Bill of 1867 extended the right to vote to
   (A) middle-class businessmen
   (B) working men in the cities
   (C) all adults
   (D) all adults living in the cities
   (E) the Catholics

   28. Ⓐ Ⓑ Ⓒ Ⓓ Ⓔ

29. The increasing number of elderly widows in America is caused by
   (A) women marrying at a younger age than in the past
   (B) women marrying husbands increasingly older than themselves
   (C) women, on the average, having an increasingly longer life span than men
   (D) all of the above
   (E) B and C, but not A

   29. Ⓐ Ⓑ Ⓒ Ⓓ Ⓔ

30. Which of the following reforms was *not* advocated by the Progressive Movement in the United States of the early 20th century?
   (A) Referendum
   (B) Recall
   (C) Primary elections
   (D) Nonpartisanship in municipal elections
   (E) The removal of restrictions on Negro voting

   30. Ⓐ Ⓑ Ⓒ Ⓓ Ⓔ

31. In the history of the presidency until 1974, there had never been an instance of
    (A) a Vice-President becoming President
    (B) a President failing to be elected by the electoral college
    (C) the election of a President by the House of Representatives
    (D) the resignation of a President
    (E) the assassination of a President

31. Ⓐ Ⓑ Ⓒ Ⓓ Ⓔ

32. Which amendment to the Constitution abolished slavery?
    (A) 12th   (B) 13th   (C) 14th   (D) 15th   (E) 16th

32. Ⓐ Ⓑ Ⓒ Ⓓ Ⓔ

33. "The American expansionists and imperialists of the 1890s appealed to biological evolution and economic and social history to support their views. We are suffering today because of the hangover from their nonsense." The person saying this would have particularly disliked the
    (A) Federal Reserve Act   (B) Civil War
    (C) Kellogg-Briand Pact   (D) Spanish-American War
    (E) Russo-Japanese War

33. Ⓐ Ⓑ Ⓒ Ⓓ Ⓔ

34. The interest which Russia historically manifested in the Dardanelles arose from a desire to have an outlet to the
    (A) Black Sea   (B) Yellow Sea   (C) North Sea
    (D) Mediterranean Sea   (E) Red Sea

34. Ⓐ Ⓑ Ⓒ Ⓓ Ⓔ

35. "L'état, c'est moi." This statement is attributed to
    (A) Louis XVI
    (B) Louis XV
    (C) Louis XIV
    (D) Louis XIII
    (E) Louis X

35. Ⓐ Ⓑ Ⓒ Ⓓ Ⓔ

36. After the Franco-Prussian War, the German Imperial constitution
    (A) made the Prussian king the new emperor
    (B) was a generally democratic instrument
    (C) declared the equality of all member states
    (D) declared the ruler of Austria to be Emperor of the Empire
    (E) made Roman Catholicism the state religion

36. Ⓐ Ⓑ Ⓒ Ⓓ Ⓔ

37. In The Prince, Machiavelli counsels a ruler that
    (A) it is better to be feared than loved
    (B) it is better to be loved than feared
    (C) he need not worry about arousing the hatred of his subjects
    (D) it is best to be both feared and hated
    (E) it is better to be truthful with one's subjects

37. Ⓐ Ⓑ Ⓒ Ⓓ Ⓔ

38. "In Hegel's writings, dialectic stands on its head. You must turn it right way up again if you want to discover the rational kernel that is hidden away within the wrappings of mystifications." Who said this?
    (A) Charles Darwin   (B) Friedrich Nietzsche
    (C) Sigmund Freud   (D) Karl Marx   (E) Max Weber

38. Ⓐ Ⓑ Ⓒ Ⓓ Ⓔ

39. Freud criticized Marxism on the basis that   39. Ⓐ Ⓑ Ⓒ Ⓓ Ⓔ
   (A) class struggle encouraged man's aggressive tendencies
   (B) it disregarded the evolution of institutions
   (C) it was still bound by Hegelian idealism
   (D) it left untouched the real causes of human aggressiveness
      and anxiety
   (E) it attacked traditional religion

40. When historians use the title *Augustus* they are referring to   40. Ⓐ Ⓑ Ⓒ Ⓓ Ⓔ
   (A) Julius Caesar
   (B) Octavian
   (C) Marcus Aurelius
   (D) Claudius
   (E) Trajan

41. In the U.S., the function of the family *least* transferred to outside   41. Ⓐ Ⓑ Ⓒ Ⓓ Ⓔ
agencies is the
   (A) economic
   (B) educational
   (C) recreational
   (D) religious
   (E) emotional

42. The Standard Oil trust was originally organized by   42. Ⓐ Ⓑ Ⓒ Ⓓ Ⓔ
   (A) Carnegie
   (B) Morgan
   (C) Vanderbilt
   (D) Rockefeller
   (E) Gould

43. What issue or issues in France were significant in the Dreyfus Affair?   43. Ⓐ Ⓑ Ⓒ Ⓓ Ⓔ
   (A) Anti-republicanism
   (B) Anti-Semitism
   (C) Anti-clericalism
   (D) A and B, but not C
   (E) A, B, and C

44. Bismarck, after 1851, believed that Germany could become strong and   44. Ⓐ Ⓑ Ⓒ Ⓓ Ⓔ
united only if
   (A) Austria was excluded from German affairs
   (B) she became a republic
   (C) Austria became the leader
   (D) Italy remained divided into small states
   (E) colonies could be gained for Germany

45. The Maoris are   45. Ⓐ Ⓑ Ⓒ Ⓓ Ⓔ
   (A) Bantus who fought the Boers in South Africa
   (B) the aboriginal peoples of Australia
   (C) the French Protestant settlers in South Africa
   (D) a people who lived in New Zealand before the coming of the
      British
   (E) a group of Irish revolutionaries

46. An increase in the amount of money available
    (A) always means an increase in the level of prices
    (B) never has an effect on the level of prices
    (C) always means a decrease in the level of prices
    (D) may cause no change in the level of prices under certain conditions
    (E) always acts to expand economic production and activity

46. A B C D E

47. Which of the following programs of social reform would be, according to the thought of Malthus, based on a correct analysis of the problem of poverty?
    (A) Universal education at public expense
    (B) Guaranteed minimum wage
    (C) Social security
    (D) Consumer subsidies
    (E) Aid to dependent children

47. A B C D E

48. If people do not consume all their income, but put the unspent amount into a pillow or buy an old security with it, in national income and product terms they are
    (A) saving but not investing
    (B) investing but not saving
    (C) both saving and investing
    (D) neither saving nor investing
    (E) saving, but investing only to the extent that they buy old securities

48. A B C D E

49. Which of the following is *least* common in man's various societies?
    (A) Group marriage
    (B) Divorce
    (C) Illegitimacy
    (D) Intercourse before marriage
    (E) Homosexuality

49. A B C D E

50. Compared to 1960, yearly executions of convicted criminals in the U.S. had, by 1968,
    (A) doubled
    (B) stayed about the same
    (C) increased 25%
    (D) decreased slightly
    (E) dropped to a level of zero

50. A B C D E

51. When sociologists talk of "social mobility," they usually have in mind
    (A) horizontal mobility
    (B) interracial marriage
    (C) vertical mobility
    (D) rapid social retrogression
    (E) moral progress

51. A B C D E

52. The use of the canoe and the moccasin by whites is an example of cultural
    (A) invention
    (B) mobility
    (C) simplicity
    (D) diffusion
    (E) management

52. Ⓐ Ⓑ Ⓒ Ⓓ Ⓔ

53. Which statement about the corporation is false?
    (A) It can secure capital with greater ease than other forms of economic organization.
    (B) It can delegate authority and managerial duties to individuals who are experts in their fields.
    (C) Since it is an artificial or fictitious person, it is not expected to conform to all laws.
    (D) The owners of corporations enjoy limited liability.
    (E) It can issue bonds as well as stock.

53. Ⓐ Ⓑ Ⓒ Ⓓ Ⓔ

54. Which of the following was Veblen's attitude toward marginal utility economics? He considered it
    (A) analytically proper
    (B) overly inductive and oriented to biology
    (C) collectivist in its implications
    (D) overly deductive, individualistic, and static
    (E) too strongly oriented to the labor movement

54. Ⓐ Ⓑ Ⓒ Ⓓ Ⓔ

55. In the eyes of Keynes, the ultimate responsibility for full employment rested with the
    (A) natural forces of economic variables
    (B) good will of businessmen
    (C) central government
    (D) divinity
    (E) gold-producing countries

55. Ⓐ Ⓑ Ⓒ Ⓓ Ⓔ

56. "Cost of production determines supply; supply determines final degree of utility; final degree of utility determines value." This idea would be found in the work of
    (A) Adam Smith
    (B) Jeremy Bentham
    (C) David Ricardo
    (D) Karl Marx
    (E) William Stanley Jevons

56. Ⓐ Ⓑ Ⓒ Ⓓ Ⓔ

57. States with relatively high per capita incomes (by U.S. standards) include
    (A) Tennessee, Texas, North Carolina
    (B) Texas, Kentucky, North Dakota
    (C) Texas, California, Georgia
    (D) Connecticut, Virginia, Texas
    (E) Connecticut, Delaware, Nevada

57. Ⓐ Ⓑ Ⓒ Ⓓ Ⓔ

58. In 1971 approximately what percent of the American population was
    residing and working on farms?
    (A) 50%
    (B) 33%
    (C) 25%
    (D) 15%
    (E) 6%

58. Ⓐ Ⓑ Ⓒ Ⓓ Ⓔ

59. In 1971 the states which had the largest representation in the House
    of Representatives were
    (A) Texas, Massachusetts, Virginia
    (B) California, Texas, Alaska
    (C) New York, Pennsylvania, New Jersey
    (D) California, New York, Florida
    (E) California, New York, Pennsylvania

59. Ⓐ Ⓑ Ⓒ Ⓓ Ⓔ

60. In 1960 the average Congressional district contained the following
    number of people:
    (A) 110,000
    (B) 210,000
    (C) 410,000
    (D) 1,050,000
    (E) 3,500,000

60. Ⓐ Ⓑ Ⓒ Ⓓ Ⓔ

61. In which of the following elections was the electoral college vote 523
    for the winner (name given first), and 8 for the loser?
    (A) Roosevelt, Hoover
    (B) Johnson, Goldwater
    (C) Eisenhower, Stevenson
    (D) Nixon, Humphrey
    (E) Roosevelt, Landon

61. Ⓐ Ⓑ Ⓒ Ⓓ Ⓔ

62. Alexis de Tocqueville's *Democracy in America* had as its basic subject
    (A) American political institutions during the presidency of Andrew
        Johnson
    (B) modern democracy and an alleged trend toward equality of condi-
        tions
    (C) effects of the Industrial Revolution upon America and Europe
    (D) amazing prophecies about the future political development of
        America and France
    (E) a contrast between English and American democracy

62. Ⓐ Ⓑ Ⓒ Ⓓ Ⓔ

63. Most countries with high per-capita incomes (above $4,000 per year)
    have
    (A) death rates above 20 per 1000 per year
    (B) illiteracy rates of above 50%
    (C) more than half their workers in agriculture
    (D) birth rates below 20 per 1000 per year
    (E) none of the above

63. Ⓐ Ⓑ Ⓒ Ⓓ Ⓔ

Part II

Number of Questions: 62

Time: 45 minutes

Directions: Each of the questions or incomplete statements below is followed by five suggested answers or completions. Select the one that is best in each case.

64. The Huguenots were
    (A) a French family which claimed the throne
    (B) a party which opposed the king's powers in England
    (C) French Protestants
    (D) a fleet which Philip II sent to invade England
    (E) alchemists

64. Ⓐ Ⓑ Ⓒ Ⓓ Ⓔ

65. Which of these nations came into being as a result of a war for independence during the time of Philip II?
    (A) Portugal
    (B) Dutch Netherlands
    (C) Sweden
    (D) Burgundy
    (E) Switzerland

65. Ⓐ Ⓑ Ⓒ Ⓓ Ⓔ

66. The peace and unity of the Frankish empire was disturbed in the 9th century by the invasions of the
    (A) Vikings   (B) Huns   (C) Vandals   (D) Byzantines
    (E) Britons

66. Ⓐ Ⓑ Ⓒ Ⓓ Ⓔ

67. When we measure part of the cost of education by giving a value to the output not produced by students while attending schools, we have taken account of costs termed
    (A) direct   (B) personal   (C) subsidized
    (D) opportunity   (E) interest

67. Ⓐ Ⓑ Ⓒ Ⓓ Ⓔ

68. Correlations between educational enrollments and GNP per capita in various countries tend to be positive and high. This shows that
    (A) rich countries like to spend more resources on education
    (B) education acts to help make countries richer
    (C) education is a consumer good which rich countries can afford
    (D) there is a relation between the two
    (E) none of the above is true

68. Ⓐ Ⓑ Ⓒ Ⓓ Ⓔ

69. George Herbert Mead's theory of the origin and functioning of self is best represented by which of the following statements?
    (A) The social self is comparable to Freud's id.
    (B) We must be others if we are to be ourselves.
    (C) The self is unrelated to social control.
    (D) All of the above.
    (E) None of the above.

69. Ⓐ Ⓑ Ⓒ Ⓓ Ⓔ

70. In an experiment using a control group
   (A) change is induced in the control group only
   (B) change is induced in the experimental group only
   (C) more change is induced in the control group than in the experimental group
   (D) less change is induced in the control group than the experimental group
   (E) none of these

70. Ⓐ Ⓑ Ⓒ Ⓓ Ⓔ

71. In which of the following job categories in the U.S. has there been an absolute decline over the past thirty years?
   (A) Professional   (B) Managerial   (C) Skilled
   (D) Service   (E) Farm

71. Ⓐ Ⓑ Ⓒ Ⓓ Ⓔ

72. Norms are sometimes rejected because
   (A) they are not considered important   (B) they are not understood
   (C) some are flexible   (D) all of these   (E) none of these

72. Ⓐ Ⓑ Ⓒ Ⓓ Ⓔ

73. Louis XIV tried to extend France to its "natural boundaries." Which boundary could be realized only at the cost of a series of wars?
   (A) Pyrenees   (B) Alps   (C) Mediterranean
   (D) Rhine   (E) English Channel

73. Ⓐ Ⓑ Ⓒ Ⓓ Ⓔ

74. Between 1865 and 1965, Congress admitted fifteen new states, all west of the Mississippi. Which of the following was one of these states?
   (A) Nevada
   (B) California
   (C) Iowa
   (D) Missouri
   (E) Oklahoma

74. Ⓐ Ⓑ Ⓒ Ⓓ Ⓔ

75. "The government bets you can't live on the land for five years and if you can, you win the land." This statement refers to
   (A) the Northwest Ordinance
   (B) veterans' preference after World War II
   (C) the Homestead Act of 1862
   (D) all of the above
   (E) none of the above

75. Ⓐ Ⓑ Ⓒ Ⓓ Ⓔ

76. Railway mileage in the U.S. increased most in absolute amount during which of the following decades?
   (A) 1840s   (B) 1860s   (C) 1880s   (D) 1950s
   (E) 1960s

76. Ⓐ Ⓑ Ⓒ Ⓓ Ⓔ

77. The largest state in area and the smallest in population among the following is
   (A) Nevada   (B) Texas   (C) Montana   (D) Maine   (E) Alaska

77. Ⓐ Ⓑ Ⓒ Ⓓ Ⓔ

78. "He could no longer draw a north-south line in the continental United States, on one side of which the population was less than two persons per square mile and on the other side it was more." This statement refers to the census director of which year?
   (A) 1820   (B) 1860   (C) 1890   (D) 1930   (E) 1940

78. Ⓐ Ⓑ Ⓒ Ⓓ Ⓔ

79. An immigrant arriving in the U.S. in the period 1885-1914 was most likely to be
(A) a young woman   (B) an older man   (C) a child
(D) a young man   (E) an older woman

79. Ⓐ Ⓑ Ⓒ Ⓓ Ⓔ

80. Southern landowners in the decades following the Civil War evolved, as a dominant system for getting work accomplished, the system of
(A) sharecropping   (B) migrant labor   (C) paid farm labor
(D) A and B, not C   (E) none of the above

80. Ⓐ Ⓑ Ⓒ Ⓓ Ⓔ

81. In 1790, the most populous and influential U.S. state was
(A) New York   (B) South Carolina   (C) Maryland
(D) Virginia   (E) Massachusetts

81. Ⓐ Ⓑ Ⓒ Ⓓ Ⓔ

82. The most populous state in the United States in 1860 was
(A) Virginia   (B) Massachusetts   (C) Illinois
(D) South Carolina   (E) New York

82. Ⓐ Ⓑ Ⓒ Ⓓ Ⓔ

83. In the 1960s and 1970s one group which had not previously utilized the strike began to do so. Which one?

(A) Dentists
(B) Auto workers
(C) Truck drivers
(D) Army officers
(E) Teachers

83. Ⓐ Ⓑ Ⓒ Ⓓ Ⓔ

84. The proportion of students in private colleges to all college-going people in the U.S. is

(A) increasing rapidly
(B) increasing slowly
(C) decreasing and increasing in various years
(D) decreasing rapidly
(E) staying the same

84. Ⓐ Ⓑ Ⓒ Ⓓ Ⓔ

85. "We must . . . admit that there is a much wider interval in mental power between one of the lowest fishes . . . and one of the higher apes, than between an ape and a man; yet this interval is filled up by numberless gradations."
(A) Pascal   (D) Locke
(B) Darwin   (E) Bentham
(C) Nietzsche

85. Ⓐ Ⓑ Ⓒ Ⓓ Ⓔ

86. In which year would the difference between U.S. gross national product and disposable personal income be the least?
(A) 1929   (B) 1941   (C) 1945   (D) 1965   (E) 1970

86. Ⓐ Ⓑ Ⓒ Ⓓ Ⓔ

87. The opposite of Adam Smith's "invisible hand" would be a "visible hand." Which of the following could be considered the "visible hand"?
(A) God   (B) Competition   (C) Price warfare
(D) Population increase   (E) Government

87. Ⓐ Ⓑ Ⓒ Ⓓ Ⓔ

88. The importance of Thales of Miletus rests in the fact that he
   (A) taught a system of morals based on reason
   (B) pictured an ideal society in which philosopher-kings would govern
   (C) first asked questions about the nature of beauty
   (D) advanced a naturalistic explanation for the physical universe
   (E) advanced the application of mathematics to practical problems

88. Ⓐ Ⓑ Ⓒ Ⓓ Ⓔ

89. Which of the following is a part of communist theory about capitalist states?
   (A) Capitalist states will eventually go to war with one another in an effort to secure control of foreign markets.
   (B) In a capitalist state, there must sooner or later occur a class war, with the rich on one side and the poor on the other.
   (C) In a capitalist state, a few people will gain control of the economic resources and the great mass of the population will grow steadily poorer.
   (D) All of these are parts of communist theory.
   (E) None of the above.

89. Ⓐ Ⓑ Ⓒ Ⓓ Ⓔ

90. The increased flow of precious metals from the New World to Europe in the 15th and 16th centuries
   (A) caused prices to decrease   (B) caused prices to rise
   (C) had no effect on price levels   (D) discouraged speculation
   (E) encouraged small-scale agriculture

90. Ⓐ Ⓑ Ⓒ Ⓓ Ⓔ

91. The term "sociology" (sociologie) was coined by which of the following thinkers?
   (A) François Quesnay   (B) Saint-Simon
   (C) Emile Durkheim   (D) Louis Blanc   (E) Auguste Comte

91. Ⓐ Ⓑ Ⓒ Ⓓ Ⓔ

92. Which of the following taught the observance of caste rules as a religious obligation?
   (A) Islam   (B) Buddhism   (C) Taoism
   (D) Hinduism   (E) Judaism

92. Ⓐ Ⓑ Ⓒ Ⓓ Ⓔ

93. "The President's opposition to the reconstruction policy of Congress led to an effort to impeach him." Who was the President?
   (A) Andrew Jackson   (B) Abraham Lincoln   (C) U. S. Grant
   (D) Andrew Johnson   (E) Franklin D. Roosevelt

93. Ⓐ Ⓑ Ⓒ Ⓓ Ⓔ

94. Louis XIV of France was a member of which royal family?
   (A) Hapsburgs   (B) Bourbons   (C) Tudors
   (D) Romanovs   (E) Orleans

94. Ⓐ Ⓑ Ⓒ Ⓓ Ⓔ

95. In which of the following cities would there be more Baptists in proportion to the population?
   (A) Atlanta   (B) Minneapolis   (C) Salt Lake City
   (D) New York City   (E) Boston

95. Ⓐ Ⓑ Ⓒ Ⓓ Ⓔ

96. Which of the smaller states of Europe had considerable imperial holdings in Africa before World War I?
    (A) Netherlands (B) Belgium (C) Denmark
    (D) Norway (E) Switzerland

97. The Roman world suffered shock in the year 410 when the city of Rome was taken by the
    (A) Vandals (B) Huns (C) Franks (D) Visigoths
    (E) Normans

98. "Implied powers" are the powers of the national government which are necessary to
    (A) amend the national Constitution
    (B) prevent the state governments from expanding their powers beyond those given to them by the Constitution
    (C) allow the national government to do the jobs given to it by the Constitution
    (D) allow speedy governmental action in a war
    (E) none of these

99. The Supreme Court has upheld certain tax-supported benefits going to parochial school children on the basis of the
    (A) "general welfare" clause
    (B) First Amendment
    (C) Fourteenth Amendment
    (D) Fifth Amendment
    (E) Tenth Amendment

100. Of the following, all are consumer goods *except*
    (A) transport trucks
    (B) family automobiles
    (C) a performance by the National Symphony Orchestra
    (D) a painting by Rembrandt
    (E) apples sold at the supermarket

101. Factors which operate to reduce geographical mobility in the labor market include
    (A) most pension plans
    (B) seniority in labor union contracts with business
    (C) government welfare programs
    (D) none of these
    (E) all of these

102. The typical American corporation of today is likely to be largely controlled by
    (A) two or three men, who own most of the stock
    (B) a large number of people, each of whom owns a small amount of stock
    (C) managers, who are subject to much pressure from the stockholders
    (D) managers, who are given a very free hand by the stockholders
    (E) a dominant figure who controls the majority of stock

103. Which of these people would have been apt to join one of the unions in the American Federation of Labor?   103. Ⓐ Ⓑ Ⓒ Ⓓ Ⓔ
   (A) An automobile assembly line worker in 1937
   (B) A brick mason in 1939
   (C) A department store clerk in 1950
   (D) A nurse in 1965
   (E) A school teacher in 1945

104. After he came to power in Turkey, Mustapha Kemal   104. Ⓐ Ⓑ Ⓒ Ⓓ Ⓔ
   (A) attempted to restore traditional Turkish ways
   (B) introduced many modern reforms
   (C) began a war to reconquer the Arab sections of the old Turkish empire
   (D) restored the caliph to power
   (E) tried to reconquer the Balkan peninsula

105. Henry George's "single tax" was to be applied to   105. Ⓐ Ⓑ Ⓒ Ⓓ Ⓔ
   (A) homes   (B) income   (C) sales   (D) land
   (E) imports

106. In 1971, the greatest number of American women workers were employed in   106. Ⓐ Ⓑ Ⓒ Ⓓ Ⓔ
   (A) social work   (B) clerical work   (C) accounting
   (D) real estate   (E) libraries

107. David Ricardo used Malthusian ideas to indicate the basic wage. To   107. Ⓐ Ⓑ Ⓒ Ⓓ Ⓔ
   him, the reason this wage always tends toward bare subsistence is that
   (A) employers are mean
   (B) workers dislike ostentation
   (C) society is unfair
   (D) workers will always reproduce the labor supply to the maximum
   (E) unions are prevented by the state from militant action

108. Which of the following did not take part in the 18th-century partition   108. Ⓐ Ⓑ Ⓒ Ⓓ Ⓔ
   of Poland?
   (A) Sweden   (B) Austria   (C) Prussia   (D) Russia
   (E) All of the above

109. Which of these peoples were not Germanic?   109. Ⓐ Ⓑ Ⓒ Ⓓ Ⓔ
   (A) Visigoths   (B) Vandals   (C) Huns   (D) Lombards
   (E) Franks

110. The Negro proportion of the U.S. population was greatest in   110. Ⓐ Ⓑ Ⓒ Ⓓ Ⓔ
   (A) 1870   (B) 1900   (C) 1910   (D) 1930   (E) 1940

111. Emile Durkheim found that suicide was relatively high among all the
   following except people
   (A) in military organizations, where honor is very important
   (B) who are rootless and uninvolved
   (C) with a highly individualistic success ethic
   (D) subject to highly developed ideas of individual responsibility
   (E) in extended kinship family structures with religion emphasizing
      group meaning

111. Ⓐ Ⓑ Ⓒ Ⓓ Ⓔ

112. Which of the following titles carried with it the *least* power in the
   17th century?
   (A) King of England   (B) King of France   (C) King of Spain
   (D) Holy Roman Emperor   (E) King of Sweden

112. Ⓐ Ⓑ Ⓒ Ⓓ Ⓔ

113. A fief was
   (A) a person who swore fealty to a lord
   (B) a grant, usually of land, made in exchange for promised services
   (C) a person bound to the soil
   (D) an oath of loyalty
   (E) a tariff on trade

113. Ⓐ Ⓑ Ⓒ Ⓓ Ⓔ

114. One of the first things which the Bolsheviks did in Russia when they
   came into power was to
   (A) have the Tsar removed from office
   (B) begin negotiations for peace with the Germans
   (C) make Stalin the head of the state
   (D) drive the Germans completely out of Russian territory
   (E) collectivize the land

114. Ⓐ Ⓑ Ⓒ Ⓓ Ⓔ

115. Stress and strain in adolescence are most characteristic of
   (A) all known societies   (B) preliterate societies
   (C) peasant societies   (D) modern industrial societies
   (E) frontier societies

115. Ⓐ Ⓑ Ⓒ Ⓓ Ⓔ

116. Which of the following methods of social science goes deepest into
   the motivation and problems of people?
   (A) Statistical survey   (B) Document research
   (C) Interviews   (D) Case study   (E) Behavioral model

116. Ⓐ Ⓑ Ⓒ Ⓓ Ⓔ

117. In "Federalist #10," James Madison
   (A) shows how the American republic is protected against domina-
      tion by any one faction
   (B) shows the merits of democratic government
   (C) sets forth an explanation of the contract theory of government
   (D) argues the need for a Federal Bill of Rights
   (E) indicates the value of the clergy

117. Ⓐ Ⓑ Ⓒ Ⓓ Ⓔ

118. Of the following, which is most clearly an example of reducing the domain of ascribed status?   118. Ⓐ Ⓑ Ⓒ Ⓓ Ⓔ
    (A) A young man giving his seat to an older man on a bus that is crowded
    (B) Women who devote their time to their homes and church activities
    (C) Women serving in the armed forces of the United States
    (D) Members of certain racial groups sitting in the back of a bus
    (E) Young people beginning compulsory education at an earlier age

119. The Supreme Court   119. Ⓐ Ⓑ Ⓒ Ⓓ Ⓔ
    (A) does not allow unconstitutional laws to pass in Congress
    (B) reviews all appellate cases brought by citizens
    (C) renders advisory opinions on proposed legislation
    (D) all of the above
    (E) none of the above

120. Karl Marx reacted to the capitalist economic system of his time in a famous tract written in 1848. The title of this work was "The Communist Manifesto." He contended that capitalism was   120. Ⓐ Ⓑ Ⓒ Ⓓ Ⓔ

    (A) an artificial conspiracy imposed on society by greedy people
    (B) a necessary but temporary stage in the evolution of society
    (C) a retrogressive system which had as its main fault the creation of a proletariat
    (D) going to improve by reforms instituted through state action
    (E) incompatible with Christian morality

121. The election which had most to do with establishing the hold of the Republican and Democratic Parties on the sentiments of their followers for generations was held in   121. Ⓐ Ⓑ Ⓒ Ⓓ Ⓔ
    (A) 1824   (B) 1852   (C) 1860   (D) 1880   (E) 1892

122. During the Middle Ages, the history of Spain was part of the story of the war between   122. Ⓐ Ⓑ Ⓒ Ⓓ Ⓔ
    (A) the Holy Roman emperors and the Popes
    (B) Western Christians and the Byzantines
    (C) Christians and Moslems
    (D) the Guelphs and the Ghibellines
    (E) Protestants and Catholics

123. If, following a reapportionment, a state becomes entitled to additional Representatives, and the legislature fails to redistrict the state, the additional Representatives are   123. Ⓐ Ⓑ Ⓒ Ⓓ Ⓔ
    (A) lost to the state until the next decennial census
    (B) elected from the state as a whole
    (C) lost to the state until the legislature does act
    (D) not elected, but the remaining Representatives acting as a group cast the extra votes to which the state is entitled
    (E) given observation powers only

124. Judicial self-restraint as applied to the Supreme Court can be described as

(A) a reluctance on the part of the justices to file a dissenting opinion except in rare cases

(B) an awareness of the need for dignity and propriety in courtroom proceedings

(C) a careful consideration of the wisdom and social impact of disputed laws

(D) a careful consideration of the motives of Congress in enacting the disputed laws

(E) a proper concern for the role and judgment of the legislative branch of government

124. Ⓐ Ⓑ Ⓒ Ⓓ Ⓔ

125. Which is not an essential step in making a national law?

(A) A bill is submitted on the floor of either house.

(B) A congressional committee considers it.

(C) The bill passes both houses of Congress.

(D) The bill is presented to the President.

(E) The bill is referred to the United States Supreme Court.

125. Ⓐ Ⓑ Ⓒ Ⓓ Ⓔ

ANSWER KEY—SAMPLE EXAMINATION 2

Part I

1. E	12. B	23. C	34. D	44. A	54. D
2. E	13. A	24. C	35. C	45. D	55. C
3. D	14. C	25. A	36. A	46. D	56. E
4. B	15. D	26. D	37. A	47. A	57. E
5. C	16. C	27. E	38. D	48. A	58. E
6. C	17. C	28. B	39. D	49. A	59. E
7. E	18. B	29. C	40. B	50. E	60. C
8. A	19. E	30. E	41. E	51. C	61. E
9. D	20. E	31. D	42. D	52. D	62. B
10. E	21. E	32. B	43. E	53. C	63. D
11. C	22. C	33. D			

Part II

64. C	75. C	86. A	96. B	106. B	116. D
65. B	76. C	87. E	97. D	107. D	117. A
66. A	77. E	88. D	98. C	108. A	118. C
67. D	78. C	89. D	99. A	109. C	119. E
68. D	79. D	90. B	100. A	110. A	120. B
69. B	80. A	91. E	101. E	111. E	121. C
70. B	81. D	92. D	102. D	112. D	122. C
71. E	82. E	93. D	103. B	113. B	123. B
72. D	83. E	94. B	104. B	114. B	124. E
73. D	84. D	95. A	105. D	115. D	125. E
74. E	85. B				

SCORING CHART—SAMPLE EXAMINATION 2

After you have scored your Sample Examination 2, enter the results in the chart below; then transfer your Raw Score to the Progress Chart on page 00.

Total Test	Number Right	Number Wrong	Number Omitted	Raw Score
Part I: 63				
Part II: 62				
Total: 125				

ANSWER EXPLANATIONS—SAMPLE EXAMINATION 2

Part I

1. **E.** Vidkun Quisling (1887–1945), Norwegian army officer and founder of the Norwegian Nazi party, collaborated with the German invasion of Norway in 1940. His name has become a synonym for traitor.

2. **E.** The Rumanian territory of Bessarabia was taken by the USSR in 1940. It had been detached from tsarist Russia at the end of World War I.

3. **D.** Greece and Italy were at war on Albanian soil in 1941. Albania had gained its independence from the Ottoman Empire in the Balkan Wars of 1912–13. In April 1939, Mussolini took over Albania. Greece sided with Britain against Italy and Germany in World War II.

4. **B.** Thomas Robert Malthus (1766–1834), English economist, in his *Principles of Population* wrote that population tends to increase in geometric ratio and food supply in arithmetic. The economic law of diminishing returns holds that if one factor in production remains constant, less is produced per unit, by applying other factors. Thus, the relatively constant production from land is outstripped by burgeoning population.

5. **C.** A holding company is a corporation that holds stock in another company. This is permitted by law, even though a holding company may not produce any goods or services.

6. **C.** The Securities and Exchange Commission (SEC) was established by Congress in 1934 under the New Deal to protect investors. The SEC prevents illegal stock market dealing such as prevailed prior to the great depression of the 1930's.

7. **E.** Youth-parent tensions in American society result, in part, from rapid change in our society as well as from the development of a youth subculture which has tended to obliterate the traditional demarcation between youth and adult status.

8. **A.** The term "secular" means worldly or temporal, in contrast to ecclesiastical. In Medieval European history, the king or emperor exercised "secular power"; the church exercised ecclesiastical authority.

9. **D.** In the election of 1928, Republican candidate Herbert Hoover promised two chickens in every pot if he were elected. His election to the presidency was soon followed by the great depression of the 1930's when there were no chickens in most pots.

10. **E.** The population of the United States in 1790 (the first census) was 3,929,214. In 1970, the population of Tennessee was 3,926,018; New York 18,241,391; California 19,971,069; Illinois 11,110,285; Nevada 488,738.

11. **C.** The Social Security Act was passed in 1935 under the Democratic Administration of Franklin D. Roosevelt. The abolition of slavery came in the Republican administration of Abraham Lincoln; the Pendleton Act in 1883 under Republican President Arthur; the Merrill Act in 1862 under Lincoln; and the Pure Food and Drug Act in 1906 under Republican President Theodore Roosevelt.

12. **B.** The ancient Persian Empire was the largest. It extended throughout the area we now call the Middle East from Asia Minor in the West to India in the East and from the Caucasus Mountains in the North to the Arabian Sea in the South.

13. **A.** Arabic is not an Indo-European language. It is one of the Semitic language group. Other languages in the Semitic group are Aramaic, Hebrew, and Ethiopic.

14. **C.** Monetary policy in the U.S. is administered by the Federal Reserve Board of Governors. The seven-member Board of Governors of the Federal Reserve system in Washington exercises control over the nation's money supply and credit conditions. This is referred to as "monetary policy."

15. **D.** Most of the major rivers in Soviet Asia flow north from the mountainous regions to the plains and into the seas adjoining the Arctic Ocean.

16. **C.** Reincarnation, the return of the soul after death in a new living body, is part of the teaching of Hinduism.

17. **C.** The total value (in dollars) of all goods and services produced in the American economy during a given year is called the gross national product (GNP) for that year. If we subtract depreciation (the using up of capital equipment), we have net national product (NNP).

18. **B.** In sociology and psychology, "drives" are factors which incite behavior in the individual. The term "drive" indicates an internal force or push which seeks an outlet. In psychoanalysis, "drive" is regarded as an instinct. Examples are thirst, sex, and hunger.

19. **E.** Indonesia was conquered in 1595 by the Dutch and ruled by the Netherland East India Company until 1798. The Netherland government ruled the colony until 1945 when Indonesia became an independent republic.

20. **E.** Tibet was ruled until 1959 by a Buddhist religious leader called the "Dalai Lama." In 1959, the Dalai Lama fled from Tibet. The country is under control of Communist China.

21. **E.** In the 1950's, Indo-China split into Laos, Cambodia, North Vietnam, and South Vietnam.

22. **C.** In the 1950's and 60's, the Supreme Court did not incline toward "judicial activism" in presidential control over foreign policy. Some felt that it did in civil rights (Brown v. Board of Education, 1954), legislative reapportionment (Baker v. Carr, 1962), unlawful search and seizure (Mapp v. Ohio, 1961), and right of counsel (Gideon v. Wainwright 1963).

23. **C.** Max Weber (1864–1920), German sociologist, opposed Marxism. He was concerned with the problem of social stratification. He noted that the pre-industrial test of "family" was replaced by "the certificate of education" under capitalism.

24. **C.** Pakistan, which had previously been governed by Great Britain as a part of India, became a Dominion in the British Commonwealth of Nations, as did India under the provisions of the Indian Independence Act of 1947. There was a mass movement of Moslems from India into Pakistan, and of Hindus from Pakistan into India. After Israel gained its independence (1948), Jews from many countries migrated to Israel.

25. **A.** In a free market economy, price is determined by an equilibrium between supply and demand. When the quantity supplied increases more rapidly than the quantity demanded, the effect is a decline in price.

26. **D.** Sweden is the only one of the five countries whose per capita income is anywhere near $8,000 per year in U.S. dollars. Similarly, the birth and death rate in Sweden is much closer to that of the U.S. (birth 15.9 per thousand; death 8.7 per thousand) than any of the others. In infant mortality, the U.S. (14 per thousand) does not do as well as Sweden.

27. E. The agricultural revolution of the 19th and 20th centuries in the U.S. is due to many factors. Among these are the growth of the use of tractors and an increase in the use of electric power. Farm production did not decline; it increased substantially.

28. B. The English Reform Bill of 1867, sponsored by Conservative Prime Minister Benjamin Disraeli, extended the right to vote to working men in the cities. The right to vote had been extended previously to middle-class businessmen by the Reform Bill of 1832.

29. C. Women in America, on the average, have a longer life span than men, though the gap seems to be narrowing as women assume more taxing positions in business and industry. Life expectancy in 1980 was 77.5 years for females and 69.8 for males.

30. E. All of the first four were included in the program of the Progressive Movement in the U.S. in the early 20th century. The removal of restrictions on blacks voting received major impetus after World War II, culminating in the Voting Rights Act of 1965.

31. D. In the history of the presidency until 1974, there had never been an instance of the resignation of a President. When Richard M. Nixon resigned in 1974, impeachment in the House of Representatives was imminent, and there was every indication that he would be removed by the Senate.

32. B. The 13th amendment to the Constitution abolished slavery (1865). It provided: "Neither slavery nor involuntary servitude . . . shall exist within the United States, or any place subject to their jurisdiction."

33. D. The person making this statement was obviously opposed to the expansionists and imperialists of the 1890's. The latter groups were strong supporters of the Spanish-American War and of American hegemony in Puerto Rico, Cuba, and the Philippines which that war achieved.

34. D. The Dardanelles are part of the passageway between the Black Sea (dominated by Russia) and the Mediterranean Sea, to which Russia does not have direct access. Hence, Russia has had a historic interest in the Dardanelles.

35. C. Louis XIV of France, who inherited the throne at the age of five in 1643, assumed power in 1661 at the age of 23. He ruled until his death in 1775. He was greatly admired and was called "Le Grand Monarque" or Louis the Great. He is supposed to have said, "L'etat, c'est moi" (I am the state).

36. A. The German Imperial Constitution was adopted after the Franco-Prussian War in 1871. By its terms, King William I of Prussia became Emperor William I of the newly created German Empire.

37. A. Niccolo Machiavelli (1469–1527), Italian political philosopher, is best known for his book, *The Prince*. In it, he counsels a ruler on the best way to acquire and hold political power. In a cynical vein, he advises that it is better to be feared than loved.

38. D. Karl Marx (1818–1883) and Friedrich Hegel (1770–1831) were both German philosophers. Hegel contended that Germany was the fruition of a process by which opposing forces produced a new and better civilization. Marx taught that the opposing classes would end in the liquidation of all but the working class. Hence, Marx said Hegel's view of history made dialectic stand on its head.

39. D. For Sigmund Freud (1856–1939), Viennese founder of psychoanalysis, the real causes of human aggressiveness and anxiety were lodged deep in the recesses of the mind. The failure of Marx to take account of psychiatric forces was fatal to his theories, according to Freud.

40. B. When historians use the title *Augustus*, they are referring to Octavian, the first Roman emperor. After he became the ruler of Rome, the Senate gave him titles—"imperator" (general), from which we get "Emperor," and "Augustus" (revered), by which title he is generally known.

41. E. In the United States, the emotional function of the family, if not satisfac-

torily performed, devolves on psychological or psychiatric help which, if available, is generally quite costly. Outside agencies, often included in the United Way, may help with economic needs; public schools with educational; parks and playgrounds with recreational; and churches and synagogues with religious.

42. D. The Standard Oil Trust was originally organized in 1882 by John D. Rockefeller. The story is told by Ida Tarbell in *The History of the Standard Oil Company* (1904).

43. E. The Dreyfus affair began in France in 1894 with the charge that Captain Dreyfus, a Jew, had sold military information to the Germans. He was sentenced to life imprisonment on Devil's Island. Dreyfus protested his innocence. Anti-republicans, anti-Semites, and many leaders of the Church lined up against him. His innocence was finally proven, and he was reinstated as a major in the army.

44. A. Otto von Bismarck (1815–1898), leader of German unification, believed Germany could become strong and unified only if Austria were excluded from German affairs. Bismarck was at heart a Prussian. He feared that Austria, if included, would dispute power with Prussia.

45. D. The Maoris are a branch of the Polynesian race. They migrated to New Zealand from the Eastern Pacific before and during the 14th century. The British came to New Zealand during the 18th century. By a treaty in 1840, the Maori chiefs agreed to British sovereignty, and New Zealand became a British colony.

46. D. An increase in the amount of money should, theoretically, bring a corresponding increase in the level of prices. However, when production levels continue to rise rapidly, the level of prices may remain constant despite the increase in the money supply.

47. A. Thomas Malthus (1766–1834), English clergyman and philosopher, was deeply perturbed at the rapid increase in population and the relatively slower increase in the food supply. He foresaw war, plagues, and famine unless population were kept in check. Universal education at public expense offered some hope. The others would only exacerbate the problem.

48. A. If people do not consume all their income, the part not spent is technically saving, no matter what they do with the money. Investing, however, requires that the money be put to work to create new wealth. In national income and product terms, consumption and investment go hand in hand.

49. A. Group marriage, several men and several women living together and cohabiting, is a relatively rare social phenomenon. Each of the other four is far more common in man's various societies.

50. E. During the period 1950–1959, there were 717 executions for crime in the U.S. The number dropped to 181 for the period 1960–64; to 10 for the period 1965–67. There were no executions for crime in the U.S. in 1968.

51. C. When sociologists talk of "social mobility," they usually have in mind vertical mobility, moving from the socio-economic level into which a person was born into a higher socio-economic level. In an open society, marked by widespread opportunity, this phenomenon is relatively common.

52. D. The use of the canoe and the moccasin, adopted by Europeans from the Indian culture with which they came in contact, is an example of cultural diffusion.

53. C. The corporation is an artificial person and *is* expected to conform to the law. The other statements about the corporation are true.

54. D. Thorstein Veblen (1857–1929), American economist and social philosopher, considered marginal utility economics overly deductive, individualistic, and static. Marginal utility economics teaches that the extra utility added by each last unit of a good will be decreasing, although *total* utility will rise with consumption. In his *Theory of the Leisure Class*, Veblen held that, in an affluent society, most goods are useless except for display to establish status.

55. C. In his *General Theory of Employment, Interest and Money* (1936), the English economist, John Maynard Keynes, stated that the economy could not,

of itself, maintain a viable level of employment. This, he said, required and demanded the intervention of the central government.

56. E. William Stanley Levons (1835–1882), English economist, wrote *The Theory of Political Economy* (1871). He developed the theory that value is determined by utility.

57. E. According to the census of 1980, Connecticut, with a per-capita income of $11,720, was second to Alaska ($12,790), Nevada was 6th, and Delaware was 9th. The other states mentioned finished as follows: California 3rd Texas 18th, Virginia 22nd, North Dakota 33rd, Georgia 36th, North Carolina 41st, Tennessee 44th, and Kentucky 46th.

58. E. In 1971, less than 6% of the American population was living and working on farms. The percentage has continued to decline during the past 15 years. The census of 1980 showed a farm population of less than 4%.

59. E. Representation in the House of Representatives by states is based on population. According to the census of 1970, the states in this question ranked as follows: 1. California, 2. New York, 3. Pennsylvania, 4. Texas, 5. New Jersey, 6. Florida, 7. Massachusetts, 8. Virginia, 9. Alaska.

60. C. In 1960, the average Congressional district contained 410,000 people. To obtain this figure, divide 179,323,175 (the population of the U.S. in 1960) by 435 (the number of members in the House of Representatives).

61. E. In the election of 1936, Franklin D. Roosevelt, Democrat, received 523 electoral votes. The Republican candidate, Governor Alfred M. Landon of Kansas, received 8 electoral votes. He won only the states of Maine and Vermont.

62. B. Alexis de Tocqueville (1805–1859), French writer, traveled throughout the United States in 1831 as an agent of his government. He described his findings in a famous book, *Democracy in America*. In it he wrote: "Nothing struck me more forcibly than the general equality of conditions."

63. D. Most countries with high per-capita income have birth rates below 20 per thousand per year. These include U.S. 15.9, Canada 15.5, Denmark 11.2, France 14.8, Sweden 11.7, Switzerland 11.9. By contrast, the figure for Mexico is 34.0 and for Ethiopia it is 49.9.

Part II

64. C. The Huguenots were French Protestants. They were followers of Calvin and Swiss Protestantism. Persecution in France led many Huguenots to flee to England, Holland, and America.

65. B. During the time of Philip II, the Dutch Netherlands came into being as a result of a war for independence. The Dutch rebelled against Philip II, whom they regarded as a Spanish foreigner attempting to subjugate them. The war for independence which started in 1576 saw the destruction of the Spanish Armada at the hands of British sea-dogs.

66. A. In the 9th century, Scandinavian invaders (Vikings or Norsemen, as they were called on the Continent) overran France and captured London, Cadiz, and Pisa as well.

67. D. Opportunity cost is an economic term which describes the cost represented by the opportunity lost in doing one thing rather than another. Thus, the cost of educating a student includes not only the actual expenditure on the education but the value of what he or she might have produced were they not in school (the opportunity lost).

68. D. In statistical terms, the coefficient of correlation describes the extent of the relationship between two phenomena. When the coefficient is positive and high, as it is between GNP per capita and educational enrollment, it shows there is a strong relationship between the two.

69. B. George Herbert Mead (1863–1931), American philosopher and social psychologist, in his *Mind, Self, and Society* (1934), held that the self arises as a result of social experience and that the individual experiences himself

indirectly from the standpoint of others of the same group. In Freud's psychology, the id is completely unconscious, as is the self prior to conscious development.

70. **B.** In an experiment, change is induced in the experimental group only. The control group is used to determine the amount or effect of the change on the experimental group.

71. **E.** There has been an absolute decline in farm employment during the past 30 years. In 1955, there were 8,381,000 people employed in farming. Thirty years later (1985), the number was 3,750,000.

72. **D.** Social norms are guides to appropriate social behavior. Time, place, age, sex, and circumstances are factors in established norms of behavior. A norm may be rejected because it is not considered important or not understood. If a "norm" is flexible, it does not exercise control over acceptable behavior as does a rigid norm.

73. **D.** Louis XIV (1638–1715) became ruler of France in 1661. He came into conflict with the German states over the Rhine as a "natural boundary." The War of Devolution (1667), the Dutch War (1672), the War of the League of Augsburg (1668), and the War of the Spanish Succession (1702–1713) all involved the eastward expansion of France to the Rhine.

74. **E.** Oklahoma entered the Union November 16, 1907; Nevada entered October 31, 1864; California September 9, 1850; Iowa December 28, 1864; and Missouri August 10, 1821.

75. **C.** The Homestead Act of 1862 granted 160 acres of land free to settlers who would live on the land and farm it for a period of five years.

76. **C.** Railroad mileage in the U.S. increased from 3,000 in 1840 to 190,000 by 1900. The increase by decades was as follows: 1850, 9,000; 1860, 30,000; 1870, 53,000; 1880, 80,000; 1890, 164,000. Thus, the greatest increase in absolute amount was in the 1880's.

77. **E.** Alaska: area, 589, 757 square miles; population, 400,481
Texas: area, 267,338 square miles; population, 14,228,383
Montana: area, 147, 138 square miles; population, 786,690
Nevada: area, 110,540 square miles; population, 799,184
Maine: area, 33,215 square miles; population, 1,124,660.

78. **C.** The census of 1890 showed that the population of the least settled area of the United States (the Rocky Mountain area) exceeded 2 persons per square mile. This meant that by 1890 the frontier (fewer than 2 per square mile) had ceased to exist in continental United States.

79. **D.** During the years 1885–1914, a torrent of 20 million immigrants arrived in the U.S., chiefly from Eastern and Southern Europe. Many were young men fleeing Europe to escape the great war which they knew was coming. Others were young men who hoped to make their fortune and return home.

80. **A.** The sharecropper worked the land. The owner provided him with credit for seed, tools, living quarters, and food. When the crop was harvested, the owner gave the sharecropper a percentage of the value of the crop minus the amount of the loan and interest. Since little was left for the sharecropper, he was *economically* in a situation not much better than slavery.

81. **D.** According the the census of 1790, Virginia was the most populous state, with 821,287 people (slaves were counted as ⅗). The next largest state was Pennsylvania, with 434,373. Virginia was most influential, too. Four of our first five presidents—Washington, Jefferson, Madison, and Monroe — were Virginians.

82. **E.** The most populous state in the United States in 1860 was New York, with 3,880,735. In 1860, the population of Virginia was 1,596,318; Massachusetts 1,231,066; Illinois 1,711,951; and South Carolina 703,708 (slaves in Virginia and South Carolina were counted as ⅗). West Virginia was still part of Virginia in 1860.

83. **E.** Teachers have two unions, the National Education Association (NEA) and the labor-oriented United Federation of Teachers (UFT). Prior to 1960, there were few teachers' strikes, but, during that decade and increasingly in the 1970's, teachers' strikes, particularly in urban areas, have become commonplace.

84. D. The proportion of students in private colleges to all college-going people in the U.S. is increasing rapidly. In 1965, there were 3,970,000 in public colleges and 1,951,000 in private colleges. By 1980, the relative figures had changed drastically. In that year, there were 9,475,000 in public and only 2,640,000 in private colleges.

85. B. The finding is set forth by Charles Darwin (1809–1882) in his pioneer work *The Origin of Species* (1859), in which he describes his discoveries from biological studies resulting in the theory of evolution.

86. A. The Gross National Product for 1929, the year of the economic collapse ushering in the Great Depression, was $95 billion, Disposable personal income was such as to leave no margin for saving. Hence, the difference, zero, was least of the other years.

87. E. Adam Smith (1723–1790) wrote a classic analysis of economic forces entitled *An Inquiry into the Nature and Causes of the Wealth of Nations* (1776). He referred to the unimpeded force operating in the marketplace as "the invisible hand." Government intervention in the free market would be the "visible hand."

88. D. Thales of Miletus (640 B.C.–546 B.C.) is called the first Greek philosopher. He advanced a naturalistic explanation for the physical universe based on water as the origin of all things. He predicted the total eclipse of the sun in 585 B.C.

89. D. Communist theory about capitalist states, as developed by Marx, holds that modern wars are fought over markets, that an ongoing class war pits the working class against the bourgeoisie, and that, as ownership becomes more concentrated, the masses are steadily ground down.

90. B. The increase in precious metals constituted, in effect, an increase in the money supply. Other things being equal, this steady and substantial increase in coinage was certain to cause an increase in prices.

91. E. The term sociology (sociologie) was coined by the French social philosopher Auguste Comte (1798–1857). Comte's teacher, Saint Simon (1765–1825), believed the industrial revolution necessitated a new science of social progress. Comte named it sociology.

92. D. Hinduism, the chief religion of India, developed prior to the 6th century B.C. The caste system became an integral part of Hinduism. Each individual was born into a caste. Four major castes, with many subdivisions, were Brahmans (priests), military, farmers and merchants, and laborers. A lowest group, pariahs (untouchables), were without caste.

93. D. Andrew Johnson (1808–1875) became president on the death of Lincoln, April 15, 1865. Johnson, a Tennessee Democrat, attempted to carry out Lincoln's more liberal reconstruction policy in defiance of Congress. The House of Representatives impeached him, but the Senate, by 1 vote (May 1868), failed to remove him from office.

94. B. Louis XIV of France was a member of the Bourbon family, which ruled France, Spain, and parts of Italy. The family traces its roots to a 9th-century French nobleman whose castle was named Bourbonnais.

95. A. The predominant faith of church members in many parts of the South, particularly in Georgia, is Baptist. In Minneapolis it is Lutheran, in Salt Lake City it is Mormon, in New York City all religions share the spectrum with a large Jewish group, and in Boston there is a large Catholic population.

96. B. Prior to World War I, Belgium was a major imperial power in Africa because of her control of the Congo, a rich territory extending over 331,850 square miles in Central Africa. The other major imperial powers in Africa prior to 1914 were Britain, France, Germany, Italy, Spain, and Portugal.

97. D. The Visigoths (or West Goths), one of the chief groups of the Germans, came into conflict with the Romans. In 395 A.D., Alaric I was proclaimed king of the Visigoths. In 410, his army entered Rome and sacked the city.

98. C. The Constitution, in Article I, Section 8, specifically enumerates 17 of the powers of Congress. Then, in clause 18, it gives Congress power "to make

all laws which shall be necessary and proper" to do the job given to it by the Constitution. These are called "implied powers."

99. A. The preamble to the Constitution states the reasons for its establishment. One of the reasons is "to promote the general welfare." The Supreme Court looked to this clause in approving public funds for parochial school children.

100. A. Transport trucks are capital goods used primarily to create new wealth as they are used. The others in the question are consumer goods used primarily for the benefit of the consumer.

101. E. Geographic mobility in the labor market refers to workers' moving to different locations for employment. Workers tend to remain where they are for fear of losing their pensions, or in order to retain their seniority, or if they are receiving government welfare payments.

102. D. In the typical American corporation of today, the managers who control the corporation are given a free hand by the stockholders. Rarely, except for the relatively small corporations, is the majority of the stock held by one or a few individuals.

103. B. The American Federation of Labor was established during the 1880's under the leadership of Samuel Gompers. His purpose was to organize skilled workers into craft unions. Brick masons were organized as one of the constituent unions in the AF of L. The rival union organization, the CIO, organized entire industries such as automotive. It came into being in 1935.

104. B. Mustapha Kemal Ataturk, (1880–1938), Turkish army officer, came into power after World War II. He carried out a revolution in which both the sultanate and the caliphate were abolished and complete separation of church and state instituted in a new Turkish Republic. Universal suffrage, a parliament, a ministry, and a president were established. Women gained a new freedom.

105. D. Henry George (1839–1897), American economist, wrote *Progress and Poverty* (1879). He believed a "single tax" on land would provide for all the necessary costs of government and even leave a surplus.

106. B. In 1971, the greatest number of American women, 73.6% of all women workers, were employed as clerical workers.

107. D. David Ricardo (1772–1823), British economist, wrote *Principles of Political Economy and Taxation* (1817). He maintained that wages cannot rise above the lowest level necessary for subsistence. Workers reproduce to provide a labor supply which keeps wages at this level. Malthus had previously noted the increase of population in geometric ratio.

108. A. There were three partitions of Poland during the 18th century. These occurred in 1772, 1793,and 1795. The nations that participated were Austria, Prussia, and Russia, but not Sweden.

109. C. The Huns were nomadic horsemen from north central Asia. They occupied China for several centuries. During the 4th century, they invaded the Volga valley of Russia, driving the Visigoths before them. The Visigoths, Vandals, Lombards, and Franks were Germanic peoples.

110. A. The Negro proportion of U.S. population was 12.7% in 1870, 11.6% in 1900, 10.7% in 1910, 9.7 in 1930, and 9.8% in 1940.

111. E. Emile Durkheim (1858–1917), French sociologist, published a study called *Suicide* (1897) and another entitled *The Elementary Forms of Religious Life* (1912). He found a relatively low incidence of suicide in extended kinship family structures in which group meaning is strengthened by religion.

112. D. In the 17th century, the Holy Roman Empire extended from Poland and Hungary to the North Sea. The various countries in the Empire constituted a loose union, but the Emperor exercised little power. It has been said that the Holy Roman Empire, which was finally dissolved by Napoleon in 1806, was neither holy, nor Roman, nor an empire.

113. B. A fief in medieval Europe was an estate over which a nobleman exercised control. The grantor would receive a promise of protection or other service in return for the land.

114. B. In November 1917, the Bolsheviks in Russia, led by V. I. Lenin (1870–1914), overthrew the government and came into power. They immediately began negotiations for peace with the Germans. Lenin regarded the war as an imperialist adventure. He thought both sides—the Germans and the Allies—would destroy each other.

115. D. Anthropologists point to excessive stress and strain in adolescence as a characteristic of modern industrial societies. The anthropologist Margaret Mead studied the non-industrial society of Samoa and reported the relative untroubled adolescence of its members in her *Coming of Age in Samoa* (1928). Her findings have recently been challenged.

116. D. The case study, a method used in the social sciences, delves deeply into the motivation and problems of its subjects.

117. A. In "Federalist #10, " i.e., the tenth of the 85 Federalist Papers published in 1788, which appeared in New York newspapers, signed Publius, Madison shows how the Constitution would protect the American republic against domination by any one faction. The other items are not to be found in the Federalist papers.

118. C. The traditional domain ascribed to women in industrial society is that of homemaker. Women serving in the armed forces of the United States constitute a sharp and symbolic break with this ascribed status.

119. E. The Supreme Court has no authority to dictate or prohibit Congressional legislation. It reviews only those federal cases which it wishes to review. It does not render advisory opinions.

120. B. In *The Communist Manifesto*, Karl Marx (and his co-author Friedrich Engels) contended that capitalism was a necessary step in the evolution of society to communism. Marx thought that the inevitable struggle between the capitalists and the proletariat would end in the victory of the latter (communism). Hence, capitalism was a necessary stage in the evolution of society.

121. C. In the election of 1860, the chief contenders were the Republican, Abraham Lincoln, the northern Democrat, Stephen A. Douglas, and the southern Democrat, John C. Breckenridge. A fourth party nominated John Bell. Lincoln won without carrying a single southern state. He led the North through the Civil War. So the "solid South" remained Democratic and the North Republican for generations after the war.

122. C. The Moors of North Africa converted to Islam in the 8th century and became fanatic Moslems. They crossed into Spain in 711 A.D., overran the country, and spread into France. Christians and Moslems vied for control of Spain from the 11th to the 15th centuries, culminating in 1492 when the Moslems were driven from Spain.

123. B. If, following reapportionment, a state becomes entitled to additional Representatives, and the legislature fails to redistrict the state, the additional Representatives are elected from the state as a whole. It is not unusual to have a Representative-at-large. States with small populations, such as Alaska and Wyoming, have one Representative, elected by all the voters of the state.

124. E. Judicial self-restraint as applied to the Supreme Court can be described as a proper concern for the role and judgment of the legislative branch of government. The Court prefers not to overrule an act of Congress if it can see any way of finding the act compatible with the Constitution.

125. E. The United States Supreme Court plays no part in the making of a national law. The others are essential steps in the national law-making process.

SAMPLE EXAMINATION 3

Part I
Number of Questions: 63
Time: 45 minutes

Directions: Each of the questions or incomplete statements below is followed by five suggested answers or completions. Select the one that is best in each case.

1. Which of the following percentages comes closest to describing the proportion of the world's population living in the United States?
   (A) 6%   (B) 13%   (C) 20%   (D) 33%   (E) 45%

   1. Ⓐ Ⓑ Ⓒ Ⓓ Ⓔ

2. In the case of *McCulloch* v. *Maryland* the Supreme Court held that the
   (A) states could tax the national government
   (B) taxing power of the national government was limited by due process of law
   (C) limitations of the Bill of Rights did not apply to federal regulation of interstate commerce
   (D) powers of Congress might be extended beyond the express grants of power in the Constitution
   (E) national government could not invalidate state action dealing with the internal affairs of a state

   2. Ⓐ Ⓑ Ⓒ Ⓓ Ⓔ

3. The Taft-Hartley Act
   (A) outlawed the closed shop
   (B) restricted the union shop
   (C) indicated a determination to regulate labor unions
   (D) all of the above
   (E) none of the above

   3. Ⓐ Ⓑ Ⓒ Ⓓ Ⓔ

4. A new employee must belong to the union in order to be hired. This is
   (A) a closed shop   (B) an open shop   (C) socialism
   (D) a "yellow-dog" contract   (E) a union shop

   4. Ⓐ Ⓑ Ⓒ Ⓓ Ⓔ

5. Sampling theory is most commonly used in
   (A) historical research   (B) monetary theory
   (C) botanical categorization   (D) opinion polls
   (E) business accounting

   5. Ⓐ Ⓑ Ⓒ Ⓓ Ⓔ

6. A synonym for the word "proletarian" in a capitalist society would be, for the Marxist, which of the following
   (A) union leader
   (B) shopkeeper
   (C) free citizen whose income comes from wages
   (D) wage slave
   (E) serf

   6. Ⓐ Ⓑ Ⓒ Ⓓ Ⓔ

7. Economic value is created when
   (A) iron ore is converted to steel
   (B) corn is moved from an Iowa farm to a Milwaukee mill
   (C) strawberries are frozen in summer and stored until winter
   (D) A, B, and C
   (E) A and B, but not C

   7. Ⓐ Ⓑ Ⓒ Ⓓ Ⓔ

8. Which of the following status situations suggests a combination of low prestige with high esteem?
   (A) A good doctor
   (B) An inefficient corporation president
   (C) A good street cleaner
   (D) A lawyer who wins few cases
   (E) A ineffective janitor

8. Ⓐ Ⓑ Ⓒ Ⓓ Ⓔ

9. Apes and other primates, in their social organizations, share all but one of the following characteristics with civilized humans. Which one?
   (A) Organization into family groups
   (B) A means of vocal communication
   (C) A high degree of specialization of work
   (D) Some learned behavior
   (E) A system of hierarchy

9. Ⓐ Ⓑ Ⓒ Ⓓ Ⓔ

10. Which of the following German parties lost most votes (as the Nazis grew) between 1928 and 1932?
    (A) (Catholic) Center Party
    (B) Communist Party
    (C) Conservative Party
    (D) Center parties of the middle class
    (E) None of the above

10. Ⓐ Ⓑ Ⓒ Ⓓ Ⓔ

11. Since World War II, which American industry has grown at the fastest rate?
    (A) Steel   (B) Cigarettes   (C) Coal mining
    (D) Railroads   (E) Airlines

11. Ⓐ Ⓑ Ⓒ Ⓓ Ⓔ

12. Early in the 5th century B.C., the Greek city-states faced an invasion form the
    (A) Egyptians   (B) Assyrians   (C) Macedonians
    (D) Persians   (E) Romans

12. Ⓐ Ⓑ Ⓒ Ⓓ Ⓔ

13. The Progressive Movement's attitude toward monopoly was one of
    (A) advocating a cooperative economy
    (B) advocating the end of corporate privileges in government and the regulation or destruction of trusts
    (C) encouraging the progressive development of trusts which had a social conscience
    (D) ignoring the subject as of minor importance in comparison with dishonest politics and corrupt morals
    (E) desiring the institution of profit-sharing

13. Ⓐ Ⓑ Ⓒ Ⓓ Ⓔ

14. Eighty percent of her people live within eighty miles of her southern border, an area not more than ten percent of her total area. This country is
(A) Sweden   (B) France   (C) Japan   (D) USSR
(E) Canada

14. Ⓐ Ⓑ Ⓒ Ⓓ Ⓔ

15. A major cause for the decline of Italian commerce in the 16th and 17th centuries was
(A) the lack of national unification
(B) a shift in the spawning ground of herring
(C) the new sea routes to India and America
(D) the religious wars
(E) the Crusades

15. Ⓐ Ⓑ Ⓒ Ⓓ Ⓔ

16. Henry VIII of England took the first steps towards a break between the Church of England and Rome because
(A) he had been an enthusiastic follower of Luther from the very beginning
(B) of a controversy about the respective legal powers of church and state
(C) most Englishmen were becoming Protestants and Henry wanted to keep their loyalty
(D) Christian teaching and practice, he thought, should be purged of error
(E) of Scottish pressure, supported by followers of Knox

16. Ⓐ Ⓑ Ⓒ Ⓓ Ⓔ

17. In the period between 1865 and 1900, Japanese education was greatly affected by all of the following *except*
(A) educational exchange with Europe and America
(B) gifts of private philanthropists
(C) revision of the traditional classical curriculum
(D) compulsory education laws
(E) importation of American school books and equipment

17. Ⓐ Ⓑ Ⓒ Ⓓ Ⓔ

18. Which of the following is not a part of our capital assets?
(A) Virgin grazing land
(B) Shoe machines
(C) Steel bars stored in a warehouse
(D) Office buildings
(E) Corporate research laboratories

18. Ⓐ Ⓑ Ⓒ Ⓓ Ⓔ

19. The Federal Reserve Board is in a position to
(A) influence interest rates
(B) provide public work programs
(C) make payments to the unemployed
(D) balance the federal budget
(E) insure bank deposits

19. Ⓐ Ⓑ Ⓒ Ⓓ Ⓔ

20. Adam Smith believed that tariff restrictions on trade
    (A) decreased a nation's total productivity
    (B) gave a nation more real wealth
    (C) were necessary if any nation were to raise itself above the lowest level of common poverty prevailing in the world
    (D) encouraged high standards of production
    (E) were necessary in infant states

20. Ⓐ Ⓑ Ⓒ Ⓓ Ⓔ

21. "The efficacy of the sentiments in producing social cohesion in no way depends upon the understanding of the function of religion by the members of society. In fact the sentiments prove more effective if they are not scientifically understood by the average person." This statement implies that attachment to religion is probably
    (A) stronger if based on extended reason
    (B) weaker if based on faith
    (C) weaker if exposed to scientific investigation
    (D) essentially an exercise in logic
    (E) unrelated to current matters

21. Ⓐ Ⓑ Ⓒ Ⓓ Ⓔ

22. As Sigmund Freud saw it, there had been three great revolutions which had changed man's view of himself. The last of the three revealed that
    (A) man is part of the animal world and subject to its laws
    (B) there is no object positively true, even in the realm of physics
    (C) men are not wholly masters of their own minds
    (D) men are naturally selfish
    (E) all primeval instincts could be abolished with the advance of rationalism

22. Ⓐ Ⓑ Ⓒ Ⓓ Ⓔ

23. "Men who upset a throne and trample on a race of kings bend more and more obsequiously to the slightest dictate of a clerk." This refers to the growth of
    (A) democracy   (B) centralized bureaucracy
    (C) the powers of the clergy   (D) popular education
    (E) retail trade

23. Ⓐ Ⓑ Ⓒ Ⓓ Ⓔ

24. According to Max Weber, the "democratization" of society had led to
    (A) the mass of people taking an increasingly active share in government
    (B) the growth of a class of professional administrators and bureaucrats
    (C) administration's falling into the hands of local amateurs
    (D) the decline of bureaucracy
    (E) a rise of "high" culture and art

24. Ⓐ Ⓑ Ⓒ Ⓓ Ⓔ

25. In the case of the American family, the "in-laws" of the husband are
    usually
    (A) given preferential treatment over the "in-laws" of the wife
    (B) thought to be of primary importance in decision making
    (C) only regarded less than highly favored uncles of the husband
    (D) completely ignored
    (E) treated equally with the wife's "in-laws" and given as little authority

25. Ⓐ Ⓑ Ⓒ Ⓓ Ⓔ

26. Horace Walpole's statement "that no great country was ever saved
    by good men because good men will not go the lengths that may be
    necessary," is most in accord with which of the following works?
    (A) *The Prince*
    (B) *Candide*
    (C) *The Spirit of the Laws*
    (D) *Two Treatises of Civil Government*
    (E) *Utopia*

26. Ⓐ Ⓑ Ⓒ Ⓓ Ⓔ

27. Which best describes the position concerning priests taken by Luther
    in *An Appeal to the Ruling Class of German Nationality*?
    (A) He declared that Christians should have no priests.
    (B) He argued that only nobles should be admitted to the priesthood.
    (C) He said that priests differed from other Christians only in that
        they did different work.
    (D) He said that priests were wholly independent of secular power.
    (E) He said that Germans were relegated to the lowest of the Roman
        Church.

27. Ⓐ Ⓑ Ⓒ Ⓓ Ⓔ

28. The Congress of Vienna signalled the end of the
    (A) Napoleonic Era
    (B) Thirty Years War
    (C) Holy Alliance
    (D) French Revolution
    (E) Austro-Hungarian Empire

28. Ⓐ Ⓑ Ⓒ Ⓓ Ⓔ

29. Herodotus' history deals with the
    (A) wars between Athens and Sparta
    (B) Persian wars
    (C) siege of Troy
    (D) legendary wars among the gods
    (E) conquests of Alexander

29. Ⓐ Ⓑ Ⓒ Ⓓ Ⓔ

30. The highest of the large castes or orders of Hindu society were the
    (A) Brahmans   (B) Kshatriyas   (C) Vaisyas
    (D) Sudras   (E) Gurkas

30. Ⓐ Ⓑ Ⓒ Ⓓ Ⓔ

31. Energy in the U.S. derived from falling water makes up about what
    proportion of all energy sources?
    (A) 70%   (B) 50%   (C) 30%   (D) 20%   (E) 3%

31. Ⓐ Ⓑ Ⓒ Ⓓ Ⓔ

Questions 32–36 pertain to Map A.

32. Which area was taken from Poland by the USSR in 1939?   32. Ⓐ Ⓑ Ⓒ Ⓓ Ⓔ
    (A) 14   (B) 1   (C) 10   (D) 2   (E) 4

33. Which country was invaded and annexed by Italy in 1939?   33. Ⓐ Ⓑ Ⓒ Ⓓ Ⓔ
    (A) 13   (B) 25   (C) 17   (D) 9   (E) 7

34. Which country now has the highest economic standard of living?   34. Ⓐ Ⓑ Ⓒ Ⓓ Ⓔ
    (A) 25   (B) 13   (C) 22   (D) 7   (E) 6

35. Which area did Czechoslovakia lose to the USSR in 1945?   35. Ⓐ Ⓑ Ⓒ Ⓓ Ⓔ
    (A) 10   (B) 14   (C) 2   (D) 4   (E) 26

36. Which country surrounds the city of Berlin?   36. Ⓐ Ⓑ Ⓒ Ⓓ Ⓔ
    (A) 1   (B) 23   (C) 14   (D) 10   (E) 21

37. Which river served as one of the boundaries of the Roman empire for   37. Ⓐ Ⓑ Ⓒ Ⓓ Ⓔ
    much of its history?
    (A) Rhine   (B) Po   (C) Seine   (D) Rhone   (E) Thames

38. Much history is associated with rivers and river valleys. Near which river were the early Sumerian and Mesopotamian cities?
   (A) Nile   (B) Indus   (C) Euphrates   (D) Yangtze
   (E) Danube

38. Ⓐ Ⓑ Ⓒ Ⓓ Ⓔ

39. Which British party, a major party before the First World War, declined most decidedly after 1919?
   (A) Conservative   (B) Labor   (C) Liberal
   (D) Unionist   (E) Nationalist

39. Ⓐ Ⓑ Ⓒ Ⓓ Ⓔ

40. Which of these came earliest?
   (A) Seven Years' War.   (B) American Revolution
   (C) Reign of Louis XIV   (D) Reign of James I of England
   (E) French Revolution

40. Ⓐ Ⓑ Ⓒ Ⓓ Ⓔ

41. Which of the following was a period of deflation in U.S. history?
   (A) 1930-33   (B) 1893-98   (C) 1873-77
   (D) 1837-40   (E) all of these

41. Ⓐ Ⓑ Ⓒ Ⓓ Ⓔ

42. Perhaps the single most important factor increasing life expectancy in Western Europe and America over the last century was the work of
   (A) Malthus
   (B) DeFoe
   (C) Newton
   (D) Pasteur
   (E) Einstein

42. Ⓐ Ⓑ Ⓒ Ⓓ Ⓔ

43. Which of the following did not occur between 1866 and 1900?
   (A) The first federal anti-trust act was passed.
   (B) The Sioux Indians were subdued.
   (C) The Fourteenth Amendment was used by the courts to protect the rights and privileges of corporations.
   (D) The Federal Reserve Banking system was founded.
   (E) The forty-fifth state was admitted to the Union.

43. Ⓐ Ⓑ Ⓒ Ⓓ Ⓔ

44. The Kulaks in Russia were
   (A) a political party
   (B) well-to-do peasants who opposed the collectivization of agriculture
   (C) the workers in the cities
   (D) intellectuals
   (E) agents of the secret police

44. Ⓐ Ⓑ Ⓒ Ⓓ Ⓔ

45. Plato found in Sparta the model for many of his social prescriptions. Which of the following is non-Spartan?
   (A) Exposure of unfit infants
   (B) Co-educational gymnastic exercises
   (C) Common meals among the citizens
   (D) Philosopher-kings
   (E) Hierarchy

45. Ⓐ Ⓑ Ⓒ Ⓓ Ⓔ

46. Sun Yat-sen was
    (A) a defender of the old imperial rule in China
    (B) a conservative army leader who tried to overthrow the Chinese republic during the First World War
    (C) a leader in the establishment of the Chinese Republic
    (D) the Chinese leader who lost the war against the Chinese Communists
    (E) the man who introduced the federal system to China

46. Ⓐ Ⓑ Ⓒ Ⓓ Ⓔ

47. Which of these countries became a center of Moslem civilization in the Middle Ages?
    (A) Italy   (B) Greece   (C) Spain
    (D) France   (E) England

47. Ⓐ Ⓑ Ⓒ Ⓓ Ⓔ

48. The importance of the Magna Carta rests in the fact that it
    (A) established the principle that the law was above the king
    (B) gave the English trial by jury
    (C) established parliamentary control over the purse
    (D) gave all Englishmen equal rights
    (E) set forth the rights of the lowest orders

48. Ⓐ Ⓑ Ⓒ Ⓓ Ⓔ

49. The characteristics of a caste system include
    (A) unlimited occupational choice
    (B) caste exogamy
    (C) maintenance of ritual avoidance
    (D) normlessness
    (E) all of the above

49. Ⓐ Ⓑ Ⓒ Ⓓ Ⓔ

50. Primogeniture was the
    (A) requirement that a man's first loyalty was to his king
    (B) requirement that a man's first loyalty was to his immediate feudal lord
    (C) rule that the eldest son inherit the entire estate
    (D) primitive means of agriculture still used in the Middle Ages
    (E) idea that the first minister was the prime minister

50. Ⓐ Ⓑ Ⓒ Ⓓ Ⓔ

51. In which of the following legislative bodies is party discipline greatest?
    (A) U.S. Senate
    (B) U.S. House of Representatives
    (C) British House of Lords
    (D) British House of Commons
    (E) New York State Assembly

51. Ⓐ Ⓑ Ⓒ Ⓓ Ⓔ

52. Only one President was elected to office more than twice. Which one?
    (A) Woodrow Wilson   (B) Grover Cleveland
    (C) Franklin Roosevelt (D) Dwight Eisenhower
    (E) Abraham Lincoln

52. Ⓐ Ⓑ Ⓒ Ⓓ Ⓔ

53. Between 1824 and 1844 one man was a significant candidate for President three times, yet failed to be elected. Who was he?
    (A) Van Buren   (B) Webster   (C) Fremont
    (D) John Quincy Adams   (E) Clay

53. Ⓐ Ⓑ Ⓒ Ⓓ Ⓔ

52. If marginal revenue equals price at all levels of production, a firm is operating under
    (A) monopolistic conditions
    (B) monopolistic competition
    (C) oligopoly   (D) pure competition
    (E) pure oligopoly

54. Ⓐ Ⓑ Ⓒ Ⓓ Ⓔ

55. In the day-to-day life of most societies, the most pervasive feature is
    (A) conflict   (B) latent conflict   (C) complete consensus
    (D) cooperation   (E) active competition

55. Ⓐ Ⓑ Ⓒ Ⓓ Ⓔ

56. The Soviet Union changed its policies in August 1939 when it
    (A) signed a non-agression pact with Germany
    (B) announced its hostility toward Hitler
    (C) joined an alliance against Hitler
    (D) announced demands for Czech territory
    (E) invaded Bulgaria

56. Ⓐ Ⓑ Ⓒ Ⓓ Ⓔ

57. The guild system of the Middle Ages
    (A) discouraged competition
    (B) encouraged the introduction of new ideas and processes
    (C) made little effort to regulate standards of work
    (D) was always open to any who wished to enter a particular craft
    (E) forced non-guild workers into the factories

57. Ⓐ Ⓑ Ⓒ Ⓓ Ⓔ

58. In Utopia, as Thomas More described it, there was no
    (A) religion
    (B) government
    (C) private property
    (E) family life
    (D) city life

58. Ⓐ Ⓑ Ⓒ Ⓓ Ⓔ

59. Which one of the following functions of the Vice-President is specified by the Constitution?
    (A) Serving as president of the United States Senate
    (B) Making good-will tours to foreign nations
    (C) Relieving the President of a part of his work load
    (D) Acting as chairman of cabinet meetings
    (E) Acting as party chairman

59. Ⓐ Ⓑ Ⓒ Ⓓ Ⓔ

60. By giving the President authority to be commander-in-chief of the armed forces, the makers of the Constitution tried to make sure that
   (A) there would be civilian control of military forces
   (B) the executive branch of the government would have supreme power over the legislative and judicial branches
   (C) the national government would be able to dominate the states
   (D) only the executive department could declare war
   (E) war would be waged efficiently

60. Ⓐ Ⓑ Ⓒ Ⓓ Ⓔ

61. Justices of the United States Supreme Court are aided in making independent decisions by the fact that they
   (A) have lifetime tenure during good behavior
   (B) are prohibited from belonging to political parties
   (C) achieve their office through winning a nonpartisan election
   (D) cannot be impeached by the United States Congress
   (E) are not allowed to buy stocks

61. Ⓐ Ⓑ Ⓒ Ⓓ Ⓔ

62. In order to operate legally, business corporations must obtain their charters from the
   (A) municipal government
   (B) local Chamber of Commerce
   (C) county government
   (D) National Association of Manufacturers
   (E) state government

62. Ⓐ Ⓑ Ⓒ Ⓓ Ⓔ

63. The famous Eugenic Protection Law which legalized and subsidized abortion in Japan was passed in
   (A) 1925
   (B) 1935
   (C) 1948
   (D) 1968
   (E) 1962

63. Ⓐ Ⓑ Ⓒ Ⓓ Ⓔ

Part II

Number of Questions: 62
Time: 45 minutes

Directions: Each of the questions or incomplete statements below is followed by five suggested answers or completions. Select the one that is best in each case.

64. Which of the following describes the appointment and dismissal of a Secretary of State?
   (A) He is appointed by the President with the consent of the Senate but can be dismissed by the President alone.
   (B) He is appointed by the President with the consent of the Senate and can be dismissed by the President if the Senate consents.

64. Ⓐ Ⓑ Ⓒ Ⓓ Ⓔ

(C) He is both appointed and removed by the President without the consent of the Senate.

(D) He is appointed by the President and cannot be removed from office once appointed.

(E) He is both nominated and appointed by the Senate with the consent of the President but can be dismissed by the President alone.

65. When the electoral college fails to choose a President, the President is selected by the

    65. Ⓐ Ⓑ Ⓒ Ⓓ Ⓔ

(A) House and Senate sitting jointly, each member having one vote

(B) House only, with each member having one vote

(C) House only, with each state having one vote

(D) Senate only, with each member having one vote

(E) House, which chooses from a list compiled by the Senate

66. The judicial concept of "previous restraint" is most important in relation to

    66. Ⓐ Ⓑ Ⓒ Ⓓ Ⓔ

(A) freedom of the press   (B) freedom of religion

(C) double jeopardy   (D) the writ of habeas corpus

(E) self-incrimination

67. Fiscal policy designed to curb inflation might include

    67. Ⓐ Ⓑ Ⓒ Ⓓ Ⓔ

(A) raising taxes

(B) drives to sell government bonds to individuals

(C) cutting government spending

(D) all of the above

(E) none of the above

68. Face-to-face social groups in which people treat others as ends and not means are usually referred to as

    68. Ⓐ Ⓑ Ⓒ Ⓓ Ⓔ

(A) reference groups

(B) secondary groups

(C) personal groups

(D) categoric groups

(E) primary groups

69. Social scientists, in studying mate selection, have verified that

    69. Ⓐ Ⓑ Ⓒ Ⓓ Ⓔ

(A) opposites attract

(B) women will be more successful in finding mates in the East than in the West

(C) "love at first sight" is especially characteristic of the urban lower classes

(D) like tends to marry like

(E) religion is an insignificant factor

70. Which of the following would most clearly be an ascribed status in our society?

    70. Ⓐ Ⓑ Ⓒ Ⓓ Ⓔ

(A) The president of a corporation   (B) A college professor

(C) A first grade student   (D) A salesman   (E) A mayor

71. Which of the following writers considered that land speculation was the root cause of economic inequality and poverty?
   (A) Henry George   (B) Henry Thoreau   (C) Jacob Riis
   (D) Woodrow Wilson   (E) Edward Bellamy

71. Ⓐ Ⓑ Ⓒ Ⓓ Ⓔ

72. All of the following factors contributed to the large increase in the American urban population during the 1920s *except*
   (A) falling farm prices
   (B) cutbacks in federal subsidies to the farmer
   (C) a construction boom in cities
   (D) agricultural rationalization
   (E) improvement in industrial technology

72. Ⓐ Ⓑ Ⓒ Ⓓ Ⓔ

73. The veto power in the UN refers to the
   (A) practice of having each government agree upon any important issue
   (B) power of the Assembly to veto any action of the Security Council
   (C) requirement that all having permanent seats in the Security Council must agree
   (D) power of the Secretary General to veto any Assembly action
   (E) veto power of many small states

73. Ⓐ Ⓑ Ⓒ Ⓓ Ⓔ

74. When the British cabinet loses the support of the majority in the House of Commons on an important bill, it will
   (A) continue in office until the king dismisses it a year later
   (B) ask for a new parliamentary election
   (C) suspend Parliament and govern by decree
   (D) serve out the remaining time of the five year term
   (E) hand the power of government to the loyal opposition

74. Ⓐ Ⓑ Ⓒ Ⓓ Ⓔ

75. During serious economic depressions one of the following things does not occur:
   (A) borrowing declines   (B) interest rates rise
   (C) prices fall   (D) unemployment increases
   (E) investment declines

75. Ⓐ Ⓑ Ⓒ Ⓓ Ⓔ

76. Which one of the following lived before the others?
   (A) Alexander the Great   (B) Hammurabi
   (C) Julius Caesar   (D) Marcus Aurelius   (E) Hannibal

76. Ⓐ Ⓑ Ⓒ Ⓓ Ⓔ

77. The population of which area is now growing most rapidly?
   (A) Europe   (B) USSR   (C) North America
   (D) South America   (E) Australia

77. Ⓐ Ⓑ Ⓒ Ⓓ Ⓔ

78. In Max Weber's *Protestant Ethic and the Spirit of Capitalism*, the particular type of Protestantism that is especially analyzed is
(A) Calvinism   (B) Anglicanism   (C) Unitarianism
(D) Mormonism   (E) Christian Science

78. Ⓐ Ⓑ Ⓒ Ⓓ Ⓔ

79. An ascribed status might be assigned a person because of his
(A) sex   (B) age
(C) race   (D) grades in college
(E) A, B, and C

79. Ⓐ Ⓑ Ⓒ Ⓓ Ⓔ

80. Which of the following is an example of role conflict?
(A) A career woman working diligently at her job
(B) A confused woman driver maneuvering in the midst of heavy traffic
(C) A judge judging a fellow American
(D) None of the above
(E) A and C of the above

80. Ⓐ Ⓑ Ⓒ Ⓓ Ⓔ

81. Factors keeping unhappy marriages together in the past were
(A) moral and religious convictions of the evils of divorce
(B) social control of the extended family and neighborhood
(C) economic interdependence
(D) all of the above
(E) none of the above

81. Ⓐ Ⓑ Ⓒ Ⓓ Ⓔ

82. The American Constitutional Convention of 1787 was dominated by
(A) backwoods farmers and frontiersmen
(B) men having large property holdings or commercial interests
(C) inflationists and speculators
(D) officers and enlisted men of the Continental Army
(E) artisans and mechanics

82. Ⓐ Ⓑ Ⓒ Ⓓ Ⓔ

83. Lenin's New Economic Policy in 1921 provided for
(A) the re-establishment of limited private ownership of property
(B) the collectivization of agriculture
(C) the immediate socialization of all productive wealth
(D) the building up of heavy industry through the first five-year plan
(E) establishment of the gold standard

83. Ⓐ Ⓑ Ⓒ Ⓓ Ⓔ

84. The samurai were
(A) Japanese scholars
(B) a people from Central Asia which invaded Japan
(C) a Buddhist sect in Japan
(D) a Japanese warrior class
(E) Japanese industrialists

84. Ⓐ Ⓑ Ⓒ Ⓓ Ⓔ

85. Which economist originated the concept "propensity to consume"?
(A) Keynes   (B) Veblen   (C) Marshall   (D) Marx
(E) Malthus

85. Ⓐ Ⓑ Ⓒ Ⓓ Ⓔ

86. Who developed a theory of human development with the three following stages: theological, metaphysical, scientific?
(A) Comte (B) Hegel   (C) Marx (D) Saint-Simon   (E) Bentham

86. A B C D E

87. The mercantilists believed
(A) that the government should not regulate trade or business
(B) in spite of their name, that trade weakened a country
(C) that a nation which would be politically powerful should import
more than it exports
(D) that a nation should try to acquire a stock of precious metals
through trade
(E) in laissez-faire

87. A B C D E

88. A plan for the government of territory east of the Mississippi and
north of the Ohio River, drawn up in 1787, was called the

(A) Great Compromise
(B) Connecticut Plan
(C) Treaty of Greenville
(D) Northwest Ordinance
(E) National Plan

88. A B C D E

89. Thomas Jefferson would probably have been *least* likely to have agreed
with which of the following statements?
(A) "The aim of all political association is the conservation of the
natural rights of man."
(B) "The state must grant men liberty and life, in order that they
may more fully develop themselves."
(C) "Nothing then is unchangeable but the inherent . . . rights of
man."
(D) "All men have certain God-given rights and can not justly be
denied them."
(E) "The state is obliged to protect its citizens from disorder and
subversive notions."

89. A B C D E

90. "The line of boundary between the territories of the United States and
those of Her Britannic Majesty shall be continued westward along the
forty-ninth parallel." This provision relates to which of the following?
(A) Gadsden Purchase   (B) Louisiana Purchase
(C) Oregon Territory   (D) Northwest Ordinance
(E) Mexican War

90. A B C D E

91. The main basis of Pakistani nationalism in the 1940s was
(A) language
(B) race
(C) religion
(D) economics
(E) geographical attachments

91. A B C D E

92. The first atomic bomb was exploded in
(A) Japan   (B) Guam   (C) Bikini   (D) New Mexico
(E) Russia

92. Ⓐ Ⓑ Ⓒ Ⓓ Ⓔ

93. "Prowess and exploit may still remain the basis of award of the highest popular esteem . . . but for the purposes of a commonplace decent standing in the community these means of repute have been replaced by the acquisition and accumulation of goods." Which of the following writers is well known for his elaboration of these viewpoints expressed above?
(A) Keynes   (B) Ricardo   (C) Veblen   (D) Bentham
(E) Quesnay

93. Ⓐ Ⓑ Ⓒ Ⓓ Ⓔ

94. Each of the following Presidents had to deal with challenges made by certain states to the ultimate sovereignty of the federal government *except*
(A) Lincoln
(B) Jackson
(C) Eisenhower
(D) Kennedy
(E) Coolidge

94. Ⓐ Ⓑ Ⓒ Ⓓ Ⓔ

95. A newspaper with a strong laissez-faire principle and very anti-Communist and pro-states-rights posture would have probably reversed its attitudes toward the Supreme Court's power of judicial review between
(A) 1876 and 1900   (B) 1900 and 1927   (C) 1927 and 1937
(D) 1937 and 1965   (E) none of these

95. Ⓐ Ⓑ Ⓒ Ⓓ Ⓔ

96. Unification of Germany and the creation of the German empire occurred under the leadership of
(A) Austria (B) Bavaria (C) Prussia (D) Saxony (E) Hamburg

96. Ⓐ Ⓑ Ⓒ Ⓓ Ⓔ

97. Veblen argued that the price system and double-entry bookkeeping are reflected in
(A) progressive education in the school
(B) the credit and grading system in the school
(C) the attachment of educators to classical subjects
(D) the ideal of the teacher as a servant of higher values
(E) the movement to include entertainment in the school program

97. Ⓐ Ⓑ Ⓒ Ⓓ Ⓔ

98. To Max Weber, bureaucracy necessarily implies all of the following *except*
(A) authoritarian structure
(B) specialization
(C) standardization
(D) formal rules
(E) humane policies

98. Ⓐ Ⓑ Ⓒ Ⓓ Ⓔ

99. The most important source of revenue for local governments is the   99. Ⓐ Ⓑ Ⓒ Ⓓ Ⓔ
    (A) personal income tax   (B) corporation income tax
    (C) general property tax   (D) sale of bonds
    (E) corporate income tax

100. That the marriage contract is something more than an ordinary con-   100. Ⓐ Ⓑ Ⓒ Ⓓ Ⓔ
    tract is shown by the fact that in most countries
    (A) it generally cannot be altered by simple mutual consent
    (B) often, marriages are recognized which were not contracted ac-
        cording to the law
    (C) one becomes a different legal person by contracting marriage
    (D) A and B, but not C
    (E) A, B, and C

101. Class lines in the U.S. are blurred by   101. Ⓐ Ⓑ Ⓒ Ⓓ Ⓔ
    (A) mass communications
    (B) geographic mobility
    (C) racial, religious, and ethnic heterogeneity
    (D) all of the above
    (E) none of the above

102. In the Spanish colonies, the *mestizos* were   102. Ⓐ Ⓑ Ⓒ Ⓓ Ⓔ
    (A) people of mixed race (Spanish and Indian)
    (B) Indians
    (C) people of European descent born in the Americas
    (D) Europeans who had migrated to the colonies
    (E) Negro slaves

103. The term "life chances" refers to   103. Ⓐ Ⓑ Ⓒ Ⓓ Ⓔ
    (A) the statistical probability of living the normal life span
    (B) the physical hazards normally encountered by all human beings
    (C) the process of maturation
    (D) the likelihood that given events will happen to a person
    (E) none of the above

104. The number of presidential electors coming from each state is deter-   104. Ⓐ Ⓑ Ⓒ Ⓓ Ⓔ
    mined by
    (A) the number of votes cast by the state in the last general election
    (B) the number of Senators and Representatives to which the state is
        entitled in Congress
    (C) the population of the state in proportion to total U.S. population
    (D) Congressional act
    (E) the party elders

105. Most of the members of which of the following groups have voted   105. Ⓐ Ⓑ Ⓒ Ⓓ Ⓔ
    Democratic in the majority of American presidential elections since
    1932? I. Negroes, II. Catholics, III. Protestants, IV. Jews, V. Busi-
    nessmen.
    (A) I and II only   (B) II and III only   (C) II and IV only
    (D) I, II, and IV only   (E) I, III, and V only

106. The banking system created by the American government in 1913 is
known as the
   (A) Federal Intermediate Credits System
   (B) Land Bank System
   (C) Federal Reserve System
   (D) National Banking System
   (E) World Bank

107. In waging war against Rome, Hannibal
   (A) launched a great fleet against Roman sea power
   (B) built up military power in Greece
   (C) tried to wear the Romans down by drawing them to fight in
       North Africa
   (D) attacked Rome by land from bases in Spain
   (E) used masses of Teutonic mercenaries

108. The assertion that the family is a cultural universal
   (A) represents an obsolete anthropological attitude
   (B) means that all families everywhere are much the same
   (C) means that the family as an institution exists in all cultures
   (D) means that all culture is dependent upon the family
   (E) means that universal values are embodied in the family

109. Recent sociological studies have usually found that boys in American
public high schools admire and give most recognition to
   (A) athletic ability   (B) religious devotion
   (C) scholarly achievement   (D) activity leadership
   (E) artistic achievement

110. "Relative surplus-population is therefore the pivot upon which the
law of supply and demand works." This viewpoint is to be found in
the thought of
   (A) Malthus   (B) Ricardo   (C) Marx   (D) Veblen
   (E) Keynes

111. Quotas based on "national origin" had to do with the
   (A) "Gentleman's Agreement" with Japan in 1907
   (B) Oriental Exclusion Act of 1882
   (C) Immigration Law of 1965
   (D) immigration laws passed in the 1920s
   (E) Smith Act of 1940 which restricted Communist actions

112. "We hold these truths to be self-evident, that all men are created
equal, that they are endowed by their creator with certain inalienable rights, that among these are life, liberty, and the pursuit of
happiness. That to secure these rights governments are instituted
among men, deriving their just powers from the consent of the
governed." This is a quotation from the
   (A) Constitution of the United States   (B) Mayflower Compact
   (C) Articles of Confederation   (D) Declaration of Independence
   (E) United Nations Charter

113. The role played by Cavour in Italy was similar to that of which of the following in his own country?
    (A) Napoleon III   (B) Bismarck   (C) Gladstone
    (D) Metternich   (E) Lincoln

113. Ⓐ Ⓑ Ⓒ Ⓓ Ⓔ

114. The ruler of the Holy Roman Empire in 962 was
    (A) the Pope
    (B) a French king
    (C) the Emperor at Constantinople
    (D) a German king
    (E) an Italian king

114. Ⓐ Ⓑ Ⓒ Ⓓ Ⓔ

115. Population growth and economic changes in the United States during the last fifty years have contributed to the growth of all of the following *except*
    (A) metropolitan governments   (B) county government
    (C) special districts   (D) regional planning units
    (E) quasi-judicial regulatory bodies

115. Ⓐ Ⓑ Ⓒ Ⓓ Ⓔ

116. Which of the following countries did not lose land to the USSR because of World War II?
    (A) Germany
    (B) Poland
    (C) Finland
    (D) Czechoslovakia
    (E) Austria

116. Ⓐ Ⓑ Ⓒ Ⓓ Ⓔ

117. If one wishes to convert family income (expressed in current dollars) to a figure which takes inflationary trends into account, one looks at the index of
    (A) manufacturing
    (B) consumer prices
    (C) grain production
    (D) wholesale prices
    (E) car loadings

117. Ⓐ Ⓑ Ⓒ Ⓓ Ⓔ

118. "Why can the deer run so fast? Because the slow deer were eaten, leaving only swift ones to reproduce." This way of thinking is associated with
    (A) Plato   (B) Aquinas   (C) Newton   (D) Darwin
    (E) Pascal

118. Ⓐ Ⓑ Ⓒ Ⓓ Ⓔ

119. The creative potential of personality is accounted for by
    (A) stimulus-response psychology
    (B) situational psychology
    (C) drive psychology
    (D) trait psychology
    (E) none of these

119. Ⓐ Ⓑ Ⓒ Ⓓ Ⓔ

120. China was forced to sign treaties opening itself to European nations
as a consequence of its defeat in a war in 1839-42 with
(A) Britain   (B) Japan   (C) Russia   (D) Germany
(E) France

120. Ⓐ Ⓑ Ⓒ Ⓓ Ⓔ

121. Which of the following nations was forced out of its colonial holdings
in North America in the 17th century?
(A) Netherlands   (B) Spain   (C) France   (D) England
(E) Portugal

121. Ⓐ Ⓑ Ⓒ Ⓓ Ⓔ

122. Regarding exogamy and endogamy, indicate the least valid statement.
(A) In some historical instances, the ban on brother-sister marriage
has been lifted.
(B) In many places in the U.S., first cousins may not marry.
(C) In-laws as well as blood relatives have at times been forbidden
to marry.
(D) Exogamous practice is more common in feudal society.
(E) Human inbreeding does not inevitably cause physical degenera-
tion of offspring.

122. Ⓐ Ⓑ Ⓒ Ⓓ Ⓔ

Questions 123–125 relate to TABLE X.

TABLE X

U.S. CURRENT AND REAL OUTPUT, 1939-42

	Gross national output measured in current prices	Price index	Gross national output calculated in 1939 prices
1939	$ 90 billions	100	$ 90 billions
1940	100	101	99
1941	125	106	118
1942	160	114	140

Source: U.S. Department of Commerce.

123. In TABLE X, using your knowledge of the period, the increase in gross
output between 1939 and 1942 can be attributed mainly to
(A) price increases
(B) the New Deal
(C) an increase in foreign trade
(D) military expenditures which put millions, unemployed in 1939,
to work by the end of 1942
(E) the gains in unionism made after 1938

123. Ⓐ Ⓑ Ⓒ Ⓓ Ⓔ

124. Considering only the data in TABLE X, which one of the following
characterized the period 1939-42?
(A) Deflation
(B) Decreased government activity
(C) Inflation
(D) Much improved government services, such as education
(E) Increased real investment by business

124. Ⓐ Ⓑ Ⓒ Ⓓ Ⓔ

125. Considering TABLE X, real output increased by well over 50% in only four years. This phenomenon also occurred during what other similar time period?

125. Ⓐ Ⓑ Ⓒ Ⓓ Ⓔ

(A) At the start of World War I
(B) At the end of the Civil War
(C) At the high point years of the 1920s
(D) In the early Kennedy years of the 1960s
(E) Such an increase in four years is unique in American history

ANSWER KEY—SAMPLE EXAMINATION 3

Part I

1. A	12. D	23. B	34. E	44. B	54. D
2. D	13. B	24. B	35. E	45. D	55. D
3. D	14. E	25. E	36. A	46. C	56. A
4. A	15. C	26. A	37. A	47. C	57. A
5. D	16. B	27. C	38. C	48. A	58. C
6. D	17. B	28. A	39. C	49. C	59. A
7. D	18. A	29. B	40. D	50. C	60. A
8. C	19. A	30. A	41. E	51. D	61. A
9. C	20. A	31. E	42. D	52. C	62. E
10. D	21. C	32. E	43. D	53. E	63. C
11. E	22. C	33. E			

Part II

64. A	75. B	86. A	96. C	106. C	116. E
65. C	76. B	87. D	97. B	107. D	117. B
66. A	77. D	88. D	98. E	108. C	118. D
67. D	78. A	89. E	99. C	109. A	119. B
68. E	79. E	90. C	100. E	110. C	120. A
69. D	80. D	91. C	101. D	111. D	121. A
70. C	81. D	92. D	102. A	112. D	122. D
71. A	82. B	93. C	103. D	113. B	123. D
72. B	83. A	94. E	104. B	114. D	124. C
73. C	84. D	95. D	105. D	115. B	125. E
74. B	85. A				

SCORING CHART—SAMPLE EXAMINATION 3

After you have scored your Sample Examination 3, enter the results in the chart below; then transfer your Raw Score to the Progress Chart on page 14.

Total Test	Number Right	Number Wrong	Number Omitted	Raw Score
Part I: 63				
Part II: 62				
Total: 125				

ANSWER EXPLANATIONS—SAMPLE EXAMINATION 3

Part I

1. A. The world's population is approximately 4½ billion; the population of the U.S. is nearly 250 million. The proportion of the world's population living in the United States is 6%.

2. D. In McCulloch v. Maryland (1819) the Supreme Court decided that Congress had the power to create a national bank even though the power is not specifically granted to Congress in the Constitution. Said John Marshall, Chief Justice: "Let the end be within the scope of the Constitution . . . all means which are appropriate are constitutional."

3. D. The Taft-Hartley Act (1947) sought to limit the growing power of organized labor. Among other provisions it outlawed the "closed shop" and restricted the union shop. In its general tone and provisions, the Act indicated a determination by Congress to regulate labor unions. The Act was passed over President Truman's veto.

4. A. In a closed shop contract a new employee must belong to the union in order to be hired. A union shop is one in which a recognized union is the bargaining agent but employees are free to join or not. An open shop has no recognized union. A "yellow dog contract," now outlawed, in one in which an employee agrees not to join a union as a condition of being hired.

5. D. Between World War I and World War II sampling theories based on probability began to be used in opinion polls. The result of each such poll is released with an accompanying probability of error either way, depending on the percentage of the sample relative to the total population studied.

6. D. For the Marxist a "proletarian," or member of the working class, was nothing but a wage slave. The workers (non-owners) in industry and agriculture were, according to Marx, ineluctably bound to their labor and beholden to their capitalist-employer.

7. D. Economic value is created in each of the examples. Steel has greater economic value than iron before it is processed. When corn is moved from farm to mill its greater economic value is due to place. When strawberries are available in winter, the greater economic value is one of time.

8. C. Esteem means high regard. The street cleaner (but not the corporation president, lawyer, or janitor) would be held in high regard by his colleagues and others. Prestige means status in the community. The occupation "street cleaner" has low status generally. The good doctor would enjoy both prestige and esteem.

9. C. Unlike civilized humans, apes and other primates, in their social organization, do not exhibit a high degree of specialized work. They do, however, exhibit the other four characteristics here described.

10. D. The depression which hit Germany with 6 million unemployed between 1928 and 1932 caused wide discontent in the middle class. Both the National Socialists (Nazis) and the Communists gained following. In 1928 in the Reichstag the Nazis went from 12 seats to 107, the Communists from 54 to 77. This was at the expense of the center parties of the middle class.

11. E. Airlines have shown phenomenal growth since World War II. Revenue rose as follows: 1945, $215 million; 1950, $558 million; 1960, $2.1 billion; 1970, $7.1 billion. Railroads went from $9 billion in 1945 to $12 billion in 1970. Steel has had an even poorer growth rate. Cigarettes too have tailed behind airline growth.

12. D. The Persian invasion of the Green peninsula in the 5th century B.C. is memorialized by the famous Battle of Marathon 490 B.C. There a Persian army of 15,000 sent by Darius was defeated by the Athenians led by Miltiades. News of the victory at Marathon was carried more than 26 miles to Athens by the runner Pheidippides who fell dead after delivering the message.

13. B. The Progressive Movement of the early 20th century advocated the end of corporate privileges in government and the regulation or destruction of trusts. Such books as Ida M. Tarbell's *History of the Standard Oil Company* (1903), Thomas R. Lawson's *Frenzied Finance* (1902) and Gustavus Meyers' *History of the Great American Fortunes* (1910) laid the groundwork for the Progressive program.

14. E. Canada, a land of 3,850,000 square miles has a population of 25 million people, 80% of whom live within eighty miles of her southern border. Canada is the world's second largest country, next to the U.S.S.R. Canada's Northwest Territories, encompassing one-third of her land area, are virtually unsettled.

15. C. Prior to the 16th century, merchants of Genoa and Venice had control of trade with the East by overland routes. In the 16th and 17th centuries, following the discoveries and voyages of Spanish, Portuguese, Dutch, English, and French navigators, sea routes to Asia and Africa diverted this trade from the Italian cities.

16. B. Henry VIII, King of England (1509–1547) had no intention of questioning religious doctrines of the Church. But the refusal of the Pope to annul his marriage led to a controversy which culminated in the 1534 Act of Supremacy declaring the English king to be "Protector and Only Supreme Head of the Church and Clergy of England."

17. B. The Meiji era (1868–1912), when a new emperor (Mutsuhito) ruled, was the great era of Westernization. It was marked by all of the four items here mentioned except gifts of private philanthropists.

18. A. Virgin grazing land is not part of our capital assets because no capital value can be attributed to them until they enter the economy in a productive capacity. The other four choices are capital assets according to this criterion.

19. A. By controlling the amount of lending that member banks can do, the Federal Reserve Board may increase or decrease the money supply and thereby the availability of credit. A tightening of the reins will cause interest rates to rise. A loosening has the reverse effect.

20. A. Adam Smith (1723–1790), Scottish economist, believed that the economic welfare of a nation was best served by a policy of "laissez-faire"; i.e. no government restrictions on the operation of the market. Tariff restrictions, he believed, decreased a nation's productivity because they interfered with the free flow of economic goods.

21. C. The statement makes the point that "the sentiments prove more effective if they are not scientifically understood by the average person." Presumably they would be less effective if understood. If attachment to religion be

considered a sentiment, then it probably is weaker if exposed to scientific investigation.

22. C. Sigmund Freud (1856–1939) showed that the events of childhood have lasting effects upon the individual's capacity to adapt to changing circumstances and to learn new ways.

23. B. The term "clerk" in this quotation symbolizes the authority of forms and records in centralized bureaucracy. Form becomes more important than substance and the creative members of society must defer to the keeper of the records.

24. B. Max Weber (1864–1920), German sociologist, called bureaucracy "man's greatest social invention." Essential bureaucratic characteristics, he said, included carefully defined positions or offices, a hierarchical order, technical or professional qualifications, rules and regulations, and security of tenure.

25. E. In the case of the American family, the "in-laws" of the husband are usually treated equally with the wife's "in-laws" and given as little authority.

26. A. In his famous work, *The Prince*, Niccolo Machiavelli (1469–1527), Italian statesman, counsels the young Florentine on the principles of effective government. He cynically advises the ruler to be circumspect rather than good and to do whatever is necessary to attain and retain power.

27. C. In "An Appeal to the Ruling Class of German Nationality" Martin Luther (1483–1546), professor at the University of Wittenberg, declared that the clergy were no different from the laity except in their work. He urged people to find Christian truths in the Bible for themselves.

28. A. The Congress of Vienna (1814–1815) met in September 1814. Napoleon had been defeated and exiled to the island of Elba. The Bourbon monarchy in the person of King Louis XVIII had been restored in France. Now a great congress assembled in Vienna signalizing the end of the Napoleonic Era.

29. B. Herodotus (484 B.C.–425 B.C.), Greek historian, wrote his *History* (449 B.C.) giving a detailed account of the Graeco-Persian War 490 B.C.–479 B.C. ending in victory for the Greeks.

30. A. In traditional Hindu society, the highest of the major castes were the Brahmans, or priests. The Kshatriyas were the military, the Vaisyas the farmers and merchants, the Sudras the laborers. The Gurkas (not a caste) were an ethnic group from Nepal, many of whom served in the British colonial army.

31. E. Energy derived from falling water (hydroelectric) makes up less than 4% of all U.S. energy sources. Major energy sources are coal 32%, natural gas 31%, and crude oil 29%. Nuclear and geothermal make up less than 4%.

32. E. The area marked #4, East Poland, was taken by Russia at the outbreak of World War II. The German armies invaded Poland September 1, 1939. A secret treaty between Germany and Russia provided for the partition of Poland. The Russian army moved into East Poland two weeks after the Germans struck in the west.

33. E. The area marked #7 on the map, Albania, was invaded and annexed by Italy in 1939. Albania had become an independent kingdom after The Balkan Wars of 1912–13. In 1939 after Hitler took Czechoslovakia, his partner Mussolini invaded and took Albania.

34. E. Sweden (#6) now has the highest economic standard of living in Europe. Per capita income is over $10,000. Industries are steel, machinery, instruments, autos, shipbuilding, shipping and paper. Sweden, a land larger than California, has a population of 8½ million people (California has 25 million).

35. E. Czechoslovakia lost the area of Ruthenia (#26) to the U.S.S.R. in 1945. The Soviets came to control this area along with most of Eastern Europe as Russian armies drove the Germans westward in the closing months of World War II.

36. A. East Germany (#1) surrounds the city of Berlin. At Potsdam, near Berlin, in July 1945, after the collapse of Hitler's Third Reich, President Truman met with Stalin and Churchill (later replaced by Attlee). Germany was

divided, with the USSR in virtual control of East Germany except for Berlin which was itself divided into 4 sectors—American, British, French and Russian.

37. A. The Rhine River (in today's West Germany) served as one of the boundaries of the Roman Empire for much of its history. It separated the states under Roman control from the Germanic tribes to the East. Ultimately, the Empire collapsed as a result of invasions from the East.

38. C. The early Sumerian civilization c. 3500 B.C. flourished in the valley of the Tigris and Euphrates Rivers. By 2500 B.C. the Mesopotamian civilization was well into the bronze age when Europe was only entering the stone age. Mesopotamia means between the rivers (Tigris and Euphrates).

39. C. During the 19th and early 20th century the Liberal Party in Great Britain alternated with the Conservative Party in governing the country. A new party, the Labour Party, came into being in the early 20th century and replaced the Liberal Party after World War I as one of Britain's two major parties.

40. D. The reign of James I of England (1603–1625) came first. Louis XIV of France (1643–1715), the Seven Years War (1756–1763), the American Revolution (1776–1783) and the French Revolution (1789) followed in that order.

41. E. Each of these periods in U.S. history, 1837–40, 1873–77, 1893–98, and 1930–33 were periods of financial panics and economic collapse. Mass unemployment accompanied by a sharp decline in consumer buying helped cause deflation in each of these periods.

42. D. Louis Pasteur (1822–1895), French bacteriologist, developed the germ theory of disease. Pasteurization of milk, the method of killing harmful microorganisms, a result of Pasteur's research has saved countless lives. He also produced a successful vaccine against the dread disease rabies (hydrophobia).

43. D. The Federal Reserve System was established by Act of Congress in 1913. The Sherman Anti-trust Act was passed in 1890. The Sioux Indians were subdued in 1891. The Supreme Court first used the Fourteenth Amendment to protect corporations in the Slaughterhouse Cases of 1873.

44. B. The Kulaks in Russia were well-to-do peasants (farmers) who opposed the collectivization of agriculture. During the first Five-Year Plan (1928–32) the Kulaks were liquidated. Hundreds of thousands of Kulaks and their families were killed. Others were sent to labor camps in Siberia.

45. D. Plato (428 B.C.–348 B.C.), Greek philosopher, wrote "dialogues." In *The Republic* he considers the problem of government and concludes that the best form of government is an oligarchy ruled by philosopher-kinds.

46. C. Sun Yat-sen (1866–1925), Chinese hero, led a revolution against the corrupt Ch'ing dynasty. Under his leadership the first Chinese Republic was proclaimed in 1911.

47. C. The Moslem Moors of North Africa entered Spain in the 8th century A.D. and controlled the country until they were evicted by the Christians in 1492. A high degree of civilization including literature, science, and the arts, flourished in Spain when the rest of Europe was in the Dark Ages.

48. A. In 1215, a group of English lords and high churchmen joined by representatives of the City of London, forced King John to sign the Magna Carta. In it he confirmed and guaranteed their historic liberties.

49. C. Membership in a caste system is fixed for life and is hereditary. Caste is closely tied to occupation. Occupational shifts, when tolerated, are between callings at the same level of "ritual purity" or "impurity."

50. C. Primogeniture, the exclusive right of inheritance belonging to the eldest son, was a characteristic of feudal societies. It persisted in England and parts of the American colonies and was abolished in the United States after independence was gained.

51. D. Party discipline is greatest in the British House of Commons. Under the parliamentary system, the majority party must prevail on every important measure that comes before the House of Commons. If the majority (party in power) loses a vote on a major bill, the government falls, and a new election must be held. Hence party discipline is paramount.

52. C. Franklin D. Roosevelt is the only one who was elected president more than twice. He was elected four times—1932, 1936, 1940, and 1944. The 22nd amendment to the Constitution, adopted in 1951, provides that "No person shall be elected to the office of the President more than twice . . . "

53. E. Henry Clay (1777–1852), a leader of the Whig party, was a candidate for President in 1824, 1832, and 1844. Martin Van Buren was elected President in 1836. He ran for President unsuccessfully in 1840 and 1848. Daniel Webster never secured the nomination for President. John C. Fremont ran unsuccessfully in 1856 as the first presidential nominee of the newly organized Republican Party. John Quincy Adams was elected President by the House of Representatives in 1824 but was defeated by Jackson in 1828.

54. D. If marginal revenue equals price at all levels of production a firm is operating under pure competition. In a monopolistic situation, marginal revenue exceeds price because the seller is able to bring about an artificial (contrived) scarcity of the product.

55. D. In the day-to-day life of most societies, a pervasive feature is cooperation. There is rarely complete consensus. We tend to notice conflict and competition which, of course, exist. But voluntary compliance with the laws, customs and traditions, i.e., cooperation pervades our daily life.

56. A. The policy of the Soviet Union, in the decade prior to 1939, was uncompromising opposition to fascism. Hence the world noted a turnabout in Soviet foreign policy when Stalin negotiated a non-aggression pact with Hitler in 1939.

57. A. The guild system of industry and business prevailed in Europe during the Middle Ages. The guild comprised a group of members of the same craft (jewelers, tanners, weavers, etc.). By controlling entry into the craft or business, the guilds discouraged competition.

58. C. The name *Utopia*, which has become synonymous with an ideal or visionary society is the title of a book written by Sir Thomas More (1478–1535). In More's *Utopia* there was no private property and no poverty.

59. A. The Constitution (Article I, Section 3, clause 4) reads as follows: The Vice-President of the United States shall be president of the Senate . . ." This is the only function of the Vice-President of the U.S. specified in the Constitution other than succeeding to the Presidency upon removal, death, resignation, or disability of the President.

60. A. The Constitution in Article 2, Section 2, Clause 1 specifies: "The President of the United States shall be Commander in Chief of the Army and Navy of the United States . . . " The Founders were trying to make sure that there would be civilian control of military forces. The above clause made possible President Truman's relieving General MacArthur of command of U.S. troops in Korea in 1951 in a dispute over our China policy.

61. A. The Constitution (Article 3, Section 1) states: "The judges, both of the Supreme and inferior courts, shall hold their offices during good behavior . . . " This lifetime tenure means that the justices may make independent decisions without regard to politics, personal relations or other possible prejudicial factors.

62. E. The power to grant charters to business corporations is impliedly granted to the state government by the 10th amendment. This amendment reads: "The powers not delegated to the United States by the Constitution, nor prohibited by it to the states, are reserved to the states respectively or to the people."

63. C. The Eugenic Protection Law of 1948 in Japan legalized and subsidized abortions and birth control measures including sterilization of women. A phenomenal decline in birth rate occurred between 1947 and 1960—from 33.6 per thousand population to 17.2.

Part II

64. A. All members of the President's cabinet are appointed by the President with the consent of the Senate but can be dismissed by the President alone. The Tenure of Office Act (1867), by which the radicals in Congress attempted to prevent President Johnson from dismissing his Secretary of War was repealed in 1887 during the administration of President Cleveland.

65. C. Amendment 12 (adopted in 1804) provides; "If no person have a majority [in the electoral college], then from the persons having the highest numbers not exceeding three on the list of those voted for as President, the House of Representatives shall choose, by ballot, the President. But in choosing the President, the votes shall be taken by states, the representation from each state having one vote.

66. A. The judicial concept of "prior restraint" is most important in relation to freedom of the press. This is illustrated by the case of the Pentagon Papers, a highly classified 3,000-page report on the Vietnam War. A Federal judge ordered the New York Times to desist from publishing any more of the report (prior restraint). The Supreme Court upheld the right of the New York Times and the Washington Post to continue publication.

67. D. Each of these procedures—raising taxes, selling government bonds to individuals, and cutting government spending would cut down on consumer purchases and thus have the effect of a down pressure on prices.

68. E. Primary groups, as defined in sociology, are groups having an intimate, generally long-lasting relationship. The family is a prime example. Other examples might include close friends or even a closely knit neighborhood. A workplace association does not constitute a primary group.

69. D. It is not really surprising to find, as sociologists have, that like tends to marry like. People associate with those of their class and of their economic and professional levels. Association is also affected by religion, race, and ethnic group.

70. C. An ascribed status is different from an achieved status. An ascribed status results from a person's age, sex, or color—something over which he has no control. A first grade student is an ascribed status. The other examples in this question illustrate achieved status.

71. A. Henry George (1839–1897), American economist and reformer, wrote *Progress and Poverty* (1879). He believed that land speculation was the cause of the inequality and poverty he saw everywhere. He argued that the unearned increment resulting from the increase in land value should be taken by the government. This "single-tax" would make for social justice.

72. B. Causes for the large increase in the U.S. urban population in the 1920s include: falling farm prices, a construction boom in the cities, large scale introduction of machinery in agriculture, and an urban boom in industry. Federal subsidies to farmers were not only cut back but were extended in several acts such as the 1922 Capper-Volstead Act.

73. C. There are five permanent members on the Security Council of the U.N.—China, France, United Kingdom, the United States and U.S.S.R. All five must approve any (except purely procedural) acts before they can be implemented. Thus any one of the five has a veto power in this most important of all UN bodies.

74. B. Without the support of the majority in the House of Commons the British prime minister and cabinet cannot govern. Hence if they lose the support of the majority in the Commons on an important bill, they must call for a new election.

75. B. During a serious economic depression unemployment increases, prices fall (no buyers), investment declines (no confidence). Then borrowing declines. When borrowing declines, there is less of a demand for money and interest rates fall.

76. B. The dates are as follows: Hammurabi 1950 B.C.; Alexander the Great 356 B.C.–323 B.C.; Hannibal 247 B.C.–182 B.C.; Julius Caesar 102 B.C. –44 B.C.; Marcus Aurelius 121–180 A.D.

77. D. Annual demographic growth rates for the five areas expressed in percentage figures are as follows: Europe, 0.4; USSR, 0.9; North America 1.1; South American, 2.4; and Australia 1.4

78. A. In his *Protestant Ethic and the Spirit of Capitalism*, Max Weber (1864–1920), German sociologist, identified the rise of capitalism with the strict self denial that characterizes Calvinism.

79. E. An ascribed status, something over which the individual has no control, is illustrated by age, sex, or race. Grades in college, on the other hand, are examples of achieved status.

80. D. None of these are examples of role conflict. An example of role conflict arises when a businessman must decide whether to risk profits by being ethical or make profit by dishonest dealing. Another arises when a legislator must choose between his belief and his fear of losing votes.

81. D. All of the above were factors keeping unhappy marriages together in the past. The relaxation of moral and religious conviction, the decline in social control formerly exercised by the extended family and neighborhood, and the economic emancipation of women all contribute to the rapid increase in the divorce ratio.

82. B. Of the fifty-five delegates to the American Constitutional Convention of 1787, over half were lawyers. The remainder consisted of well-to-do planters like Washington, prominent merchants like Robert Morris of Pennsylvania, and a few physicians and college professors.

83. A. A severe famine in 1920 in the Soviet Union and a mutiny in the Navy caused Lenin to introduce a New Economic Policy (NEP) in 1921. Private trading for profit was allowed and peasants were permitted to sell farm products for private income.

84. D. The samurai were members of an aristocratic warrior class in Japan. Each wore a long and short sword at his side. This class, established at the beginning of the Tokugawa regime in 1600 was abolished by the new Meiji regime in 1868.

85. A. John Maynard Keynes (1883–1946), English economist, wrote *The General Theory of Employment, Interest, and Money*. He showed the relationship of income to saving and coined the phrase "propensity to consume" to describe the point in income where saving begins.

86. A. Auguste Comte (1798–1857), French philosopher, wrote *Course of Positive Philosophy* (1842) in which he asserted that the mental evolution of the race consisted of three stages: the theological, the metaphysical, and the positive or scientific.

87. D. Mercantilism of the 17th and 18th centuries was a doctrine underlying colonialism. The mother country would import raw material from the colonies and export manufacturers to them. The balance, favoring the imperialist nation, would come to it in the form of gold and silver.

88. D. The Northwest Ordinance of 1787 was adopted by the Congress of the Confederation as a plan of government of the then Northwest Territory. It provided for the admission of 3 to 5 new states (ultimately, Ohio, Indiana, Illinois, Michigan, and Wisconsin), prohibited slavery, and proposed encouragement of public education.

89. E. The germ of the first four statements is contained in the Declaration of Independence. The fifth statement, however, could be used to justify oppression by the state. This danger was allayed by the adoption of the Bill of Rights (1791) which Jefferson strongly supported.

90. C. The dispute between Britain and the U.S. over the Oregon Territory was settled by a treaty in 1846. The forty-ninth parallel of north latitude, constituting the then existing boundary between the U.S. and Canada to the Rockies, was extended to the Pacific.

91. C. During World War II, the British promised independence (dominion status) to India. The Moslem League demanded separation of predominantly Mos-

lem Pakistan from the rest of India which was chiefly Hindu. In 1947, Pakistan was made a separate dominion. A religious war broke out between Moslems and Hindus in which 1,000,000 people died.

92. D. At dawn on the morning of July 16, 1945, the first atomic bomb was detonated in the desert at Los Alamos, New Mexico. Through their dark glasses, the scientists and military men saw a blinding flash, a fireball, and then "the mushroom" that reached 41,000 feet through the clouds.

93. C. Thorstein Veblen (1857–1929), American economist, emphasized the pecuniary motives of society. In his *Theory of the Leisure Class* (1899), he used the term "conspicuous consumption" to describe the motivating factor behind much economic activity.

94. E. Lincoln met the most serious threat against the sovereignty of the federal government in the secession of the southern states. Jackson contended with the South Carolina Ordinance of Nullification of the Tariff of 1832. Eisenhower confronted the refusal of the southern states to abide by the Supreme Court Decision for the school desegregation in Brown v. Board of Education (1954) and Kennedy faced opposition to his Civil Rights program from southern states.

95. D. During the period between 1937 and 1965 the Supreme Court took an activist position. It interpreted the Fourteenth Amendment to mean that the guarantees of the Bill of Rights applied to the states. It struck down some attempts of the Un-American Activities Committee of Congress to prosecute alleged communists.

96. C. Prussia, under the guidance of premier Otto von Bismarck took the lead in German unification. In a war against Denmark (1864) Prussia took Schleswig and Hollstein. Then in the Austro-Prussian War (1866) Austria was eliminated as a rival. Finally in the Franco-Prussian War (1870–71) Prussia took Alsace and Lorraine and proclaimed the new German Empire.

97. B. In *The Higher Learning in America* (1918) Thorstein Veblen described American education as "a merchantable commodity to be produced on a piece-rate plan, rated, bought and sold by standard units, measured, counted and reduced to staple equivalence by impersonal, mechanical tests." This comes close to describing the price system and double-entry bookkeeping.

98. E. Max Weber (1864–1920) described the characteristics of bureaucracy in his *Essays in Sociology*. They encompassed an authoritarian structure, specialization, standardization and formal rules. He found humane policies eminently missing.

99. C. The most important source of revenue for local governments is the general property tax. In 1977, for example, all local taxes in the U.S. amounted to $74.8 billion of which $60.3 or 80.6% consisted of property taxes.

100. E. The statements in A, B, and C are true. In the U.S., for example, a court proceeding is necessary for divorce or annulment. Common law marriage is recognized. For some purposes, man and wife become one entity in law.

101. D. Clan lines have never been firm in the U.S. but in the 20th century they have become even more blurred by the mass media, ease of geographic mobility, and dilution of racial, religious and ethnic homogeneity.

102. A. In the Spanish colonies, the mestizos were people of Spanish and Indian mixture. The word "mestizo" in Spanish means mixed.

103. D. The term "life chances" refers to the likelihood that given events will happen to a person. In mathematical terms an event will be realized with relative frequency corresponding to its probability.

104. B. The Constitution (Article 2 Section 1 Clause 2) states: Each state shall appoint, in such manner as the legislature thereof may direct, a number of electors, equal to the whole number of Senators and Representatives, to which the state may be entitled in the Congress.

105. D. Most Negroes, Catholics, and Jews have voted Democratic in the majority of American presidential elections since 1932 Voting pattern of ethnic and religious groups is determined by comparing vote tallies in specific areas

with the ethnic and religious groups that predominate as residents in those areas. More recently exit polls have also been used.

106. C. The Federal Reserve System of banking was created by an Act of Congress in 1913. There are 12 Federal Reserve Banks, one in a major city in each part of the country. A Federal Reserve Board, whose members are appointed by the President of the U.S., exercises overall control over the banking system.

107. D. Hannibal commanded the Carthaginian (North African) forces in the Wars against Rome in the 3rd century B.C. He crossed into Spain from Africa and used his bases in Spain to lead a powerful army, with elephants to transport supplies and armaments, across the Alps into Italy.

108. C. The family as an institution is a cultural universal; that is, it is found in all cultures. However, great differences exist with respect to the family among cultures. In the U.S., especially in the traditional middle class family, the kinship group consists of parents and children, whereas in many primitive societies, there is a much more inclusive kinship group.

109. A. Boys in American public high schools admire and give more recognition to athletic ability than they do to academic or other extra curricular excellence. The traditional male role is reinforced by the support of school authorities who provide scholarship, pep rallies, school letters and honoraria for athletes.

110. C. Karl Marx (1818–1883), German social philosopher and economist, maintained that labor received in wages only a portion of what it produced. The excess he described as surplus value. Surplus population would serve to exacerbate this inequity by forcing wages down to bare subsistence according to the law of supply and demand.

111. D. In the 1920's, U.S. immigration laws introduce a quota system. The Act of 1921 limited immigration from any country to 3 percent of that country's nationals residing in the U.S. in 1910; the 1924 act, to 2 percent in 1890. The act of 1929 shifted the base to 1920 but limited total immigration to 150,000 in any one year.

112. D. This a direct quotation from the Declaration of Independence as written by Thomas Jefferson in June 1776 and approved by the Second Continental Congress, meeting in Philadelphia, July 4.

113. B. Otto von Bismarck (1815–1898) premier of Prussia, was the father of German unification. Count Camillo di Cavour, premier of Sardinia, was the father of Italian unification.

114. D. In 962 A.D. the Saxon (German) Otto I was crowned Holy Roman Emperor by Pope John XII. The Empire was not finally dissolved until 1806 when Napoleon conquered most of Europe.

115. B. There are some 3000 counties (called parishes in Louisiana) in the 50 states. They continue to perform governmental services (legal and educational). However, they have become less important during the past fifty years as population and economic changes have concentrated power in metropolitan areas and in state capitals.

116. E. Austria, farthest from the Soviet Union of the five countries specified, is the only one that did not lose land to the USSR because of World War II. Austria became an independent republic July 22, 1955 by agreement with Britain, France, the United States and the USSR.

117. B. The consumer price index, published monthly by the Bureau of Labor Statistics (BLS), reports the changes in prices paid by a worker's family. Thus, if the index goes up 6.2% over a year and the workers wages go up only 5%, he or she has taken a pay cut in absolute terms. If wages go up faster than the index, the reverse is true.

118. D. Charles Darwin (1809–1882) set forth the theory of evolution in his seminal *On the Origin of Species* (1859). One aspect of evolution is "the survival of the fittest." This is the basis for the statement about the fast deer surviving while the slow deer cease to exist.

119. B. The creative potential of personality, often called personality assessment, may be determined through the use of various techniques and tests over a period of days. This is a doctrine of situational psychology resulting from studies of H. Shartshorne and M. A. May in the late 1920's.

120. A. In the Opium War of 1839–1842, Britain went to war because China attempted to stop British imports of opium from India into China. China was defeated, forced to cede Hong Kong to Britain and open Shanghai, Canton, and other cities, called "treaty ports," to European nations.

121. A. The Dutch colony of New Netherland, extending from New Amsterdam (New York) along the Hudson River to and beyond Albany, and their colony on the Delaware River, were a threat to the English. The latter sent a fleet in 1664 and forced the Dutch to give up their holdings to the British.

122. D. Exogymous practice, marriage outside of a specific group as required by tradition or law, was taboo in feudal society. Nobility married only nobility, commoners only commoners, and clergy were celibate. Endogamy means marriage within a specific group.

123. D. Military expenditures put millions to work during World War II. From 1939 to 1945 the government spent $300 billion to fight the war. In 1940 four million Americans were looking for work (unemployed), while 50,000,000 were at work. By 1945 the number of employed had risen to 64,000,000.

124. E. The figures in Table X apply only to items A (deflation) and C (inflation). The price index rose 14 points between 1939 and 1942 indicating a 14% inflation, since the increase is measured from a base of 100.

125. E. The increase at the start of World War I was about one-fourth of that at the start of World War II. At the end of the Civil War the nation was prostrate and economic recovery was slow. At the high point in the 20s, the output was little more than it had been in World War I and in the Kennedy year of 1963 it was not even that high. The four year increase in World War II is unique in American history.